Site Planning

Site Planning

International Practice | Gary Hack

The MIT Press | Cambridge, Massachusetts | London, England

This book was set in Neue Haas Grotesk and Arnhem by
the MIT Press. Printed and bound in Canada.

Library of Congress Cataloging-in-Publication Data

Names: Hack, Gary, author.
Title: Site planning : international practice / Gary Hack.
Description: Cambridge, MA : The MIT Press, 2018. | Includes
    bibliographical references and index.
Identifiers: LCCN 2017029083 | ISBN 9780262037389 (hardcover :
    alk. paper) | ISBN 9780262534857 (pbk. : alk. paper)
Subjects: LCSH: Building sites — Planning. | Architectural practice.
Classification: LCC NA2540.5 .H33 2018 | DDC 720 — dc23 LC
    record available at https://lccn.loc.gov/2017029083

10 9 8 7 6 5 4 3 2 1

Contents

Preface

This international edition of *Site Planning* continues a long tradition of compiling and distilling the experiences of designing settlements on the land, as a guide for students and practitioners of the art of site planning. It emphasizes the importance of sustainability, cultural attitudes, and emerging technologies that can overcome the sameness that afflicts so much development today. Sites, and the way we inhabit them, support the sense of localism that we must not lose.

In his preface to *City Planning, with Special Reference to the Planning of Streets and Lots*, the first American textbook on site planning, Charles Mulford Robinson wrote:

A book of this kind, whatever its other deficiencies, must not be one of fine-spun theory. It must be practical, if it is to be serviceable. It must depend for value upon what it can draw from the experience of many cities and many nations, and from the thoughts of many practitioners. It must represent the slow fruition of years devoted, not to introspective study, but to research in places and books and records—and among the men who are doing the actual work of city building. (Robinson 1916)

Robinson, the first professor of civic design at an American university, drew together knowledge gained from almost half a century of progress and experimentation, from Olmsted's remarkable plan for the village of Riverside, Illinois (1859) to the prosaic suburban subdivisions that were proliferating on the fringes of every Midwest city. Much of the knowledge of land planning then, as today, resided with individual consultants; the Olmsted firm alone planned over 50 residential developments across the US. *City Planning*, together with Robinson's earlier tract *The Width and Arrangement of Streets* (1911), conveyed best practices and served as manuals for planning new streets, lots, parks, and centers. They also became textbooks for educating the growing number of professionals in city planning, landscape architecture, architecture, and civil engineering.

Other books from Europe also became widely used in the US in the early decades of the twentieth century, especially Raymond Unwin's *Town Planning in Practice: An Introduction to the Design of Cities and Suburbs* (1909), rooted in the garden city experience. And texts for site planning continued to evolve after Robinson's pioneering volumes, each updating the state of the art. F. Longstreth Thompson's *Site Planning in Practice* (1923), which includes a preface by Unwin, drew together the salient issues in the planning of housing estates. It was the first book to use the term site planning in its title, and covered topographic issues, street types and dimensions, the form and aesthetics of housing areas, and infrastructure for sites.

Thomas Adams, also a veteran of the garden city movement, covered some of the same territory in his book *The Design of Residential Areas* (1934), adding Canadian and US examples, including his work in the reconstruction of Halifax, Nova Scotia after the great explosion of 1917. Adams designed the new planning curriculum at MIT, and during the 1930s site planning became a required course in most architecture and planning programs in US universities. Robinson's and Adams's books were the favored textbooks. In 1939, the US government also got into the act with the highly influential guidebook *Design of Low-Rent Housing Projects: Planning the Site*, issued by the United States Housing Authority.

Kevin Lynch began teaching site planning shortly after he arrived at MIT as a junior faculty member in 1949, sharing notes and ideas with Hideo Sasaki who taught a similar course at Harvard, and inheriting materials assembled over the years by Draveaux Bender on planning site infrastructure. Gradually the subject evolved to reflect Lynch's special passion for the value of landscape and his lifelong interest in how people sense and experience places. His first edition of *Site Planning* was published by the MIT Press in 1962, reflecting these sensibilities while not shying away from the analytics, rules of thumb, and technical detail required to create a practical site plan. A second edition followed in 1972, and I had the pleasure of joining him in preparing a third edition, published in 1984. In it we sought to expand the scope of site planners' knowledge beyond the physical aspects of sites to include issues of economics, logistics of site construction, and public engagement in the planning of sites. The contents of the book were largely drawn from the North American experience. Nonetheless the book was translated into several languages, and to my dismay continues to be widely used in other societies without accounting for cultural differences. I hope to compensate for that in this international edition.

Much has changed since the publication of the last edition of *Site Planning*. Issues of sustainability have become critical, reflecting the existential threat of climate change. We are learning how to predict and minimize the environmental effects of site development. Lessening the draw on unrenewable resources, including energy, materials, and water, has become an imperative in both building and maintaining sites. Infrastructure technologies have improved dramatically, loosening the dependence on large public systems. We know much more today about how people use and value public spaces, and the cultural differences that shape activities in common spaces. Public engagement has become a norm in decisions about site development, and predictions about site impacts are important in the debates about what should be permitted. The emergence of hyperdensity in many cities across the globe, and the growing preference for mixing work, living, shopping, and recreation, demand new ways of thinking about site development. Currently some of the most innovative site planning and development projects may be found in Asia and the Southern Hemisphere, where growth rates outdistance those in older cities of the West. And, of course, planners work quite differently today: using digital tools, drawing resources from the Internet, collaborating electronically, and moving seamlessly from site data to concepts to detailed plans for sites. Many of the tasks done by hand three decades ago have been reduced to apps that reveal results in an instant.

The format of this book is a response to the fast-changing nature of the practice of site planning. Each of its 40 chapters covers a discrete subject, organized in five broad areas: values and visions that guide site planning, site analysis techniques, site planning processes, site infrastructure, and prototypes of site development. This modular format will allow new information and examples to be added to the electronic version of the book, and to reissues of the print edition. Much as automobile models are improved through continuous change, my intent is to initiate an ever-evolving volume on site planning.

I am deeply indebted to many people who have contributed to the knowledge reflected in this new edition. Kevin Lynch taught me about the field of site planning and how to teach it, and his passion for discovering the meaning and potentials of sites and places continues to be a guiding light. Much of what I know about innovative development I learned from another mentor, William Teron, while working with the Canadian government's housing and urban development agencies. My professional partners, Stephen Carr and James Sandell, were wonderful collaborators on projects that sought to improve the public realm, and many of the results are included here. Over the years, my co-teachers of site planning, case studies, and design for development courses at MIT and Penn, including Rick Lamb, Steve Ervin, Dennis Frenchman, Jinai Kim, Martha Lampkin-Welborne, Walter Rask, Tom Campanella, Greg Havens, Tsing-Wei Chung, Peter Brown, Khaled Tarabieh, Zhongjie Lin, Melissa Saunders, Paul Kelterborn, Sisi Liang, and others before them, brought new insights to the subject. The Penn site planning class of 2010 compiled a fine catalog of sustainable infrastructure technologies and techniques for employing them that helped launch the site infrastructure section of this volume.

As with each of its predecessors, the book would not have been possible without the generous contributions of the professionals whose work is cited and illustrated in it. Dennis Pieprz's inspiring work at Sasaki Associates has had an outsized influence on the book, as is evident from the number of the firm's projects I have included. His colleagues Fred Merrill and Mary Anne Ocampo also helped immeasurably. Joe Geller of Stantec, L. Bradford Perkins of Perkins Eastman, and others in their firms helped me understand the NewBridge case and provided illustrations. Ellen Lou of Skidmore, Owings and Merrill, Tsing-wei Chung, and Albert Chan Kain Bon and Michael Hsiung Shu Pon of Shui On Development were invaluable in compiling information on the Taipingqiao development. Literally hundreds of professionals in firms breaking new ground allowed me to publish illustrations of their work. I was not turned down by a single professional firm or development organization from which I requested information. And professional photographers extended the courtesy of allowing me to use their images, many without a fee. Adam Tecza's creative work in preparing the illustrations helps set the tone for the book and explains concepts far better than words alone.

Several chapters benefited from the close reading and suggestions of individuals more knowledgeable about their subject than I could ever hope to be. Martin Gold helped me understand land regimes internationally, as did John Keene. Susan Fine greatly aided my appreciation for land regulations. Chuck Lounsberry and Joe Geller of Stantec helped expand my knowledge of the use of digital media in today's practice, and provided many of the images that I have included. Barbara Faga, then of EDAW, introduced me to their working methods and influenced what I have written. Donna Walcavage of Stantec helped me think about how to distill the subject of landscape planning and focus it on site decisions. Steve Tiesdell and David Adams gave Lynne Sagalyn and me the opportunity to explore the relationship between urban design regulations and the value of sites in the chapter we published in their book *Urban Design and the Real Estate Development Process* (2011), and this work is reflected in chapter 17.

Roger Conover and Victoria Hindley oversaw the talented team at the MIT Press that made this book a reality. Matthew Abbate, my editor, was invaluable in clarifying ideas, and skillfully managed the process of organizing the materials. Mary Reilly took charge of the illustrations. Emily Gutheinz, the designer, found a way to assemble it all creatively on the pages of the book. I thank all of them, and others too numerous to mention, for helping publish this volume.

Books such as this reflect the accumulation of understandings gained through years of visiting sites, often speaking with site designers and listening to their descriptions of how they were inspired to create places of lasting value. My family has tolerated regular diversions of trips to see this or that project, for which I thank them. Lynne Sagalyn, my wife and intellectual partner, has shared much of the journey, tutoring me on the hidden hand of economics that has shaped what I am looking at, while patiently tolerating my discourses on aesthetics and materials. She provided the encouragement that brought this book to fruition. I thank them all for their support.

Great Wass Island, June 2017

Part 1 | The Art of Site Planning

Site planning is the art of designing settlements and activities on the land, and planning the essential infrastructure they require. It is an important activity at all scales, from laying out an individual building site to creating a cluster of buildings to planning an entire new community. It draws on knowledge and understandings developed over centuries, but is deeply rooted in contemporary values and patterns of behavior. Sites are often built upon quickly, yet structures and landscapes usually outlive their designers and builders. The site planner needs to anticipate change and create a framework for constant adaptation of a site.

Site planning is an activity shared by architects, engineers, landscape architects, city planners, and a variety of other specialized professions. Too frequently the work of each professional is layered on the work of others—one plans how the land is to be broken up, another creates roads and sewers to serve the parcels, a third locates and designs the buildings, and landscape is added later by still another designer. Great sites, however, seldom result from such a disjointed process. Creativity flourishes when the elements of a site are conceived in unison, taking a synoptic view of land, property, buildings, outdoor spaces, and the utilitarian elements serving them.

Thinking synoptically about sites requires many kinds of knowledge. A site is at once part of a natural system, an economic commodity, an aspect of a community, the extension of man-made roads and infrastructure, and a territory that must serve its occupants. Legal issues of ownership and subdivision must be mastered, and many sites require a lengthy process of public discussion and approval before they can be developed. What occurs on the site will have consequences for the surroundings: demands will be created for water, sewer, and electrical service; traffic will be added to roads; children may need to be accommodated in schools; water may drain off the site into nearby streams, and so on: few projects are without impacts. All of these issues will need to be analyzed and taken into account in making plans.

With such complexity, there is no single formula for how to go about planning sites. Precedents can be instructive, and many techniques have been devised to help analyze the consequences of site arrangements. Regulations and manuals of good practice bound what is possible. Rough guidance can be set down about the activities of site planning, but creating a fine site is ultimately an art. The best sites are acts of invention, forward-looking and shaped by a vision of what is uniquely possible on this land. And site planning does not stop when the land is occupied, since those who use it continue to reshape the legacy they have inherited.

1 | **Values and Visions**

Often the first question we ask strangers is "Where are you from?," and we quickly form conclusions about them from the response. We assume that they have been shaped by climate, landscape, a way of life, circles of interaction, economic status, and a host of other local influences where they grew up. Of course humans are far more complicated, and we are never simply a product of the places of our childhood or even adulthood, but the belief that we are rooted in a *sense of place* is fundamental to how we understand others.

The sense of place is the product of traditions, aspirations, and values as well as geography, a fact that is well recognized by those who survive on the land. The vignerons of the Burgundian hillsides understand their vineyards in terms of *terroir*—the subtle blend of landform, orientation, soils and subsoils, rainfall, and growing season. But the terroir of a wine is also the result of human processes, including the long and evolving traditions of how to plant, harvest, and maintain vineyards and vines, decisions about which varieties to plant, and techniques of making wines from the fruits of the land. In great vineyards, such as Le Montrachet, natural and human processes are intimately intertwined, as they are in every well-planned site (Wilson 1999).

At the Sea Ranch development on the Pacific shore of California north of San Francisco, the planners created a distinctive terroir responding to the unique topography and landscape of the site, integrating human uses with nature. The varying ecologies of the Sea Ranch site offered cues for the uses and building forms serving a mixture of year-round and seasonal residents. Along the ocean, houses hug the margins of wooded ravines that slope to the shore, avoiding the grassy meadows once grazed by sheep. Roads and walkways are carefully sited to minimize the disruption of the shoulder-high natural grasses on the meadows. On the steeper wooded hillsides rising up from the coastal promontories, houses are carefully inserted between the trees, raised up from the ground to minimize their footprints. Horse farms and active recreation areas are sited in the clearings in the forest, where topographic changes can be best accommodated. Residents of Sea Ranch value the fact that nowhere else on the California coast can they be so closely in touch with nature yet part of a living, thriving community (Halprin 2002; Lyndon and Alinder 2014).

Recognizing that *places* have *value* is fundamental to site planning. But what values should guide the planning of a site?

Sustainability

Site planning begins with an appreciation of the site, out of which grows a vision of what is possible. Exploiting the site's potentials in a way that is *sustainable* should be the highest value.

When we occupy a site we inevitably change it, even if the greatest care is taken to protect a valuable landscape. A virgin site is altered as it is developed, with hard-surfaced roofs, roads, and driveways replacing natural ground cover that absorbed rainfall, forcing changes to natural drainage patterns. Clearing portions of a site may jeopardize the wind firmness of the remaining trees. Smoothing out topography will necessitate locations for surplus soils, while disturbing the land cover may pose dangers of erosion. We sometimes

Terroir

Used with reference to the character of wines from a particular locale, the term terroir means loosely the sense of place. While its origins are in describing the distinctive ground of a vineyard – soils, geology, drainage patterns, and groundwater – it also includes the orientation, sunlight, rainfall, seasonal temperatures, day-night differential in temperatures, and traditions of cultivation of vines. Human actions are intertwined with natural features, and over time ground and culture become one.

Nowhere is this more evident than in the Montrachet vineyard in Burgundy, straddling the towns of Puligny and Chassagne, source of the world's finest white wines. The small close, 7.99 ha (19.7 ac), is subdivided into 18 parcels, and each of the owner-producers creates a unique interpretation of the distinctive Montrachet terroir. The distinction begins with the soils and subsurface geology, formed by the erosion of the limestone on the southwest-facing slope of Mont Rachet. The finest chardonnay grapes are grown on a 3% grade in the Montrachet vineyard. Adjacent, excellent vineyards separated by geological fault lines are used for Batard-Montrachet (1% grade on the slopes below) and Chevalier-Montrachet (15% grade above) wines, each with their own unique terroir.

Site planners need to understand their sites as intimately as the vignerons of Montrachet understand theirs. Expressing the terroir of a site can create distinctive character, leaving plenty of room for interpreting how it is expressed.

1.1 Photograph of Le Montrachet vineyard. (Jonathan Caves/ Wikimedia Commons)

1.2 Section through Le Montrachet hillside. (Courtesy of Catherine Ponst-Jacquin/ James E. Wilson)

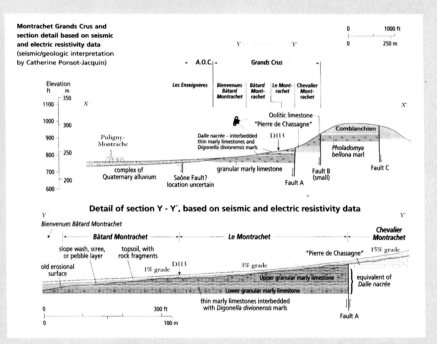

3

1.3 Aerial view of Sea Ranch, California.
(Courtesy of Breakers Inn)

1.4 Locational score for Sea Ranch.
(Lawrence Halprin Collection, Courtesy of The Architectural Archives, University of Pennsylvania)

1.5 Houses along edges of tree-lined creeks, with meadows left open, Sea Ranch.
(Gary Hack)

1.6 Hillside houses, Sea Ranch.
(Gary Hack)

think that the natural ecology of a site needs to be preserved, but that is never really possible. The objective is to re-form a site in a way that creates a new *balanced ecology* where humans and other natural species coexist, and natural systems are in equilibrium.

Thinking of a site as a *closed loop* helps in formulating a plan that is sustainable. In a closed loop, the export and import of materials, energy, and water from the site is minimized. The ideal is finding ways to recycle or convert all the byproducts of building and to occupy the site to its fullest. Where it is possible to generate energy on a site by exploiting wind or solar power to produce electricity or heat, tapping geothermal sources, or harvesting waste heat from industrial processes or sewage, these should be explored. Composting waste or burning it to convert it to energy can also be part of the solution. Equally important is selecting materials for a site that minimize the need for energy, chemical fertilizers, and other imported materials for ongoing operations and maintenance (Wheeler and Beatley 2014).

Sustainability also requires attention to the *resilience* of a site. Is it planned to cope with extreme weather events, prolonged droughts, or natural disasters such as earthquakes? Is it protected from hazards originating beyond the site—flooding of adjacent rivers or oceanfronts and landslides, as examples? Does the plan of the site create hazards for surrounding areas by reducing protection from storm surges, reducing wetlands, or exporting silt? Does the development of a site make it more vulnerable to wildfires?

Metrics are important to achieving site sustainability. Minimizing *greenhouse gas (GHG) emissions*, principally carbon dioxide and methane, is critical, and there are methods for estimating these impacts. Minimizing energy consumption is sometimes a useful surrogate, although not all energy is equal in its *carbon footprint*. Exploiting passive solar arrays or locally generated wind energy turbines affects the atmosphere far less than drawing energy from the grid. Greenhouse gases can also be used on a site, as by tapping methane from underground landfills, or can be *sequestered* through tree-planting programs.

Adopting a *zero net criterion* is an important target in promoting sustainability. Water discharges from a site should be limited to predevelopment rates (measured by total quantity or runoff rates); no earth should be exported or imported; demolition materials from prior development should be reused on the site; traffic generated by site development should be offset by reduced travel off site (such as by reducing trips through mixed-use development). While it is seldom possible to achieve zero net GHG emissions, paying attention to the ways that emissions may be offset by reduced off-site travel (for example) can lower the *carbon footprint* of a site's activities. Each of these measures is essential if sustainability is to be more than rhetoric.

Efficiency

Sites also must serve the purposes of their owners and occupants. Sometimes these are congruent, but often the insistence of owners and developers that the site be efficient will trump the long-term necessities of users. *Efficient use* of a site *is* important, although measuring efficiency is often more an art than a science. It usually means *minimizing the distance* people and goods must

1.7 Neighborhood energy utility serving the Southeast False Creek neighborhood, Vancouver.
(Gary Hack)

1.8 BedZed EcoVillage, Sutton, England, aims at zero net energy consumption.
(Bill Dunster/Ted Chance/Wikimedia Commons)

1.9 Hammarby Sjöstad, Stockholm, collects and filters all rainfall on the site before reusing it.
(Gary Hack)

travel, both on the site and to points beyond. There will always be many ways of achieving this through setting the density of development as high as possible, mixing uses, and clustering activities. *Promoting multiple use* of costly infrastructure, by sharing parking areas or consolidating loading docks, is another strategy. Efficiency may also mean *optimizing the development process*, minimizing the time it takes for the first facilities to be completed, and allowing each portion of the site to be developed without disturbing the others. In deciding upon the objectives in planning a site, the site planner needs to arrive at an operational definition of efficiency.

The goal of efficiency usually implies *economizing on the infrastructure* needed, and *minimizing operating and maintenance expenditures*. This does not automatically mean paring initial expenditures to the bone, since prudent initial investments may result in economies of *life cycle costs*. It will be important to arrive at an implied or explicit *discount rate*, allowing future savings to be traded off against present costs (see chapter 17). For developers who plan to exit a project once it is completed, the discount for saving on future costs may be high, although in this case they may be tarred by a reputation for constructing projects that soon deteriorate. As a counterbalance, public bodies often adopt extremely low discount rates, requiring durable construction and minimizing infrastructure maintenance costs that will become public responsibility once a site is occupied.

1.10 The Rise, Vancouver, demonstrates the virtues of mixed-use development, combining large-format stores with neighborhood services and housing.
(Courtesy of Grosvenor Americas)

Human Needs

Sites must be planned with the developer's economic aspirations in mind, but ultimately they need to serve the needs and habits of their human occupants. The outdoor areas of sites are especially important in promoting *human contact.* Meeting people face to face in public, or simply observing passersby, roots us in our society, maintains friendships, and helps form communities. The way we organize paths and the density of use of public spaces will affect the number of serendipitous contacts we experience, and may also be critical to economic activities such as shopping or selecting an eating place. In creative districts, the opportunity for casual contact may be the crucial spark for innovation.

How places are organized, we now know, can be an important determinant of perceived (and often actual) *safety* and *security.* While perceptions are heavily shaped by culture, forlorn and abandoned areas almost never seem as safe as places where there are many eyes on the street. The plan of a site establishes a pattern of private, semipublic, and public zones, and through the filter of culture we understand what may legitimately go on in each. In a more prosaic sense we also plan environments to separate hazards from people, keeping pedestrians from stepping out into fast-moving traffic or falling into rushing water, and providing escape routes for crowds in times of emergency. A good environment provides the cues, subtle and explicit, for how we safely inhabit our world.

1.11 Rockefeller Park at Battery Park City, New York, draws visitors and users of all ages for active and passive recreation.
(Gary Hack)

1.12 A neighborhood shopping street, Toronto, provides eyes on the street while promoting socialization.
(Gary Hack)

1.13 Olympic Sculpture Park, Seattle, provides accessibility for all by creatively navigating the sloping hillside that covers rail lines and highways.
(Courtesy of WEISS/MANFREDI Architecture/Landscape/ Urbanism / Ben Benschneider photo)

1.14 Millennium Park, Chicago, provides natural beauty in the heart of the city, combining casual and programmed activities.
(Gary Hack)

Children and elderly people who have limited mobility are especially affected by the layout of sites. With their diminished range of travel, it is important that places be organized so that those with restricted (or exceptional) physical abilities can get around. Often the kinds of pathways needed by the elderly serve parents with children equally well. Children need nearby environments that challenge and promote *development of their mental and physical abilities.* The needs change with each age group, and may be something as simple as a safe paved area that can be adapted for street hockey or other games. But younger children may need fixed installations or creative play spaces that go beyond catalog equipment. Easy surveillance of children's areas may also be a requisite, but for teens, usually neglected in planning places, exactly the opposite may be needed.

Perhaps the highest human need is experiencing *beauty* in everyday settings. This does not mean cluttering the environment with public art, although the work of artists can surely make contributions to distinctive places. Rather, it means capturing the essence of the emotions being served. In a place that is filled with activity and people, dialing up the stimuli may be the route to creating a memorable place (think Times Square in Manhattan). In another place that is a respite from a crowded city, the winning formula may be screening out noise, reducing the distractions, and offering a simple palate of nature blessed with sunlight. Memorable streets elevate the sense of procession under a generous canopy of trees, while a town common anchors our image of place by collecting the important institutions around its edge. These are created by the inspired planning of sites, beginning with an aspiration to seek beauty.

Compatibility

Few sites are islands. Almost all are a portion of a larger setting, a river edge, valley, town, city neighborhood, or distinctive region. Making sure that a site is compatible with its surroundings is a valued objective, but tricky to define and judge. We also want sites to be unique and identifiable in their own right. Sameness isn't necessarily a virtue.

In lightly settled areas, *compatibility* with the natural setting will be the objective. Usually nature will dominate

1.15 Haystack Mountain School, Maine, sits gently on the rocky sloping site, with structures connected by decks. (Gary Hack)

1.16 The whitewashed structures of Cáceres, Spain, unify the town while emphasizing the natural form of its site. (Gary Hack)

the site, and we will not wish to detract from its valued qualities. If the site slopes dramatically, particularly if trees and vegetation are important for stabilizing hillsides, it will be important to organize roads and buildings so that they flow with the land, while exploiting views to the distance. Keeping structures below the tree line and avoiding hilltop development will ensure that the site seems undisturbed. Of course, there are times when siting structures in contrast to the natural setting heightens the experience of nature, but this is not a general license to disregard the powerful form of the land.

The norm in urban areas is usually compatibility with the pattern of man-made surroundings. But which surroundings? In most cities there are mixed signals, and a rationale can be constructed for almost any approach to a site. Start with the prevailing pattern of streets and blocks—are they long and narrow, or rectangular? Are the dimensions of blocks adequate for creating courtyards or private outdoor spaces? Local traditions are often responses to the urban form of cities. Look for the character-defining elements of a city—consistent street walls or heights or architectural elements or materials or colors, ways of handling the automobile, and so on. Respecting views to, from, and across sites is an important form of respect for surroundings. Aligning utilitarian functions such as pedestrian routes, the hierarchy of streets, locations of roadway intersections, and mass transit stops will also continue the fabric of a community.

But what if the surroundings are a hodgepodge of forms and patterns, or are in the midst of change, as so many urbanizing suburbs and exurban areas are today? Then the onus may be on the site planner to establish the pattern that may be emulated by others. Compatibility can also mean providing a generic example of the form of future development.

Making a site compatible with its surroundings also implies dealing with more prosaic issues of *impacts*—ensuring that adjacent neighborhoods are not flooded with traffic or parked cars, protecting fragile commercial areas from overwhelming competition, balancing the costs of increased public services with the new revenues flowing to local governments, and a host of other issues that can fuel "Not in My Backyard" (NIMBY) objections. The solution usually involves both the physical and financial program for a site.

Economic Value

In market economies, sites are *economic units*—one element in the triad of labor, capital, and land. Even in countries where the land is the responsibility of the state, sites are a component in the shadow economy that focuses on the *productivity of locations*. Considerations of a site's economics cannot be detached from decisions about its form.

Site arrangements and form can have a profound effect on the economic value captured by those involved in developing them. Location of a park on a site will immediately raise the value of properties surrounding it. Increasing the number of houses or office spaces with views of a river or distant mountains will similarly raise the value of rents. Mixing uses so that there is a built-in market for commercial spaces will customarily raise the value of a site. Site arrangements can also lower costs, as by locating a parking structure that is shared by office workers in the day, restaurant patrons in the evening, and overnight hotel guests (Hack and Sagalyn 2011).

Most site owners seek to maximize the economic value of their properties, but there are important differences in how this is operationalized. It may be advantageous to mix several uses on a site—housing, shopping, workplaces—because it will allow the developer to market the entire site more quickly than if only one use were located there. For another developer, slow and steady development may be a virtue, if they are looking for long-term appreciation in value. Whether the developer will maintain a long-term stake in the development can become a determining factor in how they regard the economics of the site. End users of a site will also favor particular economic values, as residents do when they look for appreciation in their home values, or compatible neighbors, or proximity to good schools. Public regulations also affect the economics of a site, by limiting heights of buildings to ensure they are compatible with existing structures, or retaining historic structures, or requiring ground-floor spaces to be given to retail uses to maintain the continuity of streets, or requiring a proportion of affordable housing units on the site, even though some of these may require internal subsidies.

At the point of departure on any site planning process, the planner needs to identify as precisely as possible the economic expectations of clients, end users, public bodies, and others who will need to provide a green light for development. Questions to ask include: What would constitute an adequate return? How large an investment in infrastructure can be financed? How long a marketing or startup period will be tolerated? Are particular uses considered loss leaders or amenities, to be paid for by other occupants of the site? Some of the answers can be obtained easily, others may require comparisons with other projects, and still others will only emerge as the plans evolve.

Other site planning projects may be less driven by immediate returns on investments. A university campus planning project, as an example, will generally have a long time horizon, and the economic issues will have more to do with the *opportunity costs* of devoting a site to one set of uses rather than another, and the capacity to attract donors or raise money for a project. A corporate headquarters may be more attuned to the image it projects than to the market value created in buildings and site improvements. But the discipline of viewing the tradeoffs through the lenses of each of the affected parties— owner, user, and the broader public—remains a useful way of calibrating economic values.

1.17 The High Line, New York, has stimulated investments in new structures, while providing a respite above the street for the Chelsea neighborhood.
(Gary Hack)

Adaptability

No site is ever static. As soon as it is developed, the owners and users begin to contemplate changes. Some of these involve completing the missing elements— adding seating to popular public spaces, moving merchandise out into streets or squares in commercial areas, paving paths worn by pedestrian desire lines, or creating venues for festivals and events. *Adaptability* needs to be considered before plans are firmed up, and the planner needs to contemplate both short- and long-term changes.

There are advantages to planning sites so they can be easily adapted, including the fact that many of the needs only become apparent once the residents or users inhabit the site. Too many outdoor spaces are finished prematurely, with a cliché of unoccupied benches, unvisited (and unmaintainable) fountains, children's playgrounds ordered from catalogs, and landscaped planters. If left to the occupants' decisions, more imaginative places could surely result. Parking areas are customarily sized and planned for worst-case accumulations of vehicles, then sit empty most of the time; a better strategy would be to reserve the land and pave only the minimum needed at the outset. The land should be planned so that if expected demands fail to materialize parcels can be shifted to other uses. In street-oriented housing areas, purchasers will immediately begin personalizing their yards and contemplating additions, and site plans need to anticipate such changes. Higher-density areas will also change but over a longer cycle, and plans need to think in terms of second and third lives of sites.

The rate of change of site uses varies considerably. Academic institutions such as universities plan in terms of many decades, even centuries, while their counterpart medical institutions are constantly in flux, responding to changing medical technologies and treatment protocols. Strictly commercial enterprises, such as retail shopping outlets, reinvent themselves every ten or twenty years in response to shifting fashions and sales strategies. Housing, particularly in dispersed ownership, may last for long periods, although slowly changing through individual initiatives. As a general rule, it is important to plan sites so that there are varying rates of change, with some uses providing stability while others are constantly being modified.

1.18 Quinta Monroy Social Housing, Iquique, Chile, is designed for adaptability so that every house can be doubled in size by its occupants. (Cristobal Palma Courtesy of © Elemental)

Adaptability is valuable, but so is its counterpart, *continuity*, which anchors the sense of place and maintains human memories of it. Preserving a historical record on the ground by incorporating valued landscapes, buildings, and artifacts is an important value in site planning. Maintaining the natural divisions of a site, such as hedgerows that predominated when it was an agricultural landscape, or man-made artifacts such as remnants of the site's industrial past, not only provides a unique identity but adds value to newly created places.

Identifying and reconciling the values, and understanding the choices among them, is a puzzle that will preoccupy the early stages of a site planning project. Conversations with owners, public officials, marketing agents, and possible tenants and occupants of the site and its surroundings will make clear some values, both implicit and explicit. And they will reveal the conflicts—a developer wishing to maximize the proportion of a site devoted to housing while a municipality seeks commercial tax revenues; nearby residents wishing to protect a much-used playing field from development; a marketing agent wishing to reproduce a hot-selling form of development on a site where it will be inappropriate; or a developer who may have paid too much for the land and needs to find a way to recover the economic value over time.

To these concerns must be added the values of the site planner, who may be the only voice of the human needs of eventual occupants of the site, and may be thinking in terms of future adaptability and change. The site planner needs to aim for a fair and equitable solution. Does it broaden choice? Do all income levels benefit from the common goods? Do the impacts fall disproportionately on those with lowest resources? Reconciling these competing desires requires creativity, including the ability to reframe the problem in ways that none of the protagonists has imagined. It is what makes the responsibility of planning a site interesting and fulfilling.

2 | Examples of Fine Sites

There are many well-worn and recently created places that can serve as exemplars for site planning. Three are presented here, and each illustrates an important set of values that have guided its creation. The NewBridge community, located on the Charles River in Dedham, near Boston, is devoted to care of seniors and education of youth and is rooted in a set of values of sustainability and caring for the land. Taipinqiao in Shanghai, a new city district, illustrates how creative reuse of historic *shikumen* houses, attention to the scale and character of the city's traditional streets, along with developing a large new park, can establish a distinct character for an area that sets it apart from other large developments. Battery Park City, in New York, is also a new city district that combines work, living, and leisure along Manhattan's waterfront. Its accomplishments include integration with the surrounding city fabric and a public realm without parallel. Each of these new places sets new standards for developing environments.

NEWBRIDGE ON THE CHARLES
Dedham, Massachusetts

Located in a suburb of Boston, NewBridge is a stellar example of a how a unique site can result from a creative response to site constraints, a strong vision of community, and a commitment to sustainability. The developer and its planners wanted to create a comprehensive, thoughtful, and sustainable campus for 750 aging adults in settings ranging from independent and assisted living to full nursing care, as well as the Rashi

School, an independent school for 450 kindergarten through eighth grade day students. The concept of an intergenerational campus where the seniors and students could congregate in a central community facility for casual and programmed interaction was at the heart of the project.

Hebrew SeniorLife, a nonprofit organization concerned with serving the needs of its community, developed the site. Many of the residents of NewBridge and their families have longstanding ties to the surrounding communities, and many of the students in the school live in these towns and cities.

The Site
The 162 ac (66 ha) site was formerly a family farm and more recently a polo grounds. Over the years, as farming was abandoned, many of the fields became reforested. When purchased for its current use, pine and spruce trees with a few clearings covered much of the site, with the exception of two large meadow areas that served as polo fields. One of the site's difficulties was its limited access possibilities. With only about 400 ft (120 m) of frontage on West Street adjacent to access ramps to Interstate 95, Boston's first ring road, it was difficult to create an intersection to serve the needs of the site. A second access road through the adjacent subdivision, Common Street, proved impractical because of neighbors' objections to increased traffic on their residential street.

Located on a meandering elbow of the Charles River, 60 ac (24 ha), over one-third of the site, consists of wetlands, areas in the 100-year flood zone, protected riverfront areas, and other protectable lands. The

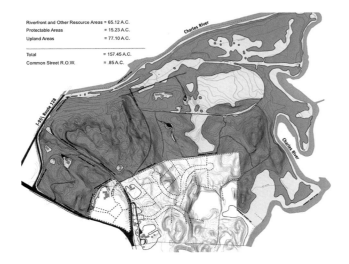

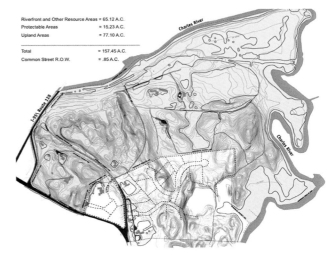

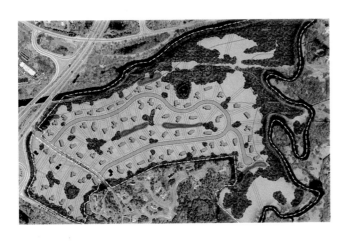

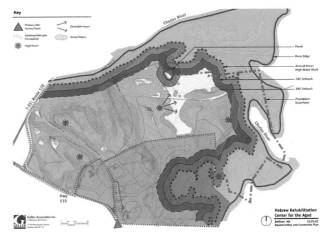

remaining upland areas were zoned for single-family detached housing, which would allow for about 75 individual housing lots, similar to the areas recently developed south of the site. Protests from these neighbors and others in the town over any increased density made the process of rezoning the site onerous.

After a two-year debate, the town allowed clustered higher-density development. In exchange the developers agreed to a number of site restrictions, including setting back any institutional buildings 200 ft (60 m) from the property line, maintaining a vegetated buffer of at least 100 ft (30 m) along the border with adjacent housing, minimizing the amount of impervious paving and runoff from the site, creating a new access point from West Street as far as possible from the interchange, and increasing the amount of on-site green spaces beyond what was first proposed. All of these conditions, along

2.1 (top left) NewBridge on the Charles, predevelopment site indicating vegetated areas.
(Courtesy of Stantec)

2.2 (top right) Topography of the site prior to development.
(Courtesy of Stantec)

2.3 (bottom left) Site plan of what existing regulations permitted.
(Courtesy of Stantec)

2.4 (bottom right) Site analysis mapping wetland areas, steep slopes, views, and current access routes.
(Courtesy of Stantec)

with the commitment to maintain the conservation lands and pay *exactions* and annual taxes to the town, provided a basis for proceeding.

The site has other features that created planning challenges. Surprisingly steep slopes and ledge hidden below the tree canopy needed to be reflected in the layout of roads, but also served as natural divisions between areas of the site. Once trees were felled, several promontories provided views to the distance. And a number of structures on the land were able to be repurposed, as reminders of past histories.

The Program

The largest component of the site is residential-care facilities, where residents can age in place, couples with different service needs remain on one campus together, and ties to children and others in the larger community combat the isolation so often felt by the elderly. The living accommodations include cottages, villa apartments, independent-living apartments, traditional assisted-living apartments, memory support rooms, and a resident health center housing 220 long-term-care residents and 48 subacute patients.

The Rashi School consists of a fully equipped elementary and middle school for 450 students. It includes classrooms, labs, a library, art and music studios, an auditorium, a gymnasium, a cafeteria, and community spaces for prayer and holiday celebrations. Sports fields, an outdoor amphitheater, and two playgrounds are provided near the school.

Since public transit access is distant, approximately 1,000 parking spaces needed to be accommodated on the site. To avoid seas of parking, the decision was made to locate 456 of these in a below-ground parking structure mostly under buildings, and the rest topped by a landscaped courtyard. The cottages have attached garages.

Conservation lands along the Charles River serve as a unique resource for residents and students on the site, but also for the wider community. The planners were determined to make the open space as connected as possible with people in the surrounding neighborhoods.

Table 2.1 | Site program, NewBridge on the Charles site

Use	Units	Gross floor area	
		sq ft	m²
Residential-care community			
Independent-living apartments	182	235,440	21,873
Independent-living villas	24	50,400	4,682
Independent-living cottages	50	389,905	36,223
Assisted-living units	51	62,460	5,803
Memory support units	40	27,367	2,542
Health center and nursing beds	268	246,000	22,854
Total		1,011,572	93,978
Parking	695		
Rashi School	450 students	82,000	7,618
Parking	205		
Playing fields		292,000	27,128
Overall site area		7,056,720	655,591
Net buildable area		4,443,120	412,779
Approximate floor area ratio (based on net buildable area)		0.25	

The Plan

The site plan for NewBridge evolved along with its program and the form of the dominant residential-care community. It made sense to locate the structures with large footprints on the generally flat land on the eastern half of the developable site, and devote the wooded sloping areas on the west half to independent-living apartments, villas, and cottages. Several possible site plans were sketched and debated for the main complex and school, ranging from creating a single linked complex of buildings to clustering the buildings around an enclosed winter garden to hybrid schemes with structures grouped around a series of courtyards. Ultimately, it was decided to create an interlinked complex for the residential-care complex, and to locate the school north of it on its own site, adjacent to open space and playfields which made effective use of the floodplain.

A single parkway access road begins at West Street near the southwest corner of the site and curves gracefully to the center of the site, becoming a loop road that encloses the residential-care complex. A community green reminiscent of the original meadows on the site serves as the centerpiece of the complex, and is surrounded by recreation, dining, and other common facilities. The independent cottage housing is located on its own loop off the parkway, navigating the topography and providing the addresses for 12 housing clusters.

A series of nature trails connect each of the structures to the open space that surrounds the site and to

2.5 (top left) Sketch plan of possible configuration of senior care facilities. (Courtesy of Perkins Eastman)

2.6 (top middle) Sketch of another possible configuration of senior care facilities. (Courtesy of Perkins Eastman)

2.7 (top right) Alternative sketch plan of senior facilities. (Courtesy of Perkins Eastman)

2.8 (bottom) Final site plan. (Courtesy of Stantec/ Perkins Eastman/Chan Krieger)

the nature trail system along the Charles River which abuts adjacent town- and state-owned conservation lands. There are also connections to streets in the bordering neighborhoods. Common Street is retained as a pedestrian pathway and emergency access route to the site, but closed to general traffic.

Green Infrastructure

The site's commitment to sustainability begins with green infrastructure and extends to every aspect of the development. Roadway widths were minimized as much as possible, which required the town to adopt new standards. Stormwater runoff from roadways and parking areas is retained on the site, filtered through vegetated swales into above-ground detention areas, or infiltrated through large subsurface infiltration basins. Roof runoff is collected in a separate system and stored

2.9 (top left) Site during construction, showing installation of underground detention areas.
(Courtesy of Stantec)

2.10 (top right) Geothermal wells being drilled adjacent to senior care facilities.
(Courtesy of Stantec)

2.11 (bottom left) Detention tanks.
(Courtesy of Stantec)

2.12 (bottom right) Vegetated swale.
(Gary Hack)

in 170,000-gallon underground cisterns, where it is used for irrigation of the landscape. Wherever possible, permeable paving is employed. Over 400 geothermal heat transfer wells have been installed to assist in the heating and cooling of building spaces, resulting in an overall reduction of fuel use of 50% and a 34% reduction of CO_2 emissions—amounting to 9,000 fewer tons of greenhouse gases each year.

While much of the forest has been retained, new landscaping has been designed to reinforce the bands of vegetation and domesticate the landscape nearest the buildings. Native plant materials are widely used to minimize maintenance and enhance the existing native landscape. Courtyards throughout the site are designed to encourage socialization among residents and their visitors. Programming brings students into contact with the elderly, and outsiders who use the site for recreation and events are welcomed into the heart of the complex.

Planning Team

Planners
Perkins Eastman
Chan Krieger Associates (now NBBJ)
Geller Associates (now Stantec)

Architects
NewBridge Center: Perkins Eastman
Cottages: Chan Krieger Associates (now NBBJ)
Rashi School: HMFH Architects

Site engineering, entitlements, and landscape architecture
Stantec

2.13 Aerial view of completed senior care complex.
(Courtesy of Perkins Eastman)

2.14 Aerial view of Rashi School, senior care complex, and cottages.
(Courtesy of Perkins Eastman)

2.15 Pathways linking each of the areas of the site.
(Gary Hack)

2.16 Landscaped courtyard in life care complex.
(Gary Hack)

2.17 NewBridge on the Charles, cottage area.
(Gary Hack)

2.18 Rashi School with freshly mowed meadow.
(Gary Hack)

2.19 Playfields.
(Gary Hack)

TAIPINGQIAO
Shanghai

The Tapingqiao development project, in the former French Concession of Shanghai, demonstrates that selective preservation of historic structures and the creation of amenities open to all can provide a unique identity for an area while enhancing its financial prospects. Combining old and new, mixing business, commercial, and residential uses, and moderating high-density development through generous open spaces, the area has become a livable and much-loved district in the new Shanghai. It is a model for creative urbanism.

The project was developed by Hong Kong-based Shui On Land Ltd., a publicly listed company with a long record of major land development projects in China. It is headquartered in Shanghai and served as master developer for Taipingqiao.

The Site
In 1997, the 52 ha (129 ac) Taipingqiao site consisted of 23 city blocks, occupied by the rundown remnants of *shikumen* ("stone gate") houses from the 1920s. They were typically two or three stories, many on narrow midblock alleyways. Over the years they had been subdivided and were in very poor condition.

The developer, working closely with the municipal government and its urban designers and architects, planned the area as a comprehensive redevelopment for both private and public uses. The master plan for Taipingqiao serves as the controlling document, and is updated periodically to reflect current market conditions.

The Program
The development, on leased land, was approved for 1.5 million m² (16.1 million sq ft) of commercial and residential uses in 1997, although the entitlement was subsequently reduced to 1.25 million m² (13.5 million sq ft). The developer sought to create a mixed-use development that would be attractive to international businesses, shopping, and entertainment uses, catering to local and expat residents who were looking for an attractive urban environment.

2.20 Historical view of Taipingqiao area, Shanghai.

总平面图

2.21 Master plan for Taipingqiao redevelopment project. (Courtesy of Shui On Development)

Table 2.2 | Program, Taipingqiao redevelopment project, Shanghai

Use	Units	Gross floor area	
		m² (000)	sq ft (000)
Xintiandi historic area			
Retail, food, and beverages		47,970	516,340
Offices		4,710	50,700
Parks		3.45 ha	8.5 ac
North development sites			
Hotels		62,000	630,540
Offices		254,000	2,733,040
Retail, food, and beverages		58,000	624,080
South development sites			
Retail, food, and beverages		13,607	146,411
Residential	904	534,000	5,745,840
Future development sites (to be determined)			
Retail, food, and beverages			
Offices			
Residential			
Hotels			
Public and institutional			
Overall project entitlement		1,500,000	16,100,000
Site area		520,000	5,597,000
Floor area ratio		2.88	

Prior residents of the area were relocated in new housing in other parts of the city, or received cash compensation.

The Plan

The plan seeks to integrate a wide range of uses in a traditional urban environment of walkable streets and blocks. The prevailing grid street pattern was largely kept intact. A few blocks were modified to provide larger parcels for mixed-use projects with shops at their base, topped by hotels, offices, and housing. The grid was also modified to create a large public park surrounding a lake, which has become the center-piece of the site, with underground parking below a portion of the landscaped area. While several streets were widened in line with the city's arterial street plan, internal streets were kept as narrow as possible—typically 12 m (40 ft) to 20 m (70 ft)—to encourage walking and slow vehicular speeds. Streets were lined with syca-more (London plane) trees to continue the character of the French Concession area.

Taipingqiao has two elements that create the identity for the area: the Xintiandi ("New Heaven and Earth") restoration project, and the new Taipingqiao park at the center of the development. At great cost, the developer restored and in many cases reconstructed two blocks of the historic fabric, adding new struc-tures where old buildings were not salvageable. The restored space, labeled Xintiandi, was leased generally to small tenants that include boutiques, restaurants, bars, offices, a boutique hotel, and cinema. A museum commemorating the location of the first meeting of the Communist Party of China is adjacent to these facili-ties. Within the perimeter streets the area is restricted to pedestrians, a place to stroll, enjoy an outdoor meal or drink, and watch the passersby. This project established the character of the area and brought both Shanghai residents and visitors to the area through-out the day and evening. On a typical weekday, 60,000 people come to Xintiandi, with 75,000 on weekend days. Peak crowds may be found there at 10 pm, when revel-ers from downtown office and retail areas flock there for nightlife activities.

Two hotels and a shopping complex (Hubindao) have been built on the northernmost blocks, and are linked by overhead bridges. The intention is to connect

2.22 Aerial view, Xintiandi, office and residential areas.
(Courtesy of Shui On Development)

2.23 Local street in Taipingqiao area.
(Gary Hack)

2.24 Pedestrian street in Xintiandi.
(Courtesy of Shui On Development)

2.25 Xintiandi at night.
(Courtesy of Shui On Development)

2.26 Museum of the First Meeting of the Communist Party of China, Xintiandi.
(Gary Hack)

all of the uses in this area with aerial or underground links, a system that extends to the city's prime retail street along Huaihai Road. Parcels north of the park (Corporate Avenue) are designed for mixed-use projects, with offices above retail and restaurant uses. All of the commercial projects strictly hold the street line, although sidewalks are widened in the densest areas, providing active street frontages with uses that range from international-brand shops to luxury automobile showrooms.

At the southwest corner of the site, a mixed-use project connects directly into the Metro line. Two stories above ground and two below form the plinth of the site, with mid-rise and high-rise housing above. Xintiandi Style, as the retail area is called, also has shops accessible from the street, integrating it with the larger environment. An upper-level bridge connects the development to the historic blocks. And on the east frontage of the block, residential apartments have a direct street access.

As is common practice in most Asian cities, the Lakeville residential blocks, south of the park, feature gated automobile access to the internal green courtyards, where amenities serving the residents are located. Parking, throughout the site, is located below grade. A mixture of mid- and high-rise housing provides alternatives, and a number of the structures facing the park are kept deliberately low so that taller structures behind them can share the fine views of the Taipingqiao Park. Where possible, the perimeter of the residential blocks has been lined with retail uses facing the street, reinforcing the continuity of the public realm.

Future development of the Xintiandi site will complete the blocks east of the park and south of Xizhong Road. Originally this was to have been the site of a tall office structure marking the end of the open space, but to satisfy the vigorous opposition the plan has been modified to retain and restore structures lining the historic Dongtai Road antiques market, hopefully breathing life into this long-declining area. It will be surrounded by smaller office, recreation, and hotel structures. A large new middle school will occupy a full block along Fuxing Road, along with other residential and institutional uses.

The Taipingqiao master-planned community is a LEED-ND stage 2 Gold-certified development. Xintiandi has in a short time become a destination in a sea of

2.27 Hotel and shopping area, Taipingqiao.
(Gary Hack)

2.28 Aerial view, Taipingqiao Park, Xintiandi, and Corporate Avenue offices.
(Courtesy of Shui On Development)

2.29 Corporate Avenue at night, viewed from park.
(Courtesy of Shui On Development)

2.30 Xintiandi Style, a four-level retail complex connected to
subway and topped by apartments.
(Gary Hack)

2.31 Street-oriented shops at Xintiandi Style.
(Gary Hack)

2.32 Lakeville residential area, viewed from Taipingqiao Park.
(Courtesy of Shui On Development)

2.33 Interior courtyard of Lakeville residential complex.
(Gary Hack)

new and old developments, and the larger development is a great success in financial as well as human terms. It has been widely emulated across China and beyond in other projects that combine historic preservation with new development.

Planning Team

Planners
Skidmore, Owings and Merrill
Shanghai Urban Planning and Design Research Institute

Architects
Historic quarter:
Wood + Zapata
Tongji Urban Planning and Design Institute
Nikken Sekkei International, Ltd
Hotels:
Kohn Pedersen Fox Associates
Offices:
Kohn Pedersen Fox Associates
P & T Architects
Housing:
P & T Architects
Nikken Sekkei International, Ltd
Wood + Zapata
Park:
Peter Walker and Partners
Shanghai Landscape Design Institute

BATTERY PARK CITY
New York

Battery Park City is one of the finest examples of a site created for dense, mixed-use development by multiple developers. Planned and constructed over a 30-year period, it exemplifies the street-oriented form of traditional residential and commercial development in New York, while providing a constantly changing continuous waterfront promenade, a rich array of parks for all ages, and cultural institutions for residents and visitors. It is a living neighborhood, with schools and playfields and shopping for everyday needs. The development of every parcel was carefully shaped through design guidelines and review that covered building form, materials, and key aspects of how buildings address the street and each other.

The Battery Park City Authority (BPCA), a state entity, was created to carry out the development. It has the power to develop infrastructure and parks, paying for them through bonds it issues, lease sites to developers, and maintain the public spaces on the site. The entire site is developed through long-term land leases, since state laws do not allow sale of lands in the intertidal zone.

The Site

The landfill that became the 92 ac (37 ha) Battery Park City site began as a location to dispose of earth and rock excavated for the World Trade Center, constructed during 1966–1975 directly across West Street.

Much of the fill proved problematic and was later removed, and the balance of the site was filled using spoils, mainly sand, from harbor dredging. A relieving platform was constructed to secure the edges of the reclaimed land, and it provided the basis for a 70 ft (22 m) esplanade that extends more than 1.5 miles (2.4 km) along the waterfront.

Anticipating coastal flooding, the developable portions of the site were elevated from 9 to 15 ft (2.7–4.6 m) above mean high tide, which has stood the test of recent hurricanes. During Hurricane Sandy in 2012, Battery Park City was the only area in Lower Manhattan that was not flooded.

2.34 Battery Park City landfill site, New York City. (Courtesy of Battery Park City Authority)

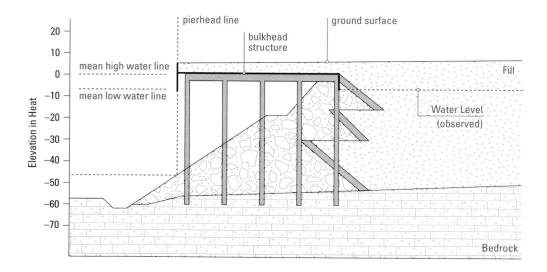

2.35 Section through relieving platform, supporting waterfront esplanade. (Adam Tecza)

2.36 Esplanade, Battery Park City. (Gary Hack)

The Program

The site was designed to accommodate a roughly equal mix of office space and housing. The intent was to create large sites for modern offices, unconstrained by the small blocks of Lower Manhattan. There was very little housing near Battery Park City when the site was planned, and it needed to achieve a critical mass capable of supporting schools, shopping, and local services. Over the years, as more residents have migrated to the adjacent Tribeca area, there has been pressure to create parks and open spaces and provide schools for the larger area. Ultimately roughly 10.7 million sq ft (990,000 m²) of office space and over 8,600 housing units have been constructed, along with shopping, two hotels, and a range of cultural facilities.

The Plan

There were two false starts before the plan for the site was arrived at. A proposal to construct a connected megastructure failed because it was too costly to be financed or borne by the site's rent-paying uses. A second plan in 1969 sited a large office area at the southern end of the site and a series of eight housing pods, each with about 1,000 units. After completion of the first residential complex, this plan failed during a serious economic recession in the 1970s. In 1979, a new plan was prepared, adopting an approach more akin to normal city building.

Table 2.3 | Development program, as built, Battery Park City

Use	Units	Sq ft	m²
Built area			
Offices and related retail (6)		10,658,611	990,217
Hotels (2)	761 rooms	950,000	88,257
Cultural facilities (4)*		200,000	18,580
Residential (30)	8,615 units	10,125,764	940,714
Schools (4)*	4,568 students	580,000	53,883
Maintenance facilities*		40,000	3,716
Total		22,554,375	2,095,369
Site area		**ac**	**ha**
Development sites		34	13.7
Streets		22	8.9
Parks and open space		36	14.6
Total		92	37.2
Gross floor area ratio		5.6	
Net development floor area ratio		15.2	
Resident population (2010)	13,386		

* Approximate areas.

2.37 First proposal for Battery Park City, known as the megastructure plan.
(Conklin and Rosant et al.)

2.38 1969 plan for Battery Park City with pods for development, only one of which was built.
(Drawing by Alexander Cooper Associates)

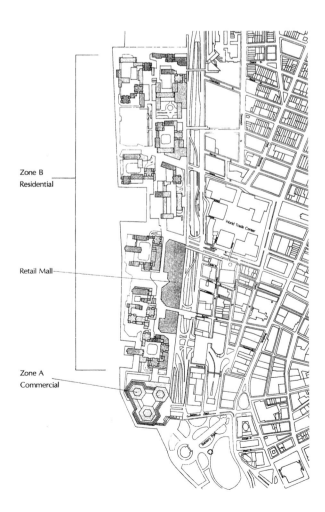

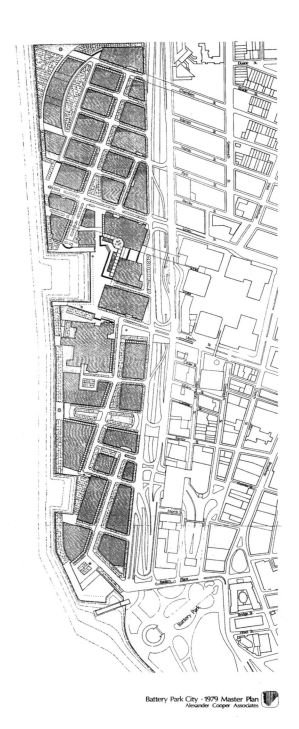

Battery Park City · 1979 Master Plan
Alexander Cooper Associates

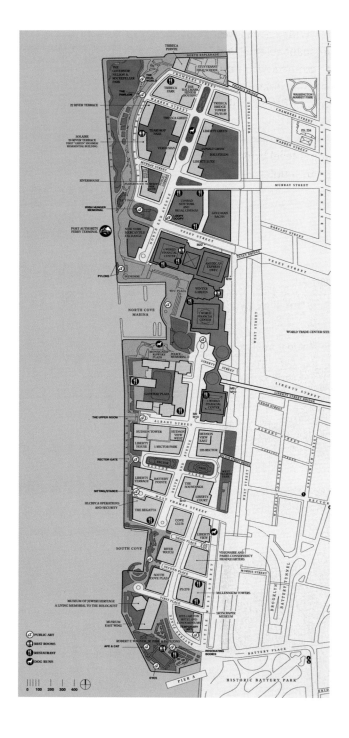

2.39 1979 plan for Battery Park City, incorporating blocks and streets.
(Alexander Cooper Associates)

2.40 Final Battery Park City plan, as built.
(Courtesy of Battery Park City Authority)

Office areas were moved to the center of the site, adjacent to the World Trade Center, where they could be connected via upper-level bridges. In this area, now called Brookfield Place, the main lobbies for offices and much of the retail space are at the second level, since elevator overrides could not be located below ground. With the reconstruction of the World Trade Center, the upper-level bridges to it have been replaced with underground links, and the commercial areas of the complex have been reconfigured to place more emphasis on the ground level.

The balance of the site was planned with small blocks, typically 200 × 300 ft (60 × 90 m) or smaller, that could support multiple developers each offering their own projects. Ultimately 30 sites were created for housing and five for offices. Local shopping was integrated into the lower levels of housing and commercial buildings, and the three elementary schools

2.41 Panoramic view of World Financial Center (now Brookfield Place) and plaza.
(Gary Hack)

2.42 South Cove Park, which anchors the South residential area.
(Gary Hack)

2.43 Rockefeller Park, which fronts the North residential area.
(Gary Hack)

are located in mixed-use residential buildings. A large site on the northern edge of the neighborhood became the new location for Stuyvesant High, New York's most prestigious public high school. The street network was connected to the city grid in eight locations. Over one-third of the site is dedicated to parks and open spaces, and each was designed for a unique set of uses, responding to the needs of adjacent residents and workers.

Open spaces on the site are designed for both active and passive use, and ensure that as many buildings as possible look out on public spaces. Hard-surface areas predominate in the intensively used central commercial area and include the year-round Winter Garden, which is used for events and performances. The South Park emphasizes the connection to the water's edge, while Rockefeller Park at the north end layers active areas for all ages on terraces overlooking a large informal green. Also in the North neighborhood, Teardrop Park is a quiet respite, just a few yards from the playing fields adjacent to West Street. The parks and open areas are generously endowed with specially commissioned in situ art.

Over the 30-year development period, the plan has been refined to capitalize on new opportunities to integrate cultural uses, meet additional office demand and housing needs, and respond to residents' pressures for more active recreation space. Nonetheless the basic principles and the structure of the plan have remained remarkably consistent.

Assuring Quality

The World Financial Center, which constitutes the centerpiece of the site, was designed through a developer-designer competition, then carefully tailored to the site through collaboration between the BPCA and the developer. A condition of any lease to developers is that they comply with parcel-specific design guidelines prepared by BPCA. The guidelines are largely based on patterns found in other New York neighborhoods, particularly the Upper West Side. Emulating traditional patterns, it is argued, will allow the new neighborhoods to seem like they have always been part of the city.

Every project goes through a rigorous design review process, and final leases are not signed until the plans are judged satisfactory. BPCA has maintained a preference for having developers use different

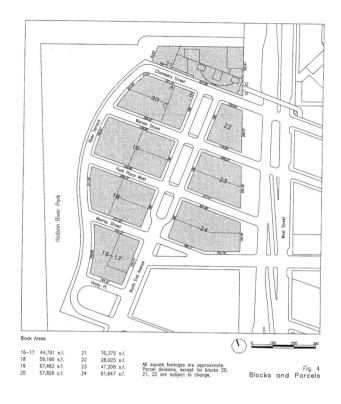

Block Areas

16–17	44,791 s.f.	21	70,375 s.f.
18	59,160 s.f.	22	28,025 s.f.
19	67,483 s.f.	23	47,206 s.f.
20	57,826 s.f.	24	61,647 s.f.

All square footages are approximate. Parcel divisions, except for blocks 20, 21, 22 are subject to change.

Fig. 4
Blocks and Parcels

2.44 North residential neighborhood blocks and parcels. (Ralph Lerner Associates)

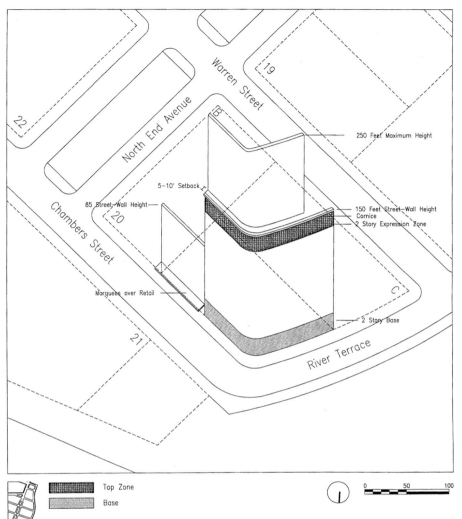

250 Feet Maximum Height

5-10' Setback

85 Street-Wall Height

150 Feet Street-Wall Height

Cornice

2 Story Expression Zone

Marquee over Retail

2 Story Base

Warren Street

North End Avenue

Chambers Street

River Terrace

19

22

18

20

21

C

Top Zone

Base

0   50   100

Fig. 28
Bulk Summary: Parcel 20A

2.45 Guidelines for Parcel 20A, showing essential massing and design features.
(Ralph Lerner Associates)

2.46 Aerial view of North neighborhood and Rockefeller Park.
(Courtesy of Battery Park City Authority)

2.47 South End Avenue, with residential blocks and ground-level commercial uses.
(Gary Hack)

2.48 North End Avenue, with linear park in median. (Gary Hack)

Planning Team

Planners
Alexander Cooper Associates
(subsequently Cooper, Eckstut Associates)
Ehrenkranz Group & Eckstut
(subsequently Ehrenkranz Eckstut and Kuhn)
Vollmer Associates
Zion and Breen Associates
Hanna/Olin
(subsequently Olin Partnership)
Alexander Gorlin, Architect
Ralph Lerner Architect
Machado and Silvetti Associates, Inc.
Hanrahan and Meyers, Architects
Carr, Lynch, Hack and Sandell

Public space design
Hanna/Olin (Esplanade)
Innocenti and Webel (Rector Park)
Child Associates with Mary Miss and Stan Eckstut (South Cove)
Carr, Lynch, Hack and Sandell with Oehme van Sweden
(Rockefeller Park)
Olin Partnership (Robert F. Wagner Park)
Michael Van Valkenburgh Associates (Teardrop Park)
M. Paul Friedberg and Balmori Associates (Winter Garden area)

Building design
Cesar Pelli and Associates
(World Financial Center, now Brookfield Place)
Pei Cobb Fried Associates (Goldman Sachs headquarters)
Over 25 architectural firms designed individual residential and
commercial buildings

architects on adjacent buildings to encourage a variety of expression, within its guidelines. BPCA oversees the design and directly constructs parks and public spaces. Its approach is to complete the public realm in an area before private development begins, so that developers are able to sell or lease their projects in a finished environment. As with the buildings, BPCA has deliberately sought a wide range of designers for its public spaces. And with residents moving to Battery Park City, they have been engaged in advising and reviewing successive plans for public spaces, sparking a spirited debate about priorities and facilities.

Part 2 | Understanding Sites

Site planning begins with a thorough understanding of the site. There is no substitute for walking a site at the start, gaining an appreciation for its orientation to the sun, land forms, vegetation, views, drainage patterns, and relationships to its surroundings. What portions of the site are buildable, and which should be preserved? Are there natural form-givers—steep slopes that separate one part from another, hedgerows that make for natural divisions, existing buildings that need to be respected? What are the logical connections to the roads and transportation serving the site? Notes will be jotted on a base map, ideas will be triggered about how land and buildings can be mated and how spaces and roads can be organized. These first impressions will help drive the process. While the designer will investigate every aspect of the site in much more detail, the initial visit will help focus on the areas and aspects that need greatest attention. An analysis that is informed by possibilities is far more effective than evenhanded coverage of a site.

The chapters that follow focus on geomorphology, natural systems, human processes, property, and regulations, all of which will need to be taken into account in coming to terms with the site. In practice they are not so neatly divided, since human processes shape the form of the land over time as they do the natural context, and property rights will need to reflect the natural conditions of a site. Nonetheless, the intellectual and research disciplines that lie behind each are sufficiently discrete to be understood in their own right. Following these topics is a discussion of how to make sense of the array of information that is accumulated through site analyses, so that it informs site planning.

3 | Site Form

Much can be learned by simply walking a site, sensing the natural and human forces that are constantly shaping it. But a true understanding of the site requires us to peel back the layers and look below the surface at a world that has been formed over millions of years.

We think of all that lies below ground as stable—except in earthquake zones, of course—but even the rocks that seem so impermeable are constantly being degraded into smaller particles. Four aspects of the site's *geomorphology* play an important role in how it is planned and developed: the *surficial geology*, *soils*, *groundwater*, and *surface form*. As we shall see, these are closely related, and are not easily separated from natural and human systems at work on a site, covered

in the next two chapters. However, when planning a site, the first step is usually to develop an understanding of what lies below the ground.

Surficial Geology

Somewhere beneath a site there is *bedrock*, native consolidated rock created by the earth's cooling and the movement of the tectonic plates. Its depth, stability, and the deposits that lie above it will determine the feasibility and cost of providing foundations for structures on the site, and will affect the layout of buildings and open areas. Ledges of bedrock may be a meter or less below the surface on rocky shorelines or in mountain environments. Some cities such as New York are blessed with bedrock near the surface, making sites ideal for tall buildings, although if too close to the surface costly blasting may be required to accommodate spaces below ground. In other places, such as today's great agricultural basins that were once submerged by the waters from melting glaciers, a solid base may be hundreds of meters below ground, necessitating a careful analysis of the strata of surficial materials and their capability of supporting structures. In areas with unstable strata or materials with poor bearing capacity, it may be very costly to create foundations, limiting the scale of development—or forcing it ever higher, as in Hong Kong where tall thin buildings economize on the number of deep piles required.

The surficial geology of a site will affect many things beyond the adequacy of foundation support. Rock outcroppings will limit where roads may be economically constructed. Groundwater will be channeled

3.1 Site for ecological city development, Russia. (Carr Lynch Hack and Sandell)

**Sources of
Geologic Data**

In the US, the United States Geological Survey (USGS) provides maps and databases in paper form that may be useful. See http://ngmdb.usgs.gov/ngmdb/ngmdb_home.html.

For a general explanation of geologic maps and coding, see http://www2.nature.nps.gov /geology/usgsnps/gmap/gmap1.html.

For many US states, information is also available in GIS form. See, for example, http://pubs .usgs.gov/of/2005/1325/. Symbols and color coding for maps may be found at http://pubs.usgs .gov/of/2005/1314/.

Many US states have supplemented national data with separately compiled materials. For example see California, www.conservation.ca.gov/cgs/information/geologic_mapping/Pages /index.aspx, or the Great Lakes Geologic Mapping Coalition, http://igs.indiana.edu/GreatLakes Geology, or Maine's site on bedrock geology, http://www.maine.gov/doc/nrimc/mgs/explore /bedrock/index.htm.

Many countries have parallel programs of compiling geologic maps, although public availability varies widely. Exemplary data sources include:

Canada, http://atlas.nrcan.gc.ca/site/english/maps/environment/geology
Australia, http://www.ga.gov.au/cedda/maps/1084
Sweden, http://www.sgu.se/sgu/eng/geologi/index.html
Japan, http://gsj.jp/Map/index_e.html.

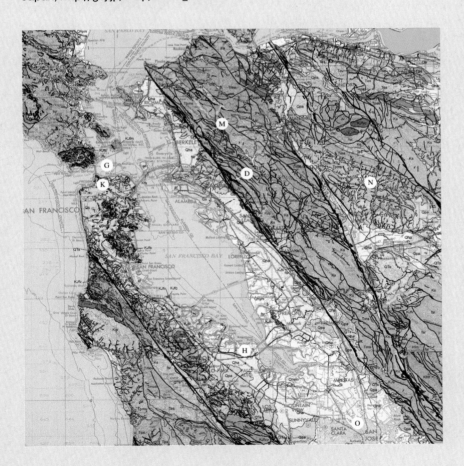

3.2 Geological survey map.
(USGS)

by the bedrock profile and layers of unconsolidated rock above it, affecting where wells might best be located. Shallow depths of bedrock—and high water tables—will limit the potential for disposal of septic wastes. And the presence of rock near the surface will greatly influence where ponds or other watercourses may be created.

There are many sources of information on the surficial geology of a site. At the macro scale, national or state governments have compiled and make available maps of geologic data in either paper or digital form, or both. For large sites, these will provide a useful first approximation of the areas where building is easiest and other portions where it should be avoided. For a small site, published sources of information may not be adequate or dependable, and *test borings* will be necessary. If the site is to be lightly developed, a sample of borings where buildings are likely to be sited will be adequate. Sites that will be intensively used may require a regular grid of test locations, providing the data to map subsurface conditions. If adjacent sites have been recently developed, it is always useful to consult with engineers who have tested or designed foundations on these sites before deciding on how much additional sampling is necessary.

Knowledge about the surficial geology of a site is usually captured in the form of a profile identifying the material at each depth below the surface. Information from test borings also will identify the types of soil that overlay the solid base, and begin to paint a picture of issues that must be faced in planning the site.

Soils

The materials we call soil are a mixture of mineral matter, organic matter, and water, separated by air. Mineral matter is the result of millennia of decay or erosion of the rock that once covered the earth, a process that involves water, wind, oxidation, bacterial and animal organisms, movements of the earth, glaciation, and other forces. Organic matter is constantly being deposited at the surface and penetrates the layers of soil below as the roots of plants reach down to retrieve water; they eventually die, decay and are added to the mineral material. Hence, shallow soils are different from deep soils, and the layers, or *horizons,* will be revealed in a soil boring.

Soils are typically made up of five or six horizons. On some sites, these may be distributed over a depth of a hundred meters or more, while in others with bedrock near the surface they may be compressed into a meter or less. Sites that have been used for agriculture may have distinct horizons, except where pumped irrigation or the construction of levies for *sheet irrigation* (rice growing, for example) has altered the groundwater and profile of the soil. In urban areas, soil borings frequently encounter a more exotic mixture of soil materials that may include remnants of previous construction, paving materials, soils transported to the site to raise its elevation and alter surface drainage, garbage or ash used for landfill, and contaminated soils. Conducting archival research on the prior uses of the site can be a useful exercise in identifying what may be encountered.

As a matter of convention, we typically divide the mineral matter of soils into three basic types: *sand*, *silt*, and *clay*. They are distinguished by their particle size, with sand particles typically more than ten times larger than those of silt and a hundred times larger than those of clay. Sand particles are large enough to allow water to move freely between them, so they promote drainage. Clay particles, at the opposite extreme, are so small that they trap water between them, becoming *quick* when saturated. They are stiff and cohesive when dry, but when water is added clay soils will slip, swell, and soften, capturing the water. Silt particles are stable when dry or damp, but will compress under a load and become unstable when wet.

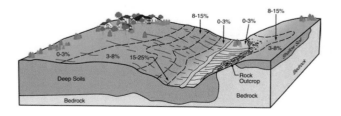

3.3 Profile of soils and underlying geology.
(USDA Natural Resources Conservation Service)

Soil Horizons

O horizons are formed by the accumulation of fresh and decayed plant materials such as leaves, needles, branches or trunks, crop roots and stems, grasses, and animal materials. In areas that have hosted plant colonies for long periods, this horizon may be referred to as *humus*, particularly in forested or wet areas. It is usually dark in color.

A horizons are immediately below the humus and are made up of mostly mineral material, with some organic matter. Much of the iron, clay, and aluminum has been removed by plants in this horizon, while organic matter has been added. The soil is usually dark in color, and is commonly referred to as *topsoil*.

E horizons, or *eluvial* soils, commonly appear in forested areas, where plant life has removed much of the clay, iron, organic matter, and other minerals. They are white or lighter in color than horizons above them.

B horizons are typically referred to as *subsoil*. Located below A or E horizons, these soils typically have an accumulation of clay, iron, aluminum, and other compounds. This horizon is generally lighter in color than the soils above it.

C horizons or the *substratum* are composed of partially weathered or *disintegrated parent material* from the rock below, or transported there by glaciation, underground water flows, or other processes. It may include boulders, or unconsolidated rock materials, and evidence of organic processes will be slight.

R horizons refer to the *bedrock*, often the *parent material* for soils in this location.

Source: Scheyer and Hipple (2005).

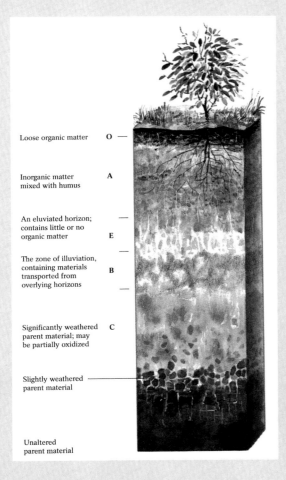

Loose organic matter — O

Inorganic matter mixed with humus — A

An eluviated horizon; contains little or no organic matter — E

The zone of illuviation, containing materials transported from overlying horizons — B

Significantly weathered parent material; may be partially oxidized — C

Slightly weathered parent material

Unaltered parent material

3.4 Soil horizons. (Portland Community College)

Sidebar 3.3

Soil Types

Classified by Grain Size

Type	Grain Size (diameter)	Description
Gravel	>2 mm	Course particles with no cohesion
Sand	0.05 to 2 mm	Finest grains visible to eye, gritty feel
Silt	0.002 to 0.05 mm	Grains invisible but can be felt, smooth not gritty
Clay	<0.002 mm	Smooth and floury or in stiff lumps when dry, plastic and sticky when wet

Common Classes of Soils

Type	Composition	Description
Clean gravel	Gravel with <5% silt or clay	May be classified as well-graded or poorly graded depending upon compaction
Silty and clayey gravels	Mostly gravel with >10% silt or clay	
Clean sands	Sand with <5–10% silt or clay	May be well or poorly graded
Silty and clayey sands	Mostly sand with >10–12% silt or clay	
Nonplastic silts	Inorganic silts or very fine sands	Liquid limit <50 (i.e., flows like liquid with <50% water)
Plastic silts	Inorganic silts	Liquid limit >50
Organic silts	Silts with substantial organic matter	Liquid limit <50
Nonplastic clays	Inorganic clays	Liquid limit <50
Plastic and organic clays	Inorganic clay or silt or clay with organic matter	Liquid limit >50
Loam	40–50% silt, 5–15% clay, 50–70% sand	Common use for landscape soil and final grading
Peat and muck	Predominantly organic matter	If plant remains are visible (peat) or soil is saturated

3.5 Relative sizes of soil particles. (Adam Tecza/USDA)

3.6 Types of soils.

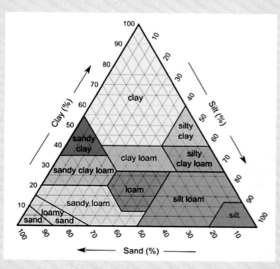

Most soil consists of a mixture of the three basic types of mineral matter with organic matter and water added. Determining the precise mixture will require laboratory analysis techniques, although a rough guess of the predominant content can be made in the field. *Gravel* (a special class of sand) is self-evident if the material is granular and typical particles are larger than 2 mm (⁵⁄₆₄ in) in size. If the particles are smaller but still visible to the naked eye, sand is the predominant material. Silt and clay can be distinguished because the latter can be formed into a ball or horizontal thread when wet, while the former cannot. The presence of large amounts of organic matter will confound the rules of thumb and require further analysis.

A variety of names have been devised to describe specific mixtures of soil, and a soil textural triangle helps us understand the distinctions. Near the intersection of the three basic materials is *loam*, the preferred soil for surface plant materials, particularly if it is blessed with a significant organic content. Sandy soils are highly desirable for foundations, since they allow water to drain through their pores, even when compacted. Plastic and organic silts, and particularly clays, create difficult conditions for foundations, since they will shrink and swell with changes in their moisture content. Water may penetrate these soils from rainfall or seasonal snowmelts, and may be extracted by trees and vegetation that lower the water table. A single fast-growing tree may draw down the water table below it by several cm in a year. The result of changes in water content of clayey soils can be foundations that crack or tilt and roadways that break up. Deep winter frost penetration in silty or clayey soils, or frequent freeze-thaw cycles in spring and fall, are a special problem, causing soils to swell and shrink, producing frost heaves on roads and cracked foundations. Plastic clays are particularly hazardous on hillsides, where slippage from added moisture can contribute to landslides.

The differing size of soil particles, and their characteristics when wet, affect the ability to hold a slope. We refer to the natural angle of the sloping walls of a soil type as its *angle of repose*. Sand has the least friction and will naturally settle to an angle of about 33°. Loam, if well drained, will repose at 35–45°, even steeper if the hillside is secured by forests or vegetation. Loose clay, if saturated with water, will slide until it settles to only 15–25°, but if compacted and well drained it will hold a much steeper slope. Bedrock, as we know from unique natural formations of Monument Valley, Arizona and Guilin, China, can maintain a completely vertical profile.

Data on soil types is readily available in many countries from national and state government sources in the form of paper maps and their digital counterparts. There is a long tradition of mapping soils for agricultural purposes, employing a classification scheme that allows predictions to be made about the productivity of the soil. Since soils vary both vertically and horizontally on a site, standard classification systems tend to incorporate the geographic region where they originate, then the predominant type of soil at or near the surface, then usually the slope of the zone. As an example, one of the soil types identified on the site shown in figure 3.9 mapped by the USDA is "Chester silt loam, 3–8% slopes, abbreviated CeB, which covers approximately 18% of the area of interest." The accompanying lexicon of soil types indicates that it is well

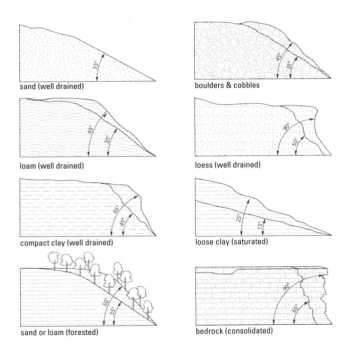

Figure 3.7
Angles of repose for various soil types.
(Adam Tecza)

Sources of Soil Data

The most common source of soil data is agencies concerned with agriculture.

For the US, the Natural Resources Conservation Service (NRCS) of the US Department of Agriculture (USDA) makes available data on soils in several formats:

The Web Soil Survey (WSS) provides data for small areas for planners and the public in a prepackaged stand-alone form, not requiring GIS software. See http://websoilsurvey.nrcs .usda.gov/app. Customized soils reports are created by the website, including maps and data on each of the soil types identified.

The Soil Data Viewer (SDV) provides data for larger areas for planners and the public, but requires GIS software and some experience with its use. Data can be downloaded and colors modified to suit the planner's preferences. See http://soildatamart.nrcs.usda.gov. Soil Data Viewer software is available at http://soildataviewer.nrcs.usda.gov.

Similar surveys are available for many countries in the world. The International Soil Reference and Information Center (ISRIC) website includes a world soil database and information on international standards for soil classification. See http://www.isric.org.html.

For Canada, see http://sis.agr.gc.ca/cansis/nsdb/index.html.

For Australia, see http://www.asris.csiro.au/index_other.html.

For the UK, see http://www.landis.org.uk.

Data on urban soils is more difficult to come by, since urban development and spoils frequently modify the predevelopment soils of the area. The International Committee for Anthropogenic Soils (ICOMANTH) has proposed soil classification systems, and the international group Soils of Urban, Industrial, Traffic, Mining and Military Areas (SUITMA) has made progress in knowledge and classification systems. Some individual cities have conducted soils surveys and make them available. An example is New York City's *Reconnaissance Soil Survey*, http://www.nycswcd.net/soil_survey.cfm.

3.8 USDA Soil Data website.
(USDA Soil Conservation Service)

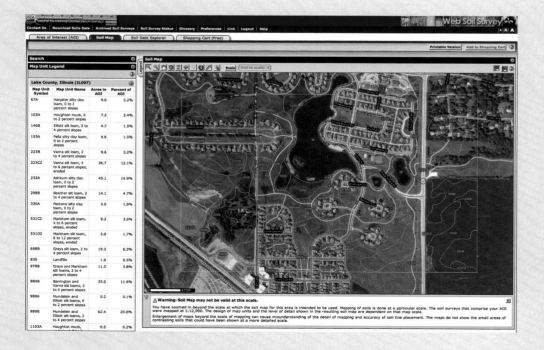

3.9 Soil map, Philadelphia site. (USDA Soil Conservation Service)

Table 3.1 | Distribution of soil types for the site in Philadelphia. (USDA Soil Conservation Service)

Map unit symbol	Map unit name	Acres in area of interest	Percent of area of interest
CeB	Chester silt loam, 3–8% slopes	17.1	9.9
Ha	Hatboro silt loam	0.5	0.3
MaB	Manor loam, 3–8% slopes	11.9	6.9
MaC	Manor loam, 8–15% slopes	4.9	2.8
MbD	Manor extremely stony loam, 8–25% slopes	52.6	30.3
McE	Manor and Chester extremely stony loams, 25–50% slopes	42.2	24.4
UdB	Urban land-Chester complex, 0–8% slopes	17.9	10.3
UdC	Urban land-Chester complex, 8–15% slopes	17.2	9.9
UrA	Urbana silt loam, 0–3% slopes	4.9	2.8
W	Water	4.2	2.4
Total		173.5	100.0

Table 3.2 | Soil bearing capacity, New York (New York City Building Code)

Class of materials	Allowable foundation pressure	
	Tonnes/m²	Tons/sq ft
Bedrock, hard and medium (gneiss, schist, marble)	475–710	40–60
Bedrock, intermediate and soft (shale, sandstone)	95–235	8–20
Sandy gravel and gravel, well compacted (GW, GP)	70–120	6–10
Granular soils, gravelly or sandy (GC, GM, SW, SP, SC)	35–70	3–6
Clays (SC, CL, CH)	25–60	2–5
Silts and silty soils (ML, MH)	20–35	1.5–3

Source: New York City Building Code, table 1804.1
Notes: GW = well-graded gravel, GP = poorly graded gravel, GC = gravelly clay, GM = gravelly silt, SW = well-graded sand, SP = poorly graded sand, SC = clayey sand, CL = lean clay, CH = fat clay, ML = silt, MH = elastic silt

drained, with a depth to water table of more than 2 m (6.6 ft) and a typical depth to bedrock of 1.8–2.5 m (6–8 ft). The typical soil horizons are also noted. Data such as this is often very useful for initial site analysis, but there is a caveat: since it is mapped at a scale of 1:15840, boundaries between soil zones cannot be taken literally. Certainly the zones are not sharp-edged, but gradually morph from one to another.

Soil maps created for agricultural purposes typically do not reflect the effects of urbanization—the presence of imported fill, demolition debris, buried pavement or concrete, and various forms of soil pollution. Nonetheless, areas with good agricultural soils tend also to be good areas for low- and moderate-intensity urban development—unfortunately, in the competition between them, urban uses usually win. Stable soils that are well drained, free of large boulders or outcroppings of rock, and allow the infiltration of water tend to be sought by both.

The first step in developing a site is to remove and stockpile surface loam and organic materials (horizons A and O) that will later be useful for final landscaping. Rough grading of the site can then take place, with erosion protection measures that protect the exposed layers (see chapter 32). The extent of excavation and types of building foundations will depend upon the soil profile and the elevation of the water table. Sand and gravel may need to be imported to ensure that the foundations are well drained, and the design of foundations will take account of the bearing capacity of the soils they rest on. If spread foundations or a foundation mat are inadequate to transfer loads from buildings to the soil, piles or caissons will need to be designed. Soils are only one factor that will shape the pattern of development, but selecting locations wisely can have a measurable impact on costs and practicality.

Groundwater

Life on earth depends upon the presence of water, both on the surface and below ground. *Groundwater*, which occupies the pores of soil and the fractures of rock formations, represents about 20% of the earth's fresh water supply, and about the same fraction of all water used in the US each day (Kenny et al. 2009). In many countries not blessed with clean water from lakes and streams, it can be the predominant source of drinking water. It is also a significant issue in developing and using sites.

Groundwater can take several forms. Below the surface and above any rock strata or impermeable layer it forms a saturated zone, an *unconfined aquifer*, the top of which we refer to as the *water table*. It is recharged by the hydrologic cycle through rainwater and snow or glacial melt, and it may gain water from or discharge water into streams and lakes. Groundwater is constantly flowing, so that any pollution penetrating the water table will be transported as a plume in the direction of the flow. Groundwater maintains a relatively

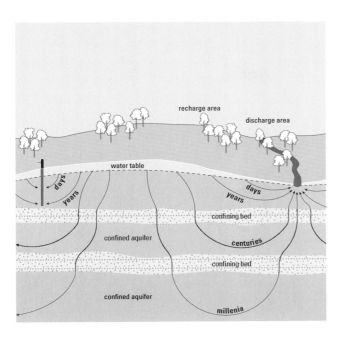

3.10 Typical groundwater flow.
(Adam Tecza/USGS)

constant temperature of about 10°C or 50°F in temperate climate zones, allowing it to serve as a geothermal medium for heating and cooling (see chapter 30). The water table generally mimics the topography of a site, meeting surface water at the edges of streams, rivers, wetlands, and ocean shores. There, saltwater may penetrate the groundwater supply, producing brackish water that is not useful for drinking or irrigation.

Below impermeable layers of clay or rock, sometimes hundreds of meters below the surface, other sources of groundwater may flow as *confined aquifers*. They may be recharged slowly from surface water sources hundreds of kilometers away, and may provide an essential supply of potable water, particularly in areas near ocean shores, or in dry environments where the unconfined supply is very deep or inadequate. Deep aquifers can be as much as 1 million years old. Overreliance on historic aquifers for irrigation or industrial use can endanger these supplies and lead to subsidence of land. The metropolitan area of Bangkok is today below sea level as a result of subsidence triggered by pumping groundwater for urban uses.

A high water table can also pose hazards and challenges for urban development. Soils that are saturated cannot accept septic discharges, forcing individual septic fields to be constructed above ground (with mounds covering them), or effluent to be pumped to disposal sites at higher elevations. Generally, septic disposal pipes need to be at least 30 cm (12 in) above the water table, and in cold climates they also need to be below the typical frost line.

Constructing foundation walls below the water table can be costly, and may require the construction of *slurry walls* to hold back the water as well as pumping until the foundation is sealed. Water pressure will tend to cause a structure that extends below the water table to float upward, like a ship in the sea, which must be counterbalanced by the weight of a tall structure above, or a very thick foundation mat. Structures that extend below the water table will also tend to dam the flow of groundwater and can have downstream effects on other structures and landscape, particularly in clayey soils that shrink as the water is diverted away from them. In Boston, construction of a deep basement below the John Hancock Tower caused Trinity Church, next door, to settle 10 in (25 cm) because the water table was lowered—necessitating costly repairs and stabilization efforts.

The depth of the water table and capacity of the water-bearing strata to deliver water can be ascertained by drilling test wells. Ideally, for development sites a water table 2–3 m (6–10 ft) below ground will assure adequate foundation depth and close enough proximity to the ground to support trees and other vegetation. The objective should be to develop the site in a way that assures that *infiltration* balances out *withdrawals* from the aquifer, taking account of the areas of site that will be covered by impermeable materials. In that way, the water table will remain relatively stable over time. We deal with this subject further in chapter 25.

Topography

It is important to understand what lies below the surface of the ground, but ultimately the most critical influence on the planning of a site is the *topography* of the ground surface. We have a rich vocabulary to describe what we see on the ground—hill, hillside,

Topographic Signatures of Common Features

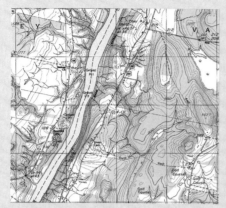

3.11 Valley, Vassalboro, Maine. (USGS)

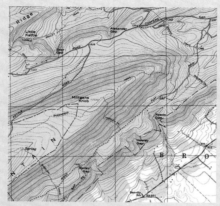

3.12 Ridge, Barryville, Pennsylvania. (USGS)

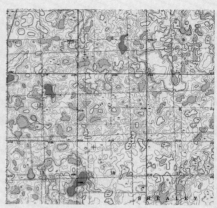

3.13 Flatland, Flatland Plaza NW, North Dakota. (USGS)

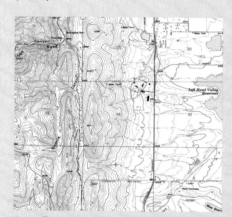

3.14 Escarpment, Boulder, Colorado. (USGS)

3.15 Peak, Pisgah Forest, North Carolina. (USGS)

3.16 Rock outcrops, Laguna Cañoneros, New Mexico. (USGS)

3.17 Canyon, Cathedral Canyon, Utah. (USGS)

3.18 Marsh, Bombay Hook, Delaware. (USGS)

3.19 Estuary, Ipswich, Massachusetts. (USGS)

**Sources of
Topographic Maps**

Aerial photo maps from Google Earth are available for much of the world, and are a useful place to begin an analysis of sites. National and local governments prepare and make available topographic maps of areas in their jurisdiction at a variety of scales.

For the US, the national geological survey maps are available via the Internet at the USGS Store, http://store.usgs.gov. A booklet describing the available maps is at http://egsc .usgs.gov/isb/pubs/booklets/usgsmaps/usgsmaps.html. These include: *7.5 minute maps* at a scale of 1:24,000, or 1 in = 2,000 ft; *15 minute maps* for portions of the US, at a scale of 1:62,500 or approximately 1 in = 1 mi, and *1:100,000 scale maps*, or approximately 1 in = 8,333 ft. Contour intervals vary, but generally are at 10 ft on 7.5 minute maps. A simple navigation toolbar available from USGS, TeraGo Toolbar for Windows, allows the user to measure distances, identify locations, and perform other functions on encoded geospatial PDF files.

For selective portions of the east coast of the US, *orthophotoquad maps* are available at a scale consistent with 7.5 minute maps. However, aerial photo maps available from Google Earth are generally of better quality, and have embedded topography.

For Canada, see http://geogratis.cgdi.gc.ca/geogratis/en/index.html. Maps are available for most of the country at 1:50,000 and 1:150,000 scales, as well as thousands of other maps of thematic and historical value.

For Australia, see http://www.ga.gov.au/topographic-mapping.html. Topographic maps and data are available in printed, digital, and geodata formats for GIS. Maps are at 1:50,000 scale (portions of the country) and 1:100,000 scale with 20 m contour intervals, and 1:250,000 scale.

For the UK, the Ordnance Survey provides maps at www.ordnancesurvey.co.uk/oswebsite /products/os-mastermap/topography-layer/index.html. The OS MasterMap topography layer provides a highly detailed view of towns and open landscapes, including individual buildings, roads, and areas of land, downloadable in a variety of formats. Scales include 1:1,250 and 1:10,000. Its Land-Form Profile file provides contour data at a 5 m interval.

Wikipedia maintains an inventory of publishers of national topographic map series. See http:// www.en.wikipedia.org/wiki/Topographic_map.

3.20   7.5 minute series topographic map, with a scale of 1:24,000, or 1 in = 2,000 ft (1 cm = 240 m), Ariel Quadrangle, Washington. (USGS)

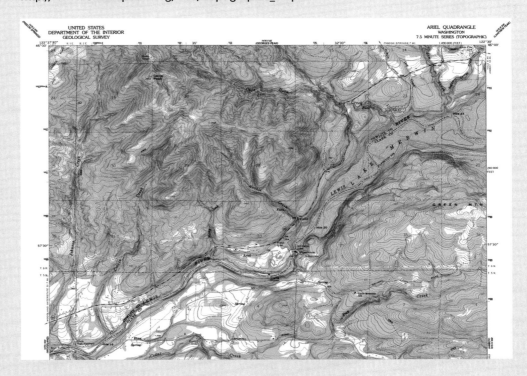

valley, vale, canyon, ridge, mesa, summit, plain, bowl, promontory, escarpment, vista, and a hundred other descriptors that conjure up associations with the places we know—each with a unique topographic signature. Capturing and understanding the form of the ground plane is critical to discovering how it might be used.

Most analyses begin with a *topographic survey*, often available from national or local government mapping agencies in digital or paper form. Such maps come in a variety of scales, although they are easily enlarged or condensed if in digital form. In the US, United States Geological Survey (USGS) maps are available for most areas at scales of 1:24,000 (7.5 minute), equivalent to 1 in = 2,000 ft. They map level contours at 10 ft (3 m) intervals, which may be adequate for rough analysis and planning but is usually too crude for final design. Since these maps are today compiled automatically from aerial photography, a gridded digital terrain array of elevations may also be available, which allows a three-dimensional digital or physical model to be constructed. A number of states and cities also provide quite accurate topographic maps that are useful as a point of departure for site planning.

Ultimately, a more precise contour map will be needed, which may necessitate a field survey. The traditional method uses transit instruments and rods, measuring the elevation in relationship to a benchmark of a known elevation somewhere on or near the site. The site will be gridded on a regular interval, such as 20 m or 50 ft—the steeper and more irregular the slope, the smaller the grid interval needs to be. Then

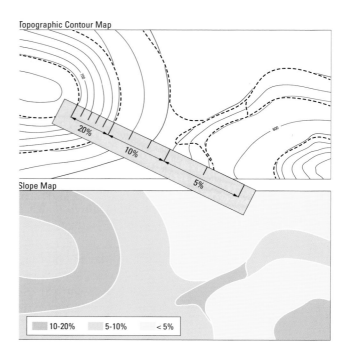

3.22 Technique for estimating slopes. (Adam Tecza)

the elevation of each intersection of the grid will be measured, key elements on the site (such as large trees, or rock outcroppings, or remnant structures or foundations) will be located with their elevations noted, and existing infrastructure (curbs, sewer catchment basins, electrical lines, and the like) will be located and spot elevations noted.

Today most site surveys are done using laser techniques commonly known as *lidar* (or LIDAR or LiDAR), an acronym for light detection and ranging. A variety of technologies share this label, but for site surveys they fall into two categories: airborne lidar systems (ALS), and terrestrial lidar scanning (TLS). The former uses aircraft or drones that interpret the return signals they receive to compose a model or map of topography and objects on a site. The latter employs a 3D survey instrument mounted on a tripod, on several locations in a site, to sense objects and the ground form at high resolution, often with an accuracy of less than a centimeter. The technique is precise enough that the details of buildings on a site can be recorded, and a 3D model can be constructed. Such surveys are costly, and it

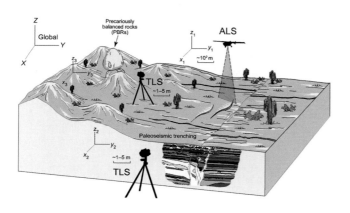

3.21 Lidar sensing techniques for site surveys. (Swiss Lidar)

Table 3.3 | Maximum gradients of typical site uses

Site use	Maximum gradient (%)
Roadway, cross section slope (paved)	2
Roadway, cross section slope (gravel)	4
Roadway, longitudinal grade (with snow and ice)	7
Roadway, longitudinal grade (no icing)	12
Roadway, sustained grade for truck	17
Parking area, cross grade	5
Walkway, longitudinal grade	10
Walkway, short pedestrian ramp	15
Walkway, handicapped ramp	8
Walkway, stepped ramp	8
Public stairs	50
Railway spur or mass transit line	2
Residential area, step down one-story front to back	25

may make sense to defer them until the rough pattern of roadways, walkways, and development has been sketched. The detailed survey can then focus on those areas where the ground form will likely be modified.

Topographic maps help the planner visualize the distinct zones of the site—particularly when overlaid with a map of the pattern of vegetation (see chapter 4). But they can also be deceptive, and a useful exercise is to analyze the average slopes of the site, distinguishing between areas that are easily developed and served and other areas likely to create problems. Typically, for a slope analysis the site is broken into areas that are:

0% to 5%—FLAT areas where almost anything is possible,

6% to 15%—SLOPE areas where movement up and down the slope is more difficult, but possible with some modification of topography,

16% to 25%—STEEP SLOPE areas where development will need to be reached at different levels on the upside and downside of slopes, and where slopes will need to be vegetated,

Over 25%—VERY STEEP SLOPE areas where sloping land will need to be protected from erosion by substantial vegetation or retaining walls.

Computer programs are available that can quickly divide a site into zones within each of these ranges, based on the input of a digital terrain array. However, the site planner also needs to develop an intuitive understanding of the site, which is often gained by analyzing the site by hand. Comprehending the topography by analyzing the slopes can be a revealing exercise. A simple technique is to create a graphic scale that can be overlaid on a contour map that interprets the spacing of contour lines assigning the slope to a gradient range.

In considering what is possible in each zone, keep in mind the maximum gradients shown in table 3.3. The ability of vehicles to navigate slopes is often a determining factor. Of course, it is always possible to create switchbacks on roads to navigate steep slopes, but these are costly and may not be suitable in winter climates or if large volumes of traffic are required. A slope analysis will help the planner rapidly discern areas to be focused upon for development, and other areas that need to be avoided or protected because of their steep gradients.

Having identified the steep areas, it is also useful to divide the site into natural *watersheds* or *drainage basins*, since ultimately sewers and other gravity-driven infrastructure will need to be designed with these basins in mind. Also consider the views—which areas of the site are outward-looking, and which are inwardly focused? Run your hands over the site map imagining the ridges and valleys, and how they might be used. When one really understands the topography of a site, it is possible to summarize it in a small sketch, about the size of the palm of your hand.

Sites Altered by Humans

So far we have viewed sites as the product of long geological processes and the erosion of surface forces, but much of the land that will need to be planned for urban development has been used for generations (even millennia) for agriculture and other productive uses. The uses may have left behind soils that are contaminated (*brownfields*), mountains of discarded materials (*slag heaps*, *tailings mounds or ponds*, and *landfill areas*), and precarious slopes from the extraction of materials. These are sometimes called *drosscapes*, and may require substantial remedial action before they can be occupied or used. And some of the land may have

3.23 Conversion of quarry lands into water recreation environment, Cotswold Water Park, UK. (Courtesy of © Bob Bewley, Aerial Photographic Archive for Archaeology in Europe APAAE)

3.24 Clay quarry converted into environmental and recreation center, Eden Project, Cornwall, UK. (Jürgen Mattern / Wikimedia Commons)

been created by humans through reclamation projects or significant regrading of hillsides or mountains (Berger 2007).

Abandoned quarries are among the most important areas of drosscape encountered as urban areas expand. It matters, of course, whether the material extracted was sand and gravel, stone, or clay, as does the depth and slope of the quarry's surface walls, and whether it is now filled with water. Often such sites' best use is for recreation purposes, capitalizing on the water (if present) and steep walls as a relief from nearby urban development. The Cotswold Water Park in England is perhaps the most spectacular conversion of a former gravel quarry, with dozens of lakes, beaches, water activities, bird and nature sanctuaries, and other recreation lands combined with sites for recreational housing development. This required the selective reshaping of shorelines and their protection from erosion, and some filling of water bodies to construct roadways for access.

If the bottom of a former quarry is dry, it may be a good site for a specialized institution, as with the Eden Project in Cornwall, England, an environmental and recreation center built in a former clay quarry. Consolidating the hillsides and adapting them for recreation purposes was necessary to take advantage of the unique setting.

3.25 Stone and gravel area mined for reclamation fill, Anderson Road Quarry, Kowloon, Hong Kong.
(Planning Department, Government of the Hong Kong Special Administrative Region)

3.26 Rendering of proposed development of Anderson Road Quarry, Hong Kong.
(Planning Department, Government of the Hong Kong Special Administrative Region)

3.27 Quarry Village, San Antonio, Texas, built on a mining and waste dump site.
(Property Solutions)

3.28 Johannesburg mine tailings, currently being remined.
(Courtesy of Dorothy Tang)

3.29 Hong Kong harbor land reclamation.
(bricoleurbanism/Creative Commons)

Many urban areas are located on steeply sloping lands that have been mined for landfill and reclamation areas, leaving drosscape that needs to be reshaped to make it usable for urban development. The Anderson Road area of Hong Kong is an excellent example, adjacent to high-density urban areas. With high densities, site preparation can easily be afforded. The current plan is to protect the steepest slopes while creating a series of benches for urban development. With recontouring, the land needs to be stabilized to protect against landslides, but it offers the potential of parks with wonderful prospects to the distance. These benefits can be obtained at lower densities as well.

Other sites face unconsolidated piles of mining overburden that is both a hazard and unsightly. Large areas of Johannesburg, South Africa have lived with mountains of tailings from now-abandoned gold mines, laced with cyanide and constantly eroding. In coal mining areas, mounds of fine coal dust are frequently left behind, and in steel-making communities dumps with slag and ash may be encountered. These may create erosion hazards, particularly after heavy storms, and may need to be recontoured and vegetated, adding organic materials. Complicating matters, many of these areas are being remined, employing new technology to extract minerals, or in the case of ash, being used for paving and other applications. On development sites, they will need to be compacted and stabilized to avoid subsidence, with careful attention to the water table and to avoiding erosion.

Lands created by reclamation of the oceanfront or riverfronts also require compaction and protection before they are used. A significant amount of the land now occupied by oceanfront cities, especially New York, Boston, the San Francisco Bay area, Tokyo, and Hong Kong, has been obtained by filling marshes and tidal areas to make room for new development. Much of the Netherlands, of course, occupies land that was once under sea. Many of the iconic developments in Dubai and other Gulf States were created on made land, as was the 73 ha (180 ac) site for the new downtown of Beirut. The Kansai Airport serving Osaka, Japan is built entirely on reclaimed lands.

In the past, hills were cut down and gravel transported to the waterfront to raise the elevation of the land; a railway was built in Boston for the filling of the Back Bay. Since tidal wetlands were filled in Boston, streets needed to be elevated to account for possible subsidence, and structures were built on wooden piles driven to the stable gravel underlay. Piling or caissons remain an imperative for tall structures in reclamation areas today, but dredge materials also must be compacted and consolidated before being occupied.

Most reclamation today involves creating a *cofferdam* at the outer perimeter of the landfill, either by driving sheet piles or, in shallow waters, by excavating the bottom material and filling with rock and other materials to the desired elevation. Dredge materials, the most common form of fill, are then pumped into the enclosure, and the area must be dewatered. Conventional dewatering processes include surcharging the land with additional fill for several years, installing dewatering wells (wick drains) and pumping the moisture out of the soil, and employing vacuum or electrokinetic methods. If the bottom soil is highly plastic, consolidation of the fill may require injections of concrete or piles in addition to dewatering.

Reclaimed lands are often areas that have been used for salt evaporation cells, and the highly saline soil introduces another level of complexity. Highly saline soil can make development difficult by corroding pipes, damaging pavement, limiting the use of groundwater, and retarding the growth of many trees and plants. Salinity levels may be reduced by installing porous subsurface drains and flooding the surface with freshwater, or by leaching the salt by planting deep-rooted perennials, such as lucerne (alfalfa), which absorb the salt. Since salt dissolves in water, it is important to carefully control the flow of underground water to reduce possible subsidence.

Reclaimed land is subject to liquefaction in earthquake zones, just one of many reasons why the filling of land on waterfronts should be considered with caution. More importantly, valuable habitat zones are destroyed in the intertidal zone, the most productive portion of the ocean. In the US, the Clean Drinking Water Act prohibits the filling of coastal lands, unless there is no other practicable alternative. This has put a stop to most of the reclamation of coastal lands.

4 | Natural Systems

Every site is a part of a larger natural system that shapes and is shaped by the way the site is planned and used. Sites *are* natural phenomena, no matter how urbanized their surroundings. Even in the densest built-up areas, they receive water from rainfall, benefit from the sun's rays, host vegetation, emit and consume greenhouse gases, and import and export the materials of everyday life, all part of natural processes. Large sites may encompass critical areas such as wetlands, riparian corridors, wildlife habitats, and other landscape zones that respond to climate and locale. There is nothing immutable about these aspects, and in most parts of the world natural systems that evolved over centuries have been modified by agriculture and recent occupancy of the land. Sites need to be understood as part of an ever-changing ecology that extends well beyond their boundaries.

Any parcel of land is at the center of a web of natural (larger and smaller than human) influences that we outline here. Site planners are often encouraged to preserve or protect "nature" on a site, so that it doesn't change as new uses are added. Stability is the objective, but that is a chimera. On some sites, minimizing damage to fragile ecologies is critical. Building structures on barrier dunes, as an example, not only exposes them and their residents to extreme storms but also interferes with the natural processes of forming and eroding the sand that is essential for protecting upland

4.1 Undisturbed site with a mixture of wetlands and uplands. (Courtesy of Brook Wallis/One World Conservation Center, Bennington, VT)

4.2 Terraced hillsides, Douro Valley, Portugal. (Gary Hack)

areas. Dunes are constantly changing—as are most ecologies, if less dramatically. Human use of the land can accelerate or slow down processes of change, but can seldom stop them. The task of the site planner is to ensure that change does not endanger human conditions. Ecological succession needs to be planned, just as do the structures that occupy the land.

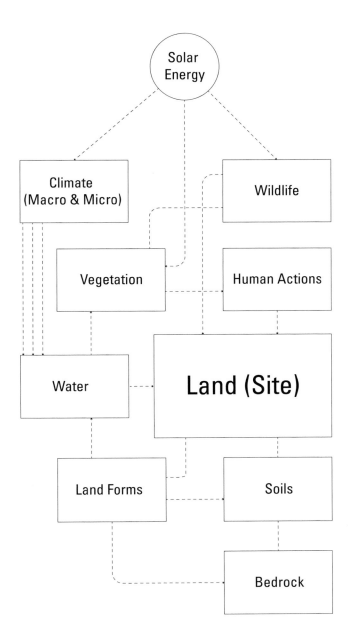

4.3 Key elements in an ecological model. (Adam Tecza/Gary Hack)

Sunlight

Natural systems begin with the sun and the radiant energy it delivers to the earth. Orientation to the sun affects climate, vegetation, and the amount of daylight buildings receive, and should be a major influence in organizing activities on a site.

At any moment, the angle of the sun can be described in terms of its local *altitude* and *direction* or *azimuth*. Both vary over the course of the day and year. Altitude is measured in degrees above the horizon, and azimuth is usually expressed in terms of compass direction. The earth's 23.5° tilt means that in the Northern Hemisphere the sun reaches its highest apogee at noon on about June 21 during the summer solstice, and its lowest about December 21 at the winter solstice (the opposite is true in the Southern Hemisphere). In June, the sun rises well north of east and sets north of west, while in the winter its path begins and ends well south of east and west.

Sun charts for any location are easily retrieved using readily available programs on the Internet. (SunEarthTools, University of Oregon, and NASA ESRL are examples for the US.) Two different formats are used to express the results—a spherical diagram and a horizontal matrix. For Bangor, Maine (44.8° N, 68.8° W), shown on these charts, the altitude of the sun reaches 70° in summer, while at the winter solstice it barely exceeds 20°. In midsummer the sun rises and sets 35° north of east and west, while in winter the sunrise is 32° south of due east, and sunset its equivalent to the west. As a consequence, the north sides of buildings receive sunlight for significant portions of the morning and evening in summer, but never in the winter.

The contrast between northerly and more southerly locations is evident from a comparison of the diagrams for Bangor, Maine and Miami, Florida (25.8° N, 80.2° W). In near-tropical Miami, the sun reaches an altitude of 87°, almost directly overhead, in midsummer, and the north sides of buildings enjoy close to 5 hours of sunshine in morning and afternoon. Even at the winter solstice, sunrises and sunsets are slightly north of east and west.

Knowing the altitude and azimuth of the sun on a site, one can estimate the shadows cast by buildings and natural features such as steep hills. There are many automated programs that will predict the extent

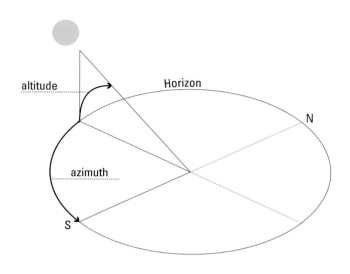

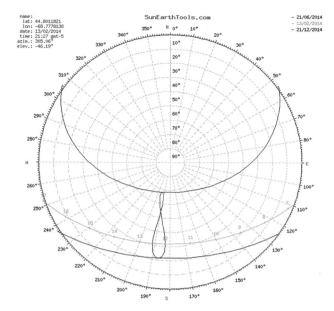

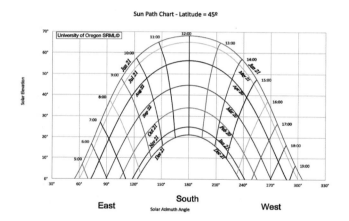

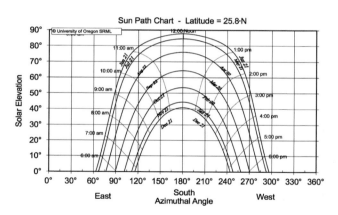

4.4 (top left) Sun diagram indicating altitude and azimuth.
(Adam Tecza)

4.5 (top right) Spherical sun diagram, Bangor, Maine, plotted using SunEarthTools.
(Gary Hack/SunEarth Tools)

4.6 (bottom left) Sun diagram, Bangor, Maine, plotted using Solardat.
(Courtesy of © University of Oregon SMRL)

4.7 (bottom right) Sun diagram, Miami, Florida, plotted using Solardat.
(Courtesy of © University of Oregon SMRL)

of shadows when buildings have been located on a site. But when is sun exposure a virtue and when is it not? It depends upon the purpose. For outdoor spaces in temperate climates, people gravitate to the sun, particularly in fall and spring, when it provides warmth in times of cooler temperatures; in the hot midsummer they may prefer shade. In winter, particularly in snowy climates, they may not spend as much time outdoors, although a sunny spot for outdoor recreation will always be valued. Sun exposure of a site at the spring and fall equinoxes (March 20 and September 22) may be especially relevant, since it can help to extend the warm seasons by several weeks. In tropical climates, by contrast, shade may be more valued at midday, while sun is welcomed in mornings and evenings.

4.8 People sunning on a spring day in Bryant Park, New York. (Gary Hack)

Sunlight warms the earth and all the surfaces exposed to it. Its greatest effect is on surfaces perpendicular to the direction of the sun's rays, which has special importance for siting and designing solar panels. Sunlight hitting the earth at an altitude of 30° delivers only half the energy that it would if it were directly overhead. Even small differences in the slope of the surface receiving sunlight can have important effects. Snow melts first on hillsides facing the sun and on the sloping banks beside roadways, a sign that they receive more radiation than flatter areas. Land that slopes at a 10% grade receives as much radiation as flat land 6 degrees closer to the equator—equivalent to the difference between Portland, Maine and Richmond, Virginia, or between London and Venice. Wise gardeners and vignerons understand the value of slopes for accelerating their growing season, and good site planners look for places on the site where sunlight will deliver a warm climate for outdoor activities.

The type of surface that sunlight strikes also has an impact on how much of the sunlight is reflected or absorbed. The term *albedo* refers to the fraction of the total radiant energy that is reflected back into the atmosphere rather than absorbed. A mirror would have a perfect 1.0 albedo, reflecting all of the sunlight that falls on it, while a matte black surface may approach 0.0, absorbing all the radiation that falls on it. Albedos are affected by the wavelength of radiation and will

vary depending on whether the criterion is the visible spectrum or an infrared band, but average albedos of surfaces have been computed for the purpose of estimating the heat gained. Light surfaces typically absorb less than dark surfaces. Because of their low albedo, the temperature of water bodies tends to remain relatively even over the day, while surfaces such as asphalt pavement absorb most of the energy directed at them, warming during sunlight periods and releasing heat during the night. Altering the surface albedo is a critical factor in controlling the heat island effects of urban sites, as we discuss below.

Also important are the *specific heat* and *thermal mass* of the materials receiving the sun's radiation, which will determine how much is stored in the form of heat. Materials with high specific heat warm up when the sun is falling on them, and may return this heat to the atmosphere as temperatures fall in the evening. Earth typically has a lower thermal mass than stone or synthetic materials such as concrete, although its higher albedo means that it may absorb more energy.

In dense urban areas, exposure to the sky may be the important issue, as it affects the daylight available to structures and determines how much heat the facades of buildings and ground surfaces will gain. Methods have been devised to measure the fraction of the total sky dome that is available for any spot on a site, ranging from complete visibility of the sky (1.0) to only a tiny fraction (0.1 or less in urban canyons). A *sky view factor* (SVF) of 0.5 is not unusual in Hong Kong, and in most cities sites can be expected to range from 0.3 to 0.8. There are a variety of methods for estimating SVF, both photographic and computational. One method uses a fish-eye lens and measures the area of the total sphere occupied by the sky, which produces accurate measurements but is very time-consuming. A faster method involves computing the SVF using commercial 3D databases, which allows larger sites to be modeled efficiently (Brown, Grimmond and Ratti 2001).

The issue of sky exposure is of increasing importance, for several reasons. Research in Hong Kong has found a high correlation between daytime temperatures of areas of the city and the SVF—with less sky exposure, the temperature is lower. The differences are significant, and suggest that tall urban clusters shelter the street spaces from energy gain. But it also highlights an important tradeoff between receiving sunlight

Table 4.1 | Albedo estimates for typical surfaces

Surface	Albedo
Mixed forest	0.5–0.10
Conifer forest	0.09–0.15
Deciduous trees	0.15–0.18
Fresh asphalt	0.04
Worn asphalt	0.12
New concrete	0.55
Granite paving	0.3–0.35
Grass	0.05–0.3
Sand	0.2–0.4
Snow	0.06
Soil	0.05–0.3
Urban areas (averaged)	0.05–0.2

Source: Various, including *Science World*, Rees (1990), Weast (1981).

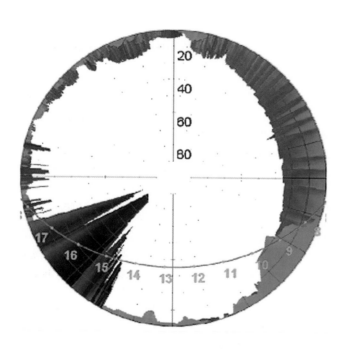

4.9 Sky view factor (SVF) = 0.69, Freiburg, Germany. (Courtesy of Olaf Matuschek and Andreas Matzarakis)

at street level and promoting daylight in buildings, on the one hand, and wishing to minimize heat island effects, on the other.

Heat island effects are, of course, the result of many factors, including the albedo of materials on the ground, discharges of heat from building air conditioning systems, and heat discharged from vehicles using the roads. Studies in many locations have found that the annual mean air temperature in a city with one million or more people can be 1–3°C (1.8–5°F) warmer than in the surrounding country side (Oke 1997). On a clear calm night, this difference can be as much as 12°C (22°F) (Environmental Protection Agency 2016). Changing the ground and roof surfaces—trading pavement for grass, employing porous pavement, shading areas with trees, resurfacing playgrounds with green matting, painting rooftops white, among other steps— can make a significant difference in reducing heat islands. Studies have estimated that every 10% increase in reflectivity of ground materials could lower surface temperatures by 4°C (7°F), and that if pavement reflectance throughout a city were increased from 10% to 35%, the air temperature could potentially be reduced by 0.6°C (1°F) (Pomeranz et al. 2002). Of course, it is also possible to cover large paved areas such as parking lots with solar collectors, which protect the cars from the hot sun and make positive use of the solar radiation the collectors receive.

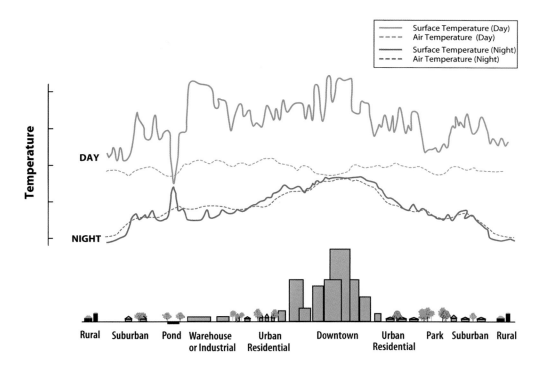

Temperature

DAY

NIGHT

Rural Suburban Pond Warehouse Urban Downtown Urban Park Suburban Rural
       or Industrial Residential Residential

4.10 Temperature profile of an urban area. (US EPA)

A high level of sky exposure is also important for the operation of GPS systems on city streets, as vehicles increasingly depend upon them. And protecting sky exposure is critical to the installation and long-term viability of solar panel installations on buildings.

Whether occupants of property own the rights to sunlight has long been debated, and societies have come to different conclusions. The English common law principle of *ancient lights* prevents an owner or occupier of an adjoining structure from building or placing on his land anything that blocks light to a building that has enjoyed light continuously for at least 20 years. Dutch building codes typically require that the principal facade of a structure must receive 3 hours of direct sunlight each day between the spring and fall equinoxes. In China, a longstanding rule in designing housing areas mandates that one room in each unit must receive at least 2 hours of sunlight a day. In northern latitudes in China this results in widely spaced structures. In the US, California passed a law in 1978, the Solar Shade Control Act, that bans trees and shrubs on adjacent properties from shading solar panels between 10 am and 2 pm, if they were planted after the panels were installed. Other states, including Massachusetts, have granted local governments the right to adopt laws protecting the solar rights of properties. Rules such as these can have a profound impact on how sites are planned.

A century and a half ago, the urban engineer Ildefons Cerdà advocated that street grids in urban areas would best be oriented 45° from north-south, to assure maximum sunlight in intersections and along streets. His plan for the Eixample area of Barcelona was motivated by this view, which Cerdà amplified by creating enlarged areas at each intersection to invite more sunlight into places designed for public contact—and to smooth traffic flows. Cities such as Tokyo and New York that employ *view planes* in building or zoning ordinances also promote greater sunlight on sidewalks of densely built-up areas.

The amount of sunlight that reaches a site is, of course, determined by larger climate regimes, which vary considerably across the globe. They are affected by upper-level wind patterns and the presence of large water bodies as they interact with temperatures, producing clouds, rainfall, and weather events. Parts of the US, including the Pacific Northwest, have cloud cover much of the year, while the sunbelt in Southern California, Arizona, and South Texas enjoys clear skies almost constantly. The resulting hours of sunlight greatly affect

4.11 (right) Block orientation, l'Eixample, Barcelona.
(Google Earth)

4.12 (middle) Worldwide average hours of bright sunlight
each year.
(H. E. Landsberg and M. Pinna/Wikimedia Commons)

4.13 (bottom, left) Mean annual sky cover, sunrise to sunset, US.
(NOAA)

4.14 (bottom, right) Insolation factors, US.
(US DOE)

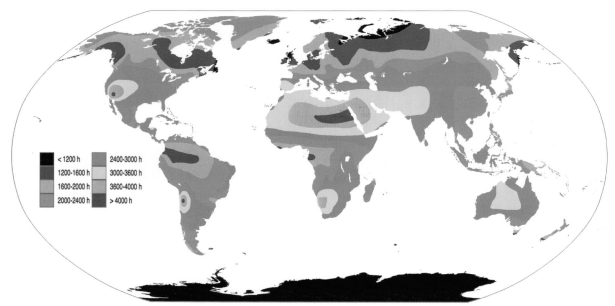

< 1200 h	2400-3000 h
1200-1600 h	3000-3600 h
1600-2000 h	3600-4000 h
2000-2400 h	> 4000 h

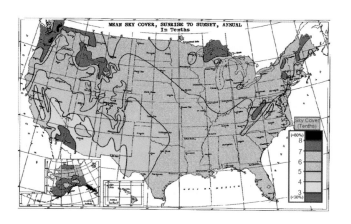

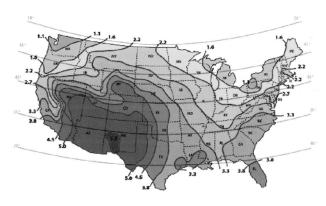

the viability of sites for harvesting energy through passive design and active solar panels. *Insolation* (incident solar radiation) charts are available that estimate the amount of energy that may be gained per m² per day. Figure 14.14 indicates the insolation factors for December, in most US locations one of the cloudiest months of the year. In Southern California, you could expect approximately 4 kWh of energy per day per m² of surface optimized to capture the sun. Similar charts are available for many parts of the world.

Wind

Sunlight is important in influencing the climate of a site, but it is only one of many factors. A continental site will have quite different weather than a coastal site at the same latitude, and the relationship of the site to mountain ranges and prevailing atmospheric patterns will often trump localized conditions. Toronto is roughly the same latitude as Northern California, but you would never know that from temperature and weather statistics. However, within each site there can also be dramatic microclimatic differences, the result of landforms, vegetation, and the pattern of buildings that are placed on the land.

Weather patterns are becoming increasingly variable, but it is useful to begin with long-term average conditions for the area of the site. *Wind* patterns are an important place to start because winds greatly modify the perceived temperature: they can sharply intensify the sense of cold in winter (hence the use of "wind-chill" estimates) while cooling the heat of a warm summer's night. Wind patterns tend to recur in predictable ways and are mapped by local meteorological services, often located at airports. While it is possible to take wind readings on a site using a hand-held anemometer, or wind speed meter, the variability of wind over the course of a day or week confounds drawing conclusions. A better solution is to consult sources of information made available by national weather services, usually accessible on their web sites (National Weather Service, n.d.).

The common way of expressing wind direction is through a *wind rose* diagram, which indicates the monthly or yearly frequencies of each wind direction and speed. In most locations, patterns vary over the

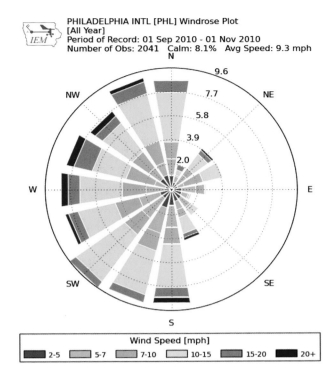

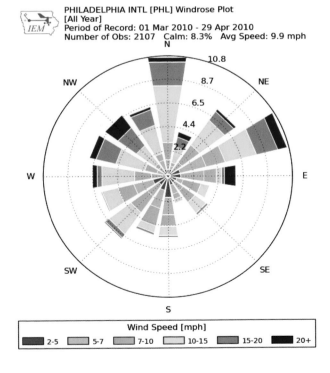

4.15 Fall and spring wind patterns, Philadelphia. (Courtesy of IES Iowa State University)

course of the year, reflecting changes in upper-level wind conditions. As figure 4.15 indicates, in Philadelphia prevailing winds in the fall are predominately from the southwest, while in spring there are a substantial number of days with northeast winds. Taking account of this in planning the site, we will want to block the winter winds with structures of tall trees, while opening the site to summer breezes.

Winds vary according to the topography and as a result of vegetation on a site. Boundary-level wind speeds that are relatively constant occur at a height of about 500 m (1,500 ft) on plains—although higher if there are mountains nearby—and the friction of land forms, buildings, and trees slows the winds to the levels experienced on the ground. Wind speeds on the crest of a hill can be 20–30% higher than in an adjacent valley, while in urban areas, buildings can channel winds so that they greatly exceed the reported wind speed. Nearby bodies of water can also affect wind

patterns and help condition a site. On the edge of an ocean or large lake, even on a day reported as windless, there will be an afternoon breeze blowing onto the land, and a night breeze blowing out to sea. This is the result of a shift in the relative temperatures of land and water, as land warms in the day and cools in the evening. Local depressions at the foot of long slopes or in valleys can also collect cold air if they are not well ventilated by breezes, in some cases freezing before other upland areas.

When wind strikes an obstruction, such as a building or dense stand of trees, it creates a high-pressure zone in front of the object and a low-pressure zone behind. Air rushes over or around the object to equalize the pressure, creating a vortex of higher-speed air. In the case of buildings, wind is actually drawn down to the ground on the front side of the structure, and high-speed winds will be experienced at its sides. On the opposite side, a wind shadow is created, with protection from the winds. This is the principle of creating windbreaks, which shelter areas of 20 times the height of the hedges. If there is snow in the air, it will be deposited at the front of the object.

It will be important to analyze and predict the wind patterns on a site once buildings and landscape have been sketched out, and there are a variety of modeling techniques for making such predictions. But in analyzing sites the important issue is understanding the direction and intensity of winds the site is likely to experience, and how these might need to be modified

4.16 Wind pressure on buildings.
(Adam Tecza/Gary Hack)

4.17 Wind shadow distances from wind breaks.
(Adam Tecza/Iowa State University)

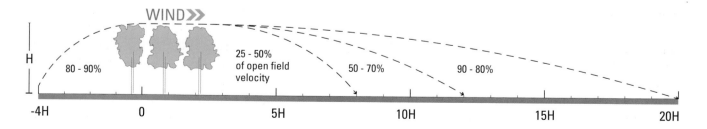

Table 4.2 | Wind effects on human activities

Wind speed, m/sec (mph)	Effects
2 (4.5)	Wind felt on face
4 (9)	Newspaper reading difficult; dust and paper raised; hair disarranged
6 (13)	Begins to affect control of walking
8 (18)	Clothing flaps; progress into wind slowed
10 (22)	Difficult to use umbrella
12 (27)	Difficult to walk steadily; unpleasant noise on ears
14 (31)	Almost halted walking into wind; tottering downwind
16 (36)	Difficulty with balance
18 (40)	Need to grab railings and supports to walk
20 (45)	People blown over
22 (50)	Cannot stand

or mitigated through the way the site is planned. There are common guidelines that should be kept in mind for acceptable winds for various types of outdoor activities. Predicting wind conditions is a tricky task, made more complicated by the fact that the wind patterns vary constantly and have a periodicity. In urban areas such as Boston, winds increase and decline on about 90-minute cycles, while in more tropical locations the significant cycles are daily, with winds increasing in the afternoons as the air temperature rises, and calming in the evenings. Local knowledge of climate is sometimes a more reliable indicator than average statistics.

Rainfall

Every location has a unique rainfall signature, established by the climate and geography of its region. We think of Seattle as a place where it seems to drizzle constantly and Boston as a city with bright skies and thunderstorms, but on average each city receives about 37 in (940 mm) of rainfall each year. (Boston receives another 4 in (100 mm) of precipitation from snowmelt.) Some places receive most of their rainfall in one season, while in others it is spread out over the year, which makes it deceptive to draw quick generalizations.

The water that falls to earth has at least three basic origins. *Convection rainfall* occurs, particularly in tropical areas, where the hot sun promotes evaporation that cools as it rises, resulting in rainfall, often in the afternoons. *Frontal rainfall* is the result of weather fronts moving across a location, when warm air fronts collide with colder air. *Relief rainfall* originates when prevailing winds pick up moisture as they travel across large water bodies, such as oceans, and deposit it when they encounter mountains or hills on land. The opposite sides of these hills experience a rain shadow, with little or no precipitation. A very large site may have features that affect how much rainfall is received, and the form of the site will certainly affect what happens to the water when it reaches the ground, but for the most part the total rainfall will be constant across a site.

Average annual and monthly rainfall data is available in most places from national climatological agencies, based on long term data monitoring. In areas above 40° north and south of the equator, some of the precipitation will come in the form of snow—with many variations from hail to slush to fluffy snowflakes. The rain content of snow (depth of snow proportional to equivalent depth of rain) averages 10:1, but in snow that is too dry to make snowballs it can be 30:1, and in wet slushy snow it can easily be 6:1. Snow management in many northern cities is the largest item in the streets department's budget.

Heavy periods of rainfall are categorized in terms of their probable frequency in any given year. Ten-year

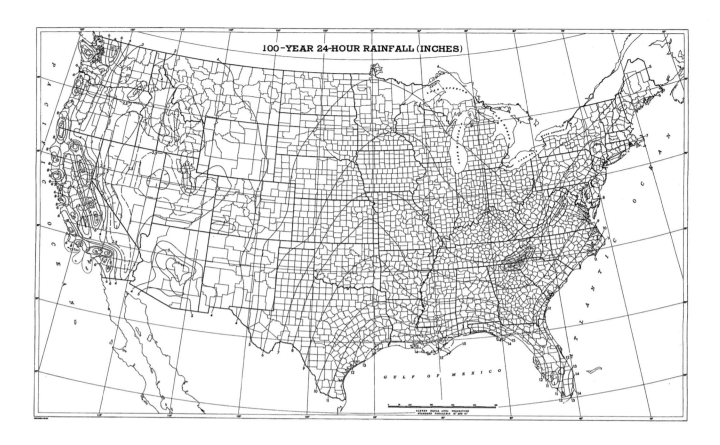

100-YEAR 24-HOUR RAINFALL (INCHES)

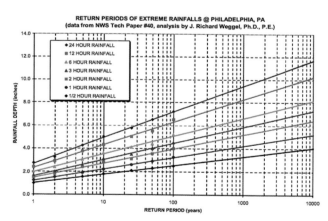

RETURN PERIODS OF EXTREME RAINFALLS @ PHILADELPHIA, PA
(data from NWS Tech Paper #40, analysis by J. Richard Weggel, Ph.D., P.E.)

4.18 100-year, 24-hour rainfall events, US. (NOAA)

4.19 Rainfall events, Philadelphia. (Courtesy of J. Richard Weggel)

storms have a 0.1 probability of occurring, 100-year storms have a 0.01 chance, and 500-year storms a 0.002 chance in any year. Of course, the fact that a 100-year storm occurred last year doesn't reduce the chance that one might again occur this year. Usually the amount of rainfall that can be expected in any storm event is reported over a 24-hour period, but storm data tables can be found for periods ranging from 1 hour to 10 days. As an example of how storm events vary, in Philadelphia a 100-year storm can be expected to yield slightly over 7 in (178 mm) of rain in 24 hours, while a 10-year storm will yield about 5 in (127 mm) and a typical maximum 1-year storm will yield just under 3 in (76 mm).

Local communities frequently adopt the 100-year storm as a design parameter for planning drainage systems and protection from flooding. This has become a matter of convention; in the case of irreplaceable buildings or cultural artifacts, it is probably not stringent enough, while in areas with inexpensive or expendable buildings it may be too conservative. Nonetheless, flood zone maps are created showing the areas that might be inundated by a 100-year storm, based on

4.20 100-year flood event map, Montgomery County, Texas. (US Federal Emergency Management Agency)

fairly complicated estimates of the fraction of rainfall that will be absorbed by the soil, how quickly water will reach streams and wetland areas, and how much is detained locally. Alternatively, the flood maps may be based on actual measurements of the elevations of water in streams and water bodies after a storm of 100-year intensity. In the US these maps indicate areas prone to flooding where the main floor of structures needs to be elevated above flood levels to qualify for flood insurance (Federal Emergency Management Agency, n.d.). Many cities prohibit any construction in 100-year flood zones and the filling of land that would limit its capacity to absorb or store water.

Flood zone maps are often misinterpreted, however, since development can affect flood hazards. Accumulated water can easily exceed the projected 100-year flood zone line as an area adds more pavement and impervious surfaces. Because of changes in the watershed, flood zone maps need to be revised regularly. Climate patterns are also changing, and with ongoing climate change, more intense storms will likely be occurring more frequently in many locations.

Global climate change will likely disrupt historical patterns of rainfall, and in northern climates will affect snow cover. The impacts will vary across the continents,

but northern latitudes are projected to become wetter, particularly in the winter and spring. Less of the precipitation will come in the form of snow, with correspondingly less snow cover. Heavy downpours such as 20-year flood events are likely to occur every 4–15 years by 2100, depending upon location (US Global Change Research Program 2009). Sites on coastlines will be among the most affected, with estimates of sea level rise of as much as 1.5 m (6 ft) by the end of this century.

In analyzing a site, it is useful to map its *watersheds*, which constitute one of the natural divisions of a site. Many cities and towns have mapped local watersheds, which can be helpful in situating a site in its larger environment. As we explain later, these divisions will help determine the layout of any underground pipes, and understanding the natural drainage directions

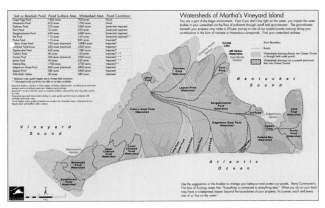

4.21 Map of watersheds, Martha's Vineyard, Massachusetts. (Courtesy of Martha's Vineyard Commission)

4.22 Dry stream, Tsavo East National Park, Kenya. (Christopher T. Cooper/Wikimedia Commons)

will help avoid problems from having runoff course from one person's land to another's. Water always runs perpendicular to the contours of the land. It is also useful to calculate the amount of water entering and leaving the site overland via streams and gullies in peak rainfall periods. Some of these watercourses may be dry much of the year; in other cases small streams will flow constantly, with the stream spreading out during peak periods of flow. Usually the height of peak flow is evident from the vegetation and erosion on banks, and the capacity can be estimated by the profile of the stream. If the site planner aspires to create no new net runoff from the site (or the local government mandates this), the capacity of streams will be a critical determinant. More will be said about this in chapter 25.

Landscape Ecology

At first glance, the landscape of a site that has been idle for some time is a jumble of constantly varying plants draped over a topographic field. On a closer look, we notice that particular species dominate in some areas and may be largely absent in others, and that the edges of areas have a more diverse set of plants than the centers. And this is a static view; had we visited a year or two ago, we would notice how the landscape has subtly changed in the meanwhile. How should we classify and describe the natural systems that seem to be at work?

The ecology of a site is the product of water, soils, sunlight, climate, historical species common to an area, wildlife, and human exploitation of the land. The vegetation of a gully, blessed with running water each time it rains, will be different from that of the meadows it borders; the forest edge will differ from areas 100 m within the forest. The two main structural elements of a landscape are *patches* and *corridors*. Patches (or *land units*) are relatively uniform areas where one or a set of species dominate, and are usually characterized by consistent soils, orientation, and slopes. Over time a distinct *biotic community* will develop in these patches. Corridors, such as valleys or riverbanks, are usually the product of watercourses, but may also be upland areas with unique soil strata or steep slopes. Areas between patches and corridors that remain very much in flux—sometimes as a result of

4.23 (top) Patch and corridor ecology, Nevada. (Gary Hack)

4.24 (middle and bottom) Site ecology before and after exploitation for vineyards, Mendoza, Argentina. (Gary Hack)

human activities such as agriculture—are commonly labeled the *matrix* of a site. Their landscape ecology is constantly being altered, and it is useful to understand what it was before alteration. The vineyards of Mendoza, Argentina, as an example, were largely an arid steppe, dominated by grasses and *solum*, a bush adapted to droughts; the productive landscapes we see today are largely the product of irrigation. In using the land, the native materials should be kept in mind to minimize the necessary human maintenance.

The transition areas between biotic communities are called *ecotones*, zones of contention where various species are competing for dominance. It may be narrow or wide, and can be a sharp break or a gradual transition from one community to another. This is usually the place where the broadest array of species may be found. It is also the place most vulnerable to change through human occupancy of a site—the place where invasive species can get a foothold most easily and where trees are most vulnerable to wind damage. The term ecotone is also used to describe regional shifts in landscape, such as mountain ranges that separate one type of landscape from another or the zone where a coastal landscape becomes an upland plain.

The easiest way to map the landscape ecology of a site is to begin by plotting distinct patches and corridors on aerial photographs, following up with field investigations detailing the species that predominate. The soils they depend upon can be easily discerned by taking hand-drilled core samples. And it will be clear which corridors are heavily dependent upon water by the marks of water coursing along them. Where the site is large and many critical environments are discovered, a landscape ecologist may be essential to fully understand the dynamics of the site.

In thinking about how to use a site, special respect needs to be given to mature landscape ecologies, or *climax communities*, which have developed over long periods of time and cannot easily be replicated. A mature New England forest of maples and beeches probably began many centuries ago as lichens and mosses covering the rocky surface left by glaciers as they receded. Sufficient organic material will have built up after that to support ferns and grasses, then as these added to the topsoil, shrubs and woody plants grew up. Small animals will have found this a hospitable environment, and they will have become the agents

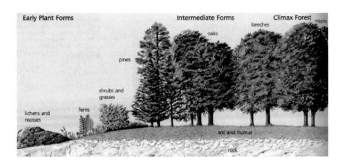

4.25 Forest succession.
(Courtesy of Earth Talk)

of change, spreading seeds from area to area. As the depth of soil and humus increased through leaves and decaying branches, the first pines will have pioneered in the area, followed by birches, oaks, and other deciduous trees. Natural forces such as lightning will have ignited the forest, hastening the succession of the landscape. Ultimately the great stalwarts of the region replaced the earlier species, creating a canopy that captures much of the sunlight and efficiently uses the organic material deposited through leaves and falling trees for its own growth processes, supporting wildlife as an integral part of the system.

Of course, few climax forests remain in New England, where original growth was felled to create fields and acquire timber for ships and construction of settlements. We refer to today's wooded areas as second- or third-growth forests, with only a few legacy stands remaining in steep valleys and other areas where it was impossible to log. Most forested areas are in some stage of evolution, and humans have been agents to that succession. Newly planted areas require the constant input of water, fertilizer, and fungicides, and may require tilling or forest management to remove competition to accelerate the processes of achieving a landscape that looks "natural."

The ultimate mature ecology will be quite different from place to place, partly by accident of history but more because of variations in climate, soils, drainage, and topography. Regional landscapes are broken into *biogeoclimatic zones* differentiating the direction of evolution. British Columbia in Canada has at least 10 such zones, ranging from the alpine tundra zone in the north to the ponderosa pine–bunchgrass zone in the interior to the coastal Douglas fir zone. Within each zone there are many local landscape ecologies: the ponderosa pine–bunchgrass zone includes Palouse prairie, ponderosa pine parkland, cottonwood-dominated alluvial communities along streams, and other ecologies (Valentine et al. 1978). Inventories of landscape ecologies have been published or are available on the Internet for many of the world's regions, and this is a place to begin in creating a classification of natural systems on a site.

Wildlife Ecology

While sites serve human purposes today, they inevitably have already served the purposes of other animal species for thousands of years. Wildlife ecology is inextricably linked to landscape systems; disturbing the latter will inevitably displace wildlife that depend upon it, or will invite other species to take up residence. Urban areas have much higher bird populations than the countryside, because of the abundance of food sources, the warmer climate, and the reduction of natural predators. Many species adapt their behavior to urban conditions, becoming nocturnal as a strategy to avoid danger, changing their diets, even evolving rapidly to deal with human-induced stress (Ditchkoff, Saalfeld, and Gibson

2006). On the other hand, built-up areas generally have reduced aquatic populations, are hostile to large migratory species, and are inhospitable to species that require darkness, such as owls. Maintaining diversity in wildlife species is an important objective.

The largest threat to wildlife in areas in the path of urban development may be the fragmentation of their habitats. While every species has its own minimum size of habitat—and size is highly dependent on food supplies, the character of the environment, and other factors—it is critical that sufficient habitat area be maintained as sites develop. Beyond that, ecologists have argued that creating *habitat corridors* is an effective strategy to provide options for wildlife. Such corridors have several advantages: they provide access to new food supplies when areas previously exploited become depleted; they allow for seasonal migration; and they allow interbreeding with animals in other areas to maintain genetic diversity. Many regional habitat corridors have been established, including the European Green Belt, the Ecologische Hoofdstructuur in the Netherlands, the Ontario Greenbelt, and hundreds of riparian corridors. At the site level, it is also possible to include habitat corridors connecting fragmented wildlife environments.

How wide should a wildlife corridor be? The short answer is as wide as possible; but as a practical matter

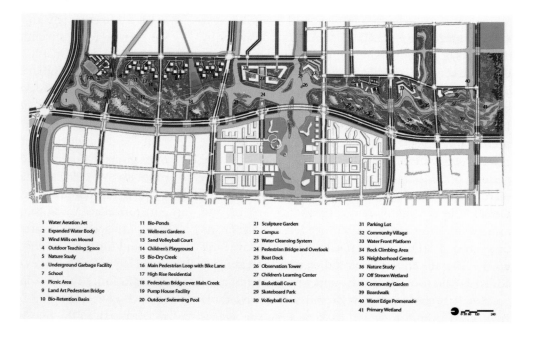

1 Water Aeration Jet	11 Bio-Ponds	21 Sculpture Garden	31 Parking Lot
2 Expanded Water Body	12 Wellness Gardens	22 Campus	32 Community Village
3 Wind Mills on Mound	13 Sand Volleyball Court	23 Water Cleansing System	33 Water Front Platform
4 Outdoor Teaching Space	14 Children's Playground	24 Pedestrian Bridge and Overlook	34 Rock Climbing Area
5 Nature Study	15 Bio-Dry Creek	25 Boat Dock	35 Neighborhood Center
6 Underground Garbage Facility	16 Main Pedestrian Loop with Bike Lane	26 Observation Tower	36 Nature Study
7 School	17 High Rise Residential	27 Children's Learning Center	37 Off Stream Wetland
8 Picnic Area	18 Pedestrian Bridge over Main Creek	28 Basketball Court	38 Community Garden
9 Land Art Pedestrian Bridge	19 Pump House Facility	29 Skateboard Park	39 Boardwalk
10 Bio-Retention Basin	20 Outdoor Swimming Pool	30 Volleyball Court	40 Water Edge Promenade
			41 Primary Wetland

4.26 Ningbo eco-corridor, China. (Courtesy of SWA Group)

4.27 Wildlife bridge crossing major highway, Banff, Alberta. (Qyd/Wikimedia Commons)

a corridor of a few hundred feet is likely to be too small to encourage wildlife to make it their home, particularly if the corridor is also a walking route for humans or is near roadways. A minimum of 300 m (1,000 ft) is better. The critical issue is continuity of the corridor, which in urbanized areas will require crossings of roadways. Box culverts of at least 3.5 m (12 ft) or overpasses that continue the natural ground surface are essential. If that is not possible, level crossings protected by speed bumps on either side of the corridor and wildlife crossing signs, avoiding overhead illumination, will help encourage the flow.

Critical Environments

One rule of thumb is that development is most easily accommodated on land that is most suitable for agriculture—soils are most often well drained, topography is generally flat, there are not major impediments to movement, and the site usually has favorable orientation. Like all rules of thumb this has exceptions, and the exceptions often create value for a site. Such value may come from views of nearby water bodies, mature wooded areas, streams running through a site, bluffs and steeply sloped areas with good prospects, and other special features. Thus, the site designer is faced with having to balance protection of the natural features with exploiting their presence.

Several types of natural areas can be singled out for special attention, and need to be studied closely.

Coastal areas

Coastal areas range from beaches to granite-lined shores, from mangroves to estuarine mudflats, and a hundred more variations, making it difficult to generalize about how they should be addressed. But regardless of their form, the essential natural systems invariably need to be understood and carefully managed. This was not always done: mangroves were cut down and channels filled for the resorts of Florida, cities like New York and Hong Kong expanded by "reclaiming" land from the sea, barrier islands were developed along the coasts of North Carolina and New Jersey, hillsides were scaled with structures in the Amalfi coast and Newfoundland, all a testimonial to the high value that comes with being close to the water. Each of these actions does some violence to the natural systems at work, and may endanger the activities they intended to accommodate. Recent storms have made plain the folly of overlooking nature, and rising sea levels pose new threats to those who locate on the shore.

The *intertidal zone* is the most productive area of any shoreline ecology. Its twice-daily inundation creates an environment where marine and shoreline plants interact with marine life and onshore wildlife, receiving sunlight, oxygen, the freshwater runoff from the land, and nourishment from microscopic and visible plants. Fishes and birds flock there, clams and other marine life spend their most vulnerable years protected on the shallow bottom, crustaceans attach themselves to the rocks, and the area is teeming with life. Tidal marshes are the most active intertidal zones, but even in urban areas, under piers and along bulkheads, a productive ecosystem thrives. There is good reason to restrict intrusions into this zone. In the US, the Clean Water Act and a number of state acts prohibit all filling of coastal waters, unless there is no other practicable alternative (33 USC 1344, sec. 404). In practice this means restricting the use of coastal waters to maritime purposes.

Coastal zones serve as the first line of protection for more vulnerable areas behind. *Mangrove* areas provide protection against storm surges in most tropical and subtropical areas of the world and are highly productive habitats. They are also effective carbon sinks, sequestering carbon over long periods. The mangrove biome consists of trees and large shrubs (over 100 types) that thrive in saline environments, sometimes with highly concentrated salinity as seawater evaporates in brackish pools, and low-oxygen soils. Many of the plants have multiple stems, intertwining to provide a web that is well braced for high winds and storms. The loss of mangroves to aquaculture and urbanization has made both extremely vulnerable.

In temperate regions, *salt marshes* are the equivalent of mangroves and are among the world's most productive plant communities. They can extend just a few meters along the shoreline, or several kilometers in low-lying coastal areas. Halophyte species dominate these areas, typically cordgrasses, reeds, and glassworts that are able to survive in areas with high salinity by taking their oxygen from the air. Salt marshes are the breeding grounds of small crabs, periwinkles, and other forms of life that feed on the decaying plants, drawing herons, gulls, and other birds to prey on them. They also serve an important purpose of trapping sediment from runoff or streams as they reach the ocean, and increasingly absorbing excess nitrogen from agricultural fields. These marshes are often a prime candidate for landfilling, but the loss of important habitat makes this unconscionable. They provide a needed margin for protection of the upland areas against the vagaries of natural hazards.

The ecology of *dunes* is also an important protection for areas behind. While the ocean is constantly eroding and replenishing dunes, and their profile changes year by year, dune grasses and plants provide stability. On the ocean-facing side, American beach grass, sword grass, marram grass, sand couch grass, sea rocket, and other fast-growing pioneer species help bind together sand grains and trap windblown sand. Behind the dunes, where there is greater protection, heathers, wattles, *Rosa ragusa*, blackberries, and other woody shrubs provide a more secure anchor for the

4.28 Coastal salt marsh, Maine.
(Gary Hack)

4.29 Coastal mangroves, Panama.
(Courtesy of Martin E. Gold)

4.30 Bride Brook salt marsh, Connecticut.
(Alex756/Wikimedia Commons)

4.31 Dunes, Virginia Coastal Reserve.
(Courtesy of S. T. Brantley)

sand. Dune vegetation is easily disrupted by humans beating paths to the water, and must be protected by installing wooden walkways and restricting pathways. Coastal marshes and other fragile communities are often found behind dunes, so the zone of protection may extend a considerable distance inland.

Barrier dunes, as we have noted, are critical lines of protection for a much larger region. Building on them, or paving them over for roads, has several implications: it disrupts the capacity of the dunes to absorb heavy storm impacts; accelerates erosion by reducing the supply of sand; creates runoff that can erode sand areas, reducing birds and other wildlife that are an essential part of the ecosystem; and increases foot traffic to the shore with harmful effects on the ecology. The best strategy is to avoid development; second best is to maintain the coastal dunes and restrict development to areas well behind the lee side of the dunes. Restoration efforts can be helpful in promoting vegetation, and the introduction of wind fences can be of value in increasing the deposits of wind-driven sand along the line of the dunes.

Erosion of the coastline is an issue not simply in areas of shifting sand. Even along granite-armored shorelines, wave motion during storms can erode the line of soil and vegetation at the margin of the land. Freshwater is usually the culprit, coursing above the rock and loosening the hard won vegetation that covers it. In these and most coastal areas, structures should be set back 15 m (50 ft) or more, to avoid disrupting the water table and compromising the pattern of ground cover.

Freshwater Wetlands

Wetlands are a crucial aspect of the way a site deals with water, and often a most important habitat for vegetation and wildlife. They store rainfall and put it to productive use in nourishing plants and other forms of life, and in many places also recharge the groundwater supply. Wetlands may be seasonal, absorbing the snowmelt in the spring or large quantities of water in rainy seasons, then slowly dissipating over the year, or they may function as year-round detention or retention areas. Most permanent wetlands will be obvious as one walks a site and discovers standing water or mushy soils, but seasonal wetlands may only become evident through more studied analysis. There are two things to look for: the presence of *hydrophytic vegetation* or obligate wetland species such as ferns, sedges, or cattails (Typha); and *hydric soils*, formed under conditions of saturation or flooding, that have anaerobic conditions in their upper horizons. Hydric soils vary by region, but typically the upper horizon that is regularly exposed to water is dark and shows signs of muck or peat or decayed roots, and it is underlaid by lighter materials (often gley, gray or bluish gray) such as sand or clay where the organic matter has been depleted (Natural Resources Conservation Service 2010). Wetlands highlight the important

4.32 Headlands coast, Great Wass Island, Maine. (Gary Hack)

4.33 Paunacussing Wetlands, Buckingham, Pennsylvania. (Courtesy of Natural Lands Trust)

way that water, soil, and vegetation interact to become part of the landscape ecology of a site.

In the past, before the ecological values of wetlands were understood, they were often seen as an unattractive nuisance that needed to be drained, filled, and forgotten. However, the loss of storage area for stormwater was soon felt through flooding, lower groundwater levels had long-term effects on vegetation, and there was a significant decline of wildlife. Filling wetlands is now prohibited by many environmental agencies, and in planning a site wetlands need to be accommodated, which also means maintaining the ecosystem that supplies water to them, and to the

wildlife that are critical in their functioning. Wetlands may obtain their water from subsurface, surface, or tidal sources, and this needs to be respected if they are to continue to function.

Some loss of wetlands may be unavoidable, however, as when they must be crossed by a roadway to connect two parts of a site. To mitigate this, it is possible to construct new wetlands or enlarge existing wetlands to compensate for losses. This requires the careful matching of soils and plant species, and tending of the new marsh until it is established.

More ambitious wetlands may be constructed to deal with the increased runoff of new development,

4.34 Constructed wetlands, Providence Estate, Greenvale, Victoria, Australia. (Courtesy of Programmed Property Services)

4.35 Constructed wetland detention area, Qun Li new town, Harbin, China. (Gary Hack)

allowing it to recharge the groundwater while providing a recreational resource. Such areas are now required by many local governments to detain rainfall. Typically they have three areas: an *inlet zone* which is an open water sedimentation pond that allows stormwater to flow out of a watercourse into a wetland; a *macrophyte zone* with aquatic plants growing under or out of the water which further trap sediment and algae and bacteria that help treat the stormwater; and an *outlet area*, with greater depth to allow finer particles to settle and sunlight to kill unwanted bacteria. One design challenge is the need to deal with storm surges, which are lowered slowly through infiltration, evaporation, and runoff. Constructed wetlands need to be maintained, since they will over time accumulate sediment that limits their capacity and flow. As plants mature, they become a part of the site ecology, and can be a beautiful addition in all seasons.

4.36 Barton Springs Pool, Austin, Texas. (Downtown Austin/Wikimedia Commons)

Ponds

Freshwater or *liminal ponds* are a special form of wetlands that are usually valued for their scenic and recreational possibilities more than for their ability to cleanse runoff or contribute a rich ecological environment. Maintenance of water quality is usually the top concern. Where ponds exist naturally, they depend upon being supplied with clear or relatively uncontaminated water from streams or underground springs. In that sense, they are the opposite of the kinds of wetlands just described: water quality needs to be managed beyond their shorelines by assuring that humans do not degrade the water.

A stellar example of a much-valued pond is Barton Springs Pool in Austin, Texas. Three ac (1.2 ha) in size, it is fed by underground springs at an average temperature of 70°F (21°C), and attracts swimmers and bathers through much of the year. Maintaining water quality is a constant struggle, and the pool has had to be closed on several occasions as a result of polluted runoff and pollution of underground water sources. It is also the home of the Barton Springs salamander, an endangered species, which coexists with humans using the water body.

Maintaining water quality in ponds generally requires strict control of surface runoff in the area surrounding them, ensuring that sediment is largely removed in streams before reaching the pond, restricting use of salt on roads nearby, and prohibiting fertilizers, pesticides, and other contaminants in landscaping on adjacent properties. The dangers are *acidification* from acid rain and other sources, and *eutrophication*, the promoting of plankton blooms from high concentrations of phosphorus or nitrogen, generally from fertilizers. In developed sites, the edges need to be designed to minimize erosion, and the water surface may need to be skimmed to remove accumulations of leaves and other organic matter. Many ponds also employ artificial aeration to improve water quality, through the installation of air diffusers on the bottom, or floating surface aerators, or jet spray fountains.

Riparian Corridors

Riparian corridors are transition zones between terrestrial and aquatic environments. Most often they contain streams that trap sediment, nutrients, and contaminants, while providing water for vegetation and wildlife. The streams are bordered by permanent bands of trees, shrubs, and ground cover, sometimes called buffer strips, which also serve important ecological functions. Often they connect habitats for wildlife, and for humans they are choice locations for hiking and cycling paths, fishing, and recreation areas. Their continuing viability depends upon maintaining natural systems in the corridor.

How wide does a riparian corridor need to be to be effective? The evidence varies, but for water quality purposes, it is clear that buffer strips on first-, second-, and third-order streams (the upstream portions) have much greater benefit than buffers on downstream reaches. Continuous buffer strips are important in maintaining stream temperatures. Research has found that 75–90% of sediments and a large fraction of suspended phosphorus and nitrogen are removed in buffers between 9 and 30 m (31–100 ft) in width, and that wider dimensions add little to performance (Fischer and Fischenich 2000).

As important as the width of a riparian corridor is the type of vegetation that lines it. Woody pants and deep-rooted trees stabilize stream banks and help minimize erosion during flood stages. Farther back from the bank, vegetation diversity is important to support wildlife, and ground cover helps filter runoff before it reaches the stream. The addition of paths for human and wildlife movement must be done with care so that natural watercourses feeding the stream are not blocked and erosion is minimized.

Steep Hillsides

Areas of steep (15–25%) or very steep (>25%) slope need to be identified in the site survey, since they will limit how the site can be used and have a major bearing on the design of roads and infrastructure. They may also pose landslide hazards, particularly if the natural vegetation is disturbed as the site is developed. But they offer the prospect of marvelous views from a site, and are well worth the added costs and cautions to make them livable.

Landslides are a particular hazard in areas with fine clay soils that are subject to swelling and slippage when saturated. When the weight of the saturated layer exceeds what can be held in place by friction, the land will begin to slump and eventually slide. There are a variety of computer models that can help predict vulnerability of slopes to landslides (US Army Corps of Engineers 2003). Vegetation with deep roots is essential to hold the upper layers of soil in place and absorb some

4.37 Riparian corridor, Bear Creek, Story County, Iowa. (USDA/Wikimedia Commons)

4.38 Steep slope hillside, Atamai Village, New Zealand. (Courtesy of Permaculture)

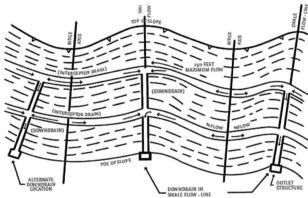

4.39 Ridgeline stabilization with irrigation.
(Courtesy of Gordon Peabody © Safe Harbor Environmental Services)

4.40 Landform grading technique, Los Angeles.
(Emily Gabel/Los Angeles Department of Planning)

4.41 Landform drainage swales, with undisturbed hillsides at rear, Los Angeles.
(Courtesy of Emily Gabel)

of the runoff. In California, chaparral plants serve this purpose on many hillsides, but in periods of drought they can also pose wildfire risks. Securing the tops of slopes is especially critical, since runoff can both erode the surface of the hillside and begin the process of land slippage during periods of heavy rainfall.

In an ideal world, very steep areas should not be disturbed. But in some places, including land-constrained Hong Kong, there is no choice but to build on hillsides, and the preferred strategy is to employ deep piles to protect against slippage and to limit the footprint of buildings. In Los Angeles and other California cities, use of the mountainsides allows the city to be more compact and capitalizes on spectacular views, but requires major recontouring of hillsides. Most cities with steep slopes have local regulations that limit the amount of development allowed on them, and limits on roadway gradients and other infrastructure will tightly constrain how the site is planned. Areas with at least a 25% gradient and at least a 15 m (50 ft) change of elevation are typically classified as environmentally sensitive lands.

A variety of techniques are available to stabilize steep slopes. The tops of slopes may be protected by *recontouring* the land so that water runs away from the slope, and by planting the crown to stop it from sliding. In dry climates this may require irrigation to ensure that roots develop quickly. The steep slopes themselves may need protection to minimize the penetration of water and reduce the chance that runoff erodes the hillside. A set of techniques, referred to as *landform grading*, may be the right strategy (Los Angeles Department of City Planning 1983). This involves creating horizontal swales across the face of the slope, lining them with impervious material, and connecting them to vertical drainage courses that transport the water to detention areas at the bottom of the slope. If the hillsides are planted with deeply rooted shrubs, the swales may be largely invisible from below.

Forests

Forests can contribute to a site in so many ways that we are reluctant to clear a single tree. They add a visual and recreational amenity, create a windbreak, humidify the air, stabilize the soil, help create microclimates, and support wildlife. They may be a productive resource,

4.42 Old-growth forest, Alaska.
(Henry Hartley/Wikimedia Commons)

and not least are important carbon sinks that sequester the carbon dioxide we humans add to the atmosphere. But, alas, if other uses are to find a place on a site, we may need to clear areas in a way that does not destroy the virtues of the forest.

We have emphasized that any forest is constantly in a state of evolution, and understanding its current state will be essential in deciding how to use it wisely. Mature old-growth forests have a multilayered canopy with surviving large trees, standing dead trees, and gaps where rapidly growing smaller ones will ultimately take their place. Fallen leaves and tree trunks provide the fuel for lower growth and create protected areas for wildlife. Well-managed forests replicate this natural pattern by removing closely spaced trees to allow others to thrive. Forests can achieve this state in

about two generations, 120–150 years in eastern hardwood forests, longer in western coniferous stands.

Of course, few forests in areas of urban development remain undisturbed for such long periods. They have been logged indiscriminately, if not clear-cut, leveled by wildfires (part of nature's succession strategy), or left to grow without management. The result is often growth that is too dense, where trees reach for the sky but must depend upon each other for wind-firmness, or monocultures that are susceptible to disease. A decision to maintain a forest area may require practices that manage it to become healthier and more diverse.

Some general strategies will help in maintaining forested areas that must be shaped to accommodate development. The shape of the area is important; it is better to maintain compact areas at least 50–100 m (165–330 ft) across than narrow bands of forest that will be susceptible to wind damage. While the idea of maintaining the forest edge near structures is attractive, it is rarely successful to put development features within the width of the trees' crown, since the groundwater regime and root structures will generally be disturbed. A better strategy may be planting a new edge to the forest. In a similar way, roadways through the forest inevitably disrupt the root patterns, unless roots are preserved below the roads, using pervious materials for the roadbed. Finally, it is important to avoid domesticating the forest floor by removing the understory of decaying trees and leaves, low pioneering plants, and succession species. While it is possible to introduce pathways and adapt the forest for human enjoyment, it needs to be done with a recognition that a forest is a living ecology, not simply a collection of trees.

5 | Context and Surroundings

Every site has a time and place. While we begin developing our understanding of a site by focusing on the land and its natural systems, we must overlay on this a knowledge of how it has been used in the past, and how its new occupants will engage the larger settlement that surrounds them. This means compiling the facts on the ground, but also learning about its associations and memories, and the habits of mind and body that inform them.

We ask: What is the larger entity this site is part of? How is it known? How has it been used, and does any evidence of the past remain? How does one get there? Are there public systems in place that would support use of the site? What man-made buildings and structures could be reused? Are there important pathways along or across the site that need to be recognized? These and other questions about the human context will provide cues for the future form and character of the site.

Locale

A useful departure point is to place the site in its built-up surroundings. Is it part of a known district, or is it large enough to be its own separate domain? Are there surrounding features that the site is associated with? How would you describe the route to get there?

Studies over the years have identified a set of common mnemonics that are used widely to construct mental maps of cities and towns. Kevin Lynch suggested that the most common elements of a city image are *landmarks*, *nodes*, *paths*, *edges*, and *districts* (Lynch 1960). Landmarks serve as points of reference to locate oneself; they are usually natural features or structures visible from a distance, but a curiously shaped building, or a building with special meaning (such as a town hall or school), may also be important as an orientation device. A church steeple, a building at the end of a long avenue, the span of a suspension bridge seen from afar, and a distant mountain peak are obvious examples. Nodes are the human equivalent of landmarks—collecting points, places of convergence, spots that are instantly recognizable by their form or activities or because of the structures that surround them. European squares are the first examples that come to mind, but important multilegged intersections or traffic circles may also be nodes, whether we like them or not. In Boston it is said that the main criterion for a place being called a square is that it is not square.

Important paths are the armatures of our understanding of the structure of a settlement. We use them each day to get from place to place, moving from landmark to node and gradually filling in our understanding of the places between. They are the essential routes we name when providing instructions about how to get from one place to another. Paths, particularly if they are heavily trafficked routes, can also be the edges of the territories of a city, divisions between the various districts we identify by name. Thus, traveling along Commonwealth Avenue from Newton to Boston (or running, since this happens to be the last third of the Boston Marathon), we pass by Waban on the right, Newtonville on the left, then Newton Center on the right, then Boston College on the left and Chestnut Hill on the right, both straddling the invisible boundary between Boston and Newton, and so on, neighborhood by neighborhood divided by this gracious avenue culminating at the Boston Public Garden. Of course, major

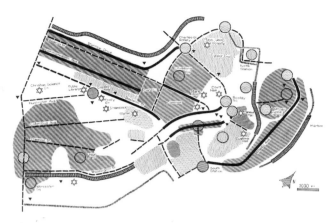

5.1 Image of downtown Boston in the field, c. 1958.
(Kevin Lynch)

5.2 Park Street Church spire, a landmark in downtown Boston.
(Gary Hack)

5.3 Meeting place, kiosks at Harvard Square, Cambridge,
Massachusetts.
(Gary Hack)

paths need not be dividers; they can also be *seams* knitting together districts on either side, as Commonwealth Avenue is when it reaches Cleveland Circle, an important node, or Kenmore Square, further along. And there are many other kinds of edges to districts: water bodies, rail lines, abrupt changes of use such as a wall of industry adjacent to a residential area, parks and forests, among others.

Every person will have a somewhat different mental map of a place, and the way a place is mapped in the mind may vary between cultures, and may be dependent on the form of the landscape and the pattern of roadways (Appleyard 1976). Living in a gridiron city leads to different orientation skills than living in a city with a linear pattern of parallel but diverging or sometimes crossing roadways, as in Boston. For a city spread out along a river, views to the water may be the essential orientation feature rather than more conventional landmarks. A cul-de-sac-dominated suburban world may force reliance on subtle landmarks (the green house on the right, the apartment building on the corner) to get around. Of course, signage plays a crucial role, especially for visitors, in reinforcing what is on the ground. With increased reliance on GPS maps, mental maps may have less importance in directional orientation than they used to, but continue to shape perceptions.

Why is it important to understand the mental map of a place? One reason is that the shape of the site the planner is given may not match the pattern of the city as local people understand it. Entrances to the site located off several major roadways may result in confusion. A large site may be part of several districts, each with its own connotation and prestige, which it is useful to know. One part may be more associated with higher-income areas, another associated with nearby warehousing or businesses; the trick is knowing how to parse the site into its logical domains. Often these differences will be obvious when one speaks with residents, asking them what words they would use to describe the site. Realtors have an especially acute sense of differences in location, and how sites draw their influences from their surroundings. They can be valuable informants.

Consistencies are as important as differences in the surroundings of a site. A city that is largely a three-story red brick built environment will generally demand recognition of this when a site is developed. Places

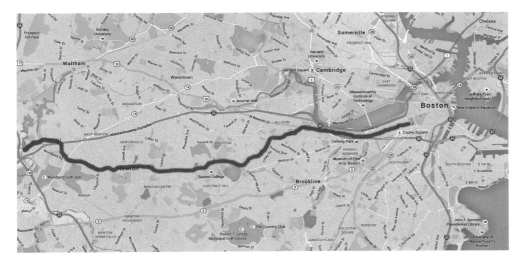

5.4 Route of Commonwealth Avenue from Newton to Back Bay, Boston.
(Gary Hack)

5.5 Commonwealth Avenue at Kenmore Square, Boston, on Marathon Day.
(fenwaypark100.org)

5.6 New infill development in Society Hill, Philadelphia, with scale and materials consistent with historic structures.
(Gary Hack)

graced by generous boulevards lined by double rows of trees will take exception to site plans that have buildings hugging the roadway. These are obvious, but more subtle differences in densities and scale of structures may also be important to creating a harmonious environment, and smoothing the way to acceptance of plans.

Analyzing the locale of a site also involves the more prosaic task of mapping surrounding uses, roadways, open spaces, public facilities, and other features that will be needed by future users of a site. Equally important is mapping potential detractors to the smooth flow of gaining approval of site plans, and beginning to imagine how their objections will be addressed. The site may also provide solutions to traffic bottlenecks or other issues in the area surrounding the site, and bring needed facilities such as shopping or schools to

the area. All this will become obvious through a careful analysis of the surroundings.

Memories of the Landscape

Next we focus on the character of the site itself: how is it known? As Wilson's farm? A part of a spruce forest? A place with island views? The edge of a historic Swedish Village? A spot along the rocky shore? This is not simply an exercise in discovering or inventing a brand—although marketers will appear soon enough to do so—but a way of asking what aspects of a site's character should be highlighted. If the site was previously used for agriculture, there will be artifacts left behind: hedgerows or stone walls bordering fields, remnants of orchards, abandoned farm structures, detention ponds

5.7 Hedgerows provide structure for a site, Ireland. (Courtesy of Kelly Brenner)

5.8 Old ranch structures and fences that remained at Sea Ranch. (Gary Hack)

that supplied water to the fields and flocks. Sea Ranch on the Sonoma coast of California, shown in chapter 1, is an environmental poem created out of the fields and structures that were once a working sheep ranch. If a site is currently forested, the type of trees and their scale will influence how to clear areas for development. Views from a gradually sloping hillside to mountains or the sea will suggest corridors that should remain undeveloped. Or on an urban site, the scale and use of surrounding structures will provide cures about how the edges of the site should be handled.

All of this needs to be mapped and photographed so that the essential elements of the site are kept in mind as we plan. We are motivated less by nostalgia, more by the search for the unique logic of how the site might be developed. Some of that may be revealed by how the site was previously used. Farmers of the land will have created roadways that remained dry year-round; their siting is not accidental. Buildings, we discover, were located with their backs to the wind and porches were built toward the sun. New uses will make their own demands, but there is also value in retaining memories of the past, which add to the richness of the terroir.

Views

There is a long Chinese tradition of incorporating views toward distant landmarks in a site design, creating *borrowed landscapes*. Distant views have a strong hold on the imagination in most cultures and have practical economic consequences. In North America, buyers of condominiums pay a substantial premium for upper floors in buildings if they have views over adjacent structures—2.5% more for each higher floor in Vancouver, by one estimate, to assure a view of the mountains—when they are not obscured by fog (Hack and Sagalyn 2011). Views of parks and water command smaller but significant premiums, as does the sight of landmark structures.

It is interesting to speculate about why views are so valued. They connect undistinguished locales to aspects of the larger setting that are widely admired. A site that is well back from the edge of a sea or lake will seem connected to it if it is visible. Views offer a respite from smaller and more confined spaces, particularly in urban environments. Apartments that face Central Park in New York, or even tiny Louisburg Square in Boston, are considered special because of their identification with the open spaces. In the hills of the Bel Air area of Los Angeles, or the mid slopes of Hong Kong, the land is contoured and buildings are sited to assure every home a distant view. Buildings that are built parallel to a waterfront or that block views to hills are often lightning rods of public protest, even by individuals who do not directly benefit by views. Maintaining open views at the end of public streets is generally considered a matter of equity.

In surveying a site, it is useful to locate the most prominent viewpoints and map the viewsheds that may be seen from them, taking account of trees, structures, and other obstructions. This can be done on the ground

5.9 Borrowed landscape at the Summer Palace, Beijing. (Gary Hack)

5.10 Louisburg Square houses, Beacon Hill, Boston. (Gary Hack)

for a modest-sized site, although it is difficult on sites carpeted by forest that may be selectively cleared. On urban sites, the eye is the best detector of views on the ground, although other methods will need to be employed for views on upper levels of buildings or terraces not yet built.

There are a variety of techniques available to aid in identifying viewsheds from particular locations on a site. Computer mapping programs have now largely replaced stereoscopic air photo methods, once common. Most GIS systems have programs to compute the *prospects* that can be seen from a designated point.

The same programs also allow the *aspects* of a site to be identified—buildings or structures on the site that can be seen from particular locations off the site. These programs have been particularly effective in helping inform debates about tall buildings, wind generators, and high-voltage transmission lines.

Of course, not all views are equal. A long-distance view to mountains or water may be present but may occupy so little of one's view frame that it is not worth much. Or the opposite: a wind farm on the far horizon may be nearly invisible but is still a distraction, while one nearby will feel oppressive. Some views call out to be screened, such as rock-quarrying operations, while in other cases we may wish to clear corridors to desirable landmarks. Objects have connotations that must be kept in mind, as the debate over offshore wind turbines demonstrates. We are interested in both the negative and positive views from the site, and each needs to be treated differently.

Plans

So far we have looked at the site as if it existed in a governmental vacuum, which usually is far from the truth. Most communities have plans and policies that will have a great bearing on how a site may be developed, establishing key infrastructure locations and prescribing the kind of development that is permitted. However, on the fringe of metropolitan areas where sites are rapidly undergoing conversion to urban uses, such plans may lag behind the needs, and part of the site planning process may involve a negotiation over specific plans for the locale.

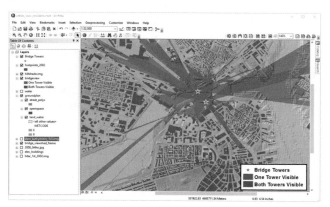

5.11 Viewshed analysis from Olana House, Columbia and Greene counties, New York.
(Courtesy of C. T. Male Associates)

5.12 Visibility of towers of Leonard Zakim Bridge, Boston, using viewshed analysis software.
(Courtesy of Paul B. Cote)

In an ideal situation, the local government has a *comprehensive plan* (or *general plan*, *master plan*, *master development plan*, or more recently *strategic development plan*) that describes its desired future in terms of its development objectives, the pattern of land uses, open spaces, and major infrastructure, and conservation policies. In the Western US, and in most Canadian, Australian, and European cities, such a plan will be essential in analyzing a site. Many communities with respected traditions of planning also have *consistency requirements*, mandating that all development be aligned with the comprehensive plan, necessitating a lengthy process of changing the plan if the site owner wishes to depart from it. But in older US cities, the plan may be out of date if it exists at all (New York City has no comprehensive plan underlying its zoning regulations), and many local governments on the edges of metropolitan areas maintain agricultural designations for land about to be urbanized, in the belief that it gives them more leverage over developers when new uses are proposed. In fast-growing Asian cities, development usually runs well ahead of the capacity of public authorities to plan for it.

Comprehensive plans seldom deal with sites in sufficient detail to resolve all the issues that will be faced. However, many local planning agencies also prepare, and governing bodies adopt, *specific area plans* (or *district plans*, *secondary plans*, *area plans*, *neighborhood plans*, *or master control plans*) that are quite prescriptive and may lead to design guidelines for individual sites. These plans may also detail the type and timing of infrastructure the local government expects to construct. *Concurrency requirements* may force a site owner to pay for or finance infrastructure off the site if he wishes to develop in advance of the government's timetable. Specific area plans will also locate major roads and infrastructure that will need to be accommodated on the site to serve others beyond it, and will usually be quite specific about lands to be conserved from development.

Plans and regulations are intimately connected—or should be. Chapter 7 outlines in greater detail the kinds of subdivision and development regulations that may affect the site. Here, as we consider the impacts of plans on the pattern of uses, we outline the specific requirements of infrastructure needed to serve the site's future occupants.

Access

Roadway access is a critical requisite for developing a site. Sites typically cannot be subdivided unless every parcel has access to a public roadway, either directly or through easements. And most sites larger than 1 ha (2.5 ac) require at least two points of access, providing for emergency access in the event that the main access route is blocked. Finding a way to assure site access is an early planning task.

The initial site analysis will identify the logical access points to the site, taking account of the capacity and design of surrounding roadways, the topography of the site, and desired lines of movement. Later, as the site's road network is sketched out and the uses become clear, detailed transportation analyses will be done using techniques that are spelled out in chapter 21. However, to begin the site planning process, we will need to make quick assumptions about the traffic volumes that will be generated, and test these against the available capacities of surrounding roads. Will the estimated numbers of vehicles be able to flow smoothly in and out of the site without the creation of new controlled intersections? If new signalized intersections will be necessary, how much distance will need to be maintained from current intersections on the surrounding roadways?

We begin by mapping surrounding roadways, noting their right-of-way dimensions and current number of lanes. These roadways are part of a local network, and will be classified by the local authority as arterial, collector, or local streets, which telegraphs their role in the system. Current traffic volumes during the peak hours are then assembled or extrapolated from 24-hour counts—typically the peak hour will represent 10–15% of the average daily traffic (ADT) volumes. Moving traffic through controlled intersections will be the key constraint, and a quick check can then be made of the available roadway capacity by using the rule of thumb that about 600 vehicles per hour per lane can flow through a typical intersection, if the light is timed equally in each direction. Using another rule of thumb, access onto an adjacent street through an intersection without traffic signals is generally difficult if there are more than 300 vehicles per hour per lane on that street. All of these figures will need to be revisited when there are more detailed plans, but they allow some first-cut assumptions to be made about feasibility and the number of access points that will be necessary.

Topography will play a role in establishing access points. Sight lines at any access points should be adequate to allow a motorist to brake when encountering a vehicle entering a roadway. On a roadway signed for 50 kph (30 mph), a vehicle traveling that speed would need 33 m (109 ft) to brake, which suggests that the minimum sight distance should be at least 50 m (165 ft), providing a 50% margin of safety for drivers moving faster or not fully attentive. Thus, the entrances to a site should be at least that distance from the crown of a hill, or from a curve on the approach to a site. These sight lines are doubly important for pedestrians crossing the street at access points to reach a bus stop or get to a destination on the other side of the road.

Local authorities will typically have standards or conventions about how closely intersections may be spaced. Some localities prohibit signalized intersections on arterial roads closer than 200 m (650 ft), which unfortunately encourages fast-moving traffic. A common convention is to require streets intersecting with collectors or arterials to be spaced at least 30 m (100 ft) from streets entering on the opposite side of the roadway, to avoid crosscutting traffic. A conversation with the local transportation department will surface the formal and informal rules that will affect access to the site.

People arriving at a site on foot, on bicycle, and via transit also need to be considered from the start. If access to local bus or mass transit is at the edge of a site, mapping the radius of access within 10 minutes' walk—typically 800 m (0.5 mi)—will help establish the area where higher densities and uses dependent on transit should be located. This radius will of course be extended by those using bicycles (owned or shared) to make the final leg of their trip. Many places have developed a network of bicycle lanes, and we need to identify how these can be connected to systems we will design on the site. Having a clear pathway system to reach transit and safe ways to cross major streets needs is at least as important as providing uncongested access points for motor vehicles.

Finally, in planning large sites, the roadways, pedestrian links, and bicycle ways crossing the site may be critical links in the citywide system of movement. We should remember that few trips (other than recreational cycling and teenage cruising in automobiles) are taken strictly for pleasure; most trips satisfy a need to reach important shopping, workplace, educational, social, and cultural destinations. Thus, in mapping the surrounding access system we should be attentive to the most important destinations they are intended to serve, mapping destinations along with surrounding uses. As we plan the site, this map will help resolve the probable flows of people and vehicles across and off the site.

Infrastructure

Parallel to analyzing the access system, we need to inventory the public services the site will depend upon. These include the infrastructure: water supply, sewers and sewage treatment facilities, piped and overland storm drainage systems, electrical supply, telecommunications systems, towers providing cell phone and internet service, district heating and cooling systems, and waste transfer and recycling facilities.

We are especially interested in the nearest location and available capacity of each of the systems that will serve the site. As with the access system, rough calculations need to be made of the possible magnitude of demands that developing a site will make on the infrastructure systems, flagging systems that may need upgrades. Some of the systems, such as electrical service, are easily upgraded (unless major new transformer capacity is needed), while other systems such as sewer service may necessitate lengthy and costly processes to construct new plants. Alternatively, many of the current systems may be able to be augmented by package plants on the site. Knowing which of these are essential at the outset will shape the mix of uses and have a large bearing on the capital investments needed for the site.

Part 4 discusses in detail each of these systems and the available options for on-site as well as off-site infrastructure and facilities. Final choices of site service systems must, of course, await the programming of the site, the financial framework, and the planning ideas. But the initial site analysis will provide the framework for making these choices. It will also identify the customary requirements imposed on the developer of a property to contribute to the costs of off-site facilities that will be dedicated to serving the site. In some instances these will be included in an impact fee charged upon approval of a development; in other cases the developer will be required to construct new facilities beyond the site.

Social infrastructure also needs to be identified in the initial inventory of the site's surroundings. This includes: educational facilities, child care and crèches, medical facilities, social service facilities, religious institutions, cultural institutions, parks and recreation facilities, socialization and meeting spaces (commons), libraries, and makerspaces.

The importance of each will, of course, depend upon the intended uses for the site. Depending upon the size of the site, local authorities may require land to be set aside for needed facilities (Callies, Curtin, and Tappendorf 2003). In the US and Canada, many communities have requirements that site developers contribute their fair share of the land (and sometimes the buildings and landscaping as well) for essential facilities. Since the future occupants of most sites provide only a fraction of the numbers needed to support a school or local park, developers are generally allowed to contribute funds to a common funding pool that will acquire the facilities. If they provide a site for a school but create demands for only half of the seats in it, they will be compensated for half the value of the land.

Parks and open spaces are difficult to distribute among sites in a city, since not every site has potential recreation lands, and some facilities serve purely local needs while others attract users from a broad region. The city of Vancouver, Canada provides for dedicating up to 10% of all sites over 20 ac (12 ha) for park and recreation purposes at the time that they are subdivided, with the specific choice of lands to be negotiated between the parks department and the developer. It also imposes a requirement on developers of all properties that they provide for 2.75 ac (1.1 ha) of publicly accessible open space per 1,000 people living in an area, through a combination of on-site facilities and contributions to a fund that will be used to acquire sites and create parks in other locations (City of Vancouver, n.d.).

In other parts of the world, there are blanket requirements regarding the amount of land to be set aside for streets, parks, and public facilities. In Saudi Arabia, as an example, it is customary for the local development authority to require developers to contribute 25% of their land area for roads, parks, and public facilities, in locations that are mutually agreed upon.

Legacy Structures

Many sites are blessed with structures that have historic meaning, often laced with nostalgia for local residents. Legacy structures can help shape the character and identity of a site, and may provide valuable space that can be adapted to other uses. In many cases, it is obvious that they ought to be saved, or even restored to their original splendor. But in other situations the structures are in an awkward location that will restrict the use of a site, or may be in such poor condition that preservation would largely require reconstruction, or may have no particular meaning to anyone. In some communities legacy structures will have been designated as historic places, prescribing what can be done with them, but in far more cases the decision will be left to negotiations between the site owner and local authorities. Adding complications, neighbors who resist any development of a site routinely seize on the historic significance of existing structures to block their demolition and slow down projects. How then to decide whether individual structures should be retained?

Legacy structures can be positioned on a ladder of significance, with interesting old structures of no wider consequence at the base and nationally recognized *historic structures* at the top. The terms for historic structures vary from city to city and across countries; they are sometimes called *landmarks*, *cultural monuments*, *heritage structures*, or *historical buildings*, and in some places are graded in terms of significance. In the US, local, state, and federal governments have programs for designating historic structures. While the processes differ, the qualities that distinguish registered *historic structures* are quite similar. To be designated, a structure must generally qualify under at least one of several criteria: it must either be associated with events that have made a significant contribution to local, regional, or national history; or be associated with the lives of persons important to that history; or embody or exemplify the distinctive characteristics of a type, period, region, or method of construction or

represent the work of a master or possess high artistic values; or have the potential to yield important information about the prehistory or history of the local area (California State Parks 2017). Typically a building must be more than 50 years old before being designated, although the threshold varies, and some local governments have begun considering much younger fine structures for designation to forestall their demolition.

Before designation, a historic structure report is prepared documenting the origins, form, and significance of a structure, and these are a valuable resource for a site investigation. Once it is designated, there are generally restrictions on demolishing a structure or altering its exterior appearance. On the positive side, recognition as a historic structure may make the owner eligible for tax credits or relief and favorable loans that can aid in returning a building to use. Even if it is not officially designated as a historic landmark but is eligible for designation, it may qualify for these benefits.

Most structures that remain on a site do not rise to the level of listed historic structures. However, they remain as reminders of past times, and may have significant value for the new use of the site. Barns can become community centers or the base for community farming operations. A sturdy factory structure can be adapted for apartments or startup businesses or a retail outlet. Millstones or industrial artifacts such as cranes can become sculptural objects to admire while commemorating past uses. Future uses may not be obvious at the outset, as with the hulking grain silos that are costly to demolish as well as to adapt to other uses. But keeping them standing leaves open the possibility that others may find innovative opportunities in the future, and the cost of removing the rubble of demolition is avoided.

Structures on a site may be important because they are part of a larger cluster of buildings that represent a

5.13 Street in Nantucket Historic District, Massachusetts. (Gary Hack)

5.14 Shipping cranes retained as sculptural objects, Puerto Madero, Buenos Aires, Argentina. (Gary Hack)

5.15 Abandoned grain silos retained for future uses, Puerto Madero, Buenos Aires, Argentina. (Gary Hack)

historic district, even though they would not qualify separately as historic structures. Within the boundaries of a designated historic district, structures are usually designated as *contributing* or *noncontributing*, with the latter usually not restricted in terms of demolition. They may contribute to the streetscape or the overall character of an area, and in some historic districts individual structures are graded on a scale of significance.

Historic places need not be individual buildings, but can be ensembles of structures of special significance or other landmarks. Many areas have also begun to designate important *cultural landscapes* and afford them special protection. These may be gardens and cultivated landscapes, but also may include open areas of natural landscape that have particularly treasured views or landmark natural features—the view to a river valley or ridge line, spectacular coastlines, or even scenic drives. Whether or not they are protected by regulations, a site survey needs to identify them. In urban areas wonderful tree-lined streets, public squares, cobblestoned streets, promontories, and monuments of all sizes will need to be recognized as significant elements in planning a site. Their form and pattern may be extended into the site, providing an intimate connection to the surroundings.

Nuisance and Noise

Not all aspects of a site's surroundings will be positive. The presence of derelict buildings, or waste disposal sites, or areas with unrestricted dumping or surface mining operations (*drosscapes*, as we have discussed in chapter 3) may require reclamation if they are on the site, or substantial buffers for separation if they are nearby (Berger 2007). Nearby railroad yards, highways, or transit lines may provide both an unattractive visual environment and noise that is incompatible with a peaceful residential environment. Nuisances need to be identified at the outset, since they may drive the planning approach.

Dealing with off-site noise is more straightforward than dealing with drosscape. Its sources may be from above the site (aircraft) or from highways, rail or transit lines, or industrial uses adjacent to the site. For urban or large fringe sites, noise-generating functions may be located within the site's boundaries. While the measurement of sound levels is well understood, quantitative measures do not account for the meaning of sound. We refer to sound as noise if it is considered undesirable (trucks on a nearby highway), while the same sound levels may in other cases be considered pleasurable (music in an outdoor concert). Loud sound levels may be tolerable if they are infrequent (although startling), but intolerable if they are constant. High-pitched sounds, such as the screech of mass transit vehicles on constrained curves, are more obnoxious than lower-pitched sounds at the same level. Hence, predicting the impacts of sound must account for the frequency of sounds and their periodicity as well as their absolute volume.

Sound levels are generally measured in terms of decibels (dB), and can be obtained with specialized sound level meters or inexpensive smart phone apps. Technically, a decibel is a measure of the difference between the energy level of the pressure wave of the sound and some reference sound. The reference sound is one that is just barely audible to a good human ear, and the decibel scale begins at 0 and runs to about 135, at the threshold of pain. Since the scale is logarithmic, each interval of 10 decibels represents sound energy that is 10 times greater than before, which the human ear distinguishes as being roughly twice as loud. Since the human ear doesn't hear sounds at all frequencies equally, an A-weighted scale (dBA) has been developed that adjusts for high- and low-pitched sounds to best approximate hearing. This scale is commonly used for transportation noise studies and other site analyses.

Common levels of outdoor and indoor sound are indicated in figure 5.16.

Noise levels have important human health effects and affect social relationships, worker productivity, and comfort. In 1974, the US Environmental Protection Agency established 70 dB as the upper level of environmental noise that can be endured without any measurable hearing loss over a lifetime. Levels of 55 dB outdoors and 45 dB indoors were set as upper limits on acceptable sound to avoid interference with conversations and other activities (Moudon 2009). In outdoor conversation standing 1 m (3 ft) apart, individuals usually speak at about 60–65 dB. Ambient noise levels in many cities are well above these levels, risking health and safety and stressing the population. The US Department of Housing and Urban Development

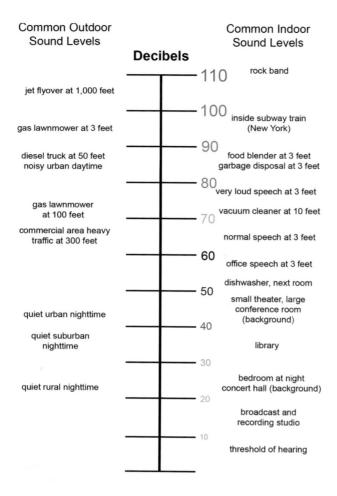

Common Outdoor Sound Levels   Common Indoor Sound Levels

Decibels

110 — rock band

jet flyover at 1,000 feet

100 — inside subway train (New York)

gas lawnmower at 3 feet

90

diesel truck at 50 feet
noisy urban daytime

food blender at 3 feet
garbage disposal at 3 feet

80
very loud speech at 3 feet

gas lawnmower at 100 feet

vacuum cleaner at 10 feet

70

commercial area heavy traffic at 300 feet

normal speech at 3 feet

60

office speech at 3 feet

dishwasher, next room

50

small theater, large conference room (background)

quiet urban nighttime

40

quiet suburban nighttime

library

30

quiet rural nighttime

bedroom at night
concert hall (background)

20

broadcast and recording studio

10

threshold of hearing

5.16 Common outdoor and indoor sound levels. (FTA 1995)

(HUD) has established 65 dB as the maximum acceptable site-average sound level for residential sites, but allows up to 75 dB to be used for housing based on a stringent environmental review and attenuation measures (Department of Housing and Urban Development, n.d.). Canadian housing standards are somewhat stricter, setting 60 dB as the maximum outdoor noise level on residential sites and 35 dB as the limit for interior spaces used for sleeping, although a slightly different methodology for measurement is used. As a general rule, HUD requires all sites located within 15 miles (24 km) of a military or civilian airport, 1,000 ft (305 m) of a major highway, or 3,000 ft (915 m) of a railroad to be scrutinized for noise attenuation.

Aircraft noise is difficult to assess, since noise levels are high when planes land and takeoff but low or nonexistent between flights. The volume of flights therefore matters, as does the distribution between day and night, since such noise is more tolerable when people aren't sleeping. Aviation authorities generally publish aircraft noise contours for approaches to runways, and local regulations typically restrict the use of sites within these contours. Criteria and methods of measurement have been standardized throughout much of the world, based on guidelines published by the International Civil Aviation Organization and the US Federal Aviation Administration (FAA).

The FAA's integrated noise model is considered the state-of-the-art tool for measuring aircraft noise impacts, taking account of the duration of the flyover, peak sound levels, tonal characteristics of the sound, and the number of daytime and nighttime aircraft movements. Noise levels are usually expressed in dB as the day-night average sound level (DNL) or the community noise equivalent level (CNEL). Both measures reflect the cumulative sound levels averaged over a 24-hour period, and the differences between the two are subtle, with the DNL accounting for day and night levels and CNEL adding a third evening period.

Current practice in planning around airports focuses on areas within the 65 dB CNEL contour as the *noise impact area*, where residences of all types, public and private schools, hospitals and convalescent homes, and places of worship cannot be located. Building codes typically set 45 dB as the maximum sound level for environmental noise reaching interior spaces, which serves as a target for building noise abatement.

Roadway noise levels are affected by many factors, including the speed allowed, the mix of vehicles using the road (percentage of trucks, age of the vehicle fleet, types of tires), the type of surface on the roadway, roadway geometrics, the terrain, and the micrometeorology of the area. At low speeds, stopping and starting of trucks at intersections and navigating steep grades can be major sources of roadway noise. Levels of highway traffic noise generally range from 70 to 80 dB at a distance of 15 m (50 ft) from the roadway edge. Another set of factors affects how noise spreads, including atmospheric effects, ground surfaces, and the presence of objects that reflect sound.

Noise levels are affected by distance from the source. Noise levels from a line source, such as a roadway, decrease by about 3dBA with each doubling

2006 EXISTING CONDITIONS & 2020 NO BUILD NOISE CONTOURS

LEGEND

2006 EXISTING CONDITION NOISE CONTOURS

2020 NOISE CONTOURS WITHOUT RUNWAY EXTENSION

AREAS OF DECREASE COMPARED TO 2020 WITHOUT EXTENSION

AREAS OF INCREASE COMPARED TO 2020 WITHOUT EXTENSION

Source: THE LPA GROUP INCORPORATED, ESA & CITY OF JACKSONVILLE (2006)

5.17 Noise levels, Jacksonville Executive Airport, existing and 2020. (Jacksonville International Airport)

of the distance. Thus, noise levels of 65 dBA at 100 ft (30 m) from a roadway would drop to 62 dBA at 200 ft (60 m) and to 59 dBA at 400 ft (120 m). Greater attenuation of sound will require some form of barriers that absorb the sound energy.

A common misconception is that densely planted buffers of trees can reduce noise levels. While these may mask the view of the highway, they will do little to reduce sound levels, since they screen out only the high-pitched sounds, and little of those. One thousand ft (300 m) of thick woodland will decrease noise in the audible range by only 20 dB more than the result of the distance alone. The energy of sound waves is most effectively reduced by berms of earth that interrupt the sight lines between a roadway and the site. Heavy concrete or masonry walls will also do the trick, although adjacent property owners who dislike their appearance often resist them. Nonetheless, tall concrete barriers may reduce the noise on a site by 5 to 10 dB, cutting the perceived loudness of the noise by one half (Corbisier 2003).

Many of the same issues are present in planning sites near railroads or mass transit lines, although transit in most cities does not operate 24/7. Railways, on the other hand, often come with significant vibration as well as noise, making control difficult. And the introduction

of high-speed trains has added aerodynamic noise as a factor that must be considered when speeds reach 300 kph (185 mph). The most effective way to deal with these issues is within the right-of-way through a combination of vehicle and isolation techniques. In the US, federal railway standards limit noise emissions to 70–90 dB, depending on the type of equipment. French TGV trains typically emit 85 dB when traveling at 100 kph and 95 dB at 350 kph. There are limits to how much these levels can be reduced through heavy sound barriers, and the fact that most high-speed rail lines are elevated makes isolation difficult.

In limited areas, noises can also be masked by the introduction of pleasurable sounds. Water is the equivalent to white noise in outdoor spaces, the result of both physical characteristics and mental perception. Studies have found that water sounds at 55 dB, roughly similar to the traffic noise level, can be an effective way to improve urban outdoor spaces. Low-frequency water sounds that are characteristic of fountains were found to be preferred to waterfall sounds. Nonetheless, the gentle cascade at Paley Park in New York is a respite from the sounds of the busy street it faces, and fountains in large public spaces contribute greatly to the sense of separation from urban surroundings.

6 | Sites as Property

One of the purposes of site planning is creating usable *real property*. When roads, blocks, lots, and buildings are arranged on a plan, there is an implicit division of the land into territories that will be under the control of particular individuals and groups. Before the site is developed, legal agreements will be entered into about the rights, responsibilities, and ownership of each area of the site. This process creates developable property, lots or parcels which become the economic basis for securing financing, and ultimately generate the revenues that will pay for developing and improving the site.

Use of Property

Property ownership and control is one of the most durable relationships between individuals in any society. Private ownership of property and the security it provides are considered a fundamental right in many societies. Some have argued that ownership derives from "natural law" (Locke 1988), while others describe the idea of private property as a constantly evolving form of contract between individuals and the state (Field 1989). Property rights are enshrined in the UN Universal Declaration of Human Rights, the US Constitution, the French Declaration of the Rights of Man and the Citizen, the European Convention on Human Rights, and the constitutions of many countries and states. In most societies, ownership of property is not absolute—it can be taken by the state for specific public purposes and can be regulated through zoning and environmental laws—but it conveys a relatively stable set of rights to those who hold the land.

The owner of a parcel of land is allowed to enjoy its use, exclude others from it, construct structures on it, and otherwise benefit from the property. He has the right to sell or exchange it, pledge it as collateral (such as a mortgage) for a loan, or rent it to others. Ownership represents a form of wealth, conveys obligations, and creates economic opportunities. Hence, a fundamental concern of site planning is allocating the rights to a site in a manner that will be effective for long-term development and use of the land. Site planners should not just think of the initial ownership of the land but also the subsequent ways it may be used.

The type of ownership established when a site is developed will have a direct bearing on how it can be planned. A site that will remain in a single ownership allows a great deal of flexibility in the location

6.1 Privately owned agricultural land, Bangkok, subdivided by families into ever narrower strips.
(Gary Hack)

of structures and common spaces. At the opposite extreme, a site that is broken into many small parcels, distributed among a large number of private owners, must be planned with lot lines in mind and with careful disposition of any spaces that are to be shared. It may require restrictions on adjacent lots to assure that development is compatible. Making the type of ownership a consideration of site planning can help avoid later conflicts between use and ownership.

It is important that there be an alignment between the "natural" territories of a site and the legal definition of properties. A site arrangement that subtly encourages people to cross a private property to reach a public open space will undoubtedly lead to conflicts. Lot drainage patterns that discharge runoff from one property onto the next will inevitably pit neighbors against each other. While lot lines may often be invisible, the responsibilities that come with them are quite real and will affect the quality of community life.

Property Regimes

The mechanisms and rules governing the ownership and control of property vary considerably around the globe. While they owe their origins to several historical types of property regimes, in every country these have been modified and codified to fit social and political conventions and powers. The principle of *lex rei sitae*—the law where the property is situated—governs. Nonetheless, it is worth understanding some things about major legal systems.

English Common Law

Much of modern property law in the English-speaking world derives from the notion of an *estate* in English common law. An estate consists of a recognized bundle of rights and duties that are communicated through deeds to property. While there are at least six types of estates recognized in law, by far the most common are *fee simple absolute* and *life estate* (Sprankling 2000). Fee simple roughly corresponds to a layperson's understanding of full ownership, and implies that a property may be sold, passed along to heirs, mortgaged or conveyed through leases or other grants of rights to others, without limitation. Over 99% of property owned in the

United States is in fee simple ownership. Life estates convey all the rights of use and enjoyment of property, but only during the lifetime of a designated individual, after which it passes to someone else. When the federal government purchased land for national parks, the owners were often provided with life estates so that they could continue to enjoy their property during their lifetimes, but with all rights transferring to the government when they passed away.

It is possible for the fee simple owner to *lease* land for long periods, conveying to others for a time virtually all the rights that the owner normally enjoys, referred to as a *leasehold*. Large portions of the UK, including much of central London, consist of hereditary estates that are leased for periods of 100 years or more to those occupying the land. In many societies, the state owns the "fee" to all or portions of the land, and leases it to individuals and groups for very long terms.

In many countries, constitutions and laws modify common law in providing protection against the taking (or *expropriation* or *condemnation*) of land by governments, and limiting the kinds of restrictions that may be imposed on the lands. In the US the Fifth and Fourteenth Amendments to the Constitution limit the right of governments to take property from individuals without due process and obligate the payment of just compensation when it is taken. These amendments also limit the government's ability to impose regulations that overly restrict the use of land, so-called *regulatory takings*. State laws set additional limits on condemnation in the US.

Napoleonic Code

In countries that owe their origins to English common law, it is assumed that private ownership of property conveys absolute rights, and that the burden rests with the state to demonstrate that these should be limited through rules created to protect the public interest. Countries with Napoleonic law traditions explicitly recognize the right of governments to set the parameters of ownership. Article 554 of the Napoleonic Code considers ownership to be "the right to absolutely free enjoyment and disposal of objects, provided that they are not in any way contrary to the laws and regulations" (UN Department of Economic and Social Affairs 1975). Now called the *Code Civil*, it represents a civil

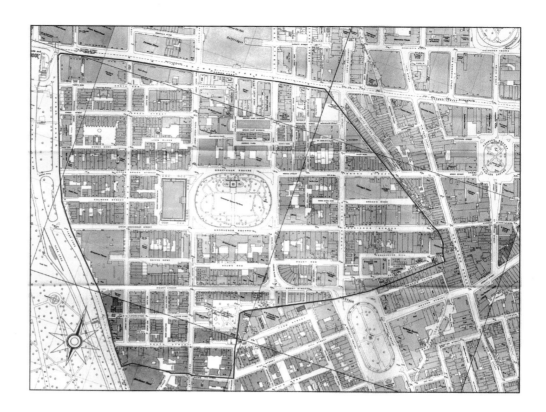

6.2 Grosvenor Estate, central London, subdivided in the eighteenth century for leasehold development. (London County Council)

law tradition that has been carried forward in many former French dependencies, but also plays a role in Quebec and Louisiana. The Napoleonic Code (and its preexisting Roman roots) influenced in important ways the laws of Latin American countries, such as Chile and Puerto Rico, as well as Spain, Belgium, the Scandinavian countries such as Norway and Denmark, and many other countries.

The differences between the common law and civil law traditions are subtle, and vary with the laws of each country. They can affect the way properties are defined and conveyed. The French civil code recognizes five types of rights to land: freehold ownership (*plaine propriété*), usufruct (*usufruit*), bare ownership (*nue-propriété),* co-ownership (*co-propriété*), and three-dimensional unit divisions (*division en volumes*) (Global Legal Group 2008). In Luxembourg, property ownership (*propriété*) is only achieved where the *usus, fructus,* and *abusus* (i.e., the right to use, the right to enjoy the fruits of, and the right to dispose of) are held by the same person (Global Legal Group 2008). In addition to ownership, other rights to real estate may be granted, including long-term leases (*droit d'emphytéose*),

building rights (*droit de superficie*), usufruct, or easements. In Poland, another civil law country, there is a distinction between ownership and perpetual usufruct (approximating a perpetual lease), where buildings may be owned but not the ground on which they are located.

Because of the wide variation among civil law countries, it is important to understand the particularities of the legal system before planning the subdivision of property and rights.

Islamic Law

In countries in the Middle East and parts of North Africa that derive their legal basis for ownership from Ottoman Empire laws, land is differentiated into four categories of ownership, each with elaborate rules governing use, transfer, and ultimate disposition (Darin-Drabkin 1971). *Mulk* properties represent private holdings that are owned individually, with full property rights. *Miri* land is state-owned land that may nonetheless be used by individuals as under the right of *tassruf* (usufruct)—under which the land is not diminished through its use. The right may be inherited but not divided, and the property returns to the state in the absence of an heir. Land designated as *waqf* is a special category, intended as an endowment for charitable purposes—to support hospitals, schools, mosques, libraries, and other institutions, and for housing indigent families. Any proceeds from such lands flow to the intended purposes, and waqf land cannot be alienated. Finally collective holdings are considered under *musha*—where members of a group each hold parcels, but where ownership may be redistributed periodically to maintain equality of holdings. This land tenure may be found mainly in rural areas.

Property regimes based on Islamic traditions have been modified in most of the countries that employ them through the addition of civil law codes. Many countries in the Middle East have modernized their property laws to encourage foreign investment and development, so that there is a significant convergence internationally in forms of ownership, ways of dividing up interests in land and buildings, and property registration practices.

Customary Law

A number of African and Asian countries recognize regimes of customary law that govern the holding and transfer of property. In Uganda, the Land Act of 1998 allows customary land ownership that is governed by the conventions and rules of local communities. Rights to land are rooted in local traditions and differ considerably (Foley 2007). In the Acholi regions, ownership is based on clans and land is largely communally owned or held by individuals for the benefit of the community. In other regions property is held individually and passed along to heirs, with disputes arbitrated by local councils of elders.

Most customary legal regimes are not codified and evolve to meet the challenges of the times (Payne 1996). Native North Americans inhabited the land as hunters and gatherers, observing local conventions of fairness and range. While a myth has grown up of communal ownership by First Nations members, anthropological research has led to the conclusion that many groups observed a form of undocumented private ownership and control (Steward 1938). By tradition, privately occupied land in the Acoma Pueblo in New Mexico cannot

be sold, passing upon death of the matriarch of a family to the eldest woman in the next generation. If there is no direct descendent, the cacique (tribal council) is responsible for reallocating it to other families. While customary regimes differ, generally they provide an individual right of occupation and use, but property can only be sold with the consent of the community enjoying these rights (Payne 1996).

In Indonesia and Malaysia, *Adat* is the customary law of the land that prevails in many areas, often alongside codified land registration systems in urban areas. There are wide variations in Adat systems throughout the countries—there are over 20 discrete indigenous legal systems in Indonesia—based on their histories, and the spread of Islamic law has added further complexity. In the Aceh province of Indonesia, as an example, customary law provides a form of land ownership but provides that land being sold must be offered first to neighbors, cannot be sold to community outsiders, is subject to neighbors' and other community members' legitimate rights of access, and may be appropriated by the community for community purposes (Gold and Zuckerman 2015).

Customary law traditions often coexist with more modern property laws, leading to a great deal of uncertainty about property rights. It is not unusual for a person to acquire a property, recording a deed with the official property registrar, only later to discover that there are a variety of customary law servitudes that still must be dealt with. The new owner may then have to purchase the rights of people to pass over the land or use it for hunting grounds, and the good graces of the spirits that are believed by the community to inhabit the site (Gold 1977).

Forms of Ownership

The wide variation of property laws around the world makes it impossible to speak with precision about all circumstances (Payne 1996). Nonetheless, there are underlying generalities that are broadly recognized, even if the names they are given vary and their application is rooted in local practices.

It is possible to speak of at least four forms of ownership of property (Sprankling 2000). One option is *no ownership*—no individual has any rights to the area in question. Many indigenous societies did not recognize ownership and fall within this realm, as do vast remote areas on a number of continents that have not been claimed by individuals and are beyond governmental control. Urban squatters' settlements in many less developed countries come close to this situation, although individuals in the favela will have informally recognized patterns of use and control.

A second possibility is *common property ownership*, where everyone has equal rights in the parcel. Colonial societies often created common property for common functions such as grazing lands, and the New England town commons in the US remain as an example of this format. Common property can also occur at a more local scale, as where a number of owners have undivided rights to the use of a property. Communal ownership is a fundamental organizing principle in tribal areas of many African countries, and continues in many of the burgeoning urban areas.

A third form of ownership is *state property*, where the government owns all rights in the land. Streets, parks, and public buildings are common examples. Many socialist societies nationalized all lands in order to control their use and retain their value. Even as countries such as China, Poland, and Ukraine have opened their economies to private initiatives, they have chosen to retain much of the land in state ownership (Bourassa and Hong 2003). In the US, the federal government owns a substantial proportion of the land nationwide, particularly uninhabited wilderness, national parks and forests, military reservations, and land below the water. And public entities, such as port authorities or state development entities, often own large portions of waterfronts, airports and their peripheral lands, and other current and former public facilities. In some instances, they may be precluded from selling them to private entities and must rely on leasing for development.

European countries such as Sweden, Finland, and the Netherlands, along with Israel, have pursued policies of public ownership of urbanizing areas in order to maintain tight control over development and benefit from land value increases over time. National capital cities often are built on publicly owned land; Canberra and Brasília are notable examples. All of Hong Kong and much of Singapore are developed on state-owned property, leased to individuals. In China, all property belongs to the state and in recent years has been leased to individuals or corporations for development, usually through prepaid leases extending for up to 70 years. Ground leases in these countries typically prescribe the amount and type of development that will be allowed on a site, serving as a substitute for other development regulations. The leases on state-owned property may be bought and sold, but the underlying property remains with the government.

6.3 Informal community, Rio de Janeiro, where land rights are unregistered.
(Gary Hack)

6.4 Town Common, Cohasset, Massachusetts, which has served as common land since the founding of the settlement.
(Wwods/Wikimedia Commons)

Private property is the fourth and most dominant form of ownership of land in modern societies. We refer to sites and all that is attached to them—buildings, roads, trees, and the like—as *real property,* distinguishing this form of ownership from tangible *personal property*, such as books or cars or other portable objects (also referred to as *chattels*) or *intangible personal property*, such as stocks, bonds, licenses, or *intellectual property*, such as patents or trademarks. Individuals, corporations, or other legal entities in most societies may own private property.

In higher-density developments, *cooperatives* and *condominiums* (also referred to as *strata title* entities) are special forms of ownership that provide for dividing the responsibilities of ownership into those elements that individual occupants are responsible for and those that are the collective responsibility. In cooperatives, owners do not actually own their units but are shareholders of the entity that owns the land and the building, and they have a proprietary lease on their personal spaces. Most cooperatives must consent to the transfer of shares to new owners. In condominiums, by contrast, owners each have fee simple ownership of their three-dimensional space and have an undivided interest in common areas including the grounds, rooftops, elevators, lobby, and common spaces. More will be said of the implications of these differences in chapter 16.

We generally think of ownership in terms of conveying a "bundle of rights." The most important of these are the right to exclude others from the property, the right to transfer the property for compensation or considerations, and the right to possess and use it or give others such rights. As a practical matter, governmental regulations may severely restrict how a property may be used—land use regulations, subdivision regulations, coastal zone restrictions, environmental regulations, and other rules. Ownership does not imply unlimited rights to exclude others: aircraft may fly over a site, so long as they maintain permitted altitudes, and police may enter a property if they have a warrant, or if there is an imminent public danger.

Unbundling Property Rights

The rights of ownership may be restricted to certain time periods, as in *time-share* or other *fractional ownership*

6.5 Canberra, Australia, a city developed on land leased from the national government.
(Government of Australia)

6.6 Straw Hill, a residential condominium in Manchester, New Hampshire, contrasts with adjacent homes with fee simple ownership.
(Google Earth)

arrangements, where several owners have the right to use and enjoy the same property during different times. In many jurisdictions, owning a property may not include ownership of the resources below the ground, such as *oil* or *mineral rights*.

It is possible to "unbundle" the rights to a property and sell some while retaining others. In some jurisdictions, the *development rights* attached to a property may be sold or transferred to other sites, while the owner of the property retains the right to use it for agricultural or recreation purposes. Other localities, notably New York City, allow the sale of *transferable development rights* (*TDR*)—the unused rights of development under a zoning law, such as those attached to designated landmark structures. In arid locations, where *water rights* are the critical prerequisite for development, these may also be transferred. A site without water rights may have limited potential for use.

When subdivided land is sold or leased, specific rights and obligations pass from one individual to another. The sale agreement is generally registered or recorded in the land title registry. A subsequent sale or lease agreement between owner and lessee would embody that agreement. The manner by which these conditions are conveyed has important consequences for the planning of a site.

The simplest site plan involves subdividing the land only into private lots and public streets. Normally, street frontage is required for every lot that is to be developed, so that owners have access to their land. However, alternative forms of access such as an *easement* across another private property may be recognized as adequate access. If the lots are sold, then the new owners may acquire a *fee simple freehold estate*. This means that all the claims by others on their property have been discharged, and that all the fees for the use of the land have been paid. The owner is, of course, subject to public laws and regulations such as zoning that affect the use of his land and must pay taxes, so not all obligations have been removed. But no other private party may impose requirements on the owner.

Easements and Covenants

The title to a property may record commitments made by the new owner of a property to the person he has purchased it from. Technically, a seller "reserves" these rights and responsibilities in the deed when it is conveyed to a new owner. Two common forms of commitments are *easements* and *covenants*, and they may cover a variety of circumstances.

Easements convey to a person who does not own a parcel of land the right to use it for limited purposes. The most common form of easement is a *right-of-way* granted to allow passage across a site. The owner of a back lot may have an easement allowing him to travel across the front lot to reach his land. Two adjacent owners may share a driveway, partially on the property

of each, through *cross-easements*. Easements may be granted to utility companies to enter a property to maintain pipes or wires below or above the ground. Where buildings are built right on the lot line, as in zero lot line housing (see chapter 33), the owner may be provided with a *maintenance easement* that allows him to enter the adjacent property for the purpose of maintaining or repairing the abutting side of his structure.

Easements may involve conveying rights other than physical access to a site: a *view easement* may oblige the owner of one property to maintain sight lines across his land for the benefit of adjacent property owners. Conversely, a *privacy easement* may be created to prohibit any windows on one property that look out on a particular space on an adjacent property. A *conservation easement* may require that portions of a site remain in an undisturbed state to protect the ecosystem of the area, or may simply restrict an area from certain developments. A *solar easement* may prevent an owner from constructing buildings or planting trees that shade all or parts of an adjacent property. A *facade easement* may grant to others—often a city agency or nonprofit organization—the right to approve any changes to the face of a building, including its demolition.

Some types of easements, and even the right of ownership, may be established by means other than the consent of an owner. A longstanding principle of English common law recognizes *prescriptive easements* and rights of ownership established by *adverse possession*. Thus, an adverse easement right to continue to walk across a property may be established by a longstanding pattern of use, not sanctioned by the owner. The standards to assert such rights are high; it generally must be proved that the person claiming a right must have openly and continuously used the land for a lengthy period (in some jurisdictions this is 20 years), without the permission of the owner, and the owner must have made no efforts to prohibit such use. As a practical matter, while such claims are difficult to prove, they can provide a nuisance in the planning of a site, and need to be investigated.

Easements pass from owner to owner as land is sold and are not easily removed from titles. Removal generally requires the consent of all the beneficiaries, or a court finding that the purposes are no longer relevant.

Covenants may also run with the land, binding successive owners to make good on promises concerning

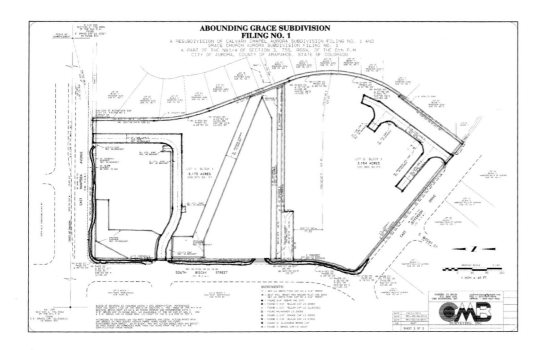

6.7 Multiple easements affecting parcel of land, including drainage easement, rights-of-way, utility easements, and slope easements. (Courtesy of CMB Land Surveying)

the use of land. As an example, a covenant may limit the use of a property to residential uses. Once it is accepted in a deed to a property, the beneficiary of the covenant, usually the individual who inserted it, is the only one who may remove it.

Promises created through covenants may run the gamut of purposes. Often they are used to ensure that property owners, over time, conform to community standards, and the enforcement is assigned to a homeowners' association or other entity that has a stake in community interests. As an example, a covenant may oblige an owner to have plans for buildings or renovations approved by a design review committee comprised of owners of property in the area. Covenants in planned developments often regulate changes in great detail, including the colors of doors and windows. But there are limits—generally covenants may not be used to discriminate against individuals or groups, or to force actions that may be a hazard to the larger communities.

One general rule is that while negative covenants may only run with the land and bind successive owners, positive covenants (taking an action or expending money) apply only to the next owner, unless additional legal devices are employed. Thus, covenants may prevent an owner of a property from destroying a hedge or stone wall on the property line, or may restrict the location of building on a site, or may prevent an owner from changing the exterior colors of his house without consent of the homeowners' association, but may not require successive owners to expend money such as to build a roadway to serve others. This rule against positive covenants running with the land is in keeping with the principle that fee simple ownership means that obligations ("fees") have been discharged at the time of purchase. It forces the planner and developer to look to other means to fund the long-term maintenance of shared properties.

Cadastral Systems

With the complexity of ownership, easements, and covenants in most societies (other than customary law areas), there is a need to memorialize the ownership status and commitments in a legally recognizable form. Cadastral systems have been developed both to describe property boundaries and to provide a template for conveying the level of ownership. These generally take one of three forms.

In a *deeds registration system* or more technically *juridical cadastre*, the transfer document (the deed) itself is registered. The juridical cadastre normally consists of two parts: The first part is a written record or register with information on each parcel, such as owner and the rights of the land, while the second part includes a detailed description of the parcel in the form of a map or survey measurements. The written deed, in itself, does not prove the ownership, and the chain of ownership has to be traced back either by lawyers or the land registration authority. Often a system of title insurance is employed to provide security that the chain of title is adequate.

In a *title registration system* the certificate itself is the proof of ownership. This system was developed in the United Kingdom and exists in many Anglo-Saxon countries and countries whose legal systems were modeled on Britain. However, in some countries with such a system, land registration is not compulsory or is only required when land is sold or subject to long lease (e.g., England and Wales). The *Torrens system* is a variant of the title registration system developed in Australia. The advantage is that there are two certificates to each parcel and the original is kept at the land registry. An ownership transfer is merely endorsed on the back of both the original and duplicate. Variations of this system have been adopted in countries such as Thailand, Malaysia, and Kenya.

The *private conveyance system* is the most common system in developing countries. While a system to register deeds often exists, in Bangladesh and Pakistan (as examples) only 10–20 percent of transactions are actually registered. In these countries, the remaining transactions are conveyed either formally or informally, often without a person with legal training involved (Farvacque and McAuslan 1992). A practice has gradually developed in most societies requiring the land transaction to be written and witnessed by a disinterested party.

A number of countries have made attempts to introduce new tenure systems to deal with widespread squatting on disputed lands in informal settlements. The certificate of rights in Botswana and the occupancy licenses in Zambia are two examples, which can be transferred to others. In other countries, such as Thailand and India, slum dwellers are able to lease their plots from private or public landowners, even improve and transfer them, while remaining the equivalent of a tenant at will. Nonetheless, it is difficult to displace them because of the political repercussions (Payne 1996).

The necessity of secure title is a fundamental condition for obtaining loans or mortgages to purchase property. Gradually, cadastral systems are being harmonized across the globe, as capital moves across borders. Nonetheless, the peculiarities of each country (or community, in the case of varied land tenure systems) need to be understood by the site planner, as detailed plans are made to subdivide the rights on a site.

7 | Site Development Regulations

Owning a site or holding a leasehold interest creates the right to use and enjoy a site, limited only by the easements, covenants, and other restrictions that pass with the deed. However, governments generally prescribe what may be built on a property and set the rules for planning the site. These rules will be contained in codes and regulations, which go by a variety of labels: *zoning and subdivision regulations* (in the US and Canada), *land use zoning* (Japan), *development control plans* (Australia), *building control regulations* (Thailand), *development control regulations* (Malaysia), *city planning and management regulations* (China), or *development regulations* (in much of the rest of the world).

In many countries, development regulations are mandated by the national government (Germany and France, as examples), in others the national government establishes the categories of development regulations and these are mapped onto the ground locally (Japan), and in other places, development regulations are the responsibility of state or local governments (US, Canada, Australia, UK). In some countries development regulations are embedded in building codes, while in the majority of cases they are distinct bodies of law.

However imposed, development regulations have a direct bearing on what can be built on a site, and ultimately on the site's value. However, large development parcels are frequently zoned inappropriately, since urban development often involves the conversion of land to new uses—agricultural land becoming urban; institutional or governmental sites converting to a mixture of urban uses; formerly industrial areas becoming residential and commercial areas, and other changes. In these situations, obtaining the right to build often means changing the development regulations that apply to a site, a process that usually involves public hearings, negotiation, and concessions. In most cities, an army of lawyers exists to plead on behalf of property owners for favorable interpretations of development regulations, seek variances from them, or write proposals for new regulations.

Most development codes regulate by creating a series of land use categories, each with unique requirements that are mapped on the land. The number and typology of categories is a national or local convention, but also reflects the degree of separation of uses that is considered desirable in urban areas. In most of Japan, there are only eight land use categories, and a great deal of mixing of housing with other uses is encouraged. Except for one exclusive low-rise residential zone, shops and businesses are permitted in all other areas of a city. By contrast, many North American cities have dozens of land use districts, restrict commercial uses in most housing areas, and segregate different housing types.

Allowable Densities

On residential sites, the amount of development allowed is generally limited by minimum *lot sizes* and dimensions, or by restrictions on the density of development (no more than x dwellings per ha or ac). A 400 m² (4,300 sq ft) minimum lot size will restrict development to about 25 dwellings per hectare (10 per acre). Establishing a 5 m (16 ft) minimum frontage for dwelling lots will have the practical effect of limiting densities to about 75 units per ha (or 30 units per ac) if each unit must accommodate parking on site. These figures are expressed in terms of *net density*—the number of units divided by the area of property actually

7.1 Zoning map for Vancouver, Canada, consisting of seven use-based zoning districts, three historic districts, and seven comprehensive development districts with custom-tailored standards. (City of Vancouver)

devoted to the use, excluding public roads, parks, and other lands not attached to the property. In other circumstances, such as in planning large sites, density may be expressed as *gross density*, generally meaning the entire site area divided by the number of residential units or the amount of residential space on the site.

For uses other than housing, the amount of development on a site is generally limited by a maximum *floor area ratio* (FAR), also known as the *plot ratio*, or *floor space index* (FSI). Thus an FAR of 6, or 6:1, or 600% (depending on the local convention) would allow a building to be constructed that has a floor area 6 times the area of the site. The definition of what is included in built space must be carefully studied, and in high-density cities such as New York, code consultants work with developers to harvest every allowable square foot under the zoning code. In some cities, underground space is not included in the calculation, and a number of cities, including Vancouver, Canada, only include enclosed parking areas if they are above ground. These rules have the effect of pushing more uses below ground.

A further restriction on development may be imposed through a maximum *site coverage ratio*, or its inverse, a minimum *open space ratio*. Some codes impose such restrictions implicitly, by requiring setbacks from streets and property lines or by prescribing usable open spaces. In other situations, such as the development control regulations in Dhaka, Bangladesh, FAR and site coverage ratios are tightly linked. In a residential area that allows an FAR of 3.0, ground coverage is restricted to 65%, while in an area with an FAR of 3.75, coverage is limited to 60% (Khan and Mahmud 2008). For lower-intensity uses, such as local shopping areas, the most powerful regulation affecting site capacity may be the on-site *parking requirements.* More will be said of the dominant impact of parking in part 5.

Beyond controlling the uses and intensity of development of a site, most development codes also create a building envelope that defines the opportunity for development. Maximum *height limits* are common in Europe and much of the US, although in New York there are no height limits in office districts, which sanctions a race to the sky. Setback requirements, intended to guarantee adequate sunlight at ground level and into interior spaces, become the controlling factors in many development codes. They are especially pernicious, creating vast amounts of waste space along roadways and streets. In Japan and other parts of the world development is limited by creating a *setback plane* or *slant plane* from front and rear property lines. In most residential zones in Japan, the street face of buildings may not be higher than the street is wide; above that height it must step back 1 m for each 1.25 m of additional height. The result is the proverbial Japanese "pencil building," shaped by development regulations. New York's setback requirements influence the amount of development that is possible in an equally powerful way. Other cities have negotiated similar setback schemes, some adopting sophisticated *sky plane exposure requirements* that affect heights, the placement of buildings, and ultimately the amount of development.

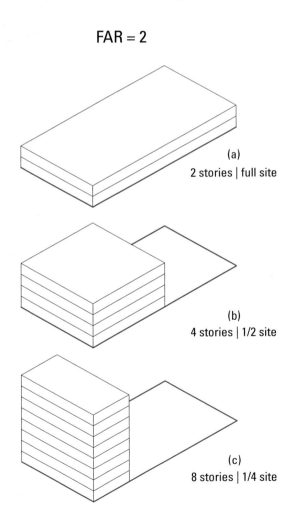

FAR = 2

(a)
2 stories | full site

(b)
4 stories | 1/2 site

(c)
8 stories | 1/4 site

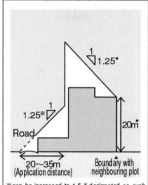

[Slant Plane Restriction]

● Residential Land Use Zone

1
1.25*

1
1.25*
Road
20m*

20~35m
(Application distance)

Boundary with
neighbouring plot

※can be increased to 1.5 if designated as such by the local government building authority with the approval of the City Planning Council.
★can be increased to 2.5 and 31 m respectively if designated as such by the local government building authority with the approval of the City Planning Council.

● Other Zones

1
2.5*

1
1.5
Road
31m*

20~50m
(Application distance)

Boundary with
neighbouring plot

※can be exempt from restriction in areas designated by the local government building authority with the approval of the City Planning Council.

7.2 (left) Alternative ways of deploying the same floor area.
(Adam Tecza/Gary Hack)

7.3 Slant plane restrictions in Japan that require setbacks when buildings are taller than the width of the adjacent street.
(Ministry of Land, Infrastructure and Transport, Japan)

7.4 Sky plane restrictions force upper levels of Tokyo buildings to step back.
(Gary Hack)

Incentives are sometimes built into development codes, allowing tradeoffs of greater density in exchange for creating public goods. New York's zoning code has elevated this practice to a high art, offering bonuses for including affordable housing on a site, creating plazas or open spaces in dense districts, renovating transit stations on or adjacent to the site, or contributing to the construction of transit or open spaces nearby. In other cities, added density is often the result of negotiations over such items. Still other cities, including Boston, require the payment of impact fees to support public objectives (job training, creating social infrastructure, subsidizing affordable housing), or to pay for off-site improvements to roadways, sewer and water lines, and open spaces.

An increasing number of cities in the US are adopting *form-based zoning* codes that regulate what may be built explicitly rather than implicitly, by setting limits on building form. Such codes often prescribe the locations of buildings on the site, minimum and maximum heights, locations of parking areas, and even the required architectural character. Where such codes are in effect, the form of buildings and their placement will provide the point of departure for site planning.

Environmental regulations, embedded in development codes or in separate regulations, can also have a powerful influence on a site's capacity for development. Many cities have special requirements for *wetlands areas*, *coastal zones*, areas with steep slopes, areas subject to *subsidence*, or other areas of special environmental hazard or concern. The uses of *brownfield* sites may be limited by the requirement to clean up the site if the surface is disturbed.

Specific Design and Planning Requirements

Urban design regulations can also have a shaping influence on what may be built on a site, and its corresponding economic value (Punter 1999). Vancouver, Canada, regulates towers by setting dimensional limits on tall buildings: structures should be no more than 85 ft (23 m) on a side and separated from other towers by at least 80 ft (24 m). An accepted development rule in the northern half of China is that every residential unit must have sunlight for at least two hours a day; the effect is that residential densities are limited to an FAR of about 2.25. Many cities seek to encourage

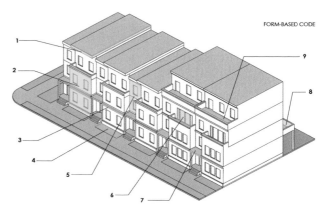

7.5 Form-based zoning code, downtown Woodbury, New Jersey, that prescribes massing and form of structures. (City of Woodbury/Courtesy of Group Melvin Design)

continuous street walls by imposing "*build-to*" requirements, generally prescribing that a high percentage of the structure must be located along the property line at the street. Or they may require or provide incentives for just the opposite—the creation of plazas along streets—a step that is only appropriate in the densest urban centers.

In some cities, *specific area plans* (also known as *secondary plans*, *district plans*, *neighborhood plans*, or *urban design plans*) have been adopted that tightly regulate building heights, locations, and relationships, leaving little discretion to the landowner about what may be constructed. Urban design regulations may be imposed through development *overlays*—rules that apply on top of normal zoning or development regulations—or they may come into play in cases where there is discretionary review. A city may impose more restrictive

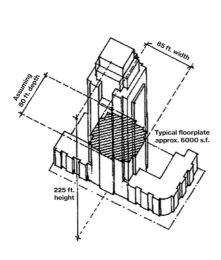

85 ft. width

Assuming 80 ft. depth

Typical floorplate approx. 6000 s.f.

225 ft. height

Lower, wider tower configuration floorplate.

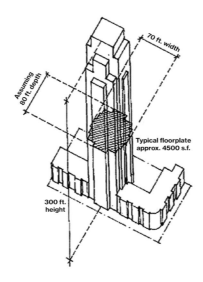

70 ft. width

Assuming 80 ft. depth

Typical floorplate approx. 4500 s.f.

300 ft. height

Higher, slimmer tower configuration with larger configuratin with smaller floorplate.

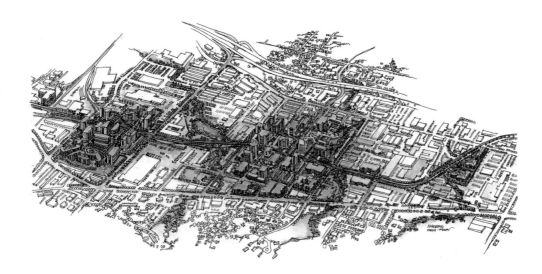

7.6 Residential tower dimensional requirements, Vancouver, Canada. (City of Vancouver)

7.7 Transfer of development rights (TDR), King County to Bellevue, Washington, allowing the shift of unused development rights from conserved land in the county to the Bel-Red subarea of the city. (King County, Washington)

7.8 By purchasing TDR from lands that are conserved, and constructing affordable housing, the city of Bellevue can increase the allowable FAR in the Bel-Red area from 1.0 to 4.0. (King County, Washington)

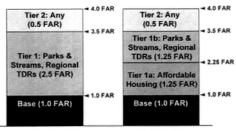

Within Nodes
(MO-1, OR-1, OR-2, RC-1, RC-2, RC-3)

Tier 2: Any (0.5 FAR) — 4.0 FAR	Tier 2: Any (0.5 FAR) — 4.0 FAR
— 3.5 FAR	— 3.5 FAR
Tier 1: Parks & Streams, Regional TDRs (2.5 FAR)	Tier 1b: Parks & Streams, Regional TDRs (1.25 FAR) — 2.25 FAR
	Tier 1a: Affordable Housing (1.25 FAR)
Base (1.0 FAR) — 1.0 FAR	Base (1.0 FAR) — 1.0 FAR
Non-Residential Development	**Residential Development**

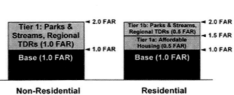

Outside Nodes
(R and CR Zones Only)

Tier 1: Parks & Streams, Regional TDRs (1.0 FAR) — 2.0 FAR	Tier 1b: Parks & Streams, Regional TDRs (0.5 FAR) — 2.0 FAR
	Tier 1a: Affordable Housing (0.5 FAR) — 1.5 FAR
Base (1.0 FAR) — 1.0 FAR	Base (1.0 FAR) — 1.0 FAR
Non-Residential Development	**Residential Development**

requirements (height limits, required cornice line, street walls, material requirements, etc.) to promote uniformity in special districts such as along a major boulevard, even if taller buildings are generally permitted in the larger zoning district it passes through.

Historic preservation provides an especially powerful set of tools for public bodies to restrict what may be built on a site. Individual buildings may be *landmarked* (or listed on a local historic register), or an entire area may be designated as a historic district, worthy of special protection, as a way of preserving cultural resources of a city. The powers of *historic commissions* (or *landmark commissions* or *heritage commissions*) to enforce these regulations vary widely, but many have the ability to block the demolition of structures, and have the power to review and approve any additions or changes. Regulations may limit the size, height, location, and appearance of any new structures added on sites within a historic district, over and above any zoning or other development rules that may apply. Since the owner of a designated historic structure may not be able to make full use of the development rights, some cities including New York now allow the transfer of development rights to other sites, creating a market for purchase and sale of such rights. Most historic districts create procedures for *discretionary review* and approval of projects within the areas of their jurisdiction, which may be applied with few or no formal guidelines.

As of Right vs. Discretionary Approval

Development review procedures tend to fall into one of two camps: *as-of-right* systems, where the owner of the site is entitled to a building permit to construct a structure if it meets the zoning and other regulations applicable to its site; and *discretionary review* systems, where a project must obtain permission from a review officer or pubic body before the project is allowed to proceed. In New York and many American cities, Japan, and many Canadian cities, the majority of new development is approved as of right. However, development review procedures that go beyond quantitative requirements and scrutinize the aesthetic character of proposed buildings are being adopted by an ever-increasing number of cities. The best of these jurisdictions also adopt *design review guidelines* to provide a

level of certainty about what is acceptable, while others operate purely from precedent of what has been successful—and not so successful.

Many cities allow smaller projects to proceed as of right, while subjecting large projects to greater scrutiny because of their potentially large impacts. All projects in Boston larger than 50,000 sq ft (4,650 m²) are required to report on their impacts, which opens them to discretionary review. Most cities set higher thresholds, while some cities such as San Francisco have discretion in deciding when a project may potentially have impacts that warrant discretionary action. Obtaining relief from normal development regulations, through variances or changes to the zoning, will in many cities trigger discretionary review of the project. Most large projects require some form of variance, and in many cities development regulations are unfortunately antiquated, forcing developers to submit to discretionary review. An increasing number of cities have created design review bodies that review the aesthetics of all large projects, or their impact on the public realm; these are generally advisory to the decision makers, unless the project involves public funding.

Most landowners recoil at the thought of going through a discretionary review that places their fate in the hands of neighbors, planning staff members, and unpredictable public officials, and will settle for less development rather than test fate. However, there is a positive side to discretionary review procedures as well: they offer greater flexibility in planning sites, the ability to move densities around, and the ability to phase developments. *Planned development area* procedures, also called *planned unit development* (*PUD*) rules, allow normal development rules to be suspended in favor of a master plan for a site and development agreement (contract) which control what is built on the site over time. Once an agreement is reached on what can be built on a site and the rules that will apply, these are referred to as an *entitlement*. These may be passed along to new owners in most circumstances. Entitlements usually have a time dimension, with the requirement that construction begin within a specified number of years.

In countries where *development permit* systems are the norm, such as England and Australia, discretionary review is an accepted fact of life. Achieving entitlements for development may require many months or

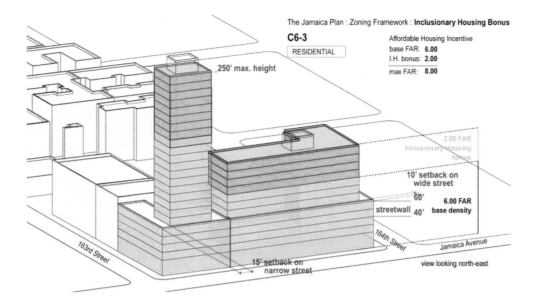

C6-3

RESIDENTIAL

250' max. height

Affordable Housing Incentive
base FAR: **6.00**
I.H. bonus: **2.00**
max FAR: **8.00**

2.00 FAR
Inclusionary Housing
bonus

10' setback on
wide street

60'

6.00 FAR
base density

streetwall 40'

164th Street

163rd Street

Jamaica Avenue

15' setback on
narrow street

view looking north-east

7.9 Building massing study, Jamaica, Queens, New York, complying with existing zoning and indicating effects of inclusionary zoning bonus. (New York City Planning Commission)

years, and a great deal of planning and negotiation to arrive at the agreed-upon program and plan. Without entitlements, it is not possible to develop a site.

In the UK, the process involves applying for *planning permission* by submitting a detailed description of what is proposed for a site. The application is reviewed by the planning authorities, who consult with the dozens of other agencies and local bodies that have authority over the development, from city departments to English Heritage, the local highway and environmental authorities, and interest groups both broad and specific (such as the Ramblers Association which may have interests in footpaths across a site). The public, particularly neighbors, will be consulted, and an open *public inquiry* may be held. In response, the planning officials may propose *planning conditions* and *planning obligations* (such as inclusion of low-income housing or paying a community infrastructure levy). Negotiations will ensue, and ultimately the planning committee of the local council will rule on approval of the development with agreed-upon conditions that must be met by the developer. All of this makes for a lengthy (and costly) process, and until conclusions are reached (or appeals are ruled on) the owner of a site must live with a high level of uncertainty about the site program and plans.

Each country has its own unique processes for determining what may be permitted on a site, and the site planner needs to become familiar with them to avoid the risk of pursuing an approach that ultimately may prove impossible to get approved. We have described situations where regulations have been adopted to guide development, but in many cities there

are no such regulations; proposed plans for development are simply compared to the overall master plan of the city (usually a land use diagram), and judgments are made about whether to approve them. The fine-grained negotiation may occur much later, in discussions with agencies on plans for roadways or links to sewer and water systems.

Determining Site Capacity

Before beginning the process of making plans, it is essential to analyze the amount of development permitted on the site, whether conforming to the current regulations or to changes in the regulations made to fit the objectives of the landowner and planning team. The analyses can take a variety of forms: a site plan laying out the site as currently permitted (the as-of-right plan); an envelope study showing the outer limits of the development as shaped by the setbacks, sky planes, and other regulations; a statistical analysis of how much traffic will be generated by uses currently permitted; and so on. They will serve as a benchmark for comparing the effects of any changed regulations. Such a study was compelling in the NewBridge project described in chapter 2, in helping persuade the city that higher-density institutional uses would yield more public open space than carpeting the site with low-density development. It will also help the owner begin to create a financial model for the project, and will expose the decisions that need to be made about the program for the site. This analysis marks the start of the process of designing a site.

8 | Interpreting Site Knowledge

Even a cursory look at the form, natural systems, context and surroundings, property issues, and regulations affecting a site will reveal the complexity of the area that needs to be planned. A more detailed analysis will cry out for some system of making sense of the accumulated information. Not all issues and factors are equally important, and some of them will have relevance only later in the process once first-cut decisions are made. How can the site planner sift through what he has learned and condense the influences into the essentials?

The traditional way to accomplish this is to construct a diagram of important site factors. Making such a diagram forces the planner to become clear about the critical natural factors (orientation, winds, microclimates, important ecologies), immovable or unchangeable elements on the site, the big opportunities, the critical access points, the regulations and policies that will shape the form of development, views and aesthetic relationships, and other things that will express the unique terroir. In all cases, the site planner asks, How will this impact the configuration of the site? This is the first step in creating a site plan.

Site analyses can take many forms, and they are best understood through examples.

Small Site – Just the Essentials

This shorefront site analysis has been reduced to the essentials—sunlight, winds, topography, large trees to be preserved, location of adjacent buildings, water views from the site, and the nuisance of heavy traffic on the edge of the site. Hand-drawn, its evocative qualities convey an appreciation for the natural form of the site, which is intended as an access base to Seattle's Lake Union.

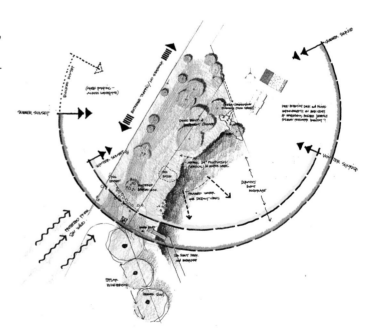

8.1 Site analysis diagram, Lake Union shoreline access base, Seattle, Washington.
(Courtesy of Windrose Landscape Architecture)

Sensitive Site – Sea Ranch Expansion

Chapter 1 recalled the guiding vision for the Sea Ranch development in California, where nature and buildings now harmonize to provide a unique environment. There have been a variety of proposals over the years to complete and expand the uses on the site, including this proposal for an expansion of Sea Ranch Lodge. The site analysis maps the essential natural features, the topography, and views to the water, and identifies sites for new structures.

8.2 Site analysis drawing, Sea Ranch Lodge expansion project. (Courtesy of Bull Stockwell Allen)

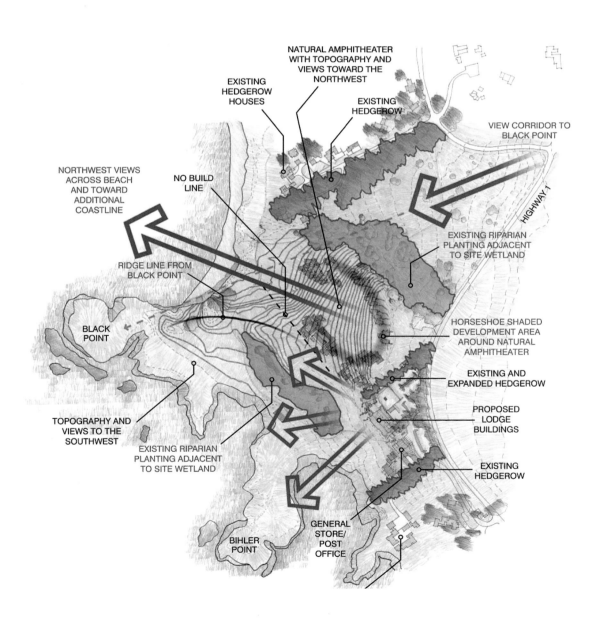

More Complex Site

Urban sites are generally more complex than greenfield sites beyond the edge of current development. There is a need to account for man-made influences (adjacent development, potential access points, utility easements, and altered topography, among other influences) as well as natural features. Compiling the essential elements on one drawing is a challenge.

Large Complex Site

This large site in Hawaii is intended for multiple hotel and resort uses, and the site analysis is done with an eye to key locations for siting facilities. Views are paramount, as are breaks in topography that could serve to separate the site into distinct zones. Notes are an essential part of the diagram.

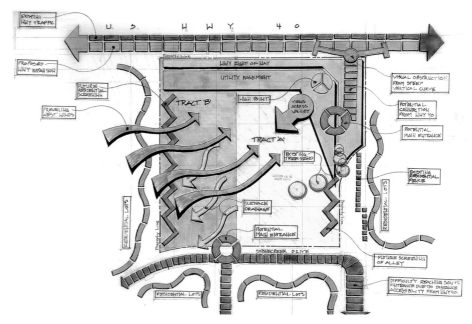

8.3 Site analysis diagram of an urban site for future church and educational campus. (Courtesy of © Williams Spurgeon Kuhl & Freshnock Architects)

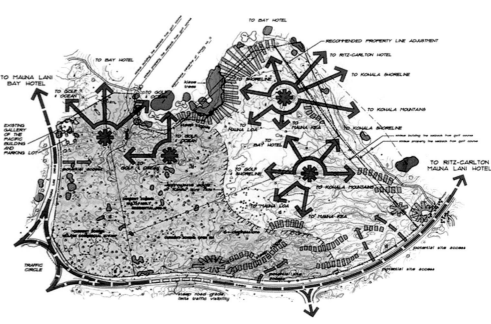

8.4 Analysis of Mauna Lani resort site, Hawaii. (Courtesy of David Evans and Associates)

Site for a Large New University

Hills, two natural ravines, steep slopes, existing structures, and potential access points are singled out as key
influences on this site for a new university in Indonesia.
At the time of this plan, a number of sites remained to
be acquired, which consigned them to later development. The area within a 10-minute walking distance
from the center of the site is mapped, indicating where
the main concentration of facilities should be located.

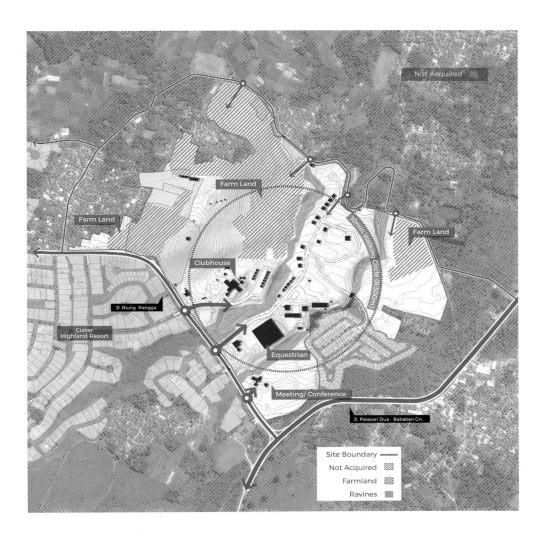

8.5 Existing conditions
diagram, West Java
New University, Subang,
Indonesia.
(Courtesy of Sasaki
Associates)

Fragmented Urban Site

In some circumstances, site analysis is the vehicle to determine potential sites for development and how they might be linked. This analysis, of the Harbor Point area of Baltimore, Maryland, recognizes the potential of a procession of uses and open spaces from Fells Point on Broadway to Thames Place on Harbor Point.

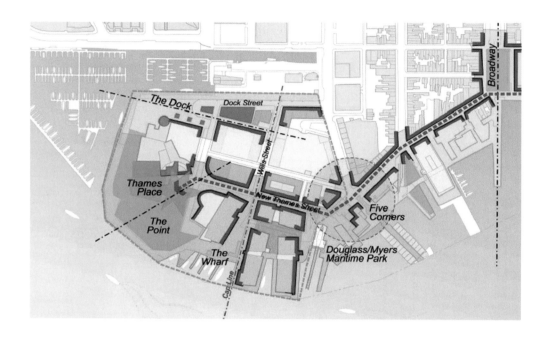

8.6 Site framework analysis, Harbor Point, Baltimore.
(Courtesy of Ehrenkranz, Eckstut & Kuhn)

Multifunctional GIS Synthesis

The dream of site planners for half a century has been to automate the analysis of sites, synthesizing the data available in a GIS format. Ian McHarg pioneered this work long before GIS systems were available, and applied it using layers of transparent paper in the planning of The Woodlands, a new community north of Houston, Texas. Five factors were singled out as limiting the location of development: 100-year flood zones, drainage ways, primary open space areas to be preserved, soils critical to recharge of groundwater supply, and soils important to maintaining the water table. When these were overlaid, the areas between them became the sites for urban uses. Implicitly each of them was equally important. As a practical matter, however, it was difficult to make the translation from maps to plans. Sharp boundaries on the map turned out to be wide bands on the ground, requiring considerable effort in confirming the logical locations to limit development. Nonetheless, the studies served as a rough guide to determine development areas.

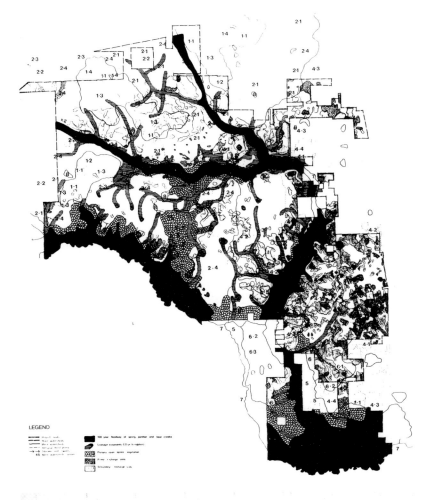

LEGEND

8.7 Synthesis of important factors, The Woodlands new town site, Houston, Texas. (Wallace McHarg Roberts and Todd/ Courtesy of WRT Design and Anne Spirn)

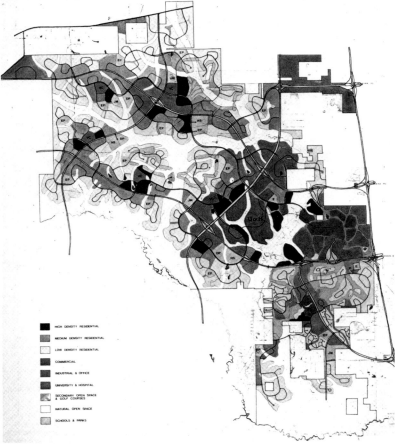

HIGH DENSITY RESIDENTIAL

MEDIUM DENSITY RESIDENTIAL

LOW DENSITY RESIDENTIAL

COMMERCIAL

INDUSTRIAL & OFFICE

UNIVERSITY & HOSPITAL

SECONDARY OPEN SPACE & GOLF COURSES

NATURAL OPEN SPACE

SCHOOLS & PARKS

8.8 Site development plan, The Woodlands. (Wallace McHarg Roberts and Todd/ Courtesy of WRT Design and Anne Spirn)

Most GIS systems today have programs making possible a synthesis of data on separate layers. Special-purpose algorithms have been devised to weight the data and allow an aggregate suitability factor to be computed (Andris, n.d.). Two difficulties challenge their effectiveness: continued reliance on data for mapping of soils, vegetation, and other factors that is less than precise, and the value-laden decision on how to weight the different factors. As a result, such techniques are more relevant for large-scale, regional policy decisions than for planning individual sites. They can also be effective in identifying sites for specific forms of development, such as airports.

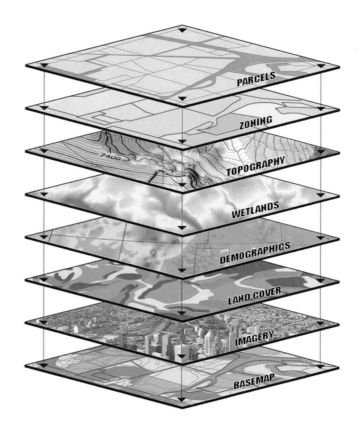

8.9 Site layers diagram for GIS analysis.
(Courtesy of Adam Gage)

8.10 Multifactor analysis of potential airport sites, Griffin, Georgia.
(Courtesy of Clio Andris/ LPA Group/Michael Baker International)

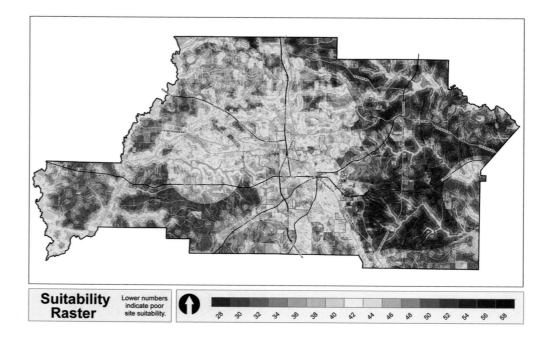

Suitability Raster Lower numbers indicate poor site suitability.

28 30 32 34 36 38 40 42 44 46 48 50 52 54 56 58

Part 3 | Planning Sites

Creating a plan for a site demands a subtle blend of creativity, persuasion, and technical skills. No two paths to a plan are ever identical, but it is possible to discern practices that can lead to fine sites more often than not. Experienced site planners draw upon a repertoire of techniques, allowing them to decide quickly on the process that is likely to yield a successful plan, and the actors who will need to be engaged along the way.

Scale and location make a great deal of difference. For small sites, it may be possible to move rapidly to design, based on a quick site analysis and a limited range of possible uses of the site. Planning large sites usually forces a more deliberate process combining the skills of many specialists, and requires a longer schedule. Sites in built-up cities and towns, regardless of size, generally involve greater consultation with nearby residents, interest groups, and officials, drawing out the process, while greenfield sites may be planned by professionals working independently or even in confidence, with only occasional outside reviews.

In this part of the book we examine each of the components of the site planning process. A prototypical model of the site planning process is presented, with the understanding that each project will have its own critical path. Ideas for engaging stakeholders and users are presented, as well as other ways of learning about users. Then methods are explored for arriving at a program for the site. A critical choice the planner faces is what media to use for planning, whether traditional or digital. Sites can be designed in many different ways, and with the help of examples we explore how to decide upon the best approach. This part also focuses on the analytics of site planning: measuring performance against criteria, analyzing the economics of changes, and predicting impacts.

Like site planning itself, there is no single ideal way to navigate through this part. Chapter 9 provides an overview of the many tasks that may be needed, and is a useful place to begin. The balance of part 3 should be seen as a set of resources to be consulted as needed.

9 | Site Planning Methods

A useful way to think about the site planning process is as parallel steams of activity, each rooted in a discipline, becoming increasingly aligned as the project moves toward construction of the site. The streams need to be joined and will ultimately arrive at their destination with specific products: a definitive program and plan for a site, an infrastructure plan, a subdivision plan, a financial plan, a landscape plan, and ultimately the documents needed to guide construction of site infrastructure, public spaces, and facilities. Many of these products will need to be approved by local authorities, and the developer of the site will need to assemble the financial resources, marketing and construction expertise, and management team to carry the project forward.

Site planning is not a lockstep process, but one of expanding and narrowing possibilities as new information is revealed. Backtracking is common; assumptions will need to be tested and revised, ideas will need to meet the test of markets, public approvals, and citizen support, and as external conditions change it is not unusual to discard initial plans in favor of other approaches. Nonetheless, there is forward motion, and a site planning process usually moves through several increasingly specific stages from preliminary studies to schematic plans to refined plans to construction documents.

A typical process is illustrated in figure 9.1, based on a generic site 40 ha (100 ac) or larger, intended for multiple uses.

The Preliminaries

The first steps in the site planning process, which we label the *preliminary stage,* will usually involve *identifying clients, users, and stakeholders* (1a), discerning their objectives, hopes, and aspirations and the outer bounds of what they will find acceptable. This may be the beginning of a *public engagement process* (1b) that will extend through much of the planning process. The most important conversations will be with the paying client and with potential users, but the first weeks of a planning process, before the first ideas are generated, are not too soon to begin discussions with those who will have a say in whether the plan is approved. Chapter 10 outlines techniques for engaging stakeholders and the public, and considerations of users are included in chapter 11.

An *initial site analysis* (2a) will be made, which may consist of simply compiling available aerial photographs, data, urban plans, and base maps and transcribing the results of a site visit (notations on a map, photographs, etc.). To be useful, this information needs to be digested, noting the natural territories of the site, important site features, views, contextual influences, potential access locations, infrastructure available to serve the site, and regulations that affect its development, as we have noted in chapter 8.

Sites with special circumstances, such as those bordering on waterfronts or containing protected landscapes, may require a deeper analysis at the outset, but the general rule is to plumb existing information before embarking on costly site studies. Ultimately, the types of uses to be located on a site will help determine the detailed site information needed, so analysis should not outpace these decisions.

In parallel with the site studies, an initial *sketch program* (3a) will be drawn up, working in dialogue with the paying client. It will be based on the informed

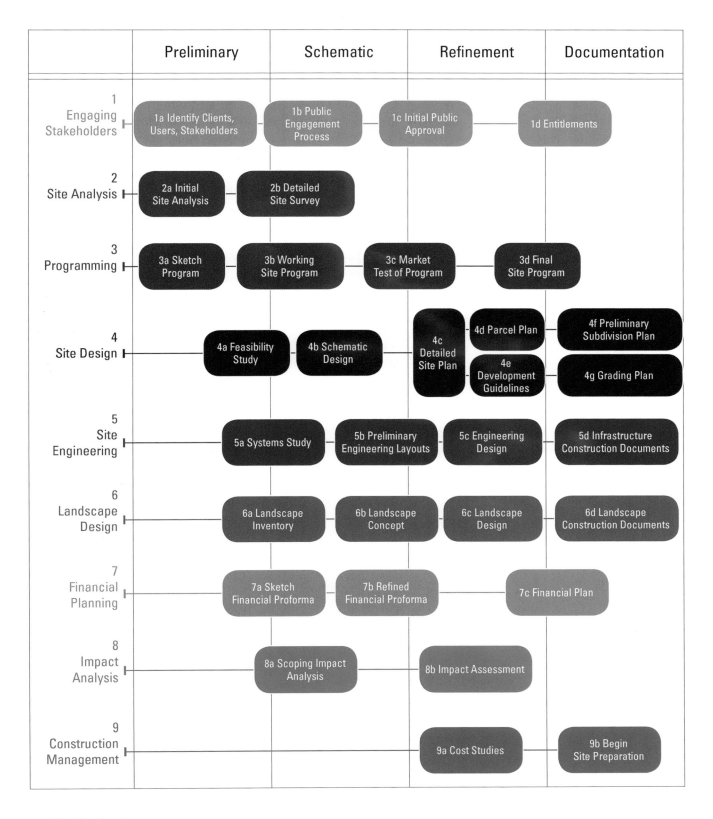

	Preliminary	Schematic	Refinement	Documentation
1 Engaging Stakeholders	1a Identify Clients, Users, Stakeholders	1b Public Engagement Process	1c Initial Public Approval	1d Entitlements
2 Site Analysis	2a Initial Site Analysis	2b Detailed Site Survey		
3 Programming	3a Sketch Program	3b Working Site Program	3c Market Test of Program	3d Final Site Program
4 Site Design	4a Feasibility Study	4b Schematic Design	4c Detailed Site Plan	4d Parcel Plan / 4f Preliminary Subdivision Plan / 4e Development Guidelines / 4g Grading Plan
5 Site Engineering	5a Systems Study	5b Preliminary Engineering Layouts	5c Engineering Design	5d Infrastructure Construction Documents
6 Landscape Design	6a Landscape Inventory	6b Landscape Concept	6c Landscape Design	6d Landscape Construction Documents
7 Financial Planning	7a Sketch Financial Proforma	7b Refined Financial Proforma	7c Financial Plan	
8 Impact Analysis	8a Scoping Impact Analysis		8b Impact Assessment	
9 Construction Management			9a Cost Studies	9b Begin Site Preparation

9.1 The site planning process.
(Adam Tecza/Gary Hack)

guesses of those who know about local markets (or demands for space), the economics of development, and the social and environmental aspirations the client and designer have for the site. The program may be as simple as specifying the number of housing units within a particular price range, along with the open space and facilities needed to support them. Or it may be more elaborate, outlining the objectives, performance expected of the site, and innovations to be attempted in its design and development. It needs to be adequate to permit the first studies of how the site might be planned, but not so detailed as to be a straitjacket. Creative design studies uncover possibilities for using the site that were not imagined at the outset, and these will be reflected in more detailed programming as the process moves forward. The site program is the subject of chapter 12.

All the information in this preliminary stage needs to be brought together in a *feasibility study* for the site (4a). This is both a creative look at the potentials of the site and a test of the initial site program. It will expose the immediate choices that need to be made and address many questions: Can the site uses contemplated actually fit on the site? Will they be too dense, or is there room for other uses? Does the site itself suggest other uses? Are the access possibilities and infrastructure likely to be adequate? What innovations are possible? If it is a large site, what are the logical ways to think of phasing development? And so on. Several alternative sketch plans will be drawn for the site and discussed and debated. The site owner may wish to share these with local officials and the public, seeking their input before planning progresses too far. A first *sketch of a financial pro forma* (7a) will be made to judge the comparative merit of the several possibilities. The purpose of this step is to make first-cut decisions that will allow definitive planning to move forward. Techniques of financial analysis are covered in chapter 17.

Completion of the feasibility study is a time to pause, take stock, and make decisions about the basis for proceeding. An immediate task will be to develop a *working site program* (3b) that captures the decisions on the uses for the site, important criteria to be met, standards to be used, and the timetable for the balance of the process. The working program is often a bridge to the *schematic phase* of the project.

Creating a Schematic Plan

Preparing a *schematic plan* for the site (4b) involves retracing many of the preliminary steps but in much greater detail, and adding new information and skills into the process. A more *detailed site survey* (2b) will be necessary, supplementing the information previously available. It may include preparing a careful topographic survey, determining the precise location of wetlands and special site features, and soil borings to determine the capacity of areas of the site considered likely candidates for development. Where there are areas that may need remediation, detailed soil testing will need to be done.

While the feasibility study may have been done largely based on hand sketches, the shift to schematic design will require data to be reconciled in a digital format that will become the working medium for the balance of the project. The choice of system will be important: it must be precise, but also robust enough to allow quick exploration of plans and three-dimensional presentations of proposals. Chapter 13 presents the most common digital platforms for site planning.

Engineers will be brought aboard to do a *systems study* of infrastructure (5a) to help determine the roadway and transit capacity surrounding the site, the capacity of streams and soils to absorb runoff, and the presence and capacity of nearby sewer, water, electrical, and telecommunications services. This is also a time for a creative look at infrastructure possibilities: Should the site tie into citywide systems or develops its own systems? What are the potentials of green infrastructure? Is it large enough to create district heating or cooling systems? How can the demand for travel be minimized? Will electrical and telephone service be located above ground or below, in streets or easements? Answers to each of these questions will help guide the site designers as they develop a schematic plan. And as that plan unfolds, the engineering team may test it by preparing *preliminary engineering layouts* (5b) of infrastructure, roadways, and other elements. Cost estimates will be made for these based on typical unit costs from other projects. Part 4 details the site infrastructure systems that may be required.

This stage of the process is the time to begin thinking about the ultimate landscape character of the site, and to assure that these ideas are central to the conceptual plans, not an afterthought. Where the site has existing vegetation or a landscape history, these need to be documented in a *landscape inventory* (6a), with advice on what it will take to maintain existing elements. The site needs to be placed in its broader ecological context. Collecting examples of fine landscapes that seem relevant to establishing the site's character is also useful at this point.

Developing a schematic design will require creative exploration of the form of roadways, open spaces, and development prototypes, always searching for solutions that emphasize the unique characteristics of the site. The objective is to create a powerful sense of place. But the scheme must also be practical, accommodating the site program—and suggesting how it might be revised advantageously—and always maintaining an eye to what public decision makers and other stakeholders may be persuaded to accept. Many site designers prefer to work by developing and comparing widely different alternatives before settling on a preferred direction. Others prefer to begin with a known site development prototype, fitting it to the site, and then distorting and reinventing it to reflect the current potentials. Still others work by analogies that are more abstract—using metaphors as generative ideas, or reacting to the generic characteristics of the site's form. Whatever the approach, collaboration of the entire team in both generating and assessing ideas is essential; they allow the site to be seen through different lenses, and it is never obvious which view will lead to a truly creative solution. Chapter 14 focuses on design methods that can help arrive at an inspired design for the site.

Large sites will require a variety of impact analyses as part of the public approval process. It is not too soon to begin the *scoping of the impact analysis* (8a) as the schematic plans are being prepared. This discipline establishes useful metrics (the amount of runoff from the site, the reduction of traffic generated, etc.) that can help shape the design and serve as benchmarks of progress as it evolves. Chapter 18 outlines the contents and procedures for conducting impact assessments.

The schematic phase of the process generally concludes with a full presentation of the plan and the studies on which it is based. Persuasive illustrations of the intended character of the site are essential, since many who will need to decide on the plan will not easily envision how the site will look and feel from two-dimensional plans. Constructing a physical model may be warranted, although today's visualization tools allow ground-level and aerial views of a site to be created quickly, and with alarming accuracy. Animating the views is more costly, but simple walk-throughs or flyovers are increasingly possible. The danger that lurks in visualization is that lay individuals take what they see literally, hating (or falling in love with) the architectural or landscape character of the illustrations, when the point is deciding on the overall layout of the site. Nonetheless, fine sites only come about because clients and stakeholders are inspired by the possibilities, and the illustrations of the plan are essential for creating such sentiments. An example of a compelling presentation of a site plan is included in chapter 19.

Completion of the schematic plan allows important decisions to be made about a project. The paying client will need to decide whether to proceed further, based on a blend of emotion and practicality. He may wish to do a *market test of the program* (3c), to judge whether assumptions in the *refined financial pro forma* (7b) are reasonable. The plan and pro forma will be used to assemble the financial resources to proceed. It will also be essential at this point to receive some form of *initial public approval* (1c). This may take the form of rezoning a site, approval in principle by a planning body or chief executive of a local government, or an agreement on the terms of moving forward.

Refining the Plan

With a decision to proceed, detailed planning can begin. The objective is to arrive at a *detailed site plan* (4c) that will serve as the blueprint for development over time. On a large site, there will be inevitable refinements after the initial phases of development are complete, but the detailed site plan serves as the constitution for the site, establishing its character and guiding the main decisions. To arrive at this plan, the infrastructure will need to be designed, the landscape character set, and rules established for buildings and other aspects of development on the site. While schematic plans could remain accurate within 10 m (30 ft), the detailed site plan needs to be accurate at the level of 1 m (3 ft) or less. Refining plans to this level requires close collaboration between the site designer and each of the specialized professionals on the team.

The detailed plan will include a parcel plan (4d), accounting for all the property on the site. It will specify the areas to be developed (by the owner, or sold to others as development sites), the land that will become public land for roadways, parks, and public facilities, and any lands that will be retained in collective ownership for common use. Areas that will be protected by easements or covenants will be specified. While this aspect of the plan will later be translated into a legal subdivision plan, a parcel plan is essential for receiving approval to proceed with the development. Chapter 16 focuses on the subdivision process.

On large sites that are constructed over many years, detailed site plans may concentrate on the framework of major streets, parcels, and infrastructure, while becoming more detailed for the early development phases. In market-driven development, it is difficult to predict what will be marketable in 10 years, and it is important to make plans that offer flexibility without compromising the character-giving elements of the site. A useful exercise is spinning out multiple scenarios of how development might occur over time. What are the essential, unchangeable aspects of the site design that should be retained whatever the ultimate uses?

Each of the elements of the infrastructure for the site will need to be designed, bearing in mind that these will not all be constructed at once. The *engineering design* (5c) will specify the sizes, geometry, location, and capacities of each of the systems that will serve the site. This is still short of the detailed design—sizing all pipes, designing precise roadway profiles, and the like—that will go into the construction documents for the systems, but it will allow dependable cost estimates to be made, and will create the framework for designing individual projects, or "packages" as they are often called.

During this stage, the *landscape concept* (6b) will be developed, working closely with the site planner and engineering team. Because landscape has such a powerful impact on the visual character of sites, landscape architects often take the lead in site planning. Whether they are leading or collaborating, however, the plan of streets, open spaces, development sites, and shared facilities needs to be informed by a landscape vision. In planning green infrastructure such as a swale or rain garden, engineering, planning, and landscape design are tightly coupled. Later, when the main elements of the plan are fixed, it is time to begin the detailed *landscape design* (6c) to define the form of important open areas on the site and typical landscape materials, details, and planting conditions. Many of the possibilities for the site's landscape are discussed in chapter 32.

Before the plan is submitted for public approval, many jurisdictions require a detailed environmental impact assessment (8b) or study (EIS), projecting the impacts of the site's development on its surroundings. The report will outline the alternatives considered, and will compare these to the baseline of the current site or a "no-build" alternative. Subjects will include impacts on traffic, infrastructure, the natural environment, air quality, the use of nonrenewable resources, and other topics usually spelled out in local regulations. Specialized studies may be required to prepare the EIS, including traffic, runoff, and wind modeling. In some US states, developments that will have significant regional impact are subjected to other tests. Local jurisdictions may require a *fiscal impact study* (FIS) to be prepared, spelling out the revenues and costs that governments may be burdened with if the site is developed, and setting the stage for negotiations with the developer. A smaller number of places now require a *health impact study* (HIS), outlining how the proposed development of the site will contribute to (or prevent) obesity, healthy lifestyles, and social contact. The format for such studies is discussed in chapter 18.

Finally, the detailed plan is not complete without a set of *development guidelines* (4e) that spell out the key aspects of the built environment of the site. These can take various forms—minimal rules on setbacks, heights, uses allowed, locations of entrances, and the like; or more robust requirements that specify the intended form and character of buildings and materials, with important principles for their design ("continuous retail across this frontage," or "step buildings back above 30 feet"); or full pattern books that offer a repertoire of building types, forms, materials, and details that must be followed. Design guidelines are particularly important when a site is to be broken into parcels and developed by people other than those involved in creating the site plan. They assure that the intentions are carried out, set quality standards, and provide the security of knowing what will be next to them for each purchaser of a site. Chapter 15 covers the range of guidelines, criteria, and standards for a site.

With this increased level of detail, the flashy presentations and models of the site will be refined to become the essential props for explaining the final site plan to the public, decision makers, potential investors, and ultimately purchasers of land and buildings. The illustrations and technical studies will be bundled together for public consumption. A website may be an essential vehicle for making the plans known and receiving comments on them.

The detailed site plan provides the essential materials for securing the *entitlements* (1d) for developing a site. These will usually include the approval of any public roads and rights-of-way, a signal of the willingness of the local government to accept and maintain any public parks or facilities, agreements on the pattern of infrastructure for the site, and any adjustments to local development regulations that must be made to facilitate development. There are an infinite set of variations as to how entitlements are granted, based on local custom for controlling development. Some cities and towns sign formal development agreements, binding the developer and them to specific actions and a timetable for developing the site. Others act by passing local ordinances or resolutions. In some instances, particularly if the development is large, higher levels of government may need to approve the plans. In the US, if wetlands are involved, the US Army Corps of Engineers needs to approve the plans. A variety of boards and commissions may get involved—environmental commissions, historical commissions, regional commissions, air quality boards, coastal commissions, and so on. Local circumstances and the receptivity toward development will determine how long this process will take. If the planners have done their homework and responded to the issues raised by the stakeholders, the plan may sail through the entitlements process; but more often than not, modifications to the plan will be required to gain all the necessary signatures.

Preparing for Construction

An approved site and development plan allows the project to shift gears and move ahead quickly into construction. If there are changes in the plans that have been agreed to during the entitlement process, these need to be reflected in the *final site program* (3d) and the *financial plan* for site development (7c). Initial *site preparation* (9b) may begin in advance of having the final construction documents—removing structures on the site, remediating contaminated soils, extending utility lines to the site, and other tasks that will be needed before the site can be developed. But before the topography can be altered and roads and other infrastructure built, a number of technical tasks will need to be completed.

The parcel plan will need to be translated into a precise *subdivision plan* (4f), with dimensions, bearings, and radii for each parcel. Surveyors who install a series of monuments as reference points will eventually map the subdivision plan on the ground. Despite the improvements of GPS technology, in most places field surveys will be required to validate the boundaries and key reference points. This task of subdividing the site can't be completed without close coordination with the engineering consultants who will be designing and preparing *construction documents* (5d) for roads, utility lines, and other infrastructure. Precise alignments will be established, along with the profile and elevations of each link. The subdivision plan and engineering designs allow the third key technical document to be prepared—the *site grading plan* (4g).

There is an art to orchestrating how sites are parceled, infrastructure is designed, and sites are graded. How a roadway is handled on a side slope, whether its alignment is a series of arcs and straightaways or a continuous curve, how it navigates up and down a slope—these decisions are essential to the experience of using a site, and are too important to leave strictly in the hands of an engineer guided by convention. Similarly, the precise size and shape of parcels has a large influence on how buildings may be sited, and whether the space around buildings is usable or wasted—not really the expertise of surveyors. Sticking as closely to the site's current topography, and worrying about how the land will need to be modified while resolving technical issues, will ensure that the final grading plan is not an afterthought.

The same can be said about the landscape plan—landscape is not what one worries about after all the other key decisions have been made. Maintaining mature vegetation on a site will depend upon not drastically modifying the runoff patterns, and new impervious surfaces will need to be balanced with natural materials that can absorb the increased flows. Landscape designers need to be the fourth section of the orchestra, preparing the *landscape construction documents* (6d) in concert with planners, surveyors, and engineers.

The process we have outlined is conventional for most locations in the US and Canada, but will vary in other parts of the world depending upon local circumstances. In countries with development permit systems, more detail may be required in the schematic phase to receive entitlements. In other places, public entities may plan and construct the infrastructure of a site, once the schematic plan has been agreed upon, although this is generally an invitation to use generic standards that neglect the special qualities of a site.

More will be said about each of these steps in the process of planning sites in the chapters that follow. There is never just one possible plan for a site, but finding the best plan involves intense collaboration of the many disciplines involved in a project. When built, if it has good terroir, a site will seem like it was inevitable.

10 | Engaging Stakeholders and the Public

The site planner is rarely the exclusive user of a site, except perhaps when planning their own home or vacation retreat. Even then, families and significant others need to be accommodated, the planner will worry about how the design will be seen by neighbors, and a host of people will need to sign off on the plans—mortgage companies, building permit officials, design review boards, among others. From the outset of any site planning project, much of the planner's effort will need to be devoted to understanding the aspirations of clients, determining who the users will be and what they need, and seeking ways to satisfy the many other stakeholders who have a say about what gets built on the site. In large and small projects, the site planner will also need to serve as surrogate for many of the eventual users of the site who may not be present, or may not even be known. They will need to have conversations with and ultimately persuade a bewildering array of individuals who will need to agree to the plan, or who have the ability to block it from becoming a reality.

Clients, Users, and Stakeholders

The first task is identifying whose views and needs need to be satisfied. It is important to distinguish between *clients, users, and stakeholders*.

The planner has a direct and often contractual responsibility to *clients*—they are the people who hired them, need to agree to the plan, and will need to make further financial and legal commitments to accomplish the overall development. Nothing will occur unless the clients are satisfied. Sometimes the clients

are also the ultimate users of the site, but more often than not they depart the scene when the site is completed. A developer may plan a site, see it through the approvals process, and then sell individual properties to builders or other developers. When the infrastructure, streets, and open spaces are completed and all the sites are sold, their work is complete. Or a governmental building authority may plan and construct a campus for a university, exiting the scene when it is turned over to the university administration. In such cases, the site planner has a special responsibility to serve as the advocate for the ultimate *users* of the site, while also satisfying the formal clients.

Determining who will be the *users* of the site is not entirely straightforward. When the site is a commercial development and will be sold to end users, the market will determine who actually occupies it. And this may change over the years, as the area of the site evolves, businesses change, and inhabitants grow older. Residential sites are particularly tricky. The target market may not materialize, and the initial assumptions may need to be rethought. As first residents arrive and mature, their needs and desires will change. Houses may be added to or renovated for other kinds of households. This is not a reason to disregard users, but a call to be as precise as possible, make projections of possible changes over time, and provide flexibility for needs not yet anticipated.

Even if the users can be pinpointed, and the planner has a good handle on how they will change over the years, every site has a diversity of users with often-divergent interests. The sports teams that use a park regularly will have desires quite different from the casual user; the family inhabiting a street will see it differently from the express parcel delivery agent who visits occasionally, or the fire department official who needs to assure its safety. Unfortunately, individuals involved in maintenance and protection of places often have disproportionate weight in planning decisions, resulting in environments that are easy to operate but dull to inhabit. The planner has to work hard to keep the interests in balance.

Clients and users have the most direct interest in the planning and design of sites, but many other *stakeholders* will also have a say. These include the public bodies or authorities that will need to approve the uses or development of the site, the elected officials who will take credit or be blamed for approving site development, and many agencies at higher levels of government who may need to sign off on it. Other interest groups will weigh in to advocate particular ways of planning the site—environmental groups promoting the preservation of unique or fragile lands, neighbors seeking to prevent increased traffic from using their streets, users of paths across the site who wish to ensure that their rights are maintained, residents of adjacent areas who want land to be set aside to serve their recreation needs, and so on. Often such groups have no direct role in the decision process, but they may have the ability to delay the process by appealing

Sidebar 10.1

Range of Clients for Site Planning

Formal clients
Direct sponsor of project (paying client)
Current investors in site development
Owners of the site
Any holders of easements or rights to the site

Users
Ultimate purchasers or lessees of portions of the site (houses, commercial space, offices, institutions)
Those who will inhabit or use the site routinely (including groups like children, those differently abled, and others not usually represented)
Those who will use the site on special occasions
Those who will operate and maintain the site
Those responsible for protection of a site – police, fire protection, hazard and disaster recovery officials
Future generations of users
Animals who will inhabit the site

Stakeholders
Potential investors in site development
Public bodies that must approve site development – elected council and chief executive, planning, roads and infrastructure, conservation agencies, schools, recreation, parks, etc.
Elected officials whose support will be essential

Other Interest Groups
Neighbors of site and owners of adjacent sites
Pro-development advocacy groups – chamber of commerce, public interest groups
Environmental advocacy groups

decisions or filing suits to block the project. The lack of ownership or control only increases the determination to influence the project.

A successful planning process usually begins with drawing up a robust list of clients, users, stakeholders, and other interest groups. Then a strategy is needed to learn where each stands and to vet the plans as they emerge. Some individuals (especially owners and politicians) will require one-on-one conversations to get straight answers; others may be more amenable to roundtable discussions or large-group events. Where the decision-making group is limited in size and know each other well, regular weekly or monthly meetings to review plans and discuss and deal with issues may be all that is needed. Large and complex projects, where interests are conflicted and strategies need to be devised to come to a consensus, may require several parallel tracks of consultation and negotiation.

Organizing Public Engagement

Many projects require that multiple interest groups and a large cross section of the public be engaged in discussions and ultimately support the plans that emerge. Without transparency and efforts to develop trust from the outset, the projects run the risk of cultivating uncertainty and opposition. An organized *public engagement* process is one way to build positive momentum for a project.

The purposes of public engagement include: identifying all the interest groups that need or wish to have a say in the planning of a site; surfacing their interests and aspirations early enough in the process so that they can be taken into account in plans; identifying

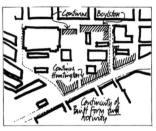

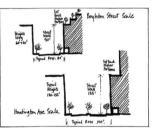

OBJECTIVE 2:

NEW DEVELOPMENT AT PRUDENTIAL CENTER SHOULD BE IN SCALE AND CHARACTER WITH ITS SURROUNDINGS

10
DEVELOP RING ROADS TO CONTINUE ADJACENT STREETSCAPES

The original plan for Prudential Center included a ring road to distribute traffic around the perimeter of the site and to separate vehicles entering parking or dropping off passengers from traffic on surrounding streets. Whatever the original merits, the scheme had the effect of separating Prudential Center from its surroundings, creating a vacuum of disused spaces, hostile to pedestrians because of the maze of service roads. The pattern also breaks the street walls along Boylston and Huntington. With the extension of the Hynes Auditorium out to Boylston Street, the north ring road no longer functions as such. And because there is only one level of parking below the ring road, this 95 foot wide strip provides an ideal site for new development. Similarly, several acres of unused land along Huntington should be developed to provide a new face along the avenue.

11
BOYLSTON STREET DEVELOPMENT SHOULD BE SYMPATHETIC TO ITS SURROUNDINGS

Street facing retail uses in new development along Boylston are important to ensure that the street is active along its length, and to integrate Prudential Center with its surroundings. While there is considerable variation in the height of structures along Boylston, the appropriate street wall height for new development appears to be an average of about 90 feet — roughly the same as the Hynes Auditorium and somewhat lower than the 125 foot

10.1 Engaging stakeholders through public meeting, Fourth Ward redevelopment project, Houston, Texas. (Gary Hack)

10.2 Agreed-upon principles for development, Prudential Center redevelopment project, Boston. (Gary Hack)

10.3 Task force presenting its recommended development principles for Prudential Center to the mayor, Boston. (Gary Hack)

Engaging Stakeholders and the Public

conflicting objectives, and having discussions of these among the contending parties so they recognize the tradeoffs that must be made; airing planning approaches, and ultimately conceptual plans for reactions, and dealing with the comments in subsequent presentations; and ultimately seeking a consensus on the project. Depending on the actors and local climate of opinion, this process may be contentious or a welcome give-and-take among all involved. It is a distinctly political process, and needs to be crafted with local traditions in mind.

Where the site is in a built-up area, with many organized interest groups, it may take many meetings to resolve differences and agree on a site plan. In Boston, the planning of the redevelopment of the Prudential Center, a 26 ac (10 ha) urban site at the seam of four neighborhoods near downtown, required over 200 meetings and two years of intensive effort to reach agreement (Hack 1994). Fourteen interest groups, several with longstanding conflicts among them, were represented on the task force appointed by the mayor to help shape the plan, and ultimately all endorsed the development proposal.

There are several keys to a successful process of public engagement (Faga 2006). One is to develop a working group or task force or steering committee that can fairly reflect the breadth of views that need to be reflected. A group of 10–20 individuals is a workable size, providing enough airtime for each. While members should be chosen to reflect interests, they should not be seen as simply the conduits for positions held by groups. It is important to appoint individuals who are respected, and who are at ease in dealing with conflicting views. There needs to be a *facilitator* or *animateur* for the engagement process who is even-handed, comfortable with wading into conflicts, and enjoys dealing with stakeholders of all kinds. The facilitator's role is to help build a consensus on the plan.

With the working group in place, the second key to success is to begin with large *workshops* to educate the wider constituencies on possibilities and options. These may take the form of *design charrettes* (see below) or may be structured as a series of conversations over the length of the project. An early conversation might focus on precedents, examples drawn from other places or cities that have some relevance to the site being planned. It is often salutary to have members of

the public attempt to make a plan for the site as a way of surfacing their values, and educating them about the opportunities and constraints of the site. This can be done with kits of parts resembling buildings, streets, and other urban elements, which force people to set aside their conventional ways of thinking about things. Developing a common language and common examples helps frame the discussions of the project.

On high-visibility, symbolic projects, large public meetings may be essential so that all groups feel they have a voice in the matter. In 2002, in the early planning of the redevelopment of the World Trade Center site in New York, a "listening to the city" session was held, attracting some 4,500 residents. Possible approaches to the plan were vetted, aided by technology that allowed instant voting and display of the tallied votes. As a result of the session, the decision was made to hold an ideas competition to expand the range of possibilities for the site (Sagalyn 2016).

A third important strategy is ensuring that there is *forward progress* and that public engagement avoids an endless loop of the same discussions. Targets need to be set and met: agreeing on the *principles* or *objectives* or *metrics of success* at an early point; agreeing on the *scope* of an EIS or other type of impact assessment (chapter 18) before it is begun; agreeing on the *positives and negatives* of alternative approaches; agreeing on the *refinements* or *changes* that need to be made as the plan evolves; and ultimately *endorsing* the plan.

The Internet can be an invaluable aid to public engagement. There are now dozens of platforms that can be used for posting principles, alternatives, and plans, soliciting views and comments, and carrying on real-time dialogues (Horose 2015). Web clips of meetings and presentations can also be posted; it is always surprising just how many people view these. Compiling an email list of all individuals who attend workshops or public presentations can ensure that subsequent information gets out to those who cannot attend follow-up meetings, helping avoid one of the most distressing qualities of engagement processes—people wanting to reopen issues because they missed the previous discussion.

These strategies describe common practice in the US and much of Canada, where there are long traditions of direct citizen engagement. In some places, the process of public engagement has been institutionalized and

projects cannot be considered by local commissions or councils without public input. Often it is organized as a quasi-judicial hearing process, with public comments submitted in advance. In the UK, the *public inquiry process* serves this purpose, as do the hearings before the Ontario Municipal Board (in Canada) on adoption of secondary plans. In the UK and in Germany, plans are sometimes submitted to a *citizens' jury,* composed of a cross section of ordinary citizens who cross-examine experts and debate the merits of a plan. The *planning cell method* used in Spain and *Planungszelle* in Germany are variations of this approach adapted to their particular planning cultures. There are as many variations as there are political cultures; what they share is a desire to surface differences so that they can be dealt with while avoiding excessive delays.

10.4 User-generated model of their ideal community.
(Courtesy of James T. Rojas)

10.5 Listening to the City, public engagement session in the planning of the World Trade Center redevelopment, 2002.
(Jacqueline Hemmerdinger/Courtesy of The Civic Alliance)

10.6 Engaging Plans interactive platform for sharing and debating new projects.
(Courtesy of Urban Interactive Studio)

10.7 Citizens jury debating impacts of climate change on development.
(Courtesy of Jefferson Center)

Design Charrettes

One way of avoiding delays in a project, and ensuring that there is a forum for individuals and groups to voice their concerns, is to assemble the interests in one room at the beginning, rather than waiting until plans are firmly established. This can take the form of a *design charrette*. The term *charrette* has been co-opted from the architects' practice of working intensively to come up with an *esquisse* or concept, which dates back to one-day competitions at the Ecole des Beaux-Arts in the nineteenth century. As employed in planning, it is usually a several-day process aimed at arriving at a concept for a project and getting agreement among the important stakeholders before proceeding to more detailed work (Lennertz and Kutzenhiser 2006). A design charrette can

Sidebar 10.2

Typical Six-Day Charrette Schedule

Day 1
Public meeting for all participants (morning)
Introductions, expectations, schedule, ground rules
Precedents – good outcomes in other similar cases
Air time for all who wish to speak on the issue
Site visit of all key stakeholders and their consultants
One-on-one interviews with key stakeholders to discuss their ideas for the project
Design team begins to explore alternatives

Day 2
Continue interviews with key stakeholders
Narrow down alternatives to a handful of important choices
Meeting of key stakeholders to discuss alternatives (evening)

Day 3
Design team incorporates feedback on alternatives
Discussions with key stakeholders whose issues will be difficult to resolve – ascertain what opportunities there are for convergence
Prepare sketch presentation on alternatives
Public meeting to discuss refined alternatives (evening)

Day 4
Based on feedback on alternatives, make choice of preferred direction
Design team works on refinement of preferred direction
Begin to prepare images and presentation materials
Review work in progress with key stakeholders (evening)

Day 5
Refine presentation materials
Dry run with key stakeholders
Public presentation of recommendations

Day 6
Design team takes stock of charrette
Outline next steps to implement agreements reached

be an important tool when there are many conflicting interests that need to be served, and when there is a need for creative imagination in breaking through past deadlocks. Charrettes are often organized for replanning neighborhoods or debating public policy choices, but they can also be an effective way to accelerate the process of planning an individual site.

Charrettes need to be designed with the context in mind. They can vary in length from a single day to a week or more; the length will be determined by the ability to get all the key decision makers and interest groups together, and to some extent by the ambitions of the charrette. The best charrettes are intensive enough to build and hold the interest of participants, and just long enough to permit people to make considered judgments about the plan. A typical six-day charrette is outlined in sidebar 10.2. Ideally, the activities should be located in a single accessible place near the site. The space should have plenty of room for meetings of large and small groups, and display space to post drawings or photographs of other sites that serve as good examples. It should be equipped with technology and drawing boards at which ideas can be sketched and shared with others.

Effective charrettes depend upon excellent preparation. An agreement needs to be reached with the sponsors (landowner, developer, city, or others who have control over the site) on the expectations for the charrette, and on which issues are open to debate and which are not. The data needed to make a plan needs to be assembled, digested, and displayed. All of the key actors need to be interviewed in advance to learn their *priors*—the points of view they bring into the project—and to flag any conflicts that will take special efforts to resolve. A team of experienced designers and other experts (on traffic, engineering, markets, etc.) needs to be assembled and briefed so that they can get off the mark quickly. Publicity can help inform the process if done carefully so it doesn't get in the way. If opinions from a broad cross section of the public are sought, a website may be needed where events can be podcast and comments solicited. All of this needs to be done in a way that establishes a spirit of openness and a desire for participation, recognizing that not all key stakeholders will be willing to reveal their cards in public.

The charrette team needs to have exceptional skills and a willingness to work long into the night

10.8 Experts and residents creating a low-energy community, Seattle.
(Dwell)

to produce ideas and plans. The team needs to have all the technical knowledge to make a plan, and a willingness to rethink conventional solutions. There need to be people with skills at visualizing and presenting ideas in graphics, three-dimensional images, and words. Even in a time when computer-generated images are the norm, skills in sketching ideas quickly can be a real asset—allowing quick cycling of ideas. Many hands will be needed to create final presentations, and this is sometimes an opportunity to recruit design and planning students to aid in the process while observing how work gets done in an intense professional setting. Team members need to be passionate about the work, but not hard-headed—many good ideas will need to be discarded along the way.

One day or one week will, of course, not result in a detailed plan; much will be left to follow-up studies. Plotting the strategy for further studies and implementation will need to be an important outcome of the process. But if the charrette is successful, a working consensus will be gained on the direction the plan should take, and a supportive constituency will be formed to help in its implementation. In some cases it will make sense to reassemble all the key stakeholders who participated for periodical updates and feedback on the plan.

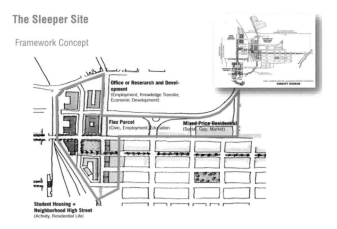

The Sleeper Site

Framework Concept

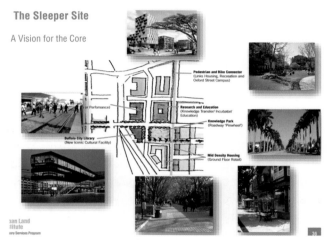

The Sleeper Site

A Vision for the Core

10.9 Proposed organization of Sleeper Site, Buffalo City, South Africa, results of a one-week charrette.
(Courtesy of Urban Land Institute)

10.10 Illustrations of character of site development, Sleeper Site.
(Courtesy of Urban Land Institute)

10.11 Design team leader presenting results of charrette to public, Fourth Ward project, Houston.
(Gary Hack)

Not all situations lend themselves to design charrettes. There may not be sufficient openness from the paying client to discuss the important issues publicly. It may prove impossible to get enough of the key actors together in one place. The issues may need detailed technical studies that cannot be completed before the team begins work. And charrettes are costly; the benefit of shortening the time to get an early agreement on a plan needs to be weighed against the resources needed to mount a charrette.

Design Competitions

Public and private clients are increasingly recognizing that organizing a design competition can be helpful in planning a site. Like design charrettes, competitions can take may different forms, and the devil is in the details (Collyer 2004; Nasar 2006).

There are four main types of competitions, each with somewhat different purposes. *Idea competitions* are intended to enlarge the range of possible ideas for a site, and are commissioned without a firm commitment to implement any of the entries received. The main purpose may be to provide publicity for a project, or to produce ideas that can be debated publicly, or to break through conventional ways of viewing a project, or to build a coalition of support for a project (Sagalyn 2006). Such competitions are commonplace in China and other rapid-growth places, where developers are seeking a unique identity for their project. Sometimes these are *open competitions*, without the requirement that entrants be capable of carrying through on what they propose, and the main benefit to competitors is the prize offered and recognition for the work. Idea competitions can have important political benefits for sponsors by conveying the willingness to entertain ideas that go beyond what is usually expected.

A second type of competition is the opposite: a *definitive building* or *site competition* whose winning entry a sponsor intends to implement. In many European countries, particularly Scandinavia, all major public buildings and projects must be designed through competitions, a practice that has been adopted in Korea, Taiwan, and other parts of Asia. These competitions are usually governed by strict procedures and rules of assessment. Typically, the sponsor distances

10.12 Idea competition for the West Side Waterfront, New York, 1988. (Courtesy of Municipal Art Society)

himself from the selection process by appointing a *jury* with the responsibility of selecting a winner, or in some instances a set of the top two or three candidates (this is common in China). A *professional advisor* oversees the preparation of a program for the building or site, sets the submission requirements, handles any questions that are submitted by the competitors and makes available the responses to all, and oversees the logistics of the jury process. There may be a second *technical jury* that examines in detail the competition entries in terms of whether they meet the terms of the competition, are capable of being implemented, and fall within the cost parameters. While the technical jury's findings are rarely decisive, if entries do not fall within the rules, the professional advisor or the jury may reject them, and the technical analysis will surely influence the way the jury views the entries.

Definitive competitions may be open to all or restricted to a shortlist who have been prequalified based on their experience and past projects. In an open competition, all who meet the professional qualification requirements may register and submit entries, and they are usually judged *anonymously*. Sometimes these competitions are organized in two stages: during the first stage entries are anonymous and the jury singles out a handful to go on to a second stage, where the competitors are provided with modest resources to produce more detailed proposals. An *invited competition* will provide assurance that teams have the capacity to carry things through to completion, but it can also screen out emerging talents or people who will bring fresh perspectives to the project.

A third type of competition is a *team selection competition*. The emphasis here is on selecting the best team to create plans for a project, a choice the sponsor wishes to make with an indication of each team's approach to the planning of the project. Team selection competitions usually provide only a few weeks for the competitors to prepare their ideas, and the program offered to them may not be firmly established. Once selected, the team works closely with the clients, users, and stakeholders to produce a program for the site and a plan, which often departs considerably from the initial ideas submitted. In this type of competition, qualifications and ideas are considered together, and the sponsor usually makes a balanced choice, usually with professional advice from the selection committee.

There are also hybrids of these approaches. A set of competitors may be selected based on qualifications, with each then working in parallel on schemes for the project, punctuated by several conversations with the sponsor or clients—a *mediated competition*. This can help avoid the situation in which competitors simply misjudge the situation and submit proposals that are

10.13 Winning entry, West Kowloon park and cultural center competition. (Courtesy of © Foster + Partners)

completely out of bounds. The final selection may be made by a jury, or more often by a group with representatives of the clients and professional experts. The World Trade Center ideas competition was organized in this way (Goldberger 2005; Sagalyn 2016). Or a handful of competitors may be preselected based on their sterling reputation, while others may need to compete openly for a slot in the competition. This is sometimes done in Korea.

Competitions need not exclusively center on design. In the US, public bodies are increasingly turning to *developer-design competitions* for key sites. In these, teams that include development interests and design professionals make combined two-part proposals: for the plan they would carry out and the financial proposition they are prepared to offer. The sponsor, sometimes aided by professional advisors, balances the two and makes a selection. Two of the most highly visible recent projects in New York and Los Angeles, the Columbus Circle–Coliseum redevelopment (now Time Warner Center) and the Grand Avenue Project, were planned in this way. The results are not always satisfactory. Sometimes the strongest development team does not submit the most inspired planning and design proposal, and the sponsor is inclined to try to broker a new marriage of

the best designers and strongest developers—usually an invitation for problems (whose views will carry the day?) Other times the sponsor opts for the highest financial return regardless of the plan being proposed, hoping that a poor plan can be remedied later. The record, however, is not encouraging.

When is it worth entertaining a design competition for a site? And if so, how does one decide on the form of competition? Several things may guide this choice.

If the program for the site is not precisely defined, it is difficult to conduct a definitive competition, since the jury will be forced to compare apples and oranges (and pears and cherries). If the purpose of the competition is to help establish the program for the site by looking at a broad array of alternatives, an independent jury is probably not the appropriate body to make a programmatic decision. In these situations, a team selection competition may be the best strategy, allowing the sponsor to sample alternative approaches while setting the stage for continued exploration of ideas about the program and design with the selected team.

For sites where the program is clear and the sponsor wants to entertain the most innovative new approaches, for competitive reasons or because he is unsatisfied with conventional solutions, there may be value in holding an open competition. If public officials or agencies are the barrier to innovation, they can be co-opted by inviting a representative to serve on the jury, and the buzz of the competition can elevate the sights of all who must agree to the project. Open definitive competitions are costly and take considerable time to organize properly—at least six months for the competitive period and up to a year of preparation and publicity. But they can also pay dividends by discovering a unique approach.

Competitions, which are a unique feature in the planning and design worlds, raise a number of ethical dilemmas. Competitors are being asked, in effect, to proffer their ideas in the hope of being selected, some-thing that no other professionals outside of the world of advertising are willing to do. Who do these ideas then belong to? Can they be used in the subsequent plans by the winning team? How much should be expected of a competitor who is not being compensated? In limited competitions, a small stipend is usually provided to the competitors, which helps blunt the criticism that they are being asked to work for no fee, but typically it costs competitors many times what they receive to prepare their proposals. Young and emerging professionals, however, are constantly seeking a breakthrough project; winning a competition and seeing it realized has created more than one firm.

10.14 Selected entry, World Trade Center redevelopment idea competition, New York.
(Courtesy of Studio Libeskind/photo © Jock Pottle)

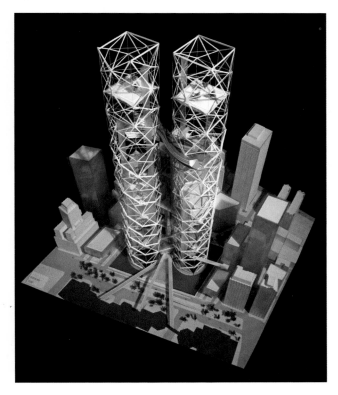

10.15 Runner-up, World Trade Center redevelopment idea competition, New York.
(Courtesy of THINK team)

11 | Learning about Users

Planning a site involves an extended dialogue between the potentials of the land and the needs, aspirations, and patterns of its users. But how does one discern what users will expect of a site and how they will use it, especially since users are not always identified as planning begins? What does a planner or designer need to know about users to create a plan?

The preferences of homeowners, shoppers, and resort visitors can often be inferred from consumer choices. But markets are not perfect predictors, since market choices are limited to the options available and can only be made by those with resources. In marketing housing, "curb appeal" does not always translate into satisfaction with the home and neighborhood. People make choices for many reasons. Housing buyers often have an eye on the resale value of the homes they are considering, rather than what will satisfy their needs as residents. Prestige figures heavily in consumption decisions—the cachet of owning a brand, the ability to brag about where one has been. Such forms of satisfaction are often transitory, and when one is planning long-lasting neighborhoods and communities, or even commercial centers that may function as community gathering places, a more far-reaching understanding of needs, preferences, and behavior is essential.

Demographic Analysis

The first step in user analysis is a *demographic analysis*: predicting who will use the site and how they will be distributed across groups of individuals (Murdock et al. 2015). While ultimately every individual has a unique set of preferences, there are broad similarities in behavior and preferences among groups of similar age, gender, ethnicity, social class, and lifestyle.

Age and stage in the life cycle are generally the most powerful predictor of preferences and patterns of use. Adolescents clearly use a residential street in ways that differ (and may conflict with) seniors; play spaces for young children are totally at odds with the team sports of their older siblings. Gender is especially critical for space use in societies that segregate the sexes, but the preferences of men and women for public space are almost always divergent. Ethnicity plays an important role in determining activities in public; in US cities, streets and parks in Latino neighborhoods are likely to be teeming with activity, while the same spaces may be deserted in middle-income white neighborhoods, where the residents make other choices for socialization and recreation. Immigrant neighborhoods in most cities are distinguishable from the mainstream of city life by differences in the use of public space. Social class is also a powerful determinant of use and activity on sites, and as individuals move up the income ladder they often shed past behaviors and adopt new ones. Socializing on the front porch in contact with neighbors often characterizes tight-knit low-income communities, in contrast to higher-income groups where there is often a preference for private gatherings in backyards (Michelson 2011).

Lifestyle is an important point of convergence between site planners and marketers. Marketing experts target lifestyle categories that describe clusters of people sharing similar activities, interests, and opinions (Plummer 1974). A lifestyle category is described by a combination of behavioral and demographic attributes, including age, social relationships, patterns of

11.1 Shopping areas vary as a response to lifestyle and ethnic differences: Boyle Heights, Los Angeles, a center of the Latino community.
(Gary Hack)

11.2 Rockridge serves as a center for the college and professional communities in Oakland and Berkeley, California.
(Gary Hack)

activity and dress, attitudes, and preferences (Giddens 1991). Claritas, a market research firm, has categorized US households into 66 types, attaching labels that include "urban elders," "beltway boomers," and "Mayberry-ville" (Claritas, n.d.). Acorn has categorized the UK's population and residential lifestyles into 62 demographic types (Acorn 2013). Marketing experts in other countries have followed suit.

"Young influentials" (previously referred to as yuppies in the US) and "upper crust" (retired urban boomers who have moved back to the city) may be the target markets for a housing development. This decision offers immediate cues for location, facilities, and arrangements of houses. The site planner may visit an arts-oriented residential community in the Netherlands and an edgy neighborhood in New York and conclude that residents of Toronto would be attracted to similar lifestyles. One way to begin the programming of a project is to imagine a set of lifestyle categories that need to be accommodated, then use these as a test of the adequacy of plans that emerge.

How then does the planner learn about behavior, needs, and preferences in enough detail to create a site plan that is responsive to users? A number of techniques can aid in this effort, drawn from the social sciences and the study of environmental behavior. The following sections are short of an exhaustive inventory of methods, but outline techniques that have proved effective in developing the essential understandings.

Study of Precedents

The place to begin is almost always in looking for examples that can serve as useful models for the site about to be planned. Almost no site planning assignment is totally unprecedented, and while none will be totally similar, the art is in finding examples that share as many important characteristics as possible. If the project is a mixed-use commercial area, look for cases that have similar densities, in similar climates, located roughly the same place in the city, and with mixes of uses that resemble the mix being contemplated. If broadly similar examples can't be found, look for paired comparisons: similar densities, even if in different locations; similar mixes of uses, even if the densities vary; and so on.

A good case study gauges how different users relate to such a place—tenants, shoppers, residents, and visitors—at different times of the day and year. Even more fundamentally, identify who the users are: Which merchants have considered it a good location, and how have they done? Who feels comfortable living over a retail area? What do rents say about each area compared to others? Do the residents of the area actually shop there? Are other users attracted to the area as well? How do people use the outdoor spaces in the area? Digging deeper, in what ways does the physical form of the area influence its success economically and

Examples of Claritas® PRIZM Lifestyle Categories, focused on high-consumption households (courtesy of © Claritas, Inc.)

01 Upper Crust

The nation's most exclusive address, Upper Crust is a haven for wealthy empty-nesting couples over the age of 65. This segment has a high concentration of residents earning over $100,000 a year and many possess a postgraduate degree. They have an opulent standard of living – driving expensive cars and frequently eating out and traveling.

02 Networked Neighbors

Networked Neighbors is a family portrait of suburban wealth, a place of million-dollar homes and manicured lawns, high-end cars and exclusive private clubs. This lifestyle is characterized by married couples with children, high technology use, graduate degrees, and six-figure incomes earned by business executives, managers, and professionals.

03 Movers & Shakers

Movers & Shakers is home to America's business class, a wealthy suburban world of dual-income couples who are highly educated, typically between the ages of 45 and 64. Given its high percentage of executives and white-collar professionals, there's a decided business bent to this segment as they enjoy reading business publications and visits to business oriented websites.

04 Young Digerati

Young Digerati are tech-savvy and live in fashionable neighborhoods on the urban fringe. Affluent and highly educated, Young Digerati communities are typically filled with trendy apartments and condos, fitness clubs and clothing boutiques, casual restaurants and all types of bars, from juice to coffee to microbrew. Many have chosen to start families while remaining in an urban environment.

05 Country Squires

The wealthiest residents in exurban America live in Country Squires, an oasis for affluent Baby Boomers who've fled the city for the charms of small-town living. In their bucolic communities noted for their recently built homes on sprawling properties, the families of executives live in six-figure comfort.

06 Winner's Circle

Among the wealthy suburban lifestyles, Winner's Circle is the youngest, a collection of mostly 35- to 54-year-old couples with large families in new-money subdivisions. Surrounding their homes are the signs of upscale living – recreational parks, golf courses, and upscale malls. With a median income over $100,000, Winner's Circle residents are big spenders who like to travel, ski, go out to eat, shop at clothing boutiques, and take in a show.

07 Money & Brains

The residents of Money & Brains seem to have it all – high incomes, advanced degrees, and sophisticated tastes to match their credentials. Many of these city dwellers are married couples with few children who live in fashionable homes on small, manicured lots with expensive cars in the driveway.

08 Gray Power

Gray Power consists of upscale older couples typically living just beyond the nation's beltways. This segment is a haven for white-collar professionals drawn to comfortable homes and apartments within a manageable commute to downtown jobs, restaurants, and entertainment. They enjoy traveling and watching golf on television.

09 Big Fish, Small Pond

Older, upper-class, college-educated professionals, the members of Big Fish, Small Pond are often among the leading citizens of their small-town communities. These upscale, empty-nesting couples enjoy the trappings of success, including belonging to country clubs, maintaining large investment portfolios, and spending freely on computer technology.

10 Executive Suites

The residents of Executive Suites tend to be prosperous and active professionals who own multiple computers, large-screen TV sets, and are above average in their use of technology. Executive Suites also enjoy cultural activities, from reading books to attending theater and watching independent movies.

11 Fast-Track Families

Fast-Track Families lead busy, active lives often centered around the schedules and interests of their children. Always on the go, they are frequent restaurant diners, drive larger SUVs, visit Pinterest, and tend to shop in bulk at wholesale clubs.

12 Cruisin' to Retirement

With their children mostly grown and out of the house, these older couples are Cruisin' to Retirement. They remain in the neighborhoods where they raised their families, enjoying the suburban lifestyle. They vacation often, watch golf on television, and listen to talk radio.

13 Upward Bound

Upward Bound are often upscale families boasting dual incomes, college degrees, and new homes. Residents of Upward Bound are above average technology users who own multiple computers and frequently research and purchase all types of products online.

14 Kids & Cul-de-Sacs

Upper-middle-class, suburban, married couples with children – that's the skinny on Kids & Cul-de-Sacs, an enviable lifestyle of large families in recently built subdivisions. This segment is a refuge for college-educated, white-collar professionals with administrative jobs and upper-middle-class incomes. Their nexus of education, affluence, and children translates into large outlays for child-centered products and services.

15 New Homesteaders

Young, upper-middle-class families seeking to escape suburban sprawl find refuge in New Homesteaders, a collection of small rustic townships. With a mix of jobs in white and blue-collar industries, these dual-income couples have fashioned comfortable, child-centered lifestyles; their driveways are filled with campers and powerboats, their house with the latest technological gadgets and hunting gear.

16 Beltway Boomers

The members of the postwar Baby Boom are all grown up. One segment of this huge cohort, college-educated, upper-middle-class, and home-owning, is found in Beltway Boomers. Like many of their peers who married late, many of these Boomers are still raising children in comfortable suburban subdivisions while beginning to plan for their own retirement.

17 Urban Elders

Urban Elders, a segment located in the downtown neighborhoods of such metros as New York, Chicago, Las Vegas, and Miami, are more likely to be renters than other households in their age cohort. They enjoy the cultural options available to them in their communities, frequently attending musical performances and other live events.

18 Mayberry-ville

Like the old Andy Griffith Show set in a quaint picturesque burg, Mayberry-ville harks back to an oldfashioned way of life. In these small towns, upscale couples prefer outdoor activities like fishing and hunting during the day, and stay home and watch TV at night. Overall, their use of technology trails that of others at their same asset level.

19 American Dreams

American Dreams residents are found in upper-middle-class multilingual neighborhoods in urban areas. They are heavy grocery and convenience store shoppers, opting to prepare meals at home more than their urban counterparts in other segments.

20 Empty Nests

With their grown-up children out of the house, Empty Nests is composed of upper-middle income older Americans who pursue active, and activist, lifestyles. Most residents are over 65 years old, but they show no interest in a rest-home retirement. They travel frequently, enjoy golf, and many are active in their country clubs or fraternal groups.

Source: Claritas MyBestSegments (www.MyBestSegments.com) 2017

as a setting for everyday life? How has the area changed since it has been completed, and what does that say about the initial assumptions? And, of course, what are its shortcomings; what has not worked as intended?

Good comparative data is important to inform judgments about the ingredients for success. Studying a precedent, the planner will calculate as precisely as possible the floor areas, density and intensity of development, number of households and children, number of parking spaces provided (categorized by type), critical dimensions (shop frontages, width of streets, etc.), foot traffic on streets at various times of day, and other relevant data that can be discovered. An ideal case study involves both indirect data drawn from published sources and studies and *direct observation.* Consulting the Internet, and reading carefully any blogs that make reference to the site, can reveal a great deal. Archival information on older projects can provide useful insights about their origins (see Urban Land Institute development case studies, http://uli.org/publications/case-studies/; Rudy Bruner Award publications, http://www.rudybruneraward.org/winners/). But visiting the site, speaking with users, and observing their patterns brings all the senses into play, and provides a depth of information that cannot be duplicated vicariously.

Looking at a handful of precedents raises issues of selection bias and randomness of results, which is why many social scientists shy away from studies involving a small number of cases. Ideally, one should look at paired examples that are successes and failures to understand the sources of each. As an example, compare an area with no human contact on the street with one teeming with activity to really understand the role of the environment and the habits of occupants in supporting street life.

Direct Observation

Looking closely, aided by a camera, notebook, and tape recorder, an alert observer can learn a great deal about a place even in a relatively short visit. Better still, by making repeat visits at several times of the day and night, and in different seasons, the observer can learn about the rhythm of occupants and ways that the place changes over a longer cycle. Direct observation is not without bias—observers can miss things they are not attuned to seeing—but if approached with an open mind, the direct evidence provides a firm foundation for understanding users.

Direct observation yields a mountain of data and impressions—what should one count, photograph, and record? Our eye is attuned to seeing unique things, while it may be the sheer humdrum of repeated use that needs to be documented. And what aspects of the environment should be recorded? The observer never knows in advance what will be important. Per Anselm Strauss's advice, field studies can usefully be done in stages that become increasingly precise (Glaser and Strauss 1967; Corbin and Strauss 2007). Begin with unstructured observations, simply "hanging around," which will yield hunches about what is occurring; follow up by collecting more precise data to test those hunches; then get inside people's heads by interviewing or discussing what you have found to validate your understandings.

To be useful to site planning, observation needs to find a connection between people's activities and the environmental situation. By studying use patterns from a similar environment, we hope to be able to infer habits so powerful that they are likely to be carried over to other places. The form of the environment will, of course, have some influence on people's behavior, but it is not likely to be deterministic. Roger Barker's idea of *behavior settings* is a useful way of thinking about the relationships between environments and activities (Barker 1963). He argues that any large environment can be divided into an array of spatial and temporal units, each with understood rules and relatively consistent behaviors that are adapted to their surroundings.

Constructing a map of behavior settings, and cataloging the written and unwritten rules (scripts) for their occupants, is a useful way to structure a study of activities in an environment. Are there natural territories in a place, each with its own occupants, coexisting in a sympathetic way? Or do these territories overlap, with some groups feeling threatened? What kinds of individuals are attracted to each setting, and what are the routines in each?

William H. Whyte's classic studies of the use of public spaces in New York identified routines and users in parks and plazas, and provided a template for the design of successful spaces (Whyte 1980). His studies of Bryant Park identified the hegemony of undesirable characters using the park as a behavior setting, protected by perimeter landscape that hid their activities. The fear they engendered was reinforced by the park's lack of attractions for a more diverse user group. Based on the recommendations of this observational study, Bryant Park has been redesigned and is now one of the most heavily used public spaces in New York.

Much can be inferred from careful observation of people using public spaces, if the observer has an eye for detail. Do the users seem comfortable in the space, or are they tentative or frustrated or confused? Do people adapt the space to better suit their purposes, such as by moving chairs around or setting up tentative territories? How does the place change from day to night, summer to winter? Watching the progression of the sun in the space and where users locate themselves can indicate whether sunlight (or shade) is an important determinant of use. Plotting wind patterns and places people avoid can help determine the conditions in which people feel comfortable. Observational studies are particularly important in improving existing public spaces, but they can also provide solid guidance for planning and designing new spaces.

One fruitful technique is to observe and catalog *environmental traces*, which sometimes tell a great deal about how places are used and regarded. Paths cutting across lawns can signal important connections; window grilles may indicate security concerns; ornaments and decorations in windows may suggest how residents want to be seen by passersby, as do areas appropriated outside their front door for flowers and furniture; a new car at the curb may be an extension of the resident's personality; and graffiti can tell a great deal about what is valued. The observer needs to be cautious about jumping to conclusions from such evidence, but repeated sightings can add support to one's hunches.

11.3 A classic behavior setting, Qingdao, China.
(Gary Hack)

11.4 Based on observational studies, the edges of Bryant Park, New York have been opened up to surrounding streets and lined with activities, encouraging people to visit the park.
(Gary Hack)

11.5 An environmental trace: a well-worn path in London leads to the bus stop.
(Kake/Creative Commons)

Plotting and understanding movement on sites presents its own challenges. While many activities occur in fixed places, a great deal of time is spent moving from place to place. It is often useful to know the routes people take, and what activities they participate in along the way. When people visit shopping areas, do they move from end to end, or seek out particular clusters of shops? Are there very different ways to use a public park? What are the routines of mothers with young children in a neighborhood over the course of the day? Knowing about such behaviors can be very helpful in designing environments that accommodate their users.

Patterns of movement through fixed spaces can be captured with time-lapse photography taken from the tops of nearby buildings, or by the myriad of surveillance cameras that have been installed in public spaces. Where time lapses are 3 seconds or less, the recording can be played back and offer a clear impression of movement patterns at different times of the day (or week). Invasions of privacy are a real issue with such studies, but can be minimized if the resolution is low enough that individuals can't be identified (usually the opposite of the reason the cameras have been installed!). Time-lapse studies are especially valuable in analyzing the use of public spaces, such as urban parks and plazas, in analyzing pedestrian behavior on streets, and in disentangling the interaction of pedestrians and vehicles at street intersections or crosswalks (https://vimeo.com/138382675). The studies often yield new insights into how the environment can be modified to improve safety or use.

Where filming is not possible, flows can be counted at cordon lines in key locations, from which a model can be constructed of the overall pattern of movement. A study of this kind, made on the Boston Common, identified a disparity between the width of pathways and movement patterns—several of the narrowest paths carried the largest volumes of pedestrians, leading to many conflicts between slow-moving strollers and fast-paced commuters. Based on this, a program of rebuilding walkways adjusted the environment to more closely match user patterns.

Pedestrian cordon studies can account for the numbers of individuals moving past a fixed point, but they tell nothing of the routes taken to and from that location. How do pedestrians move from parking garages to their office work place? Why are so few pedestrians walking on a particular block? Is there an opportunity to divert them through a site you are planning? Each of these involves an understanding of patterns of travel, and the ways individuals make decisions about which route to take.

One obvious approach is to follow a sample of individuals as they move from point A to B and ultimately to their destination, but this risks creating a threatening situation if the subjects do not know why they are being tracked. Asking their permission at the beginning is likely to elevate the sense of threat, or result in a skewed sample of those who agree to be followed. If data on pedestrian flows is available, the researcher can reconstruct likely routes and walk these herself, observing carefully the environments along the way—noting stretches that are dull, threatening, filled with sidewalk displays, occupied by interesting people, and otherwise noteworthy. Better still, sketch the key points along the route, as Gordon Cullen did in his landmark study of townscape. Sophisticated *serial notation techniques* have been developed to structure the recording and analysis of route experiences, but in most instances they yield more information than is needed for making site decisions. Routines and habits of navigating through environments are often driven by learned behaviors and unconscious calculations that may need to be disentangled by others.

An alternative is to combine observations with interviews, in which individuals can be asked to make a map of the route they took that day, and to discuss why they walked that way and what they saw. This approach was adopted in a study of the use of streets in downtown Washington; the results revealed the dead spots in the experience of the city, and areas that were avoided by pedestrians concerned with security (Carr et al. 1992).

Interviewing

Conversations are usually the best way to get inside people's heads. These may be *unstructured dialogues*, or may involve a series of questions designed to elicit a stream of comments. As any good interviewer knows, getting to the heart of the matter requires careful and persistent probing.

Most successful interviews begin with a handful of well-formulated questions to guide the conversation.

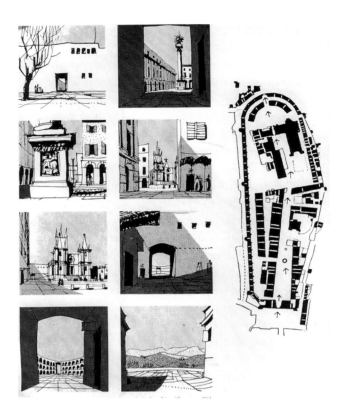

11.6 Sequence of views on a route through a walled city, by Gordon Cullen.
(Gordon Cullen, *Townscape*)

since the software will not have been trained for each subject's voice patterns. Notes made by the interviewer or an assistant sitting in on the conversation can help correct transcription errors.

Most unstructured or loosely structured interviews reveal how the subjects think about the questions, but after a dozen interviews, the planner will find that she has too much raw data to keep track of views. The responses can be grouped into categories ("postcoding") and the results tallied. A careful content analysis of the words and phrases used by subjects can offer ways of naming or framing issues. Illustrative stories can be extracted from the interviews and used to characterize attitudes. All of this will provide anecdotal evidence, but the sample of those interviewed is usually

Several techniques are important for getting useful answers: explaining the purpose of the interview and how the comments will be used, to allay any fears of the subject; outlining the topics to be covered so that subjects don't feel the need to respond to the first question with everything on their mind; maintaining a nonjudgmental but interested tone; avoiding questions that will lead to obvious answers or preclude possible responses; using plain jargon-free language to ensure questions are understood; following up with probes that extend the line of thought rather than slavishly ticking off preset questions; and offering an opportunity at the end for the subject to speak about other things that he feels are relevant, but haven't been covered. The interviewer can take notes, or capture the comments in tape recordings. Voice recognition software can provide a quick transcript of the interview, although this will require considerable editing,

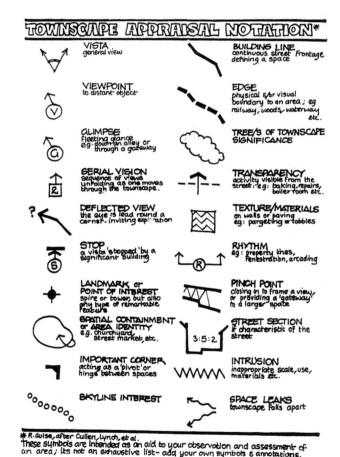

11.7 Serial notation system for urban spaces.
(Courtesy of Richard Guise)

not large enough for dependable generalizations. In a site planning process, however, not all opinions are weighed equally—interviews with even a small number of clients, opinion makers, public officials, and others with a stake in the outcome can be vitally important.

There are occasions when it is important to sample larger groups to obtain statistically significant responses to important questions. The larger the sample, the lower the probability that the responses will err, assuming that the sample is truly random, mirroring the demographics (and often the geography) of the larger population that one wishes to understand. The survey may be done through telephone interviews, Internet survey programs (some of which are free), a mailed questionnaire, or face-to-face interviews. Each method has its pluses and minuses, and poses its own difficulties in achieving a good random sample (Roper Center, n.d.). The relatively low cost of Internet surveys has increased their popularity, although ensuring a good cross section of respondents is a challenge.

Structured surveys require that the question be easily understood and unambiguous. They are best done when the issues are clear and one is seeking to calibrate the weight of opinion on one side or another, or when there are clear alternatives that need to be polled. Sliding-scale responses—"strongly agree–agree–neutral–disagree–strongly disagree"—can measure the intensity of feelings as well as the general direction. The value of such surveys is that they can be analyzed quantitatively, and results can be cross-tabulated for groups in the population. Structured sample surveys are, nonetheless, costly to do, and should only be initiated when it is possible to be precise about the questions.

Focus Groups

Sometimes the best way to learn about preferences or needs or to solicit opinions on choices is to compose groups of representative individuals and have them meet together for discussions of the issues. *Focus groups*, which are widely used in marketing studies, can be an effective tool for surfacing issues and requirements in planning a site (Greenbaum 2000). The challenges are in deciding the size and composition of the groups and how to structure the dialogues.

Focus groups work best when they are fairly homogeneous demographically (middle-aged middle-income homeowners, teenagers, working singles, etc.), which often avoids the conversation-stopping disputes of polar opposites. Having a good range of groups can ensure the desired diversity of opinions. The groups need to be small enough to provide airtime for all—usually fewer than a dozen participants. And the dialogue is often aided by having various props available—photos of a site, examples of similar developments elsewhere, illustrations of possible designs, models of the project, etc.—so that group members share similar knowledge. Clear and tangible questions need to be outlined at the beginning of the session, a clear time to wind up the session needs to be established, and the conversation needs to be mediated by a skilled interlocutor who can keep it on track and moving toward conclusions.

Technologies that provide instantaneous polling of responses can both calibrate and greatly expand the potential size of focus groups. These include handheld devices that allow participants to select among several choices, sometimes also allowing them to signal how strongly they feel about their choice. Or they may use computer terminals where possibilities are shown and participants vote their preferences. Interactive town meetings organized by America Speaks have allowed intense dialogues among groups as large as 4,500 (see figure 10.5).

11.8 Focus group discussion of LEED design priorities. (Courtesy of Stantec)

Visualization Techniques

Most of the choices in planning sites involve decisions about the physical character of what will be built or preserved, and many lay individuals feel inadequate in translating their reactions to the visible world into words. In learning about and from users, it is often useful to work directly with visual data. A wide range of techniques is available to assist in the dialogue.

One approach is to have users reveal things about themselves through images. The use of cameras (which could be the cameras in their smart phones) allows users to document the important places in their daily routines and can help pinpoint the most important aspects of a site. In preparing a campus plan, students' visual diaries can be eye-opening. A simpler technique is asking individuals to make a map of where they have been that day and the most important places along the way.

A second approach, the *visual preference study*, involves showing users or their surrogates examples of possible environments, or renderings of alternative plans, and asking for their reactions in free-flowing or structured form. Doing so involves many choices of viewpoint, which can subtly bias the dialogue. A poor photograph of even the best environment can dampen enthusiasm for it, while a well-situated illustration can exaggerate a plan's virtues or avoid obvious problems it faces. Nonetheless, with care on the part of the planner, useful data can be obtained. Asking respondents to react to examples on a sliding scale can provide data that allows preferences to be calibrated. Showing paired examples that differ along one or more critical dimensions can help get at the subtleties of differences—two streets that vary slightly in their dimensions, two areas developed at different densities, public spaces with different character, and the like.

Participants can be asked to step beyond what they know or are shown and enter into the realm of what they can imagine. Users can be asked to draw a picture of their "ideal" neighborhood, and the results are often revealing if one looks beyond the childlike depictions of houses and shops and schools, for which the artists inevitably apologize. Residents of a Cambridge, Massachusetts neighborhood responded to this challenge with exuberant visions of a future inner-city environment. A variant on this is to ask individuals or groups of users to construct an ideal settlement using a kit of parts provided by the planner—Lego blocks, odds and ends, or shapes that symbolize various buildings or urban simulacra.

Going one step further, the game of constructing an ideal environment can include the task of making tradeoffs, recognizing that real life is never unconstrained. Users can be given a budget to construct their neighborhood, which can be used to purchase objects representing land, buildings, recreation spaces, shops,

11.9 Visual preference survey, in which participants were asked to rate the images as positive or negative by placing green or red dots beside each. (Courtesy of Sustainable Development Program, Augusta, Georgia)

SINGLE-FAMILY RESIDENTIAL
Image Preference Survey
August 2012

Look at these images and consider their appropriateness for the priority corridor area in the future. Please put two green dots on the two images that you find the most appropriate and two red dots on the two that are least appropriate.

11.10 Results of a group exercise in planning an ideal city. (Courtesy of Benoit Colin/ EMBARQ/World Resources Institute)

and other elements, each with a price. They may purchase more private land for home sites and smaller buildings or common spaces, or small schools nearby with higher property taxes, or other combinations. Computer games such as Sim City can also serve as tools for gaming user preferences, as several players compete for scarce locations and resources. While the players' behavior can be revealing, one should not put too much stock in the outcomes, since these are as likely the product of the rules of the game, the pricing of actions, and the competitive strategies of players.

Experiments

On rare but important occasions, it may be possible to learn about users by conducting experiments that expose them to changed environments. One example is a study, conducted in Norfolk, Virginia, of the appropriate pattern and standards for street lighting at night in residential neighborhoods (William Lam Associates 1976). About a dozen residential and arterial streets were selected for a carefully controlled experiment, in which portions of the blocks were fitted with new lighting fixtures that varied in type, spacing, intensity, and color. Over 100 randomly chosen residents (from this and other neighborhoods) were asked to walk the blocks and score their impressions along a number of semantic differential scales, as well as in words. From an analysis of the data a clear set of preferences emerged, and standards were estimated for such improvements. Such experiments are possible where the number of variables is small, the cost of an investment is large, and there are users available who are willing to participate. Temporary closures and traffic-calming measures on residential streets often yield excellent information on the residents' tolerance of circuitous traffic patterns.

A more common source of information is from "natural experiments," observing the results of changes made for other reasons. When families move from high-rise apartments to ground-oriented housing with backyards, do they use their newfound space, and in what ways? When buses are rerouted, how many of the individuals who must walk further to a bus stop shift to taking their cars to work? Baseline information is important for analyzing such changes, and other variables must be able to be ruled out.

In large-scale site developments, it is also possible to plan in a series of experiments—*pilot projects*, they are often called—to test the efficacy of departures from conventional practice. Developing a small portion of the site with common parking some distance from housing units could be an excellent test of

11.11 Test of concept for converting a lifeless parking lot in Silver Lake, California into a pedestrian plaza, using paint and inexpensive materials.
(Courtesy of Kenneth A Wilson/flickr)

this arrangement's marketability and fit with residents' desires. Creating a small prototype of shared courtyard housing as a demonstration project, as Tsinghua University did in the hutongs of Beijing, can be a useful test of its suitability for the kinds of families that wish to locate in infill sites in the inner city. Installing an experimental multifuel district heating package plant may be the best way to test its technical and economic performance, and whether users can maintain it, before committing to larger systems. The problem of scaling up will always bedevil such experiments, as will the risk of unique circumstances that cannot be duplicated, but having some data is usually better than relying on speculation.

User Advocates

Sometimes the best way to have user preferences reflected in site planning is by engaging a user advocate, who serves as intermediary between planners and users. The advocate begins by identifying the constituency whose views need to be represented, meets with it, and formulates a set of desires and parameters by which to judge the plans for the site. As plans emerge, the advocate shows them to the users, elicits views, and translates these into a series of suggestions for the planning team. Where plans are at loggerheads with

the desires of users, the advocate will be the agent of the users in negotiating a successful outcome.

The best user advocates have a solid understanding of planning and design issues, and an ease of communicating in often-contentious situations. Theirs is a tightrope act, balancing responsibility to users with an understanding of the constraints the planners face. At times they may need to sketch ideas and plans to assist the designers, while other times helping users envision what the site might be like. A user advocate was an essential participant in the planning of Rockefeller Park at Battery Park City, New York, making sense of the disparate desires of residents of Tribeca and the residential and working populations of the area. The result is a diverse set of environments, and possibly the best-used park in the city.

Self-Analysis

Ultimately, the planner's ability to engage users may be constrained by having too little time, too small a budget, or a need to work in secrecy because of sensitivities in seeking approval for the development. Or the project may be too distant, unprecedented, with uncertainty about future users, or a prototype to be located in many places. In such cases it falls to the planner to immerse herself in the question of how the site will be valued and used by potential users. They may need to their own experiences and imag-ination to test whether plans will be responsive to user needs.

The techniques used by method actors to prepare themselves for roles on stage or screen have lessons for planners who need to understand users well enough to make judgments on their behalf. The root of many others' responses may be found in our personal life experiences, if one reaches deeply enough, but one needs also to be highly sensitive to how culture and circumstance shape our views and behavior. Hanging around people who might be like the eventual occupants of a site, reading about them, seeing movies that are relevant (often made by actors and directors who have done their homework), observing places currently occupied, spending a day or two in a comparable place—all can help develop a deeply ingrained sense of use and value. Faced with quickly creating and discarding possibilities, the planner needs to develop an instinct for how eventual users might react.

12 | Programming Sites

The site *program* sets down understandings about the scope, purposes, and qualities of site improvements: What uses should be included, and how much of each? For whose use? Patterned how? Built and maintained by whom? At what cost? On what timetable? A program usually emerges out of a dialogue among the owners, users, planners, designers, financiers, public officials, and other stakeholders in the project.

A program, called in some countries a *brief* or *project scope,* may be drafted by the owner as a way of establishing objectives at the beginning of a project, or by the planners once engaged as a way of confirming their understanding of what is expected. Programs are never static, however, changing as new possibilities are discovered, external circumstances change, and purposes are redefined. The initial assumptions of the program may prove infeasible when possible plans are studied, and surely will need to be refined once all the participants have a better understanding of the capacity of the site.

Some situations demand comprehensive program documents—as the basis for a design competition, for example—while in other cases a few pages in outline form may suffice. The program can be used to memorialize agreements among multiple clients, and can be useful to avoid slippage or retracing steps when responsibility for the site is passed from one entity to another. Public land development agencies often include detailed programs when calling for proposals from private developers. Local authorities in the UK sometimes present briefs for sites ripe for development, spelling out the issues that the site planner must take account of. On phased developments, the program can serve as the reminder of original intentions as development resumes after a gap of a few years. Approval of a phased development by a governmental agency is often tied to hitting targets in the site program. Thus, there are many reasons why preparing an explicit development program is a good investment.

Even on small sites, preparing a program can provide the impetus to think in fresh ways about environmental character. Siting a new school in a built-up area is an example. School boards have adopted rigid minimum site area requirements, ruling out many inner-city locations because they are too small. But if the real purposes of open space are considered and specified in terms of activities, ways may be found to overlap activities, use portions of the building (such as rooftops) for outdoor play, and use other nearby vacant spaces to accomplish the program. Difficulty can be turned to advantage, producing a unique design response.

The contents of a program can be expressed in many forms: lists of objectives and design criteria; estimates of the types and numbers of people to be housed; charts of responsibility for the project; schedules of spaces or activities to be included and their desired characteristics; diagrams of linkages between activities, timetables for construction; financial pro formas; photographs or drawings of other projects that can serve as exemplars, among others. A useful strategy is to agree on the outline of the program, and then use it as the format for discussions among the various groups that need to be consulted. A first draft of the activity program for a common space in a residential area will immediately stimulate debates on what is missing, what activities are appropriate, and what others should be avoided. A first sketch of the *financial*

The Program for this Hybrid Housing project is a suggestion of a set of different environments and typologies for a wide range of people (couples, friends, professional profiles, families, elderly people, disabled people) that reflect on the contemporary housing demands. The challenge is to think not only in square meters of each cell, public spaces but also to express the relationship between housing cells, open spaces and the urban fabric. A successful design must factor in these conditions, as well as consider new configurations of the required program. Future needs, social, functional and spatial necessities can also be taken into consideration to generate a distinct and more meaningful proposal.

RESIDENTIAL

This competition aims for an experiment in different types of domestic space, exploring its programmatic potential and spatial richness. Here, are included people with different backgrounds and different permanence times in the city, permanent residents (families / elderly people) and semi-permanent (students).

Housing Cells Typologies:
- Four University Students: *30 units, 80-90 m2 each.*
- A Couple with two or more children: *30 units, 90-100 m2 each*
- A Couple with one child: *30 units, 70-80 m2 each*
- A Couple with no children: *30 units, 60-70 m2 each*
- An Elderly Couple: *30units, 60-70 m2 each*
- A Single-person studio: 50 units: *30-40 m2 each*

Community Private Areas:
Laundry Rooms / Fitness Room / Terraces / Rooftop terraces / Music Room / Youth Room / Resident Community Room / Communitarian rooms for students /Bicycle Parking / etc.
These communal spaces should be considered, as to help foster a vital community of residents. Deliberately, there are no area limitation here assigned, they are left to the consideration of the Participant Team. Nevertheless, they are included in the Maximum Total Area of the Residential Program.

The Residential Program should not exceed the Maximum Area of 15000m2

12.1 (this and facing page) Hamburg hybrid housing competition brief.
(Courtesy of CTRL+SPACE)

pro forma will allow decision makers to focus on financial objectives and the level of investment they are prepared to entertain. When agreements are reached, these are assembled into a working program. It will serve as a temporary constitution for the project that needs to be tested and informed by planning studies.

Assembling a program involves delving into at least four subjects, which for convenience can be thought of as the *four P's*:

Populations

Who will inhabit the site? Often this is thought to be a closed issue. A campus is to be built for an estimated student population of 10,000 and faculty of 800, and there are many examples to draw upon to specify what they need. But is the campus to be designed as well for the 600 staff—what are their needs? And will the student population remain the same in the future, or will there be more midcareer individuals returning for short periods and distance education students spending part of their time on campus, and what will their needs be? Or on a site focusing on workforce housing, what will the full range of residents be? How many will have elderly family members living in? How large will their families be? Are there likely to be ethnic groups with special patterns of activity? The first step in creating a program involves constructing a profile of the population that goes beyond the statistics and begins to account for the variety of needs to be addressed on the site.

COMMERCIAL

The presence of Commercial facilities, apart from responding to the concrete needs of the site, can also have a benefic contribution in its overlapping and combination with the residential function. In the Commerce sector, functions that not only relate to the residents needs but also bring added value to the neighborhood, can be considered.

The Commercial Program can include a series of functions:

Shopping — Bookstore / Design store / Art Gallery / Pharmacy / Souvenir shop / Hair Salon / Health food shop / Bicycle repair shop / Convenience store;

Offices — Small offices / collaborative working space;

Entertainment — Music clubs / Bars / Restaurants

These can help activate the urban space and act as buffer between the different sectors of the building. There is no fixed area for any element. The total areas, as with which elements will compose this sector are left to the discretion of the Participant Team. Other functional need that the participant team detects as lacking in the urban context shall also be accepted.

Backpacker's Hostel — 500m2

The central location in the city requires the answer to the need of temporary accommodation. A midpoint between the Commercial and Residential function, the presence of this element reinforces the heterogeneous community spirit.

Functionally, it should be comprised of 20 mixed-sex bedrooms for a total of 100 people. A communal space for Reception and Leisure is also included in this total Area. Toilet facilities should be present one in each floor and in effective functional quantity.

The total of Commercial facilities, which includes the Backpackers Hostel, should not exceed the Maximum Area of 2000m2

EXTERIOR PUBLIC SPACE

This would ideally be a space where social relations can be enhanced. The needs of the neighborhood children and elder citizens that are most likely to benefit from this new public space should be kept in mind. Ludic activities, children playground, games and sportive activities, like Basketball, Tennis, water features or swimming pool can be also integrated.

The Exterior Public Space should account for 60% of the Ground Floor.

CIRCULATION

For both Commercial and Residential sectors of the building, the areas for interior circulation are not assigned, but should preferably not exceed 20% of the overall building. Exterior circulation is not accountable.

PARKING

Even though it is not the main focus of this exercise, parking facilities could be considered. Underground parking is restricted to one level and can be able to contain up to 200 vehicles. The vehicle Parking is an optional element that may bring value to the proposal.

SUSTAINABILITY

In a project with this dimension, sustainable approaches: waste management, energy production and consumption, could be taken into account.

There are no height restrictions, but the overall proposal must be harmonious with its surrounding. Structurally, no engineering calculation is to be presented, but structural elements should be represented in order to provide some degree of realism and feasibility to the project.

MAXIMUM TOTAL AREA: 17.000m2

Here are excluded all exterior areas and Underground Parking.

Development Briefs: West of High Sparrowmire, Kendal
Draft Constraints and Opportunities Map   December 2015

12.2 Development brief, South Lakeland District Council, Kendal, Cumbria, UK.
(South Lakeland District Council)

Space Type Institution Mission	FTE Enrollment			
	Fewer than 3,000 students	3,000 to 6,000 students	6,000 to 10,000 students	Greater than 10,000 students
Classrooms and Service	applied to Non Dist Ed FTE	applied to Non Dist Ed FTE	applied to Non Dist Ed FTE	applied to Non Dist Ed FTE
Community College	13 ASF/FTE student	13 ASF/FTE student	12 ASF/FTE student	12 ASF/FTE student
Baccalaureate/Masters	12 ASF/FTE student	12 ASF/FTE student	11 ASF/FTE student	11 ASF/FTE student
Research University	11 ASF/FTE student	11 ASF/FTE student	10 ASF/FTE student	10 ASF/FTE student
Teaching Laboratories and Service **General Academic Instruction**	applied to Non Dist Ed FTE	applied to Non Dist Ed FTE	applied to Non Dist Ed FTE	applied to Non Dist Ed FTE
Community College	16 ASF/FTE student	16 ASF/FTE student	15 ASF/FTE student	15 ASF/FTE student
Baccalaureate/Masters	15 ASF/FTE student	15 ASF/FTE student	13 ASF/FTE student	12 ASF/FTE student
Research University	14 ASF/FTE student	13 ASF/FTE student	12 ASF/FTE student	11 ASF/FTE student
Teaching Laboratories and Service **Auto/Construct Trades Instruction**	applied to Non Dist Ed FTE	applied to Non Dist Ed FTE	applied to Non Dist Ed FTE	applied to Non Dist Ed FTE
	*Existing ASF/FTE for campuses not increasing Auto/Construction Trades instruction			
Community College	6 ASF/FTE student	6 ASF/FTE student	5 ASF/FTE student	5 ASF/FTE student
Baccalaureate/Masters	5 ASF/FTE student	5 ASF/FTE student	4 ASF/FTE student	4 ASF/FTE student
Open Laboratories and Service				
Community College	8 ASF/FTE student	7 ASF/FTE student	6 ASF/FTE student	5 ASF/FTE student
Baccalaureate/Masters	8 ASF/FTE student	7 ASF/FTE student	6 ASF/FTE student	5 ASF/FTE student
Research University	8 ASF/FTE student	8 ASF/FTE student	8 ASF/FTE student	8 ASF/FTE student
Research Laboratories and Service				
Baccalaureate/Masters	35 ASF/FTE faculty	35 ASF/FTE faculty	35 ASF/FTE faculty	35 ASF/FTE faculty
Research University	475 ASF/FTE faculty	475 ASF/FTE faculty	475 ASF/FTE faculty	475 ASF/FTE faculty
Office and Office Service				
Community College	150 ASF/FTE employee	150 ASF/FTE employee	150 ASF/FTE employee	150 ASF/FTE employee
Baccalaureate/Masters	170 ASF/FTE employee	170 ASF/FTE employee	170 ASF/FTE employee	170 ASF/FTE employee
Research University	195 ASF/FTE employee	195 ASF/FTE employee	195 ASF/FTE employee	195 ASF/FTE employee
Libraries	15,000 ASF minimum			
Community College	7 ASF/FTE student	6 ASF/FTE student	5 ASF/FTE student	4 ASF/FTE student
Baccalaureate/Masters	9 ASF/FTE student	9 ASF/FTE student	7 ASF/FTE student	7 ASF/FTE student
Research University	14 ASF/FTE student	14 ASF/FTE student	14 ASF/FTE student	12 ASF/FTE student
Special Use Space				
Community College	3 ASF/FTE student	3 ASF/FTE student	3 ASF/FTE student	3 ASF/FTE student
Baccalaureate/Masters	3 ASF/FTE student	3 ASF/FTE student	3 ASF/FTE student	3 ASF/FTE student
Research University	3 ASF/FTE student	3 ASF/FTE student	3 ASF/FTE student	3 ASF/FTE student
Physical Education			35,000 ASF minimum	
Community College	35,000 ASF minimum	35,000 ASF minimum	4 ASF/FTE student	3 ASF/FTE student
Baccalaureate/Masters	35,000 ASF minimum	35,000 ASF minimum	4 ASF/FTE student	3 ASF/FTE student
Research University	35,000 ASF minimum	35,000 ASF minimum	4 ASF/FTE student	3 ASF/FTE student
General Use Space				
Community College	15 ASF/FTE student	13 ASF/FTE student	11 ASF/FTE student	10 ASF/FTE student
Baccalaureate/Masters	15 ASF/FTE student	13 ASF/FTE student	11 ASF/FTE student	10 ASF/FTE student
Research University	15 ASF/FTE student	13 ASF/FTE student	11 ASF/FTE student	10 ASF/FTE student
Support Space				
Community College	4 ASF/FTE student	4 ASF/FTE student	4 ASF/FTE student	4 ASF/FTE student
Baccalaureate/Masters	6 ASF/FTE student	6 ASF/FTE student	6 ASF/FTE student	6 ASF/FTE student
Research University	8 ASF/FTE student	8 ASF/FTE student	8 ASF/FTE student	8 ASF/FTE student
Land Grant Mission Addition	+6 ASF/FTE student	+6 ASF/FTE student	+6 ASF/FTE student	+6 ASF/FTE student

ASF- Assignable square feet
FTE- Full-time equivalent

12.3 Utah space standards for higher education institutions of various sizes (Utah System of Higher Education)

Package

One will then have to decide on the types and quantities of elements to be provided: the number of housing units and size of each type; the commercial square footage and number of parking spaces; the list of outdoor activities; community facilities to be included, and so on. Usually this takes the form of a spreadsheet of requirements, with their estimated sizes and characteristics, but it may also be represented graphically so that the relative scale of each is evident. During the initial feasibility study, the package will be tested by making quick design sketches laying out the uses of the site, and by constructing a rough pro forma of costs and revenues (or sources of funding, when profit is not the motive).

How the package is described can greatly affect the planner's and designer's flexibility in organizing the site. Open space on a site can be prescribed in quantitative terms (25% of the site, or a 5 ha open space, or a playground of such and such dimensions) or, better, by listing the activities to be accommodated (little league baseball, cricket, an area for Frisbee play, a play area for children under five, an exercise loop, etc.). The former ties the planner's hands, while the latter leaves open many possibilities, including several open areas linked by paths, or the use of other spaces (such as schoolyards) to meet some of the recreation needs. The package of activities needs to be open to unique uses that emerge from creative planning of the site.

Performance Requirements

Effective leaders know that "you can only manage what you can measure," which applies equally to planning: you can only know whether you've accomplished your objectives if you have a way to measure them. Programs usually begin with lofty objectives—encourage public transit use, promote mixing of diverse household types, create safe public spaces, minimize runoff into adjacent streams, and the like—but these need to be operationalized in the form of performance statements. What levels of transit use would be considered a success, and how do these compare to other similarly situated areas? How would we know if households are in contact with others? What activities would we like to preclude from public spaces? What will our runoff

standard be? No net runoff? Runoff rates that don't exceed predevelopment rates?

There is usually an advantage to performance goals that can be judged quantitatively, and our goals must allow us to discriminate between alternatives. "Maximize the number of houses that have south-facing living rooms" allows the planner to put a figure on performance, making comparisons between plans on this dimension. But performance goals can also be a strait-jacket: "all south and west facades should be shaded by trees" leaves little room for other solutions. And subtler qualities should not be lost in the rush to adopt measurable objectives. The best way to specify performance is to link the human dimension with the standard: "create streets that allow pedestrians to cross without fear of accidents, with no more than an average delay of ten seconds," as an example. Performance objectives should not overlook the special qualities of the site, capturing the views, important natural systems, visual linkages, and paths across the site to be maintained, along with important values.

Patterns

Patterns serve as the bridge to design. Few site problems are totally without precedent, and so a useful program can identify workable examples. Patterns can

OBJECTIVE 3:

THERE SHOULD BE A SEQUENCE OF OPEN SPACES CLEARLY CONNECTED TO PUBLIC WAYS

15
CREATE DISTINCTIVE OPEN SPACES ON THE SITE

While building footprints currently occupy only about one quarter of the site, the open spaces between them are extremely similar in character (or characterless) and are largely devoid of uses. There needs to be a more pronounced sense of greenery, in contrast to the hard surfaces of the surrounding streets. In redeveloping the site, the objective will be to create a series of distinctive open spaces, each with a special character, and each clearly defined by buildings and bordering activities.

16
BETTER CONNECT OPEN SPACES WITH PEDESTRIAN ROUTES

Open spaces on the deck need to be better connected to the street level, through stairs and ramps that are secure and inviting. In one or two places, grand fountains or cascades, landscaping and stair forms can make a feature of the need to move from street to deck. There also needs to be an easy flow from pedestrian ways travelling through the center into open spaces. Where possible, outdoor paths through open spaces should offer an alternative to walking indoors across the center. However, for security, large open spaces should be capable of being closed-off during evening hours.

17
ENSURE THAT OUTDOOR OPEN SPACES HAVE FAVORABLE MICROCLIMATES

In Boston's climate, the presence of sunshine and the

absence of wind can extend the period of use of outdoor spaces by two months. Shaded open spaces on the north side of tall structures should generally be avoided; where existing buildings create such conditions, enclosure of all or parts of the spaces should be considered. In a similar vein, new structures should be located and should be of a form to minimize shadows on outdoor spaces especially in the hours between noon and 2 PM. Building forms should deflect high winds away from ground level outdoor spaces.

18
ENLIVEN OPEN SPACES THROUGH ACTIVE BORDERING USES

The activities which border open spaces give them their life and provide the surveillance to ensure that they remain safe. While existing open areas are often visible from indoor spaces there are no uses which spill out into outdoor spaces. Activities now in the center which could do this -- such as the child care center, sidewalk cafe, or common spaces of the apartment structures -- are poorly related to outdoor areas. In renovating the Prudential Center, the object should be to ensure that each outdoor space is rimmed by activities that give life to the space.

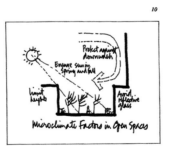

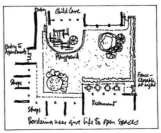

12.4 Patterns for redevelopment of Prudential Center, Boston. (Carr Lynch Hack and Sandell)

range from solutions to a single requirement ("locate parking areas 0.5 m below pedestrian walks," which is designed to reduce the obtrusiveness of autos) to complex prototypes that encapsulate many objectives ("sustainable housing clusters"). They may highlight aspects of the context of the site that deserve attention ("continue the six-story street façade" or "set houses at the margins of the woods so the fields aren't disturbed") or may focus on issues of grouping ("create a central open quadrangle and locate new college buildings around it"). Environmental patterns can be suggested at scales from the immediate ("create a semipublic space between the street and the building entrance") to the extensive ("organize streets as an orthogonal grid").

Patterns are most persuasive if diagrams accompany them, with the key aspects clearly labeled, and illustrations or sketches of the patterns as they have been tried elsewhere. Case examples that embody many of the desired patterns for the site should be

12.5 Patterns for public spaces, Pattern Language. (Courtesy of © Christopher Alexander)

included in the program as reference sources. Compiling a computer file of valuable patterns is an essential resource for site programming and planning. Designers often mine their sketchbooks for useful examples, and those who take photographs during site visits have found ways of coding them to reflect their environmental attributes so that they are not lost in the digital abyss. Some designers argue that tried and true patterns provide the essential ingredients for inventions, and that knowledge of environments ought to be codified as a language of patterns (Alexander et al. 1977).

Programming Processes

The four domains of programming—population, package, performance, and patterns—are, of course, closely related. It does no good to assemble a catalog of patterns that are inappropriate because they assume the wrong population inhabiting the site or are beyond the resources or management of the project. Choices made in one domain inevitably affect the others. There is no foolproof beginning point for programming, and no obvious end (it is always possible to compile more examples or be more precise in specifying performance objectives).

How then to begin? The original assignment by the client will offer the first clues. The clients may be interested in repeating an earlier development that they consider successful, perhaps a housing project already built or visited. The first step might analyze that development, isolating what patterns made it successful, constructing a profile of its population and how they use the site, making an estimate of the development package, if not a search through the financial records of the project. Transposed onto the current site in a feasibility study, the first cut may make a poor fit. It may seem impossible to attract the same residents, so a modified population profile will be drawn up. The price paid for the current site may be higher, or its intrinsic character may be different, suggesting a modified development package. This in turn may suggest new patterns. Since it is difficult to juggle all aspects simultaneously, one makes reasonable assumptions about as many aspects as possible and explores the remaining areas.

Standards and norms can be the point of departure for programming. In higher education planning, there

Student Housing

EXISTING CIATER PROGRAM

The existing Ciater program currently allocates 83,354 GFA for student housing within the "Dormitory" category, which translates into a space factor of 8.09 GFA per bed.

CEFPI MODEL

The CEFPI model assumes 100% of students will live on campus. A sample dormitory with double rooms, a single common bathroom on each floor, and modest community space resulted in an average space factor of 14.3 GFA per bed or 9.3 ASM per bed at 65% efficiency. Taking this information into account, the CEFPI model generates a space need of 147,269 GFA to accommodate 10,300 students. The difference between the existing Ciater program and the CEFPI model is a deficit of 63,915 GFA.

RECOMMENDED PROGRAM

The recommended program for student housing is 147,269 GFA.

Employee Housing

EXISTING CIATER PROGRAM

The existing Ciater program allocates 9,320 GFA for "Employee Housing".

CEFPI MODEL

The CEFPI model assumes 100% of lecturers will live on campus and bases projections upon 40 GFA per lecturer for a studio-style apartment. This translates into 30 ASM per lecturer when using an efficiency of 75%. Taking this information into account, the CEFPI model projects the need for 9,320 GFA at 75% efficiency to accommodate 233 lecturers. The Ciater program and CEFPI model generate the same space need.

RECOMMENDED PROGRAM

The recommended program for employee housing is 9,320 GFA and maintains the existing Ciater space program.

Master Plan Program Summary

In total, the recommended master plan program at full build-out with 10,300 students, 233 lecturers, and 109 back-office staff approaches 260,000 GFA, with the most significant space need associated with housing. Space needs across all categories are summarized on the following table:

Space Type	Recommended GFA	Ciater GFA	CEFPI GFA	Difference
Instructional	46,026	44,026	54,115	- 10,089
Office Space	5,700	4,875	6,372	- 1,497
Study Space	10,000	1,154	10,944	- 9,791
Sports	14,000	14,132	17,587	- 3,455
Student Life	13,700	9,185	13,721	- 4,536
Support	13,000	-	13,070	- 13,070
Healthcare	642	46	642	- 596
Student Housing	147,269	83,354	147,269	- 63,915
Employee Housing	9,320	9,320	9,320	-
Total	259,657	166,091	273,039	-106,948

12.6 Building space program for West Java New University, Subang, Indonesia, comparing recommended areas with accepted standards.
(Courtesy of Sasaki Associates)

are well-researched norms for the amount of space needed for the range of education and research activities. Many governments also set standards to ensure that campuses built with public money are not gold-plated—although the amount of space is only roughly correlated with costs (TEFMA 2009; Paulien and Associates 2011). Types of academic programs vary considerably in the amount and types of space needed. Liberal arts programs that rely on classroom teaching may require only half the space of professional programs in architecture or laboratory-based fields. Site requirements are much more elastic: fine universities can exist both in dense urban areas and in bucolic small towns. However, the program will generally begin with the best estimates of what is required, drawing on the research and standards that are available, and the initial plans for the site will constitute a test of the program.

For projects with no obvious precedents, programming might begin by listing objectives and then translating these into performance statements. Special experts may be needed to help frame the program from their different perspectives. In planning a new town, bring together professionals with understandings of community sociology, sustainable infrastructure, innovative infrastructure planning, marketing, and finance, and ask each to outline how they would specify the performance of a well-planned community. They will help identify appropriate examples and patterns, which may then be translated into first drafts of the development package. But programs can just as easily begin from dreams and utopian schemes, and become more precise as these are translated into measurable criteria.

Sometimes the logic of the site will be so compelling that it will suggest many aspects of the program.

Steeply sloping areas may need to be devoted to low-density development or open space, limiting the overall package of uses on the site. Spectacular views may argue for keeping buildings low so that they do not block the views from other parts of the site. Possible access patterns may constrain the number of people that can be accommodated on the site. All of this may force adjustments to the package. As we noted in chapters 4 and 5, the journey between program and site analysis is not a lock-step march.

13 | Media for Site Planning

Site planning requires graphic media for recording site information, constructing a model of the site, representing ideas of how it might be developed, testing those ideas, and communicating what the site might be like if developed as proposed. Ultimately, site development also involves the design and preparation of detailed plans and specifications for infrastructure, defining property lines, and documenting landscape construction. Separate media and conventions have evolved for each of these activities, driven by professional disciplines—planners do layouts of the site, traffic engineers design and specify the roadways, sanitary engineers design the underground piping systems, and so on—each with their tried and true ways of going about their task. Much of the task of learning to do site planning has involved mastering these separate conventions. But, to paraphrase Marshall McLuhan, the media used also shape the methods of planning. The ongoing transition to digital media has opened up a world of possibilities, including a more seamless convergence of site planning techniques among the various specialists involved.

Traditional Media and Methods

Traditional working methods of site planning—which evolved slowly over the twentieth century—employ cameras, paper and writing instruments, materials for hand construction of models, and calculators for analyzing infrastructure needs. Planning a site using traditional media is a time-consuming process, involving a great deal of duplication of drawings. It requires the ability of a planner to imagine the site's character based on lines on a page and physical models.

The customary first step, after visiting and photographing a site, is constructing a *site model*. The common technique involves laboriously cutting contours out of cardboard or wood and layering them on each other. The finished product serves as a working model, offering cues to where buildings and infrastructure might be sited. Building the site model offers the added advantage of getting to know the lay of the land, and allowing one to see it from every direction and altitude.

The process of site analysis and design begins by creating a base map that records boundaries, contours, and other essential elements as we have described in chapter 8. Then semitransparent tracing paper (translucent drawing paper, bumwad) is rolled out over the map and sketching begins. A possible network of roads may be the point of departure, recognizing topography and the landscape of the site. Possible buildings

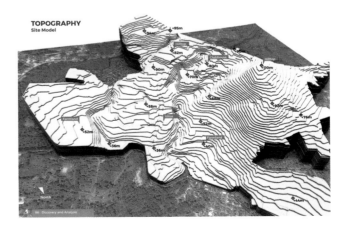

13.1 Working model of site topography, West Java New University, Subang, Indonesia.
(Courtesy of Sasaki Associates)

will be added, or the process may be reversed, with locations of structures determining where roads are necessary. Knowing when to be sketchy and when to become precise is at the heart of the design process. The site planner moves back and forth in scale, from tiny diagrams of site organization to detailed layouts of portions of the site, working at first in two dimensions. Then three-dimensional relationships of structures on the site will be tried, and the two-dimensional plans adjusted from what is learned. Site planners are attached to their instruments—some prefer wax pencils or crayons or charcoal sticks for the broad strokes at the start while reserving sharp pencils and precise pens for later; others work with colored markers, varying the broadness to reflect the level of certainty.

Other site designers prefer to work in the opposite direction, using a kit of parts to try various relationships of structures on the site model, then sketching a two-dimensional plan. Where the topography is steep and views are at a premium, this may be the most effective strategy. Three-dimensional modeling may also be essential for exploring the fit with an urban context. The advantage of combining modeling and sketching is that many ideas can be tried out quickly—and discarded equally quickly if their faults are obvious. It is also easy to move from a palm-sized diagram to a more detailed idea for portions of the site. One or more ideas will emerge as candidates for the concept plan.

Other techniques and new media need to be employed to depict or *render* a plan so that decision makers, investors, and potential purchasers can understand the site issues and the character of the developed site. Site analysis drawings sketched loosely will be tidied up or redrawn to show how the program can be accommodated. Three-dimensional sketches will be created to convey how the site will be seen on the ground or in an aerial view, sometimes by montaging buildings, roads, and new landscapes on photographs of the site. Presentation drawings such as these are often the work of skilled watercolorists or illustrators. And the site model will be modified to show the built form of the completed site.

Once the concept is decided upon, the plan will need to be hardened up, using pens or pencils on paper, but employing a variety of new tools and conventions adopted by each of the engineering and design disciplines involved. Precise horizontal and vertical

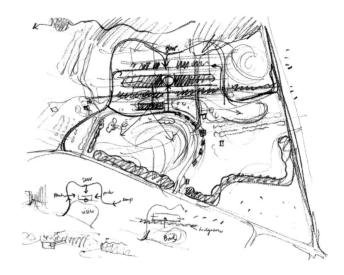

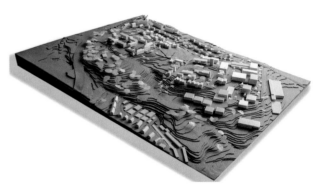

13.2 Quick diagram of site plan, ARCO Research Center (now SAS headquarters), Newtown Square, Pennsylvania. (Courtesy of Laurie Olin)

13.3 Model study of reuse of Bredtet prison site, Groruddalen, Norway. (Courtesy of Vardehaugen Architects)

alignments of roads will be drawn, composed of curves and tangents, and a rough plan of land grading will be sketched to establish the key elevations. Alignments will then need to be tested in terms of cross sections, and estimates of the quantities of cut and fill will be made to quantify possible costs for site works. Each element of infrastructure will be designed based on the key elevations determined on the grading plan, with hand calculations employed to determine the adequacy of the proposed systems. Once the roads are fixed, property lines will need to be precisely delineated,

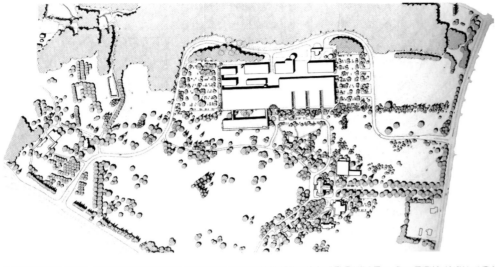

13.4 Preliminary site plan,
ARCO Research Center.
(Courtesy of Hanna/Olin)

13.5 Conceptual rendering
of site development,
Santa Monica, California.
(Courtesy of John Kaliski
Architects for the City
of Santa Monica/rendering
by William Block)

establishing points where iron stakes or monuments will be placed, the lengths of each tangent, and the angles between them. (See part 4 for each of the infrastructure elements.) This stage of design will typically result in several sets of drawings, meeting the professional standards of each discipline. Coordination is inevitably difficult: laying drawing over drawing may not entirely expose the contradictory information. The site planner is left to arbitrate differences.

This process is only rarely practiced today, since digital media have become the gold standard. Traditional methods continue to be used for small remote sites, by some small firms, and in countries lagging in computer technology. And much can be said for having done the process manually at least once, since it helps in understanding the conventions built into computer routines. Contemporary site planning can command a vast array of computer software and programs that allow for easy assembly of site data, real-time collaborative planning, reduction of the drudgery of hand calculations, more precision in the translation of design ideas into plans, and effective visualization of the site.

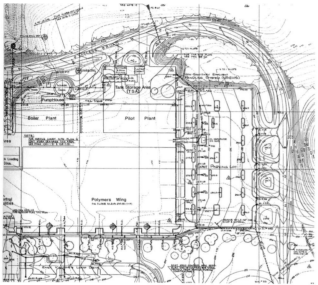

13.6 Site concept model, Prudential Center redevelopment, Boston.
(Carr Lynch Hack & Sandell/Sikes Jennings Kelly & Brewer)

13.7 Portion of final grading and site drainage plan, ARCO
Research Center.
(Courtesy of Hanna/Olin)

Contemporary Media

In an ideal world, a single software platform would accommodate all the tasks of the site planner and enable solutions for sites of all sizes and purposes. Unfortunately, and despite the claims of those purveying computer systems, this utopia has not yet arrived. Partly this is the result of different hardware capabilities—*raster-based technologies* vs. *vector-based programs*, as an example—but it also highlights the broad array of techniques required for site planning. Conceptual thinking requires fuzzy logic, and precision needed in the latter stages of a project can be counterproductive at the beginning. Many planners skilled in computer techniques set their machines aside and use a pen on paper for conceptual sketching, then scan their sketches and use them as the base for more detailed digital work. Physical models have also not lost favor, even though digital models can be constructed more rapidly and allow a flyover or walk-through to be created quickly for a site. Computer-driven milling devices can make a base model in a fraction of the time it once took, and with minimal human effort. So while practices have shifted, and much for the better, the digital revolution remains a work in progress, and many planners work in hybrid ways.

The choice of the platforms for site planning is critical. Currently three different types of platforms are essential: a system for capturing and combining site data; systems for sketch planning and visualization of plans; and a precise system for creating site engineering and construction documents. While data and drawings can be moved from one system to another, no single software suite currently supports all of these functions equally well. The various disciplines involved in site planning each have their preferences for systems, and early decisions on systems will allow data to be migrated easily and collaboration to occur effectively.

Instructional videos for the use of digital platforms are now widely available on the Internet, particularly on YouTube, and we will not duplicate instructions here. Digital platforms change regularly, and the best suggestion for keeping abreast of current techniques is to use online resources.

Data Capture

Much of the site data available resides with agencies or organizations that use *geographic information systems* (GIS), so the site planner will need to have at his disposal the software to capture this data. The information includes: geospatial imagery and data from national or local governments or private sources; mapping of underground utilities from public agencies or private corporations providing sewer, water, electricity, telecommunications, and other services; population data from census and other sources; and other specialized data such as soil contamination, flood zones, and traffic flows from a variety of public agencies. The most widely used GIS systems are supplied by esri®, particularly ArcGIS, although other competitors offer compatible products. Versions of ArcGIS can be obtained for desktop, online, and server applications.

GIS systems capture data in layers, which can be switched on or off and combined to view relationships. A number of built-in and freestanding applications also support analytics such as analyzing solar exposure, predicting noise levels from adjacent roadways, and plotting view planes from points on the site. Thus, the GIS

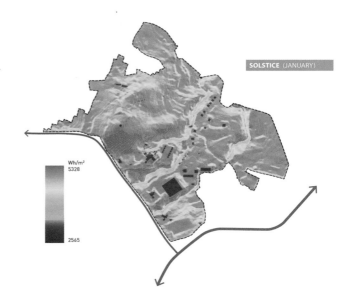

13.8 Solar exposure map for West Java New University, Subang, Indonesia, created using ArcMap.
(Courtesy of Sasaki Associates)

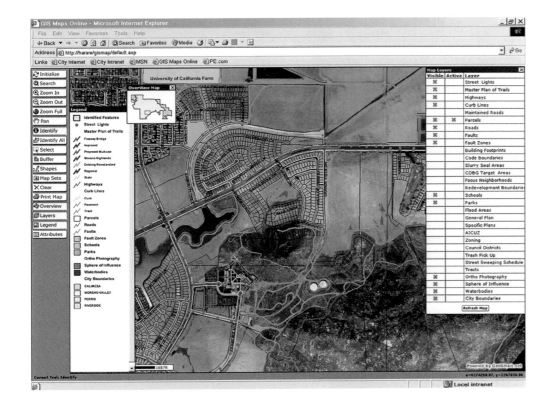

13.9 Example of ArcGIS base map, Moreno Valley, California, with data that can be toggled on or off. (Courtesy of esri)

system is customarily used as the medium for the site analysis phases of a project.

Sketch Planning and Visualization

The media for visualizing, creating plans, and communicating them to others requires platforms that allow the planner to quickly sketch possible ideas for site development in two and three dimensions. As the designs become more specific, such platforms allow for translation of sketch plans into quick renderings of the site. These platforms sit between GIS systems that can handle large data sets and precise computer-aided design (CAD) programs, which are too specific and prove cumbersome for early-stage planning. A single program will probably not suffice: with today's state of the art, there is advantage in being eclectic.

The current software of choice for sketch planning is SketchUp, which provides for easy manipulation of roads, buildings, and other elements of a site, and

13.10 SketchUp study model on Google Earth base map. (Courtesy of Henriquez Partners/Wendy Wen.)

13.11 Modelur, a SketchUp extension for parametric urban design that provides instantaneous calculations of the amount of development on the site. (Courtesy of Modelur)

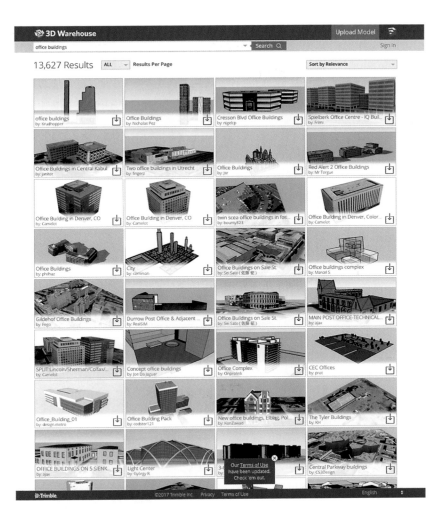

13.12 3D Warehouse collection of downloadable office buildings which can be inserted into SketchUp study model. (Courtesy of 3D Warehouse/Trimble)

offers cartoon views in 3D. Many site planners begin by importing a Google Earth aerial photograph of their site, which has topography embedded for some parts of the world. One should check the resolution of Google Earth photographs, however, which can vary from 15 cm (6 in) to a meter (3 ft) or more. Site plans can then be sketched over the image; when a satisfactory plan emerges, three-dimensional elements can then be added to the plan. A number of plug-ins have been created to augment the capabilities of SketchUp, including Modelur, which assists in calculating the amount of development being sketched on a site.

SketchUp comes with an open source catalog of building and landscape elements, 3D Warehouse, a collection of millions of models contributed by users. Custom models of buildings, walls, and other elements

13.13 3D site model for West Java New University, Subang, Indonesia, created with SketchUp. (Courtesy of Sasaki Associates)

can be created quickly, through extrusions of plan forms or by aggregating volumes. A quick but compelling 3D sketch of site development can be made using the kit of parts—roads, buildings, and landscape elements—moving them over the surface of the site to form the desired pattern of site development. And the plan can then be viewed from any location desired. If more detail is desired, this can be easily added to a quick model.

Planning a site using a virtual model has its advantages, especially the ease in making changes and ability to layer in detail as ideas are firmed up. Some site planners, however, prefer to work in parallel with both virtual and physical models. The latter are sometimes easier to comprehend by those not skilled in 3D design, and can reveal features in a complicated terrain that are easily missed in a virtual model.

Topographic data can be used to create a physical site model using one of two computer-driven methods. The first employs a laser cutter and duplicates the traditional hand construction process of creating layers for each contour level, starting from the bottom contour elevation and attaching each successive layer. The second technique employs a computer numerical control (CNC) milling machine that duplicates the digital model in solid materials. A variety of light foam materials that are easily milled are preferred, although some species of wood are also acceptable. The process involves cutting the material down, contour by contour, beginning at the top, until it resembles the terrain of the site. The model may be left as stepped contours, which help identify elevations if it is used as a study model, or may be sanded to resemble the actual topography on the ground. In creating a model, the topographic data generally needs to be cleaned up by removing extraneous lines that would confound the computer and clarifying steep areas where the topographic lines may merge. Digital models are fed into the system in .dwg form or other acceptable formats, and CNC machines typically have proprietary software that drives their 3D cutting heads. While CNC machines have become relatively inexpensive, there are also a variety of services that promise rapid delivery of models from files transmitted over the Internet.

Study models of a site can be made on the topographic base, with wooden blocks, foam core, cardboard, and paper (cut to the shape of roadways), all easily modified as the ideas evolve. When a final plan for a site has

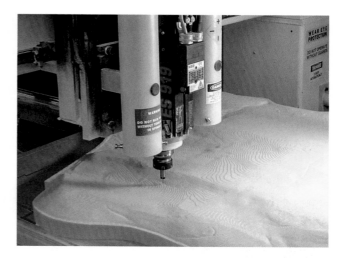

13.14 Base model being created by CNC router. (Courtesy of Landform.com)

13.15 Illustration of site plan montaged into photo of site using Illustrator, University Park, Gwinnett County, Georgia. (Courtesy of Stantec)

13.16 Photoshop illustrations with proposals inserted into existing image, Delhi Pike, Cincinnati, Ohio, over three phases of change. (Courtesy of Stantec)

been settled upon, a more finished model will need to be constructed, with the topography modified to reflect the final grading plan and more finished elements added to represent the types of buildings and landscape being proffered. Quick plans and 3D sketches will also need to be refined into presentation materials. These can be done in SketchUp or by employing Adobe Illustrator and Photoshop. One useful technique is montaging a SketchUp perspective of the new development into a photograph taken of the site, using Photoshop. This avoids having to model and render the site's surroundings, and gives a realistic sense of how the new development will relate to what is currently on the ground.

Precise Plans

A computer-aided design platform will be required for preparing the precise plans that will be needed to construct infrastructure, stake and register properties on the land, and install landscape improvements. Though it will become the principal medium only as layouts are decided upon, it needs to be selected earlier so that materials can be ported into the system as they become available along the way.

There are two dominant CAD systems, each widely used in the US and throughout the world. AutoDesk's AutoCad has the largest installed base, and a variety of capabilities essential for site planning and engineering are included in its application Civil3D. Many clients also wish to have construction documents provided using Revit, AutoCad's 3D building information and modeling (BIM) system, which is becoming widely used in building design and construction. An equally robust alternative platform is Bentley Systems' Microstation suite of products, which support 2D and 3D BIM modeling and drawing production. Microstation has a broad array of application programs that cover all aspects of site surveying and infrastructure design. There are, of course, many additional platforms capable of handling some or all of the tasks of site planning, including VersaCAD, Vectorworks, Archicad, and ZWCAD, among others, and one of these may be the local standard. The difference between platforms is often subtle, and IT professionals, working in consultation with public agencies, should make the choice. Previous use may tilt the decision one way or another: local transportation and infrastructure agencies may have standardized

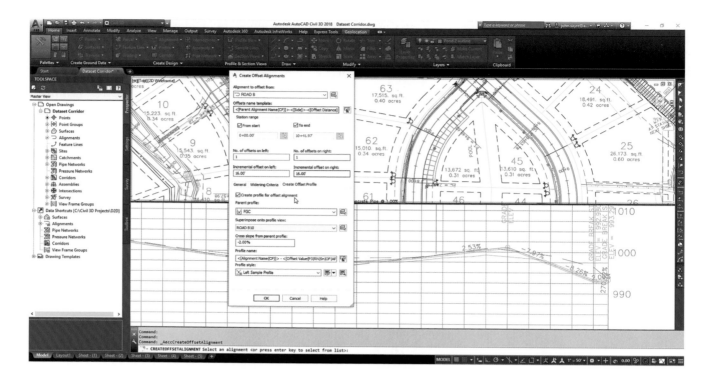

13.17 CAD desktop working environment.
(Courtesy of AutoCad 3D Civil)

their internal documentation of systems with one of the systems; or the planners may have a substantial history with and investment in one platform, with a large library of compiled models and details.

The use of CAD systems has greatly routinized the process of creating the drawings necessary to guide site development, and saves a great deal of time, particularly when changes need to be made. For site planners, this can also be a source of frustration: nothing is finally settled until construction begins, and sometimes even after. With documents being shared among the many individuals and firms working on the project, real-time collaboration is possible. CAD systems also come with application modules that cover most of the tasks required for detailed site planning, including constructing base maps, laying out parcels, the design of roadways, transit lines, piped systems, and runoff channels, grading design, survey layouts, and utilities design. There are also freestanding software

applications that handle specific aspects of site planning. For storm runoff, HydroCAD and StormCAD are widely used by site planners, and WRKS is an efficient program for sizing piping. Landscape designers often use landF/X because of the ease it offers in locating and specifying landscape surfaces and materials, and its easy interface with CAD systems.

While the best CAD systems offer the capability of constructing 3D renderings of a site development, computer systems designed specifically for visualization provide greater power and ease of application. These include Maya, which is particularly effective for rendering flowing surfaces and provides for the construction of flyovers and drive-throughs with relative ease, and rhino3D, which is effective in capturing 3D terrain and reflecting it in computer renderings. A common process is to use AutoCAD or Microstation to construct the basic model, then export it to one of these programs or 3DStudio for rendering.

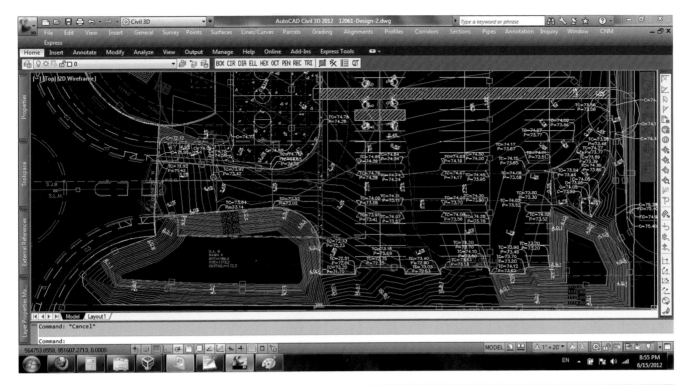

13.18 Example of CAD application for grading.
(Courtesy of Thomas Gail Haws)

13.19 Rendered site "image using 3D Studio,
Petronelli Way, Brockton, Massachusetts, with new development
montaged into existing photo and rendered using filters.
(Courtesy of Stantec/MassDev/TDI)

Mix and Match

The site planner need not cast his lot exclusively with hand methods or digital media. As we have noted, many planners who are accomplished in working in the virtual world find it more effective to shift to hand diagrams, or even quick sketches of the site, because of the speed or ease of these methods. Even after plans have been hardened, there may be a place for hand drawings. Many planners and clients resist photorealistic renderings because they leave little to the imagination of the viewer. They can be coldly precise, with little affect. So, while CAD systems may be used to construct the view, skilled delineators or watercolorists may be enlisted to render the image in fuzzier but more approachable terms.

Media evolve constantly, and site planners need to be constantly experimenting with new techniques to advance the state of their art.

14 | Design Methods

Design and programming go hand in hand in the site planning process. A program, however rough, provides the springboard for design, by which we mean the search for appropriate forms for a site. In turn, design explorations may reshape the program, as new possibilities are revealed and some of the program needs prove impractical. Both are essential aspects of the larger process of planning and decision making that result in a project on a site.

A common misconception is that design involves a flash of creative genius and is not something easily dissected. A second error is the belief that the skill of designing is an innate ability which simply can't be learned. Designers do have special skills, including the ability to quickly sketch ideas, creating and discarding possibilities at a rapid pace. But on close inspection, the strategies that designers use and the skills they need are clearly capable of description and can be learned. Site design is not a singular process, but one that involves working back and forth with many types of knowledge.

People who have an intimate knowledge of form possibilities design fine places. They have the capacity to constantly reframe the problem in search of new arrangements, and to move quickly between developing conceptual ideas and trying them out in concrete form. They may work using sketches, study models, or computer representations, alone or in combination. If developing a hillside for housing proves impractical when studied in detail, the designer diagrams another possibility with a terraced hillside garden on the steep slopes, and higher-density housing on the hilltop above it. Quick plan sketches are made and a rough massing model tried. Another possibility occurs to the designer: a stack of housing located on the lower areas of the slope, entered from bridges to the upper levels. Each

new idea will need to be tested with real dimensions to know whether it is feasible. After many such explorations, a preferred direction tends to emerge. Revelations appear by the inch and the foot, rarely by the mile. Particular methods and strategies, learned by experience, help the designer make this journey of discovery.

Designers develop a preference for a particular way of structuring their process of design and have strong attitudes about what is appropriate. Some believe that there are many possible approaches to any problem, and that the best choices are made when a broad range of alternatives has been developed. Others see design as a process of constant refinement where small but important changes are made on each successive scheme, even if the general approach does not change. They may begin with a "dumb possibility" or "straw man," then in successive schemes explore how it might be improved, always comparing it to the original scheme to sense progress. Still others may create an abstract model or find a metaphor for the problem, then apply it to the site. "This site is about flows," the designer may observe, and sketches make these tangible by showing strands of infrastructure and buildings that follow the natural patterns of the site.

Developing a personal style of designing, or a shared style among members of a design team, reduces the anxiety of dealing with an unfamiliar problem and offers an immediate way to proceed. Design strategies may be organized into several categories:

Adapting Prototypes

The most common design method involves adapting a known solution to the particularities of the site. This approach offers efficiency, since it usually begins with known methods of building, established cost structures, and proven markets for a project. If the sites are sufficiently similar and past examples are in digital form, portions of many of the drawings and details may be reusable. Being able to point to similar examples (taking care to ensure they have been successful) can help smooth the process of receiving public approval. Private developers understandably prefer the certainty this approach offers, even if the designer may be bored with repeating familiar forms, and concerned about producing "generic environments."

Pattern books and published *case studies* provide prototypes that can be a point of departure (Souza 2008).

14.1 Quick SketchUp study of possible site plan for high-tech Nottingham Medipark, UK, constructed using space modules. (Courtesy of Moko3D Production Studio)

Fabric Types for Al Dhahiyah Al Gharbiyah

14.2 Prototype patterns of development at increasing densities, Al Dahiyah Al Gharbiyah structure plan, Makkah, Saudi Arabia. (Courtesy of DPZ Partners)

F-1 Low Intensity Fabric Type: *This is the lowest intensity fabric typology. It consists of low density, single-family lots, defined by sideyard houses, duplexes and villas exclusively at a gross density of 11 du/Ha.. It has the smallest variety of building types and does not include any commercial or mixed-uses.*

F-2 Medium Intensity Fabric Type: *This is a low to medium-density residential fabric typology, consisting exclusively of low density, single-family lots, defined by villas, sideyard houses, duplexes, townhouses and a small percentage of small multi-family dwellings, at a gross density of 16 du/Ha. It includes no multi-family, commercial or mixed-uses.*

F-3 High Intensity Fabric Type: *This is a high-density residential fabric typology, consisting predominantly of multi-family and mixed-use buildings, with few sideyard houses, duplexes and townhouses, at a gross density of 61 du/Ha. It includes some retail uses at grade, but no fully commercial or office buildings.*

C-1 Low Intensity Center Type: *This is a medium-density mixed-use fabric typology, consisting of the greatest mix of building types as it include villas, sideyard houses, duplexes, townhouses, multi-family and mixed-use buildings, at a gross density of 37 du/Ha. While less dense than F-3, it includes more commercial uses (10,000 sm).*

C-2 Medium Intensity Center Type: *This is a high-density mixed-use fabric typology, consisting of a large mix of attached building types, ranging from townhouses, multi-family and mixed-use buildings, at a gross density of 74 du/Ha. This Fabric type excludes any single-family detached villas. It also includes a significant amount of commercial uses (20,000 sm).*

C-3 High Intensity Center Type: *This is the highest density mixed-use fabric typology, consisting exclusively of multi-family and mixed-use building types, at a gross density of 82 du/Ha. This Fabric type excludes any single-family detached villas, sideyard houses and duplexes. This Fabric type includes a significant amount of commercial uses and is the only type to also include office uses. (30,000 sm and 60,000 sm respectively).*

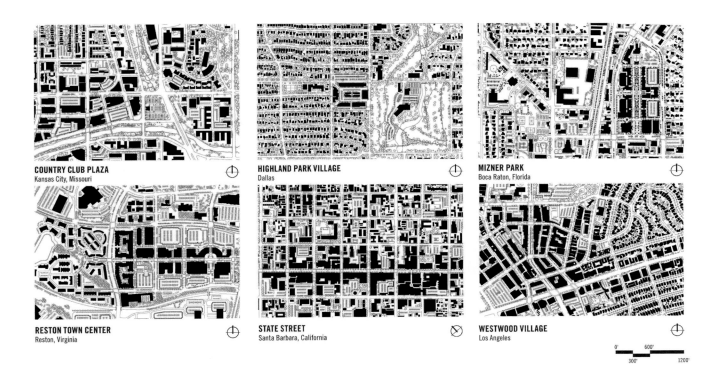

COUNTRY CLUB PLAZA
Kansas City, Missouri

HIGHLAND PARK VILLAGE
Dallas

MIZNER PARK
Boca Raton, Florida

RESTON TOWN CENTER
Reston, Virginia

STATE STREET
Santa Barbara, California

WESTWOOD VILLAGE
Los Angeles

0'   600'
   300'   1200'

14.3 Figure-ground studies of iconic US commercial centers. (From *Grid/Street/Place*, © 2009 by and reproduced courtesy of the American Planning Association and RTKL Associates, Inc.)

The Urban Land Institute's development case studies, now accessible on the Internet, provide dozens of examples of virtually every building type, as do their many publications on residential and commercial development (Urban Land Institute 2004). There is a wealth of resources on the Internet providing examples of sustainable developments (Commission for Architecture and the Built Environment, n.d.), public space design (Project for Public Spaces 2009, n.d.), traditional housing development (Urban Design Associates 2004, 2005), university campuses (Ayers Saint Gross Architects 2007), and other uses. Dozens of awards programs offer leads to exemplary developments, and often provide links to the project websites.

A familiarity with past forms is essential knowledge for designers, and often yields a useful springboard for a project. The *new urbanism* movement has refocused attention on historic American town plans and early twentieth-century subdivisions, and has attempted to codify the essential characteristics of these places (Duany, Plater-Zyberk, and Alminana 2003; Thadani 2010). Oglethorpe's original town plan for Savannah offers an enduring urban pattern, as does Thomas Holme's plan for Philadelphia as it evolved with tree streets and alley streets. The European tradition of *morphological analysis* has yielded many examples of fine urban textures that can be consulted as possible approaches to urban form (Moughtin et al. 2003). The lessons are often more conceptual than literal, since it is seldom possible to reproduce medieval or nineteenth-century streets and houses in an era of automobiles on streets and houses without servants. Every designer needs to compile their favorite examples of fine places, with scale plans and illustrations, ready for mining when the appropriate project comes along.

Working from Patterns

Rather than beginning with fully formed prototypes, it is possible to assemble designs from the elements of an environment that seem to work well—probing with the vocabulary of place rather than its syntax. Most designers remember dozens of patterns that have delighted them, often anecdotes: the long bench against the sunny wall in North Square, Boston, occupied by all ages on a fine day in spring or fall; the arcade fronting shop houses in Guangzhou, offering shelter on a blustery day while allowing merchants to move their wares into the street on a good day; the axial view in Ludlow, England, terminated by the town hall that is asymmetrical, inviting the pedestrians around the corner to the market; the orthogonal pattern of streets in the Glebe in Ottawa, Canada, which have similar houses along each street but allow diversity across the grain; and so on (see chapter 40). These may trigger ideas about how to organize a site. Clients and users also think in these terms, and can speculate about what makes places special as part of a design dialogue. The design pattern strategy begins with collecting as many images, sketches, and diagrams as possible that capture the desired qualities of place. Fitting them together, however, requires considerable creativity and ultimately a willingness to give up many possibilities that conflict or simply cannot be accommodated.

Several attempts have been made to create *pattern languages*, codifying valuable patterns that can be assembled to aid design. The most ambitious is by Christopher Alexander and his colleagues and originated in the Center for Environmental Structure at the University of California, Berkeley and is now maintained by the nonprofit group Pattern Language (Alexander et al. 1977). Working from many cases and the available literature on the subject, they have extracted environmental configurations that seem well matched to particular human needs. Each pattern is explicitly normative, rooted in values for the environment that the authors make clear. Several of the patterns deal with the program for the site, including "Pattern 22—Nine Percent Parking: Do not allow more than 9 per cent of the land in any given area to be used for parking." Other patterns prescribe specific arrangements for streets: "Pattern 3—Looped Local Roads: Nobody wants fast through traffic going by their homes."

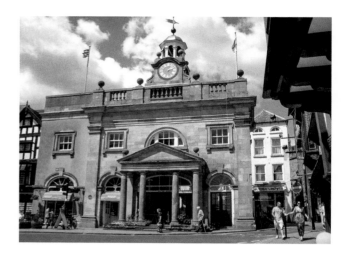

14.4 The asymmetrical town hall, Ludlow, England, guides the eye around it to the market and commercial spaces behind. (Tony Grist/Creative Commons)

Several of the patterns are delightfully quirky and remain to be tested in practice, including the prescription for long parallel streets uninterrupted by cross roads, apparently based on the unique pattern of Bern, Switzerland. Nonetheless, *A Pattern Language* is a useful sourcebook for beginning to assemble a design.

Another fruitful source of patterns is the work of the Center for Applied Transect Studies, headed by Andres Duany and Elizabeth Plater-Zyberk (Center for Applied Transect Studies, n.d.). Their fundamental organizing idea is the rural-to-urban *transect*. Patterns, they argue, must be appropriate to the urban situation, which may be organized into six degrees of urbanization: the natural zone "T-1," the rural zone "T-2," the suburban zone "T-3," the general urban zone "T-4," the urban center "T-5," and the urban core "T-6." As an example, the appropriate transition from street to building will vary from generous winding paths (T-1) to urban arcades (T-5 and T-6). The *SmartCode* captures the full range of patterns essential to the design of sites in all six contexts. It also offers a catalog of public spaces ranging from parks to playgrounds, noting their appropriate sizes. Building on the work of the wider

49 LOOPED LOCAL ROADS**

260

. . . assume that neighborhoods, house clusters, work communi-ties, and major roads are more or less defined—LOCAL TRANSPORT AREAS (11), IDENTIFIABLE NEIGHBORHOOD (14), PARALLEL ROADS (23), HOUSE CLUSTER (37), WORK COMMUNITY (41). Now, for the layout of the local roads.

✧ ✧ ✧

Nobody wants fast through traffic going by their homes.

Through traffic is fast, noisy, and dangerous. At the same time cars are important, and cannot be excluded altogether from the areas where people live. Local roads must provide access to houses but prevent traffic from coming through.

This problem can only be solved if all roads which have houses on them are laid out to be "loops." We define a looped road as any road in a road network so placed that no path along other roads in the road network can be shortened by travel along the "loop."

The loops themselves must be designed to discourage high volumes or high speeds: this depends on the total number of houses served by the loop, the road surface, the road width, and the number of curves and corners. Our observations suggest that a loop can be made safe so long as it serves less than 50 cars. At one and one-half cars per house, such a loop serves 30 houses; at one car per house, 50 houses; at one-half car per house, 100 houses.

Here is an example of an entire system of looped local roads designed for a community of 1500 houses in Peru.

Looped local roads in Lima.

261

14.5 Pattern 49: Looped local roads.
(Courtesy of © Christopher Alexander)

new urbanist community, the center has compiled desirable patterns and an image library that is publicly accessible for streets, low-impact urbanism, and other subjects.

Work on the transect continues a long tradition of compiling catalogs of urban elements that dates from Camillo Sitte's nineteenth-century compendium of European squares, streets, and gardens (Sitte 1945), and Werner Hegemann and Elbert Peets's *American Vitruvius,* an inventory of 1,200 examples of important civic spaces (Hegemann and Peets 1996), which has recently been imitated by a contemporary update, *New Civic Art* (Duany, Plater-Zyberk, and Alminana 2003). Pattern

books for the layout of housing areas have also been published for many decades. Early examples include Thomas Adams's surveys of housing design in the 1920s (Adams 1934), and more recent examples include Urban Design Associates' various pattern books and manual for their use (Urban Design Associates 2004, 2005).

Design that begins with patterns drawn from the past is inherently conservative, and runs the risk of carrying forward forms and practices that have lost their social meaning. It is the preferred method of designers who believe in the virtues of familiarity, and that truly great environments are the product of accumulated understanding.

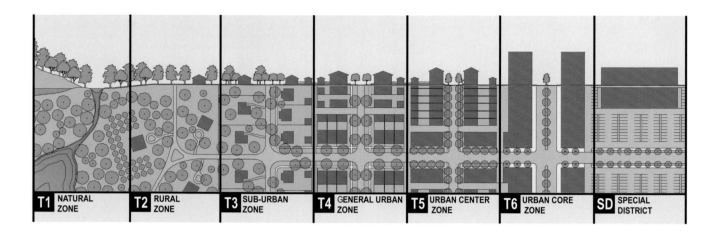

| T1 NATURAL ZONE | T2 RURAL ZONE | T3 SUB-URBAN ZONE | T4 GENERAL URBAN ZONE | T5 URBAN CENTER ZONE | T6 URBAN CORE ZONE | SD SPECIAL DISTRICT |

14.6 The transect, from rural to urban zones. (Center for Applied Transect Studies)

14.7 Desirable frontages vary depending on the urban zone, as prescribed by SmartCode. (Center for Applied Transect Studies)

SMARTCODE

Municipality

TABLE 7. PRIVATE FRONTAGES

TABLE 7: Private Frontages. The Private Frontage is the areas between the building Facades and the Lot lines.

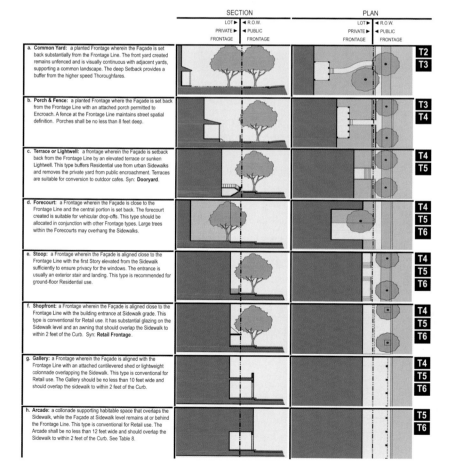

	SECTION	PLAN	
a. Common Yard: a planted Frontage wherein the Façade is set back substantially from the Frontage Line. The front yard created remains unfenced and is visually continuous with adjacent yards, supporting a common landscape. The deep Setback provides a buffer from the higher speed Thoroughfares.			T2 T3
b. Porch & Fence: a planted Frontage where the Façade is set back from the Frontage Line with an attached porch permitted to Encroach. A fence at the Frontage Line maintains street spatial definition. Porches shall be no less than 8 feet deep.			T3 T4
c. Terrace or Lightwell: a frontage wherein the Façade is setback back from the Frontage Line by an elevated terrace or sunken Lightwell. This type buffers Residential from urban Sidewalks and removes the private yard from public encroachment. Terraces are suitable for conversion to outdoor cafes. Syn: **Dooryard.**			T4 T5
d. Forecourt: a Frontage wherein the Façade is close to the Frontage Line and the central portion is set back. The forecourt created is suitable for vehicular drop-offs. This type should be allocated in conjunction with other Frontage types. Large trees within the Forecourts may overhang the Sidewalks.			T4 T5 T6
e. Stoop: a Frontage wherein the Façade is aligned close to the Frontage Line with the first Story elevated from the Sidewalk sufficiently to ensure privacy for the windows. The entrance is usually an exterior stair and landing. This type is recommended for ground-floor Residential use.			T4 T5 T6
f. Shopfront: a Frontage wherein the Façade is aligned close to the Frontage Line with the building entrance at Sidewalk grade. This type is conventional for Retail use. It has substantial glazing on the Sidewalk level and an awning that should overlap the Sidewalk to within 2 feet of the Curb. Syn: **Retail Frontage.**			T4 T5 T6
g. Gallery: a Frontage wherein the Façade is aligned with the Frontage Line with an attached cantilevered shed or lightweight colonnade overlapping the Sidewalk. This type is conventional for Retail use. The Gallery should be no less than 10 feet wide and should overlap the sidewalk to within 2 feet of the Curb.			T4 T5 T6
h. Arcade: a collonade supporting habitable space that overlaps the Sidewalk, while the Façade at Sidewalk level remains at or behind the Frontage Line. This type is conventional for Retail use. The Arcade shall be no less than 12 feet wide and should overlap the Sidewalk to within 2 feet of the Curb. See Table 8.			T5 T6

Formal Explorations

The ultimate product of design is the form of roads, paths, and buildings on the ground, and the shape and character of spaces between them. There is value in beginning design with more abstract explorations of form, focusing on the geometries and dimensional relationships that create the matrix for inhabiting the site. Adopting this approach, the designer selects from the many languages of form and begins sketching how things might be organized, not worrying greatly at the start about the details of uses and precise layouts of elements of the site. Usually the exploration focuses on site circulation systems and the experienced form of the site; buildings and spaces follow later.

There is a long tradition of exploring organic analogies to give structure to a site, seeking an affinity with the underlying topography and natural areas. The design study may begin with the recognition that nature evolves through a series of "corridors" (rivers, paths, fronts) and "patches" (forests, fields, marshes, heaths), the ecological model, and that settlement of the land might also follow this form. Hence, the logical corridors, both natural and man-made, are identified and traced, circumscribing the patches to be developed. Circulation or infrastructure systems might also emulate nature by laying out smoothly curving roadways and pedestrian ways that mount the topography gradually, organized in branch-and-spoke patterns like streams or trees. Frederick Law Olmsted's influence immediately comes to mind, in his magnificent designs for the Riverside community near Chicago and the Roland Park neighborhood in Baltimore. But this approach is not confined to suburban development, as the dense urban areas in the historic center of Bern, Switzerland and the urban form of Venice, Italy attest.

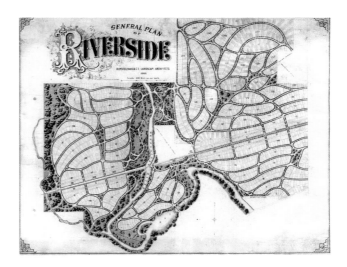

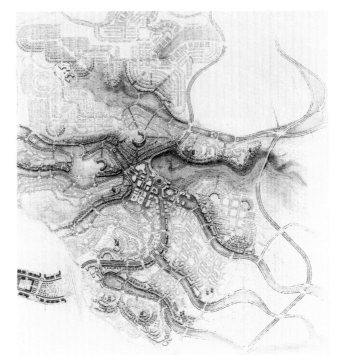

14.8 Plan of Riverside, Illinois.
(Olmsted, Vaux & Co., 1869)

14.9 Conceptual sketch of new town following the valleys, Modi'in, Israel.
(Courtesy of Moshe Safdie)

14.10 Concept plan, Modi'in, Israel.
(Courtesy of Moshe Safdie)

The design of the new town of Modi'in, Israel, planned by Moshe Safdie, is closely aligned with the natural form of hills and valleys. There is a renewed interest in organic forms, spurred in part by the ease of *parametric modeling* that aids in the generation and construction of complex geometries and smooth flowing forms.

There are, of course, many other geometries that can be used as a point of departure. One approach is to emulate the forms of the surrounding urban pattern. *Space syntax* offers an approach to analyzing the spatial structure of areas, including the geometries of streets and clustering of important places. Such an analysis can be useful in arriving at a geometric layout for a site (Hillier 1996). Gridiron patterns—strictly orthogonal, or distorted to fit the topography (as in Milton Keynes, England) have many advantages, including flexibility (by omitting streets for larger blocks, or altering the spacing of them) and multiple choices in travel

patterns. Circular forms create a powerful centrality, particularly as seen from the air, but have the disadvantage of being disorienting on the ground. Linear patterns, with uses strung out along a main access way (road, rail, transit, pedestrian way), can have powerful advantages where sites are located between important poles. The designer may canvass these and other possibilities, seeking to reveal which geometry provides the best fit for a site.

Formal explorations need not focus only on the plan form of roadways and access routes. They can work with the built form of the place, responding to orientation, topography, and internal patterns simultaneously. In China, the tradition of ensuring that every unit of housing has sunlight for at least two hours a day suggests alignments of buildings on east-west axes, progressing from the tallest to the lowest structures from north to south edges of the site. Ralph Erskine's site

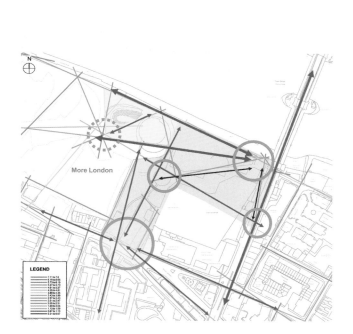

14.11 Space syntax analysis of Potters Field, London, identifying locations for clustering activities and key linkages. (Courtesy of Anna Rose/Space Syntax)

14.12 Warped 1 km grid, Milton Keynes new town plan, 1970. (Llewelyn-Davies, Weeks, Forestier-Walker and Bor/Milton Keynes Development Corporation)

14.13 Byker housing estate with housing wall to shield noise and capture sunlight, Newcastle, UK.
(Owen Humphries/Press Association)

14.14 MOMA linked hybrid housing complex, Beijing.
(Courtesy of Steven Holl Architects/© Shu He)

plans for the center and residential areas of Svappavaara, Sweden and the Byker redevelopment in Newcastle-upon-Tyne, England adopt the idea of a massive wall sheltering the development (from cold winter winds and from noise, respectively) while capturing the sun, with smaller housing in its wake (Collymore 1994). Another approach views the built form as a compositional problem, locating structures so that they are well spaced from others, with sun-filled open areas between, and create a sense of separation of the site from surrounding areas. Two Beijing housing complexes—the Grand MOMA, designed by Steven Holl, and the Jian Wah

SOHO development by Riken Yamamoto—are notable examples. In both, site planning and architectural composition are one and the same.

Symbolic Form

Many cultures have long traditions that shape the design of places, often codified as a set and influenced by metaphysical interpretations. Perhaps the oldest system that still bears influence is the Indian system of *Vastu Shastra* that originated around the tenth century BC (Chakrabarti 1998). Vastu Shastra, literally the "text of embodied energy," deals with the choice of a site, its shape, siting issues, relationships between activities and uses, orientation, and other matters. It applies to city form, sites, buildings, and even the movable furniture within them. Because of the complexity of the system and the many principles that must be observed, many designers use Vastu consultants to advise them on the propriety of locations, orientation, and plans.

In the Vastu Shastra system, the objective is to optimize the flow of life energies through the five elements: earth (Bhumi), water (Jalu), air (Vayu), fire (Agni), and space (Akasha). The *mandala* becomes the fundamental way of organizing and diagramming a plan, oriented in the cardinal directions and connecting the topography of the site to the cosmos through the route of the sun and stars. Mandalas come in various increments—from a single divided site (Sakala) to 100 squares (10 × 10, the Aasana), although the nine-square plan (3 × 3, the Pitha) and the 81-square plan (9 × 9, the Paramasaayika) are most common in city plans. Jaipur was planned with the mandala as its guide, but today the influences are subtler, affecting the placement of centers (along the central register), orientation of buildings (toward the southwest if possible), and other detailed choices.

Chinese geomancy, *Feng Shui*, has its origins in Indian cosmology, and has developed over three thousand years to reflect the climates, geographies, and relationships of Chinese society. Originally called Kan Yu ("the Tao of heaven and earth"), Feng Shui (literally "wind-water" after the famous third-century passage, "*qi* rides the wind and scatters, but is retained when encountering water") seeks to harmonize the flow of life energy through the arrangements of sites, buildings,

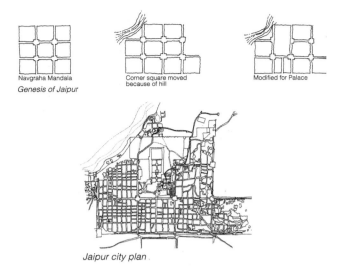

Navgraha Mandala
Genesis of Jaipur

Corner square moved
because of hill

Modified for Palace

Jaipur city plan

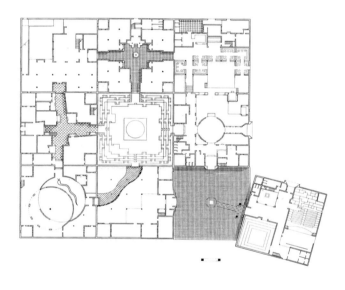

14.15 Plan of Jaipur, India, derived from the 3 × 3 Navagraha mandala, modified to reflect topography and social hierarchy.
(Courtesy of Charles Correa Foundation)

14.16 Plan of Jawahar Kala Kendra, a multi-arts center built in honor of Nehru, based on the Navagraha mandala and modeled on the original plan of Jaipur.
(Courtesy of Charles Correa Foundation)

and elements in relationship to natural phenomena (Hwangbo 2002). As the practice has evolved and been elaborated over the centuries, the prescriptions require a detailed understanding of the belief system, usually acquired by hiring a Feng Shui expert, whose numbers have mushroomed in recent years. There are a variety of schools of thought (the "eight mansion" approach, the "Black Hat Sect," the "compass school," among others) and many charlatans. Most Chinese do not take the practice seriously, although it has greater currency in Hong Kong, Taiwan, and Vancouver. But the fact that some do, and that rumors of bad *qi* can have negative impacts on a project, mean that receiving the blessing of an expert can be valuable. The location of the main gates to Hong Kong's Disneyland was shifted by 12° to satisfy Feng Shui considerations, and the walkway from the train station to the entrance was bent to ensure that positive energy did not slip by the park and out into the ocean (Holsum 2005). Meeting these needs was considered important for attracting local residents.

Many of the tenets of Feng Shui make intuitive sense in a north temperate climate, such as the prescription that buildings be oriented on a north-south axis, with south-facing courtyards and entrances on the southeast corner, an arrangement designed to capture the sun and protect against northwest winter winds. The notions of axiality and progression have deep cultural connotations. However, the origins of many Feng Shui principles must simply be accepted. Where sites or buildings have unfavorable characteristics, there are often remedies to be had. One Hong Kong high-rise apartment solved the problem of not capturing unfavorable energies, flowing down from a nearby mountain, by designing the structure to allow them to escape through a multistory gap in the building.

In Western cultures, there are few similar codified systems of thought that can provide the framework for design of a site. The *Laws of the Indies* (Leyes de Indias), developed by King Philip II in 1573, came close, providing 148 ordinances to guide the planning of Spanish settlements in the Americas and the Philippines. Hundreds of settlements from California to Argentina were founded based on their principles. The ordinances prescribed the layout of the town, the location and proportions of the main public square, the uses that could be located on it and the number of

Excerpt from the
Laws of the Indies

112. The main plaza is to be the starting point for the town; if the town is situated on the sea coast, it should be placed at the landing place of the port, but inland it should be at the center of the town. The plaza should be square or rectangular, in which case it should have at least one and a half its width for length inasmuch as this shape is best for fiestas in which horses are used and for any other fiestas that should be held.

113. The size of the plaza shall be proportioned to the number of inhabitants, taking into consideration the fact that in Indian towns, inasmuch as they are new, the intention is that they will increase, and thus the plaza should be decided upon taking into consideration the growth the town may experience. [The Plaza] shall be not less than two hundred feet wide and three hundred feet long, nor larger than eight hundred feet long and five hundred and thirty feet wide. A good proportion is six hundred feet long and four hundred wide.

114. From the plaza shall begin four principal streets: One [shall be] from the middle of each side, and two streets from each corner of the plaza; the four corners of the plaza shall face the four principal winds, because in this manner, the streets running from the plaza will not be exposed to the four principal winds, which would cause much inconvenience.

115. Around the plaza as well as along the four principal streets which begin there, there shall be portals, for these are of considerable convenience to the merchants who generally gather there; the eight streets running from the plaza at the four corners shall open on the plaza without encountering these porticoes, which shall be kept back in order that there may be sidewalks even with the streets and plaza.

116. In cold places, the streets shall be wide and in hot places narrow; but for purposes of defense in areas where there are horses, it would be better if they are wide. ...

118. Here and there in the town, smaller plazas of good proportion shall be laid out, where the temples associated with the principal church, the parish churches, and the monasteries can be built, [in] such [manner] that everything may be distributed in a good proportion for the instruction of religion.

119. For the temple of the principal church, parish, or monastery, there shall be assigned specific lots; the first after the streets and plazas have been laid out, and these shall be a complete block so as to avoid having other buildings nearby, unless it were for practical or ornamental reasons. ...

121. Next, a site and lot shall be assigned for the royal council and cabildo house and for the custom house and arsenal, near the temple, located in such a manner that in times of need the one may aid the other; the hospital for the poor and those sick of noncontagious diseases shall be built near the temple and its cloister; and the hospital for the sick with contagious diseases shall be built in such a way that no harmful wind blowing through it may cause harm to the rest of the town. If the latter be built in an elevated place, so much the better.

Excerpt from *Ordinances from the Laws of the Indies Addressing the Planning of Settlements* (compiled in 1680). English translation by Axel Mundigo and Dora Crouch from "The City Planning Ordinances of the Laws of the Indies Revisited, I," *Town Planning Review* 48 (July 1977), 247–268.

14.17 Feng Shui considerations helped decide the location of major activities and the appropriate termination of the central axis of the Olympic site, Beijing. (Courtesy of Tsinghua Urban Planning and Design Institute)

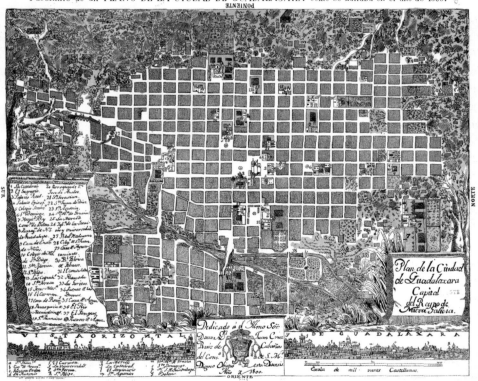

Facsimile de un PLANO DE LA CIUDAD DE GUADALAJARA como se hallaba en el año de 1800.

14.18 Spanish colonial city of Guadalajara, Mexico in 1800.

streets that led outward from it, the location of commercial uses, the size of lots, and other important matters determining the settlement. It urged settlers "as far as possible to have the buildings all of one type for the sake of the beauty of the town." The impact of these ordinances can be seen today in Santa Fe, New Mexico, and Puebla, Mexico, and in dozens of mission communities throughout Latin America.

Symbolic templates greatly simplify the task of designing settlements, although there remains scope for creativity in responding to specific topography, views, and natural features of sites.

Problem Solving

Some designers adopt the view that design is essentially a process of problem solving and capitalizing on site opportunities. They begin by identifying the issues to be addressed and the influences on the site that require a response, and study what would constitute an optimal solution for each. Land form, microclimate, views, and orientation are good points of departure. When the responses to these are overlaid, the rough outlines of a site plan may emerge. Compatibility with neighboring uses may suggest the most appropriate locations for each element of the program. Linkages with surrounding streets and places where access is possible may provide the point of departure for the road network. Topographic conditions and the capacity to service areas of the site may suggest where higher densities should be located. The necessity of phasing the development will have a bearing on the pattern. And so on. This pragmatic approach should not be dismissed as unimaginative; there is room for creative responses to each of these issues. Moreover, a collection of localized responses isn't necessarily wrong: land ownership patterns are often a historical accident, and it may be incorrect to assume that a site should be planned as a single unified whole, if the land suggests it is several distinct areas.

Rather than parceling the site geographically, a designer may explore optimal solutions to each of the critical issues, one by one, asking: What would be the ideal solution for creating walkable access from housing to the commercial area? For capturing and treating runoff before discharging it into the streams? For

14.19 Notes by Lawrence Halprin on the genesis of the plan for Sea Ranch, California.
(Lawrence Halprin Collection, Courtesy of The Architectural Archives, University of Pennsylvania)

14.20 Lawrence Halprin's notes on the importance of the hedgerows and ravines on the Sea Ranch site.
(Lawrence Halprin Collection, Courtesy of The Architectural Archives, University of Pennsylvania)

protecting the wetlands? For buffering the residential areas from highway noises? With the problem disaggregated in this way, the process becomes more transparent to clients and officials. Assumptions can be challenged, and the weighting of each issue can be debated.

Many designers seek to portray design as a process of *rational choice* among competing approaches. Half a dozen or so creative alternatives are developed, from different points of departure. A matrix of evaluation criteria is constructed with weighting for each criterion. Then the several alternatives are scored and are ranked from best to worst. The devil is in the details, of course, particularly in the weighting assigned each criterion. Not everyone will agree on the criteria or the weighting, producing a robust debate about the importance of the factors that are being considered. If there are multiple decision makers, each can assign individual weights to each criterion, and it is often useful to see whether the results differ substantially if divergent weights are assigned. Since the human mind generally has the capacity to integrate criteria more quickly than any process of scoring alternatives, a useful exercise is to work backward: beginning with a plan generally judged superior to others, ask what weighting would be needed to predict such an outcome? This is, of course, heresy to rational thinkers, but the results of evaluation matrices ultimately must pass the test of common sense as well as of logical reasoning.

How to choose among the many different design strategies? The project itself may suggest the optimal approach. The client may wish to emulate a successful past project, or one that he has seen and admires. Development regulations and natural conditions, such as wetlands or steep slopes, may dramatically limit the range of alternatives that can be considered. In both such cases, there may be merit in quickly developing a single solution that can be refined as other factors weigh in. Designers also carry their past explorations into each project; they may wish to explore further an idea that worked well for them elsewhere—indeed, they may have been hired because of a successful project— or they may wish to try an approach that they could not carry out in a previous project.

Ideally, designers should be aware of a range of design strategies, and should have some flexibility in their approach to suit the circumstances. Working with a team, they need to make the approach explicit and establish a timetable for reaching decisions. There are always additional avenues that can be explored, new technologies that can be considered, and better drawings that can be made. The trick is to chart the course that makes best use of the time and resources available.

15 | Guidelines, Criteria, and Standards

Creative site planning needs to be responsive to an array of standards, prohibitions, and requirements that delimit what is possible on a site. Many of these are adopted by local, regional, or national governments as codes or regulations, but they also include rules of thumb, professionally sanctioned norms of practice, governmental policies, design guidelines, and a growing number of voluntary programs certifying that a plan meets criteria of excellence. Standards and review criteria profoundly influence the range of possibilities for a site, and site planners have joined the scrum in reforming and framing the rules.

Standards cover almost every aspect of site planning. As we have noted in part 2, the area of the site available for development will be influenced by wetlands regulations, restrictions on the use of steeply sloping lands, set-asides for agricultural lands, restrictions on the cutting of trees, required setbacks from streams or water edges, buffers required alongside major roadways or hazardous areas, and requirements that certain portions of lands be reserved for open-space and public uses. Some of these requirements may be arbitrary, others are created to reflect community expectations or aesthetic preferences, but most will be rooted in broadly accepted professional or policy norms. Chapter 7 has outlined the often determinative role played by local and regional plans, land use regulations, limits on density or intensities, setback requirements, and a variety of special regulations such as view plane protections or restrictions on use of historic resources. The infrastructure of the site will need to be designed within a framework of local requirements (minimum widths of streets, parking requirements, local design standards, sustainability regulations) as well as powerful engineering standards created by professional bodies. These standards are presented for each infrastructure component in part 4. Ultimately, the form of the new uses will also be shaped by local design traditions and design review processes, and by requirements and underwriting standards acceptable to lenders who provide the capital for development. As an example, financial underwriters for retail and office projects customarily require more parking spaces than do local government regulations.

Increasingly, clients and designers are voluntarily agreeing to plan their sites to meet standards for energy and sustainability set by organizations such as the US Green Building Council, the Green Building Initiative, BRE Global, the Sustainable Sites Initiative, and dozens of other organizations that certify buildings and sites. Meeting these criteria can be of considerable value for marketing and publicity. Some national or local governments have mandated these standards for all new development, or for development that is sponsored or financed by governmental organizations.

The bewildering array of standards sometimes leaves the impression that there is little room for innovation, unless the planner is willing to work to bend the rules to allow a uniquely appropriate plan. Ultimately this may be necessary if no good solutions can be found, or the program may need to be reshaped to allow smooth passage of the site through the regulatory process. But it is also true that meeting minimum standards does not guarantee a well-planned site. That requires aspirations that go beyond those codified in laws or regulations.

Aspirational Criteria

In planning Sea Ranch (chapter 1), Lawrence Halprin convened a series of *take part workshops* among the first and future residents of the site. They outlined their aspirations:

Nature predominates, *not* buildings,
Rural setting, *not* suburban,
Home size modest, *not* enormous,
Exteriors simple, *not* showy,
Design guidelines, *not* "anything goes,"
Sense of community, *not* "statement" houses,
Aesthetics valued, *not* disregarded (Gordon 2004).

Criteria such as these serve as metaobjectives, ways of judging whether particular standards or criteria are appropriate. At Sea Ranch, a proposal that each owner be given a large fenceable lot might be seen as too suburban, although with further thought the offender might be the type of fencing, not the size of the lot. There are leading objectives, and others that logically follow from them.

The essential question the site planner needs to ask at the outset is, "How will I judge whether I have created a satisfying place?" Sidebar 15.1 presents comments of the planners of the three sites illustrated in chapter 2. For the planner of the NewBridge site, the overriding aspiration was to create a multigenerational community set in the landscape in a way that reflected the values of *tikkun olam* (repairing the world) and *bal tashchit* (do not destroy). Shanghai Taipingqiao's planners framed their hopes quite differently, reflecting the very different context. They sought to create a place that was the product of the unique history of the site but which also introduced a new set of attractions, including a lake and park in the middle of the city. And at Battery Park City, the immediate threshold was to get a community built, as the participants had seen the development corporation go bankrupt trying to implement several previous schemes. Creating a uniquely New York environment was the way to accomplish that, a place that recognized the best qualities of older neighborhoods but was a modern addition to the city.

Aspirations such as these become the leading ideas behind a plan, and from them follow a number of logical moves. At NewBridge, the extensive investment in green infrastructure was the obvious projection of the core idea of healing the landscape, although one that would require a great deal of analysis to ensure that each system made economic sense. At Battery Park City, creating modest-sized blocks with buildings fronting on streets, and connecting streets to the existing network, were logical deductions from the desire to make the area uniquely New York, and to create a development system that could function within the framework of local builders and owners.

Compiling a list of benchmarks of success is an important bridge between analyzing a site and making the plan. The list deserves to be widely discussed among the stakeholders, and once agreed upon, it needs to be prominently displayed as a reminder of the planning mission.

Urban Design Guidelines

Public bodies, interest groups, and those impacted by a development also have their wish lists. Many of these are codified in zoning, subdivision, and other regulations that are publicly adopted (as noted in chapter 7), although it is sometimes difficult to disentangle the purposes from the actual standards. But there are a variety of other statements of hopes, policies, and aesthetic preferences that go beyond formal requirements.

15.1 Design guidelines and the oversight of a town architect assured that buildings were consistent in form and character along Main Street, Kentlands, Maryland.
(Gary Hack)

Sidebar 15.1

**Planners' Aspirations:
NewBridge, Taipingqiao,
and Battery Park City**

**NewBridge on the Charles,
Dedham, Massachusetts**

The overriding objective was to create a
senior community that changed the existing
paradigm for senior living in an elegant
and environmentally sensitive way.

The three most important aspirations were:

Design a community that provided seniors
with an apartment for life, included many
lifestyle options, and replaced existing long
term care beds with a state of the art facility.

Take advantage of the unique landscape
and site features of the Newbridge site in a
sustainable manner that reflected the
Jewish customs of Tikun Olam (repairing
the world) and Bal Tashchit (do not destroy).

Integrate into the community an
intergenerational program that provides
casual interaction and would not rely on
forced programing.

These aspirations fostered many of the
design solutions. The integration of the long-
term care, assisted living and independent
living facilities centered around the Village
Center, the many sustainable elements
of the project including low impact design
techniques, the geothermal system
and water recovery, and the inclusion of
the Rashi School and its reliance on
the larger senior community for support
and interaction.

Joe Geller, landscape architect and
site planner

**Taipingqiao (including Xintiandi),
Shanghai**

We wanted to create a place that is inspired
by the site, but was also something new. …
We thought through conserving the fabric
that was uniquely Shanghai, we could give
context to the First Meeting House of
the Communist Party of China, and provide
identity to the entire area. … By introducing
the Lake Park, we provided needed
outdoor space and a community focus, and
recognized that there used to be a creek
running through the area. …

The most important aspirations were:

Create a memorable sense of place in
Xintiandi (XTD) through the conservation
and regeneration of Shikumen Style houses.
Manage density and human scale by
retaining the 2 block conservation area and
introducing the Lake Park to relieve the
density of new development.

Create liveable communities by providing
a shared open space, well-defined public
realm, fine-grain street pattern and walkable
community.

Develop a visionary yet implementable plan,
by converting historic structures for viable
contemporary uses, not preserving them as
a museum.

Leverage the developer's interests to provide
public benefits from private development
projects, by introducing amenities that
improve the community while generating
higher profits for the developer.

Because of the success of this project,
almost every major Chinese city wants to
build an XTD.

Ellen Lou and John Kriken, site planners

**Battery Park City,
New York**

The overriding objective was getting it built.
The project was bankrupt and many talented
architects had tried but failed to produce
realistic designs.

The three most important aspirations were
(and continue to be):

To design a whole district that is a destination for both city residents and visitors —
as popular as Rockefeller Center, Central
Park, the Brooklyn Bridge, and other iconic
places that define New York.

To create an area with the look and feel of
city, without replicating any other location —
a uniquely different evolution of a modern
New York.

To employ buildings as a means for making a
lasting urban fabric and exciting public places.

From these aspirations flowed a number of
other objectives that guided the planning:
creating sites for successful real estate
projects, connecting to and enhancing adjacent Lower Manhattan streets and districts,
creating successful new parks, mixing uses,
forming a dramatic waterfront esplanade,
and many more.

Stanton Eckstut, co-designer/planner
(with Alexander Cooper)

These may come into play in *design review* requirements, or through the negotiations over approval of a project.

Compatibility is at the heart of most *design guidelines*. Public design guidelines relate a project to its larger context—the district where it is set, the special form of the landscape, nearby land uses, and the network of connections between the site and its surroundings. A public or private owner who has planned a site may also use design guidelines to enforce internal compatibility, conveying the intended character of the site plan to the ultimate developers of parcels, safeguarding against inappropriate buildings and projects. Sometimes these parcel requirements are memorialized in deed restrictions, or in contracts that accompany the sale or leasing of properties. In many cases, a design review process is established to judge whether the letter or spirit of guidelines has been met.

A number of conventions have evolved that capture the experience of successful projects. The best guidelines are insistent about the essential qualities sought for a place, while leaving room for creativity in how these are created. A fine balance needs to be struck, avoiding the twin pitfalls of being too prescriptive or so vague as to have little effect. If the guidelines are to be self-enforcing, they will need to leave little to interpretation; if coupled with a dependable review process and trusted reviewers, they can leave much more to be decided in a dialogue about plans.

THE MIXED-USE CORE: A CONCENTRATION OF OFFICES, RETAIL, HOUSING AND CIVIC AMENITIES WITHIN WALKING DISTANCE OF THE TRANSIT STATION

15.2 Mixed-use core development form promoted in the Envision Utah transit-oriented development guidelines. (Envision Utah)

Types of Design Guidelines

General design guidance may be found in published urban design studies (in print or on the Internet) for the city where the project is located. Often these are not officially adopted, because of the difficulty of translating subjective matters into legal language (and agreeing upon it), but they guide local actions nonetheless. As an example at the regional scale, Envision Utah has developed a compelling vision for the future development of the Wasatch Valley that includes Salt Lake City, staking out general principles for development (transit-oriented, increased densities, protecting watercourses, among others) and conveying an ethos for planning sites. Because the program involved thousands of citizens of the region, its principles for development enjoy broad public support and serve

as a touchstone in the planning of any sensitive site (Envision Utah, n.d.).

Specificity is an important issue in design guidelines. The most basic guidelines are simply *statements of intent*:

"Multifamily, commercial and office structures should be designed to be compatible with single family residential structures in the community" (Germantown, Tennessee Design Guidelines),

"The lower two levels of buildings, where they face the street, should be made highly transparent, through the use of windows or fixed glass panels" (Austin Urban Design Guidelines), or

Organize mixed uses so that office workers can
walk to restaurants, entertainment venues and
everyday shopping.

Statements that are useful need to be unambiguous
and have direct implications for the plans of a site or
buildings that will occupy it. *Quantitative guidelines* go
one step further by offering a way to measure whether
the guideline has been met:

Residential units should be located within 10 minutes
of a bus stop, accessible by direct sidewalks,
Buildings along Main Street should form a consistent
street wall and be 4–6 stories in height, or
There should be 2.75 ac of public open space for each
1,000 people expected to live on the site (Vancouver
Urban Development Guidelines).

Guidelines such as these are generally adequate where
design review bodies will review the plans as they
evolve. Through discussion, a working understanding
will be reached of what is meant by "compatible with
single family residential structures," or "highly transparent" or "a consistent facade." Such common law
understandings are impermanent resolutions, however,
requiring continuity of both the project team and the
reviewers. They can easily evaporate with a changing
cast of characters.

Many planning ideas are better described through
diagrams or graphic examples than by words. Three-
dimensional notions of relationship, scale, detail, and
form fall into this category. Design guidelines may need
to be richly illustrated, always avoiding the trap of having
schematic diagrams taken literally. They should create
an envelope for what is being sought, not the final object.

One of the best examples of using *graphic guidelines* to shape a large-scale site development may be
found at Battery Park City in New York (see chapter 2).
The site developer, Battery Park City Authority, created
a site plan that established streets and the public
realm—parks, a waterfront esplanade, recreation
areas, plazas, museum sites, schools, and public buildings. Areas to be developed privately were divided into
parcels, and detailed design guidelines were established for each. Developers made financial bids on the
parcels, understanding that their design would need
to conform to the guidelines and would be reviewed

by the authority's staff. While the overall intent was to
create a harmonious district of buildings, each developer was encouraged to be creative in interpreting the
guidelines. The result is a rich texture of buildings that
form a coherent community. While several generations
of leaders took charge of the development and over
50 developers with their designers built projects, the
design guidelines supplied the continuity over the 25
years it took to build Battery Park City.

Local urban design plans that affect sites directly
are usually the product of planning agencies working
with affected communities. Many downtown areas have
urban design plans that focus on how buildings should
meet streets, the uses along major walkways, how
parking should be handled, and other issues. Sometimes they are purely narrative, like Portland, Maine's
downtown guidelines that discourage street closings
and upper-level pedestrian passageways, urge proponents to concentrate attention on the first 35 ft (10 m)
of height closest to pedestrians, and encourage the use
of brick and complementary materials in structures for
compatibility with existing fabric. The city's namesake
in Oregon publishes a comprehensive set of guidelines
for its central city, heavily illustrated by examples of
good practice drawn from Portland and beyond (City
of Portland 2001). Some cities such as Toronto focus
their efforts on areas likely to undergo change in the
foreseeable future, seeking to ensure that the transition
doesn't overwhelm the valued structures and character
of the area. Criteria for these areas typically include
height planes and criteria on the form of tall buildings.
In setting the planning expectations for a project, understanding these guidelines will be critical.

In the UK and other countries where discretionary
review is required before receiving planning permission
for a site plan, planners need to pay special attention
to urban design guidelines. An excellent example is
the city of York's urban design plan, which presents an
urban framework and set of valued criteria for development and change. These are then applied to 10 sites
critical to the future development of the city, including
the British Sugar site. Suggestions include maintaining public access to the river and green wedge beyond,
embracing the ring road and initiating its change into
a boulevard, creating a central avenue through the
site, and reproducing York's typical historic pattern of
streets and squares.

Provide Plazas in High Use Areas

Issue

Urban plazas should be designed with public use as a priority. The use of public open space is often dependent on the real estate maxim of "location, location, location." Therefore, it is important to analyze the location of a proposed plaza in terms of the existing plazas in the area, the linkage to a downtown pedestrian and transit system, the primary population to be served, and the diversity of potential users. Creating open space in a dense development without coordinating the size and use with other nearby plazas can result in declining use in the others. Conversely, areas with too few outdoor spaces will generally be overused. Care should be taken to coordinate plazas with their catchment areas.

Values Supported

Density
Humane Character
Diversity
Sustainability
Connection to the Outdoors

Recommendations

- Consider the need for a new urban plaza based on the catchment area of potential users. The catchment area extends 450 feet in all directions from the center of the proposed plaza.
- Review the need for a high use corner location versus the oasis potential of a mid block cul-de sac or pedestrian thoroughfare.
- Consider the number of potential workers in the catchment area to ensure a lunchtime clientele.
- Provide diversity in ground level retail to encourage daytime use by workers, tourists, and shoppers.
- Design the plaza as a catalyst to enhance urban pedestrian and transit circulation patterns.
- Link the plaza to an urban open space plan which provides and encourages safe pedestrian walkways.

Coordinate the location of new urban plazas with their catchment areas

56 · urban design guidelines for Austin

15.3 Austin, Texas urban design guidelines, aimed at creating plazas in commercial development areas. (Austin Design Commission)

2. COMMUNITY CHARACTER

Over the past three decades, Germantown has evolved from a rural fringe area to an established community that is home for more than 33,000 residents. Through its careful control over development, it has maintained many of the qualities which originally made it an attractive place to locate, while allowing a diverse range of housing, services and facilities to locate within the City boundaries.

2.1 PRINCIPLES
The fundamental design principles that have governed this transition are:

1. **Dominant landscape.** Nature should be the dominant visual characteristic of the City, even in commercial areas. Buildings should be framed by the landscape. Streets should take their character from the landscaping which frames them. At boundaries between land uses, dense planting should provide the separation necessary to avoid conflicts.

2. **Domestic scale.** While a broad mix of housing and commercial opportunities are encouraged in Germantown, structures generally should be domestic in scale and appearance and should not detract from single family housing areas.

3. **Public vs. private domains.** All that is visible from public streets and open spaces should be carefully controlled, while individuality is encouraged in more private areas.

4. **Respectful diversity.** While a diversity of architectural styles is encouraged, individual buildings should not shout for attention. Materials and colors should mirror those of nature and be compatible with existing buildings in the immediate area of the project.

5. **Restraint in public communications.** Public signage and advertising should be restrained and not detract from the sense of a continuous landscape.

15.4 Guidelines for community character, Germantown, Tennessee. (Carr Lynch Hack and Sandell)

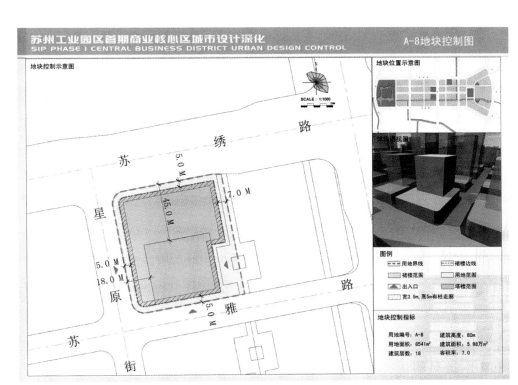

图 8　城市设计对中央商务区内的每一个地块均制定详细的形态指标
（图片由苏州工业园区管委会提供）

15.5 Parcel development guidelines, Suzhou Industrial Park, Suzhou, China. (China-Singapore Suzhou Industrial Park Development Co. Ltd.)

C 7 DESIGN CORNERS THAT BUILD ACTIVE INTERSECTIONS

BACKGROUND

The Central City's 200-foot block structure creates many street intersections and subsequent building corners. These frequent intersections and building corners create unique spaces of concentrated activity where pedestrians, bicyclists, and motorists come together.

Enhanced building corners can include characteristics such as large windows, canopies, marquees, or signs. The location of stairs, elevators, and upper-floor access toward the middle of the block frees sidewalk-level building corners to be activated by retail opportunities.

Buildings that are set back from property lines at corner locations create spaces for active outdoor uses such as café seating, sidewalk vending, or the provision of public art or water features. Active intersections developed by building corners on opposite sides of public rights-of-way also provide a framework for gateways. A cohesive design strategy that integrates the building design with the right-of-way design adds to these corner environments. Enhanced building corners and their adjacent right-of-way systems contribute to the vitality of the Central City's pedestrian network.

Thiele's Square at the intersection of W Burnside and 23rd

GUIDELINE

Use design elements including, but not limited to, varying building heights, changes in facade plane, large windows, awnings, canopies, marquees, signs, and pedestrian entrances to highlight building corners.

Locate flexible sidewalk-level retail opportunities at building corners.

Locate stairs, elevators, and other upper floor building access points toward the middle of the block.

This guideline may be accomplished by:

1. Orienting building corners toward transit alignments. This corner of the Nordstrom's department store (in the background) at SW Morrison and Broadway, is set back from the intersection and faces a primary downtown MAX stop at Pioneer Courthouse Square.

2. Emphasizing the corner with signs or marquees. The Kitchen Kaboodle retail store, at the corner of SW 6th Avenue and Washington, creates a point of interest with its unique sign.

3. Locating upper floor access toward the middle of the block. Upper floor access at Jackson Tower is located in the middle bay, freeing up space at the corner for retail opportunities.

BRITISH SUGAR
CITY BEAUTIFUL RECOMMENDATIONS

15.7 Guidelines for planning and development of the British Sugar site, York, UK.
(York New City Beautiful)

The British Sugar site, a significant area of brownfield land within the existing defined area of the city, is a major economic asset. The site must be cherished, and should not be developed for uses of low value in terms of either design or economics. Development at British Sugar will guide the future perception and standards for the city.

The proposals for an urban eco-settlement for York Northwest, with a pilot scheme on part of the British Sugar site, will contribute to this approach, and ensure that innovation and high standards of sustainable development are pursued. The design and delivery of the pilot scheme will be a benchmark for further development on this site and in the wider city.

The site, currently being master planned, will come forward before York Central. As its development is likely to represent the starting point of the wider redevelopment of York Northwest, proposals for British Sugar and York Central will need to complement and provide benefit to each other.

To achieve the aspirations of the plan, proposals for the British Sugar site must:

- Create direct access to the river and historic green wedges.

- Explore the potential for a central avenue to link to the Great Street, which incorporates on the York Central Site and extends into the city core.

- Provide strong pathways and linkages to the wider countryside and the new country parks.

- Embrace the ring road and commence its transformation into an avenue.

- Explore sustainable street designs that reinforce the pedestrian and cycle connections to the station and city centre.

- Promote foot, cycle and mobility scooter movement between the site and the city centre.

British Sugar is a strategic housing site with a capacity of 1,300 units, located on the important north-western approach into the city. Linked to the York Central site to the south, the two development opportunities offer long-term scope to create a new employment and residential community that can fulfill the city's needs for the next 20 years. The site supports economic growth objectives, providing the opportunity to create a new residential area, designed with high environmental credentials to attract high-value individuals working in the technology, science and creative sectors. In terms of construction impacts, the site could employ more than 400 people, generating £0.1 billion of value for the local economy during the construction period.

DEVELOPMENT SITES
4. BRITISH SUGAR

The British Sugar site, along with the York Central site, forms the York Northwest development area. This regionally significant investment priority will play a vital role in York's future.

Located on the western edge of the city, with wonderful views of the Minster and the River Ouse, this site provides extraordinary potential to deliver York's New City Beautiful plan. Its location between the core and countryside provides the opportunity to create a new twenty-first century neighbourhood.

 CITY RIVERS The site lies south and west of the River Ouse. Proposals should provide leisure and amenity opportunities by direct access to the river through identified pathways and connections. These river pathways should be developed from green routes and spaces across the site, linking into both the city core and the wider countryside.

 CITY WALLS AND GATEWAYS The site should connect to the city walls by way of the new arterial avenue through the York Central site, through the railway station into the new city wall gateway.

 CITY STREETS, PLACES AND SPACES Streets and squares within the British Sugar site should reinterpret those of York's traditional neighbourhoods. A central avenue should be extended through the site as a spine of connected neighbourhood squares.

 CITY AS PARK This site has the potential to deliver a section of the proposed linear park (running parallel to the current ring road). Direct connections should be established into the proposed country parks. This will enable the creation of a new pathway connection to the countryside and direct access to proposed a park-and-go country park. This will create an opportunity to reduce private vehicle use within the outer ring road area, creating a more sustainable and healthy environment. Connections should also provide seamless pathway access along the river to Museum Gardens (as the future cultural park), one of York's proposed great city parks, effectively linking the site to the city core.

Often special interests predominate in design guidelines. In Australia, there has been a proliferation of water-sensitive design guidelines, a tribute to the strong advocacy groups throughout the country. These organizations amplify the guidelines by providing examples of best practice, and even drawings of typical designs for accommodating water on sites—suggestions that are relevant on other continents as well (South East Queensland Healthy Waterways Partnership 2007).

Design Review

Design guidelines and design review go hand in hand. As a general rule, fewer design guidelines are needed if they are backstopped by an effective and respected review process. Design review can take account of changing tastes and the experience of building, marketing, and using sites over time, refining the rules based on results. But even a loosely structured review process requires some general guidelines so that it doesn't lapse into completely arbitrary decisions. Where a public body oversees the review process, due process requirements also demand some written rules in advance of decisions (Scheer and Preiser 1994).

Design review can be done by a variety of entities. The simplest approach is to put the responsibility in one person's hands. Many European cities have city architects who must sign off on everything that is built within their boundaries. The developers of large new communities sometimes appoint a town architect to serve in an oversight role, with a degree of independence to safeguard them from the inevitable pressures of sponsors and designers. Many US universities have campus architects or planners, who nominally report to the president and trustees but have sufficient leverage to assure that poorly conceived projects never make it to the senior decision makers. Private development organizations typically assign design review to a single individual within the organization (a vice president for design and development); if there is sufficient commitment to assuring high quality, this can be an effective arrangement. The successful Battery Park City project was handled in this way.

Establishing a single design "czar," however, can have many downsides. The individuals so empowered may have personal preferences that blind them to some types of innovation. They may subconsciously wish to design the project themselves, and force constant redesign efforts until the project architect gives up and yields to the reviewer's preferences. Hans Stillman, the German senator who oversaw Berlin's development for two decades, is legendary for his battles with strongminded developers and their architects, but the reconstruction of the city clearly shows his iron hand.

Creating a *panel of experts* is a second strategy, opening the door for more diversity in outcomes. These panels may be ad hoc, tied to a specific project, or may be standing committees that continue over several years. When the Central Artery in Boston (an elevated highway) was rebuilt as a tunnel, a design advisory panel was created to review all proposals for use of the newly liberated surface space—parks, walkways, structures, streetscape elements, and the like. It consisted as a mix of professionals, architects, planners, landscape architects, and artists drawn from Boston and beyond. All projects were reviewed multiple times as they moved from conceptual plans to detailed construction documents, and the panel was disbanded when all immediate projects were approved.

Standing design review panels may continue over many years and offer the advantage of continuity of perspective. The Baltimore Urban Design and Architecture Review Panel reviewed and provided professional advice to all projects in urban renewal areas for over 30 years, with several members serving through much of its history. As projects wound down, it was reconstituted as a citywide panel dealing with signature sites. Cleveland's University Circle design review panel has also functioned for over five decades, with remarkable continuity of membership. The 40 institutions in that area voluntarily committed to submit their plans for design review and advice in the interest of assuring the orderly development of the district they share. Many universities have design review panels that review and provide advice for all building projects on campus, examining their consistency with the plans of the university and the quality of their contribution to the campus environment.

Design review committees (or commissions, boards, or advisory committees) are publicly chartered organizations that seek to improve the quality of the public realm and the built environment of cities. The Boston

Civic Design Commission (BCDC) and the Cincinnati Urban Design Review Board are only two of hundreds of such organizations in the US. Their scope may be defined geographically (within design review districts, or fronting on important streets), by the scale of projects (all projects over a certain area), or by projects seeking exceptions (requests for zoning variances.) Their powers are similarly varied. Many commissions in historic districts have the absolute right to turn down projects that they consider inappropriate—the Philadelphia Historical Commission is an example. More often they serve as advisory groups with the power of persuasion and publicity on their side. While the BCDC is only advisory, the mayor or Boston Redevelopment Authority (now the Boston Planning and Development Agency) can only overturn its rulings if they state their reasons for doing so in writing.

Design review committees may also be established at the neighborhood level by homeowners' associations, enforcing covenants in the deeds to property that require submission of all modifications and plans for buildings or additions. At the (not so new) community of The Woodlands, Texas, the residential design review committees are organized and run by volunteers, who also evaluate violations of established standards and seek constructive resolutions. The responsibilities and scope of such organizations need to be established at the time of planning the site, since this will affect the marketability and long-term stability of the neighborhood or district created.

Design review practices vary considerably from country to country. The conceptual design of large-scale sites in China is often done through invited competitions. The jury for the competition may serve as the ad hoc design review panel, both selecting the most promising approach and offering advice for its improvement. In the UK, *public inquiries* are organized to review planning and design proposals, particularly ones surrounded by controversy, opening them to comments and suggestions from professionals, interest groups, and neighbors. At Paju Book City in Seoul, the planners and urban designers prepared architectural guidelines for the entire site, and sector architects were appointed for each area to review projects and ensure that they conformed to the plan.

Regardless of the method of design review, there is much to be gained from inviting outside eyes to view and provide suggestions on the overall plans and parcel designs. There are several keys to success:

Start reviews as early in the process as possible, before ideas and attitudes are frozen,

Use design guidelines to structure the discussion and protect against arbitrary comments,

Create a design review capacity that is respected (composed of citizens as well as professionals) and is free of self-interest conflicts,

Visit completed projects and learn from them for subsequent projects.

Sustainability Criteria

A variety of voluntary systems have been developed to judge the sustainability of site plans, buildings, and landscapes. Their premise is simple: provided with reliable information about the sustainability of projects, the market will choose those that are rated highest, creating a premium in their valuation. For the most part this has been true, and a number of studies have found that highly rated developments command a premium in price and sell or lease more quickly (Institute for Building Efficiency 2011). The first rating systems were developed for individual buildings in the UK (Building Research Establishment Environmental Assessment Method, or BREEAM) and the US (Leadership in Energy and Environmental Design, or LEED). They quickly became adopted and spawned many similar systems across the globe, responding to the perception that the values and weightings that informed them were not universally applicable. There are now dozens of systems, some particular to individual countries, others focused on specialized building types such as medical centers or retail complexes, or adapted to interiors or to reuse of existing structures.

Most sustainability scoring systems designed for new construction include criteria that account for site location and planning, typically representing 20–30% of the weight of scores. However, when sites contain multiple buildings and involve major commitments to infrastructure, they deserve to be assessed in their own right. We outline here two systems of criteria that can aid the planner in designing a site, and mention others that may have relevance for projects in particular places.

Table 15.1 | Sustainability assessment systems

Name	Sponsor	Country	Scope	Reference
BCA Green Mark	Singapore Building Construction Authority	Singapore	New buildings and land-based housing developments	http://www.bca.gov.sg/greenmark /green_mark_criteria.html
BEAM Plus	Hong Kong BEAM Society	China (HK)	New buildings, with approximately 25% of points awarded for estate issues	http://www.beamsociety.org.hk /files/download/download -20130724174420.pdf
BREEAM Communities	BRE Global Ltd.	UK	Moderate or large-scale mixed-use developments, comprehensive environmental and sustainability analysis	http://www.breeam.org /communitiesmanual/
BREEAM GULF	BRE Global Ltd.	Middle East	Building-oriented rating system specifically tailored to Gulf states, with approximately 30% of points awarded for site issues	http://www.bream.org
CASBEE Urban Development	Institute for Building Environment and Energy Conservation	Japan	Urban development projects, assessing groups of buildings, site design, and quality of public spaces	http://ibec.or.jp/CASBEE/english /download/CASBEE _UDe_2007manual.pdf
EarthCraft Communities	Southface Energy Institute	US	New residential communities of at least 35 homes	http://www.earthcrafthouse.com
EnviroDevelopment Standards	EnviroDevelopment/ Urban Development Institute of Australia	Australia	Comprehensive branding system that assesses the environmental quality of developments	http://www.envirodevelopment .com.au/_dbase_upl/National _Technical_Standards_V2.pdf
Evergreen Sustainable Devrelopment Standard	Department of Commerce, Washington State	US	Sustainability standards that must be met to receive state assistance for affordable housing	http://www.commerce.wa.gov /Documents/ESDS-2.2.pdf
GBCS Korea	Ministry of Land, Infrastructure and Transportation and Ministry of Environment, Korea	Korea	Assessment and certification system based on sustainability and energy considerations	http://greenbuilding.re.kr
Green Communities	Audubon International	US	Existing and new communities; broad-based environmental and community assessment	http://www.auduboninternational .org/Resources/Documents /SCP%20Fact%20Sheet.pdf
HQE – Haute Qualité Environnementale	Cerway, representing Certivia (nonresidential) and CERQUAL (for housing)	France and international	Broad-based assessment of environmental quality, including urban development track	http://www.behqe.com /tools-and-resources
LEED-NC India	India Green Building Council	India	India-specific standards for sustainable communities and housing	http://www.igbc.in
LEED-ND	US Green Building Council	US	Site planning for sites up to 320 ac (130 ha)	http://www.usgbc.org/resources /leed-neighborhood-development -v2009-current-version
MINERGIE	MINERGIE Building Institute	Switzerland and Lichtenstein	Energy performance of new and existing buildings with a special emphasis on housing	http://www.minergie.ch

Name	Sponsor	Country	Scope	Reference
QSAS	Gulf Organization for Research and Development (GORD)	Qatar, Gulf states	Comprehensive system for assessing environmental and energy performance in buildings in the Middle East	http://www.gord.qa/uploads/pdf/GSAS%20Technical%20Guide%20V2.1.pdf
SITES	Sustainable Sites Initiative	US	Site planning with emphasis on natural, cultural, and environmental factors	http://www.sustainablesites.org/report/Guidelines%20and%20Performance%20Benchmarks_2009.pdf
Three Star Rating System	Ministry of Housing and Urban-Rural Development and China Academy of Building Research	China	Environmental and energy performance of residential, office, hotel, and commercial development projects	http://www.cabr.com.cn/engweb/Standards.htm

LEED-ND

LEED for Neighborhood Development is designed to assess the sustainability of site development or redevelopment projects ranging in size from a few buildings to complete neighborhoods of up to 1,500 ac (607 ha). It is aimed mainly at the planning of residential areas, although it may have relevance to neighborhood commercial developments and mixed-use areas. The system was developed recognizing that, no matter how sustainable individual buildings may be, much of an area's energy consumption is in transportation, and many of the environmental impacts relate to areas beyond the buildings. The Congress of New Urbanism, Natural Resources Defense Council, and US Green Building Council jointly developed LEED-ND, and the values incorporated are largely those that prevail in the US and Canada, although it may have applicability elsewhere for developments that aspire to be walkable, energy-efficient, and sustainable. It is not specifically oriented to large institutional sites such as universities, military bases, central business districts, or industrial areas, although several sites in such areas have obtained certification, as have sites beyond North America. By 2014, over 350 projects were listed as meeting LEED-ND standards, and these are useful precedents for sustainable site panning (US Green Building Council 2013).

LEED-ND consists of a scoring system with a maximum of 110 points (including bonuses) that certifies sites as meeting Certified (40 points), Silver (50), Gold (60), or Platinum (80) standards. The criteria for earning points are quite detailed, but the overall categories (LEED-ND v.4 listed in figure 15.8) fall into five areas:

Smart location and linkage (28 points)—criteria that encourage compact urban development and diverse access possibilities. There are five prerequisites that sites must meet: contiguity with existing development (or infill), avoiding sites that harbor imperiled species, minimizing impacts on wetlands, conserving prime agricultural land, and avoiding development in flood plains. Points in this category are weighted toward locations where it is possible to reduce automobile dependence and minimize the need for travel. One critique of LEED-ND is that with such heavy weighting of location factors, preferred sites are well on the way toward achieving certification before they are planned—which is, of course, the point of the standards.

Neighborhood pattern and design (41 points)—criteria that emphasize walkability, easy access to shopping, recreation, and local institutions, and diverse communities. The three prerequisites are employing walkable streets, attaining adequate densities to support transit and locating near it, and creating multiple connections with adjacent areas. These criteria rule out most gated developments and promote roadway plans with multiple routes to a destination. Walkable streets, easy access to transit, and compact development patterns are the touchstones of this category.

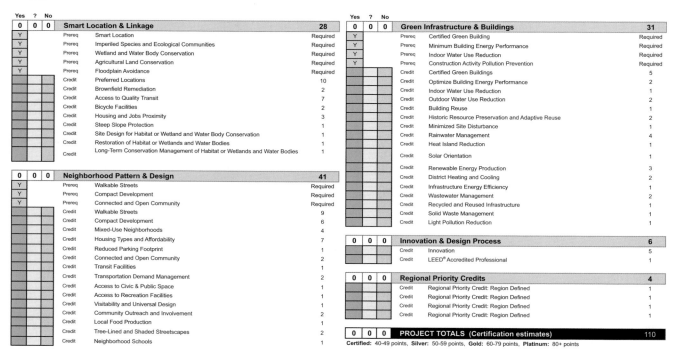

15.8 LEED-ND scorecard outlining criteria and their weights, 2013. (Courtesy of Green Business Certification Inc.)

Green infrastructure and buildings (31 points)—sites are given credit for including certified green buildings and adopting best practices of providing green infrastructure. Sites must include at least one LEED-certified building, or structure certified by a comparable rating entity. Other prerequisites include meeting energy and water use reduction standards and adopting best practices for site construction. Additional points are earned by incorporating specific technologies on the site such as district heating and renewable energy sources, and by adopting techniques that reduce heat island effects, better manage solid wastes, and reduce light pollution.

Innovation and design process (6 points)—projects are awarded bonus points for including innovative features, or adopting innovative site planning processes, that go beyond the items specified in the LEED-ND manual. A bonus is also offered when LEED-accredited professionals are employed in the process.

Regional priority credits (4 points)—additional credits are awarded to projects that are responsive to regional or national sustainability priorities. For the US these priorities are differentiated by region and metropolitan area, reflecting climatic, urban pattern, and landscape differences. In other countries the priorities vary according to national or local policies. As examples, in San Jose, California, extra credits emphasize energy conservation, wetlands preservation, and brownfields redevelopment, while across the continent in Portland, Maine the emphasis is on reducing auto dependence, conserving existing

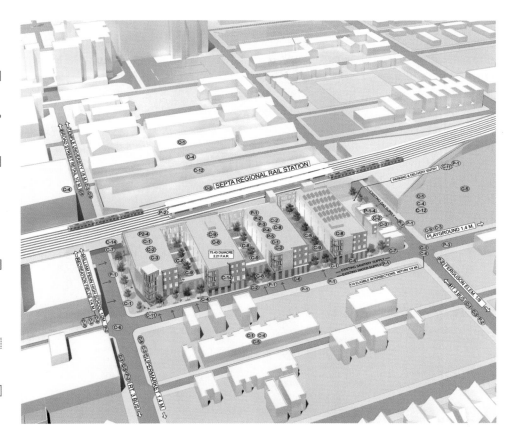

LEED NEIGHBORHOOD DEVELOPMENT CREDITS

SMART LOCATION & LINKAGE

- SMART LOCATION
- IMPERILED SPECIES CONSERVATION
- WETLAND AND WATER BODY CONSERVATION
- AGRICULTURAL LAND CONSERVATION
- FLOOD PLAN AVOIDANCE
- PREFERRED LOCATION- INFILL SITE-PREVIOUSLY DEVELOPED
- BROWNFIELD REDEVELOPMENT
- REDUCED AUTOMOBILE DEPENDENCE
- HOUSING & JOBS PROXIMITY
- STEEP SLOPE PROTECTION
- SITE DESIGN FOR HABITAT & WATER BODY CONSERVATION

NEIGHBORHOOD PATTERN & DESIGN

- WALKABLE STREETS
- COMPACT DEVELOPMENT
- CONNECTED AND OPEN COMMUNITY
- WALKABLE STREETS
- COMPACT DEVELOPMENT
- MIXED USE NEIGHBORHOOD CENTERS
- MIXED INCOME DIVERSE COMMUNITIES
- STREET NETWORK
- TRANSIT FACILITIES
- ACCESS TO CIVIC & PUBLIC SPACE
- ACCESS TO RECREATION FACILITIES
- VISITABILITY & UNIVERSAL DESIGN
- COMMUNITY OUTREACH & INVOLVEMENT
- TREE-LINED AND SHADED STREETS
- ↑ BUILDING ENTRIES ON STREET FACADE

GREEN INFRASTRUCTURE & BUILDINGS

- CERTIFIED GREEN BUILDINGS
- MINIMUM BUILDING ENERGY EFFICIENCY
- MINIMUM BUILDING WATER EFFICIENCY
- CONSTRUCTION ACTIVITY POLLUTION PREVENTION
- CERTIFIED GREEN BUILDING
- BUILDING ENERGY EFFICIENCY
- BUILDING WATER EFFICIENCY
- WATER EFFICIENT LANDSCAPING
- STORMWATER MANAGEMENT
- HEAT ISLAND REDUCTION

INNOVATION & DESIGN PROCESS

- EXEMPLARY PERFORMANCE - SLL C-3
- EXEMPLARY PERFORMANCE - NPD C-11
- EXEMPLARY PERFORMANCE - GIB C-9
- LEED ND EDUCATION
- LEED ACCREDITED PROFESSIONAL

REGIONAL PRIORITY CREDITS

- SLLC-2 BROWNFIELDS REDEVELOPMENT
- SLLC-5 HOUSING & JOB PROXIMITY
- NPDC-4 MIXED INCOME DIVERSE COMMUNITIES
- GIB-2 BUILDING ENERGY EFFICIENCY

15.9 Features of Paseo Verde that qualify it as a LEED-ND Platinum affordable housing project.
(Courtesy of WRT Design)

buildings, and jobs-housing proximity; in China extra credits are awarded for district heating systems, among other priorities, while in Finland on-site alternative energy sources are favored. Priority credits may be found in the USGBC Credit Library (http://www.usgbc.org/rpc).

This brief description of LEED-ND hardly does justice to what has become a font of good site planning practices. Whether or not site planners are aiming for certification, the LEED-ND manual is worth having at their side (US Green Building Council 2013). It provides rules of thumb, target dimensions, and standards that are based on dozens of exemplary pilot projects. LEED-ND standards must of course be adapted to the particular locale, culture, and level of development, but offer a useful set of objectives for planning a site.

15.10 View of Paseo Verde, Philadelphia.
(Courtesy of Halkin Mason Photography LLC)

SITES

The Sustainable Sites Initiative has created an assessment system (*SITES*) that complements LEED-ND by emphasizing in greater detail site planning and maintenance practices that respect the land and create sustainable landscapes. The guidelines and performance standards were the product of an interdisciplinary collaboration led by the American Society of Landscape Architects, the Lady Bird Johnson Wildflower Center at the University of Texas at Austin, and the United States Botanic Garden, with the cooperation of the US Green Building Council. Green Business Certification, Inc., the sister organization of the US Green Building Council, acquired SITES in 2015 and is now certifying projects under SITES version 2. The LEED-ND standards emphasize the built environment, while SITES begins with the natural character of the site, and the additions and changes to it that result from land uses. SITES can serve as a useful accounting of highly developed sites, but it can also provide guidance and an assessment of sites developed for recreation and open-space uses that have only minimal built structures (Caulkins 2012).

The guiding perspectives of SITES are that a site provides useful ecosystem services for its occupants and their wider region, and that the combination of natural and man-made systems can be planned so that

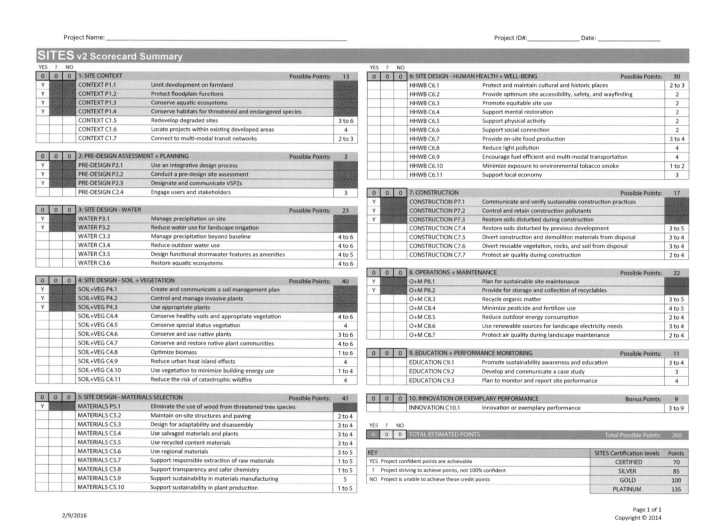

15.11 SITES criteria.
(Courtesy of Green Business Certification, Inc.)

**Ecosystem Services
of a Site**

Global climate regulation
Maintaining balance of atmospheric gases at historic levels, creating breathable air, and sequestering greenhouse gases

Local climate regulation
Regulating local temperature, precipitation, and humidity through shading, evapotranspiration, and windbreaks

Air and water cleansing
Removing and reducing pollutants in air and water

Water supply and regulation
Storing and providing water within watersheds and aquifers

Erosion and sediment control
Retaining soil within an ecosystem, preventing damage from erosion and siltation

Hazard mitigation
Reducing vulnerability to damage from flooding, storm surge, wildfire, and drought

Pollination
Providing pollinator species for reproduction of crops or other plants

Habitat functions
Providing refuge and reproduction habitat to plants and animals, thereby contributing to conservation of biological and genetic diversity and evolutionary processes

Waste decomposition and treatment
Breaking down waste and cycling nutrients

Human health and well-being benefits
Enhancing physical, mental, and social well-being as a result of interaction with nature

Food and renewable non-food products
Producing food, fuel, energy, medicine, or other products for human use

Cultural benefits
Enhancing cultural, educational, aesthetic, and spiritual experiences as a result of interaction with nature

(SITES)

they serve current occupants without compromising future generations. It seeks to balance environmental, economic, and social considerations. The guidelines are applicable to virtually any form of site development: open spaces, parks, utility corridors, transportation rights-of-way, conservation areas, botanical gardens, industrial, retail and office areas, residential and commercial developments, campuses for education and research, streetscapes and plazas, airports, and military complexes.

SITES guidelines provide a useful agenda for site planning, particularly for siting structures and infrastructure on the land, and for planning and maintaining the outdoor spaces that humans occupy (Sustainable Sites Initiative 2009). The guidelines can serve as benchmarks of good practice and as a checklist of considerations that need be taken into account. SITES also provides a rating system with four tiers: Certified (attaining at least 100 of 250 possible points, or 40%), Silver (125 points or 50%), Gold (150 points or 60%), and Platinum (200 points or 80%). Achieving these levels requires a combination of meeting prerequisites and achieving points based on projected performance.

SITES requirements are organized in nine categories that mirror the stages of site planning and development and the critical concerns in achieving a sustainable site, with extra points for innovation or exemplary performance. Seven of the nine categories have prerequisites, and many of the requirements have variable point scores depending on the level of achievement. Criterion 1: Site Context closely mirrors the concerns of LEED-ND, including the prerequisites (which is by intent, since efforts have been made to synchronize the two assessment systems). On the other hand, SITES's treatment of water, soil and vegetation, landscape materials, and human health and well-being is far more detailed than that of LEED-ND. Criterion 8: Operations and Maintenance adds entirely new dimensions to the consideration of site planning, and the post-completion monitoring of site performance included in Criterion 9 goes well beyond other site assessment systems.

Over 45 sites have been certified as achieving the standards of SITES with over 50 more in the pipeline, many in the site-monitoring stage (Sustainable Sites Initiative 2017). The majority are open-space and recreation projects and university campuses, with a broad range of

15.12 Novus International Headquarters, St. Charles, Missouri, an example of a three-star SITES-certified site (now Gold certification). (Courtesy of SWT Design)

15.13 View of completed site, Novus International Headquarters. (Courtesy of SWT Design)

15.14 Wetland detention area, Novus International Headquarters. (Courtesy of SWT Design)

other types as well. Few sites have been able to achieve the highest ratings, which speaks to the demanding criteria. Nonetheless, striving for certification is a worthy objective; using the criteria as guidelines for site planning will greatly improve practice. As of this writing, LEED and SITES have announced an agreement to integrate SITES criteria into LEED assessment systems.

Other Site Sustainability Rating Systems

There are a number of other sustainability rating systems that are widely used in countries beyond the US and Canada, and these may be the best choice for a project depending on its location. Each comes with an emphasis on the issues that prevail where it was developed. There is no natural law that determines the weighting of particular factors: these are matter of policy and represent choices of emphasis.

BREEAM Communities is the UK counterpart to LEED-ND. Sponsored by BRE Global, it is intended for moderate to large mixed-use developments, particularly those with significant housing components. It is an early-stage assessment method using an interactive website where project proponents are asked a series of questions and the project is rated accordingly. Questions cover five categories: governance (9%), social and economic well-being (42%), resources and energy (22%), land use and ecology (13%), transport and movement (14%). The assessment system is coordinated with UK planning and environmental impact assessment requirements, and provides for third-party validation. As with other BREEAM assessment schemes, projects are rated from pass (30% or more) to outstanding (85% or more) (BRE Global 2012). BRE also employs a bespoke methodology for projects in other countries, and has specifically tailored rating systems for the Middle East (BREEAM GULF) that places greater emphasis on conservation of water and mitigating heat effects, among other local concerns.

The University of Pennsylvania, working with BARWA in Qatar, has developed a comprehensive assessment system, QSAS (Qatar Sustainability Assessment System), now fully implemented in that country and used in several others. Its site assessment criteria deal with issues critical to development in hot, arid climates, including ecological protection, vegetation and shading, desertification, rainwater runoff, heat island effects, and

adverse wind conditions. Together with standards for energy, water, transportation, emissions, and cultural factors, these requirements provide an underlay for each of the family of assessment manuals that cover commercial development, schools, residential development, and spectator sports facilities. The sports facilities manual is now widely used for facilities intended for World Cup, Olympics, and regional athletic meets (Gulf Organization for Regional Development, n.d.).

The CASBEE (Comprehensive Assessment System for Built Environment Efficiency) assessment tool for urban development, developed by the Institute for Building Environment and Energy Conservation (IBEC) in Japan, is one of a family of sustainability rating systems that extend from individual buildings to clusters of buildings to heat islands to complete cities (Murakami, Iwamura, and Cole 2014). CASBEE for Urban Development differentiates its assessment scales between buildings with a floor area ratio over 500% (FAR = 5 or more) and those below that threshold, since the factors to take into account and their weighting need to vary accordingly. The assessment system is complex. Three broad categories are assessed: effects on the natural environment (microclimates and ecosystems), impacts on public service systems (water, transportation, disaster and crime prevention, convenience of daily life), and contribution to the local community (history, culture, scenery, and revitalization). In addition, projects are assessed in terms of the load reductions beyond the boundaries of the site: environmental impacts on microclimates, facades, and landscape; social infrastructure; and management of the local environment. Scoring sheets compute the score of a project and weight it according to whether it is above or below the 500% threshold. The results are displayed in a series of graphs so that the planners can see where they have succeeded and where fallen short. Perhaps the most useful aspects of the CASBEE for Urban Development manual are the detailed explanations of the criteria for good practice and the catalog of site plans complete with explanations of achievements and shortcomings (Japan Sustainable Building Consortium and Institute for Building Environment and Energy Conservation 2017).

There are a number of Australian site-oriented rating systems that can be effective guides to site planning criteria. One of the most ambitious is the

EnviroStandards program, originated by the Urban Development Institute of Australia. EnviroStandards provides criteria for assessment and certification of sites, buildings, and components. Its technical standards are parsed into nine categories that include master-planned communities of up to 1,500 homes and supportive businesses, residential subdivisions of up to 1,500 units, senior living areas, multiunit residential areas, mixed-use developments, industrial areas, retail projects, educational campuses and buildings, and health care facilities. While there is some overlap in the standards across the project types, they also reflect the special requirements of each use and the probable environmental impacts. They are organized under six general criteria: ecosystems, waste, energy, materials, water, and community. The certification process is driven by the planners of the site, with the guidance of technical experts. It also involves a site visit by an independent assessor, and annual renewal of the certification (Urban Development Institute of Australia 2013).

Housing sites have been a special focus of sustainability assessment systems. One of the most interesting US site planning assessment programs is EarthCraft Communities, the product of collaboration between the Southern Energy Institute, the Greater Atlanta Home Builders Association, the Urban Land Institute Atlanta District Council, and the Atlanta Regional Commission (www.earthcraft.org). Originally written to promote positive environmental practices in land and housing development in projects of over 35 homes in the Atlanta region, the criteria have been adapted for Piedmont Communities and Coastal Communities to reflect the special environmental qualities of each site locale. The guidelines constitute a valuable compendium for low- and moderate-density housing. Their use has spread to a large number of communities in the southeastern US. Projects that meet the threshold are labeled as Certified EarthCraft Communities.

Organizations in other US regions have created their own sets of sustainable development standards, some of which are mandated as a requirement for financial assistance or public approval. Washington State's Evergreen Sustainable Development Standard applies to all affordable housing in the state that receives public assistance (Washington State Department of Commerce 2013). The Pennsylvania Standards for Residential Site Development present a comprehensive set of planning and design standards for residential sites, reflecting best practices in the mid-Atlantic region (Brown, Foster, and Duran, 2007).

Finally, a number of the building-specific rating systems have substantial components relating to site issues. LEED New Construction allocates 25% of its points to site issues; BREEAM New Buildings weights the site roughly the same. Measured by building areas assessed, the widest-used system in the world is the BEAM Plus system that originated in Hong Kong and is now widely used in the balance of China as well. If buildings are part of an estate, the performance of the entire site is taken into account, and 25% of the points relate to site issues. The LEED-NC system in India allocates 29% of its points to site planning issues, with particular emphasis on water conservation, alternative transportation, and reduction of disturbance to the natural site (India Green Building Council, n.d.). There appears to be a convergence of views on the sustainability value of sites in building assessments.

Sustainability criteria are most effective when they are used as guides throughout the site planning process, rather than as items that need to be scored at the end of the process in hopes of qualifying for certification. Minor adjustments then may raise scores above minimum thresholds, but only substantial commitment to sustainability principles will qualify a site for the top rank.

16 | Subdivision and Land Assembly

Subdivision involves dividing a site into parcels of land that can be sold or leased or transferred to organizations for common use. Rights of access and use are established in a subdivision plan, in line with the property rights regime that prevails.

The subdivision process may leave few visible marks on the land, but it represents one of the most powerful actions affecting the pattern of settlements. War or hurricanes cannot erase the invisible pattern of landownership; lots and streets routinely reappear in identical form when areas are reconstructed because of the difficulty of wiping out the past and starting fresh. The dimensions of lots influence the type of structures that can be constructed on a site, even as uses change over the years. Parcels may be subsequently resubdivided, but it is extremely difficult to reverse the process and reassemble a site that has been divided and is owned by several people.

Subdivision

The process of *subdividing* a site into *lots* or *plats*, sometimes called *platting*, creates properties that will become the grounds for buildings and other uses. These lots are given precise dimensions and are mapped on the ground by installing stakes or monuments on the boundaries. The subdivision process also establishes the size and shape of land to be used for common purposes, such as roads, open spaces, or access ways. In many locations in North America, the developer of the land is required to install essential services on the site being subdivided—water lines, storm and sanitary sewers, roadways, and sometimes underground electrical lines—before being allowed to transfer property to others or obtain a building permit. While not all sites go through a subdivision process, large areas that will ultimately be developed, financed, or owned by multiple parties will undoubtedly need to be broken into individual parcels. It is the legal parcel (or lease on a parcel) that provides security to lenders: buildings, roadways, or other items added on a site are considered improvements to the land.

The process of subdivision is usually prescribed in municipal, state, or national statutes and regulations, which may also set down the minimum standards for lot sizes and shapes, road and right-of-way widths, land that must be reserved for public purposes, and other important decisions (Listokin and Walker 1989).

16.1 Property lines represent the invisible plan for a site: a subdivision near Dallas, Texas. (Gary Hack)

Generally, a plan of subdivision must be approved by a planning board, or other agency charged with ensuring that the standards are met, before a landowner can provide a buyer with a deed for a lot.

Where developers are required to install services, the subdivision process typically has two distinct steps. Initially, a *draft plan* or *preliminary plan of subdivision* will be approved, which establishes the pattern and dimensions of lots and streets, lands to be conveyed to the municipality, and the design of services to individual parcels. Approval of this plan may be accompanied by a long list of conditions that the developer must meet before final acceptance of the subdivision, including the mitigation of many on- and off-site impacts. When all the services are in place, boundaries and lots

are permanently staked, all impact fees have been paid, and the developer has discharged all their obligations to the local government, the *final plan of subdivision* will be approved and recorded in the local land title office. After final approval, the developer transfers streets and other public land to the local municipality, and is free to sell or transfer titles to other lands on a discretionary basis. The developer may need to post a *performance bond* guaranteeing the functioning of the infrastructure on a site for a specified period beyond when they have exited the scene.

An additional step may be added to the process in the case of large developments carried out over long periods of time. Before a preliminary plan of subdivision for a portion of the site is submitted, an overall

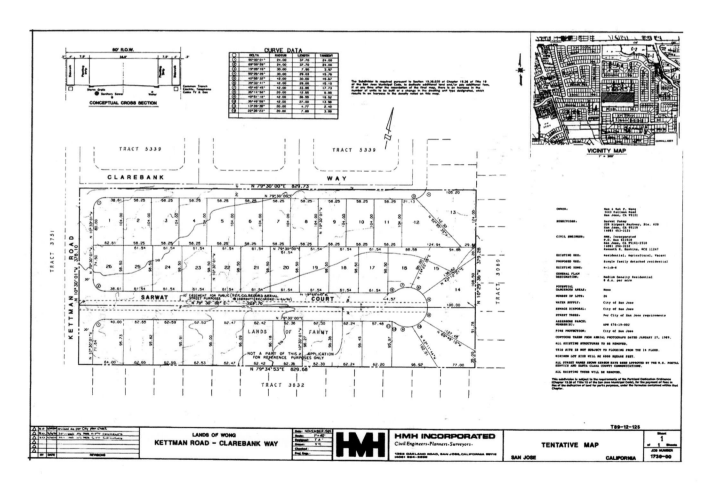

16.2 Preliminary plan of subdivision, San Jose, California. (Courtesy of HMH Inc.)

development concept plan or *master site plan* for the entire property will be approved, and a *development agreement* will be signed. Together, they will specify the amount of built space or number of housing units that will be allowed on each area of the site, the location and size of open spaces, the public facilities that must be constructed by the developer, any contributions which the developer must make to pay for public utilities or facilities beyond the site, and the schedule for completing each phase of the development and public facilities. Preliminary and final plans of subdivision for each phase will then be considered by the municipality within the framework of the development agreement. The form of the master plan and development agreement is generally prescribed in a *planned*

unit development (PUD) or *planned development* (PD) section of the local zoning, subdivision, or development code. In parts of Canada, these plans are called *secondary plans* and must be approved by provincial as well as municipal authorities.

Most cities and towns also have a simplified set of procedures for two- or three-lot subdivisions served by existing roadways and public facilities. These usually dispense with elaborate review procedures and allow immediate approval of a final plan of subdivision. There may be restrictions on the number of small lot subdivisions that a landowner can create on a property over a five- or ten-year period, to avoid this becoming a loophole by which the developer escapes normal review processes.

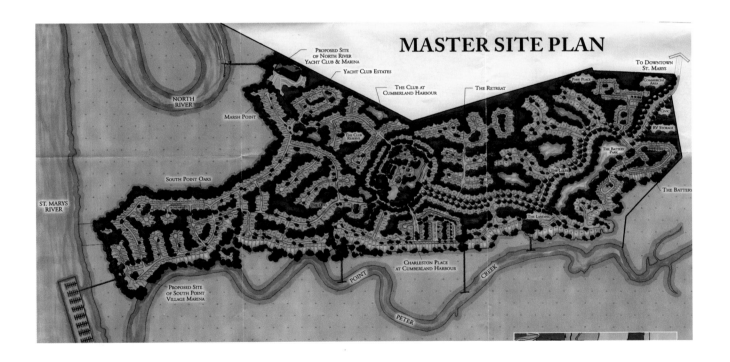

16.3 Master development plan for a phased development, Cumberland Harbour, St. Mary's, Georgia. (Courtesy of Atlantic Development Group)

Common Property and Facilities

When land is subdivided, it often makes sense to reserve certain properties for common use. These may include recreation areas, undevelopable sites that are preserved for their ecological value, or public facilities for recreation or community use. The issue of paying for their maintenance must be addressed at the time of subdivision, particularly in a residential area where there will be many owners with diverse needs. One obvious solution is to dedicate or transfer such lands and facilities to the local government. But this may require locating them so that they are accessible to the wider community, which may conflict with the local residents' desire to discourage traffic or outside use.

The local government also may be unwilling to accept the areas or facilities as public property because of the excessive maintenance costs of scattered properties, or because their standards do not meet municipal norms. Local governments have become wary of accepting left-over parcels of land that are not easily accessible to the larger community.

In some cases, shared driveways may provide access to several sites, but the developer may not wish to make them public streets in order to avoid burdensome city development standards. In such circumstances, variations on fee simple ownership and the use of covenants may need to be explored. Figure 16.4 shows several possibilities. One is to offer each fee simple owner an *undivided interest* in the common driveway through a

16.4 Alternatives for common areas on a site: (top left) dedicate roadway area to local government or other entity; (top right) give each property owner an undivided interest to be managed consensually or through a homes association; (bottom left) create a condominium or strata title corporation; or (bottom right) create a cooperative with title to entire surface area and proprietary leases for private areas. (Adam Tecza/Gary Hack)

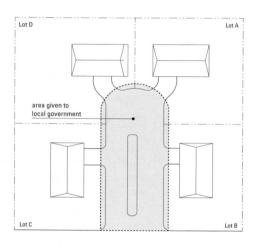

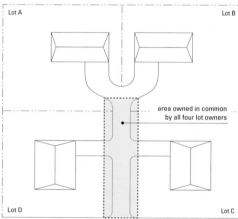

Home associations may be created to take responsibility for undivided area

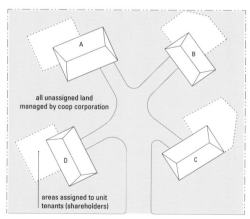

Site and units owned by cooperative corporation

provision in the deeds that passes the interest along to successive owners. Since positive covenants are not enforceable beyond the initial owners, the system relies on a sense of obligation among current owners to maintain the roadway.

Undivided interests are only workable if the ownership group is small and close-knit, the costs of ownership are minimal, and the interests in maintaining the common facility are equal and apparent. Five homeowners may share a wooded ravine at the rear of their lots, viewing it as an extension of their outdoor living areas and having no ambitions to change its character. But where the facility demands more upkeep and attention, we must look to other arrangements.

Most jurisdictions permit the creation of *mandatory homes associations*, a second way to manage shared facilities in residential areas. The names of these organizations differ; it may be a *homeowners' association*, *property owners' association*, *community association*, *civic association*, *property board*, *property committee*, *property trust*, *owners' corporation*, or *common interest realty association*, among other names. Membership in the association is automatic upon purchasing a lot or home in the development area. By vote of the membership, annual maintenance charges are levied against all property owners. If these charges are not paid, the association can place a lien on the owner's property, collecting unpaid charges upon sale of the property. The rules and regulations of such associations are usually governed by specific statutes of a state, province, or country.

Large developments give their homes association permanent responsibility for many facilities—open spaces, lakes, clubhouses, golf courses, and the like. They can, if so chartered, offer services beyond maintenance, such as programming social events, publishing a newspaper, or sponsoring educational programs. The Columbia Association has responsibility for one-third of the land area and most of the shared facilities in that Maryland new town and is a powerful social force among the residents. Since Columbia itself is not a municipality, the association serves as a surrogate form of local government for recreation areas and services that go beyond what the county provides.

A third solution to holding and maintaining common facilities is *condominium* ownership, also called *strata title*, *commonhold*, *syndicate of co-ownership*,

16.5 Open spaces and recreation facilities surrounding the town center of Columbia, Maryland are maintained and programmed by the Columbia Association, a homeowners' association. (Maryland Department of Commerce)

or *co-propriété*. In a residential situation, a condominium corporation (or *strata council*, *commonhold association*, *body corporate*, *owners' corporation*, or *syndic*) typically has responsibility for the common facilities, including the land on which the housing sits and, if apartments are included, the structure, elevators or stairways, common spaces, and roofs of the buildings. Condominium ownership was originally devised as a form of fee simple ownership for apartment dwellers, and allows the subdivision of property in three dimensions. More recently, condominium tenure has spread to moderate-density townhouses, semidetached, and even detached housing in cases where consistently high maintenance is desired for all building exteriors and grounds, such as in exclusive resort and retirement developments. More limited condominiums have also been devised to deal with common facilities in commercial development areas.

Owners of condominium units must meet at least annually to agree on the budget, level of maintenance, maintenance contractors, and specific capital investments for the coming year. The condominium association also sets regulations for use of common properties, to ensure that their investment is safeguarded and the quality of life is protected. All of this can be quite divisive, particularly if members regard their property or housing units differently.

While the practical size of a residential condominium depends on what is to be shared (how many units are needed to afford a swimming pool or warrant a full-time maintenance person?), experience has shown that beyond about 150 housing units it is extremely difficult to maintain a cohesive ownership group. Many professional managers favor projects of no more than 50–75 units, or even fewer if possible. Coupling high-rise apartments (whose elevators are prone to breakdown) with low-rise townhouses (which front on open spaces that need to be manicured) is a sure formula for resident conflict. And when large numbers of the units are rented rather than owner-occupied, there are frequent conflicts. Many condominium associations are given the right of approval for any unit rentals.

A variety of other issues and conflicts prevail in commercial condominiums, or in areas where housing and commercial uses are mixed within a building or on a site. A common solution is to structure each commercial unit as a separate condominium—separating offices from retail areas, as an example, or housing from retail uses—each with its essential common spaces and facilities attached. *Fractional ownership* is another solution, where individual entities own outright the ground or airspace they occupy but have obligations to the entire entity as well. In commercial condominiums it may be practical to contract with one or more of the owners or large tenants for maintenance of the common spaces and facilities, thereby reducing the condominium association to largely a financial entity.

In the case of housing, another tenure option for maintaining common spaces and facilities is structuring the development as a *cooperative corporation*, a further step in the direction of collective ownership. In a cooperative, all land and buildings are held in common, and "owners" are shareholders in the corporation. Each member has a *proprietary lease* that outlines the obligations and rights of owners, the subdivision of the property among owners, and the procedures for setting and collecting assessments for the maintenance of facilities. One feature of cooperatives is that the board generally reserves the right to approve any transfers of shares through the sale of units, providing substantial control over the occupants of a building or site. This encourages discrimination—current members of a residential cooperative can exclude anyone they regard as socially below them on the grounds that all owners will need to share the financial responsibilities of the corporation. But it can also be a formula for discriminating in positive ways, such as by ensuring that units are reserved for low- and moderate-income people, through a *nonprofit limited dividend cooperative*.

Cooperatives are common in New York City, where they predate adequate condominium laws and are maintained as a means of social segregation. In Canada *limited equity cooperatives* have been used as a vehicle for providing and maintaining low-income housing. Individuals or families purchase shares in the coop at a modest price, and upon leaving resell the shares to the coop at a price that reflects only modest gains, thereby preserving access to the unit for people of similar income. In many European countries coops (*asunto-osakeyhtio* in Finland, *bostadsrattsförening* in Sweden, *borettslag* in Norway, *mutual housing associations* or *building societies* in the UK) have been encouraged for social reasons, as a practical way to buffer housing from market forces and promote shared responsibility. In India, *cooperative housing societies* are popular as a means of ownership of urban *flats*.

Combinations of forms of tenure are of course possible, particularly for large sites. A residential development may consist of lots that are variously developed for fee simple, condominium, and cooperative ownership, with an umbrella homes association responsible for common facilities beyond individual sites. Thus, two levels of common lands and facilities may be necessary: those on individual sites (such as a swimming pool for the condominium or homes association members) and those shared with people on other sites (such as a large athletic field or sports facility), each with a separate entity responsible.

Leaseholds

Leasehold tenure is being used increasingly as an alternative to ownership for large-scale site developments where long-term maintenance of common spaces is required. A very long-term leasehold (say 99 years) is almost indistinguishable from ownership of a site. In the case of commercial development, leasing the land may make no practical difference to the initial owner, particularly if leases are prepaid.

Buildings may be owned on land that is leased. Annual land lease payments can be structured to include the costs of maintaining common roads or facilities, and the lease can be written so that these are reset periodically to reflect increased costs. At Battery Park City in New York (chapter 2), the maintenance of common outdoor spaces is funded through such an arrangement and carried out admirably through the Battery Park City Parks Conservancy. While leasehold condominiums are generally not permitted in New York State, exceptions have been made in cases where public benefit corporations own the underlying land.

Lease periods must be long enough to provide the security needed for mortgaging the owned property (typically lenders require a lease term at least 50% longer than the mortgage), and so that there is an incentive for continued maintenance. Lease terms of 50–60 years are common, but many commercial buildings have been developed on sites leased for as few as 35 years—long enough to provide lender security and allow the lessee to reap the bulk of the tax benefits for depreciation, while allowing the owner of the property to realize the appreciation or residual at the end of the lease term.

The ability to reset lease rates has led many public bodies and nonprofit organizations such as universities to adopt a policy of leasing their land instead of selling it. This can be an effective strategy in locations where land values are currently low but might rise dramatically as a result of a changing environment or the ongoing growth of the city (Sagalyn 1993). Leasing can provide a mechanism for *value recapture*, often referred to as the *unearned increment*—any increase in land value that is not due to improvements made by individual property holders (Ingram and Hong 2012). A portion of this increment of value may be captured by periodically raising lease rates to reflect the general rise in land values.

Leasing land at favorable rates, or creating a schedule of lease payments that begins with a very low rate and escalates over time, can also be a way of lowering the initial development costs, thereby encouraging forms of development that might otherwise not be feasible. Leasing residential lots can make housing more affordable to lower-income residents. But there are many political and practical difficulties with leasehold development of public lands, particularly for housing:

ground lease rates seldom keep pace with inflation because of the impact on those least able to pay; it is virtually impossible to evict tenants or homeowners at the end of the lease term, even if the land is needed for public purposes; and a long period of uncertainty, even disinvestment, can precede the expiration of the lease. The city of Vancouver, which has developed many thousands of units on publicly owned leased land, has favored prepayment of ground leases to avoid some of these problems.

Dealing with the end of the lease term is critical to making leasehold tenure an acceptable development tool. During the final years of a lease, with no chance of renewal, there is little incentive for leaseholders to maintain the property or reinvest in it. Residential properties will face a sharp decline in value beginning 25–30 years before the expiration of the lease term, when it becomes difficult to find buyers for structures with an uncertain future, or to obtain mortgages for their purchase. The result will inevitably be disinvestment or abandonment.

There are a variety of solutions to the end-of-term issues. One, common in commercial properties, allows the landowner to step in and cost-share or pay for improvements during the final years of the term. Another solution is to have lengthy notification times in the event that a lease will not be renewed. Most difficulties arise when property has appreciated substantially in value between the original lease and renewal time, jeopardizing the economics of a development.

Using a ground lease as a mechanism for providing for common spaces and facilities places a large burden on the lease document. It must provide a clear definition of what is covered and what is not, and there should be no ambiguity about who has maintenance responsibility for each space on a site, particularly if security is an important issue.

Land Assembly and Readjustment

Sensible planning of a site may require one to look beyond the boundaries of individual properties. This is particularly true in areas of intensive agriculture on the urban fringe, where individual properties may be small and shaped by the history of prior use. In the areas surrounding Bangkok, as an example, families subdivided

16.6 The random pattern of property ownership, the legacy of agricultural uses, creates difficult sites for urban development: Bangkok, Thailand.
(Gary Hack)

rice-growing lands into ever-narrower strips to accommodate each generation's desire for an independent farm. Developing each long narrow strip individually does not result in a sound pattern of urban development, forcing the government to consider ways of reassembling properties into larger sites.

A variety of techniques have been developed to facilitate land assembly in rapidly developing urban areas, both on the urbanizing fringe and in central areas. These include *land pooling*, *land sharing*, *compulsory land readjustment* procedures, *public taking* of lands, and the creation of *land assembly districts* with special powers to consolidate and redevelop land. Variations of these are widely employed in Japan, Korea, Taiwan, Australia, Israel, the Netherlands, and Germany, and they have been practiced on a more limited scale in the US, Canada, and portions of the Middle East. Generally these techniques require specific enabling legislation at the state or national level, and there are as many variations as there are local situations where they are employed.

Land Readjustment

Land pooling (as it is called in Australia) or land readjustment (as it is called in much of Asia) or land sharing (in Bangkok) generally is aimed at three objectives: assembling parcels of land that are large enough to allow planned development, thereby overcoming fragmented

historical ownership patterns; allowing development to occur in a timely manner, without the risk of holdouts; and self-financing the installation of infrastructure, so that it doesn't lag the development. About 30% of Japan's urban land has been developed through over 11,000 land readjustment projects, and similar projects comprise a large fraction of urban development in Taiwan and Korea (Hong and Needham 2007).

Generally, the procedures work as follows:

A local government prepares a scheme for developing a site that is currently in multiple ownership and a logical location for development. The plan indicates the future layout of roads and other infrastructure, the ultimate parcelization of the development, and the pattern of sites that will be required for parks, schools, community buildings, and other facilities. A financial plan is also prepared for the project, estimating public development costs for roads, services, and facilities.

The financial and development plans are approved by the local government council or other relevant agency. In some countries, all the owners of the land included must agree to the arrangement, a difficult hurdle. In other places, owners of a majority of the land area must vote to approve the readjustment scheme, still a significant hurdle. In both Germany and Israel, there are two tracks to land readjustment—a

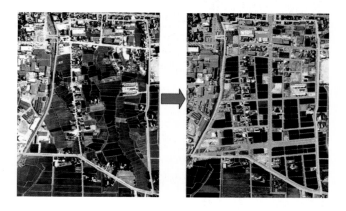

16.7 Aerial view of site, before and after land readjustment, Japan.
(Metropolitan Area Planning Council, Boston)

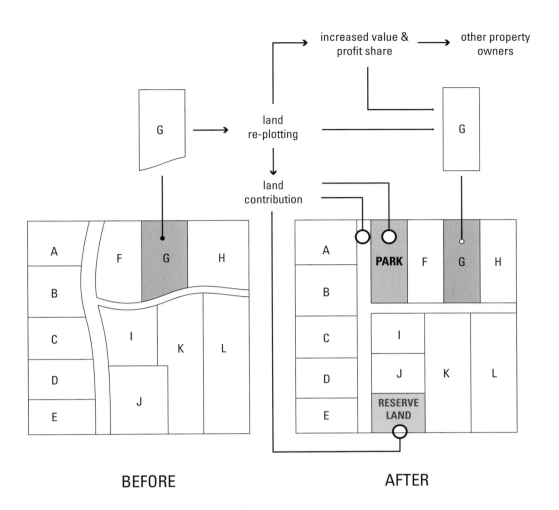

increased value &
profit share → other property
owners

land
re-plotting

G → G

land
contribution

BEFORE

AFTER

16.8 Basic model of land readjustment in Japan. (Adam Tecza/Hideki Satou-Minoru Matsui, JICA)

16.9 City Hall and surrounding Xinyi district of Taipei, Taiwan, created through land readjustment project by pooling small parcels. (Lord Koxinga/Wikimedia Commons)

full-consent route and a less-than-full-consent route—each with separate procedures (Alterman 2007). In Saskatoon, Canada, where a vote by owners of at least 51% of the land area is necessary for replatting, the municipal government makes a practice of acquiring enough land in a target area to assure that they have control over readjustment plans. In still other places, such as in Taiwan, an effort is made to reach a general consensus (80–90% of owners) before proceeding with land readjustment schemes.

An independent assessment is made of the values of each existing property and of each ultimate development parcel. Under some schemes, current owners are offered the opportunity to sell their property at the assessed value or exchange it for equally valued property in the new subdivision; in other cases they are only allowed to exchange existing for new properties. They can, of course, sell the new parcels they receive on the open market, even before the project is completed.

Some countries are explicit in prescribing the rules of redistribution of lands. In Israel, as an example, three principles guide the allocation of the new plats: proximity (as close as possible to the original plot); proportionality (as close as possible to the relative value of the original plots); and balancing fees (allowing for compensatory payments if proportionality cannot be achieved) (Alterman 2007). Reallocation arrangements are never entirely satisfactory to original owners, but efforts to achieve fairness can help make land readjustment processes acceptable.

The local government (or land development entity) generally retains and sells a fraction of the resubdivided properties, with the proceeds used to cover the development costs and installation of infrastructure and services. Some countries limit the amount of land that may be retained for public use and sale—in Taiwan, it cannot exceed 40% of the total area. Nonetheless, with rising land values as the land makes a transition from agricultural to urban uses, each current owner will generally obtain a generous financial return on their property, even if they exchange it for sites that are roughly half as large as those they currently own.

There are many examples of successful land readjustment projects, both central and peripheral. The Xinyi district in Taipei, site of the city's new City Hall and dense mixed-use development, is one such area. Large portions of Fukuoka, Japan have been redeveloped using land readjustment. At the opposite extreme, land pooling projects have provided the basis for installing essential services and reconstructing slums in Bangkok and Chang Mai, Thailand.

Compulsory Purchase

Many of the same objectives may, of course, be obtained by *expropriation* or the *exercise of eminent domain* or *compulsory taking* of property followed by public development of the land. In most countries, local governments or public development entities (such as national housing corporations) are entitled to purchase land for public purposes, with or without the consent of the owner, under urban renewal or urban development laws. There may be restrictions on the use of these powers. In some countries and jurisdictions, land so acquired may only be reused for public development projects, and agencies are prohibited from reselling the land to other private parties. In other places, its use is restricted to housing. In the US, a long succession of court rulings has established that "public purposes" include not only the construction of public facilities and removal of blight, but also the promotion of economic development of areas (Kelo 2005).

Expropriation can be a powerful tool for allowing sites to be planned in ways that are not overly influenced by the vagaries of past property and parcel boundaries. However there have been many abuses in exercising these rights, including widespread displacement during urban renewal in the US, and scandals over inflated appraisals or favoritism in the acquisition and disposition of properties in many countries. These have made public bodies cautious in exercising expropriation rights. In many places, public bodies will only authorize compulsory taking of land to round out the parcels of important development projects, where holdout owners block private developers from moving forward. In the East Cambridge (Massachusetts) Redevelopment Project, the city authorized public taking of land to carry out the project but did not need to exercise the right: the threat of expropriation was enough to encourage private landowners to collaborate in developments that conformed to the plan. Such "surgical" use of expropriation may be the norm in the future.

Public acquisition of land shifts the entire burden for acquisition and carrying costs and installation of infrastructure to the public entity, along with all the risks (and rewards) of the development. This may be the preferred (or only) strategy to create logical development parcels in areas that are largely abandoned or with absentee owners. The city of Philadelphia, as an example, is taking over 15,000 parcels, mostly vacant, originally occupied by narrow-front row houses, and replatting them for newer forms of development. This will allow full blocks or larger areas to be developed without regard for current lot lines and street patterns (McGovern 2006).

It is possible to lower the public financial commitment and risk by shifting the cost of installing much of the infrastructure to the ultimate developers of the replatted land. An example is the redevelopment of 42nd Street (Times Square) in New York City, where the high (and unpredictable) cost of renovating extensive subway stations was borne by the developers of the sites located above them (Sagalyn 2001). Coupled with the surgical use of expropriation, public-private partnerships can be effective in land assembly and development.

Land Assembly Districts
There is growing interest in the creation of *land assembly districts*, where entities are created to aggregate lands and interests and oversee their redevelopment,

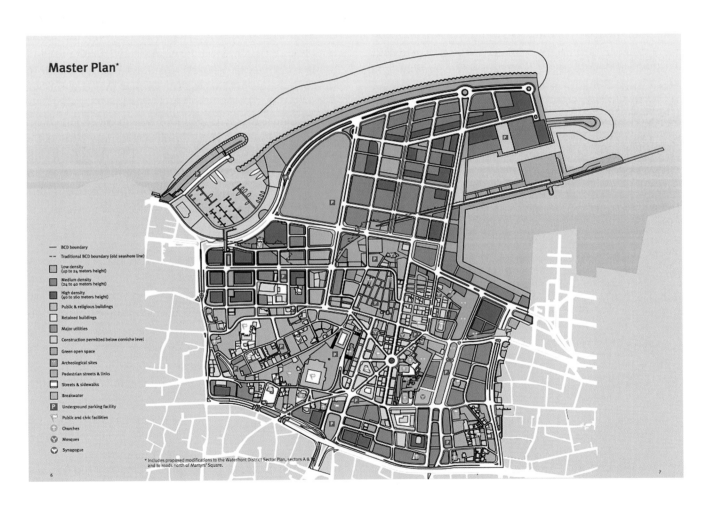

Master Plan*

— BCD boundary
-- Traditional BCD boundary (old seashore line)
Low density (up to 24 meters height)
Medium density (24 to 40 meters height)
High density (40 to 160 meters height)
Public & religious buildings
Retained buildings
Major utilities
Construction permitted below corniche level
Green open space
Archeological sites
Pedestrian streets & links
Streets & sidewalks
Breakwater
P Underground parking facility
Public and civic facilities
Churches
Mosques
Synagogue

* Includes proposed modifications to the Waterfront District Sector Plan, sectors A & and to roads north of Martyrs' Square.

16.10 Master plan for central Beirut, implemented through a land assembly district.
(Courtesy of Solidere)

as an alternative to public assembly of land (Heller and Hills 2009). In the Middle East these take the form of publicly *chartered real estate investment companies* or trusts (REICOs). The best-known and most successful example is Solidere, which is overseeing the redevelopment of central Beirut. There are several other working examples in Saudi Arabia and in other countries.

The land assembly district concept involves the compulsory exchange of lands and rights to lands for shares of an entity that will oversee the redevelopment of those lands. The company may also sell shares to investors who are not landowners in order to obtain development capital. Depending on how the land assembly entity is established, landowners may be given the opportunity to trade in their shares for development parcels once the land has been aggregated and resubdivided and after infrastructure has been installed. Or they may maintain their shares and be repaid, like other investors, through the proceeds of the land development activities, often realizing an excellent return on their capital.

In Beirut, two classes of shares were created in Solidere. Class A shares were given to original owners in exchange for their interests in the property (which included land, buildings, and leasehold interests). These shares may be exchanged for developable property or leases on redeveloped property, or they may be maintained as shares earning dividends. Class B shares were offered to outside investors to raise capital for the project; these provide only dividends, but may be bought or sold at prices established by the market. While the development has faced many challenges, the results of its efforts are impressive, and offer an effective counterpoint to land readjustment or public expropriation efforts in other countries.

Land assembly districts may also be voluntary. In neighborhoods with rapidly rising land values, owners have on occasion joined forces and pooled their lands in order to offer them to developers, with all owners sharing the proceeds. For this "buy-out" strategy to work, the financial incentives must be high: the value of the aggregated land parcels must be much greater as a redevelopment site than the sum of the individual parcel values. This form of land pooling requires all owners to participate, since rights-of-way, streets, and covenants must be adjusted to allow new development. In the Netherlands, there are examples where developers purchase adjacent properties and ask the municipality to serve as the pooling agent, so that the area can be developed more efficiently than if each site was developed independently (Hong and Needham 2007). Often the motivation is to ensure that the municipality delivers the needed infrastructure for the development. The number of such public-private developments is likely to increase as sites require joint efforts of governments and developers (Sagalyn 2007).

17 | Economic Value of Sites

The *economic value* of a site is determined by the uses that can be made of it. This simple statement masks an important paradox: uses determine a site's market value, but the purchase price of a site determines the range of uses that can be considered for it. Ultimately, market values of land approximate use values for the *highest and best use* of a site.

Land Markets

The value of a site is generally established by land markets, in which buyers and sellers negotiate an appropriate price for the site. The *fair market value* is defined as the price a willing buyer and a willing seller would agree upon, assuming each is reasonably knowledgeable and under no pressure to buy or sell. A look at comparable prices that have recently been paid for land in the vicinity of the site can offer an indication of its market value.

Each site is, of course, unique, so the prices of other sites (*comparables*) are never entirely comparable. Size of the site, access, physical characteristics, and orientation all matter, as do the reputation of the area, character of surroundings, and growth trajectory of the community. The allowable uses on the site (and the willingness of the local government to entertain other uses) will help determine the value, and the market for those uses will be important. Estimates of future price rises for land in the area will be *capitalized* into the sale price, and the value will be discounted for estimated time it will require to plan and get approval for development.

The land price will also take into account extraordinary costs and circumstances. A brownfield site, where there may be cleanup responsibilities, will be *discounted* to reflect this uncertainty. The price of sites with poor foundation conditions, or with wetlands that make portions impossible to develop, will reflect these added costs or limitations. Sites with rock outcroppings that will be difficult to service will be priced accordingly. Conservation restrictions or other easements on a site will need to be factored into the price.

Land *appraisals* will weigh each of these items, and seek to price each of the deviations from the comparables. Ultimately, a large measure of judgment will be needed to arrive at an estimate of the value of a parcel of land.

Determining Site Value Based on Uses

A site may have *intrinsic value* to an owner, based on the pleasure of controlling it and enjoying its use in an undeveloped state. In most cases, however, its economic value is determined by what can be earned by using it. These earnings may materialize through developing and selling the site, by creating uses on the site that return annual revenues, or some combination of the two.

Land value is the residual of the earnings obtained from a site less what it costs to make a productive use of it. Simply put:

$$LV = R - DC,$$
where
LV = land value,
R = revenue a site will produce,
DC = development cost to make the site productive.

Table 17.1 | Annual compound interest tables at 10%

Years	Amount of $1 at compound interest	Accumulation of $1 per period	Sinking fund factor	Present value of reversion of $1	Present value ord. annuity $1 per period	Installment to amortize $1
1	1.100000	1.000000	1.000000	0.909091	0.909091	1.100000
2	1.210000	2.100000	0.476190	0.826446	1.735537	0.576190
3	1.331000	3.310000	0.302115	0.751315	2.486852	0.402115
4	1.464100	4.641000	0.215471	0.683013	3.169865	0.315471
5	1.610510	6.105100	0.163797	0.620921	3.790787	0.263797
6	1.771561	7.715610	0.129607	0.564474	4.355261	0.229607
7	1.948717	9.487171	0.105405	0.513158	4.868419	0.205405
8	2.143589	11.435888	0.087444	0.466507	5.334926	0.187444
9	2.357948	13.579477	0.073641	0.424098	5.759024	0.173641
10	2.593742	15.937425	0.062745	0.385543	6.144567	0.162745
11	2.853117	18.531167	0.053963	0.350494	6.495061	0.153963
12	3.138428	21.384284	0.046763	0.318631	6.813692	0.146763
13	3.452271	24.522712	0.040779	0.289664	7.103356	0.140779
14	3.797498	27.974983	0.035746	0.263331	7.366687	0.135746
15	4.177248	31.772482	0.031474	0.239392	7.606080	0.131474
16	4.594973	35.949730	0.027817	0.217629	7.823709	0.127817
17	5.054470	40.544703	0.024664	0.197845	8.021553	0.124664
18	5.559917	45.599173	0.021930	0.179859	8.201412	0.121930
19	6.115909	51.159090	0.019547	0.163508	8.364920	0.119547
20	6.727500	57.274999	0.017460	0.148644	8.513564	0.117460
21	7.400250	64.002499	0.015624	0.135131	8.648694	0.115624
22	8.140275	71.402749	0.014005	0.122846	8.771540	0.114005
23	8.954302	79.543024	0.012572	0.111678	8.883218	0.112572
24	9.849733	88.497327	0.011300	0.101526	8.984744	0.111300
25	10.834706	98.347059	0.010168	0.092296	9.077040	0.110168
26	11.918177	109.181765	0.009159	0.083905	9.160945	0.109159
27	13.109994	121.099942	0.008258	0.076278	9.237223	0.108258
28	14.420994	134.209936	0.007451	0.069343	9.306567	0.107451
29	15.863093	148.630930	0.006728	0.063039	9.369606	0.106728
30	17.449402	164.494023	0.006079	0.057309	9.426914	0.106079
31	19.194342	181.943425	0.005496	0.052099	9.479013	0.105496
32	21.113777	201.137767	0.004972	0.047362	9.526376	0.104972
33	23.225154	222.251544	0.004499	0.043057	9.569432	0.104499
34	25.547670	245.476699	0.004074	0.039143	9.608575	0.104074
35	28.102437	271.024368	0.003690	0.035584	9.644159	0.103690
36	30.912681	299.126805	0.003343	0.032349	9.676508	0.103343
37	34.003949	330.039486	0.003030	0.029408	9.705917	0.103040
38	37.404343	364.043434	0.002747	0.026735	9.732651	0.102747
39	41.144778	401.447778	0.002491	0.024304	9.756956	0.102491
40	45.259256	442.592556	0.002259	0.022095	9.779051	0.102259
41	49.785181	487.851811	0.002050	0.020086	9.799137	0.102050
42	54.763699	537.636992	0.001860	0.018260	9.817397	0.101860
43	60.240069	592.400692	0.001688	0.016600	9.833998	0.101688
44	66.264076	652.640761	0.001532	0.015091	9.849089	0.101532
45	72.890484	718.904837	0.001391	0.013719	9.862808	0.101391
46	80.179532	791.795321	0.001263	0.012472	9.875280	0.101263
47	88.197485	871.974853	0.001147	0.011338	9.886618	0.101147
48	97.017234	960.172338	0.001041	0.010307	9.896926	0.101041
49	106.718957	1057.189572	0.000946	0.009370	9.906296	0.100946
50	117.390853	1163.908529	0.000859	0.008519	9.914814	0.100859

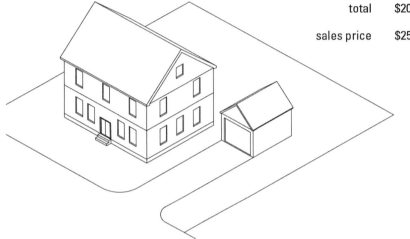

SINGLE HOUSE ON ONE LOT

cost to build home & garage	$150,000
marketing costs	$10,000
interest during construction	$12,000
taxes during construction	$4,000
total cost	$176,000
profit expected	$26,400
total	$202,400
sales price	$250,000

17.1 Single house on one lot.
(Adam Tecza/Gary Hack)

However, since revenues seldom appear instantaneously, and a site owner needs to invest money before obtaining returns, the cost of capital must be accounted for. Thus, the revenue a site produces must be discounted to determine its *present value,* accounting for the fact that $1 received a year from now is not the same as $1 received today. Annual compound interest tables, widely available on the Internet, provide factors for both accumulations for investments and present value of funds obtained in the future.

Pro Forma Financial Analysis

When development of a site extends over several years and the cost of capital must be accounted for, a *spreadsheet* is a useful tool for constructing a *pro forma financial analysis.*

Consider the simplest case, shown in figure 17.1. A builder wishes to purchase a lot to construct and sell a single house. He estimates that the cost of producing the house, including interest and taxes, will be $202,400, and believes it can be sold for $250,000, within the year it was built. The site, based on the residual value, has an estimated worth of $47,600.

A slightly more complex case is shown in figure 17.2. A developer wishes to purchase a 3.6 ac (1.5 ha) site to develop 10 houses. He estimates it will require almost three years to construct the houses, and that all will be sold by the end of year 3. He constructs a simple spreadsheet to ascertain the present value of his net revenues, and therefore what he can afford to pay for the site. As pro forma 1 (table 17.2) reveals, based on his initial assumptions, the site would have a present value of roughly $170,000, or $47,000 per ac ($116,000 per ha).

17.2 Schematic plan of 3.6 ac (1.5 ha) site with 10 houses.
(Adam Tecza/Gary Hack)

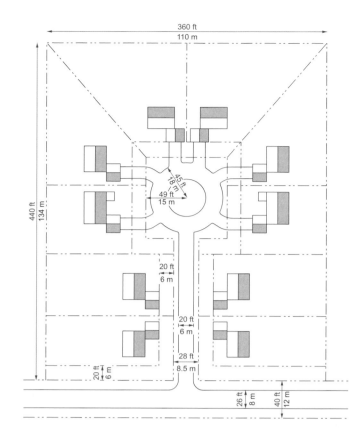

Table 17.2 | Pro forma 1 for 10-house development

	Total	Year 1	Year 2	Year 3
Number of units completed	10	3	6	1
Number of units sold	10	2	5	3
Costs				
Infrastructure	150,000	150,000	–	–
Unit construction	1,500,000	450,000	900,000	150,000
Marketing and sales	90,000	27,000	54,000	9,000
Taxes	57,000	19,000	26,000	12,000
Insurance	26,000	6,000	14,000	6,000
Interest on construction work in progress	153,585	48,900	104,685	–
Total costs	1,976,585	700,900	1,098,685	177,000
Revenues (sales proceeds)	2,500,000	500,000	1,250,000	750,000
Revenues – costs	523,415	(200,900)	151,315	573,000
Less development fee and profit	296,488	–	–	296,488
Net revenues	226,927			
Outstanding loan balance		200,900	49,585	–
Year-end position		(200,900)	(49,585)	226,927
Present value of revenues	170,494			170,494
Residual value of land				
Present value per sq ft	1.08			
Present value per ac	46,839			

Note: All figures in US dollars. Simplifying assumptions: total project cost is financed with loan at 15% interest; deficits are financed; development fee and profit at 15% of total costs taken when loan is repaid; present value at 10% discount rate.
Source: Lynne Sagalyn/Gary Hack.

The spreadsheet also allows other assumptions to be entertained. Suppose the asking price for the site is considerably higher than his initial pro forma reveals. The developer wonders what the results would be if he were able to sell the houses for 10% more, or $275,000 per unit, rather than the $250,000 previously estimated. Pro forma 2 (table 17.3) indicates that the value per acre would rise considerably to about $115,000 ($283,000 per ha). Thus, a 10% increase in revenues implies a 64% increase in the land price that can be paid! Or, the developer wonders, what would the value be if the $250,000 sale price prevailed but I lowered my development fee and profit expectations from 15% to 10%? Pro forma 3 (table 17.4) estimates, on this basis, that the site would be worth $67,000 per ac ($165,000 per ha)—a more modewst increase than if the sale price of the units is higher.

The spreadsheet allows the developer to consider other possible forms of development as well, plugging in new data for construction costs, sale prices, and schedules of development. The developer can quickly answer: What if I were to construct 20 semidetached housing units on the site rather than the 10 detached units considered thus far? This may mean lower costs of construction for the smaller units, and lower sale prices, but how would it affect the value of the site? Estimates such as these, even if done crudely, will help avoid mistakes in purchasing sites and establishing programs for them.

Table 17.3 | Pro forma 2 for 10-house development, with higher sale price

	Total	Year 1	Year 2	Year 3
Number of units completed	10	3	6	1
Number of units sold	10	2	5	3
Costs				
Infrastructure	150,000	150,000	–	–
Unit construction	1,500,000	450,000	900,000	150,000
Marketing and sales	90,000	27,000	54,000	9,000
Taxes	57,000	19,000	26,000	12,000
Insurance	26,000	6,000	14,000	6,000
Interest on construction work in progress	100,815	48,900	51,915	–
Total costs	1,923,815	700,900	1,045,915	177,000
Revenues (sales proceeds)	2,750,000	550,000	1,375,000	825,000
Revenues – costs	826,185	(150,900)	329,085	648,000
Less development fee and profit	288,572	–	–	288,572
Net revenues	537,613			
Outstanding loan balance		150,900	–	–
Year-end position		(150,900)	178,185	359,428
Present value of revenues	417,296		147,252	270,043
Residual value of land				
Present value per sq ft	2.63			
Present value per ac	114,642			

Note: All figures in US dollars. Simplifying assumptions: total project cost is financed with loan at 15% interest; deficits are financed; development fee and profit at 15% of total costs taken when loan is repaid; present value at 10% discount rate.
Source: Lynne Sagalyn/Gary Hack.

Table 17.4 | Pro forma 3 for 10-house development, with lower profit expectations

	Total	Year 1	Year 2	Year 3
Number of units completed	10	3	6	1
Number of units sold	10	2	5	3
Costs				
Infrastructure	150,000	150,000	–	–
Unit construction	1,500,000	450,000	900,000	150,000
Marketing and sales	90,000	27,000	54,000	9,000
Taxes	57,000	19,000	26,000	12,000
Insurance	26,000	6,000	14,000	6,000
Interest on construction work in progress	153,585	48,900	104,685	–
Total costs	1,976,585	700,900	1,098,685	177,000
Revenues (sales proceeds)	2,500,000	500,000	1,250,000	750,000
Revenues – costs	523,415	(200,900)	151,315	573,000
Less development fee and profit	197,659	–	–	197,659
Net revenues	325,757			
Outstanding loan balance		200,900	49,585	–
Year-end position		(200,900)	(49,585)	325,757
Present value of revenues	244,746			244,746
Residual value of land				
Present value per sq ft	1.55			
Present value per ac	67,238			

Note: All figures in US dollars. Simplifying assumptions: total project cost is financed with loan at 15% interest; deficits are financed; development fee and profit at 10% of total costs taken when loan is repaid; present value at 10% discount rate.
Source: Lynne Sagalyn/Gary Hack.

Estimating Investment Return

So far we have used a pro forma analysis to estimate the residual value that may be paid to acquire a site, assuming a specific program for its use. The same form of analysis may also be used in reverse: given a specific asking price for a site, what would the returns to a landowner be if particular uses were developed on the site? There are a variety of metrics for assessing the return on a site development project. The simplest is to compare the net revenues for the project to the total net cost of the investment, which indicates the *unleveraged return on investment* (ROI). But this nominal return may be misleading, since there is a time value to money; a better measure is the *present value ROI*—discounting revenues to reflect when they are received and costs to reflect when they are incurred. This return metric estimates the gain as if the developer was investing the entire cost of purchase and improvement of the land without taking a loan for the project. However, since most developers are likely to finance a portion of their costs with debt, the more meaningful measure may be the *leveraged return on investment* or *return on equity* (*ROE*).

To calculate the ROI, enter the acquisition and development costs of the site and structures built on it in the cost portion of the spreadsheet, along with any operating costs for each year. Revenues are then inserted, each year's net revenues or costs are then calculated, and the present value of the returns is computed, using an appropriate *discount rate*.

Then:

ROI = PV returns/PV capital invested.

This analysis is shown in simplified form in table 17.5, using the 10-unit subdivision of homes shown previously. Assuming that the site is purchased for $180,000, the estimated unleveraged nominal ROI is 17.7%. But when revenues are discounted to reflect the year they are received, the return is negative. Hence the caution about assessing the investment return by comparing the nominal costs and revenues.

But what if the developer had supplied only part of the equity needed, borrowing the remainder, using what developers call leverage? If the developer had supplied only 25% of the necessary equity, our analysis

Table 17.5 | Estimating ROI for 10-house development

	Total	Year 1	Year 2	Year 3
Number of units completed	10	3	6	1
Number of units sold	10	2	5	3
Costs				
Purchase of site	180,000	180,000	–	–
Infrastructure	150,000	150,000	–	–
Unit construction	1,500,000	450,000	900,000	150,000
Marketing and sales	90,000	27,000	54,000	9,000
Taxes	57,000	19,000	26,000	12,000
Insurance	26,000	6,000	14,000	6,000
Total costs	2,003,000	832,000	994,000	177,000
Revenues (sales proceeds)	2,500,000	500,000	1,250,000	750,000
Revenues − costs	497,000	(332,000)	256,000	573,000
Less development fee (6%)	120,180	–	–	120,180
Net revenues	376,820			
Outstanding loan balance		200,900	49,585	–
Year-end position		(332,000)	(76,000)	376,820
Return metrics, unleveraged analysis				
Nominal return on investment (ROI)	17.7%			
Present value of year-end position	(81,484)	(301,788)	(62,806)	283,111
Present-value ROI	negative			
Return metrics, leveraged ROE (75% loan)				
25% equity	568,351			
Interest on construction work in progress	150,225	62,400	74,550	13,275
Total project costs	2,273,405			
Nominal return on equity (ROE)	39.9%			
Present value of revenues	2,050,986	454,500	1,033,000	563,486
Present value of costs (including interest on construction work in progress)		813,010	883,050	233,249
Present value of net revenues	121,677			
Present-value ROE	21.4%			

Note: All figures in US dollars. Assumptions: interest rate for construction work in progress 15%; discount rate 10%.
Source: Lynne Sagalyn/Gary Hack.

suggests that the nominal ROI would increase to 39.9%. In present value terms, the project would turn from a negative investment to one with a ROE of 21.4%. It should not be surprising that most developers seek to leverage their capital on every project.

On many sites, the return is not received immediately through sales, but through lease revenues that continue for long periods of time. At the end of the lease period, the site will have a *residual or terminal value* that may be significant—representing what it could be sold for upon expiration of the lease. This also must enter the equation in order to compute a present value. It is worth noting that the present value of funds received 30 years in the future is quite small, particularly if the discount rate is high—about $0.06 for each dollar received at the end of the lease term with a 10% discount rate. It nonetheless contributes to the bottom line.

Financial Rules of Thumb

Rules of thumb are dangerous necessities. Often decisions need to be made quickly to avoid wasting time on possibilities that are unlikely to prove feasible. Many developers have a sense of the rough parameters of site value, and apply them in advance of more precise financial analyses. These are highly specific to city and location, and since most developers are locally rooted (and if they are not, they will draw upon local expertise), they will have rules of thumb at their fingertips.

An example is the fraction of end costs that site costs should represent. Typically for suburban or outlying residential developments in the US, site acquisition typically should not exceed 25–30% of the end cost of a unit. Of course, for downtown development, the site costs may be a larger fraction, as it will be for high-prestige areas where buyers will pay a premium for location. Conversely, for high-density development, where construction costs are higher, site acquisition may also need to be a smaller fraction. On sites where office development is being contemplated, the intensity must be factored in. Developers often speak in terms of the *FAR value*—the amount that it would be appropriate to pay for the right to build 1 sq ft of office space on a site. If that value is $30 per FAR-sq ft, and (as in a suburban development) the expected FAR = 0.35,

then a site value of $10 per sq ft would be justified. On a downtown site, the comparable figure might be $50 per FAR-sq ft, and with an expected FAR = 8 the justifiable site value would be $400 per sq ft. In the largest US cities, such as New York, the FAR value can be $800 per sq ft or higher for residential sites.

Such figures vary enormously from country to country. While land is relatively inexpensive in the US because there are fewer barriers to development, in Europe and Asia land constitutes a much larger fraction of the final cost of a project. In Japan, site costs are often 80% of the cost of development, and in Korea 70%. In Europe they may be as high as 60% of the total development costs, although there is great variation. In many European cities, governments write down the costs to encourage development, so there may be several distinct land markets from city to city.

The site planner would be wise to acquire rules of thumb for specific areas of practice to help in first-cut judgments about the economics of site development. For large projects, it is critical to collaborate with professionals who have a detailed sense of the market for land and space.

Financial Planning for Site Development

The financial analyses explained here can help determine whether a site is worth purchasing, and the forms of development that are feasible for it. Financial analysis should proceed hand in hand with site design. At the earliest conceptual stage when maps and physical models are being created, their equivalent financial model consisting of a spreadsheet should be developed using rough estimates of costs and revenues. As the plans evolve and become more precise, the model will be elaborated into a full financial pro forma.

The ultimate objective is to produce a pro forma that can be translated directly into a plan for managing the development. The *financial plan*, along with the logic of the site plan, will determine the timing of infrastructure and development phases. As the project accumulates the experience of contracting for site improvements and marketing or constructing the structures on the land, the financial plan will need to be fine-tuned. Large development projects will undoubtedly need to navigate through economic storms, and by constantly adjusting the financial plan to reflect the realities of expenditures and best estimates of the future, the project can avoid flying blind. The financial plan may reveal that the site plan also needs to be refined to reflect shifting markets and opportunities.

Figure 17.3 is a site plan for a proposed *traditional neighborhood development* (*TND*) that indicates the allocation of land and layout of the site. Figure 17.4 is the corresponding financial pro forma for the site, indicating the expenditures necessary to install infrastructure and the expected revenues from the sale of lots. Since this project is a partnership between the original landowner and the developer, raw land is moved into the venture as lots are serviced, a practice that is becoming more common to buffer the risks of delay and market cycles. As the pro forma indicates, the project is expected to yield an *internal rate of return* (*IRR*) of 85.9%. As fate would have it, the lots came to market in the midst of a financial crisis for housing, and the pro forma has needed to be reworked several times.

One important discipline in creating a financial plan for a large land development project is based on the recognition that such a project is inevitably two separate projects—creating the sites for development

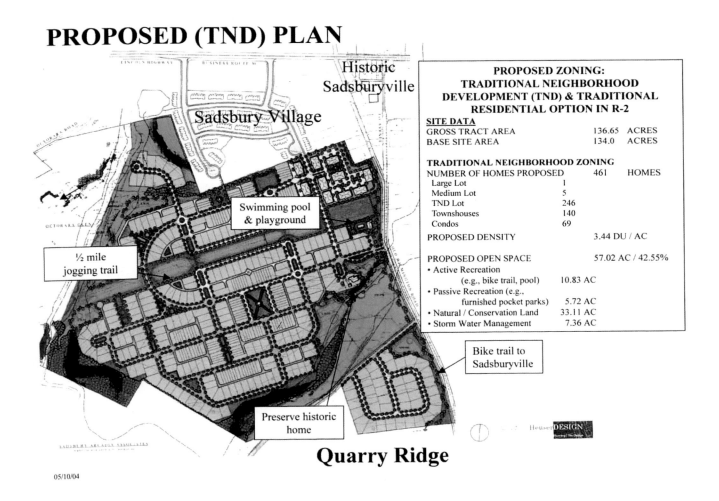

17.3 Site plan, Sadsbury traditional neighborhood development, Pennsylvania, with allocation of land uses.
(Courtesy of W. Joseph Duckworth/Arcadia Land)

	Per Lot	Total	Year 2003	Year 2004	Year 2005	Year 2006	Year 2007	Year 2008	Year 2009	Year 2010	Year 2011	Year 2012	Year 2013
REVENUE													
Unimproved lot sales	Per Lot (2004)	41	0	0	41	0	0	0	0	0	0	0	0
Large Lot	$ -	$ -	$ -	$ -	$ -	$ -	$ -	$ -	$ -	$ -	$ -	$ -	$ -
Medium Lot	$50,000	100,402			100,402								
TND Lot	$50,000	1,957,835			1,957,835								
Townhouses	$ -	-											
Condos	$ -	-											
Total		2,058,237			2,058,237								
Improved lot sales	Per Lot (2004)	420	0	0	0	22	49	84	83	67	84	31	0
Large Lot	$85,000	87,795				87,795							
Medium Lot	$85,000	311,958					94,089			217,869			
TND Lot	$85,000	21,193,985				1,874,098	3,339,397	3,506,798	3,581,356	2,252,215	4,059,601	2,580,520	
Townhouses	$60,000	9,972,384					800,232	3,300,515	3,465,579	2,406,058			
Condos	$50,000	4,570,725								772,077	3,184,001	614,647	
Total		36,136,647				1,961,893	4,233,719	6,807,313	7,046,935	5,648,219	7,243,602	3,195,167	
Sale of existing farm buildings		50,000			$50,000								
Gross revenue		38,245,084			2,108,237	1,961,893	4,233,719	6,807,313	7,046,935	5,648,219	7,243,602	3,195,167	
Settlement costs		572,926			30,874	29,428	63,506	102,110	105,704	84,723	108,654	47,927	
Net Revenue		37,672,158			2,077,364	1,932,464	4,170,213	6,705,203	6,941,231	5,563,496	7,134,948	3,147,239	
COST OF GOODS SOLD													
Land acquisition	Per lot (2003)	461	0	0	94	0	123	119	0	125	0	0	0
Large Lot	$20,000	20,827			20,827								
Medium Lot	$16,800	97,393			34,989		18,821			43,582			
TND Lot	$14,400	4,066,466			1,364,564		790,503	902,780		1,008,619			
Townhouses	$10,000	1,625,615					817,839	807,776					
Condos	$7,500	671,245								671,245			
Total		6,481,545			1,420,379		1,627,163	1,710,555		1,723,447			
Site improvements													
Fees and Permits		386,975			33,523	27,428	112,068	60,435	49,447	104,075			
Survey		227,138			19,676	16,099	65,779	35,473	29,023	61,088			
Erosion Control		273,238			23,670	19,366	79,129	42,673	34,914	73,486			
Clearing		67,300			5,830	4,770	19,490	10,511	8,600	18,100			
Site Excavation		2,119,000		50,000	224,900	143,100	584,700	315,315	257,985	543,000			
Sanitary Sewer System		1,177,750			102,025	83,475	341,075	183,934	150,491	316,750			
Storm Sewer System		1,682,500			145,750	119,250	487,250	262,763	214,988	452,500			
Water Distribution System		1,346,000			116,600	95,400	389,800	210,210	171,990	362,000			
Public Utilities		1,009,500			87,450	71,550	292,350	157,658	128,993	271,500			
Site Lights and Signs		336,500			29,150	23,850	97,450	52,553	42,998	90,500			
Curbs		538,400			46,640	38,160	155,920	84,084	68,796	144,800			
Paving - Interior Roads		1,682,500			145,750	119,250	487,250	262,763	214,988	452,500			
Paving - Exterior Roads		117,775			10,203	8,348	34,108	18,393	15,049	31,675			
Sidewalks / Aprons		302,850			26,235	21,465	87,705	47,297	38,698	81,450			
Dedication		841,250			72,875	59,625	243,625	131,381	107,494	226,250			
Site Maintenance		286,025			24,778	20,273	82,833	44,670	36,548	76,925			
Site Landscaping		1,177,750			102,025	83,475	341,075	183,934	150,491	316,750			
Amenities		1,250,000			50,000		700,000		100,000	400,000			
Hard cost contingency		1,477,245		5,000	121,708	95,488	460,161	210,404	182,149	402,335			
$ 25,221,059 Total		16,299,696		55,000	1,388,786	1,050,371	5,061,766	2,314,449	2,003,640	4,425,683			
Sewer fees/AIM reimbursement - EDU		2,439,819			447,187	-	622,252	646,994	-	723,386			
Sadsbury Twp Bldg and Garage		1,050,000			850,000	-	-	-	200,000	-			
Total cost of goods sold		26,221,059		55,000	4,056,353	1,050,371	7,311,181	4,671,998	2,203,640	6,872,516	-	-	-
Gross margin		11,451,099	-	(55,000)	(2,028,989)	882,094	(3,140,968)	2,033,205	4,737,591	(1,309,020)	7,134,948	3,147,239	

projects by installing infrastructure and receiving approvals, followed by constructing buildings on individual lots. The site developer may build on the lots or may sell them to others realizing their market value. This approach avoids the pitfall of assuming that cost overruns on land development will be made up by overperformance of the commercial projects, or conversely that land parcels can be repriced to account for underperformance of commercial projects. More than one large development has floundered as a result of failing to distinguish between the two aspects of site development.

Enhancing the Value of a Site

Site planning needs to be mindful of the requisites of a fair return from site development, but it can also enhance the value of a site through the skillful planning of buildings and public spaces. Many ideas about value creation have long been incorporated into the site planner's toolkit, and public policies have been designed to create the incentives necessary to induce developers to deliver public goods (Hack and Sagalyn 2011). Some of the most important *value creation* strategies include:

	Total	Year 2003	Year 2004	Year 2005	Year 2006	Year 2007	Year 2008	Year 2009	Year 2010	Year 2011	Year 2012	Year 2013
SOFT COSTS												
Architecture	$ 80,147	$ -	$ 5,997	$ 11,150	$ 3,300	$ 7,350	$ 12,600	$ 12,450	$ 10,050	$ 12,600	$ 4,650	$ -
Charitable Contributions	$ 4,650	$ -	$ 650	$ 500	$ 500	$ 500	$ 500	$ 500	$ 500	$ 500	$ 500	$ -
Engineering - Site	$ 603,847	$ -	$ 104,797	$ 113,700	$ 129,150	$ -	$ 124,950	$ 131,250	$ -	$ -	$ -	$ -
Engineering - Geotechnical Studies	$ 40,000	$ -	$ -	$ 10,000	$ 10,000	$ -	$ 10,000	$ 10,000	$ -	$ -	$ -	$ -
Engineering - Plan Sets	$ 9,500	$ -	$ 500	$ 3,000	$ 2,000	$ -	$ 2,000	$ 2,000	$ -	$ -	$ -	$ -
Engineering - Pump Station	$ -	$ -	$ -	$ -	$ -	$ -	$ -	$ -	$ -	$ -	$ -	$ -
Engineering - Sewage Treatment Plant	$ -	$ -	$ -	$ -	$ -	$ -	$ -	$ -	$ -	$ -	$ -	$ -
Entitlements Consultant	$ -	$ -	$ -	$ -	$ -	$ -	$ -	$ -	$ -	$ -	$ -	$ -
Environmental	$ 27,712	$ -	$ 12,712	$ 15,000	$ -	$ -	$ -	$ -	$ -	$ -	$ -	$ -
Fiscal Impact Studies	$ 4,110	$ -	$ 4,110	$ -	$ -	$ -	$ -	$ -	$ -	$ -	$ -	$ -
Government Fees - Other	$ 24,280	$ -	$ 9,280	$ 15,000	$ -	$ -	$ -	$ -	$ -	$ -	$ -	$ -
Government Fees - Sadsbury Township	$ 97,028	$ -	$ 82,028	$ 15,000	$ -	$ -	$ -	$ -	$ -	$ -	$ -	$ -
Insurance	$ 73,862	$ -	$ 250	$ 6,085	$ 4,774	$ 23,008	$ 10,520	$ 9,107	$ 20,117	$ -	$ -	$ -
Land Planning - Township Building	$ 3,500	$ -	$ 1,000	$ 2,500	$ -	$ -	$ -	$ -	$ -	$ -	$ -	$ -
Land Planning - Other	$ 63,911	$ -	$ 63,911	$ -	$ -	$ -	$ -	$ -	$ -	$ -	$ -	$ -
Landscape Architecture	$ 35,329	$ -	$ 5,329	$ 30,000	$ -	$ -	$ -	$ -	$ -	$ -	$ -	$ -
Legal Fees	$ 182,575	$ -	$ 53,575	$ 51,000	$ 12,000	$ 12,000	$ 12,000	$ 12,000	$ 12,000	$ 12,000	$ 6,000	$ -
Market Research	$ -	$ -	$ -	$ -	$ -	$ -	$ -	$ -	$ -	$ -	$ -	$ -
Marketing and Public Relations	$ 8,173	$ -	$ 3,173	$ 5,000	$ -	$ -	$ -	$ -	$ -	$ -	$ -	$ -
Office Supplies	$ 9,725	$ -	$ 125	$ 1,200	$ 1,200	$ 1,200	$ 1,200	$ 1,200	$ 1,200	$ 1,200	$ 1,200	$ -
Postage/Shipping	$ 3,387	$ -	$ 987	$ 300	$ 300	$ 300	$ 300	$ 300	$ 300	$ 300	$ 300	$ -
Professional Fees	$ 28,280	$ -	$ 1,280	$ 3,000	$ 3,000	$ 3,000	$ 3,000	$ 3,000	$ 3,000	$ 3,000	$ 3,000	$ 3,000
Property/Project Management	$ 57,500	$ -	$ 1,500	$ 4,500	$ 24,500	$ 9,000	$ 4,500	$ 4,500	$ 9,000	$ -	$ -	$ -
Property Taxes	$ 50,000	$ -	$ -	$ 10,000	$ 10,000	$ 10,000	$ 10,000	$ 10,000	$ -	$ -	$ -	$ -
Reference Material	$ 2,035	$ -	$ 2,035	$ -	$ -	$ -	$ -	$ -	$ -	$ -	$ -	$ -
Reimbursable Expenses	$ (5,203)	$ -	$ (5,203)	$ -	$ -	$ -	$ -	$ -	$ -	$ -	$ -	$ -
Reproduction and Presentation	$ 9,783	$ -	$ 5,783	$ 2,000	$ 500	$ 500	$ 500	$ 500	$ -	$ -	$ -	$ -
Traffic	$ 26,817	$ -	$ 11,817	$ 15,000	$ -	$ -	$ -	$ -	$ -	$ -	$ -	$ -
Travel & Meals	$ 3,046	$ -	$ 2,246	$ 800	$ -	$ -	$ -	$ -	$ -	$ -	$ -	$ -
Total soft costs	$ 1,443,995	$ -	$ 367,883	$ 314,735	$ 201,224	$ 66,858	$ 192,070	$ 196,807	$ 56,167	$ 29,600	$ 15,650	$ 3,000
Cash flow from operations	$ 10,007,104	$ -	$ (422,883)	$ (2,343,725)	$ 680,869	$ (3,207,826)	$ 1,841,135	$ 4,540,784	$ (1,365,187)	$ 7,105,348	$ 3,131,589	$ (3,000)
FINANCING												
Bank fees and loan closing costs	$ 600,000	$ -	$ -	$ 150,000	$ -	$ 150,000	$ 150,000	$ -	$ 150,000	$ -	$ -	$ -
Loan balance (beg of period)	$ -	$ -	$ -	$ -	$ 3,240,351	$ 3,050,626	$ 7,552,113	$ 7,489,005	$ 4,629,515	$ 7,669,115	$ 2,558,863	$ 219,047
Loan draws	$ 25,116,059	$ -	$ -	$ 3,206,353	$ 1,050,371	$ 7,311,181	$ 4,671,998	$ 2,003,640	$ 6,872,516	$ -	$ -	$ -
Interest accrued	$ 2,219,133	$ -	$ -	$ 33,998	$ 231,324	$ 365,595	$ 370,379	$ 422,071	$ 403,248	$ 322,449	$ 56,559	$ 13,510
Debt service	$ (27,102,635)	$ -	$ -	$ -	$ (1,471,419)	$ (3,175,289)	$ (5,105,485)	$ (5,285,202)	$ (4,236,164)	$ (5,432,701)	$ (2,396,375)	$ -
Loan balance (end of period)	$ 232,557	$ -	$ -	$ 3,240,351	$ 3,050,626	$ 7,552,113	$ 7,489,005	$ 4,629,515	$ 7,669,115	$ 2,558,863	$ 219,047	$ 232,557
Capital calls from LPs	$ 715,408	$ -	$ 435,000	$ 280,408	$ -	$ -	$ -	$ -	$ -	$ -	$ -	$ -
Cash flow after financing activities	$ 8,085,935	$ -	$ 12,117	$ 993,036	$ 259,820	$ 778,066	$ 1,257,648	$ 1,259,222	$ 1,121,165	$ 1,672,646	$ 735,214	$ (3,000)
AH fee paid (9% of net rev)	$ 3,385,994	$ -	$ -	$ 182,463	$ 125,968	$ 423,273	$ 603,468	$ 624,711	$ 500,715	$ 642,145	$ 283,252	$ -
Capital distributions to LPs	$ 4,700,041	$ -	$ -	$ 734,535	$ 139,289	$ 337,612	$ 654,180	$ 634,512	$ 620,450	$ 1,030,501	$ 454,463	$ 94,500
IRR	85.90%											
Net change in cash during period	$ (100)	$ -	$ 12,117	$ 76,039	$ (5,437)	$ 17,181	$ -	$ -	$ -	$ -	$ (2,500)	$ (97,500)
Cash account (beg of period)	$ 100	$ 100	$ 100	$ 12,217	$ 88,256	$ 82,819	$ 100,000	$ 100,000	$ 100,000	$ 100,000	$ 100,000	$ 97,500
Cash account (end of period)	$ -	$ 100	$ 12,217	$ 88,256	$ 82,819	$ 100,000	$ 100,000	$ 100,000	$ 100,000	$ 100,000	$ 97,500	$ -

17.4 (this and facing page) Pro forma financial plan for Sadsbury traditional neighborhood development, showing 11-year development period.
(Courtesy of W. Joseph Duckworth/Arcadia Land)

Urban Design

Approved master plans offer an assurance of stability that can enhance the value of sites. When developers face uncertainty over their entitlements for a site, they customarily discount its value to reflect the risk of reaching an agreement with local authorities. A lengthy approvals process can affect the timing of development and can cause developers to miss favorable periods in the economic cycle, increasing the costs of holding the site. The possibility that future development on an adjacent site might block views or access, or take away market advantage by flooding the market with competitive uses, will also be reflected in what developers are willing to pay for a site. They dislike uncertainty even more than costs that are substantial but certain.

For large sites that will be built out over many years, obtaining entitlements for future phases will add considerable value. Coupling this with design guidelines will offer future developers the predictability they are seeking. Lots at Seaside, Florida sold for several times the amounts of their counterparts in nearby developments, despite the fact that they were smaller in area, came with detailed requirements for the form and

17.5 Certainty of the future built environment and consistency of requirements greatly enhanced site values at Seaside, Florida. (Gary Hack)

nature of what could be built, and had significant annual fees to pay for maintenance of the common spaces. As development proceeds and is shown to be successful, site developers reap the increasing value of future sites. Hence a common strategy is to leave the best sites to the final phases, where the greatest appreciation can be achieved.

Density

Increasing the amount of building allowed on a site is the surest way to create value that can be tapped to offset the cost of public spaces and amenities. In New York City and many other American cities, *incentive zoning* offers the opportunity to increase the allowable floor area ratio in exchange for specific public purposes—improving a subway station, creating a public open space, incorporating affordable housing, preserving a historic structure, preserving or creating a legitimate theater or other cultural venue, among others. In the best of such schemes, the amount of additional development allowed more than covers the costs of the public goods, making it advantageous to elect the bonus (Kayden 1978).

Zoning recently passed for the Hudson Yards District of midtown Manhattan introduced a sophisticated system of incentives aimed at accomplishing the site development plan adopted by the city. On the most intensively used sites, developers can increase their allowable FAR from the base level of 10 to as much as 33 by purchasing additional development rights (a "District Improvement Bonus") at $113 per sq ft of additional buildable space, a figure that rises with inflation,

17.6 Site plan for Hudson Yards, New York City, includes open spaces, transit extensions, and cultural amenities paid for by bonus FAR that developers may purchase. (NYC Department of City Planning)

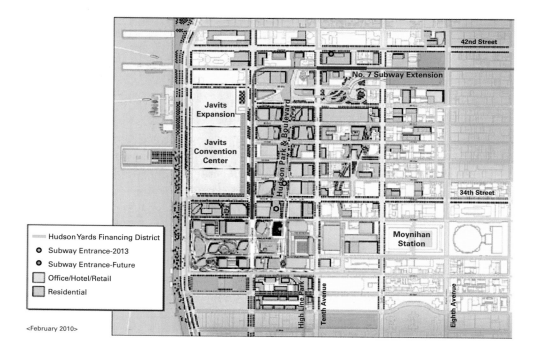

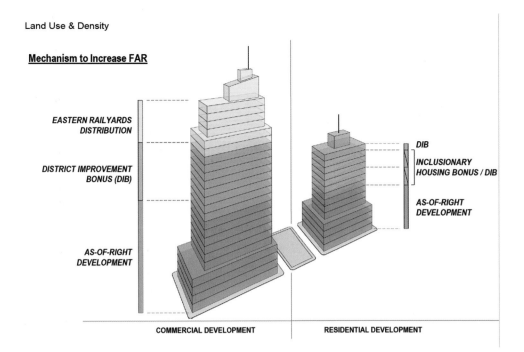

with the funds paid going directly into the creation of open spaces, a grand boulevard, infrastructure, and transit facilities in the area. Bonuses are offered for inclusionary housing, and developers may also purchase and transfer rights from other lower-density areas to increase their development from a base FAR of 6.5 to as much as 12. Through this system of transfers and purchases of development rights, the built form, infrastructure, and amenities needed to make Hudson Yards a viable and lively district of the city will largely be self-financed.

Building Heights and Views

Even if the intensity of development is strictly regulated, allowing buildings to be taller can have a powerful impact on the value of a site. A review of office leasing prices in US cities suggests values increase in direct proportion to height, especially for space above the height of adjacent structures that block views. In midtown New York, a rule of thumb is that office rents rise $.50 per sq ft per floor, increasing from about $45 at the base of a 60-story building to $75 at the top, an increment of 68%. Iconic views can command even greater rents: a view of

Central Park can push rents to $100, a 122% increment. In other American cities, height similarly increases office value: 20–45% in Chicago, 20–50% in Boston, 20–30% in San Francisco—in all cases, the value gain depends upon the type of views and the height of surrounding buildings.

Height can add considerable value to residential buildings as well. In New York, the value of apartments increases by 0.5–2% on each higher floor, depending upon the quality of views. In Vancouver, the comparable figure is 2.5% per floor. In Bellingham, Washington, single-family houses with full ocean view were priced almost 60% higher than comparable houses without the view (Benson et al. 1998).

The experience in other countries is similar. In Hong Kong, the sale value of residential units with distant views was found to be only 3% higher than units with no views, but units facing mountains directly behind the development were discounted by 6% (Jim and Chen 2009). In the Netherlands, a house with scenic views of water could attract a price 10–12% above those without (Luttik 2000). In the old town of Guangzhou, China, houses with a river view were priced 6% higher than those without.

17.8 Development regulations in North False Creek, Vancouver, Canada encourage tall buildings to be located to maximize views to distant mountains and open spaces provided by the developer. (Gary Hack)

17.9 Houses that face Louisburg Square, Boston, have a value 60% greater than nearby houses not facing green spaces. (Darling Kindersley Ltd/Alamy Stock Photo)

Open Spaces

There is plenty of both anecdotal and empirical evidence on the value of open spaces as an amenity. Housing in the blocks facing Central Park in New York commands a significantly higher value than that even one block distant—perhaps 10–20% more. Units facing the park typically are valued at least 20% more than units in the same building without park views. This has led to an explosion of super-tall towers in New York, some rising to over 100 stories to command views of Central Park. Researchers in Turkey found that the price of a house was increased by 20–33% by the presence of 7–14 m² of green space per capita on a housing site (Altunkasa and Uslu 2004), a figure comparable to what many cities call for in their regulations. Finnish studies pegged the incremental value lower, with apartments adjacent to open spaces selling for about 7% more than units 500 m away, although this may reflect the generous amount of open space surrounding the city studied (Tyrvainen 1997; Tyrvainen and Miettinen 2000). Where the adjacent open space is a golf course, a California study found that it added 7.6% to property values on average (Do and Grudnitski 1995). Earlier studies of the value of undeveloped land in Philadelphia and Boulder, Colorado suggested that the value could be as much as 10 times higher if the land is adjacent to an open space with a stream, and that values decline with every foot away from the amenity (Correll, Lillydahl, and Singell 1978).

Even small open spaces can make a very large difference. The value of houses facing Louisburg Square in Boston, roughly an acre in size, is as much as 60% more per sq ft than the average on Beacon Hill. At Battery Park City in New York, fingers of open space such as Rector Park and Teardrop Park, which connect to the more extensive waterfront esplanade, allow units to be marketed as "facing the park" rather than facing streets. Substantial boulevards, such as Commonwealth Avenue in Boston or Park Avenue in New York, confer the same advantages.

Mixed Uses

A site plan that incorporates mixed uses can be favorable to developers, offering flexibility in what they build and allowing them to spread their risks across several markets for space. On large projects, it may also allow the developer to create an internal market for other uses—housing that generates retail demands and offices that create the opportunity for restaurants and shops. Mixing uses is also considered a public good, reducing the need for travel, generating life on streets through more of the day and night, and, where housing is included, helping create a sense of community.

In many cities, incentives are offered to promote mixed uses. In New York City, several new theaters have

17.10 Permission to increase heights and the amount of prime commercial and residential space at the Woodward's site in Vancouver, Canada, allowed the developer to cross-subsidize affordable housing, neighborhood facilities, and new facilities for a university. (Courtesy of Henriquez Partners/© Bob Matheson)

17.11 Transfer and sale of development rights along the High Line in New York City helped pay for the elevated walkway that provides an amenity for residents of new buildings. (Gary Hack)

17.12 Multifamily housing in suburban Kentlands, Gaithersburg, Maryland, which echoes the form and character of older housing and commercial areas, commands a premium. (Gary Hack)

been built by developers in exchange for added rights to build additional office or residential space above. The Woodward's Project in downtown Vancouver, a complex 1.1 million sq ft project of mixed uses, includes space for a university school for contemporary arts, 200 affordable housing units, a supermarket, office space for nonprofit organizations, office space for federal and city agencies, and a child-care center, as well as 536 market-rate condominiums. The project was made possible by granting the developer the right to build more space on the site, exceed the site's prior height restrictions, and enhance the development rights on another site the developer owns elsewhere in downtown (Enright and Henriquez Partners 2010).

A similar strategy has been adopted in the West Chelsea area of New York, where the High Line park threads its way through a jumble of old warehouses and new designer chic buildings. The city allowed transfer of development rights from the elevated park to adjacent sites and, in line with newly enacted special district zoning, sold enhanced development rights to cover a large portion of the costs of constructing the park. The award-winning park has become a magnet for development, helping West Chelsea evolve into a unique mixed-use district anchored by galleries, restaurants, shops, offices, and housing (James Corner Field Operations and Diller, Scofidio & Renfro 2015).

District Identity

A central purpose of site planning is often to create neighborhoods or districts with a unique and memorable character. A single building cannot do this; creating identity requires consistency among many buildings in an area. It may be achieved through the form of streets, open spaces, and buildings, through consistency of materials and details, and through the uses that are attracted to the area.

Districts with *distinct identity* can have greater economic value than faceless or confused areas. A Turkish study found that harmony between the building facades and colors was the most effective factor in promoting high land values, and that consistent and interesting architectural features ranked just behind this (Topcu and Kubat 2009).

Identity is the central theme of new urbanist communities, which are governed by prescriptions that range from the form of streets to architectural

17.13 Taipingqiao in Shanghai is a mix of old and new, low and high structures that share materials, similar scale, and a pedestrian orientation. (Gary Hack)

details. A study of the value of this bundle of character-giving features has found that buyers are willing to pay a premium of about 11% for single-family homes in such communities (Eppli and Tu 1999). While the study did not disaggregate the contributions to this premium, it is fair to assume that overall identity plays a role. Of course, new urbanist communities are not for everyone: market studies have found that about one-third of US households are prepared to accept a smaller lot size and adopt the form of housing that predominates in such communities (Hirschhorn and Souza 2001; Bohl 2002).

The value of district identity is at the core of the success of Taipingqiao in Shanghai (see chapter 2). The restoration of traditional houses and their conversion to shops, restaurants, boutiques, and entertainment venues, coupled with the creation of park space, differentiates this development from all others in central Shanghai. The costs of these moves have been repaid several times by the dramatically increased rents and values of the high-rise hotels, offices, housing, and commercial spaces that look down on the amenities. The creative site planning and development not only enhance the quality of life but have proved to be profitable.

18 | Impact Assessment

In most places, site planners are required to conduct an assessment of the impacts of developing a site if it is above a specific size threshold, or in a critical location, or draws upon irreplaceable resources. Environmental impact assessment emerged in the 1970s as a way to disclose impacts before decisions are made, and to allow the public to comment on and provide input about developments. Since then, other forms of impact assessment have emerged—notably fiscal impact assessment, health impact reporting, and climate impact reporting. The site planner needs to be familiar with these, as they often drive the process of seeking approval of projects.

Impact assessment assumes that it is impossible to pin down all the important criteria for a site before plans are made, and that tradeoffs will need to be made based on a careful analysis of alternatives. Most assessment procedures are aimed at informing decisions, not ruling out possibilities. Many projects run aground or are delayed when their planners fail to reveal their impacts, leaving opponents to make claims about the negative effects. Once disclosed, impacts can be debated and weighed against other considerations, and mitigation actions can be proposed to counteract negative impacts. Impact assessment procedures often mandate the time frame of the comment period and timetable for making decisions, providing predictability in a process that could otherwise drag on indefinitely.

Environmental Impact Assessment

Assessment of the environmental impacts of a project goes by a variety of names: *environmental impact assess-*

ment (*EIA*) in the US, Hong Kong, and India; *environment assessments* (*EA*) in Australia, Canada, and China; *strategic environmental assessment* (*SEA*) in the European Union and many of its member states; *assessment of environmental effects* (*AEE*) in New Zealand; and the *environment effects statement* (*EES*) process in Victoria, Australia, among other labels. Such assessments are generally mandated by national governments; in some federal states, national requirements may only apply in cases where the senior level of government is taking an action. They may be paralleled by state or provincial requirements for assessments, and in some places local governments may also mandate a process of disclosing impacts.

In the US, the National Environmental Policy Act (NEPA) requires that environmental impact statements (EIS) be prepared for all federal actions (policies as well as projects) that are likely to have significant environmental impacts. Most US states also require environmental analyses for projects that rise above specified thresholds—the New York State *environmental quality review* (*SEQR*) and California's *environmental quality assessment* (*CEQA*) are examples. Individual cities follow suit; Boston requires that all projects over 50,000 sq ft (4,645 m²) submit a *project impact report* (*PIR*), and as a practical matter most large projects in New York City must go through its *uniform land use review procedure* (*ULURP*) that requires a full airing of the impacts. In instances where EISs are required by several levels of government, consolidated reporting may be permitted.

Environmental impact review processes generally involve six steps: screening a project to discover whether there are likely to be any significant impacts;

scoping the environmental analysis; conducting the analysis and preparing a *draft impact report*; circulating the report for agency and public comment; preparing a final impact report; and deciding on whether the project may proceed. Within this broad framework, the local customs and variations in the process are too numerous to catalog. Instead, we focus here on the typical contents of an environmental impact analysis.

The process is cumulative, with each step building on those it follows. Thus, the screening may reveal that there are no likely significant environmental impacts, which will relieve the necessity for further study. This is not a likely outcome for most site developments, but could be the case where structures on a site are replaced in kind, not significantly altering the environment. A finding that there may be significant impacts triggers the scoping process. When the environmental study is completed, based on the agreed-upon scope, comments are solicited, and the adequacy of *mitigation measures* is scrutinized. The final impact report addresses the comments received, and may result in alterations to the plan or the mitigation schemes. Only after this can it be decided whether the project should proceed. If the scope of the project changes significantly during the process of implementation, a supplemental EIS (SEIS) may be required, recycling the earlier process. Developers of sites work hard to avoid triggering an SEIS, because of its potential for delaying or stopping a project in midstream.

Contents of an Environmental Impact Report

Environmental impact reports address the broad range of impacts that a project may have on its natural, man-made, cultural, economic, and social environment. They are concerned with both on-site and off-site impacts. A checklist of possible types of impact is given in sidebar 18.1. Not all of these areas will be relevant for every project, of course, and the specific contents may be prescribed by the agency receiving the assessment. The following sections are included in most environmental impact reports:

Project objectives and plan. The environmental impact report begins by spelling out in some detail the necessity of the project and the planning and development objectives. It outlines the regulatory and other constraints that have influenced the approach taken in planning the site. Next the report describes the proposed plan in considerable detail, including plans, images, and statistics necessary to provide decision makers with a basis for judging the project's desirability.

Alternatives considered. The report documents the range of alternatives that were considered, beginning with the *"no-build" alternative* of leaving the site in its current condition. This constitutes a baseline against which the plan and other alternatives can be considered. Alternatives will typically include plans with more or less development and plans that address obvious impacts of the proposed plan. While the range of possible alternatives is infinite, a "rule of reason" should apply, selecting alternatives that will allow a reasoned choice to be made. A responsible EIS avoids alternatives that are impractical or impossible on their face.

Environmental impacts. The report then documents each of the categories of impacts, comparing the proposed action to the alternatives considered, relying upon the scientific and analytic materials assembled. It catalogs direct and indirect impacts, distinguishing between short- and long-term effects. It identifies any conflicts with local and national policies, including energy conservation, protection of historic resources, avoidance of depleting irreplaceable resources, and economic development objectives. Using a matrix, it indicates how the impacts vary across the alternatives considered. Where there are significant environmental impacts, the report comments on whether they are temporary or irreversible. Understandably, this section is the core of the impact report. There are a number of excellent manuals that can help guide the analysis of environmental impacts, including New York City's CEQR Technical Manual (New York City Mayor's Office of Environmental Coordination 2014).

Mitigation measures. This section identifies ways of counteracting or compensating for environmental impacts. As an example, loss of wetlands may be mitigated by the creation of artificial wetlands elsewhere on the site or in other locations. Traffic

A Checklist of Environmental Impacts

Land alteration
Alteration of topography
Import and export of soil materials
Slopes, erosion, landslides, and subsidence
Rehabilitation of mining areas
Contaminated soils
Shoreline alteration and impacts on
    intertidal zone
Dredging and filling of land below water

Water resources
Alteration of water table and groundwater
    hydrology
Groundwater recharge
Contamination of groundwater
Changes in runoff, quantities, rates, and
    contamination
Impacts on current watercourses
Eutrophication
Snowfall accumulation and melting
Changes in chemical and biological
    composition of water
Future impacts of climate change and
    sea level rise

Vegetation
Impacts on trees, tree cover, and species
Wetlands loss or degradation
Alteration of ground cover
Impacts on unique and threatened species
Invasive species
Effects on agriculture and natural
    food sources

Wildlife
Effects on habitat and food chain
Impacts on migration patterns
Introduction of new predators

Climate
Wind patterns
Solar exposure
Heat island effects
Humidity changes
Snow drifting and accumulation
Ambient air quality, dust, particulates
Microclimatic effects — sunlight, wind,
    topography
Impacts of global warming

Noise
Attenuation of on- and off-site sound

Airport sound cones
Relationship to recommended human
    sound levels

Transportation
Travel options
Quality of movement corridors for all modes
Trips generated by site, modal split
Effects on adjacent roadways and
    intersections
Mass transit demands
Logistics and delivery transportation
Bicycle movement
Walkways and pathways

Wastes
Quantities and mix of solid wastes
    generated on site
Collection methods and disposal locations
Liquid effluent processing and discharge
Septic systems
Discharge of cooling water

Energy
Energy demands, conservation measures
On-site energy generation
Energy distribution networks

Aesthetics
Views to and from site
Skyline effects
Visual privacy
Compatibility with existing development
Relationships of structures to pedestrian
    environment
Impacts on landmarks and historic
    structures

Economy
Jobs created — during construction and
    beyond
Tax revenues and costs to local
    governments
Support for public facilities and activities

Cultural
Demographics of site occupants
Demands created for educational,
    recreation, and other public services
Affordability of facilities on site
Contribution of new recreation and cultural
    facilities on site

impacts may be counterbalanced by improvements to intersections around the site. The measures may include physical construction, ecological actions, and financial payments in compensation for losses, all of which may be made conditions for proceeding.

List of preparers. All of those participating in the preparation of the EIS and their qualifications should be listed, and all meetings with the public or interested parties cataloged. This provides review agencies with an understanding of the expertise and interests the report reflects.

Environmental impact statements inevitably become weighty documents, and there is virtue in separating the summary materials from the vast amounts of detail used to reach conclusions. Traffic counts and analyses, wind studies, catalogs of ecological conditions, economic studies, and other detailed analyses should be organized as appendices, to be read by those specifically interested in the subject. As the final impact report is compiled, reflecting any changes in response to agency and public comments, the record of commentary should also be included in an appendix.

Approval of Environmental Impact Report

Local, state or provincial, and federal or national agencies that are obliged to consider environmental impacts before approving projects must address two questions when they receive the final EIS. First, is the EIS adequate? Is it lacking important information, has it failed to consider possible alternatives, or is the assessment inadequate? A satisfactory EIS is the prerequisite to any decisions, and not meeting this threshold is one of the most frequent causes of delay of projects.

With an adequate EIS in hand, the question becomes whether the impacts and mitigation efforts proposed are acceptable. The US EPA rates impact statements in four categories: LO (lack of objections); EC (environmental concerns); EO (environmental objections); EU (environmentally unsatisfactory) (Environmental Protection Agency 2017). While it would be unusual to proceed with a project that received an EU rating, other considerations might weigh in favor of moving ahead with projects rated EC or EO, with adequate mitigation measures or conditions (Environmental Protection Agency 2012b).

Other countries or localities have their own criteria in deciding whether to proceed. In Canada, the project can only proceed if the Minister of the Environment concludes that it is unlikely to cause any significant adverse environmental effects, or if the federal cabinet determines that such impacts are justified. In California, CEQA states that a public agency cannot approve a project unless one or more findings are made for each of the significant impacts. Findings may include changes or alterations to the plan that lessen the environmental impacts, mitigation measures, or compensating actions. In other places, considerable discretion is provided to the decision makers, and case law may be the most reliable predictor of outcomes.

Fiscal Impact Assessments

Fiscal impact reports are mandated by many local governments in the US as a way of disclosing the costs and revenues they are likely to experience if a site is developed. Such studies are a peculiarity of the US governmental system, where the costs experienced by cities, counties, service districts, and states as a result of development don't necessarily match the revenues they receive from local taxation, fees, exactions, sales taxes, and income taxes. Some new uses, such as family-oriented housing, generally cost local governments more than they yield in property tax revenue because of school costs, and the local council will be interested in whether this is offset by additional income or sales taxes from those living in a new development. While individual developments may provide all the on-site infrastructure needed, they may trigger the need for new trunk lines leading to the site or require additional capacity in a sewage treatment plant, money which cannot be recovered fully through user fees. Rather than speculate on the flows of resources, a fiscal impact analysis predicts the costs and revenues to particular governmental entities. It will also help in setting and defending *exactions* imposed on the developer to ensure that the government and current residents are kept whole.

Fiscal impact studies usually focus on one governmental unit, but if several governments or service districts have to approve a development, it may make sense to expand the analysis to construct a balance sheet for each.

Estimating Costs

Making an estimate of the financial burdens a governmental unit will experience is a tricky exercise, since costs will include annual *operating expenditures* for services, and may also require lumpy *capital expenditures* that are required to expand capacity. Accommodating a dozen or two new students in schools with excess capacity will require one or two new teachers, but if several hundred students are added to the system, additions to an existing school or an entire new facility may be needed. Capital facilities are generally financed through grants and bond proceeds, paid off over time. So it is essential that operating expenditures be separated from capital expenditures in the analysis.

There are a variety of methods of estimating annual expenditures. The simplest is to simply adopt the local *average cost per capita*, dividing the total annual expenditures for a particular service by the number of people served. This figure can be seriously off the mark if the population projected for a site doesn't match the existing demographics of the community. A site for senior housing will obviously yield few schoolchildren but require higher medical service costs than the average. Those served by public services include people working in, studying in, and visiting a local area, not simply those who live there, so it is an error to allocate to a residential development the cost of policing commercial and industrial areas, or to burden commercial areas with school costs. Thus, unbundling the costs to reflect the types of development on a site makes common sense, a technique sometimes called the *disaggregated per capita costs* method.

These two techniques can also be used to arrive at an estimate of the off-site capital costs that flow from a development. For each service system—police, fire protection, schools, hospitals, libraries, sewers, water supply, etc.—the replacement costs of sites, buildings, infrastructure, and capital equipment (with a life of more than 5 years) is divided by the population served to obtain a figure that will apply to the development. This has all the potential errors just noted for operating costs. An alternative is to relate the capital costs to the design capacity of each system. Thus, if a fire station is required for each 10,000 residents or jobs, its cost can be divided by that number to arrive at a per capita cost, which is then used for the site. Since most local governments use bonds to pay for these facilities (net

of grants), the relevant figure is the annual *debt service cost*. In some cases, a specific capital cost may already have been incurred, building in excess capacity to serve the site being analyzed. A sewer trunk line may have been installed in an adjacent street and partially paid for by other developments. In such a case, the capital cost can be apportioned to the site by determining the fraction of the ultimate capacity that a site will be using.

Adding the debt service costs to the annual operating costs, a projection can be made of the cost burden to a governmental entity serving a new development. The relevant question in the fiscal analysis then becomes what revenues the government will receive to offset its costs.

Estimating Revenues

Estimating future *governmental revenues* requires a wider view of how a development will impact the local economy. A commercial or retail development may generate local sales or income taxes (if there are any), some of its employees may live in the community and pay additional taxes and fees, and some of their incomes will be spent locally, generating further revenues to the government. The recirculation of incomes is referred to as the *multiplier effect*, typically 3 to 8 times the income received directly, depending upon the opportunities to buy goods and services locally. A distinction also needs to be made between the construction impacts and the recurring fiscal impacts of a development. Communities receive a bump in revenues during the period of construction when sales and income taxes are collected from the builders and their employees, then revenues settle down to a more stable level once it is occupied. The revenue sources will also shift. In a residential development, property and personal income tax revenues will replace the initial sales and income taxes and fees once the houses are occupied.

In estimating the revenues, each of the sources (and the governmental units receiving the revenue) should be accounted for. Intergovernmental transfers of revenue need to be taken into account: a portion of the sales taxes received by a county may be sent back to local governments to pay for schools, or the transfer may go in the other direction. It is legitimate to use a multiplier to reflect the actual revenues received. A household spending $40,000 a year locally, and paying

Cumulative Absorption (Year)

Revenues	1	2	3	4	5	6	7	8	9	10	11	12	13	14	15
Property Taxes	$245,547	$533,052	$654,976	$668,898	$683,074	$697,780	$713,031	$728,838	$745,218	$762,185	$779,760	$797,962	$816,805	$836,307	$856,486
Property Transfer Tax	$63,008	$72,514	$23,665	$6,769	$6,913	$7,062	$7,217	$7,377	$7,543	$7,715	$7,894	$8,078	$8,270	$8,468	$8,673
Sales and Use Taxes	$78,394	$184,215	$230,095	$234,242	$238,471	$242,785	$247,186	$251,674	$256,252	$260,922	$265,685	$270,543	$275,499	$280,554	$285,709
Prop. 172 Public Safety Sales Tax	$3,753	$8,819	$11,015	$11,214	$11,416	$11,623	$11,833	$12,048	$12,267	$12,491	$12,719	$12,952	$13,189	$13,431	$13,678
Municipal Service Tax	$16,901	$41,614	$53,745	$54,820	$55,916	$57,034	$58,175	$59,339	$60,525	$61,736	$62,971	$64,230	$65,515	$66,825	$68,161
Parks Maintenance Tax	$10,290	$23,976	$33,203	$33,203	$33,203	$33,203	$33,203	$33,203	$33,203	$33,203	$33,203	$33,203	$33,203	$33,203	$33,203
Public Safety Tax	$13,302	$35,711	$51,817	$52,854	$53,911	$54,989	$56,089	$57,211	$58,355	$59,522	$60,712	$61,927	$63,165	$64,428	$65,717
Transient Occupancy Tax	$0	$0	$0	$0	$0	$0	$0	$0	$0	$0	$0	$0	$0	$0	$0
Business License Tax	$0	$8,121	$19,301	$19,880	$20,476	$21,090	$21,723	$22,375	$23,046	$23,737	$24,449	$25,183	$25,938	$26,717	$27,518
Franchise Fees	$3,953	$9,342	$13,444	$13,848	$14,263	$14,691	$15,132	$15,586	$16,053	$16,535	$17,031	$17,542	$18,068	$18,610	$19,168
Property Tax In-Lieu of Vehicle License Fees	$92,872	$201,614	$247,729	$252,995	$258,356	$263,919	$269,687	$275,666	$281,861	$288,278	$294,926	$301,810	$308,937	$316,313	$323,946
Gas Tax Revenues	$13,900	$32,850	$47,277	$48,695	$50,156	$51,660	$53,210	$54,807	$56,451	$58,144	$59,889	$61,685	$63,536	$65,442	$67,405
Community Services Revenue	$8,711	$20,586	$29,627	$30,516	$31,432	$32,375	$33,346	$34,346	$35,377	$36,438	$37,531	$38,657	$39,817	$41,011	$42,241
Fines and Forfeitures	$254	$601	$865	$891	$918	$945	$973	$1,003	$1,033	$1,064	$1,096	$1,129	$1,162	$1,197	$1,233
Discount Rate 3.2%															
Sub-Total Revenues	$550,885	$1,173,013	$1,416,760	$1,428,823	$1,458,504	$1,489,157	$1,520,804	$1,553,471	$1,587,184	$1,621,970	$1,657,865	$1,694,900	$1,733,103	$1,772,505	$1,813,139
Percentage change from prior year		53.04%	17.20%	0.84%	2.04%	2.06%	2.08%	2.10%	2.12%	2.14%	2.17%	2.19%	2.20%	2.22%	2.24%
Discounted Total		$1,136,641	$1,330,261	$1,299,988	$1,285,846	$1,272,161	$1,258,911	$1,246,078	$1,233,644	$1,221,590	$1,209,908	$1,198,581	$1,187,594	$1,176,932	$1,166,582
Expenditures	1	2	3	4	5	6	7	8	9	10	11	12	13	14	15
Public Works	$36,808	$64,560	$75,156	$78,084	$81,126	$84,287	$87,570	$90,982	$94,527	$98,209	$102,036	$106,011	$110,141	$114,432	$118,891
Community Development	$13,111	$31,214	$45,253	$46,953	$48,718	$50,548	$52,448	$54,419	$56,464	$58,585	$60,787	$63,071	$65,441	$67,900	$70,452
Community Services	$29,781	$65,451	$89,160	$92,509	$95,984	$99,590	$103,331	$107,212	$111,240	$115,419	$119,754	$124,253	$128,920	$133,763	$138,788
Asset Management	$94,542	$256,095	$323,930	$336,483	$349,523	$363,068	$377,138	$391,754	$406,935	$422,706	$439,087	$456,103	$473,779	$492,139	$511,211
Police	$115,721	$275,420	$399,181	$414,065	$429,504	$445,519	$462,132	$479,363	$497,237	$515,778	$535,010	$554,959	$575,651	$597,116	$619,381
Fire	$70,410	$167,327	$242,152	$250,804	$259,765	$269,046	$278,659	$288,615	$298,927	$309,608	$320,670	$332,128	$343,994	$356,285	$369,015
General Government	$32,020	$70,486	$96,172	$99,945	$103,865	$107,939	$112,173	$116,573	$121,146	$125,898	$130,837	$135,969	$141,302	$146,845	$152,605
Sub-Total Expenditures	$392,394	$930,554	$1,271,003	$1,318,842	$1,368,485	$1,419,998	$1,473,451	$1,528,919	$1,586,476	$1,646,203	$1,708,180	$1,772,493	$1,839,230	$1,908,481	$1,980,343
Percentage change from prior year		57.83%	26.79%	3.63%	3.63%	3.63%	3.63%	3.63%	3.63%	3.63%	3.63%	3.63%	3.63%	3.63%	3.63%
Discounted Total		$901,699	$1,193,403	$1,199,924	$1,206,483	$1,213,079	$1,219,713	$1,226,384	$1,233,094	$1,239,841	$1,246,628	$1,253,452	$1,260,316	$1,267,219	$1,274,162
NET GENERAL FUND BALANCE	$158,491	$242,460	$145,757	$109,980	$90,020	$69,159	$47,353	$24,553	$708	-$24,233	-$50,315	-$77,593	-$106,127	-$135,976	-$167,204
Discounted value Net GF Balance	$158,491	$234,942	$136,858	$100,063	$79,363	$59,082	$39,198	$19,694	$550	-$18,251	-$36,720	-$54,872	-$72,722	-$90,287	-$107,580
Cumulative Discounted GF Balance	$158,491	$393,433	$530,291	$630,355	$709,718	$768,799	$807,998	$827,692	$828,242	$809,991	$773,271	$718,399	$645,677	$555,390	$447,810

Key Development Assumptions

Inflation			Turnover %		
General Rate of Revenue Inflation:	2.0%		Single Family	4.0%	
Inflation for Personnel Costs:	3.7%		Multi Family	5.0%	
Inflation for Non-Personnel Costs:	4.0%		Non Res.	3.0%	

Annual Real Estate Market Price Appreciation	Study Years		
	1-5	6-10	11-15
Affordable for-sale units	2.0%	3.0%	3.0%
Residential for-sale units	2.0%	3.0%	3.0%
Multifamily rental units	2.0%	3.0%	3.0%
Non-residential properties	1.0%	2.5%	3.5%
Prop 13 annual increase (no turnover/sale)	2.0%	2.0%	2.0%

	Units
Total Residential	547

Non-Residential	Square Feet
Retail	63,790
Office	55,800

Parks and Open Space	Acres
Park	5.77
Greenbelts	5.6
Habitat	7.5
Streets	Linear Ft.
Two-Lane Arterial	1,478
Collector Street 1	1,109
Collector Street 2	1,182
Residential Lane	15,259

18.1 Fiscal impact analysis for the Cannery Development, Davis, California. (City of Davis)

sales taxes on a portion of it, may induce an additional $120,000 in local expenditures as resources are recirculate through the community. Revenue estimates are best reported in a matrix that distinguishes the source of revenues and the governmental body receiving them.

When developers report the fiscal impacts of their project, there is an incentive to inflate revenues while minimizing the costs to governmental units. One common error is to assume that all tax revenues are incremental to the community. Some revenues will simply *displace* current revenues—new retail outlets paying taxes that erode the sales taxes of existing stores, as an example. A second error is to assume that new residents will spend all their resources within their community, while in fact much of this spending might leak out into adjacent municipalities. For large projects it is also misleading to portray revenues as if they will materialize overnight, when the reality is that they will be phased in over many years. This could put a governmental or service entity in a bind, as it has to lay out immediate expenditures to upgrade its facilities while waiting many years for revenues that will pay for them.

With all of these caveats, a fiscal impact analysis, like a broader environmental analysis, can aid the process of debate and approval of a project by bringing objective data to the table as a basis for proceeding. A number of consultants have developed models that allow them to quickly estimate the fiscal impacts of projects, and it is not unusual to find local governments and developers with competing estimates of impacts, each provided by their consultant. There are also a number of open-source impact assessment models, including Envision Tomorrow, a model that is calibrated for US usage (Fregonese Associates, n.d.).

Health Impact Assessments

Health impact assessments (HIAs) focus on the human health consequences of policies and actions, and are gradually being recognized as valuable around the world. Most often they are applied to programs or policies (creating neighborhood-based clinics rather than expanding emergency rooms in hospitals, or lowering the fares on mass transit to discourage automobile use, as examples), but they have also been mandated or encouraged in a number of cities to examine the health effects of development projects. Several international agencies, including the International Finance Corporation of the World Bank, require HIAs for all of their large development projects. In some places they are an alternative to environmental impact assessments, while in others they represent a parallel requirement.

Health impact assessments can take a variety of forms, from a simple checklist to a full assessment that parallels the process of an EIA. In a small community, a checklist may reveal areas of concern from a project and suggest areas where evidence on health effects

---

CHARTER TOWNSHIP OF MERIDIAN
HEALTH IMPACT ASSESSMENT

Please provide written responses to each applicable question. For those questions which are not applicable, please indicate so on the form. Attach additional sheets if more space is necessary to respond fully to the questions. Submit completed form with your project/development application.

Project Name:_____, Address/Location: _____ Case # _____
Type of Project: ☐ Residential ☐ Commercial ☐ Office ☐ Public

Water Quality Considerations/Impacts

YES NO
What is the source of water for the proposed project/development?_____
What is the estimated daily water demand? _____
☐ ☐ If public water, is there available capacity to handle this project in the municipal facilities?
☐ ☐ If private well, is the water considered potable (safe)?
☐ ☐ Is the project/development within existing municipal service areas?
☐ ☐ Are there nearby sources of potential water contamination? IF YES LIST _____
☐ ☐ Are there underground storage tanks? IF YES LIST_____
☐ ☐ Are their gasoline or oil pipelines? IF YES LIST _____
☐ ☐ Is there a nearby known source of contaminated soil? IF YES LIST _____
☐ ☐ Are there abandoned wells on the site? IF YES LIST _____
☐ ☐ Will the water supply require on-site treatment, such as iron removal?
☐ ☐ Are there any wetlands on the site?
☐ ☐ If YES what is/are the size(s) of the wetland(s)? _____
☐ ☐ If wetlands are being impacted, is adequate mitigation being proposed?
☐ ☐ Is the project located in a known floodplain?
☐ ☐ Will the proposed project affect groundwater recharge?
What percentage of the parcel is covered by impervious surfaces? _____
☐ ☐ Does the project affect the overall percentage of impervious surfaces in the watershed?

Wastewater Considerations/Impacts

YES NO
☐ ☐ Does the project/development require an on-site wastewater system?
☐ ☐ If YES, are the soils appropriate to support a septic system?
☐ ☐ Is project/development within the service area of the municipal sewage system?

Air Quality Considerations/Impacts

YES NO
☐ ☐ Does the project/development entail demolition activities?
☐ ☐ If YES, has the site been examined for asbestos and/or lead?
☐ ☐ Are there plans for mitigating dust?
☐ ☐ Will the project/development result in increased stationary air emissions?
☐ ☐ If YES, are emissions controlled contaminants? PLEASE LIST_____
☐ ☐ Has the applicant obtained necessary permits?
☐ ☐ Will the project result in increased air emissions from cars?
What is the increase in traffic volume projected for peak hours? _____
☐ ☐ Is the proposed use compatible with adjacent uses?
☐ ☐ Is the site near known areas affected by radon?

Solid & Hazardous Waste Disposal

YES NO
☐ ☐ Is the proposed project/development located near any facility handling or disposing of hazardous waste?
☐ ☐ Is there historic evidence of solid or hazardous waste disposal or releases on or adjacent to the site?
☐ ☐ Are there plans in place to prevent the release of hazardous materials into the environment in the case of fire?
If YES describe_____
☐ ☐ Does the project entail hazardous waste disposal?
☐ ☐ ____ If YES is the proposed waste handling or disposal activity compatible with adjacent use and/or zoning?
☐ ☐ Is the proposed waste handling or disposal activity compatible with the Ingham County Solid Waste Management Plan?
☐ ☐ Is the facility near vulnerable resources (e.g. nursing homes) that may require contingency planning for extra protection in the event of an on-site fire? IF ANY LIST_____

Noise Considerations/Impacts

YES NO
☐ ☐ Is the project/development likely to generate noises that will create a nuisance to neighboring uses?
If YES please list type of noise(s) and hours _____
☐ ☐ Are there engineered or non-engineered measures that can be employed to mitigate nuisance noises?
If YES please list _____
☐ ☐ Does the generated noise violate the noise ordinance?

Social Capital

YES NO
☐ ☐ Does the project/development promote interaction between neighbors?
If Yes please list_____
☐ ☐ Is the physical design of the project harmonious with the overall neighborhood?

Physical Activity and Injury Prevention

YES NO
☐ ☐ Does the project/development provide mobility options for those who cannot drive?
☐ ☐ Does the project/development have sidewalks that lead to local destinations?
If YES what is the proposed width of the sidewalks?
☐ ☐ Does the project/development have or connect to a trail system for walking or biking?
☐ ☐ Does the project/development contain elements that enhance the feeling of neighborhood safety?
☐ ☐ Are local streetlights being provided?
☐ ☐ Are houses oriented toward the street to provide "eyes on the street"?
☐ ☐ Can a child walk safely to school?
☐ ☐ Are there sidewalks/pathways along the route to the school(s)?
☐ ☐ What is the walking distance to the area's schools?
☐ ☐ Is the visibility at intersections good?/Can drivers see short children?
☐ ☐ Does the route contain known dangerous intersections?
If YES please list_____
☐ ☐ Are there crossing guards at these intersections?
☐ ☐ Will the project/development contain a significant elderly population?
☐ ☐ Can the elderly walk to important destinations (i.e. banks, post office, and library)?
What is the walking distance to these destinations?
☐ ☐ Are there sidewalks/pathways along the routes to these destinations?
☐ ☐ Does the route contain known dangerous intersections?
☐ ☐ Does the project contain design elements to calm traffic such as speed humps, extended corners, raised street crossings, or similar features? IF ANY LIST
☐ ☐ Does the project/development present unsafe conditions or deter access and free mobility for the physically handicapped?
☐ ☐ For projects/development on arterial streets does the plan include pedestrian crossing signals and/or mid-street islands?
☐ ☐ Is public transportation available?
If YES where and how close is the nearest bus stop? _____
☐ ☐ Does the nearest bus stop have a shelter?
☐ ☐ Does the nearest the bus stop have a bench?

Health Equity/Food Systems (HOUSING PROJECTS ONLY)

YES NO
☐ ☐ Does the project provide for a diversity of housing types to accommodate a variety of income groups?
What is the square footage of the smallest dwelling unit?
What is the estimated market price? _____
☐ ☐ Does this price represent an "affordable house" given the area median income?
☐ ☐ Is the proposed project/development located in an area that provides easy access to healthy foods?
What is the distance to the nearest full service grocery store?_____
What is the distance to the nearest convenience store?
☐ ☐ Does the neighborhood have a disproportionate number of liquor/party stores?
☐ ☐ Is the project/development located in a neighborhood or region characterized by concentrated poverty?
☐ ☐ Are affected residents involved in the planning process?
☐ ☐ Are disadvantaged populations at greater risk of exposure to environmental hazards?

Growth Objectives/Regional Growth Project

YES NO
☐ ☐ Is the project located within the designated growth area of the Tri-County Regional Growth Project?

18.2 Checklist of health impacts.
(Meridian Township, Ohio)

needs to be compiled. A more elaborate process will specify issues to be addressed in detail by a project sponsor, such as safety (avoidance of motor vehicle accidents, pedestrian safety), combatting obesity (encouraging walking and transit use, mobility options, having fresh food outlets nearby, promoting active recreation), interaction (promoting neighboring, mixing incomes and ages, providing nearby schools and community facilities), or reducing environmental hazards (water quality, flooding, air quality, exposure to pollutants) (Harris et al. 2007).

Health impact analyses adopt a broad definition of *health*, encompassing physical, mental, and social well-being. The *distributional impacts* of plans and policies across incomes and ethnic groups in a community are critically important and need to be the focus of every HIA. *Vulnerable populations* such as the elderly, young children, those with chronic diseases, those who lack resources, and those who require mobility aids need special attention in assessments.

Full-scale HIAs typically mirror the process of conducting EIAs: screening, scoping, assessment, reporting, deciding, and monitoring a completed project (Horton 2010; Harris et al. 2007). The first step in the assessment is agreeing on a set of health indicators, using available local data. Sidebar 18.2 lists possible *indicators* and determinants of health, not all of which will be relevant to a particular project. Some of these are surrogates for healthy environments; others are indicators of stress or illness. In all cases, the linkages between health and environmental conditions are complex, since humans are resilient and may prosper even in suboptimal conditions. While it may be desirable to be within a 30-minute walk or commute to a primary health care facility, a community may provide transportation and services that compensate for longer distances. Nonetheless, all else being equal, proximity is a desirable objective.

There are a mountain of studies on health and the environment, and it is sometimes bewildering to explain why studies come to opposite conclusions. Professionals knowledgeable about the field of health and the environment can help access and interpret the available evidence, but there are also many excellent Internet sites that provide links to published sources. The US National Institutes of Health provides a searchable database through its PUBMED site (www.ncbi.nim .nih.gov/pubmed), and the World Health Organization has compiled data and analyses on subjects including urban health, road safety, and obesity (World Health Organization 2014b). Other nonprofit organizations provide systematic reviews on the Internet of the linkages between health and the environment, including the Cochrane Collaboration and the Campbell Collaboration.

Whether addressed through HIAs or EIAs, issues of health and the planning of sites are of growing concern and need the attention of site planners.

Climate Impact Assessments

Assessing the *climate impacts* of development projects is the newest form of impact assessment. In most situations it involves two separate questions: How will the project affect the local and global climate? And how will predictable and unpredictable changes to climate affect the site? While they are conceptually linked, the first generally involves *mitigation* of climate effects, while the second is concerned with *adaptation* to climate change. We are only just learning how to address these questions. However, a number of local, state, provincial, and national governments have mandated the reporting of climate impacts, and tools have been developed to assist in these efforts (Condon, Cavens, and Miller 2009). Notably California, Washington State, and British Columbia all have mandated reductions of gas emissions that contribute to climate change, and reporting protocols have been established to determine whether new projects are on target. Other governments have mandated that climate impacts be covered in environmental impact statements (New York City Mayor's Office of Environmental Coordination 2014).

Climate Impacts

A site development can impact climate in two ways: at the macro scale by discharging *greenhouse gases* (GHGs) into the atmosphere, contributing to long-term global warming and climate changes; and at the micro scale by modifying the climate on a site, such as by creating a heat island effect, modifying humidity levels, discharging heat exhausts from on-site mechanical systems, or

**Examples of
Health Status and
Health Determinants
Indicators**

Livelihood

Proportion of area residents employed

Proportion of area residents living in relative or absolute poverty

Share of jobs that meet health-supporting criteria: self-sufficiency incomes, paid sick leave, health insurance, etc.

Housing

Ratio of median income to median cost of housing

Proportion of population living in overcrowded conditions

Proportion of households without adequate heat, water, or sanitary services

Transportation

Vehicle miles traveled per capita

Proportion of households commuting to work by public transit

Number, type, and location of traffic collisions

Retail and public services

Proportion of population within one-half mile of a full-service grocery store or fresh produce market

Proportion of population within a 30-minute transit or walking commute of a primary care public health facility

Proportion of population within one-half mile of regional transit stop and one-quarter mile of local public transit stop

Proportion of residential units within one-quarter and one-half mile of public elementary and middle schools

Access to parks and natural space

Proportion of population within one-quarter mile of neighborhood or regional park, open space, or publicly accessible shoreline

Acres of neighborhood parks and natural habitats per capita

Proportion of land area under tree canopy

Access to primary health services

Proportion with government-provided health services or health insurance

Proportion of households within one mile of a health care center or primary care services

Environmental quality

Proportion of population living a safe distance from roadways and industries emitting hazardous pollutants

Capacity of drinking water supply

Proportion of population living with ambient noise levels below 65 decibels

Acres of cultivatable land

Per capita waste generation

Social cohesion

Proportion of voting age population participating in elections

Perceived level of safety and "trust" of neighbors

Rates of violent and property crimes

Residential segregation by race/ethnicity and income

Source: After Mark B. Horton

Item	'Sutton average'	'BedZED average'	'BedZED keen'
	Average data from the REAP software	Data acquired through the 2007 monitoring period	BedZED average data modified to assume a resident making a significant effort to reduce impact. Also modified to represent the energy supply as originally intended.
Energy and home	Electricity 3.9kWh pp per day Other fuel 18.2 kWh per day	Electricity: 3.4 kWh pp per day 20% electricity from PV Heat and hot water: 5.2 kWh pp per day	Energy demand classed as zero due to planned renewables meeting all capacity.
Personal travel in private car	5,282 km/year	2,015 km/year	0 km/year Also 0 km/year by taxi
Private vehicle ownership	1.6 cars per household	0.6 cars per household	0 cars per household
Train	897 km/year	4992 km/year	4992 km/year
Bus	465 km/year	676 km/year	676 km/year
Air travel	3,245 km/year	10,063 km/year	0 km/year
Consumable items Includes clothing, furniture, tools, appliances, personal care etc.	100% of UK typical consumption. *Reflects 'typical western style' consumption patterns.*	100% of UK typical consumption. *Replacing clothes and other items when they are worn out and need replacing as well as occasional other purchases.*	41% of UK typical consumption *Replacing clothes and other items when they are worn out and need replacing.* - tobacco and jewellery to zero - audio-visual equipment reduced by 75% - clothing, furniture, textiles & personal care reduced by 50% - household appliances, tools, utensils, maintenance, and recreational items reduced by 20%
Diet	Typical diet from REAP	25% of veg, fruit, meat and diary are organic	Healthy vegetarian diet, further reduction calculated in line with SEI food report.
Food waste	0% reduction compared to average UK consumption.	20% reduction in fruit and veg compared to average UK consumption	30% reduction compared to average UK consumption.
Private services Includes hospitals, clinics, postal services, water supply, education, catering etc.	100% of UK typical use Water services Sutton average 171 litres per day	100% of UK typical use. Water services reduced to 87 litres per day	100% of UK typical use apart from specified categories: - Water services reduced to 65 litres per day - Mobile phone bills & eating out reduced by 50% - Private medical treatment reduced to zero
Government and capital investment	100% of UK typical	100% of UK typical	100% of UK typical
Carbon footprint	11.2	9.9	6

18.3 Aerial view of BedZED low-energy development, Sutton, UK. (Google Earth)

18.4 View of BedZED, Sutton, UK. (Tom Chance/Wikimedia Commons)

18.5 Analysis of ecological and carbon scenarios, BedZED. (Courtesy of Bioregional Development Group)

capturing radiation from the sun. Each type of impact needs to be analyzed, and there are tools to aid the site planner in this analysis.

It is by now incontrovertible that the accumulation of GHGs in the atmosphere contributes to global temperature rise by trapping heat in the atmosphere. While there will always be year-to-year fluctuation, the long-term trend has been one of rising average temperatures and greater extremes. The four most important GHGs contributing to global warming are *carbon dioxide*, *methane*, *nitrous oxide*, and *fluorinated gases*; of these the first two have the greatest impacts on climate change. Carbon dioxide is discharged whenever fossil fuels are burned, in power plants, automobiles, industries, heating systems, and oil extraction and refining, and constitutes 82% of US GHG emissions. Methane, which has far more potent greenhouse effects and accounts for 9% of US emissions, is emitted by coal processes, agricultural uses, and the decay of organic waste in solid waste landfills. Most national governments have set ambitious targets of reducing per capita GHG emissions by 2040, or reducing the carbon

Sidebar 18.3

**Sources of GHG
emissions**

Operations emissions

Direct emissions from on-site boilers used for heat and hot water, on-site electricity
generation, industrial processes, and fugitive emissions

Indirect emissions from purchased electricity or steam generated off-site and consumed
on-site

Indirect emissions from solid waste generated on-site, including transportation, treatment,
and disposal of solid wastes

Energy usage on site for maintenance of landscape, operation of infrastructure serving the
site (such as street lighting), and protection

Mobile source emissions

Direct mobile source emissions from fleet or private vehicles of occupants of the site

Indirect mobile source emissions from vehicle trips to or from the site during its operation

Construction emissions

Direct emissions resulting from the operation of construction vehicles and equipment

Emissions resulting from the manufacture or transport of construction materials used for
the project (especially steel and concrete)

Based on New York City Mayor's Office of Environmental Coordination 2014

---

intensity of their national economies. Reducing emission levels below the norm in all new site development is an important component of all programs.

An analysis of GHG emissions from a site development project will need to focus on two main sources, energy use on site and transportation, while not neglecting smaller contributors. Both direct and indirect emissions need to be assessed. Drawing a boundary around the project is one of the trickiest issues. A site plan for a university campus clearly requires an accounting of the energy consumed on campus and in regular commuting travel to and from the campus. But does it also include faculty travel to conferences on aircraft, which are among the largest GHG sources? Campus facilities, such as telepresence opportunities, may have a modest effect on long-distance travel, but a useful guide in drawing the boundary is whether a

particular aspect of the project can significantly impact emissions. If not, it is fair to exclude this aspect.

A second important issue is the assumptions made about human behavior that will effect emissions. The performance of an office building that is designed for natural ventilation will only meet its targets if occupants actually exploit this capability. A landscape of natural grasses, designed to minimize maintenance, can be subverted if occupants of a site dislike the appearance and mow the grasses regularly. Most low-emissions environments require changes to normal patterns of behavior—avoiding the purchase of a gas-powered automobile in favor of electric vehicles, car sharing, using mass transit for commuting rather than driving alone, setting thermostats lower, and so on.

The difference human behavior can make is illustrated in the BedZED housing development in the London borough of Sutton, designed for live-work

TABLE 2

Indicators for Existing Benchmarks and Project Objectives

INDEX Indicators	Units	Citywide Existing	Station Area Objectives	Station Area Design Scenarios A	B	C
Demographics						
Population	residents	3,324		6,868	5,882	7,441
Employment	employees	948		3,151	5,893	3,551
Land-Use						
Use Mix	0-1 scale	0.19	0.50 or more	0.40	0.57	0.36
Use Balance	0-1 scale	0.71	0.90 or more	0.87	0.89	0.81
Housing						
Dwelling Unit Count	total DU	1,306		3,276	2,895	3,664
Single-Family Dwelling Density	DU/net acre	2.60	14.00 or more	16.00	14.62	16.00
Multi-Family Dwelling Density	DU/net acre	8.22	28.00 or more	26.61	26.39	28.65
Single-Family Dwelling Share	% total DU	76.6		38.5	10.9	12.5
Multi-Family Dwelling Share	% total DU	21.3		61.5	89.1	87.5
Amenities Proximity	avg walk ft to closest grocery	4,952	2,000 or less	1,906	3,048	3,110
Transit Proximity to Housing	avg walk ft to closest stop	2,909	1,000 or less	952	928	1,146
Employment						
Jobs to Housing Balance	jobs/DU	0.73	0.90 to 1.10	0.96	2.04	0.97
Employment Density	emps/net acre	21.04	70.00 or more	49.92	52.82	60.09
Commercial Building Density	avg FAR	0.20	0.65 or more	0.54	0.56	0.59
Transit Proximity to Employment	avg walk ft to closest stop	1,384	1,000 or less	731	959	1,087
Recreation						
Park/Schoolyard Space Supply	acres/1000 persons	19.8	3.0 to 8.0	4.0	4.9	5.9
Park/Schoolyard Proximity to Housing	avg walk ft to closest park/schoolyard	2,144	1,000 or less	1,725	1,319	1,165
Travel						
Street Segment Length	avg ft	658	300 or less	315	399	452
Street Network Density	centerline mi/sq mi	6.8		27.6	24.8	18.9
Transit Service Coverage	stops/sq mi	1.0	10.0 or more	22.6	18.1	13.6
Transit-Oriented Residential Density	DU/net acre w/i 1/4 mi of stops	4.03	28.00 or more	21.90	23.71	27.95
Transit-Oriented Employment Density	emps/net acre w/i 1/4 mi of stops	15.78		49.92	51.52	61.32
Pedestrian Network Coverage	% of streets w/sidewalks	91.9	100.0 or more	99.7	99.7	100.0
Street Route Directness	walk distance/straightline ratio	1.84	1.40 or less	1.38	1.33	1.36
Bicycle Network Coverage	% street centerlines w/bike route	33.16	50.00 or more	44.29	49.41	27.67
Home Based VMT Produced	mi/day/capita	25.0		20.6	20.9	20.2
Non-Home Based VMT Attracted	mi/day/emp	15.0		12.4	12.5	12.1
Climate Change						
Residential Building Energy Use	MMBtu/yr/capita	50.92		45.51	41.69	41.84
Residential Vehicle Energy Use	MMBtu/yr/capita	41.51		34.18	34.66	33.59
Residential Total Energy Use	MMBtu/yr/capita	92.42		79.69	76.35	75.43
Non-Residential Building Energy Use	MMBtu/yr/emp	45.66		43.34	42.47	11.85
Non-Home Based Vehicle Energy Use	MMBtu/yr/emp	24.90		20.51	20.80	20.15
Non-Residential Total Energy Use	MMBtu/yr/emp	70.56		63.85	63.26	32.00
Residential Building CO2 Emissions	lbs/capita/yr	6,462		4,561	4,735	3,634
Residential Vehicle CO2 Emissions	lbs/capita/yr	6,340		5,221	5,294	5,130
Residential Total CO2 Emissions	lbs/capita/yr	12,802		9,781	10,029	8,764
Non-Residential Building CO2 Emissions	lbs/emp/yr	7,286		4,343	4,823	1,029
Non-Home Based Vehicle CO2 Emissions	lbs/emp/yr	3,804		3,132	3,176	3,078
Non-Residential Total CO2 Emissions	lbs/emp/yr	11,090		7,476	7,999	4,107

18.6 Climate change indicators, Station Area Development, Elburn, Illinois. (Courtesy of Lincoln Institute of Land Policy)

arrangements, use of public transit, natural ventilation, and passive solar heating, among a long list of innovations. A study of BedZED in operation revealed that it reduced overall emissions by about 12% with people living conventional lifestyles on the site, but the study also pointed to a potential 47% reduction through behavioral changes that would include recycling office paper, giving up private automobiles, and changing diets (Hodge and Haltrecht 2009).

Finally, there is the issue of what benchmarks to use in comparing site emissions levels. One approach is developing alternative site plans representing different mixes of uses and site forms, then comparing these to the preferred plan. Another benchmark might be the known emissions levels of other developments in the geographic area of the site—if a residential development, other nearby neighborhoods; if a commercial site, other projects that have been approved recently. In a city that requires disclosure of GHG emissions levels, past climate impact studies may offer good comparative data. Estimates of site emission levels may also be compared to citywide averages for a similar mix of uses. Some cities that track their GHG emissions levels provide data on the average carbon intensity of typical structures that may serve as a benchmark (New York City Mayor's Office of Environmental Coordination 2014).

Once calculations have been made of projected carbon emissions, they need to be arrayed on a spreadsheet that allows for easy comparisons. Figure 18.6 is an example, drawn from a study of potential station area development in Elburn, Illinois. Projections of GHG emissions levels were made using Criterion's INDEX GHG estimation tool (Condon, Cavens, and Miller 2009).

18.7 Residential area in Tuckerton, New Jersey, inundated by storm surge following Hurricane Sandy. (US Coast Guard)

Responses to Climate Change

The second aspect of a robust climate impact analysis concerns how a site has been planned to respond to likely changes in climate over the coming years. Scientists predict that some of the impacts will include rising average temperature levels, greater climate extremes (fluctuations in temperature that include higher and lower temperatures, more and less precipitation and snowfall), melting glaciers, more extreme wind events (including tornados and hurricanes), rising sea levels, and melting of permafrost, among other changes. The standard 100-year storm event that has been used for planning will become a moving target. Local issues will, of course, differ. Sites along rivers or oceans will need to plan for added protection; sites in high-sunshine cities in warm climates will need to be especially sensitive to heat island effects. Whether sunshine is to be exploited for heating or shielded to reduce temperatures will depend upon geographic location and the local climate. Increasing the resilience of a site to deal with long-term climate change is an essential planning objective.

Two difficulties in planning for climate change are the variability of impacts from year to year and the lack of precise forecasts of their magnitude. An example is sea level rise along coastlines: a 2.5°C (4.5°F) rise in global mean temperatures is likely to result in a 1–2 m (3–7 ft) rise in ocean levels, but this could increase to 7 m (23 ft) or more with the accelerating melt of the Greenland and West Antarctic ice sheets (Intergovernmental Panel on Climate Change 2007). Setting a design parameter for adapting to sea level rise is difficult; as a practical matter, designing for 2 m (7 ft) sea level rise makes sense today, with the possibility that protection may need to be expanded in the future. This will also assure a margin of safety for ocean surges resulting from hurricanes.

Adaptation planning should not be an afterthought; it will affect the overall layout of a site. Constructing a sea wall around a site on the ocean will disrupt views at ground level, making it desirable to raise the main pedestrian movement level above the top of the barrier. Storing site runoff during times when adjacent streams or water bodies are high will require detention areas to be set aside, or installation of underground cisterns. Many of these adaptations may make sense for other reasons—they make an underground service and parking level possible, or allow runoff to be used for landscape irrigation—so that adapting to climate change can work in favor of producing a better site design. Elsewhere in this volume we discuss these benefits more fully.

19 | The Site Proposal

Analyses, programming, and plans for the form, infrastructure, and landscape converge in a proposal for the site. It will provide the client with enough detail to make decisions, develop a financial plan for the project, and begin assembling the human resources to make it a reality. Public officials and citizens will be able to envision the look and feel of the developed site, and stakeholders will be able to judge whether their aspirations are being met. Ideally, all will have had glimpses of the proposal as it was being prepared, so many of the ideas will not come as a surprise. However, a fully documented site plan will bring together all the threads of a project, with a presentation that is inspiring while addressing the practical issues.

As with every aspect of site planning, there is no single formula for how to present the site proposal. However, we can the learn how to think about presentations from successful examples. The case study presented here offers many lessons.

ANANAS COMMUNITY
Silang, Philippines

ACM Landholdings, Inc., a Philippines land and housing developer, has partnered with Philippine Transmarine Carriers, Inc., one of the country's largest maritime crew management companies, to create housing and communities for returning seafarers. ACM's vision is "to create vibrant communities that promote a new approach in sustainable living while maintaining a distinctive Filipino identity" (ACM Homes, n.d.). ACM engaged Sasaki Associates, Inc. to plan for their new community in Silang, Cavite province, about 30 km from central Manila. All illustrations in this chapter are from the Sasaki project report (Sasaki Associates 2015), and used by courtesy of the firm.

The Ananas site, which ACM acquired many years ago, consists of 247 ha (610 ac) of prime farmland, currently used for pineapple plantations and other products. ACM is seeking to "infuse 'soul' into the experience of everyday life, preserving the agricultural heritage of the site and promoting the sensitive integration of ecological systems" (ACM Homes, n.d.). The area around the site is rapidly urbanizing, and this will accelerate upon completion of the new metropolitan ring road, the Cavite-Laguna Expressway (CALAX), that will be located on the northern edge of the site. Business parks, industries, and residential development are already developing in a scattered pattern around the site.

The Site

The site itself is largely flat tableland, edged by steep ravines and rivers on its eastern and western sides. Intermittent streams with dense vegetation, fed by the monsoon rains that restore the water table, drain the center of the site. Two existing communities and several tree groves and plantations are also found on the site. Current access is via an entrance roadway that bisects the site.

Taking account of lands that need to be set aside for protection of the ravines and rivers, and water quality drainage buffers, the site planners estimate that 195 ha (480 ac), or about 79% of the site, is buildable.

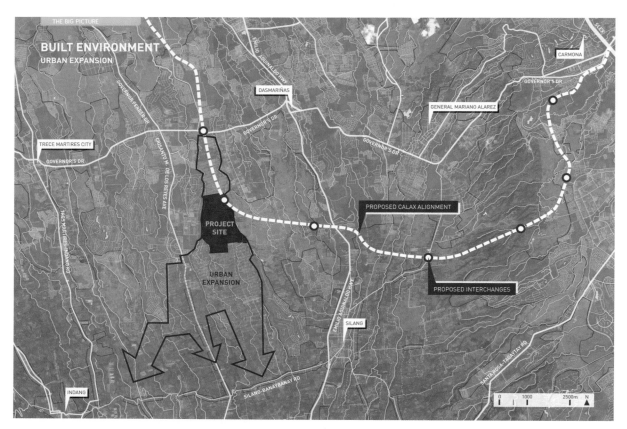

BUILT ENVIRONMENT
URBAN EXPANSION

THE BIG PICTURE

CARMONA

DASMARIÑAS

GENERAL MARIANO ALAREZ

GOVERNOR'S DR

TRECE MARTIRES CITY

GOVERNOR'S DR

GOVERNOR'S DR

GOVERNOR'S DR

GOVERNOR FERRER DR

CRISANTO M. DE LOS REYES AVE

TRECE MARTIRES-INDANG RD

EMILIO AGUINALDO HWY

PROJECT SITE

PROPOSED CALAX ALIGNMENT

URBAN EXPANSION

PROPOSED INTERCHANGES

EMILIO AGUINALDO HWY

SILANG

SANTA ROSA-TAGAYTAY RD

INDANG

SILANG-BANAYBANAY RD

SLEX

0   1000   2500m   N

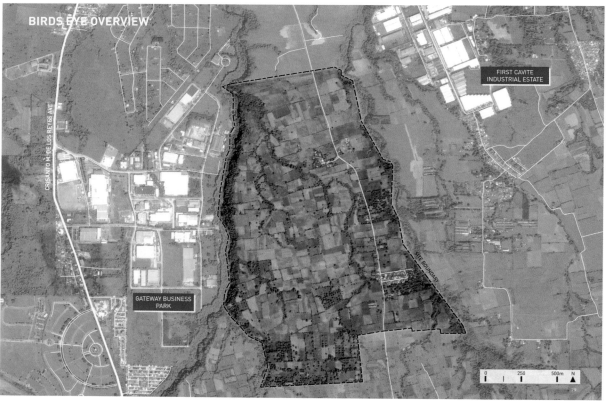

BIRDS EYE OVERVIEW

FIRST CAVITE INDUSTRIAL ESTATE

CRISANTO M. DE LOS REYES AVE

SITE BOUNDARY

GATEWAY BUSINESS PARK

0   250   500m   N

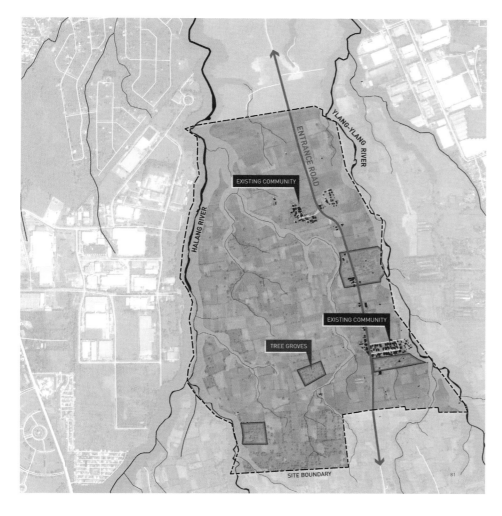

All illustrations courtesy of
Sasaki Associates

19.1 (facing page, top)
Location of Ananas site on
the urban fringe of
Manila, Philippines.

19.2 (facing page, bottom)
Aerial view of site and
surroundings.

19.3 (this page, top)
Current site conditions.

19.4 (this page, bottom)
Net buildable land area.

NET BUILDABLE LAND AREA

Based on the preceding analysis, the adjacent map illustrates the area most
favorable for development. This identifies areas deemed most suitable for
development, excluding areas of steep slope, ravine and waterway buffers,
and water quality considerations.

As a result, a total of 195 hectares (78.8%) of the 247 hectare site is
recommended as suitable for development. While not directly developed
as saleable areas, the ravines and stream areas hold significant landscape
amenity and value for the community, and may be integrated as functional
elements of the Ananas open space system.

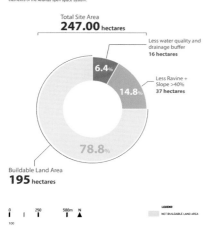

Total Site Area
247.00 hectares

Less water quality and
drainage buffer
16 hectares

6.4%

Less Ravine +
Slope >40%
37 hectares

14.8%

78.8%

Buildable Land Area
195 hectares

The Concept

The site plan is rooted in a "big idea." Rather than sheet urbanization, which continues to push agricultural uses further outward, the idea is to interleaf urban uses with intensive agriculture, creating an agripolitan town. This is a concept that is easily remembered and makes tangible the client's desire to infuse "soul" into everyday life.

The next step is to create a structure for the site plan that applies the concept to the land. Four major structuring devices create the framework for development: creating a central park and east-west streets that respond to the microclimate of predominant winds; integrating food production and sales systems along the east-west corridors; creating a great street that links the community and provides a sense of place; and promoting resilience by maintaining and augmenting current natural systems.

CURRENT PARADIGM

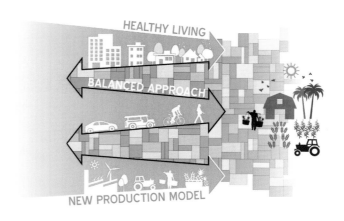

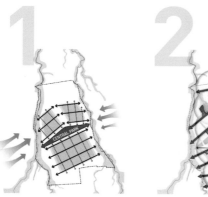

1

CREATE A COMFORTABLE MICROCLIMATE BY MAXIMIZING WIND CAPTURE

2

INTEGRATE FOOD SYSTEMS BY INTRODUCING NOVEL URBAN AGRICULTURE STRATEGIES

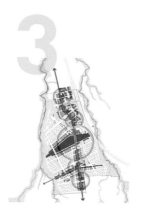

3

CREATE A SENSE OF PLACE BY PROVIDING GREAT PUBLIC SPACES

4

CREATE A RESILIENT COMMUNITY BY INCORPORATING NATURAL SYSTEMS IN THE DEVELOPMENT

19.5 (top left) Conventional development pushes agriculture out.

19.6 (top right) The new paradigm: balancing urban and agricultural development.

19.7 (bottom) Four main structuring elements for the plan.

Master Site Plan

The overall plan for the site elaborates the concept and lays out the streets, agricultural and ecological corridors, uses, and prototypical forms of development. The ideas are conveyed through an illustrative plan, an aerial view of the three-dimensional model, and diagrams that explain each of the systems that provide the armature of the site. The emphasis is on the quality of the public realm, not on defining the precise form of the buildings. These will come much later, but now the critical issues are the heights, relationship of structures to streets and open areas, and the sense of place that is intended.

The hierarchy of roadways needs to be diagrammed, along with other key elements of infrastructure. Special attention is given to the prototypical cross sections of each type of street. The great street will be the linear spine of the community and needs to be planned in coordination with bordering uses. Local residential streets have been narrowed to favor pedestrians over cars and are designed to absorb runoff in bioswales. The street views illustrate how multipurpose drawings can both provide a sense of the spatial character and indicate the innovative infrastructure that is embedded in the street profile.

19.8 Master site plan for Ananas community.

```
0      1000       2500m  N
I  I   I         I   I   ▲
```

MASTER PLAN FRAMEWORK

1 CULTURAL HUB AND PLAZA
2 CENTRAL PARK
3 MUSEO PAMBATA (CHILDREN'S MUSEUM)
4 INDOOR SPORTS CENTER
5 TENNIS CLUBHOUSE
6 AGRICULTURAL RESEARCH
7 PRIMARY SCHOOL
8 MERCADO ANANAS (FARMER'S MARKET)
9 MIXED-USE RETAIL HUB
10 MIXED-USE COMMERCIAL HUB
11 MIXED-USE EDUCATIONAL CENTER
12 NATURE CENTER
13 CULINARY SCHOOL
14 FOOD HUB AND RESTAURANTS
15 MAIN CHURCH
16 FOOD FOREST PARK
17 SECONDARY SCHOOL
18 RETAIL PAVILION
19 NEIGHBORHOOD CENTER
20 POLLINATOR PATHS

19.9 (this page, top)
Aerial view of community from 3D model.

19.10 (this page, bottom)
Proposed street hierarchy.

19.11 (facing page, top)
Urban boulevard cross section and adjacent uses.

19.12 (facing page, bottom)
Illustration of character and infrastructure of urban boulevard.

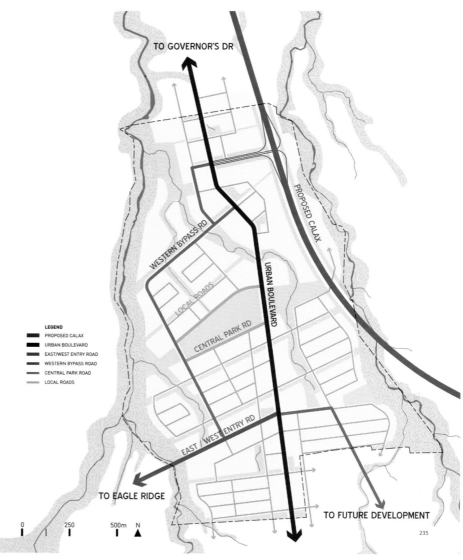

TO GOVERNOR'S DR

PROPOSED CALAX

WESTERN BYPASS RD

LOCAL ROADS

URBAN BOULEVARD

CENTRAL PARK RD

EAST / WEST ENTRY RD

TO EAGLE RIDGE

TO FUTURE DEVELOPMENT

LEGEND
PROPOSED CALAX
URBAN BOULEVARD
EAST/WEST ENTRY ROAD
WESTERN BYPASS ROAD
CENTRAL PARK ROAD
LOCAL ROADS

0   250   500m   N

235

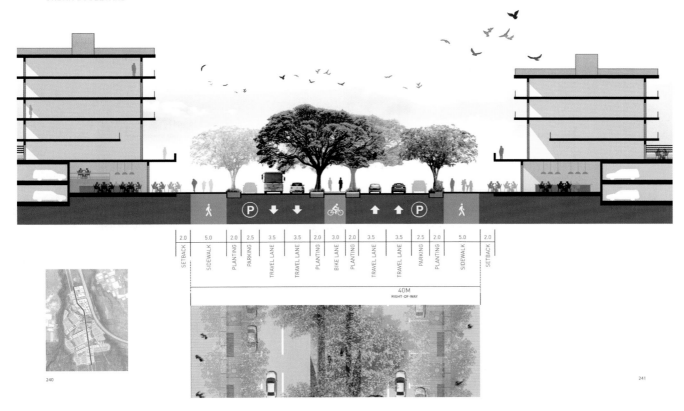

SETBACK	SIDEWALK	PLANTING	PARKING	TRAVEL LANE	TRAVEL LANE	PLANTING	BIKE LANE	PLANTING	TRAVEL LANE	TRAVEL LANE	PARKING	PLANTING	SIDEWALK	SETBACK
2.0	5.0	2.0	2.5	3.5	3.5	2.0	3.0	2.0	3.5	3.5	2.5	2.0	5.0	2.0

40M
RIGHT-OF-WAY

240

241

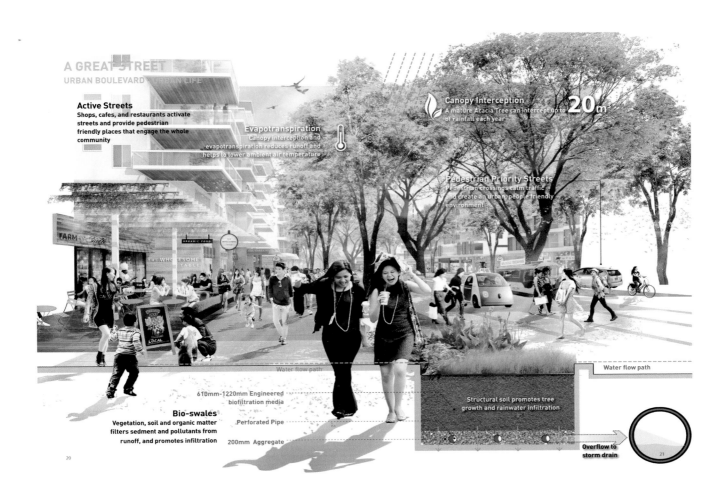

A GREAT STREET
URBAN BOULEVARD

Active Streets
Shops, cafes, and restaurants activate streets and provide pedestrian friendly places that engage the whole community

Evapotranspiration
Canopy interception and evapotranspiration reduces runoff and helps to lower ambient air temperature

Canopy Interception
A mature Acacia Tree can intercept up to **20m** of rainfall each year

Pedestrian Priority Streets
Pedestrian crossings calm traffic and create an urban, people friendly environment

Water flow path

Water flow path

610mm-1220mm Engineered biofiltration media

Perforated Pipe

Bio-swales
Vegetation, soil and organic matter filters sediment and pollutants from runoff, and promotes infiltration

200mm Aggregate

Structural soil promotes tree growth and rainwater infiltration

Overflow to storm drain

20

21

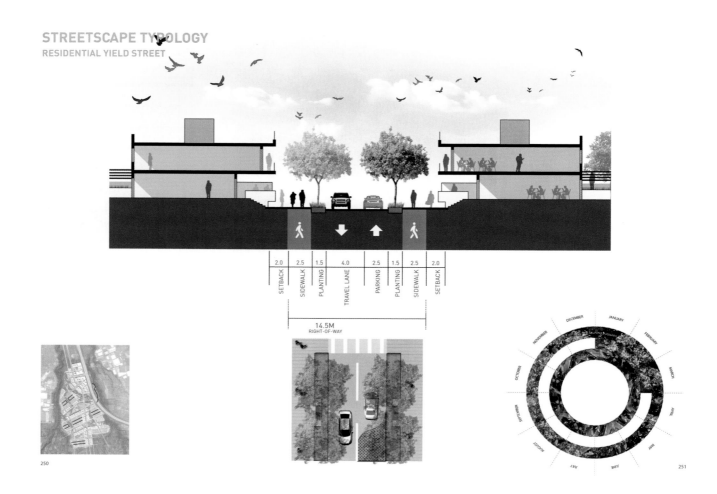

2.0	2.5	1.5	4.0	2.5	1.5	2.5	2.0
SETBACK	SIDEWALK	PLANTING	TRAVEL LANE	PARKING	PLANTING	SIDEWALK	SETBACK

14.5M
RIGHT-OF-WAY

250

251

19.13 Local residential street cross section and adjacent uses.

19.14 Illustration of character and infrastructure of local residential street.

Native Street Trees
Strong rooted and adapted to the seasonal climate, native tree species withstand seasonal variations & typhoon winds

Heat Island Reduction
Abundant street trees help to keep neighborhoods cool and reduce ambient air temperatures as much as 3°C

Bicycle Friendly Streets
Slow streets and abundant multi-use paths make Ananas the perfect place to bike for fun and to get around

50,000m²
Less Pavement = More Place
Narrow streets lower vehicle speeds making neighborhoods more safe and help to reduce excess stormwater runoff
22

150,000m³
Reduction in Stormwater Runoff
Directing stormwater runoff into street planters filters runoff, reduces flooding, and promotes groundwater recharge

20km
Pedestrian Oriented Walkways
Every neighborhood and amenity is easily accessible by foot or bike, reducing short vehicle trips, and easing congestion
23

Elaborating the Site Plan

Several areas of the plan are singled out for special attention, and the viewer zooms in on greater detail. The central park is the social and cultural center of the community, and the plan provides a possible spatial program for activities and facilities that might accompany it. This is not an attempt to design the park, but to create the program for it that will allow discussions with institutions that might consider locating there. Words and images are fused in describing places. However, it is also important to illustrate the look and feel of places in the park, and drawings of the cultural hub and sheltered basketball courts in the sports center offer a look at what they might become.

The predominant use of land on the site will be for residential areas, and the site planners have made studies of prototypical residential clusters and their relationship to the matrix of urban agriculture. The blocks are sized to permit many possible internal arrangements, only one of which is shown here, fronting on a pollinator path devoted to urban agriculture. Residential blocks are large enough to allow internal spaces for parking, clothes drying, and other activities that homeowners wish to screen from public streets. A major issue for residential development in the Philippines is whether residential areas should be gated for security, which is preferred by many builders and homebuyers. However, gating communities discourages walking by requiring circuitous routes and limiting access to across-the-street neighbors. The site

19.15 (top left)   Aerial view of central park.

19.16 (bottom left)   Diagram of uses of central park.

19.17 (top right)   Close-up of program for cultural hub and recreation area.

19.18 (this page, top)
Illustration of cultural hub.

19.19 (this page, middle)
Covered courts in recreation area.

19.20 (this page, bottom)
Prototypical layout of residential cluster and pollinator path.

19.21 (facing page, top)
Cross section of residential cluster.

19.22 (facing page, bottom)
Illustration of pollinator path and residential area.

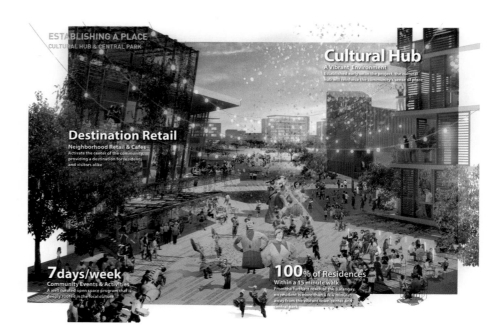

ESTABLISHING A PLACE
CULTURAL HUB & CENTRAL PARK

Cultural Hub
A Vibrant Environment
Established early on in the project, the cultural hub will reinforce the community's sense of place

Destination Retail
Neighborhood Retail & Cafes
Activate the center of the community, providing a destination for residents and visitors alike

7 days/week
Community Events & Activities
A well curated open space program that is deeply rooted in the local culture

100% of Residences
Within a 15 minute walk
From the furthest reach of the barangay, no resident is more than a few minutes away from the vibrant town center and central park

ESTABLISHING A PLACE
SPORTS CENTER

Sheltered Courts
Year-Round Activities
Covered courts allow for active use under harsh heat or heavy rain conditions

11,000 m²
Indoor Sports Center
Sports Center includes basketball courts, a gym, multi-purpose rooms, and an olympic pool

Basketball
13 Outdoor Courts
A sports destination in Ananas and the region

Tennis
6 Outdoor Courts
Courts and clubhouse create a venue for tennis camps

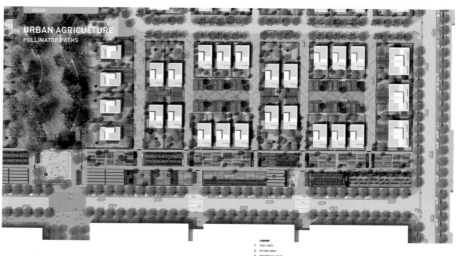

VISION
URBAN AGRICULTURE
POLLINATOR PATHS

8.3 hectares
Organic Farmland On-site
On-site community garden plots and orchards provide food security and a rooted connection to the local landscape.

LEGEND
1 TOOL SHED
2 SITTING AREA
3 RESIDENTIAL PLOT
4 COMMUNITY PLOT
5 COMMERCIAL PLOT
6 GREENHOUSE
7 BASKETBALL COURT
8 PLAYGROUND
9 PICNIC AREA

0   1000   2500m

WORKING WITH THE CLIMATE
RESIDENTIAL BLOCK TYPOLOGIES

4x more energy efficient
Simulation has shown that the proposed cluster arrangement maintains comfort level for 60% of the year. A typical development can only rely on natural ventilation for 15% of the year.

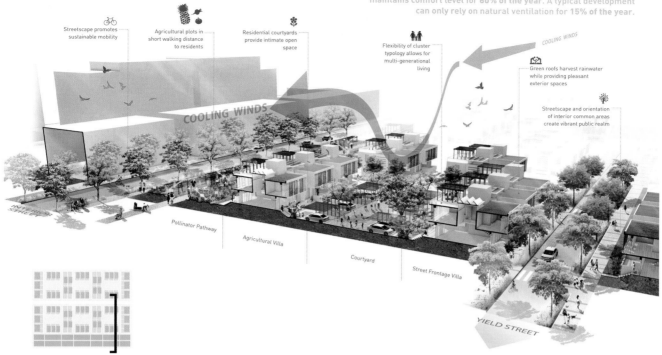

Streetscape promotes sustainable mobility

Agricultural plots in short walking distance to residents

Residential courtyards provide intimate open space

Flexibility of cluster typology allows for multi-generational living

COOLING WINDS

Green roofs harvest rainwater while providing pleasant exterior spaces

Streetscape and orientation of interior common areas create vibrant public realm

COOLING WINDS

Pollinator Pathway

Agricultural Villa

Courtyard

Street Frontage Villa

YIELD STREET

URBAN AGRICULTURE
POLLINATOR PATHS

Rainwater Harvesting
Wet-season capturing of rainfall from residential buildings helps to offset demand of groundwater for irrigation during the dry season

Wet Season

MONSOON PROTECTION

PERMEABLE PAVING

9M COMMERCIAL PLOT

8M COMMUNITY PLOT

CISTERN

UNDERDRAIN

KANG KONG

CARROTS

POTATO

Water Sensitive Street Design
A combination of narrow streets, enhanced canopy coverage, infiltration strips, and permeable sidewalks allow capture of rainwater for irrigaton that helps to reduce runoff and promote groundwater recharge

HYDROPHILIC VEGETABLES

ROOT VEGETABLES

Seasonal Crop Rotation
Garden swales function as wet gardens during the wet-season, provide positive drainage for mounded root vegetables, and protect sensitive crops from excessive wind and evaporation during the dry season

SECURITY
STRATEGIES FOR AN EVOLVING CULTURAL LANDSCAPE

The master plan establishes a hierarchy of larger public and smaller
private residential streets that offer flexibility to accommodate
the security needs of each residential neighborhood as the new
community is established.

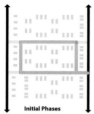

Initial Phases　　　**Future**

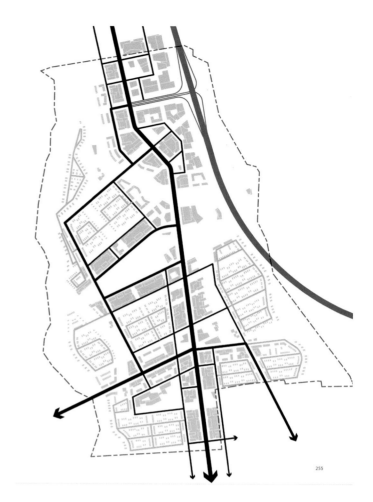

0　　250　　500m　N

LEGEND
▬▬ PUBLIC STREET
▨ PRIVATE DRIVE
⌐¬ GATED ENCLAVES
→ GATES

254

255

ESTABLISHING A PLACE
THE CENTRAL PARK & MARKET

8.3 hectares
Organic Farmland On-site
On-site community garden plots and
orchards provide food security and a
rooted connection to the local landscape

Farm-to-Table
Supporting the Local Economy
Produce sold on-site and used in local
cafes is locally grown and harvested,
supporting local farmers and their
families

10,000 local farmers
In Silang & General Trias
One of the most productive agricultural
areas near Manila, Cavite Province is
known for its high quality produce

planners, who advocated more open street networks, indicated how the option could be left open until the time of development, or even altered after the residential clusters are occupied.

Urban agriculture also needs a place to sell produce, and the plan illustrates the possible locations of several market centers along the main spine of the community. The streams and valleys on the site have been carefully protected as ecological corridors, which can be an asset to the community. The plan illustrates how they can be integrated with development while continuing to serve hydrological functions.

INTEGRATE NATURAL SYSTEMS
ECOLOGICAL CORRIDORS

Evapotranspiration
Canopy interception and evapotranspiration reduces runoff and helps to lower ambient air temperature

Open Space Frontage
Residential apartments define and activate open spaces, while maximizing real estate value

Ecological Corridors
Offer landscape amenity while accommodating the site's hydrology requirements

Pedestrian Trails
Provide for active and passive recreational uses and connect various neighborhoods to create a whole community

19.23 (facing page, top)   Options for security of residential areas.

19.24 (facing page, bottom)   Produce market at central park.

19.25 (this page)   Integrating ecological corridors with development.

Program and Phasing

Site planning projects generally begin with a rough program of uses, but these need to be validated and refined as the plan is produced. The proposed program for the site plan is included here. Based on it, it is possible to estimate the total floor area of the community at 1,225,300 m² (13,188,900 sq ft) and the ultimate population of the community at about 30,000.

Communities of that size do not get built overnight—except perhaps in China—and a phasing plan is a practical necessity. The plan for the Ananas community imagines five stages, beginning with the creation of the central park, portions of the core and recreation areas, and residential areas north of them, which will collectively signal the identity of the community. Then development would begin south of the central park, awaiting the completion of the CALAX highway. Once complete, the mixed-use commercial center would capitalize on the new interchange with the highway, and development would begin to become more linear in the north-south direction. The area would fill out as demand materializes in successive phases.

19.26 Site development program.

DEVELOPMENT SUMMARY
FULL BUILD-OUT

GROSS FLOOR AREA (GFA)

■	RESIDENTIAL = 708,247 m² (63%)	
■	RETAIL = 178,953 m² (16%)	
▨	DENOTES GROUND FLOOR RETAIL IN RESIDENTIAL BUILDING	
■	OFFICE = 123,972 m² (11%)	
■	EDUCATION = 41,354 m² (4%)	
■	HOTEL / CONFERENCE = 31,715 m² (3%)	
■	SPORTS = 26,717 m² (2.5%)	
■	CIVIC = 18,009 m² (1.5%)	
■	NEIGHBORHOOD CENTERS = 5,877 m² (0.5%)	
	TOTAL GFA = 1,225,293 m²	

RESIDENTIAL

■	APARTMENTS	= 197,828 m² (36.6% of total units)
	# OF UNITS	= 2,198 (BASED ON AVERAGE UNIT GFA OF 90 m²)
■	TOWNHOMES	= 286,669 m² (43.4% of total units)
	# OF UNITS	= 2,606 (BASED ON AVERAGE UNIT GFA OF 110 m²)
▢	SINGLE FAMILY	= 223,750 m² (10% of total units)
	# OF UNITS	= 1,206 (BASED ON NUMBER OF DETACHED HOMES)
	TOTAL RESIDENTIAL GFA	**= 708,247 m²**
	TOTAL # OF UNITS	**= 6,010**
	TOTAL # OF PEOPLE	**= 30,051 (ASSUME 5 PEOPLE PER UNIT)**

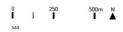

0   250   500m   N

345

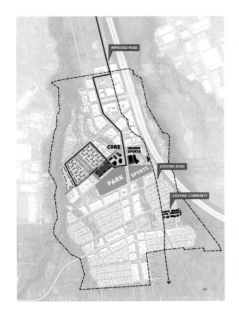

19.27 Phase 1 development.

19.28 Phase 2 development.

19.29 Phase 3 development.

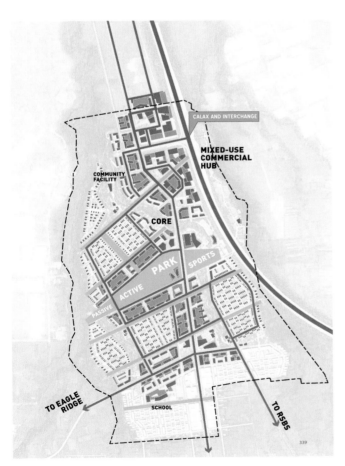

19.30 Phase 4 development.

19.31 Phase 5 development.

Summing Up

The site proposal needs to capture the attention and enthusiasm of those who are viewing it, communicate a way of thinking about the site's development, and provide both conceptual and detailed information about how to develop the site. Effective presentations combine drawings, diagrams, and words for maximum effect. They establish the key structural elements while avoiding premature excursions into architectural and landscape detail. The proposal is one step in designing the site, allowing the site to move through the approval process and be broken into parcels and the design of major infrastructure to begin. It needs to establish the character of the site, inspiring continued creativity in its planning and design.

Part 4 | Site Infrastructure

Infrastructure makes it possible to inhabit a site. It provides access, supplies a site's essential public services, and removes its wastes. The term *infrastructure* originally referred to permanent installations for military purposes, but today it encompasses the full range of a settlement's visible and invisible services, ranging from underground pipes and conduits to roads, transit systems, and traffic control devices, to cell phone installations and even satellite downlinks. Keynesian economics popularized the term *infrastructure*, defining it as public assets that support private production, but in recent years the line has been blurred between public and private goods. Today, public services are often supplied by private organizations licensed and regulated by public bodies, or by joint public-private enterprises that share risks and rewards.

Infrastructure planning has often been left to engineers, since it is largely standards-driven and rooted in the experience of installing and maintaining equipment and technologies. The result, however, is that much infrastructure is overdesigned and costly, unattractive, and compromises the ability to create other things on a site. Roadways are too wide and favor automobiles over pedestrians, cyclists, and transit; storm drainage is placed underground in costly pipes that sit empty most of the time but are unable to accommodate intense storms; electrical and communication cables are placed underground below roadways and constantly need to be dug up to deal with new demands or technologies. It is better to think of infrastructure decisions in terms of policy choices—how to balance smooth flow of automobiles against the safety of pedestrians, whether to decentralize the treatment of wastes or transport them to central processing plants, whether to rely on central energy production or local production, and so on.

There have been significant advances in infrastructure systems and their corresponding economics, particularly through real-time monitoring, on-demand supply, decentralization and miniaturization of facilities, and closed-loop recycling. Taking advantage of this innovation generally requires better synchronization of infrastructure design with planning the uses of a site and the form of its buildings. It also generally requires new financial arrangements and a new division of responsibilities between site developers, owners, and local governments.

The site planner can often envision possibilities that specialized consultants overlook. Infrastructure planning invites innovation, but also requires a thorough grounding in conventional methods. This part of the book offers both the conventions and the emerging possibilities.

Developing a site usually requires installing infrastructure both within its boundaries and beyond. On greenfield sites, roadways, sewer and water lines, and communications infrastructure may need to be extended out to a site, and drainage courses may need to be modified to transport runoff away from it. If the site is large, there is usually the option of creating freestanding infrastructure systems that serve just the site, but small sites need to rely on larger public systems. The need for infrastructure may be minimized by creative site design that reduces runoff, reuses water, keeps the size of roadways to a minimum, and lowers site maintenance through the use of indigenous vegetation. Local engineering standards usually spell out what is normally permitted, and exceptions will need to be negotiated.

Infrastructure Investments

The cost of installing infrastructure is a significant financial hurdle, often equaling or exceeding the cost of acquiring a site. Who pays for the infrastructure is a matter of local convention. In many places, the developer must install all infrastructure, designed to meet government standards, prior to transferring land to those who will occupy it. In other places, sewer, water, roadways, parks and open spaces, and other essential services are installed by local governments and paid for out of fees charged to the site developer, or through bonded capital raised by the local government, repaid from taxes or user fees. In some places, electrical and telephone lines are installed by the local service companies, with costs charged to the developer or covered as part of the utility's rate base. If infrastructure beyond the site—such as sewer treatment facilities or water treatment plants or arterial roads—must be expanded, frequently the local government or utility company will do so, charging the site developer for the incremental costs. Off-site systems may have been oversized in anticipation of a site's development, with the developer reimbursing the local government for its fair share of earlier investments.

Regardless of who pays for it, infrastructure always implies two types of costs: immediate capital costs to construct or install it, and long-term operating and maintenance costs incurred over its life. There are often tradeoffs between the two. Placing electrical lines on poles may be far less costly than installing them in trenches below ground, but maintenance and replacement costs will be higher, especially in locations with high winds and freezing rain, not to mention the intangible value of avoiding unsightly poles and lines above ground. Transporting water away from roads in large storm pipes is far more costly than creating swales on the sides of roadways, but the latter may require more land to be devoted to rights-of-way and will necessitate regular maintenance. When alternatives are considered, they should be analyzed in terms of life cycle costs:

$$LCC = IC + PV(AM) + PV(RC)$$
where
LCC = life cycle costs,
IC = initial capital costs,
PV = present value discounted at borrowing cost rate,
AM = annual maintenance costs,
RC = replacement costs.

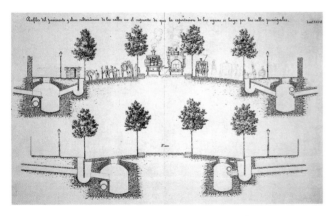

20.1 Underground sewers proposed in 1865 by Ildefons Cerdà for l'Eixample (the expansion) of Barcelona, one of the earliest examples of planning infrastructure in advance of development. (Ildefons Cerdà)

20.2 Sewers, water, drainage, and sidewalks being installed in Rio de Janeiro's hillside favela.
(Gary Hack)

The lifetime to be valued should equal the expected life of the most durable component, although as a practical matter the present value of expenditures required 50–75 years into the future is very small (see chapter 17).

In situations with very low resources available, such as rapidly urbanizing areas of developing countries, infrastructure may need to be created over time as resources permit rather than at the outset of the development. Initially, only the rights-of-way may be established, then overhead electrical lines installed, with other infrastructure added later. Most North American cities were developed in this way: in residential areas, gravel roads lined by ditches, wooden sidewalks, overhead electric and telephone lines, and minimal underground water lines were installed in most cities in the nineteenth century, replaced later by paved streets, underground storm drains, concrete sidewalks, larger-diameter water mains with hydrants for firefighting, and, sometimes, underground electric and telephone lines. This process of upgrading, common today in many barrios and favelas, is a practical way to provide services without excluding low-income people from urban areas.

Rights-of-Way for Infrastructure

Infrastructure is usually installed in a public right-of-way, usually a street, although it may cross private lands where easements have been granted for access, maintenance, and replacement (see chapter 6). Since many types of infrastructure must share the right-of-way, it is essential that the location of infrastructure—above, on, and below ground—be carefully organized, keeping in mind that most systems will require regular maintenance. Most cities have conventions for the precise location of each infrastructure system. Water pipes are typically located on the opposite side of the street from the electrical and telecommunications lines, to avoid damage in the case of a water line break. Storm and sanitary sewer lines, usually the largest and most costly systems, are generally in the center of the street, where they can easily serve inlets from either side. Underground lines are generally spaced away from tree roots that can easily damage them. Cities provide infrastructure planners with standard street profiles that they are obliged to follow, making it easy for emergency workers to quickly locate a line that needs to be repaired.

Street profiles in rapidly urbanizing countries reflect the necessity of using less costly infrastructure systems. Many cities use combined sewer systems that are less costly to install, collecting sewage in drainage trenches located below sidewalks or at the edges of properties, rather than providing individual building hookups to the sewer lines. Where storm drainage systems are in place, they customarily are limited to roadway runoff.

20.3 Typical low-density suburban street cross section, with conventional infrastructure. (Courtesy of Bolton & Menk, Inc.)

20.4 Standard cross section with location of infrastructure, Santa Monica, California. (City of Santa Monica)

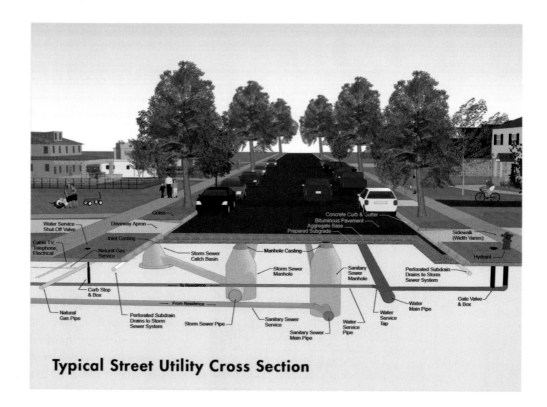

Typical Street Utility Cross Section

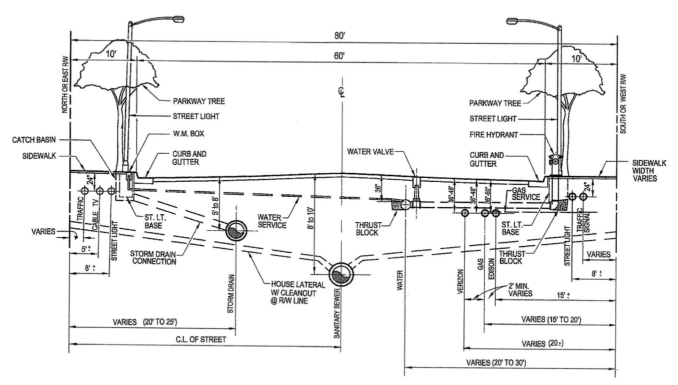

TYPICAL STREET CROSS SECTION

SCALE: N.T.S.

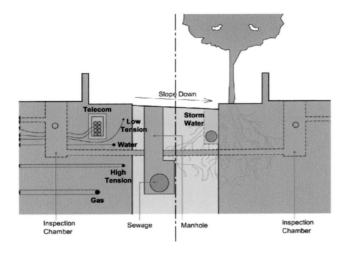

20.5 Recommended street cross section in India, relying on utility trenches for collection of wastes.
(Courtesy of Environmental Planning Collaborative/Institute for Transport and Development Policy)

Historically, the width of a street right-of-way has been largely determined by the number of lanes required to move traffic and accommodate parked vehicles, but other factors also play a role. The desire to introduce landscape to absorb runoff, provide shade, or simply to add beauty to the street can add to its width, as can the need for generous sidewalks in dense urban areas. The disruption of digging up streets has led to the installation of common utility boxes or trenches in some dense urban areas, sometimes located below sidewalks, but other times occupying a separate portion of the right-of-way width. Wide rights-of-way may also reflect the desire to maintain flexibility for the future, keeping the option open to add dedicated mass transit lanes along a street, or to expand the moving lanes as traffic grows in an area. Such possibilities should be carefully scrutinized, however, since overly wide streets can discourage walkability and waste scarce land resources.

Rights-of-way in US and European cities typically occupy 20–30% of the land resources of a city, while in dense older areas of Asian cities they may only occupy half that amount or less (Vasconcellos 2001). As income rises in a country, automobile ownership rates increase, and there is a corresponding rise in the amount of land devoted to roadways. One study suggests that the elasticity is 1: for every 1% increase in national income, the length of roadways (and area occupied by them) rises by 1% (Ingram and Liu 1997). Nonetheless, limiting the area devoted to rights-of-way to less than 20% of the land available is a reasonable target, requiring ingenuity on the part of the site planner.

Since roadways are generally laid out first on a site, there is a tendency to err on the side of making rights-of-way overly generous. Most of Manhattan was developed with 60 ft (18 m) rights of way on east-west streets and 100 ft (30 m) on north-south avenues and major crosstown streets. It has evolved from a city of townhouses to one where tall apartments and office buildings predominate, but continues to exist comfortably at high densities within its original framework. Streets in New York represent over 26% of the surface area of the city. Many of Philadelphia's charming "alley streets" are as narrow as 30 ft (9 m). At the other extreme, new Chinese cities are commonly built with rights-of-way of 80 to 150 m (262–492 ft) for major arterials, and 18 m (60 ft) for local streets. These streets are excessively wide for the number of vehicles currently using them, and planners justify them through future projections of traffic and vehicle ownership, which may or may not materialize. Residential subdivisions in the US often require 60 ft (18 m) street widths, even in the lowest-density areas, also far in excess of what is required.

20.6 Use of a common trench for the diverse and constantly changing telecommunications technology simplifies the replacement costs.
(Gary Hack)

Complete Streets and Context-Sensitive Design

Since much of the infrastructure is housed in streets, we typically begin site planning with their design. The layout of streets and rights-of-way is often seen strictly as an engineering problem of how to most effectively organize infrastructure to minimize installation costs and operating problems. Each system is optimized within the available right-of-way, and conventions have evolved for typical types of streets. A better approach, however, begins with a list of the human needs to be served by the channels being constructed. The list might include:

Moving autos, buses, and trucks,
Space for children to play,
Access to frontages,
Space for pedestrians to walk,
Parking space for cars,
Shade for pedestrians,
Safe bicycle travel,
Allowing pedestrians to cross streets safely,
Potable water,
Mail delivery,
Water for firefighting,
Incorporating ornamental landscape,
Piped natural gas,
Absorbing most runoff to support landscape,
Electrical service,
Draining excessive storm runoff,
Cable service for TV and telephones,
Accommodating snow removal and storage,
Safe bus stops,
Street sweeping and cleaning,
Lighting for pedestrian safety.

20.7 Streets of 60 ft (18 m) laid out in Manhattan for townhouses.
(Gary Hack)

20.8 Streets of 60 ft (18 m) continue to function for high-density office uses.
(Gary Hack)

20.9 Philadelphia alley street with 30 ft (9 m) right-of-way.
(Gary Hack)

20.10 Arterial street, 80 m (260 ft) in width, Qun Li New Town, Harbin, China.
(Gary Hack)

Satisfying all these demands may create conflicts, particularly in dense urban situations with constrained rights-of-way. Thus it is important to get priorities straight in order to guide tradeoffs. New York City has publicized its priorities for traffic moving over city streets: (1) pedestrians, (2) bicyclists, (3) bus riders, and (4) motorists (New York City Department of Transportation 2009). Other conventions hinge on safety issues, such as allowing adequate space between sewer and water lines or between gas and electric lines. Unfortunately, issues of aesthetics and use, such as where trees can be planted or whether sidewalks are widened at intersections, are hamstrung by a host of engineering decisions.

The *complete streets* movement has emerged as an effort at rebalancing the use of streets to better reflect the needs of a diverse set of users. It is also rooted in considerations of public health and the realization that the decline of walking and cycling is in part a result of inhospitable streets (Seskin and McCann 2012; Seskin et al. 2012). Typically, the objectives of a complete streets program are "to ensure that the safety and convenience of all users of the transportation system are accommodated, including pedestrians, bicyclists, users of mass transit, people with disabilities, the elderly, motorists, freight providers, emergency responders and adjacent land users ..." (Bloomington, Indiana, MPO 2009). Most complete streets programs only deal with organizing

the surface of the street—the moving and parking lanes, pedestrian walks, crosswalks, medians, and landscaped areas of the street. A truly comprehensive street program would, of course, take into account what occurs below and above ground as well.

Complete streets encourage safe walking and cycling, even if doing so reduces vehicle capacity or speeds or requires a reduction of on-street parking. In the US, half the trips in metropolitan areas are of three miles or less, and 20% are of one mile or less, yet the vast majority of trips are taken by automobile (Federal Highway Administration 2008). Shifting short-distance trips to walking or cycling, or longer-distance trips to transit, can more than offset any delays that may occur as a result of devoting a greater share of the roadway corridor to pedestrian, bicycle, or bus usage. Better pedestrian facilities can also promote safety: over 40% of pedestrian fatalities occurred on roads where no crosswalks were available, with more than half occurring on fast-moving arterial roads (Ernst and Shoup 2009). The most vulnerable groups are those who have no options for travel, including many of the elderly, children, and people with disabilities. European countries have generally adopted a more balanced approach to the use of street space, and comparative studies have shown that pedestrian death rates in Germany and the Netherlands are typically half to one-sixth the rates in the US per km traveled (Jacobsen 2003).

20.11 Example of a complete street proposed for Redmond, Washington, balancing the needs of motorists, transit riders, pedestrians, cyclists, and adjoining properties.
(Courtesy of Crandall Arambula PC)

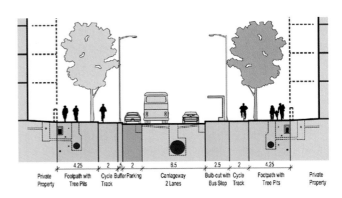

20.12 Proposed 24 m (80 ft) complete street in India.
(Courtesy of Environmental Planning Collaborative/Institute for Transport and Development Policy)

European cities have pioneered many complete streets solutions, particularly in integrating safe bicycle and pedestrian ways, dedicated or shared transit routes, and vehicular traffic in streets. Hundreds of US cities have adopted complete streets strategies, converting existing streets and revising standards and prototypical layouts of new rights-of-way. A common theme is revisiting standards to offer the flexibility needed to respond to the varying needs of streets. Traffic planners have pursued a parallel approach, seeking *context-sensitive solutions* that differentiate design standards based on their location (Institute of Transportation Engineers 2006). Many of these approaches have been integrated in the chapters that follow.

Surprisingly, there has been less innovation in below-ground infrastructure. Streets continue to need constant excavation to add new lines, replace obsolete ones, and repair breaks and damages. The evolution of telecommunications technologies has required many streets to be dug up for installation of cable, fiber optic, and other data conduits. Underground pipes are subject to routine blockages, although the problem is slowly being reduced by the use of curved pipes and continuous conduit. Nonetheless, underground infrastructure remains vulnerable to damage by tree roots, high water tables, poorly planned excavations, and other hazards. Some of this can be solved by intelligent organization of underground infrastructure.

One approach is limiting the area of disruption through the use of *common trenches* for certain infrastructure elements. On newly planned sites, common trenches are often located between the public right-of-way and the building face in a public *utility easement*, and are generally at least 0.5 m (18 in) wide and 1.4 m (54 in) deep. Accommodating half a dozen lines in this area requires careful planning, to allow subsequent access for upgrades or repairs. Trenches are filled as lines are added with fine-grain backfill material, often sand, that is nonabrasive and easily excavated. A common trench may contain some combination of cables for gas, TV, fiber optic, telephone, primary and secondary electric, and street lighting. Some cities limit what can be included in common trenches by requiring a minimum of 1 m (3 ft) horizontal spacing between gas, domestic sewer, storm sewer, and water lines.

In dense urban complexes, or areas undergoing rapid development, it may be worthwhile to take the

20.13   Common utility trench, Prince William Street, St. John, New Brunswick, Canada, combining all electrical and telecommunication conduits.
(Courtesy of A. J. Good/Streetscape Canada)

next step of creating a continuous utility tunnel below ground, where infrastructure can be organized and worked on without disrupting the surface. Dense development may also necessitate large vaults below ground for switching, telephone connections, and transformers, fed by the utility tunnel. In addition to traditional infrastructure, steam, hot water, and chilled water lines may run through such utility tunnels. Medical complexes and universities often expand utility tunnels so that they are capable of serving as underground passageways for building services (removal of wastes, transporting goods received) or even as internal passageways for patients and professionals. If planned in advance, such passageways could be located either above ground or below.

Green Infrastructure

Cables, pipes, moving-vehicle lanes, lighting, and walkways are the infrastructure we are most familiar with. However, natural processes can provide an alternative for some forms of infrastructure. Runoff can be accommodated on a site through *rain gardens* or *rainwater detention areas*, rather than transported away in large

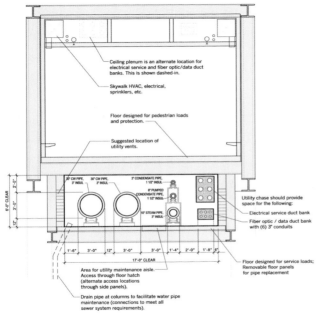

20.14 Utility tunnel, Gujarat International Finance Tec-City (GIFT), India, with ample room for expansion as the city grows. (Atul Tegar/Wikimedia Commons)

20.15 Proposed skywalk with utilities, Texas Medical Center, Houston. (Courtesy of Skidmore, Owings and Merrill/Texas Medical Center)

pipes. *Solar panels* or *wind turbines* can generate electricity locally, powering buildings or streetlights, rather than relying on large amounts of electrical power generated remotely. *Composting* and *recycling* at the scale of a site can reduce the transport of wastes to landfills, and on large sites waste may provide the raw materials for energy generation. Water used on a site can be recycled for landscape irrigation (as *gray water*) or purified for reuse. Trees and other landscape elements can absorb greenhouse gases, humidify the air, and temper the climate, thereby reducing the need for air conditioning. All of these moves need to be considered as a system of *green infrastructure*, which can complement or displace the need for *gray infrastructure* on a site.

An essential idea behind green infrastructure planning is creating *closed loops* on a site. Resources consumed on a site are reused or returned to a usable state on site, thereby minimizing the impact of the site on its larger environment. An excellent example is the new community of Hammarby Sjöstad in Stockholm, which serves as a model for integrating a range of green environment systems (see chapter 40). The essential loops in a community include:

Water loops—for domestic consumption, wastewater, storm runoff, irrigation, use in production, use in tempering outdoor spaces;

Energy loops—for heating and cooling, for movement to and from and around site, for lighting, for production;

Carbon loops—consumption of resources, discharges to the atmosphere, absorption and sequestration of carbon;

Materials loops—products for use in homes and businesses, recycling processes, reuse processes.

Hammarby Sjöstad uses a combination of green technologies and up-to-date mechanical systems that serve the residents, businesses, and industries of the new district. The results are constantly monitored, and operations are adjusted to remedy problems.

Among the closed-loop systems, water loops are among the easiest to put in place on almost any site. In most places, water is too valuable a resource to use only once, and a combination of conservation and recycling is needed. There is a long history of harvesting rainwater for purposes of supporting landscape, reprocessing water for reuse, using water for recreation, and celebrating water through fountains and water bodies. Today, carbon loops are at least as important, requiring low-carbon strategies and sequestering carbon emissions. And green infrastructure often serves several purposes. Large groves of trees can improve both water and carbon loops while improving local climate, creating a more attractive place to live, and offering recreation opportunities.

Green infrastructure has potential at all scales, from whole communities to individual sites. High-performance buildings such as the Visionaire in Battery Park City, New York reduce the dependence on public infrastructure by generating significant quantities of energy within the structure, harvesting rainwater, recycling a large fraction of the domestic water used in the building, and reducing energy consumption through the building's skin and systems. At lower densities, absorbing all the rainwater on a site can obviate the need for major storm sewers, at significant savings of infrastructure costs. Often, however, the savings flow to others or to the broader public. Charging the owners of buildings and sites for water discharged into storm sewers is one way to create an incentive to invest in retention infrastructure.

Intelligent Infrastructure

The technology of infrastructure has changed slowly over the past century, and many of the systems in the ground today are only slight improvements over systems installed many decades ago. Roadways today are only subtly different from what they were half a century ago; storm sewer technology may now use precast elements rather than clay or steel pipes but has improved very little. Regulations have stalled innovation in infrastructure, and there is little incentive for governments to try new arrangements that may fail.

20.16 The Visionaire, a high-efficiency residential building, Battery Park City, New York.
(© Jeff Goldberg/Esto)

20.17 Sustainability systems in the Visionaire, Battery Park City, New York.
(The Albanese Organization/Pelli Clarke Pelli)

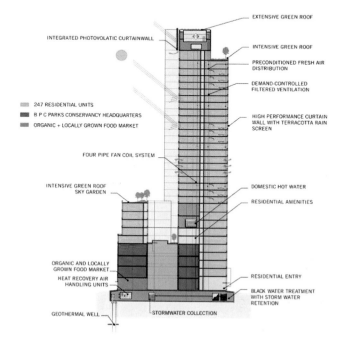

However, new technologies and materials offer the potential of adding intelligence to public services in urban areas. The innovations include new sensing and control devices, self-adapting systems, robotic maintenance equipment, real-time information systems, wireless communication systems, GPS technologies, new transmission and conduit materials, and sophisticated human-systems interfaces. The addition of new software is making it possible to change the hardware.

The chapters that follow outline some of the potentials on the horizon for the individual components of site infrastructure. Taken as a whole, they have as objectives:

More effective use of fixed resources—better utilization of roadways through improved flows of vehicles, diverting traffic in the case of breakdowns, better scheduling of public facilities, demand-sensitive routing of buses, managing distributed parking inventories, and car-sharing systems;

Load balancing—balancing energy loads across a network, shifting the sources of district heating over the day and year, and managing stormwater flows to reduce their effects;

Better predictions of failure—systems monitoring to detect potential failures, and rerouting around failures;

Improving safety—collision avoidance systems, automated vehicles, and surveillance systems to prevent crime;

Improving information for personal decisions—telepresence systems that help avoid travel, real-time transport information systems, location reports, and rerouting algorithms on personal devices;

Reducing maintenance and operating costs—automated reading of meters, detection systems for waste disposal needs, and robotic maintenance systems.

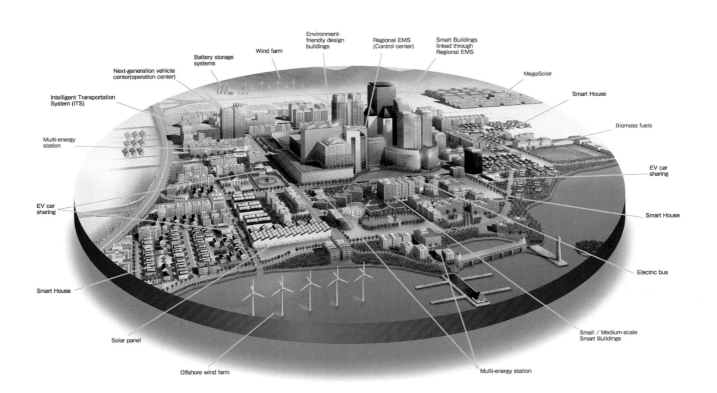

20.18 Emerging intelligent city components. (Ministry of Urban Development, India)

Intelligent environments depend upon wired or wireless communications that link displays with sensors, and sophisticated software and hardware to store

20.19 City operation center, Rio de Janeiro. (Gary Hack)

data and make estimates of the future. Every major systems corporation has produced its image of how intelligent cities should be organized, favoring of course devices and programs where they have a comparative advantage. It will take a while for experience to guide standardization, and in the meantime many thousands of partial solutions are being implemented. The chapters that follow discuss approaches to intelligent infrastructure in greater detail.

Most intelligent infrastructure systems also require people inhabiting sites to change their everyday patterns. A car-sharing system can significantly reduce the need for parking spaces and stretch roadway capacity, but also requires individuals to change their habits of car use. A distributed energy generation system which employs arrays of panels on individual houses requires individuals to participate in the maintenance of the system. Nonetheless, intelligent systems offer plenty of benefits to compensate, and infrastructure offers plenty of scope for technological development, large and small.

21 | Motor Vehicles

Over the past century, motor vehicles have dominated the site planning agenda. Even as we strive for greater balance in access—favoring transit, walking, and two-wheeled vehicles—the demands of automobiles, trucks, and other motor vehicles largely shape how we inhabit the land. They determine the widths of rights-of-way, the geometry of the environment, and patterns of movement. How vehicles are handled largely determines the character of the public realm. Areas devoted to roadways and parked vehicles represent a large fraction of space in urban areas, affecting climate and runoff patterns. There is room for innovation in every aspect of planning for motor vehicles.

The geometry of movement has traditionally been driven by conventions, standards, and simulation techniques, elevated to a science in recent years. There is detailed research to be consulted on almost every aspect of transportation planning. While precision is ultimately important when it comes to engineering the system of roadways on a site, during the initial planning stages simplified tools and rules of thumb will often suffice. Behind every standard are a host of assumptions and policy decisions, whose appropriateness to the situation at hand needs to be determined.

The infrastructure for motor vehicles always needs to balance multiple objectives:

Providing as direct access as possible to desired
 destinations,
Allowing choice in modes of travel,
Minimizing travel time,
Avoiding congestion,
Promoting safety,
Minimizing the land area devoted to vehicles,
Minimizing costs over the life cycle of facilities,
Creating a public realm that is pleasurable,
Fitting with the uses that border on a roadway or
 parking area,
Minimizing impacts on the ecology of the area,
Building in future flexibility for the use of facilities.

These objectives are not always compatible, forcing planners to make choices. Should an extra lane be added to a roadway to reduce peak hour congestion, at greater cost for the roadway, while making it more difficult for pedestrians to cross? Should the geometry of a roadway be designed to lower vehicle speeds for pedestrian and bicycle safety, or to smooth the flow of automobiles? Should parking areas be designed for the convenience of self-parkers, or to minimize the area devoted to impermeable surfaces? And so on—every choice needs to be rooted in broader values for site development, not simply traffic and transportation.

21.1 Street serving multiple purposes, at Columbus Circle, New York. (New York City Department of Transportation)

Travel Demand

It is worth remembering that all movement is an *induced activity*—the result of how we arrange activities in space. We are able to reduce the need for travel by creating an efficient pattern of land uses—mixing uses on a site, for example, or ensuring that workplaces are close to residences. Most people regard time spent in travel as wasted (although recreational travel appeals to some), so that minimizing it, and making it a pleasant experience if it remains necessary, are the twin objectives of roadway design. The paradox is that construction of a new road or transit link, usually intended to reduce travel time, also encourages activities to spread further apart and induces more travel. Land uses and forms of access must be planned in tandem.

Sizing and designing roadways requires an estimate to be made of the number of trips likely to be generated by a set of uses contemplated for a site. There are rules of thumb for most cities, usually expressed as trips per unit of housing, or trips per 100 m² (or per 1,000 sq ft) of space devoted to a commercial use. While the total number of trips generated in a day has some consequences, the more important number is how many trips are generated during the peak hour of travel—usually on a weekday morning or late afternoon hour. As an example, a typical single-family detached dwelling unit in a US suburban location generates 9.6 roadway trips over a 24-hour period. On average 8% or 0.8 of these trips are during the morning peak hour (one hour between 7 and 9 am), and 10.7% or 1.0 of them are during the afternoon peak hour (one hour between 4 and 6 pm) (Martin and McGuckin 1998). Thus, the afternoon peak hour figures, which are higher, provide the basis for estimating the maximum volumes that must be accommodated on an access roadway. Data such as these are available in many countries based on national or local surveys. In the US and Canada, the routine source is the Institute of Transportation Engineers' *Trip Generation* manual, which is updated every decade and broadly averages trip generation rates across many cities (Institute of Transportation Engineers 2017).

Table 21.1 | Average trip generation rates for different site types, for US and Canadian cities

Land use	Daily vehicle trip rate	per	Percent of total daily vehicle trips		ITE code
			AM peak	**PM peak**	
Residential					
Single-family	9.55	Dwelling unit	8.0	10.7	210
Apartment	6.47	Dwelling unit	8.6	10.7	220
Condo/townhouse	5.86	Dwelling unit	7.5	9.2	230
Mobile home park	4.81	Occupied dwelling unit	8.9	12.1	240
Planned unit development	7.44	Dwelling unit	7.8	9.7	270
Retail (shopping center)[1]					
Under 100,000 sq ft	70.7	1,000 sq ft GFA	2.3	9.2	820
100,000–500,000 sq ft	38.7	1,000 sq ft GFA	2.1	9.5	820
500,000–1,000,000 sq ft	32.1	1,000 sq ft GFA	2.0	9.3	820
1,000,000+ sq ft	28.6	1,000 sq ft GFA	1.8	9.1	820
Office					
General[2]	11.85	1,000 sq ft GFA	13.8	13.1	710
Medical	34.17	1,000 sq ft GFA	10.0	13.0	720
Office park	11.42	1,000 sq ft GFA	16.1	13.2	750
Research and development center	7.70	1,000 sq ft GFA	16.0	13.9	760
Business park	14.37	1,000 sq ft GFA	11.3	10.3	770

Land use	Daily vehicle trip rate	per	Percent of total daily vehicle trips		ITE code
			AM peak	PM peak	
Restaurant[3]					
Quality restaurant	96.51	1,000 sq ft GFA	6.6	10.1	831
High-turnover (sit-down)	205.36	1,000 sq ft GFA	8.7	15.5	832
Fast food without drive-through	786.22	1,000 sq ft GFA	9.7	13.7	833
Fast food with drive-through	632.12	1,000 sq ft GFA	9.5	7.3	834
Bank					
Walk-in	140.61	1,000 sq ft GFA	13.7	0.4	911
Drive-through	265.21	1,000 sq ft GFA	13.3	19.3	912
Hotel/motel					
Hotel	8.7	Occupied room	7.5	8.7	310
Motel	10.9	Occupied room	6.7	7.0	320
Parks and recreation					
Marina	2.96	Berth	5.7	7.1	420
Golf course	37.59	Hole	8.6	8.9	430
City park	2.23	Acre	NA	NA	411
County park	2.99	Acre	NA	NA	412
State park	0.50	Acre	NA	NA	413
Hospital					
General	11.77	Bed	10.0	11.6	610
Nursing home	2.6	Occupied bed	7.7	10.0	620
Clinic	23.79	1,000 sq ft GFA	NA	NA	630
Educational					
Elementary school	10.72	1,000 sq ft GFA	25.6	23.2	520
High school	10.90	1,000 sq ft GFA	21.5	17.8	530
Junior/community college	12.57	1,000 sq ft GFA	17.2	8.2	540
University/college	2.37	Student	8.4	10.1	550
Airport					
Commercial	104.73	Average flights/day	7.8	6.6	021
General aviation	2.59	Average flights/day	10.4	12.7	022
Industrial					
General light industry	6.97	1,000 sq ft GFA	14.5	15.5	110
General heavy industry	1.50	1,000 sq ft GFA	34.0	45.3	120
Warehouse	4.88	1,000 sq ft GFA	11.7	12.3	150
Manufacturing	3.85	1,000 sq ft GFA	20.3	19.5	140
Industrial park	6.97	1,000 sq ft GFA	11.8	12.3	130

Source: Martin and McGuckin (1998).

[1] Rates given are for high end of indicated range. Weekend rates for shopping centers are significantly different from the weekday rates given here.

[2] The rate given here is for a 200,000 sq ft general office.

[3] Rates are given for the number of seats in the restaurant.

Many cautions must be voiced about using national average data to estimate travel demand. Studies have found that there is considerable variation in travel behavior from city to city, from outlying areas to city centers, and even among income groups within a city. One important variable is the fraction of individuals who drive as opposed to walking or taking mass transit. For residential units, the number of individuals in each household affects the number of trips. The size of the city also influences travel demand: in the US, residents in cities of over 1 million take 8% fewer trips than their counterparts in communities of less than 200,000 population. Spatial patterns of urban areas can also have an effect. One study of a *traditional neighborhood development* found that households made, on average, 1.5 fewer trips a day beyond their neighborhood, a 16% reduction compared to residents of other types of neighborhoods, and took significantly fewer vehicular trips within their neighborhood (Khattak and Stone 2004). For all these reasons, local survey data is a more reliable source for estimating trips generated on a site. National averages may be useful for

Table 21.2 | Variation in daily person-trips by household size and size of city

Autos owned	Persons per household					Weighted average
	1	2	3	4	5+	
Urbanized area of population 50,000–199,999						
0	2.6	4.8	7.4	9.2	11.2	3.9
1	4.0	6.7	9.2	11.5	13.7	6.3
2	4.0	8.1	10.6	13.3	16.7	10.6
3+	4.0	8.4	11.9	15.1	18.0	13.2
Weighted average	3.7	7.6	10.6	13.6	16.6	9.2
Urbanized area of population 200,000–499,999						
0	2.1	4.0	6.0	7.0	8.0	3.1
1	4.3	6.3	8.8	11.2	13.2	6.2
2	4.3	7.5	10.6	13.0	15.4	10.1
3+	4.3	7.5	13.0	15.3	18.3	13.5
Weighted average	3.7	7.1	10.8	13.4	15.9	9.0
Urbanized area of population 500,000–999,999						
0	2.5	4.4	5.6	6.9	8.2	3.4
1	4.6	6.7	8.8	11.0	12.8	6.4
2	4.6	7.8	10.4	13.0	15.4	10.3
3+	4.6	7.8	12.1	14.6	17.2	12.9
Weighted average	4.0	7.3	10.2	13.0	15.4	8.7
Urbanized area of population 1,000,000+						
0	3.1	4.9	6.6	7.8	9.4	4.1
1	4.6	6.7	8.2	10.5	12.5	6.3
2	4.6	7.8	9.3	11.8	14.7	9.7
3+	4.6	7.8	10.5	13.3	16.2	11.8
Weighted average	4.2	7.3	9.3	12.0	14.8	8.5

Source: Martin and McGuckin (1998).

Table 21.3 | International comparative data on mobility

	China (Shanghai, Beijing, Guangzhou)	India (Mumbai)	Latin America	Africa	Middle East	Eastern Europe	Western Europe	Singapore, Hong Kong	Australia, New Zealand	US	Canada
Modal split of all trips (%)											
Nonmotorized modes	40**	64**	31	42	27	26	31	28	16	8	10
Motorized public modes	33*	32**	34	26	18	47	19	30	5	3	9
Motorized private modes	27**	5*	35	32	56	27	50	42	79	89	81
Private motor vehicles											
Passenger cars per 1,000 persons	140**	68**	202	135	134	332	451*	78*	647*	640*	522*
Motorcycles per 1,000 persons	22**	123**	14	5	19	21	32	88	13	13	9
Motor vehicle passenger car units[1] per 1,000 persons	146**	112**	205	136	139	337	459*	99*	650*	643*	524*
Private mobility											
Passenger car passenger-km per capita	3,017**	3,021*	2,862	2,652	3,262	2,907	5,130*	1,334*	12,447*	18,703*	8,495*
Motorcycle passenger-km per capita	289	684	104	57	129	19	119	357	81	45	21
Infrastructure											
Freeways per person (m/1,000 persons)	6**	<1	3	18	53	31	89*	27*	83*	156*	157*
Parking spaces per 1,000 CBD jobs	17	77	90	252	532	75	241*	121*	298*	487*	319*
Land use											
Urban density (persons/ha)	133**	314**	75	60	119	53	42.5*	217*	15.4*	25.8*	14.0*
Proportion of jobs in CBD (%)	51	17	29	15	13	20	18*	9.2*	12.7	8.2*	15.0*

Source: Kenworthy and Townsend (2002) (1995 data); Kenworthy (2013) (2006 data); Kenworthy (2015) (2012 data).

Note: All data from 1995 except as noted: * = 006 data; ** = 2012 data.

[1] Motor vehicle passenger car units = cars + (motorcycles × 0.25)

first approximations, but careful planning of roadways ultimately requires locally validated data.

When estimating the demand for vehicular travel, we need to make assumptions about the modal split between automobiles, transit, cycling, and walking. This may be the largest source of variation between locations. In Lower Manhattan, only 8% of trips are made in private automobiles (although others are made in taxis and buses that also travel the roads), while in many suburban areas where there are no real transit alternatives, over 90% of trips are made by automobile. This also accounts for the considerable variation internationally in the number of vehicle trips taken. Table 21.3 shows comparative modal splits in cities around the world. In China and low-income Asian countries, trips by private vehicles represent 16–35% of all trips, compared to 42–50% in Western Europe and high-income Asian cities, and 79–89% in Australia, New Zealand, and North America.

Using the best available data on trip generation rates and modal splits, the site planner makes a first estimate of the traffic volumes likely to be created during peak hours by a proposed development. An important issue is which peak hour will serve as the "design peak." If the roadway is designed to carry the flows in the highest peak hour of the year (in the US, often the final shopping days before Christmas), the roadway will be underused through most of the year. Typical standards in the US are that the roadway must serve the 50th-highest peak hour of the year without congestion, although other benchmarks are often used, including the 30th-highest hour (Texas, Nebraska, Asia) and the 100th-highest hour (Florida). Volumes then need to be apportioned based on the various directions of flow—predicting the likely destinations of those leaving the site, and likely origins of those arriving. Once the entry and exit volumes are pinned down, flows can be estimated for the local roads on the site. Finally, the site planner is now in a position to deal with the types of vehicles that need to be accommodated, and to estimate the size of roadways required.

Roadways Needed

Several assumptions and policy decisions are needed to convert estimates of travel demand into the required size of internal site roadways and the impacts of site development on surrounding roads. One is the mix of vehicles that will be using the roadways. Clearly trucks and buses using roadways occupy more space, and limit the capacity of roadways by their slower startups at intersections and greater difficulties in turning. As Asian cities attest, motorbikes and similar motorized vehicles (tuk-tuks, motorized rickshaws, three-wheeled delivery vans, etc.) make smaller demands on a roadway, because of their smaller size and maneuverability. In some countries, nonmotorized vehicles such as bicycles, human-powered rickshaws, and even horse-drawn carts also affect the flows. One way to account for these differing demands on roadways is to convert projected traffic volumes into *passenger car equivalents* (PCEs, also referred to as *passenger car units*, PCUs). Table 21.4 outlines conventional PCEs in use in the US and in Asia. Using the US figures, a roadway with 400 peak hour automobiles, 10 motorcycles, 20 light trucks and 10 heavy trucks, and 6 buses would have a PCE of 475 vehicles/hour, compared to the 446 vehicles actually using the road.

Table 21.4 | Passenger car equivalents

Vehicle type	Passenger car equivalent (US)	Passenger car equivalent (Asia)
Passenger car	1.00	1.00
Motorcycle	0.33	0.50
Light/medium truck	1.75	1.00
Minibus	1.00	1.00
Heavy truck	2.25	3.00
Large bus	2.25	2.00

Sources: Transportation Research Board (2000); Adnan (2014).

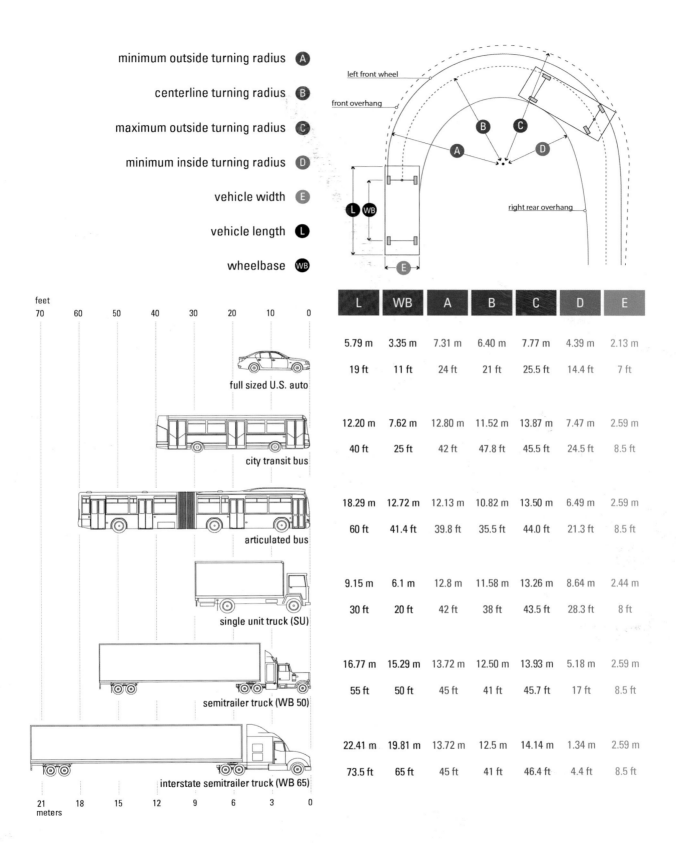

minimum outside turning radius (A)

centerline turning radius (B)

maximum outside turning radius (C)

minimum inside turning radius (D)

vehicle width (E)

vehicle length (L)

wheelbase (WB)

left front wheel

front overhang

right rear overhang

L	WB	A	B	C	D	E
5.79 m	3.35 m	7.31 m	6.40 m	7.77 m	4.39 m	2.13 m
19 ft	11 ft	24 ft	21 ft	25.5 ft	14.4 ft	7 ft
12.20 m	7.62 m	12.80 m	11.52 m	13.87 m	7.47 m	2.59 m
40 ft	25 ft	42 ft	47.8 ft	45.5 ft	24.5 ft	8.5 ft
18.29 m	12.72 m	12.13 m	10.82 m	13.50 m	6.49 m	2.59 m
60 ft	41.4 ft	39.8 ft	35.5 ft	44.0 ft	21.3 ft	8.5 ft
9.15 m	6.1 m	12.8 m	11.58 m	13.26 m	8.64 m	2.44 m
30 ft	20 ft	42 ft	38 ft	43.5 ft	28.3 ft	8 ft
16.77 m	15.29 m	13.72 m	12.50 m	13.93 m	5.18 m	2.59 m
55 ft	50 ft	45 ft	41 ft	45.7 ft	17 ft	8.5 ft
22.41 m	19.81 m	13.72 m	12.5 m	14.14 m	1.34 m	2.59 m
73.5 ft	65 ft	45 ft	41 ft	46.4 ft	4.4 ft	8.5 ft

feet
70   60   50   40   30   20   10   0

full sized U.S. auto

city transit bus

articulated bus

single unit truck (SU)

semitrailer truck (WB 50)

interstate semitrailer truck (WB 65)

21   18   15   12   9   6   3   0
meters

21.2 Dimensions and turning radii of typical urban vehicles.
(Adam Tecza/AASHTO 2004)

A second important decision is what should constitute the *design vehicle*—which will govern the standards adopted for roadway geometry, turning radii, curvatures, speeds, and other factors. In the case just cited, the passenger car is the likely candidate, since the volume of larger vehicles is limited. However, in an industrial area or commercial area where there are significant volumes of deliveries, a large semitrailer truck may be the design vehicle, and on arterial roads, buses and trucks may determine the standards. Figure 21.2 illustrates the dimensions of typical vehicles of each type. One immediate implication of the choice of design vehicle is the width of lane, or carriageway, needed to accommodate flows. While there are differences in standards across the globe, in general urban roadways where automobiles predominate can easily function with 3 m (10 ft) lanes, but where there are significant volumes of truck or bus traffic a width of 3.4 m (11 ft) is preferred, and on higher-speed arterials and limited-access highways 3.7 m (12 ft) is typical.

The third policy choice that will affect the need for roadways is the density of flows that is acceptable in the peak hour, or, its opposite, the level of congestion that will be tolerated. This is a cultural decision, with widely varying attitudes about congestion. Nonetheless, transportation engineers have reduced this to a single index: the *level of service* (LOS) provided by the roadway. Level of service is determined by comparing vehicle volumes and the capacity of roadways:

LOS = V/C,

where

V = number of vehicles (PCEs),

C = capacity of roadway.

As table 21.5 illustrates, LOS is scored on a scale ranging from A (very light traffic) to E (heavy traffic with minor slowing). LOS F represents a roadway that is failing, with congested heavy traffic involving slowing and stopping. The important policy decision is the LOS used in design. Many communities strive to design all their roadways so that they function at LOS D or better, a practical policy that ensures that roadways are largely uncongested. However, smaller auto-dominated cities sometimes require LOS B, resulting in an excessive amount of pavement, and dense existing urban areas may simply settle for keeping their roadways at LOS E or better.

In urban areas, the real determinant of traffic capacity is the ability to move vehicles through intersections. The capacity of roadways varies depending on the presence and timing of traffic signals and other impediments. Assuming that signals are timed to equalize the flow in each direction of an intersection, traffic volumes that can be handled per lane are reduced to about 45% of the theoretical volume per lane, accounting for some loss of time in startup and slowdown of vehicles. If the signal timing is different, the volume in each direction needs to be adjusted to reflect the green time available in that direction. Capacities of roadways may be further reduced as a result of vehicles waiting to turn, heavy pedestrian flows that block traffic, cabs or vehicles dropping off passengers, breakdowns of vehicles, double-parked vehicles, vehicles maneuvering into parallel parking stalls, and a host of other conditions. Some of these conditions may be mitigated by the design of the roadway, by creating left or right turn bays, introducing bus stop bays, increasing the width of the parking lane so that parkers do not block traffic, creation of loading zones, and phased signal timing to allow turning traffic to clear intersections before the opposing traffic begins to move. Unfortunately, many of these moves to smooth traffic flows also affect pedestrians crossing streets. Free right turn lanes, designed to allow motorists to short-circuit red lights, can be extremely hazardous for pedestrians.

21.3 Streets in rapidly growing cities, such as Dhaka, Bangladesh, need to accommodate a wide array of vehicles as well as loading and unloading.
(BDNews24.com)

Table 21.5 | Level of service (LOS) for vehicles on urban roadways

Level of service	V/C ratio	Average travel speed, mph (km/hr)[1]	Traffic volume, pc/lane/hr[2]	Intersection delay, sec	Description
A	0.00–0.35	> 35 (56)		< 10	Very light traffic, free flow
B	0.35–0.58	> 28 (45)		10–20	Light traffic
C	0.58–0.75	> 22 (35)	275	20–35	Moderate traffic
D	0.75–0.90	> 17 (27)	700	35–55	Moderate to heavy traffic without significant slowing
E	0.90–1.00	> 13 (21)	850	55–80	Heavy traffic with minor slowing
F	> 1.00	< 13 (21)	> 850	> 80	Congested traffic involving stopping and slowing

Various sources.
[1] Based on Class II arterials or local streets.
[2] Based on streets with frequent signal-controlled intersections.

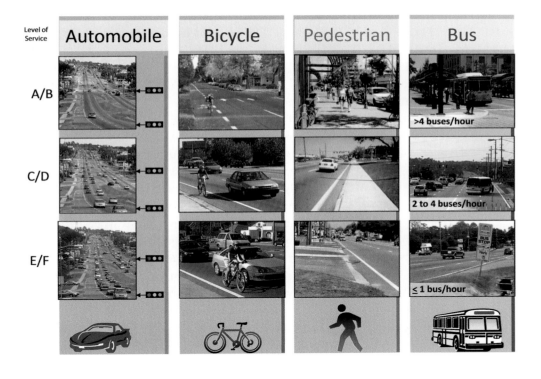

21.4 Comparison of levels of service for vehicles, cyclists, pedestrians, and buses. (Florida Department of Transportation)

Because of the many contingencies in any existing urban area, traffic planners generally use an alternative method of determining LOS based on the time required to drive from point to point. This can be converted to average speed, then LOS. The impacts of new developments are then overlaid on current conditions. For final impact studies this level of precision may be necessary, but in planning sites table 21.5 is useful for sizing roadways.

As an example, assume that 1,000 PCEs are predicted for the peak hour (one direction) on a new collector street, and that the policy adopted is to maintain at least LOS D for peak hour traffic. Consulting table 21.5, two lanes would be required in each direction. With two lanes, the actual LOS would be between C and D, leaving room for future increases in travel or new development.

Ultimately, the capacity of a roadway depends on a host of other factors including the width of lanes, roadway surface, alignment, gradients, and edge conditions, as well as characteristics of the traffic including the mix of vehicles, speed, and driver skills. Theoretical capacities need to be adjusted upward or downward to reflect these factors. Computer models allow traffic engineers to factor into the equation all of the contingencies and arrive at a precise figure for LOS. This may be overkill at the early stages of a project, when roadways are being planned. Many planners use a rule of thumb that a single lane of urban roadway is capable of carrying about 600 vehicles per hour (which implies that they operate at an LOS between C and D), leaving more precise calculations to later stages.

The LOS concept emphasizes automobile flow without equal concern for how roadways function for pedestrians, bicyclists, and transit. Parallel LOS calculations have been developed for cyclists, pedestrians, and buses, and attempts have been made to develop multifunctional LOS indicators. This is a tricky task, however, since much depends upon how the planner values each type of mobility—there is no natural law that will decide the weighting. Being attentive to this problem is the first step in finding a balanced solution.

Roadway Standards

Conventions for roadway design usually begin with the driver's interest in mind, aiming at roadways that are safe, convenient, and effective in moving traffic. These objectives need, of course, to be balanced against competing goals that include minimizing the pavement area, reducing dangers to pedestrians, and avoiding the separation between sides of the street and neighborhoods created by wide heavily trafficked roadways. The precise standard agreed upon will be the product of discussion with local authorities, developers, and (if they exist) residents of a site.

Lane and Roadway Width

Variations in roadway and lane width standards between countries (and cities) often reflect the differing size and mix of vehicles, roadway use practices (such as bus and car loading at the curb), and climatic differences (such as snow removal needs). Table 21.6 compares international standards for roadway lane width. While many traffic engineers press for the widest possible lanes, wider isn't necessarily better. Wide lanes encourage drivers to speed, make crossings more difficult, and encourage motorbike riders to scoot in and out of traffic dangerously.

Design Speeds

The *design speed* adopted for a roadway will determine allowable curvatures, location of driveways (based on sight distances), and other aspects of a roadway, so it is an important choice. Most studies show that drivers regularly exceed posted speed limits (if roads are uncongested), so a margin of safety needs to be built into roadway designs. However, this can be self-defeating, since roadways designed for speeds higher than thought desirable will encourage even faster driving. Thus, safety margins are important for higher-speed roadways, but less critical on urban roads.

Design speeds need to relate to posted speeds on streets and highways. However, many places have no

Table 21.6 | Recommended roadway widths

Roadway type	US		Germany		Australia		Japan		Canada	
	ft	m	m	ft	m	ft	m	ft	m	ft
Limited-access highways	12	3.66	3.75	12.3	3.50	11.5	3.50–3.75	11.5–12.3	3.50–3.75	11.5–12.3
Urban arterials	11	3.35	3.50	11.5	3.30–3.50	10.8–11.5	3.50	11.5	3.75	12.3
Urban collectors	10	3.05	3.25	10.7	3.00–3.30	9.8–10.8	3.25	10.7	3.50	11.5
Local streets	10	3.05	2.75	9	3.00	9.8	3.25	10.7	3.50	11.5

Various sources.

Table 21.7 | Typical urban roadway design speeds

Roadway type	US		EU	
	km/hr	mph	km/hr	mph
Local roads	32–48	20–30	30–60	19–37
Collector roads	48–64	30–40	30–60	19–37
Arterial roads	48–80	30–50	50–80	31–50
Limited-access highways	80–113	50–70	100–120	62–74

Sources: Institute of Transportation Engineers (1999); Federal Highway Administration (2001).

posted speeds (German autobahns, for example), and in many others congestion makes speed limits impossible to attain. In still other places (New Zealand and the, Netherlands, among others) speed limits are variable, signaled to motorists through electronic signboards, and set taking account of roadway conditions—rain, snow, high winds, accidents, etc. Nonetheless, adopting a design speed is important for the layout of roadways. Often it is established by determining the 85th percentile speed—the speed that 85% of drivers typically do not exceed. Typical design speeds in the US and Europe are shown in table 21.7. The range of design speeds varies considerably, as does the relationship of roads to pedestrian routes and buildings (Institute of Transportation Engineers 1999; Federal Highway Administration 2001).

There is now compelling evidence that the rate of serious pedestrian injuries increases greatly when vehicles are traveling greater than 40 km/hr (25 mph). The average risk of severe injury is 25% when struck by a vehicle traveling at 37 km/hr (23 mph), 50% at 50 km/hr (31 mph), 75% at 63 km/hr (39 mph), and 90% at 74 pm/hr (46 mph). In addition, higher speeds require longer lead times to stop a vehicle, leading to a greater number of accidents (Telft 2011). The Vision Zero program for pedestrian safety advocates lower speed limits; among other places, New York City has reduced its maximum speed limit on all roads except limited-access parkways to 25 mph (40 km/hr) (New York City 2017).

Grades

Travel speeds are affected by the grade of the roadway, as is safety. The opposite is also true: the speed of a vehicle affects the grade it can conquer, and its

21.5 Filbert Street, with 32% grade, San Francisco.
(Robbie Sell)

21.6 Lombard Street, San Francisco.
(Gary Hack)

ability to stop. Passenger cars have difficulty navigating roadways that are continuously above 7%, while a large truck must shift down on sustained grades of more than 3%. A 17% sustained grade is the limit of most trucks' climbing ability in low gear. Most localities limit grades on local streets to 7–8% and aim for no more than 5% on arterials, although these may be exceeded in short sections at low speeds. Snow and ice are serious constraints on the grade of streets. Where drivers are not accustomed to winter driving, grades as low as 3–4% can cause slipping and sliding.

There are nonetheless many steeper streets in cities, including Filbert Street and 22nd Street (31.5%) in San Francisco and East Roy Street (21%) in Seattle, all lengthy streets, and Dornbush Street (32%) and Canton Avenue (37%) in Pittsburgh, Baxter and Fargo Streets (32%) in Los Angeles, and Baldwin Street (35%) in Dunedin, New Zealand, shorter streets used by few people (for good reasons). When Seattle regraded many of its hills to make them inhabitable, it adopted a limit of 20% grades, and the city has many streets that nudge against this extreme. In San Francisco, Lombard Street was built with a switchback alignment—running one way down the hill—to allow motorists to travel its steepest portion. Cities in mountainous settings often need to make exceptions to the norms.

Alignments

Roadways are planned by laying out the centerline of the moving lanes in a pattern that is safe to the driver, pleasurable, and requires minimum steering motion. The alignment must meet acceptable standards in both the horizontal and vertical directions. In both cases, the road alignment will consist of straight sections joined by parabolic or circular curves.

The vertical alignment needs to assure that forward sight distances are adequate to allow a driver to stop in time to avoid a road hazard, and avoid the unpleasant weightlessness of going over a hill too fast. The vertical alignment is conventionally shown as a series of profiles, or continuous sections of the centerline drawn to an exaggerated vertical scale and flattened out on the plane of the drawing as if the centerline were straight in plan. By convention, grades are shown as positive percentages if they are ascending, and negative on the descent.

Designing the roadway profile is as much an art as a science. Straight grades are connected to parabolic curves on the hills and valleys, creating a roadway that feels fluid and continuous. The length of the parabolic curve depends upon the speed—as it increases, the curve must be longer to assure sight lines. Table 21.8 indicates the minimum length of vertical curves.

Table 21.8 | Alignment standards and design speed

Design speed		Minimum radius of horizontal curves		Minimum length of vertical curve for each 1% change of grade		Minimum forward sight distance		Maximum grade (percent)
km/h	mph	m	ft	m	ft	m	ft	
20	15	25	85	2.75	9	40	130	12
30	20	30	100	3	10	45	150	12
40	25	50	165	5	16.5	55	180	11
50	30	80	260	6.5	21	65	210	10
60	35	120	395	9	29	75	245	9
70	40	170	550	15	49	95	310	8
80	50	230	750	22	72	115	380	7
90	55	290	950	30	98	135	440	6
100	60	370	1,200	45	150	160	525	5
110	70	460	1,500	60	200	180	590	4

Various sources.

Studies have found that drivers slow down both on the crest of the hills and on sag sections, particularly if the curve is too short, and this is a major contributor to congestion on high-speed highways. Grades are also important at intersections, where ideally there should be a flat area of at least 12 m (40 ft) before drivers meet the cross traffic lanes to allow them to see oncoming cars and be seen by them.

Planning the horizontal alignment of a roadway also involves joining straights and curves, although the determining factors are different. Curves should not be so abrupt that vehicles lean dangerously, although on slow-moving minor streets small radii are a warning to motorists to slow down. Table 21.8 also includes recommendations for acceptable radii of horizontal curves. Horizontal curves should be circular in form, allowing drivers to transition from straight to curve with one motion of the wheel. Broken-back curves, where the curve begins with one radius then shifts to another in the opposite direction should be avoided; they have proved dangerous. Where it is impossible to create an adequate radius of horizontal curvature, superelevation of the roadway (banking the outer side of the roadway) of up to 4% may be a solution. On high-speed roadways with broad curves, superelevation is the norm for all curvatures, and may be as great as 6%.

Horizontal and vertical alignments must, of course be considered together, since vehicles travel in three-dimensional space. And they must be viewed from the height of a driver's eyes. Small dips and bumps make for an awkward roadway; dips just before a curve can be disorienting. For reasons of safety, sharp horizontal curves should be avoided on high summits, in deep cuts, or at the foot of steep grades. Curves need to be avoided at the entrance to underpasses or tunnels, where drivers must adjust to lower (or higher) light levels. The general rule is to avoid curves when drivers must be attentive to other factors such as entering traffic or scenic views.

Fortunately, there is excellent software to help the planner in designing roadways, including programs that allow for easily converting sketch designs into horizontal and vertical profiles. These programs compute the required curvatures to fit the topography and design speeds, and calculate the balance between cuts and fills to minimize earthwork. But one should be cautious of the built-in assumptions of the program,

which too often are a "black box." Skilled roadway designers develop an intuitive sense of good roadway design that allows them to spot situations where the assumptions built into computer routines are too conservative. And they do not account for the sensuous feel of driving a roadway. Simulation software, however, will allow the planner to do a simulated drive-through of a roadway, to test the roadway experience.

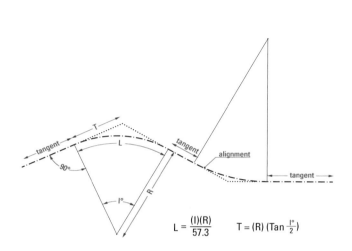

$$L = \frac{(I)(R)}{57.3} \qquad T = (R)\left(\text{Tan } \frac{I°}{2}\right)$$

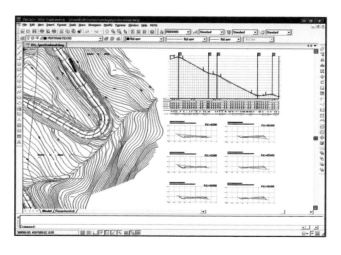

21.7 Elements of roadway curves.
(Adam Tecza/Gary Hack)

21.8 Computer-drawn horizontal and vertical curvatures.
(ZWCAD)

Roadway Types

Regardless of the geometric pattern, it is generally necessary to organize roadways into a hierarchy, from the smallest local street to the high-capacity limited-access highway. A site will seldom have all the types of roadways, unless it is very large, but every roadway must be planned mindful of the role it will play in the area-wide movement system. Because each type of roadway carries with it opportunities (volumes of individuals passing by, presence or absence of mass transit, etc.) and nuisances (noise, dust, safety hazards, etc.), there is a logic about the uses that should be located along it. The *roadway hierarchy* and the hierarchy of land uses go hand in hand.

Most cities have conventions that determine their hierarchy of roadways, which differ in subtle ways from those in other places (Jacobs 1993; Federal Highway Administration 2013a). But as a general rule, the hierarchy includes *local access streets*, *collector streets*, *arterials*, and *limited-access highways*. Table 21.9 indicates the approximate average daily traffic (ADT) volumes that each of these roadway types carries. The ADT ranges may in practice overlap, and the critical issue is generally the peak hour volume, which will determine the safety and functioning of the system. The design considerations, and possibilities, for each type of street are quite different.

Local Access Streets

Local access streets can take the form of grid streets, loops, cul-de-sacs, alleys, mews, auto courts, and other roadways fronted by houses, institutions, open spaces, and uses that generate low volumes of traffic. Usually pedestrian sidewalks parallel the roadways, although if the traffic is strictly local, as in a mews or alley, pedestrians may share the roadway with vehicles. Parking is often accommodated in the rights-of-way of minor streets, either parallel to the moving lanes or in small head-in parking lots. Curb cuts are made as needed, but in higher-density areas frequent driveways eliminate the possibility of on-street parking. If the properties served are narrower than 9 m (30 ft), they may be paired with alleyways that provide access to garages at the rear of lots.

The pavement of local streets can be as narrow as 2.4–3.0 m (8–10 ft), as in Philadelphia's alley streets, or as wide as 12 m (40 ft), which allows for two generous moving lanes and parking at each curb. However, a 12 m (40 ft) roadway is a social separation and can be an invitation for speeding, so traffic calming devices need to be considered (see below). Traditional residential streets are often 8–9 m (26–30 ft) (Kulash 2001), which causes some inconvenience for motorists meeting oncoming vehicles when curbs are occupied by parked vehicles, but if the volumes of traffic are low, this is a reasonable compromise between maintaining a residential scale and providing for access. They can be narrowed to 6.7 m (22 ft) if parking is restricted to one side. If traffic flows in only one direction, 6 m (20 ft) is an adequate width, with parking limited to one side. The final width of pavement too often is decided by the need to maneuver emergency vehicles, such as fire trucks, although the width requested by emergency officials must be scrutinized carefully, not taken on faith. Depending on the number of lanes and width of

Table 21.9 | Typical elements of the urban roadway hierarchy, United States

Roadway type	ADT (veh/24 hr)	Access condition	Typical lane width, ft (m)
Interstate expressway	35,000–129,000	Fully controlled	12 (3.66)
Other freeway	13,000–55,000	Partially/fully controlled	11–12 (3.35–3.66)
Major arterial street	7,000–27,000	Partially controlled/uncontrolled	11–12 (3.35–3.66)
Minor arterial street	3,000–14,000	Uncontrolled	10–12 (3.05–3.66)
Collector street	300–2,600	Uncontrolled	10–12 (3.05–3.66)
Local street	80–700	Uncontrolled	8–10 (2.44–3.05)

Source: Federal Highway Administration (2013a).

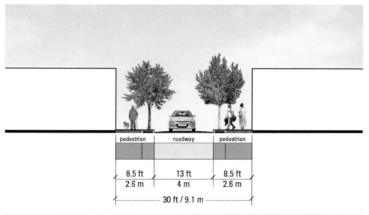

sidewalks, local streets can require rights-of-way of 9–18 m (30 to 60 ft). Local development standards usually prescribe the minimum dimension of rights-of-way.

There are a variety of devices to narrow the apparent width of local streets as *traffic calming measures*, discussed below. Topography and climate will also play a role in shaping the width and design of local streets. On a steep side slope, it is possible to locate the directions of traffic on different elevations, with a landscaped median taking up the slope between. In areas of high snowfall, portions of roads may need to be wider to allow snow to be piled until it is taken away, and will need to be designed so that snow banks do not restrict drainage. The use of salts for ice melting will also limit the type of vegetation that can be placed near the roadway, and will affect the location and type of drainage provided.

To keep traffic volumes within a tolerable range, local streets need to be limited in length, and designed to direct through traffic to higher-volume links in the system. The maximum total length of a loop drive is usually given as about 500 m (1,600 ft) and that of a cul-de-sac as perhaps 150 m (500 ft). The maximum allowable block length might be put at 500 m (1,600 ft). All of these standards are based on the same reasoning: as block, loop, and cul-de-sac increase in length, general circulation becomes more indirect, service deliveries longer, and emergency access more liable to misdirection. These rules are commonly held as reasonable. Not all site planners agree with them. The rules would not apply where through circulation is

21.9 (left) Local street cross sections. (Adam Tecza/Gary Hack)

21.10 (top right) Alley street, with 12 ft (3.7 m) pavement and 30 ft (9.1 m) right-of-way, Rittenhouse Square area, Philadelphia. (Gary Hack)

21.11 (bottom right) Local street with 30 ft (9.1 m) pavement and 50 ft (15.2 m) right-of-way, Chestnut Hill, Philadelphia. (Gary Hack)

already blocked for other reasons, as on a narrow peninsula, ridge, or pocket of land.

A minimum turnaround at the end of a cul-de-sac should have a 12 m (40 ft) outside radius free of parking so that vehicles such as fire engines can negotiate it. This requires a large circular right-of-way, and may defeat the economic and visual purpose of small cul-de-sacs. A T-shaped terminus or shunt is an alternative way of providing for backing turns on very short dead ends, but the backing of a vehicle always includes the possibility of overrunning a small child who is out of sight. The wings of the shunt should be at least a car's length deep on each side, exclusive of the width of the street, and at least 3 m (10 ft) wide exclusive of parking.

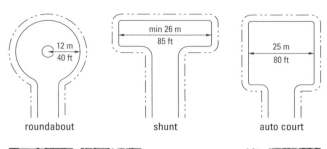

21.12 Cul-de-sac turning heads.
(Adam Tecza/Gary Hack)

21.13 Traditional woonerf in the Netherlands, where automobiles are slowed to pedestrian and cyclist speed.
(Courtesy of Canin Associates)

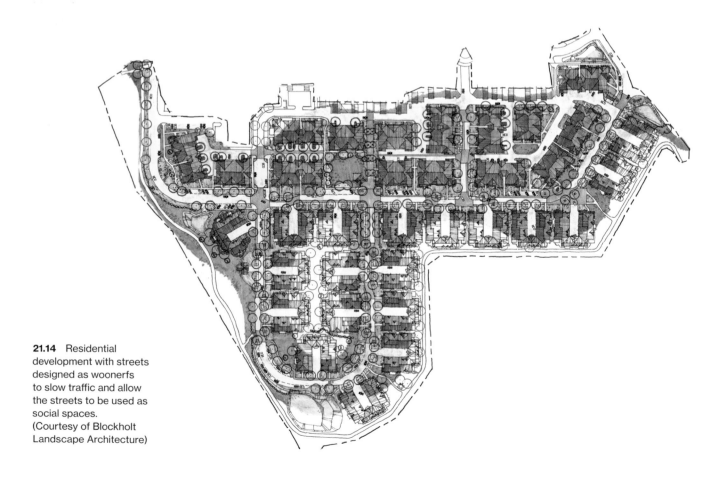

21.14 Residential development with streets designed as woonerfs to slow traffic and allow the streets to be used as social spaces.
(Courtesy of Blockholt Landscape Architecture)

21.15 Conversion of Charlotte Street, Morice Town, Plymouth, UK into a home zone.
(Courtesy of Adrian Trim/Plymouth City Council)

The inside curb should have a 6 m (20 ft) radius. As long as these turning requirements are provided for, free of obstacles, a small short residential cul-de-sac need not adhere rigidly to these shapes. A freely formed parking and arrival court may be quite desirable.

Local roadways should not be considered purely utilitarian devices for moving traffic and storing vehicles. Where there is little or no through traffic, they can also be significant hard-surface play areas for pick-up games of basketball, street hockey, stick ball, or touch football. They can serve as the location of street fairs, community cookouts, or square dances. Vehicles are not a hazard if

they move at pedestrian speeds; with barriers to rapid movement, the street will welcome other users. The Dutch *woonerf*, literally the "living yard," is a wonderful example of how a street can serve multiple purposes. In other countries, these multipurpose streets are called *living streets* or *home zones*, that have relevance to both residential and local commercial areas.

Collector Streets

One step up in scale from the local access street is the *collector street*. It serves a variety of purposes. In residential areas, collector streets gather traffic from the local streets and channel it to arterials if it is destined for other parts of the city. The collector street is also the logical location for local shops and services, higher-density housing that generates significant traffic volumes, and institutions such as high schools or recreation centers. Collector streets will typically have parallel parking, providing access for fronting uses, and will be the location of public transit routes through the neighborhood. Collector streets are also important in employment areas, commercial districts, and other zones of the city where the mix of traffic is divided between service vehicles and commuters.

Collector streets generally have one to two moving lanes in each direction, as well as curb parking, resulting in a width of 11–17 m (36–56 ft), and a right-of-way of 18–24 m (60 to 80 ft). With a 24 m (80 ft) right-of-way, it is possible to provide one moving lane in each direction, a second 3 m (10 ft) moving lane that alternates

pedestrian	verge	bus & parking	drive lane	median	drive lane	bus & parking	verge	pedestrian
15 ft		20 ft		10 ft		20 ft		15 ft
4.5 m		6 m		3 m		6 m		4.5 m

80 ft / 24 m

21.16 Collector street cross section.
(Adam Tecza/Gary Hack)

between curb parking and bus loading areas and is wide enough to allow cyclists to use the road safely, as well as a modest median and sidewalk zones. While a single lane in each direction is often adequate, if there are heavy public transit flows with large buses it may be necessary to add a second lane, as well as bus loading zones. Alternatively, with light rail or streetcars or heavy flows of buses, it may make sense to dispense with the median and locate the transit in the center. Generally the location of access driveways is carefully controlled on collector streets, so as not to interfere with the significant volumes of traffic using the road. Traffic signals will generally be located at all key intersections, with stop signs on local streets leading to the collector. Controlling the speed of vehicles and assuring that pedestrians are able to cross safely are a significant design challenge.

One way to limit the amount of pavement is to eliminate curb parking, but this is not a good strategy. Collector streets that consist solely of moving lanes invite higher-speed travel. Cars parked at the curb buffer pedestrians from the movement lanes, and tend to provide a friction at the edges of the roadway that slows traffic. A center boulevard on a collector street can provide a refuge for pedestrians when crossing. It also reduces the apparent width of the roadway, although it will require an increased right-of-way. Once established, the boulevard needs to be guarded against erosion for turning lanes that are hardly ever essential on collector streets. Treating the parking as an indentation, rather than a continuous zone, can also reduce the intersection crossing distance.

In residential areas, collector streets typically make up 5 to 10 percent of the total street mileage. No residential location should generally be more than half a mile (or 1 km) from a collector street, which in the

21.17 Neighborhood collector street, Garrison Woods, Calgary, Alberta.
(Gary Hack)

21.18 Town center collector street, without median to minimize distances between buildings, Reston, Virginia.
(Gary Hack)

21.19 Amsterdam collector street, with transit and bus lanes in center.
(Courtesy of Charles Siegel)

US is also the maximum range for attracting people to public transit. Collector streets provide the shared identity for those living in a neighborhood, and should be landscaped in ways that express the special identity of the place. They mark the point of arrival, are the route to schools and local shopping areas, and are likely to have significant foot traffic, even in low-density areas. They are also critical routes for cyclists, and must be designed with them in mind (see chapter 23).

Arterial Streets

If the collector street provides the identity to neighborhoods and districts, the *arterial* is critical to the citywide image. Arterials can take many forms: *arterial streets*, *parkways*, *multiway boulevards*, and *grand avenues* among them. They balance competing purposes—smoothing crosstown traffic, providing access to adjacent properties—and may weight one more than the other. They provide the shared perceptual structure for an urban area, and their appearance signals the look and feel of the city. Unfortunately, many collector streets have evolved in stages by widening local roadways, and have never really been designed. Large-scale shopping centers, automobile dealerships, and a world of outlets desiring visibility gravitate to arterials, and the result is too often an ugly and disordered commercial strip. But it need not be so.

Arterials have a history that dates to the first attempts to deal with congestion and social disorder in nineteenth-century European cities. Paris's boulevards, Regent Street in London, and Washington's radial avenues stand as lasting reminders that it is possible to carry large volumes of traffic yet produce streets that

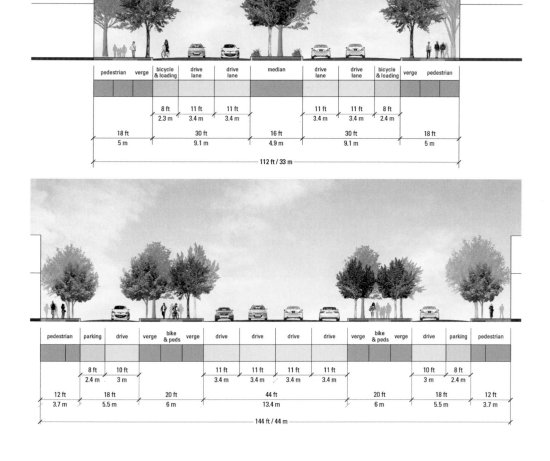

21.20 Arterial street cross sections. (Adam Tecza/Gary Hack)

21.21 Typical suburban arterial street, Surrey, British Columbia, with restricted access.
(City of Surrey, British Columbia)

21.22 Hudson River Boulevard, New York City, which replaced an elevated highway and carries traffic along the western edge of Manhattan.
(Gary Hack)

21.23 Commonwealth Avenue, Boston, an urban arterial with transit running in the median.
(Courtesy of Phil Goff)

have grace and character. In some cases, like the Ringstrasse in Vienna that replaced the historic city wall, transit ran below the grand avenue and it became the address for many of the city's great cultural institutions. In the US, the parkways of New York, Buffalo, Kansas City, Houston, and many other cities arrived with the City Beautiful movement, as a way of creating a civic realm in cities that were exploding with development. Parkways provided new traffic capacity while also creating recreation spaces for the communities they traversed. Chicago's boulevards, snaking their way through the city, offered a linear recreation spine for communities while diverting through traffic away from the local street grid. All of these can serve as prototypes for contemporary arterials.

Arterial streets generally have two or three lanes of moving traffic in each direction, although there is often pressure to expand to wider dimensions. Pedestrians resist crossing roadways with more than two moving lanes in each direction, and a median or refuge needs to be provided when the extent of traffic increases to three lanes each way. Parallel parking at the curb may be incorporated, and it will provide a degree of separation between sidewalks and the moving traffic lanes. Traffic engineers often object, however, since parking interferes with the flow in outer lanes. One solution to this is providing 3 m (10 ft) wide parking lanes that allow for maneuvering. (The danger is that they can easily be converted to an additional travel lane in the future.) Bus loading zones will also need to be provided at the curb, and many arterial streets are now designed with reserved bus lanes. An arterial street of six moving lanes, parking at the curb, and a median will typically require a right-of-way of 30 m (100 ft) or more.

There is usually great pressure to restrict, even prohibit, vehicular access to adjacent properties from arterial streets, in the interest of reducing or avoiding conflicts with the flow of traffic. There is also some evidence that accidents increase in areas with commercial diversions to the driver (McMonagle 1952). Restricting access usually means turning housing away from the arterial street; in commercial areas a parallel service road is then often required, and signage is restricted. The effect is to deaden the street for pedestrians and create long distances between active uses and the roadway. Such tendencies need to be challenged, since streets without active uses encourage speeding and may become more, not less, dangerous to both pedestrians and motorists. Carefully planned access is not incompatible with moving large numbers of vehicles at reasonable speeds. But it does require careful controls on access points, and planning of adjacent properties to prohibit vehicles from backing onto the street and ensure that that they are visible.

The *multiway boulevard* provides a fine solution to the challenge of moving traffic while creating active frontages along arterials (Jacobs, Macdonald, and Rofe 2002). A multiway boulevard consists of a central roadway, intended to carry through traffic, bordered by smaller roadways on either side that provide access to uses along the street (see figure 21.20). The earliest of such roadways appeared in Paris during the nineteenth century; the form is exemplified by Avenue Montaigne, Avenue Marceau, and Avenue Charles de Gaulle in Paris, the Passeig de Gràcia in Barcelona, and Via della Conciliazione in Rome. The Champs-Élysées, once the grand example of a multiway boulevard, has in recent years been transformed by eliminating the access roadways in favor of wider pedestrian zones. Many American cities also have examples, which include the Benjamin Franklin Parkway in Philadelphia, portions of Commonwealth Avenue in Boston, K Street in Washington, Ocean and Eastern Parkways in Brooklyn, and the Esplanade in Chico, California. Examples in other countries include Ratchadamnoen Klang Road in Bangkok, Nanjing East Road in Taipei, and St Kilda Road in Melbourne. Often these arteries serve as processional routes, connecting important symbols of the city or nation. The multiway boulevard balances the often-competing objectives of the arterial by creating separate environments for pedestrians and for local traffic and through traffic, separated by tree-lined medians.

While there are successful examples of multiway boulevards, they are often resisted by traffic engineers and others who argue that their confusing movements at intersections are dangerous, and that they require too wide a right-of-way. But studies have shown that they are no more dangerous than other types of arterials, and that motorists, realizing that intersections are more complex, pay greater attention to their driving. And they can be shown to work within the dimensions of many conventional rights-of-way for arterial streets, within as little as 120 ft. Their advantages are that they offer

21.24 Avenue Charles de Gaulle, Paris boulevard street. (cocoparisienne/pixabay)

21.25 Octavia Street, San Francisco, a new multiway boulevard, originally scheduled to be an expressway. (Steve Boland/flickr/Creative Commons)

21.26 Rock Creek and Potomac Parkway, Washington, DC. (AgnosticPreachersKid/Wikimedia Commons)

street-oriented retail opportunities and allow pedestrians to cross roadways that are manageable in size.

Parkways are a third form of arterial, and are weighted in favor of through traffic. The classic American parkway consists of moving lanes separated from any development by broad bands of open space at their margins. The width of right-of-way varies but may average 200 ft, and often it is integrated with parks on one or both sides. Storrow Drive, Memorial Drive, and the Fellsway in and around Boston are three examples, as are Allen Parkway in Houston, Colonel By Drive in Ottawa, Rock Creek Parkway in Washington, DC, and Martin Luther King Jr Drive in Cleveland.

Parkways were originally intended as pleasure routes—for carriages first, then automobiles—and were usually limited to one or two lanes in each direction. Roadway alignments are sinuous, designed to fit the topography, with opposing lanes diverging if necessary to preserve important stands of trees or rocks. The roadway and its equipment—barriers, signs, lighting, bridges, and walkways—are intended to blend into the landscape. Intersections are generally limited to one or two per mile, and if pedestrians must cross more frequently, pedestrian bridges are provided. Unfortunately, as traffic volumes have increased, many parkways have been widened, grade intersections have been "improved" with underpasses, and today they are clogged with commuters. However, some parkways continue to prohibit commercial traffic, and revert to their original functions as pleasure drives on weekends.

Limited-Access Highways

Many parkways have become *limited-access highways*, which is the fourth general category of urban roadways. The Ottawa River Parkway in Ottawa and Riverside Drive in Manhattan are two of many examples of urban roadways that have parkway character but serve as long-distance limited-access roadways. Most *expressways* (or *freeways*, or *motorways*) are less generous to the driver and adjacent properties. As volumes and speeds increase on roadways, and as the mix of vehicles includes trucks, buses, and other large vehicles, issues of noise, air pollution, dust, light, and toxins spill over into adjacent neighborhoods.

The best urban expressways are isolated from their neighbors—placed below grade, covered or uncovered, separated by sound walls, or incorporated into slopes or placed below structures that allow adjacent uses to see over them. If they are located on grade, distance

21.27 Urban expressway depressed to form a deck park connecting neighborhoods on either side, Phoenix, Arizona. (© Tim Roberts Aerial/ Dreamstime.com)

can help isolate them and trees can mask them from views, but the only sound reduction strategy requires mass materials, such as earth berms. From a driver's perspective, elevated roadways offer relief from confining walls (if the guardrails are not too high), but they too often leave the areas under the expressway in need of uses. It is generally better to elevate roadways 35 ft or more above the ground, so that they are less disruptive of views along streets below and allow greater choice in the use of space below. Many cities have used areas below expressways for parking decks, while in Tokyo many types of retail uses may be found under expressways (and rail tracks), providing continuity with adjacent retail districts.

The most difficult issue in integrating expressways into the development fabric of cities is dealing with intersections, entrance and exit ramps, service roads, and toll plazas, all of which demand a considerable amount of space and can disrupt the urban fabric. Roadway configurations designed for the open countryside have often been adopted in urban expressways, and cities are now eyeing the possibility of reclaiming this land for urban uses. A variety of strategies can be used to minimize the intrusion of expressways. One may question whether a free-flowing roadway is even necessary, particularly in downtown areas that represent destinations and where frequent access is important. An expressway link intended to cross San Francisco was eliminated in favor of the Embarcadero, a waterfront esplanade and boulevard; the same occurred in New York City, where the West Side Highway became Hudson River Boulevard (see figure 21.22), with little loss of roadway capacity and great environmental gains. If expressways must cross urban areas, slip ramps will minimize the land needs for access links, direct-flow three-level interchanges demand less land than cloverleaf configurations, braided access ramps can provide frequent access in minimal dimensions, and rotaries below or above expressways can provide multidirectional access in an efficient manner. The use of transponder technology should, over time, obviate the need for most toll plazas.

Urban expressways need to be designed as civic infrastructure, with bridges, ramps, retaining walls, sound walls, and other elements designed as significant elements in the urban landscape. Today these are usually created from standard prototypes, with little conscious effort to fit them to their surroundings. However, expressway bridges can help orient motorists, if they contain visible elements of the neighborhoods nearby or become recognizable landmarks. Planting in medians and on expressway walls can help moderate the harsh roadway environment. Lighting can be designed with cutoff fixtures to minimize the overspill onto adjacent buildings and streets. And sound barriers can be transparent to minimize their dimension, or can become integrated with adjacent buildings. The designer should always be on the lookout for devices that improve the experience for both the driver and those who inhabit spaces next to the expressway.

Intersections

The shape and pattern of intersections greatly affect traffic flows on a site and the sense of orientation of drivers. To navigate safely through an intersection, drivers must be able to see oncoming traffic. A clear sight triangle is needed for vehicles entering an intersection, and the dimensions should be keyed to the speed of cross traffic. Streets should ideally meet at an angle close to 90°, and if needed be bent to improve the angle so that it is within 20° of perpendicular.

T-intersections have the advantage of making it clear which direction has precedence, naturally reinforcing the pattern of primary and secondary roadways. There is some evidence that they have safety advantages, with a small number of points of collision. Because of this, they have been the favorite of roadway designers for several generations, and account for many of the curvilinear subdivision plans that dominate US suburbs. Points of entry need to be spaced at least 50 m (165 ft) apart to avoid dangerous cross traffic flows. T-intersections are best employed when local streets meet collector streets.

Four-way intersections are the norm for local streets in a grid plan. If one of the two streets dominates the flow, the opposite direction should be signed so that drivers stop before entering the intersection. Four-way stops can also be instituted, but cultural factors—such as the propensity for "rolling stops" and a general disregard for traffic controls—can diminish in their effectiveness. When traffic volumes average 100–150 vph in the peak hour on the minor street, it is worth

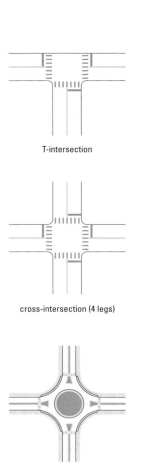

T-intersection

Y-intersection

cross-intersection (4 legs)

five or more legs (not circular)

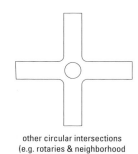

roundabout

other circular intersections
(e.g. rotaries & neighborhood
traffic circles)

non-conventional intersection
(e.g. super-street, median U-turn, &
displaced left turn)

21.28 Types of local street intersections.
(Adam Tecza/US Federal Highway Administration)

considering the installation of traffic control signals (Federal Highway Administration 2003). They may also be justified by the need to accommodate pedestrian crossings safely.

When more than four directions of travel must be accommodated in an intersection, it is worth considering a *roundabout* (also called a *traffic circle* or *rotary*). Roundabouts have advantages as well in keeping traffic flowing at four-way intersections with high volumes and significant turning movements. They can serve as an important punctuation point on roadways, signaling arrival and departure, and are a favorite transition point between highways and local street systems at the entry to many European towns and cities. For many years they were shunned in the US, although they are witnessing a revival. They have been found to be safer than signalized intersections, reducing crashes and injuries by about 30% when intersections were converted to roundabouts (Federal Highway Administration 2000). They use far less space than equivalent grade-separated interchanges.

Table 21.10 outlines some important characteristics of roundabouts, including their minimum dimensions. While roundabouts make it easier for heavy vehicular volumes to flow through an intersection, they inconvenience pedestrians who must walk around. Pedestrian crossings must generally be pulled back from the edge of the circle to allow vehicles to queue for entering the traffic flow, and to avoid speedy exiting traffic. Pedestrian

21.29 Roundabout, Forest Lake, Minnesota, accommodating heavy flows on arterial streets as well as pedestrians.
(Washington County, Minnesota)

Table 21.10 | Roundabout dimensions and flows

	Mini roundabout	Urban compact	Urban single-lane	Urban double-lane	Rural single-lane	Rural double-lane
Recommended entry design speed	25 km/h 15 mph	25 km/h 15 mph	35 km/h 20 mph	40 km/h 25 mph	40 km/h 25 mph	50 km/h 30 mph
Maximum number of entering lanes per approach	1	1	1	2	1	2
Typical inscribed circle diameter[1]	13–25 m 45–80 ft	25–30 m 80–100 ft	30–40 m 100–130 ft	45–55 m 145–180 ft	35–40 m 115–130 ft	55–60 m 180–200 ft
Typical service volumes on 4-leg roundabout (veh/day)	10,000	15,000	20,000	Depends on operations	20,000	Depends on operations

Source: Federal Highway Administration (2000).

[1] Measured to outer edge of circulating lane(s).

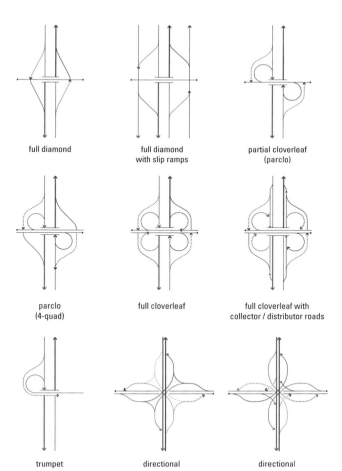

full diamond

full diamond with slip ramps

partial cloverleaf (parclo)

parclo (4-quad)

full cloverleaf

full cloverleaf with collector / distributor roads

trumpet

directional

directional

21.30 Expressway interchange diagrams. (Adam Tecza/Gary Hack)

refuges may be necessary to allow safe crossings of heavy traffic flows. A variety of sophisticated simulation techniques can aid in the design of effective roundabouts (Federal Highway Administration 2000).

Where through traffic volumes are quite high relative to turning volumes, it may make sense to create an underpass or overpass for through flows, combined with a roundabout for other movements. The disadvantage of these configurations, which are used in Washington, is the long distance it takes to ramp up or down, which typically deadens long distances of the roadway. However, roundabouts can provide an effective surface-level alternative to land-hogging cloverleafs and other interchanges between high-speed roadways and local street systems.

The most difficult intersection design problem is how to integrate urban expressway interchanges into the urban fabric. Too often space-hogging configurations are adopted that separate communities and make local automobile and pedestrian routes impossible. Many cities are rediscovering the space of cloverleaf intersections by substituting slip ramps for broad deceleration curves and braided ramps from service roads. Figure 21.30 offers a catalog of urban expressway intersection types and compares the amount of space they occupy. Ultimately, the best interchange is no interchange at all: bringing express roadways down to the surface as they move through urban areas, or if through movement is heavy, placing it in tunnels belowground with a minimum of connections to the surface.

Roadway Networks

It is important to consider every portion of roadway in its next largest context: a local residential street is part of a neighborhood network; a neighborhood street layout is part of a citywide system; and so on. The system must meet multiple tests: Is it legible, allowing people to navigate easily and understand their location in the network? Does it distribute traffic in ways that avoid congestion in a few places? Is there redundancy in case of accidents or other incidents? Does it minimize the time spent and distance traveled getting to and from important destinations?

Does it encourage choice of modes, including walking, cycling, driving, and taking mass transit? As a practical matter it is never possible to optimize along all of these dimensions, so tradeoffs need to be made. The design of roadway networks is as much a policy challenge—deciding the objectives to be favored—as it is a technical task of arriving at the most effective solution.

Roadway networks are generally more legible if they follow a consistent pattern. There have been many studies of roadway structure and an equal number of typologies proposed (Marshall 2005). Four generic patterns frequently appear: grids, radial patterns, branching systems, and linear networks. These, of course, emulate common patterns in nature, with all of the advantages and disadvantages attending each.

Grids

The uniform *gridiron plan* (*grid*) is the most commonly employed network pattern. It allows traffic to be spread, is capable of being employed at a variety of scales, is legible to those using it, and results in parcels that have access from multiple directions—all advantages over other systems. Grids are usually rectangular, but

21.31 Grid pattern on the North Side of Chicago, the result of subdividing the mile-square grid into quarters, then into four long blocks by eight short blocks.
(Google Earth)

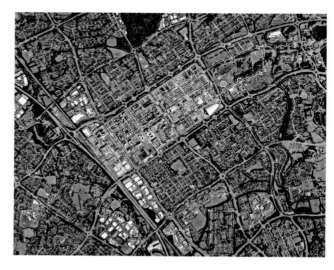

21.32 Grid pattern, Milton Keynes new town in England, averaging 1 km square, distorted to take account of topography and natural features.
(Google Earth)

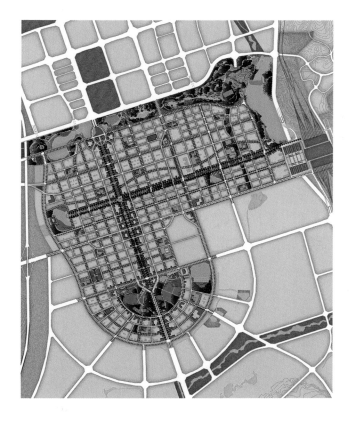

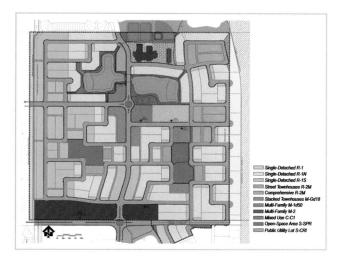

21.33 Grid pattern of the center of Chenggong New District, Kunming, China, breaking from recent practice by creating small blocks and a generous public realm.
(Courtesy of Calthorpe Associates)

21.34 Fused grid pattern for a proposed subdivision in Calgary, Alberta, breaking the grid pattern by creating open spaces in the center of each of the quadrants.
(Genesis Land Development Corporation/CMHC)

hexagonal patterns have also been employed, and have their devoted advocates. The even rectangular grid is often criticized for its insensitivity to landscape, and for the lack of differentiation between heavily and less traveled ways. But it is possible to distort the grid to reflect the topography, introducing variety while retaining all its advantages. The grid pattern may be at the scale of individual blocks of houses or buildings, as in Philadelphia's Center City, Manhattan, or most of the Midwest and western cities in the US and Canada, or may be at the level of collector or arterial roadways, as in the new town of Milton Keynes in England. Nothing in the grid pattern precludes the differentiation of streets by varying the right-of-way width and roadway capacity or by making local streets discontinuous.

Grid street patterns are usually more costly than other alternatives, because of the multidirectional access they provide, but this must be weighed against the need for redundancy and choice of routes. The frequency of intersections, and necessity of ordering flows through them, also creates the need for many traffic control devices when volumes approach half or more of intersection capacity.

Faced with undesirable through traffic, many neighborhood groups located in gridiron subdivisions have transformed their street pattern to slow vehicles or encourage through traffic to use perimeter routes. A variety of traffic calming devices has been employed, and some neighborhoods have gone further to create a *precinct traffic pattern*. This may include changing the direction of streets to create circuitous through routes, selectively closing streets, creating loops that do not connect at intersections, and curving the alignments of roadways. One virtue of these arrangements is that they are generally reversible; in the future they may be removed or changed again as the neighborhood changes its character and seeks other objectives.

The grid may be modified to overcome some of its disadvantages. A common modification is creating one-way flows on alternating streets, which simplifies intersections, makes pedestrian crossings safer, and increases the capacity of the system. While motorists may need to travel greater distances and reverse direction to reach their destination, one-way grids are by now well-understood systems. A variation on this is the installation of a steady-flow system, in which movement is directed clockwise and counterclockwise around adjacent blocks so that flow in any one direction requires diversion in the route. The advantage is that there are no direct crossings of traffic, only weaving movements, as in a rotary. The system works for small blocks, but makes lengthy trips exceedingly tedious. Blocked grids or fused grids are other variations, often created at the neighborhood scale, to discourage through traffic. By creating an orthogonal pinwheel pattern, most intersections have an obvious bias in favor of traffic moving in the through direction, so that stop signs are rarely needed. The disadvantage is the mazelike quality of the pattern, which can easily confound those visiting for the first time.

Radial Patterns

A second general pattern is the *radial* form, in which roads spread outward from a common origin. They may also be connected by circumferential routes, becoming a *radial-concentric* pattern. This pattern is frequently employed at the city scale, where a loop surrounding the central area serves to connect major routes leading outward, and distributes traffic to its destinations on each side of the core. While this system works well when there is a dominant center, it does not easily deal with a situation of multiple centers. And as the area to be served multiplies, distances on circumferential roadways can become daunting; one wishes for more direct access across the area. At the neighborhood scale, this pattern takes the form of crescents and sometimes full circles with common facilities at the center. Navigating a circumferential street can be thoroughly disorienting, since it lacks an obvious way of measuring one's position in space, and views to distant landmarks are limited by the curvature of the street.

Branching Patterns

Branching layouts are a third general pattern, sometimes flowing from a single center but more often from multiple origins. They have the advantage of clarity of direction, and allow streets to be decreased in size as

21.35 Radial plan of Sun City, Arizona, with highest densities and commercial spaces at its center.
(© Tim Roberts/Shutterstock)

21.36 Branched pattern of development, Pacific Palisades, California, necessitated by the steeply sloping hillsides.
(Google Earth)

the traffic drops off. Streets at the end of the system are safe and dead-ended, and can become outdoor extensions of the properties that face them. A notable example of a branching layout is the plan for Riverside, Illinois, planned by Olmsted and Vaux in 1869. Designed for carriages, roads slide gently with the slopes, weaving their way across the landscape (see figure 14.8). It remains a fine testimonial to organic planning.

The common complaint of branching systems is the difficulties they create for emergency or delivery vehicles, which may travel to the end of the street only to discover they are not at the desired location. Lacking redundancy of route, they are also vulnerable if a route is blocked by an accident, road construction, or a broken water main. In steep topography, however, a branching pattern may be the only feasible way to provide access to all the properties. And in cases where controlled access is essential, branched networks may be the most desirable pattern.

Linear Patterns

Linear systems have a long history and are a fourth general pattern. The system may consist of a single line of movement, with all secondary streets accessible from it, or two or more parallel routes. Such patterns have grown up without conscious planning, centered on canals, railroads, streetcars, and highways. They imply a hierarchy, with the through route serving as the spine of the system and secondary routes branching from it, as loops or cul-de-sacs. The spine need not be strictly linear; the pattern may curve or fold back on itself, but it will retain the differentiation between the main route and its subsidiaries.

Linear roadway systems have an obvious advantage in routing buses or other forms of public transportation. The highest densities of destinations, if not of development, are logically located along the spine. One

such pattern, found in the Rome suburb of Spinacento, consists of a couple of parallel roadways extending for several kilometers, one-way in each direction, with commercial uses and apartments between them and lower-density housing beside. The new district of Ørestad, in Copenhagen, is a linear development centered on an arterial roadway and a new mass transit line. In the Scottish new town of Cumbernauld, the commercial core of the city is located directly over the linear transportation spine. The linear pattern has also proved effective for airports, with both the Houston International and the Dallas–Fort Worth airports organized along linear spines.

Geometric patterns may, of course, be combined. A 1 km or 1 mi grid may be the used for the arterial system, with internal streets organized in branched or radial patterns. Much of the fabric of modern Chinese cities was organized as grid of superblocks accommodating *danweis*, the live-work units that were fundamental to the socialist economy, with internal networks branching from the gates. Superblocks have been much criticized of late, because of the high traffic volumes they create on arterials and circuitous travel routes they make necessary, but they have significant virtues if the areas inside the blocks are largely devoted to pedestrians.

A radial plan may be overlaid on a grid pattern, as in Washington, DC, Detroit, Venice (Florida), and countless

21.37 Linear development of Ørestad, Copenhagen, with central spine consisting of an arterial roadway, mass transit line, major drainage canal, and trunk infrastructure for the area. (Courtesy of CPH City & Port Development/Ole Malling)

new urbanist projects. But such hybrids often confuse those navigating through the pattern, and can result in odd-shaped properties that are difficult to develop. A far better approach is to work within a coherent pattern and stretch it to its limits.

Network Connectivity

The issue of street connectivity has been much debated. In many countries, private streets have been created with security barriers or guards screening those entering. The motivation is a combination of security and exclusivity, often more perceived than real, but important nonetheless. Studies in the US have concluded that crime rates are not very different in gated and ungated developments with similar socioeconomic status (Blakely and Snyder 1997). Nonetheless, in the US there are at least 20,000 gated communities, large areas of central Manila are walled neighborhoods, gated residential compounds are the norm for much new housing in Brazil, and large new developments in China and Thailand have adopted this approach.

There are other reasons for preferring disconnected neighborhoods. Cul-de-sacs or local streets gained only through circuitous routes are often seen as a way of reducing through traffic volumes, making streets safe for children's play (see the following section of this chapter). In some cases, limited site entrance and exit routes are the unwitting result of traffic engineering regulations that limit intersections on collector or arterial roads. Regardless of the reasons, the effect is generally longer driving and walking distances (compared to a simple grid pattern), more concentration of traffic on arterials and collectors (and wider roadways for them), and considerable separation of districts of a city.

On the other side of the debate, open and accessible public streets are advocated as democratizing influences, where people are free to enter and leave at will and casual encounters can occur. There is also evidence from the US that street patterns with a greater density of intersections (i.e., more connections) have fewer accidents, promote walking, and reduce the distance of travel. Studies of 24 California cities show significantly fewer injuries and fatalities on streets in neighborhoods where there is a higher density of intersections (Marshall and Garrick 2008). Safe cities, with lower accident rates, had on average 38% more intersections per km^2 than less safe cities. Part of the reason for lower accident rates may be the reduction of total vehicle miles traveled. Simulations of travel patterns have demonstrated that there could be reductions in vehicle miles traveled of as much 57% within neighborhoods in areas with highly connected streets (Kulash, Anglin, and Marks 1990), although only a small proportion of travel is neighborhood-oriented. Other studies have projected total reductions in automobile travel and significant increases in walking by those living in connected street areas (Frank and Hawkins 2008). Of course, self-selection will play a role: people who enjoy walking or cycling will gravitate to areas where it is easy and safe to do so. But the connection between safety and connected streets seems positive.

How should street connectivity be measured? The simplest measure is *intersection density* per km^2 or sq mi, computed by dividing the number of nodes or intersections by the relevant area. Cul-de-sacs or dead ends may be included in the total number of nodes, or the count of nodes may be limited to real intersections—consistency is the important issue. A typical grid subdivision has an intersection density of about 150 per sq mi, while modest-density suburban subdivisions with little connectivity average about 50.

A more nuanced index of connectivity is the *connected node* ratio (CNR),

Figure 21.38
Street corners are the locations for casual encounters and socialization, as in Boyle Heights, Los Angeles.
(Gary Hack)

21.39 Comparison of block sizes – Irvine, London, Los Angeles, and Manhattan. (From Allan Jacobs, *Great Streets* [Cambridge, MA: MIT Press, 1993]; courtesy of Allan Jacobs)

CNR = RI/TI,

where

RI = number of real (non-dead-end) intersections per km^2 or sq mi,

TI = total number of intersections including dead ends per km^2 or sq mi.

This ratio offers a good indication of what fraction of streets offer at least two directions of travel to destinations. A ratio of at least 0.75 is considered desirable, and some US state and local governments have begun requiring this level of connection (Handy, Paterson, and Butler 2003).

Finally, it is often useful to weigh the length of road segments as well as the number of intersections in determining connectivity, since small blocks also promote connectivity and may also reduce traffic speeds. A simple way to do this is to compute the *roadway density* (RD) per

km^2 or sq mi, by dividing the number of roadway segments by the relevant area. A more sophisticated ratio is the *link:node ratio* (LNR),

LNR = R/TI,

where

R = number of road segments per km^2 or sq mi,

TI = total number of intersections including dead ends per km^2 or sq mi.

A consensus seems to be forming that an LNR of about 1.4 is essential for a linked development (Ewing 1996).

There are a number of strategies for promoting connectivity of street and pedestrian networks. Some jurisdictions have banned cul-de-sacs outright or severely limited their length. If cul-de-sacs are used, pedestrian walkways connecting their ends to adjacent streets can obviate the need to walk long distances to get to nearby locations. Substituting loops for dead end streets can modestly improve connectivity. Small blocks produce more intersections and choices of direction. On longer blocks, midblock alleys or pedestrian ways (as in Midtown Manhattan) can minimize travel or walking distances. These measures need to be seen in combination with the organization of uses on a site, since the ultimate objective is to increase choice within easy range of people.

Traffic Calming

Traffic calming techniques have become an essential part of the toolkit for livable streets. The name is a literal translation of the German term *Verkehrsberuhigung*; it is also called *traffic mitigation* or *traffic abatement* in parts of the US, *stille veje* (silent roads) in Denmark, *tempo 30 zones* in Germany, and *local area traffic management* in Australia, among other terms. They refer to the combination of mainly physical measures that seek to alter the behavior of drivers and improve conditions to benefit pedestrians and nonmotorized street users (Ewing 1999). Unlike speed limits or traffic signals that require regulations and monitoring, traffic calming measures are intended to be largely self-enforcing.

Traffic calming has several purposes. It seeks to get drivers to slow down and be more attentive to pedestrians, children playing, and cyclists. In residential areas, it generally aims to reduce the volumes of cut-through traffic, especially trucks. A frequent benefit is the reduction of accidents and improved safety of streets. There is considerable evidence that even small reductions of speed can have significant impacts on safety: European studies found that reductions of speeds by only 5% will reduce injury crashes by 10% and fatalities by 20% (OECD 2006). As we have noted, US studies have concluded that the risk of death or incapacitating injury in pedestrian-vehicle accidents rises considerably at speeds greater than 25 mph (41 km/hr) (Leaf and Preusser 1998). And, if well designed, traffic calming also results in improvements to the character and appearance of streets and roadways.

Many of the strategies that fall under the traffic calming umbrella have been used for more than half a century, and are commonsense if not routine practice. The first *woonerven* were installed in Delft in the 1960s.

These efforts were soon expanded to cover whole districts in Germany, Denmark, and Sweden, as well as the Netherlands. In the US, traffic calming began as efforts to modify grid street layouts to make through traffic circuitous if not impossible—creating precinct traffic plans—while reclaiming paved areas for landscape and pedestrian use. Berkeley and Seattle neighborhoods were among the first to adopt these strategies, and experiments in the Stevens neighborhood of Seattle provided encouraging data to demonstrate that overall traffic could be reduced (by 56%) and accidents totally eliminated (Ewing 1999). Experiments in area traffic calming have been conducted throughout the world, particularly in Europe, Japan, Australia, and Israel, and it is now routine practice in most of these countries.

Changing Pavement Profile and Texture

Speed bumps are the best-known strategy for slowing motorists, sometimes as an act of desperation by residents along a street. They are also a sign of failure of other ways of tempering speeds, and should be a last resort. They come in various forms, the simplest of which is a short area of raised pavement that forces drivers to slow to 10–15 km/hr (6–10 mph) to avoid damaging the undercarriage of the vehicle. Rubberized prefabricated speed bumps (often using recycled materials), 10–15 cm (4–6 in) high by 0.3–1 m (1–3 ft) long, are now widely used. *Rumble strips*, three or more parallel narrow rubberized strips, avoid damage to vehicles and warn drivers to slow down for upcoming hazards. A more integrated way of changing the pavement profile is the use of a *speed table*, or *speed hump*, usually coinciding with a crosswalk, a broad raised area with a texture and color (often brick) that signals that motorists are passing through a pedestrian zone. Or an entire intersection may be raised 10–15 cm (4–6 in) above the normal height of the driving lanes, and paved with unit pavers in crosswalks and cobblestones where pedestrians do not walk. It is also possible to landscape the center of an intersection or raise it further, creating a form of mini-roundabout for motorists.

Speed bumps and other systems of raising the street profile create difficulties for drainage and an impossible condition for snowplows in winter months, good reasons why other measures need to be pursued for slowing speeds.

21.40 Rubber speed bump, designed to slow traffic but not destroy vehicles.
(Traffic Safety Store)

21.41 Speed table, or speed hump, installed on major route passing through a town in France, signaling pedestrian crossing zone.
(Gary Hack)

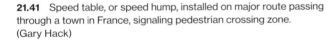

Narrowing Pavement Widths

Wide clear lanes encourage motorists to speed, so the simplest traffic calming strategy is *narrowing lane widths* from 3.65 m to 3 m (12 ft to 10 ft), which also cuts down on impervious surfaces. On existing roadways, this may be part of a *road diet* program, involving reducing the number of lanes from 2 to 1 (or 3 to 2) along with the introduction of striped bicycle lanes. *Curb extensions*, which narrow the pavement at intersections to reduce the walking distance of pedestrians, can have a powerful effect on the appearance of streets and roadways, not to mention reducing the scale of pavement at intersections. Coupled with this, pervious materials such as cobbles, unit pavers, or compacted gravel can be used for parallel parking lanes, recharging the water table

21.42 Curb extensions, Madrid, emphasize the priority of pedestrians while slowing vehicles to walking speeds.
(Gary Hack)

21.43 Vehicles and trees share the parking lanes in this Vienna street.
(Gary Hack)

21.44 Small roundabouts at intersections in Kitsilano, Vancouver slow speeds and force drivers to pay attention to pedestrians and other vehicles.
(Courtesy of Justin Swan/City Clock Magazine)

21.45 Sunnyside Piazza, Portland, Oregon, a neighborhood-initiated project to convert an intersection into a community gathering place through the annual springtime place-making festival, the Village Building Convergence. (Courtesy of Anton Legoo, Portland Street Art Alliance/Village Building Convergence)

while reducing the apparent width of the street. Curb extensions (also called *pinchers* or *chokers)* can also be planned for midblock or other locations where pedestrian crossings are anticipated, as well as for traffic islands where parking is not allowed.

Older residential areas in Vienna and other cities where streets were built before automobiles sometimes have trees in the parking lanes, making for a delightful arch of leaves over the width of the street. New urbanist developments have mimicked this feature, which narrows the apparent width of the street. Spacing trees about 12 m (40 ft) apart will allow two cars to park in each bay between them. Trees, of course, need to be protected from drivers who park by touch, and driveways and access ways need to be coordinated with the tree and parking zones.

A variation on these measures is shifting the alignment of lanes from side to side, allowing parking on only one side. The shift point is sometimes called a *chicane*, or *diverter*, and it can be lushly landscaped or may signal a midblock crosswalk. Installation of small roundabouts at the intersections of local streets will force drivers to slow and take notice before entering the intersection. An interesting reversal is to make intersections into gathering places, signaling this through paint and seating, so that drivers understand that they are entering a special precinct. Neighbors who invest in their creation have a special reason to respect such places.

Medians and Boulevards

The traffic calming strategies just mentioned have greatest value in local streets and collectors, although curb extensions may be equally relevant on arterials and at the point of contact between limited-access roadways and local streets. The taming of fast-flowing arterials with three or more lanes in each direction may require larger moves. One is the introduction of central landscaped medians, both to narrow the apparent width of roadways and to provide a refuge for pedestrians. Or a true boulevard street may be considered, separating zones for local use on the outer edges from faster-moving through traffic in the center. Alternatively, the moving lanes may be separated to make room for mass transit in the center, with diversions that require pedestrians to cross the full width of the corridor in two lights.

Parking

Parking makes immense demands on the land and imposes very large costs on residents, businesses, and institutions. The equivalent of half the living space of a house may be required to garage and park the cars of its residents; in suburban office areas, the areas devoted to parking and driveways will far exceed the work spaces; and in retail areas that depend on the automobile, parking typically overwhelms the floor area of shopping space by 50% or more. Large paved parking areas sit awaiting crowds at stadiums, beaches, and racetracks, used relatively few days of the year, to say nothing of the vast parking garages in downtown areas that are idle at least two-thirds of the 24-hour day. The high cost of constructing parking garages (*carparks*) in central areas of cities tilts the economic equation in favor of developing outlying sites where surface parking (albeit more of it) can be provided cheaply on the ground. Finding a

21.46 Downtown Mesa, Arizona, where a majority of space is occupied by parking areas.
(© Tim Roberts Photography/Shutterstock)

way to satisfy legitimate parking needs is important, but parking arrangements are one of the best candidates for innovation in site development.

Parking Needs

Most local governments have strict parking standards, usually designed to ensure that all the needs of a site are taken care of on-site rather than spilling over onto surrounding roads. These standards are routinely set to deal with the worst case, making site innovation difficult. They usually have scant empirical basis; when put to the test of field studies, they have been shown to overshoot dramatically the actual accumulations of cars (Shoup 1997). The effect of these standards is to inflate the cost of site development by requiring more land and structures to accommodate vehicles.

The amount of parking needed is a function of the types and mix of uses on a site, their location and arrangement, the presence (or not) of mass transit, the cost of parking, and the operation of parking facilities—a complex equation, not easily captured in simple standards. The best data on parking needs is obtained locally, by surveying the accumulation of parked cars at locations of comparable uses. This is costly, but on large site development projects could result in considerable savings compared to simply applying conventional standards (Dunphy et al. 2000). It is important to understand the dynamics of parking

needs. Demand varies over the day, week, month, and year, particularly for uses such as shopping. In the US, the need for parking spaces in suburban shopping areas is likely to be 35% lower on average in January than in the preceding month, and 25% lower at 5 pm on a Saturday than at 2 pm (Barton-Aschman Associates 1982). If parking is provided for the peak hour of the peak day—usually 2 pm the Saturday before Christmas—it will require about 50% more spaces than during any day in a month other than December—spaces that will sit idle unless there are other uses on the site that can absorb the surplus. Within the category of retail uses there is also considerable variation in the number of parking spaces required, from the quick-turnover convenience store to the home furnishings outlet where shoppers stay for several hours.

Because of the many variables, parking needs on a site should be determined in steps, always seeking to find ways to efficiently manage the demand. Figure 21.48 illustrates a recursive process that involves eight sets of activities.

The point of departure is the list of proposed uses on a site and the floor space devoted to each (1). This need only be a tentative estimate, as it will be affected by the requirements of parking in terms of land and cost, and will surely need to be revisited. The second important starting point is identifying local parking practices and requirements (2), some of which may be found in local ordinances or codes, while others will become clear from a look at competitive or comparable projects. In some instances, the requirements of prospective tenants for the site may take precedence; retail chains and office space users often have minimum acceptable parking standards, unless they can be shown that they will not be harmed by lower numbers.

The first decisions that need to be made are on the parking policies for the site (3). Among the policies are decisions (4) on the design day—will it be the peak hour of the year, the average over the day (meaning that there will be shortages each day), or some other figure? For retail uses, often the tenth- or fifteenth-highest peak hour will be used, meaning that over the Christmas season, not all seeking parking will be able to find it unless other steps are taken. There are a variety of ways to manage peak demands, including valet parking to remote locations and acquiring overspill space for peak days. At shopping centers, 10–15% of the need for

SHARED PARKING TABLE

Parking Requirements may be met with On-Street or Off-Street parking.

Land Use	Parking Requirement	Estimated Ratio	Estimated Sq. Ft.	Estimated Stalls	Weekdays 7AM - 10 AM	Weekdays 10 AM - 3 PM	Weekdays 3 PM - 6 PM	Weekdays 6 PM - 10 PM	Weekends 7AM - 10 AM	Weekends 10 AM - 3 PM	Weekends 3 PM - 6 PM	Weekends 6 PM - 10 PM	Land Use
Single-Family Residential*	0.5 Per Unit	1:4000 SF	2000	1									Single-Family Residential*
Multi-Family Residential**	1.5 Per Unit	1:600 SF	1000	1.5									Multi-Family Residential**
Retail	1 Per 300 SF	1:300 SF	20000	67									Retail
Convenience Store	1 Per 400 SF	1:400 SF	1000	5									Convenience Store
Restaurants	1 Per 150 SF	1:150 SF	3000	20									Restaurants
Office	1 Per 300 SF	1:300 SF	2000	7									Office
Medical Office	1 Per 200 SF	1:200 SF	20000	100									Medical Office
Banks	1 Per 500 SF	1:500 SF	2000	4									Banks
Elementary School	2 Per Classroom	1:700 SF	40000	57									Elementary School
Daycare/ Nursery	1 Per 3 Children	1:300 SF	2000	7									Daycare/ Nursery
Library, Museum or Art Gallery	1 Per 500 SF	1:300 SF	9000	18									Library, Museum or Art Gallery
Worship	1 Per 3 Seats (Primary Room)	1:100 SF	10000	100									Worship
Community Center	1/ 50 SF Floor Area Primary Room	1:250 SF	10000	40									Community Center
Hotels & Motels	1.12 Per Room	1:500 SF	60000	120									Hotels & Motels
Theaters	1 Per 50 SF	1:50 SF	10000	200									Theaters
Health & Athletic Club	1 Per 200 SF	1:200 SF	30000	150									Health & Athletic Club
Park/ Play Fields	NA	30:Field	2 Fields	60									Park/ Play Fields

Capacity legend: 0% - 25% Capacity | 25% - 50% Capacity | 50% - 75% Capacity | 75% - 100% Capacity

* Single-Family Residential requires two garage parking stalls per detached or attached single-family home. An additional 1/2 parking stall is required for each home within 1000 feet of the home.

** Multi-Family Residential (Apartments or Condos within one larger building) requires one parking stall within 200 feet of the home and an additional 1/2 parking stall within 1000 feet of the home.

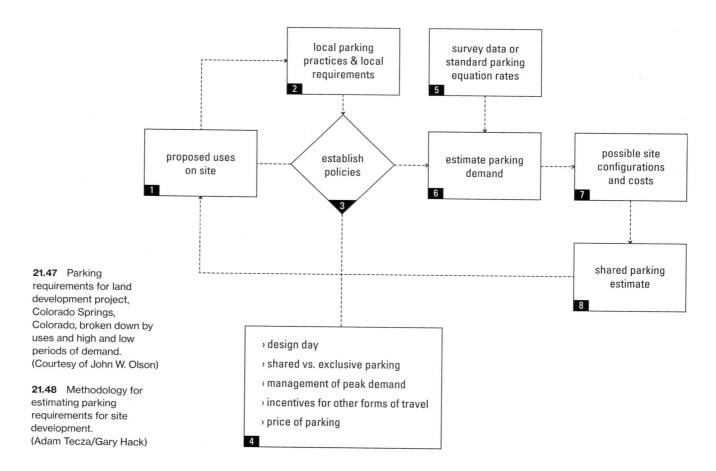

21.47 Parking requirements for land development project, Colorado Springs, Colorado, broken down by uses and high and low periods of demand. (Courtesy of John W. Olson)

21.48 Methodology for estimating parking requirements for site development. (Adam Tecza/Gary Hack)

parking is for employee cars, which can be relocated during peak periods with the help of shuttle service. In hospital or medical areas, off-site employee parking might be acquired for daytime shifts, when visitors and patients need to park near the facility, while employees are allowed to park nearby during night shifts. Another important policy issue is whether to embark on a transportation management program to lower demand for parking. By subsidizing transit passes for employees or encouraging carpooling or providing minibus service to areas where employees live, businesses could lower the demand for parking substantially, paid for through savings on parking facilities. Decisions on the pricing of parking will also play a role in determining parking need and encouraging the use of alternatives to automobiles. Finally, it is useful to consider whether parking will be a common resource among users or dedicated to specific tenants or individuals, since this will affect the flexibility in the use of parking.

With at least tentative decisions about site uses and parking policies, the analysis now moves to estimating parking demand. Survey data may be used as the basis for estimating parking generation rates, or standard factors may be employed (5). In the US, the sources include the publication *Parking Generation* (Institute of Transportation Engineers 2004). These figures need to be used with caution, since they are national averages and may not be in tune with local habits, and are often based on small samples, invariably in suburban locations. Adjustments will need to be made to reflect the share of people who arrive by walking, cycling, or taking mass transit instead of in their automobiles, including any shifts in the mode share that may result from policies adopted on the site for reducing parking demand. For sites with several uses, one can construct a simple spreadsheet of uses, parking generation coefficients, mode shares, and estimated parking needs, allowing quick adjustments to be made in successive passes.

The first estimate of parking needs (6) should be tested on the site, looking for ways that parking for one use could be shared with others (7). Shared parking is one of the most effective methods for lowering the amount of the site occupied by pavement or parking structures. Figure 21.47 indicates that there are clear opportunities for sharing parking spaces if the right activities are located together. It is not accidental that

retail spaces and cinemas often share a site, since the peak accumulation of parkers for shopping usually is at about 2 pm, while cinemas peak in the early evening. Hotel use of parking is also a good fit with shopping. Institutions such as churches that need parking only on weekends may be able to share with offices that are closed then. Good combinations of uses may also lower the demand for parking by encouraging people to walk from place to place—housing beside shops, offices, or restaurants, offices beside restaurants, and so on. There might also be opportunities to share parking with activities beyond the site, or to use on-street parking for part of the need.

The shock of seeing just how much land parking consumes will undoubtedly spur ideas for changing the site program or the parking policies to reduce parking needs, which will require a new round of estimates for parking demand. Or it may prompt the site planners and their sponsor to seek relief from local requirements. It may take several rounds of analysis to arrive at a final figure for the parking needed on a site. Never lose sight of the objective of reducing the amount of pavement that goes unused.

Accommodating Parked Vehicles

A full-grown road monster requires a parking stall of 2.75 by 6 m (9 by 20 ft) and adequate space to maneuver it into place. Before the recent explosion of SUVs, it was possible to make parking stalls 2.5 or 2.6 m (8 or 8.5 ft) wide and 5.5 m (18 ft) deep, but a better strategy today may be to reserve a fraction of narrow stalls for compact cars while providing ample full-sized stalls for their cousins on steroids. In Europe and Asia, where the vehicle mix is shaded to smaller vehicles, the narrower parking stalls may be used. The prospect of rapid growth of minicars (Smart Car, Tata Nano, and their imitators) offers the promise of dramatically downsizing the size of parking stalls to 2.2 by 3.7 m (7 by 12 ft). Many cities in Europe and Canada have begun to create on-street parking spaces of these dimensions, and soon it will make sense to reserve portions of parking lots for minivehicles.

Every parking area should have spaces set aside for handicapped individuals, with 1.5 m (5 ft) aisles providing access to these spaces. While requirements vary, typically at least 4% of parking spaces should be reserved for handicapped in lots of fewer than 500

Table 21.11 | Handicapped parking requirements in various countries

	US	UK	Australia	Japan
Required number of spaces	< 500 in lot: 4%	Existing employee area: 2%	1–4% depending on use and location	< 200 in lot: 2%
	501–1,000 in lot: 2%	New employee area: 4%		> 200 in lot: 1%
	> 1,000 in lot: 1%	Shopping area: 6%		
Minimum parking stall	8 ft (2 m)	2.4 m	3.2–3.8 m	3.5 m
Minimum access aisle	5 ft (1.5 m)	1.2 m		
Minimum van parking stall	8 ft (2 m)			
Minimum van access aisle	8 ft (2 m)			

Various sources.

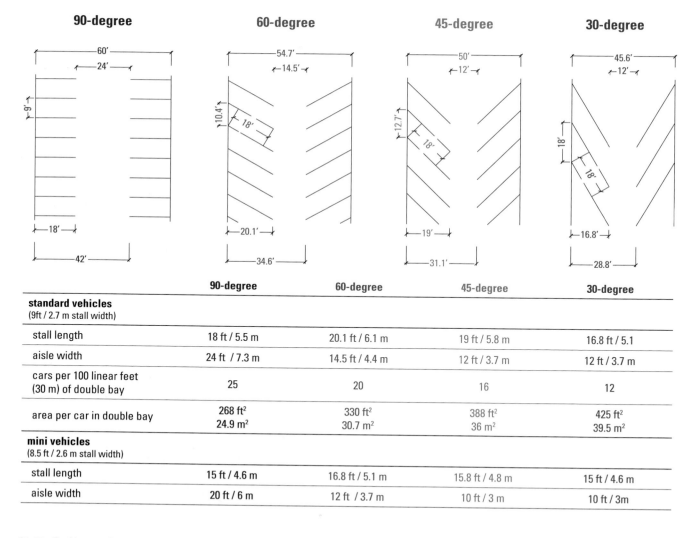

	90-degree	60-degree	45-degree	30-degree
standard vehicles (9ft / 2.7 m stall width)				
stall length	18 ft / 5.5 m	20.1 ft / 6.1 m	19 ft / 5.8 m	16.8 ft / 5.1
aisle width	24 ft / 7.3 m	14.5 ft / 4.4 m	12 ft / 3.7 m	12 ft / 3.7 m
cars per 100 linear feet (30 m) of double bay	25	20	16	12
area per car in double bay	268 ft² 24.9 m²	330 ft² 30.7 m²	388 ft² 36 m²	425 ft² 39.5 m²
mini vehicles (8.5 ft / 2.6 m stall width)				
stall length	15 ft / 4.6 m	16.8 ft / 5.1 m	15.8 ft / 4.8 m	15 ft / 4.6 m
aisle width	20 ft / 6 m	12 ft / 3.7 m	10 ft / 3 m	10 ft / 3m

21.49 Parking configurations.
(Adam Tecza/Gary Hack)

spaces (with a minimum of 1 in every lot); above that size the proportion can drop to 2%. About 1 in 8 of the handicapped parking spaces must be van-accessible, with an access aisle of at least 2.5 m (8 ft) beside its 2.5 m (8 ft) parking space, and a clear height of 2.5 m (8 ft) for the taller vehicles that use it. It goes without saying that handicapped parking spaces should be located to minimize the distance and obstacles to the parker's destination, and must be fully accessible. These figures are based on US disability laws; other laws in other countries will vary.

Parking may be parallel to driving lanes, perpendicular (90°), or at various angles (typically 45°, 60°, or 75°). Each has its virtues and disadvantages. Parallel parking can be squeezed into the narrowest spaces but is the least efficient in the use of space, typically requiring 48 m² (520 sq ft) if it has one-way aisles. At the opposite extreme, 90° parking configurations are often the most efficient in using space and allow two-way movement, but require a width of 18.3 m (60 ft) for two parking stalls and access lanes. Perpendicular parking creates difficulties for some parkers, and typically 15% of the spaces are lost to people parking improperly. A narrower module of width is possible with angled parking, and experience has shown 75% to be an optimal angle for ease of parking. All angled parking requires one-way movement, which creates difficulties in organizing parking structures on tight sites. Finding the right pattern for a site is generally a process of trial and error. Planners of large sites generally opt for perpendicular parking because it offers the greatest flexibility over time to modify widths of bays and patterns of movement.

Depending on the configuration chosen, the meanest parking lots usually require 25–30 m² (275–325 sq ft) per vehicle. With amenities added to make them tolerable—trees, landscaping, infiltration gardens, walkways for pedestrians, waiting areas at elevators, etc.—they can average 37 m² (400 sq ft) per vehicle. The efficiency of a parking area can be greatly enhanced by parking vehicles two or three deep, which requires attendants to shuffle cars to free those trapped behind others. Where valet parking is used, as in hotels, exclusive shopping areas, and entertainment venues, or where land values are high as in the center of cities, this can be an effective way to intensify parking, lowering the amount of space required to 21 m² (230 sq ft) per vehicle.

Types of Parking Facilities

The simplest and easiest way to accommodate parked vehicles is in paved surface parking areas. If the cost of land is low, they are also the least expensive way to satisfy parking needs, and offer the flexibility of being future sites for development. However, surface lots are also the most damaging to the environment, creating large volumes of runoff often polluted by chemicals and salts, blocking infiltration of water into the groundwater, raising the air temperature through the solar energy absorbed by the pavement, and encouraging sprawl. For much of the day or year, most surface parking lots sit empty, begging for other activities

There are creative ways to address these challenges. Large lots or unused corners of them may be used for temporary activities such as farmer's markets, flea markets, auto meets, fairs and festivals, basketball tournaments, performances, and outdoor merchandising. The amount of pavement can be dramatically reduced by substituting permeable surfaces such as reinforced grass, unit pavers, or gravel in the parking areas, which reduce the heat island effects and allow water to percolate into the soil. Generous planting of trees can provide shade for vehicles and paved areas, while improving the appearance of the area. Lush rainwater detention areas can slow the runoff, filter the water, and allow some of it to penetrate the soils. Landscaped walkways can allow parking areas to connect adjacent uses rather than serving as separators. And laying out parking areas as a gridiron of streets and lots can provide for future conversion

21.50 Weekend auto show in unused high school parking lot, Huntington Beach, California.
(Huntington Beach High School Car Show)

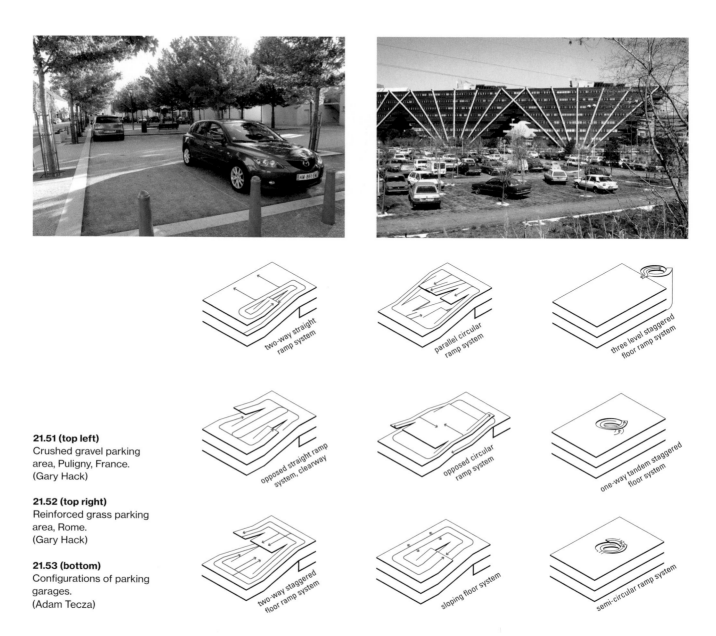

21.51 (top left)
Crushed gravel parking area, Puligny, France.
(Gary Hack)

21.52 (top right)
Reinforced grass parking area, Rome.
(Gary Hack)

21.53 (bottom)
Configurations of parking garages.
(Adam Tecza)

two-way straight ramp system

parallel circular ramp system

three level staggered floor ramp system

opposed straight ramp system, clearway

opposed circular ramp system

one-way tandem staggered floor system

two-way staggered floor ramp system

sloping floor system

semi-circular ramp system

of lots into development sites, by devoting other lots to parking garages.

As land prices increase, multistory *parking garages* (also called *multilevel carparks*, *parking structures*, *parking ramps*, *parking decks*, *parking podiums*, or *parkades*) become a costly but necessary evil. The least expensive form is a single deck, which in sloping topography can often be built with independent entrances to each level. Most parking garages, however, consist of concrete or steel structures that are either continuous ramps or flat floors connected by ramps. Sloping ramps are the most efficient in the use of space, but require sites of

at least 37 by 43 m (120 by 142 ft). Sites as narrow as 33.5 m (110 ft) can also be designed as ramped-floor garages, with one-way flows, but these require additional length, usually 62 m (204 ft), to accommodate a double-threaded helix (Chrest, Smith, and Bhuyan 1989). There is a limit of about 10 stories to a ramped garage configuration, determined by drivers' tolerance for circulation and the accumulation of volumes entering and leaving on the lower floors that makes it nearly impossible to use spaces on those levels. Much of course depends upon the uses of the garage. If it serves uses with heavy peak demands, speed ramps may be necessary to clear the exit

21.54 Parking structure with street-level activities and green facade, Miami Beach, Florida. (Gary Hack)

21.55 Parking structure wrapped by active uses. (Adam Tecza)

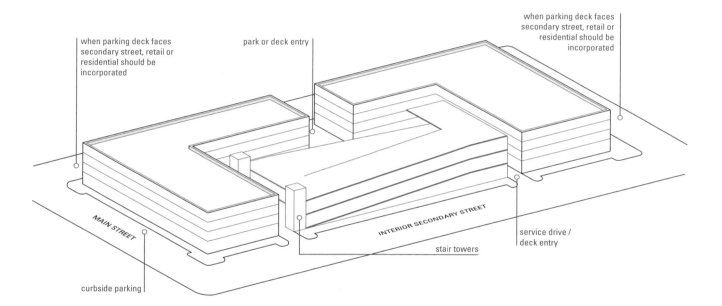

when parking deck faces secondary street, retail or residential should be incorporated

park or deck entry

when parking deck faces secondary street, retail or residential should be incorporated

MAIN STREET

INTERIOR SECONDARY STREET

service drive / deck entry

stair towers

curbside parking

volumes with modest waits. Very large garages, such as at airports or regional shopping centers, are generally best handled with huge flat floors connected by ramps.

The dream of every site planner is to do away with visible parking by creating underground parking garages. Some cities such as Vancouver require all structured parking to be below grade in downtown, as do many European cities. In many cities, areas below public squares have become public parking structures. This is a costly solution, with parking typically costing double the price of aboveground parking or more, depending on groundwater conditions and the

landscape that is created above, but is well worth the investment. A large portion of the added cost results from the need to mechanically ventilate underground garages, a problem that may be lessened with the advent of electric vehicles. Exhaust locations need to be carefully sited, and an added challenge is locating ramps so that they do not disrupt pedestrian flows to the space above, or traffic movement patterns.

Aboveground parking structures can be made attractive, of course, by integrating them into the streetscape, cladding them with high-quality finishes, or through greening. They can be wrapped with active uses so that

21.56 Parking structure and event space, Lincoln Road, Miami Beach, Florida.
(Phillip Pessar/Flickr)

21.57 Automated parking garage.
(© Paha_l/Dreamstime)

they are nearly invisible. Since many parking structures, like their counterpart lots, sit idle on weekends or evenings, another approach is to design them for additional uses. Rooftops can become tennis courts on weekends or can be topped by housing. By designing the structure with additional floor height, they can be transformed into event spaces when not used for parking.

In many dense urban areas it is impractical to develop any form of parking with ramps connecting levels because of the small sizes of sites. A host of new technologies have come to the rescue. In Tokyo, automated elevator systems raise or lower cars and file them into slots on floors with as few as two cars per floor. Turntables allow cars to be turned before reentering the streets. Robotic garages handle the filling of cars without human intervention, and have become a hit in New York. Automated garages are a costly if good solution to parking below residential towers that have small footprints. Because of their efficient use of space—they typically increase parking by up to 100% by sliding cars closer together and dispensing with driving lanes—they are often a cost-effective solution.

Vehicle Sharing

Many car owners use their vehicles only occasionally for a trip out of town or to pick up and deliver items, relying on mass transit or walking for everyday routines. Parking these cars is costly, not to mention the costs of ownership, insurance, and maintenance. Car share programs cater to these drivers' needs while reducing the number of cars on the roads and in parking lots. Experience in central Philadelphia indicates that each

21.58 Autolib car sharing service, Paris.
(Gary Hack)

car share vehicle has substituted for 15 privately owned vehicles. Current technologies allow Internet booking of cars, dispensing with the need for contact with an agent.

Many cities now require that parking lot operators set aside spaces near the entrance to their facilities for car share vehicles. Another critical location is along transit lines, particularly at the ends of lines, where shared vehicles can transport passengers to their ultimate destination. An added virtue of car sharing is that it supplies users with precisely the type of vehicle they need—a small truck for deliveries, a minicar for short distances, a minivan for taking a crew to a game, a sporty car for a two-day excursion. Car sharing has gained favor with urbanites in areas with good mass transit, college students, large businesses making occasional service calls, and public employees needing to make trips into the field. In the future, it is likely to multiply to many other groups, and each of the major automobile manufacturers has a program to place its vehicles in the field for car share use.

The Future of Motor Vehicles

Car sharing is an example of the radical changes in mobility that will affect both the hard and soft infrastructure needed for motor vehicles. There is evidence that fewer young people in Europe and the US desire to own automobiles if there are other options available when they need one. Some developers are already integrating car share opportunities in their projects, which could result in a significant reduction in the amount of parking spaces they need to provide. Access to car sharing may become a competitive advantage for projects.

Access on demand using smartphones is already affecting the mix of traffic on the roads, adding to and possibly displacing current taxi and courier services. With the ability to match vehicles to needs, the types of automobiles, trucks, and buses are likely to continue to increase, particularly at the smaller ends of the scales. Fixed bus routes in low-density areas may be abandoned in favor of custom routes that pick up passengers near where they are and deposit them near their destination. On high-volume routes, scheduling may be optimized to accommodate peak demands created by events and occasions.

Electric vehicles are becoming commonplace, and will require widely distributed infrastructure for charging—in homes, workplaces, shopping areas, and general parking facilities. Two-way batteries may make it advantageous to couple solar arrays with charging facilities, allowing batteries to be charged during the day and used for electric power in the house they are attached to during the evening.

The most radical changes in mobility, however, will result from the arrival of autonomous vehicles. The immediate effect will be to allow driverless taxis and small buses to pick up and deliver passengers, then move on to the next customer. This will reduce the need for parking spaces, which could have a large impact on places where parking is costly, as in dense urban centers. For those who ride in a vehicle they own to a destination, the car will go on to park itself, awaiting a signal hailing it from the owner's smartphone. Parking garages will want to be optimized for many vehicle types that can be differentiated between long- and short-term parking, and there will be a preference for flexible flat-floor arrangements.

As autonomous vehicles become ubiquitous, the roadway infrastructure will need to change to capitalize on the new opportunities. Roadways will handle more vehicles, since collision avoidance systems will allow them to follow others more closely without danger. Roadways with flexible lanes will be able to reprogram the number of lanes in each direction in response to

21.59 Electric car sharing service, Cité Lib by Ha:mo project, by Toyota, Grenoble, France.
(Toyota)

sensor data on flows. This may suggest the possibility of doing away with lanes entirely, allowing vehicles to move to places on the roadway that are underoccupied.

The fluidity of flows on roadways and ability to avoid collisions will also affect the way pedestrians and vehicles interact. Some have suggested that it will be possible to reprogram portions of roadways for other uses in off-hours, such as events and gatherings, while maintaining flows for the number of vehicles that must use the route. This will require a remarkable change of mindset for a field that has been devoted to channeling flows in regimented ways.

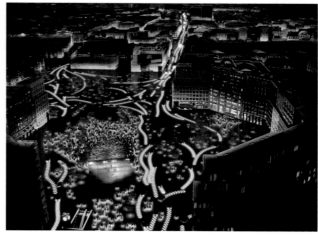

21.60 Driverless POD taxi service, Milton Keynes, UK.
(Catapult Transport Systems)

21.61 Google's Waymo self-driving car prototype.
(Google)

21.62 Driverless buses currently operating in Rotterdam, Netherlands.
(Maurits Vink)

21.63 Plasti-city, with driverless cars and pedestrians sharing street space of Berlin.
(Courtesy of BIG – Bjarke Ingels Group)

21.64 Potsdammer Platz, Berlin, shared by pedestrians, performers, driverless cars, and bicycles.
(Courtesy of BIG – Bjarke Ingels Group)

22 | Transit

Shared mobility can take the form of voluntary car sharing, use of a taxi or jitney, private or public bus service, as well as more established forms of transit including trolleys, monorails, streetcars, and light and heavy rail systems. In European cities, using mass transit is the norm, and large new development areas customarily include links to the public transit network. North American cities are playing catch-up, installing transit systems where possible, hampered by sprawling development patterns that are difficult to serve. In rapidly urbanizing countries of Asia and Latin America, mass transit provides the backbone of mobility, supplemented by a wide array of paratransit services. In much of Africa, paratransit is the only option.

Whatever form it takes, transit needs to become the sine qua non of all future site development plans. Reduction of energy use and greenhouse gas emissions depends on sharing transportation. During peak hours, a medium-sized car consumes more than twice the energy of a minibus per average passenger served, and over three times the energy of a conventional bus, light rail, or heavy rail system. Even in off-peak periods, when mass transit systems are not near capacity, they use less than half the energy per passenger compared to private automobiles (Potter 2003). But more than energy is at stake: as the populations age in many countries, shared transportation modes are critical for mobility; and access to cultural, social, and employment opportunities in increasingly fragmented cities depends on having activities concentrated near public transit.

Planning for transit is best done on a regionwide or systemwide basis, since few sites are large enough to support an independent transit system beyond buses. Nonetheless, given a range of possible transit services, the way streets are arranged and their dimensions will affect the types of transit service that may run on them, and exclusive rights-of-way need to be set aside for higher-volume mass transit systems. Orienting development to locations that can be served by transit will help build patronage, and assuring that there are adequate densities along transit corridors will make for economical operations. On a small site near a transit stop, providing direct and convenient walkways and sheltered places to wait may be the key. As sites increase in scale, the design of rights-of-way for effective transit circulation becomes the planner's challenge. At airports and on large campuses, specialized forms of transit may be possible, such as automated guideway systems and monorails that provide rapid and convenient circulation between terminals and buildings. And in the future, the emergence of driverless cars and new types of vehicles will blur the line between transit and private vehicles.

There are many excellent texts on planning transit systems (see especially Vuchic 2007; Grava 2002), which give detailed information on technologies and operational issues. Here the focus is on the choices available to site planners, and effective ways of planning sites to support transit use.

Transit Modes

Selection of a transit mode is more a matter of policy and economics than an imperative of the technologies involved. If cost is no object, private transit service can be provided to all addresses in a community, and indeed it is in some cities, through dial-a-bus services and taxis hailed through smartphones. Rail-based transit service can be provided for a line just a few hundred meters long, as at the US Capitol, speeding elected representatives in a minute from their offices to vote on the floor of their legislative chambers. But in most circumstances, capital and operating costs are a key factor in decisions about transit modes, as are acceptable levels of public subsidies and transit fares, the capacity to operate and maintain systems, the level of technology available, and local traditions of public and private supply of transit services.

Transit modes fall into three broad categories: those that operate on roadways shared with automobiles, trucks, and other vehicles; those that have exclusive rights-of-way, on the surface, above, or below; and special-purpose modes that provide for circulation on limited properties, traverse difficult terrain, or move people across water. There is an exponential difference in costs between roadway-based transit and lines on dedicated routes, mainly reflecting the need to acquire rights-of-way and provide grade separations and transit stations. However, reserving transit corridors as sites are developed can narrow the differences considerably, even if transit is installed a decade or more later.

The types of vehicles and traditions of providing transit vary considerably around the world, and technology is constantly evolving. This brief review of planning considerations should offer the site planner a point of departure for more detailed investigations.

Roadway-Based Transit

There are many obvious advantages to using roadways to provide transit service, not the least that they provide access to virtually every site in the city. They offer flexibility in accommodating the hundreds of types of vehicles available, at little cost beyond the vehicles. Rubber-tired vehicles are not bound to specific routes (except *trolleybuses*), and can be rerouted and rescheduled as demands shift. There may be no choice but to use roadways: in low-density areas, rubber-tired vehicles are the only practical way to provide transit service; and in low-income countries that lack the capital to install mass transit systems, *paratransit* vehicles fill the gap. Vehicles providing transit on streets can range in size from three-person taxis to double-articulated buses and streetcars with 200 passengers. Each has unique requirements. (See table 22.1 for their dimensions and capacities.)

Taxis

Taxis are not normally thought of as part of a community's transit system, but they provide a critical "last-mile" link from other types of transit to and from destinations. In cities with poor transit opportunities they may also serve the "first mile," for trips up to 15 km (9 mi) in length. During nighttime, taxis may be the only way to get from place to place, or may be preferred for safety reasons. Taxis have many advantages, but they are also the most expensive form of mass transit, with high labor costs for each passenger mile. They remain nonetheless essential in any large city.

Since taxis join the normal flow of traffic, they make no extra demands on roadway planning. However, areas for queuing are critical at major transportation terminals (airports, rail stations, mass transit stops) and large generators of taxi demands (sporting venues,

22.1 Light rail sharing the streets with vehicles, Portland, Oregon. (Courtesy of © Tim Jewett)

Table 22.1 | Roadway-based transit

Mode	Length, m (ft)	Vehicle capacity[1]	Maximum operating capacity, passengers/hour[2]	Assumed headways[3]	Lane width required, m (ft)	Turning radius required for 90° turn, m (ft)	Outside turning diameter required for 180° turn, m (ft)
Minibus	7 (23)	14/20	1,200	1 min	3 (10)	8 (26)	16 (52)
Jitney jeepney	7 (23)	11/16	864	1 min	3 (10)	8 (26)	16 (52)
Mobility transit (wheelchairs)	6 (20)	4/6	N/A	N/A	3 (10)	7 (23)	14 (46)
Shuttle bus (midi-bus)	10 (33)	38	684	3 min	3 (10)	8.8 (28)	17.5 (57)
Standard US bus	12 (39)	55/85	1,530	3 min	3.35 (11)	14.4 (47)	29 (94)
Articulated bus	18 (60)	70/105	1,890	3 min	3.5 (12)	11.6 (38)	23 (76)
Trolleybus	12 (39)	55/85	1,530	3 min	3.35 (11)	13 (43)	26 (86)
Double-decker bus	12 (39)	78/90	1,620	3 min	3.35 (11)	10.4 (34)	20.7 (68)
Double-articulated bus	25 (82)	120/200	3,600	3 min	3.5 (12)	12 (39)	24 (78)
Tram/streetcar (superlight)	15 (49)	40/130	2,340	3 min	3.35 (11)	11 (36)	22 (72)
Articulated streetcar	20 (66)	30/150	2,700	3 min	3.5 (12)	18 (60)	36 (120)

Sources: Vuchic (2007); manufacturers' data.

[1] Seats/total capacity including standing.

[2] Assumed headways operating at 90% capacity.

[3] Assumed for capacity estimate; actual headways based on operations and demand.

hotels, performing arts centers). Often this requires little more than a curb lane reserved for taxi use, and a stacking area (a *taxi queue*, *rank*, *cab*, or *hack stand*) where taxis may wait to be called. In places with surges of demand, multiple loading bays may be required. A good example is Hong Kong's Airport Station, which is designed to accommodate over 1,000 taxi boardings per hour.

Local traditions determine the most effective way to find a taxi. In some cities—particularly low-density areas—they must be booked over the telephone or Internet, while in others taxis cruise the streets looking for fares—a strategy that requires a high density of destinations and large number of taxis to be effective. Most cities provide some form of taxi stands where taxis wait for passengers, and a modest amount of curb space for several taxis to queue. Providing shelter from the weather helps encourage people to gather in these locations to wait for taxis. The taxi queue problem may be solved in the future by the advent of *driverless taxis*, which remain in motion or parked remotely until called on a smartphone.

22.2 Taxi waiting area, Hong Kong IFC Airport Station. (WiNG/Wikimedia Commons)

22.3 Taxi queue, Kowloon waterfront, Hong Kong.
(Diego Delso/Wikimedia Commons)

Paratransit

One step up from taxis in efficiency is the variety of paratransit modes that serve up to 20 passengers at a time, on demand, on fixed routes, or roaming. These include:

Carpooling,
Commuter vans,
Dial-a-ride services,
Handicapped-access vehicles,
Airport shuttles,
Touring vehicles,
Transit feeders,
Jitneys,
Community-service vehicles,
Jeepneys, públicos, colectivos,
Party vehicles, marshrutkas, etc.,
Flexible transport.

In many cities, paratransit is the mainstay of the access system. In Johannesburg, a city that lacks an effective mass transit system, privately operated mini-buses serve the bulk of the demand for commuting from outlying townships. The government has provided low-cost loans for the purchase of vehicles. Entrepreneur-operators establish routes and compete for the loyalty of their passengers. Públicos in Puerto Rico provide a similar service, as do marshrutkas in Russia and Eastern Europe, colectivos in Bogotá, wonderfully decorated jeepneys in Manila, and a host of services

in other Asian cities. In Hong Kong, there is a system of public light buses that fills the gaps between mass transit and double-deckers that ply the main routes. Whether publicly or privately operated, paratransit is highly responsive to transit needs, self-organizing, and capable of serving populations that would undoubtedly be neglected by more formal systems.

Paratransit services can serve commuter needs well, even in dispersed cities, and they cannot be overlooked in planning new developments. They need locations to idle for pickups and at central destinations such as downtown areas, and they need large areas to lay over between the main commuting hours; without these they clog the streets and curbs. The city of Johannesburg has constructed exemplary minibus taxi loading and parking structures in downtown and at the entrance to Soweto. These include well-designed boarding areas, public markets, and other retail outlets catering to the thousands of commuters who flow through these facilities.

Similar facilities are needed for paratransit in advanced countries, particularly at airports, tourism centers, and other concentrated destinations. Since many paratransit services involve waiting for customers or lengthy boarding times—airport shuttles, car rental shuttles, tourist minibuses, circulator shuttles, and the like—a good strategy is often to separate their flows from normal traffic, to avoid congesting regular streets.

Dial-a-ride service—or on-demand service using smartphones—is provided using minibuses in many communities with low-density development, using vehicles specially equipped for the handicapped, and they operate even in the densest cities in response to US government mandates to assure mobility for all residents. Many handicapped residents need to be picked up at their door, but for other customers, one way to improve efficiency and service is to designate service locations within easy walk of all residential areas. Service can then be provided among a dense set of nodes distributed across an urban area, or via a central transfer station employing a hub and spoke system (Cervero 1997). While computer matching of origins and destinations can help increase the occupancy of vehicles, it remains a costly service to operate. The largest cost of these services is the labor cost, and there may be hope on the horizon in the form of *driverless buses*. Several cities are currently experimenting with such services.

22.4 Colectivo, shared bus service, Bogotá, Colombia.
(Gary Hack)

22.5 Minibus terminal and market, Soweto, Johannesburg,
South Africa.
(Soweto Urban)

It is often cost-effective to encourage carpooling, as a way of reducing the number of vehicles on the road and the required number of commuter parking spaces. Some employers provide free parking in preferred locations for carpools, instead of devoting several parking spaces for the group involved. Where parking is costly (as in center city locations), employers may find it is even worth their while to supply vans for carpool groups, and to valet them to remote locations during working hours. Privately organized carpools require all their members to leave and arrive at the same time, which may be difficult on occasion (due to child care

responsibilities, emergencies, medical appointments, etc.), and function best when there are alternatives available, such as mass transit service and day-parking when needed. New carpooling services such as Lyft can overcome this hurdle by providing a large pool of potential customers to be matched with vehicles.

Buses

Buses traveling on fixed routes are the mainstay of public transit in North American cities, and they serve a large proportion of trips around the world. Most buses travel in mixed traffic with automobiles and trucks, although increasingly cities are dedicating bus lanes on roadways, and creating *bus rapid transit* (BRT) lines that serve the most intense commuting corridors. Buses typically accommodate 40–80 passengers, with *articulated vehicles* and *double-articulated megabuses* handling up to 300. Bus service also varies in prestige, from the luxury private motor coaches that carry commuters to New York City and other major metropolitan areas to broken-down, un-air-conditioned and jam-packed buses that crawl along congested streets in Dhaka, Cairo, and other developing cities, and everything in between.

Public subsidies bring bus fares into a range where they are accessible to most residents of cities. Nonetheless, in most US communities it becomes impractical to provide transit service in residential areas where the density is less than 8 dwelling units (du) per ha (3 du per ac) or 2,200 people per km² (5,800 per sq mi) (Edwards 1992). One starting point for planning bus routes is that daily volumes of 1,800–2,000 vehicles are necessary to establish a bus corridor, with at least 150–200 in the peak hour (Giannopoulos 1989). Typically, this will require about four buses per hour in peak periods, and two per hour during other parts of the day.

Evidence indicates a strong resistance among Americans to walking more than 0.5 mi (0.8 km) to a transit stop, which suggests that transit lines should be spaced about 1 mi (1.6 km) apart. Use of transit service increases significantly when both origins and destinations are within a 10-minute walk of bus stops, without transfers between lines. With the ongoing dispersal of employment locations on the fringes of US cities, it is increasingly difficult to achieve that target without inordinate subsidies for transit.

22.6 Standard and articulated buses, Santiago, Chile. (Art Konovalov/Shutterstock)

Desirable walking distances vary around the world. Studies in Toronto found that around 60% of transit users live within a radius of 0.3 km (0.2 mi) of a stop, although a significant minority walks longer distances. London's design criterion for its expensive bus system (mainly employing *Routemaster double decker buses*) is to provide service within a 5-minute walk (approximately 0.4 km or 0.25 mi) of every resident, if possible, depending on roadway configurations. Bus service on Beijing's grid of major roadways means that most residents are never more than 10 minutes from a bus line. In the planning of the new city of Milton Keynes in the UK, the grid of collector roadways was spaced approximately 1 km (0.6 mi) apart so that all residents were within 10 minutes' walk of a bus stop.

Ultimately walking distances are largely determined by density of development near transit lines. In Curitiba, Brazil, which has an exemplary BRT system using double-articulated buses, and an array of smaller buses on shared roadways, development policies have promoted the highest densities of new buildings on streets served by high-frequency transit. The majority of residents of the city are within a few short steps of a bus stop. Transit-oriented development is the key to effective transit, as well as to minimizing carbon emissions from transportation.

The spacing of bus stops also makes a difference. Frequent stops, which minimize walking distances, need to be balanced against the speed of travel, which also encourages transit usage. The general consensus among operations specialists is that bus stops should be spaced 275–600 m (900–2,000 ft) apart, but in practice in the US, the typical spacing is 200–240 m (650–800 ft) (Li and Bertini 2008). On high-capacity routes with short *headways*, skip stops are often the solution to lengthening the distances between stops without eroding service, assuming that buses can pass others in the driving lanes. This is the practice in Beijing and other cities. Detailed models have been developed that determine optimal spacing of bus stops based on a variety of factors, including the size of loading areas, average dwell time, the timing of traffic signals, and time required for buses to join the traffic flow (Kittelson & Associates 2003).

Electronic information systems at bus stops can play an important role in aiding the bus user by indicating the expected arrival time of oncoming buses, and their routes. There is at least anecdotal evidence that people are willing to wait longer if they know when the bus will arrive. On streets with multiple bus routes, electronic information systems can lower the anxiety over which bus to take.

Bus stops are typically located on the *near side* or *far side* of an intersection, and there are strongly held preferences for each practice. Locating bus stops on the near side of signalized intersections can make effective use of red light waiting times, but interferes with right turns (or left turns in countries where traffic travels on the left) by other vehicles, particularly in locations where right turns are permitted on red. Locating stops on the far side can avoid some of this delay, and has the logic of allowing buses to easily pull into the parking lane for loading. Far-side loading requires smaller loading bays, since it avoids lengthy deceleration distances. An alternative to either practice is the creation of *bus bulbs*, where the walkway is widened to the edge of the curb-parking lane. This has many advantages including providing adequate space for waiting and bus shelters, although it disrupts travel in one lane.

Creating *dedicated bus lanes* adjacent to the curb, where automobiles are prohibited during peak hours or throughout the day (except for those making right turns), can help smooth the flow of transit in high-demand areas. These may be coupled with a signalization system that allows buses to advance the green phase and avoid

22.7 Real-time bus information system, New York City. (New York City Department of Transportation)

22.8 Bus bulb on New York City street. (NACTO)

22.9 Dedicated bus lane, New York City. (NACTO)

intersection delays. Since a single bus may carry 20–30 times the average number of passengers in automobiles, buses running on four-minute headways in dedicated lanes will more than replace the number of motor vehicles that would otherwise use the lane. The more difficult issue, in most US cities, is whether to displace *parallel parking* at the curb with dedicated bus lanes, or whether to maintain it and tolerate the interference of parking movements (and double parking!) in bus lanes.

Curb parking is less practiced in countries beyond North America, making dedicated bus lanes (or express bus lanes—see below) more common. Some Asian cities with heavy directional flows have created counterflow (or reverse flow) bus lanes on major streets, borrowing unused capacity to speed buses in and out of cities. These are tricky to establish, require signalization systems to warn drivers moving in the opposite direction, and require buses with doors that open on both sides.

Trams and Streetcars

Most North American cities had *streetcars* shuttling passengers along city streets until the 1950s, when trolley buses and diesel buses replaced them (Slater 1997). A few cities resisted the abandonment of street railway systems, and others simply paved the rails over in case that they were needed in the future. Toronto (streetcars), San Francisco (*munis*), Philadelphia (*subway-surface lines*), and Boston (*trolleys*) are among the cities that have operated streetcars for over a century, several placing them in tunnels within central areas. Over the past two decades, several cities, notably Portland, Oregon, have installed new streetcar (now dubbed *superlight vehicle*) lines in their central areas.

Many European cities also employ active fleets of rail vehicles, usually called *trams*, *tramcars*, or *interurbans*, that share the streets with automobiles and other vehicles. In the 1980s, St. Petersburg, Russia had the largest tram system in the world, although Melbourne, Australia currently claims the title. It has invested in updating its tram system and has converted several downtown streets into exclusively pedestrian and tram domains. Strasbourg was among the first cities to introduce modern glassy vehicles, and today many cities around the world have introduced low-floor trams,

22.10 The Portland streetcar, connecting the downtown with the rapidly emerging Pearl District.
(Schw4r7z/flickr/Creative Commons)

22.11 Melbourne, Australia tram system on a priority street in the central city.
(Gary Hack)

22.12 Low-rise tram in mixed traffic, Milan, Italy.
(Gary Hack)

which allow passengers to board directly from slightly raised curbs, including Melbourne, Milan, Dublin, and Houston. Many modern trams are articulated vehicles, and streets in both North America and Europe have been closed to allow them to run and board efficiently in dense urban centers, and make the necessary turns. Double-decker trams continue in use in Hong Kong.

Streetcars are energy-efficient and are much loved by their users, particularly the new versions. Single cars typically accommodate up to 120 passengers (seated and standing) and are capable of making turns at intersections in a radius similar to those of light trucks. Articulated versions, which can accommodate 150 passengers, require slightly larger radii, but offer greater flexibility for peak loads. Typically they require 4 m (13 ft) lanes to operate, and must be carefully integrated with flows of pedestrians and other vehicles.

There are three basic choices for how to integrate streetcars in mixed traffic. Historically they were located in the center lanes of four-lane streets, as they continue to be in Toronto and portions of Philadelphia. This location is least disruptive to local traffic, allowing loading, parking, right turns, and other activities unimpeded, but requires pedestrians to cross a moving lane of traffic to board the streetcar. In Toronto this works in part because of strict rules that give pedestrians the right of way from the moment they step off the curb. Some streetcars are designed for boarding on the left from a median platform, which improves pedestrian safety. This alternative is especially appropriate where wide medians exist.

The second alternative is to locate streetcars in the curb lane, eliminating parallel parking while loading passengers along the street. This is ideal for pedestrians, but otherwise disruptive of street access to shops or other facilities along the street. A third alternative is to locate streetcars adjacent to the parking and loading lane, with the sidewalk bumped out at streetcar stops to meet the vehicles, much as with bus stops previously mentioned. In most cases this will be the preferred location.

When streetcars run in the curb lane, catenaries can be easily supported on arms from utility poles located on the sidewalk. Vehicles running in center lanes require that *catenaries* be attached to suspension wires that run across the street, a more difficult—and more obtrusive—arrangement. Both situations require a high degree of coordination of utility poles, arms, suspension cables, signage, transit shelters, and street lighting, to avoid clutter and assure that each element serves its purpose.

Transit in Dedicated Rights-of-Way

Transit that runs in mixed traffic ultimately has only a small advantage over other vehicles, although transit riders can use the time to do other things. Dedicating one lane of a roadway to the exclusive use of street-cars or buses can advantage transit during congested periods, and sometimes these lanes are also made available to cyclists and taxis. However, the use of exclusive rights-of-way for transit greatly increases travel speed and the capacity of transit systems.

The traditional locations of a dedicated right-of-way are in the median of a wide street or in a corridor separate from other traffic. Typically, the right-of-way will require a width of 10–11.6 m (33–38 ft), plus an additional 3 m (10 ft) at stations for boarding areas. In the centers of dense urban areas, specific streets may be dedicated to transit and pedestrian use, with private vehicles banned, although during specific hours commercial loading may be allowed. People and transit vehicles may not need to be rigidly separated in bus arrival areas where buses are traveling at slow speeds, allowing the streets to become lively and convenient places.

In most cases, the critical issue is separating the transit lanes (whether for trams or for buses) from the grid of local streets. Overpasses or underpasses may be the best way to allow transit vehicles to avoid stopping at major intersections, and may also be required to transport passengers across streets to transit stations.

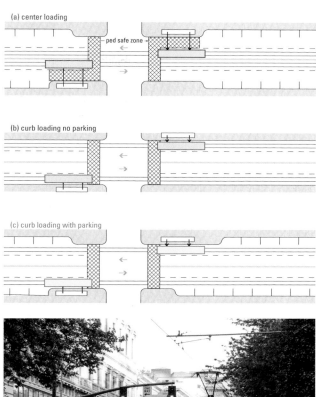

22.13 Options for streetcar loading.
(Adam Tecza/Gary Hack)

22.14 Portland streetcar, employing arms from poles on sidewalk to support catenaries.
(BeyondDC/flickr/Creative Commons)

22.15 Buses and trams converge on the transit interchange in the center of Bern, Switzerland, which also connects to retail and intercity trains.
(Gary Hack)

Table 22.2 (this and facing page) | Transit on dedicated rights-of-way

Mode	Vehicle type	Individual vehicle length, m (ft)	Vehicle capacity[1]	Assumed number of vehicles	Maximum operating capacity, passengers/hour[2]
Bus rapid transit	Single-articulated	18 (59)	49/85	1	18,360
	Double-articulated	25 (82)	72/130	1	28,080
Light rail systems	4-axle single	15 (50)	120	2	12,960
	8-axle articulated	30 (100)	250	2	27,000
Rapid transit	Rail	20 (65)	170	6	27,540
	Rubber-tired	19 (62)	160	6	25,920
Regional commuter systems	Rail	25 (85)	360	6	38,880

Sources: Vuchic (2007); manufacturers' data.
[1] Seats/total capacity including standing.
[2] Assumed headways operating at 90% capacity.
[3] Assumed for capacity estimate; actual headways based on operations and demand.

Abandoned railway rights-of-way are often an ideal solution, since they usually have grade separations at major streets. It may be possible to integrate transit with express roadways, but this is difficult after a roadway has been constructed if the right-of-way has not been reserved.

Bus Rapid Transit

Buses can serve as mass transit systems if they run on exclusive rights-of-way and are provided with high-speed boarding and off-board ticketing systems. Two of the earliest BRT systems were created in Curitiba, Brazil and Ottawa, Canada. Currently there are more than 150 systems throughout the world.

The Curitiba system runs largely in broad medians along major corridors in the city. Buses are provided with two exclusive lanes in each direction to maintain the flow, and to allow through buses to bypass others stopped at local stations. A variety of vehicles are used, but on express routes double-articulated buses are typically employed, with six loading doors for quick entry and exit of up to 270 passengers. Tubelike stations allow fares to be collected prior to boarding, reducing loading

times to an average of 15–17 seconds. Buses operated by 10 separate bus companies can run on headways as low as 90 seconds, carrying up to 18,000 passengers per hour in the corridor.

The Curitiba system and the subsequent Bogotá TransMilenio BRT and Guangzhou's BRT system, each of which improve upon it, have proven successful in part because buses originate on or connect to other routes beyond the high-speed corridors. In Guangzhou, the 22.5 km (14 mi) trunk line along Zhongshan Avenue carries 850,000 passengers a day. For dispersed cities, aggregating local buses on trunk lines provides a high level of service throughout the city.

In Ottawa, Canada, a 35 km (22 mi) transitway has been created that operates above or below the level of the normal streets. Most buses are articulated vehicles that travel at up to 90 km/hr (56 mph). Transit terminals are provided at the main intersection points, and stations are spaced between 600 m (2,000 ft) near the center and 1,000 m (0.6 mi) in outer areas. In the downtown area two streets have exclusive bus lanes, and the curbs in these areas are devoted to boarding and *layover*. Unfortunately, this creates extreme congestion in the downtown area, but

Assumed minimum headway[3]	Right-of-way width required for two-way operation, m (ft)	Curvature radius required, m (ft)	Assumed minimum design speed, km/hr (mph)	Optimal distance between stops, central area/ outlying area, m (ft)	Maximum gradient, %
15 sec	11.6 (38)	90 (300)	50 (30)	300/500 (100/160)	15
15 sec	11.6 (38)	90 (300)	50 (30)	300/500 (100/160)	15
1 min	10 (33)	82 (270)	65 (40)	360/1,600 (1,100/5,280)	15
1 min	10 (33)	82 (270)	65 (40)	360/1,600 (1,100/5,280)	15
2 min	11 (36)	150 (500)	70 (44)	500/200 (1,640/6,500)	6–8
2 min	11 (36)	125 (410)	70 (44)	500/200 (1,640/6,500)	8–10
3 min	14 (45)	175 (575)	100 (60)	1,200/7,000 (3,960/22,965)	7–9

22.16 (top left)   Central spine of the Curitiba BRT system.
(World Bank)

22.17 (top right)   Stations on the Curitiba BRT system.
(Mario Roberto Duran Ortiz/Wikipedia Commons)

22.18 (bottom)   Bogotá TransMilenio BRT station, integrated with major expressway.
(Jorge Lascar/Wikipedia Commons)

22.19 Guangzhou BRT system along major arterial street. (Transmilenio SA)

22.20 Ottawa transitway, Westboro station. (Radagast/Wikimedia Commons)

there is significant opposition to closing these streets entirely to automobile traffic. Peak capacity of each of the grade-separated lines is 10,000 passengers per hour each direction. The success of the system has led to replacing the central trunk line with a light rail system to increase capacity.

Light Rail Systems

European cities have long favored *light rail transit* (LRT) for its flexibility in routing, energy efficiency, and comparatively minor environmental impacts when operating

in dense urban areas. These systems go by a variety of names, including S-Bahn or Stadtbahn (Germany), city rail (UK), and bybane (Norway.) In North America, only a few light rail systems survived the demise of streetcars, notably in Boston, Philadelphia, Pittsburgh, and San Francisco. During the past two decades, however, over 25 new light rail systems have been created in North America, and many dozens more throughout the world. It has become the transit of choice for cities with between 0.5 million and 5 million residents, and an essential component of many larger cities.

Light rail transit differs from streetcars by generally traveling on its own right-of-way outside of central areas, utilizing two to four connected articulated vehicles, and stopping at defined stations where fares are usually taken prior to boarding. Vehicles generally travel at ground level, although they may be routed in tunnels or onto elevated structures in dense areas, and are generally electric-powered using catenaries. Typical vehicles range in size from dual-section vehicles with 60 seated to triplex vehicles with 85 seated to five-section vehicles (Stuttgart) with 150 seated. Generally, 100–200% more can be accommodated standing, depending on the configuration of vehicles. Vehicles are typically 2,700 mm (8 ft 10 in) wide. Standard vehicles have a floor height of 480–830 mm (19–32.7 in) above the rails, necessitating an elevated platform to provide universal accessibility, while low-floor vehicles

22.21 Tramway running in central median of major boulevard, Strasbourg. (Bernard Chatreau/Wikipedia Commons)

with floors 197–360 mm (7.8–14.2 in) above the tracks are easier to access.

Most European LRT lines use *standard gauge* tracks, which are spaced 1,435 mm (4 ft 8 ½ in), although several cities maintain narrow gauge lines of 1,000 mm (3 ft 3 ⅓ in) since these are better able to navigate narrow streets or rights-of-way. North American LRT installations also use standard gauge tracks, although in several cities embedded tracks in streets forced other standards—Philadelphia 1,588 mm (5 ft 2 ½ in), Toronto 1,581 mm (5 ft 2 ¼ in). Employing standard gauge LRT vehicles allows the shared use of railway lines, such as in the Edmonton system.

The preferred geometry of tracks may vary slightly depending on the vehicles being employed, but there are several general standards that may be used in site planning:

Gradient:

Desirable maximum = 4%
Maximum, short section (<500 m or 1,500 ft) = 6%
Maximum in embedded section = 6%
Maximum with special vehicles = 10% (Stuttgart)
In station = 0.5%

Horizontal alignment:

Minimum radius in yard = 25 m (80 ft)
Minimum radius, slow sections = 35 m (115 ft)
Minimum radius, fast sections = 150 m (500 ft)

Tangent:

General rule:

minimum radius = (0.58 × V) m, where V = design speed in km/hr
minimum radius = (3 × V) ft, where V= design speed in mph

Vertical alignment:

Minimum length of constant-profile grade between vertical curves = 30 m (100 ft) or 0.58 × V in km/hr (3 × V in mph), whichever is greater.

While the requirements will differ somewhat from system to system, a general rule is that tracks should be at least 4,250 mm (14 ft) apart, centerline to centerline, to

22.22 Light rail system, Minneapolis, with side-loading platforms. (Minneapolis Star Tribune)

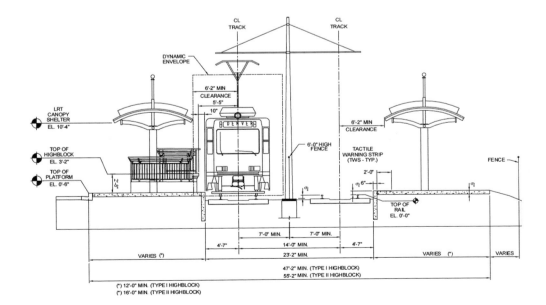

22.23 Recommended LRT cross section with side-loading platforms. (Denver Regional Transportation District)

allow supports for the catenaries to be located between the lines, and there should be a clear zone of 3,000 mm (10 ft) from the side of tracks to any immoveable objects or fences. As a practical matter, this means a right-of-way of at least 11.65 m (38 ft) for a light rail line. In corridors where LRT lines run parallel to moving traffic lanes, the outer face of the curb of the adjacent traffic lane should be at least 2,500 mm (8 feet) from the centerline of the LRT lane.

Planning stations on LRT lines will require the greatest creativity. Where lines run in both directions in a corridor, there are two basic configurations: side-loading platforms for each direction, and a center-loading platform serving both directions. Each poses important challenges.

Center-loading platforms minimize the width of corridor required, allow ticket gates, concessions, and information to be centralized, and allow some transfers to occur across the platform when multiple lines use the tracks. This configuration is often adopted for cost reasons, and where rights-of-way are restricted. Depending upon boarding volumes, a platform width of 5 m (16 ft) may be adequate, which may add only 2–3 m (7–10 feet) to the right-of-way requirements in the station area. The difficult problem is getting people to the platform safely. In stations where vehicles are moving slowly and rails are embedded, pedestrians may simply wander across the tracks, an advantage of low-floor vehicles. Another solution may be gated crossings that stop pedestrians when trains are approaching.

But where vehicles enter at high speeds, over- or underpasses will be necessary, which are costly if accessibility standards must be met and escalators are installed to ease the flow. A central platform also makes transfers to buses or automobiles inconvenient.

The alternative is providing dual *side-loading platforms*, which solves half the interface problem with other forms of transportation but may not totally obviate the need for protected crossings. Platforms are typically 3.5–4 m (11.5–13 ft) in width. Where trains run in a median, safety protection is essential for passengers waiting for trains; thus, the right-of-way requirement for a dual side-loading station is typically at least 15.4 m (50.5 feet). This may increase with

22.24 Opening day of Union Station stop on Denver's LRT, with center-loading platform. (Ken Schroeppel/Denverurbanism.com)

22.25 Recommended LRT cross section with center-loading platform. (Denver Regional Transportation District)

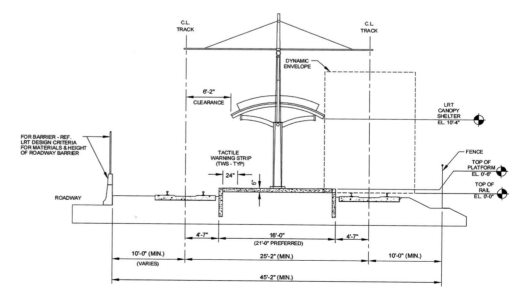

22.26 Long Beach, California transit gallery.
(Tisoy/Wikimedia commons)

standard-height vehicles where ramps and stairways are necessary to elevate passengers to boarding level.

In either type of station, weather protection for waiting passengers is essential. Allowing light in and air to circulate through stations, and creating heated spaces in cold climates, will make waiting for a train more tolerable. Many cities have created kits of parts that can be customized for individual stations, including roof structures, signage, benches, furnishings, and platform materials.

Where several light rail lines converge on the center of a city, it may be impractical to create enough platform space at ground level to serve peak loads. This may argue for running the LRT line underground in the center, as in Seattle, or devoting a street solely to transit and pedestrians (as in Denver, San Diego, San Jose, and Long Beach). This may allow easy transfers between LRT and bus lines, and can be a stimulus for businesses lining the streets.

Mass Transit Systems

A step up from LRT systems are true *mass transit systems*, also called in various cities *heavy rail*, *rapid transit*, *metro lines*, *métropolitaine*, *subterráneo*, *U-Bahn*, *S-Train*, *subways*, *the Underground*, *rapid railway*, or by their branded titles, *the T, MTA, CTA, SkyTrain, MRT, MetroTrain, MetroRail, MARTA, the El*, and so on. They provide the highest-capacity service among all public transport modes, and have a profound impact on the growth patterns of cities.

Mass transit systems are as varied as the cities that have installed them. Vehicles are almost always custom-designed and built to local standards, and in older cities traditions of station design will have evolved over many decades. The place to begin when the site planner confronts the need to integrate mass transit into a project is by consulting the local standards manual compiled by the entity operating the transit system. Inevitably there will be templates for stations and standards for rail alignments, separations, and safety protection. Since mass transit systems require complete separation from automobile traffic, they are often elevated or placed in tunnels or located below grade in depressed sections. Each city has its own unique policies on whether stations can be connected directly into adjacent development, and how stations function in relationship to other transportation modes.

The most successful mass transit systems are well integrated with their surroundings. The right-of-way width for two tracks running at grade needs to be at least 8–10 m (25–33 ft), depending on how catenaries, controls, and safety protection are provided. If elevated, the typical running platform is generally 7 m (23 ft) wide, supporting two tracks, although there is an increasing preference for separating the tracks and supporting them on individual structures, which allows more sunlight to penetrate the space below. Elevating

22.27 Washington Metro station at Pentagon City.
(Wikimedia Commons)

them to 15 or 20 m (50 or 65 ft) will also make them less of a barrier at ground level, and creates opportunities for the use of the *underspace*.

The internal dimensions of underground tunnels or structures are typically 5,700 mm (19 ft) for a single track or 9,500 mm (31 ft) for double tracks. While the dimensions vary based on the types of cars, considerably more clearance is required when power is drawn from overhead catenaries. Many mass transit systems receive their power from third rails, which lowers the required tunnel height. Coordinating this active corridor with what occurs above, beside, and below it is the challenge.

Integrating elevated structures for mass transit with surrounding uses offers both challenges and opportunities. If the platform structure is just high enough to allow road traffic to pass beneath it, or worse still if it is lower where there are sections without road crossings, it can create a dark and disused space below. The natural impulse in dealing with an elevated line is to create a linear park below it, compensating nearby residents for the noise and nuisances they must suffer, and maintaining visual connections between the areas on either side. At main streets, it is possible to continue commercial uses under the line, so that the retail frontage is not interrupted. At the new town of Ørestad, in Copenhagen, the elevated transit line and watercourse below it serve as the spine for the linear community, with major parks located at each of the transit stops. Where a transit line bisects a campus, as at the Illinois Institute of Technology in Chicago, placing the student center below the station helps make it a magnet for activities. But there are other possibilities as well: inserting two parking decks, creating an area for open-air markets or other occasional activities, or filling in

22.28 Proposed underline park below mass transit lines, Miami.
(Courtesy of James Corner Field Operations)

22.29 Street activities below Bangkok Skytrain.
(© somdul/Dreamstime.com)

22.30 Development under SkyTrain line at Commercial-Broadway station, Vancouver.
(Courtesy of Stephen Bohus/City Hall Watch.ca)

22.31 CTA Station at Illinois Institute of Technology, Chicago, with Student Center below.
(Philippe Ruauld/Courtesy of OMA Architects)

22.34 Los Angeles Metro kit-of-parts station entrance.
(Los Angeles Metro)

22.32 Transit stations in central Montreal are generally incorporated in large-scale development projects.
(Société de transport, Montréal)

22.33 The Toronto subway is directly accessible from the lower levels of Eaton Centre, helping to activate the multilevel retail space.
(Andrew Bardwell/flickr/Creative Commons)

the area with artisanal shops and artists' spaces, as in the Viaduc des Arts in Paris where the rail lines above have been abandoned and replaced by a public garden.

Another strategy is integrating elevated transit lines within large-scale development projects so that they are hardly visible. However, the complexities of property ownership and necessity for cross easements that allow buildings and transit lines to function effectively over time make such integration difficult, unless the site is controlled by the transit authority. Linking transit and urban development is often simpler when lines are located belowground and development occurs on the air rights over a station or adjacent to it. There is a long history of such development in London and New York, and in the more recent past Montreal, Toronto, Washington, and Shanghai have created many station area developments that serve or capitalize on transit accessibility. Eaton Centre in Toronto is a stellar example of a development that capitalizes on the flows from the transit line and station that parallel the complex.

Not all transit stations lend themselves to joint development, and there is a need for simple *headhouses* to provide access to the underground and well-designed public spaces that surround them. The Los Angeles Metro has adopted a kit-of-parts approach to its station entrances, allowing light to penetrate to the escalators and platforms below, providing an identifiable marque but one that doesn't shout for attention. As sites mature as development areas, these entrances are easily removed and even reused in other locations.

Circulator Systems

Special-purpose transit systems have been installed in many airports and some downtown areas to serve the needs of those circulating within the area. In the case of airports, they may simply allow flyers to move from one end of a terminal to the other quickly, as in Detroit International Airport, or may connect several terminals and remote parking areas, as in Newark and Chicago O'Hare airports in the US and Birmingham in the UK. Detroit and Miami in the US, Singapore, Guangzhou, and Perugia, Italy have created *people mover* systems that circulate through their central business districts, independent of larger mass transit systems. In downtown Seattle, the *monorail* constructed for its World's Fair to connect downtown to the Seattle Center continues to operate. Sydney, Australia has also created an elevated monorail system in its downtown. Disney operates monorails in its theme parks in Florida and

22.35 (top left)　Detroit International Airport ExpressTram people mover.
(Danleo/Wikimedia Commons)

22.36 (top right)　Singapore Crystal Mover transit system.
(Calvin Teo/Wikimedia Commons)

22.37 (bottom left)　Downtown terminal of the Seattle Monorail, connecting downtown to the Seattle cultural district.
(Razvan Socol/Wikimedia Commons)

22.38 (bottom right)　Downtown circulator monorail, Sydney, Australia.
(Gary Hack)

California. And in several locations, including Düsseldorf airport and Dortmund's H-Bahn, suspended cars hanging from guideways shuttle people from location to location.

Industries and cities continue to experiment with the concept of people movers, which began as a visionary idea of moving sidewalks whisking people from place to place in dense urban centers, and has over time evolved into automated small-car circulator transit networks operating on guideways. Every installation has been largely a proof-of-concept experiment. Circulator systems are costly to operate and maintain, even if they are automated, and depend on having an institution or other entity that sees benefit in their subsidy. In Las Vegas, casino owners have collaborated in creating a circulator system to connect their enterprises, which has an obvious benefit. Each system is attuned to the market it serves, making it hard to generalize about them, but they fall somewhere between light rail systems (or streetcars) and personal transportation systems.

Personal Transit Systems

Personal rapid transit (PRT) systems have been the dream of planners for at least half a century, but only recently has the technology matured to the point that they are a practical possibility. One of the earliest installations was in Morgantown, West Virginia, serving the downtown and West Virginia University, which began functioning in 1975. Each vehicle accommodates up to eight seated and four standing, making it more of a people mover than a PRT. The single route has accommodated up to 31,000 riders a day between five stations. It operates in three modes depending on the time of day: demand (typically passenger-activated with a 5-minute delay to collect any additional passengers, typically in evening hours), scheduled (during peak hours), and circulation (during low-volume hours, when the vehicles stop at all stations). An automated guideway transit system has also been functioning on a limited basis in Las Colinas, a large suburban center near Dallas, Texas.

The first truly operational PRT systems without fixed guideways are at Masdar, the high-tech eco-community in Abu Dhabi, and at Heathrow Airport in London. The electric-powered vehicles accommodate

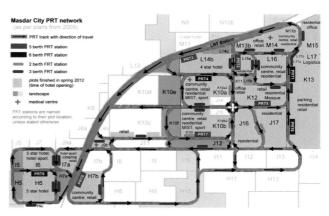

22.39 One of the earliest PRT systems, in Morgantown, West Virginia.
(Michlaovic/Wikimedia Commons)

22.40 PRT vehicle in Masdar, Abu Dhabi, United Arab Emirates.
(Masdar City)

22.41 Proposed PRT routes in Masdar.
(Kat Logics)

two passengers seated (plus two standing) and allow riders to select their destination. At Masdar, vehicles travel on roadway routes and are guided by electronic cables below the surface. Parking docks accommodate 4–6 vehicles and serve as charging stations. At Heathrow, quite similar driverless vehicles on the Heathrow Pod are used to transport passengers between Terminal 5 and remote parking locations.

It is hard to estimate the capacity of PRT systems, but it falls below that of minibuses on fixed routes, and above personal automobiles over short distances. Their advantage is in responsiveness to users, and they seem most suited to locations where vehicles will have rapid turnover. In the not too distant future, PRT systems are likely to be overtaken by driverless car and taxi technology, which offers greater flexibility and is capable of reconfiguring the location of vehicles in real time.

Funiculars

For over a century, *funiculars* (also called *inclines*, *cliff railways*, and *cog railways*) have been installed where topography is too steep for cable cars, streetcars, or even bus systems. Funiculars typically have gradients between 48% and 78%, with the Scenic Railway at Katoomba Scenic World in Australia rising at a bone-chilling 128%. Many cities rely on funiculars for everyday transportation—Valparaiso, Chile has 15 in operation, and they are important parts of the transportation systems in Pittsburgh, Pennsylvania, Wellington, New Zealand, Lugano, Switzerland, Lisbon, Portugal, and many other places. Other funiculars are mainly confined to tourism and ski resorts, providing spectacular views as they rise above the city or base camp. They are costly to maintain, if inexpensive to operate, and gradually have been replaced by other transportation systems. Pittsburgh, which once had 15 inclines, now relies on only two, the Duquesne Incline and the Monongahela Incline.

While the cars of funiculars are often ungainly, struggling to brace themselves against the slopes, there is elegance in the continuous rope mechanism that allows them to use very little energy in operation. To accomplish this, two cars are typically counterbalanced, one ascending, the other descending. They usually operate on two parallel sets of tracks (four tracks), although two- and three-track systems are also

22.42 Funicular in Lisbon, Portugal, also a favorite target of local graffiti artists.
(Gary Hack)

22.43 Duquesne Incline, Pittsburgh, Pennsylvania, which navigates a 30° (58%) hillside, now largely a tourist attraction. (Plastikpork/Wikipedia Commons)

22.44 Architect Renzo Piano's personal funicular, to reach his hillside home office in Genoa, Italy. (Maspero Elevatori)

common, particularly for long runs, with passing zones at the center point of the system. While every system is a unique creature, large funiculars have been built in recent years at ski resorts in Switzerland, Austria, and Utah. An example is the Davos Parsenn Bahn, which rises (in two sections) 1,106 m (3,628 ft) over a 4,048 m (13,280 ft) run, traveling at 10 m/sec (nearly 2,000 ft/ min) with 200 passengers in a car. It has the capacity to move approximately 2,000 persons per hour.

Funiculars may also be the solution for abrupt changes in elevation at the scale of individual buildings. Private funiculars are common in Wellington, New Zealand and have been installed in several hotels on mountainsides, including the St. Regis Resort in Park City, Utah. The architect Renzo Piano has installed a personal glass-sided funicular to reach his hillside office and home overlooking the Mediterranean near Genoa, Italy.

Escalators and Moving Sidewalks

An alternative to funiculars is the installation of *escalators* that can transport large numbers of people up slopes as steep as 58% (30°). They are costly to build and operate, but if the volume is high, they may be more cost-effective than funiculars or running buses on several miles of switchback routes. They require a benign climate and must be protected by canopies in areas of high rainfall.

The longest outdoor escalator system is in Hong Kong, traveling over 800 m (2,600 ft) and climbing 136 m (443 ft). Daily traffic exceeds 55,000 people on the 20 escalators and moving walkways that span between 13 streets. To accommodate high peak directional volumes, the system generally runs downhill in the morning and uphill in the evening rush hours. Shorter escalators have been installed in Medellín, Colombia and Caracas, Venezuela to transport people to the base of elevators or cable cars that scale the steep hillsides of settlements.

Typically, escalators are either 80 cm (32 in) or 122 cm (48 in) in width, and travel 0.5 m/sec (100 ft/min). Their capacity is approximately 2,300 and 4,500 passengers per hour respectively (Dionne, n.d.).

For slopes less than 9% (15°), *moving sidewalks* are another alternative. Moving sidewalks have a

22.45 Moving sidewalk section of Cochrane Street escalator, connecting central Hong Kong to the Mid-Slopes.
(Wing Luk/Wikipedia Commons)

22.46 Yebisu Skywalk, Tokyo.
(Y. Kanazawa/flickr/Creative Commons)

22.47 Mechanical ramps, enclosed in glass and stainless steel, connecting the old town to the new city center, Vitoria-Gasteiz, Spain.
(Courtesy of Roberto Ercilla, Architect)

long history, having been unveiled at Chicago's 1893 World's Columbian Exposition, where they could move 31,000 passengers per hour. But they never took hold for general circulation, and today are mainly used in airports and other large complexes. In Tokyo, the Yebisu Skywalk connects Ebisu Station with the Ebisu Garden Palace complex, nearly 1 km (0.6 mi) away, with its hotels, museums, and entertainment places. It consists of a series of moving walkways with short landings between.

Although they come in many sizes, the maximum practical length of an individual motorized walkway is about 300 m (1,000 ft), and they typically travel at 0.45 to 0.65 m/sec (90–130 ft/min). A conventional sidewalk also needs to be provided to cope with periods when the moving sidewalk is being serviced, and they must be protected from weather. Typically moving sidewalks are employed in large complexes under unified ownership where large volumes of people must be moved quickly. However, an excellent example of a public moving walkway is in Vitoria-Gasteiz, Spain, consisting of seven segments that parallel a traditional cobblestone street, connecting the old town with the new city.

Aerial Tramways

Once considered a novelty and found only in ski resorts and recreation areas, aerial tramways are increasingly being installed to serve development on steeply sloping hillsides. Roosevelt Island, a residential community in the East River, is connected to Manhattan by an aerial tramway, which was a practical necessity since the island had no subway service when it opened in 1976. Each cabin has a capacity of up to 110 people and makes 115 trips per day across the 945 m (3,100 ft) length of the cables. The tramway has remained so popular that it was continued after the completion of subway service to the island.

Medellín, Colombia has created a very effective aerial tramway system, which it calls Metrocable, serving several densely settled hillside communities. The steep slopes and unplanned form of the settlements made it practically impossible to provide any other form of access up the hillsides. Three routes are in operation, ranging in length from 2 km (1.2 mi) to 4.6 km (2.9 mi). The detachable gondolas can

22.48 Tramway connecting the growing neighborhood on Roosevelt Island to Manhattan, New York City.
(Gary Hack)

22.49 Medellín Metrocable system connecting hillside communities to the main public transportation systems.
(Jorge Lascar/Wikipedia Commons)

22.50 Aerial tram connecting the waterfront with a new health and science university, Portland, Oregon.
(Cacophony/Wikimedia Commons)

accommodate 8 passengers, travel at up to 22 km/h (14 mph) up the slope, and can deliver 2,000–3,000 people per hour. Medellín has integrated transit with the upgrading of communities, creating much-needed commercial and community facilities with the tramway terminals.

Aerial tramways require custom design and careful installation. They are sensitive to high winds, and scheduling maintenance remains an issue for facilities that are heavily used. Nonetheless, they may be the most cost-effective way to provide access to communities on hillsides, or divided by water from their neighboring areas. Portland, Oregon has installed an aerial tram system to connect its South Waterfront residential area with the sprawling new Oregon Health and Science University. It travels 3,300 ft (1 km) and navigates a 500 ft (1,400 m) vertical slope, and is operated as an integral component of the city's public transport system.

Ferry Systems

Ferries are the oldest form of mass transportation, and play a vital role in the everyday functioning of many cities including New York, Hong Kong, Seattle, Sydney, Istanbul, and Halifax, Canada. They are lifelines for many island communities, and can shorten the distance of travel by connecting shore points in congested areas. Circular Quay in Sydney is the front door of the city for a large fraction of those working downtown, as well as the point of arrival and departure for millions of tourists each year. The technology for waterborne movement ranges from simple walk- or drive-on barges to water taxis to large ships carrying dozens of automobiles and trucks and a thousand or more passengers. High-speed catamarans can whisk passengers to a resort (such as the Hong Kong–Macau lines) in a fraction of the time it would take by any other mode. The vast majority of boats are specially designed to serve the particular needs of the routes they serve. With such a great range, few generalizations can be made about the landside needs.

With all ferry operations, quick loading, unloading, and servicing is of utmost importance. Landside patterns of movement need to be designed to minimize the conflicts between those arriving and those leaving, and to queue passengers and vehicles for rapid loading.

Advance booking and locating ticket validation at the point of first arrival can help avoid congestion near loading areas.

For ferries that accommodate walk-on passengers only, the connection with transit and parking areas will be critical. Ideally the parking areas can be located a short distance from the waterfront to avoid its being dominated by pavement. There is a need for protective cover for those waiting to board, and a transparent structure will help reduce the intrusiveness of the terminal. An excellent small-scale example may be found at Battery Park City in New York. For high-capacity operations that involve truck and automobile service, there will be a need for marshaling lots where vehicles can line up and wait for loading. There may also need to be locations for ferries to berth when not in scheduled service, since demands will vary across the day. Terminals for high-capacity operations begin to resemble waiting areas in modest-sized railway stations and airports, with dual-level loading that separates passengers from vehicles. Such operations also require accommodations for large numbers of employees and offices for logistics and operations management.

Transit-Oriented Development

Any effective transit system requires dedicated riders from the areas it serves. The most effective way to lock in riders is to concentrate housing and workplaces near transit stops. In Washington, DC, ridership surveys indicate that transit is used by 46% of all metropolitan residents if their workplace is near a transit stop or station, and by 55% of all who live near one, compared to 13% and 36% of people, respectively, who are half a mile or more away. People who both live and work near transit stations are the most likely to use transit (Washington Metropolitan Area Transit Authority 2006).

Transit also needs to have densities great enough near transit stations or stops to make transit operations viable. There is no one answer to how much density is required, since it depends on the level of subsidy provided, level of service, and many other factors. However, US studies suggest that densities of 45 people per gross ac (18 per gross ha) are required for heavy rail transit to run cost-effectively, and 30 people per gross ac (12 per gross ha) for light rail transportation. The same studies

22.51 Circular Quay, Sydney, the front door to the city for millions of commuters and tourists.
(Peter L. Johnson/Wikimedia Commons)

22.52 Ferry terminal, Battery Park City, New York, serving New Jersey commuters and tourists visiting the Statue of Liberty.
(Gary Hack)

suggest that transit is most patronized if jobs are within 0.25 miles (400 m) of the transit station and residential locations are within 0.5 mile (800 m) (Cervero and Guerra 2011).

Creating *transit-oriented development* (TOD), where people are encouraged to walk to transit, has advantages that go well beyond support for the system. It can

Lower the cost of providing parking by encouraging people to give up their vehicles, and promotes shared parking,
Promote security in and around transit stations,
Encourage commercial development nearby, reducing the need for travel,
Promote use of bicycles for traveling to and from the station, including bicycle sharing, and
Encourage physical exercise by walking or cycling.

Greater density also has social advantages by encouraging face-to-face contact and reinforcing community activities.

There are many excellent examples of TOD throughout the world at all scales. The Fruitvale Transit Village in Oakland, California, developed by a neighborhood-based nonprofit organization, mixes housing, neighborhood retail, community services, and commuter parking on a 9 ac (3.6 ha) site beside a BART station and its adjacent bus interchange area. The development is mixed vertically, with retail outlets on ground levels, offices and services above, topped off by affordable housing. The draw of people to and from BART provides a ready clientele for commercial services and community activities. Two future sites, now used for parking, will greatly expand the development, which has already become the center of the adjacent neighborhoods.

With a superb transit system that is constantly being improved, Tokyo's large-scale development projects are routinely connected to transit stations. In the Roppongi district, Tokyo Midtown has underground connections to two subway lines, while sweeping escalators connect Roppongi Hills to its nearby station. At Midtown food and restaurant areas are located belowground near the point of arrival, and office workers and residents of the development pass through these to get to transit. Roppongi Hills celebrates the uphill climb through an arrival area that also showcases the nearby cinemas.

22.53   Aerial view, initial phase of Fruitvale Transit Village, Oakland, California.
(Microsoft Virtual Earth)

22.54   Fruitvale Village viewed from BART Station, Oakland, California.
(Gary Hack)

22.55 Entrances to underground shopping and subway, Tokyo Midtown.
(Gary Hack)

22.56 Escalators from subway to main shopping, entertainment, and office levels, Roppongi Hills, Tokyo.
(Gary Hack)

Encouraging this form of transit-oriented development requires that transit systems be planned from the outset with connections to future buildings and complexes in mind. Some cities demur from direct connections of stations to privately owned developments on the ground that it gives the latter commercial advantages over their neighbors. On the private side, there are also security issues that need to be accommodated when connections are made to transit stations, particularly where housing, hotels, and other sensitive uses are adjacent. However, TOD encourages transit ridership as well, and connections can be planned so that they are not exclusively through private buildings, and separated from private lobbies and elevator cores. Ultimately, everyone benefits from well-planned transit-oriented development.

23 | Cycling

Cycling serves many purposes in urban areas: commuting to work or school, getting to or from the nearest transit stop, pleasure riding, running errands, providing fast courier services, even competitive racing. In some cities cycling is a necessity, in others a matter of choice. The practicalities of steep slopes, difficult climate, and dangerous roads make it impossible in some cities. But over 80% of Amsterdam residents own a bicycle, and on a typical weekday 55% cycle to their workplaces if they are less than 7.5 km (4.7 mi) distant. Residents of Copenhagen are close behind, with an average of 36% commuting to work by bike each day, even in the winter. Until recently, cycling was the preferred way to get around in Beijing, but mass transit and private automobiles are slowly displacing it. At the same time, New York, Vancouver, and thousands of other North American cities have seen a resurgence of cycling, and efforts are being made to create safe and effective citywide bicycle routes.

Cycling has many virtues, not the least its health benefits, the energy saved, the comparatively small amount of road and parking space cycles occupy, reduction of noise, and the ease of combining cycling with public transit and other modes of travel. Among college or university students, it is often the preferred way to get around. For those below legal driving age, or living in low-density suburbs, it may be the only option for extended mobility. Safety is the foremost deterrent to wider use of cycling, especially where cyclists must share the roads with automobiles, buses, and trucks. Retrofitting roads to provide safe bicycle lanes can be difficult, and often requires a painful reallocation of pavement available for vehicle travel or parking. However, in new developments it is possible to establish optimal

23.1 Cycling, Amsterdam.
(Alfredo Borba/Wikimedia Commons)

conditions at the outset, avoiding difficult tradeoffs. The habit of using bicycles is best acquired at the initial occupancy of a site.

Bicycle Dimensions

A typical bicycle with a rider is 0.75 m (2.5 ft) wide and 1.75 m long (5.8 ft), and travels within a 1 m (3.3 ft) wide band along a roadway. North American standards generally prescribe dedicated cycle lanes of 1.2–1.8 m (4–6 ft) in width, with 1.4 m (4.5 ft) commonly cited (American Planning Association 2006). However, surveys indicate that most cyclists in US cities feel uncomfortable cycling in a lane that is less than 1.5 m (5 ft) in width (Kroll and Sommer 1976), and lanes 1.5 to 1.8 m

(5–6 ft) are more accommodating of cyclists' needs. AASHTO standards recommend a minimum of 1.5 m (5 ft) (AASHTO 1999). This assumes a one-way operation of a *dedicated bicycle lane*; where two-way cycling is planned, the dimensions needed are typically 3.0–3.5 m (10–11.5 ft). The increasing use of cargo bikes, bicycles with trailers, and recombinant bikes and trikes justify the wider dimensions.

Australian standards are similar to those in the US (New South Wales Roads and Traffic Authority 2003), while European standards tend to be more generous. In the Netherlands, lane widths of 2 m (6.5 ft) are suggested (C.R.O.W. 1994), so that cyclists can ride side by side, and 2.5 m (8 ft) is recommended when peak

hourly volumes exceed 150 bicycles, so that cyclists can pass each other.

Choosing the Type of Bicycle Route

Studies in the US suggest that over 90% of cyclists feel that a street is safer when there are areas reserved for bicycle users (Kroll and Sommer 1976). For many, fear of danger is a significant deterrent to their use of bicycles on urban streets. A study in Portland, Oregon found that only 8% of city residents were confident and enthusiastic about cycling, while 60% were interested in cycling but concerned over their safety on the roads

23.2 Bicycle dimensions and width of bicycle lanes. (Courtesy of Keri Caffrey/ American Bicycling Education Association)

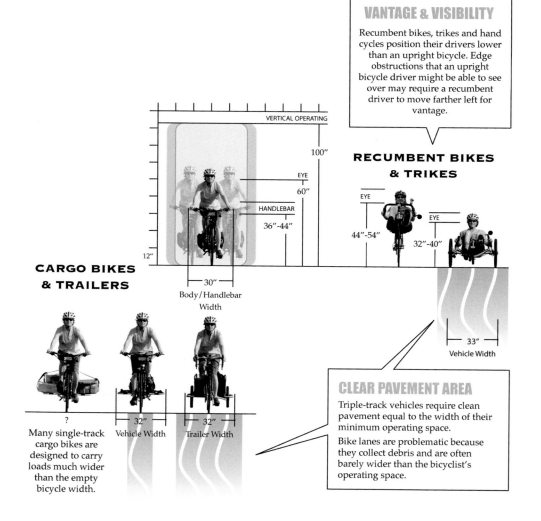

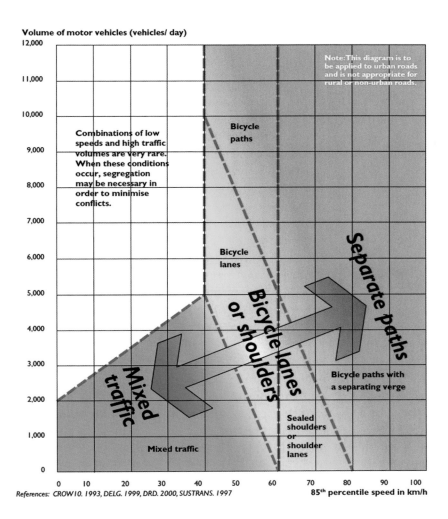

Volume of motor vehicles (vehicles/ day)

Note: This diagram is to be applied to urban roads and is not appropriate for rural or non-urban roads.

Combinations of low speeds and high traffic volumes are very rare. When these conditions occur, segregation may be necessary in order to minimise conflicts.

Bicycle paths

Bicycle lanes

Separate paths

Bicycle lanes or shoulders

Mixed traffic

Bicycle paths with a separating verge

Mixed traffic

Sealed shoulders or shoulder lanes

References: CROW10. 1993, DELG. 1999, DRD. 2000, SUSTRANS. 1997

85th percentile speed in km/h

23.3 Preferred types of bike lanes based on traffic volumes and speeds. (New South Wales Bicycle Guidelines)

(Geller, n.d.). One way to provide greater confidence is to create a network of bicycle routes, with areas for cyclists signed and delineated.

Bicycle lanes can take several forms. In rural areas, a paved shoulder or widened lane at the outside edge may be adequate. *Wide curb lanes* (WCLs), where the width of the outer lane is increased to 4.2 m (14 ft), allow motorists to pass cyclists while remaining in their lane (AASHTO 1999). A number of studies have confirmed the safety advantages of WCLs, but they have serious operational problems often stemming from confusion between drivers and cyclists as to who has the right of way in making turns (Hunter et al. 1998). Some US states including Maine require that drivers maintain at least 4 ft (1.2 m) clear space when passing a cyclist. If the vehicle passing is a large truck, even this dimension can be very scary because of the large draft of the passing vehicle.

Routes with heavy traffic volumes and high driving speeds require a clearer delineation of areas reserved for bicycles. Figure 23.3 suggests a framework for making choices between the most common types of bicycle lanes, based on Australian experience. In the Netherlands, separate bicycle paths are recommended when motor vehicle speeds exceed 50 km/hr (30 mph) or when traffic volumes exceed 1,200 vehicles per hour (Diepens and Okkema Traffic Consultants 1995).

Designated cycling lanes may take several forms. The most common arrangement is striping a portion of the roadway, usually at the curb, and marking it as reserved for cyclists. This arrangement allows the flexibility of using the lane for dropping off passengers, with a temporary disruption of cyclists—although this is also its disadvantage. If parking is allowed at the curb, the *designated bicycle lane* may be moved to the area between the parked vehicles and the driving lane.

This can be accomplished by creating a striped bicycle zone or by reserving an extra-wide zone for parking and cycles, typically 3–3.5 m (10–11.5 ft). The advantage of this arrangement is that it allows cars to park without disrupting traffic, but it creates a serious safety hazard for cyclists—especially from drivers who open their doors or pull out of parking spots without looking for passing cyclists. A third condition is where the curb lane is reserved for bus transit or streetcars. While a curb cycle lane can be designed to jog around buses or streetcars discharging passengers at designated stops, a better arrangement is to locate the bicycle lane between the transit lane at the curb and the first traffic lane. Or bicycles may be combined with buses in a lane that is 3–3.7 m (10–12 ft) wide, as in Toronto. Studies in that city indicate that cyclists feel comfortable riding in combined cycle-bus lanes (Egan 1992). One caution about combining cycling and streetcar lanes is the danger of bicycle wheels crossing recessed rail tracks; rubberized inserts along the tracks can help lessen the hazard. Such shared lanes are often called *sharrows* (a combination of "shared" and "arrows"), signaled by a distinctive marking. Sharrows can also be streets where bicycles share a roadway lane with vehicles, distinctly a last resort if there isn't land available for separate

cycle lanes, and appropriate only in areas where traffic volumes are low.

Instead of striping a bicycle lane, a *rumble strip* (consisting of cobbles or other textured surfaces) may be inserted between the bicycle and moving lanes as a reminder to motorists that they are leaving their zone. Or a curb or median may be inserted to physically separate driving lanes from cycling lanes. Drainage and snow removal must be carefully considered in such bicycle lanes. Catch basins need to be flush with the cycling surface, and ponding needs to be avoided, particularly in climates where frost is a danger. Where a curb separates the driving and cycle lanes, separate drainage basins may be necessary. Cycling lanes cannot become the repository for snow removed from the street; they must be capable of being plowed if winter cycle use is encouraged.

An alternative configuration, often preferred in European cities, is to integrate the cycle lane with pedestrian walkways paralleling the roadway. In this arrangement, a cycle path is located at the same elevation as the walking surface, and the two are differentiated by markings or different surface textures or colors. There can be danger in the close proximity of pedestrians walking at a slow speed and cyclists

23.4 On-roadway options for providing bike lanes. (FHWA)

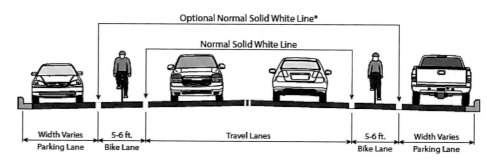

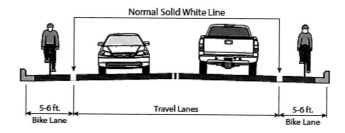

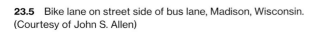

23.5 Bike lane on street side of bus lane, Madison, Wisconsin.
(Courtesy of John S. Allen)

23.6 Combined bus and bike lane, Mannheim, Germany.
(Courtesy of Martin Hawlisch)

23.7 Sharrow on local street, Los Angeles.
(Joe Linton/Streetsblog)

23.8 Bike lane separated from traffic, 9th Avenue, New York.
(New York City Department of Transportation)

23.9 Separated two-way bike lane, Paris.
(Gary Hack)

23.10 Bike lane combined with pedestrian sidewalk,
Malmö, Sweden.
(Gary Hack)

traveling faster, particularly at intersections (or with tourists unaccustomed to paying attention to cyclists). This can be solved by separating the two as they approach intersections, or by providing a continuous landscape strip between the pedestrian and bicycle zones.

Where cyclist volumes are heavy, bicycle lanes may be located in a separate right-of-way paralleling the roadway. Cycle ways such as these are located on many major roadways in Beijing, together with grade-separated overpasses at major intersections threaded between the surface roadway and vehicle overpasses. At grade-level intersections, separate phasing of traffic signals may be necessary to allow vehicles to make right turns across bicycle lanes and bicycles to cross driving lanes for left turns. Parallel bicycle roadways only make sense in urban areas with heavy bicycle traffic, although an increasing number of cities have constructed separate bicycle overpasses over expressways, arterial roads, and waterways.

Bicycle paths, of course, need not parallel roadways. In planned developments with continuous open-space corridors, they may follow their own course, arriving at important destinations having to cross only a few roadways. They may double as pleasure riding loops, gently traversing the site, with places to stop and enjoy the natural features. They may be combined with walking routes, but it is important to signal regularly whether pedestrians or cyclists have the right of way. A typical two-way combined walkway-cycle path should be at least 2.5–4 m (8–13 ft) in width

Ultimately the design of cycling lanes will need to address several issues:

The purpose of cycling—commuting, running
    errands, pleasure riding, etc.,
The types of cyclists—schoolchildren and youths,
    college students, occasional adult cyclists,
    hardened regular users,

23.11 Separate bike lanes, Hudson River Boulevard, New York City.
(Gary Hack)

23.12 Copenhagen Bicycle Snake, providing a short-cut across Copenhagen harbor.
(Courtesy of DISSING + WEITLING Architecture/Rasmus HjortshØj-COAST)

23.13 Cycling trail in Catalunya, Spain.
(Anon/Wikimedia Commons)

Destinations—school, work, mass transit stops, commercial areas,
Traffic volumes on roads,
Right-of-way dimensions,
Opportunities for off-road cycle routes,
Topography,
Climate.

Gradients and Geometry

The steepest hills will not deter hardened cyclists, but not all who wish to cycle will have the strength (or persistence) to climb steep grades, or the bicycles with gears that make it possible. Generally, the average cyclist prefers grades that are similar to those prescribed for vehicle roadways. They should be kept within 5%, except in circumstances where topography does not allow it. If the grade must be greater, the length of the steep section should be limited, as follows (AASHTO 1999):

5–6% for up to 240 m (800 ft),
7% for up to 120 m (400 ft),
8% for up to 90 m (300 ft),
9% for up to 60 m (200 ft),
10% for up to 30 m (100 ft),
11+% for up to 15 m (50 ft).

Horizontal alignments of cycle ways can also closely parallel those of driving routes that in most instances they run alongside. Most turns will be made at intersections where cyclists will need to slow down or stop. However, when bicycle paths run on their own rights-of-way or are combined with pedestrian routes, they need to be designed to accommodate the intended design speed of cyclists. In turning, cyclists lean into the curve, typically about 15°. The minimum horizontal radius is as indicated in table 23.1.

There is considerable experience in synchronizing bicycle and motor vehicle movement systems, and the conventions tend to differ between countries. In many countries, national guidelines will prevail; absent them, local ordinances or manuals prepared by bicycle advocacy groups will offer guidance. While improvements are always possible, there is no need to reinvent the wheel.

Designing bicycle routes is not exclusively about safety and engineering. For cycling to become a pleasurable activity, the designer needs to imagine the sensuous form of moving along a roadway or through a landscape. The cyclist views the world in motion, often in the company of others traveling the same route. Without undue risk, it should be possible to have a conversation, window-shop, or enjoy the natural environment. There need to be places to stop and rest, adjust an ailing bicycle, or gain temporary respite from a sudden downpour. And at important destinations, finding a place to park is the next challenge.

Bicycle Parking

Ranked just below personal safety on the list of cyclists' concerns is the fear of having one's bicycle stolen or damaged when it is parked. As a result, cyclists routinely try to take their bicycle as near as possible to where they are headed. They will chain their bike to trees outside stores, take it up elevators to their workplace (if allowed), and park it on the balcony of their apartment. None of these are good solutions; a better approach is to provide secure parking at or near destinations. Parking areas are as much a part of the bicycle system as the lanes required for movement.

Table 23.1 | Desirable minimum radii for independent bicycle paths

Design speed, km/h (mph)	Minimum radius, m (ft)
20 (12)	12 (40)
30 (20)	27 (89)
40 (25)	47 (154)
50 (30)	74 (243)

Source: AASHTO (1999), p. 38.
Note: Based on 15° lean angle.

A typical bicycle parking space is 0.6 by 1.8 m (2 by 6 ft), with a 1.5 m (5 ft) aisle providing access. Thus, 1.5 m² (16 sq ft) per bicycle needs to be allocated to parking in a standard format. Vertical format bicycle parking can reduce this requirement to 1.2 m² (13 sq ft) per vehicle. A variety of manufactured bicycle racks are available for parking, permanently secured or movable as circumstances demand. One key feature is the ability to accommodate cables, chains, or locks, securing not only the frame but also removable wheels. There are also a number of lockable bicycle closets that provide protection from the weather as well as security.

Short-term bicycle parking—for shoppers, visitors, messengers, and those attending events up to two hours or so in length—needs to be located as near as possible to the destination, preferably within eyesight of the entrance. Along a commercial frontage, the most convenient arrangement may be distributing parking racks along the street, rather than asking cyclists to walk to and from larger parking areas. There needs to be adequate clearance for pedestrians. Cover is highly desirable. In lots of 10 or more vehicles, at least half the parking should be covered; and since cyclists will seek out arcades and other covered areas in bad weather, it makes sense to incorporate bicycle parking into their design.

Long-term bicycle parking is designed for those spending at least half a day at a destination. These cyclists include commuters to work, residents seeking overnight parking, train and mass transit passengers seeking parking at the station, students attending schools and colleges, and recreation cyclists at trail heads. Security is of utmost concern, suggesting electronic surveillance or, if the area is large enough, human attendants. Protection from rain and snow and good drainage are also critical: other concerns are keeping bicycles warm in cold weather and the ability to remove snow that accumulates. For those commuting to work, the optimal solution may be an indoor bicycle room, with showers nearby to allow cyclists to change before going to their workplace.

Innovative *bicycle garages* have been constructed in a number of cities, near business districts or railway stations. These one-stop service centers include various combinations of high-density storage areas, lockers, concessions for repairs and tune-ups, equipment and sales outlets, bicycle rentals, bicycle touring services, showers

23.14 Bicycle storage cabinets, Los Angeles Metro station. (Gary Hack)

23.15 Bicycle parking near entrance to supermarket, Washington, DC. (Zoning DC)

23.16 Covered bicycle parking, New York City. (Jim Henderson/Wikimedia Commons)

23.17 Bicycle garage and center, Freiburg, Germany.
(Gary Hack)

23.18 Bicycle storage area, bicycle garage, Freiburg, Germany.
(Gary Hack)

and washrooms, and coffee shops for the start or end of a journey. The Velo Center in Freiburg, Germany, located near the city's main train station, includes many of these services as well as a car share rental outlet. In Chicago, the McDonald's Bicycle Center at Millennium Park, adjacent to the business district, is a full-service outlet for cyclists, and also includes facilities for skateboarders and in-line skaters. Members who join the center also have access to bicycle sharing and car sharing. Some colleges and universities have invested in bicycle centers, and many US cities require bicycle parking to be set aside in all indoor parking garages that they license.

Bicycle Sharing Systems

Bicycle sharing programs have their origins in Amsterdam's White Bicycle Plan created by Luud Schimmelpennink in 1965. The idea was to distribute bicycles throughout the city and invite residents to use them as needed, leaving them at their destination for others' use. Within a month, most of the bicycles had disappeared, but the idea had traction and spread to other European cities, and more recently to Canada and the US. Several hundred cities currently have bicycle sharing programs in some form.

Three basic systems have proved viable. One is *community bicycle sharing* operated by a nonprofit entity, or cooperative unit, making bicycles available to its members. Several universities have created such programs, notably the University of Wisconsin at Madison. The Community Bicycle Network in Toronto created a highly successful BikeShare program with over 400 members, and similar groups operate programs in many cities. In Europe, many cooperative housing programs offer shared bicycles to their members. These systems typically have a limited geographic range, and members are obliged to return bicycles to designated locations. The fundamental problem of such systems is the high maintenance and administration costs which are unlikely to be covered by membership fees, forcing organizations to turn to grants, advertising, and sponsorship revenues. Nonetheless, it remains a valuable tool for community mobility.

A second type of system is operated as a commercial enterprise, sometimes after an initial capital grant to get the system running. The Paris Vélib' system is one such prototype, put in motion by an advertising agency that benefited from the buzz it created. With 20,000 specially designed bicycles distributed among 1,450 locations across the city, it aims to have a bicycle available within 200 m of every door. Its widespread success led to programs in many other cities, some sponsored by municipalities, others run privately (with or without subsidies), still others as public-private partnerships, or sponsored by business improvement districts. They are offered under various names—Vélo'v (Lyon), Bixi (Montreal), Bycyklen (Copenhagen), City Bikes (Stockholm), Bikabout (Portland, Oregon), Call

a Bike (Berlin, Munich), Bicing (Barcelona), OYBike (UK), Citi Bike (New York), SmartBike (Washington, DC), HZBike (Hangzhou), Bicicletas Públicas (Chile), to mention just a few. Each has a unique format. A deposit is generally charged (credit card or cash) when a bicycle is picked up and refunded when it is returned; typically there are hourly charges for use. Automated bicycle racks secure vehicles, and some systems allow bicycles to be reserved using cell phones or the Internet.

A newer format for commercial systems dispenses with the automated bicycle racks, substituting *dockless shared bicycles* with transponders that can be controlled by a smartphone. The systems originated in China, where Shanghai has seen over 500,000 dockless bicycles flood its streets, closely followed by Hangzhou and Beijing. The rapid introduction of these systems has exposed a variety of problems, including inadequate budgets for maintenance, massive accumulation of bicycles in a few locations, and abandonment of bicycles with problems. Nonetheless, similar systems are being introduced in other cities of the world.

The third type of bicycle sharing system operates as an adjunct to other activities. Some mass transit systems have made available rental or sharing systems at their stations; cycling is seen as an extension of the reach of transit. OV-fiets bicycle rentals, offered by the national railway, are available at over 200 locations in Dutch cities and towns, some via automated bike dispensers. The Call a Bike system is operated by Deutsche Bahn, the national railway, at several of its largest stations, and is attractive to tourists or commuters. In Europe, car park operators have begun to offer free bicycle use to their patrons, thereby extending their attractiveness to a broader audience.

Incorporating bicycle sharing as an integral part of a system of bicycle routes will become an important strategy for the future. Attractive locations need to be dedicated to bicycle sharing bases, and convenient short-term storage locations with lockable facilities will encourage the use of the system.

23.19 Toronto Community Bicycle Network station. (Secondarywalz/Wikimedia Commons)

23.20 Citi Bike station, New York City. (Gary Hack)

23.21 Dockless bicycle sharing, Shanghai. (Gary Hack)

23.22 OV-fiets bike dispenser, Utrecht, Netherlands. (Apdency/Wikimedia Commons)

24 | Pedestrians

Every journey begins and ends on foot. After a century of trying to minimize walking, substituting motorized movement for foot power, planners are rediscovering the virtues of being a pedestrian. Walking (or jogging or skateboarding or traveling in a wheelchair) is often the best way to get from place to place, enjoy the sights, and meet others in public. Walking is also the most energy-efficient form of travel, with the added benefit of preventing obesity. Being in public also serves the important social purpose of promoting face-to-face contact in a world where communication is increasingly vicarious.

A well-planned pedestrian network is essential for a sustainable community. Use of mass transit requires an effective system of pedestrian ways leading to bus or tram stops and transit portals. Many suburban areas in North America lack any sidewalks, making travel on foot dangerous, particularly after dark. Even where there are walkways, they are often discontinuous, stopping at property boundaries, and may require pedestrians to travel circuitous routes to their destination. In the rapidly developing areas of China, sidewalks are almost nonexistent, or cluttered with automobiles or bicycle parking lots. Thus, the challenge of planning for pedestrians is creating networks of routes that connect desire lines.

Basic Criteria

Pedestrian spaces must be tailored to human capabilities, cultural attitudes, and the purposes they serve. Ordinary people are limited by kinesthetic abilities that change as they develop and age, and spaces for walking ought to be safe and comfortable, even pleasurable. Culturally acquired norms affect when we feel crowded, how we behave in public spaces, and our ability to respond to our surroundings. Planning of pedestrian areas begins with acquiring an awareness of the abilities of those who will inhabit the spaces, and their attitudes and behavior.

Space in Public

Humans employ social distance as a way of warding off danger and signaling our intentions to others. Edward T. Hall (1966), who pioneered the study of *proxemics,* proposed that we think about distance as a series of concentric zones. Nearest to the human body is the zone of *intimate space,* for the average Westerner roughly 60 cm (24 in) on either side of us, 70 cm (28

24.1 State Street, Chicago.
(Gary Hack)

24.2 Proxemic distances in North America.
(Adam Tecza/Gary Hack)

INTIMATE SPACE   PERSONAL SPACE   SOCIAL SPACE   PUBLIC SPACE

2 ft / 60 cm   4 ft / 120 cm   4-12 ft / 120 - 260 cm

in) in front and 40 cm (16 in) behind. Only family and friends (and medical personnel) may comfortably penetrate this zone, although we are often forced to surrender our intimate space while riding crowded subways or sitting in a movie theater or other place of assembly. We adapt to such situations by avoiding eye contact with our neighbors unless we know them well and by selectively screening them out of our consciousness. Beyond this is a second zone, *personal space,* which extends to about 1.2 m (4 ft) from the body. This is the zone where we greet others, shake their hands, have conversations with them, and feel connected. A third zone is *social space,* extending roughly 1.2–3.7 m (4–12 feet) from us, beyond arm's length, where we communicate in more impersonal ways, transact business, or make presentations to people. Areas beyond about 3.7 m (12 ft) we consider to be *public space* over which we have little control, where we are only observers of (and observed by) others inhabiting the space.

Culture determines the precise dimensions of these zones. Southern Europeans greet others by a hug and bus (on both cheeks), communicating an intimacy that Northern Europeans, Asians, and most North Americans consider overly familiar. In the Middle East, standing close enough to experience the breath of your friend is considered respectful, and holding hands is a sign of social grace. At the same time, greater distances are observed between opposite sexes, except one's relatives. In India and much of Asia, jostling or bumping people in crowds, or standing close behind them in lines, is an accepted norm, and necessary personal space is smaller. Many Westerners feel claustrophobic in such situations.

Examples of people observing social distance can be found in any park, on ocean beaches, and in public squares. Individuals will distribute themselves quite precisely along continuous benches, closer to those they know, further away from strangers, and avoiding open spots that do not allow for adequate personal space on either side. The distance sought is cultural. Typically Americans place their beach blanket 183 cm (6 feet) from another beachgoer's (if they have a choice), while French beachgoers will average 135 cm (4.4 ft) and Germans 165 cm (5.4 ft) (Smith 1981). A line of beach chairs will mitigate closeness by offering an assurance that a neighbor will move no closer (as does an arm rest on a park bench, movie, or concert hall seat). These cultural norms affect the dimensions of walkways, public spaces, and gathering places and make it hazardous to borrow precedents from other cultures.

Space for Walking

People moving on a public walkway also expect others to respect their intimate space, except when they are walking hand in hand with friends. At any moment a pedestrian occupies an elliptical area about 50 cm (20 in) by 60 cm (24 in), roughly 0.3 m² (3.2 sq ft). To avoid contact with those they meet or pass on a walkway, pedestrians also expect a *walking buffer zone* (also called a *shy distance*), so one should plan on about 0.75 m² (8 sq ft) per pedestrian when they are walking.

Studies have found that pedestrians typically maintain a space of 0.45 m (1.5 ft) from walls, 0.35 m (1.1 ft) from fences, and 0.3 m (1 ft) from occasional obstacles such as streetlights, trees, benches, and hydrants (Stucki, Gloor, and Nagel 2003). Two people walking side by side or passing each other while traveling in opposite directions typically take up a space of 1.4 m (4.7 ft). While they can be accommodated on a 1.5 m (5 ft) walkway, a more adequate dimension is 1.8 m (6 ft) (Fitzpatrick 2006), and where there are large numbers of groups walking together, 2.3 m (7.5 ft) has been suggested (Pushkarev and Zupan 1975b).

When does a space feel too crowded? Crowd safety experts generally conclude that when *pedestrian densities* are between 0.5 m² (5.2 sq ft) and 0.85 m² (9.1 sq ft), regardless of speed of flow, pedestrians feel comfortable (Huat, Ma'soem, and Shankar 2005). Densities with space at the low end of that range are possible in Asian cities, while in North America pedestrians expect larger amounts of space. In either case, below the cultural minimum pedestrians feel constricted, and flows along sidewalks may stop or be delayed. Studies in New York found that all pedestrian movement effectively stopped when the amount of space available to each pedestrian fell below 0.2 m² (2 sq ft) per person, and below 0.3 m² (3 sq ft) per person contact is unavoidable and only shuffling is possible (Pushkarev and Zupan 1975b).

24.3 Lunchtime scene, Avenue of the Americas, New York City. (Gary Hack)

24.4 Sunning on Pier 45, New York City. (Gary Hack)

24.5 Crowded European beach. (Stefano Guzzetti/Shutterstock)

24.6 Sidewalk, Reston City Center, Virginia. (Gary Hack)

Walking Speeds

Pedestrian *walking speeds* range considerably by purpose, age, and culture. For planning purposes, an average of 1.2 m/sec (4 ft/sec) has been a rule of thumb for the average speed of walking. But studies have found significant variation, as shown in table 24.1. Walking speeds are highest in Tokyo and lowest in Southeast Asia among the countries sampled, with North American and European speeds falling in between. Women tend to walk slightly slower than men. Tourists taking in the passing scene tend to strike a slower pace than locals determined to get to their destination. People in groups tend to walk more slowly than those traveling alone. The elderly tend to walk slower than younger people, and pedestrians with disabilities may only walk at half the speeds of those who are fully abled. And studies in New York found that lunch hour pedestrians tend to walk significantly slower than those rushing to and from work.

Translating walking speeds into distances, the average pedestrian will cover approximately 800 m or half a mile in 10 minutes. This is often used as a guideline for locating essential local facilities and for planning local public transportation. However, surveys in North America indicate that few actually walk these distances each day. Residents of center city districts tend to walk more often than those who live in suburban areas, since there are more destinations within easy walking range.

Topography also affects walking speeds and the distances pedestrians are willing to travel. Walking speeds are 20% lower when gradients reach 10% (1:10), and the willingness to navigate such slopes declines markedly. Walking speeds also decline when pedestrians are distracted: in New York, about 13% of pedestrians were observed talking on the phone, listening to headphones, using a PDA, smoking, eating, or drinking (New York Department of City Planning 2003).

Pedestrian Flows on Walkways

The capacity of a walkway is limited by the width available, volumes of pedestrians, any obstructions that may block those walking or slow their speed (such as sidewalk vendors or pedestrians waiting for a bus), and other factors. However, during planning it is useful to

Table 24.1 | Walking speeds of pedestrians

Type	m/sec	ft/sec	Distance traveled in 10 min	
			m	ft
Rule of thumb[1]	1.22	4.00	732	2,400
New York male[2]	1.32	4.42	792	2,652
New York female[2]	1.25	4.10	750	2,460
Calgary male[3]	1.43	4.70	858	2,820
Calgary female[3]	1.35	4.43	810	2,658
Colombo male[3]	1.35	4.43	810	2,658
Colombo female[3]	1.30	4.27	780	2,562
Tokyo average[4]	1.56	5.11	936	3,066
Thailand average[4]	1.22	4.00	732	2,400
With crutches or cane[5]	0.80	2.62	480	1,572
With walker[5]	0.63	2.07	378	1,242
With wheelchair[5]	1.08	3.55	648	2,130

[1] Generally accepted.
[2] New York Department of City Planning (2006).
[3] Morrall, Ratnayake, and Seneviratne (1991).
[4] Mateo-Babiano (2003).
[5] Federal Highway Administration (2006).

be able to predict how well a walkway might function, so that accommodations can be made to deal with expected flows. Several rules of thumb help with such estimates.

It is useful to think in terms of walking lanes, each about 1 m in width, which accounts for body width and space to pass or meet other pedestrians. In the US, the approximate capacity of a walkway is 3,600 pedestrians per hour per m of width. This assumes a front-back buffer zone of about 0.75 m (2.5 ft) between pedestrians walking in the lane, and a pedestrian speed of 1.25 m (4.0 ft) per second. The formula from which this is derived is:

$V = S / M$,
where
V = flow or volume,
S = speed,
M = pedestrian area module (or 1/density).

The *pedestrian area module* consists of the pedestrian spacing + 0.5 m (1.6 ft) assumed space occupied by the pedestrian (Huat, Ma'soem, and Shankar 2005). These figures are approximate, since field studies have found that pedestrians tend to travel in platoons as crossings at corners, buses discharging passengers, and other forces cluster the flow. Studies in other countries have found that a higher volume of pedestrians can be accommodated in each meter of walkway width, since pedestrians there are comfortable with closer pedestrian spacing. A variety of simulation models will provide more precise estimates of pedestrian flows (Stucki, Gloor, and Nagel 2003; Still 2000). However, few

24.7 Diagram of walkway densities for LOS levels. (Adapted from Transportation Research Board 2010)

walkways reach their capacity for sustained periods of time, and a quick estimate will confirm whether simulations are necessary.

Level of service guidelines have been developed for pedestrian flows, emulating similar guidelines for roadways and bicycle routes. The LOS range is from free-flowing (LOS A) to completely stopped (LOS F) (Federal Highway Administration 2003). It is not unreasonable to experience an hour or two of LOS C or D each day, or even to reach LOS E during short periods. The art is in setting the level of performance desired. Crowded walkways a few times a year for parades or holiday shopping are tolerated by most people, but hated if they are a regular occurrence.

Table 24.2 | LOS guidelines for pedestrian walkways

LOS	Space		Flow rate		Average speed		v/c ratio
	m²/ped	ft²/ped	ped/min/m	ped/min/ft	m/s	ft/min	
A	≥5.6	≥60	≤16	≤5	≥1.3	≥255	0.21
B	3.7–5.6	40–60	16–23	5–7	1.27–1.30	250–255	0.21–0.31
C	2.2–3.7	24–40	23–33	7–10	1.22–1.27	240–250	0.31–0.44
D	1.4–2.2	15–24	33–49	10–15	1.14–1.22	225–240	0.44–0.65
E	0.75–1.4	8–15	49–75	15–23	0.75–1.14	150–225	0.65–1.0
F	≤0.75	≤8	var.	var.	≤0.75	≤150	var.

Source: Transportation Research Board (2010).

Accommodating Other Walkway Users

Not all users of walking spaces are individuals or couples purposefully headed for their destination. Some will be walking at a slower pace with children in hand, while others will be rubbernecking to see the sights or window-shopping. Dog walkers are a regular occurrence on walkways or paths. Joggers will be competing for space with slower pedestrians. Wheelchair users will need special attention in terms of walking lanes, places to stop, and ramps whenever height must be navigated. An increasing number of motorized wheelchairs and scooters need to be accommodated. Rollerboarders and in-line skaters will demand a clear alley for their faster speeds. Where the walkway is used for loading—for shops, taxis, buses, express mail deliveries, etc.—the walkway dimensions will need to be adequate for handling these functions as well.

Access guidelines and requirements have been adopted in most countries, although the practices of how to meet them vary in subtle but important ways. From a site planning perspective, providing *universal access* means observing some basic parameters:

Maintain a clear width for walking of at least 0.9 m (3 ft) for all pathways, which is adequate for wheelchairs.

Ensure that there are closely spaced places for wheelchairs to pass and places to turn a full circle, particularly at doorways and corners, which require 1.5 m (5 ft).

Limit the running grade of surfaces to no more than 8.3%, and the cross slope to no more than 2%.

When running slopes exceed 5% provide handrails for the assistance of those with walking limitations.

When running slopes are over 5%, provide a 1.5 m (5 ft) flat landing area every 12 m (40 ft), and at 8.3% provide landings every 9.1 m (30 ft).

Provide sloped ramps at curbs, stairways or any location where steps must be negotiated. Curb ramps should not exceed 1:12, with side slopes not more than 1:10.

Install detectable warnings along pathways to help guide those with sight deficiencies.

Many places restrict rollerboarders, in-line skaters, and blade runners to bicycle lanes and encourage joggers to use them as well, because their speeds make

24.8 Motorized wheelchair traveling in mixed traffic, North Michigan Avenue, Chicago.
(Gary Hack)

for an uncomfortable mix with pedestrians. Where they share pedestrian pathways, it is essential that those paths are wide enough for passing, and that respite zones be provided for slower traffic.

Stairs

When slopes greater than 12–15% must be navigated, stairs need to be considered. Stairs also provide a psychological sense of separation, breaking the pace of movement and heightening the processional sequence. Temples, capitols, shrines, courthouses, and public buildings are often raised above surrounding streets as a way of emphasizing their stature, although in recent years continuous warped walking surfaces have gained favor as a way of breaking down the barriers between institutions and citizens. If a pathway is to be accessible to all, stairs and ramps need to be thought of in integrated ways.

The shift from walking on the flat to navigating stairs needs to reflect ergonomics. A typical male stride is 760 mm (2.5 ft), and for females is 670 mm (2.2 ft). The gait is shortened when moving up or down stairs, and the rate of movement slows. The relationship between the length of a stairway tread and the height of rise is inverse: the higher the rise, the shorter the tread should be. One early study suggested that two times the height of the riser plus the length of the tread should equal the typical length of a stride (Blondel and

Patte 1771). Over the years this relationship has been refined into the formula:

$$2R + T = 630 \text{ mm or } 25 \text{ in,}$$
where
R = height of riser,
T = length of tread.

Thus, for an outdoor stairway with a 150 mm (6 in) riser, the length of tread should be 330 mm (13 in). If the riser is 178 mm (7 in), the tread should be 274 mm (11 in). In cases where the running grade is just above a walkable slope, it may prove impossible to conform to the ideal relationship. For example, with a 20% running grade—equal to the steepest roads in San Francisco—sidewalks need to be stepped. To match the roadway slope, a 152 mm (6 in) riser must be matched with a 762 mm (30 in) tread—not ideal since it is too long for all but the tallest to climb by placing one foot on each step. A better solution would be 178 mm (7 in) risers with 890 mm (35 in) treads, allowing for two short steps on each tread.

Other factors are as important as getting the proportion of stairs right. Single risers must be strictly avoided; they are frequently missed by pedestrians and cause falls. Risers that are not exactly equal will surely cause people to trip. And handrails should be available on at least one side of all stairs to provide assistance in climbing. This is often difficult on long runs of steps, but is doubly important in climates with snow or frequent frosts.

Pathways

The simplest pedestrian way is the pathway separated from motorized vehicles, running across open land. It may be a busy walkway connecting two sides of a park, a recreation trail, a waterfront promenade, or some other place of convenience and enjoyment. The pathway may be reserved for pedestrians (and dog walkers and joggers), or may be shared with bicyclists or low-speed electric vehicles. Each situation will call for a subtly different approach to its design.

While midblock pedestrian ways in residential areas may be as narrow as 1.2 m (4 ft), and a recreation trail through wilderness may be no wider than a single hiker, a typical multipurpose pedestrian way functions best if it is 2.4 m (8 ft) in width. This will allow couples walking together to pass each other, allow joggers or cyclists to pass by pedestrians, and will be wide enough to allow maintenance vehicles to travel along the route to collect trash, clear snow, and make needed repairs. For high-density usage, the way might be expanded to 3 m (10 ft), or if the bicycle lanes are striped, 3.7 m (12 ft).

Effective drainage of pedestrian ways is essential, particularly in climates where there are freeze-thaw cycles. It is best to crown the pedestrian way or provide a slight slope (2%) to the side to allow water to drain

24.9 Stairway on Broadway, Russian Hill, San Francisco. (San Francisco Days)

24.10 Stairway interlaced with ramp, Robson Square, Vancouver. (Gary Hack)

24.11 Permeable pathway through wetland reserve, Prairie Crossing, Illinois.
(Gary Hack)

24.12 Mixed-use pathway, Battery Park City, New York City.
(Gary Hack)

quickly. Ideally, storm runoff will percolate into the soil or drain overland, but if catch basins are needed they should be off the walkway surface. Pedestrian ways may be paved or consist of compacted gravels. Paved roadways are not ideal for joggers, and where there is space it is best to parallel them with a narrow 0.7 m (2.3 ft) jogging path surfaced with *fines*.

Pedestrian pathways should be lined with lighting that is scaled to pedestrians, preferably not higher than 3.7 m (12 ft). Such lighting should be closely spaced and have enough of a horizontal throw that the faces of oncoming pedestrians are visible. Studies have shown that evenness of lighting is far more important than the absolute illumination level, since it takes time for the human eye to adjust to changing levels of light.

The well-designed pathway also is equipped with seating every 60–80 m (200–260 ft), located particularly at places where there are views to admire, and placed at least 1 m (3.3 ft) off the pathway to avoid blocking movement. Adequate bicycle racks are also essential if the pathway has joint use.

Sidewalks

Sidewalks are the essential connective tissue of cities. The presence of sidewalks may be the most important signal that an area is urban rather than rural, asserting that there are destinations within walking distance and that pedestrians have equal claims on rights-of-way. Two or more tons of metal matched against 100 kilos (220 lb) of flesh and bone is not a fair competition, so in planning streets pedestrians must be given highest priority.

Sidewalks, also called *pavements*, *pathways*, *footpaths*, *platforms*, or *footways* in various parts of the world, occupy the space between roadways (or *carriageways*) and built frontages of streets. They are never the sole occupants, sharing the space with light standards, signs, parking meters, fire hydrants, mailboxes, newspaper vending racks, trash receptacles, benches, transit shelters, kiosks, and a variety of other equipment. Increasingly, as we have noted, the zone between the roadway and buildings is also being called upon to serve as a water detention area and drainage course, a place for landscape and shade trees, and the location of bicycle routes. And sidewalks are not simply passageways for walking; they provide places for children's play, vending and outdoor merchandise areas, sidewalk cafés, street theaters, even a tableau for sidewalk artists' work.

The purposes of sidewalks will differ greatly depending upon the context. In a residential area, they may simply be a place for everyday walks to transit, schools, and nearby shops. In commercial hubs they may be the place to be and be seen, particularly in evenings and on weekends. In many Latin countries, the evening paseo is a ritual of daily life. Clarifying the program is the first step in planning an appropriate sidewalk. However, there are several common aims that guide the planning of all sidewalks. They should be:

Planned as part of a connected system of paths
beyond any particular site,
Wide enough to accommodate peak flows, leaving
room for other uses off peak,
Equipped to support everyday life, with places
to wait, purchase essentials, mail letters, and
store bicycles,
Shaded for pedestrians and offering cover during
storms, if possible,
Flexible, allowing for occasional and future uses,
Easily maintained, and capable of storing
snow removed from streets in cold climates,
Well-lit for pedestrian safety and security,
Provided with clear wayfinding directions.

24.13 Cross section through sidewalk, parking, bicycle, and traffic zones.
(Michele Weisbart/LA County)

24.14 Frontage zone of sidewalk, used for outdoor dining, Broadway, New York City.
(Gary Hack)

24.15 Greengrocer with outdoor display and sales area, Broadway, New York City.
(Gary Hack)

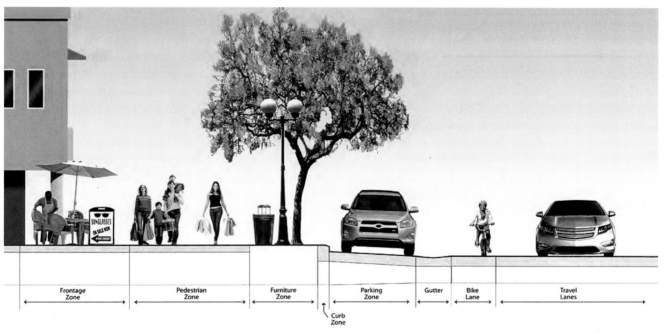

Most sidewalks have three distinct zones. The *curb zone* or *furniture zone* (sometimes both), nearest the traffic, is the logical location for the utilitarian functions of the sidewalk—the place for light, electrical, and signage standards (poles), the place to collect storm drainage, the location of street trees, hydrants, newspaper racks, and other street furniture. Typically a 1.2 m (4 ft) band will accommodate these elements, with those that are a traffic hazard (trees, vertical poles, etc.) offset 0.6 m (2 ft) from the driving surface. In dense urban areas, this zone may need to be expanded to 1.8 m (6 ft) to accommodate bicycle racks, bus shelters, vending kiosks, information kiosks, and other more substantial equipment. Even larger zones may be required for subway portals or stairways to upper-level crossings, or if bicycle lanes are placed on the same plane as the walkway. A generous curb zone will also allow for benches and planting between the structures, as figure 24.8 shows. As much as possible of this zone should be permeable, both to irrigate street trees and minimize storm runoff.

The opposite edge of the sidewalk is the *interface zone* or *frontage zone*. Here the dimensions and character will be determined by the uses that exist or are proposed, bearing in mind that streets generally outlive their initial bordering uses. Where the bordering uses are shops with display windows, an area of 1 m (3.4 ft) should be reserved for pedestrians who wish to window-shop, without stopping other walkers. This will allow merchants to occasionally move their wares out into the street. If there is an expectation that restaurants may occupy the frontage, the interface zone needs to be widened to 1.5 m (5 ft) to allow four-person tables or 4 m (13 ft) for a double row of tables for outdoor dining, without intruding into the walking zone.

If there are likely to be active uses, the frontage zone should be covered with roll-down or permanent awnings or canopies. In areas with tall structures, well-designed canopies have the added advantage of deflecting downdrafts away from the sidewalk. During bad weather, pedestrians can walk in this zone, as it is unlikely to be used for sidewalk merchandise or dining. An alternative, most common in Asia and Europe, is to create an interface zone through a street-facing arcade. Sometimes these are wide enough to cover a broad walking area as well, although (as we will note in chapter 34) there are commercial disadvantages to such

arrangements. Nonetheless, elegant two-story arcades line many of the iconic streets of the world.

Between the frontage and curb zones is the *pedestrian zone*, which needs to be dimensioned to provide adequate space for walking, both now and in the future. While it is possible to enforce minimum dimensions, planners need to err on the side of more generous walkways. Over time, the great streets of the world have held their value because of the flexibility offered by their oversized dimensions.

In residential areas where there are no commercial uses, the interface zone merges imperceptibly with the yards of houses or is the opportunity for a second row of trees to arch across the sidewalk. Where private spaces are fenced, there is a need to maintain space in this zone for placing garbage containers on pick-up days and adding planting that will soften the harshness of the interface. Even in the densest residential areas, the interface zone is critical, with elevation differences providing a much-needed separation from the street. In these areas, there is a need to expand the pedestrian space at corners and in drop-off areas that are likely to be congested.

Constant vigilance is needed to maintain the true walking zone of sidewalks. Poorly conceived or managed curb and frontage areas can squeeze this. In many cities, such as Dhaka, vendors and hawkers set up shop on the sidewalk, gradually forcing pedestrians to walk in the streets. In Paris, Philadelphia, and other cities, sidewalk cafés have all but crowded pedestrians off the sidewalks. Utility companies place their poles, transformers, and switching boxes in the walking zone, with little regard for how pedestrians navigate by them. The offenses are legion, and the presence of more than minimum dimensions will allow for some forgiveness.

Pedestrian Bridges and Underpasses

Traffic engineers, not wanting to slow the movement of vehicles in areas with heavy pedestrian flows, have insisted on the construction of pedestrian bridges or underpasses. These are costly and universally loathed by pedestrians who resent having to climb 5.5 m (18 ft) of steps, particularly if they are carrying parcels or pushing children's prams. Underpasses are disliked for other reasons, often the fear of dark places or having

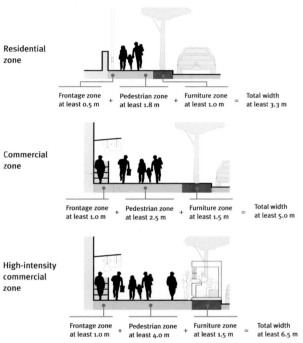

Residential zone

Frontage zone at least 0.5 m + Pedestrian zone at least 1.8 m + Furniture zone at least 1.0 m = Total width at least 3.3 m

Commercial zone

Frontage zone at least 1.0 m + Pedestrian zone at least 2.5 m + Furniture zone at least 1.5 m = Total width at least 5.0 m

High-intensity commercial zone

Frontage zone at least 1.0 m + Pedestrian zone at least 4.0 m + Furniture zone at least 1.5 m = Total width at least 6.5 m

24.16 Two-story arcade with shops lining the Rue de Rivoli, Paris.
(besopha/Wikimedia Commons)

24.17 Footpath standards proposed for India.
(Courtesy of Institute for Transportation and Development Policy)

24.18 Sidewalk shaded by a double row of trees, Riverside, Illinois.
(Gary Hack)

24.19 Sidewalk along Kentlands Boulevard, Kentlands, Maryland.
(Gary Hack)

24.20 Sidewalk separated from houses by fences and steps, South End, Boston.
(Courtesy of Juliene Paul)

to navigate areas with vendors and beggars. Making overpasses fully accessible generally involves constructing lengthy ramps (67 m or 220 ft at the steepest slopes allowed) or escalators coupled with elevators, all costly.

Before deciding to create a grade-separated crossing, a careful analysis should be made of the costs and benefits of stopping traffic so that pedestrians can cross at grade. No bridges were included in the construction of Hudson River Boulevard, south of 42nd Street along the west side of Manhattan, a major traffic artery that replaced an elevated highway. It was determined that the loss of traffic capacity would be minimal with crossings every three blocks (so pedestrians would never need to walk more than a block out of their way) and with automated traffic signals that responded to current traffic conditions.

While the first choice should be to avoid bridges or underpasses, there are clearly situations where they make good sense. On very high-speed highways,

24.21 (top left)   Pedestrian bridge at Arad Bay, Muharraq, Bahrain, mimicking the form of the traditional dhow.
(MSCEB Architects/Open Buildings)

24.22 (top right)   Footbridge over the Yarra River, Melbourne, Australia, connecting Flinders Station with the South Bank developments.
(Gary Hack)

24.23 (bottome left)   BP Pedestrian Bridge at Millennium Park, Chicago.
(Frank Gehry/Torsodog/Wikipedia Commons)

24.24 (bottom right)   Tunnel, United Airlines Terminal, Chicago O'Hare Airport.
(Michael Hayden, artist/Chicago at Night).

the danger of motorists missing traffic signals may be greater than the inconvenience, and pedestrians may feel safer crossing on bridges. Topography sometimes works in favor of over- or underpasses: with a significant side slope, or where the roadway is in a cut, bridges may be a natural extension of pathways on at least one side of the roadway. The need to cross over a roadway, railway, or river can also be an occasion for a significant ramped structure, celebrating the procession of moving from side to side, as examples from Melbourne, Australia and Chicago's Millennium Park illustrate.

Pedestrian bridges are best if they become significant places as well as serving their utilitarian function. Historical bridge structures such as the Rialto Bridge in Venice and the Ponte Vecchio in Florence—both of which incorporate shops along their length—offer possibilities. The 150 m (500 ft) long Chihuly Bridge of Glass in Tacoma, Washington, which connects the downtown to the waterfront across a busy interstate highway, provides an introduction to the city's Glass Museum and traditions of glassmaking. Dynamic works of art can also humanize underpasses, as Chicago's O'Hare Airport United Airlines tunnel shows.

Pedestrian Promenades

Barcelona's La Rambla demonstrates that it is possible to develop linear pedestrian streets over time that become the centerpiece of whole districts. Its 1.2 km (¾ mile) pedestrian promenade is lined with clusters of activities—a flower market, bird market, bookstalls, artist galleries, restaurants, and the ubiquitous human sculptures that claim prime spots along the walkway. The promenade is located in a broad 18 m (60 ft) median at the center of a street lined with hotels, restaurants and shops, at the heart of the Barri Gòtic. La Rambla succeeds because it connects two of the city's prime attractions, the Plaça de Catalunya (with its fountains and meeting spots) and the historic seaport, Port Vell. Tourists quickly join local residents each evening, promenading the length of La Rambla, stopping to buy flowers or inspect the goods in kiosks, finally alighting in a restaurant for their midnight meal. The walking zone is quite narrow, often only 3 m (10 ft) wide, and can become quite crowded during peak evening hours, slowing movement to a crawl. But La Rambla was never intended to be a quick throughway.

Not every city can support a promenade as lengthy or active as La Rambla, which depends upon the density of surrounding residents and workers and the concentration of tourists. But pedestrian promenades can take many other forms, each uniquely responding to local opportunities. In Boston, the 30 m (100 ft) central median of Commonwealth Avenue in the Back Bay provides a seven-block promenade that is a quiet place to stroll and sit, away from the busy streets around. Covering the Central Artery, recently placed belowground, Boston has created a second promenade, the Rose Kennedy Greenway. Its 60 m (200 ft) average width offers enough space for programmed events, seating and socializing, fountains, ponds, and children's play as well as a meandering pathway for strolling. Over time, new kiosks and uses will undoubtedly be added to the greenway, as residents and visitors are attracted to it.

Promenades need not be at street level. In San Antonio, Texas, the Riverwalk consists of over 5 km (3 mi) of walkways lining an elbow on the San Antonio River, one story below the surrounding streets. Built as part of a flood control project 70 years ago and extended over the years, it is now lined with hotels, restaurants, shops, and entertainment places, sharing an intimate relationship with the slow-flowing river. An ambitious contemporary example is the Cheonggyecheon Stream greenway project in central Seoul, Korea,

24.25 Flower market block of La Rambla, Barcelona. (Gary Hack)

24.26 Commonwealth Avenue Mall, Boston.
(Gary Hack)

24.27 Rose Kennedy Greenway, Boston.
(Gary Hack)

where a historic stream that had long been covered over was reopened to the sky and transformed into a recreation corridor. Nearly 6 km (3 3/4 miles) in length, the greenway allows pedestrians to walk along the sides of the stream, shaded by trees and cooled by the water. It is among the most visited attractions of central Seoul.

Wonderful pedestrian promenades can also be created above ground level, providing prospects to the distance and offering a respite from traffic-clogged streets. New York's High Line, created on the structure of an abandoned industrial rail line, offers a 2 mi (3 km) walkway with unparalleled views of Manhattan buildings and the Hudson River waterfront. It is also a place

24.28 Riverwalk along the San Antonio River, San Antonio, Texas.
(Gary Hack)

24.29 Cheonggyecheon Stream walkway and park, Seoul, Korea.
(Smiley.toerist/Wikimedia Commons)

24.30 High Line Park, on a repurposed elevated railway structure, Chelsea, New York City.
(Gary Hack)

to stop, sip a coffee, or lounge in the sun (or get out of the rain in a downpour). The generous landscaping was designed to provide interest in four seasons. The planners of the High Line could only guess at the number of users that might be attracted to this unusual walkway, which varies in with but is only 2 m (6.6 feet) wide in many sections. Its success has meant that it is often overcrowded, although slowing down pedestrians also encourages people to stop and linger.

Pedestrian Zones

The idea of converting the street space of city centers into *pedestrian zones* has its origins in the post-World War II reconstruction of European cities. These car-free areas, also called *pedestrianised zones* (UK), *pedestrian precincts* (New Zealand), *zones piétonnes* (France), *Fußgängerzonen* (Germany), and *zonas peatonales* (Spain), are often coupled with the introduction of tram and subway systems and parking garages below the main squares or at the edges of central areas. The Liijnbahn in Rotterdam, opened in 1953, was the first European street planned entirely for pedestrians, and many large reconstruction projects followed suit. The first British new town, Stevenage, inaugurated in 1959, was built around a car-free center.

Of course, some cities have never had vehicles on their streets. Venice's uniqueness is inseparable from its devotion to canals and vaporette, and squares and streets where you can hear footsteps rather than motor vehicles. The streets of many walled medieval cities were too narrow to accommodate cars and trucks, including portions of Dubrovnik, Ghent, San Sebastián, and Edinburgh. Other cities including the Cinque Terre in Italy, the Old Town of Rhodes, and Bellagio had streets too steep for vehicles, so became natural pedestrian realms. And many resorts have eschewed vehicles in favor of more leisurely ways of getting around, including Mackinac Island in Michigan, Fire Island in New York, Sark in the English Channel, Krabi in Thailand, and the alpine resorts of Gstadt and Zermatt. New resorts often take their cues from these successful destinations, and substitute electric carts for larger motor vehicles.

While many large new developments, such as Norrmalmsregleringen in Stockholm and La Défense in Paris, are centered on spaces reserved for pedestrians, the most successful European pedestrian zones are in the old city centers. Few places match Strøget in Copenhagen, a 1.1 km (2/3 mi) car-free zone extending from the Town Square and City Hall to Kongens Nytorv, the city's cultural center. Strøget actually consists of portions of five separate streets, with widths varying from 10 m (33 ft) to 30 m (100 ft), linked together to form a coherent path through the central retail and cultural district. It was constructed in stages, beginning with temporary closures of streets in the 1950s, made permanent in 1962 by removing cars and repaving an area of 15,800 m² (170,000 sq ft), and expanded step by step as each link proved successful to an area of 100,000 m² (1.1 million sq ft) in 2000 (Gehl and Gemzøe 2006). Over the years many of the local shops have turned into tourist-oriented outlets, but Strøget retains a healthy mix of department stores, boutiques, showrooms, specialty stores, restaurants, and entertainment places. Other streets in the area have recently been closed to automobiles or become pedestrian-priority areas.

People arrive at Strøget on foot, by bicycle, on trams, and via the subway; the small number who drive to the area park in underground parking structures at the edge of central Copenhagen. Nearby hotels, universities, offices, and housing provide it with built-in patronage, as does Tivoli Gardens, a short walk away. At the height of the summer tourist season, 80,000

24.31 Strøget, Copenhagen, the central spine of the city's shopping district.
(Gary Hack)

pedestrians walk Strøget each day, and even in the depths of winter, 48,000 find their way there (Gehl and Gemzøe 1996). Equally important, the number of people standing or seated in the city center at any midday time has more than tripled, from 1,700 in 1968 to 5,900 in 1995. While the reputation of Strøget as the place to be undoubtedly draws many to it, one can't overestimate the importance of its location at the transit hub of the city and center of both tourism and employment. Pedestrian zones need a stable built-in clientele to prosper.

German cities have been aggressively limiting or removing private vehicles from city centers, often in concert with transportation improvements. In Hannover, placing streetcars belowground so they connect directly to mass transit became an occasion to reconsider all movement in the city center. Much of the truck deliveries were placed belowground, along with large areas of parking for cars, allowing the streets to be freed from traffic. The belowground transit level along Bahnhofstraße was opened to the sky and lined with shops to become the Niki-de-Saint-Phalle-Promenade. A spiderweb of pedestrianized streets reaches out from Kröpcke Square, the historic center of Hannover, to exclusive shopping areas and the Altstadt with its towering Market Church. The result is one of the largest and healthiest pedestrian zones in Europe. It is never better than in Christmas season, when the pedestrian streets become a Weihnachtsmarkt, crowded with Hanoverians and visitors enjoying the special treats and grog.

Freiburg, Germany is an example of a smaller city that has transformed its image through pedestrianization of its historic core. Like Strøget, this pedestrian zone was constructed in increments beginning with closing of streets around the Town Hall and cathedral. Over two decades Freiburg, which bills itself as the solar capital of Europe, extended its tram (light rail) network to serve outlying areas of the city, developed one of the most extensive bicycle networks in any city of its size, and constructed several large underground parking garages (for 5,000 cars) around the perimeter of the historic city. This allowed it to repave the streets of the area and restrict their use to trams, bicycles, and pedestrians. A unique feature of the pedestrian zone is the open channels, typically 20–50 cm (8–20 in) wide by 5–10 cm (4–6 in) deep, called *Bächle*, which allow runoff to pass through the center of the city. They have been

24.32 Bahnhofstraße and the Niki-de-Saint-Phalle-Promenade, Hannover, Germany, with connections to transit and truck servicing on lower level.
(Courtesy of Patrick Scholl/flickr)

carefully placed to create a distance between pedestrians and trams, and allow the winter snowmelt to be carried away without underground pipes. No expense has been spared in creating a delightful street surface of cobbles, small stones composed into patterns, and stone bands marking the edges of merchants' zones.

Every European pedestrian zone has its unique virtues, and there are many lessons to be learned. Among them are the importance of:

Creating networks for bicycles and transit, and perimeter parking facilities, in concert with the program of removing vehicles from the streets,
Starting small and expanding pedestrian zones as they prove popular and merchants accept them,
Arranging uncluttered pedestrian zones that are capable of being used for events such as festivals and performances, street markets, and cafés, as well as everyday strolling,
Connecting major attractions that create a draw through the pedestrian zone,
Accommodating truck deliveries and messengers, while restricting them to defined hours of the day,
Using building facades for lighting, or suspending lights on catenaries, rather than cluttering the street with light standards.

In North America, pedestrian zones have most often taken the form of downtown malls, created in the hopes of reviving fading Main Streets of older cities. Largely the invention of Victor Gruen, who also pioneered the enclosed shopping center, downtown malls sought to attract shoppers and visitors by providing generous areas for pedestrians and space for merchandizing and events. Over 200 large and small cities in North America closed streets in their downtown areas between 1959, when Kalamazoo's pioneering Burdick Street Mall opened, and 1990, when the trend had largely run its course. Only a minority of the projects had the intended economic effect, although the lack of success probably had more to do with the difficulty of competing head to head with regional malls and big box retailers, the changing demographic of central cities, and evolving shopping habits of North Americans. Over the past decade, many of the pedestrian malls have been modified to reintroduce automobiles for all or part of the day or have become streetcar corridors. An excellent example is Santa Monica's Third Street Promenade, where the orientation of downtown shopping has also been shifted to emphasize specialty, restaurant, and entertainment uses rather than general merchandising.

The width of downtown pedestrian malls is usually determined by the width of streets being closed—typically 15, 18, or 24 m (50, 60, or 80 ft). Where new pedestrian links are created, they should conform to the commercial logic of the pedestrian way (see chapter 34). On existing rights-of-way, underground utilities and the loading needs of shops will influence how much of the street space must be kept open. Typically, a meandering 3 m (10 ft) path needs to be maintained for vehicles, with areas for stopping. When a 24 m (80 ft) right-of-way is available, there may be room for two pathways with landscaping, water elements, shops, or kiosks between, and there may be an opportunity to excavate areas near shops to provide two levels of active space, as in the Pearl Street Mall in Boulder, Colorado.

What makes for a successful downtown pedestrian mall? Perhaps not surprisingly, many of the most successful US malls are in college towns—in Boulder, Charlottesville, Burlington, Santa Cruz, among other places. If the college is nearby, students walk or cycle to the mall for their latte, or take their parents there for a visit when they are in town, or go there to seek out

24.33 Pedestrian zone, Freiburg, Germany, with *Bächle* for drainage.
(Gary Hack)

24.34 Third Street Promenade, Santa Monica, California, closed to traffic during weekends and evenings.
(Gary Hack)

the unique shops not usually found in regional malls. A nearby residential population or sizable office concentration can also help sustain a downtown pedestrian zone, particularly if it has made the transition to entertainment and restaurant uses. In short, a pedestrian mall needs a nearby clientele, and the transportation to get them there. If it reaches beyond these groups, parking rimming the perimeter of the area is essential, as in European cities.

A second ingredient for success is developing a unique identity. The Church Street Marketplace in Burlington, Vermont does this by bringing the larger landscape into the mall—enormous granite rocks, slabs of stone, and golden maple trees that celebrate the seasons. Surveys have found that Americans feel most comfortable in spaces that are filled with greenery, unlike their European counterparts. The Main Street Mall in Charlottesville is characterized by its deep red brick, recalling the historic houses of the region, by magnificent oak trees that arch across the mall, and by carefully restored shop fronts. The total environment needs to be unique and memorable.

Pedestrian malls also need to have the flexibility to accommodate an ever-changing schedule of events—markets, festivals, concerts, street performances, vendors, and more—that bring life to an area. This third ingredient of success requires a management system with creativity and skills to make the mall an attraction. Such an entity is also essential for high-quality maintenance, and may be important for mounting a security presence on the mall during off hours.

Fourth, every Main Street mall also needs byways or alleys for lower-rent and experimental uses. It needs to incubate its enterprises and activities, since a large part of its appeal is that it is not dominated by national retail chains that can be found anywhere.

The final lesson is shared with European examples: start small and add to the pedestrian zone as the number of pedestrians grows. It is better to have a small activity-filled space than a large empty one. Unfortunately, many American cities did the opposite, seeking a single transformative move that failed to deliver enough pedestrians to fill the spaces created. By trial and error, several cities have hit on a solution of recreating a pedestrian zone that changes its character across the day and week—open to traffic and transit during daytime hours, but car-free in evenings and on weekends, on market days, or for special events.

24.35 Downtown mall, Charlottesville, Virginia. (Courtesy of Alison Yeung/Daily Moves and Grooves)

24.36 Golden maples, rocks, and traditional brick in Church Street Marketplace, Burlington, Vermont. (Courtesy of Matt Sutkoski)

24.37 Famous Dave's 5th Annual BBQ & Blues Festival, Peavey Plaza off Nicollet Mall, Minneapolis. (Courtesy of Sharlene Hensrud)

24.38 Nanjing Road, Shanghai, linking People's Park and the Bund. (Gary Hack)

In Asian cities, pedestrianization of streets is often motivated by the opposite problem: too much foot traffic. In the early 1990s, sidewalks along Nanjing Road, Shanghai's main commercial street, were so crowded that a rope needed to be installed along the centerline to separate the directions of traffic and avoid total pedestrian gridlock. Volumes were so great that elaborate bridges had to be created connecting the four corners of key intersections. Closing Nanjing Road to traffic and removing the bridges has made it the top place to meet others in the shopping district of Shanghai, a place to stroll, window-shop, and take children on an outing on a hot summer night. The pedestrianization of the Ximending district of Taipei has made it that city's hot spot for young people, attracted to the area because of its bustling night market and concentration of movie theaters. Most Asian cities are developing pedestrian zones that emulate these efforts.

Pedestrian Concourses Above and Belowground

Many projects and districts of cities have developed extensive walkway systems above and belowground. These go by various names: skyway, catwalk, sky bridge,

24.39 Map of the upper-level Minneapolis Skyway system and the ground-level Nicollet Mall. (Skyway Directory)

Minneapolis Skyway System

or skywalk if they are aboveground, and concourses, underground city, *ville souterraine*, 地下城, catacombs, pedways, paths, underground shopping streets if they are belowground. Minneapolis boasts 11 km (7 mi) of skyways, connecting 69 blocks in its downtown area, developed over a period of 40 years. Calgary's +15 walkway system now contains 16 km (10 mi) of walkways connecting most blocks of downtown. Hong Kong has several such systems, connecting projects in each of its commercial hubs. Mumbai has many skyways, which are gradually being connected into an integrated system. Upper-level walkways connect the main office towers, hotels, the convention center and its annex, and mass transit stations in the new town of Makuhari Messe in Chiba, Japan, allowing free flow of crowds through much of the center. In Montreal and Toronto, large portions of the downtown are connected by belowground passageways, which also connect to mass transit stations. It is possible to move throughout most of Houston's downtown in air-conditioned belowground concourses. The most extensive underground shopping streets may be found in Tokyo, where many such areas, crowded with shoppers, span between nearby metro stations. Across the globe, over 50 cities have some form of multiblock passageways, separated from the level where automobiles flow (Montgomery and Bean 1999).

The motivations for creating such systems are a combination of pedestrian comfort, protection from the climate (cold, hot, or rainy), expansion of the amount of commercial frontage in an area, and a desire to smooth the flow of traffic on roadways by reducing the conflicts with pedestrians. They are costly to create, represent a major long-term commitment to movement in an area, and are not always a success. Many cities do not have the density and flow of pedestrians to support both street-level and upper- or lower-level shopping, and usually it is the street level that suffers. The hope that vertical separation of pedestrians will solve street-level vehicle conflicts is often elusive, since some pedestrian functions (access to buses; hotel and housing entrances) will generally remain on the street level, necessitating sidewalk crossings of roads. Often skyway systems are disorienting, as they pass through blocks constructed at different times and with varying materials. Maintenance and security responsibilities for such systems are a regular challenge. Nonetheless, they can allow downtown areas to capitalize on the

24.40 IDS Place, Minneapolis, where ground-level and upper-level pedestrian paths connect.
(Gary Hack)

24.41 Makuhari Messe upper-level pedestrian network, Chiba, Japan.
(Gary Hack)

24.42 Upper-level walkway connecting Southern Cross Rail Station to Docklands urban development, Melbourne, Australia.
(Gary Hack)

24.43 Three-level pedestrian bridge on Stephen Avenue, Calgary, that connects vertical elements on the Plus 15 skyway system. (Courtesy of Tracy Santink)

24.44 The ground-level Nicollet transit mall, Minneapolis, supports restaurants and shops for transit patrons. (Gary Hack)

flows from mass transit and parking garages, provide shelter and comfort to pedestrians even in the worst of weather, and can integrate dense urban areas into coordinated centers.

Several principles are essential in planning pedestrian ways above and belowground:

Set systemwide standards for width of walkways, running grades, and climate conditioning. Typically, pedestrian ways should not be narrower than 4 m (13 ft), but widths should be established by an analysis of projected flows.

Make visible connections to the street through multilevel spaces where pedestrian ways are visible from sidewalks. These help in orientation, and provide punctuation points on the system for pedestrians to meet others and stop for a respite. Make secondary connections through multilevel retail outlets with frontages on both pedestrian ways and streets.

Design the system so it can operate 24/7, even during hours when stores or the buildings it passes through are closed. This is essential to maintaining a system during retail holidays, and through retail relocations.

Differentiate retail activities between street level and the separate pedestrian level. Cities such as Minneapolis have found that restaurants, clubs, and entertainment venues prefer street-level frontage, as do smaller specialized shops, while frontage on the pedestrian ways is essential for high-volume, convenience and larger-scaled retail uses.

Provide universal access at all key points of entry to the system. This access needs to be separated from building elevator systems to maintain security.

Create an effective wayfinding system.

Organize a management entity that can oversee development and operation of the skyway or concourse system, establish access hours, oversee security, set maintenance standards, and guide in design of extensions to the system.

Well-planned and managed skyway and underground concourse systems can be an important infrastructure element in areas with dense urban development, but must be carefully planned and designed.

25 | Surface Water

Water is essential for all forms of life, from bacteria to plants, animals, and humans. How it is managed on a site directly affects the quality of life, and in extreme situations can affect the survival of residents. Water shortages limit growth in many settled areas, while in other cities annual or occasional flooding rules out large areas for development. In urban areas that can afford it, rainfall is quickly captured in underground storm sewers and transported to large water bodies—out of sight and out of mind. This usually shifts problems downstream, and many localities have concluded that they need to manage runoff within their boundaries, rely on overland drainage, and limit the flows they discharge. This means adopting improved site planning and management practices.

Water can also be a focus of civic life. The fountains of Rome not only provided a supply of potable water for residents, but also cooled the air, celebrated mythology, and became focal points for neighborhoods. Freiburg, Germany's drainage channels, the *Bächle*, reminded residents that the city spans between mountains and rivers. Artificial lakes in Tempe, Arizona (Rio Salado), Austin, Texas (Lake Austin), and Regina, Canada (Wascana Lake) have become the centerpieces of urban recreation, while also managing flooding by storing runoff. Lakeside cities are especially revered in China, with Hangzhou's West Lake and the lakes area of Nanjing representing destinations for every citizen. Most cities are located along oceans, rivers, or streams and need to husband their water resources so they can continue to provide drinking water, recreation, and beauty while absorbing the runoff from the city.

Sustainable site development practices begin with a systems view of water on a site. Sites that have never

25.1 Wascana Lake and provincial legislative buildings, Regina, Canada.
(Gary Hack)

25.2 Xuanwu Lake, Nanjing, the centerpiece of the urban area.
(Chu Yu/123rf)

been developed have evolved into an ecology where rainfall, groundwater, and vegetation are in balance. Rainfall or snowmelt percolates into the soil, replenishing the water drawn down by the roots of trees and plants, with a portion becoming part of the groundwater regime. Quantities beyond what can be absorbed by the soil travel across the land, filtered along the way, into wetlands where they are detained, further filtered, and support aquatic and plant life, or into streams where their nutrients serve downstream plant and human communities. When sites are exploited for agriculture over long periods, their ecology evolves through the addition of drainage areas, irrigation ditches, and detention ponds, remaining in balance.

Not all sites have stable natural systems prior to development, and ecologies are also in a constant state of evolution. Hillsides may be eroding, and where humans occupy these, as in many informal settlements in less developed countries, the water management task will include remediating the hazard of landslides and soil loss. Informal settlements that lack any organized sanitary sewer systems may rely on overland drainage to dilute human wastes, creating the additional challenge of preventing waterborne diseases. Well-planned drainage systems can help reduce dangers, even if they also require human cooperation for their maintenance.

Principles for Site Runoff

When urban uses are added to a site, the first objective of the planner should be to emulate natural outcomes—creating a *stable ecology* that balances use and exploitation of water and limits water transported beyond the site to quantities that can be safely absorbed in existing streams and rivers. Usually this means a policy of *zero net runoff*: no more water should be discharged from a site than in its predevelopment state. As a practical matter, this is usually defined as not increasing the rate of runoff per hour, by detaining water on a site so that it is used or exported over a longer period. Some cities mandate retention of a portion of the water falling on a site: in Philadelphia, all development sites must be planned to detain the first 1 in (25 mm) of rainfall (Philadelphia Water Department 2011). The city of Austin, Texas requires on-site

25.3 On-site retention, mandated by Philadelphia rules, may include green roofs, permeable parking areas, and detention areas for infiltration into groundwater.
(Philadelphia Water Department)

25.4 High water table and inadequate sewers result in severe pollution of groundwater, Bangkok.
(Gary Hack)

control of the runoff for all two-year-return storms (City of Austin, n.d.). Full detention of rainwater is rarely possible, necessitating downstream improvements that increase the capacity of streams or ponds receiving a portion of runoff from a site.

Another important objective is maintaining the *water table* at acceptable levels. If it falls too low or fluctuates greatly, soils may shrink or shift, impacting buildings and pavements, and trees and plants may be difficult to maintain. If the water table rises to or near the surface, soils will become saturated quickly, runoff will increase, and areas planned for recreation uses may never dry out enough to be properly usable. Groundwater flows like surface water (but more slowly), and development of a site, particularly with underground structures, may unwittingly dam flows, resulting in unexpected drops in levels downstream. Managing the groundwater level may mean using surface water to recharge the groundwater supply, or constructing drains to transport it from areas of a site where the water table is too high. In cites that lack adequate sanitary sewer systems (such as outlying areas of Bangkok and many Saudi Arabian cities), vast quantities of untreated sewage are released into the groundwater, causing its level to rise. It is a reminder that surface water, groundwater, and water supply are tightly linked.

Improving or maintaining *water quality* is a third important objective. Remedying point sources of pollution is an obvious goal, but a more common issue is impurities absorbed by surface water in the course of draining off land. Rainfall that falls on roadways and parking lots often absorbs petroleum wastes, salt and sand deposited during winter months, and other substances emitted from exhaust pipes. Nitrates are absorbed by water running off lawns and landscaped areas and can create efflorescence or algae bloom in lakes or streams. Lead, arsenic, and other hazardous materials may leach from soil and be transported by runoff, particularly from once-industrial sites. Even natural substances may be hazardous if they are deposited into sensitive water bodies, as with organic materials that foster the growth of toxins in bays ("red tide"), affecting shellfish. A variety of techniques can help filter runoff as it makes its way to water bodies.

Reduction of hazards of all kinds is a critical objective in its own right. This includes reducing flood hazards to people and property, preventing erosion and landslides, avoiding siltation of streams reducing their capacity to convey runoff, and avoiding disruption of traffic because of flooding and dangerous conditions in winter freeze-thaw conditions. One of the most vulnerable periods is during construction, when pavement, ground covers, and drainage liners are not in place and loss of soil and vegetation can have many consequences.

The opposite issue is equally important: providing for dry seasons by *conserving water* from year to year. It may be critical for irrigated sites, reservoirs,

or areas with water recreation. In desert climates, the planner may need to minimize evaporation from lakes or streams by configuring them so that they have large volumes but small surface areas.

Finally, an essential attitude is conserving water for productive uses on a site. Rainwater is largely free of impurities, and therefore a treasured commodity that can be used for domestic purposes. In low-rainfall areas it may be too valuable to use for irrigation, and gray water (water that has been purified after human use) may be best for such purposes (see chapter 27). Where rainfall is plentiful, creating productive uses near where it lands is a useful pursuit. Examples include rooftop cisterns, allotment gardens, urban agriculture, evaporation basins, and even micro energy installations.

Establishing Parameters

Planning an effective surface water management system on a site requires data on rainfall, soils, and water flows in surrounding streams and rivers. It is best done with sketch plans in hand, since the density of development, how the site might be arranged, the areas of impervious surfaces, and the potentials for water movement across the site will all greatly affect the design of systems. Most importantly, a policy needs to be established about the severity of flooding that may be tolerated in the most extreme weather events. Many local or national governments have established these standards, and meeting them will affect whether the property is insurable against flooding or storms. The owner of the site always has the option of going beyond what is required, and in many circumstances this may be the best course.

Typically, coping with a 100-year flood is the standard adopted for on-site drainage (see chapter 4), although its more accurate term is *100-year rainfall return event*. Many governments provide maps of the estimated flood levels along streams and lakes for 100-year storms. These represent extrapolations of storm data making assumptions about ground cover and the other factors that will affect the flooding of streams and water bodies. A variety of computer programs are available for mapping flood contours for flood events, using GIS systems (National Research Council, 2007). Flood maps are important particularly because they

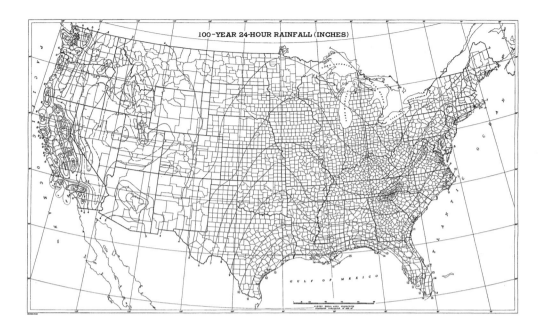

100-YEAR 24-HOUR RAINFALL (INCHES)

PDS-based point precipitation frequency estimates with 90% confidence intervals (in inches)[1]									
Duration	Average recurrence interval (years)								
	1	2	5	10	25	50	100	200	500	1000
5-min	0.326 (0.292-0.366)	0.389 (0.347-0.437)	0.473 (0.423-0.531)	0.539 (0.480-0.603)	0.625 (0.553-0.698)	0.691 (0.609-0.771)	0.759 (0.664-0.845)	0.829 (0.721-0.921)	0.927 (0.797-1.03)	1.00 (0.854-1.11)
10-min	0.507 (0.453-0.569)	0.608 (0.542-0.683)	0.736 (0.657-0.825)	0.832 (0.741-0.931)	0.956 (0.846-1.07)	1.05 (0.923-1.17)	1.14 (1.00-1.27)	1.24 (1.08-1.38)	1.36 (1.17-1.51)	1.46 (1.24-1.62)
15-min	0.621 (0.555-0.698)	0.743 (0.663-0.835)	0.903 (0.807-1.01)	1.02 (0.911-1.15)	1.18 (1.05-1.32)	1.30 (1.14-1.45)	1.42 (1.24-1.58)	1.54 (1.34-1.71)	1.70 (1.46-1.89)	1.82 (1.55-2.02)
30-min	0.822 (0.735-0.923)	0.994 (0.888-1.12)	1.24 (1.10-1.39)	1.42 (1.26-1.59)	1.67 (1.48-1.86)	1.85 (1.63-2.07)	2.05 (1.79-2.28)	2.25 (1.95-2.50)	2.52 (2.17-2.80)	2.73 (2.33-3.03)
60-min	1.00 (0.897-1.13)	1.22 (1.09-1.37)	1.55 (1.39-1.74)	1.81 (1.61-2.02)	2.16 (1.92-2.41)	2.44 (2.15-2.72)	2.74 (2.40-3.05)	3.05 (2.65-3.39)	3.48 (3.00-3.87)	3.83 (3.27-4.26)
2-hr	1.14 (1.01-1.29)	1.39 (1.22-1.56)	1.76 (1.55-1.99)	2.06 (1.81-2.32)	2.49 (2.18-2.79)	2.85 (2.47-3.18)	3.22 (2.79-3.59)	3.63 (3.11-4.04)	4.23 (3.58-4.70)	4.72 (3.96-5.25)
3-hr	1.23 (1.10-1.38)	1.49 (1.33-1.67)	1.88 (1.67-2.11)	2.19 (1.95-2.46)	2.65 (2.34-2.95)	3.03 (2.65-3.36)	3.44 (3.00-3.81)	3.89 (3.35-4.30)	4.54 (3.87-5.02)	5.09 (4.30-5.62)
6-hr	1.52 (1.37-1.70)	1.83 (1.65-2.05)	2.28 (2.05-2.55)	2.66 (2.38-2.96)	3.20 (2.85-3.55)	3.65 (3.23-4.04)	4.13 (3.62-4.56)	4.65 (4.04-5.13)	5.42 (4.66-5.97)	6.06 (5.15-6.67)
12-hr	1.89 (1.71-2.10)	2.27 (2.05-2.52)	2.81 (2.54-3.13)	3.28 (2.95-3.63)	3.95 (3.52-4.36)	4.52 (4.00-4.97)	5.14 (4.51-5.63)	5.82 (5.06-6.36)	6.83 (5.85-7.45)	7.68 (6.50-8.37)
24-hr	2.25 (2.09-2.43)	2.70 (2.51-2.92)	3.36 (3.11-3.63)	3.90 (3.61-4.21)	4.69 (4.32-5.05)	5.36 (4.91-5.76)	6.09 (5.54-6.54)	6.89 (6.21-7.38)	8.06 (7.18-8.64)	9.05 (7.97-9.70)
2-day	2.61 (2.42-2.84)	3.13 (2.90-3.40)	3.88 (3.59-4.21)	4.50 (4.16-4.88)	5.42 (4.97-5.86)	6.20 (5.65-6.68)	7.04 (6.38-7.60)	7.97 (7.16-8.59)	9.33 (8.27-10.1)	10.5 (9.19-11.3)
3-day	2.78 (2.58-3.01)	3.32 (3.08-3.61)	4.11 (3.80-4.45)	4.76 (4.39-5.15)	5.71 (5.24-6.17)	6.52 (5.95-7.03)	7.39 (6.71-7.97)	8.34 (7.51-9.00)	9.74 (8.66-10.5)	10.9 (9.60-11.8)
4-day	2.94 (2.73-3.19)	3.52 (3.27-3.82)	4.34 (4.01-4.70)	5.02 (4.63-5.43)	6.00 (5.52-6.48)	6.84 (6.25-7.38)	7.74 (7.04-8.35)	8.72 (7.86-9.41)	10.2 (9.05-11.0)	11.4 (10.0-12.3)
7-day	3.46 (3.24-3.72)	4.13 (3.87-4.43)	5.03 (4.70-5.39)	5.75 (5.37-6.16)	6.77 (6.29-7.26)	7.61 (7.04-8.15)	8.50 (7.82-9.11)	9.44 (8.63-10.1)	10.8 (9.76-11.6)	11.9 (10.7-12.8)
10-day	4.00 (3.76-4.28)	4.75 (4.47-5.08)	5.71 (5.36-6.10)	6.48 (6.06-6.92)	7.55 (7.05-8.07)	8.43 (7.83-9.00)	9.34 (8.63-9.98)	10.3 (9.45-11.0)	11.7 (10.6-12.5)	12.7 (11.5-13.7)
20-day	5.55 (5.23-5.90)	6.54 (6.16-6.95)	7.63 (7.19-8.11)	8.49 (7.99-9.02)	9.64 (9.05-10.2)	10.5 (9.87-11.2)	11.4 (10.7-12.1)	12.3 (11.5-13.1)	13.5 (12.5-14.4)	14.5 (13.3-15.4)
30-day	6.97 (6.61-7.37)	8.17 (7.74-8.63)	9.39 (8.88-9.91)	10.3 (9.76-10.9)	11.6 (10.9-12.2)	12.5 (11.8-13.2)	13.4 (12.6-14.2)	14.4 (13.4-15.2)	15.6 (14.5-16.5)	16.5 (15.3-17.5)
45-day	8.86 (8.43-9.34)	10.4 (9.85-10.9)	11.8 (11.2-12.4)	12.8 (12.2-13.5)	14.1 (13.4-14.9)	15.1 (14.3-15.9)	16.0 (15.1-16.9)	16.9 (15.9-17.8)	18.0 (16.9-19.0)	18.8 (17.6-19.9)
60-day	10.7 (10.2-11.2)	12.5 (11.9-13.1)	14.0 (13.3-14.7)	15.1 (14.4-15.9)	16.5 (15.8-17.3)	17.6 (16.7-18.4)	18.5 (17.6-19.4)	19.4 (18.4-20.4)	20.6 (19.4-21.6)	21.4 (20.2-22.5)

[1] Precipitation frequency (PF) estimates in this table are based on frequency analysis of partial duration series (PDS).

Numbers in parenthesis are PF estimates at lower and upper bounds of the 90% confidence interval. The probability that precipitation frequency estimates (for a given duration and average recurrence interval) will be greater than the upper bound (or less than the lower bound) is 5%. Estimates at upper bounds are not checked against probable maximum precipitation (PMP) estimates and may be higher than currently valid PMP values.

Please refer to NOAA Atlas 14 document for more information.

25.5 100-year 24-hour rainfall map, US. (NOAA)

25.6 Precipitation frequency estimates for Philadelphia. (NOAA)

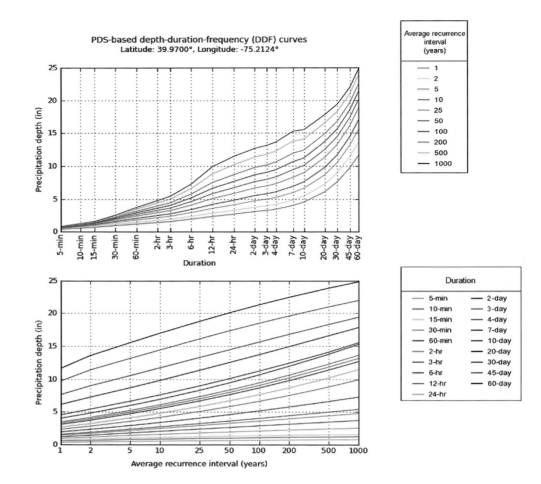

25.7 Comparison of precipitation for various return dates, Philadelphia. (NOAA)

establish benchmark elevations for inhabited spaces and facilities, and indicate areas where typically any intrusion of structures or loss of capacity to absorb floods needs to be compensated for by replacement areas. They are also widely used by insurance companies to decide what risks they are prepared to cover.

In the US, the National Oceanic and Atmospheric Administration (NOAA) makes available data on rainfall levels expected for various rainfall return events. Its interactive website provides data for most urban locations. Rainfall charts are available from most national meteorological services for urban areas.

The first and most important step in designing a site to accommodate runoff is deciding on the design event. Local governments are often excessively cautious in setting the design standard, since they have only to lose from flooding and the costs for preventing it are borne by others. Some require that developers design for a 500-year storm event, imposing large burdens

on the developers. More common is planning for a 100-year storm event. But site planners also need to focus on more routine storms in the 10–15-year range, ensuring that the site is not disturbed by frequent occurrences.

In the US, common standards are to use the 10- or 15-year/24-hour storm event for designing underground piping systems on small sites, the 25- or 100-year/24-hour storm event for planning sites larger than 640 acres (259 ha), and the 100-year/24-hour storm event for planning detention areas or open channels.

Estimating volumes of water

A portion of the water that falls on a site will be absorbed immediately by the soil. How much will depend upon the ground cover, soils, and the slope of surfaces. Ultimately the duration and amounts of rainfall will also affect runoff, since as the soil or other ground surfaces become saturated, further penetration will be limited. Almost all the water falling on an impermeable rooftop or roadway will need to be accommodated as runoff, while typically 20% will run off a lawn or domesticated landscape, and there will be almost no runoff from woods or sandy areas. On a vegetated sloped surface, water will sheet-drain for about 100 m (320 ft), but by 150 m (500 ft) will begin to cut rivulets. Managing runoff so that soil is not lost is an important objective.

As a first cut, a quick estimate can be made of the runoff from a site using average coefficients of runoff for typical urban development types. A more accurate estimate of runoff requires parsing the footprint of the site by surface materials. Remember that the site is also part of a larger drainage basin, with water from adjacent sites being added to the site's drainage requirements. The peak rate of runoff for the site itself can be computed using the *rational method*:

$Q = ciA$,
or with metric measurements,
$Q = ciA / 360$,
where
Q = peak rate of runoff in cubic feet per second (or m^3/sec),
c = runoff coefficient,
i = average intensity of rainfall for the time of concentration (T_c) for a selected design storm in in/hr (or mm/hr),
A = drainage area in ac (or ha).

Most sites have several types of surfaces—roofs, paved areas, areas of planting, and undeveloped areas—and to make an accurate projection of runoff a composite coefficient (C) needs to be calculated. Determining the average intensity of rainfall (i) is a matter of climate and policy, and local government engineering offices are the source. If there is no official policy, tables may be consulted that indicate the intensity for storms lasting between an hour and 24 hours.

With these numbers in hand, it is simple to compute the amount of water that must be accommodated on a site using the rational method. The rational method has been used for over a century and tends to be reasonably accurate in watersheds of less than 200 acres (80 ha) in which natural or man-made storage is small.

Table 25.1 | Typical runoff coefficients

	Runoff coefficient (C)
By type of area	
Business district	
Downtown	0.70–0.95
Neighborhood	0.50–0.70
Residential area	
Single-family	0.30–0.50
Semidetached	0.40–0.60
Attached townhouses	0.60–0.75
Large-lot single-family	0.25–0.40
Apartments	0.50–0.70
Industrial area	
Light industry	0.50–0.80
Heavy industry	0.60–0.90
Parks, cemeteries	0.10–0.25
Playgrounds	0.20–0.35
Undeveloped land	0.10–0.30
By character of surface	
Pavement	
Asphalt and concrete (standard)	0.70–0.90
Porous asphalt	0.25–0.35
Brick on asphalt	0.75–0.85
Brick or block on sand	0.30–0.35
Open-cell grass pavers	0.15–0.40
Lawns, sandy soil	
Flat, <2% slope	0.05–0.10
Average, 2–7% slope	0.10–0.15
Steep, >7% slope	0.15–0.20
Lawns, heavy soil	
Flat, <2% slope	0.13–0.17
Average, 2–7% slope	0.18–0.22
Steep, >7% slope	0.25–0.35
Roofs, asphalt or membrane	0.75–0.95
Green roofs	
Depth <10 cm (4 in)	0.45–0.55
Depth 10–20 cm (4–8 in)	0.30–0.45
Depth 20–40 cm (8–16 in)	0.20–0.30
Vegetated areas	
Flat, <2% slope	0.10–0.15
Average, 2–7% slope	0.15–0.20
Steep, >7% slope	0.20–0.25

Various sources.

Estimating Runoff from a Site

Computing the peak rate of runoff using the *rational method*:

As an example, for a 10 ac site with 20% coverage by impermeable rooftops, 15% coverage by driveways and parking areas, 25% coverage by lawns, and 40% wooded areas, the separate runoff coefficients (C) would be:

2 ac × 0.85 = 1.70,
1.5 ac × 0.80 = 1.20,
2.5 ac × 0.18 = 0.45,
4 ac × 0.10 = 0.40,

and the combined runoff coefficient for the site would be:

3.75 / 10 ac = 0.38.

If the 10-year design storm has a 24-hour depth of 5.3 in, the average intensity of the design storm is 0.16 (from an intensity chart). Then

Q = 0.38 × 0.16 × 10 = 0.608 cfs.

If the entire volume of water falling on the site in a day (beyond what is absorbed) needs to be retained on the site, the size of a retention area would need to be:

1 cfs for 24 hours = 1.9835 acre-ft,
0.608 cfs = 1.2 acre-ft,

or slightly more than one acre filled to a depth of one foot.

25.8 Estimating runoff from a site. (Adam Tecza/Gary Hack)

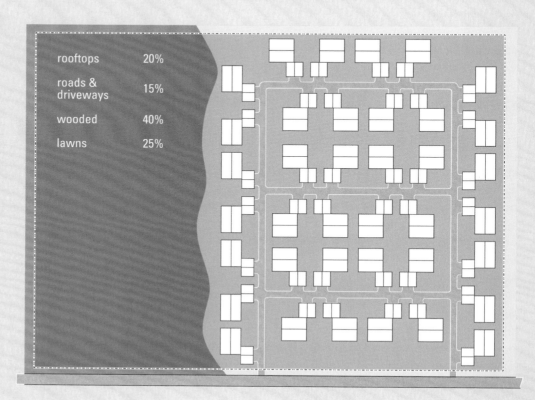

rooftops	20%
roads & driveways	15%
wooded	40%
lawns	25%

The art of planning for runoff involves striking a balance between water that is retained for recharge into the groundwater, used for irrigation of landscape, and detained or retained in water bodies created on the site. Retaining water indiscriminately can be hazardous, as on roadways that freeze in the evening, or can prevent use of sites, as on playfields that turn into mud bowls after each storm. Hence, a minimum slope should be provided for most surfaces on a site. Planted areas or broad paved areas should have a slope of 1%, although broad open areas where some ponding is tolerable could be sloped as little as 0.5%. Streets and other paved surfaces that are laid to exact elevations may also have a minimum grade of 0.5%. Land should slope away from buildings at a minimum grade of 2%, to allow for some settlement of soil after construction. Planted drainage swales and open ditches also should have a minimum grade of 2% to drain properly, and should not exceed 5% to prevent erosion. Lawns and grass banks can have a maximum slope of 25%; steeper slopes are not only subject to soil loss but also difficult to maintain. When unmowed planted slopes exceed 50%, cribbing or retaining walls need to be considered.

Overland Drainage Systems

Once the quantity of water to be handled on a site has been estimated, a network of channels needs to be designed to transport it to storage areas, *infiltration zones*, or *discharge locations*. These channels may be above or belowground, but there are many advantages to transporting water overland. Using *vegetated swales* as channels allows water to be cleansed as it flows, and the swales themselves are able to hold runoff and slow the rate of discharge from a site. Swales can irrigate the areas along them, supporting vegetation and wildlife. Like any water bodies, however, large drainage courses can pose hazards to children, and may need to be designed so that they can be closed off following large storms.

Drainage channels should be laid at a grade of at least 1%, and should have sides with a slope of 2:1 or flatter, preferably at least 3:1. Where the grade exceeds 2%, check dams may be needed to slow the flow and allow for infiltration of water into the ground. While the size of drainage channels may vary from modest

25.9 Vegetated swale, NewBridge community, Dedham, Massachusetts.
(Gary Hack)

25.10 Qian'an Sanlihe Greenway, a drainage channel serving the surrounding developments in Qian'an, Hebei Province, China.
(Courtesy of Turenscape)

25.11 Drainage course designed to slow water flow rate and filter it on a steep hillside, Bel Air Crest, Los Angeles.
(Gary Hack)

ditches at side of a roadway to large watercourses that retain water much of the year, they should typically have flat bottoms at least 60 cm (2 ft) wide to allow for maintenance. Geotextiles may need to be installed to prevent erosion of the channel while the vegetation is becoming established. Strategic placement of check dams along the channel will assist in removing sediments from the water, and slow its movement when slopes exceed 2%. In areas of excessive slope, it may be necessary to line the entire cross section with rock (riprap) to prevent the erosion of the channel and slow the flow.

Where overland watercourses cross roadways, culverts or bridges will need to be installed to maintain the flow. Normally culverts are made of steel-reinforced plastic or corrugated metal and are circular in cross section, although when very large an oval shape may be preferred. They should typically cross a roadway at right angles, and their inlets and outlets need to be finished with rock to prevent water from undermining the roadway. Where possible, culverts are laid with a minimum grade of 0.5% and a maximum grade of 8–10%. They need to be sufficiently below the roadway and covered with crushed rock to prevent being destroyed by vehicles passing above.

Detention and Retention

The best strategy for managing water on a site is always putting it to productive use. If it is captured and stored in sanitary tanks, it can become the source of potable water, which is especially important in locations that lack reliable and affordable water supply. Another obvious use is recharging the groundwater system. Rainfall may also become the source of water for irrigation, either directly or by storing it from wet to dry periods. Water can be used for cooling or heating occupied spaces (see chapter 30), or stored in ponds for recreation or agriculture. Many of these purposes require land to be set aside for storage, which can have an important influence on the plan for a site.

In sizing detention areas and drainage channels, the amount of water falling on the site needs to be converted into an estimate of the amount that would accumulate over a day. The rational formula above provides an estimate of the flow rate, and a rough equivalence between rates of flow and volumes is:

25.12 Rain garden allowing infiltration of runoff from roadway, Los Angeles.
(Los Angeles Department of Water and Power)

25.13 Bioswale, Kronsberg residential area, Hannover, Germany.
(© Atelier Rambol Dreisetl)

1 m³/sec = 43,200 m³ per day or 4.3 ha-m per day,
1 cu ft/sec = approximately 43,200 cu ft per day or 11.9 ac-in per day.

Some cities specify the fraction of rainfall that must be retained, or the rate of discharge of stormwater from a site. As we have noted, Philadelphia's requirement that the first 1 in (25 mm) of rainfall be retained on a site inevitably forces most urban sites to employ some form of storage. Other cities limit runoff from a site to predevelopment rates, and the volume of water that must be retained to be discharged later can be estimated by using the rational method and comparing predevelopment and after-development coefficients of runoff.

Centralized storage is not the only option for retaining water on a site. Water may be used to recharge the groundwater through trenches or recharge wells. Other possibilities focus on retention close to the sources of runoff by creating green roofs, rain gardens near roofs, parking areas, and roadways, or vegetated bioswales. Properly designed, each of these can become an element of the landscape of a site.

Permeable Pavement

Recharging the groundwater on a site is an important objective, since buildings and pavement that occupy sites limit the opportunities for water penetration, and newly planted trees and vegetation make demands on subsurface water. One of the simplest ways to recharge groundwater is to switch from impervious to pervious pavements. The materials used must meet the tests of carrying the loads on them (vehicles and people), maintenance and replacement, all so simply solved when conventional concrete is poured or asphalt laid.

There are many types of permeable materials that serve this purpose, including:

Permeable concrete—concrete created with little or no fine aggregate, so that water can penetrate through the voids. It is suitable for modest traffic loads, as in residential areas.

25.14 Permeable asphalt, unit pavers, and rain garden eliminate the need for storm drainage system in parking area, Phipps Conservatory, Pittsburgh.
(Courtesy of Phipps Conservatory)

Porous asphalt—asphalt created with coarse aggregate so that water penetrates. It can be used on roadways, where it improves safety because of its coarse texture. It is widely used on sidewalks in Japan.

Compacted gravel—compacted large-aggregate gravel or stone chippings without any binder is adequate for low traffic volumes, parking areas, and parallel parking lanes along roadways. Dressed with gravel dust, it makes for an excellent pedestrian way.

Unit pavers—made of concrete, brick, or asphalt, these can carry surprisingly heavy traffic volumes. A large variety of shapes and colors are available.

Recycled-glass porous pavement—elastomeric-bound postconsumer glass with binding agents is available as an alternative to conventional paving.

Reinforced grass—a variety of systems are available to reinforce turf so that it can bear the weight of traffic, including concrete lattice blocks, PVC matrixes, and belowground metal or plastic fabric. They make an excellent surface for parking areas, and have the added advantage of counteracting heat island effects.

Green Roofs

Green roofs (also known as *living roofs*) serve the several purposes of insulating the structure below from heat and cold, absorbing and using rainwater, and reducing the heat island effect in urban areas. They are also a delight to look at from above, and can make a rooftop an amenity. They come at a price, however: the expense and trouble of building and maintaining a rooftop compared to considering it out of sight and out of mind.

Creating and installing green roofs is by now a well-refined art, with specialized materials available to provide a membrane and matrix for planting (ZinCo, n.d.). The challenges include supporting the added weight of soil, vegetation, and the water they store; keeping vegetation alive in climates with lengthy dry spells or with heavy seasonal monsoons; and dealing with climate extremes of cold or heat. Generally, there are two approaches to sustainable roofs: *extensive green roofs* that aim for a planting regime that is consistent across the surface and capable of being maintained with

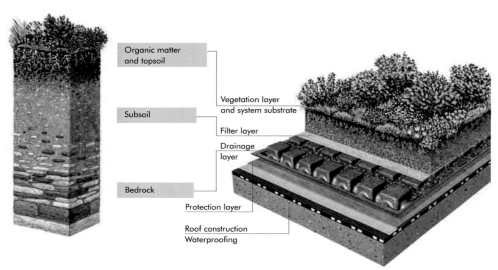

25.15 Extensive green roof covering 10.4 ac (4.2 ha), River Rouge plant, Ford Motor Company, Detroit, Michigan. (Courtesy of Xero Flor America)

25.16 Intensive green roof over shopping area, International Finance Center, Chengdu, China. (Gary Hack)

25.17 Reproducing the natural profile of soil in green roof installation. (Courtesy of © ZinCo GmbH)

Organic matter and topsoil

Subsoil

Bedrock

Vegetation layer and system substrate

Filter layer

Drainage layer

Protection layer

Roof construction
Waterproofing

minimal human effort; or *intensive green roofs*, with lush landscape that creates a garden-like environment.

Extensive green roofs typically employ perennials capable of growing in dry or semidry climates, such as alpine conditions, or on rock outcrops. These include, for the US, sedums, prickly pear, yarrow, phlox, and various wildflower blends. In Europe, sedums are also widely used, along with stonecrops, iceplants, and native wildflowers. There are a variety of methods for creating a green roof, but each typically includes a roof barrier, then a protection mat, then a drainage element to allow excess moisture to be collected, then a filter sheet, then 7–12 cm (3–5 in) of engineered soil which provides the medium for growth (Weiler and Scholz-Barth 2009). Studies have demonstrated that a green roof with such composition can retain 50% or more of annual precipitation (Berhage et al. 2009).

Intensive green roofs require considerably more soil, although it may be engineered to minimize its weight, in order to support more lush vegetation. Typically they incorporate grasses and other perennials that may require irrigation to sustain them. Hence, they may be designed with rain collection and storage systems, ensuring that no water is wasted. Usually, intensive green roofs are designed to be occupied as decks or places for enjoyment.

Cisterns and Tanks

Cisterns are used for storage of water that is dedicated to landscape irrigation or heating and cooling of buildings, or for detention of stormwater that will ultimately be discharged into watercourses. They can be aboveground tanks capturing roof runoff, which allows irrigation with little or no pumping. This may be the best solution for small structures, or for large buildings in dense urban areas (where they are enclosed within the structure). But for larger sites they are typically located belowground and usually constructed

25.18 Stormwater storage area under recreation area, Los Angeles.
(Los Angeles Department of Water and Power)

25.19 Stormwater storage installation under parking area in shopping center.
(Courtesy of CULTEC Inc.)

of concrete, sometimes with steel lining to minimize maintenance. A good location is often below parking areas, tennis courts, or playfields where they can be easily reached for maintenance and repair.

Subsurface areas can also be used for temporary storage of storm drainage, then emptied in dry seasons when rivers or streams are flowing below capacity. If a site development cannot avoid displacing wetlands or areas within the 100-year storm line, installing belowground storage areas can offset the capacity of the area displaced.

There are dozens of manufactured systems available for this purpose. In simplest form, ganging together corrugated metal pipes can serve the purpose. More sophisticated systems include modular precast concrete boxes, PVC pipes that can be bent to form a continuous coil, and modular PVC elements.

Infiltration

If the soils are adequate, a good solution for runoff is injecting the water into the soil matrix. Since soil cannot absorb intense rainfall—which is why it runs off—it is necessary to create a storage chamber that detains water and allows it to infiltrate into the soil over an extended period of time.

An *infiltration basin* or *bioretention basin* is an apparently simple solution, but it is wickedly difficult to design. It will only work in permeable soils that allow between 1 cm and 8 cm (0.5 and 3 in) infiltration per hour. The soils should have no more than 20% clay content and less than 40% silt/clay content. The bottom of the infiltration basin should be kept at least 1.3 m (4 ft) above the seasonal high groundwater elevation to reduce the risk of contamination. Accommodating runoff from parking lots or major roadways through *vegetated swales* can also deal with the impurities that find their way to their surfaces. Typically they are designed to absorb a 25 mm (1 in) storm, while allowing the 10-year stormwater to move through the swale without causing erosion. Water should generally not exceed 450 mm (18 in) in depth, and where the slope of a swale is more than 3%, check dams need to be designed to assure that solids are filtered and to prevent erosion. Swales may be grassed or may be

treated as linear wetlands, trapping sediments and pollutants.

A well-designed grass swale can remove over 90% of suspended solids and nitrogen (fertilizer runoff), 67% or more of phosphorus, and 80–90% of metals (Claytor and Schueler 1996). In areas where salt and sand are used on roadways in winter, species need to be selected that are salt-tolerant or that have phytoremediation properties. Roadway swales are less expensive to build and maintain than curbs, gutters, and underground piping, and are generally effective for drainage areas of 2 ha (5 ac) or less. Ultimately the most difficult problem is how to deal with safety issues of an area that quickly may fill to dangerous depths (short of fencing it), and how to make an area attractive that may be dry much of the year while wet at other times. One solution is planting grasses that absorb the water while providing an attractive cover (New Jersey Department of Environmental Protection 2016).

For infiltrating small or modest volumes of water, another good solution is a *dry well*, consisting of a vertical concrete or PVC pipe with perforations, filled with and surrounded by coarse gravel. Dry wells also must be kept at least 1.3 m (4 ft) above the high water table, to ensure that impurities are filtered before entering the groundwater. In small spaces, such as alleyways, it may be possible to inject all the runoff directly into the soil, obviating the need for storm drainage.

Greater capacity for infiltration may be gained by installing an *infiltration trench*, or filter *drain*, or *French drain*. Located just below the surface, it collects water from pervious surfaces and pipes it along the trench so that it infiltrates the soil over an extended distance. A variation is an infiltration trench that receives surface water along its length through pea gravel or compacted sand at the surface. This may underlay a pathway or parking area, doing double duty. Using perforated pipe

25.20 Bioretention pond, absorbing runoff from parking areas and roadways.
(Courtesy of Enviro-utilities, Inc.)

25.21 Dry well infiltration system for alleyways, Philadelphia.
(Philadelphia Water Department)

25.22 French drain system, or infiltration trench, created along major pathways on a site.
(chiroassociates.us)

laid in several parallel rows in an infiltration bed, a substantial quantity of water can be disposed of.

All of this assumes that the soils are adequate to accept the quantities of water that will be injected, and that the water reaching the trench or field has been largely purged of silt and fine particles that will clog the system over time. Soils must be tested to assure that they are adequate, and a simple method can be used to test initial feasibility. This involves placing a 5 in diameter 36 in casing to a depth 24 in below the proposed facility bottom and monitoring the rate of absorption, averaging several trials. This rate should be at least 10 mm (0.4 in) per hour, or double that rate to provide a margin of error. Not all soils are adequate for infiltration—the soils may be too weighted toward clay or silt, the water table may be too high, or large trees may have root structures that prevent installation of trenches. Climates with frequent freeze-thaw reversals, or locations where the ground freezes to a depth of 1 m

(3 ft) or more may not be appropriate, since the trench will not be available for infiltration during the spring melt, when it is most needed.

Underground Storm Drainage

Despite the advantages of managing stormwater through green infrastructure, the majority of large sites continue to install underground piped stormwater systems to meet all or part of their needs. In dense urban areas these may be the only practical alternative for dealing with excess water beyond what can be used on the site. For most site development projects, stormwater facilities are the largest single infrastructure investment.

The technology of underground storm drainage has changed little over the past century, although new materials make installation and maintenance less costly

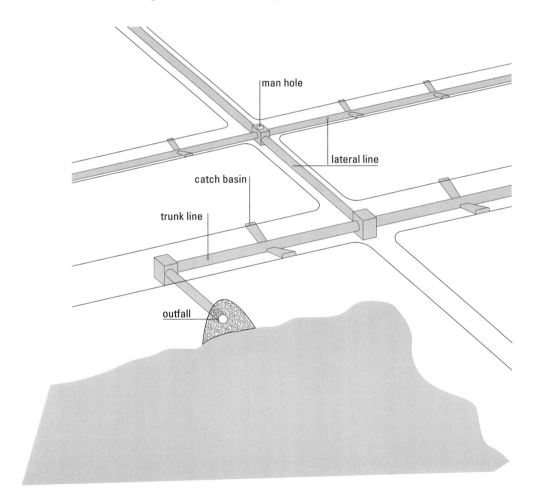

25.23 Diagram of typical underground storm drainage system. (Adam Tecza/Gary Hack)

and more efficient. The typical system consists of *catch basins* on streets, paved areas, and low-lying locations, *lateral lines* which accept the water from these sources, *drain lines* or *conduits* that transport it, *manholes* at key junction points that provide access to the system, and *collector sewers* which transport the water to *outfalls* along water bodies. Storm sewer systems normally function by gravity and typically require at least a 0.5% slope to operate, which creates the burden on the site planner to align the underground network with the topography of a site. It is possible to create pumping stations that move stormwater from one watershed to another, but these are costly to build and operate.

Catch basins

With a generous crown and a good gutter (or vegetated swale) along a roadway, water can flow some distance before being collected in a catch basin or trapped inlet. Usually this should not exceed 250–300 m (800–1,000 ft), and water should not have to flow across intersecting roadways before reaching the inlet. While the normal layout collects water from each side of a roadway and locates the storm drainage conduit in the center, for narrow roads it is possible to place catch basins on only one side, and in climates without excessive rain or the threat of freezing, water may be collected at the center of the roadway. Catch basins have a grate to block large debris from entering, and may be designed with traps to collect solids before water drains into the system.

In many countries with heavy rainfall and modest resources, shallow *drainage boxes* are located along the curb, accepting water continuously. Covered with precast concrete lids, they are easy to clean out and serve the purpose well.

Conduits

Storm sewer lines have historically been constructed of 1–2 m segments of vitreous clay or concrete pipes, joined to form straight or gently curving conduits, with the curves at least 60 m (200 ft) in radius. Newer materials include PVC pipes that can extend for much longer distances and curve more tightly around corners. However, large collector lines are invariably made of concrete sections with a minimum dimension of 300 mm (12 in).

25.24 Underground storm sewers, such as this PVC line being installed in Mexico, are generally the most costly infrastructure element on a site.
(© Thomas Castelazo/Wikipedia Commons)

In cold climates, lateral and collector lines need to be at least 1.2 m (4 ft) below the surface to avoid freezing. They need to have a minimum slope to ensure that the pipe is kept clean by flows. The slope depends upon the roughness and dimensions of the pipe, but in general laterals should have at least a 0.3% gradient and main lines at least 0.5%. As a starting point, the minimum velocity of flow should be taken as 60 cm per sec (2 fps) when flowing full, which will provide for sufficient speed when lines are only partially full, and the slope should not yield velocities of over 3 m per second (10 ft/sec), to avoid scouring the pipe lining.

One approach to designing underground storm lines, which may seem counterintuitive, is to oversize pipes and use them to store storm runoff so it can be discharged into rivers or streams gradually over time. While this adds to the cost, in dense areas where detention basins are not possible, it may be a cost-effective solution for meeting zero net runoff regulations.

Manholes

Underground pipes require access for inspection and cleaning, usually via a manhole. Manholes also are critical when lines change direction and can be clogged by deposits, and in locations where higher-level pipes enter the system and water must be dropped to lower-level pipes. The elevation of the lowest level on the internal surface of a pipe is generally referred to as the *invert*, and as a system is laid out, the inverts will provide the means for estimating slopes and flow rates.

Manholes are typically 1 m (3 ft) in diameter, and usually made of precast concrete with metal tops. Most communities seek to standardize their design for convenience of maintenance, although drop manholes may need to be custom-ordered. The maximum manhole spacing is generally set at 120 m (400 ft) for pipes up to 600 mm (24 in), while with larger pipes they can be spaced up to 180 m (600 ft) apart. Some communities allow them to be 240 m (800 ft) apart for 600 mm pipes, and as much as 610 m (2,000 ft) for pipes 1,370 mm (54 in) or larger. The variability has much to do with the necessity for cleanout—in snowy climates where sand is used on streets in winter, cleaning of storm sewer lines will need to be more frequent. Many municipalities use automated equipment to inspect and clean storm drainage lines.

Discharge Outlets

Storm sewer systems are designed as branching networks with increased pipe sizes as water is collected, mimicking the streams and rivers they replace. In areas with little topographic variation, the designer will need to work backward from the elevation where water will be discharged to establish the inverts of branches of the network. If it is not possible to create reasonable gradients, lift stations may be required before water is discharged. Where water is discharged into a stream or river, the design will need to take account of seasonal or storm fluctuation of the water line of the receiving body. In extreme situations, such as in New Orleans or Bangkok, where much of the settlement is below the high-water mark in rivers, a sophisticated system of detention and pumping will be required to handle major storms. Under any circumstance, stormwater outlets need to be protected from intrusion by people and wildlife, while providing access for equipment to survey and repair major trunk lines.

Underground storm drainage systems do not enjoy the benefits of improving water quality that are provided by open-air bioswales and other natural drainage courses. In some situations the quality of the storm drainage may need to be improved before discharging it into lakes or streams. This is a demanding problem, made even more difficult by the surges of runoff at the outlet of systems. The Sherbourne Common treatment facility in Toronto is an example of how this can be accomplished, while also providing much-needed recreation facilities for a neighborhood. The treatment system consists of two belowground UV reactors with a combined capacity of 140 l/sec (3.2 Mgd); above is a multiuse community park that features the treated water before it is discharged into Lake Ontario. Three delightful play sculptures are a constant reminder of the special role that water plays in the city.

25.25 Headhouse for stormwater treatment facility, Sherbourne Common Park, Toronto.
(© Randall Croft/Wikimedia Commons)

25.26 A thin veil of treated water cascades down from three art sculptures, then passes through a 240 m long biofiltration channel before being discharged into Lake Ontario, Sherbourne Common Park, Toronto.
(© Stephen Allen/Wikimedia Commons)

26 | Water Supply

Adequate and safe drinking water is among the basic necessities of life, along with food and shelter. How much water and how it is delivered vary considerably across the globe as a result of differences in climate, lifestyle, culture, technology, and the economy of settlements. Water can be supplied from backyard wells, cisterns harvesting rainwater, or by large public systems employing desalination, storage reservoirs, treatment plants, and piped water networks. With water shortages throughout the world and climate change making supplies of water increasingly unreliable, cities are looking to conservation and reuse to reduce water needs. Much can be accomplished through sustainable approaches, on all scales of sites.

Water Needs

Water consumption levels vary considerably across the globe, driven by availability, pricing, and cultural differences. Even within countries there can be large variation. To put things in perspective, in the US the generation of thermoelectric power uses 45% of the water consumed each year, followed closely by agriculture and aquaculture at 35%. Urban and household uses consume about 13% (Barber 2014).

Across the US, indoor domestic water consumption averages about 70 gallons per day per person (gpd/p) (265 lpd/p) for food preparation, drinking water, bathing, laundry, and other uses. However, there are large differences between cities in the consumption of water on residential sites as a result of use of water in cooling, landscape irrigation, car washing, street cleaning, maintaining swimming pools, and other activities. These can easily double the consumption per capita. Older dense urban areas such as New York and Philadelphia average around 85 gpd/p (322 lpd/p) in total daily consumption, while in sprawling new metropolitan areas such as Denver or Phoenix, domestic consumption averages 160–180

Table 26.1 | Typical US daily household consumption of water (US EPA)

Activity	Rate of water use	gpd/p	lpd/p
Indoor			
Shower	1.5 g/min (5.7 l/min)	12	45
Laundry	28 g/load (106 l/load)	15	57
Toilets	1.6 g/flush (5.7 l/flush)	19	72
Sinks	6 g/sink (23 l/sink)	11	42
Leaks and other		13	49
Outdoor, all uses		30	114
Daily total		100	379

Source: EPA, "Water Sense," http://www3.epa.gov/watersense/pubs/indoor.html.

Table 26.2 | Comparative residential water consumption

City	l/p/d	g/p/d
US		
New York	327	86
Philadelphia	318	84
Houston	273	72
Phoenix	671	177
Salt Lake City	682	180
Seattle	326	86
Boston	155	41
San Francisco	216	57
Denver	682	180
Canada		
Waterloo	284	75
Toronto	257	68
Vancouver	295	78
Australia		
Melbourne	200	52
Sydney	215	56
Countrywide urban areas	270	65
UK		
Cambridge	149	39
London	157	41
Wales	157	41
Denmark, Copenhagen	131	35
Norway, Oslo	200	53
Germany, countrywide urban areas	115	30
Israel, Jerusalem	119	31
China		
Tianjin	89	23
Beijing	138	36
Hong Kong	219	58
Japan		
Tokyo	236	62
Fukuoka	202	53
Singapore	160	41
Vietnam, urban areas	70	18

Sources: Heaney, Wright, and Sample (2000); Hughes (2000); Walton (2010); International Water Association (2010), Zhang and Brown (2005).

gpd/p (606–682 lpd/p) (Walton 2010; Maupin et al. 2014). Residents of detached single-family houses typically consume much more water than their counterparts in multifamily units. In Toronto, as an example, single-family residents consume an average of 320 lpd/p (84 gpd/p) while multifamily residents average only 191 lpd/p (50 gpd/p) (City of Toronto 2002). In most cities residential water consumption represents 40–60% of total water use, the balance consumed by industry, institutions, service establishments, and maintenance of the public realm. "Non-revenue water," even on well-managed systems, can average 15–20% for purposes that include street cleaning, parks, irrigation, firefighting, sewer rehabilitation, illegal connections, as well as water lost through system leakage or breaks. The consumption of water also varies considerably across the year. Where there are distinct climate differences between summer and winter, demand peaks during summer months and can easily be 150–170% of daily needs averaged over the whole year.

About 70% of the water delivered to users finds its way into the sewer system or into on-site treatment facilities or disposal systems. In most communities, water is too valuable a commodity to be used only once, and recycling is now broadly accepted—but only occasionally practiced.

On-Site Water Sources

Internationally, about half the water used in urban areas comes from *surface water* sources, about half is from *groundwater*, and a small fraction is created through *desalination*. However, in any particular community, the sources will depend upon natural resources and the willingness to make capital investments to obtain, store, treat, and distribute water.

If densities are low and the soil or air is not contaminated, the simplest way to obtain water is to exploit resources on a site. Rainwater may be collected from rooftops and stored in tanks or cisterns for use by occupants of the site. If it is used for human consumption, the collection surfaces will need to be free of bacterial contamination. Water collected from parking areas or other runoff will generally not meet this test, but can be used for irrigation and other purposes.

If on-site water is the only source, enough water needs to be collected and stored to account for periods

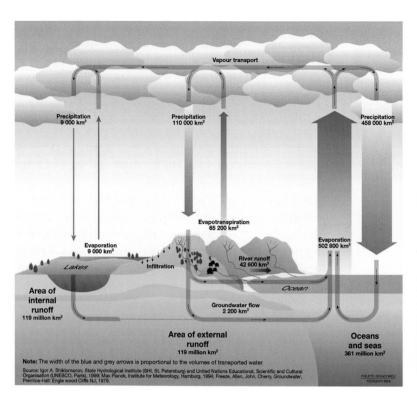

of prolonged drought—one standard is to provide for the equivalent of a *100-year-occurrence drought*. Local climate data will help establish the minimum annual rainfall over long periods, and this can be compared to the capacity to collect water from rooftops and estimates of consumption. Ideally, the amount of water that can be collected and stored and consumption estimates should be modeled over several years including a prolonged drought. However, a quick check can be made by employing the following formula:

$$V = RA \times AAR \times CR \times 0.5,$$
where
V = approximate volume of water to be accumulated in gallons,
RA = roof area in sq ft,
AAR = average annual rainfall in inches,
CR = capture rate accounting for evaporation, typically 0.62 gal/sq ft/in of rainfall on roofs,
0.5 = 50% rule providing for storage of half of the water that can be collected in an average year (based on experience).

26.1 The water cycle.
(UN Environment Program)

26.2 Harvesting rainwater from rooftop, Lanxmeer, Culemborg, Netherlands.
(Gary Hack)

On large sites, particularly with uses that have large roof areas with low consumption (such as industrial or office uses in a mixed-use development that includes housing), it may make sense to create shared *storage reservoirs*, *cisterns*, or water tanks that serve the entire site. This means installing a water collection system as well as a water distribution network.

The other source of water on a site is groundwater tapped through wells. This may also be done on an individual or a collective basis, depending on densities and the cost of extracting groundwater. Wells are typically drilled and lined with metal or concrete pipe, and powered by submersible pumps.

In low-density residential areas, individual wells may be practical, although they must be sited carefully both to exploit groundwater and to ensure they

26.3 Rainwater harvesting cistern, Monterrey Institute of Technology.
(Monterrey Institute of Technology and Higher Education/ Wikimedia Commons)

are away from sources of contamination. Typically a residential well needs to be capable of extracting 35 to 190 lpm (10 to 50 gpm), although with conservation efforts these figures could be 30% lower. Wells need to be sited on relatively high points to avoid contamination from runoff, and should be at least 30 m (100 ft) from any *septic disposal field* and 15 m (50 ft) from the high-water mark of a surface water body or stream. For sites located on salt water, wells should be located as far as possible from the shoreline and need to be deep enough to draw water from strata well below those with saltwater intrusion.

Wells extracting more than 200 lpm (50 gpm) need to be further away from potential contaminant. They should be 200 ft or more from any disposal field, at least 75 ft from the high-water mark of surface water bodies, and need to be protected from any source of pollution.

Public Water Supply

Public water supplies commonly tap water resources from rivers and lakes, drawing on water basins located many miles from the settlements being served. Since the Romans, water has been transported hundreds of miles to cities via *aqueducts* and underground pipes. Phoenix and Tucson draw much of their water supply

from the Colorado River, via the 330 mi (530 km) long Central Arizona Project canal; and the Colorado River Aqueduct traverses 242 mi (390 km) to provide water to Los Angeles and Southern California. Safeguarding the quality of water at the source and while it is transported is a major preoccupation of all public water systems. Use of salt on roadways is generally prohibited or restricted near reservoirs, and development regulations commonly restrict the use of nitrogen and other compounds that might find their way into the water supply.

Other cities draw their water from nearby streams and rivers, although the water quality of urban rivers is usually not high enough to use directly. The tradeoff for saving money on transporting water to a community is the necessity of *water treatment.*

Many communities use wells to provide their water supply, often in locations some miles from settlements to protect the quality of water. The wells may tap aquifers well below the surface, and depending upon the strata of soils they pass through, may impose a risk of subsidence. Some areas of Bangkok that rely on wells for water supply and industrial operations have experienced *subsidence* of 5 to 10 cm (2 to 4 in) per year, damaging structures and roads and confounding the city's ability to deal with storm drainage during annual monsoons. Large-scale pumping needs to be calibrated to the ability to recharge *aquifers* through penetration of water through the surface layers.

26.4 Central Arizona Project canal.
(Arizona Department of Water Resources)

26.5 Al Shuaibah FO-RO (forward osmosis/reverse osmosis) hybrid desalination plant, Shuaibah, Saudi Arabia. (Doosan Heavy Industries and Construction)

26.6 Reverse osmosis package plant by Quimpac de Colombia, S.A. (Paola Archila/Wikimedia Commons)

26.7 Small-scale desalination plant run by solar power, Oman. (Courtesy of Robert Kyriakides)

Many locations have neither adequate rainfall nor groundwater resources to support settlement. Large portions of the Middle East as well as islands such as Aruba rely upon *desalination* for all or portions of their water supply. There are several processes to convert salt water to freshwater, including *distillation*, *ion exchange*, *reverse osmosis* and other membrane processes, and *solar desalination*. What they have in common is the need for large amounts of energy and expensive infrastructure, making desalination the most costly way to acquire water. Use of solar energy for desalination is gradually changing the equation. Until recently, it was only cost-effective to construct large plants for desalination, but recent advances in reverse osmosis and distillation technologies have resulted in small-package systems that have been installed in hotels, campgrounds, city parks, institutions, and industrial areas. These systems typically provide 60–1,000 m³/d (15,000–250,000 gpd) of water of drinking water quality. They are frequently used for temporary water supply in construction areas, but may also serve as permanent facilities for hotels, residential developments, and institutions.

Water Treatment

Water that is drawn from polluted streams or contaminated runoff or is recycled will need to be purified before it is adequate for consumption. Depending on the composition of the water and what it is to be used for, it may require physical processes such as *filtration* and *sedimentation*, *biological processes*, *chemical treatment*, or *electromagnetic radiation*. Municipal water treatment plants typical employ several of these processes.

Screen filters are used to remove large debris from water that is drawn from rivers, and storage in reservoirs will allow some of the heavy materials to settle out before treatment. Usually groundwater does not need this coarse screening. Water that is excessively hard will be adjusted by adding sodium carbonate (soda ash) or by employing reverse osmosis membranes. Fine or slow sand filters will remove the small particles that remain. Removing harmful microbes generally requires water to be chlorinated or subjected to ozone; the latter is more costly but produces fewer dangerous byproducts. In many areas, fluoride is also added to help prevent tooth decay among the population being

26.8 Residuals processing center at Delecarlia Reservoir, supplying water to Washington, DC.
(US Army Corps of Engineers)

served. All of these processes are housed within large municipal water treatment plants, and water emerges to be distributed to consumers who have little knowledge of what it has taken to produce it.

It is also possible to decentralize water treatment to smaller water treatment plants that require minimal operator supervision. Package plants may be installed to provide 1,000–4,000 m³/d (0.250 to 1 million gpd). They employ technologies tailored to the water quality issues, including aeration, detention, filtration, *flocculation*, *UV disinfection*, and chemical processes. Package plants are especially useful for hard-to-reach locations such as resorts and industrial plants, but are also widely used in areas where the capacity of the water system cannot keep pace with development. Some institutions and hotels have installed package plants for final treatment of government water supplies that are not adequate to their standards of taste and smell.

Water Storage

Water awaiting distribution to consumers is typically stored in cisterns, reservoirs, or water tanks, above or belowground. Many houses in the Middle East, South Asia, and Brazil collect and store water in tanks on their rooftop, where it may also be heated by the sun. Apartment houses in New York also generally have water tanks that are filled by pumping from the municipal water system, providing a ready supply of water with

good pressure for use of the residents and for fire safety. Where there is a high-elevation location capable of housing a water tank or reservoir, this will suffice for an entire community. Lacking this, most small towns and cities construct water tanks that become their symbol on the skyline.

The *hydrostatic pressure* of water is 1 kilopascal (0.145 psi) of pressure for every 10.2 cm (4 in) of water. Thus elevating water to the height of 30 m (96 ft) produces roughly 300 kPa (43.5 psi), which is minimally adequate for most domestic water and distribution purposes. Many municipal codes require 310 kPa (45 psi), and New York requires 85 psi (586 kPa) in high-rise buildings. Accounting for line losses in pressure over long-distance distribution lines, water towers should probably be a minimum of 50 m (165 ft) high. Alternatively, booster pumps at the building or community level can supplement water pressure.

26.9 Rooftop water storage, Dharavi, Mumbai, India.
(Courtesy of David A. Smith/Affordable Housing Institute)

Where cisterns or water tanks are located belowground, they will need to rely on pumps to deliver water at adequate pressures. Underground cisterns have a long history dating to Neolithic sites of the Levant and Lebanese storage chambers that aided dry-land farming. There were huge underground chambers in Istanbul in the sixth century, and the Moors transported the techniques to Portugal and Spain. After a long period of neglect, cisterns are being rediscovered for rainwater harvesting in sustainable developments.

Contemporary cisterns are typically constructed either of reinforced concrete, sometimes with metal liners or acrylic surfaces, or out of PVC materials. The tanks may be coupled with water filters to ensure that no contamination is introduced. They need to be inspected regularly, and the quality of the water stored needs to be carefully monitored. They can serve as the primary water supply source, or as a backup source for irrigation and firefighting purposes.

26.10 Examples of local water tanks.
((top) Courtesy of Tank Engineering; (middle) Noblevmy/Wikimedia Commons; (bottom) schaoyz/Panoramio/Creative Commons)

26.11 Underground water storage tank.
(Courtesy of Buildipedia.com)

Distribution Systems

Water is distributed to end users through a network of pipes, valves, and meters. Historically the pipes were of wood, cast iron, or other metals; in recent years these have been supplanted by plastic or concrete. Plastic pipes have the advantage of being able to bend around corners, obviating the need for joints that are prone to leakage. In cold climates where the ground freezes, pipes need to be buried at least 1.2 m (4 ft) below the surface, and they should be located at least 3 m (10 ft) horizontally from lines carrying sewage or stormwater. Positive pressures in the water line help protect against intrusion of contaminants. Typically, main water lines are at least 10 cm (4 in) in diameter, although lateral lines serving individual houses or structures will be smaller, sized to the demand.

A well-designed water distribution system will be organized as a series of loops so that each user can be served from two directions. There are a variety of strategies for creating loops. In the event of a break in a water line, shutoff valves, spaced every 300 m (1,000 ft) or so, will allow water in the broken line to be shut off, and service shifted to the opposite direction. Water mains also provide service to hydrants for firefighting purposes. These are spaced no more than 300 m (1,000 ft) apart to allow hoses to reach any site, although some local governments limit these distances to 150 m (500 ft). Much will depend upon the type of equipment used for firefighting.

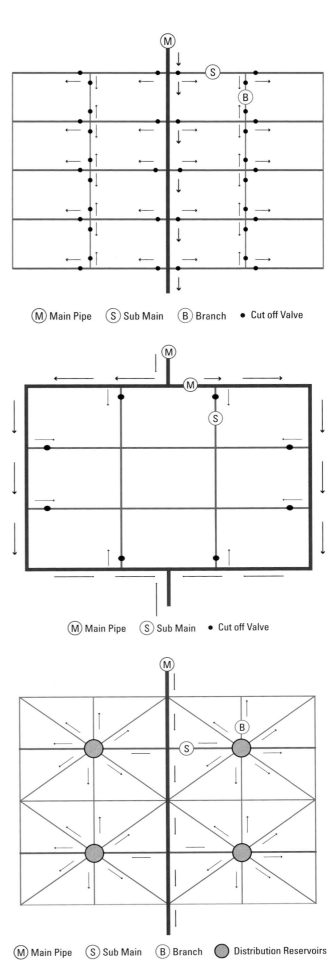

26.12 Water distribution loop strategies. (Adam Tecza/Gary Hack)

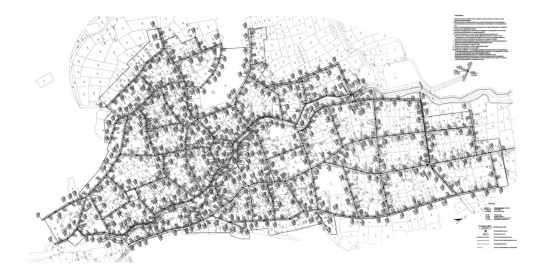

26.13 Water distribution network, Debrashtica village, Bulgaria. (RC Design)

Dual-Pipe Water Supply

Reclaimed water (*gray water*) from sewerage and water from runoff that may not meet drinking water standards can be a valuable resource for landscape, construction, agricultural, and other industrial purposes. If the water is of sufficient quality, it may also be used for toilet/urinal flushing, cooling towers, and fire protection systems. Its use requires the installation of a second water distribution network, and a careful monitoring system. Although expensive to install, a *dual-pipe system* can be important in areas where water restrictions limit development, and for serving heavy water users such as golf courses, greenhouses, parkways, and industrial uses. Dual-pipe systems are widely used in Australia, and several have been installed in the United States.

The main issues in planning for a dual-pipe system are how to apportion demand, the need to differentiate the two pipe systems (usually by color and signage), the location of each in a crowded street right-of-way (usually on opposite sides), and the need to provide adequate water pressure in each system. One disincentive to dual systems is minimum pipe standards in many communities that are larger than needed when water is supplied in two separate conduits. However, *purple pipe systems*—the usual color labeling of gray water pipes—represent the future of sustainable water supply (EPA Victoria 2005).

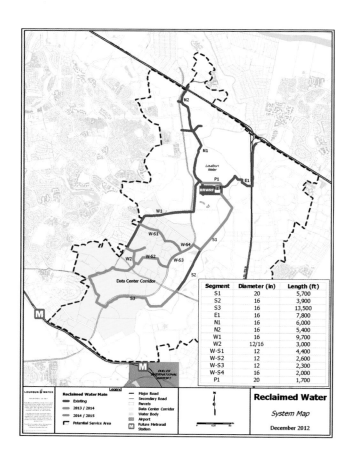

Segment	Diameter (in)	Length (ft)
S1	20	5,700
S2	16	3,900
S3	16	13,500
E1	16	7,800
N1	16	6,000
N2	16	5,400
W1	16	9,700
W2	12/16	3,000
W-S1	12	4,400
W-S2	12	2,600
W-S3	12	2,300
W-S4	16	2,000
P1	20	1,700

Figure 26.14 Reclaimed water system map, Loudoun, Virginia. (Loudoun Water Company)

26.15 Multiple residential water lines: standard hot and cold (red, blue), standard waste (white PVC), gray water (purple). (Courtesy of Terrano Plumbing)

An ideal use of gray water is for *drip irrigation*, in lieu of using potable water. In the simplest of applications, on residential lots, water is drawn off the tops of septic tanks after solids have settled out. It is then pumped through perforated pipes set in trenches with 150 mm (6 in) of gravel above and below, and covered by geotextile fabric. Above it sandy loam and seeded or sodded grass or other ground covers draw their nourishment from the gray water. Such systems are most appropriate in climates where temperatures do not go below freezing (Sustainable Sources 2014).

Effective water conservation involves both reduction of use and the most efficient ways of accomplishing its purposes.

27 | Wastewater Systems

We depend upon water for survival, but human life also requires an effective and safe way of disposing of our wastes. Much of it is in liquid form, collected from toilets, sinks, showers, and washing machines in the home, and through drains in industrial and commercial establishments. In urban areas it is collected in sewers and transported somewhere to be disposed of. The capacity for collection and disposal is a critical issue in planning sites. Many projects flounder on not having trunk lines available to connect to, or because the capacity of public waste treatment plants is inadequate to accommodate the development proposed. Planning for wastewater disposal needs to be a foreground issue, not an afterthought.

On-Site Disposal

Where the density is low and the disposal requirements are relatively light, liquid wastes may be taken care of on the site. The most common practice is the construction of a *disposal field* that allows the leaching of liquids into the soil. This involves two stages. Wastewater is deposited in a *septic* or *Imhoff tank* where the heavier materials settle out and less dense materials such as fats and oils float to the top. Then the liquid in the middle (gray water) is distributed through a network of perforated pipes into an underground disposal field where it bonds with the soil, and natural populations of soil microorganisms destroy any pathogens. Disposal tiles will typically be surrounded by 300–450 mm (12–18 in) of gravel, topped by 150 mm (6 in) of vegetated soil. Alternatively, the effluent may supply a drip irrigation system serving a wider area.

Septic systems are engineered to meet the demand and reflect the absorption capacity of the septic field. Soils in the field are tested by digging a test pit to the depth the infiltration tiles will lie, then filling it with water and timing its drop. There are a number of manuals and codes that correlate the absorption times with the size of the disposal field required (Gustafson and Machmeier 2013; Greywater Action, n.d.; South Australia Health Commission 1995). Typically disposal fields must be at least 600 mm (2 ft) above groundwater

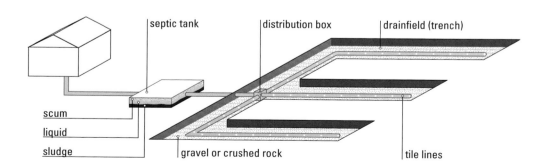

27.1 Domestic septic disposal system. (Adam Tecza/Gary Hack)

septic tank

distribution box

drainfield (trench)

scum

liquid

sludge

gravel or crushed rock

tile lines

27.2 High-capacity septic infiltration tiles. (Courtesy of Southern Water and Soil, Inc.)

in the wet season, and at least 1,000 mm (3.3 ft) above bedrock or ledge, which means that in shallow soils the septic field may be elevated above the ground. While the most common disposal tiles are perforated round PVC pipes, a number of newer infiltration tiles and pipes have been patented, and their greater efficiency reduces the amount of cover needed and the overall size of the septic field. These systems are essential for disposing of waste from commercial facilities such as restaurants, or for systems that serve multiple homes.

In cases where it is not possible to find a site with the capacity for absorption and there is no public sewer system available, wastes (*septage*) may be stored in a sewage holding tank (or *black water tank* or *cesspool*) and periodically pumped into trucks for transport to a sewage treatment plant, or into a landfill. This is a costly arrangement over time, and should be considered a last resort. Nonetheless, holding tanks are widely used in many low-income settlements that lack the resources to create a centralized collection and sewage treatment system. A better solution is to invest in a small package plant to process wastes (discussed below). Originally designed for construction sites and remote areas where no public sewers exist, these are becoming competitive for regular installations.

Traditional Sewer Systems

Sewer systems (also referred to as *sewerage systems*) in cities have a 3,000-year history, beginning in Iran and

Crete, where some original systems remain in working condition. Roman towns and garrisons in first-century Britain had fully functional sewer networks, using hollowed-out logs to collect wastes. Wastes were disposed of in nearby rivers and streams, relying on dilution for treatment. In the second half of the nineteenth century, with massive urbanization, the municipal sanitation movement grew up as a reaction to the spread of diseases, particularly in London, where cholera and other epidemics were associated with the lack of adequate disposal of wastes. The installation of piped-in water systems in the large cities of Europe and North America also greatly multiplied the need for some system of collecting and disposing of liquid wastes. In the US, the new field of sanitary engineering began to be established in universities after the Civil War and developed the scientific basis for designing systems. Many of the choices made then and the practices that were developed for the first sewer systems remain the underpinnings of current municipal engineering. Not all for the better, though: the early decision to construct combined (storm and sanitary) sewer systems, made largely because it was more economical and would allow storm water to dilute wastes, continues to plague efforts to clean up streams and rivers (Burian et al. 2000).

Today, virtually all new sewer systems separate *sanitary wastes* (an ironic twist of the term, since they are quite unsanitary) from storm water, both of which need to be disposed of in urban areas but by quite different methods. Storm drainage, as we have noted, generally requires minimal treatment, although it may be costly if put into pipes because of their size. Much of storm runoff can be treated through natural processes before the water reaches drainage channels or pipes (chapter 25). Unlike storm sewers, sanitary sewers are closed systems not connected to open inlets, in the interest of sealing off odors. Wastes generally flow by gravity through lines of increasing size until they reach the treatment plant. Many local and higher-level governments have published criteria for the design of gravity flow sewer systems. While there is some variation—usually a response to special problems of soils and slopes—their requirements show considerable overlap (Environmental Protection Agency 2002a; City of Carlsbad 2006; Gold Coast City Council et al. 2013).

Design of a sewer system requires engineering expertise, since it involves navigating complex regulations, local practices, and the specifics of a site. However, it is possible to quickly sketch a sewer layout for a site which may be adequate for identifying the challenges in servicing the uses contemplated for the land, and may allow the planner to make a rough estimate of costs. The first step in laying out a sewer system is estimating the discharges. Table 27.1 provides average discharge rates for various uses of a site in the US. Discharge rates are available for many other countries, either in published form or on the Internet (British Water 2009; Gold Coast City Council et al. 2013; Hong Kong Government 1995). With a rough estimate of discharges for each area of the site, we are ready to sketch possible layouts of the sewer system.

Since *gravity sewers* depend on downhill flow, we look for the natural drainage basins of the site—areas where lines can easily join and make their way downhill. At the upper ends of lines, liquid wastes are collected in drains and transported from houses or businesses or other locations through *laterals*, lines made of cast iron or PVC, at least 100 mm (4 in) in size but preferably larger. They must be buried well below the frost line, and bend in the direction of flow before they meet the *collector lines* to avoid blockage. Collectors, which are typically 200–250 mm (8–10 in) in size, aggregate the wastewater from a number of houses or buildings and carry it downhill. Ultimately *trunk lines* that are often 760 mm (30 in) or larger transport the waste from several collectors to the sewage treatment plant. Where several lines intersect or lines change direction, *manholes* are required to allow access for maintenance and to avoid blockages. These are typically 1.2 m (4 ft) in diameter for lines up to 610 mm (24 in). They may be made of precast concrete rings, designed to adapt to the depth of the lines, or of preformed fiberglass units. On straight runs manholes are also required for cleanout every 90 to 180 m (300 to 600 ft), although robotic cleaning equipment has stretched the distances.

The critical factor in laying out the system is attaining an optimal slope for lines. Engineers strive for a Goldilocks solution: not too steep, not too flat. The ideal

Table 27.1 | Approximate sewage discharges by use (US)

Use	Unit	Liters/day	Gallons/day
Housing			
General	per person	378	100
Single-family	per unit	1,400	370
Townhouse	per unit	1,135	300
Apartment	per unit	1,135	300
Commercial			
General	per ac	7,570	2,000
	per ha	18,700	4,940
Motel	per unit	490	130
Office	per employee	75	20
Industrial (varies by industry)			
General	per ac	37,855	10,000
	per ha	93,500	24,700
Warehouse	per ac	2,270	600
	per ha	5,605	1,480
Schools, general	per student	60	16

Source: Environmental Protection Agency.

27.3 Sketch plan of sewer layout for subdivision. (Adam Tecza/Gary Hack)

is to achieve a flow of at least 0.6 m/s (2 ft/sec) that will ensure that lines are self-cleaning. Velocities higher than 3 m/s (10 ft/sec) need to be avoided, however, since they can cause erosion of the pipes and backup at manholes. Table 27.2 indicates the minimum and maximum slope for typical sizes of pipes. The velocity of flow will ultimately determine the capacity of pipes to transport sewage. There are a variety of ways of estimating flows when the pipe size and slope are known, but the simplest method is to use one of several calculators that are available on the Internet (see Calctool, n.d.; Engineering Tool Box, n.d.; Springfield Plastics, n.d.).

The necessary gradients of the sewer lines will have a large bearing on the pattern of streets, assuming that lines run below the travel way. A 300 m (1,000 ft) line with a 300 mm (12 in) dimension will need to

slope at least 0.7 m (2.3 ft) over its length, and not more than 14 m (48 ft). The constraints are much narrower as pipe sizes increase: for a 900 mm (36 in) pipe, the slope will need to be between 0.2 m (0.6 ft) and 3.4 m (11 ft). Achieving a match between the gradients that sewers need and the slopes that are navigable by vehicles may be difficult, and manholes may be used to make transitions.

It may be difficult to provide sewers to portions of a site because of topographic barriers such as hills, or because areas are low-lying and impossible to drain or because of ledge or rock close to the surface. One solution is to install *pumping stations* that raise the elevation of the sewage. These can be as simple as a manhole with a submersible pump, or a more elaborate holding tank that allows the pumping process to even out the

Table 27.2 | Maximum and minimum slopes by pipe size

Pipe diameter		Minimum slope	Maximum slope
mm	in	m/100 m or ft/100 ft	m/100 m or ft/100 ft
100	4		
200	8	0.40	
250	10	0.28	
300	12	0.22	4.88
350	14	0.17	
375	15	0.15	3.62
400	16	0.14	
450	18	0.12	2.84
600	24	0.08	1.94
750	30	0.06	1.44
900	36	0.05	1.12
1,050	42	0.04	0.92

Source: Great Lakes-Upper Mississippi River Board of State and Provincial Public Health and Environmental Managers (2004).

peaks or flows. Installation of a pumping station may be less expensive than construction of a lengthy line to connect two watersheds. Another solution may be installation of an effluent sewer system, also known as a *septic tank effluent pumping* (*STEP*) system, a hybrid that combines septic tanks with a collection system. In this arrangement, each home or business has a buried collection tank that is used to separate solids from the liquid effluent. Only the liquid portion is then pumped through pipes typically 40–100 mm (1.5–4 in) to downstream trunk lines. Because the line is pressurized, it can follow the contours of the land, and can even be close to the surface if well insulated.

Sewage Treatment Facilities

The ultimate destination of sewer flows is the sewage treatment plant, where effluent is treated before being released into rivers or other water bodies. Sewage treatment plants span the range between legacy facilities that are quite basic and have been operated and adapted for decades, and new high-tech facilities using advanced methods. The site planner is unlikely to design a sewage treatment facility, but it is helpful to have an understanding of the intent, methods, and scale of typical facilities.

Water quality standards distinguish between three levels of treatment: *primary*, *secondary*, and *tertiary*. Primary treatment consists of holding sewage in a settling basin where heavy matter can settle to the bottom while oil, grease, and lighter solids rise to the surface. The surface materials are then skimmed off and the sludge at the bottom is removed, leaving the remaining liquid to be discharged or moved on to secondary treatment.

Secondary treatment removes the dissolved and suspended biological matter, through *aerobic biological processes* or other methods. The most critical components are disease-carrying pathogens, but a variety of other elements and compounds such as heavy metals must also be removed. Secondary processes may include the use of surface-aerated lagoons or basins, filter beds, activated sludge techniques, membrane bioreactors, and biological aerated filters. After secondary treatment, many of the harmful materials in sewage should have been removed, but the water quality still

27.4 Thames Water Sewage Works, Deephams, North London. (Courtesy of Thames Water Co.)

may not be high enough to allow release into an open environment of streams and other water bodies.

Tertiary treatment usually involves removal of nitrogen and phosphorus which could cause eutrophication of lakes and streams, disinfection to quell most of the organisms that remain, and filtering over activated charcoal to remove remaining suspended particles that discolor the liquid. Lagooning in manmade ponds can also be an effective treatment method. Disinfection almost always involves chlorination, and is the final step of the process.

The remaining water may be of drinking-water quality after tertiary treatment. Singapore, which has few natural sources of water, will soon be relying upon recycled water for 50% of its water supply. Even if not recycled within the same community, water that is discharged into lakes and streams will surely be tapped by the next community down the line for its water supply.

One of the byproducts of the sewage treatment process is *sludge*, the heavy materials that have been filtered out of the liquid. Most often they are simply disposed of in landfills, but they clearly have value as biosolids. For almost a century, the city of Milwaukee has dried its sludge and marketed it as fertilizer under the brand name Milorganite. Dozens of other cities in the US and abroad have followed suit. A drying process is required to take advantage of the residue, and a number of commercial dryers are available for

this purpose (Environmental Protection Agency 2006). One estimate suggests that 800–1,000 sludge dryers are currently in operation, most intended to simplify the process of disposal.

Another strategy is to use the organic matter as fuel for district heating or electric generating stations, for which again the sludge must first be dried. Dried sludge can also fuel combined heat and power (CHP) facilities, and there are many examples that demonstrate that it is cost-effective. Sixteen percent of Thames Water's electricity needs are currently being met by burning sludge, reducing the utility's overall cost base. The ECO-Springfield Facility in Massachusetts and the North Wastewater Treatment Plant in Menands, New York, just outside Albany, burn sludge as part of CHP operations. Dried sludge is also being used in the cement industry as a low-cost fuel. Another way to harvest the potential of sludge is to convert it to biogas, either to fuel heating and cooling facilities or for use in vehicles (Levlin 2009).

Constructed Wetlands Treatment Systems

The use of *engineered wetlands* for secondary and tertiary treatment may in some circumstances be a good alternative to constructing hardened technology-driven sewage treatment plants. Such wetland systems require considerable land area, and if used for secondary treatment need to be fenced for health reasons. If used for tertiary treatment, they may be made accessible as a visual resource. Sewage needs to have primary treatment before being piped into the wetlands; a settling pond may be adequate, with a skimmer to remove floating substances (Environmental Protection Agency 2000a; UN Environment Programme 2004; Gustafson et al. 2002).

Engineered wetlands are of two types: *free water surface* (*FWS*) *wetlands* (or *surface flow* [*SF*] *wetlands*), which resemble natural wetlands in appearance and function, and *vegetated submerged bed* (*VSB*) *wetlands* (or *subsurface flow* [*SSF*] *wetlands*), where effluent makes its way through gravel beds below the water. Both systems will typically be created in a basin or channel, surrounded by a barrier of gravel and soil. A FWS wetland will typically employ engineered reed beds that perform phytoremediation. In warmer

constructed wetlands in wastewater treatment train

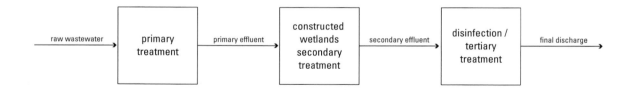

elements of a free water surface (FWS) constructed wetland

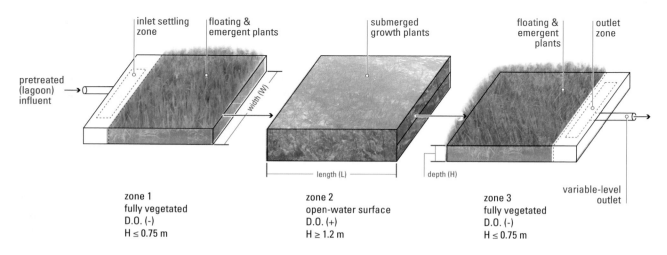

zone 1
fully vegetated
D.O. (-)
H ≤ 0.75 m

zone 2
open-water surface
D.O. (+)
H ≥ 1.2 m

zone 3
fully vegetated
D.O. (-)
H ≤ 0.75 m

elements of a vegetated submerged bed (VSB) system

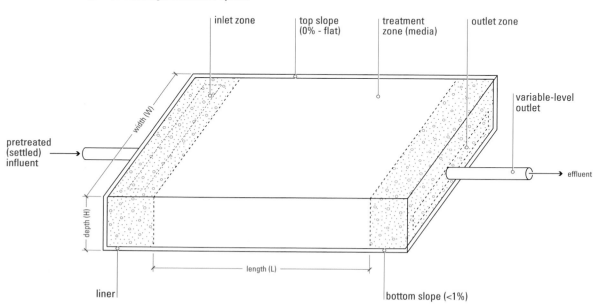

climates, hydroponic plants such as lotus may be employed, rooting in a shallow layer of sand. The water depth should be 0.5–1.5 m (20–60 in), deeper in the case of cold climates where the water will freeze. While the wetland will continue to function under the ice, it will be at a much reduced rate.

In VSB wetlands, the pattern is reversed. Effluent enters a crushed-stone bed, typically 0.5–1.5 m (20–40 in) thick, providing the nutrients for plants that grow in the matrix, and the water level hovers just below the surface of the bed, which may be covered by a thin layer of soil. This has advantages in mosquito-prone places, but the system is also more susceptible to freezing in cold climates. As the water makes its way through the system, which has a slight slope, it is filtered and the roots of plants absorb organic matter. VSB systems are best suited to smaller flows, typically less than 40,000 l/d (10,000 gal/day), and may serve an individual home or a cluster of a few houses or a small resort.

The size of constructed wetlands will depend upon the flow but is also affected by temperatures, composition of effluent, and type of pretreatment it receives. In colder climates, wetlands should be sized for a minimum detention time of 10–13 days for treatment, while in warm areas 7 to 10 days may be adequate. Because of the many variables, the approximate area needed for this purpose has wide brackets. An FWS wetland may range from 3 to 25 m² (32–270 sq ft) per person, while a VSB wetland may require 1–10 m² (11–110 sq ft) per person.

Adequate land areas are necessary for wetlands treatment of wastes. Urban applications require innovation but are also worth considering; they require wetlands to be integrated into public spaces in ways that protect those using the spaces from contamination. One stellar example of an urban system may be found in Portland, Oregon in the city's Lloyd District.

27.5 (facing page) Vegetated wetlands sewage treatment.
(Adam Tecza/US Environmental Protection Agency)

27.6 Constructed wetlands for secondary treatment of wastewater.
(Courtesy of Bauer Water GmbH)

27.7 Subsurface-flow wetlands.
(Courtesy of Laren Roth Venu, Roth Ecological Design International)

Package Plants

In recent years, the use of small sewage treatment package plants has become a practical possibility, as technology has improved and costs have come down. Small package plants are especially applicable in situations where long lines would be needed to connect to central plants, where topography would require extensive pumping of sewage, where central facilities lack the capacity to handle a development's projected output, or where there is no system to connect to. Package plants typically handle flows of 38–950 m³/d (0.01–0.25 Mgd) (Environmental Protection Agency 2000c).

A variety of technologies are used for package plants, including extended *aeration, sequencing batch reactors, oxidation ditches,* and *membrane bioreactors* (Environmental Protection Agency 2000c). Small prefabricated plants often combine processes in a single

**Natural Waste
Treatment in
an Urban Setting:
Hassalo on Eighth,
Portland, Oregon**

Natural waste treatment is generally found in outlying sites where there is plenty of land to devote to wetlands. With some creativity, it can also be a solution in urban areas. The Hassalo on Eighth project, designed by GBD Architects with the assistance of Place Studio and developed by American Assets Trust, demonstrates how a linear plaza for a district can also become a functioning wetland for waste treatment. The NORM (natural organic recycling machine) system accepts 45,000 gallons per day from toilets, sinks, domestic and commercial kitchens, and appliances in four buildings in the Lloyd District, processing it to meet Oregon Class A reuse standards. The process includes an anoxic reactor, trickling filter, a series of wetlands, and final filtration and disinfection. Wetlands line NE Eighth Avenue and are an integral part of the landscape.

27.8 Linear pedestrian plaza with parallel vegetated wetlands trays, Hassalo on Eighth, Portland, Oregon. (Courtesy of GBD Architects/American Assets Trust)

27.9 Plan of one block of Multnomah Street, Hassalo on Eighth. (Courtesy of GBD Architects/American Assets Trust)

27.10 Ground-level view of pedestrian plaza and wetlands trays, Hassalo on Eighth. (Courtesy of GBD Architects/American Assets Trust)

27.11 (facing page) Diagram of NORM (natural organic recycling machine) system, Hassalo on Eighth. (Courtesy of GBD Architects/American Assets Trust)

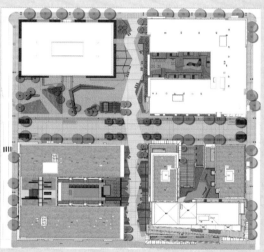

SO HOW DOES THIS WORK?

NORM DIAGRAM IN MOTION

Every used drop of water from sinks, toilets, showers and laundry (black and grey wastewater) is collected and stored by NORM. NORM then uses innovative treatment technologies to reduce nutrient loads and natural constructed wetlands to further process the wastewater. NORM's high tech filtration and disinfection system creates the highest quality of reclaimed water at a level of clarity appropriate for residential reuse.

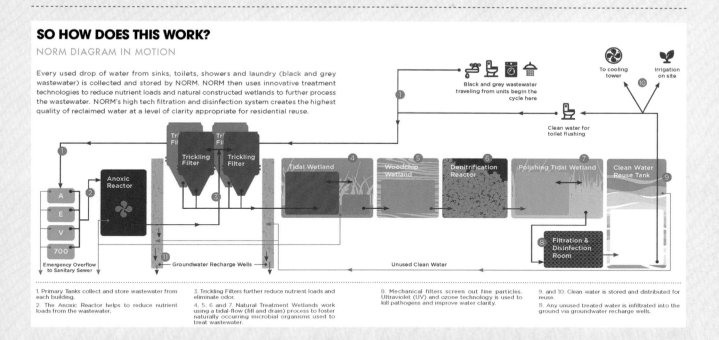

1. Primary Tanks collect and store wastewater from each building.
2. The Anoxic Reactor helps to reduce nutrient loads from the wastewater.

3. Trickling Filters further reduce nutrient loads and eliminate odor.
4, 5, 6 and 7. Natural Treatment Wetlands work using a tidal-flow (fill and drain) process to foster naturally occurring microbial organisms used to treat wastewater.

8. Mechanical filters screen out fine particles. Ultraviolet (UV) and ozone technology is used to kill pathogens and improve water clarity.

9. and 10. Clean water is stored and distributed for reuse.
11. Any unused treated water is infiltrated into the ground via groundwater recharge wells.

---

assembled unit. A typical unit employs four steps. First, the sewage moves through a comminutor or *bar screen* that removes the gross solids. Then it is mixed with an active biomass in a rolling action within an aeration tank. The effluent is then clarified through an injection of air and through filtration. In the final step, the treated water is disinfected through chlorination or ultraviolet rays. If a higher quality of discharge is required, final stage filtration may be added to the process (Pollution Control Systems 2014). While each manufacturer employs a somewhat different set of processes, their products have been tested and come with warrantees that give comfort to small operators.

Package plants are generally located on their own site away from activity areas, where they are accessible to service vehicles. They may be in the open or enclosed, since odors are minimal. They may also be located belowground to make them less obtrusive.

Figure 27.12 Small wastewater package plant, Camp Aldershot, Nova Scotia.
(Courtesy of Newterra, Inc.)

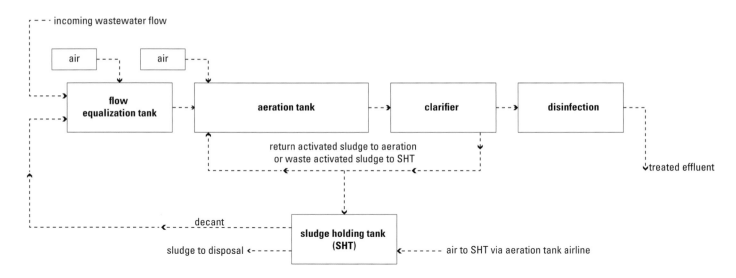

incoming wastewater flow

air → air

flow equalization tank → **aeration tank** → **clarifier** → **disinfection**

return activated sludge to aeration
or waste activated sludge to SHT

↓treated effluent

decant

sludge to disposal ← **sludge holding tank (SHT)** ← air to SHT via aeration tank airline

27.13 Treatment process flow chart, small package plant.
(Adam Tecza/Gary Hack)

27.14 Belowground wastewater package plant, Suffolk County, New York.
(US Environmental Protection Agency)

Vacuum Sewer Systems

A number of site conditions may make it difficult to create and operate a gravity sewer system. The land may be flat, requiring a large number of pumping stations to provide for gravity flows—oceanfront reclamation areas are an example. It may have a high water table, making deep excavation difficult, or have ledge or rock close to the surface making it costly, or may be in an ecologically sensitive area where any excavation will disturb the groundwater regime. Or it may be a seasonal settlement, or a facility (such as a Formula 1 racetrack) that is used only occasionally, risking sedimentation of pipes because of low flows when it is not being used. A *vacuum sewer system* may be a cost-effective technology in any of these situations.

There are a number of proprietary vacuum sewer systems, each of which takes a slightly different approach to collecting sewage. A typical system has three components: a *holding tank* near the source, *pressure-sealed collection lines*, and a *vacuum station* with a *collection tank*. Wastewater from a home or other source is drained into the holding tank or *sump tank*. When the effluent reaches a predetermined level, a valve is opened and the liquid is sucked into the collection line by differential pressure. Traveling at a fast speed, typically 4.5–5.5 m/s (15–18 ft/sec), it reaches a collection tank in the vacuum station. It is then pumped to the main leading to the treatment plant.

Vacuum sewer systems are typically designed to serve up to 2,000 homes along lines up to 3–4 km (2–2.5 mi) long. They have been installed in a number of residential subdivisions in the US, including Bay Creek in Cape Charles, Virginia, an oceanfront community with flat topography, a high water table, and sensitivities over pollution of groundwater (Gibbs 2005). Portions of Bernalillo County, New Mexico and Hooper, Utah are serviced by vacuum sewer installations (RUMBLES 2009). Yas Island in Abu Dhabi and the Seeb coastal area in Oman are both served by vacuum sewer systems.

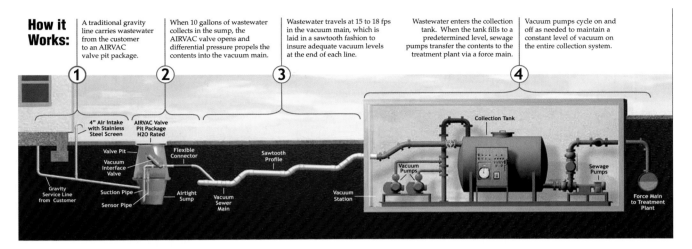

How it Works:

1. A traditional gravity line carries wastewater from the customer to an AIRVAC valve pit package.

2. When 10 gallons of wastewater collects in the sump, the AIRVAC valve opens and differential pressure propels the contents into the vacuum main.

3. Wastewater travels at 15 to 18 fps in the vacuum main, which is laid in a sawtooth fashion to insure adequate vacuum levels at the end of each line.

4. Wastewater enters the collection tank. When the tank fills to a predetermined level, sewage pumps transfer the contents to the treatment plant via a force main.

Vacuum pumps cycle on and off as needed to maintain a constant level of vacuum on the entire collection system.

4" Air Intake with Stainless Steel Screen

AIRVAC Valve Pit Package H2O Rated

Collection Tank

Valve Pit

Vacuum Interface Valve

Flexible Connector

Sawtooth Profile

Vacuum Pumps

Sewage Pumps

Gravity Service Line from Customer

Suction Pipe

Airtight Sump

Sensor Pipe

Vacuum Sewer Main

Vacuum Station

Force Main to Treatment Plant

27.15 Vacuum sewer system diagram. (Courtesy of AIRVAC Systems)

27.16 Palm Jumeirah community, served by vacuum sewer collection system. (© Mklg/Dreamstime.com)

The large Palm Jumeirah development in Dubai relies on a vacuum collection system to serve its 2,300 villas, located on narrow strips of land, and the large collection of hotels and resorts on its palm-shaped island. The system, which is the largest in the world, includes 40 km (25 mi) of pipeline network and may have been the only way to provide sewers to this (thoroughly unsustainable) community. At Masdar, in Abu Dhabi, vacuum sewage collection serves the Masdar Institute of Science and Technology, and will be an integral part of the infrastructure layer of this technology-intensive zero energy community.

Vacuum sewer systems have many advantages, but also involve significant capital and operating costs. Some of the capital costs may be offset by lower costs for excavation, decreased pumping, smaller sizes of pipes, and lower maintenance costs. Vacuum systems require no manholes and have greater flexibility in installations. They may be the only practical way to serve many large-scale developments.

28 | Solid Wastes

The handling of *solid wastes* (more conventionally, *garbage* or *refuse* or *trash*) on a site can be among the most visible of public service needs. Most systems, however, are designed to make the process as invisible as possible: local rules usually require waste materials to be stored in places that are out of sight and restrict the number of hours they may be placed on the curb awaiting pickup; once removed, they disappear into landfills and other disposal facilities. Employing more advanced technologies such as vacuum collection systems makes the process even more invisible. However, solid waste management represents a large fraction of public expenditures—typically 30–50% of the municipal budgets in developing countries and only slightly less in developed cities if all the costs are accounted for. And the waste stream includes a great deal of valuable material that can be recycled or reused both on the site and beyond. In planning a site, the choices need to be spotlighted, not hidden.

There are five components to most solid waste management systems: storage of wastes at the source, collection systems, transfer stations, recycling and reuse systems, and disposal systems. We will deal with each in turn. The downstream activities are usually beyond what can be accommodated on individual sites, although if the site is large enough, facilities for composting of wastes, incinerating waste materials to produce energy, and production of biogas may be located within the boundaries.

Waste Generation

The point of departure is understanding the magnitude and composition of solid wastes. In the US, on average 4.38 lb (2 kg) of waste are generated per person per day, of which 1.42 lb (0.64 kg) are recycled or composted, and the balance is either disposed of in landfills or incinerated. The total quantities vary considerably by country: they are higher in Canada and about half the US rate in Japan, where reusable packaging and recycling have been elevated to fine arts.

The amount of solid wastes generated on a site varies depending on the use of buildings and management practices. In housing areas it also depends on the type of household, its income and lifestyle, exemplified by the fact that residents of single-family homes typically generate twice as much waste as those living in apartments. A California accounting of the composition of residential wastes indicated that the largest components are organic materials, paper, and plastics (mostly containers), together accounting for almost three-quarters of the materials placed at the curb or in a dumpster. These items have been the focus of recycling efforts along with glass and metal, which represent an additional 10% of residential solid wastes (Cascadia Consulting Group 2008). Construction debris and demolition materials are also a significant component of wastes in the US and are usually subject to special rules for disposal. Materials disposed of vary over the course of the year, with yard wastes constituting a large component in summer and fall and paper peaking at Christmastime and other holidays when gifts are given.

The composition of wastes is also affected by the uses served. Restaurants generate large amounts of organic wastes, while offices generate large quantities of paper, as might be expected. Institutions such as universities and hospitals, which generally must pay to dispose of their wastes, have greater incentives to

Table 28.1 | Waste generation rates by land use type, United States

Land use	Measurement unit	English measure	Metric measure
Single-family residential	lb (kg) per household per day	9.8–12.3	4.4–5.6
Multifamily residential	lb (kg) per unit per day	3.6–8.6	1.6–3.9
Commercial, retail	lb per 1,000 sq ft per day (kg per 100 m² per day)	2.5–6.0	1.1–2.5
Commercial, shopping center	lb per 1,000 sq ft per day (kg per 100 m² per day)	5.0–6.0	2.1–2.5
Commercial, supermarket	lb per 1,000 sq ft per day (kg per 100 m² per day)	31.0	13.1
Offices	lb per 1,000 sq ft per day (kg per 100 m² per day)	10.0	4.2
Restaurants	lb (kg) per seat per day	1.0	0.4
Hotels	lb (kg) per room per day	2.0–4.5	0.8–1.9
Schools	lb (kg) per student per day	1.0	0.4

Source: CalRecycle (2010), http://www.calrecycle.ca.gov/wastechar/WasteGenRates/

Material Class	Est. Percent
Paper	19.6%
Glass	2.4%
Metal	4.0%
Electronics	0.7%
Plastic	9.2%
Other Organic	48.6%
Inerts and Other	11.2%
HHW	0.3%
Special Waste	1.5%
Mixed Residue	2.5%
Total	**100%**

28.1 Composition of residential solid wastes, California. (© 2008 California Integrated Waste Management Board)

Numbers may not total exactly due to rounding.

reduce or recycle solid wastes and generally do better at it than residential users. However, there are also cultural differences: some cities have developed an ethos and effective programs for avoiding disposal, and some countries do better than others. In the US, San Francisco diverts almost 80% of its wastes to recycling and composting, compared to the US average of about 35% and laggards such as Houston at 17% and San Antonio at 4%. Internationally, EU countries have aggressively

sought alternatives to the use of landfills, promoting recycling, composting of organic wastes, and waste-to-energy incineration. Germany is the leader in diverting materials in its waste stream, with less than 1% of its solid wastes disposed of in landfills.

While developed countries focus on the ultimate disposition of wastes, the problem in less developed countries is often the small fraction of wastes that are actually collected. In low-income countries, it is estimated that only 41% of wastes are removed from the places where they are generated, in contrast with OECD countries where the figure is 97%. The mix of materials also varies significantly from that in more developed countries, making disposal efforts more difficult. In South Asia including India, approximately half the waste stream is organic material, and at least one-quarter is ash from cooking and heating. In much of Africa, fully 57% is organic materials, while 22% is plastic and paper materials. These differences have consequences for storage and potential recycling or composting efforts (Hoornweg and Bhada-Tata 2012).

The mantra for solid waste management is *reduce, reuse, and recycle*. The best strategy seeks to reduce the amount of waste created—by employing land-scape materials that do not require constant pruning, eliminating paper plates and plastic bottles, avoiding printing out materials received in a digital form, and a thousand other ways of reducing throwaway materials. The next best is to favor reusable items, such as reusable glass containers and office supplies, or construction materials that can be repurposed. Where neither reducing nor reusing is possible, recycle—by composting organics, recycling plastics, glass, metal, and paper products, recovering materials from televisions and computer terminals, and converting wastes to energy through pyrolysis or incineration. Accomplishing this requires accommodations on the site and within buildings.

Waste Storage

In the simplest situation, residential wastes from individual houses will be stored in airtight containers to protect against foraging animals and minimize odors, in inconspicuous locations beside the house or in a garage. With recycling, there may be several containers, and the contents are taken to the curb on pickup day. Many European cities and some in the US mandate specific containers that can be automatically dumped into collection vehicles. The use of compactors will minimize the volume that must be taken to the curb. In row house developments where there is limited inside storage space, architecturally compatible outdoor storage enclosures will need to be designed.

28.2 Household refuse containers, Richmond, Virginia. (City of Richmond)

Recycling programs that require *source separation* often necessitate the use of several pickup vehicles delivering to transfer stations and landfills, which can be an inefficient process. In Europe, a widely practiced alternative is creating common *recycling points* or locations, which avoids the need for each household to store recyclable materials. They need to be convenient but out of sight of individual houses, and easily accessible by pickup vehicles. Some systems employ *underground storage chambers* to minimize the size of the aboveground collection elements. New technologies allow a signal to be transmitted when the container is nearing capacity, allowing separate scheduling of pickups. Separate storage containers can also be located in public spaces, and emptied on a schedule that reflects the rate of accumulation.

In multistory residential developments, wastes may be collected from units via chutes and stored in lower levels where they are compacted. Some systems allow for separation of wastes before they enter the chute; in others they may be separated when they arrive in the storage area. Usually wastes are stored in *dumpsters* or *automatic dumping hoppers*, which may require access to the storage area by the collection vehicles. Alternatively, a small forklift vehicle may be used to transport the dumpster or hopper to the collection vehicle a short distance away. An alternative is to use

28.3 Recycling collection point, New Byth, Scotland.
(Anne Burgess/Wikimedia Commons)

28.4 Waste collection with underground storage containers, employing special-purpose vehicles for pickup.
(Courtesy of Kliko Systems)

28.5 Waste collection containers with sensors that trigger automatic collection.
(Smart Santander)

28.6 Automated waste hopper, Torino, Italy.
(Gary Hack)

28.7 Recycling bales of crushed metal materials, Austria.
(Blahedo/Wikipedia Commons)

a vacuum collection vehicle that attaches to a pipeline at the curb. Restaurants, office areas, and other structures that fall below the threshold of requiring loading docks generally employ some form of dumpster or container that can be loaded onto a vehicle for removal.

Larger commercial areas require dedicated space for assembling, shredding, storing, and compacting of wastes. A common strategy is to allocate one bay in a loading area to removal of wastes, served from an adjacent waste storage space. This will allow storage and separate pickup of organic, paper/cardboard, glass and metal recycling, and bulkier materials such as furniture and computer equipment.

Waste Collection

There are three basic methods to collect and transport solid wastes: *self-transportation* by households and businesses to a transfer station; use of *collection vehicles* on roadways; and belowground *vacuum collection systems*. Self-transportation is a viable solution in areas of scattered settlement, or in resort communities where the seasonal demand cannot justify purchase and operation of collection equipment. The regular trips to the *collection point* (or *tip*) can be an important social occasion in such communities, as well.

Most solid wastes in urban areas are collected using special-purpose collection vehicles that travel over city streets. The typical US vehicle is quite large, typically 2.4 m (8 ft) wide, 11.3 m (37 ft) long, and 3.8 m (12.5 ft) high, has the capacity to compact wastes, and will carry up to 16 tonnes (18 tons) to a transfer station or receiving site. Vehicles of this size are difficult to accommodate in narrow urban streets, and because they often require two driving lanes for operations, they inevitably create congestion. A variety of scaled-down vehicles have been created for urban situations. The smallest are electric powered, typically 1.5 m (5 ft) wide, 3.8 m (12.6 ft) long, and 2.2 m (7.3 ft) high, with a capacity of 1,000 kg (1.1 tons).

Collection vehicles come in a variety of formats; the most common is rear-loading, with a single storage chamber and the ability to mechanically empty waste containers. The storage chamber may be subdivided to allow general waste and recyclables to be collected in the same vehicle, but in most communities recyclable materials are collected separately. Side-loading vehicles are widely used in Europe, where every customer must use special waste containers and there is no curb parking. Front-loading vehicles are most appropriate for areas where volumes of waste generated by users are quite large and access to them is difficult. Waste stored in special containers is lifted hydraulically over the cab of the vehicle and dumped into the storage area behind. There are strong local preferences and a variety of mandated work rules that prescribe the options permitted for waste collection vehicles. Labor costs are a significant factor, which generally drive the quest for larger vehicles and greater automation in collecting and dumping of wastes.

The dream of most planners in large communities is to dispense with the use of vehicles entirely, using

28.8 Standard US garbage collection vehicle.
(Zena/Wikimedia Commons)

28.9 Mini electric collection vehicle, China.
(Suzhou Eagle Electric Vehicle Manufacturing Co., Ltd.)

28.10 Intermediate-size side-loading collection vehicle, Aardenburg, Netherlands.
(Charles01/Wikimedia Commons)

underground pipes and vacuum technology to transport wastes to central collection stations. Many *automated waste collection systems* (AWCS) have been installed in district-scale developments in at least 30 countries. Among the first general-purpose vacuum collection systems was one at Roosevelt Island in New York City that began operation in 1975. Other large systems have been installed at Makuhari Messe in Chiba, Japan, Hammarby Sjöstad in Stockholm, Sweden, Reflections at Keppel Bay in Singapore, Mecca, Saudi Arabia, Yas Island in Abu Dhabi, UAE, the Disney World Resort in Orlando, Florida, and

Le Quartier des Spectacles in Montreal, among other places. Modern vacuum collection systems are said to have been invented by Envac, a Swedish company that designs, manufactures, and installs systems across the globe using proprietary technologies.

The earliest systems, such as Roosevelt Island's, employ a single set of vacuum pipes, collecting waste from each floor of residential buildings and transporting it to the AVAC center at 60 mph (27 m/sec) where it is compacted, then transported for disposal to other locations. More recently, systems with up to five pipes have

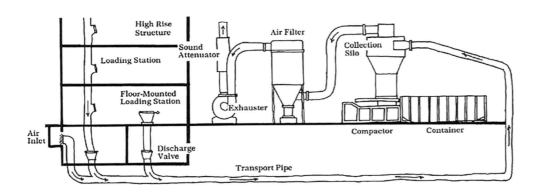

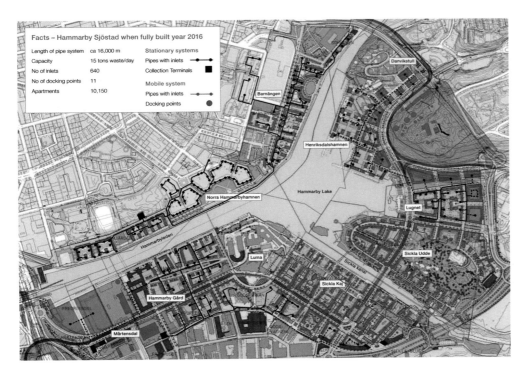

28.11 Roosevelt Island automated waste collection system, New York City. (Warusu)

28.12 Layout of vacuum waste collection systems, Hammarby Sjöstad, Stockholm, Sweden. (Stockholms Stadsbyggnadskontor, Sweden)

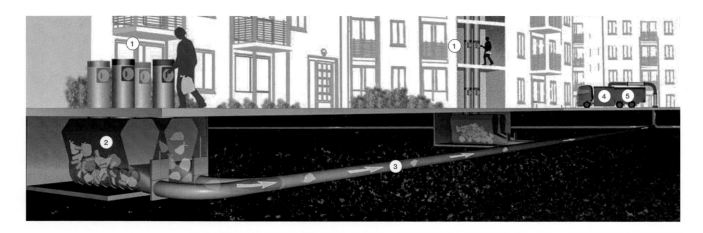

Mobile systems are suitable for small residential areas	1. The waste is thrown into a disposal chute. It is possible to extend the system by adding more inlets, e.g. inlets for more fractions. 2. Containers are emptied one at a time and the process is computer controlled. 3. All waste is sucked through the same system of pipes at a speed of 90 km/h.	4. A vacuum pump creates the pressure that conveys the waste via the docking point to the vehicle. 5. The air is passed through filters to remove any impurities before being expelled outdoors.

28.13 Mobile waste collection system, Hammarby Sjöstad. (Courtesy of Envac)

28.14 Mobile vacuum collection vehicle, Hammarby Sjöstad. (Gary Hack)

been installed to accommodate the desire for recycling, although this is costly. Typically, materials are collected in unique colored bags and stored in the basements of buildings, or collected via portals in the public environment, then loaded into a single vacuum pipe in tranches for transport to a receiving center. These are called stationary systems; an alternative is the use of mobile vehicles to collect the wastes from portals at the curb, where vacuum pressure sucks wastes from the basement storage areas. Hammarby Sjöstad, in Stockholm, employs both systems as part of its objective of recycling or reusing all wastes generated on its site.

Most stationary systems supplied today are designed for source separation.

1. Waste is disposed off into ordinary refuse chutes. One for each fraction.
2. The waste is stored for a short while on a valve, which opens when the computer-controlled emptying process starts. One fraction is emptied and collected at a time.
3. All waste fractions are transported through the same pipe system at a speed of 70 km/h.
4. Fans create the partial vacuum that sucks the waste to the collection station.
5. The waste is guided to the correct container.
6. The transport air is cleaned through filters before being released.
7. The largest fractions are compressed.

28.15 Stationary waste collection system, Hammarby Sjöstad. (Courtesy of Envac)

28.16 Stationary vacuum collection ports, Hammarby Sjöstad. (Courtesy of Envac)

Transfer Stations

In small communities, wastes are transported directly to the disposal field or purchaser of the recycled materials. Where distances are long, however, and the scale of operation is large, intermediate collection points are often created. These facilities, sometimes called *transfer stations*, often are combined with materials recovery facilities. They can serve several purposes—separation of recyclable materials from waste to be incinerated or sent to solid waste landfills, compacting or crushing of recyclable materials (such as metal, glass, or plastics) for more efficient transport to recycling receivers, drying of wastes, and loading of wastes onto long-distance vehicles. For seasonal wastes, such as yard wastes or Christmas trees, or for hazardous wastes such as paints, chemicals, and batteries, collection points allow materials to be segregated and handled separately (shredding and composting landscape wastes, as an example.) In cities on the water, collection points are often at the water's edge to take advantage of barge transportation, reducing the demands on roadways.

Collection facilities come in all shapes and sizes, depending on the combination of purposes served, the technologies employed, and ultimate disposal methods. In a small community, those delivering wastes may self-sort them, and the station may be primarily designed for storage, compacting, and reloading for the final destination. In large urban areas, sorting may occur through a combination of mechanical and human processes, with a constant flow of receiving and outbound vehicles. In the US, mechanized receiving stations need to have a throughput of at least 450 tonnes (500 tons) per day to be economical (equivalent to serving about 100,000 households), and need to be at least 24 km (15 miles) from a landfill. With shorter distances it is generally more economical for collection vehicles to deliver directly to the landfill (Applied Economics 2003).

An excellent example of a large transfer station and material recovery station is the North Gateway facility in Phoenix, Arizona that began operations in 2005. Located on a 17.4 ha (43 ac) site, the main processing facility consists of 16,720 m² (180,000 sq ft) devoted to separation of materials, compacting and loading, administrative offices, and visitor areas. A separate structure serves as a driver assembly area. The facility has the capacity to process 4,000 tons of solid wastes per day and 400 tons of comingled recyclables.

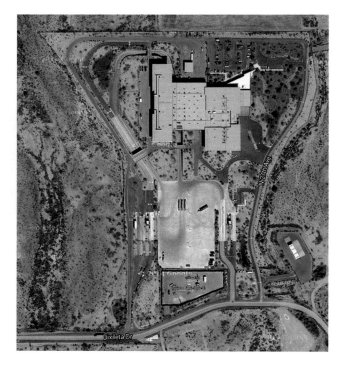

28.17 Aerial view, Phoenix North Transfer and Materials Recovery Station, Phoenix, Arizona.
(Google Earth)

28.18 Phoenix North transfer and materials recovery station, Phoenix, Arizona.
(Courtesy of HDR Architects/JRM&A Architects and Engineers)

28.19 Interior, Phoenix North Transfer and Materials Recovery Station, Phoenix, Arizona.
(Edythe30/fansshare)

Recycling and Reuse Systems

Reusable materials are typically separated from wastes to be disposed of either at the source or at materials recovery stations. Actual reuse depends on there being markets for the materials recovered, at a price that justifies the investments in labor and technology for separation. The US has a substantial surplus of recycled glass and paper, much of which is exported to countries including China where it is reused. Where labor costs are low, as in many low-income countries, separation of many valuable components may be justified, including building materials, electronic components, mechanical devices, cloth, furniture, and other household goods, in addition to the routine categories of glass, plastics, paper, and metal. In countries with high labor costs, source separation and mechanization are the key to reducing the costs of recycling. At some point in the future, many materials may be labeled with scannable tags or designed for easy sorting in an organized cradle-to-cradle system of material use. Once they have reached the end of their useful life, they become either biological or technical nutrients for their next life (McDonough and Braungart 2002). Thinking in advance about the ultimate reuse of materials used in site development can also influence the choices of materials and components.

Organic materials are an obvious target for recycling through *composting*. Composting consists of the controlled decomposition of organic materials by microorganisms, mainly bacteria and fungi, into a stable *humus* material that is dark brown or black and has an earthy smell (Environmental Protection Agency 1994). A well-organized composting program can yield valuable material for gardens and landscape. California estimates that 32% of the materials disposed of in landfills in the state are compostable organic materials, and several of its cities, notably San Francisco, have taken the lead in creating composting programs. In San Francisco, most of the organic materials are food wastes, while in suburban areas landscape wastes constitute a much larger fraction. Nationally, 18% of the waste stream consists of yard trimmings. The techniques of composting vary depending upon the mix and scale

CradletoCradle

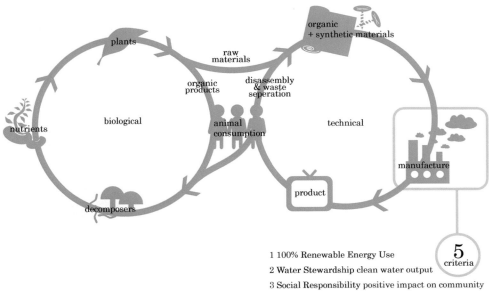

28.20 Cradle-to-cradle materials loops. (Zhiying Lim/Wikimedia Commons)

of materials, and there are a variety of technologies that can accelerate the composting process. While individual backyard compost bins may be an adequate solution in low-density residential areas, in most cities some form of collective composting is an essential.

For large sites, creating a composting area is a way of promoting a sustainable site, and an area should be planned at a minimum for composting of landscape materials. Larger-scale facilities run by local governments or their contractors will require a considerable site to allow excavators to be able to create, manage, and distribute the organic wastes. A preprocessing area is needed to screen out nonorganic materials, particularly metal and glass; this can be done by visual inspection as wastes are dumped, or through the use of magnets or other separators. Then there are several choices for the composting process: using passive piles, turned windrows, aerated static piles, or in-vessel systems, listed roughly in order of the amount of space they will consume (Environmental Protection Agency 1994).

How much space should be set aside on a site for a composting operation? Estimates vary considerably depending upon the technique employed and the materials being processed. As a rough guide, use from 5,700 to 11,400 m³/ha (3,000–6,000 cu yd/ac) for the processing operation. This represents about 2,750–5,500 tonnes/ha (1,200–2,400 tons/ac) of processing capacity. One reason for the broad range is that organic materials vary considerably in weight—food wastes can run more than three times the weight of yard clippings. Local regulations typically require processing areas to be at least 1.5 m (5 ft) above the high water table to avoid contaminating groundwater, and at least 75

28.21 Yard compost heap.
(© Andrew Dunn/Wikimedia Commons)

28.22 Food composting yard, Carson City, Nevada.
(Courtesy of First Circle Soils & Compost/BioCycle Magazine)

28.23 Windrow turner, compost facility.
(Courtesy of Midwest Bio-systems)

m from wetlands or watercourses. They also generally require that processing areas be set back from the site boundaries at least 30 m (100 ft) and from residential areas at least 75 m (250 ft) as a protection against unpleasant odors. Depending on the scale of the operation, these setbacks can double the area required for a composting operation, and they generally mean that sites are sought in areas of industrial or commercial development.

Finally, many items are too good to dispose of and don't lend themselves to material recycling. Books are an obvious example—their value is in the ideas they contain, not the paper on which they are written. But there are many other household items, like children's toys, furniture, and clothing, that should be passed along when no longer needed. Creating *exchange centers* where valuable goods can be deposited, to be taken away at low or no cost, can facilitate this. Within housing complexes these can be a valuable addition to the sense of community. Remainder centers for obsolete models can be established by local businesses, and restaurants often contribute foods left unserved at the end of the day to local charities or meals-on-wheels programs.

Disposal Systems

There are two basic strategies for disposing of common wastes that cannot be recycled or composted: depositing them in engineered landfills, and incinerating them or otherwise harvesting the embodied energy they contain. New landfills are unlikely to be located on development sites, since they are specialized operations requiring plenty of land and significant protections against the migration of pollutants. However, some infill sites in urban areas may contain historical landfills that may discharge methane or carbon dioxide gases, which can be tapped for generating electricity or heat. Gases from a historical landfill at Hammarby Sjöstad are piped to the central energy plant in that community.

Waste-to-energy facilities are becoming increasingly common, particularly in Europe and Japan where they

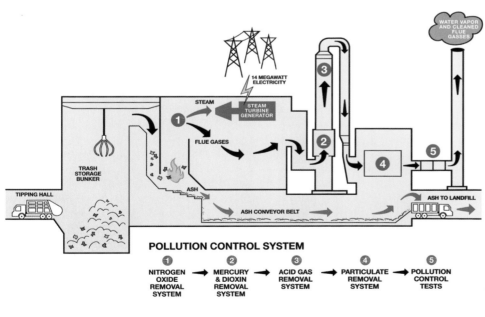

28.24 Waste-to-energy process diagram promoted by ecomaine, a quasi-government waste management company. (Courtesy of ecomaine)

28.25 Amager Resource Center, waste-to-energy facility, Copenhagen.
(Courtesy of BIG – Bjarke Ingels Group & MIR)

28.26 Spittelau district energy facility, Vienna, Austria.
(Lukas Riebling/Wikimedia Commons)

most often serve the dual functions of generating electricity and supplying hot or chilled water for district heating systems. In the US there are 86 operating waste-to-energy facilities, most in the eastern states (Environmental Protection Agency 2014). Incineration of wastes will reduce their volume by 70–80%, leaving ash to be disposed of in landfills. A typical incineration process will generate 600 kwh/tonne (550 kwh per ton) of waste. There are a variety of other processes that produce heat, gas, and solids from waste, including *pyrolyzation, anaerobic digestion, gasification,* and *plasma arc gasification. Combined heat and power* (CHP) facilities are explored further in chapter 30.

Integrating a large waste-to-energy facility into an area of urban development can be a challenge. The facility is bulky, requires significant exhaust stacks, and needs to receive hundreds of large vehicles each day delivering waste and removing ash. There may also be significant noise issues that require isolation from surroundings. One approach is to locate the facility in a recreation area, using the buffer area for active and passive outdoor uses. Or the integration may be tackled directly, by locating the facility in a commercial area and compressing roadways and ramps to connect with the local street system. In either case, the facility can become an asset through careful planning, but certainly cannot be hidden.

There is an understandable aversion to planning ahead for waste disposal. Waste is generally considered to be smelly, dangerous to health, and above all useless. But there is no sharp divide between waste and useful. Think of waste instead as materials we have not yet found a way to use.

29 | Electrical Energy

Providing electrical service to homes, businesses, and institutions is a fundamental infrastructure requirement. While it is possible to live without electricity in a remote rural area, and individual generators are a possibility, urban areas cannot function without common electrical generation and transmission systems. For many years this meant large generating plants and lines that delivered their products to individual consumers. Today, however, generation systems have become much more diverse, and sophisticated power line grids both receive and distribute electrical energy. Sites are becoming the source of energy as well as its consumers.

Centralized Networks

We start with *centralized generation* and the *distribution systems* attached to it, still the backbone systems in most communities. Large *power generating stations*, fueled by coal, natural gas, oil, or nuclear fission, produce electrical power by converting water to steam and using it to drive turbines that in turn (so to speak) drive electric generators. Hydroelectric power is the second largest source of power, and in places where underground *geothermal energy* is abundant (as in Iceland) it too may be tapped to drive the turbines. And an increasing number of waste-to-energy facilities are another source of power for central generation plants. In all cases except hydro, waste energy is produced, which must be cooled, or better still may be tapped for district heating or cooling, as we discuss in chapter 30. And a significant quantity of greenhouse gases are emitted from the smokestacks of fossil fuel-fired generating plants.

From the generating plant, electricity is transmitted to consumers on *extra high voltage lines*, typically 265–275 kV, as *alternating current* (AC) or occasionally as *high voltage direct current* (HVDC). Major *transformers,* usually at the edge of urban areas, then reduce the current to lower voltages so that it may be safely distributed to customers on 50 kV lines. Inevitably, these substations emit noise and need to be located a distance from occupied spaces. The electrical current is then transformed further in smaller distribution centers, then finally on individual sites or blocks and supplied to customers at 110 V in North America and 220 V in Europe, much of Asia, and the rest of the world.

High-Capacity Transmission Lines

High-capacity transmission lines are usually carried on steel lattice or truss structures with one or several sets of arms, considered by some elegant engineering marvels, and by others unsightly blemishes on the landscape. This is a place where engineering design matters, and scores of designers have tried their hand at improving upon standard engineering prototypes.

Rights-of-way for high-capacity transmission lines are often 30–90 m (100–300 ft) wide, representing substantial swaths of land that often go unused. There has been a long and inconclusive debate over whether *electromagnetic fields* (EMFs) associated with these lines can have health effects on those living nearby or using spaces below them, with many research studies addressing the subject. Those who urge caution point to studies that have associated childhood leukemia with long-term exposure to EMF radiation. However, the general scientific consensus is that this remains

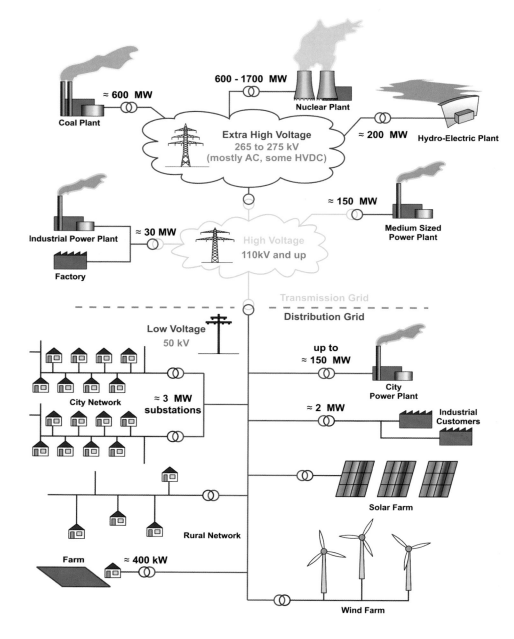

unproven in the case of power lines, and the effect is likely to be extremely rare if it occurs at all (Environmental Protection Agency, n.d.; World Health Organization, n.d.).

Since these rights-of-way need assured access for maintenance and pose dangers in the event of broken cables, they typically must remain free of buildings. However, they are ideal locations for bicycle and walking trails and can become fine linear parks benefiting the adjacent properties. Planting needs to be

kept to modest heights to avoid interfering with the lines draped between standards.

A frequent question is whether high-capacity transmission lines can be put underground so that they are out of sight, reducing right-of-way requirements. This is an extraordinarily costly proposition and is generally only done where there are no other choices, as when the line must cross a long stretch of open water. Underwater cables have been installed throughout the world in lengths up to 580 km (360 mi) from the

(a)

(b)

(c)

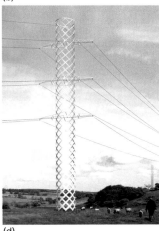

(d)

29.2 (top left)   Standard high-capacity pylon.
(Yummifruitbat/Wikimedia Commons)

29.3 (top right)   Alternative high-capacity pylons, RIBA Pylon
Design Competition. (a) © Knight Architects/Roughan &
O'Donovan/ESB International; (b) Gustafson Porter + Bowman with
Atelier One and Pfisterer; (c) AL_A & Arup; (d) New Town Studio
(Chris Snow), Engineer: Structure Workshop.
(All images courtesy of the firms submitting proposals)

29.4 (bottom left)   Albertson Parkway trail, San Jose, California.
(City of San Jose)

Netherlands to Norway, and are common over short distances. However, on land they require cooling of the line using pumped fluids, they have significant *capacitance* that may reduce their effectiveness, and breaks in the line are difficult to identify and repair. In dense urban areas, special tunnels are constructed for high-capacity cables. No utility company welcomes underground high-capacity lines.

Local Distribution

Except in dense or ordered urban areas, *distribution lines* (*feeders*) and *subtransmission lines* are generally located aboveground. They are attached to concrete, metal, or wooden utility poles, typically 12 m (40 ft) high, spaced 38 m (125 ft) apart in urban areas, and up to 90 m (300 ft) in the countryside. In the US they will typically carry 3 wires or *phases* on a horizontal cross-arm, with a second arm sometimes added to increase the capacity. The standard may also carry telephone and cable TV lines on an additional cross-arm or directly mounted to the pole. If located along a street, utility poles may also be the supports for streetlights. Aboveground transmission lines need to be protected against the falling limbs of tall trees, providing a license for power companies to aggressively prune or fell nearby trees, to the consternation of many property owners.

The final transformers to reduce the voltage to residential or commercial levels will also typically be mounted on the utility pole. North American and European practices in placing transformers tend to differ: North American systems' low-voltage step-down transformers tend to serve 7–11 homes in a suburban setting, or a single apartment building, while in Europe with higher domestic voltage they will tend to supply a complete neighborhood.

Placing overhead utility lines along the street and stringing lines to individual houses and buildings can be unsightly and restricts the location of and types of trees that can be planted, giving a veto over trees to utility companies. An alternative in residential areas is to locate electric and communication lines at the rear of lots, which is easily done if there are rear alleys or if properties back on an open space. If not, a maintenance easement will need to be provided, which will complicate the use of rear yards and fencing.

29.5 Standard utility pole, US.
(Gary Hack)

29.6 Tree conflicts with overhead utility lines, Pottstown, Pennsylvania.
(Courtesy of Thomas Hylton)

The best solution is to place local distribution lines underground, and many communities require this for all new subdivisions. This has been common practice in central areas of large North American cities for some time. Overhead utility lines are rarely sighted in European cities, although in Japan and much of Asia they are still a common part of the streetscape. Typically, underground electrical lines are installed in continuous flexible tubes, 1 m (3 ft) below the surface in narrow trenches created by excavators specially designed for this purpose. Cables are then "pulled" through the tubes. They need to be in an accessible location in the case of breaks in the line, away from heavy roadway loads and well away from water and sewer lines. Transformers will be located aboveground in lower-density areas, and the challenge is to locate them so that they are not the most visible objects, or minimize their obtrusiveness on the street. In dense urban areas, underground vaults will be constructed for the transformers, and larger ducts carrying multiple lines will connect between them.

Underground utility lines have many advantages, particularly in areas subject to freezing rain and severe windstorms. The cost of underground lines in lower-density areas can be from 4 to 14 times as much as that of overhead lines, depending upon excavation costs, capacity needed, and other factors. Some of these costs will be offset by lower maintenance costs of lines in the event of storms, but on a present-value basis it will take many years or a very low discount rate to recover the added costs (Alonso and Greenwell 2013). Where local governments require the developers of land to install underground utilities, the purchasers of property will absorb the costs, and their general willingness to pay for this improvement speaks to its aesthetic value. Regulated electric suppliers generally resist undergrounding power lines unless the users cover the excess capital costs.

29.7 Overhead wires, Harajuku, Tokyo, Japan
(Gary Hack)

29.8 Playa Vista transformer in disguise.
(Courtesy of Josh Callaghan)

29.9 Ice storm damage to electrical lines, Rothesay, New Brunswick, Canada.
(Courtesy of Alan Good/Streetscape Canada)

Distributed Energy Networks

Diversifying energy production to facilities beyond large generating plants has added a new dimension to planning for electrical service: the need to collect energy as well as distribute it to customers. There are several reasons for this shift, including the difficulty and costs of building large generating plants, the rising cost of fuel, restrictions on emissions, difficulty in getting high-capacity distribution lines approved, and, perhaps most important, the search for more environmentally friendly sources of power and national desires for energy independence. A number of alternative energy sources are now approaching *grid parity*, where they will be able to deliver energy to the electrical grid at unit costs that approximate those of large centralized generating facilities.

Alternate energy sources today include *photovoltaic (solar) panels*, *wind turbines*, local *waste-to-energy plants*, *cogeneration plants*, *micro combined heat and power installations* (*micro-CHP*), *biomass incineration*, and *low-head hydropower*. The challenges of installing these sources include the fact that they seldom create enough electrical capacity to serve an entire area, and that they depend upon sunshine and winds that are intermittent. Owners of systems are often better served selling their power to the grid rather than directly to local consumers. Many governments have passed laws guaranteeing local producers the right to sell energy to the grid at a fair price, but in many places the issue of assured customers remains difficult. However, a likely scenario for the future is that electrical networks will consist of many suppliers and many consumers sharing a sophisticated electrical grid (see figure 29.1). Electricity will be flowing into the network locally as well as being drawn down from distant plants. Advanced monitoring and control systems will be the essential mechanisms for managing this new pluralistic system.

Distributed networks also have direct consequences for site planning. As we discuss contributions that local sources of electricity can provide, a useful benchmark is the average energy consumption of a typical household. Table 29.1 indicates just how varied consumption levels are internationally, with Canada and the US leading the pack at more than double the consumption levels of most European countries and 9 to 12 times the consumption levels of China, Brazil, and India.

Table 29.1 | Household electricity consumption

Country	kWh/year
Canada	11,879
US	11,698
Australia	7,227
France	6,343
Japan	5,513
UK	4,648
South Africa	4,389
Spain	4,131
Germany	3,512
World average	3,471
Italy	2,777
Russia	2,419
Brazil	1,834
Mexico	1,809
China	1,349
India	900
Nigeria	570

Source: Enerdata via World Energy Council.

Photovoltaic Systems

Photovoltaic (*PV*) *panels* are widely installed on rooftops, building faces, and as freestanding structures to generate electricity locally. As their technologies improve, the price continues to drop to the point that they approach grid parity. Photovoltaic panels can be installed on individual structures and managed by their owners independently or as part of an area-wide scheme that benefits a collective entity (such as a condominium, homeowners' association, or master property owner.) The advantage of a collective scheme is that it can utilize lands or building faces and rooftops most effectively. Large flat roofs on apartment buildings may be a better location for solar panels than the rooftops of individual houses, which can become shaded by trees. Unoccupied rooftops of large commercial or industrial structures can be an ideal location for panels that supply nearby residential areas. Of course, if electricity is being supplied to the grid, any potential source can make a contribution.

We have noted in chapter 3 that the productivity of solar orientation varies considerably by geography and climate of an area. The optimal orientation of a photovoltaic panel in the Northern Hemisphere is due south at midday, taking into account the position of a site's location in a time zone. Solar position calculators are available to assist in calculating the exact orientation and tilt based on a site's longitude and latitude (National Renewable Energy Laboratory, n.d.; Solar Electricity Handbook 2013; GreenerEnergy, n.d.). As an example, in New York City the optimal tilt (from the vertical plane) is 26° in midwinter, while in midsummer it is 72°. If the difference is split, a logical angle for photovoltaic panels is 49°. In Dallas or Fort Worth, Texas, the optimal tilt is 33°, 51° in Calgary, Alberta, 40° in Beijing, and 53° in Berlin. Several of the solar calculators also estimate the *solar radiation* that will be received at each location, expressed in *peak sun hours* (PSH) in kilowatt-hours per square meter per day, or kWh/m²/day.

By making a number of assumptions it is possible to quickly estimate the size of a PV array that will be required to serve a site's needs. A residential customer in Dallas, consuming electricity at the average US rate (caution: new residential units may far exceed the averages), will require about 32 kWh per day. Solar panels at that location will be exposed to a PSH of 5.46 kWh/m²/day. Dividing the first figure by the second, we would need 5.86 m² of solar panels if the solar panels were operating at 100% efficiency, converting all the sunlight they receive into electricity. However, the very best panels deliver up to a 40% conversion efficiency, and average ones deliver 30%, assuming that the panels are optimally oriented to the sun in all seasons. There will also be a 15% line loss in conveying the electricity. Thus, with average-efficiency panels optimally oriented, the actual size of the solar array needed will be about 22.5 m² (242 sq ft). This is, of course, a theoretical calculation, and installers of solar panels will increase the areas by at least 30% to account for decreased solar gain during winter months because of the low sun angle, losses during heavy storms, and other contingencies. That would result in a solar array of about 30 m² (323 sq ft).

While PV panels come in many sizes and their performance characteristics vary, calculators are available on the Internet that will allow a quick approximation of the size and number of solar panels needed in a specific location. (See Wholesale Solar, n.d.; GoGreenSolar.com, n.d.; Solar Power Authority, n.d.) Supposing we are employing a standard commercial 250 W panel, 1,490 by 668 mm (59 by 26.3 in) in size, one such calculator suggests that 31 of these panels would be required to meet the electricity demands of a single household in Dallas. Or stated differently, 29 m² (312 sq ft) of solar panels will be required, probably within the area available on a modest two-story pitched-roof house. For comparison, the typical household in Berlin would require a 3,738 W system, or 15 panels, while one in Beijing would need an 825 W system with 4 panels—assuming average electrical consumption remains at today's levels. Of course, it is important to use data for the actual needs of those who will be located on a site, rather than national averages.

It is generally not possible to meet all the electricity needs of housing areas through PV installations, although in modest-density areas they may come close by using roofs of housing, garages, and carpark areas. A network of locations allows the best use of all the potentials on a site. By utilizing rooftops of garages and taller structures, solar panels may serve the dual purpose of shading as well as generating electricity. In

New York City
optimum tilt of solar panels by month

Jan	Feb	Mar	Apr	May	Jun
33°	41°	49°	57°	65°	72°

Jul	Aug	Sep	Oct	Nov	Dec
65°	57°	49°	41°	33°	26°

figures shown in degrees from vertical

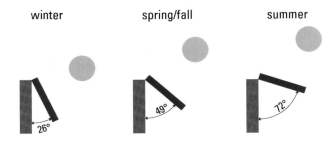

29.10 Optimal angle of solar panels.
(Adam Tecza/calculations from my-diysolarwind)

dense urban areas, the most promising locations may be on vertical surfaces, particularly at the tops of buildings, or on blank faces surrounding elevator shafts. And at the community scale, it may be possible to site arrays of PV panels in areas such as buffer zones along major roadways, which may otherwise be underused.

The fundamental problem of any PV system is the fact that electricity is generated during daylight hours, while much of the demand is during the hours of darkness. For a small installation, an array of batteries may provide storage, and rapid improvements in battery technologies may mean that storage is soon possible

29.11 (top left)   Crescent Park, affordable housing with solar panels, Richmond, California.
(Courtesy of Crescent Park Apartments)

29.12 (top right)   Villa Verde rooftop panels, Bronx, New York.
(© David Sundberg/Esto)

29.13 (bottom left)   Solar parking garage, Vauban, Freiburg, Germany.
(Gary Hack)

29.14 (bottom right)   Mechanical penthouse with photovoltaic panels, Visionaire, New York City.
(© Jeff Goldberg/Esto)

29.15 Vertical photovoltaic installation, 502 Colorado, Santa Monica, California.
(Oliver Seely)

29.16 Photovoltaic array on margin of arterial street, Tianjin Eco-City, China.
(Gary Hack)

even for large developments. But for the moment, larger systems require other methods of storing energy. Water may be heated using PV generated power during the day, stored in well-insulated tanks, and used for space heating in the evening. Of course, it may be more effective to use liquid-based solar panels if this is the intention. Water may also be pumped to higher-elevation tanks or reservoirs using daytime electricity, and then used to drive turbines generating electricity in the evening or night. Hydroelectric plants have been using pumped storage systems since the 1920s in the US, where 38 facilities can store just over 2% of the country's electric generating capacity. In Europe and Japan the capacity is much larger, 5% and 10% respectively

(Energy Storage Association, n.d.). All of these methods involve considerable reduction of efficiency. Ultimately, supplying electricity to the grid during the daytime may be the most effective method, since it allows for reducing production at large generating facilities when they are not needed.

Solar Arrays

Large projects that wish to reduce dependence on centralized supply of electricity may look to construction of a solar array that serves as a local generating station. There are now dozens of such facilities in operation throughout the world generating from 50 MW to 350 MW, serving substantial cities and towns or as part of supply grids. Many have been located away from settlements, in desert areas with favorable sunlight. The experimental zero-carbon city of Masdar in Abu Dhabi constructed a 10 MW solar PV plant, delivering 17,500 MWh of clean electricity annually, providing power for construction of the new city. The 87,780 modules cover 210,000 m² (21 ha or 52 ac). The facility will be expanded greatly to provide a large fraction of the electricity needs of the entire settlement.

While arrays of PV panels are the most proven alternative source, larger solar facilities may be more efficient if they employ *parabolic reflector* technology or *heliostats* that beam radiation to the top of a tower. Parabolic reflectors have proven effective in concentrating the sun's rays at a variety of scales from individual panels to large dishes. Two large parabolic arrays, Andasol 1 and 2, have been in service since 2008 and 2009 in Granada, Spain, supplying electricity to the grid. They employ long rows of parabolic mirrors, curved and tilted upward so that they look like troughs. These capture and concentrate solar irradiation, generating intense heat in the fluids in tubes that pass through the trough. The steam that is produced turns a turbine to produce electricity. Andasol 1 generates 175 GWh/year, enough to satisfy the electricity needs of over 25,000 average Spanish households or almost 15,000 in the US.

Heliostat systems harvest the extreme heat (over 500°C) at the focal point of a tower surrounded by reflectors. They transport the energy in the form of molten salts to heat exchangers, then in the form of steam that drives generator turbines. Gemasolar, an experimental plant on a 185 ha (457 ac) site near Seville,

29.17 Masdar solar photovoltaic facility, Abu Dhabi.
(Masdar City)

29.18 Andasol 1 and 2 solar power facilities, Grenada, Spain.
(© Flagsol GmbH)

29.19 Gemasolar heliostat energy facility, Seville, Spain.
(Courtesy of SENER/Torresol Energy)

Spain, employs 2,650 heliostats. The use of hot salts for storage allows the facility to generate steam for up to 15 hours without any incoming solar radiation and up to 6,500 hours a year, 1.5 to 3 times more than other renewable sources. The plant is rated at close to 20 MW, and can deliver 110 GWh/year. This is enough to satisfy the needs for over 16,000 average households in Spain, or 9,400 in the United States.

Wind Turbines

Wind turbines have been used since 200 BC for raising water from wells, grinding grain, maintaining the water levels in canals, and pumping water over dykes. In the late nineteenth century they were used in Scotland to charge batteries and began to be used in the US to provide electricity, particularly on farms and in remote locations. The technology has greatly advanced in recent decades with the production of large wind turbines employing optimized blades and efficient generators. While the majority of installations are *horizontal-axis wind turbines* with vertical blades and high-capacity generators, mounted on their own towers, there are also smaller lower-capacity turbines that can be installed on the tops of buildings. *Vertical-axis wind turbines* occupy less ground area and are especially suited to urban areas, both as freestanding generators and mounted on buildings.

Horizontal-axis turbines come in a wide range of sizes, and the general rule is that the larger the capacity for generation of electricity, the taller the structure must be. Small-scale generators, of the type that may power an individual home or small commercial building (1.5 kW) in the US, might have a rotor diameter of 4 m (14 ft) and be mounted on a tower of 20–35 m (65–115 ft). The size may be more or less than this depending on the average wind speed and the size of structures being served. One rule of thumb is that the rotor needs to be at least 10 m (35 ft) higher than any trees or structures within 150 m (500 ft) of it. At the opposite extreme are gigantic commercial wind turbines generating as much as 7.5 MW, with rotors 125 m (410 ft) in diameter, mounted on towers 140 m (460 ft) high. Wind turbines of this size are generally confined to offshore locations. The 1.5 MW turbine produced by GE, one of the most common in the world, has an 82.5 m (270 ft) diameter rotor and is mounted on an 80 m (262 ft) tower.

29.20 Horizontal-axis wind turbine farm, Shepherds Flat, Oregon. (Steve Wilson/Wikimedia Commons)

29.21 Wind turbines on roof of Twelve West Building, Portland, Oregon. (Courtesy of ZGF Architects LLP/© Timothy Hursley)

Vertical-axis wind turbines are much more varied in their design and functionality. In general, they are less efficient than horizontal-axis turbines (19–40% versus 56%), but also less costly per unit of rated power, and they occupy less space, making them more suitable for urban uses. The two most common types are the *Darrieus rotor* that employs a continuous curving blade, and the *Savonius* design that resembles a corkscrew. Other types include H-rotors with straight blades, vertical sail machines, Venturi wind turbines, and various types of hybrids (Ragheb 2013). Among the advantages of vertical-axis turbines, beyond size and cost, is that they generally emit less noise, respond to quickly changing wind conditions, and are generally easier to brake in times of high wind speed. The Quietrevolution QR5 wind turbine has been specifically optimized for urban environments where wind speeds are lower and change directions frequently.

In the US, optimal land-based locations for wind turbines tend to be in places distant from the largest metropolitan areas. As figure 29.25 indicates, average wind speeds in much of the central plains average over 10 m/s (22 mph), while on the east and west coasts where many of the largest cities are located they average only half those speeds. However, offshore sites along the coasts offer a great deal of potential, and locations can often be found along ridge lines near major development sites. Unfortunately, both these types of site are highly visible and spur intense opposition from those who do not wish to see mechanical intrusions into natural landscapes. While siting is easier in more remote areas, these often lack the grid capacity to transport power to the places where it is consumed.

The use of wind turbines raises a number of environmental and health issues that have a bearing on their siting. Sound exposure is the most significant, but opponents of wind turbines also customarily claim that there are dangers of EMF radiation exposure or interference, shadow flicker and blade glint, ice throw or ice shed, and structural hazards in the case of failure of blades or supports. Underlying the objections is often an unspoken but deeply felt objection to the aesthetics of wind turbines, which are seen as despoiling natural landscapes or creating motion in otherwise still environments.

A large modern wind turbine will emit slightly over 100 dB of sound at the level of the generator. As figure

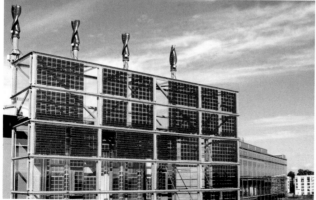

29.26 indicates, at a distance of 100 m (330 ft) at ground level the sound is about 55 dB, and at 350 m (1,150 ft) this drops to about 40 dB (Rogers, Manwell, and Wright 2006). Other studies indicate that a 10-turbine wind farm at 350 m (1,150 ft) will emit 35–45 dB at ground level (National Health and Medical Research Council 2010). These figures may be compared to the typical background noise in rural areas of 20–40 dB, and US noise standards for residential areas of 45 dB. Clearly distance can neutralize the noise impacts of wind turbines. Opponents of wind power have also raised the issue of the effects of *low-frequency infrasound*, below the hearing threshold of most individuals. Metastudies have concluded, however, that there is no reliable evidence of physiological or psychological effects of infrasound from wind turbines on humans (Chief Medical Officer of Health 2010; National Health and Medical Research Council 2010).

Similar conclusions have been reached from studies of other issues raised by objectors. Nonetheless, many local and national governments have adopted siting standards that require that wind turbines and wind farms be spaced a significant distance from any occupied structures. The standards vary considerably, as table 29.2 indicates, and they are based on horizontal-axis wind turbines. In the US a minimum spacing of 350 m (1,000 ft) from occupied structures is widely

29.22 Darrieus vertical-axis wind turbine, Heroldstatt, Germany.
(W. Wacker/Wikipedia Commons)

29.23 Four Savonius rotor vertical-axis wind turbines on the Viikki "Eco-Building," Helsinki.
(Courtesy of Oy Windside Production, Ltd.)

29.24 Vertical-axis wind turbines, 888 Boylston Street at Prudential Center, Boston.
(Courtesy of FXFOWLE)

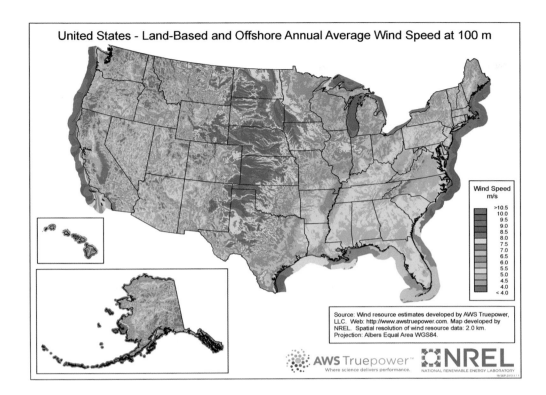

29.25 Average wind speeds at 100 m height, US. (National Renewable Energy Laboratory)

29.26 Sound levels from horizontal-axis wind turbine. (Courtesy of Anthony L. Rogers, James F. Manwell and Sally Wright/Adam Tecza)

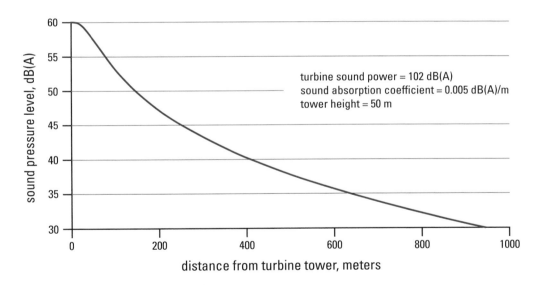

turbine sound power = 102 dB(A)
sound absorption coefficient = 0.005 dB(A)/m
tower height = 50 m

advocated by those promoting wind power, although this appears to be based on no scientific evidence and is generally well below international practice, where minimums range from 500 m (1,640 ft) to as much as 2,000 m (6,560 ft). With the variability of vertical-axis turbines, each needs to be considered on a case-by-case basis.

Wind power contributed approximately 4% of the power generated in the US in 2013 but has been growing at a rapid rate, and the target is to achieve 20% by 2030. Internationally, Denmark is one of the leaders, with 30% of its power generated by wind in 2012, followed closely by Spain with 25%. Finding ways to tap wind resources is one key to sustainable development.

Table 29.2 | Siting standards for wind turbines

Jurisdiction	Minimum distance to residential use	Maximum sound levels, dB	Shadow flicker
Irish Republic	500 m (1,640 ft)	43 night, 45 day	No flicker within 10 rotor diameters
Netherlands	1,000 m (3,280 ft)	41 night, 47 day	
Germany	Varies by state, 300 m (980 ft) to 1,000 m (3,280 ft)	35–50 night (depends on use), 45–77 day	Maximum 30 min/day, 30 hr/year
Denmark	4x turbine height or 600 m (2,000 ft)	37–44	Maximum 10 hr/year
Spain	500 m (1,640 ft)	50	
France	500 m (1,640 ft)	25	
Ontario, Canada	550 m (1,804 ft)	40	
Manitoba, Canada	500–550 m (1,640–1,804 ft)	40–53	
Victoria, Australia	2,000 m (1.24 mi)	40 or <5 above background noise	
Monterey County, California	5x turbine height		
General Electric recommendation	1.5x hub height or 400 m (1,300 ft)		

Haugen (2011); various sources.

Low-Head and Micro Hydropower

In the mid-nineteenth century, most factories located on fall lines and river rapids so they could tap the energy of rapidly flowing streams to power machines. With the advent of steam generation of electricity and fossil fuel engines, many of the penstocks and canals used to power the mills were abandoned, dams were removed, and mills fell into ruin. In the twentieth century attention turned to large-scale hydroelectric dams, and low-head hydropower was all but forgotten. But it is being rediscovered as an inexpensive source of electric power, particularly in hard-to-serve locales. With it, tapping rivers to drive turbines, and the dream of several centuries—using tidal power to generate electricity—now are becoming a reality.

Micro hydropower refers to small hydropower plants that have an installed power generation of less than 100 kW. Many such systems operate "run of the river," which means that no large dams or water storage areas are necessary. These systems simply tap a portion of the flow of a river at an upper elevation and transport it via pipes or a canal to a lower level where it drives a small turbine, then is released back into the river. Since there are significant line losses in transporting water through

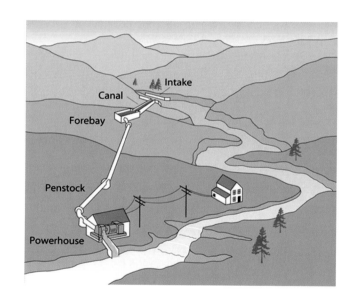

29.27 Micro-hydropower system. (US Department of Energy/Wikipedia)

pipes, micro-hydropower systems work best when they are located on streams with significant head (drop) in a short distance (Natural Resources Canada 2004).

A rough estimate can be made of the electric power potential of a stream using the formula

P = QHge,
where
P = power output in kW,
Q = usable flow rate in cubic meters per second (m^3/s),
H = gross head in meters (m),
g = standard acceleration due to gravity (9.8 m/s^2),
e = efficiency factor (0.5 to 0.7).

As an example, a turbine generator set to operate at a head of 10 m (33 ft) with a flow of 0.3 m^3/s (636 cu ft/min) will deliver approximately 15 kW of electricity, assuming an overall system efficiency factor of 50% (Natural Resources Canada 2005). Micro hydropower systems are simple to install and operate and don't require damming of rivers. Small turbines can be easily purchased and require little space to operate. The disadvantage of the system is that it depends upon constant flows. Hence, rivers must not be subject to seasonal drought or susceptible to wider drought conditions.

On wider slower-moving streams, with a head of less than 5 m (16 ft), a low-head hydro system may be more appropriate. One method involves constructing a dam in a riverbed to create a reservoir, and installing a turbine either at the base of the dam or downstream fed by a small raceway. In effect, this emulates conventional dam construction, albeit at a much-reduced scale. Another method is to install turbines directly in river current. Depending upon the river depth and its use for recreation or navigation, these may be installed on the river bottom on pilings, attached to bridge abutments, or even suspended from barges. In rivers that freeze, direct installation of turbines is a tricky affair.

Exploiting tidal power by installing turbines that run and reverse with the tides offers immense potential for generation of electricity. However, to be effective it requires a tide difference of at least 5 m (16 ft), such as in the Bay of Fundy between Maine and Nova Scotia, or a constrained channel such as New York's East River with rapid tidal flows. Such projects are capital-intensive and require connections to the grid, and are unlikely to be linked to site development efforts.

Other Sources of Electrical Power

There are other potential sources of electric power available on sites, which we note only briefly. For large-scale sites, combined heat and power (CHP) plants simultaneously generate electric power and generate heat for district heating and cooling systems. Most large institutions have such facilities, which may be powered by multiple sources—fossil fuels, natural gas,

29.28 Central power plant supplying both electricity and heat, Yale University.
(Courtesy of Michael Raso/Divisionone Architects)

29.29 Stevens Croft wood-burning plant, Lockerbie, Scotland.
(Mott Macdonald)

and combustible waste, among others. Yale University's cogeneration facility supplies 15 MW of electricity as well as steam for heating and cooling of the university and its hospital. Such facilities are best sited at the edge of a campus, where the noise and need for supply and maintenance of the facility do not disrupt the main activities.

Biomass incineration is becoming a promising source of electric power that can be developed at a variety of scales. Initially located in logging areas or near plants for papermaking or other products, it used the waste materials to fuel steam generators. Today, however, such systems are being developed with dedicated sources of fuel specifically grown for the plant or committed to it through long-term contracts. This may include straw, wood pellets, wood fiber, *Miscanthus* grasses, and agricultural wastes. As of 2013, 20 biomass power stations have been constructed in the UK, ranging in capacity from 2 MW to 44 MW, and almost twice that number are being planned. The 44 MW Stevens Croft wood-burning plant in Lockerbie, Scotland, as an example, burns sawmill coproducts, small roundwood, short rotation coppice (willow), and recycled fiber from wood product manufacturing, all sourced from within a 60 mi (97 km) radius of the plant. It provides sufficient electrical energy to serve 70,000 homes.

Lighting of Streets and Places

We began this chapter by exploring the technologies for delivering electricity to homes and other structures that occupy a site, and have explored the potentials of generating electricity on local sites. But the site itself is also a significant user of electricity, particularly for the lighting of public ways and places. Making a site safe, secure, and hospitable for use at night affects greatly the quality of life of residents, shoppers, workers, and visitors.

Lighting systems for public ways are generally planned in concert with roadways and pedestrian ways. Most local governments and some state or national governments have standards for the level of illumination that is required, and many of them also prescribe the types of fixtures that may be employed, in the interest of standardizing the equipment that must be maintained. Lighting standards are mainly the product of illumination engineering societies that respond to the advocacy of lighting manufacturers, and there is curiously little empirical research that validates recommended light levels or practices in placing fixtures. Rather, they are often a response to a rash of street crimes, or pedestrian-vehicle accidents, or neighborhood pressures to improve lighting. Few people ever pressure cities to reduce the amount of light on their streets in the evening, although recently desires to reduce energy consumption and promote dark skies have called into question prevailing standards.

Street lighting serves four purposes, each of which may suggest somewhat different choices. There is a desire to promote *safety* and prevent collisions between vehicles traveling along a street, and accidents between vehicles and pedestrians crossing. Pedestrian *security* is often equally important—ensuring that pedestrians are able to avoid people and situations that may be threatening. Lighting should create a comfortable environment that complements the uses along the street—houses, shops, parks, businesses, and institutions, each of which will need to be visible from sidewalks, but not flooded in light that distracts from their use. Finally, street lighting should aid in *wayfinding*, by giving advance warning of intersections and illuminating street signs along the way.

The general multipurpose solution for street lighting is installing lighting poles (or standards) typically 8–10 m (26–32 ft) high with arms that project over the street 1.2–2.4 m (4–8 ft) and accommodate a light fixture (New York City Department of Transportation 2016). There are an almost infinite variety of standards and fixtures, responding to the historic and aesthetic preferences of cities. Today, most cites are encouraging the use of light-emitting diode (LED) fixtures, while in the past high-pressure sodium (HPS) and compact ceramic metal halide (CCMH) fixtures were the standard. Tall fixtures do a better job of lighting the roadway than lighting the sidewalk for pedestrians, and if there are trees along the street, there may be areas of darkness below them. In the US and many other countries, vehicles drive with their headlights on, and lighting the roadway may not be as critical as providing good pedestrian illumination.

Pedestrians require the type of illumination that allows them to see approaching people and allows vehicles to see them as they cross streets. One guideline is

that pedestrians should be able to recognize the face of a person at a distance of 4 m (14 ft). This requires good illumination on vertical surfaces, not well served by tall light fixtures. Also, the human eye may not be able to react quickly enough to patches of darkness below street trees, so evenness of the light levels is more critical than its absolute level (Barr 1976). For these reasons, the best pedestrian lighting is with fixtures that are relatively low, 3–4 m (10–14 ft), with lenses that cast a broad pattern of light. Spacing poles 20–30 m (65–100 ft) apart will generally assure that the evenness is within the comfort range, depending upon the fixtures chosen.

The best street illumination pattern combines pedestrian-scale fixtures spaced relatively closely, with taller fixtures further apart along the roadway. Intersections should be lit more intensely than block lengths, to signal the important decision points and provide

29.30 Cobra head streetlights, Caihong Road, Foshan, China. (Hitech Lights)

29.31 Swanson Street pedestrian lighting, Melbourne, Australia. (City of Melbourne)

Table 29.3 | Recommended illumination standards, United States

	Average illuminance	Uniformity (max:min)
Roadways		
Collector	8–12 lux (0.84–1.11 footcandles)	4:1
Local	6–9 lux (0.56–0.84 footcandles)	6:1
Intersections		
Collector/collector	16–24 lux (1.49–2.23 footcandles)	4:1
Collector/local	14–20 lux (1.30–1.86 footcandles)	4:1
Local/local	12–18 lux (1.11–1.67 footcandles)	4:1
Plazas, walkways, and bike paths	5–10 lux (0.46–0.93 footcandles)	4:1

Source: New York City Department of Transportation (2016), based on IES standards.

added illumination for pedestrians crossing the moving lanes. Although there is too much emphasis on quantitative standards, table 29.3 presents ranges of illumination that are typically mandated in US communities. In low-density areas, the bottom of the range may be more appropriate.

Spaces planned exclusively for pedestrians offer more freedom in the introduction of lighting. Freestanding fixtures may provide the basic illumination, while emphasizing the flow of people. Or lighting poles may be dispensed with entirely and spaces may be illuminated by the uses surrounding them, supplemented by lights suspended from cables between the surrounding structures. Older European cities reduce the clutter by employing this strategy, and historic streets

throughout the world are lit entirely by reflected light. In parks, landscape may be lit from below, providing indirect light for the walkways. Lighting is a subject that invites creativity.

29.32 (top left)   Waterfront walkway, Suzhou, China. (Gary Hack)

29.33 (bottom left)   Stockholm's central shopping district is lit almost entirely by shop fronts, their signs, and suspended lights. (Gary Hack)

29.34 (right)   Nizami Street, Baku, Azerbaijan. (Urek Meniashvli/Wikimedia Commons)

30 | District Heating and Cooling

District heating and cooling systems are important for sustainable development, particularly on large sites. Increasingly they also make sense for modest-sized projects and will become essential as measures to combat global warming become drivers of development. They offer the potential of utilizing energy sources not available within individual buildings, and often can supply heat, cooling, and hot water to buildings more cost-effectively than when each building has its own system.

District heating systems have a long history, dating in the US to the eighteenth century when Benjamin Franklin created a central heating source to provide heat to several adjacent residences in Philadelphia (Commission on Engineering and Technical Systems 1985). The first commercial district heating system was installed in Lockport, New York in 1887, and Manhattan's steam generators and distribution system were created in 1882. Denver's district steam heating system, created in 1880, is the oldest continuously operated district heating system in the world (Wagner and Kutska 2008). Many European systems were created in the same era—but recent years have seen the addition of chilled water lines and a host of new sources of energy. Currently over 90% of buildings in Iceland are connected to central heating systems; in Scandinavia, 50–60% are connected, with over 90% in many urban areas; in Central Europe, 10–20%; while in the US, UK, and Canada, fewer than 10% are connected (Euroheat and Power, n.d.). However, new technologies and the rising cost of conventional fuels have put district systems within reach of many projects.

A typical district system consists of an *energy source*, *distribution lines*, and *exchangers* that transfer the energy in the form it is delivered in into heat, cooling, or domestic hot water within the building. It may also include a *heat or cooling sink* for storage of energy over a 24-hour cycle or longer periods, arbitraging the time when economical energy is available with the timing of demand. There are choices to be made for each of these elements of the system, and the capital and operating costs vary considerably. In all cases, these will need to be weighed against the aggregate costs of individual systems serving each building over the life cycle of the systems.

Energy Sources

Conventional Fuels

Burning oil, natural gas, and coal is the most common source of energy for district heating and cooling systems. With multiple boilers, it is possible to switch from one fuel to another as prices fluctuate, or bargain for favorable rates from suppliers. Rising fossil fuel costs and shortages, however, mean that conventional energy may not be the best solution. Even with clean-burning technology, coal generally emits substantial amounts of CO_2, with oil emitting somewhat lower amounts and natural gas the lowest of the three. In some areas where there is surplus hydroelectric power during evening hours (when the demand for heating is greatest) it may be an economical source of energy. However, reducing flow rates in hydro installations during off-peak times allows for a natural form of energy storage.

Conventional fuels may nonetheless be an important element for meeting peak demand in systems that use more economical sources to meet the bulk of their needs. This tiered approach—using least-cost energy sources first and supplementing them with higher-cost fuels—is an important strategy in district heating and cooling.

Cogeneration

Use of waste heat in cogeneration facilities is one of the most cost-effective methods of fueling district heating systems (see chapter 29). Typically, up to half the energy used in a dedicated electric power plant is wasted as condensate is cooled and gases go up the stack. Tapping these can be a cost-effective source of heat for district heating or cooling facilities. Fully 98% of the city heating in Copenhagen is supplied by district heating, and 70% of the energy for the district heating comes from combined heat and power plants (CHPs), supplemented with a series of small dedicated boilers that are employed only in peak periods. The most recent of its cogeneration facilities uses multiple fuels, including wood pellets, straw, and other fuels, and reaches 94% energy efficiency (C40 Cities 2011).

It is now possible to install package cogeneration plants to serve districts, rather than relying on city-wide systems. Many universities in the US and Canada

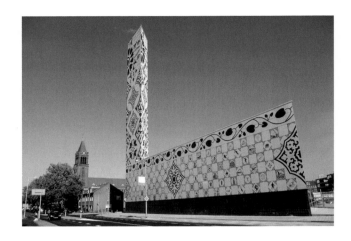

30.1 Enschede cogeneration facility, Delft, Netherlands, powered by natural gas and generating 60 MW of electricity, with thermal output used for district heating.
(© Hansenn|Dreamstime.com)

30.2 Process diagram for University of Calgary CHP facility.
(Courtesy of Solar Turbines)

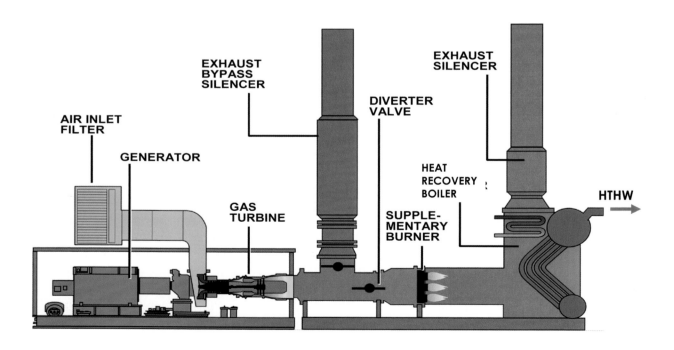

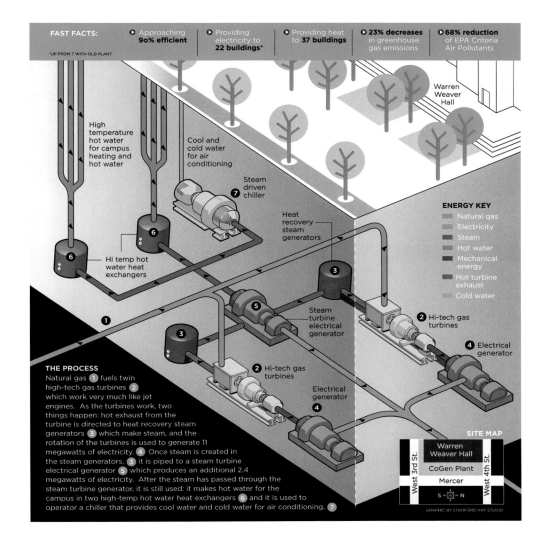

Warren Weaver Hall

High temperature hot water for campus heating and hot water

Cool and cold water for air conditioning

Steam driven chiller ❼

ENERGY KEY
- Natural gas
- Electricity
- Steam
- Hot water
- Mechanical energy
- Hot turbine exhaust
- Cold water

Heat recovery steam generators

Hi temp hot water heat exchangers ❻

❻ ❻

❸

❶

❸

❺

Steam turbine electrical generator

❸

❷ Hi-tech gas turbines

❷ Hi-tech gas turbines

❹ Electrical generator

Electrical generator ❹

THE PROCESS
Natural gas ❶ fuels twin high-tech gas turbines ❷ which work very much like jet engines. As the turbines work, two things happen: hot exhaust from the turbine is directed to heat recovery steam generators ❸ which make steam, and the rotation of the turbines is used to generate 11 megawatts of electricity. ❹ Once steam is created in the steam generators, ❸ it is piped to a steam turbine electrical generator ❺ which produces an additional 2.4 megawatts of electricity. After the steam has passed through the steam turbine generator, it is still used: it makes hot water for the campus in two high-temp hot water heat exchangers ❻ and it is used to operator a chiller that provides cool water and cold water for air conditioning. ❼

SITE MAP

West 3rd St.	Warren Weaver Hall	West 4th St.
	CoGen Plant	
	Mercer	
	S – ☉ – N	

GRAPHIC BY STANFORD KAY STUDIO

30.3 Underground cogeneration facility, New York University, New York City. (Courtesy of Stanford Kay Studio)

have found it advantageous to create CHP facilities. In India, where central electric generating capacity lags far behind demand, developers are offered incentives to build and operate such facilities as part of large development projects. The energy of waste heat can be converted into chilled water for nearby buildings.

Geothermal

Groundwater below about 30 m (100 ft) maintains a relatively constant temperature throughout the year, influenced only by geothermal heat gradients. In the eastern United States, it averages about 13°C (55°F), although in northern states it can be as low as 9°C (48°F), rising to over 23°C (73°F) in southern Florida.

Groundwater can vary from 4°C (39°F) to over 100°C (212°F) in locations around the globe. In geologically active areas, such as Iceland and parts of Japan and Italy (look for areas with hot springs and natural spas), groundwater temperatures may be as high as 132°C (270°F). Virtually all structures in Reykjavik, Iceland are heated today by district heating powered by geothermal sources.

The difference between groundwater and outdoor air temperatures can be exploited to shoulder all or part of the heating or cooling load. When outdoor temperatures are hovering near freezing (0°C, 32°F), use of 13°C (55°F) groundwater for heating can provide much of the heat to reach indoor temperatures of 21°C (70°F). Or when temperatures are over 32°C (90°F) the much lower groundwater temperature can provide much of the needed cooling.

There are several techniques for utilizing geo-thermal temperature differentials. The simplest, the *open-loop system*, involves creating wells and pumping groundwater to the surface where it heats or cools water circulating through an exchanger, then return-ing it back into the ground. *Closed-loop systems* involve placing U-shaped vertical tubes (or for small installa-tions, horizontal tubes) filled with water, glycol, or

a refrigerant into the ground, where it is warmed or cooled by the groundwater. The heat is then trans-ferred to the heating or cooling medium for buildings (typically air or water) via a heat exchanger. Another alternative is to pump air through the tubes, heating or cooling it as needed.

Closed-loop arrays may involve hundreds or thou-sands of tubes to obtain the needed heating or cooling capacity for a district heating system. One estimate sug-gests that approximately 140 m (450 ft) of 25 mm (1 in)

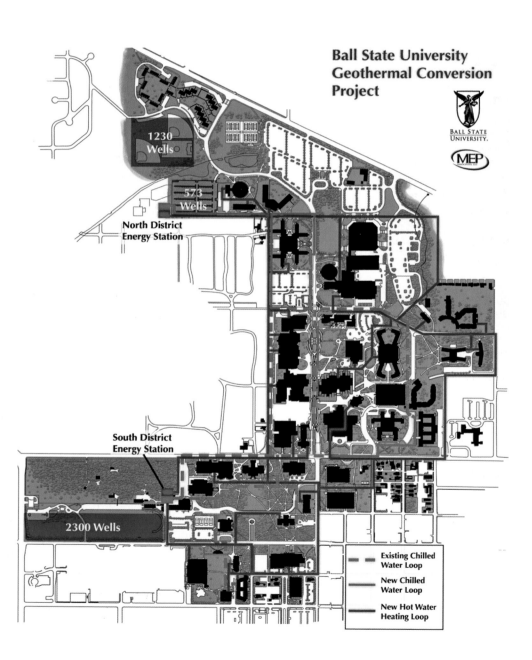

30.4 Geothermal wells installed below parking lots and playing fields have become a main source of heating and cooling: Ball State University, Muncie, Indiana.
(Ball State University)

30.5 Geothermal wells being created below playing field, Ball State University, Muncie, Indiana.
(Ball State University)

30.6 Geothermal lake cooling system, with 12 tons of coils placed on bottom of water body.
(© Mark Johnson/Wikimedia Commons)

tubing is needed to provide the 36,000 BTU/hr (3 tons) of heating or cooling needed by an average home in the US (Lund 1990). It makes sense to aggregate arrays for ease of maintenance and conversion, and many college and university campuses now employ geothermal energy for part of their heating and cooling needs.

District heating or cooling systems can also capitalize on temperature differentials between the temperature of oceans, lakes, ponds, or man-made water bodies and the air temperature around. Open- or closed-loop systems can be used, pumping water through an exchanger and returning it to its source, or placing closed-loop arrays at the bottom of the water body. Care must be taken not to alter the ecology of the water body: placing the array can disrupt the ecology of the bottom, and raising the water temperature significantly can affect organisms of all kinds, from plankton to migratory birds.

The world's largest *deep lake water cooling* (*DLWC*) *system* is in Toronto, where 4°C water is drawn at a depth of 83 m from Lake Ontario, and with a heat exchanger is used to supply chilled water to the city's largest downtown commercial complexes. The water is then filtered and treated for the city's potable water supply (www.enwave.com/district_cooling_system.html). Ocean water can also be an economical source of cooling. At Purdy's Wharf, a 65,000 m² (700,000 sq ft) office and retail complex on the waterfront of Halifax, Nova Scotia, a deep seawater cooling (DSWC) system draws on 7°C seawater to cover cooling needs for 10 ½ months of the year. During peak summer months, it needs to be supplemented by electrical chilling.

Biomass

Biomass is an alternative to using conventional fuels to power a district heating or cooling system. Biomass refers to carbon (along with other residues) recently derived from plant or animal sources. (Oil, gas, and coal are of course also from the same sources, but millions of years old.) Typical forms of biomass include virgin wood, byproducts from forestry, energy crops grown specifically for energy applications, agricultural residues, food wastes, postconsumer wastes such as paper, and industrial wastes. Materials may be pelletized before use or used directly, and are converted to energy using *combustion*, *pyrolysis*, or *gasification*. Biomass systems often employ cogeneration, with waste energy used for heating and cooling of homes.

Using biomass in community heating or cooling systems puts in sharp relief the ecological footprint of settlements. Trees, plants, and other biomass materials grow by absorbing CO_2 from the atmosphere; when they are converted into energy, a portion of the CO_2 is released back into the air. The ideal, of course, is achieving a carbon balance, where the growth of biomass offsets the carbon released into the atmosphere. This means allocating or setting aside enough land for production of biomass materials for both the immediate energy needs and to absorb the carbon emitted in the atmosphere when it is burned. The amount of land that must be devoted to production depends upon the materials grown, the climate for growth, the efficiency of the energy conversion process, the demand for heating and cooling, and other factors. Table 30.1 shows how the productive capacity of land varies by fuel type.

How much land would need to be set aside to provide for the energy needs of a settlement? A rough (and greatly oversimplified) approximation suggests that one ha (2.5 ac) of land developed in central latitudes of the US with 25 housing units would require 18.5 GJ (17.5 million BTUs) of energy for heating each year. If fast-growing willows were cultivated and used for biomass production of heat, approximately 9.2 ha (23 ac) of land would need to be devoted to fueling a

district heating system. Not accounted for in this calculation are all the other residential uses of energy (air conditioning, light, appliances, etc.), which would bring the total to over 23 ha (57 ac) for each 1 ha (2.5 ac) developed for modest-density housing. One way of thinking about this is that the *carbon footprint* for this housing is roughly 23 times the area of housing development.

Organizing a biomass program for district heating and cooling requires several things, not the least gaining approval from agencies that regulate emissions, agriculture, and other environmental aspects. There needs to be a stable supply of fuel, owned by the operators of the system or provided through long-term contracts, preferably within 30 km (20 mi) of the facility. As with any new technologies (or in this case old technologies updated), there have to be skilled operators and backup systems in case of failure. Currently there are over 600 biomass-fueled systems in place in the UK,

Table 30.1 | Potential outputs from biofuels

Type of biomass	Net calorific value, MJ/kg (BTU/lb)	Annual yield per hectare, tonne (oven-dry tonne)/ha/yr	Annual yield per acre, ton (oven-dry ton) /ac/yr	Energy per hectare per year, GJ/ha/yr (MWh/ha/yr)	Energy per acre per year, million BTU/ac/yr (MWh/ac/yr)
Wood (forestry residues, small round wood, thinnings, etc.) @ 30% MC	13 (5,600)	2.9 (2)	7.8 (5.4)	37 (10.3)	86 (25)
Wood (SRC willow) @ 30% MC	13 (5,600)	12.9 (9)	35 (24)	167 (46)	390 (114)
Miscanthus @ 25% MC	13 (5,600)	17.3 (13)	47 (35)	225 (63)	526 (156)
Wheat straw @ 20% MC	13.5 (5,800)	4.6 (3.7)	12.5 (10)	47 (13)	110 (32)
Biodiesel (from rapeseed or canola oil)	37 (15,900)	1.1	3	41 (11.3)	96 (28)
Bioethanol (from sugar beet)	27 (11,600)	4.4	12	119 (33)	278 (82)
Bioethanol (from wheat)	27 (11,600)	2.3	6.3	62 (17)	145 (42)
Biogas @60% CH_4 (from cattle slurry)	30 (12,900)	0.88	2.4	26 (7.3)	61 (18)
Biogas @60% CH_4 (from sugar beet)	30 (12,900)	5.3	14.4	159 (44)	373 (109)

Notes: These figures are approximate and depend on geographical location, cultivation inputs and techniques, harvesting and processing, etc. While some of these fuels may be harvested annually, some are harvested on a longer cycle. Short-rotation coppice (SRC) willow is typically harvested on a three-year cycle.
Source: Biomass Energy Centre, UK, 2011.

30.7 Harvesting three-year willow woodlot for bioenergy production, New York State.
(Tim Volk, SUNY-ESF)

30.8 District energy facility using biomass and solar thermal collectors for the majority of the energy it produces, St. Paul, Minnesota.
(District Energy St. Paul)

where it is considered one key to meeting carbon reduction targets, and many systems are currently operating in Scandinavia. The biomass-fueled CHP in Gresten, Austria, which uses waste wood from local businesses, supplies a combination of electric power and district heating for a community of over 2,000 houses and businesses. In Växjö, Sweden, two-thirds of the energy for district heating comes from biomass wood and waste wood from industrial processes, all produced locally.

In the US, District Energy St. Paul (www.district energy.com) is a CHP district energy system, created in 1983 through a public-private partnership of the US Department of Energy, the State of Minnesota, and the downtown business community. Its hot and chilled water lines provide heat for more than 185 buildings and 300 single-family homes and cooling for 95 buildings. Originally fueled by coal, the plant was converted to burning wood from the regional waste stream in 2003, reducing its coal reliance by 70%, reducing particulate emissions by 50%, and significantly reducing GHG emissions. The system is twice as efficient as the previous steam heating system in downtown St. Paul.

Sewer Heat Recovery

Sewer systems also have a large supply of embodied energy in the temperature of the wastes that are moving through them. When water from a washing machine or dishwasher or shower enters the drain, all the energy that was required to heat the water literally goes down the drain with it. It is possible to harvest some of this energy through a heat exchanger attached to sewer lines and recycle the energy for heating buildings. The Southeast False Creek Neighborhood Energy Utility in Vancouver, British Columbia was the first facility in North America to do this, and sewer heat energy supplies 70% of the heading demand of the district (Sauder School of Business 2011).

At the False Creek facility, circulating coolant water is warmed as it moves through a heat exchanger past municipal sewage, never mixing with it. It is then pressurized and circulated throughout the district to heat exchangers in each building. This system provides the bulk of heating, augmented by natural gas when the energy demand is high (Roger Bayley, Inc. 2010). Similar systems are in use in Oslo, Norway and Tokyo, Japan.

Neighbourhood Energy Utility
Heat Pump

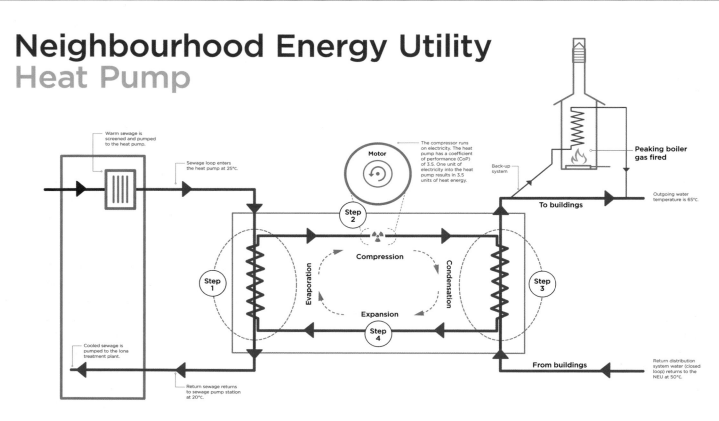

Warm sewage is screened and pumped to the heat pump.

Sewage loop enters the heat pump at 25°C.

The compressor runs on electricity. The heat pump has a coefficient of performance (CoP) of 3.5. One unit of electricity into the heat pump results in 3.5 units of heat energy.

Motor

Peaking boiler gas fired

Back-up system

Outgoing water temperature is 65°C.

To buildings

Step 2

Compression

Condensation

Step 3

Evaporation

Step 1

Expansion

Step 4

Cooled sewage is pumped to the Iona treatment plant.

Return sewage returns to sewage pump station at 20°C.

From buildings

Return distribution system water (closed loop) returns to the NEU at 50°C.

Step 1:
Heat Absorption

Refrigerant in the loop absorbs sewage heat causing it to vaporize into a gas.

Step 2:
Compression

The refrigerant has expanded. It is then run through a compressor which increases the refrigerant pressure, making it into a hot gas.

Step 3:
Heat Transfer

Thermal energy from the heat transfer loop is transferred to the NEU distribution system pipes.

As it cools, the refrigerant gas condenses into a liquid.

Step 4:
Cycle Starts Again

The condensed refrigerant gas returns to a liquid form before it starts the heat absorption process again.

CITY OF VANCOUVER

30.9 Sewer heat exchange, Southeast False Creek Neighbourhood Energy Facility, Vancouver. (City of Vancouver)

30.10 Exterior view of Southeast False Creek Neighbourhood Energy Facility, Vancouver. (Gary Hack)

Landfill Waste Gas

Methane gas from landfills is customarily vented into the atmosphere, wasting a valuable energy source and contributing significantly to GHG levels—since by weight methane is 10 times as harmful in the atmosphere as CO_2. A number of projects and cities have recognized the resource and integrated it into their district energy systems. The system at the University of California, Los Angeles draws 35% of its fuel from methane gas harvested from a landfill located 4.5 miles (7.2 km) away. This move alone offsets 36% of the GHG emissions on campus.

Industrial Processes

Some communities have the option of using waste heat from local industries to fuel district heating and cooling networks. Waste heat from oil refineries is an excellent source, as is gas turbine exhaust, both of which are conventionally wasted into the atmosphere. The temperature of industrial waste heat may not match the optimal temperature for circulating hot water or steam, necessitating a process heat recovery exchanger.

Recovery of waste heat from solid waste incineration can also be an important source of energy for district heating and cooling. In Denmark, over 20% of the energy used by district heating systems is from municipal incinerators. In Sheffield, UK, waste heat from two incinerators is circulated to serve most of the buildings in the center of the city. To cope with wide fluctuations in demand for heat, it is supplemented by a conventional boiler, used only in peak periods. Advanced flue gas purification technology is essential for controlling emissions.

Nuclear Power

Nuclear power stations generate an immense amount of heat, which is generally wasted as steam condensate. Typically, it is released in cooling towers or cooled through a closed loop system often using nearby water bodies. While nuclear facilities are often located distant from urban areas because of perceived hazards, and worries over radiation generate resistance to circulating water that has gone through an exchanger in a nuclear power plant, there may be circumstances where transport of waste energy is justifiable. In Helsinki, a proposal to pipe high-temperature steam 77 km (48 mi) from the Loviisa nuclear power plant indicates that it could reduce Finland's GHG emissions by 6% (High Tech Finland 2010).

Solar Energy

The most abundant source of energy in any community is from the sun. Virtually every rooftop is a potential location for solar hot water collection, along with expanses of roofs on industrial and commercial buildings. Since the capacity to capture solar energy usually does not match the heating or cooling requirements of a structure, there is advantage in integrating solar energy into a larger district heating system. The solar district energy system in Marstal, Denmark covers 32% of the city's heating needs and currently serves 1,500 customers. Seven types of collectors, totaling 18,365 m² (198,000 sq ft) in area, are coupled with 14,000 m³ (18,000 cu yd) of storage to serve the community (Solarge, n.d.). District Energy St. Paul has recently created a 21,000 sq ft (1,950 m²) solar array on the roof of the city's convention center, St. Paul RiverCentre, which is integrated into the city's district heating system (see above). In addition, the array serves the hot water needs of the convention center itself.

Use of solar energy as a source for district heating brings to the fore the need to create a system of energy storage, since collection of solar energy peaks in the daytime, while heating demands generally are greatest at night.

Thermal Storage

Conserving energy in the form of heat, or reducing the need to convert it to chilled water, can be important components of a district heating or cooling system. The most common *thermal storage systems* arbitrage day and night temperatures, using sources of energy available cheaply during one period to benefit other periods of demand. In locations where hydropower is available at low rates during the night, or *time of use (TOU) tariffs* are used for pricing of electricity, ice making may be employed to create a chilled medium that is used for air conditioning during the day. Or where solar energy is plentiful during the day and there is a need for heating during the night, heat may be stored in insulated water reservoirs and used to supply a district with heat. More ambitious systems are designed to store heat or cool temperature media over the course of several months, evening out changes in the availability of solar or other energy over the course of the year.

Several media are available for thermal storage. Water is by far the most common. In its simplest form such a system consists of underground storage tanks that store warm or chilled water for use when required. University campuses are among the best candidates for such facilities, since they can be constructed below playing fields, parking areas, or other large open spaces. Georgetown University has created a 1M gal (3,800 m³) tank under a parking garage; New Mexico State University has a 3M gal (11,300 m³) tank under a parking lot; and Yale University has a 3M gal (11,300 m³) chilled water storage tank buried below a parking lot, tennis court, and green space. The University of Arizona employs 205 ice storage tanks aboveground, each storing 1,600 gal (6,057 l) of water that is frozen at night and melted during the day as it is used in cooling. In all these cases the storage allows off-peak energy to be used to chill water for use during peak hours of cooling need, thereby saving significantly on cooling costs.

While water (in liquid or ice form) is a logical candidate for dealing with the daily energy cycle, it can also be employed for seasonal storage. In Munich, Germany, a solar-assisted district heating system employs a 5,700 m³ (1.5M gal) water thermal energy storage tank to allow energy to be carried over from summer to winter. The solar collectors charge heat into heat storage during the summer, and the stored heat is used to maintain the temperatures in the 300 apartments, in 11 structures, during the winter months (Schmidt, Mangold, and Müller-Steinhagen 2004).

Ice is a more effective way to store energy because of water's large heat of fusion. One metric ton of water, just 1 m³, can store 334 MJ (317k BTUs, 93kWh, or 26.4 ton-hours) of energy—in fact, this is the original source of a "ton" of cooling. This is the average amount of energy required to cool a typical Boston-area house of 280 m² (3,000 sq ft) during a summer day. One strategy for cost-effective cooling is to run a chiller at an even rate 24 hours a day; during the night it produces ice for storage, and during the day it chills water for air conditioning, augmented by water running through the

melting ice. Such a system typically runs in ice-making mode for 16 to 18 hours a day, and in an ice-melting mode for the balance. Capital costs are reduced by 50–60%, with an equally large reduction in operating costs, depending upon the climate.

Rocks can also be an effective medium for storing energy. They are cheap and readily available, and have good heat transfer characteristics with air at low velocities. Their main disadvantage is their high ratio of volume per BTU stored compared with water, which means a larger volume needs to be devoted to such a system (Ataer 2006). A number of individual buildings have employed rock storage technology, including the EcoBox headquarters of Fondación Metrópoli in Madrid (Fondación Metrópoli 2008). Use of gravel is also a possibility for storage, particularly in gravel-water storage systems. A solar-assisted district heating system in Steinfurt-Borghorst, Germany utilizes a 1,500 m³ (1,962 cu yd) gravel-water heat store as seasonal storage in serving 47 flats (Bauer, Heidemann, and Müller-Steinhagen 2007).

Finally, energy may be stored through geothermal means, which can be particularly effective for seasonal storage. Several German experiments, including a residential development in Crailsheim-Hirtenwiesen, use borehole loops to heat groundwater and store energy for use in other seasons (Schmidt, Mangold, and Müller-Steinhagen 2004).

Distribution Systems

The system for distributing heated or chilled water (or both) is the third component of a district heating and cooling system. Typically this employs insulated underground pipes that transport steam or water to exchange units in individual buildings. Older systems use single-pipe systems, wasting water or condensate once it has served its purpose. Using a single pipe to deliver heat and cooling requires that it be devoted to one function or the other at a time, with the switchover usually made twice a year. Invariably users are treated to a spell of cold weather just after the switchover to chilled water for the cooling season, or a hot spell crying out for cooling just after the heating season begins.

New distribution technologies operate with at least two pipes to conserve water, and sophisticated new

30.11 University of Arizona ice storage tanks.
(Courtesy of University of Arizona Facilities Management Utilities System)

30.12 Examples of preinsulated flexible district heating piping. (Courtesy of Thermaflex International)

30.13 Installation of preinsulated district heating pipe, Flanders, Belgium.
(Courtesy of Klaas de Jong/Energieprojecten)

preinsulated pipe clusters may contain as many as 5 pipes within a single insulated sleeve. This allows for delivering both hot and cold water, returning the condensate or used water, and adding to the supply during peak periods. While high-pressure or high-temperature pipes are typically made of steel, lower-temperature water pipes may be made of PVC or other synthetic materials. This allows pipes to be curved where they need to change course, saving on the installation costs of fittings.

Most layouts are branched networks, particularly in low-density areas. In higher-density locations, loop systems offer the redundancy to operate the system if one link must be taken off line, or in case of emergency breaks. In very dense areas (such as medical complexes, urban university campuses, or downtown areas), high-pressure steam lines may run within buildings or in common *utility tunnels,* allowing easy access for maintenance or replacement (chapter 20). Utility corridors also tend to minimize line losses by avoiding direct contact with the earth.

31 | Communications

For a century and a half from the invention of the telegraph, communications infrastructure consisted of copper wire cables, strung between poles alongside roadways or in cables in dense urban areas and under water. Change was slow: wires used for telegraphy were followed by telephone lines, more sophisticated cables were developed, and gradually new technology was added to increase capacity and the speed of transmission and switching. Coaxial cables were added in the 1980s to allow television signals to be transmitted. But over the past 25 years, with the introduction of fiber optics and wireless networks and the increasing sophistication of integrated systems of hardware and software, the possibilities of communications technology have exploded. Systems have been layered on older systems, with sometime bizarre results. Today, communications infrastructure is as essential as water, sewer, and transportation links to the operations of modern settlements.

While there is much debate about wired versus wireless communication, both are essential for the intelligent city of the future. Technologies are evolving so quickly that it is difficult to predict the infrastructure needed a decade or two from now. Television broadcasting began as a wireless medium with fixed points of distribution, then was largely captured by cable service, and today shows signs of migrating back to wireless service via satellites, laptop computers, and handheld devices. This rapid evolution is likely to accelerate, not stabilize. How then should a site planner think about communications infrastructure?

Three aspects of communications infrastructure are likely to require choices and investment in the foreseeable future. There will be the continuing need for *cabling systems* to support *broadband communication*. At

31.1 Overhead communications and electrical infrastructure, Tokyo, Japan.
(Gary Hack)

the same time, wireless systems, both from local points and satellites, will continue to proliferate. And systems within urban areas will become more integrated as cities and service providers move to *embedding intelligence* in other infrastructure systems and the environment. Each makes demands on the planning of a site (Agrawal 2002).

Cabling Sites

Trunk lines serving wide areas of cities are increasingly migrating to *fiber-optic cables*, because of their broad *bandwidth* (up to 100 Gbit/sec), carrying capacity (a million or more telephone lines), long-distance transmission capabilities (100 km or 62 miles with ease), speed of transmission (the speed of light), low line loss, and resistance to electromagnetic interference (they carry no electricity). Although there is no such thing as a typical installation, a trunk line serving a residential area with 1,000 households would consist of one or more strands of fiber protected by a polymer cover and armored in steel, accompanied by a variety of devices for transmission, regeneration, and reception.

The significant choice to be made concerns how to handle the last mile of service, a decision that will likely be determined by the local provider of telecommunication services. The ideal arrangement is to deliver fiber directly to the home or business network (FTTH or FTTN). In Korea, Singapore, large portions of Australia, parts of the US, and many European countries, FTTH and FTTN are expected in new developments. An alternative is to provide fiber to the curb or to a receiving cabinet located outside the structure (FTTC), using copper telephone wire to serve the remaining distance, a distinctly inferior arrangement but acceptable for homes or businesses equipped with *very-high-bit-rate digital subscriber line* (VDSL) service.

Despite the advantages of fiber-optic technologies for trunk lines, some areas do not have the required infrastructure, and others stubbornly cling to copper wires and DSL service, which is more easily distributed on overhead wires. Because the signal degrades far more quickly, repeaters and amplifiers are needed to maintain service, adding to the equipment that needs to be accommodated on poles or in cabinets on the ground.

A number of computer media can assist the site planner in laying out communications cables for a site, automatically tallying line lengths and other elements. Cables are typically directly buried in the ground, using special excavators that create narrow trenches. Local governments generally specify where they must run in the right-of-way and the depths of the cable, in order

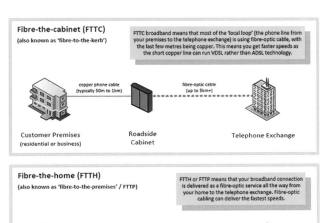

31.2 Installing underground communications infrastructure. (Courtesy of Long Wavelength Array/University of New Mexico)

31.3 Options for fiber-optic connections. (Courtesy of thinkbroadband.com)

31.4 Installing direct-buried cables, Rockland, Idaho. (Courtesy of Direct Communications, Inc.)

Communications

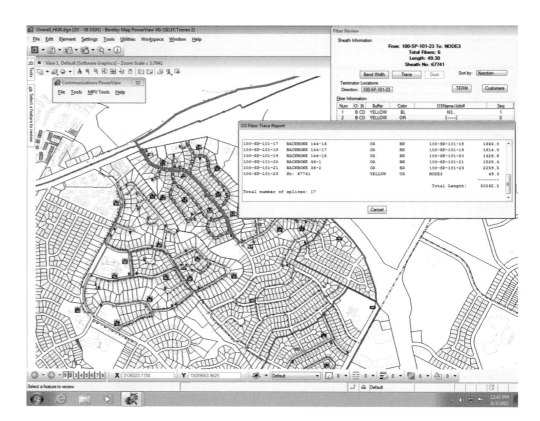

31.5 Media for mapping cable networks. (Courtesy of Bentley Systems)

to coordinate with other infrastructure in the street. The rapid evolution of technology over the recent past has resulted in streets needing to be opened up several times, with unpleasant results if the lines are located under pavement. An alternative to excavation is plowing the trench, and horizontal boring may be necessary to cross below other infrastructure, railroad tracks, or other impediments. In densely built urban areas, conduits may be laid with sufficient capacity for several lines and the flexibility to accommodate new technologies in the future. These may be coordinated with electrical conduits, since fiber-optic technology is not affected by electromagnetic charges.

Wireless Communications

Much of the growth of communications technology has been the result of ubiquitous wireless service. Most of the inhabited areas of the US and Europe are served, and much of Asia are now covered by cellular service. Many developing countries have made the leap from having few landline telephones to universal cellular service, and the ownership of smartphones has multiplied. Cellular transmission sites may be located on radio towers, mountaintops, specially constructed towers, or tall buildings. Most cell service requires line-of-sight propagation of signals, which will be disrupted by topography and concentrations of buildings and may be affected by dense landscape, depending upon the strength of the signal. *Cell towers* typically host antennas, transmitter/receivers, digital signal processors, GPS receivers, and backup electric power in case of failure of grid-based power. They may also be the link to longer-distance communication, housing microwave antennas and down- and up-link transmitters and receivers. Most local governments have sought to coordinate the equipment of all local providers on combined *base transceiver stations* (BTS) or *sites*, because of local opposition to the siting of such facilities. They can be a significant source of revenue for the property owners, and even rooftop antennas are often sought by building owners because of their revenue potential.

There is no general rule about the spacing of cell towers; it will depend upon the power of their signal, the height of the tower, topography, sources of interference, and the uses of the signal. In less settled areas they may be spaced as far as 30–40 km (20–25 mi) apart, but in urban areas as near as 1 km (0.6 mi). A less obtrusive solution than large consolidated cell stations is the construction of a *distributed antenna system*, consisting of a series of antenna nodes indoors or outdoors below the clutter level. These are commonly employed in mass transit subways that have difficulty in receiving service from towers aboveground, and by universities, research parks, and other institutions where a system with blanket coverage can be installed. The Shard, a recently constructed office building in London, has a distributed antenna system throughout its height.

The proposal to locate a cell tower nearby generally elicits a wave of opposition. Assertions about the health effects of nearby towers always accompany such debates, and a mountain of studies has addressed this subject. The concern is that *radio frequency radiation (RFR)*, one form of electromagnetic frequency (EMF) energy, may cause cancer. While negative scientific findings do not obviate future discoveries, it is the general consensus of the World Health Organization EMF Project, the International Agency for Research on Cancer, the American Cancer Society, and the vast majority of researchers on the subject that cell towers do not elevate the risk of cancer (American Cancer Society, n.d.). This matches the findings on EMF radiation for another nemesis, wind turbines, outlined in chapter 29.

Two other objections are commonly voiced to proposals for cell towers. Nearby property owners assert that their property values will be affected negatively by the presence of a tower. Only a few studies have addressed this. Opinion surveys conducted in Christchurch, New Zealand found a wide variation in views about whether properties within 30 m (100 ft) of a cell tower were less valuable than those 1 km (0.6 mi) away—the range was from no effect to about 20% decrease in value. Transaction studies in the same city indicated that properties would be devalued 12–20% by the presence of a nearby cell tower. An empirical study in Orange County, Florida in 2004 found that there was a statistically significant but minimal impact on property values as the result of construction of a cell tower, of less than 2% and diminishing with distance (Bond 2007). Thus, objectors are not wrong in asserting that property values

31.6   Cell phone tower, Palatine, Illinois.
(Joe Ravi/Wikimedia Commons)

will be impacted, but the size of the impact may be determined by cultural values.

Aesthetic preferences are behind many of the objections to cell towers, and are not to be taken lightly. Placing towers on hilltops, many believe, will ruin the natural landscape; others object to changes in the skyline, or the clutter of mechanical objects intruding into ordered surroundings. Disguising the paraphernalia as natural objects can sometimes mute these objections, although this is seldom successful. Or the transmission devices may be installed within enclosures, such as church steeples, cupolas, clock towers, or bell towers, or in false floors or penthouses of structures, which may be a more satisfactory solution. The aesthetic objections seem not to be an issue for very tall towers, where antennas are often integrated into the design—think Empire State Building, Tokyo Tower, Toronto's CN Tower, among other symbols of cities. Perhaps the most creative solution is to design cell towers as works of art, as objects in the landscape that people can admire.

Satellite disks, which have become ubiquitous as subscriptions to satellite TV service multiply and as many businesses install direct satellite links, pose

31.7 Cell phone tower disguised as fake tree, Annandale, Virginia (Courtesy of Ellie Ashford/Annandale blog)

31.8 Cell phone tower concealed in cupola, Ocean City, New Jersey. (Courtesy of Stealth ® Concealment Solutions, Inc.)

31.9 Cell tower as public sculpture, Piazza Matteotti, Treviso, Italy. (Roberto Pamio + Partners)

another kind of aesthetic challenge. Their placement is restricted to locations where there is clear line of sight to multiple satellites, ruling out locations where tall trees or buildings obstruct the signal. Thus they are almost always visible, and are not easily overlooked. One approach is making them creative objects on the face of buildings or in the landscape. However, a better solution is to organize common reception points on rooftops, or behind walls, networked to all the users in an area or building. Fabric covers can be installed around the satellite both to protect it from dust and weather and to improve the appearance of the equipment.

Cities throughout the world are seeking to blanket their public realm with hotspots, so that residents and visitors are always within range of an Internet connection. Some places are converting now obsolete public telephone booths into Internet sites, while others have designed new forms of streetscape to accommodate wireless transmitters. In open spaces, new options are available to locate equipment belowground, easily accessible through hatches.

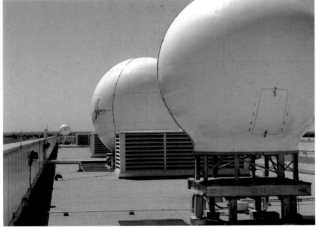

31.10 Collection of satellite dishes, Amsterdam.
(Peter Doeswijk, artist)

31.11 Satellite dish enclosure, University of Texas, Austin.
(Courtesy of University of Texas, Austin)

31.12 Free WiFi via sidewalk hotspot, New York City.
(Courtesy of LinkNYC)

31.13 Underground wireless hotspot.
(Oldcastle Precast)

Intelligent Cities Infrastructure

It takes only a short leap to envision urban areas with high-speed fiber connections to every door and street, combined with satellite access, and where public systems are fully integrated and adapt to human needs in real time. This vision is a reality in cities with automated traffic control (ATC) systems, but the new generation of cities being built across the globe goes far beyond. These include New Songdo in Korea, Lusail in Qatar, Masdar in Abu Dhabi, King Abdullah Economic City in Saudi Arabia, Gujarat International Finance Tec-City in India, among dozens of new developments that label themselves "smart cities" or "intelligent cities" or "smart connected cities." Older cities are racing to catch up, including Copenhagen, Santander, Barcelona, and other European cities. Intelligent cities are being promoted by large software and system integration companies and the makers of devices, including IBM, Siemens, Cisco, Libelium, and other firms, many of which are behind the well-publicized pilot projects. The visions differ, of course, based on the comparative expertise of the technological partners.

31.14 One vision of an intelligent city, laced with sensors. (Courtesy of Libelium)

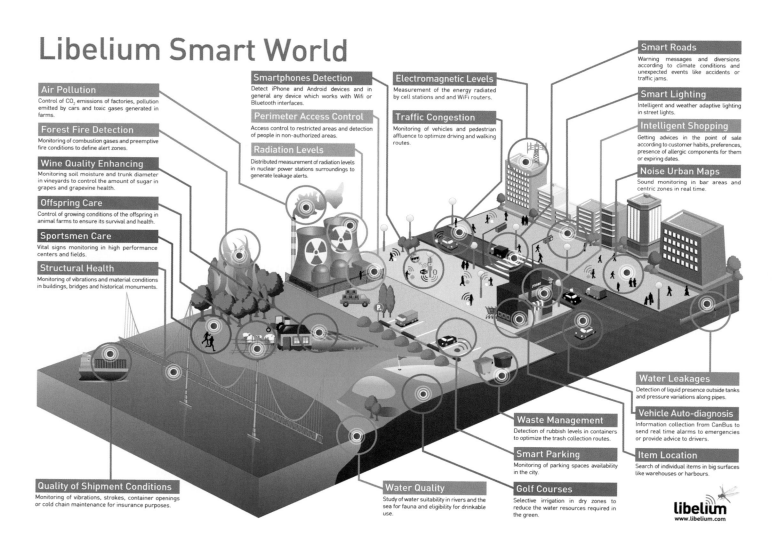

Libelium Smart World

Air Pollution
Control of CO₂ emissions of factories, pollution emitted by cars and toxic gases generated in farms.

Forest Fire Detection
Monitoring of combustion gases and preemptive fire conditions to define alert zones.

Wine Quality Enhancing
Monitoring soil moisture and trunk diameter in vineyards to control the amount of sugar in grapes and grapevine health.

Offspring Care
Control of growing conditions of the offspring in animal farms to ensure its survival and health.

Sportsmen Care
Vital signs monitoring in high performance centers and fields.

Structural Health
Monitoring of vibrations and material conditions in buildings, bridges and historical monuments.

Smartphones Detection
Detect iPhone and Android devices and in general any device which works with Wifi or Bluetooth interfaces.

Perimeter Access Control
Access control to restricted areas and detection of people in non-authorized areas.

Radiation Levels
Distributed measurement of radiation levels in nuclear power stations surroundings to generate leakage alerts.

Electromagnetic Levels
Measurement of the energy radiated by cell stations and and WiFi routers.

Traffic Congestion
Monitoring of vehicles and pedestrian affluence to optimize driving and walking routes.

Smart Roads
Warning messages and diversions according to climate conditions and unexpected events like accidents or traffic jams.

Smart Lighting
Intelligent and weather adaptive lighting in street lights.

Intelligent Shopping
Getting advices in the point of sale according to customer habits, preferences, presence of allergic components for them or expiring dates.

Noise Urban Maps
Sound monitoring in bar areas and centric zones in real time.

Water Leakages
Detection of liquid presence outside tanks and pressure variations along pipes.

Vehicle Auto-diagnosis
Information collection from CanBus to send real time alarms to emergencies or provide advice to drivers.

Item Location
Search of individual items in big surfaces like warehouses or harbours.

Quality of Shipment Conditions
Monitoring of vibrations, strokes, container openings or cold chain maintenance for insurance purposes.

Water Quality
Study of water suitability in rivers and the sea for fauna and eligibility for drinkable use.

Waste Management
Detection of rubbish levels in containers to optimize the trash collection routes.

Smart Parking
Monitoring of parking spaces availability in the city.

Golf Courses
Selective irrigation in dry zones to reduce the water resources required in the green.

libelium
www.libelium.com

Intelligent cities have five basic components. *Sensors*, both electronic and video, are the key to gathering and feeding real-time information on conditions on the ground. The information may be collected in video form (as with traffic flows or monitoring of places), as numeric data (temperature, numbers of people crossing an intersection, level of trash in a container, water pressure), as binary data (whether or not a parking spot is occupied), or as a readout from a complex meter (water quality, air quality). Sensors may be mounted on vertical poles, attached to buildings, or embedded in structures or roadways. The data they collect can be transmitted through cable or wireless networks. A number of cities are developing a series of wireless nodes that are capable of assembling data collected by a variety of sensors and transmitting them to a their ultimate destinations.

The second component is *displays*—data is of little use without an operations interface. A number of cities, including New York and Rio de Janeiro, have created sophisticated operations centers staffed by representatives of all the city's agencies. This allows an immediate discussion of incidents or looming disasters as soon as they appear on the displays, and agencies can quickly react and alter their service patterns. Large institutional sites, such as university campuses, and integrated development projects have similar operations centers monitoring security, energy use, and a variety of other indicators of performance. Displays may also be directed at users of an environment—as with directional or caution signs on roadways, news boards, or displays of energy use intended to encourage conservation. The adoption of LED traffic signals

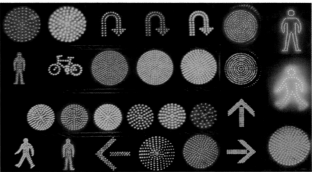

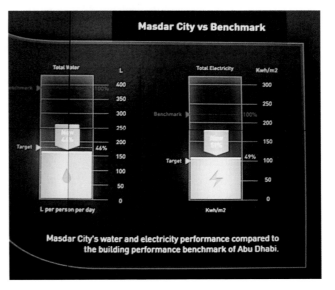

31.15 Operations center serving all city agencies, Rio de Janeiro.
(Gary Hack)

31.16 LED traffic signal menu allowing for custom control of traffic.
(Unidentified)

31.17 Real-time reporting of energy and water consumption, Masdar, Abu Dhabi.
(Gary Hack)

Communications

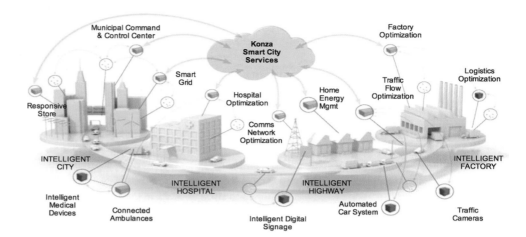

31.18 Data centers as hubs of an intelligent city. (Courtesy of Konza Techno City)

allows more fine-grained management of traffic movement, with signal timing and allowable moves displayed lane by lane. At Masdar, temperature, energy and water use, and other data are displayed conspicuously in indoor and exterior public information kiosks, comparing consumption to predicted levels and the norm for other such developed areas. Data may also be displayed on handheld devices, such as smartphones with apps to retrieve information.

Not all operations require human intervention: models allow traffic signal timing to be recalibrated based on the volumes sensed in the field, and energy sources can be switched automatically to optimize costs and loads. Thus, the third component of the intelligent city is the *data center* with its programs that not only display information (geographically, or compared to norms, or in time sequence) but use artificial intelligence to adapt their operations. The accumulation of large volumes of data from multiple sources in a data center can allow analyses that may uncover patterns not apparent by observing a single source. Comparing data on school attendance, shopping, and transit ridership, as an example, may reveal neighborhood patterns that have consequences for traffic and roadway management. The larger vision is that the data center will become the hub of public and private intelligence, a new form of public utility used by an entire community.

The fourth component is *mobile information devices* that are both originators and users of the data. The most common one is the smartphone, which has become a vital link in the emergency response system of most cities—reporting accidents or incidents, sending images about flooding or other natural disasters. They are also, as we have noted, essential portals to information from operating agencies, allowing residents to find out when the next bus will arrive, order a taxi, find the location of a service agency or restaurant, and plot the shortest route to a destination, among a thousand other tasks that rely upon data that is centrally assembled. In the future, self-driving automobiles will also have built-in intelligence functions, reading signal phases at intersections and avoiding collisions with pedestrians and other vehicles, and will have the capability to return to a parking area without an occupant. Other forms of intelligent mobile devices will also evolve.

Finally, an essential component will be intelligence *embedded* in the environment that may be directly sensed or reached using mobile devices. One example is the use of *quick response (QR) codes* to provide access to knowledge connected to the visible environment. A QR code may provide access to the history of a place, may introduce one to all the occupants of a building without requiring the glare of signage, or could provide the basis for a museum or a shopping place without

artifacts. Other devices that both sense the presence of a person or object and transmit meaningful data might be embedded in the pavement of cities. One speculation is that the combination of sensor/transmitters and smart vehicles might make it possible to have pedestrians and automobiles share the same spaces in a city. As discussed in chapter 20, dissolving the rigid separation of vehicles and pedestrians along a street, in a way that is safe, would be a truly revolutionary breakthrough in site design.

31.19 QR code in pavement linking to the history of Almere, Netherlands.
(Gary Hack)

31.20 QR codes on facade of office building, Teletech Campus, Dijon, France.
(Courtesy of MVRDV/Philippe Rualt)

31.21 Smart tiles and smart vehicles could make it possible for pedestrians, cyclists, and vehicles to share streets and plazas.
(Courtesy of © BIG – Bjarke Ingels Group)

THIS *PLASTICITY* WILL REPLACE THE STATIC CITY CAST IN CONCRETE, WITH A FUTURE CITY THAT DYNAMICALLY TRANSFORMS AND ADAPTS TO THE LIFE BETWEEN BUILDINGS...

32 | Site Landscape

The form and landscape character of a site are what users ultimately experience as they arrive or go about their daily rounds. The space between buildings creates a sense of place, along with the structures on the land. It may seem unusual to be including landscape as an element of the infrastructure of a site. However, landscape is not an afterthought, not cosmetics added to spruce up leftover spaces on a site, and surely not simply a foil to show buildings in their best light. Consideration of landscape form begins with the first moves to locate things on a site, and ends with the completed site landscape plan. In truth, it never really ends, since landscape is a living phenomenon that constantly changes and is in need of attention.

As we have noted in chapter 2, the form of the land and its landscape ecology are the point of departure for site planning. Roads, buildings, and public spaces will be added to the terroir in ways that capitalize on its natural qualities, respecting views, drainage patterns, areas of fine vegetation, and longstanding man-made features. Inevitably the topography will need to be altered to allow workable gradients for the roadways, walkways, and structures. As more hard surfaces are added to the site, runoff will increase. These changes will in turn create new demands on the landscape, to protect slopes from erosion, stabilize hillsides, define public spaces, and guide the eye through the site. A conceptual plan for the landscape will be needed, followed shortly by a grading plan that defines the new topography of the site. While the process begins by considering the existing landscape ecology, design of the new ecology of the site is among the most creative opportunities of site planning.

32.1 Memorial park at the World Trade Center, New York City, where memory and repose combine to leave an indelible impression on visitors. (Gary Hack)

The most memorable sites are sometimes those where the new construction appears to have been there forever, as at Sea Ranch (chapter 1) or NewBridge on the Charles (chapter 2). But sites are also man-made artifacts, accommodating activities added to the land, and bear the marks of those who have shaped them. Choices must be made about the geometry of outdoor spaces and elements, their materials, and how they will be used. There are long traditions of creating gardens and outdoor spaces where the prevailing landscape has been totally reshaped to provide a narrative about nature and human experience. Memory and human nature are also essential to landscape form.

Landscape Concepts

The term *landscape* originated with the Dutch *landschap* (also *landsceap* and *landscipe* in Old English, and *landschaft* in German), joining the concepts of ground or soils (land) with shape (scape)—literally the shape of the ground and the process of shaping it. Its meaning has changed over time to encompass the addition of plant materials, walls, and artifacts that are anchored to the earth. Painters use the term more expansively, encapsulating all that is visible to the observer—everything that is "out there"—from snow-topped mountains to structures on the land to the trees and ground cover. Many urban scenes contain few natural elements, yet hard-surfaced streets and buildings are still referred to as urban landscapes.

The most obvious approach in creating the landscape of a site is to take cues from what existed before. Frederick Law Olmsted advocated *completeness*, by which a created landscape seemed to belong to the

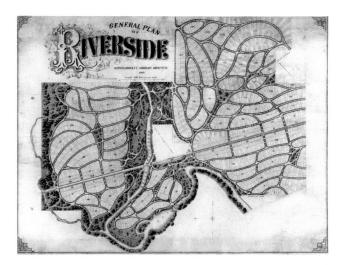

32.2 Riverside, Illinois, which created a template for nature-centered planning.
(Olmsted, Vaux & Co.)

32.3 Minghu Wetland Park, Liupanshui city, Guizhou province, China.
(Courtesy of Turenscape)

32.4 The constructed landscape of Central Park, New York City.
(Gary Hack)

32.5 Constructed hillside at Olympic Sculpture Park, Seattle.
(Courtesy of WEISS/MANFREDI/Ben Benschneider photo)

wider landscape of the region. In his planning of Riverside, Illinois, he employed curvilinear forms for streets that mimic the gentle hillsides of the area. The form of a braided river is the geometry employed in the Minghu Wetland Park in Liupanshui, China, planned by Turenscape. Both forms have practical advantages in avoiding sharp turns, with the streets in Riverside smoothing the flow of horse-drawn carriages (now automobiles), and the flow of water in Liupanshui cleansing the industrial wastes of the previous brownfield site. Creating a landscape in harmony with the wider ecology may limit the needed changes to a site, but we are reminded that Olmsted's best-known landscape, Central Park in New York (planned with Calvert Vaux), involved moving millions of cubic meters of soil and rock to fill marshes, create level playing grounds, and expose rock walls, not to mention displacing over 1,300 site residents. And in other instances, such as the Olympic Sculpture Park in Seattle, site and building are formed to resemble a hillside that may (or may not) have once existed, providing a sense of continuity of landscape.

Connections with the wider landscape may be direct or through symbolic associations. Native plant materials can provide instant identification with the local ecology, knitting newly planted areas with areas that are untouched. When a site borders on a large forest or wetland, the margins may be planted with native species to provide a stable or seamless transition. Often such moves are necessary to repair previous human modifications, which may have created slopes that are too steep, or armored with concrete that eliminates their ecological function or exposes mature landscape areas to threats of erosion.

But the landscape idea usually must go beyond simply repairing the landscape. The *picturesque tradition* of landscape may be the guiding aesthetic. At its apex in the nineteenth century, it emphasized peaceful, gentle landscapes surrounded by unspoiled, often rugged panoramas—the contrasts sought out by painters of the day. Romantic landscapes were not wedded to local plants; many were designed to exhibit exotic species from around the world. Olmsted was inclined to create picturesque landscapes, and it remains a popular aesthetic today, offering landscapes worthy of photos, with or without subjects in the foreground.

In the long evolution of Japanese and Chinese garden traditions, one of the enduring themes has been *compressing landscape* forms found in the larger region, so that they can be experienced in a leisurely walkabout or from a single vista from a pavilion. References to wider landscapes need not be literal. Japanese master gardeners frequently symbolize iconic landscapes through abstract forms, as at Ginkaku-ji temple in Kyoto, where the sea and mountains are represented in meticulously raked sand. The forms can be appreciated

32.6 Restored wetlands at Houtan Park, Shanghai. (Courtesy of Turenscape)

32.7 The romantic landscape of Stourhead Garden, Wiltshire, UK. (Lechona/Wikimedia Commons)

on several levels of consciousness—as platonic forms, admired for their precision and placement; as representational objects, symbolizing the iconic mountains and seas of Japan; or as neutral forms that strip away redundant thought and allow the mind to be reset.

Ultimately, all made landscapes are the product of human minds, and all materials placed on a site are unnatural, even plants, since they have been uprooted to become part of a new ecology. They may also depend upon irrigation and human labor for survival and growth. Many designers take this as a license to use landscape as a form of *symbolic expression*, voicing themes that go beyond the site's original terroir. In an urban area lacking any larger landscape references, the forms may be totally abstract or may reference historic landforms. Or they may recall the preurban landscape, as in Shenyang Architectural University, which celebrates the centuries of rice culture that preceded the site's appropriation for modern uses.

Landscape also celebrates the dimension of time. The rice fields at Shenyang are different in spring when they are being planted, summer as they mature, and fall or winter when the rice is harvested. Tall grasses planted along a walkway have a similar cycle, and they stimulate the tactile senses when their crops bend in the wind and brush against people walking the edge of the path. Some landscapes are designed to be edible, creating an entirely different connection with the land. Their stewards are not passive observers; they feel responsible for the crops that will mature in fall. And as winter arrives in snowy climates, plants provide color and offer the hope that nature will return in the spring. We understand seasons and the cycle of regeneration by marking time through nature.

32.8 Moss garden, Saihou-ji shrine, Kyoto.
(Ivanoff/Wikimedia Commons)

32.9 Sand garden, Ginkaku-ji temple, Kyoto.
(Gary Hack)

32.10 Plaza with drumlins, Federal Courthouse, Minneapolis.
(Courtesy of Sifei Liu)

32.11 Central space, Shenyang Architectural University, Shenyang, China.
(Courtesy of Turenscape)

32.12 Edible landscape, large-scale potager at Château de Villandry, France.
(Manfred Heyde/Wikimedia Commons)

Landscape ideals will guide the planning of the site. However, the site planner must also deal with several practical issues that will influence site form, beginning with ensuring that the site is safe for human occupancy.

Remediation of Contaminated Sites

Remediation of sites contaminated by hazardous materials has become an important issue as the scarcity of land in urban areas turns brownfields sites into candidates for development. In American cities these issues were either ignored in the past or considered intractable or too costly to address, leaving many sites fallow. Former industrial, petroleum, and chemical sites top the list, but capped sanitary landfills, areas with underground storage tanks that have leaked, abandoned military reservations, waste disposal areas, incinerators, rail yards, gravel pits, quarries, and mining areas remain underused in or around many American cities. In other countries, intensive agricultural zones at the edge of cities, such as abandoned shrimp farms, may have left behind soils with concentrations of chemicals and organic residues that make them unsafe for

occupancy. Fortunately, there are many new strategies and techniques that allow cleanup to go hand in hand with development.

The strategy for cleanup depends, in the first instance, on the nature of the contamination. What are the toxic substances, and what dangers do they pose? What is the extent of contamination—deposits aboveground? surface layers of soil? subsoils? groundwater? What levels of contamination are present? Are there multiple contaminants? Answering these questions involves chemical analysis, engineering testing, and public health analyses (Suthersan 2002). Often the diagnosis begins with assembling the historical record of previous uses of a site, which helps to identify the compounds that may be responsible for current conditions. Then the site must be tested and mapped to determine the chemistry and geography of the contaminants.

Hazardous materials may be located on the surface of a site or in obsolete structures that remain standing, in which case removal is generally necessary. Asbestos may have been used to insulate buildings or equipment, or structures may be laced with carbon or fibers from tire manufacturing, or hazardous chemicals may remain in tanks or other containers. Each material has its associated cleanup process, but the common issue is finding a disposal site where such materials are welcome. Some materials may be incinerated to reduce their bulk or diminish their hazard. The choice of method will depend upon technology that is available and on economic factors.

The contamination may have penetrated the soil, making contact with it hazardous or limiting the plant materials that can be supported. The soil in former railway repair yards may be saturated with substances used to wash engines, including arsenic; petroleum storage areas may have a residue of compounds from spills or discharges; areas used for snow dumps in winter may have excessive concentrations of lead, carbon fibers, and cadmium from automobiles. It will be important to determine the type and concentration of contaminants and their depth of penetration in the soil.

When hazardous substances have entered the groundwater supply, their impact may extend across or even well beyond the site in a plume that mirrors groundwater flows. Measuring the impact area is considerably more difficult, and may involve drilling test wells from which the contours of contamination can be plotted. A three-dimensional digital model of the areas below the site, including subsurface soil layers and the contours of hazardous substances, can help in visualizing possible approaches to treating the problem.

Having identified the source, location, extent, and type of contamination, there is generally a choice among four broad strategies: *containment*, *removal*, *ex-situ treatment*, or *in-situ remediation* (Suthersan 1997). The contaminants may be isolated or contained in one area of the site, or capped so that human contact is minimized. Or they may be removed and disposed of in hazardous waste landfills or in locations where they do not constitute a human danger. Ex-situ treatment involves extracting and treating contaminants through chemical processes, then returning the decontaminated material to its original location. These traditional methods of dealing with contamination remain in many instances the most cost-effective, but they can impose considerable constraints on site development and often export the liabilities to other locations. The most interesting new methods involve chemical or biological methods of in-situ treatment of hazards. Among the techniques are *natural attenuation*, *bioattenuation*, *natural remediation*, and *monitored natural attenuation*. In their simplest form they involve exposing hazardous substances to natural materials, such as air or plants or organic compounds, that over time neutralize the dangers they pose. Used alone or in combination with traditional methods, these processes can often occur while a site is occupied, and can become an opportunity for rethinking forms of site development.

In some instances the best strategy—or the only economically viable approach—is to retain hazardous materials on a site, containing them so that their impact is limited and human contact is minimized. Natural processes may, over time, result in improvements to conditions, or the hazards may be minimal if contained. As an example, for a site that will have large paved parking areas, it may be possible to cap an underlying hazard by use of the parking area's impervious surfaces. Or it may be possible to build structures over areas with lightly contaminated soil, as long as they do not have basements that disturb the hazard or come in contact with it. Some substances lend themselves to *solidification* processes, which encapsulate the waste in a monolithic solid of high structural integrity. Other compounds can be stabilized by forming them

into solid materials through the addition of Portland cement, fly ash, cement kiln dust, quick lime, or slags in various forms (Suthersan 1997). These techniques encapsulate the hazardous elements and reduce their exposure to water and humans. Many environmental protection agencies now recognize such techniques of site development as legitimate strategies for mitigation.

If the risks are higher, it may be possible to contain hazardous substances and prevent them from entering the groundwater supply by creating a concrete slurry wall around the perimeter of the contaminated area. Or in the case of a plume of contaminated groundwater, a slurry wall can limit the flow and allow the contamination to be treated near the barrier that has been created. Areas that are contained generally need to be monitored to ensure that the hazardous materials have not migrated to locations where humans are exposed to them.

Removal of hazardous materials is, of course, always an option. Soil may be so contaminated that it is not practical to remove the impurities through natural processes, or it may contain substances that cannot be removed; it will then need to be excavated and transported to landfill sites able to receive it. Quarries, exhausted mining sites, and large areas where there is little human contact, such as landfills below airport runways, are often candidates for disposal of such soils. To facilitate removal and disposal of heavily contaminated wastes, it may be necessary to vitrify the materials, using heat to convert waste materials into glass, or to encapsulate the offending substances in blocks of concrete. Sulfur wastes, as an example, can be melted and formed into solid block form.

Ex-situ site treatment of contamination is another option for many substances. For groundwater, "pump and treat" techniques are the most common approach, found on more than two-thirds of the cleanup sites in the US. There are dozens of methods, but they generally involve removing groundwater by pumping, treating the liquids to neutralize or remove offending substances, and returning the purified material to the groundwater. Constructing a treatment tower or a structure to house the treatment equipment may be necessary if the process is continuous. Or mobile units may be brought to the site on a regular schedule and connected to a series of wellheads where material is pumped, treated, and returned.

Treatment of contaminated soils ex-situ is also common when only the upper layers are contaminated. Soil is typically formed into windrows, mixed with chemical or natural substances, and allowed to react until its composition is sufficiently changed that it is safe for use. Where the quantity of soils to be treated is large enough, a processing plant may be constructed to mechanize the process. In the construction of the Central Artery/Tunnel project in Boston, millions of cubic yards of excavation needed to be treated to neutralize saline contaminants before the material was returned to the construction site as backfill.

There has been an explosion of interest in in-situ techniques for remediation of contaminated soils and groundwater over the past decade. They take many forms, but all are rooted in the use of natural processes—dilution, anaerobic and aerobic exposure, oxidation, filtration through natural materials, chemical reactions, the actions of microbes, absorption in plant roots and bodies, and other natural conversion processes—that have the ability to cleanse the environment. They are often more cost-effective and can be effective in low-permeability soils, as an example, where other techniques have had little success.

Phytoremediation, or the engineered use of plants for environmental remediation, shows considerable promise for cleaning soil with unacceptable levels of certain metals (such as nickel, cobalt, copper, zinc, manganese, lead, or cadmium) and organics (such as PAHs, chlorinated benzenes, PCBs, BTEX compounds, many pesticides, chlorophenol, carboxylic acids, and trichloroethylene). There are several different phytoremediation processes. *Phytoaccumulation*, also called *phytoextraction*, involves the uptake of metal contaminants in the soil by

Table 32.1 | Phytoremediation overview

Mechanism	Process goal	Media	Contaminants	Plants	Status
Phytoextraction	Contaminant extraction and capture	Soil, sediment, sludges	Metals: Ag, Cd, Co, Cr, Cu, Hg, Mn, Mo, Ni, Pb, Zn; radionuclides: ^{90}Sr, ^{137}Cs, ^{239}Pu, ^{238,234}U	Indian mustard, pennycress, alyssum, sunflowers, hybrid poplars	Laboratory, pilot, and field applications
Rhizofiltration	Contaminant extraction and capture	Groundwater, surface water	Metals, radionuclides	Sunflowers, Indian mustard, water hyacinth	Laboratory and pilot-scale
Phytostabilization	Contaminant containment	Soil, sediment, sludges	As, Cd, Cr, Cu, Hg, Pb, Zn	Indian mustard, hybrid poplars, grasses	Field application
Rhizodegradation	Contaminant destruction	Soil, sediment, sludges, groundwater	Organic compounds (TPHs, PAHs, pesticides, chlorinated solvents, PCBs)	Red mulberry, grasses, hybrid poplars, cattail, rice	Field application
Phytodegradation	Contaminant destruction	Soil, sediment, sludges, groundwater, surface water	Organic compounds, chlorinated solvents, phenols, herbicides, munitions	Algae, stonewort, hybrid poplars, black willow, bald cypress	Field demonstration
Phytovolatilization	Contaminant extraction from media and release into air	Groundwater, soil, sediment, sludges	Chlorinated solvents, some inorganics (Se, Hg, As)	Poplars, alfalfa, black locust, Indian mustard	Laboratory and field application
Hydraulic control (plume control)	Contaminant degradation or containment	Groundwater, surface water	Water-soluble organics and inorganics	Hybrid poplars, cottonwood, willow	Field demonstration
Vegetative cover (evapotranspiration cover)	Contaminant containment, erosion control	Soil, sludges, sediments	Organic and inorganic compounds	Poplars, grasses	Field application
Riparian corridors (non-point-source control)	Contaminant destruction	Surface water, groundwater	Water-soluble organics and inorganics	Poplars	Field application

Source: US Environmental Protection Agency.

32.13 Sunflowers for phytoremediation of toxic wastes, Centrale Nucléaire, Saint-Laurent-des-Eaux, France. (Nitot/Wikimedia Commons)

plant roots, so that they are lodged in the above-grade portions of plants. They may then be harvested and disposed of by landfilling, incineration or composting, in some instances recovering or recycling the metals. After several cycles of planting, soil contaminant levels may be brought down to acceptable levels.

Plants that are most effective in extracting metals are referred to as *hyperaccumulators*; they are usually specific to a particular metal. Table 32.2 lists a number of species that have been proved effective. Indian mustard plant, grown throughout the world for its oil seed, has been found to accumulate up to two metric tons of lead per hectare of planting (Brown et al. 1995). Sunflowers have proved effective in absorbing heavy metal substances around old manufacturing plants and radioactive substances in Chernobyl; they are also an attractive addition to the landscape. Hyperaccumlator plants are typically effective in shallow soils, up to 2 ft (30 cm) in depth. If contamination is deeper, fast-growing poplar trees have been shown to be effective for extracting heavy metals 6 to 10 ft (2 to 3 m) deep, although disposal of their leaves is an issue that must be considered.

A less understood process is *phytovolitilization*, which involves the uptake of water and inorganic compounds such as selenium or mercury, and their conversion and release into the air as less toxic gases. *Phytodegradation*, or *phytotransformation*, is a third natural process by which plants can improve soil conditions, particularly those with organic contaminants. A variety of common tree and aquatic plants are effective in degrading organic compounds.

A fourth phytoremediation process, *rhizodegradation* or *phytostimulation*, involves the acceleration of natural processes whereby microorganisms (yeast, fungi, or bacteria) in the root zone degrade organic substances such as fuels or solvents and convert them to harmless products. Natural substances released by plant roots, such as sugars, alcohols, and acids, contain organic compounds that act as nutrients for microorganisms. Plants also can loosen the soil and allow more oxygen to penetrate the root zone. Deep-rooted grasses, particularly with fibrous roots, can enhance degradation. Densely planted, the grasses and flowering crops can also make for an attractive ground cover that celebrates the seasons and gives scale to the environment.

Phytoremediation generally requires more time than removal of offending compounds or pump-and-treat methods. However, for sites that will be phased over many years or for sites that are land-banked it has considerable appeal, as it does on recreation sites where remediation planting can be an integral aspect of the design. Capped landfills, mining sites, and former industrial areas can be made attractive while they await more active development. With a small investment of resources they can be converted from derelict areas to open space resources.

Table 32.2 | Plant materials effective in phytoremediation

Common name	Scientific name	Process	Effective for
Pennycress	*Thlaspi caerulescens*	HA	Metals (zinc)
Indian mustard plant	*Brassica juncea*	HA	Metals (lead, chromium, copper, nickel)
		PV	Metalloids, metals (selenium, mercury)
Abyssinian mustard or cabbage, Ethiopian kale	*Brassica carinata*	HA	Metals (lead, chromium, copper, nickel)
Sunflower	*Tithonia diversifolia, Helianthus annus*	HA	Metals (uranium, lead, zinc
Hemp, dogbane	*Apocynum* spp.	HA	Metals (lead)
Common ragweed	*Ambrosia artemisiifolia*	HA	Metals (lead)
Aeollanthus	*Aeollanthus subacaulis* var. *linearis*	HA	Metals (copper)
Broom teatree	*Leptospermum scoparium*	HA	Metals (chromium)
Canola	*Brassica napus, Brassica rapa oleifera*	PV	Salt (selenium)
Kenaf (Deccan hemp)	*Hibiscus cannabinus*	PV	Salt (selenium)
Tall fescue	*Festuca arundinaceae*	PV	Salt (selenium)
		RD	Organics (PAHs)
Mouse-ear cress	*Arabidopsis thaliana*	PV	Salt (mercury salt)
Poplars (aspen)	*Populus* spp. (many varieties)	PT	Organics (trichloroethylene, atrazine)
Black willow	*Salix nigra*	PT	Organic herbicides
Yellow poplar	*Liriodendron tulipifera*	PT	Organic herbicides
Bald cypress	*Taxodium distichum*	PT	Organic herbicides
River birch	*Betula nigra*	PT	Organic herbicides
Live oak	*Quercus viginiana*	PT	Organic herbicides
Parrot feather	*Myriophyllum aquaticum*	PT	Organics (TNT)
Algae	*Nitella* spp. (many varieties)	PT	Organics (TNT)
Big bluestem	*Andropogon gerardi*	RD	Organic compounds, PAHs
Indiangrass	*Sorghastrum nutans*	RD	Organic compounds
Switchgrass	*Panicum virgatum*	RD	Organic compounds
Canada wild rye	*Elymus canadensis*	RD	Organic compounds
Little bluestem	*Schizachyrium scoparium*	RD	Organic compounds
Western wheatgrass	*Agropyron smithii*	RD	Organic compounds
Blue grama	*Bouteloua gracilis*	RD	Organic compounds
Crested wheatgrass	*Agropyron desertorum*	RD	Organics (PCBs)
Red mulberry	*Morus rubra*	RD	Organics (PCBs)
Crabapple	*Malus ioensis*	RD	Organics (PCBs)
Spearmint	*Mentha spicata*	RD	Organics (PCBs)
Osage orange	*Maclura pomifera*	RD	Organics (PCBs)
Alfalfa	*Medicago sativa*	RD	Organics (PAHs)
Sudan grass	*Sorghum vulgare sudanense*	RD	Organics (PAHs)

Sources: Sutherson 2002; Environmental Protection Agency 2000c.
Notes: HA = hyperaccumulator; PV = phytovolitilization; PT = phytodegradation or phytotransformation; RD = rhizodegradation or phytostimulation.
Metals include: nickel, cobalt, copper, zinc, manganese, lead, cadmium.
Organics include: polycyclic aromatic hydrocarbons (PAHs), chlorinated benzenes, polychlorinated biphenyls (PCBs), benzene, toluene, ethylbenzene, and xylene (BTEX) compounds, many pesticides, chlorophenols, carboxylic acids, trichloroethylene.

A Phytoremediation Proposal

The four illustrations show how phytoremediation can be an attractive alternative for sites that will remain fallow for a few years before being redeveloped. (a) The heavily contaminated site (fuels, petroleum residues, heavy metals) was originally created by filling a low-lying area with rubbish and garbage, and capping it with asphalt paving. (b) These materials need to be removed and relocated, with wood, concrete and other materials recycled on the site. (c) The site is then planted by a variety of species chosen to reflect the types of soil contamination, including *Agropyron repens*, *Cynodon dactylon*, *Festuca arundinacea*, *Festuca pratensis*, *Helianthus annus*, *Juniperus virginiana*, *Populus* spp., *Salix* spp., and *Typha angustifolia*. (d) Over time the vegetation fills the site while cleansing the impurities and restoring the health of the soils.

32.14 Phytoremediation proposal, Dagenham South brownfield, UK, by Anna Sieczak. (Illustrations courtesy of Anna Sieczak)

(a)

(b)

(c)

(d)

Grading the Site

The eventual shape of the site will have been on the planner's mind throughout the process of planning roads, walkways, buildings, and outdoor activities. Once these are situated, even if tentatively, it is possible to develop a sketch of the site grading plan, which will be essential in determining drainage patterns, the gradients of roadways and walks, the elevations of structures on the site, and whether existing vegetation can be maintained.

The site grading plan will also determine how much earth must be moved around the site, not a trivial financial issue. Modifying the topography of a 5 ha (12.3 ac) site by an average of 300 mm (12 in) up or down involves moving 15,000 m³ (19,600 cu yd) of earth, the equivalent of almost 2,000 10-wheeler truckloads. So a few millimeters of difference in elevations can greatly affect the amount of disruption to the site as well as costs.

If the site is undeveloped and has good-quality topsoils, the common practice is to strip and stockpile the upper layer (A and O horizons) to be eventually used to top out the areas to be planted. This will require separation of rocks, tree roots, and other materials, which usually results in a reduction of volume of 10–15%, although loosening the soil will tend to increase the volume slightly. Then the B or E horizons need to be reshaped to form the basic contours of the site (see chapter 3). Since the amount of topsoil to be removed is unpredictable, the site planner generally prescribes the final elevations of the site, leaving to the site contractor the task of determining the rough grades. Protection against erosion is essential when the site is being reshaped, since it has lost its natural protection.

32.15 Silt fences for erosion control while irrigated plants are established on regraded hillside.
(© Vadimgouida | Dreamstime.com)

An accurate contour plan of the site is the starting point for determining final elevations. On a modest-sized site, this will be created based on a ground-based LIDAR survey; on large sites, where this may be prohibitively expensive, contours derived from aerial photography or sensing will be supplemented by spot elevations at key locations. Rough estimates of future benchmark elevations will then help the planner begin to establish the new contours. Will the determining factor be the gradients of roadways, or the flows in waste sewers below them, or the base elevations of fine specimen trees to be retained, or the need to accommodate runoff?

Table 32.3 provides guidelines for minimum and maximum slopes on a site. If roadways are the limitation,

Table 32.3 | Guidelines for site grading

	Minimum slope	Maximum slope
Slope stability and drainage		
Planted or broad paved areas	1%	
Planted or broad paved areas (with ponding)	0.5%	
Backfill at building perimeter	2%	
Drainage swales and ditches	2%	10%
Mown grassed areas		25%
Unmown planted banks		60%
Unmown banks with deep-rooted ground cover		100%

Table 32.3 | Guidelines for site grading (continued)

	Minimum slope	Maximum slope
Angles of repose		
Loose, wet clay or silt		30%
Compact, dry clay		100%
Wet sand		80%
Dry sand		65%
Cobbles or dry retaining walls		70%
Forested land		100%
Gabions (up to 1 m)		100%
Roadways and walkways		
Cross section slope, concrete or bituminous	2%	
Cross section slope, earth or gravel	4%	
Cross section slope, paved walkways	2%	
Longitudinal grade, paved road (normal)	0.5%	10%
Longitudinal grade, paved road (no icing)		12%
Sustained longitudinal grade (trucks)		17%
By design speed, km/hr (mph):		
20 (15)		12%
30 (20)		12%
40 (25)		11%
50 (30)		10%
60 (35)		9%
70 (40)		8%
80 (50)		7%
90 (55)		6%
100(60)		5%
110 (65)		4%
Up-ramp, grade-separated intersection		6%
Down-ramp, grade-separated intersection		8%
On-grade intersection, for 12 m (40 ft) each side		4%
Parking area		4%
Sidewalk		10%
Accessible ramps, 1 m (3 ft) length		10%
Accessible ramps, 2 m (6 ft) length		8.5%
Accessible ramps, 5 m (16 ft) length		7%
Accessible ramps, 10 m (33 ft) length		5%
Public stairs		50%
Rail spur		2%

Sources: Various accepted standards.

**Techniques
for Estimating
Earthwork**

There are three basic techniques for estimating the earthwork required to achieve the new contours specified for a site: the contour area method, the cross-sectional method, and the terrain method. Each method begins with a new contour plan that can be overlaid on the predevelopment contours of the site.

Contour Area Method

This method of estimating the earthmoving begins by identifying the areas where the land will be disturbed by cutting or filling, differentiating between the two. This already provides an impression of whether the cuts and fills seem in balance; if they don't, the contours need to be adjusted. Then each of the contour areas where the topography is disturbed needs to be measured. Empirically, the volume of soil to be moved (C) is about ⅔ of the disturbed area, multiplied by the contour interval c. The volume of soil to be filled (F) is similarly derived from the area to be filled, and the aim is for the two volumes to be equal. For the site shown,

$$C = c \, (\tfrac{2}{3}(C1+C2+C3+C4+C5)),$$
$$F = c \, (\tfrac{2}{3} \, (F1+F2+F3=F4)),$$

and C should equal F. A rough estimate of the area can be obtained by placing a grid over the areas and counting the units, while a more accurate estimate will require a planimeter, or if in digital form, use of an area measure in the CAD program.

Cross-Sectional Method

The cross-sectional method is especially useful when only a small portion of a site will be disturbed, such as when estimating the grading necessary to construct a roadway. The method employs cross sections taken at a consistent interval, measuring the area of cut and fill in each. Then the areas are summed and multiplied by the number of intervals in which either cut or fill is necessary. Of course if a roadway navigates a cross slope, both cut and fill may be necessary in each cross section. This method provides a relatively accurate estimate of necessary earthwork, and is employed by many computer programs that accompany roadway design software.

Terrain Method

The terrain method involves sampling elevation differences between the existing and proposed topography on a grid, then multiplying these differences by the area surrounding each point. Thus, if the scale of the grid is 40 by 40 m and the difference of elevation between old and new is 2 m in one square of the grid, then about 3,200 m^3 will be displaced in this square. This method will tend to overestimate the earthmoving somewhat, but will become more accurate as the scale of the grid or contour interval is decreased. Digital terrain models are now common and provide an important interface with construction operations. Some earthmoving equipment can be programmed to undertake automatic grading, employing a digital terrain model linked to GPS benchmarks.

32.16 Estimating earthwork required: the contour area method. (Adam Tecza/ Gary Hack)

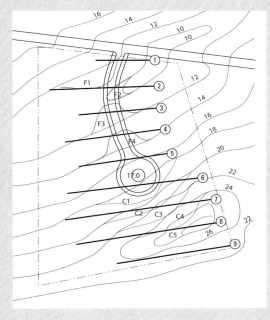

32.17 Estimating earthwork required: the cross-sectional method. (Adam Tecza/Gary Hack)

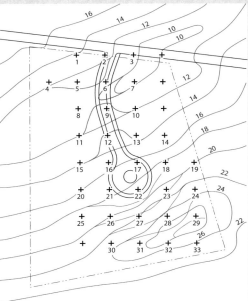

32.18 Estimating earthwork required: the terrain method. (Adam Tecza/Gary Hack)

spot elevations at the centerline (the vertical profile) will then need to be determined for the major roadways, paying attention to the underlying contours of the site. If rock is near the surface and blasting is to be avoided, roadways will need to be elevated enough to provide adequate cover for water and sewer lines located below the roadways. From the roadway profiles, the elevations of adjacent areas can be determined, and the grading plan spreads outward as roadways are pinned down, always attentive to the site drainage patterns. Some areas may be too steep to cover with grass or normal vegetated cover, and retaining walls will be added. Culverts or bridges may be needed to allow watercourses to cross roadways. Ground-floor elevations of structures will be determined, and the grading altered to ensure that runoff moves away from occupied spaces. Outdoor public spaces, parking areas, and walkways also will need to be accounted for, and graded to allow for runoff in heavy storms.

In the past, the grading plan was constructed by creating overlays on an existing contour map, with roadways and structures outlined, spot elevations noted, and new contours that departed from the original marked in colors—differentiating between areas that need to be lowered (cuts) and raised (fills). The method continues to be used to develop the preliminary grading plan, to be sure that the topography is manageable before the site plan is hardened. Visually, it will be obvious if the area of cuts is out of balance with the fill required, although this is tricky, since cuts for roadways in steep slope areas may yield large volumes of materials. If the volume needed for fill is out of balance with the volume yielded by cuts, the datum for roads or structures will need to be revised and new contours drawn. This trial and error method will avoid major earthmoving requirements. The objective is to balance the earthmoving, so that no soil needs to be imported or exported from the site. There are a number of techniques for making a more accurate estimate of earthmoving requirements, outlined in sidebar 32.2.

Today, grading and earthwork calculations are generally done using techniques embedded in engineering

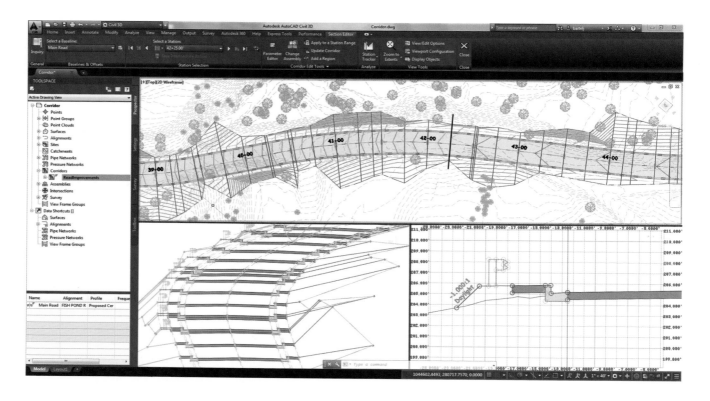

32.19 Roadway geometry and cross sections.
(Courtesy of Autodesk Inc./3DCivil)

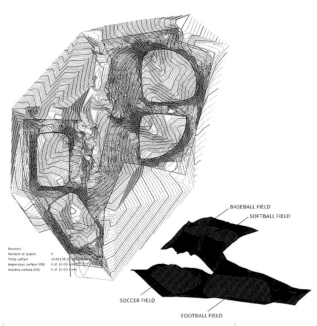

BASEBALL FIELD
SOFTBALL FIELD

SOCCER FIELD

FOOTBALL FIELD

COSTS: $697,994.79

ELEVATION BETWEEN FIELDS: 24', 18'

SCHEME THIRTEEN

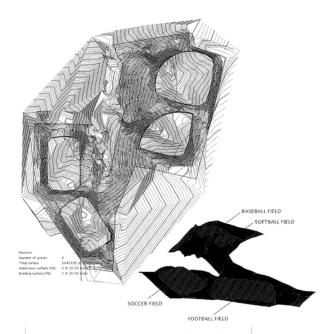

BASEBALL FIELD
SOFTBALL FIELD

SOCCER FIELD

FOOTBALL FIELD

COSTS: $736,024.99

ELEVATION BETWEEN FIELDS: 22', 8'

SCHEME FOUR

32.20 Computer-generated grading plans for alternative elevations of playing fields.
(Courtesy of Bentley Systems/SITEOPS)

CAD programs, which employ several of the techniques described here. When key elevations are input for roadways, programs will determine the optimal vertical alignments and, provided with cross sections of the roadway, will compute the cuts and fills necessary to insert the roadway into the landscape. Computer programs such as Bentley Systems' SITEOPS will automatically generate site grading plans, based on benchmark elevations that the planner inputs. This and other programs also allow the site to be visualized quickly in 3D, so that the planner can judge whether its appearance meets expectations (see chapter 13).

Grading a site is driven by aesthetic issues, as well as by technical requirements in assuring that the site functions well. The planner needs to envision what it will be like to move through the site, how vistas will unfold, how the character of the site will be revealed in the public domain, and how privacy can be assured for uses that need it. Digital simulations are quick and easy

to obtain, including drive- or walk-throughs, but many planners prefer also to construct small clay models of the site to understand and manipulate topography in a more plastic form, viewing the site as a set of textures and objects. Land form and landscape materials are inextricably linked.

Selecting a Landscape Palette

A successful site landscape must meet three tests: satisfying functional needs; furthering a set of aesthetic ideals; and being sustainable in the climate and topography of the site. Among the functional demands are stabilizing soils and slopes, creating microclimates, sheltering the site from sun and wind, defining territories, separating incompatible uses, as well as taking care of runoff and snow. There are programmatic purposes as well—providing food, absorbing CO_2, humidifying the environment, offering cutting flowers to grace interiors, among others. Celebrating the changes of seasons and the progression through the year, bringing humans into contact with natural beauty, adding color to the environment, and creating drama and mystery are among the aesthetic roles that landscape can play. And the landscape must be sustainable within the range of sunlight, rainfall, wind, temperature, and growing seasons of the site. These are the least changeable factors, and the place to begin in deciding upon a landscape palette.

Plant hardiness charts are usually the first reference. In the US, the Department of Agriculture has devised a zone system that takes into account the average annual minimum temperatures, reflecting the fact that surviving the winter cold is one of the major determinants of which species can prosper in a particular location (Department of Agriculture, n.d.). The system has been widely emulated in other countries, and maps are easily obtained for most parts of the world. The USDA zones are numbered from 1 to 12, each sometimes subdivided into a and b subzones to account for local variations. Most plants can survive in a range of zones and are rated accordingly (e.g., "Zones 3–5"). These ratings are a rough guide, with many caveats, of course. They do not reflect summer heat, which may exhaust many plant species; nor do they account for the hours of sunlight or length of the growing season, which may be inadequate even if the minimum temperatures are adequate. Thus, while central Newfoundland and Nebraska are both in Zone 7, the species that can survive in each place differ considerably. Winter snow cover and the length of the cold season are other factors to be taken into account, since inadequate or variable snow cover can result in destruction of roots near the surface, while blossoming plants may not have adequate *vernalization* (days of cold). Precipitation will also be a factor for plants that are expected to exist without constant irrigation. And with global warming, plant zones will need to be adjusted regularly.

A number of technical and popular publications (including guides from cooperative extension services or horticulture departments of local universities) have focused on smaller geographic areas and reflect the diversity of climate zones that can exist side by side (Sunset Magazine, n.d.; Davison, n.d.). Local climates will be affected by the elevation of an area, nearby water bodies, and prevailing winds as they interact with

Table 32.4 | Plant hardiness zones

Zone	Average annual minimum temperature	
	°C	°F
12	10	50
11	4	40
10	−1	30
9	−7	20
8	−12	10
7	−17	0
6	−23	−10
5	−29	−20
4	−35	−30
3	−40	−40
2	−45	−50
1	−51	−60

Source: Department of Agriculture (n.d.).

nearby mountains and hills. At the site level, the orientation of slopes and microclimates such as cold air basins and heat sinks will be a further factor affecting the choice of species (see chapter 4). More ambitious taxonomic efforts have created typologies of ecoregions internationally and within individual countries, although the boundaries between zones are generally indistinct, which complicates the interpretation of a particular site. The US *plant taxonomy* distinguishes between large *domains* (polar, humid temperate, dry, and tropical), *divisions* (tundra, prairie, steppes, deserts, savannas, etc.), and *provinces* (prairie parkland, cascade mixed forest, great plains steppe, etc.). Within an ecoregion, there is a preponderance of similar native species, and agriculture tends to specialize in a limited range of crops except where irrigation prevails. There is good reason to look closely at the vegetation that has evolved naturally in the area and to use the matrix of local perennials as the base for the planting palette. Local species trigger memories and connect people to their wider landscape. Spring has arrived in the prairies with the first sightings of crocuses, and summer is heralded by the blossoming of wild roses (*Rosa arkansana*). Native species also are naturalized and require less maintenance than others that are imported.

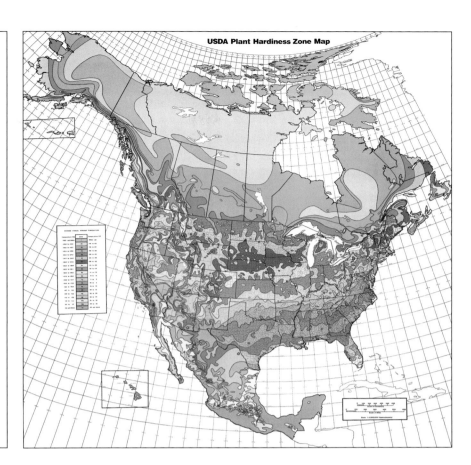

AVERAGE ANNUAL MINIMUM TEMPERATURE

Temperature (°C)	Zone	Temperature (°F)
-45.6 and Below	1	Below -50
-42.8 to -45.5	2a	-45 to -50
-40.0 to -42.7	2b	-40 to -45
-37.3 to -40.0	3a	-35 to -40
-34.5 to -37.2	3b	-30 to -35
-31.7 to -34.4	4a	-25 to -30
-28.9 to -31.6	4b	-20 to -25
-26.2 to -28.8	5a	-15 to -20
-23.4 to -26.1	5b	-10 to -15
-20.6 to -23.3	6a	-5 to -10
-17.8 to -20.5	6b	0 to -5
-15.0 to -17.7	7a	5 to 0
-12.3 to -15.0	7b	10 to 5
-9.5 to -12.2	8a	15 to 10
-6.7 to -9.4	8b	20 to 15
-3.9 to -6.6	9a	25 to 20
-1.2 to -3.8	9b	30 to 25
1.6 to -1.1	10a	35 to 30
4.4 to 1.7	10b	40 to 35
4.5 and Above	11	40 and Above

USDA Plant Hardiness Zone Map

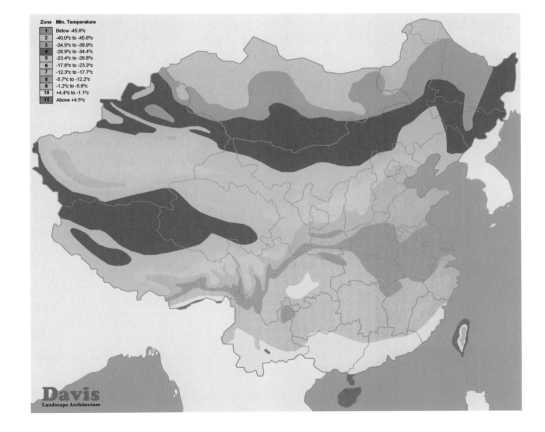

Zone | Min. Temperature
1 | Below -45.6°c
2 | -40.0°c to -45.6°c
3 | -34.5°c to -39.9°c
4 | -28.9°c to -34.4°c
5 | -23.4°c to -28.8°c
6 | -17.8°c to -23.3°c
7 | -12.3°c to -17.7°c
8 | -5.7°c to -12.2°c
9 | -1.2°c to -5.6°c
10 | +4.4°c to -1.1°c
11 | Above +4.5°c

Davis Landscape Architecture

32.21 Plant hardiness zone map of North America. (USDA)

32.22 Minimum temperature zone map, China and Mongolia. (Davis Landscape Architecture)

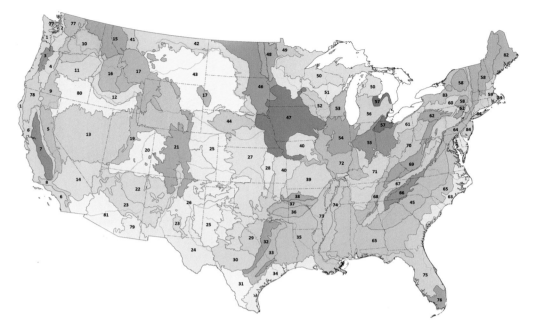

32.23 Ecoregions of the US. (US EPA/Wikipedia Commons)

Exotic plants, including annuals that can survive in a given zone, also have an important role to play in a landscape plan, even if they require greater maintenance and some irrigation (which can be captured from rainfall). They can contrast with the familiar species, add color, and celebrate passing seasons as they are replaced by other plants that reach their peak at other times of the year. Anchorage, Alaska, which suffers through months of snow and long hours of darkness during winters, is ablaze during summer when annuals are planted and display their remarkable colors. When designing the landscape of a site, the planner needs to simulate what the area will be like in all seasons—will the plants offer shade in summer? color in the winter? Which will be the first to bloom in the spring, and what will take their place as summer arrives? What will the fall colors be like as the grasses begin to decline? The High Line in New York has been designed to have color and interest throughout the year, using a blend of local and exotic perennials.

32.24 Summer planting of annuals, downtown Anchorage, Alaska. (Gary Hack)

32.25 Landscape of the High Line, New York City. (Gary Hack)

A surprising array of color is possible, even in areas with limited water resources that constitute much of the world. The practice of *xeriscaping* (*zero-scaping, xeroscaping*) aims to create landscapes that rely entirely on natural rainfall. This is now a well-developed art, and water companies and university extension services provide a wealth of materials on species and practices (Denver Water, n.d.; Klett and Wilson 2009). Several horticultural principles need to be observed: soils may need to be amended through the addition of compost to help retain water; drip irrigation is preferred for efficient use of water; species need to be matched to the amount of sunlight, wind, and moisture available; ground surfaces need to be mulched to avoid erosion and retain moisture; turf areas need to be eliminated or limited to only the essential; and planted areas need to be weeded regularly to avoid diversion of nutrients. Studies have indicated that household consumption of water decreases by about 30% when grass areas are converted to xeriscape landscaping in cities such as Las Vegas (Sovocool 2005). Xeriscape originated in Denver, and the new neighborhood of Stapleton uses low-water planting. The open spaces in Riyadh's Diplomatic Quarter are also designed for low water use, and demonstrate how the desert can be greened without depleting underground water supplies.

Ground-hugging plants are the staple of desert and prairie landscapes, but in woodland and forest ecodistricts the choice of trees is critical. They are also the most visible landscape element in urban areas. Historically, civic improvement efforts in New England towns centered on tree-planting programs, which may have been the origin of local planning (Campanella 2003). Trees are an important carbon sink, although one should be cautious about claims since it takes almost a thousand trees to absorb the average CO_2 emissions of a single urbanite. They retain moisture, helping to cool temperatures through evapotranspiration, and their shade reduces the heat island effect. Trees serve as windbreaks, slowing wind speeds in urban areas. They give definition to streets and provide cover for parks. And fully mature, they are a wonder to look at, whether in natural form or shaped by the hand of the local arborist.

Horticulturalists classify trees by *genus, species, variety, and cultivar*, hearkening to their biological origins. For planning the landscape, other issues are

32.26 Xeriscape landscape in winter, Santa Fe, New Mexico. (Gary Hack)

32.27 Low-water planting, Stapleton new community, Denver, Colorado. (William Wenk)

32.28 Desert park, Diplomatic Quarter, Riyadh, Saudi Arabia. (Gary Hack)

32.31 Pollarded trees in Golden Gate Park, San Francisco, provide an accommodating setting for tai chi.
(Courtesy of Susan Caster)

32.29 Cours Mirabeau, Aix-en-Provence, France.
(Andrea Schaffer/Wikimedia Commons)

32.32 Oak-lined street, Savannah, Georgia.
(Sean Pavone/Dreamstime.com)

32.30 Lakeside promenade, Bellagio, Italy.
(Courtesy of Douglas J. Navarick)

32.33 Honey locust canopy in fall, Cummings Corporation Park, Columbus, Indiana.
(Gary Hack)

AVERAGE ANNUAL MINIMUM TEMPERATURE		
Temperature (°C)	Zone	Temperature (°F)
-45.6 and Below	1	Below -50
-42.8 to -45.5	2a	-45 to -50
-40.0 to -42.7	2b	-40 to -45
-37.3 to -40.0	3a	-35 to -40
-34.5 to -37.2	3b	-30 to -35
-31.7 to -34.4	4a	-25 to -30
-28.9 to -31.6	4b	-20 to -25
-26.2 to -28.8	5a	-15 to -20
-23.4 to -26.1	5b	-10 to -15
-20.6 to -23.3	6a	-5 to -10
-17.8 to -20.5	6b	0 to -5
-15.0 to -17.7	7a	5 to 0
-12.3 to -15.0	7b	10 to 5
-9.5 to -12.2	8a	15 to 10
-6.7 to -9.4	8b	20 to 15
-3.9 to -6.6	9a	25 to 20
-1.2 to -3.8	9b	30 to 25
1.6 to -1.1	10a	35 to 30
4.4 to 1.7	10b	40 to 35
4.5 and Above	11	40 and Above

USDA Plant Hardiness Zone Map

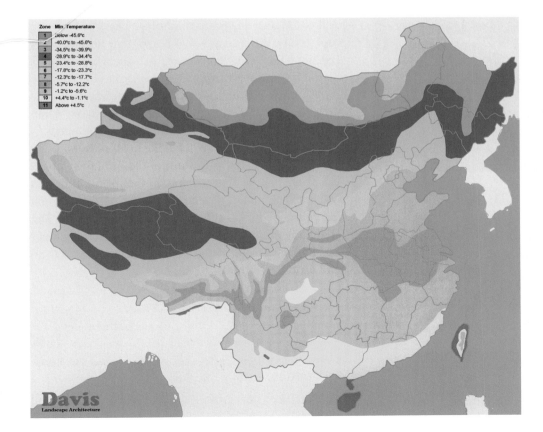

32.21 Plant hardiness zone map of North America. (USDA)

32.22 Minimum temperature zone map, China and Mongolia. (Davis Landscape Architecture)

Site Landscape

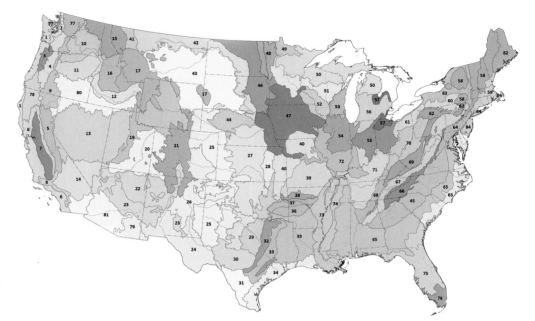

32.23 Ecoregions of the US. (US EPA/Wikipedia Commons)

Exotic plants, including annuals that can survive in a given zone, also have an important role to play in a landscape plan, even if they require greater maintenance and some irrigation (which can be captured from rainfall). They can contrast with the familiar species, add color, and celebrate passing seasons as they are replaced by other plants that reach their peak at other times of the year. Anchorage, Alaska, which suffers through months of snow and long hours of darkness during winters, is ablaze during summer when annuals are planted and display their remarkable colors. When designing the landscape of a site, the planner needs to simulate what the area will be like in all seasons—will the plants offer shade in summer? color in the winter? Which will be the first to bloom in the spring, and what will take their place as summer arrives? What will the fall colors be like as the grasses begin to decline? The High Line in New York has been designed to have color and interest throughout the year, using a blend of local and exotic perennials.

32.24 Summer planting of annuals, downtown Anchorage, Alaska. (Gary Hack)

32.25 Landscape of the High Line, New York City. (Gary Hack)

A surprising array of color is possible, even in areas with limited water resources that constitute much of the world. The practice of *xeriscaping* (*zero-scaping, xeroscaping*) aims to create landscapes that rely entirely on natural rainfall. This is now a well-developed art, and water companies and university extension services provide a wealth of materials on species and practices (Denver Water, n.d.; Klett and Wilson 2009). Several horticultural principles need to be observed: soils may need to be amended through the addition of compost to help retain water; drip irrigation is preferred for efficient use of water; species need to be matched to the amount of sunlight, wind, and moisture available; ground surfaces need to be mulched to avoid erosion and retain moisture; turf areas need to be eliminated or limited to only the essential; and planted areas need to be weeded regularly to avoid diversion of nutrients. Studies have indicated that household consumption of water decreases by about 30% when grass areas are converted to xeriscape landscaping in cities such as Las Vegas (Sovocool 2005). Xeriscape originated in Denver, and the new neighborhood of Stapleton uses low-water planting. The open spaces in Riyadh's Diplomatic Quarter are also designed for low water use, and demonstrate how the desert can be greened without depleting underground water supplies.

Ground-hugging plants are the staple of desert and prairie landscapes, but in woodland and forest ecodistricts the choice of trees is critical. They are also the most visible landscape element in urban areas. Historically, civic improvement efforts in New England towns centered on tree-planting programs, which may have been the origin of local planning (Campanella 2003). Trees are an important carbon sink, although one should be cautious about claims since it takes almost a thousand trees to absorb the average CO_2 emissions of a single urbanite. They retain moisture, helping to cool temperatures through evapotranspiration, and their shade reduces the heat island effect. Trees serve as windbreaks, slowing wind speeds in urban areas. They give definition to streets and provide cover for parks. And fully mature, they are a wonder to look at, whether in natural form or shaped by the hand of the local arborist.

Horticulturalists classify trees by *genus, species, variety, and cultivar*, hearkening to their biological origins. For planning the landscape, other issues are

32.26 Xeriscape landscape in winter, Santa Fe, New Mexico. (Gary Hack)

32.27 Low-water planting, Stapleton new community, Denver, Colorado. (William Wenk)

32.28 Desert park, Diplomatic Quarter, Riyadh, Saudi Arabia. (Gary Hack)

important—among them, whether they retain their vegetation through all seasons, their shape and spread, the type of root structure, their soil preference, and their ultimate height and lifespan. One of the creative roles of landscape designers is to discover new species that bring a fresh perspective and color to spaces on sites. Detailed descriptions of species, including their survivability, may be found in horticultural bulletins provided by governments, universities, and arbor foundations (National Arbor Foundation, n.d.; Bassuk et al. 2009; Cornell University, n.d.).

While it is possible to shape trees through pollarding and pruning, their fundamental form and character need to fit the setting. Trees that have a consistent form, such as maples and elms, lend themselves to continuous rows lining streets, while species that vary widely in shape or height, such as eucalyptus, are better suited to planting in clusters. While the shapes of London plane trees vary considerably, when mature they form a matrix of branches and foliage that resembles a continuous canopy. They are also prized for their bark, which instantly identifies them with France, despite their name. The tiny leaves of honey locusts allow dappled sunlight to reach the ground below, useful for seating areas in cool climates. Many deciduous trees reach their splendor in the fall when leaves turn golden or red—maples, aspens, locusts, and ginkgoes are especially memorable. Once they lose their leaves, the shape and color of bark and branches will remain the

32.34 Ground cover planting on steep slopes, China Vanke headquarters, Shenzhen, China.
(Courtesy of Natalie Echeverri)

32.35 Shaded areas with regular rainfall allow ground covers to define the pathway structure, Bloedel Reserve, Bainbridge Island, Washington.
(Gary Hack)

32.36 Grasses and lavender as ground cover, Lurie Garden, Millennium Park, Chicago.
(Gary Hack)

32.37 Heathers, capitalizing on the frequent rainfall of the Bloedel Reserve, Washington.
(Gary Hack)

symbol of nature, and in cold climates species may be chosen with that in mind. In spring, the glorious color of blossoming trees, such as cherries and crabapples, will signal new growth and new beginning.

Trees are selected for their aesthetic and practical contributions, but attention must also be paid to the hazards they face. The character of virtually every city in the eastern US has been ravaged by the loss of their elms as a result of sac fungi, spread by elm bark beetles (Campanella 2003). The lesson is to avoid monocultures, which leave an entire area vulnerable to disease. Far better to mix species, so that some survive as others are lost. There are other hazards to be avoided as well. Some species do better than others in polluted urban air and near roadways that are salted in winter. In ocean front locations, salt tolerance also needs to be a selection factor, while in other locations resistance to deer and other wildlife will be an issue. For deciduous trees in cold climates, the capacity to withstand ice storms may favor species with strong branching structures.

The ground surface also shapes the experience of a site. On the floor of the site, natural and man-made materials are combined and the designer has an almost infinite set of choices. Frequently decisions are made out of habit or by following conventions. Roadways are paved with asphalt, walkways made with concrete, and the spaces between filled with lawns and a scattering of annual plants. The result is prosaic, if comfortingly familiar. In many climates the green surfaces require constant watering, the roadways need to be patched every spring after the freeze-thaw cycles, and the walkways quickly become uneven and hazardous.

There are practical reasons to consider other materials, as we have noted in the discussion of xeriscape, but unique places also require a more searching examination of the ground surface. Between the intensely used spaces, there are opportunities for color and beauty through the use of mass planting and ground covers. Most ground covers are perennials, chosen to spread to form a dense cover, providing erosion control while adding texture and interest to the landscape. In shaded areas, ground covers can protect the surface in areas where lawns cannot grow, and help organize the pathway structure of a site. Gardens with grasses and perennials, if carefully planned, can provide interest throughout the year, retaining their pods as they go dormant for the next season. They can be dry landscapes or lush, taking their cues from the climate of the region. Landscape architects will ultimately lead the selection of plant materials and their placement, but the site planner can create the outdoor rooms for their creativity.

Part 5 | Site Prototypes

Very few site plans are created totally de novo. Site planners will look to precedents to see how others have addressed the issues they are facing, accounting of course for obvious differences of site form, culture, and built context. The point of departure will be the program type: is the site intended for housing, or capable of supporting mixed uses, or large enough to create a complete community? By looking for exemplars, the planner will assemble much useful knowledge about laying out the site, and a set of benchmarks against which her plan can be judged.

Over time, successful examples of types of site development emerge that become *prototypes*—models that are widely emulated and reveal fundamental ways of organizing a site. They usually cannot (and should not) be copied directly, but adapted to the current circumstance. The new *type* then improves upon the prototype and moves the field forward. Many designers and planners fear a lack of originality in consulting prototypes, but originality is only one of many virtues in site planning. It is essential in unprecedented situations—with a site that is totally unique or a program that has never been tried before. But much wisdom is captured in successful prototypes, and in most situations steady and consistent innovation is what is required.

There are dozens of books and a steady diet of print and electronic articles on the major types of urban development—housing, shopping areas, workplaces, public spaces, recreation areas, mixed-use and community developments. This part of the book focuses on identifying the major issues for each type, and offers examples from which one can begin an investigation of precedents. Fortunately, the Internet now allows access to information and images of most important projects throughout the world. Less obvious is how the projects have performed economically or in human terms—the field is rife with rumors about much-publicized projects that have failed or are unlivable. Some professional associations and awards programs serve a screening function: the ULI awards program and case studies program investigates financial performance before selecting a project, the Rudy Bruner Award program conducts field investigations of the finalists, the Landscape Architecture Foundation's case studies program looks at performance of sites in detail, and a number of universities and research institutes conduct post-occupancy studies that reveal the accomplishments and flaws of projects. Communication with the sponsors of projects is also a useful way to learn about their successes and failures.

The following chapters offer a summary of what has been learned about site development prototypes.

33 | Housing

Housing occupies over two-thirds of the developed land in most urban areas, and designing housing areas is the most frequent challenge faced by site planners. Housing areas change much more slowly than commercial or industrial zones of cities, because residents and living patterns tend to persist far longer than businesses. Hence, the design of housing sites requires a long view, with careful attention to culture, lifestyles, demographics, and values.

The *dwelling unit* is the fundamental component of residential site planning. Usually defined as space occupied by a single household, with a separate entrance and cooking facilities, it may shelter a wide range of family and nonfamily groups. In some parts of the world, extended families are the norm. In the US housing is usually designed for nuclear families with two parents and children, but over three-quarters of housing units today are occupied by single individuals, single parents with children, unrelated groups of singles, multigenerational households, or other unconventional groups. Over the life of a housing unit, it may have many types of occupants, so it is important to design for the generality of needs, within a social context.

Housing Types and Densities

In the most general sense, housing may be divided into four categories:

Detached housing: each dwelling unit is a freestanding structure on its own site. Detached housing can range from the country home on many hectares of land to small-lot housing in the city to zero lot line houses to temporary mobile homes.

Attached housing: each unit has a separate outdoor entrance and often private outdoor space, but units are joined side by side or one above another. Duplexes, semidetached units, row or townhouses, maisonettes, and stacked townhouses are the common forms.

Apartments or flats: several dwelling units share a common access and are enclosed by a common structural envelope. Depending upon the traditions and climate, the access ways may be indoors or outdoors. Apartments can be walk-up buildings, where stairs serve upper floors, or elevator buildings. A unit may be on one floor (flats) or have internal stairways to serve two or more levels. Apartments take a variety of shapes including linear slabs, towers, and units arranged around courtyards.

Mixed housing forms: two or more forms are combined, or housing is mixed with other uses. A detached house may have a granny suite or accessory apartment with a separate entrance; a tall apartment structure may devote the lower floors to self-contained units with private yards and entrances from the street; housing may be located over ground-floor shops, or may be mixed with offices or work spaces in a single structure as in live-work housing.

Each housing type can be built at a range of densities. A skilled designer can often move densities up beyond the norm, and it is always possible to develop fewer units on a site than its capacity suggests. On steeply sloping sites or places with vegetation that must be preserved, one may not be able to achieve typical densities. The ultimate density of a housing site depends on

33.1 Single-family detached houses with garages in rear, Prairie Crossing, Grayslake, Illinois.
(Gary Hack)

33.2 Townhouses near town center, Celebration, Florida.
(Gary Hack)

33.3 The Interlace housing complex, Singapore.
(Courtesy of Iwan Baan)

33.4 Mixed-use, live-work housing, University Avenue, Shanghai Knowledge and Innovation Community, Shanghai, China.
(Gary Hack)

three critical decisions: how to store the automobile (and how many must be stored); the amount of private and common open space to be provided; and regulations or norms about privacy distances.

Economics also plays an important role in determining densities. In places with efficient land markets, land values will be set by the perception of the density that can be achieved, or by the densities permitted by local zoning or regulations. Once a site becomes priced based on such an assumption, it will be difficult to justify fewer units. However, a small number of high-priced units may be possible, each absorbing a greater per unit cost for land.

In considering what is possible, a distinction needs to be made between *gross residential density* and *net residential density.* The gross density is calculated by simply dividing the area of the site by the number of housing units located on it. The figure is useful in making a first-cut calculation of the capacity of a site, but difficult to use for comparisons since the figure will depend on the amount of space set aside for roadways, open spaces, and other uses—this could be as much as 25–40%. Net residential density is more useful for comparisons, reflecting the actual area of the site used for housing divided by the number of units. A skilled site planner will know the density ranges for typical housing types.

Table 33.1 | Typical densities by housing type

Housing type	FAR	Units per ha (per ac)	
		Net density	Gross density
Single-family detached	Up to 0.2	Up to 20 (up to 8)	Up to 12 (up to 5)
Zero lot line detached	0.5	20–25 (8–10)	15 (6)
Semidetached	0.4	20–25 (8–10)	15 (6)
Duplex	0.5	25–30 (10–12)	18 (7)
Row house	0.5	40–60 (16–24)	30 (12)
Stacked townhouses	0.8	60–100 (25–40)	45 (18)
3-story walkup apartments	1.0	100–115 (40–45)	50 (20)
6-story elevator apartments*	1.4	160–190 (65–75)	75 (30)
12-story elevator apartments*	1.8	215–240 (85–95)	100 (40)
25-story elevator apartments*	2.2	280–320 (120–140)	140 (55)
40-story elevator apartments*	5.0	550–650 (220–260)	275 (110)

* In most situations, parking must be in structures.

Planning Principles

Living on a courtyard along a Paris boulevard is quite unlike life in a car-dependent American suburb, but both sets of residents share needs for light and air, a degree of privacy, nearby shopping, entertainment, and education, and, above all, human contact. Such generalities can only go so far, however, and need to be seen through the lens of cultural norms about the meaning of home, lifestyle, resources, tenure, and progression through the cycle of life.

In countries such as the US, Canada, and Australia, where home ownership rates hover between 60% and 70%, there is a greater demand for private space and for personalizing housing than in societies where rental housing is the norm. In Europe and North America, renters may satisfy their desires for personalization through weekend cottages or allotment gardens, or through elaborately decorated interiors of their apartments. The most prestigious housing in most American cities may be found in exclusive suburbs, while in most European cities it will be in the tony neighborhoods near the center. Brazilian gated enclaves provide the security sought by residents, while in Japanese or Chinese neighborhoods, and an increasing number of American cities, "eyes on the street" serve the same purpose (Newman 1972; Jacobs 1992).

These examples illustrate that, while human needs are similar, the role of housing in satisfying them varies widely. Humans are adaptable and can learn to live in a range of housing situations. They will quite likely seek different forms of housing as they move through the stages of life, from independent singles, to coupling or marriage, to childrearing, to child-free years. Some will remain single all their lives and live alone or with relatives or friends. Others may choose congregate housing arrangements. Individuals may prefer the contact and easy access to facilities and services that come with high-density living, or may regard their housing as a respite from too much human contact on busy streets or in the workplace. Thus, even within any society there will be a range of preferences for housing. Developers understand these differences and generally specialize in a narrow range of housing forms, acquiring an in-depth understanding of the housing preferences of those they serve and leaving alternative markets to others.

Privacy

Privacy is among the fundamental housing needs that must be addressed in planning sites. It can be gained through physical distance, visual separation, sound isolation, or cues embedded in the environment that signal the transition from public to private realms. Privacy is a cultural construct, shaped by perceptions of what must be shielded from others and how best to achieve this. Americans value visual privacy above all, which accounts for the preference for fences and the wide spacing of detached housing. Germans, on the other hand, value sound privacy more, and will not tolerate housing that doesn't shield neighbors from others' noises. In many Islamic societies, privacy of family life results in the bifurcation of the environment into spaces reserved for close relatives (where traditional outerwear isn't worn) and more public spaces in the house and yard where visitors are welcome.

Most traditional housing incorporates some form of a *privacy gradient*, marking the progression from a public street to a personal enclave (Alexander and Chermayeff 1965). In American suburban housing, the front lawn with its walk or driveway, the porch, a covered entrance, the parlor and living room in front are all steps en route to the more personal spaces of the home—the family room, kitchen, bedrooms, and private back yard. The traditional Chinese courtyard house is organized as a clear progression from street to entrance courtyard to public areas of the house reserved for entertainment, then to progressively more intimate courtyards and living spaces. Even in dense urban housing, the raised stoop provides psychological separation from the street, just as an entrance canopy marks the zone of transition from street to apartment lobby.

Housing spaces may be organized with subtle distinctions on the gradient between *public* and *private spaces*. There may be *group-public* or *semipublic spaces*, such as entrance courtyards in apartments, auto courts, or private streets providing shared access. Anyone may wander into such spaces from the street, but will soon become aware that these are territories belonging to a specific group of individuals. Even more private shared

33.5 Group-public space at entrance to apartment building, West Philadelphia.
(Gary Hack)

33.6 Group-private space in senior housing cluster, Lanxmeer, Culemborg, Netherlands.
(Gary Hack)

33.7 Aerial view of Bayside Village, San Francisco, with group-public and group-private spaces.
(Google Earth)

areas may be provided, such as enclosed courtyards surrounded by apartments or row houses, reached only through private lobbies or the houses that rim the space. These are often called *group-private* or *semiprivate spaces*. In high-density housing areas, these spaces may also be located on rooftops or indoors, or may be incorporated into recreation facilities. The subtle blend of group-public and group-private spaces is nicely illustrated at Bayside Village in San Francisco, a high-density, low-rise development near downtown.

Promoting Contact

Shared spaces on housing sites encourage human contact, another important need of most individuals and societies. The best shared spaces are not coercive—they provide the users of sites the opportunity to determine their level of contact with others. This is not always possible: users may have no choice whether to use entryways, lobbies, common driveways, shared parking areas, mailboxes, refuse collection areas. Experience suggests that these are most successful socially if the number of households they serve is limited. Some studies suggest that 8–12 households sharing common entries (in mid-density housing) is optimal. The exception is the growing desire for shared social spaces among young adults in apartment

33.8 Greenwood Avenue Cottages, a pocket neighborhood with eight housing units, Shoreline, Washington. (Courtesy of Ross Chapin Architects)

communities—places to mingle around the swimming pool, barbeque, and party areas—where the more the merrier is the guiding rule.

Homogeneity plays an important role in determining the willingness of neighbors to share space, and studies of the social space of neighborhoods repeatedly emphasize the importance of clustering units likely to attract people at similar stages of the life cycle, social class, and lifestyle if they are to share facilities. But exposure to differences is also an important social objective, most successfully achieved if neighbors have some things in common. Experience in mixed-income housing in the US demonstrates that households can bridge income differences if they are similar enough along other demographic dimensions. Thus, the commonality of being elderly may trump income differences, or residing in a community dedicated to active outdoor life may bridge differences of age or income. The ability to opt in or out of activities is of greater importance in socially mixed communities.

At a scale beyond individual housing clusters, there are a variety of places in larger developments that can encourage human contact—convenience stores, child care centers, car washing areas, community gardens, children's playgrounds, workout areas, and other recreation facilities. Sidewalks and walkways through open areas can be important integrators on a housing site, if designed with human contact in mind. Teenagers, often the most neglected group in planning housing sites, have the greatest need for human contact—safely away from adult eyes.

Security

Human *security* is another important preoccupation in site planning, particularly in the American context. Many crimes are opportunistic; they occur in places that are out of sight and not frequented by others. One approach is to harden the environment by eliminating shared spaces and landscaped areas where criminals might prey, building walls to protect private spaces, and adding security guards and surveillance devices to discourage crime (Newman 1972). The not-so-subtle message of this strategy is that the world beyond the house is dangerous, and ought to be avoided in off hours. The result is usually a reduction of the number of humans using outdoor spaces, particularly at night.

Increasing the number of eyes on the street is a far more desirable way to promote security, since few crimes are committed in areas where they are likely to be seen. This implies opening up a housing site to views from individual houses, and being sure that every outdoor space clearly belongs to a group who will take responsibility for its security. Maintaining sites well and removing graffiti promptly reinforces the sense of public order, and can markedly discourage crime.

Contact with Nature

People in most societies seek contact with nature in their housing environment, although the traditions of acquiring it vary widely. Americans seem to want houses that are lost in nature, and if that is not possible they will pay a substantial premium for sites that look out on parks, waterfronts, golf courses, and other areas preserved in a somewhat natural state. Tree-lined streets bordered by broad lawns are the urban counterparts for those who lack easy access to larger open spaces. In England or France, a few magnificent trees in a tiny square rimmed by houses and shops may offer a sufficient reminder of the natural world. In a dense Japanese city, a carefully tended strip of bamboo, no more than 1 m (3 ft) wide, may serve as a reminder of the larger natural world beyond the city. Residents of a Chinese city may import nature into their courtyard in the form of bonsai plants grown in ceramic vases, while the area outside their door may consist entirely of hard surfaces. And in many arid Middle Eastern cities, residents rely on painted images of lush plants on the walls of their villas, or the natural version of this, bougainvillea gracing walls and roofs, with occasional palms occupying the place of honor in their courtyards.

Immediate access to open space is for some groups a practical necessity: mothers wishing a place for children to play within sight, elderly individuals seeking places for gardening projects near their home, families with pets to exercise or other outdoor hobbies, and those seeking places for outdoor entertaining, particularly in warm climates. If resources permit, they will acquire houses with outdoor yard areas under their control. In the US and much of Europe, yards as small as 5 by 7m (16 by 22 feet) can satisfy most day-to-day needs, and there is a longstanding tradition of creating small private gardens. Where this is not possible,

33.9 Nature in high relief, Place de Furstemberg, Paris. (Unidentified)

shared spaces may serve as a substitute—garden plots, adventure playgrounds, courtyards that may be scheduled for events, nearby parks and playgrounds.

Many designers have sought to build high-density housing forms with large private spaces attached to each unit. Perhaps the most iconic is Habitat 67, built in Montreal as a demonstration project during Expo 67. More recently, The Mountain, a high-density housing project in Ørestad, Copenhagen, provides each unit with a 90 m² (970 sq ft) south-facing terrace, with considerable privacy from adjacent units.

Household structure plays an important role in the need for private open space. It is possible for millions of families in Hong Kong or Seoul or Beijing to raise children successfully in high-rise apartments, in part because they have the assistance of grandparents and others in their extended family. In high-density

American cities, a nanny or childcare helper is needed to accomplish the same. Lacking the resources for this, most families seek housing in lower-density areas, where children can play safely in backyards or nearby playgrounds while parents juggle work, home care responsibilities, and childrearing.

Accommodating Automobiles

The desire for open space on a housing site often must compete with the need to accommodate automobiles on the site, in private garages or driveways or in shared parking facilities. After the house itself, parking is the second most demanding land user. For housing at town house densities of 20 units per ac (50 units per ha), ground-level automobile parking (at 1.5 cars per unit) will consume more than a quarter of the housing site. Higher-density housing faces the choice of devoting much of the lower portion of the housing to parking ramps, or locating parking belowground at a significant cost. Most residents strongly prefer individual parking places attached to their unit or *dedicated parking* in a lot, the least efficient ways to satisfy their needs but the most convenient. When forced to use *common or shared parking* areas, the preferred arrangement is dedicated spaces, forgoing the advantages of flexibility in parking use.Shared parking areas offer the possibility of doubling up with alternative uses—as basketball or street hockey areas, or places for festivals or gatherings. Parking areas can be designed as auto courts, and need not be asphalt pads bordered by minimal landscaping. The design of parking areas is a largely neglected aspect of site planning, with considerable room for innovation (see chapter 21).

Personalizing the Environment

Beyond such practical needs, housing is for many people an important symbol of their identity and status, and signals their attitude toward neighbors and the wider community. Most residents want to personalize their home. Landscaping is one obvious way; designing or painting the exterior of their house is another. A visit to the False Creek residential area in Vancouver two decades after it was built reveals extraordinary lush landscaping added by residents in every corner of private space, as a demonstration of

33.10 Individual outdoor spaces for each unit, The Mountain, Ørestad, Copenhagen.
(Courtesy of © BIG – Bjarke Ingels Group/Dirk Verwoerd photo)

33.11 A multistory parking structure occupies the space below the housing at The Mountain, Ørestad, Copenhagen.
(Courtesy of © BIG – Bjarke Ingels Group/Mario Flavio Benini photo)

their gardening prowess but also as an expression of pride in their living environment. Puerto Rican families in the South Bronx, New York, have adapted and personalized their houses and yards in exuberant ways by adding ornamental grates and bougainvillea vines, a startling improvement on the faceless units they purchased. The sheer density and rules of a housing area may preclude this, but individuals will find small ways to telegraph their identity—pots of plants flanking their doorway, ceramic house numbers, flags over their entrance, decorations in windows, and the like.

Attitudes toward personalizing houses and sites vary considerably across cultures and social classes, and even within communities. Some American communities have anti-monotony ordinances that prevent developers from reproducing rows of identical houses. But an even larger number of local areas in the US have tough rules that enforce consistency from house to house. One community demands that only earth tones be used in exteriors, that every house have a visible roof, and that all garages be oriented to the rear or side, thus avoiding the appearance of open garage doors (Hack 1995).

Many upper-income individuals in the US have adequate ways to express themselves beyond their housing, and are content to live in units that are attractive but have anonymous exteriors. In older cities of Europe, the collective image of the housing complex is more important than symbols of family status and identity, and adaptations are frowned upon. But offered a choice in new housing, the same individuals may have sharply differing ideas about what they desire—witness their elaborate country cottages or dachas. The site planner is well advised to offer variation in the land planning, whether or not the opportunity is seized upon by housing designers.

Housing Prototypes

Detached Housing

The single-family detached house is the mainstay of housing in much of North America, accounting for half or more of the new housing constructed. Its advantages are well known: it receives adequate light and air from its four exposures and provides room for gardening, play, parking, and other outdoor uses. It enjoys direct access to the street and its own private grounds, which can be shielded from noise and view. In some traditional societies, such as South Africa, being able to walk around all sides of one's house is a way to exorcise evil spirits.

Single detached houses can be built, maintained, expanded, remodeled, bought and sold independently. With light frame materials they are economical to build, and even in countries where concrete or block construction is the norm, they remain affordable. They symbolize the autonomy of the household or family, and in many parts of the world are considered the ideal house.

The archetypal single-family detached house in the US is built at a net density of 5 or 6 per ac (12 or 15 per ha), on lots with a frontage of 60 to 75 ft (18 to 22 m). Houses are set back uniformly, often 25 ft (7.5 m) from

the front property line and a minimum of 4 to 10 ft (1.2 to 3 m) on the sides, depending on local regulations. The units may be one or two floors high, and adorned in a variety of popularly understood styles. Cars will be parked in an attached or detached garage, in the open beside the house, at the rear of the lot reached by a side driveway, or in a parking space accessible from a rear alley. Detached housing has grown in size each decade, with new houses now averaging 2,600 sq ft (242 m²), although lots have not increased commensurately.

The *villa* is the European equivalent of the detached single-family house, and it has seen renewed popularity in the outlying areas of many cities, particularly in Spain and Italy. Generally reserved for upper-income families, villas sit on lots typically 30 by 30 m (95 by 95 ft), resulting in net densities of 10 per ha (4 per ac), although they vary considerably from city to city. Cars are often parked below units, especially on sloping sites. Villas have become the aspiration of upwardly mobile families in almost every rapidly developing country.

In Japan, where land commands a great premium, single-family detached houses are being prefabricated and assembled in suburbs at densities of 40 units per ha (16 per ac), on lots that are typically 10 by 28 m (33 by 90 ft) but often as small as 10 by 15 m (33 by 50 ft). Similar housing is now being constructed in China to satisfy the demand for individual houses. There is also a growing interest in *2 × 4 houses*, with light frame

33.12 Standard single-family houses fronting on rain garden that absorbs runoff from the roofs, street, and driveways, Prairie Crossing, Grayslake, Illinois.
(Gary Hack)

33.13 Villa development with recreation spaces, suburban Bangkok, Thailand.
(Gary Hack)

33.14 Prefabricated mass housing development, Shanghai, China.
(© Biccaya/ Dreamstime.com)

33.15 High-priced villa development, Fukuoka, Japan.
(Gary Hack)

construction on small lots. Setbacks to the street are minimal, and walls assure privacy for the small areas of outdoor space on the house lots. However, in the higher-income housing areas of Japan, including Fukuoka, individual designs and generous landscaping create highly desirable districts.

There have been many criticisms of the detached house: that it is the main cause of city sprawl, which eats up rural land; that it makes public transit service uneconomical, that it is only suitable for two-parent families where one is prepared to mind the home front. These presumed liabilities have not deterred homebuyers, but the steady rise in land and servicing costs (including fees that account for the off-site costs of low-density development) has spurred a search for detached housing forms that can be built at higher densities and use less street frontage per unit.

One direct response is simply reducing the lot widths to 12 or 14 m (40 or 45 ft), which is adequate if houses are modest in size and two floors in height. Creating alleys and garages at the rear can help reduce the demands for frontage and allow houses to be set nearer the street. New urbanism communities in the US—in reality, a rediscovery of the traditional subdivision patterns of the 1920s—sometimes reduce lot sizes to 33 ft by 100 ft (10 m by 32 m), resulting in net densities of 11 units per ac (27 per ha). If *granny flats* or *accessory units* are added over rear garages, densities can be as high as 22 units per ac (55 per ha). A variety of housing forms modeled on traditional housing can be easily accommodated on small lots: Charleston side yard houses, bungalows, carpenter cottages, and shingle style gabled houses.

Another way of reducing lot size is to do away with one of the side yards, setting the house directly alongside one property line. Such *zero lot line housing* can be built at a net density of 25 to 30 units per ha (10 to 12 per ac). Maintenance easements on adjacent properties are required for painting and repairing walls located on the lot line. Because of the proximity of units, it is essential that there be covenants prohibiting windows on the lot line side wall, to avoid overlooking neighbors' spaces. Fence and driveway locations must also be controlled. If housing is designed at the same time as the lots are laid out, it is possible to create ingenious lot shapes that maximize the use of open space on individual lots, such as the Z-lot. In this arrangement, the

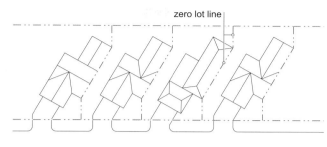

zero lot line

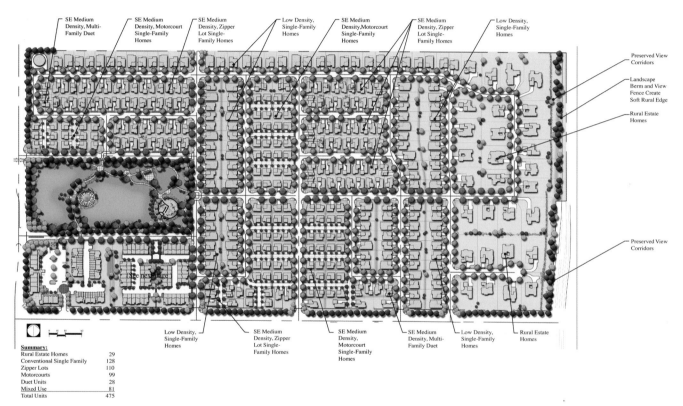

SE Medium Density, Multi-Family Duet

SE Medium Density, Motorcourt Single-Family Homes

SE Medium Density, Zipper Lot Single-Family Homes

Low Density, Single-Family Homes

SE Medium Density,Motorcourt Single-Family Homes

SE Medium Density, Zipper Lot Single-Family Homes

Low Density, Single-Family Homes

Preserved View Corridors

Landscape Berm and View Fence Create Soft Rural Edge

Rural Estate Homes

Preserved View Corridors

Low Density, Single-Family Homes

SE Medium Density, Zipper Lot Single-Family Homes

SE Medium Density, Motorcourt Single-Family Homes

SE Medium Density, Multi-Family Duet

Low Density, Single-Family Homes

Rural Estate Homes

Summary:

Rural Estate Homes	29
Conventional Single Family	128
Zipper Lots	110
Motorcourts	99
Duet Units	28
Mixed Use	81
Total Units	475

33.16 (top left) Small-lot development with garages off alleyways behind, Laguna West, Sacramento, California.
(Gary Hack)

33.17 (top right) Zero lot line plan, with lot boundaries shaped to maximize privacy in rear yards, Orlando, Florida.
(Adam Tecza/The Evans Group)

33.18 (bottom) Affordable housing development plan with small-lot, zero lot line, and attached housing, Rohnert Park, California.
(City of Rohnert Park)

claustrophobia of narrow lots is reduced by allowing outdoor space on both sides of the house. The community of Civano, near Tucson, Arizona, makes effective use of zero lot line housing and other small-lot housing forms to increase densities and create a strong sense of community.

Rather than reduce the lot size, the average frontage can be reduced by changing the lot shape. *Flag lots* are permitted in some localities. They make two tiers of development, the one served in the normal manner along the street, the second located behind it and reached by a driveway. The rear lot may have only 3 or 4 m (10 or 12 ft) of actual street frontage. Significant cost savings are possible if house utility lines are also combined for the two lots.

In some countries, such as Saudi Arabia, lots for single detached housing are bounded by high walls, within which elaborate mansions or a compound of houses for an extended family is built. Lots are typically 70 m (220 ft) square, and the enclosure wall is commonly built before construction begins on the house. A similar strategy has been used for low-income housing in South America and portions of South Asia. Once the wall is complete and a core structure with plumbing facilities is constructed within it, the house can be constructed and added to as resources permit. Owners purchase materials as they can afford them, and store them on the site until needed for construction.

In North America, *mobile homes* are a further response to the problem of delivering detached housing at an affordable price. They require less land and are considerably less expensive to build than site-framed housing because of the materials used, the lower cost of factory labor, the economies of scale, and the more lenient codes that apply to them. "Mobile" is a misnomer since most of these houses will move only once—to the site where they are first located. The trailer industry, whose products originally served summer campers and migratory workers, has evolved into a prefabricated house production system, manufacturing 12 and 14 ft (3.75 and 4.25 m) wide modules and delivering them within a range of 150 mi (240 km) of the factory. *Manufactured homes*, as they are now called, now constitute nearly 20 percent of the new single-family housing units in the US, and are delivered in modules that may be combined to form houses that are indistinguishable from site-built homes. Some are stacked to form two-story structures. Manufactured houses that look like site-built ones can easily be integrated into regular subdivisions if their construction standards meet local codes.

In the southwest US and Florida, where the winter climate is welcoming to snowbirds, large retirement and seasonal communities have been created using manufactured modules. Often they are fixed permanently to land that is sold to the occupants, and residents have elaborate shared community and recreation facilities.

Densities sometimes reach 15 units per ac (37 per ha), making both land and housing affordable. Residents add to their units, creating storage areas, covered car parking areas, children's play pools, and the like, filling the spaces between the rows of houses. The best of such projects have stringent developments standards, maintain common spaces immaculately, and provide security in off-seasons when few residents are present.

Traditional mobile home parks, on the other hand, have developed an undesirable image and are often banished to the edge of town. Frequently they are built on leased land awaiting a more permanent use. Homes are normally set on a diagonal, units have no privacy,

33.19 Seasonal community with manufactured homes, North Lake Estates, Moore Haven, Florida.
(Courtesy of Sun Communities, Inc.)

33.20 Double-wide modular home community with recreation spine, Bay Indies, Venice, Florida.
(Google Earth)

and there is little sense of responsibility for order and maintenance. This need not be so; there are also fine examples where landscaping or natural vegetation predominates, shielding the rows of banal units from view. Sometimes permanent false fronts are erected and units are inserted within them, making the mobile component hardly noticeable from the street. In a few places, automobiles have been parked at the edge of the site and electric carts are provided to each of the units, allowing roadways to be given a more intimate scale.

Mobile homes highlight the visual problem in all detached housing areas: how to avoid the appearance of endless repetition on the one hand while guarding against total disorder on the other. The problem arises from the size of the separate units relative to the development area, and to the scale of the car with its associated right-of-way. Where houses can be clustered or related across a footpath or pedestrian space, the proportions become much more pleasant, and the ground surface can be designed to unify the whole. Any reduction of the street width or the depth of the front yard always helps. Topography and color can also make a difference, as the marvelous painted Victorian structures in San Francisco demonstrate.

There are other devices for giving unity to small structures. Individual houses may be linked by means of screen walls, planting, garages, or porches. Garages may be paired or grouped in compounds to improve their proportions, although this may mean new ownership arrangements. House spacing and setback may be varied to create visual groups or modulate the street space. The Nova Scotia fishing village, with its informal grouping of structures, demonstrates that orthogonal organization is not the only alternative. And diminutive scale is not by itself unpleasant: the tiny wooden houses in Oak Bluffs on the island of Martha's Vineyard, Massachusetts are packed together along the pedestrian ways of the former camp meeting ground, and the effect is charming. But everything is in scale with these highly decorated houses: the pathways, the gardens, the vistas, and the spaces devoted to cars and service vehicles.

The town of Seaside, Florida was the first recent community to mine these lessons, which were captured in the town's urban code. Among other rules, it specifies that all houses must have metal pitched roofs with gables facing the street; there must be porches

33.21 Tiny houses built on former tent sites in the Camp Meeting Association grounds, Oak Bluffs, Massachusetts. (amis30porboston.com/Creative Commons)

33.22 Small houses with consistent details, fences, and streetscape, Seaside, Florida. (Gary Hack)

facing the street; lots must be rimmed by white picket fences; exterior materials must be predominantly clapboard; and colors must be drawn from a palate of pastels. These rules were not a deterrent to producing a great variety of house designs by many architects, including several modernist interpretations. Equally importantly, streets have been designed to be used by pedestrians as well as automobiles, and are surfaced with unit pavers. To reduce the scale of streets, parking areas along roadways were left unpaved and interrupted by trees. Similar strategies have been repeated in dozens of new urbanist communities, with results as varied as Prospect in Colorado, which has encouraged modernist housing designs, and Civano in New Mexico, which has drawn upon Southwest American vernacular traditions.

Attached Housing

In urban areas, attached housing is a practical necessity. It is simply not possible to achieve densities greater than about 30 units per ha (12 per ac) without having houses attached to their neighboring units. Older cities provide a rich array of attached housing: the Toronto semi, Philadelphia side-by-side, the Philadelphia-style duplex (in Boston), the Boston triple-decker, the San Francisco double, the Queens quads, the Montreal multiplexes, and so on, each a response to local populations and norms. Where units are stacked vertically, the owner often occupies one of the units while the others are rented out, so that houses serve different types of households. This enriches the social fabric of neighborhoods, often allowing multiple generations to remain in the same area.

There are several distinct varieties of attached housing: the *semidetached house*, with origins in England, where two units are joined side by side; the *duplex*, where one unit is over the other; *rear-lot housing*, where one unit occupies the front half of the lot, the other the rear; the *quad*, where four units are joined horizontally, and the many varieties of *row houses* which are joined on both sides, and sometimes stacked vertically. All types have individual entrances from the street and the opportunity for private outdoor open space attached to the unit, in the form of yards, porches, or balconies.

Semidetached units have all the advantages of the detached house, but can be built at higher densities because they have party walls on one side. With three

33.23 Affordable semidetached housing, Poplar Street neighborhood, North Philadelphia.
(Gary Hack)

33.24 Semidetached housing, redevelopment of abandoned public housing, Poplar Street neighborhood, Philadelphia.
(Google Earth)

33.25 Modern semidetached houses, the Cedar Lodges, Winchester, UK.
(Courtesy of Martin Gardner/Adam Knibb Architects)

exposed sides they have nearly as much light as with four, and can have private entrances, driveways, and outdoor spaces. Many traditional semis also share driveways with neighbors, further reducing the frontage needed. Although in divided ownership, they may look like one large house, especially if the entrance of one unit is tucked around to the side.

The duplex can be done at even higher densities, and with separate entrances—sometimes by way of an open-air stair and balcony to the upper unit—each unit can function independently. Good sound isolation in the floor between the units is the key to privacy. Private outdoor spaces for each unit may be obtained in several ways: one unit may be given the front outdoor space and the other the rear, or a generous balcony may substitute for ground space on the upper unit, or a roof deck may serve the upper unit while the lower unit has space on the ground. Often the two units are not equal in size, since one is intended for family occupancy, the second for child-free households. There may be a smaller ground-level unit, rented out, with a two-story unit above, or a small apartment may be located above the family unit.

The duplex and the semi are being rediscovered as housing costs increase and ways are sought to bring ownership within reach. Rear lot housing is also being reconsidered. Granny flats attached to the rear of houses are one example, popular in Australia; another is the conversion of garages in rear yards into living units. The entrance to the rear unit can be off the alleyway (if there is one), continuing the tradition of mews housing. Or, as in many San Francisco houses, it may be reached via a covered passageway from the street.

Another type of attached housing is the quad, or four-unit building, of which there are many varieties. At Frank Lloyd Wright's Suntop Homes in Ardmore, Pennsylvania, units are organized in a pinwheel pattern; each has a private yard out of sight of the adjacent units. In Quebec City, quads are widely used for new suburban housing, placed between parallel streets. While efficient in the use of land, they require more infrastructure than other units at that density, and since private yards are exposed to the street, screening is essential for privacy and to assure an ordered public environment. The Queens quad, ubiquitous in that borough of New York City, resolves this in a totally unsatisfying way by making the entire front yard an auto court. A better alternative, at a similar density, would be to build four ground-access units in a row.

The row house is the most common form of ground-access attached housing. It is the cheapest to build and maintain, and by dispensing with side yards altogether makes the most efficient use of land of any ground-access unit. Row houses can vary in width from as little as 3.5 m (12 ft) to as much as 10.5 m (35 feet); they can be two to five stories high, although in new housing two or three stories is the norm. They can be shaped to fit the street with curving rows, if

33.26 The Royal Crescent, Bath, UK, which has served as a prototype for countless row house ensembles.
(David Iliff/Creative Commons)

necessary, or organized around auto courts. Often they are thought of as working-class housing, and the term "row house" carries that connotation, but the grand crescents in Bath, England and the houses of Beacon Hill in Boston are examples of splendid row houses and pinnacles of prestige. Developers often advertise row houses as "townhouses" or "townhomes"; in England and Australia, they are called "terrace houses" or simply "terraces."

When row houses have only one street frontage, the internal arrangement will depend on cultural attitudes. Some prefer the living and dining rooms to be on the street side—this was the historic pattern in most places, when parlors for guests were separated from more private living spaces. The public entertaining areas then become the limit of how far guests will penetrate into the home—the front stage. Backstage are the kitchen and family entertainment spaces. Others prefer to locate living rooms at the rear, where activities can flow into outdoor spaces. Under either arrangement, storage and service spaces must be provided near the entrance, to accommodate clothes, bicycles, waste disposal, and other utilitarian needs. There is also the need for a direct passageway to the rear yard, since landscape materials, outdoor furniture, and all else that finds its way into the yard must arrive via the front door.

Access is made easier when there is a way to reach the unit from the rear as well as the front. Unless there are public alleyways, creating a vehicle or pedestrian way in the rear usually necessitates some form of shared ownership, obviating the simplicity of fee simple ownership with party walls. A homes association or condominium ownership can allow the form of row housing to become considerably more varied, with shared parking areas and common recreation facilities. The Society Hill townhouses in Philadelphia create elegant street fronts while grouping parking in rear parking courts. Clustering row houses tightly while preserving natural areas between is a strategy for preserving natural corridors on a site.

Most projects employing row houses consist of dozens of units, designed as a single ensemble with consistent exteriors. This was not always the case, as historic streets in Philadelphia and Amsterdam attest. Allowing each owner to custom-design their unit, within broad guidelines for setbacks and heights, can

33.27 Society Hill townhouses, Philadelphia, organized around an automobile court.
(Google Earth)

33.28 Street view, Society Hill townhouses, Philadelphia.
(Gary Hack)

33.29 Automobile courtyard, Society Hill townhouses, Philadelphia.
(Gary Hack)

result in a marvelously varied block and a test bed for new housing forms. This strategy was employed in the redevelopment of the Ghent area of Norfolk, Virginia, and more recently in portions of the Amsterdam docklands.

Another innovative form of row housing, which has its origins in Scandinavia and Germany, is the *court garden house*, where L-shaped attached units are organized around private outdoor spaces. While the densities are relatively low and each unit requires considerable frontage, every room has a view to a private outdoor space, and units can be organized to break the lockstep monotony of conventional row houses. They have been a favored form among architects, and examples may be found in Europe, Canada, and the US. However, they remain an undiscovered innovation that has as yet not caught on among the general public (Schoenauer 1962).

One of the most difficult issues in organizing row houses is dealing with the automobile. With narrow-frontage row houses, storing the automobile in garages on the street can deaden the facade with a continuous row of garage doors. If cars are parked outdoors, the street becomes a linear parking lot. One solution is to create alleyways and park the car at the rear, as many traditional townhouses do in Philadelphia, but unless the lots are very deep, this will be done at the expense of private outdoor space (although decks over the garage are a possibility). With wider frontages, 6.5 m (20 ft) or more, it is possible to retain a landscaped entrance while incorporating a garage in the structure. On sloping sites, it may be possible to locate the automobile below the unit while creating balconies above overlooking the driveway. All of this is made more difficult if there is more than one automobile per unit, an unfortunately common situation in the US.

One innovative way to accommodate the automobile is by placing it below a landscaped deck between two rows of houses. This is a common solution in Canada, where it has the added advantage of eliminating the need for snow removal in the parking area. Houses may then be entered directly from the parking garage or from the main entrance on the deck. Freestanding parking courts are another parking solution, although in North America it is difficult to persuade homeowners to park their automobiles more than a few feet from their front door.

33.30 Individually designed townhouses, Amsterdam Eastern Harbour development.
(Gary Hack)

33.31 Court garden houses with individual courtyards and shared play spaces, Albertslund South residential area, Copenhagen.
(Google Earth)

Row houses are typically built at net densities between 35 and 50 units per ha (15 and 20 per ac), but there may be as many as 75 units per ha (30 per ac) if the houses have narrow fronts of 3.5 or 4.5 m (12 to 14 ft). Higher densities usually require rethinking the form of housing and how the automobile is treated.

The *stacked row house* (or townhouse) is one higher-density form that retains private entries and outdoor spaces, and results in densities half again higher than row houses. The effect is that of a row of attached duplexes, with the same choices of access and open spaces. The upper unit, which begins on the second or third floor, is generally reached by a private stairway. Fire exit regulations usually make it advantageous to locate the smaller of the two units below, minimizing the climb to the upper unit. With stacked row houses, it is nearly impossible to make outdoor spaces that are completely private, but the creative use of roof decks and covered parking areas can provide for generous outdoor spaces. At these densities, it is no longer possible to park all the automobiles on ground level and have a site that is more than a landscaped parking lot. The preferred solution is to construct a fireproof parking garage below the housing units.

Stretching the limits of what can be put on a site, some developers have created *back-to-back row houses*, or even *back-to-back stacked row houses*, reaching densities as high as 100 units per ha (40 per ac). These units have obvious disadvantages, among them the limited frontage, lack of cross ventilation, and difficulty of accommodating the automobile. But in the eastern US, consumers seeking to purchase low-priced housing have shown a strong preference for these units over apartments constructed at the same density, where units are entered from common hallways. They are also a favored housing form in suburban Bangkok.

Gallery access can also be used to allow stacking of units, so that each retains an individual outdoor entrance. Quite innovative examples may be found in England, where they are called maisonettes, and in parts of the southwest US, where the climate favors outdoor corridors. Units entered from the outdoor corridor may be one or two stories, although fire codes often require a second egress if the outdoor street

33.32 Stacked townhouses, Woodland Village, London, Ontario. (Courtesy of Orchard Design Studio Inc.)

33.33 Clusters of stacked townhouses, with parking below central courtyards, False Creek residential area, Vancouver. (Google Earth)

33.34 Stacked townhouses with single-story ground-oriented units and two-story units above, False Creek residential area, Vancouver. (Gary Hack)

33.35 The ground floor is elevated to allow naturally ventilated parking below at Park Place apartments, Mountain View, California. (Gary Hack)

is more than one story above the ground. The most extravagant (and most costly) example of gallery-access attached housing is undoubtedly the Habitat 67 complex constructed in Montreal. There units are stacked within a frame in an irregular piled-up form, and while the densities are no higher than for stacked townhouses, there is great variation in the plans of each unit and each has light and views from all sides.

As densities increase, the cost of constructing units becomes a factor: expensive "new ground" in the form of garages and decks must be constructed to ease the demands on the site: housing footprints, automobile circulation and parking, humans at leisure, and outdoor spaces. One useful rule of thumb is that constructing decks or new ground can only be justified if the land prices per m² (or per sq ft) exceed the cost of the deck, measured similarly. Construction of stacked units is also more costly because of the need for fire protection and sound isolation between units, particularly vertically. As a result, few units of attached housing are built in North America at densities between 60 and 100 units per ha (25 and 40 per ac). The economics are somewhat different in Europe and Asia, where concrete construction is more common for low-rise construction, but high land costs in those areas tend to push densities to levels that require other forms of housing.

Apartments

The distinction between attached units and apartments is in the form of access: attached units have individual private access from the street (or a street in the sky), while apartments are reached via some form of common stairs or elevators and hallways. But apartments, or *flats* as they are called in the UK and other places, offer an infinite variety of possibilities. In many parts of the world they are the predominant form of housing.

The *walkup apartment* was at one time the cheapest kind of housing available. It would still be so today if fire laws had not banned non-fireproof construction in structures more than three stories in height, and if people had not lost interest in climbing greater distances. Two-story walkups, or three-story walkups that have their lowest floor half a level belowground, have become the most common form of inexpensive apartments in the US. They allow parking to be handled at grade, and offer excellent exposure to all rooms, particularly if organized in shapes other than rectangular blocks. Multiple stairways can allow a small number of units to share an entrance, and ground-floor units can be designed so that they have private outdoor space.

In suburban areas, walkup apartments have been rebranded as *garden apartments*, although the garden may be principally a parking lot because of high automobile ownership rates among those who rent such units. The best such developments create common courtyards between apartments, and may locate some of the parking in garages below the housing floors, as in the Park Place apartments in Mountain View, California. The term "walkup" is also becoming something of a misnomer, since inexpensive hydraulic elevators often make it economically feasible to eliminate the need to walk up stairs in buildings as low as two or three stories.

Some of the most innovative walkup units may be found in the inner city of Beijing, where they have been designed as a modern adaptation of the traditional courtyard house. Built at densities that come close to the high-rise apartments constructed nearby, they respect the traditional scale of the city's *hutongs* and have been inserted as infill housing between historic residences. Three to four stories high, they are organized around a succession of courtyards extending back from the street. Every apartment enjoys excellent light from a courtyard, which serves as a play space for children, storage place for bicycles, and common space for gatherings and casual contact.

In China, six-story walkup apartments continue to exist, as a relic of a time when constructing apartments quickly and cheaply was the objective. However, in most of the world today, apartments taller than three stories require fireproof construction, passenger elevators, and often the installation of mechanical ventilation systems. In many places in the US, if they are above 90 ft (28 m) in height, they must meet high-rise building codes, including providing sprinklers for fire protection. Above such a height, bearing wall construction is not possible, necessitating some form of fireproofed steel or concrete structure. Since these are costly items compared to light wood construction, they usually entail a significant jump of density if they are to remain competitive in price with walkups. Or if

33.36 New Siheyuan residential area in Ju'er hutong, centered on courtyards, Beijing, China.
(Gary Hack)

33.37 Costly foundations, difficult access, and exceptional views force developers to construct tall towers on Hong Kong's slopes.
(© Amadeustx | Dreamstime.com)

higher-priced, they must appeal to a market that values a doorman, urban living, and security of housing.

Elevator apartments can take many forms, and are the mainstay of new housing in most dense urban areas. They may also be the favored housing form as a way of achieving compact urban districts, or the only practical form of housing in places such as Hong Kong, where topography limits the amount of land available for development and costly foundations force it to be very tall. The basic organizing spine of any tall apartment structure is the core: elevators, fire stairs, and mechanical shafts containing building systems. The limbs of the structure are the corridors and distribution lines that extend outward from the core. These can be configured in many different ways. They can be enclosed or outdoor galleries as in the Habitat 67 housing hillside in Montreal.

In European cities, where height limits often restrict apartment structures to six or seven stories, apartments are usually organized with multiple cores, accessible from courtyards carefully watched over by a concierge who may live on the ground floor. As few as two to four apartments may share an elevator lobby on each floor and a stairway; depending on the size of the courtyard, there may be two or four vertical cores. The modern version of this often dispenses with the courtyard and creates *street bar housing* with cores distributed every 20 to 40 m (65 to 125 ft) along the street. Two to four units typically are reached from the elevator stop on each floor. Europeans favor this form of housing because it offers the possibility of cross ventilation and access to the sun for all or most units. The seven-story line of development along Java Island in Amsterdam is an excellent example of street bar housing. In Buenos Aires, 11-story housing hugging the street has become the norm, and produces a much-valued and urbane setting for urban life.

In northern China, where access to the sunlight is considered a right in all housing, 6- to 30-story slablike apartments with several vertical cores were for many years the norm. Similar housing estates were developed in Korea and other Asian countries. The sheer monotony of most housing estates built with uniform slab housing has since given way to more varied mixtures of point buildings and connected slabs. There are now examples that rise above the norm, including the Jian Wai SOHO development in Beijing. An underground infrastructure of parking and commercial spaces and a lively ground-level pattern of open spaces, restaurants, and shops provide an exciting context for the residential slabs—in reality live-work structures, since many of the apartments have been converted into offices for small businesses.

Distributed cores became the preference in luxury apartments in New York in the 1880s, and many were organized around courtyards emulating the grand buildings of Paris, Barcelona, and Vienna. The most luxurious buildings offered elevators that opened directly into apartment units, dispensing entirely with lobbies on each floor. With air conditioning, individual units could be as deep as 60 ft (18 m) from the elevator core.

Sadly, however, the norm for street-oriented elevator apartments in the US has become the double-loaded corridor building. In such buildings, units are organized on each side of a corridor that runs the length of the building. It may be a slab in form, or a multiwinged building radiating outward from a core. While they optimize the use of costly elevators, they eliminate entirely the possibility of cross ventilation, and force residents to reach their units along corridors devoid of natural light. Typical double-loaded corridor buildings are 65 to 75 ft (21 to 24 m) in width, and depending upon the fire stair configuration may

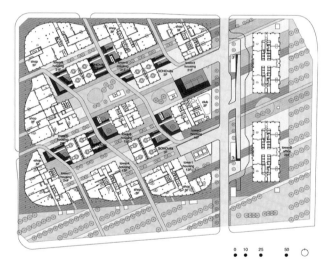

33.38 Outdoor gallery access connects individual units to elevators at Habitat 67, Montreal.
(Courtesy of Robert Michael Poole)

33.39 Street bar housing on Java Island, built in 30 m increments, Amsterdam.
(Alison Comford-Matheso © Acmphoto | Dreamstime.com)

33.40 Ground plan, Jian Wai SOHO complex, Beijing, with housing towers rimming lower offices and retail structures.
(Courtesy of Riken Yamamoto & Field Shop)

33.41 Ground-level spaces, Jian Wai SOHO complex, Beijing.
(Courtesy of Institute for Transportation and Development Policy)

be as long as 300 ft (95 m) in length. They often block views, cast powerful shadows, and adjust clumsily to terrain, but their advantage is their low cost and ease of construction.

Some of the disadvantages of the double-loaded corridor can be overcome by adopting the skip-floor system, where elevators stop ever second or third level. From the elevator, apartments are reached via corridors, or galleries, or "walkways in the sky," generally on one side of the building. One advantage is that elevator service is improved, since there are fewer stops. Floors above and below the corridor levels enjoy cross ventilation, and units may be two stories with internal stairways connecting the floors. The architect Le Corbusier was a fervent advocate of this type of unit and incorporated it in his Unité d'Habitation structures in Marseille, Nantes-Rezé, Berlin-Westend, Briey, and Firminy. Excellent examples of skip-stop configurations may be found in Toronto, at Roosevelt Island in New York, and at the Piazza in Philadelphia. The Piazza is a distinct improvement on Le Corbusier's structure, providing light into the streets in the sky and public spaces that look out onto the large courtyard that has become the center of its emerging neighborhood.

Innovative projects in Montreal and Europe have demonstrated that it is also possible economically to cluster apartments in 6- to 12-story buildings around hydraulic elevators, limiting the number of units on each floor to a handful. Most of the units can have cross ventilation. Even though elevator service is slower, residents strongly prefer such buildings to their double-loaded-corridor counterparts. Given the choice, most apartment dwellers prefer to have only a few immediate neighbors rather than dozens along a corridor.

In Hong Kong and throughout Asia, the tall residential tower is rapidly becoming the standard housing form. It originated as a way to minimize the footprint of buildings because of high foundation costs, and as a response to stringent building codes that require natural light and ventilation to all rooms, including bathrooms and kitchens. Hong Kong tower blocks are often cross- or T-shaped with many crenellations, some occupied by balconies or landings to stairways. Typical wings extend outward from the core, limited by the maximum distances that unit entrances may be located away from fire stairs. Often these residential towers are built over podiums of 3 to 8 stories which provide car

33.42 Skip-floor access to apartments provides most apartments with through-ventilation at the Piazza at Schmidts, Northern Liberties, Philadelphia.
(Tower Realty)

33.43 Aerial view, the Piazza at Schmidts, Northern Liberties, Philadelphia.
(Google Earth)

parking, shops, children's play areas, common spaces, and rooftop gardens. When grouped together with their podiums joined, they become self-contained neighborhoods, serving everyday needs just a short walk from apartment doors.

The tall apartment has advantages in addition to its usefulness at high densities. Tenants acquire some anonymity and social freedom, if that is what they seek, and they may be lifted up high enough to enjoy fine views and cleaner, cooler air. Where there are amenities such as waterfronts, residential towers avoid blocking the views to the water for those located several blocks behind. The city of Vancouver has limited the girth of residential buildings along English Bay and False Creek North to 20 m (65 ft), to allow views between them to the water. The result is a remarkable procession of slender glass towers, some with only one or two apartments per floor. These advantages have not been lost in New York City, one of the few cities without height limits, where dozens of tall thin towers (*TTTs*) are rising in residential areas and along waterfronts.

One of the difficulties of TTTs is providing parking below their footprint. Creating an adequate garage space usually requires grouping the parking for several structures. An alternative is the use of mechanical parking systems, where vehicles are taken by elevator to storage slots. In Japan such systems are common, and one such structure was recently completed in Philadelphia. In New York, a recently built tall tower lifts automobiles to the apartment floor of their owner—the ultimate in having the automobile next to your door!

Apartments are also generally more secure than ground-access housing, particularly if there is 24-hour control at the entrance. Moreover, at the densities that high apartments are generally built at, it is possible to supply special services: exercise rooms, swimming pools, squash courts, and other special recreational spaces; child care facilities; convenience stores; even catering, if they are attached to a hotel. Indeed, apartments are becoming more like hotels, even as all-suite and extended-stay hotels now look more like apartments.

Mixed Housing Forms

Different housing types can, of course, be mixed within individual buildings, or next to each other on sites. The lower floors of an apartment structure can function as townhouses, providing entranceways and yards, with the upper floors reached by elevators and corridors. To optimize the use of elevators, the lower three floors of a building may be treated as a walk-up structure, with upper floors served by bridges from an adjacent high-rise building, as is the pattern at Peabody Terrace at Harvard University. Vancouver requires continuous housing along streets, which is accomplished by mixing low-rise townhouses with tall towers. Row houses and walkup apartments for rent can easily be mixed on the same site since they are of similar scale. They appeal to different groups, and thereby broaden the occupant mix. But attention must be paid to social differences on the site as well—children's play areas or basketball courts that may be too noisy for some residents, or singles apartments areas may disturb families in the late night hours.

In New York, where a preference for tall towers has emerged and public bodies insist on continuous streetscapes, a hybrid form of housing has emerged with street bar housing of 6–10 stories topped by 30–40-story towers. The same elevators serve both; the low-rise structures generally accommodate the smaller units along double-loaded corridors, while two to four units are organized around each tower elevator floor.

33.44 Tower spacing requirements in Vancouver assure that housing units in tall buildings have distant views.
(© Leo Bruce Hempell/ Dreamstime.com)

33.45 Hybrid housing where the lower three floors function as walk-up apartments and units above are served by skip-floor elevators in the tall towers, Peabody Terrace, Harvard University, Cambridge, Massachusetts.
(Courtesy of Bruce T. Martin)

33.46 Vancouver requires that townhouses line the street with towers set back behind, to provide street activity and human scale.
(Gary Hack)

Live-Work Housing

Housing mixed with workspaces—*live-work housing*—is also becoming a widespread phenomenon, as more and more occupations can be practiced from the home. They are also a practical solution for families with young children, allowing one or both of the parents to work within the home. Accessory offices attached to homes are becoming accepted in many American suburbs, although the number of outside employees is sometimes limited, and provision must be made for off-street parking. With the opportunity to plan for home-based occupations at the outset, as was done in Celebration, Florida, housing sites can be planned with secondary entrances for the offices, and screened driveways can serve for visitor or employee parking.

Loft housing in or near downtown has become the fastest-growing housing form in most American cities. The demand is fueled by the increased numbers of child-free households who want to be within walking range of their workplaces, cultural opportunities, and amenities, but a significant number of households moving into lofts report one or more members who work out of home offices. The increased ceiling heights, typically 10 ft (3 m), glazed exterior walls, and open organization of lofts allow buildings of much greater depths to be used for housing—50 ft (16 m) or more, as opposed to typical apartment depths of 30 to 35 ft (9 to 10.5 m). This has been a boon to the conversion of older industrial buildings (from which they take their name) and obsolete office structures, but also has stimulated the construction of a new form of housing with large unencumbered floors. Often they are fitted out by the occupants, placing a premium on flexible mechanical, electrical, and plumbing systems. The system of "housing supports" devised by N. J. Habraken and his colleagues in Holland, but realized only experimentally, offers the potential of rationalizing such open building systems (Habraken 2000).

Other Housing Types

A number of emerging housing forms do not easily fit into conventional categories. Congregate housing, or cohousing, is increasing in Europe and the US and can take many forms. The fundamental concept is the desire to integrate many types of households in a single housing complex, sharing common facilities such as large living and entertainment rooms, food preparation and dining rooms, recreation facilities, child care facilities, workshops, and the like. Individual households may have small kitchens and living spaces as well, or they may be dispensed with entirely in favor of common space. The programs are as varied as the groups themselves, and usually they are created with cooperative ownership. Formally organized communes in China and Israel, and among religious communities, also adopt the approach of reducing private spaces in favor of shared facilities (McCamant and Durrett 2014).

Extended-care housing is appearing with increasing frequency as the populations of many developed countries age. Usually it involves providing a range of housing types on a site, from fully independent living in cottages or attached housing to apartments with small kitchens to full-care nursing home facilities. There will be on-site medical facilities, usually provided as part of the package of services available to all residents. They will typically share common spaces and recreation facilities, and may have the option of eating in a dining room on the site rather than dining in their units. As residents age and need greater care, they have the option of moving to facilities with higher levels of assistance. The site planning challenge is to create subcommunities on the site, where residents of each level of care can enjoy the company of others, while putting common facilities within easy reach of all.

33.47 Live-work lofts at 1310 East Union Street, Seattle, Washington.
(Courtesy of Ben Benschneider/Miller Hull Partnership)

33.48 Experimental housing unit that promotes adaptability by careful placement of service cores and exterior facade that is easily changed, units designed by 13 different architects, NEXT21, Osaka, Japan.
(Yositika, UTIDA, Shu-Koh-Sha Architectural and Urban Design Studio/Osaka Gas Co.)

33.49 Common space, cohousing area, Stichting Vrijburcht, Amsterdam-IJburg, Netherlands.
(Courtesy of Stichting Vrijburcht/Digidaan photo)

The future will surely require greater diversity in housing, new social arrangements, new forms of ownership and tenure, and the ability to adapt housing to meet rapidly changing demographics. The challenge to the site planner is organizing housing projects so that they continue to serve their residents.

Promoting Affordable Housing

Housing affordability is not linked inextricably to site planning, since any of the housing forms just discussed can be built as starter homes on a modest budget, or inflated in size and finishes for a more extravagant price. There are, however, a number of strategies that can help assure that housing on a site is accessible to a broad range of incomes. One begins with the site program: it can provide for a mix of units aimed at a range of incomes, and use cross subsidies from the higher-priced (or rental rate) units to assure that there are affordable accommodations. An increasing number of governments require that a proportion of units be set aside for households below a certain income; others provide tax relief or preferential financing in exchange for affordable units. The units themselves may not differ greatly from the market rate units, although they may be slightly smaller in size and have less expensive finishes. Mixing units for different income groups requires a delicate balance and, in the case of rental

units, careful selection of tenants to assure that residents are compatible.

A second strategy is to provide modest-sized accommodations as starter homes, designed and sited so that they can be added to over time as the income of the residents permits. Typical houses in Levittown, New York in 1963 were 750 sq ft (70 m²); over the next decade an average of 200 sq ft (18.6 m²) were added to each by finishing attics, adding rooms to the house, and converting garages to living spaces. This is a common strategy in developing countries, where very modest accommodations are provided within an enclosure wall, allowing for space to be added over time without intruding on neighbors. For single-family housing, minimizing the size of lots through zero lot lines and party wall units can result in higher densities and lower prices.

Keeping structures low so that less costly building technologies can be employed is a third approach. In North America, stick-built wood frame construction, typically limited to three and a half stories, is generally 20–30% less costly than mid-rise masonry bearing wall with concrete plank construction that can rise 6–8 stories, and at least 50% less costly than high-rise buildings. The economics of building will of course vary among cities, and in locations with a construction industry skilled in high-rise construction the gap may be narrower. Higher densities may be needed to offset high land prices, but if affordability is a goal, it is worth exploring lower-height solutions before planning the site for high-rise structures.

Finally, innovative building technology combined with site planning can directly affect the ongoing operating and maintenance costs of housing. Orienting housing to maximize passive solar gain in winter, or, in hot climates, so that large glass areas are shaded, can impact heating and air conditioning costs. Passive air movement in buildings, through operable windows or ventilation systems that capture breezes, can lower costs further. These are among the techniques common in *Passive House* (*Passivhaus* or *Mason Passive*) building systems. The Passive House organization sets several criteria to qualify for use of the name: space heating demand should not exceed 15 kWh annually or 10 W (peak demand) per m² of usable building space; space cooling energy consumption should roughly equal the heat demand figures, with

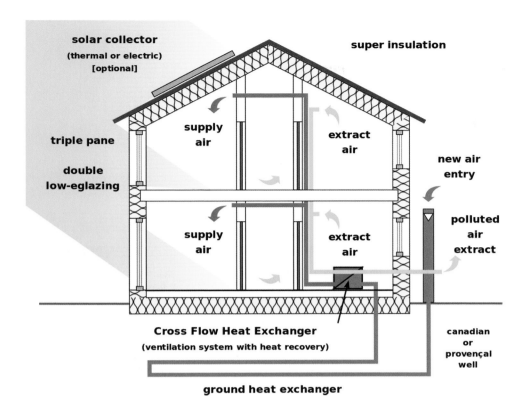

solar collector
(thermal or electric)
[optional]

super insulation

triple pane

double
low-eglazing

supply
air

extract
air

new air
entry

supply
air

extract
air

polluted
air
extract

Cross Flow Heat Exchanger
(ventilation system with heat recovery)

canadian
or
provençal
well

ground heat exchanger

33.50 Passive House scheme for single-family houses. (Passivhaus/Creative Commons)

a climate-dependence allowance for dehumidification; primary energy demand (for appliances, heating, and domestic electricity) should not exceed 120 kWh annually for all domestic applications per m² of living space; spaces should be sufficiently airtight to restrict air changes to no more than 0.6 per hour at 50 Pascals pressure; and indoor temperatures should not exceed 25°C more than 10% of the hours in any given year to assure thermal comfort. In the US, Passive House structures consume 86% less energy for heating than typical ones of the same type in their area and 46% less for cooling, a considerable saving for owners and occupants. By 2014 over 1 million m² (10.8 million sq ft) of residential space constructed across the globe met Passive House standards, including individual houses, low- and high-rise apartments, and special-purpose housing such as dormitories and institutions.

Saving energy is not the only way to reduce operating cost to make housing more affordable. Reduction of water use through xeriscape, providing low-maintenance landscape, promotion of voluntary associations that take responsibility for maintenance, and reduction of unused parking spaces by providing car share services are only a few of the possibilities for reducing annual costs. Affordability will be an essential issue in the future, and is an area wide open for innovation.

33.51 Algenhaus demonstration project at the 2013 International Building Exposition (IBA) in Hamburg, illustrating how Passive House principles can be applied to mid-rise housing. (Energieexperten/Creative Commons)

34 | Shopping

Goods and services are exchanged in shopping areas, but the significance of these places goes far beyond the commercial functions they serve. They are the locations for social encounters and important public events in the lives of cities. They help frame the identity of cities—think of Fifth Avenue or Tribeca in New York, North Michigan Avenue in Chicago, the Ginza, Omote-Sando Avenue and Harijuku in Tokyo, Mayfair in London, Boulevard Haussmann in Paris, the Galleria Vittorio Emanuele II in Milan, or other commercial high streets and complexes people instantly identify with cities. Shopping areas are the places to see and be seen, for residents and visitors alike. They are a source of pride for a town or city, conveying status by the quality of shops but also creating a sense of belonging through shared experience. Much of this is, of course, the product of image makers, advertisers, and media, intended to attract tourists and encourage locals to part with their resources. But for urban residents shopping areas are among the few common grounds for everyday life. And they are particularly important places in rapidly developing cities, where they provide the venues for interaction, events, and contact among recently arrived residents.

The physical form and design of shopping areas can have a large impact on their performance. Most people arrive at a shopping area with only a general sense of what they wish to buy, and what they return home with will be greatly affected by what they are exposed to and how it is presented. There are magnets that draw people to shopping places, and other stores or outlets that feed off their presence. Shoppers may be persuaded to stay longer in a place by the mix of opportunities—places to rest or eat, recreation areas

34.1 Galleria Vittorio Emanuele II at the Duomo, Milan, Italy. (Gary Hack)

34.2 Multilevel retail complex at Eaton Centre, Toronto.
(Courtesy of Toronto Tourism)

for their children, entertainment areas—or they may be put off by the crush of people, boredom of offerings, long walks needed to get from store to store, lack of weather protection, or a dingy environment. A great deal is known about shoppers' behavior by those who plan commercial areas, much of it not captured in guides or texts.

Shopping Programs

All else being equal, the larger the shopping area, the greater the distance from which it draws its patronage. Of course, all else is never equal, and the attractiveness of shopping areas is influenced by the mix of outlets, prestige, advertising, image, accessibility, and history; but the scale of a shopping area remains an important underlying factor that determines the distance shoppers will travel to it. Larger centers offer a greater variety of retail opportunities, and tend to accumulate their patrons from large areas. *Gravity models* can be used to predict the sphere of influence of shopping areas. By analogy to Newton's Law, they assert that the trade area of a center is directly proportional to its mass (floor area is one good surrogate). A center that is twice the size of a nearby center will attract the majority of customers until a point two-thirds of the distance between them (Reilly 1931). While it is possible to overcome scale and distance with unique offerings, those planning commercial centers overlook the gravitational pull of size at their peril. One strategy by developers is to oversize shopping centers on the urbanizing fringe to meet the future demand, hoping to discourage others from building a competing center a few kilometers down the road.

Various names have evolved to describe conventional types of shopping areas, differentiating them by size and type. At the most local level is the *convenience center*, which may include a late-hour store selling milk, sundries, and snacks, and perhaps beside it a dry cleaner or small pharmacy. One step up in size is the *community shopping center*, sometimes called a *neighborhood center*, anchored by a large supermarket, super drugstore, discount store, small department store (or some combination) and containing a range of apparel, home improvement, and other shops, and one or two eating places. *Regional shopping centers* cover the full range of retail outlets and are generally anchored by at least two mass market or discount department stores. They cater to all ages, with fashion outlets, gift and home improvement stores, electronics and toy stores, and incorporating a score of restaurants and possibly a food court and cinema area. *Superregional centers*, the largest of the planned commercial areas, will be based on multiple department stores, fashion outlets and every imaginable specialty store, entertainment centers, and even outlets selling automobiles and other high-value items.

One of the difficulties of creating very large shopping centers has been the instability of large department store chains as anchors. Department stores have fallen on tough times in North America, their market eroded by brand name boutiques at one end and large discount retailers at the other. Department

Table 34.1 | Types of shopping places

Type	Focus	Typical size	Anchor	Anchor ratio	Primary trade area
Convenience center	Daily needs	2,000–5,000 sq ft (200–500 m^2)	Convenience store	30–100%	1 mi (1.5 km)
Community center	Weekly needs	30,000–150,000 sq ft (3,000–15,000 m^2)	Supermarket, drugstore	40–60%	3–5 mi (5–8 km)
Regional center	General shopping	400,000–800,000 sq ft (40,000–80,000 m^2)	Multiple department stores	50–70%	5–15 mi (8–22 km)
Superregional center	General shopping, entertainment	800,000–3,000,000 sq ft (80,000–300,000 m^2)	Multiple department stores, entertainment outlet	40–70%	5–25 mi (8–40 km)
Power center	Category shopping	250,000–600,000 sq ft (25,000–60,000 m^2)	Multiple category killer outlets	75–90%	5–10 mi (8–16 km)
Outlet center	Off-price branded merchandise	200,000–500,000 sq ft (20,000–50,000 m^2)	High-visibility brand outlets	10–30%	20–50 mi (30–75 km)
Entertainment center	Food, movies, entertainment	50,000–200,000 sq ft (5,000–20,000 m^2)	Multiscreen cinema	30–50%	5–10 mi (8–16 km)
Fashion center	High-end clothing, home furnishings	80,000–250,000 sq ft (8,000–25,000 m^2)	High-visibility brand stores	10–30%	5–15 mi (8–22 km)

Various sources.

stores remain popular in many other parts of the world, particularly Asia (where the trading group owning the center sometimes also controls the supply chain), but even in these areas, successful department stores have largely reinvented themselves as a collection of brand name boutiques. The loss of an *anchor store* can be devastating for a center that depended upon it to draw customers, and with consolidations and reductions of the number of department stores, there are no obvious replacements. In recent years, developers have sought alternatives that have broad drawing power, but they do not put their fate in the hands of one or two anchors.

One formula has been the creation of a *power center*, composed of five to ten or more *category killers*—large outlets that dominate their business (books, linens, children's toys, outdoors equipment, etc.). Another approach is the creation of high-end *fashion centers*, aggregating dozens of brand name retailers and creating an aura of exclusivity in the environment provided. At the opposite extreme, *outlet centers* thrive by pulling together many clearance outlets of brand name merchants, who will sell their low-priced brands to customers who may be put off by the prices in their flagship stores. Other forms of *specialty centers* may be based on collections of restaurants or a large collection of cinema screens, while collateral retail opportunities appeal to those attracted.

These categories have been created for the convenience of investors and retailers and too often lead to formulaic responses, with one shopping center largely indistinguishable from another and retail chains spread evenly across the landscape. The most interesting shopping areas grow in a more organic fashion—a local shopping street filled with a mix of mostly unique local outlets with a sprinkling of chain stores; a specialty shopping district (focused on clothing boutiques or antiques, art galleries, books, restaurants, etc.) that has evolved over time, sometimes as an offshoot of one successful business; ethnic shopping areas unified by a common heritage and usually centered on food (the most persistent of all ethnic traits); entertainment districts based on restaurants and performance venues.

It proves surprisingly difficult to reproduce the richness of organic shopping areas in new development. Many local retail shops survive because their capital costs have long been amortized, and the shopkeepers may own the real estate where they are located (rents on upper stories may even be subsidizing the retail operations). Other shops can exist only at a scale where the owners and their family can cover the hours they are open; expanding to another location or getting larger will alter the basic economics of the enterprise. Still other retail uses can only exist in cheap space, such as startup restaurants, and will require subsidy in a new development. All of this may conflict with a developer's need to show secure-credit tenants to potential lenders and investors. Nonetheless, with some creativity in structuring the economics of a development, it may be possible to program a mix of tenants that rises above the banal base of tenants with nationally recognized credit.

Planning Principles

Exposure

A successful shopping area depends on the visibility of shops and merchandise—capturing the *moving eyeballs*, as retailers often say. The eyes may be in motion in vehicles passing by a retail outlet, or in pedestrians flowing by a shop. In either case, something that is attractive to the potential shopper needs to be visible, and it needs to be obvious how to enter the store or find its parking area. Thus the first principle of planning retail areas is to expose the shopping opportunities to the maximum number of potential buyers—with an emphasis on the right kinds of buyers, not necessarily the most eyeballs. For some kinds of outlets (e.g., restaurants that depend on repeat clientele) this may not require a great deal of exposure; for others, it may mean simply making visible a well-known logo or marquee; while for those that depend on constantly attracting new buyers (e.g., shoe stores, dress shops) or impulse buyers, the merchandise may need to be put in front of the shoppers' eyes. Planners of retail areas may need to differentiate the level of exposure to cater to varying types of enterprises.

Flows

A favorable location, anchor tenants, advertising, and events deliver potential shoppers to a commercial area, but the site planner needs to ensure that they reach the individual shops. The key is creating a system of flows through a site, attracting people effortlessly from one area to another, ensuring that they pass by those outlets that require direct visibility and directing them to out-of-the-way destinations by signage and other devices.

Assuming there are two prime destinations, as in many shopping centers, the route between them should be lined by stores that might not attract shop-

34.3 The Hollywood and Highland shopping and entertainment complex relies upon its visibility on Hollywood Boulevard to attract visitors to Los Angeles.
(Courtesy of Hollywood & Highland)

34.4 The Prudential arcade shops in Boston are patronized by thousands of pedestrians who pass them each day walking to work, home, conventions, and entertainment.
(Gary Hack)

pers independently. An often-cited guideline is that major destinations should not be more than 600 ft (280 m) apart to avoid shopper fatigue, although this can be lengthened if there are many interesting things along the way. Historic shopping streets in European cities are often much longer—Copenhagen's pedestrian shopping street, Strøget, extends for more than 1 km (3,000 ft) between the City Hall and Kongens Nytorv, but it changes its retail character at least five times along the way. Destinations need to be visible to entice people to keep moving. Two-sided retail areas—whether on a

34.5 Strøget in Copenhagen changes character frequently along its length.
(Dan/flickr/Creative Commons)

34.6 Dining and entertainment opportunities on the top floors of Horton Center, San Diego, draw shoppers through the vertical mall.
(Gary Hack)

34.7 Royal Arcade in Melbourne, Australia, connecting the rail station with the downtown business district.
(Gary Hack)

street or a pedestrian route—are greatly preferred since they add to the density of attractions along the way.

Like a river, the pedestrian stream can have eddies with pockets of retail outlets a short distance off the main path (although visible from it), or may have parallel streams intersecting from time to time with the main stream. While the Ginza in Tokyo is thought of as one major street lined with department stores, it is actually a district with several smaller parallel streets offering the kind of space that restaurants, boutiques, and smaller outlets require.

Creating two or more levels of shopping intensifies the number of shops within easy walking range. However, enticing shoppers to climb stairs or escalators to upper levels is difficult, and stores located there need to be visible and enticing enough to overcome the resistance of gravity. Many *multilevel retail areas* (and Japanese department stores) put eating areas at the top to encourage shoppers to navigate the height of the complex. At Horton Plaza in San Diego, rooftop food and beverage outlets have become the magnet that draws shoppers through the vertical mall. It is easier to encourage shoppers to move down than up, and another strategy is to get shoppers to enter at upper levels—such as by creating entrances from upper stories of parking garages. One rule of thumb is that in a two-floor retail area, 60% of the shoppers should enter on the second level, to balance out the resistance to moving upward.

Connections to destinations beyond the retail area can also help encourage flows. The heavily traveled route from Flinders Station to the central business district in Melbourne, Australia has stimulated the creation of a lacework of arcades, shopping streets, and complexes all capitalizing on the pedestrian flows. In Boston, Massachusetts, the Prudential Center retail area is highly successful without any anchor tenants because over 50,000 pedestrians move through the retail arcades every day to destinations beyond. Open-ended retail streets make visible the connections both within and outside the retail area.

Attracting and Retaining Shoppers

Encouraging flows provides exposure to shops, which merchants work hard to convert into sales. But the probability of success also increases when shoppers

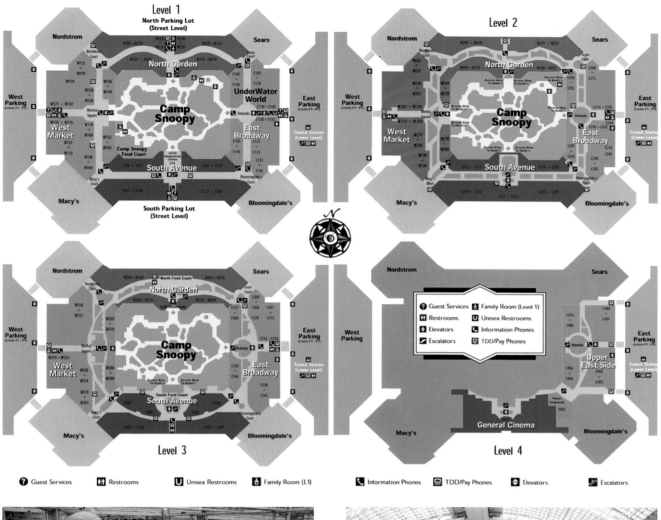

Level 1

Level 2

Level 3

Level 4

34.8 (top)
Diagrams of the four-floor Mall of America, Bloomington, Minnesota.
(Mall of America)

34.9 (bottom left)
Nickelodeon Universe (which replaced Camp Snoopy) amusement park, Mall of America, Bloomington, Minnesota.
(Mall of America)

34.10 (bottom right)
Water park at West Edmonton Mall, Edmonton, Alberta.
(Jody Robbins/West Edmonton Mall)

spend longer periods of time in the retail area. This is influenced by the mix of uses, programmed activities, and amenities provided. Superregional malls often become virtual theme parks, doubling the average time shoppers spend in them. The Mall of America in Bloomington, Minnesota is built around several enclosed amusement parks, where parents can keep their children entertained while they shop. Its precursor, the West Edmonton Mall in Edmonton, Alberta, also has an amusement park with rides for children and adults, as well as a beach covered by a large glazed roof (and a hotel overlooking it), a submarine ride, musically programmed fountains, streets with sidewalk cafés, and a practice rink for the local professional hockey team, used as a skating rink in all seasons. The center provides coat- and parcel-checking services to encourage visitors to stay longer, and has become the highest-ranked visitor attraction in its region. Not to be outdone, the Global Mall in the new Tianfu district of Chengdu, China, has a vast water entertainment complex ringed by hotels, shops, and entertainment venues. These are extreme cases only possible with mega retail complexes, but smaller centers often include botanical gardens, performance venues, public facilities such as libraries and post offices, large movie or digital screens, television production sets, and a host of other diversions intended to hold potential customers.

In many retail areas merchants collectively organize programs of events and activities designed to draw people into the retail area, while building community attachment. These can take an infinite variety of forms that include programmed entertainment, children's activities, displays, decorative planting, farmer's markets, craft or flea markets, holiday displays and markets, film screenings, and art shows, changing throughout the year. Semiprogrammed events such as street musicians, jugglers, mimes, and human sculptures can also add life and interest to a shopping area. Street fairs and seasonal festivals can draw large crowds to a commercial area, and a portion of a parking area on off days may become the location of an antique auto show or community garage sale. The point for planners is that every shared space in a shopping area—streets, alleys, malls, squares, and parking areas—needs to be designed so that it can be used in multiple ways. This involves getting the forms and dimensions right, and providing

the necessary electrical supplies, water, lighting, and surfaces to anchor temporary structures and displays.

Servicing Shopping Areas

Merchants are constantly receiving goods to restock their shelves and replenish inventories. With just-in-time supply chains, the amount of inventory is closely matched to sales, lowering the amount of floor area that needs to be devoted to storage, but this also means more frequent deliveries. Many businesses also sell via the Internet, generating outgoing merchandise that must be picked up. And a substantial amount of waste may be generated by a business—particularly restaurants and retailers that receive goods in bulk—which must be compacted, stored, and removed. Every retail enterprise has its own rhythm of receiving and dispatching materials, which is difficult to generalize. Since retail outlets change more often than the buildings they are located in, service areas need to be designed for a variety of tenants.

The simplest arrangement for loading is from vehicles parked along the street. This may be the only option if there aren't rear alleyways or loading zones. Traditionally in many US cities, goods were moved from trucks to basement storage areas via elevators or hatches with stairways, but this has proved cumbersome and unnecessary in most new street-oriented retail areas. Trucks unloading at the curb present an obvious conflict with parking for customers, and their presence on auto-free streets detracts from pedestrian enjoyment of the space outside shops. A workable solution is to restrict truck unloading to hours before shops open (before 10 am in many cities), and to schedule garbage pickup for hours after shops have closed.

Locating service areas at the rear of shops or in service courtyards is distinctly preferable. Unless the stores are very large, it makes sense to share loading docks, with service corridors providing access to the rear of each outlet. This allows the number of loading docks to be minimized, and space can be dedicated to garbage storage and recycling pickup. Locating and planning loading areas are among the most contentious issues in designing a site. Neighbors will worry about truck traffic, especially large trucks idling while waiting to unload or backing into loading areas; about the noise, odors, and pollution generated; and about the sight of loading docks and the hazards of rodents nesting in areas where garbage is stored. These issues are especially critical in mixed-use areas with residents nearby. There are solutions to each, but the loading area must be carefully planned and managed.

A loading area that can be fully enclosed behind a roll-down door is the ideal solution. Many cities, however, do not allow back-in operations, and a three-point turning radius for a large (17 m, 55 ft) semitrailer truck requires an area of at least 28 by 28 m (90 by 90 ft). This may be appropriate for a large shopping center or in suburban areas where land is plentiful, but is rarely possible in smaller urban retail areas. A costly but effective alternative is a turntable, which allows trucks to be reoriented before unloading. In very large mixed-use centers, an underground truck tunnel may be possible, or service areas may occupy portions of the ground level if retail uses are elevated one level aboveground (as in many Hong Kong podium-type developments).

Regardless of the configuration, loading docks need to be carefully managed. Deliveries need to be scheduled, and hours may need to be restricted for sites bordering on residential areas (e.g., no deliveries before 6 am or after 10 pm). Compactors can be helpful in reducing waste volumes. Trucks need to be required to turn off engines when stopped. And in

some instances—particularly for multioutlet stores—it makes sense to break down the bulk of shipments in a remote location, allowing smaller vehicles to make the final delivery.

Parking

On many shopping sites, parking occupies most of the land. Planners recognize that a great deal is to be gained by innovative approaches to the location and design of parking areas, once a dusty subject governed by local regulations and department store demands.

Innovation begins with a close look at the amount of parking needed, which varies across the day, the week, and the year. When reduced to standards, in North America suburban shopping centers are typically expected to have 4–5 parking spaces per 1,000 retail sq ft (3.7–4.7 spaces per 100 m^2). About 80% of this is for short-term shoppers, with the balance dedicated to employees and other long-term users. These standards are based on a number of assumptions: the fraction of shoppers that arrive by car (100%), the number of shoppers in each vehicle, the appropriate design day (typically the 15th highest shopping day of the year), the highest peak accumulations on the design day, and other factors. Modify any of these assumptions and the resulting parking requirements will also vary.

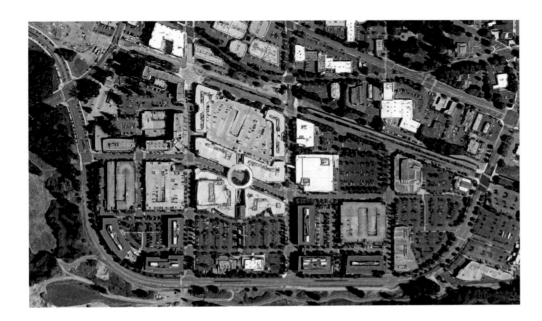

34.11 Independent blocks connected by upper-level pedestrian ways, Redmond Town Center, Redmond, Washington. (Google Earth)

34.12 View of Redmond Town Center with upper-level connections, Redmond, Washington.
(Gary Hack)

As an example, the amount of parking needed can be reduced by almost 20% by moving employee and other long-term parking off site during peak times of the year. Establishing bus routes to the center or incorporating a mass transit stop on the site can dramatically reduce the needed parking. In some cases, such as street-oriented retail where most people arrive on foot, a small number of metered parking spaces at the curb may be enough to satisfy the demand.

Parking accommodated in structures obviously requires a smaller footprint than parking in surface lots. In most situations, multistory garages only make sense if the land is valuable enough to offset the cost of structures—if it costs $50 per sq ft ($490 per m²) to build a parking structure and if three stories can be built, then it only makes sense to construct parking garages if the land value exceeds $150 per sq ft ($1,470 per m²). However, on any commercial site, parking areas should be considered as a land bank for future development and planned accordingly. Internal roadways should be established through the parking areas, and the dimensions of each area should be adequate to allow new uses to be developed on it, or to construct a multilevel parking structure replacing surface parking. Over time, shopping areas can then evolve into mixed-use areas of a shopping district.

An excellent example of this approach to planning for future development may be seen at Redmond Town Center in suburban Seattle.

Flexibility

Shopping areas change more quickly than most other uses in the city. Retail shops grow stale and need to be refreshed; inventing new merchandise is essential to continued consumption; retailing techniques change as do the business organizations; and the demographics and development patterns around retail areas change, forcing shopping areas to adapt. Retail investments are amortized over relatively short time periods, typically 15–30 years, and once debt is discharged shopping areas are ripe for reinvestment. Of course, every retail use has its own logic of longevity—restaurants turn over very quickly, anchor stores are more durable (but subject to business consolidation), and specialty shops fall between, with some lasting a full generation. When the form of a shopping area is not capable of accommodating change, it can become a drag on all its enterprises.

There are a number of strategies for dealing with change in shopping areas. The most obvious is locking in a market so that it is not easily eroded. Adding housing and workplaces to a shopping area assures a nearby market of consumers. If not at the outset, it may still be possible to provide future sites for these uses, such as through the conversion of parking areas. A second strategy is creating a hierarchy of shopping opportunities by intelligent land use planning of large sites. One of the principal motivations in developing the new town of Columbia, Maryland was to create a stable pattern of commercial centers. Its developer, the Rouse Companies, had seen too many of its retail centers eroded by larger new competing centers constructed a few miles down the road. A third strategy is deliberately planning for obsolescence. Rather than letting sites sit idle in a developing shopping area, *pop-up outlets* can be encouraged, or outdoor markets scheduled to draw people to the center. Later these can remain as incubators, or be replaced by more permanent structures as the market is proven.

Shopping areas need to be thought of as ever-changing places, where tradition and newness coexist and become embedded in the minds of their patrons.

Shopping Prototypes

Open-Air Markets

The oldest and simplest form of shopping area is the outdoor market. It dates from antiquity, and outdoor souqs and bazaars remain in cities throughout the world, but the outdoor market remains surprisingly relevant even in the most modern of cities. The past few decades have seen an explosion of green markets, farmer's markets, flea markets, antiques markets, flower markets, crafts fairs, night markets, and festival marketplaces. Holiday markets, such as the Christmas markets in most European cities, often occupy main public spaces (the Grand Place in Brussels, Piazza Navona in Rome, and Dilworth Plaza in Philadelphia, as examples). In addition, many older cities have one or more covered marketplaces that have experienced a revival as they have been discovered by a new generation of young urbanites.

The wide range of open-air markets makes it difficult to generalize about size, layout, and facilities. A temporary weekend market may require nothing more than a weather-protected folding table and place to park the truck that arrived with the items to be sold. A more organized layout allocates bays of 14 by 30 ft (4 by 9 m) where small trucks can back up to and supply a vendor stand. Permanent vendor structures, such as those found in the flower market in Paris or Amsterdam's tulip market, are elaborate structures, capable of being locked at night so that the inventory need not be removed. The most rudimentary markets require electrical services to each stall, with water and waste removal facilities provided at points on the perimeter. Large public markets generally provide refrigeration facilities (small unites for each vendor or large shared rooms) to allow meats, dairy products, vegetables, and flowers to be stored for long periods.

34.13 Roanoke Farmers Market, with back-in stalls for vendors, Roanoke, Virginia.
(Courtesy of Julie Stone)

34.14 Dairy hall, Queen Victoria Market, Melbourne, Australia.
(Gary Hack)

34.15 Pike Place Market mixes temporary and permanent stalls, Seattle, Washington.
(Gary Hack)

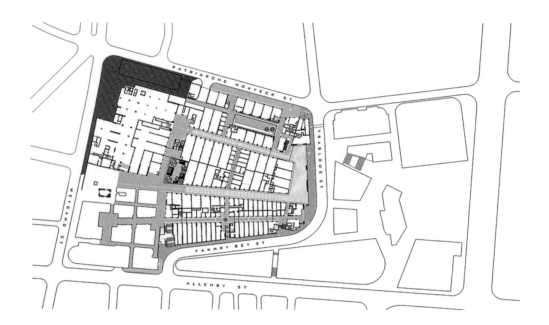

34.16 Plan of new souq, Beirut, Lebanon. (Courtesy of Studio Rafael Moneo)

The best *public markets* develop longstanding loyalties between merchants and their customers, and become social centers as well as places for transactions. They evolve over time, with merchants adding more permanent fixtures as their clientele grows. A proportion of the stalls may be permanently assigned, while other areas are reserved for daily or weekly usage. Market associations or municipal authorities commonly prescribe the hours of operation, character of tenant improvements allowed, size and type of signage, and type of merchandise that may be sold. The restrictions may go further: at Pike Place Market, vendors are limited to a single outlet and cannot be part of a chain of stores. An infamous lawsuit at Faneuil Hall Market in Boston contested the right of the market owner to restrict a merchant to selling fresh greens (specified in his lease), when it was considerably more profitable to shift to pizza and prepared foods; the owner prevailed.

Several examples illustrate the possibilities. In Beirut, Lebanon, a new clothing and jewelry *souq* has been constructed as part of a larger complex that also includes a cinema, family entertainment center, department store, and food court. It is a modern interpretation of the traditional souq, skylit, with lines of traditional shops. In the Soweto community of Johannesburg, South Africa, a public market has been integrated into the design of a multimodal transportation center,

34.17 View of new souq, Beirut, Lebanon. (Courtesy of Solidere)

allowing shoppers to purchase foods and sundries while they transfer from express to local buses. Merchants are assigned lockers to store their supplies overnight.

Large public market halls were once the pride of cities and remain important destinations for residents and visitors. The Oxford Covered Market acquired its roof in 1774 and remains today. The Central Market Hall in Budapest, Barcelona's Mercado Santa Caterina, Reading Terminal Market in Philadelphia, St. Lawrence Market in Toronto, and the Grand Central Market in

Los Angeles are examples of public markets with city-wide patronage. Smaller markets such as the waterside Old Market Hall in Helsinki, Byward Market in Ottawa, the Kitchener Market in Kitchener, Ontario, and the Lancaster Central Market in Lancaster, Pennsylvania are known for the specialty products characteristic of their regions. Several public markets, including Covent Garden Market in London, Vinohradský Pavilon in Prague, Faneuil Hall in Boston, and Pike Place in Seattle have been restored to accommodate a wider range of merchants—adding prepared foods, restaurants, crafts, and souvenirs in the main market hall, while surrounding it with boutiques and other shopping opportunities. The difficulty is retaining authentic market functions in the face of a crush of tourists who have little use for lettuce and cuts of beef. Among these, Pike Place has fared the best by being vigilant in its tenant mix, and retaining low-priced space on a lower level for unique businesses—hat blockers and barber-shops—as well as fresh seafoods and seasonal fruits and vegetables on the main floor.

Among newly constructed markets, the Granville Island Market in Vancouver is an excellent example of balancing local and tourist opportunities, permanent and temporary merchants, food and other products. It is organized around two-high spaces, with prepared foods concentrated on the water side with tables for

34.18 Aerial view of Santa Caterina Market, Barcelona. (Courtesy of Enric Miralles and Benedetta Tagliabue–EMBT/Roland Halbe photo.)

34.19 Interior, Santa Caterina Market, Barcelona. (Gary Hack)

34.20 Granville Island Public Market, Vancouver, Canada. (Gary Hack)

34.21 Interior space, Granville Island Public Market. (Gary Hack)

those who wish to pause and eat, and produce for the home kitchen located near the entrance to ease loading. Design standards control the general appearance of permanent stalls, but leave considerable room for personalization.

Convenience Shopping Centers

In new development areas, there may be a need for a small cluster of shops for the sale of convenience goods (food, drugs and sundries, and personal services), but not an established pattern of streets where these can locate organically. Creating a convenience center with shared parking is one solution; another is to use the center to establish a pedestrian realm with connections to residential areas that encourage walking. Such centers are usually anchored by a minimart or drug store selling convenience foods, and typically are smaller than 3,000 m² (30,000 sq ft). They may also include a restaurant, fast food service, dry cleaner, beauty parlor, medical or dental office, insurance agent, and other goods and services catering to local residents. In places where most people arrive by car, such centers typically require four parking spaces per 1,000 sq ft (100 m²) of gross leasable space, because of the rapid

turnover of parkers, but in areas with a large fraction of customers arriving on foot, the parking can be correspondingly reduced.

The challenge in convenience centers is making them truly convenient for people on quick trips for a few items, while not favoring motorists over pedestrians. Many chains prefer parking at the front of the store, visible from the street, which forces walk-in patrons to navigate through parked cars to reach the entrance. There are other solutions: the entrances can be placed on the side and connected to the sidewalk, or a small courtyard can be created allowing several shops to share a pedestrian space, while each has direct access to a parking area. Windows on the street should be mandated, and buildings should hold the corner of blocks if at all possible, so that entrances can provide access from two directions. Convenience centers are also better if street frontages are lined with upper-floor offices—this is an ideal location for medical, insurance, or other necessary local services. Since an ideal location for a convenience center is near a public transit stop, it may also be a good location for upper-story housing. Mashpee Commons is an excellent example of a convenience center that has been redeveloped to become a town center for its area of Cape Cod.

Mashpee Commons, Mashpee, Massachusetts

Mashpee Commons began its life as the New Seabury Shopping Center, a 62,000 sq ft convenience center anchored by a supermarket. It was redeveloped as an open-air center intended as a new town center for the area, providing sites for a wide array of new retail and public uses. Streets were introduced as frontages for the shops; parking was distributed into a number of small lots ultimately destined to be developed for housing and other uses. Over 25 years it has expanded to 110,000 sq ft, with 110 shops and businesses. Solar panels have been installed on most of the rooftops, generating 48,000 kWh of energy per year.

Site planners: Duany Plater-Zyberk Associates.

34.22 (top)
Aerial view of Mashpee Commons, Mashpee, Massachusetts.
(Google Earth)

34.23 (bottom left)
Original shopping center, New Seabury Village.
(Courtesy of Mashpee Commons LP)

34.24 (bottom right)
Aerial view of current center.
(Courtesy of Sun Bug Solar)

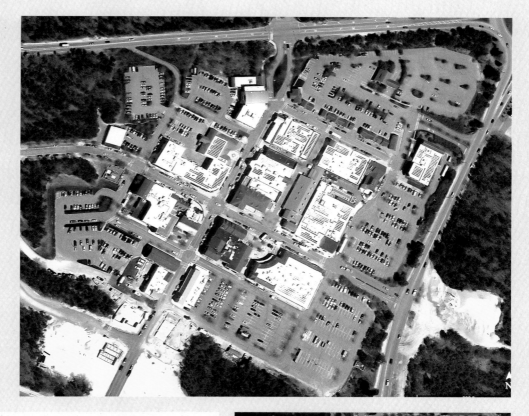

**Mashpee Commons,
Mashpee,
Massachusetts**

34.25 (top)   Current view of Mashpee Commons.
(Courtesy of Elizabeth Thomas Photography)

34.26 (middle left)   View of North Street shops, Mashpee Commons.
(John Phelan/Wikimedia Commons)

34.27 (middle right)   Mashpee Commons at night.
(Courtesy of Paul Blackmore/Mashpee Commons)

34.28 (bottom)   Long-range vision for Mashpee Commons includes housing, parks, and other retail uses.
(Courtesy of Imai Keller Moore Architects)

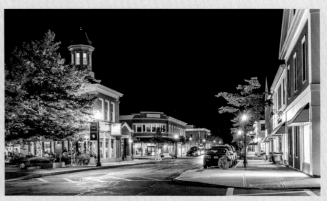

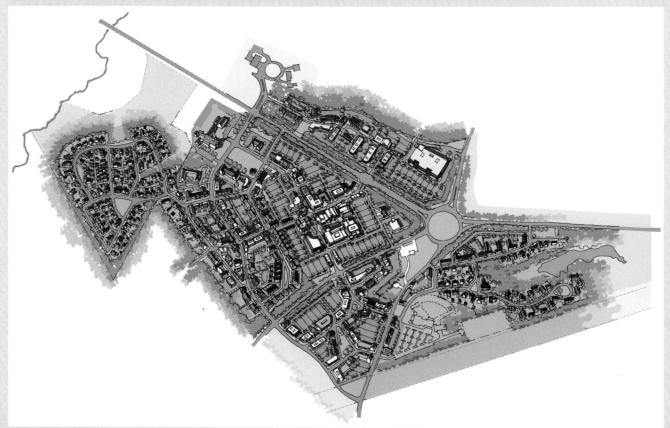

Shopping Streets

Shopping streets are the mainstays of commerce in most cities. Many of them grew up in eras when most of their customers arrived on foot or via public transportation, and not surprisingly they prosper in cities where this remains the case. In planning sites, it is often possible to create a new main street or extend a shopping street that currently exists. A look at successful street-oriented shopping can provide lessons for design.

Street-oriented shopping works best when it is scaled to pedestrian capabilities. As shoppers walk along one side of the street, they are drawn into the shopfronts they pass by window displays and the brightly lit interiors of the shops. Awnings may provide weather protection and draw the shopper closer, and tall trees will offer shade on a hot summer day. In good weather, merchants may move displays out into the street, or restaurants may appropriate sidewalk space for outdoor seating. But there is another view as well: across the street it will be the awnings, signs, and second floors that are most visible, with street traffic partly blocking the views of the sidewalk-level shop windows. Smart merchants will create upper-level displays meant to entice shoppers across the street. If pedestrian flows are constant, shoppers may wish to step out of the flow, rest, or carry on a conversation. Benches located in small eddies off the flow will offer a respite for a few moments.

With the pedestrian in mind, there are infinite ways to design a good shopping street. Ideally, it will be narrow enough that shoppers are not deterred from crossing—no more than two moving lanes of traffic in each direction, or three lanes on a one-directional street. Streets that are no more than 50 ft (15 m) between building faces can easily be designed as a unified shopping area; this can be stretched to 60 ft (18 m), but at 70 ft (21 m) it becomes difficult to entice shoppers to the opposite side. Sidewalks will be wide enough, at least 6 ft (1.8 m), to accommodate two people side by side while passing another, with additional space to handle outdoor displays by merchants or sidewalk cafés (see chapter 24). Blocks should be short enough that pedestrians can regularly navigate from side to side.

Continuity is an important factor in successful shopping streets. Areas that are broken up by driveways for hotels, entrances to parking areas, large lobbies for

34.29 Germantown Avenue, the shopping street of the Chestnut Hill neighborhood, Philadelphia.
(Gary Hack)

34.30 Shopping street, City Center, Reston, Virginia.
(Gary Hack)

office buildings, or broad facades of banks or other service institutions will lower the critical temperature of the street for shopping. If there is a choice, it is better to create narrow and deep retail spaces than broad and shallow, since it increases the opportunities along the pedestrian's route. Along Broadway in New York, shops often occupy narrow frontages on the street which entice people in; shoppers are then transported on escalators to large merchandising spaces above or below ground. It may be possible to wrap portions of larger shops behind shallow shops, much as movie houses limited the width of their passageways to the street while creating grand spaces behind adjacent shops. Use of corners is also critical, since they signal the character of the street; banks and other "dead" frontages should be avoided there.

Arcaded streets have been created in a variety of places, providing weather protection while scaling the street to pedestrians. In Bern, Switzerland, these obviate the need for snow clearance, and many of the street-level arcades are heated by underground piping. Piazza San Marco in Venice is ringed by a two-story colonnaded space, as is the Plaza Mayor in Madrid. In San Miguel de Allende and many other Mexican cities, broad arcades offer a cool environment for shoppers, and many of these spaces are wide enough to accommodate outdoor dining in the shade of the colonnade. Traditional streets in South China cities, such as Guangzhou, are lined by shop houses with covered pedestrian passageways. This pattern has been institutionalized in Taipei for new buildings along major streets, but often they are not managed well, with the unfortunate result that the pedestrian area is often overcrowded with parked motorbikes. Successful arcaded streets offer patterns that can be emulated, as they have been in the center of the new community of Celebration, Florida.

However, arcades are often not ideal for shopping, since the covered areas are generally darker than the street space and shops are less visible. In the US, deeply recessed retail spaces have become anathema to most businesses. Some of the reservations are lessened if the colonnade is two stories or more in height, but this diminishes its value for weather protection.

Accommodating parking is an important issue for street-oriented shopping. Parking at the curb may satisfy part of the need, but it needs to be restricted

34.31 Arcade along Piazza San Marco, Venice, Italy. (Gary Hack)

34.32 Arcade along Main Street, Celebration, Florida. (Gary Hack)

34.33 Parking at the rear of shops, connected to Main Street, Celebration, Florida. (Gary Hack)

to short-turnover parkers lest employees and others capture all the spaces before the shoppers arrive. For high-end retailing, valet parking at the curb may be a solution. In a new development, it may be possible to locate parking below the retail spaces, accessible from cross streets so as to avoid gaps in the line of stores. The most common solution is to locate parking areas behind the retail frontage, either in open lots or in parking structures. With people arriving from the rear, a sure way to kill street-oriented shopping is to allow direct access into shops from the parking area, as this removes the incentive to walk along the street. Rather, a passageway or arcade should be created to bring customers to the street; this is an opportunity to locate small shops along the passage as well. The same applies to underground parking (or parking above the shops): shoppers should be discharged on the street rather than deposited directly into a store. This makes sense from a security perspective as well, and allows parking areas to be used outside of shop hours.

Arcades

In many warm-weather cities, there is a tradition of draping fabric shades across streets to protect shoppers from the blazing sun. The great bazaar of Istanbul (begun in 1461) and the Cloth Hall of Isfahan (1585) were organized as a grid of covered streets and courtyards, with hundreds of market stalls. The Istanbul bazaar ultimately grew to 200,000 m² (2 million sq ft) of shops.

Beginning in the early nineteenth century, cities in rainy and cold climates began to cover streets with glass, creating some of the most intimate and special shopping environments. These evolved into the street-level arcades that may be found today in cities across the globe. Entering all shops from the same level is the characteristic that distinguishes this form, although areas on upper levels may serve as extensions of the shops, or for offices or storage. The passageway is narrow and intimate, usually less than 10 m (32 ft) wide, with the height to the glass at least twice the distance between the shops. In most cases the ends of arcades are not enclosed but offer a respite from the bustling high street environment just outside. The most successful arcades either capitalize on pedestrian desire lines or provide anchors at their ends to draw people

along their length, although exclusive collections of shops can become a destination in their own right.

The Burlington Arcade, opened in 1819 in London, remains a remarkable model for the shopping arcade. Located just behind Bond Street, the 3 m (10 ft) wide pedestrian passageway extends for 177 m (580 ft) between Piccadilly and Burlington Gardens. It is lined with 72 small 2.8 by 4.6 m (10 by 15 ft) two-story shop units, some of which have been combined into double-width shops. Curved glass shopfronts serve as sparkling vitrines for the merchandise, and the mannerist Victorian facades create an environment of exclusivity. The arcade has served an upscale market successfully for almost two centuries.

The Burlington Arcade spurred the construction of many other European arcades, including the Galerie Vivienne in Paris (1826), the Galeries Royales Saint-Hubert in Brussels (1830, the first of seven such galleries in the city), and the Passage in St. Petersburg (1848). Each outdid its predecessor, replacing intimacy with the environment of the grand salon. The idea also migrated to the cities of the new world, and among the best examples is the Royal Arcade in Melbourne, Australia (1869) (see figure 34.7). Many other arcades were constructed in Melbourne to capture the shopping potential of the thousands of commuters who rush from Flinders Station to the Collins Street business district.

The street-level arcade remains an important prototype for organizing shopping areas. At Prudential Center in Boston, windswept outdoor spaces were enclosed by creating an X-shaped pattern of arcades, connecting the main destinations beyond the site— Copley Place, the Hynes Convention Center, and the Back Bay and South End neighborhoods. The width of the arcades (typically 28 ft or 8.5 m) was determined by the spacing of columns in the parking garage below, and their capacity also limited the height of retail uses to a single story. Although larger in scale, the arcades at Prudential Center capture some of the quality of the earlier European arcades. The shopping area is among the most successful of its type in the United States (see figure 34.4).

Many Japanese cities have enclosed back streets to make shopping arcades. Among the most successful is Hondori Street in Hiroshima. An arched glass roof at the fourth-story level covers this 10 m (32 ft) wide street, lined with individual buildings and a great variety of shops ranging from boutiques to food shops, restaurants, movie houses, and mass market outlets. A number of the stores occupy multiple levels, although each has only one entrance, at street level. Department stores and large electronics stores anchor the ends of the street, located parallel to a main street of banks and institutions, served by trams. Trucks service the individual shops from the pedestrian street during off hours.

34.34 North entrance, Burlington Arcade, London.
(© Andrew Dunn/Wikimedia Commons)

34.35 Covered shopping street, Hondori Street, Hiroshima, Japan.
(Gary Hack)

Gallerias

As arcades became ever larger, they evolved into multilevel shopping complexes, sometimes incorporating offices or services on upper floors. Although they are often called arcades, we distinguish gallerias from the street-level arcades just discussed by their multiple levels of shopping (and often offices) and more expansive spaces enclosed under glass (Geist 1982). The Galleria Vittorio Emanuele II in Milan is the best-known prototype for the galleria, and has been emulated throughout the world. Opened in 1864, it faces Piazza del Duomo, the major public square of the city with its cathedral on one side, and Teatro alla Scala and its smaller square on the other side. Providing 45,000 m² (484,000 sq ft) of occupied space on seven levels, the 1,260 rooms of the complex house shops on the ground floor and mezzanine level, rented clubrooms, offices, and studios on the third level, and four levels of residential apartments. The generous 14.5 m (48.5 ft) wide public passageways total 1,150 m² (12,300 sq ft), with portions devoted to sidewalk cafés and displays. Ground- and mezzanine-level shops range from department stores, showrooms, and haute couture to coffeehouses, boutiques, and souvenir shops. The arched glass roof soars 29 m (96 ft) above the pedestrian walkway, and the central dome rises to almost 50 m (164 ft). The scale of this public space makes the Galleria the center of Milan life.

The idea of the shopping galleria spread throughout Europe and the new world during the late nineteenth century. Not to be outdone, Naples built the Galleria Umberto I across from its opera house, consisting of four glazed passageways intersecting at a grand dome even taller than Milan's. The GUM (formerly New Trade Halls) in Moscow was the most expansive arcade in Europe, occupying a full city block of 90 by 250 m (295 by 820 ft). Three major arcades and three smaller transverse passageways—all glazed above—provide access to over 1,000 shops, organized in 16 blocks. GUM was designed with two levels of shopping throughout, topped by two levels of offices.

In the US, impressive multilevel arcades were constructed in Cleveland and Providence. The Cleveland Arcade, built in 1890, accommodated over 100 shops on two levels, with three levels of offices located above. It was a retail destination, bordered by two 9-story office structures, rather than a passageway from street to

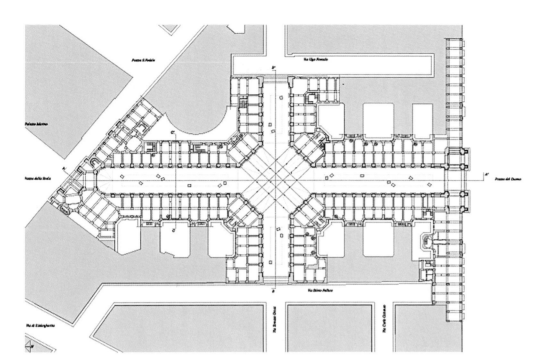

street. In recent years, the upper floors of the arcade have been converted into a boutique hotel, with lower levels remaining as specialty shops and services.

These impressive structures have provided the model for many contemporary shopping centers. Perhaps the best contemporary galleria is Eaton Centre in Toronto, a massive 145,000 m² (1,560,000 sq ft) structure with five levels of shopping concourses stretching 275 m (890 ft) and topped by a 28 m (90 ft) high glass-vaulted roof. Shoppers are drawn into the shopping levels from the underground transit concourse (level 1), through street-level entrances (levels 2 and 3), via a bridge to an adjacent department store (level 3), and

34.42 Interior galleria space, Eaton Centre, Toronto. (Gary Hack)

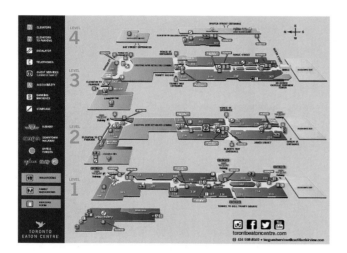

34.40 Diagram of five-level Eaton Centre, Toronto. (Courtesy of Cadillac Fairview Corporation)

34.41 Garish exterior of Eaton Centre in 2010 reflects the adjacent Yonge Street shopping district, Toronto. (Maris Luksis/flickr)

from elevators serving a 1,650-space parking structure that parallels the center (to levels 3, 4, and 5). The balancing of entrance routes assures activity on all the shopping levels. Its 250 shops run the full gamut from a large department store to mass merchandise outlets to boutiques to restaurants and services to a multiscreen theater complex. Offices line the four upper levels of the galleria, and two large office buildings and a hotel are directly attached to the complex.

Community Shopping Centers

At the opposite extreme are planned shopping centers that serve a distinctly local market. Community shopping centers are typically anchored by a supermarket or superstore that combines grocery shopping with a pharmacy and other convenience goods and services. As these outlets have grown in size, they have internalized many of the items that would otherwise have been found in independent stores and now may range from 3,000 to 10,000 m² (32,000–108,000 sq ft), and half or more of the area may be represented by the anchor store. It will require a base of at least 10,000 residents to support it.

A number of early community shopping centers continue to serve as models of human-scaled locally oriented shopping areas that are the center of community life. Country Club Plaza, opened in 1924 and modeled on a Moorish village of shops and courtyards, was an upscale early development in Kansas City, Missouri. Highland Park Village Shopping Center in Dallas, Texas, built in 1931, followed this lead. While it has been refreshed and upgraded over the years, its charming central space, graced by a fountain, and its Spanish colonial architecture continue to give it special character. River Oaks Shopping Center in Houston, Texas was among the first "modern" centers, constructed in 1937 in the deco style. Its first tenants were food and liquor stores, beauty and barbershops, a drug store, a tailor-cleaner, flower and gift shops, an electric supply store, and women's clothing outlets. It remains today an important center for the neighborhood, and while a supermarket remains the anchor, it has attracted bookstores, designer furniture stores, art galleries, fashion shops, a movie theater, and no fewer than 18 restaurants and specialty food stores—perhaps a reflection of the changing character of the surrounding area.

With anchors the size of current supermarkets or superstores, which grow ever larger each year, the site planning challenge of community shopping areas is to create a center that is more than a large box with a few shops appended surrounded by a sea of cars. There are several strategies that can help overcome this. One is to create a transit-oriented center, where a significant fraction of shoppers arrives via mass transit or buses or transfer between them. Since those arriving are already on foot in this case, grouping businesses around pedestrian areas is a logical step. An excellent example is Fruitvale Village (sometimes called Fruitvale Transit Village) in Oakland, California, serving a low-income community and planned with their considerable input. Shoppers are drawn into the center from the BART mass transit station and bus loading area, and many may make a stop before walking home or going to their parked vehicles in the park-and-ride lot. Fruitvale Village illustrates the general principles

34.43 Aerial view, Highland Park Village, one of the earliest community shopping centers, Dallas, Texas. (Courtesy of Terry Theiss Photography)

in planning effective transit-oriented community commercial centers. Mixing uses is essential, so that people coming to or passing through the center can do several things at once—see a doctor, purchase a greeting card, drop off a book at the library, as well as get their daily or weekly supply of groceries. There should be clear walking routes connecting the center with adjacent areas. And the flow should ensure that people pass by the shops en route to their automobiles, or see them while making a transfer between transit modes. There should be places to stop and grab a cup of coffee with a friend you unexpectedly met. It should be designed for all ages, from young children needing a diversion to elderly wishing to watch the passing crowd (and children). Supermarkets that cater to transit passengers and pedestrians typically are smaller in size, often 30,000 sq ft (2,800 m²) or less. And transit-oriented community shopping centers economize on parking: at transit stops in Washington, DC, supermarket operators can get away with 3 parking spaces per 1,000 sq ft (1 space per 30 m²) rather than the 5 that are typical for suburban locations.

European cities offer many examples of fine transit-oriented developments; they have been the prevailing pattern for many years, and every city with a transit or tram system has streets lined with community-oriented shopping. Where larger sites are available at key locations on transit lines, community-scale

Fruitvale Village, Oakland, California

Fruitvale Village is a transit-oriented development adjacent to the BART station, which is also an important transfer point for those taking buses. The 45,000 sq ft (4,200 m²) of retail and restaurant spaces include a supermarket, bank, coffee shop, record shop, beauty salon, bakery, and other uses. In addition, there are 45,000 sq ft (4,200 m²) devoted to offices and neighborhood services, including a library, senior center, child development center, health clinic, and a variety of local services. Rental housing is located on the second and third floors of each of the buildings. Overall, the site contains 250,000 sq ft (23,200 m²) of space, and will be extended through successive phases.

Site planners: McLarand, Vasquez & Partners.

34.44 Plan of Fruitvale Village, Oakland, California. (Courtesy of McLarand, Vasquez & Partners)

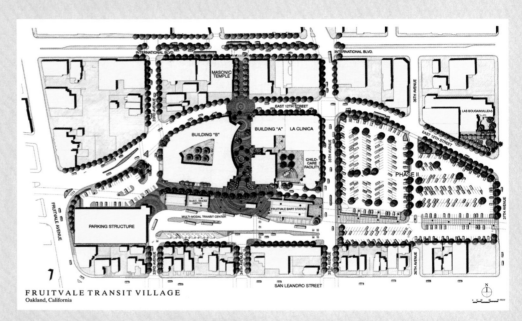

34.45 BART Fruitvale Village transit station. (Eric Fredericks/Flickr/ Creative Commons)

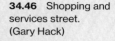

34.46 Shopping and services street. (Gary Hack)

34.47 Entrance to Fruitvale Village from neighborhood. (Gary Hack)

34.48 Close connection to shops on adjacent street. (Gary Hack)

34.49 Stairway to second-level services and housing above, also served by elevator. (Gary Hack)

shopping areas have been constructed. A nice example is the small but successful Sonnenschiff complex, built as part of the Solarsiedlung experiment in Vauban, Freiburg, Germany. Anchored by an organic super-market, it provides 1,160 m² (12,500 sq ft) of shopping and 3,800 m² (40,900 sq ft) of offices for professional services needed by the Vauban community, at the key transit stop for the neighborhood. The development is topped by residential penthouses.

A second strategy for community shopping centers is to organize them as a main street for the community with parking areas at the rear. Issues in street-oriented shopping have been discussed previously, but when planned de novo, local shopping streets can achieve a balance of retail, entertainment, services, office, and residential uses that assure synergy between the uses and a 24-hour life for the center. It is important to array the uses so that shoppers are drawn beyond their initial destination. Flows between offices, housing, restaurants, and shopping are the critical planning framework. A good example of how these might be organized is at Baldwin Park Village Center, in Orlando, Florida. This new main street consists of 212,000 sq ft (19,700 m²) of commercial space, including a super-market, drug store, restaurants, boutiques, and two large bank branches. Layered over the retail uses are 117 apartments and office space. The supermarket, located in the center of the area, has dual entrances to the main street and rear parking area, and is able to serve those who arrive either on foot or by car. Unlike most such centers, this one was built at an early stage in the development of the Baldwin Park community, to establish the commercial presence and help market the development as a full-service community.

34.50 Sonnenschiff mixed-use center at Vauban transit stop, Freiburg, Germany.
(Gary Hack)

34.51 Aerial view of downtown, Baldwin Park, Florida.
(Google Earth)

34.52 View of Main Street, Baldwin Park, Florida.
(Better Cities & Towns)

What can be done when most people arrive by automobile and there aren't sizable nearby commercial concentrations or high-density residential areas? Creating a multipurpose public space at the center of the shops is a good first step, a place that can be used as a farmer's market, venue for festivals and performances, and other important community events. The Highland Park center in Dallas illustrates just how powerfully such a space can shape a community's identity. Incorporating important civic and religious facilities, such as libraries, community recreation centers, arts centers, and religious structures, in the center will also help establish its importance beyond the commercial uses. This approach was taken in planning the village centers of Columbia, Maryland, and while the commercial uses have met with mixed success—the small supermarkets didn't fare well in competition with megamarkets farther away and have been replaced by drugstores and other uses—the centers have remained important anchors of community life. Beyond these moves, it is important to tame the parking areas through landscape that protects against heat island effects, and creative planning that allows them to be used for alternative purposes during off periods.

Regional Shopping Centers

Regional shopping centers, which became known as "malls," have their origins in the desire of department store chains to expand into the rapidly urbanizing suburbs of American cities during the 1950s. Victor Gruen, who was largely responsible for developing the prototype, saw them as social centers for suburbanites that could function equally in all weather with their covered central spaces. Southdale Center in Edina, Minnesota, opened in 1956, was the first fully enclosed modern shopping center, and the first to have two levels of retail spaces—a reinvention of the basic principles of the nineteenth-century arcades. At Southdale, about 60% of the shoppers enter at the upper level, a trick achieved by creatively regrading parking areas to alternate between sloping toward and away from the center. Within a decade, virtually every American city had its version of the suburban mall, and they have found their way around the globe wherever cities have the ability to support chains of retail outlets. Indeed, the uniformity of spaces and configurations in shopping centers made possible the growth of international retailing chains, allowing them to roll out the same products and store designs from city to city and across continents.

The earliest shopping centers typically had two department stores as anchors, which were placed at the ends of a dumbbell plan with specialty stores between. Soon centers were able to attract three or four anchors, and other configurations were needed—resulting in L or T or X shapes. When the number of anchors climbed to 6 or 8, some centers decided to create parallel connections, creating a *racetrack circulation pattern* or a figure-eight. Others simply grew longer but created kinks in the pattern to limit the perceived distance from end to end. Still other centers adopted multifloor configurations to shorten the distance between anchors. One result of layering was that the mall spaces needed to grow wider so that shopfronts on upper levels were visible to shoppers on the floor below. This, in turn created the opportunity to locate *vending carts* and *sales kiosks* in the center of the wider malls. One delightful accidental discovery was the *food court*, which owes its origins to the fact that one anchor dropped out of the mix just as the large Sherway Gardens Shopping Center was being completed in Toronto. Not wanting a dead spot, the developers installed temporary food vendors and dining tables, and these were an instant success. Today the food court is almost synonymous with the shopping center.

Conventional patterns of regional malls channel shoppers through the anchor stores that guard the ends of the pedestrian promenades, or in through minor entrances on the sides, lined with shops. This creates a sense of enclosure and control in the mall spaces, where shoppers have only retail spaces in view. The merchants may prefer this, but it contributes to a relentless commercial experience of visiting a mall. Newer regional centers strive for a greater sense of welcome by creating a grand entrance pavilion which opens up to the full range of offerings available. A good example of this is The Mall at Cribbs Causeway, in Bristol, England, where a galleria-scale entrance transports visitors into the center of the complex; from there they begin their journey to the two anchor stores and shops between.

With the proliferation of enclosed regional shopping malls in the US, Europe, and Asia, shoppers have

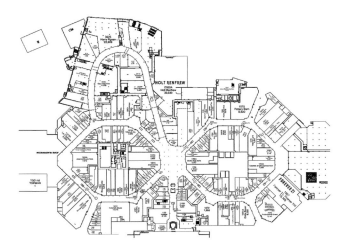

34.53 Aerial view of first enclosed two-level shopping mall, Southdale Center, Edina, Minnesota.
(Victor Gruen/Minnesota Historical Society)

34.54 Interior space, Southdale Center, Edina, Minnesota.
(Bobak Ha'Eri/Wikimedia Commons)

34.55 Figure-eight circulation path at Sherway Gardens, Toronto.
(Courtesy of Cadillac Fairview Corporation)

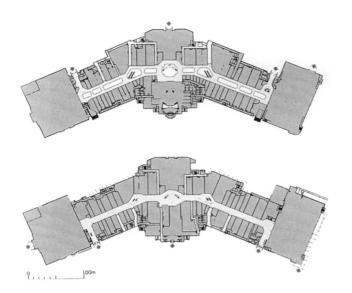

34.56 Plan, Mall at Cribbs Causeway, Bristol, UK. (M & G Real Estate Limited)

34.57 Entrance portal and atrium at Mall at Cribbs Causeway, Bristol, UK. (Valela/Wikimedia Commons)

34.58 Plan, mall with indoor and outdoor components, FlatIron Crossing, Broomfield, Colorado. (Courtesy of © CallisonRTKL)

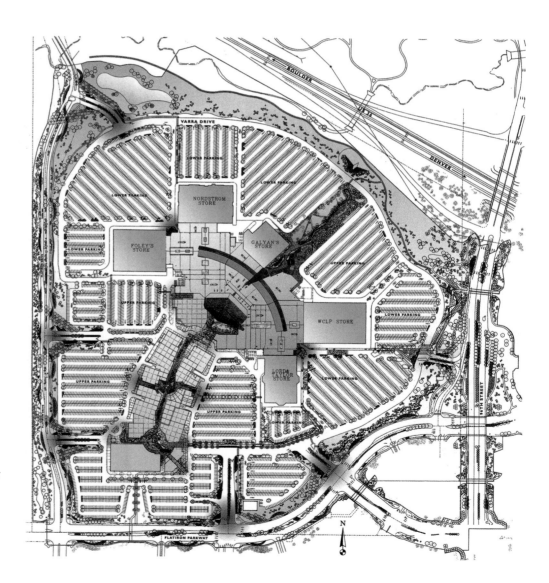

become bored with the uniformity of their appearance and the retail outlets they house—seen one, seen 'em all! Creative developers have consciously adopted layouts and materials that make reference to regional themes as a strategy for establishing a unique identity. This began at Horton Plaza in San Diego, which shunned the roof over the public space and reestablished open-air shopping, albeit on many levels, taking advantage of the city's glorious climate. In Colorado, where the winter climate can be severe, an opposite approach has proved successful: designing regional centers that remind shoppers of the magnificent mountain lodges in the nearby Rockies. Park Meadows in Littleton, Colorado was the first to do this, and it has been followed by FlatIron Crossing, a large regional resort mall in nearby Broomfield. At FlatIron Crossing, the exposed timber structure, natural lighting, wooden floors, roaring fireplaces, and the clustering of shops selling outdoors equipment provide a welcoming and informal environment.

34.59 Materials and spaces attempt to capture regional character, FlatIron Crossing, Broomfield, Colorado. (Courtesy of © CallisonRTKL)

As regional shopping centers have grown ever larger in size and pedestrian zones have multiplied in area, designers have needed to find ways to differentiate public areas by varying activities, themes, or character. This is carried to the extreme in the gigantic 482,000 m² (5.3 million sq ft) West Edmonton Mall, where each area is dominated by an activity—the Galaxyland Amusement Park, the Waterpark, the Sea Lion's rock, the Deep Sea Adventure, Europa Boulevard, the Pirate Ship, the Skating Rink, and on and on (see figure 34.10). The website for the mall offers three-day itineraries for visitors. The Mall of the Americas, by the same developer, applies this idea in a more sophisticated way, differentiating each leg of the mall by form, function, and character. Another strategy for differentiating a center is creating separate but linked areas for each type of opportunity: specialty shopping, home improvement, entertainment and dining, and so on.

The Easton Town Center in suburban Columbus, Ohio adopts a different approach to breaking down the scale of a regional center. The large (750,000 sq ft or 70,000 m²) shopping area is organized as three distinct zones: one devoted to conventional retailing, anchored by a department store and organized as street-oriented shopping; the second largely devoted to food and beverage outlets, distributed around a town square where events are held; and a third, connecting the other two, consisting of a large enclosed cinema-anchored entertainment complex. The variety of spaces, and capacity to expand each area horizontally as the demand materializes, offers the potential for organic growth and change evolving into a true commercial district.

The emergence of *big box branded* (*category killer*) retailers that prefer to locate in freestanding stores poses a problem in planning regional shopping centers. Frequently they are strung out along arteries leading to planned centers, siphoning off the demand that might otherwise be captured by the center. There is good reason to accommodate them in a regional center, but how can this be done in a way that gives the branded retailer freestanding visibility while gaining synergy by their presence alongside conventional outlets? Cracking this dilemma requires the program for regional centers to be rethought as well as their form.

Desert Ridge Marketplace in Phoenix, Arizona offers an instructive example of how a new form of regional center can be created by often-competing

**Easton Town Center,
Columbus, Ohio**

Easton Town Center was intended to be more than a shopping center, serving as a town center for the surrounding suburban area. Its large commercial areas, totaling 750,000 sq ft (70,000 m²), are organized in three clusters: an area for conventional shops fronting on streets on the north, a food and beverage area centering on the Town Square on the south, and an enclosed entertainment complex between. The area is surrounded by moderate-density housing and offices, providing a built-in clientele for the shopping.

Site planners: DGG.

34.60 Plan of Easton Town Center retail area, Columbus, Ohio. (Courtesy of DDG Architecture and Planning)

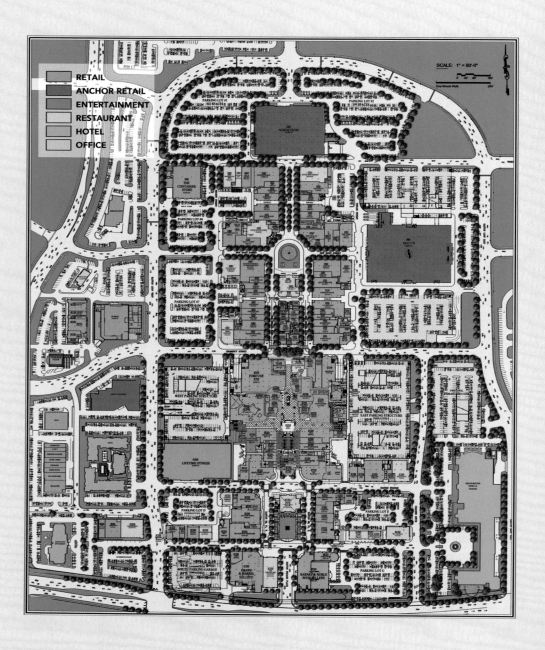

types of commercial uses. Totaling 1.2 million sq ft (111,480 m²), it combines on one site a specialty mall, power center, and neighborhood center. At the core of the site is The District, focusing on *lifestyle retailing*, entertainment, and restaurants and centered on an outdoor palm-shaded environment. This area includes a cinema, food court, outdoor video screen, live performance stage, rock climbing wall, and children's play area. This is the draw that will entice shoppers from the peripheral areas where large hard goods, health and leisure, and neighborhood convenience stores are clustered. Walkways connect the perimeter shopping to the center, and all areas share the band of parking between the two.

In Europe and Asia, fortunately, it is impossible to emulate the spread-out character of American regional centers. Land is simply too valuable to develop at such low intensities, a larger fraction of customers arrives on foot or by public transport, and public authorities exercise greater control over the siting of regional centers. As a result, multifloor centers are more the rule, as are parking structures and direct connections to transit and adjacent development areas. The challenge is to create public spaces that are memorable,

34.67 Aerial view of Desert Ridge Marketplace, Phoenix, Arizona. (Google Earth)

34.68 Entertainment area at the center of The District, Desert Ridge Marketplace, Phoenix. (Courtesy of Vestar Development)

and that entice people to walk or take escalators to shopping levels aboveground.

Some of the best recent examples of regional centers connect to and extend the streets in central areas of cities. The Beursplein in Rotterdam, Netherlands reshaped an existing street as a pedestrian zone, and provides weather-protected access to shops on two levels connecting the city's two main shopping areas. Over 70,000 passengers exit the Metro station located at the center of this street and flow toward the two ends. At the Bullring, in Birmingham, England, a new enclosed street was created, drawing customers from the three axial streets which connect with the high streets of the city. The dumbbell plan of the center includes two department stores and retail shops on three levels, taking advantage of the substantial topographic differences of the site.

In Asia, the pressures to develop high-intensity retail centers are even greater. At Canal City in Fukuoka, Japan, a new outdoor street has been created connecting the

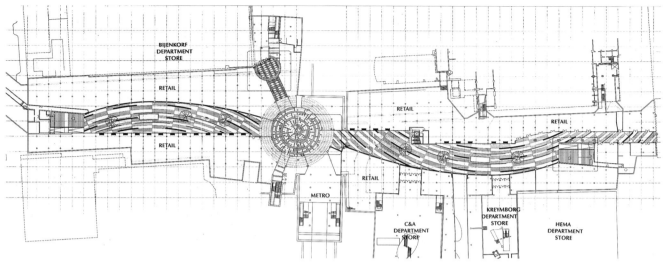

34.69 Plan of Beursplein belowground shopping concourse, Rotterdam, Netherlands.
(Courtesy of The Jerde Partnership, Inc.)

34.70 View of the Beursplein shopping concourse.
(Gary Hack)

34.71 Central space in Canal City, Fukuoka, Japan.
(Gary Hack)

business and entertainment quarters of the city. Taking its cue from the multiple canals that lace through the city, water is the central theme of the four-level central space, which is dotted with dancing water fountains, performance spaces, and public art and lined with 44,000 m² (474,000 sq ft) of retail space. The ground level along the canal is largely devoted to food and beverages, with upper levels offering a full range of comparison shopping. The five-star hotel and office development that surround the canal street, and its direct connections with the mass transit system, ensure that the center is filled with energy throughout the day and evening.

The formula of diverting potential shoppers through a commercial center, rather than leaving them on city streets, has become the tried and true approach in dense urban locations. The challenge is achieving this without deadening the streets around the complex. It is important to maintain the continuity of retail street frontages. This means identifying outlets that can function with dual entrance conditions. Department stores benefit from the flow between the street and the mall, and restaurants, food stores, and coffeehouses offer good transitional uses between indoor and outdoor walkways.

Entertainment-Based Areas

All shopping is a blend of necessity and entertainment. Of course, shopping areas have long attracted minstrels, human sculptures, street performers, sidewalk artists, vendors, and spectacles of all descriptions—offered free or with only gentle coercion to tip. The creation of festival marketplaces in American cities (a joint production of the Rouse Companies and architect Benjamin Thompson) established a new formula for retailing based on food halls, carefully screened performances, pushcarts, crafts outlets, artisanal products, bars, and restaurants, surrounded by more established merchants. These shopping areas have attracted a large following among tourists and nearby workers, and while the novelty has worn off, they remain important venues in Boston (Faneuil Hall Marketplace), Baltimore (Harborplace), and San Francisco (Ferry Plaza).

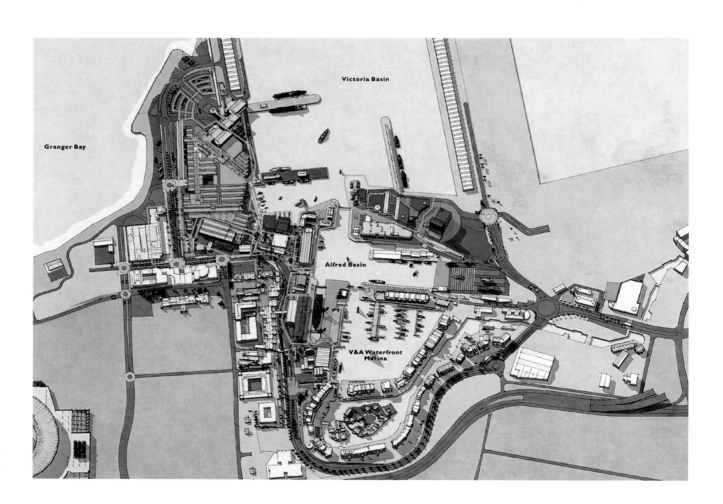

34.72 Plan of Victoria and Alfred Waterfront, with new retail complex, Cape Town, South Africa.
(City of Cape Town)

More recently the idea has taken root in China, spurred by the success of Xintiandi in Shanghai (see chapter 2). Its blend of historical architecture (mostly reconstructed), lively public spaces, outdoor cafés, top-level restaurants, and unique shops has attracted crowds of young Shanghaiese as well as tourists. Dozens of similar projects are under way in China and other Asian cities. And in Bahrain, the Souk Madinat has been developed around antiques, crafts, traditional clothes and household items, and restaurants.

The revitalization of waterfront areas has provided a wealth of opportunities to create retail complexes that mix entertainment and shopping. Waterfronts provide an instant attraction, particularly if elements of the working or recreational waterfront are kept in place, and water tempers the climate, particularly in warm-weather cities. They are a wonderful place to spend evenings, and retail programs for waterfront developments are generally weighted toward restaurants, bars, and nightclubs. One of the most successful waterfront shopping complexes is the Victoria and Alfred Waterfront development in Cape Town, South Africa. Hugging three sides of the city's former shipping basin, it adapts old buildings for retail and office uses, and a large new two-level mall has been added to accommodate international brands. An outdoor performance venue on the water attracts visitors and entertains restaurant patrons dining on the terraces which face it. The complex is designed for the cool evenings when thousands throng to the waterfront. With its constricted site, most of the parking for the complex is accommodated in parking structures that line the perimeter access road.

Universal CityWalk in Los Angeles was among the first entertainment-based shopping centers in the world created de novo. Located near Universal Studios' sprawling collection of movie production lots, performance stages, theme parks, and destination resorts, it contains 310,000 sq ft (28,800 m²) devoted to a megaplex cinema and other entertainment venues (comedy club, amphitheater for live performances, motion simulator, night spots, etc.), restaurants, and themed retail establishments, specializing in those with some relevance to movies or entertainment. CityWalk is organized along a three-block pedestrian street, something of a rarity in Los Angeles, stretching from the entrance to the Universal Theme Park to the cinema plaza and its cluster

34.73 Night view of waterfront, with outdoor dining, Victoria and Alfred Waterfront.
(Gary Hack)

34.74 Night view of Ferris wheel and walkways, Victoria and Alfred Waterfront.
(Gary Hack)

34.75 Universal CityWalk, three blocks of entertainment and food, Los Angeles, California.
(Courtesy of Visit California)

of entertainment spots. The complex topography of the site, and high opportunity costs, makes surface parking difficult, and much of the parking for CityWalk is located above the retail outlets, or provided through valet and off-site service arrangements. CityWalk has been duplicated by Universal in Orlando, Florida and other locations, and has been widely emulated by other developers including Disney.

The cinema is an important anchor for other entertainment-based retail centers. Sony Center in Berlin is organized around a large public space that is the center of the Berlin Film Festival and a place for live performances year around. A large Sony-sponsored theater complex, a museum devoted to the German cinema, and a film archive reinforce the special character of this place, which is lined with shops and restaurants. The Denver Pavilions, in Denver, Colorado, is also anchored by a large cinema complex. This 347,000 sq ft (33,000 m²) complex contains a mixture of restaurants and entertainment venues, along with leisure and lifestyle

merchants like Nike that cater to the city's attachment to outdoor living and professional sports.

The Kansas City Power and Light District is an eight-block area, once the theater district of the city, that had largely become a scene of parking lots and blighted buildings. It is being redeveloped as a restaurant, nightlife, movie, and performing arts area. The construction of the Sprint Center, an arena for basketball and other events, provides a draw to the area, which has been capitalized upon by the construction of the College Basketball Hall of Fame, bowling alleys, brew pubs, a dozen restaurants, and commercial spaces. Kansas City Live, a large covered space at the center of a key block, has become a venue for outdoor performances, and the streets in the area have been upgraded to make them pedestrian-friendly. The Kansas City Music Hall, a magnificent art deco structure next to the district, has been lovingly restored and serves as a performing arts center; the Empire Theater has been adapted to become a six-screen digital cinema. Hotels

34.76 Vision for Kansas City Power and Light District, Kansas City, Missouri.
(Courtesy of The Jerde Partnership Inc./William Cornelli)

34.77 Pregame rally for Big 12 Championships, in the plaza beside Sprint Arena, Kansas City Power and Light District.
(Courtesy of Chris Crum Photography/KC Power and Light District)

are opening in the area, which promises to become the city's hot spot for visitors and locals.

The best entertainment retail districts, as in Kansas City, make the most of local historic resources, old structures, and the archive of memories about a city's past. They are at their best when they retain an edgy quality. As the area around Pike Place Market in Seattle was being upgraded into a restaurant district, the rallying cry was "don't fix it up too much!" The French Quarter of New Orleans draws tourists from around the world; while it is safe and respectable to walk the streets and browse in the bars and shops, one does not want to look too closely at all the activities in the area. Japanese cities have succeeded in retaining restaurant and bar districts, *hanamachi*, usually near stations, which titillate but do not offend. The Kagurazaka (geisha district) and Kabukicho (red-light) areas near Shinjuku Station in Tokyo come to mind. Entertainment districts are the antidote to the sanitized shopping areas that contemporary malls have become. A new generation of consumers is seeking a better mix of authenticity and opportunity

35 | Workplaces

Workplaces are the second most important places in our lives—and for careerists, geeks, and those totally absorbed by their work, may even overshadow their homes. Work occurs in offices, factories, warehouses, research facilities, and institutions, but also in homes, shopping places, even public spaces such as libraries and parks. Much of the workaday world is custom-designed to fit the business or organization it supports. No two factories are the same, and there is wide variation in the site demands of other types of workplaces. We cannot cover all of these here, but confine our discussion to the most common repetitive forms of buildings and sites devoted to production and services.

The Changing Nature of Work

There are many ways we could typologize the workforce to help us understand the types of environments and estimate the amount of space that are needed for it. At the highest level, The International Labour Organization has created a three-digit system for classifying *occupations* which provides a useful way of comparing employment internationally, nationally, and between organizations (http://www.ilo.org/public/english/bureau /stat/isco/isco88/index.htm). These categories may be a good checklist in preparing the program for a site, although organizations that will occupy the space may have their own employment categories, managed by their human resources departments. At the simplest level we often distinguish between *white-collar workers*, who are housed largely in office environments, and *blue-collar workers*, the service and factory workers who spend their days in places of production. In recent years, *no-collar workers* have emerged as a third category—*creative workers* who work in design and artistic fields, who combine conceptual work with making products. These categories oversimplify the type of work people do, but they allow us to think about generic types of space and environments.

Every occupation is facing major changes today, the result of automation, artificial intelligence, networks for collaboration, and global *supply chains*. Many occupations that existed a decade or two ago are becoming extinct as automation replaces assembly workers on the factory floor, checkout clerks at the grocery market, and stock brokers taking orders for investment houses. Jobs are being outsourced or moved abroad, benefiting lower-cost production countries but displacing workers in more developed countries. The number of software engineers and app designers has expanded dramatically, partially offsetting this loss, and workers who remain in production roles have had to learn new skills to master their new tasks. *Artificial intelligence* break-throughs will accelerate this progress by eliminating many service workers and call centers and by simplifying diagnostic tasks. All of this change is the result of ubiquitous networks, cloud computing and data storage, and the expanded bandwidth that supports virtual presence in the work environment and beyond. Most sophisticated products today are designed, manufactured, and assembled in multiple countries, and organizations mirror their supply chains and sales patterns across national boundaries.

What do these changes mean for the planning of sites and environments for work? The obvious answer is the need for *high-capacity information networks* that can be upgraded regularly without disrupting current activities. *Adaptability* is a second characteristic—businesses, products, processes, and the types of employees change rapidly, and large open workspaces are generally preferred over smaller cubicle spaces. Adapting industrial loft buildings is one route to providing the flexibility that will be needed in the future for office or custom production work. *Organizations* are becoming *flatter*, more *lattice-like* with *less hierarchy*, and collaboration is the watchword of the day. Organization charts are changed at lightning speed to fit the urgency of the business cycle, which also favors flexible environments. Allowing for a changeable future is the third imperative.

A fourth important thrust shaping the economic landscape of workplaces is the reduction of inventories, with *just-in-time supply chains* and global production arrangements. This is most evident in the manufacturing sector, where components may originate in several countries and products may be assembled in several places before reaching their final destination. But it also results in massive *logistics warehouses* that distribute to a wide area. The basic frame of an automobile may be created in Japan, then shipped to Europe for addition of interiors and finishes, allowing deliveries within a week or two of customers' orders. The equivalent in the service sector is the large number of organizations that collaborate in carrying out an assignment using networked staff from various offices, or assembling them temporarily in one place.

Many businesses must now compete internationally, and attracting talent from a global pool becomes the key to business (or sometimes governmental) success. This places a premium on environments that promote loyalty by satisfying needs beyond the desk or workstation—offering places to enjoy lunches, workout areas for exercising or outdoor areas for team sports, even places for cultural enrichment. The best work environments deal with employees as valued participants, and planning sites with this in mind plays an important role in supporting them.

Finally, in many countries a new class of employees has emerged—the *freelancer*. Self-employed or moving between organizations, their permanent base may be in their home or in a shared work space, their conference room may be the corner coffee shop, and their file cabinet is the cloud. In the US over 25% of employees are freelancers, by choice or not, including some of the most innovative and skilled workers. Cities across the globe are creating facilities to promote freelance work, including co-working spaces and places for collaboration. Boston's District Hall, in the heart of its innovation district, is a fine example.

We will return to each of these themes as we consider the most common types of workplaces.

Offices

Buildings and sites for administrative offices are a product of the early twentieth century, when large industrial corporations grew up and differentiated their headquarters from their manufacturing functions. The first office buildings were typically located on the factory grounds, but as companies grew and created multiple manufacturing locations, being close to financial markets and attracting skilled managerial talent led to relocating administrative offices to central business districts. The emergence of large banks, insurance companies, law firms, and other service enterprises further concentrated office space in the largest cities, with iconic structures owned by brand-name companies being built side by side with speculative rental buildings owned by real estate investors. The growth of governments had a parallel trajectory, initially focusing on the construction of large civic centers that combined legislative, judicial, and administrative functions,

35.1 District Hall, Boston innovation district. (Gary Hack)

35.2 (top left) Glass facade, Reliance Co. Building, Chicago, Burnham and Root, 1890.
(Gary Hack)

35.3 (bottom left) Proposal for National Life Insurance Company headquarters, Chicago.
(Frank Lloyd Wright, 1924)

35.4 (top right) Interior atrium, Larkin Administration Building, Buffalo, New York, Frank Lloyd Wright, 1904.
(Library of Congress)

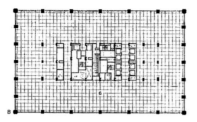

35.5 Typical office floor plan (office floor plates are smaller on higher floors), John Hancock Center, Chicago.
(Roger Sherman/Skidmore Owings and Merrill)

35.6 Use of multiple sky lobbies, Shanghai Center, Shanghai.
(Mitsubishi)

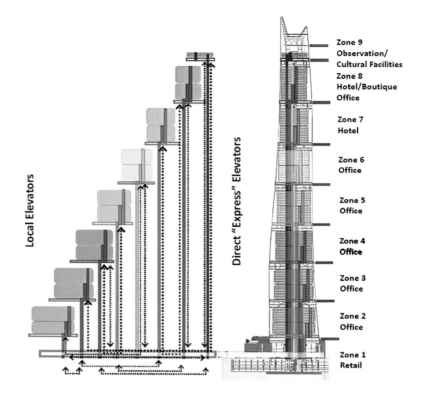

but by the 1920s in the US creating separate structures to house the growing bureaucracies.

The size and form of office buildings is the product of the social organization of work and the environmental needs of employees. The earliest office buildings were a warren of individual offices, with rooms often shared by managers and their assistants. As clerical employment grew and *Taylorism* became the management ethos, dividing office activities into repetitive tasks, larger open office areas were required. An early preoccupation was assuring adequate daylight and ventilation to the work desk, which encouraged more glass on the skins of buildings. Innovative early twentieth-century structures added *atriums* as a source of light and shaped buildings to minimize the distance from desk to windows.

By midcentury, the form of commercial office buildings had become largely formulaic, especially for leased space. Typically, a floor area of 2,300–2,800 m² (25,000–30,000 sq ft) surrounds a central core with elevators, fire stairs, and washrooms, providing office space deep enough to accommodate private offices on the window side and secretarial, service, and meeting

spaces on the inside. Dimensions from the windows to the core are routinely 12.8 m (42 ft) for tenants using primarily private offices, and 14.3 m (47 ft) for users with extensive open work spaces. The result is a rectangular structure appropriately named the *dollar bill shape* (or euro, or yen), typically 42 by 60 m (140 by 200 ft), for low-rise buildings. However, as a structure increases in height the total area of the lower floors also increases, with the added size of the core. While elevators can rise to well over 100 stories, they are typically zoned to serve a limited range of floors. If cars to each zone need to originate at the ground level, the accumulation of elevators leaves little room for occupied space in the lower levels. Very tall buildings typically employ a number of strategies to improve on this—using *double-deck elevators*, which reduces by almost half their footprint, and *sky lobbies*, which allow high-zone elevators to be stacked above low-zone elevators, among others (Al-Kodmany 2015).

35.7 (facing page) Floor plans, One World Trade Center, New York.
(Courtesy of © Skidmore Owings and Merrill)

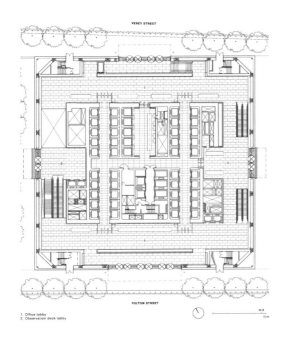

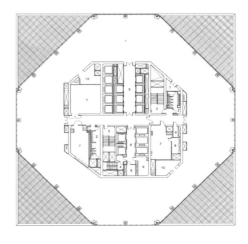

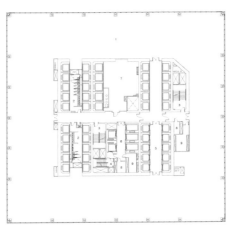

ONE WORLD TRADE CENTER — SKIDMORE, OWINGS & MERRILL LLP

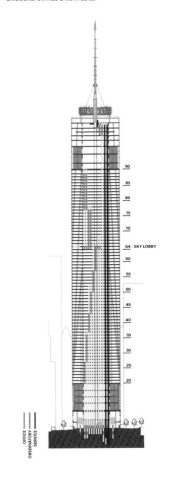

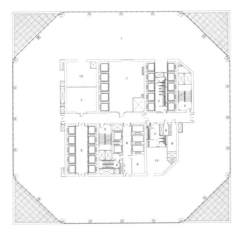

In the US, each employee in an office requires an average of 275 sq ft (25.5 m²) of office space, or slightly over 300 sq ft (28 m²) of leasable space, accounting for areas like elevator lobbies that are unusable for work. Cultural and economic factors play a role in shaping the size and form of office structures. The density of occupancy varies considerably from country to country. It is highest in Asia and lowest in the US with Europe falling between, reflecting the cost of building or renting office space per employee but also differing patterns of organization. In Asia, open office arrangements are common; sometimes a work group with half a dozen or more employees occupies a single long work space. The arrangement would be considered uncomfortably close for most US workers, and not sufficiently respectful of hierarchy in much of Europe. Each industry has its own preferred pattern of work, and space needs vary considerably. While call centers cram employees into minimal cubicles and may average only 100 sq ft (9.3 m²) for each worker, law firms require a more generous average of 400 sq ft (37 m²). Regulations also

35.8 (top left)   Office space per US worker in 2013.
(Adam Tecza/Herman Miller/CoStar)

35.9 (top right)   Office space per person internationally, 2007.
(Adam Tecza/World Business Council for Sustainable Development)

35.10 (bottom left)   Work group sharing common work space, Japan.
(Paco Alcantara)

35.11 (bottom right)   US median square feet per worker by industry.
(Adam Tecza/Herman Miller/CoStar)

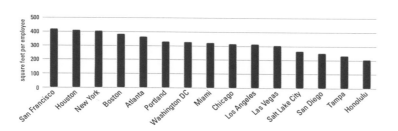

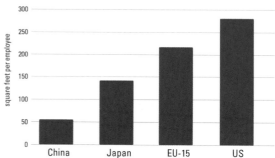

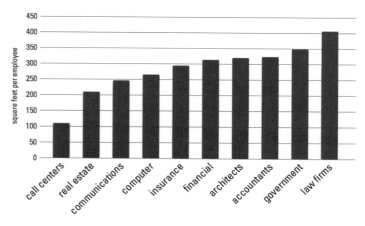

play a role. In Germany, all office spaces must have direct views of the outdoors, which results in narrow structures, often only 12–14 m (40–46 ft) in width (van Meel 2000). Wings of these dimensions can be linked by atriums to create larger buildings. In the US and Canada, setback requirements, minimum landscape standards, or open space requirements may limit the dimensions of office space that can be built on a site.

Connection to green surroundings has been a seminal idea in the location and planning of sites for offices in the US. In many US cities, half the office space created over the past several decades has been in suburban locations. Often this is in the form of *office parks* (or *business parks*), consisting of low- or mid-rise structures, typically 75,000–200,000 sq ft (7,000–18,500 m²) in area, surrounded by parking and landscape. Parking areas tend to dominate the sites, since the area required to store automobiles of workers roughly equals the built space for employees if all are commuting alone. Typical FARs for suburban office parks are between 0.25 and 0.33. There are several options to increase densities, including the construction of parking garages above or below ground. As a general rule, the land value needs to be higher than the additional cost of creating a parking structure to justify such a move.

Office parks can be deadly dull places to work if they lack lunchtime opportunities, convenience stores, or after-work recreation opportunities. Adding even modest outdoor gathering places that have been landscaped with care can provide a welcome respite, and organizing pedestrian walkways to connect structures can encourage social relationships. In higher-density areas, more extensive landscaped outdoor spaces may be possible if automobiles are stored in parking garages. The International Finance Center in Chengdu restores the meaning of an office park by literally locating offices in a park.

Where a substantial proportion of workers can reach office parks by transit, it is possible to increase densities and create an urban fabric of streets, squares, and office structures. Info-Park in Budapest, aimed at high tech offices and research firms, is a fine example. Its block structure accommodates atriums and wing structures, ensuring that there is sunlight close to every workspace. While parking is provided at a rate of 1 space for each 50 m², many of the spaces are on

35.12 Pleasanton Center office park, Pleasanton, California. (Courtesy of LBA Realty/Cannon Design)

35.13 Office buildings in a park, International Finance Center, Tianfu New District, Chengdu, China. (Gary Hack)

35.14 Park setting, International Finance Center, Tianfu New District. (Gary Hack)

35.15 Info-Park research and office park, Budapest, Hungary.
(Courtesy of Glassdoor.com)

35.16 Public square, Info-Park, Budapest.
(Courtesy of irodacsoport.hu)

streets and in small surface lots intended for visitors. Structures are 6–8 stories high, and a green public plaza serves as the centerpiece of the development.

Single-purpose office buildings continue to be a staple of urban development and have grown in size, particularly in urban centers. They have also sought to respond to the changing nature of office work. While large tenants continue to occupy full or multiple floors of buildings on long leases, there is a growing demand for smaller spaces for professional service organizations, including startups. Such firms may begin with a few employees and expand rapidly or combine with other firms, and will prefer buildings that offer the opportunity to add spaces as they grow. This has led to new prototypes for office buildings, with shared spaces for startups and modularized spaces for firms that have

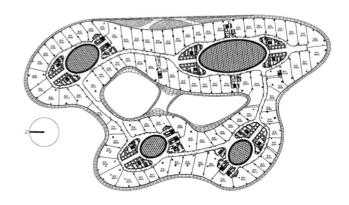

35.17 SOHO Galaxy linked office-retail complex, Beijing, China.
(Courtesy of Hufton and Crow)

35.18 Interior courtyard, SOHO Galaxy, Beijing.
(Gary Hack)

35.19 Layout of floor 5 office spaces, SOHO Galaxy, Beijing, China.
(SOHO Galaxy)

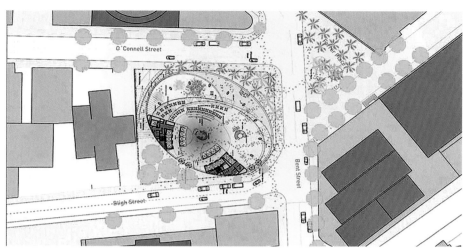

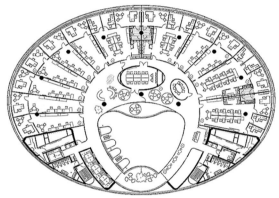

found their footing, often about 150 m² (1,600 sq ft). An excellent example is the SOHO Galaxy complex in Beijing, composed of four towers with atriums that maximize the exterior perimeter to allow for modular spaces. Rentable units range from about 140 to 250 m² (1,500–2,700 sq ft) on most of the floors, with larger units on the top floors. Many have been combined to form larger spaces. Because of its prime location, this complex also includes three levels of retail space at the base, making for a lively courtyard throughout the day.

In urban centers more of the opportunities are found in smaller sites, but it is possible to use the atrium form to create modularized spaces, particularly on corner sites. Contemporary office developers wish to offer a range of opportunities including full-floor, open-floor, and modular occupancy. A stellar example

35.20 (top left) Office tower, 1 Bligh Street, Sydney, Australia. (Gary Hack)

35.21 (top right) Site plan, 1 Bligh Street, Sydney. (Courtesy of architectus)

35.22 (bottom left) Plan with modular spaces, 1 Bligh Street, Sydney. (Courtesy of architectus)

35.23 (bottom right) Interior atrium, 1 Bligh Street, Sydney. (Photo courtesy of Cbus Property, DEXUS Property Group and DEXUS Wholesale Property Fund, co-owners)

is 1 Bligh Street in central Sydney, Australia. The oval-shaped tower, approximately 43 by 60 m (140 by 200 ft), is lifted up to create public space at the ground level and separated from surrounding buildings. An atrium opens up the interior, so that no office is more than 13 m (40 ft) from natural light. Elevators, both enclosed and exposed, and other services are clustered to one side of the floors to allow the floors to be developed as work modules or left open for open office arrangements. 1 Bligh Street and SOHO Galaxy demonstrate just how far the office prototype has evolved since its invention in Chicago.

Corporate Campuses

Headquarters offices and other purpose-built structures housing a single organization often have served as the testing ground for innovations in the arrangement of commercial office space. By removing the access core from the center of the space, the Inland Steel headquarters building in downtown Chicago, constructed in 1956, created large floor areas suitable for open office arrangements—well before such arrangements were commonly adopted. The flexibility provided by its large unobstructed spaces has allowed the structure to adapt to many subsequent tenants, including the architectural firm that designed it. At the Deere and Co. headquarters on a bucolic site outside Moline, Illinois, the company reversed the traditional arrangement, locating work areas for secretarial staff adjacent to the windows, with enclosed glazed offices for higher-level staff and conference rooms placed adjacent to the core. The complex also includes separate structures for a museum of the history of farm implements and a research and development center with large floors combining offices and workshops. This combination of administrative, research, conference, and promotional spaces is now typical of headquarters complexes. They are showplaces that symbolize a company's identity as well as housing its workaday world.

Corporations seek to create an ecology of space and interaction that is consistent with their ethos. Nike's world headquarters in Beaverton, Oregon is an entire campus devoted to innovation, fitness, health and culture, incorporating spaces for many of the sports it manufactures equipment for. Technology

35.24 Inland Steel Building, now 30 Monroe Street, Chicago. (Courtesy of Eric Allix Rogers)

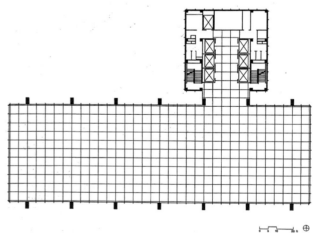

35.25 Typical floor plan, Inland Steel Building, Chicago. (Skidmore Owings and Merrill)

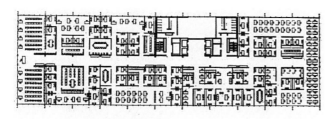

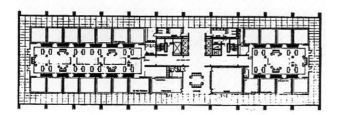

firms seek to foster informal interaction that may spark new ideas, often resulting in spaces that look disordered to outsiders but engage employees in constant dialogue and playful interaction. Facebook's West Campus, in Menlo Park, California is a single-floor continuous open space, roughly 280 by 1,500 ft (85 by 457 m) elevated over parking, built to accommodate constant flux and change. The entire range of activity is visible to each employee, and the office of the chairman is in the center of the space. The 9 ac (3.6 ha) green roof provides a half mile (0.8 km) walking or jogging loop, 400 mature trees, white boards, WiFi, and plenty of places to sit for relaxation or al fresco work. This green roof represents 40% of the 22 ac (9.9 ha) site.

A similar approach of horizontal connections has been the theme of Google's rapidly expanding campus in Mountain View, California. The corporation has added buildings as needed and currently occupies dozens of structures adjacent to Charleston Road. At the center of its campus it constructed the Googleplex (Buildings 40–43) in 2004–2006, clustering research and office spaces around an outdoor open space that is also fronted by a restaurant, child care facilities, and other shared activities. The ground level is considered the public zone, and secure spaces are connected by second-level bridges between the structures. Solar panels cover most of the roof spaces, generating 30% of the electricity required by the Googleplex. Google's proposed Charleston East structure is a more radical departure from its past buildings. Organized as a matrix of work spaces, walkways, and open areas, it seeks to create an ecology of work and interaction,

35.26 Aerial view, Deere and Company headquarters, Moline, Illinois.
(Google Earth)

35.27 View of headquarters building, Deere and Company, Moline.
(Courtesy of John Deere)

35.28 Floor plan with open office areas along windows, Deere and Company headquarters, Moline.
(Eero Saarinen Associates)

Nike World Headquarters, Beaverton, Oregon

The campus is the headquarters of the world's largest sporting goods company. Built over 30 years on a site of 213 acres (86 ha), the site has 22 buildings (each named after a sports legend — the Michael Jordan Building, Tiger Woods Building, Ronaldo Field, etc.) housing 8,000 employees. It encompasses the complete product cycle — research on ergonomics, design of products, prototype manufacturing and testing, sales management, and corporate administration. At its center are two playing fields for team sports surrounded by gymnasiums, workout spaces for corporate employees, tennis courts, track and field facilities, and a running trail looping around the perimeter of the site. As a respite from the physical activity, a manmade lake provides a centerpiece for the administrative complex, and a performing arts center serves multiple functions throughout the day and evening. Like many corporate campuses, the site is not open to the public and has security gates at its three main entrances. The original plan for the site installed a ring road on the perimeter behind berms and the jogging loop, providing access to parking areas. As the campus has expanded over the years, parking lots have been replaced by structures, allowing a second layer of buildings to be added. Many of the parking structures incorporate solar panels on their roofs, as do new structures. The flexibility provided by this arrangement will allow more than 2.3 million sq ft (214,000 m^2) be added to the campus over the coming years, and allows for future expansion beyond that.

35.29 Aerial view of Nike campus, Beaverton, Oregon. (Google Earth)

35.30 Aerial view of lake at center of Nike campus. (Nike Inc.)

35.31 Women's soccer on central green, Nike campus. (Anon.)

35.32 Gymnasium and multipurpose playing field, Nike campus. (Nike Inc.)

35.33 Lake and Nolan Ryan Building, Nike Campus. (Courtesy of TVA Architects)

35.34 Plan for future expansion on Nike campus. (Nike Inc.)

programmed and informal spaces. The entire complex will be covered by a fabric structure, largely open to the outdoors and the adjacent park.

Perhaps the most remarkable recent example of an innovative headquarters is Apple's new structure in Cupertino, California, which integrates office, research, and development activities in a single continuous four-story building surrounded by landscape. Its image is as precise and refined as the products it markets. The structure of over 1 million sq ft (93,000 m²) will house 12,000 employees in flexible space devoted to

administrative, research, and development and service activities. The central space, which houses two layers of parking and service facilities, has an outdoor court-yard for dining, socialization, and relaxation. The idea of the complex is to put all employees within walking distance of their colleagues—on an "infinite loop" that is over 1 mi (1.6 km) in length on each floor. However flexible it is inside, it is hard to contemplate how it can be expanded beyond its current form, and Apple has already taken space on other nearby sites to accom-modate activities that don't fit into its headquarters.

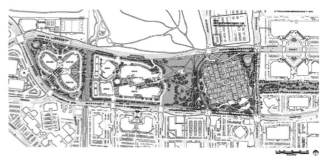

left column:

35.35 Aerial view, Facebook West Campus, Menlo Park, California.
(Courtesy of Jeff Hall Photography)

35.36 Interior view, Facebook offices, Menlo Park.
(© Spencer Lowell/Trunk Archive)

right column:

35.37 Site plan, Google headquarters buildings, Mountain View, California.
(Courtesy of © BIG – Bjarke Ingels Group/Heatherwick Studio)

35.38 Aerial view, Googleplex complex, Google Mountain View campus.
(Clive Williamson Architects/Austin McKinley photograph/Wikimedia Commons)

35.39 Plan, proposed Charleston East building, Google Mountain View campus.
(Courtesy of © BIG – Bjarke Ingels Group/Heatherwick Studio)

35.40 View of proposed Charleston East building, Google Mountain View campus.
(Courtesy of © BIG – Bjarke Ingels Group/Heatherwick Studio)

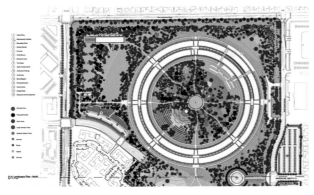

35.41 Site and landscape plan, Apple headquarters, Cupertino, California.
(City of Cupertino/Foster + Partners)

35.42 Aerial view, Apple headquarters, Cupertino.
(Apple, Inc.)

Laboratories

Many corporations and institutions require specialized laboratories for their ongoing operations or research and development efforts. Among large research hospitals, as an example, the amount of space devoted to basic and applied research can easily exceed patient care space. Pharmaceutical companies depend on new discoveries for their advancement, and the thrust in applied genetics has stimulated thousands of startup companies that require research space. Dry labs, which conduct research through data obtained elsewhere, can function adequately in office space, but wet labs require bench space and highly specialized equipment. The nature of research changes quickly as the result of new discoveries, and lab spaces need to be adapted to capitalize on the new directions. The Richards Medical Research lab,

heralded as a new paradigm for the design of medical research space when it was built in 1962 at the University of Pennsylvania, quickly became obsolete as the direction of medical research shifted from chemical to biological research. The lesson is to create buildings and sites that accommodate the fast-moving fields they house.

While the Richards lab emphasized exterior light and views for each workbench, contemporary wet labs require large amounts of space for specialized equipment, clean rooms, animal laboratories, and other purposes that can exceed the area allocated to bench

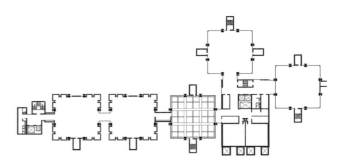

35.43 Research space and vertical service cores, Richards Medical Research Building, University of Pennsylvania, Philadelphia.
(Louis I. Kahn Collection, Courtesy of The Architectural Archives, University of Pennsylvania)

35.44 Exterior view of Richards Medical Research Building, University of Pennsylvania.
(Louis I. Kahn/Smallbones/Wikimedia Commons)

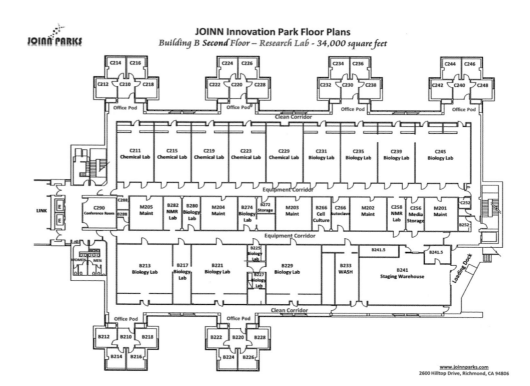

JOINN Innovation Park Floor Plans
Building B Second Floor – Research Lab - 34,000 square feet

www.joinnparks.com
2600 Hilltop Drive, Richmond, CA 94806

35.45 Floor plan, research accelerator, JOINN Innovation Park, Richmond, California. (Courtesy of JOINN Parks)

research. For many kinds of research, artificial lighting and ventilation are preferable to natural sources, to avoid fluctuation of temperature and humidity. The result is "fat" buildings, with access to labs from corridors located on the perimeter of the building and large areas of "flex" space on the interior. Buildings can be 30–37 m (100–120 ft) deep, with floor areas of 3,250–3,700 m² (35,000–40,000 sq ft). Spaces for each of the sciences will, of course, vary: physics spaces have less laboratory area and more offices, engineering research spaces may require high floors with heavy load capacity for the construction of prototypes, and so on. Academic buildings that combine research and teaching will add other dimensions.

Learning from his Richards laboratory experience, the architect Louis I. Kahn reversed the pattern in his groundbreaking plan for the Salk Research Laboratory in La Jolla, California. Here flexible laboratory space was placed in the interior of the two long research structures, with areas for offices lining the central open space and the opposite sides of the building. Along the central axis, there is a remarkable view to the adjacent bluffs and the Pacific Ocean. Because the site was constrained, there was a difficult choice about how to manage future expansion, eventually resolved by a new master plan which replaced surface parking lots at the entrance with a parking structure, making room for two future research buildings.

Land was not a constraining factor in the site planning for the Wellcome Trust Sanger Institute's campus in Hinxton, Cambridgeshire, UK. The pioneering genetics research institute sought to accommodate an expanded role in research that included laboratories, a supercomputing data center, and future laboratory support spaces as well as education in a variety of formats on its 30 ha (74 ac) site adjacent to its existing research building. It also saw advantages in finding sites for future commercial ventures based on research at the institute. The site plan established a central green for the research and academic campus and a parallel green for the innovation center. Each green spine has the

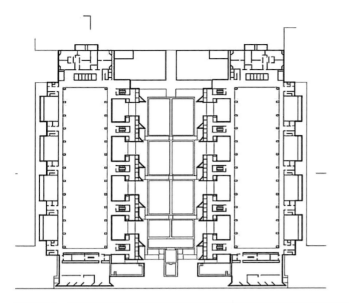

potential to accommodate growth beyond the structures shown, as the institute develops.

The fast-changing nature of laboratory-based research suggests planning a site with flexible blocks that can be developed or redeveloped without compromising the overall structure of a campus. This is the approach taken by the pharmaceutical company Novartis at its headquarters facility in Basel, Switzerland, which combines laboratories with administrative spaces. The Novartis campus is a work in progress, as it is intended to be. As science advances, the facilities required will change, but the structure of the site and its landscape should remain a constant.

35.46 Plan, Salk Institute laboratories, La Jolla, California.
(Louis I. Kahn Collection, Courtesy of The Architectural Archives, University of Pennsylvania)

35.47 View of offices along central spine, Salk Institute for Biological Studies, La Jolla, California.
(Courtesy of The Architectural Archives, University of Pennsylvania, photo by John Nicolais)

35.48 Updated master plan, Salk Institute, La Jolla.
(Courtesy of NBBJ)

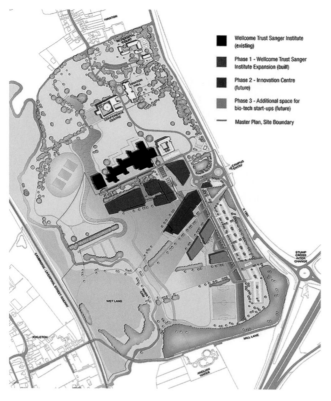

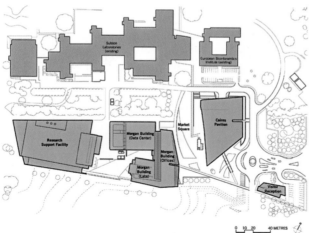

35.49 Site plan, future development of the Wellcome Trust Sanger Institute campus, Hinxton, UK. (Courtesy of NBBJ)

35.50 Site plan, research and education quadrant, Wellcome Trust Sanger Institute, Hinxton. (Courtesy of NBBJ)

35.51 Aerial view of campus development, Wellcome Trust Sanger Institute campus, Hinxton. (Genome Research Limited/Creative Commons)

35.52 Cairns Pavilion, the social hub of the Wellcome Trust Sanger Institute campus, with dining, exercise, meeting, lecture, events, and social facilities. (Courtesy of NBBJ)

Novartis Campus, Basel, Switzerland

Novartis sought to consolidate its research, development, and management activities and create an urban environment for its 5,500 employees. The plan involved repurposing the St. Johann chemical factory, overlaying a block structure, adding parks and other amenities, and creating streetscape so that the area functions as a city district. While blocks vary in size, they average about 30 by 60 m (100 by 200 ft); some of the larger blocks may be divided into two if ultimately developed for smaller structures. Well-known international architects were engaged to design individual buildings, each competing to create the perfect lab or office structure. Where streets depart from the gridiron plan, there was an opportunity to create more freely formed structures, as in the iconic offices at Fabrikstrasse 15. The formal structure of the landscape and streetscape ties together all the varied elements into a coherent urban district.

Site planner: Vittorio Magnago Lampugnani
Landscape architect and planner: PWP Landscape Architecture

35.53   Aerial view, Novartis headquarters campus, Basel, Switzerland.
(Novartis)

35.54   Master plan for Novartis campus, Basel.
(Vittorio Magnago Lampugnani, Courtesy of PWP Landscape Architecture)

**Novartis Campus,
Basel, Switzerland**

35.55   New laboratory
buildings and Fabrikstrasse
15 office building, Novartis
campus, Basel.
(Novartis)

35.56   Walkway, Novartis
campus, Basel.
(Courtesy of PWP
Landscape Architecture)

35.57   Park, Novartis
campus, Basel.
(Novartis)

Manufacturing Spaces

Manufacturing and other production spaces span such a broad array of activities that it is difficult to generalize about site planning principles for them. They range from small specialized places assembling a single item to vast plants assembling aircraft that may be as large as 10 football fields. The site planner will need to immerse himself in the production technologies and processes, materials flows, safety standards, and a host of other factors before making proposals. In the US and other countries where land is available at moderate cost, single-story structures are generally favored. Materials arrive in trucks or at a railway siding, and finished

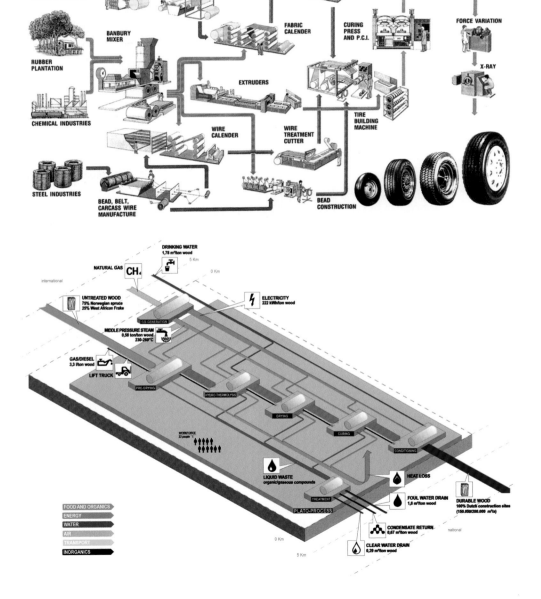

35.58 Process diagram, production of automobile tires.
(Firestone Tires)

35.59 Three-dimensional Sankey diagram of wood product process.
(Courtesy of Superuse Studios)

products depart in the same manner, unless they are aircraft or heavy trucks. Most of the employees arrive by automobile or in minibuses. In Asia and other countries that make extensive use of human labor, facilities may be many stories in height and employees often arrive by transit, or are housed nearby in worker's dormitories.

Despite the differences, there are a number of opportunities that can affect site planning and design. Materials flows are often the point of departure, using a process diagram to identify the raw materials that need to be imported and stored, the production process, and the final products. A number of computer programs that construct *Sankey diagrams* are helpful in charting the relative flows of materials (or energy or other inputs). Effective organization of flows is important, since each time material is transported, energy and labor are expended. Working with an accurate diagram, the site planner can begin to map the flows onto the site—where will the raw materials arrive? how much storage space is required? how much space will be required for the industrial processes? will the final products be inventoried or shipped immediately? And so on.

A second consideration is the rapidly automating nature of most production processes. Robots now assemble most automobiles, and in some industries handle materials from their arrival to completed product. The implication is that manufacturing facilities have evolved into large, tall multipurpose spaces with power and control grids, capable of being quickly reprogrammed and redeployed to new products. While humans control the processes and are involved in final finishes and quality control, they no longer attend to each detail. To justify the high cost of automation, production plants have grown in size and become more generic in their layouts. This results in large roof areas that offer the opportunity for solar installations, green roofs, and greenhouses. Even small structures offer the opportunity to use rooftops for urban agriculture.

Manufacturing facilities that make considerable use of water and generate contaminated wastes may also need to devote a portion of their site to remediation of effluents before discharging or recycling the water. We have outlined the prospects of using engineered natural systems for organic wastes (see chapter 27), but it is also possible to construct wetlands that remediate inorganic and complex contaminants such as BTEX, PAHs, metals,

35.60 Robotic construction of Tesla automobiles.
(Steve Jurvetson/flickr/Creative Commons)

35.61 Solar array, Boeing assembly plant, Charleston, South Carolina.
(Courtesy of Boeing)

and CVOCs. Such wetlands require a large area, and their design is a highly specialized task.

Industrial complexes and structures can become positive assets for their communities when they combine economic, environmental, and human considerations. One fine example is the Method plant on the South Side of Chicago, near Pullman (historic home of the railway car manufacturer). Its 150,000 sq ft (14,000 m²) LEED Platinum facility is consistent with the company's mission to create cleaning products that are environmentally responsible. The 22 ac (9 ha) site absorbs or retains all of its runoff and has been designed to allow the structure to be doubled in the future, while part of the site is dedicated to a park that is open to the public. Unlike most industrial plants, it has no fence on its perimeter. The plant is highly automated, producing 200 products and millions of bottles a year, making good use of its 30 ft (9 m) height for automated storage systems and mezzanines with administrative and laboratory functions. The roof of the facility is partially covered by a greenhouse (operated by New York-based Gotham Greens), and a wind turbine and solar panel installations supply energy for the plant. The planning and design possibilities of industrial uses are often overlooked, but the Method plant demonstrates that they go well beyond simply producing goods.

35.62 Green roof over manufacturing facility.
(Courtesy of American Hydrotech)

35.63 Rooftop greenhouse for Lufa Farms in industrial area, Montreal, Canada.
(Lufa Farms/Wikimedia Commons)

35.64 Engineered wetlands for remediation of industrial wastes, filtration of ore fines and other suspended solids, and detaining of stormwater runoff, Texas.
(Courtesy of Roux Associates)

35.65 Articulating solar panels, wind turbine, water detention, and rooftop greenhouses make the Method plant one of the most sustainable manufacturing facilities, Chicago, Illinois.
(© Patsy McEnroe Photography/Courtesy of William McDonough + Partners)

35.66 Manufacturing area, Method plant, Chicago.
(Courtesy of Method Home)

35.67 Stacked storage space, Method plant, Chicago.
(Courtesy of Method Home)

36 | Recreation

Spaces dedicated to public recreation occupy up to 30% of the surface area of North American cities, and their planning and management are a significant challenge for planners. Areas for recreation in the rapidly growing cities of Asia and Africa lag behind their Western counterparts, without long traditions of their use. Dedicated recreation spaces can range from small pocket parks to playgrounds to vast open-space reserves. Often new recreation spaces are acquired in the course of developing sites for other uses, but they may also be planned as additions to a city's public facilities. Each location has its own opportunities, influenced by topography, climate, and traditions in the use of outdoor spaces that provide the basis for unique site designs.

The term *recreation*, which dates to c. 1400, is something of a misnomer, originally denoting places for the recovery from illness or refreshment after exertion. To be sure, that is part of the role that recreation spaces play, but they also serve many other important purposes: promoting childhood development, social skills, and physical dexterity; encouraging neighboring; maintaining health through fitness; reinforcing family and social ties; offering a diversion from the workaday world; connecting people to nature (beyond humans); and providing a setting for public events and spectacles, not to mention their aesthetic virtues. No single label captures all these functions equally. *Open space* is too narrow a term, since the best recreation areas are often filled with equipment; *parks* are only one variant of recreation spaces; *play areas* or *playgrounds* usually refer to areas dedicated to children's play, although adults also play sports and otherwise use recreation areas. So we will stick with *recreation*

places as the generic term, and be more precise when describing the types of spaces to be planned.

Human Functions of Recreation Places

From the child's first steps, the environment is important in developing human capabilities and social and cognitive skills. While protected indoor environments may be the first places children play, by the time they are two years old they are ready to explore more open outdoor spaces under the protective eyes of their parents. Play is the way children develop their physical skills and their minds. The importance of providing places for play is enshrined in the UN Convention on the Rights of the Child, which recognizes that children have the right to "rest and leisure, to engage in play and recreational activities appropriate to the age of the child and to participate freely in cultural life and the arts" (Article 31).

Human development occurs in stages, which play spaces should support. The youngest children discover their ability to grasp objects, and develop the hand-eye coordination to be able to touch objects suspended above them. As toddlers they learn to walk to their parents' outstretched arms, and make their way on their own cautiously, holding on to a rail or bench. By the time they are three or four, they are attracted to climbing short runs of steps and enjoy the thrill of slides and crossing bridges. Collaborative play becomes the attraction when they are five or six, sharing objects and imagining possibilities with their peers. By seven or eight, they are on to pickup and organized sports, building things and participating in other forms of creative play. Children need constant challenges to push their development and are always on the lookout for new opportunities. But their environments must also be safe enough to deal with inevitable spills and falls.

Play remains important to human development when people outgrow childhood. Teamwork and collaboration are developed through organized sports, and personal esteem can come from mastering track and field events or technical climbing. Teenagers wish to develop skills that they can show off, often spending endless hours at skateboard parks, demonstrating their ability to master the pipes, or on public plazas climbing benches (while chipping away their edges). Kinship is often formed by cross-country running or walking with friends. And as young people settle into more sedentary occupations, outdoor exercise becomes an essential antidote to weight gain and flab, and the outdoor environment takes on new meaning. Cardio exercise is a life-preserving strategy for the upper years, and walking or exercise groups can be the center of elderly social networks.

Outdoor environments are doubly important for those who have restricted skills or abilities. Being able to make one's way through a recreation space in a wheelchair, stopping to exercise limbs, meet others, or simply observe activities, is a critical part of life. Differences are narrowed as developmentally disabled children join others in shared play. Recreation spaces need to celebrate differences, not frustrate those who have special needs.

Thinking of the environment as a matrix for human development is at least as important as ensuring that it functions efficiently to move traffic, or provides the spaces needed for commercial and residential facilities. Recreation is not restricted to the

36.1 Mastering the spider web.
(North Carolina Office of Public Education and Public Affairs)

36.2 Outdoor play.
(National Fund for Family Allowances, France)

36.3 Celebrating teamwork.
(GameTimeCT)

36.4 Seniors cycling.
(Kzenon/Shutterstock)

formal parks and playgrounds provided in a community; play opportunities can be found in streets, plazas, and parking lots if they are designed for that purpose, and sometimes in spite of their designs. The most creative recreation places are sometimes found where they are least expected.

Recreation Standards

How much space do communities require for recreation? A much-cited standard for the US suggests that 10 ac (4 ha) per 1,000 residents, or 40 m^2 per capita, is a desirable norm (Lancaster 1990), although the origin of the standard has been lost to time. More sophisticated measures of the adequacy of space focus on the level of service offered by available open spaces, recognizing that a mix of types of spaces is necessary, ranging from the smallest pocket parks and playgrounds to neighborhood parks, organized playfields, and large regional nature preserves. Cities across the globe vary considerably in the amount of green space they actually provide. Curitiba, Brazil provides 52 m^2 for each of its residents (equivalent to 13 acres per 1,000 residents),

while New York provides 23.1 m^2, Toronto 12.6 m^2, Paris 11.5 m^2, and Tokyo only 3.0 m^2. In general, Asian cities provide considerably less than cities in North America, with European cities in between. Cultural differences in the use of recreation spaces are an obvious source of difference, although it is hard to decide whether these are the result of not having adequate outdoor recreation space or a response to traditions of using public environments. The World Health Organization suggests a minimum of 9 m^2 per capita, roughly one quarter the amount of the (outdated) US standard (Morar et al. 2014).

The more important issue is the types of spaces required in cities. Again, these are culturally determined. Some places combine children's play facilities with schoolyards; in other cases the two are separate. Some cities, particularly in China, prefer multipurpose public spaces that can be used for dance and movement exercises in the evening and children's games in the day, while other places strictly segregate children's play facilities from places dedicated to leisure. North American cities often have norms for creating recreation spaces in newly developing areas, and expect developers to either create spaces or provide the funding for them beyond

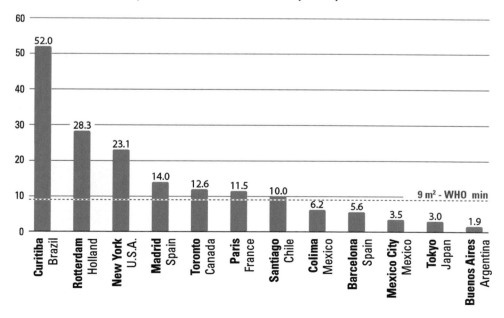

Square Meters of Green Space per Person

36.5 Per capita green areas in cities. (Adam Tecza/Sustainable Cities International Network)

Table 36.1 | Typical recreation facility standards

Facility	Number of units/population	Service radius	Minimum space requirements	Orientation
Archery range	1/50,000	30 min travel	0.65 ac (0.3 ha)	Target faces S
Badminton	1/5,000	0.5 mi (1 km)	1,600 sq ft (150 m^2)	Long axis N-S
Baseball				
Official	1/5,000	0.5 mi (1 km)	3.5 ac (1.4 ha)	Home plate to pitcher faces ENE
Little League	1/5,000	0.5 mi (1 km)	1.2 ac (0.5 ha)	Home plate to pitcher faces ENE
Softball	1/5,000	0.5 mi (1 km)	2 ac (0.8 ha)	Home plate to pitcher faces ENE
Basketball	1/5,000	0.5 mi (1 km)	8,000 sq ft (750 m^2)	Long axis N-S
Bocce (boules)	1/5,000	0.5 mi (1 km)	1,200 sq ft (120 m^2)	
Cricket pitch	1/20,000	30 min travel	5 ac (2 ha)	Bowling NE-SW
Curling (2 sheet)	1/20,000	30 min travel	6,000 sq ft (600 m^2)	
Field hockey	1/20,000	30 min travel	1.5 ac (0.6 ha)	Long axis NW-SE
Football				
US football	1/20,000	30 min travel	1.5 ac (0.6 ha)	Long axis NW-SE
Canadian football	1/20,000	30 min travel	1.6 ac (0.6 ha)	Long axis NW-SE
International football (soccer)	1/10,000	0.5 mi (1 km)	2 ac (0.8 ha)	Long axis NW-SE
Rugby	1/20,000	30 min travel	2 ac (0.8 ha)	Long axis NW-SE
Australian rules football	1/50,000	30 min travel	5.7 ac (2.3 ha)	Long axis NW-SE
Golf				
Driving range	1/50,000	30 min travel	13 ac (5 ha)	Long axis SE-NW
Pitch and putt	1/20,000	30 min travel	15 ac (6 ha)	
Full course	1/20,000	30 min travel	120 ac (50 ha)	
Handball	1/100,000	15–30 min travel	1,000 sq ft (100 m^2)	Front wall at N end
Horseshoes	1/2,000	0.25 mi (0.5 km)	500 sq ft (50 m^2)	
Ice hockey	1/100,000	30–60 min travel	0.5 ac (0.2 ha)	Long axis N-S
Running track	1/20,000	0.5 mi (1 km)	4.3 ac (2 ha)	Finish line at N end
Swimming	1/20,000	0.5 mi (1 km)	1 ac (0.4 ha)	
Table tennis	1/2,000	0.5 mi (1 km)	1,000 sq ft (100 m^2)	
Tennis	1/2,000	0.5 mi (1 km)	7,000 sq ft (700 m^2)	Long axis N-S
Volleyball	1/5,000	0.5 mi (1 km)	4,000 sq ft (400 m^2)	Long axis N-S

Adapted from Lancaster (1990) and other sources.

their sites. Vancouver, Canada, as an example, requires developers to contribute 2.75 acres (1.1 ha) of publicly accessible recreation space per 1,000 residents, or provide the funds to the city to create such spaces. The most important issue is how recreation space is distributed between local, neighborhood, and more regional facilities. One set of national standards for the US suggests that for each 1,000 residents, communities ought to have 0.25–0.5 ac (0.1–0.2 ha) of local close-to-home recreation space, 1–2 ac (0.4–0.8 ha) of neighborhood play spaces, 5–10 ac (2–4 ha) of large community recreation spaces with sports fields, and 5–10 ac (2–4 ha) of regional open spaces. These are broad ranges but represent overall aspirations for North American cities (Lancaster 1990; Moeller 1965).

Another way of thinking about recreation standards is in terms of the desirable commuting range from homes to various types of spaces. Table 36.1 offers general guidance on the need for playfields of various kinds, and their optimal distances from residential areas. Casual and organized sports obviously vary among countries, and local standards need to reflect these differences. There is also a need for places where those learning a sport can practice and where pickup games can occur (in spaces that may be quite minimal). A basketball hoop on a city street may serve these purposes, and a blank wall fronting a warehouse parking area may become a good location for honing handball or tennis skills.

Streets and Public Spaces

As a youngster growing up in Canada, I spent countless winter hours on the street playing pickup games of hockey with my friends. We had no equipment other than our hockey sticks; blocks of snow marked the goals, and a tennis ball proved easier (and less punishing) than a puck to stickhandle on the frozen street.

36.6   Street hockey, Canada.
(Arctic Photo)

36.7   Street play, Brooklyn, New York.
(© Arthur Leipzig/Courtesy of Howard Greenberg Gallery, New York)

36.8   Street basketball, Seattle.
(Joe Mabel/Wikimedia Commons)

We also had ice rinks nearby, but with half an hour to kill, it was never worth strapping on skates. In the real game of hockey, you could always tell the street hockey kids by their amazing stickhandling skills and lightning passes. In the summer the same street became our bicycle racecourse and baseball practice field, even at risk of occasional broken windows. There were few cars on the street to disrupt the flow of the games, and we felt that we owned the street.

Playing in the street has a long tradition in cities throughout the world. Stickball became New York's local version of baseball, taking account of the long narrow streets lined with stoops and the constant banter of spectators sitting on them. For younger children, hopscotch and other jump games are chalked on the pavement, and on hot summer days sprinklers magically become attached to fire hydrants to provide a cooling spray. In much of the world, skills of dribbling and ball handling a football (soccer ball) are acquired in the streets and neglected spaces, rather than in formal sports grounds. Suburban cul-de-sacs have proved to be ideal spots for neighborhood basketball hoops, and informal curfews determine when games must wrap up. Studies have found that streets, vacant lots, and other spaces near homes are used far more intensively than areas formally dedicated to recreation. So the place to begin thinking about recreation is with the underused spaces planned for utilitarian purposes—little-used roads, boulevards, parking lots, paved schoolyards, and other spaces.

The simplest strategies include painting streets and installing recreation equipment at the edges of parking lots to give them a second life in evenings and weekends. This will signal that they are more than vehicular spaces and will also slow traffic. But the functions of streets can

36.9 Painting the street, Cincinnati, Ohio.
(Courtesy of Arts Wave)

36.10 Parking lot doubles as basketball area, Williamson, Michigan.
(Anon.)

36.11 Street trampoline, Copenhagen.
(crazikyle/imgur)

36.12 La Cienega outdoor gym, Beverly Hills, California.
(City of Beverly Hills)

36.13 Shared street, San Sebastián, Spain.
(Courtesy of Heather K. Way)

36.14 Downtown court street, Detroit, Michigan.
(Gary Hack)

36.15 Skating at Nathan Phillips Square, Toronto.
(Courtesy of Michelle Shen)

36.16 Rahel-Varnhagen-Straße play street, Freiburg, Germany.
(City of Freiburg)

36.17 Dancing the tango on Sunday, San Telmo Plaza and streets,
Buenos Aires, Argentina.
(Helge Høifødt/Wikimedia Commons)

Recreation

be expanded to make them part of recreation routines. In Copenhagen, trampolines have been installed along city streets, attracting people of all ages. Many cities have created outdoor gyms along streets.

It is also possible to look carefully at existing street patterns and identify lightly used streets that can be converted to outdoor recreation areas. In European cities, this is done by dispensing with curbs and allowing streets to be closed for parts of the day or week. In a stroke of imagination, the city of Detroit has converted redundant downtown streets to outdoor basketball courts and recreation zones, drawing office and service workers at lunchtime and after work. The beauty of this strategy is that uses can be tried on a temporary basis, and made permanent if they are successful. It is also possible to make seasonal changes, as by converting ponds and water elements to skating rinks in winter. Nathan Phillips Square at the Toronto City Hall becomes a beehive of activity in winter when its reflecting pool is transformed into a skating rink.

Where there is an opportunity to design new streets, it is important to get the conditions right so that children are safe while playing. Eliminating through traffic, minimizing parked vehicles (which can be damaged or can hide children darting out into the street), providing seating along the street for parents with young children, and adding play equipment to the street are ways to create successful play streets. It is also possible to design streets so that they can be closed to traffic on weekends to encourage recreation uses while maintaining movement on adjacent streets, or to close one half of a boulevard street.

Playgrounds

Playgrounds for children are often among the least creative examples of site planning. A small plot of ground is typically set aside for play; designers immediately reach for the catalog of manufactured playground equipment, and clients order the largest assemblage the budget will permit. The result is plenty of bright colors, a safe place to play, a place adults are comfortable with but where children are quickly bored. Part of the appeal is that manufactured equipment has been designed to minimize risk and carefully tested, to minimize the threat of lawsuits over injuries. While there

are plenty of manufactured play components that are enduring, they need to be assembled in creative ways that develop children's potential. And there are alternatives to predesigned playgrounds.

One place to begin the planning process is with the developmental stages the playground seeks to accommodate. Table 36.2 lists the key steps in children's physical, socio-emotional, and intellectual development, and suggests the kind of facilities and equipment that promote each. A play area for preschool children obviously requires quite different elements than one for rambunctious seven-year-olds, but it is entirely possible to accommodate a broad range of ages on a single well-planned site. Separation and sequence are the key: young children have to be separated from older, more active kids, and need to be under the watchful eye of their guardians, and the area needed for play tends to expand as ages increase. Agreeing on the program of users and mapping the developmental stages on the site are a prerequisite to its design.

Play equipment designed for each of the stages of development should be organized as a series of "cells," with pathways and seating areas as the connective tissue. Youngest children need the most benign environments, and a sand base is ideal both for play and harmless tumbles. Safety tiles are another essential, particularly for areas with slides and climbing equipment. As children progress to larger climbing structures with hanging bridges and collaborative play wheels, these need to be separated from the young children's areas, but within sight so that youngsters can be challenged by what older children are doing. Swings will need their own separate area to prevent accidents.

Children's playgrounds need to be fenced, both to keep children from straying off the reservation and to keep dogs out and prevent contact with unwanted passersby. Parents and caretakers are also part of the playground and need to be provided with comfortable places to sit (and converse with other adults), shade for the hot summer days, and ample room to park strollers. Adding picnic tables to the playground will allow the adults to work while the children play, and accommodate hungry and thirsty playgrounders.

Water can add special magic to a playground. It cools on a hot day, adds mischief to the fun, and allows castles and other fantasies to be molded out of wet sand. Where there is room for programmable

Table 36.2 | Play facilities for child development

Age	Physical development	Social-emotional development	Intellectual development	Facilities and equipment
0–2	Swipes at dangling objects; begins to creep, crawl, and walk; begins to grip and grasp objects	Egocentric; plays alone but with adult support	Explore and discover, begins to coordinate movements	Dangling objects to strike; objects to grip and grasp; soft objects to play with such as blocks; equipment that encourages exploration; soft surfaces, separated from toddlers
2–3	Walks and talks; jumps; climbs and creeps	Plays alone but near others	Understands short directions	Surfaces for walking; climbing structures (small): safe places to jump; short slides; equipment that encourages parallel play; self-explanatory equipment; sand and water
4–5	Large motor skills being developed; need vigorous activity but lack muscular endurance; developing equilibrium and balance	Egocentric and impatient; needs approval; enjoys repetition; learning to share; transition between individual and group play	Enjoys problem solving; eager to learn; general lack of feel; sorting out differences between real and make-believe	Equipment that promotes movement; items to promote agility and flexibility; ladders and climbing structures; problem solving equipment; places for dramatic play; shallow-water fountains and hoses
6–7	Steady gains in height and weight; legs short in relation to trunk; gross motor skills developing; boys and girls equal in skills	Plays in small groups or alone, needs praise, beginning differentiation in abilities	Still short attention span, improved reasoning and memory; imaginative play sought; seeks creative opportunities	Horizontal ladders, chinning bars, climbing equipment; balance beams; creative playgrounds; places of enclosure, collaborative play opportunities

Adapted from Thompson, Hudson, and Mack (n.d.).

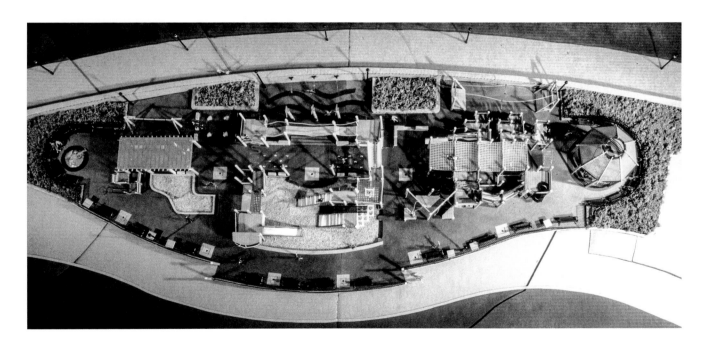

36.18 Model of playground, Rockefeller Park, Battery Park City, New York City.
(Johansson and Walcavage/Carr, Lynch, Hack and Sandell)

36.19 Sand play area, Rockefeller Park playground. (Gary Hack)

36.20 Young children's play area, Rockefeller Park playground. (Gary Hack)

36.21 Older children's play area, Rockefeller Park playground. (Gary Hack)

36.22 Swings area, Rockefeller Park playground. (Gary Hack)

36.23 Adult seating area, Rockefeller Park playground. (Gary Hack)

36.24 Picnic tables, Rockefeller Park playground. (Gary Hack)

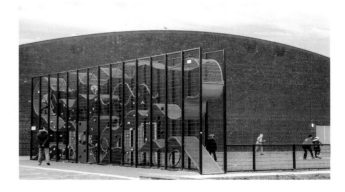

36.25 Water wall, Rockefeller Park playground.
(Gary Hack)

36.26 Water park, Granville Island, Vancouver, Canada.
(Gary Hack)

36.27 Programmed fountain, Centennial Park, Atlanta, Georgia.
(Gary Hack)

36.28 Sculpture, Rockefeller Park playground.
(Tom Otterness/Gary Hack photo)

36.29 Bob Cassilly hippo playground, Riverside Park, New York City.
(Gary Hack)

36.30 Wall-holla climbing wall structure.
(Lappset Group.Ltd)

36.31 Adventure playground, St. Kilda, Victoria, Australia.
(City of Port Phillip)

36.32 Zip line, Berkeley Adventure Playground, Berkeley,
California.
(Courtesy of Coby McDonald/California Magazine)

fountains, excitement is added in the anticipation of when the water stream will appear.

The addition of sculpture and objects that recall children's stories can be especially important for fantasy play. The very best of such works avoid transitory icons, and become works of art in their own right. Creative design of playground equipment can create objects that become a special form of sculpture.

Children can also design and construct their own play environments. The *adventure playground* movement, which emerged in the 1960s, advocated providing children with the materials and tools, and adult guidance, for them to construct huts, climbing structures, watercourses, rope lines, and other devices they dream up. Every type of material—demolition wood, tires, metal sheeting, cast-off chairs and furniture—is a legitimate resource for an adventure playground. Some such playgrounds emphasize individual or small-group collaboration—construction of huts, as an example, which then need to be maintained physically and socially. Some allow pets to be kept in the huts. Other adventure playgrounds are devoted to collective structures, heroic assemblages of materials that continue to grow as new materials are found. Bright colored paint can be the great leveler, helping forgive awkward construction.

Adventure playgrounds are usually offensive to adult eyes, hence the first step is finding a site that is out of sight, or constructing a wall that allows the designs of children to occur beyond adult scrutiny. At least one adult needs to be present during opening hours, to sign out tools, dispense nails and other consumables, and keep an eye out for obviously dangerous activities. As children grow out of the playground, decisions need to be made about playground renewal, whether to clear abandoned structures and make room for the next group of builders. Adventure playgrounds are no different in this respect from urban settlements.

Schoolyards

Schoolyards are a great underused resource for community recreation. Many urban schoolyards are simply paved areas where kids let off steam for 15 minutes or so midmorning and afternoon. There may be basketball hoops, and if the space is large enough, soccer (football) goals that are sometimes used for practice after class. Turf issues and worries about liability for accidents often mean that schools discourage after-hours and adult use of their facilities. Properly planned and equipped, outdoor spaces at schools could serve many more needs.

Painted surfaces can transform even the smallest schoolyard into a place for children's games, or ensure that a green space does not become the captive of a single sport. The addition of outdoor play equipment will help ensure that a schoolyard becomes a destination on weekends and summer breaks as well as during school hours.

A more radical transformation of the schoolyard involves creating a space for environmental learning and the production of edible products. Gardening is a remarkable recreation activity that can be enjoyed at any age, and how better to learn fundamentals of

biology than through field experiments? Many elementary and secondary schools have devoted all or parts of their open spaces to growing vegetables, flowers, and fruits. The area needs to be fenced to protect it against unwanted intruders. Creating the garden usually requires a volunteer effort among neighborhood residents working with students, which helps forge stronger ties to the school. In temperate climates, a school garden is aided by having a simple greenhouse where plants can be germinated indoors, which can become an extension of the biology lab. Use of rainwater to irrigate the gardens offers valuable lessons in water cycles, and natural fertilizers and pesticides teach about the chemistry of plant growth. Produce from the gardens can be used in the school cafeteria, and since plant growth usually doesn't recognize the school year, students and volunteers continue to tend the garden during vacation periods.

36.33 (top left)   Schoolyard pavement markings, Brooklyn, New York.
(PS 124 Brooklyn)

36.34 (bottom left)   Schoolyard markings for multiple sports, Dover College, Dover, UK.
(SSP)

36.35 (top right)   Edible schoolyard, P.S. 216, New York.
(Raymond Adams/Courtesy of WORKac)

36.36 (bottom right)   Schoolyard high tunnel, George Washington Elementary School, Putnam County, West Virginia.
(Kenny Kemp/WVGazette)

Gardening is a significant recreation activity for many people, and can be extended to other spaces in the city—to landscaped medians, allotment gardens, courtyards, and portions of public parks set aside for neighborhood care.

Playgrounds for Teenagers and Adults

The growing interest in vigorous sports by teenagers and their elders has led to the construction of play facilities for in-line skating, skateboarding, BMX riding, climbing, jumping, competitive cycling, and *parkour*, among other sports. Skateboarding parks originated as a way of moving the nuisance of boarders out of traditional parks and squares where they were ruining benches and walls and annoying others. The sport has become an art form and a way to show off skills to peers. Guidelines have been written for the design of skateboard parks, which sometimes double as BMX riding courses. A good skateboard park contains some combination of full pipes, half pipes, quarter pipes, clamshells, hubbas, pyramids, and benches, which have conventional dimensions (Poirier 2008). They are best located away from residential areas or parks where solitude is desired, and may attract boarders from a broad area. They are, of course, dangerous—which is part of their attraction—and legal issues need to be resolved before their opening, including adequate warnings and supervision.

A variety of extreme bicycle sports have also become popular and have found their way into international events. Motocross racing consists of a single track for 6–8 riders, who race over a clay and sand surface with vertical jumps, turns, and other hurdles designed to make a finish difficult. The course may also consist of a single-lane track where riders compete for the best time. BMX riders may ride not to win contests but to show off skills to their peers. Sometimes they use skateboard parks, but these are not ideal because of their hard surfaces and extreme curves. Purpose-designed BMX courses use clay-sand surfaces with occasional jumps of concrete, and they are more forgiving when riders take spills.

Rock climbing, once the province of mountaineers, has also become a popular urban sport. Rock climbing walls are now common in exercise centers but also

36.37 Pedlow Field skateboard park, San Fernando Valley, California.
(Cbl62/English Wikipedia)

36.38 BMX race, Sainte-Maxime, France.
(Fabrizio Tarizzo/Wikimedia Commons)

36.39 Cyclecross course, Gloucester, Massachusetts.
(Courtesy of Seven Cycles)

36.40 BMX bicycles at Valley Gardens Skate Park, Harrogate, UK.
(Harrogate Borough Council)

36.41 BMX course, Chula Vista, California.
(NBC 7 San Diego)

36.42 Climbing structure, CalPoly Recreation Center, San Luis Obispo, California.
(Courtesy of Cal Poly University)

36.43 Parkour, Gaza, Palestine.
(European Pressphoto Agency)

36.44 Parkour course, San Diego, California.
(Courtesy of Nerd Reactor)

Recreation

are making their appearance in outdoor parks. Vertical surfaces, generally 6–13 m (20–40 ft) in height, have handholds and belay bars attached to the surface, and rings at the top to attach safety ropes. They may be freestanding structures or attached to exterior walls. The key element is a padded safety surface at the base to break any falls, of foam or inflatable mats or a thick layer of loose materials such as wood chips.

One step up on the scale of danger is the sport of parkour, which is based on military training regimes and is becoming popular among youths. Its fundamental idea is to climb, hurdle, jump, or flip across obstacles, reaching a destination in as close to a straight line as possible. There are a variety of philosophies and conventions, and style is as important as the mastery of moves. The hazards of falling, destroying property, or injuring others are obvious and, as for skateboarding, there is a movement to create organized playgrounds to serve the sport. These are true adult playgrounds.

Playfields

Fields (or pitches) for more traditional organized sports are the centerpieces of neighborhood and citywide recreation areas. The types of sports and their social roles vary across societies, but in most places both amateurs and professionals practice them. Beginning in preteen years, learning team sports is a way to develop camaraderie, teamwork, leadership skills, and self-esteem. They are a way for adults to pass important lessons along to youngsters, while imparting the appropriate physical and mental habits. In midlife, team sports played after work in the evenings and on weekends become a way of maintaining friendships (and rivalries) while staying in shape. Australian men recreate with a passion on weekends, playing rugby, football, or Aussie rules football with their mates. Hockey, played on outdoor rinks, is the team sport of choice in cold Canadian cities, where most kids go directly to the rink after school. On Sundays, the same rinks attract skaters of all ages for pickup games. In most US cities, basketball and tennis courts, baseball and football fields, and hockey rinks are booked far in advance by the growing number of self-organized teams and leagues.

Some cities tend to adopt a sport and provide facilities for it throughout their recreation areas. Melbourne,

Australia, as an example, has a long tradition of promoting tennis at all levels, and the center of the city has a dense concentration of courts, which also can be found within a few minutes' walk of almost every home. Of course, it is also the home of Aussie rules football, and has many pitches for amateurs and professional teams. Other cities have chosen to specialize in particular elite sports: Oklahoma City aspires to become the center for rowing for its region and has developed a fine rowing basin and boathouse district. Cities frequently use the occasion of hosting an international sporting event as an impetus to develop their elite sports facilities. Many of these facilities are only lightly used after the event, although participation may grow once the city has adequate facilities (speed skating, cycle racing, ski jumping, and bobsledding are examples). It is critical that sports facilities be planned for the long future, not just the immediate event.

The success of large dedicated sports spaces depends on future growth in demand that is not entirely predictable. It also depends on the land available for sports fields, and tradeoffs usually must be made among competing desires for facilities. The first step, then, in planning a recreation site is understanding the type and number of facilities that can be accommodated on the land available. Figures 36.47 and 36.48 provide templates for the areas required by various sporting activities. The capacity of a site is easily explored by shifting paper templates around on a base plan of the site, or by moving outlines around on a digital base map. As the fields or courts are shifted to achieve an optimal orientation and provide for access and spectator areas, soon the tradeoffs become clear. Should the site contain two football fields, or only one with six tennis courts and a basketball court? It is important to consider the number of people who may be served by each—a tennis court with two or four players requires much more area per person than a basketball court.

The decision about the mix and layout of athletic fields depends on many factors, not just whether they fit on the site. Cost of maintenance will be an issue, and the presence of organized clubs that can take responsibility for the fields is another. Sidebar 36.1 illustrates some of the alternatives considered in the planning of Jefferson Park in Seattle, where many pressures weighed on the choice of how to use two reservoir areas that were becoming available for recreation use. Large recreation

36.45 Central Melbourne sports facilities. (Google Earth)

areas are also constructed and improved over time, and the site plan needs to be flexible to respond to changing trends in recreation.

Participants in team sports will need dressing rooms, places to store their street clothes, and toilets, and may need roofed areas to wait out a sudden thunderstorm. If spectators are attracted to the games, they will expect seating along the sidelines or baselines, use of toilets, and concessions for food and drinks. This set of services can become the centerpiece of the site, with walkways radiating out to the individual fields. Of course, professional teams or even aspiring amateurs will seek more than a hut, and clubs cultivating a tradition of fellowship will want lounges, bars, restaurants, and permanent storage areas for members. Whole communities are being built with sports as their theme, including LakePoint Sporting Community near Atlanta, where youngsters, parents, spectators, and professional athletes rub shoulders around the clubhouses and retail areas surrounding the playing fields.

36.46 Oklahoma City boathouse district. (Courtesy of Georgia Read/Read Studio Inc./Oklahoma City Boathouse District)

36.47 Sizes of playing courts, rinks, pools. (Adam Tecza/Gary Hack)

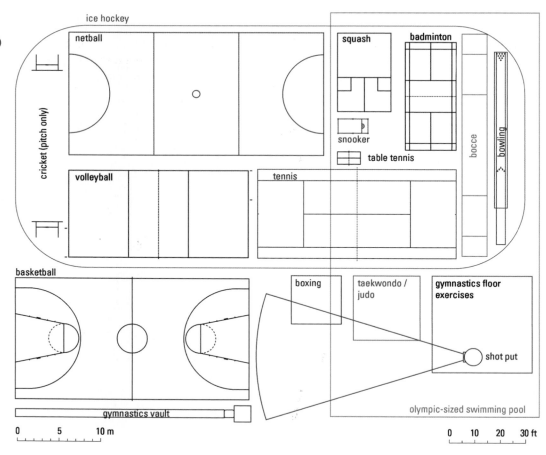

36.48 Sizes of playing fields and pitches. (Adam Tecza/Gary Hack)

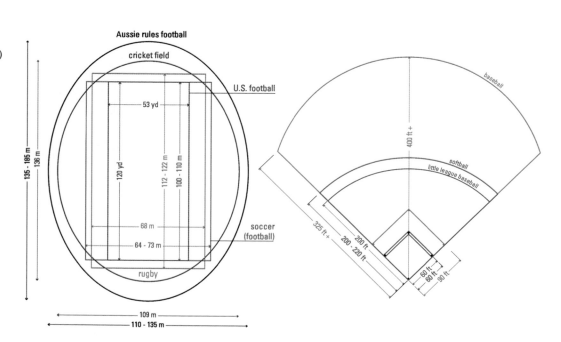

Alternatives for Jefferson Park, Seattle

Jefferson Park is a 100-year-old recreation and reservoir area in the Beacon Hill neighborhood of Seattle. Over the years, a variety of recreation uses were created on the site, including a nine-hole golf course, a golf driving range, a lawn bowling club, children's play area, and a large multipurpose field used by an adjacent elementary school. With the prospect that a 50 ac portion of the 137 ac site might become available as the two large reservoirs were

36.49 Plan of the site before development, Jefferson Park, Seattle, Washington. (Seattle Department of Parks and Recreation)

36.50 Site plan Alternative 1. (SDPR)

36.51 Site plan Alternative 2. (SDPR)

36.52 (top left) Site plan Alternative 3. (SDPR)

36.53 (bottom left) Preferred alternative. (SDPR)

36.54 (right) Long-range plan. (SDPR)

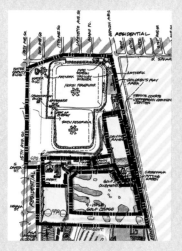
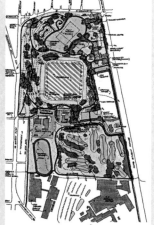
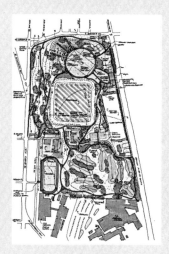
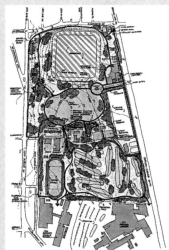

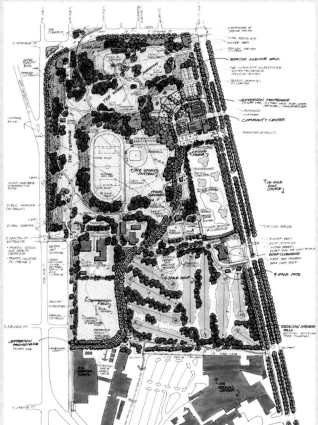

Alternatives for Jefferson Park, Seattle

abandoned (the northerly one immediately and the southern one in the indefinite future), a new plan was prepared for the site.

Many alternatives were considered, both programmatic and logistical: utilizing the north reservoir site for active sports; creating a largely passive recreation area surrounded by active uses; shifting the reservoir to the north area; and a more ideal plan, which involved capping the reservoir so that both sites could be used, with a heavy emphasis on playing fields. After much debate, cost analyses, public input, and logistical planning, a long-range plan was decided upon that balances active and passive recreation, with an understanding that it would need to be phased to account for the future of the south reservoir.

Over the past ten years, much of the plan has been implemented, including the construction of a skateboard park, a large lawn on the north reservoir site, a water play area, and improvements to the lawn bowling area and south playing fields.

36.55 Skateboard park, Jefferson Park.
(Gary Hack)

36.56 North lawn, Jefferson Park.
(Gary Hack)

36.57 Beacon Mountain water park, Jefferson Park.
(Wendi Dunlap/flickr)

36.58 Jefferson Park Lawn Bowling Club.
(Gary Hack)

36.59 Jefferson Park lighted playing field.
(SDPR)

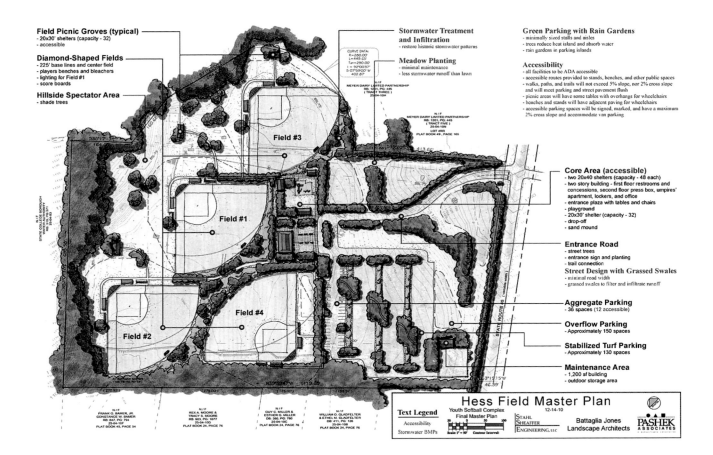

Field Picnic Groves (typical)
- 20x30' shelters (capacity - 32)
- accessible

Diamond-Shaped Fields
- 225' base lines and center field
- players benches and bleachers
- lighting for Field #1
- score boards

Hillside Spectator Area
- shade trees

Field #3

Field #1

Field #4

Field #2

Stormwater Treatment and Infiltration
- restore historic stormwater patterns

Meadow Planting
- minimal maintenance
- less stormwater runoff than lawn

Green Parking with Rain Gardens
- minimally sized stalls and aisles
- trees reduce heat island and absorb water
- rain gardens in parking islands

Accessibility
- all facilities to be ADA accessible
- accessible routes provided to stands, benches, and other public spaces
- walks, paths, and trails will not exceed 5% slope, nor 2% cross slope and will meet parking and street pavement flush
- picnic areas will have some tables with overhangs for wheelchairs
- benches and stands will have adjacent paving for wheelchairs
- accessible parking spaces will be signed, marked, and have a maximum 2% cross slope and accommodate van parking

Core Area (accessible)
- two 20x40 shelters (capacity - 48 each)
- two story building - first floor restrooms and concessions, second floor press box, umpires' apartment, lockers, and office
- entrance plaza with tables and chairs
- playground
- 20x30' shelter (capacity - 32)
- drop-off
- sand mound

Entrance Road
- street trees
- entrance sign and planting
- trail connection

Street Design with Grassed Swales
- minimal road width
- grassed swales to filter and infiltrate runoff

Aggregate Parking
- 36 spaces (12 accessible)

Overflow Parking
- Approximately 150 spaces

Stabilized Turf Parking
- Approximately 130 spaces

Maintenance Area
- 1,200 sf building
- outdoor storage area

Hess Field Master Plan
Youth Softball Complex
Final Master Plan
12-14-10

Text Legend
Accessibility
Stormwater BMPs

STAHL
SHEAFFER
ENGINEERING, LLC

Battaglia Jones
Landscape Architects

PASHEK
ASSOCIATES

36.60 Softball fields, Hess Field master plan, Harris Township, Pennsylvania.
(Center Region Parks and Recreation)

36.61 LakePoint Sporting Community, Emerson, Georgia.
(Courtesy of LakePoint Sports)

Multipurpose Recreation Areas

Team sports and other recreation activities can bring together a broad cross section of a community, breaking down barriers of income, race, age, and abilities.

Where the town square once was a community's mixing bowl, today it is more likely to be found in parks and playgrounds or along walking and biking trails. Social contact is encouraged when places offer as many types of recreation facilities as possible. As Jefferson Park illustrates, expanding the range of activities by having spaces for all ages makes for a more meaningful neighborhood center.

In urban areas, there is never enough land to cater to all recreation needs. Hence there is a premium on the flexibility of spaces—creating an open field that can be used for sports but also for a neighborhood festival or musical performance, as an example. Spaces that sit idle for part of the day or week or year may be an aesthetic plus, but they are a lost opportunity for recreation. The best new parks find ways to allow uses to overlap, which requires creative management and scheduling. At Battery Park City in New York, Rockefeller Park was designed to concentrate as many activities as possible in close range of each other, a response to the mixed clientele of the park: singles; parents with children; elementary, middle, and high school students; elderly; office workers; tourists and visitors; city residents looking for a place for an outing. Its users vary over the day and year, and it holds a special place in their hearts as a place to go in all seasons.

Rockefeller Park, Battery Park City, New York

Rockefeller Park is a 2 ha (7 ac) park constructed as part of the North Neighborhood of Battery Park City. The central idea was to accommodate as broad a spectrum of recreation opportunities as possible. Many sessions and workshops were held with Battery Park City and Tribeca residents to decide on the program and plan the park. There were many competing demands — create a passive green park while providing as much hard surface space as possible for active recreation; allow for organized sports while maintaining flexibility of uses; accommodate people of all ages while providing special environments for children; connect the park to the residential neighborhood but ensure that it feels open to the many office employees working nearby.

The park plan accomplishes these through its linear organization, with four parallel bands of activity — a riverside promenade, a continuous green space, a curving walkway that connects all activities, and a series of terraces nearest the neighborhood that provide contained environments for active and passive recreation. The green space is large enough to accommodate sports events (soccer, baseball, field hockey) but relies on removable backstops, bases, line markers, and goals so that it does not become the turf of any one group. The four terraces are devoted to social groups, active sports (basketball and handball), children's play, and quiet relaxation. The park includes two pavilions, a performance gazebo, and a park house for management, equipment storage and lending, and public washrooms.

A landscape of salt-tolerant trees and perennial species provides definition to each of the areas and ever-changing color through the seasons. The park has been voted one of the city's favorite open spaces for many years, and attracts users from a wide area.

Design team
Architects and planners: Carr, Lynch, Hack and Sandell
Landscape design: Ohme, Van Sweden Associates
Playground design: Johansson & Walcavage
Pavilion design: Demetri Porphyrios

36.62 Aerial view, Rockefeller Park, New York City. (Battery Park City Authority)

36.63 Plan, Rockefeller Park. (Carr, Lynch, Hack and Sandell)

All illustrations by Gary Hack

left column:

36.64 Riverfront promenade.

36.65 Green lawn.

36.66 Walkway spine.

36.67 Social terrace.

36.68 Noontime chess, social terrace.

right column:

36.69 Half-court basketball, active terrace.

36.70 Playground terrace.

36.71 Lily pond.

36.72 Performance pavilion.

36.73 Park house with recreation activities.

37 | Colleges and Universities

Institutions of higher education and research are increasingly the economic anchors of communities, and they need to be planned as productive and educative environments. They can also stimulate other development nearby, including shops, services, and restaurants serving the staff and students, buildings for research and startup enterprises stimulated by the institutions, and housing for those associated with them. For this reason, it is seldom possible to plan an institution without also considering its surroundings.

Universities have a long history, growing out of the monastic traditions of Europe, the Middle East, and Asia, where knowledge was cultivated and maintained within the secure walls of religious orders. In China, Taixue, the imperial academy, was created during the Han Dynasty in 3 AD. Islamic institutions were founded to transmit knowledge beginning the year after the prophet's death in 632 AD. The University of Al-Karaouine flourished in Fez in the ninth century; it and Al-Azhar University in Cairo became the centers of Arabic literature, science, and religious thought before 1000. The oldest European university is generally said to be the University of Bologna, established in 1088, followed shortly by Oxford and Paris.

Most of the earliest European institutions were located in cities and usually consisted of a few buildings along city streets. If there were outdoor spaces attached to the teaching spaces, they were typically cloistered and restricted to students and teachers. As universities grew, more buildings were added nearby until districts of the city came to be seen as the academic quarter.

The idea of creating a campus for education is largely an American invention, as is the idea that higher

37.1 University of Bologna, the oldest European university. (Gaspa/flickr)

37.2 Purdue University, West Lafayette, Indiana, a prototype of the large public multi-university. (Purdue University)

education ought to be removed from gritty cities and established in small towns in the green countryside (Turner 1984). Institutions that began as a cluster of a few academic buildings in American college towns have evolved into large multidisciplinary research universities. The form of these mass education campuses has had a large influence on the hundreds of new universities created in rapidly developing parts of the world.

Types of Institutions

While we use the term university here in a generic sense, today's institutions of higher education are remarkably varied, as are their spatial needs. Their differences are signaled by the many names they go by: colleges, universities, institutes, polytechnics, grandes écoles, tertiary schools, community colleges, technical colleges, seminaries, conservatories, and more. Many of these began as small colleges and have morphed into multipurpose institutions with diverse educational agendas. But there are prototypes that epitomize the educational missions that are at the core of the institution.

Colleges are generally focused on the education of undergraduate students, usually in the years just after secondary school. The most prestigious colleges combine living and learning, providing housing for a substantial fraction of their students within easy walk of their classrooms. Some incorporate educational spaces within a residential environment, following the model of the colleges that collectively form the larger academic institutions of Cambridge and Oxford. Yale University most faithfully replicates this model in the US. *Residential colleges* are incorporated in several Australian and Canadian universities as well. In recent years, many American universities have created *college houses*, sometimes thematic in character, which include spaces for dining, seminars, and activities that promote intellectual dialogue among the residents.

Thomas Jefferson's plan for the "academical village" at the newly founded University of Virginia (1818) offered a new model for how a college should be organized. Jefferson's idea was to construct individual pavilions for each academic discipline, connected by colonnades that lined two sides of a large lawn. The

37.3 The colleges at Oxford. (SirMetal/English Wikipedia)

pavilions were the home for the faculty associated with the discipline, and the *range* behind the pavilions contained vegetable gardens, student housing, and hotels (dining halls). At the head of the lawn, the rotunda, modeled on Rome's Pantheon, provided a place of assembly for the entire academic community and later housed the shared library. The college consisted of ten disciplines, each with a single professor, and about 100 students, all of whom lived along the lawn or ranges. Education then, as now in most colleges, involved students working under the tutelage of knowledgeable professors who provided instruction in the evolving intellectual traditions in their field.

The academical village became the iconic prototype for the campus of dozens of American colleges, even as the plan was enlarged to accommodate thousands of students and hundreds of professors. The lawn became the mall or oval or green at the center of a campus, the pavilions were replaced by large academic buildings for academic disciplines (the English building or chemistry building), the rotunda became the university auditorium or library or administration building, and student and faculty housing were pushed further afield into dormitory complexes. Over the years new buildings were added on the lawn for student or cultural activities, and as athletics became an integral part of university life, playing fields and stadiums found their place on the periphery. In recent years many large American universities have revisited

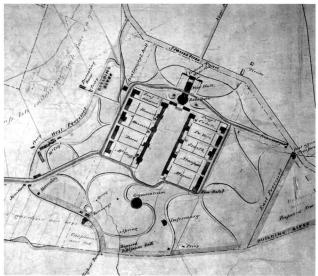

this strict segregation of uses, creating more integrated living-learning spaces, with faculty residents.

Universities differ from colleges by combining professional education and research with the education of undergraduate students in the basic intellectual disciplines. Benjamin Franklin created the first true university in North America by combining a liberal arts college and a school of medicine to become the University of Pennsylvania. The academic mission of universities is largely focused on the creation of knowledge through scholarship and research. Teaching may represent only a third of a university's budget and occupy less than half of the space required. Universities traditionally have been among the slowest institutions to evolve; throughout much of the twentieth century methods of scholarship and pedagogy remained relatively constant. While buildings were added, most campuses maintained their basic form, catering to face-to-face interaction, viewing the library as the central resource, and emphasizing classrooms, seminar spaces, and laboratories organized by disciplines. But change has accelerated, and the spatial challenge today is to keep abreast of the rapidly evolving nature of research, which emphasizes interdisciplinarity, and more recently the evolution of digital infrastructure for transmitting and storing knowledge and connecting members of the community. Flexibility is paramount in the creation of space and organization of university campuses today.

Polytechnics also combine research with education, particularly in the sciences and engineering, but the focus shifts from libraries and classrooms to research laboratories. Many specialized institutions, often called *institutes* or *academies*, share this orientation; examples include the National Institutes of Health in the US and the Academy of Sciences in China. The French

37.4 Jefferson's academical village, University of Virginia, Charlottesville.
(J. Sertz/University of Virginia Collections)

37.5 Plan of Jefferson's academical village.
(William Abbott Pratt/University of Virginia collections)

37.6 Ohio State University Oval.
(Ohio State University)

tradition of *grandes écoles* grew up around the idea of creating specialized institutions devoted to particular fields (École des Beaux-Arts, École Normale Supérieure, École Nationale d'Administration, etc.). Institutions such as the University of Paris Marie Curie (Paris VI) consist of collections of specialized institutes occupying space that can be reallocated as the importance of particular fields ebbs and flows. The Russian model of creating specialized institutions for research and teaching based on areas of application (forestry, railways, chemistry, petroleum, building, etc.), also exported to China and Eastern Europe, has produced campuses where experimental spaces (workshops, growing plots, laboratories) play a central role. Frequently they resemble industrial or business complexes more than the bucolic campuses sought for college education.

At the opposite end of the spectrum are institutions that provide technical and skill-based education, often to students who are already employed in business. They go by a variety of names, including *technical colleges*, *vocational schools* (UK), *trade schools*, *career schools* or *colleges*, *community colleges*, *business academies*, *Berufsfachschulen* (Germany), *technicums* (Europe), and *senmon gakko* (Japan). Each of these institutions has its own traditions, and curricula along with space needs vary widely. But to cater to working young (and middle-aged) adults, they are most often sited near jobs in urban areas or suburbs, near public transit, or in other accessible locations.

The new arrivals on the scene of higher education are the growing number of virtual institutions and universities with distributed campuses or no campus at all, including *open universities*, *Internet universities*, and universities organized to deliver a blend of sited and online education. For such institutions, a base campus may be visited only occasionally by students, or not at all. The planning issue may be how to create a virtual campus on the Internet, since learning involves more than simply acquiring knowledge or information. But there are many functions that still require face-to-face interaction, such as career guidance, teaching skills that require coaching, and high-touch subjects such as design and creative arts. The facility needs of these institutions are not yet clear.

People who inhabit campus-based universities often develop great attachment to the buildings and spaces of their institution. Young people spend their formative years there, and for faculty inhabiting a campus

37.7 University of Paris Marie Curie, Paris VI. (Edouard Albert et Urbain Cassan/Wikimedia Commons.)

37.8 Normandale Community College, catering to suburban workers, Bloomington, Minnesota. (© Dave Warwick)

becomes a way of life. Sports and cultural activities, special events, and patterns of behavior become institutionalized as traditions passed along to successive generations. Alums invariably return to their campuses to be photographed in front of the dormitory where they worked long into the night, before a favorite gate or sculpture, or in a space with special memories. Helping stimulate attachment is as important as functionality in designing settings for higher education.

While knowledge is constantly evolving and technologies for learning have recently been exploding, university campuses usually change much more slowly, with new buildings taking their place beside old. Look closely at them and you see the history of ideas about university education.

Sites for Education

The formal educational process involves communication between learners and the more learned, one on one in faculty offices or studios or laboratories, in groups during scheduled classes, around the seminar table, or in large events in assembly rooms. It may involve performances by students, faculty, and visitors, displays of their work, and opportunities to view films or videos or vicarious events electronically. Learners will be challenged to work individually, on computers or trolling for information in libraries and archives, and collectively in small groups. Participating in casual recreation or athletic events will develop physical skills and teach cooperation. On residential campuses, the link between living and learning opportunities will be critical, along with the opportunities for recreation and unstructured activities. Some of the education will occur off campus in coffeehouses, bars, theaters, and places for recreation and leisure. Planning a university site cannot stop at the boundaries of the property.

Universities with postgraduate and professional programs may include settings for practice—medical and dental clinics, hospitals, institutes (as in China) for the practice of architecture, research institutes often with highly specialized equipment performing contract research, and the like. Research and creation of knowledge is the central purpose of many universities, and more than half of the space will be devoted to these functions.

The site planner has an opportunity to influence the quality of education, research, and university life in three areas:

The *layout of buildings*—through the formal structure of a campus, determining what goes next to what in three dimensions, the density of development, the scale of individual structures, the openness and transparency of structures, the consistency and coherence of building materials and forms, the flexibility provided for future growth and change;

The *spaces on the site*—places of arrival (and parking), spaces for assembly, crosswalks that encourage casual encounters, places for leisure and relaxation, the surfaces, landscape, and furnishings of public spaces, and service yards that assure the smooth functioning of the university;

The *infrastructure of the site*—access and circulation routes for persons and vehicles, parking locations, security systems, communications systems, information infrastructure, service systems, and maintenance systems, all of which consume a large portion of any university's expenses.

Sidebar 37.1

- -

Purdue University West Lafayette Master Plan (Sasaki, 2009)

The master plan for Purdue's West Lafayette campus was created in dialogue with a broadly representative campus planning committee over two years. It is built on a careful analysis of existing buildings and sites available for development, a study of important environmental issues, and projections of future space needs. Five overarching planning principles were adopted to guide the plan: promote compact development, establish State Street as a collaborative center, create program synergies through strong mixed-use districts, encourage an integrated transportation system within a perimeter parkway, and preserve the western lands (figure 37.12). The master plan divided the campus into a series of districts, each with a dominant use, and indicated how green corridors could link the increasingly dispersed educational, research, and residential community. Infrastructure systems provide the backbone for future development, along with the system of roads and parking facilities.

All illustrations courtesy of Sasaki Associates.

EXISTING WELLHEAD PROTECTION ZONES - TIME OF TRAVEL

ENROLLMENT

POTENTIAL DEMAND

GRADUATE ONLY = 1.4 MILL. GSF
HISTORICAL = 3.4 MILL. GSF
EXISTING MASTER PLAN = 6.5 MILL. GSF

2005	39,228
GRADUATE	42,178
HISTORICAL	48,118
2000 MASTER PLAN	56,102

GROSS SQUARE FEET (GSF)

2005	15,099,569	
GRADUATE	16,466,860	+1,367,291
HISTORICAL	18,521,517	+3,421,948
2000 MASTER PLAN	24,594,622	+6,495,053

BIG IDEA-OVER 20 YEAR CAPACITY AVAILABLE IN CORE CAMPUS

"The University can accommodate substantial growth within the existing campus, sufficient to meet demand over the next 20 years."

37.9 (top left)
Existing campus,
Purdue University, West
Lafayette, Indiana.

37.10 (top right)
Wellhead protection
zones on and near
campus.

37.11 (middle)
Projected space needs
over 20 years.

37.12 (bottom)
Planning principles for
the campus.

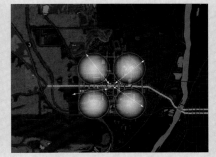

37.13 (top)
Campus master plan.

37.14 (middle)
Vision of campus
development.

37.15 (bottom left)
Campus utility corridors.

37.16 (bottom right)
Campus transportation
system.

Usually these elements are combined in a *master plan* for development of the campus, with a 5- to 20-year horizon. It will set down the location of current and proposed buildings, the main connections (pedestrian, vehicular, service) on the site, the infrastructure network, and design guidelines that will shape the form of buildings and landscapes. In a fast-growing or -changing place, the plan may need to be updated every five years, incorporating new opportunities, additional lands, and responses to changing educational techniques.

Space Needs of Universities

There is a world of variation in the types of universities and the campuses they occupy. Each campus has a unique history that reflects its evolving ideas about education and research and its success in attracting resources to realize its aspirations. Some of the key differences include: specialized institutions (such as art colleges or medical universities) versus general-purpose universities; urban campuses with constrained land resources versus expansive campuses in college towns and suburbs; residential versus commuter campuses; and undergraduate liberal arts colleges versus research-driven universities with a combination of academic and professional programs. Many US state universities are *land grant colleges*, with a mission to promote progress in agricultural and engineering practices, and their campuses include extensive fields, farm structures, and laboratories. Large urban universities often include medical schools with hospitals attached to them, used for teaching as well as medical practice. Most universities acquired their sites through government or private gifts or grants, and the site may be larger or smaller than needed for academic purposes. All of this makes it difficult to compare and generalize about site and space requirements for universities.

Table 37.1 includes data drawn from 142 university campuses mainly in the US. They are grouped into six types which capture many of the distinctions in educational mission. As the figures reveal, public universities are the largest on average, both in urban areas and college towns, with over 28,000 and 23,000 students respectively. US private universities are smaller, averaging less than half that size, with student enrollments at

technology universities even smaller. At the opposite end of the spectrum, US colleges average just over 2,200 students. The small sample of international universities more closely approximates US public universities.

While the educational agendas vary considerably, on average US public universities in urban areas provide 313 sq ft (29 m²) of built space (gross) per student. Since faculty and staff occupy much of the space, a better measure of space may be the amount provided for each person on campus, which is 232 sq ft (22 m²). As table 37.1 indicates, US private universities provide about twice as much space per student (50% more per person on campus), and US technology universities even more. US colleges, often located in more remote locations, have the highest per capita amounts of space. These figures include housing for students, which can amount to as much as 30% of the built space on campus.

Space standards for universities in other countries tend to prescribe less space per student or member of the university population. Australasian surveys indicate that about 33% of all institutions provide less than 12 m² (129 sq ft) gross space (excluding housing) per equivalent full-time student (EFTSL), while 46% provide between 12 m² and 17 m² per EFTSL, and 21% provide more than 17 m² (Tertiary Education Facilities Management Association 2009). Much of the difference is attributed to the weighting of disciplines that require special facilities, such as science laboratories or a medical school.

The mix of disciplines in an institution also shapes the kind of spaces that are needed. A survey of US universities indicates that the largest quantities of space are devoted to offices and laboratory/studio space—48 sq ft and 35 sq ft (4.5 m² and 3.3 m²), respectively, of assignable spaces per student. Libraries typically require 12 sq ft (1.1 m²) per student, and classrooms 10 sq ft (0.9 m²) (Society for College and University Planning 2003). Studies of Australasian universities reveal similar patterns (Tertiary Education Facilities Management Association 2009).

Converting the built space requirements into an estimate of site needs for universities requires assumptions to be made about the density of development that is desired, the amount of outdoor recreation and parking space to be provided, and the area that needs to be reserved for future growth and development.

Table 37.1 | University comparisons

	Large US public universities (urban)	Large US public universities (small town)	US private universities	US technology universities	US colleges	International universities[1]
Sample size	21	42	32	6	31	10
Average enrollment	28,795	23,208	10,409	7,830	2,258	26,713
Average faculty	2,765	1,661	1,351	605	203	1,761
Student: faculty ratio	14.7	16.1	10.1	13.5	11.5	17.4
Average staff	7,310	4,525	4,737	3,039	445	2,629
Average campus population	38,893	29,864	16,494	11,474	2,833	31,188
Average building area (sq ft)	9,005,618	8,527,765	6,304,673	5,453,215	1,436,222	3,284,968
Average building area (m^2)	836,622	792,229	585,704	506,604	133,425	305,174
Average building area/student (sq ft)	313	367	606	696	636	123
Average building area/student (m^2)	29	34	56	65	59	11
Average building area/campus population (sq ft)	232	286	382	475	507	105
Average building area/campus population (m^2)	22	27	36	44	47	10
Average site area (ac)	573	1,561	651	208	324	256
Average site area (ha)	232	632	264	84	131	104
Average site area/ student (sq ft)	867	2,930	2,724	1,157	6,250	417
Average site area/ student (m^2)	81	272	253	107	581	39
Average site area/ campus population (sq ft)	642	2,277	1,719	790	4,982	358
Average site area/ campus population (m^2)	60	212	160	73	463	33
Parking ratio (number of spaces/ campus population)	0.29	0.42	0.38	0.33	0.52	0.13
Campus FAR	0.36	0.13	0.22	0.60	0.10	0.29

Source: Based on data from Ayers Saint Gross Architects, "Comparing Campuses," www.asg-architects.com/2007/07/research/case-studies-research/comparing-campuses/.

[1] Includes universities in Canada, Australia, Hong Kong, and Ireland.

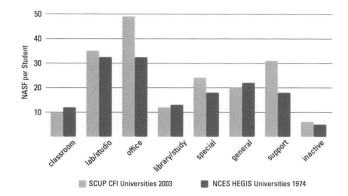

SCUP CFI Universities 2003 ▪ NCES HEGIS Universities 1974

37.17 Space use in US universities.
(Adam Tecza/Society of College and University Planners)

Table 37.2 | Distribution of space on Australasian campuses

Type of space	Average % of total space	Average usable floor area/EFTSL (m²)
Academic (teaching, research, academic offices, academic general support, dedicated classrooms and laboratories)	46.8	5.2
Central administrative (support spaces)	12.0	1.1
Centrally scheduled space (lecture theaters, seminar and tutorial rooms)	9.4	0.9
Library space (including study center, computerized student work spaces, information commons, etc.)	8.5	0.9
Student and staff services (including counseling, sport and recreation facilities, etc.)	5.9	0.6
Commercial space (bookshop, cafeterias, etc.)	4.8	0.5
Other (including transition and vacant)	5.2	0.7

Source: Tertiary Education Facilities Management Association (2009).

Using current US universities as a guide, campus FARs range from 0.1 (10%) for colleges to 0.6 (60%) for technological universities, with large urban universities typically falling between at an average of 0.4 (40%). Thus, a new US college for 2,000 students might aspire to have a site of 290 acres, a technology university of 10,000 students might seek a site that is at least 265 acres, and a new large public urban university with 30,000 students probably should have a site that is at least 540 acres. Circumstances will, of course, dictate whether this is possible.

Principles for Planning University Sites

The central tenet of any university is human contact—it is what justifies bringing people together for education, scholarship, and research.

Through human interaction, planned and unplanned, ideas are created and shared, relationships are formed, minds are changed, and worldviews are expanded. Creating opportunities for contact needs to be the key organizing idea for the campus. It will help determine which activities are central and which can be consigned to the periphery. It requires the clustering of buildings at a density high enough to promote spontaneous contact, and designing indoor and outdoor places and pathways that encourage face to face interaction. And there must be places for crowds to gather for special events.

Identity is a second important planning principle. The identity of a university is formed through the symbolic buildings and spaces on its campus—what are the focal points and what do they say about the university? What makes the campus special? Are there particular materials and styles of building that characterize the campus? Campuses such as Stanford University, Rice University, and the University of Colorado, Boulder have long maintained a consistent palate of materials to unify the image of the campus.

Individual disciplines and programs also need to have a special identity. Where does mathematics occur on the campus? Or business education? Or environmental engineering? Historically, a commonly accepted pattern was to locate the basic disciplines (English, chemistry, physics, biology, mathematics, language studies, etc.) in a central location, often surrounding a campus green, with applied fields such as civil engineering, architecture, or business in more peripheral locations. Alternatively, separate clusters might be created for the arts, engineering, and life sciences or medicine, each with their own central open spaces. Today many of the interesting intellectual breakthroughs occur at the intersections of fields. Centers for cross-disciplinary study, such as environmental studies, nanotechnology, or life sciences, have become key elements in the pattern of organization of space on campuses, forcing a reversal of thinking about the center and periphery.

Universities may change slowly but they are constantly evolving, and a third important organizing principle of a campus is its adaptability. New uses, new programs, and entities not yet invented will need to find a place on campus in the future. Campuses need to have generic space that can be adapted to many purposes over time, and swing space that new entities can move into while new space is being created. Sites need to be reserved for future buildings; the best campus plans build in flexibility. Universities allocate increasing amounts of money to adapting their campuses, and realize that renovation is as critical as new

37.18 Old Campus, Yale University, providing a shared outdoor space for interaction, New Haven, Connecticut. (Yale University)

37.19 Consistent materials and respectful buildings unify the Stanford University campus, Palo Alto, California. (Courtesy of Tom Fox/SWA)

construction in enabling them to grow and adapt to the changing intellectual environment.

A fourth principle achieving a balance among the many competing forces shaping the university. The campus wants to be a world apart, but not completely cut off from the city. It wants to minimize the distractions of everyday life so that students can focus on their studies, but also wants to provide an introduction to the wider world of work and living and culture. In practical terms, this usually means creating a car-free environment at the center of a campus, linking housing and educational opportunities and gathering places. For universities scattered across many city blocks, the burden falls on creating compelling interior

37.20 The university bookstore and shops at the edge of University of Pennsylvania campus, Philadelphia, are important meeting places.
(Gary Hack)

37.21 Rice plots have been created at the center of Shenyang Architectural University, Shenyang, China.
(Courtesy of Turenscape)

spaces that serve as the mixing bowl of campus activity. It also means that universities that are strongly oriented to interior spaces (malls, greens, walks) need to pay equal attention to their margins, where the campus meets the community. The blend of university and commercial activities is an important part of the support system for students, faculty, and staff.

University campuses, like all site uses, need to be sustainable—energy-efficient, conserving water, harnessing the sun, incorporating landscape that minimizes the draw on resources, and in other ways minimizing the carbon footprint of the campus. Rather than create

landscapes that are purely ornamental, some campuses are experimenting with productive landscapes. Such campuses can serve as an example for other areas while inculcating a sense of the value of sustainability in the minds of impressionable students (who are often the most enthusiastic advocates of campus sustainability). Universities have been among the leaders in inventorying and managing GHG emissions, and carbon impacts need to be considered for each new project on a campus.

While the planning of every campus will (and should) address objectives that are unique to its institution, attention to the five main principles—human contact, identity, adaptability, stasis, and sustainability—will assure that the site is used to its fullest potential.

Campus Prototypes

The Collegiate Form

Many of the oldest colleges sought to emulate the monastic tradition, creating cloistered worlds separated from the congested and commercial streets around. The first such colleges, including the University of Salamanca and Merton College at Oxford (1264), were planned as enclosed quadrangles housing scholars and masters in charge of their education. Undergraduate students initially lodged with families in the surrounding cities, but with the creation of New College at Oxford in

37.22 Cloister, University of Salamanca, Spain.
(Diego Delso, delso photo/Wikimedia Commons)

37.23 Plan of Cambridge colleges, many between the commercial high street and the river, Cambridge. (Cadell & Davies 1808)

37.24 King's College, Cambridge, fronting on King's Parade, the high street. (Geoffrey Robinson/Alamy Stock Photo)

37.25 The Backs at King's College, Cambridge. (RXUYDC/Wikimedia Commons)

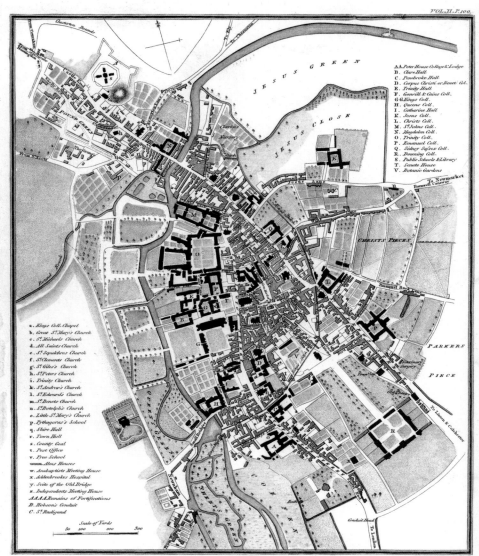

PLAN OF THE UNIVERSITY AND TOWN OF CAMBRIDGE.

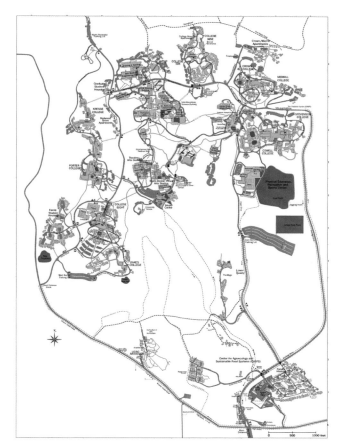

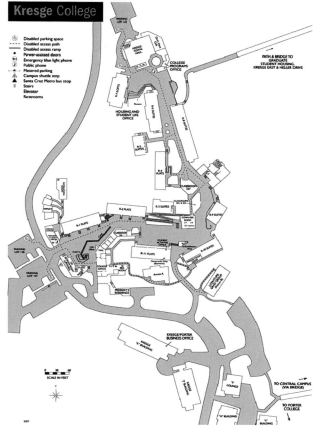

37.26 Campus plan, University of California, Santa Cruz.
(UCSC)

37.27 Baskin Engineering Complex, University of California,
Santa Cruz.
(Dynaflow/Wikimedia Commons)

37.28 Plan of Kresge College, University of California, Santa Cruz.
(UCSC)

37.29 View of Kresge College, University of California, Santa Cruz.
(BradCuppy/Wikimedia Commons)

1379, they were integrated into the cloistered environment (Turner 1984). These traditions continue at Oxford and Cambridge and have been exported to the new world, where examples may be found at the University of Sydney, Trent University in Canada, Yale University, and the University of California, Santa Cruz.

The colleges at Cambridge provide a particularly compelling example. While each college has a unique history and form, they generally have three characteristics: their front doors face a commercial street, sometimes with a green forecourt or chapel serving as the interface; their living and educational spaces are integrated around a cloistered inner courtyard; and behind the colleges is generally green space offering a respite from both the street and scholarship. Thus they span three distinct environments dominated by town, gown, and leisure. Over the years as the university has grown in stature, many more institutes, laboratories, and other facilities have been sited beyond the initial historic university area, but the heart and soul of the institution lies in its iconic form.

The University of California, Santa Cruz is a relatively new campus (opened in 1965) that builds on the Cambridge model of colleges, but is set on heavily forested hillsides above the town. The colleges and university facilities are sited so that they are as separate as possible from each other, but accessible via a short walk through the woods. Vehicular roads are mostly on the periphery of the site. Each college has been shaped by its educational theme, site opportunities, and location. They generally include housing, educational spaces, faculty residents' accommodations, a dining hall, small library, and other facilities to support student life. The colleges created in the second wave of construction also engaged students in the process of determining how they should be designed. Kresge College is a unique product of this participation. Its spine is a pedestrian street that widens to provide places for gathering, and narrows to promote the flow through the college. It has been greatly loved by several generations of students.

The Campus on the Green

Jefferson's academical village at the University of Virginia epitomizes the campus centered on a green, but it has much earlier antecedents dating from the first colleges created on American soil. Harvard's Yard, crisscrossed

37.30 The Lawn today, University of Virginia. (Courtesy of Sanjay Suchak/UVA Today)

37.31 Aerial view of the green at Colby College, Waterville, Maine. (Dave Cleaveland/Maine Imaging)

by pathways between dormitories and classrooms, took its form in the late seventeenth century (Turner 1984), a pattern that was followed at William and Mary and other early eastern colleges. Their plans evolved building by building, and today there are dozens of New England colleges with quiet greens at their center. Among the finest examples is Middlebury College in Vermont with its dual quadrangles, Colby College in Maine centered on a green, and the original college on a hill, now Brown University.

The great explosion of university building in the US occurred through the creation of land grant colleges in every state in the late nineteenth century. The Morrill Acts granted federal lands to the states to create and endow new universities, and charged them with promoting agriculture and mechanical skills. Subsequently, the mission of many of the colleges was expanded with the addition of agricultural experiment stations and extension programs. Over 70 new universities were created, and Jefferson's vision provided the template for many of their campus plans.

The University of Illinois campus in Urbana-Champaign is a literal interpretation of the Jefferson plan, scaled to a much larger university. The auditorium sits at the head of the 400 by 1,000 ft (122 by 304 m) quadrangle, facing the student center, which was added at the opposite end in the twentieth century. Classroom buildings, the main library, and the administration building line the two sides. The next layer of structures surrounding the quadrangle buildings includes laboratories, arts facilities, and other uses that require much larger spaces. As the engineering field grew rapidly, a separate cluster was created a short walk from the main quad. As professional schools were added to the campus and agricultural laboratories needed to expand, a second quad was created on the opposite side of the auditorium. In the midst of all this growth and change, a 1 ac (0.4 ha) plot, the Morrill Fields, was left undisturbed and is said to be the oldest continuously planted cornfield in the world.

Each of the green quadrangles created at the heart of the new land grant universities has a distinctly different character. The Oval at Ohio State University (see figure 37.6) is one of the largest and handsomest formal spaces, surrounded by academic, administrative, and cultural facilities. The sequence of green spaces at the center of the University of California, Berkeley retains many of the features of the hillside landscape before there was a university, including Strawberry Creek. The University of Texas mall in Austin is dominated by the towering administration building at the center of campus, on axis with the state capitol a mile away. In all these cases, everyday motorized traffic is not allowed, pedestrian paths crosscut the spaces, and

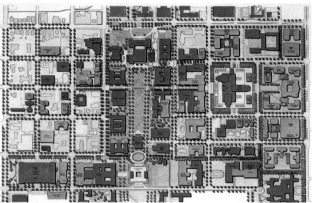

37.32 Quadrangle, University of Illinois, Urbana-Champaign. (Courtesy of Sasaki Associates)

37.33 Campus plan, University of Illinois, Urbana-Champaign. (Courtesy of Sasaki Associates)

37.34 Green heart, University of California, Berkeley. (Courtesy of philip.greenspun.com)

37.35 Mall, University of Texas at Austin. (University of Texas)

**West Java New
University,
Subang, Indonesia
(Sasaki 2016)**

Located 25 km from Bandung, the New University is planned as a residential campus for 10,300 full time students and 230 faculty. It will focus on the sciences (60%) and humanities (40%), and is intended to provide an international quality education in a living-learning-recreational environment.

The site in rolling agricultural land was previously used as an equestrian facility, with large open sheds capable of being redeployed. The campus program calls for 166,000 m² (1.8 million sq ft) of built space, approximately half of which is student housing.

The leading idea is creating a *learning valley* centered on the lushly landscaped stream that bisects the site. Nature and campus life are closely intertwined. Along the valley are the academic spaces, the student hub, recreation facilities and large public open spaces. Portions of the valley will also remain as farmland, providing food supply for the campus. Rising up from the valley are housing and a mixed use area that provides the interface between the campus and the surrounding community.

All illustrations courtesy of Sasaki Associates.

37.36 (top left)
Site for the university, West Java New University, Subang, Indonesia.

37.37 (top right)
Site area available for facilities.

37.38 (bottom)
Site concept plan.

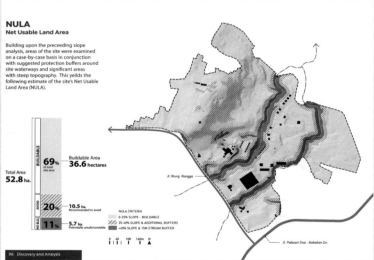

NULA
Net Usable Land Area

Building upon the preceeding slope analysis, areas of the site were examined on a case-by-case basis in conjunction with suggested protection buffers around site waterways and significant areas with steep topography. This yeilds the following estimate of the site's Net Usable Land Area (NULA).

Total Area **52.8** ha.

BUILDABLE **69%** of total site area

Buildable Area **36.6** hectares

AVOID **20%** **10.5** ha.
Recommended to avoid

NO BLD. **11%** **5.7** ha.
Potentially unsafe/unstable

NULA CRITERIA
0-25% SLOPE - BUILDABLE
25-40% SLOPE & ADDITIONAL BUFFERS
+40% SLOPE & 15M STREAM BUFFER

98   Discovery and Analysis

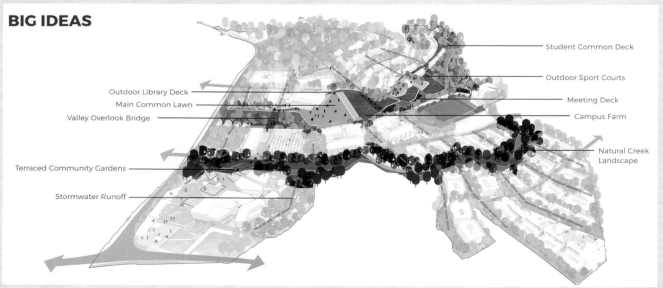

BIG IDEAS

Outdoor Library Deck
Main Common Lawn
Valley Overlook Bridge
Terraced Community Gardens
Stormwater Runoff

Student Common Deck
Outdoor Sport Courts
Meeting Deck
Campus Farm
Natural Creek Landscape

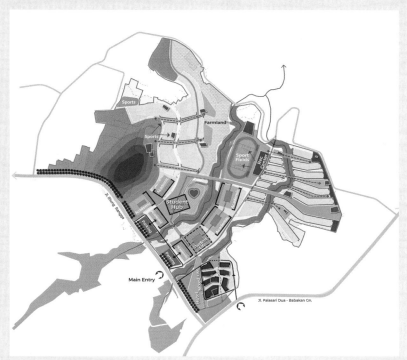

37.39 Concept for the site: the learning valley.

37.40 Illustrative plan of campus.

INTEGRATED CAMPUS PLAN

1 Library + Student Life (Student Hub)
2 Campus Green
3 Academic Buildings
4 Student Center (Equestrian)
5 Mixed-use
6 Mixed-use Arrival Plaza
7 Hotel
8 Conference Center
9 Surface Parking
10 Recreation Center
11 Sport Fields
12 Community Facilities
13 Dining
14 Multi-purpose Fields
15 Outdoor Fields
16 Student Housing
17 Faculty Housing
18 Farmland
19 Terraced Community Garden
20 Living Machine (Wastewater Treatment)
21 Service Facilities

**West Java New
University,
Subang, Indonesia
(Sasaki 2016)**

37.41 (top)
Aerial perspective of
proposed campus.

37.42 (middle)
Diagram of academic area
of campus.

37.43 (bottom left)
Student activity hub.

37.44 (bottom right)
Diagrams and section of
hillside housing.

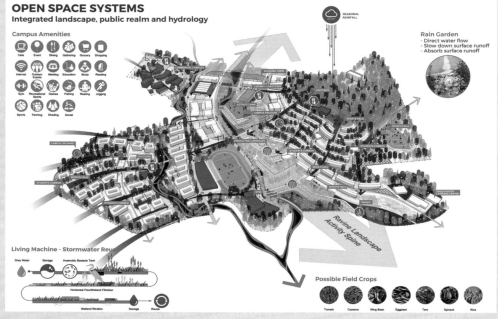

OPEN SPACE SYSTEMS
Integrated landscape, public realm and hydrology

Campus Amenities

Rain Garden
- Direct water flow
- Slow down surface runoff
- Absorb surface runoff

Living Machine - Stormwater Reuse

Possible Field Crops

HILLSIDE HOUSING
Integration with the Natural Environment

Table 37.3 | Space program for West Java New University campus (in m^2)

Space type	Recommended GFA	West Java New University GFA	CEFPI[1] GFA	Difference
Instructional	46,026	44,026	54,115	−10,089
Office space	5,700	4,875	6,372	−1,497
Study space	10,000	1,154	10,944	−9,791
Sports	14,000	14,132	17,587	−3,455
Student life	13,700	9,185	13,721	−4,536
Support	13,000	−	13,070	−13,070
Health care	642	46	642	−596
Student housing	147,269	83,354	147,269	−63,915
Employee housing	9,320	9,320	9,320	−
Total	259,657	166,091	273,039	−106,948

[1] The Association for Learning Environments.

there is ample space for students and faculty to use the lawns and shaded areas for leisure and recreation.

The campus around the green requires a super-block to be created, with automobiles limited in their penetration into the academic core. In most cases, large parking structures are located on the peripheral streets, sometimes integrated with athletic facilities. There is also logic in locating large visitor facilities—stadiums, athletic venues, museums, and institutions attracting large numbers of short-term visitors—along the perimeter access roads. Large laboratories and other facilities that are likely to change regularly are also candidates for perimeter locations. Because of the intensity of use in the core of the campus, student housing is generally located in clusters beyond the perimeter road.

Most campus planning occurs within a framework of existing roads, settlement, and infrastructure. However, in rapidly developing countries many new universities and campuses are being created de novo in the countryside, which opens up possibilities for a close integration of natural features of a site with the built environment. An excellent example is the planning of the West Java New University in Subang, Indonesia. It aspires to maintain a productive landscape while stimulating contact between students and faculty. The climate allows much of the education to occur out of doors, and the structured spaces at the center of the campus are an inventive new form for the traditional campus green.

The Polytechnic

When the Massachusetts Institute of Technology sought a model for the planning of its new campus in Cambridge on lands it had purchased in 1911, it looked to Europe for ideas. The first university that taught technology is said to have been the predecessor of today's Budapest's University of Technology and Economics, established in 1782, and by the beginning of the twentieth century there were many thriving technical universities in Europe. So it was logical that a MIT delegation visited the polytechnics of Berlin, Vienna, Darmstadt, Dresden, and others that had constructed new buildings, and returned concluding that the new

37.45 Royal Joseph Technical University, Budapest (now Budapest University of Technology and Economics). (Misibacsi/Wikimedia Commons)

MIT should consist of a single continuous building, with a building module and structural system that allowed flexible use for laboratories, classrooms, and faculty offices (Jarzombek 2004). It made no sense to construct buildings for individual disciplines, since these were rapidly evolving and would regularly change as new knowledge shaped praxis. This distinctive approach to creating a campus was a sharp departure from earlier US colleges.

William Welles Bosworth's plan for the MIT main complex that opened in 1916 went one step beyond what was ordered. The interior layout followed the original dictum, adopting a 30 by 50 ft (9.1 by 15.2 m) building module and simple concrete frame structure throughout the complex. But not content to settle for the utilitarian, Bosworth shaped the structure around a great court, clothed the sides and ends of the complex with neoclassical facades (the rear was unadorned, with the presumption that new additions would cover it), and punctuated the ensemble with a great dome devoted to the university library. Over the last century MIT has added dozens of buildings on its main campus, almost all interconnected below or above grade and modular in dimensions. Its main indoor passageway has been dubbed "the infinite corridor," and every space along it has been adapted for new uses multiple times. Housing, athletic facilities, research institutes, and spaces for its business school have been constructed a short walk from the main linked complex, but there is a constant search for ways to fill the gaps to enlarge the continuous environment.

The polytechnic plan has other stellar examples in Europe and the US, and has been adopted for both technical universities and general-purpose campuses.

37.46 The MIT main complex shortly after its completion in 1916, Cambridge, Massachusetts. (MIT Archives)

37.47 MIT campus in 2012, Cambridge. (DrKenneth/Wikimedia Commons)

37.48 Hornbostel plan for Carnegie Technical University, now Carnegie Mellon University, Pittsburgh.
(CMU Archives)

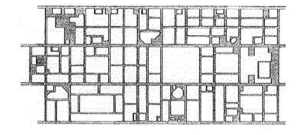

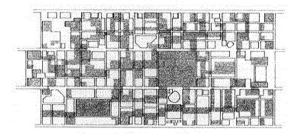

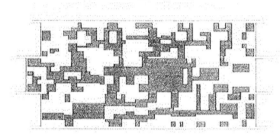

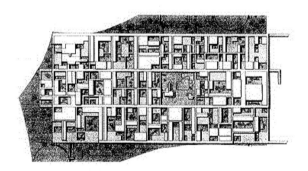

In the US, the campus plan for the Carnegie Technical Schools (now Carnegie Mellon University) in Pittsburgh, designed by Henry Hornbostel in 1900—predating MIT's campus—was an innovative arrangement of adaptable laboratory buildings connected by a horseshoe-shaped corridor around a green courtyard. The plan provided flexibility for each laboratory in size and module. Many of the original laboratories remain in educational use today.

More recent plans following this model have carried the opportunity for flexible development even further. The 1963 competition-winning entry for the new campus of the Free University of Berlin, by Candilis, Josic and Woods (with Manfred Schiedhelm), proposed an orthogonal grid of walkways and indoor corridors, with cell size roughly 65.6 by 65.6 m (215 by 215 ft); into this grid classrooms, laboratories, and other educational and research spaces of varying dimensions could be inserted over time (Domingo Calabuig, Castellanos Gómez, and Ábalos Ramos 2013). While only a portion of the campus was developed on this module—other

37.49 Mat building scheme, Free University of Berlin, Candilis, Josic and Woods, 1963.
(Domingo Calabuig, Castellanos Gómez, and Ábalos Ramos 2012)

37.50 Aerial view, Free University of Berlin.
(Courtesy of Freie Universität Berlin/Bavaria Luftbild)

portions became fully integrated buildings—it offers a glimpse of the potential of such an open planning system.

The McMaster University health sciences center in Canada, planned by Eberhard Zeidler, is the ultimate evolution of this building strategy: a three-dimensional grid of corridors and vertical circulation systems, with interstitial floors for mechanical and electrical systems. Within this armature, floors may be stacked as needed, with subsequent additions and changes in one area not disrupting the basic functionality of the institution. Over its 30-year life, it has undergone considerable change, adapting to the changing nature of health care and research.

Two- and three-dimensional circulation grids such as these are complicated, and may overestimate the need for circulation. A more common strategy is to create a central spine off which spaces for various purposes are constructed. The University of East Anglia, designed by Denys Lasdun in 1962, is among the leading examples. Following the contours of the high ground of its site, the central spine of the university connects all of its functions. The masterstroke of the plan is the cascade of student housing down the slope to the playing fields below. Every student living at the university has just a short walk under cover to all its educational spaces. The system is capable of being added to and changed over time, with new structures connected to the spine.

The Technical University of Munich has applied this strategy to several waves of new buildings at its Garching campus, constructing new clusters of research and educational spaces along spines radiating outward from the linear center of the campus, the point of arrival from the U-Bahn. The spines, no longer the infinite corridors of MIT, are designed as gathering spaces for the research communities. Those who arrive by automobile enter the spaces from the opposite end on the perimeter of the campus.

There are infinite possibilities for the polytechnic model of higher education campuses, which can be applied to research institutions as well as universities. Each distinguishes the permanent elements of the campus, usually the circulation networks and places for face-to-face contact, from the constantly changing educational and research spaces. If they can achieve a century of relevance, as MIT's original buildings have, the strategy will have succeeded.

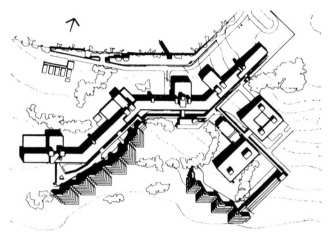

37.51 McMaster University health sciences center, Hamilton, Canada.
(Dan Zen/Wikimedia Commons)

37.52 Site plan, first phase of the University of East Anglia, Norwich, UK.
(Denys Lasdun)

37.53 University of East Anglia, Norwich, 2014.
(John Fielding/flickr/Creative Commons)

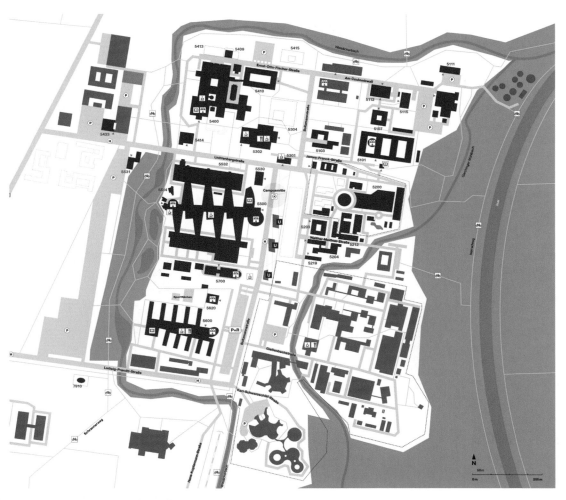

37.54 (top)
Campus plan, Garching campus, Technical University of Munich, Germany. (Edi&Sepp Gestaltungsgesellschaft/ Courtesy of Technical University of Munich)

37.55 (bottom left)
Aerial view of Technical University of Munich Garching campus. (Ernst A. Graf/Courtesy of Technical University of Munich)

37.56 (bottom right)
Atrium, Technical University of Munich Garching campus. (Church of emacs/ Wikipedia Commons)

The City University

Campuses in the densely built-up areas of cities usually don't have the luxury of spreading out as new needs arise, unless they are prepared to displace neighborhoods around them or other functions. Usually they begin as individual buildings along streets, and the notion of becoming a campus evolves over time. At the University of Pennsylvania in Philadelphia, the university tolerated a streetcar and vehicles traversing the center of its campus for almost a century. In a brilliant stroke, the streetcar was routed underground, traffic was eliminated from the streets bisecting the campus,

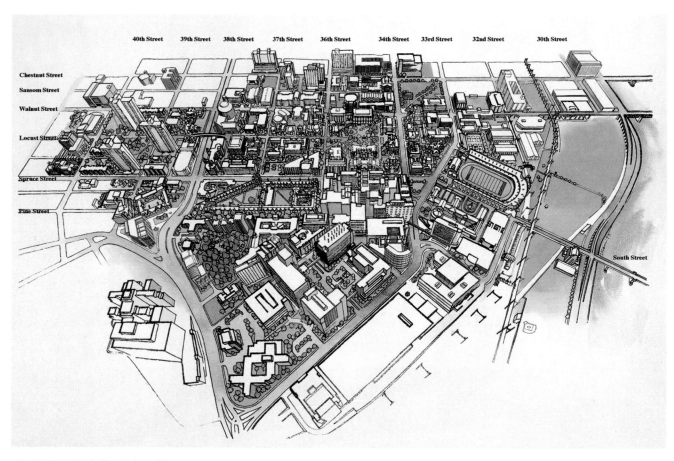

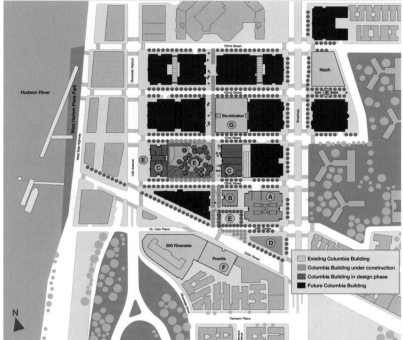

AN ACADEMIC CAMPUS BUILT FOR URBAN LIFE

(A) The Jerome L. Greene Science Center, designed by Renzo Piano Building Workshop with Davis Brody Bond as executive architect, will be home to Columbia's Mortimer B. Zuckerman Mind Brain Behavior Institute. In addition to state-of-the-art research and teaching facilities, the ground floor of the Greene Science Center will house retail space, the Wellness Center, and the Education Lab, offering a variety of programs on the brain, mental health, and neuroscience for K-12 students, teachers, and the community.

(B) The Lenfest Center for the Arts, also designed by Renzo Piano Building Workshop with Davis Brody Bond as executive architect, will not only provide a showcase for the creative work of Columbia artists in film, theatre, visual arts, and writing, it will be a venue for deepening partnerships between the School of the Arts and Harlem's vibrant cultural community. The center will be the new home of the Miriam and Ira B. Wallach Gallery—now located on the Morningside campus—for the first time allowing easy public access to the gallery.

(C) Columbia Business School will move to the Henry R. Kravis Building and the Ronald O. Perelman Center for Business Innovation. The location of these innovative buildings, designed by New York architects Diller Scofidio + Renfro in collaboration with FXFOWLE, will facilitate the business school's engagement in economic development and entrepreneurship in Upper Manhattan.

(D) The University Forum is a multi-purpose venue, designed by Renzo Piano Building Workshop with Dattner Architects as executive architect, that will provide a gateway between campus and community. It will include a 430-seat auditorium, meeting rooms, and University offices.

(E) Publicly accessible open spaces are central to Columbia's environmentally sustainable campus plan. Pedestrian-friendly streets—all of which will remain open—will provide a mix of local dining and shopping along welcoming pathways to a revitalized Hudson River waterfront.

(F) Prentis Hall, a one-time milk processing plant from Manhattanville's industrial era, houses Columbia's Center for Jazz Studies, Computer Music Center, and studios for the School of the Arts. The building next to it at 560 Riverside Drive is faculty and graduate student housing that will have a new lobby along a vibrant 125th Street.

(G) The Studebaker Building, once the site of an auto-manufacturing facility, received a LEED Silver award from the U.S. Green Building Council for Columbia's renovation, which created environmentally sustainable spaces for University administration.

37.57 (facing page, top) Sketch of campus of the University of Pennsylvania, created by selectively closing city streets, Philadelphia.
(Courtesy of University of Pennsylvania)

37.58 (facing page, bottom left) Blanche Levy Park at the center of the campus, University of Pennsylvania.
(Gary Hack)

37.59 (facing page, bottom right) Locust Walk, University of Pennsylvania, created from a city street through the campus.
(Kendall Whitehouse/Courtesy of University of Pennsylvania)

37.60 (this page, top) Main campus of Columbia University, centered on its "fields," New York City.
(Courtesy of Columbia University)

37.61 (this page, bottom) Site plan of Columbia University's Manhattanville campus, New York City.
(Renzo Piano Building Workshop/Skidmore Owings and Merrill/Courtesy of Columbia University)

37.62 Future street view, Manhattanville campus, Columbia University.
(Courtesy of FXFOWLE Architects)

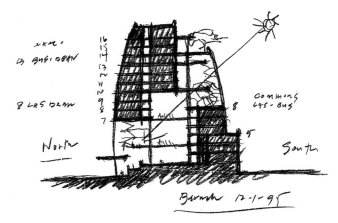

and the newly liberated spaces were combined with lawns to become a campus green and pedestrian way linking all the elements of the campus.

In a few places, universities relocated from the dense commercial centers of cities to the edge where they were able to create some breathing room, only to be engulfed again by development as the city grew. Columbia University in New York is an example, with its Morningside Heights campus designed by Charles M. McKim in 1893. Its centerpiece is its campus green, presided over by Low Library (now the administration building) and Butler Library (its replacement as the main library) at the two ends, with residential buildings on its two sides. Limited in its capacity to expand outward, Columbia has leapfrogged to Manhattanville where it is creating a satellite campus ten blocks to the north, one stop away on the subway, for its research institutes and professional schools. Baker Field, with the university's large playing fields, is located over two miles away, an accommodation that many city universities need to make.

Most city campuses are the product of the random opportunities to acquire properties for academic purposes as they become available. When large parcels present themselves, they need to be used intensively. In New York, Baruch College seized the opportunity to develop a full block adjacent to its scattered buildings, creating a vertical campus. Academic programs

37.63 Conceptual sketch for Baruch College's vertical campus, New York.
(Courtesy of William Pedersen/Kohn Pedersen Fox)

37.64 Street view of Baruch College's vertical campus.
(courtesy of Kohn Pedersen Fox)

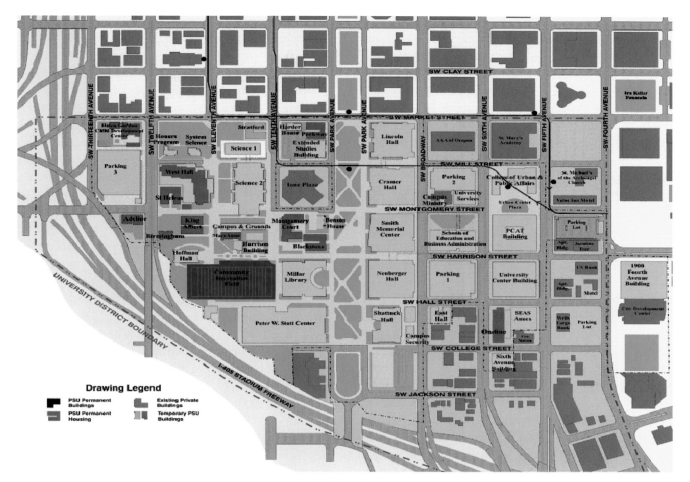

37.65 Portland State University campus plan, Portland, Oregon. (Portland State University)

37.66 Streetcar passing through campus building, Portland State University. (Portland State University)

are distributed through the full height of the 15-story campus, and places to see others, be seen, and make casual contacts surround the atria spaces. Most of the students are part-time or combine study with work, and the vertical courtyards come to life in the early evening when the campus is filled with students. While the building fills the entire block, it is shaped to allow more light to reach the surrounding streets, in deference to its neighbors. The ground level contains the college bookstore, and other retail and eating spaces to make connections with the neighborhood.

Portland State University has embraced its urban setting and designed its campus to become a working part of the city. There are no gates or security barriers, and the original block dimensions are respected for most buildings, although several large recreational facilities have needed to spill over two blocks. Several of the streets have been converted to pedestrian ways, and Park Avenue, the city's linear park, is the university's central green as it extends through the campus. The streetcar system penetrates the campus, with an important stop located directly below the College of Urban and Public Affairs. Bridges at the third level or above connect several of the buildings across streets, but only where those links are functional necessities. The Portland State campus demonstrates that a sense of identity can be created by a small number of design policies: consistent heights of buildings; compatible architectural character; a connected public realm with consistent materials; and limiting the amount of through traffic on crosscutting streets.

Virtual Campuses

Online education is currently calling into question the traditional form of university campuses. If education can be delivered anywhere via the Internet, what is the purpose of a campus? Millions of people all over the world are today taking courses without setting foot on a traditional university campus. At the same time, an unprecedented number of new universities are being established, particularly in rapidly modernizing countries. Many of these are branches of established universities that are operated in networked arrangements with the historical campus. At a minimum the new educational technologies will change the functions of campuses and the way education is delivered within them.

Higher education serves many purposes, and it is useful to parse them in order to understand those that require a fixed base of facilities and those that can be conducted in virtual space. The most basic function is acquiring knowledge, from books, lectures, demonstrations, and other sources. A second function is developing skills—how to conduct research, do design, build and test things, conduct experiments, write essays or reports, make arguments, speak in public, resolve conflicts, compete in athletics, and the like. Many of these are acquired through coaching by faculty and mentors. Still a third purpose is acquiring values, and the intellectual basis for them, along with interpersonal skills. Making friends and developing contacts and potential collaborators follow from these. And through the process of acquiring higher education, young people mature socially and intellectually and make important choices about long-term occupations. The people they encounter as faculty, visitors, and guest speakers are influential in shaping careers.

Not all of these functions require a student to be on a university campus for four years or more; in fact some purposes are better served by being in the workaday world, in the field, or in foreign places. It is not a large step to move from textbooks to online sources for the acquisition of knowledge, and the Internet is already displacing many of the functions of libraries. But the types of learning that are difficult to codify, or require coaching, or can only be acquired through intensive face-to-face interaction, surely will justify the continued presence of educational campuses. Experience with massive open online courses (MOOCs) to date suggests that they are most effective if coupled with a tutor who helps students understand and use the knowledge they are acquiring.

In coming years, we will surely see fewer large classrooms and more small-group discussion spaces. Laboratories, workshops, design studios, and performance spaces will continue to be important, although as the digital revolution affects the nature of research through widespread modeling, automation, and simulation, the kinds of spaces will need to keep pace. Places that promote human contact and exchange will be even more essential. Universities will remain places of residence and collaboration, events and socialization, even while knowledge is acquired from diverse sources.

Some universities such as Bridgewater State University in Massachusetts are reorganizing their campus around the idea of living-learning groups, where learning spaces are integrated with living areas for students and faculty. The idea of hoteling is taking root in other universities—living spaces where students come to a campus for only a few days or weeks, then return to their homes and learn through online courses. The Wharton School of the University of Pennsylvania has constructed identical case teaching classrooms, equipped with screens and cameras, in several cities (Philadelphia, San Francisco, Singapore) where a lecture-discussion can be shared across several time zones and participants can see their counterparts. These and many other innovative learning settings may signal the campus of the future.

Connecting Campuses and Their Communities

Planning places for higher education does not stop at the boundaries of the university's educational facilities. The university's role in its wider environment can take several forms: it may own or collaborate with medical centers which also provide the sites for clinical education; it may depend upon surrounding neighborhoods for student and faculty housing; semi-independent research institutes may cluster near the campus; and startup firms or large research-centered businesses may locate near the campus to tap the university's faculty and students. Much of the high tech industry in Silicon Valley, California, was a spinoff of Stanford University faculty and graduates, just as East Cambridge has become the largest cluster of biomedical research in the world as a result of its proximity to MIT and affiliated research institutes. Many universities have taken the lead in creating high-tech research parks to stimulate the commercialization of their intellectual properties, beginning with the creation of the Palo Alto research park near Stanford and the University City Science Center in West Philadelphia, both begun in the 1960s. Today, virtually every university in the US and China is a partner in a high tech research park near its campus. Many universities have also leveraged their land holdings at the periphery of their campuses to create commercial and residential projects for those who wish to live, work, shop, and be entertained nearby. In a wider sense, every university has a stake in the quality of its surroundings, which affects its ability to attract the best students and faculty.

Beginning in 1996, the University of Pennsylvania undertook a major program to improve the conditions in its surroundings, out of both enlightened self-interest and the desire to create opportunities for

37.67 Tsinghua Research Park, across from the main gateof Tsinghua University, Beijing.
(Gary Hack)

faculty and businesses to locate nearby. Large parking areas around the perimeter of the campus created a venue for crime and separated members of the university community from the residential neighborhoods where many lived. Using its land bank, the university constructed new commercial, residential, hotel, and office facilities—including a much-needed supermarket, movie theater, and bookstore—as a seam between the campus and the residential areas to its west. Two decades later, the opportunity arose to acquire a large site on the eastern side of the campus, which could fill the half-mile (1 km) gap between the university and the Schuylkill River with its bridges to Center City. The new development plan, Penn Connects, proposed four corridors to link across this site. A portion of the land was devoted to recreation spaces for the university that will be connected to the city by a new pedestrian bridge across the river. Street-level linkages will create new sites for university research spaces, a new hotel, and private office and research space. The projects are well on their way to completion.

Creating a supportive community environment is not only an urban issue. To be competitive, universities in outlying areas also need to be surrounded by opportunities for shopping, living, and connecting with the wider world. In 2004, the Universiti Teknologi Petronas completed a new campus at Seri Iskandar, Perak, Malaysia. This extraordinary campus sits in splendid isolation. As a leading institute for petro-chemical engineering, it creates a natural attraction for private corporations to locate nearby, suggesting considerable opportunities for meetings and places of contact between the campus and the surrounding areas. The university's plan for making these connections involves creating a hub at the intersection of the educational and research sites, and an environment that will attract highly skilled graduates to remain near the campus.

Hybrid educational and commercial centers are likely to multiply in the future. They are a recognition that learning and practice are closely linked, and that a rich environment for socialization is a hot spot for ideas.

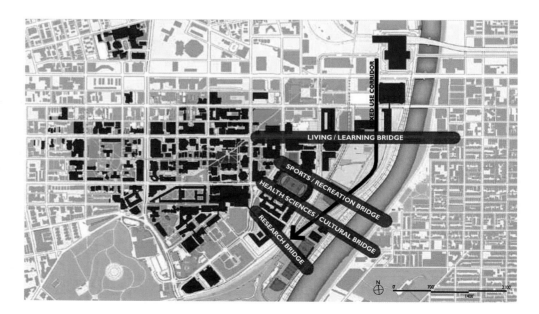

37.68 Major linkages proposed between the University of Pennsylvania campus and Center City Philadelphia. (Sasaki Associates/ University of Pennsylvania)

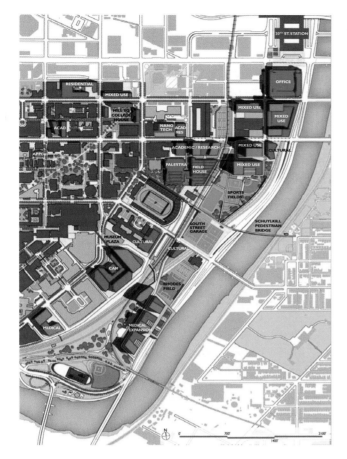

37.69 (top left) Plan of future development along Schuylkill River, University of Pennsylvania.
(Courtesy of Sasaki Associates/University of Pennsylvania)

37.70 (bottom left) Walnut Street corridor connecting the university and Center City, Philadelphia.
(Courtesy of Sasaki Associates /University of Pennsylvania)

7.71 (top right) Site plan for development of the university and adjacent research and commercial facilities, Universiti Teknologi Petronas, Seri Iskandar, Perak, Malaysia.
(Courtesy of Sasaki Associates)

37.72 (bottom right) Aerial view of proposed campus hub, Universiti Teknologi Petronas.
(Courtesy of Sasaki Associates)

38 | Public Spaces

Public spaces are the stages for human contact in cities. They are at once places to gather, see, and be seen, and places to rest, get away from crowds, and enjoy the views of the city. They take many forms: plazas, squares, pocket parks, large public gathering spaces, promenades, overlooks, or other spaces open to all. Human contact, of course, also occurs on streets, particularly in the pedestrian zones of cities, as we have noted in chapter 24, and in public recreation areas that have been dealt with more fully in chapter 36. In this chapter we take note of landscapes that make for good urban spaces.

Programs for urban public spaces vary greatly. The largest public spaces have symbolic and ceremonial purposes, such as Tiananmen Square in Beijing, the National Mall in Washington, or City Hall Plaza in Boston. Every urban area should have at least one space that can accommodate thousands of local residents, to celebrate local teams winning championships, hear the president speak, or host a local festival. These spaces run the danger of appearing empty between large events, and their landscape needs to be attractive even when not filled with people. Smaller public spaces may be principally designed to elevate the status of large public or private buildings, such as the plazas at Chicago's or San Francisco's civic centers or the Seagram Building in New York, Equitable Building in Chicago, and the ground-level public space at Hong Kong's HSBC Building. Or they may be consciously designed as a stage for public life, like Place Georges-Pompidou in Paris and Rockefeller Center in New York. They may offer a respite from the intensity of the surrounding city, as does Bryant Park in New York and the public spaces of Tokyo Midtown. Or they

38.1 Pioneer Square, Portland Oregon.
(Andy Hamilton/Pedestrian and Bicycle Information Center)

may be a quiet sanctuary to be discovered on a side street, like Paley Park in New York, Paul Revere Mall in Boston's North End, or any number of small piazzas in Venice or Rome. Some spaces become accidental places, designed for one purpose but appropriated for others, like the grand staircase at the Piazza di Spagna in Rome, which becomes an amphitheater in the summer for watching the crowds, or the steps at New York's Public Library or Vancouver's Courthouse, filled with people seated on a sunny day. The key to successful design of public spaces is deciding upon an imaginative program from the outset, while leaving room for the space to be discovered by others and used as people desire.

38.2 Boston Calling Music Festival 2013, City Hall Plaza, Boston.
(Emma-Jean Weinstein/WBUR)

38.3 Equitable Building Plaza, Chicago.
(Gary Hack)

38.4 Place Georges-Pompidou, Paris.
(© Paris Tourist Office/Amélie Dupont)

38.5 Sitting in the sun, Bryant Park, New York City.
(Gary Hack)

38.6 The waterfall, Paley Park, New York City.
(Courtesy of Jack Carman/Design for Generations LLC)

38.7 People watching, Spanish Steps, Rome.
(Gary Hack)

Successful Public Spaces

Public spaces are easily drawn on a site plan, but ensuring that they work as intended is another matter. The smart planner will also look locally for examples of spaces that are successful and draw conclusions about what contributes to their success. Project for Public Spaces, which has evaluated thousands of public spaces throughout the world, has concluded that successful spaces have four key qualities: they are accessible; people are engaged in activities there; the space is comfortable and has a good image; and they are sociable places (Project for Public Spaces 2009). When creating public spaces, the planner needs to attend to several factors.

Dimensions

Public spaces need to be large enough to preserve social distances, to avoid being appropriated by individuals or groups whose presence discourages others from entering them. As we have noted, the zone of social space typically extends 3–4 m (10–13 ft) outward from individuals standing or seated. At a distance of 20–25 m (65–80 ft) it becomes impossible for most people to read the facial expression of another individual (Gehl and Gemzøe 1996), so one becomes anonymous. Intermediate zones within larger spaces, with dimensions that range from 6 m (20 ft) to 25 m (80 ft), can be "public" while promoting social exchange.

Most successful public squares are no larger than 70–100 m (230–330 ft) in their small dimension (Gehl and Gemzøe 1996), although in high-density areas of China, activity can be sustained over an area twice that size. Much depends, of course, on the range of activities included. Copley Square in Boston was for many years considered a barren concrete wasteland, but after redevelopment with green lawns, sidewalk cafés, shaded seating areas, and fountains, it has become one of Boston's most popular spaces and is filled with people.

Flows and Eddies

The best public spaces are usually along a well-traveled route. The route may travel through the space or along its edge, with spaces for activities off the beaten path. The flow of pedestrians delivers candidates

38.8 Copley Square before reconstruction, Boston. (Gary Hack)

38.9 Fountains added to Copley Square, attracting passersby. (Gary Hack)

for activities in the space, while providing an assurance that others are passing by. A useful analogy is to imagine a public space as a river, with areas of flow bordered by eddies. Eddies need to be in scale with the flows. The most difficult public spaces have no flows—dead-end brackish pools that stagnate for lack of casual visitors.

It is also important to get the dimensions of the flow channels right. A narrow channel leading to a space lined with construction workers eating lunch may deter women from entering a space. A walkway through a space may be too narrow to allow people to stop and talk, or take advantage of the opportunities along it. While it may not be possible to limit the people entering a space, it is essential to provide adequate social distance at the entrances and along its main routes.

38.10 Eddies along walkway, Copley Square.
(Gary Hack)

Sun

In temperate climates, the presence of sun is the most important determinant of where pedestrians will perch. Sitting in the sun is a popular pastime in its own right, and the presence of good sunlight extends the active season of public spaces by months into the spring and fall. Even a slight slope will increase the sun exposure of an area. Strategically placed walls that store the warmth or reflecting surfaces that warm the air can extend the seasons even further. Sunlight can always be shaded if it is too warm, but there is no real substitute if it is absent. As a result, north-facing public spaces (in the Northern Hemisphere) are seldom as successful as those that face south. San Francisco prohibits new buildings that would reduce the sunlight falling on public spaces to less than two hours during the middle of the day.

In hot, sunny climates, shade is the condition being sought. The cafés in Piazza San Marco, Venice, charge dearly for seats under an umbrella, while in Mexico seats beneath great trees in the Zócalo are at a premium. Awnings that can be extended or retracted as the sun arcs across the sky are a splendid solution, allowing sun to warm the early morning and evening while protecting those seated during the heat of midday. It is always useful to plot the pattern of sun and shadows from surrounding buildings in deciding on the locations for activities in a space. Public spaces that include performance venues need to be sensitive to the sun direction in afternoon and evening, to avoid having the audience blinded by direct sun.

Triangulation

Regular users of a space may have no difficulty in greeting those they know or striking up a conversation with them. Casual users are unlikely to do so. Objects and activities in a space often provide the excuse for contact, however fleeting. A fountain that draws children into its pool will also draw their mothers together at the edge, and may encourage eye contact and a few words between them. The Crown Fountain at Chicago's Millennium Park is a virtual magnet, drawing children to the game of anticipating when they will be showered by water, with parents watching on the sidelines. This process of *triangulation*—using objects to bring people

38.11 Sunning on the lawn, Victoria Public Library, Melbourne, Australia.
(Gary Hack)

38.12 Crown Fountain, Millennium Park, Chicago.
(Gary Hack)

together—is a time-honored technique for creating sociable spaces (Whyte 1980).

Watching other people is often the best form of triangulation. A group of elderly men locked in a game of bocce (or boules) will undoubtedly draw a knot of casual observers, who will discuss strategy and second-guess the competitors. Chess tables unfailingly attract wannabe chess masters. A clutch of spectators will generally form at the margins of a pickup game of basketball or handball. Street musicians, human sculptures, ballroom dancers, or amateur magicians unfailingly draw a circle of viewers, trading smiles, comments, or embarrassment that they have stopped to watch. Allowing spaces to be animated spontaneously, or by audition (as one must in heavily populated places), provides the excuse for pedestrians to stop, experience, and make contact with others.

Food

The common denominator of the most successful public spaces is the presence of food. It can take many forms from formal to casual: sidewalk cafés spilling out into the space, pavilions selling food taken to nearby tables, vendors with their carts, hawkers selling treats they carry with them, and the growing number of farm stands that arrive in public spaces on particular days of the week. Introducing food has been the preferred strategy for attracting pedestrians into once-dead public spaces in New York City. At Bryant Park, a sidewalk café and concessions provide eyes on the adjacent green space. Long lines form every lunch hour, rain or shine, at the Shake Shack, a modern-day hamburger stand in Madison Square Park. At Paley Park, a small sidewalk café provides enough life to draw pedestrians into the quiet confines of the tiny jewel of a space, dominated by its water wall. In indoor public spaces, such as the bamboo forest atrium at the IBM Building in New York, a snack bar provides the excuse to linger with friends, just a few feet from the busy sidewalks.

Public spaces that double as farmers' markets, flea markets, or flower markets change their character through the course of the week. Often this is a way to assure that large spaces are inhabited during hours when they would otherwise be empty, as at Market Square in Pittsburgh or the Grand Place in Brussels. In Bangkok, many large plazas at the base of tall office

38.13 Sardine Family Circus performing at Fisherman's Wharf, San Francisco.
(© BrokenSphere/Wikimedia Commons)

38.14 Food concessions such as Shake Shack in Madison Square Park, New York City, add life to public spaces.
(Courtesy of Madison Square Park Conservancy)

38.15 Restoring the farmers' market to Market Square, Pittsburgh.
(John Altdorfer/Klavon Design Associates, Inc.)

structures undergo a transformation every evening. Large mobile kitchens, food displays, and tables with chairs are moved into the space after business hours, converting the stiff formal spaces into lively outdoor dining places. By morning, the space is again cleared, cleaned, and ready for the onslaught of businessmen.

Social Activities

Where or when there is a favorable climate, public spaces can become the outdoor living room of the city. People go to them to meet friends and converse, but they may also serve as the settings for informal or organized events. Public spaces in China are the setting for tai chi gatherings in the early morning, walking the birds later in the morning, card playing and petty gambling in the afternoon, and ballroom dancing in the evening. Large dancing clubs with their distinctive T-shirts often claim public plazas on weekends and evenings, much to the dismay of their neighbors who wish that the music would be dialed down. In good weather, tables for table tennis may be set up and used on a first come–first served basis. Large public spaces will inevitably draw children and adults practicing their kite flying skills and showing off their flyers. All of these activities help create and maintain social ties in the community, and should be encouraged.

Other activities may not be universally welcome. Teenagers are attracted to public spaces that have steps and walls and seating that will provide a challenging skateboard course; it helps to have places for their friends to perch as they show off. Such activities are hard on surfaces and generally drive others out of the space. The solution, as we have noted in chapter 36, is to create custom-designed skateboard parks. Hawkers can also be a nuisance, invading the privacy of those enjoying the public space or occupying valuable ground space with their wares. Creating a marketplace just off the main space may solve this.

Festivals and Spectacles

Regular and programmed festivals are a sure way to attract residents and visitors to public spaces, and spaces need to be designed to accommodate them. These events are also a way to showcase the special activities of the city and to bring residents and interest

38.16   Ballroom dancing, neighborhood square, Suzhou, China. (Gary Hack)

38.17   Skateboarders, MACBA Plaza, Barcelona. (Gary Hack)

groups together to meet and converse. Most cities have outdoor art fairs, European cities host Christmas markets, a regular stream of summer concerts occur in public squares in North American cities, and no Mexican Zócalo would be legitimate without its bandstand. Ferris wheels and carnival rides have become the fashion du jour in city squares, providing light and life in evening hours as well as the day. But the smaller, ever-changing events are at least as important: children's festivals, antique auto meets, postage stamp fairs, fashion shows, local musical performances, and more.

Many of these events require infrastructure that includes electrical power, water, washrooms, and waste

disposal facilities. Temporary cables and lines are dangerous; it is far better to design for events at the time the public space is being planned. Stages for performances can easily be set up and removed for a single event, using modular framing and fabric, but if performances are to be continuous they need to be incorporated into the design of the space. Stage lighting and sound systems can then be integrated into the space, and backstage and storage facilities provided.

Bordering Uses

Occasional events will bring people to a public space, but spaces that depend on programming may be empty much of the time. Great public spaces draw their energy from their surroundings. The buildings and uses surrounding a historic space such as Piazza San Marco in Venice are integral with the public space. Arcades lined with shops provide cool walkways for window shopping, restaurants spill out into the square, and crowds compete with pigeons for the large remaining central spaces. The busiest retail districts in Asia provide a seam between public and private spaces. Even in the tiniest spaces, cafés can convert a dead sidewalk into a living room.

Public spaces should be thought about in terms of three zones: the outer edge of the space that is capable of being expropriated by bordering uses during parts of the day and evening (sidewalk sales, cafés, extensions of sales area); portions of the space that are dedicated to particular groups (farmers' market, booksellers stalls, children's play area); and portions that should remain flexible and capable of hosting changeable events, performances, and spectacles. Imagining a public space as a stage for activities will help planners avoid designing forlorn spaces claimed by nobody.

38.18 Dam at night, Amsterdam.
(Jax Stumpes)

38.19 Outdoor concert, New Bedford, Massachusetts.
(Courtesy of New Bedford Whaling Museum)

38.20 Performers, Plaça de Catalunya, Barcelona.
(Courtesy of Masha Kubysina)

38.21 Performance space, Dallas Arts Square, Dallas, Texas.
(© Nigel Young/Courtesy of Foster + Partners)

38.22 Piazza San Marco, Venice.
(Gary Hack)

38.23 Pedestrian street, Causeway Bay, Hong Kong.
(Gary Hack)

38.24 Corner sidewalk café, Torino, Italy.
(Gary Hack)

Security

In many societies security in public spaces is taken for granted, and there are long traditions of sharing parks and pedestrian areas with diverse groups of people. A casual gendarme on foot may be all that is needed as a symbol of order, prodding street people to move along, stopping sidewalk hawkers from appropriating too much space, and dispersing a rowdy crowd late at night. However, the growth of drug use in public, random acts of violence or terrorism widely reported in the media, and a growing presence of homelessness has forced a new emphasis on security. Particularly in North America, where use of public space is less ritualized, many people are reluctant to enter spaces where they are unsure who and what they will encounter.

There are a number of strategies to make spaces hospitable. One is to act proactively to ensure that the homeless do not appropriate plazas and open spaces. Creating homeless shelters elsewhere, staffing them with street workers who are skilled at encouraging the homeless to move to shelters, and if necessary creating local laws that prohibit homeless from sleeping on sidewalks and public spaces are moves that have proved effective. (They are also essential in cold climates where homeless run the risk of danger from exposure.) A second move is to design public spaces so that they are visible from surrounding sidewalks and lit at night, enabling pedestrians to see the occupants before entering. Sightlines into public spaces also allow them to be patrolled more easily by security officers. The addition of activities and food outlets, as we have noted, can also attract an unthreatening population to the space, even after dark. Finally, security cameras may be installed so that the space can be monitored, and security personnel dispatched to threatening spots. Such monitoring raises thorny issues of privacy; at a minimum pedestrians should be informed that they are being monitored when they enter a space. Most public spaces are now being monitored remotely, warnings or no. And it is possible to turn the tables by showing what is being seen on the security cameras to those in the space, much as New Year's Eve celebrants in Times Square are shown on the space's Jumbotrons.

Another dimension of security currently needing attention, unfortunately, is ensuring that buildings and crowds are safe from those who would harm them with explosives or other threats. Buildings of high symbolic

38.25 Security barriers, Wall Street area, New York City. (Courtesy of Marvel Architects)

importance are obvious targets, as are governmental offices, courts, embassies, stock exchanges, markets, and other places where large crowds may gather. Creating barriers to keep vehicles out of public spaces or away from buildings is an essential measure, although many important structures are located directly on sidewalks and only human monitoring is practical. Innovative security barriers need not be oppressive; they can function as seating for pedestrians while protecting against vehicles, they can retract below the pavement when not needed, or they may be integrated into the landscape as at the Washington Monument. All of these measures only protect against the most obvious threats; ultimately the only real security protection is vigilance by those occupying spaces and maintaining public order in cities.

Local Public Spaces

Spaces set in neighborhoods or local commercial districts help anchor the identity of an area, while connecting people through casual contact. They can be as small as a tiny square with a few benches, or as large as Philadelphia's four squares that give its center city neighborhoods their names. They can be green spaces, as in Savannah's graceful residential squares, or paved areas as in many of Barcelona's residential plazas. There are many choices, but all that are successful exhibit the key qualities noted above—they are accessible, attract activities, are comfortable, and support socialization. When they are successful they

become an important third place in the lives of residents, complementing their homes (first place) and places of work (second place) (Oldenburg 1989).

Herald and Greeley Square Parks are two lush triangular miniparks in New York City, each 200 by 100 ft (60 by 30 m) created on lands that had been traffic islands for almost a century. Their form is very simple: greenery added on the perimeter to create a sense of enclosure, walkways through the center, and eddies between, with parasols and movable tables and chairs that users can group as they desire. Each park has a food concession and two public toilets, a welcome convenience in a city largely devoid of them. Although the parks are small, there is considerable area at their entrances for people to meet or to survey the passing flow. Beyond the parks there are overflow spaces on

38.26 Aerial view, Herald and Greeley Squares, New York City. (Google Earth)

Herald Square Park

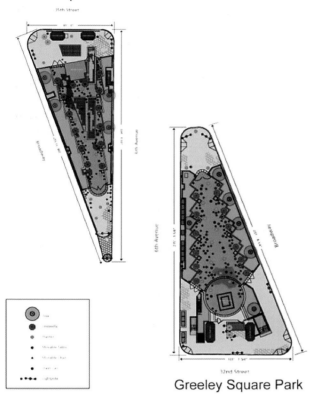

Greeley Square Park

38.27 (left)   Plans, Herald and Greeley Square Parks.
(Stantec)

38.28 (top right)   Lunch hour at Greeley Square Park.
(Gary Hack)

38.29 (middle right)   A quiet respite in Herald Square Park.
(Gary Hack)

38.30 (bottom right)   Food concession and public toilets area,
Greeley Square Park.
(Gary Hack)

the streets themselves, where traffic has been put on a diet. These small interventions in creating new public spaces have had an outsized impact on the quality of life in the area surrounded by offices, housing, and the city's largest department store.

The many pedestrians in Herald Square assure that the park is filled with people throughout the year. In a different climate and culture, St. Alekseyev Square in Harbin, China is a modest-sized (approx. 60 m or 200 ft square) local public space that anchors its neighborhood and is the center of its public life. The form of the square is very simple—a flat main space, raised 1 m (3 ft) above the surrounding sidewalks, defined by a historic church, a small performance stage, a beer garden (in summer), and landscape lining the street that creates eddies of space for separate activities. The main space is used for all manner of activities, including dancing clubs that practice and perform on many summer evenings. Residents stop to watch and may join in, mimicking the members' movements. Others come to enjoy a beer with friends or alone, meet neighbors, or make new friends. The eddies of space lining the sidewalk at the perimeter offer places for diverse interests: a traditional music group practicing their pieces, a massage specialist promising instant relief for all manner of aches, dog lovers meeting and showing off their beauties, and a bicycle mechanic tuning up vehicles. In winter, the beer garden is taken down and the square becomes a place for local ice sculptures and children's play in the snow. Residents know they can find others there throughout the year, and it is a true third place for all.

Local public squares can offer a respite as well as a setting for activity. Rittenhouse Square in Philadelphia, constructed in the nineteenth century and redesigned by Paul Philippe Cret in 1913, is approximately 475 by 550 ft (145 by 168 m), 6 ac (2.4 ha) in size. The plan is formal: its walkways encourage diagonal movement across the square between the residential neighborhood to the south and the shopping and work environment to the north, and the circular walk lined with benches provides a route within the square to meet and greet others. The tree canopy provides shade in summer and becomes a ceiling of lights during the winter holiday season. Users of the square vary throughout the day and week. Weekdays, residents bring their coffee from the shops surrounding and enjoy a chat with others

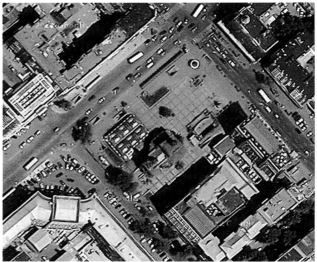

38.31 Entrance, St. Alekseyev Square, Harbin, China. (Gary Hack)

38.32 Aerial view, St. Alekseyev Square, Harbin. (Google Earth)

38.33 Dancing club, St. Alekseyev Square, Harbin. (Gary Hack)

before heading to work, at noon it is office workers who predominate, filling the benches, and in evenings families with children congregate in the areas around the fountain and play sculptures. Saturday mornings, market gardeners set up stalls along the Walnut Street sidewalk, and on a sunny weekend day the green lawns are filled with people enjoying the sun or picnicking with families or friends. Rittenhouse Square has been

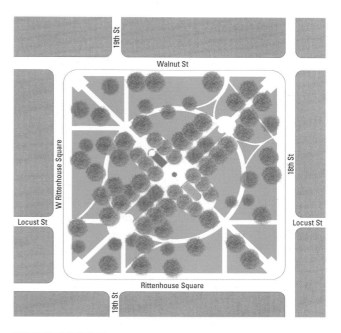

38.34 Ballroom dancing at beer garden, St. Alekseyev Square, Harbin.
(Gary Hack)

38.35 Informal music group, St. Alekseyev Square, Harbin.
(Gary Hack)

38.36 Dog admirers, St. Alekseyev Square, Harbin.
(Gary Hack)

38.37 Plan, Rittenhouse Square, Philadelphia.
(Adam Tecza)

38.38 Diagonal walkway, Rittenhouse Square, Philadelphia.
(Jeffrey M. Vinocur/Wikimedia Commons)

one of the best public spaces in the US for generations, even as the areas around it have changed, bringing new people and activities to its spaces (Jacobs 1992).

One challenge in creating new public spaces is the lack of routines of use; people are simply not yet familiar with what it has to offer. Exposure can be provided by having a location that draws people through or by the space, but sometimes this is not enough to establish it as a destination. One strategy is to use intensive *activity programming* to get people into and using the space, by creating festivals, events, and special occasions. Harbourfront, on Toronto's waterfront, spent ten years animating its public spaces through events and scheduled activities, inviting people to discover an area that many had never visited. Temporary venues were constructed for these purposes, and over time those that were successful were made permanent. A similar strategy is being used to animate Chavasse Park, the centerpiece of Liverpool's regeneration project, Liverpool One. Its gorgeous open space, undiscovered by local residents, has become a fine venue for concerts and events, using demountable structures to support activities. As more people experience the public space, it should attract return visitors seeking a respite from the dense urban surroundings, or looking for a place to socialize.

38.39 Benches lining the circular walkway, Rittenhouse Square, Philadelphia.
(Gary Hack)

38.40 Sunny spring day, Rittenhouse Square, Philadelphia.
(Mary/Philadelphia Love)

38.41 Nanny goat sculpture, Rittenhouse Square, Philadelphia.
(Boomeresque/Creative Commons)

38.42 Farmers' market on north sidewalk of Rittenhouse Square, Philadelphia.
(Courtesy of Marisa McLellan)

38.43 Amsterdam street festival, Harbourfront, Toronto. (Gary Hack)

38.44 Aerial view, Liverpool One and Chavasse Park, Liverpool, UK. (Courtesy of Grosvenor)

38.45 Outdoor concert, Chavasse Park, Liverpool. (Courtesy of Grosvenor)

Civic Spaces

Civic spaces belong to all. They are the shared provenance of all who have gone before and those who use the spaces today. They go by various names: *civic square*, city or *town square, people's (renmin) square, piazza, plaza mayor, campo, zócalo,* and others, or they are named after the founder of the settlement or its favorite son. They are the place of ceremonies, mass gatherings, and of political protests. We identify cities by the character of their civic spaces.

In medieval European towns, the civic space was most often just outside the cathedral, a relationship that was codified in the Laws of the Indies, the instructions that guided the planning of Spanish towns in the new world (Mundigo and Crouch 1977). "The size of the plaza," the Laws prescribed, "shall be proportioned to the number of inhabitants, taking into consideration ... the growth the town may experience. [It] shall be not less than two hundred feet wide and three hundred feet long [60 by 90 m], nor larger than eight hundred feet long and five hundred and thirty feet wide [240 by 160 m]." They thought of the plaza as integral with its surroundings. Article 126 of the Laws of the Indies prescribed:

In the plaza, no lots shall be assigned to private individuals; instead, they shall be used for the buildings of the church and royal houses and for city use, but shops and houses for the merchants should be built first, to which all the settlers of the town shall contribute, and a moderate tax shall be imposed on goods so that these buildings may be built.

Latin American cities generally remain centered on their plazas, surrounded by the cathedral, government buildings, and markets. During the nineteenth and twentieth centuries, when cities expanded and were rebuilt, the civic square usually fronted the city hall and courthouse or house of justice. In many US cities built during the westward expansion, the house of justice occupied the center of the courthouse square, surrounded by the main businesses of the city and civic buildings.

It is not often that new civic squares are designed, but the design leaves an indelible impression, for better or worse. San Francisco's Civic Center Plaza, built in 1915 as the centerpiece of the Panama-Pacific

38.46 Old Town Square, Prague.
(Gary Hack)

38.47 Town square, Vigevano, Italy.
(Gary Hack)

38.48 Plaza Bolívar, Bogotá, Colombia.
(Pedro Szekely/Wikimedia Commons)

38.49 Civic Center Plaza at San Francisco City Hall, San
Francisco, California.
(Supercarwaar/Wikimedia Commons)

38.50 City Hall Plaza, Boston in 1973, shortly after its completion.
(Ernst Halberstadt/US National Archives)

Sidebar 38.1

New central axis, Guangzhou, China

The master plan for Zhujiang New City, of which this is the centerpiece, consists of layers of development, both vertically and horizontally. Hotels and office buildings face directly on the public space, backed up by housing, shops, and additional workplaces. Running below the full length of the plaza is a layer of shopping, parking, and a mass transit shuttle line. Thus, people emerge from below and walk from nearby buildings to enjoy the green space and a regular diet of programmed activities. The central nexus of the public space is a crossroads linking four important cultural facilities — a new public library, a children's science center, the regional museum of art and culture, and the city's new extraordinary opera house. The central portion of the plaza is hard-surfaced and used for programmed activities that include consumer shows, children's festivals, and special events. Along the waterfront, fountains and mist makers are a welcome antidote to the hot summer days, and at night a choreographed spectacle. Further beyond, a performance stadium and the Guangzhou Tower attract millions of visitors that add to the mix in the central axis.

38.51 New central axis, Shujiang New City, Guangzhou, China. (Courtesy of OBERMEYER)

38.52 Underground shopping level, central axis, Guangzhou. (Courtesy of OBERMEYER)

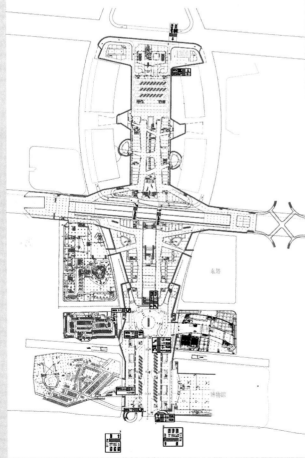

Sidebar 38.1 (continued)

**New central axis,
Guangzhou, China**

38.55   New public library, new central axis, Guangzhou.
(Gary Hack)

38.56   Children skating on ramps to New Opera House, new
central axis, Guangzhou.
(Gary Hack)

38.53   Underground shopping and subway entrance, new central
axis, Guangzhou.
(Gary Hack)

38.57   Car show, new central axis, Guangzhou.
(Gary Hack)

38.54   Children's science center, new central axis, Guangzhou.
(Gary Hack)

Exposition, serves as the venue for festivals, demonstrations, celebrations of sports victories, and everyday use as a passive open space. Its pollarded tree lines complement the neoclassical city hall but also provide shade in summer, and its soft flat surfaces, grass and compacted stone, make it an easy place to set up tables, booths, and other temporary uses.

Boston's City Hall Plaza, on the other hand, is a hard-surfaced, stepped brickyard that has bedeviled the city almost since it was opened in 1968. It is a relentless heat island in summer and windswept cold spot in winter, only coming alive when filled with people celebrating an athletic championship. The most important fault in its plan is that it gains nothing from its surroundings. It is along few people's pathways, and only a small fraction of its perimeter is inhabited by active uses. Over the years there have been various attempts to energize the square—introducing a farmers' market, programming events, setting up dining areas on the edges, among others—but the sheer size of the square, approximately 8 ac (3 ha), has defeated the efforts. It is a cautionary tale about the design of civic spaces.

The new central axis in Guangzhou couldn't be more different. Filled with people every day, it draws life from its surroundings and demonstrates how successful public space and surrounding development are intimately related. Guangzhou has built its new civic square out of activities that make it a public destination for a broad cross section of residents as well as visitors. It avoids the pitfalls of excessively formal spaces that are largely empty, and if it errs on the side of offering too many distractions, that is a small price for creating an immediate destination.

Waterfronts

Public spaces can be created in many locations in cities, but the water's edge holds a special attraction as a gathering place. It may be along the banks of a creek or river or canal, or at the ocean or lakefront. The magic of such places is primordial. Water is celebrated in song and verse, heightening its surroundings through reflection and expanding the horizon. Its presence changes the climate, cooling in summer but also sharpening the sting of winter. Being at the water's edge offers a glimpse of a workaday world of waterborne commerce

38.58 In-line skating on the esplanade, Battery Park City, New York City.
(Gary Hack)

38.59 Canal in 8 Shape Bridge neighborhood, Shaoxing, China.
(Gary Hack)

and fishing, and in favorable seasons access to boating and recreation. Cities have seized upon their waterfront resources to create unique places to gather and get away from everyday routines. In other cases, waterways are part of the natural movement systems.

Creating public spaces on the water poses several problems. How to secure the water's edge against erosion, flooding, and the longer-term threat of sea level rise? How to reconcile water-based commercial uses and the desire of waterfront residents for exclusive use of the edge with the desire for public access? How to maintain an area that is heavily used and bears the brunt of storms and seasonal changes of temperature? These and other issues create the challenges, but the

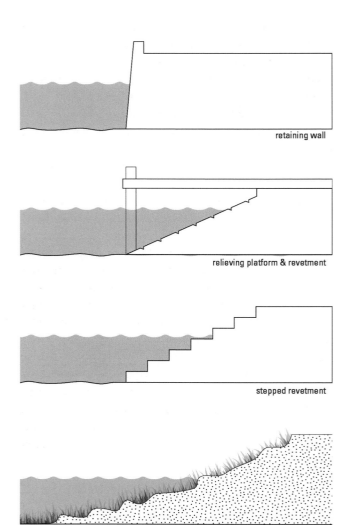

retaining wall

relieving platform & revetment

stepped revetment

natural revetment

38.60 Alternatives for the water's edge.
(Adam Tecza/Gary Hack)

38.61 Hardened edge along the Seine river quay, Paris.
(Gary Hack)

38.62 Stepped coastal protection at low tide, Margate, UK.
(Acabashi/Wikimedia Commons)

38.63 Coastline protection, Brooklyn Bridge Park, New York.
(© Elizabeth Felicella/Esto/Michael Van Valkenbergh Associates)

38.64 Natural edge, Southeast False Creek Waterfront, Vancouver, Canada.
(Courtesy of PWL Partnership Landscape Architects, Inc.)

38.65 Walkways at stream's edge, Riverwalk, San Antonio, Texas.
(Gary Hack)

river edges, since they allow the capacity of the river to expand considerably to accommodate seasonal surges in volume. Maintaining a stable water level is difficult, except where watercourses have been tamed with water control gates or diversion conduits, but it offers the opportunity for intimate contact with water, with minimal danger. The Riverwalk in San Antonio, Texas is made possible by a massive underground tunnel that diverts floodwaters around the calm stream in the center of the city.

Public spaces along the water's edge should be sized to meet expected flows, although overly wide promenades will feel empty most of the time if they are dimensioned for peak crowds. A walkway of 3 m (10 ft) will comfortably accommodate two couples meeting, but the width will need to be increased if bicycles or in-line skaters share the path. Added to this will need to be space to stop to enjoy the view or socialize. The Battery Park City esplanade is organized with a fast lane nearest the water and a slow lane a few feet above it lined with benches, which seems a good response for a heavily used public space. Where massive numbers crowd the esplanade on weekends, as along the Bund in Shanghai or at the edge of the lake in the Suzhou Industrial Park, 15–20 m (50–65 ft) may be the necessary dimension.

The experience is heightened when people are able to get as near as possible to the water. Sometimes there

potential benefits of well-planned waterfronts far outweigh them.

The first decision that must be made is the form of the interface between land and water. There are many options that include retaining walls of concrete, stone, or sheet piling, relieving platforms, stepped revetments, and natural revetments. The technology chosen will depend upon the space available, variation in water levels, danger of storms, resources, and desire to get pedestrians down to the water level. There are many advantages to natural revetments, including their support of marine and aquatic plant life in the intertidal zone. Sloped revetments are especially suited to

38.66 Walkway along Jin Ji Lake, Suzhou Industrial Park, Suzhou, China.
(Gary Hack)

is only a narrow ribbon of land available, but there remain several options. With some creativity, it may be possible to create a continuous walkway by extending the path around bridge abutments and other impediments, as Pittsburgh has done on its riverfront. Or a walkway may be constructed directly over the water, as in the Schuylkill River Walkway in Philadelphia. Floating structures may also be constructed along the waterfront, an especially good solution where there are tides that alter the water elevation. Copenhagen's floating swimming pool and deck structure is a delightful example.

The real potential of a waterfront public space is realized when activities are joined with sensitive treatment of the water's edge. Among the best recent examples is Hunter's Point South Park in Queens, New York. Constructed over multiple tunnels and sensitive conduits under the East River, the park needed to tread lightly on the land, largely respecting the existing water edge profile. Much of the site had been used for loading from barges to rail cars, and the design of its new life retained memories of earlier times. The park has large lawns for gathering and casual picnicking, children's playgrounds, seating areas, and lush areas for horticulture. Threaded through the upland area of the park is a continuous gabion wall that protects the adjacent housing areas from storm surges, a strategy that proved its worth during Hurricane Sandy, shortly after the park was inaugurated. This waterfront gem is the public commons of Queens' rapidly developing new urban neighborhoods.

38.67 Allegheny Riverfront Park walkway, Pittsburgh, Pennsylvania.
(Courtesy of Michael Van Valkenburgh Associates)

38.68 Schuylkill River Trail, Philadelphia.
(Courtesy of Lane Fike/Schuylkill River Development Corporation)

38.69 Floating swimming pool, Copenhagen, Denmark.
(Courtesy of © BIG – Bjarke Ingels Group/Julien de Smedt photo)

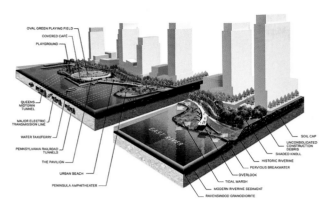

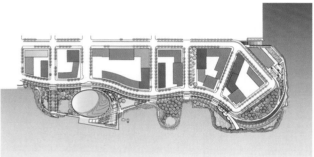

38.70 Complex relationships to natural and manmade elements, Hunter's Point South Park, Queens, New York.
(Courtesy of Thomas Balsley Associates/WEISS/MANFREDI/ARUP)

38.71 Plan, Hunter's Point South Park.
(Courtesy of Thomas Balsley Associates/WEISS/MANFREDI/ARUP)

38.72 Central green, Hunter's Point South Park.
(Gary Hack)

38.73 Remnants of railroad tracks incorporated in park, Hunter's Point South Park.
(Gary Hack)

38.74 Gabion wall providing flood protection to park, Hunter's Point South Park.
(Gary Hack)

39 | Mixed-Use Development

Cities that grow organically have a rich texture of activities, mixing residences with commercial spaces, workplaces, cultural facilities, education, and even production activities. On a single block of West 67th Street in New York—one of the most desirable places in the city, stretching between Central Park and the Lincoln Center cultural facilities—may be found exclusive residences overlooking the park, loft apartments for artists and actors, fine restaurants, a boutique, a residential college, a production center for a television company, and ordinary apartments for a wide variety of residents. This variation is sought by many people, and not only in dense urban centers. Older residential areas undergoing revival invariably include restaurants, recreation centers, shops, institutions, and schools within easy walking range of a variety of housing choices. Neighborhoods with *walkable commercial areas* typically are more valued than those that require automobiles (Hack 2013). There are long traditions of living above the shop that date to preindustrial times, and rows of *shop houses* continue to line the streets of Hangzhou, Guangzhou, Singapore, Taipei, Bangkok, and other Asian cities, many now converted to tourism districts. Behind them are alleyways filled with restaurants, convenience shops, and local services—and new apartments towering over them. These streets and alleys provide the fabric for vibrant 24-hour neighborhoods.

Nonetheless, a large proportion of new development, especially in the US, involves only a single use. The separation of uses is mostly the result of development regulations and the organization of the development industry that tends to specialize in *product lines*. Zoning in the US restricts the types of uses that can be located on sites, particularly in residential districts. In other

39.1 Mixed uses along 67th Street, New York City.
(Gary Hack)

39.2 Italian Village, now a restaurant and entertainment district, Tianjin, China.
(Gary Hack)

39.3 Shop house district, Hangzhou, China.
(Gary Hack)

countries like Japan and Taiwan this rigid differentiation does not exist, since development regulations focus on building form, not uses, a strategy that is the basis for recent US form-based codes (see chapter 15). Christopher Leinberger has identified 19 standard real estate product types that are conventions in the US development industry, including: the build-to-suit office, the office park, medical office buildings, grocery-anchored neighborhood centers, the budget motel, garden apartments, and other familiar types (Leinberger 2008). Developers know how to finance and build these uses, and may have *prototypical plans* they adapt to each new site. Residential developers tend to stick to their knitting, and developers who build commercial or office projects rarely venture into the world of residential real estate. The sources of construction and permanent financing are also different, as are the brokers selling or leasing space in completed buildings. Mixing uses is a challenge that requires working across boundaries in both design and development practices.

The virtues of mixing uses are being rediscovered in dozens of *new urbanist town centers* in the US, urban complexes in Japan and China, and urban redevelopment projects in Europe. Among the US examples is City Center in Las Vegas, which demonstrates that mixing uses vertically as well as horizontally can result in a higher-density commercial center that attracts residents as well as visitors. The much smaller center at Kentlands,

39.4 Mixed-use commercial complex, Jiang Jing SOHO, Beijing, China.
(SOHO)

39.5 City Center mixed-use area, Las Vegas, Nevada.
(Jahn Architects)

39.6 Mixed-use downtown, Kentlands Town Center, Gaithersburg, Maryland.
(Gary Hack)

in Gaithersburg, Maryland, also successfully combines shops, restaurants, and housing and is coupled with a larger shopping center beside it. There are physical efficiencies in mixing uses that include sharing expensive parking, marketing advantages in being able to sell not just a unit but a lifestyle, and internal synergies through creating patronage for commercial shops among the residents or workers above or next door. All of these make it worth the effort needed to go against the grain of separate uses.

Planning Principles

Designing effective mixed-use areas requires careful planning of access patterns, parking, and layers of privacy. In most situations, each of the components needs to function independently—commercial areas need to capitalize on the logic of shopping which is to attract passersby, while office and residential areas need strict controls over access for privacy and security. But the site also needs to harvest the advantages of co-location. This is a delicate balancing act, which requires considerable trial and error.

Horizontal versus Vertical Mixing

Visionary architects have been fascinated by the opportunity of devising *live-work buildings* that break the hegemony of single uses on a site. Frank Lloyd Wright's Price Tower, in Bartlesville, Oklahoma, completed in 1955, is a 19-story tower with offices and housing on each floor. Apartment dwellers have their own elevator that opens directly into each unit, and at least in theory the mix on each floor can be shifted over time to more housing, offices, or other uses. Part of the tower was recently converted to a hotel. A more common pattern is to locate offices below and housing on the upper floors of buildings, where they can benefit from views and return higher sales prices to the developer. Hazelton Lanes in Toronto was one of the first such examples in North America, and the elegant Edificio Pluriusi in Rome with housing over offices became an exemplar in Europe. In San Francisco, Golden Gateway Commons on Davis Street consists of a carpet of two- and three-story housing located over three stories of offices, parking, and shops.

39.7 Frank Lloyd Wright's innovative live-work building, Price Tower, Bartlesville, Oklahoma.
(Courtesy of Alex Ross)

39.8 An early mixed-use building, Edificio Pluriusi, Rome.
(Norbert Schoenauer)

**Golden Gateway
Commons,
San Francisco**

Golden Gateway Commons (renamed Embarcadero Square), near the San Francisco water-front, consists of three blocks with a carpet of housing and open spaces above two levels of retail and office space. A total of 155 condominiums have private and group-private open spaces, and the perimeter of each block is ringed by ground-level retail space and second-level offices, totaling 250,000 sq ft (23,200 m^2). Separate elevators are provided for the office and residential spaces. It is among the most treasured live-work-shop complexes in the city.

Architects: Fisher-Friedman Associates, 1976

39.9 Golden Gateway Commons, San Francisco, aerial view.
(Fisher Friedman Associates/Courtesy of NBBJ)

39.10 Section through structure.
(Fisher Friedman Associates/Courtesy of NBBJ)

39.11 Street-level view.
(Gary Hack)

39.12 View of housing courtyard.
(Gary Hack)

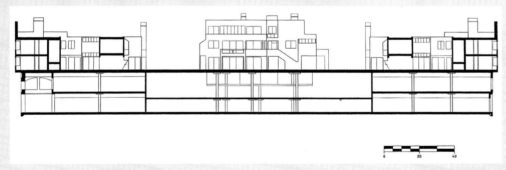

The John Hancock Building in Chicago topped all other *mixed-use buildings* at the time of its construction in 1968. Its 100-story envelope contains vertical slices for shopping, parking, offices, apartments, and other functions. With about 4,000 workers, 1,700 residents, and 4,000 visitors a day, it functions as a vertical city, smoothly transporting people from the ground to sky lobbies for each use, then on a local elevator to their ultimate destination. Only a small number of the residents work in the structure, but the mix adds immeasurably to the life and density of the area. *Vertical mixing* of uses is now the standard formula for supertall buildings, including the Burj Dubai, Jin Mao Tower in Shanghai, and Taipei 101.

One of the key challenges in mixing offices, housing, and other uses vertically is how to reconcile the differences in the preferred *building footprints* of each use. Offices in the US are typically about 45 ft (14 m) deep from elevator core to exterior wall, while it is difficult to design conventional apartments with more than 35 ft (10.5 m) depth and most hotels have a preferred depth of 25–30 ft (7.5–9 m), although suite-style hotels are deeper. There are a variety of strategies for arbitraging these differences. Housing can be stepped back from the line of the offices by inserting balconies, or the structure may be tapered. The John Hancock building tapers from base to top, with the commercial zone at its base measuring 180 by 275 ft (55 by 84 m) and typical apartment floors above only 125 by 210 ft (38 by 64 m). Housing above offices can also be reshaped to yield greater perimeter and provide more views, as has been done in the innovative Heritage on the Garden in Boston. Where hotels are stacked over offices, a successful strategy is to create an atrium in the hotel area, as in the Jin Mao Tower. In European cities, where building codes restrict the depth of offices to 8 to 10 m (26 to 33 ft), apartments fit neatly over office buildings.

Mixing housing and commercial uses in the same structure is quite common in Asia, since there is less devotion to single-use zoning and greater tolerance of sharing elevators and stairways with people in the building for different purposes. Structures may change their use over time, as the district where they are located shifts in its function. A sensible convention has evolved in Taipei: new offices cannot be established above housing. This rule reduces the nuisance of sound transmission from floors above, and the heavy

39.13 John Hancock Building, Chicago.
(Courtesy of © Royce Douglas)

demands on residential elevators by visitors. In Tokyo, where setback planes usually require upper stories to be smaller than lower ones, there is a natural gravitation of housing to the areas above offices, although the great variability in block sizes means that there is considerable mixing of functions on each floor.

Vertical mixing, even in small buildings, requires solutions to a variety of mechanical issues. If housing is over offices or retail uses, sanitary drains need to be consolidated from the many locations in apartments to a few vertical stacks, so the large open areas needed by commercial uses are not interrupted. Similarly, ventilation systems need to be segregated to avoid transmitting odors between the various uses. In very

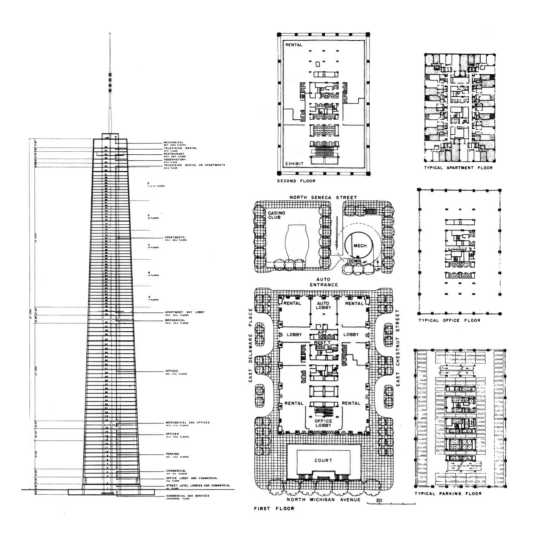

39.14 John Hancock Building, Chicago, plans and section. (Oswald Grube)

39.15 Housing stepped back from the larger office footprint below it, Heritage on the Garden, Boston. (Gary Hack)

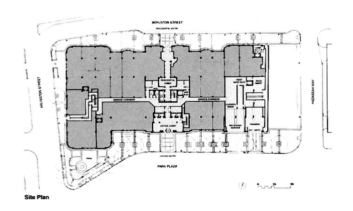

39.16 Dual elevator lobbies approached from opposite sides of Heritage on the Garden, Boston. (The Architects Collaborative)

Mixed-Use Development

large buildings, this may require dedicating floors as transfer levels. Elevator systems also need to be separated to provide the level of security needed for each use in the building, and to respect the fact that some uses are accessible 24 hours a day while others close down. Elevators to belowground parking typically terminate at the lobbies rather than connecting with residential or office floors, for security reasons.

The alternative to vertical integration of uses is sharing a site horizontally. This greatly simplifies the structural and mechanical systems, at least above any common infrastructure, and usually is more cost-effective. It may also allow the development to be more easily phased, if market conditions do not support a continuous construction process. Often a shared parking deck below or above grade will unify the complex, or there may be a 3–4-story *podium* containing shopping, restaurants, and public uses out of which tall towers rise. This formula has become conventional in Hong Kong and other Asian cities, where large blocks can accommodate two or more towers, and there is advantage in creating a network of elevated walkways from block to block. The Sanlitun SOHO complex in Beijing, Union Square in Hong Kong, Sony Center in Berlin, and Prudential Center in Boston are all excellent examples of horizontally separated mixed-use developments with a matrix of retail uses below.

39.17 Offices with hotel above, Jin Mao Tower, Shanghai (on left). (Gary Hack)

39.18 Atrium in the Grand Hyatt Hotel begins on 40th floor, Jin Mao Tower, Shanghai. (Lawrence Lavigne/Wikiimedia Commons)

Sanlitun SOHO, Beijing, China

The Sanlitun SOHO complex, located in one of Beijing's most desirable areas, is a live-work-shopping environment. It consists of five office towers and four residential towers on a foundation of three levels of retail spaces, parking, and service spaces, totaling 465,000 m^2 (5 million sq ft). Below-ground shopping covers much of the site, connected visually to the towers by generous open-air atria animated by a skating rink, performance spaces, and casual landscaped areas. The lower two floors of each tower are also devoted to shopping and services. Each tower has a distinct shape, color, and identity, rising to a maximum of 97 m (318 ft) in height. Individual entrances to the towers are located belowground in dedicated parking areas and on ground level.

Site planners: Kengo Kuma & Associates

39.19 Belowground retail space, Sanlitun SOHO, Beijing. (Courtesy of Kengo Kuma & Associates)

B1F plan   1:800

➤ retail public entrance

sanlitun soho
kengo kuma and associates

Sanlitun SOHO,
Beijing, China

F1 plan   1:800 ⊙

► retail public entrance
► office lobby entrance
► residential lobby entrance

sanlitun soho
kengo kuma and associates

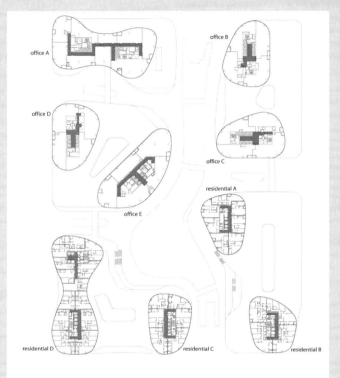

office/ residential tower typical floor plan   1:800 ⊙
(above F7)

sanlitun soho
kengo kuma and associates

39.20 (top left)
Street-level retail space.
(Courtesy of Kengo Kuma
& Associates)

39.21 (top right)
Typical floors of office and
retail towers.
(Courtesy of Kengo Kuma
& Associates)

39.22 (bottom left)
View of central entrance
to plaza.
(Gary Hack)

39.23 (bottom right)
View of lower-level
shopping area.
(Gary Hack)

39.24 International Finance Centre, Hong Kong.
(WING/Wikimedia Commons)

39.25 Street view of Sony Center, Berlin, mainly lined by offices.
(Courtesy of © Rainer Viertlbock)

39.26 Residential structure facing inward, Sony Center, Berlin.
(Courtesy of Dirk Verwoerd)

39.27 Residential and office towers with retail spaces below,
Prudential Center, Boston.
(Gary Hack)

Access

Each use needs its own doorways. Residential buildings and hotels will require drive-up access to each lobby, while in commercial areas it may be more important to limit the number of entrances to key locations along streets and make direct connections with public transit. Most large office buildings also desire independent street-level access, even if their elevator lobbies are on upper levels, in part to allow for security checks of those arriving. Where there is an adequate street dimension, a separate service road may be warranted, but this should be the exception rather than the rule, since it disrupts the continuity of street-level activities. A better solution is to locate the automobile entrance to housing or hotels on side streets, as is common in New York City. Security issues must be carefully considered so that residents' lobbies and balconies are not accessible to casual visitors; but if there are adjacent commercial areas, residents will undoubtedly wish to have weather-protected access to and from them as well. Solving the flows of people while providing adequate security is the most important access challenge.

Offices and residential uses generally desire separate lobbies and entrances. One solution in mixed-use buildings is to locate lobbies for residences and offices on opposite sides of the building while placing elevator cores back to back. The Heritage on the Garden configuration is an excellent example of how this can be handled (see figure 39.16).

Shared Parking

In dense mixed-use complexes, parking is a costly investment, particularly if located belowground, that needs to be used efficiently. An obvious advantage to combining uses is the prospect of doubling up parking use—as an example, between residents and hotel patrons who need overnight parking, and shoppers and workers who are mainly present in the daytime. But this is often frustrated by the residents' desire to have dedicated parking spaces in a protected area. It is sometimes possible to reserve spaces (say, one space per unit) on the top floor of underground garages for residents, using independent card access, while on other floors combining visitor parking and additional spaces required by residents with areas for shoppers or office workers.

Providing valet parking can also be an effective way to share expensive garage space. Since cars parked by attendants can be stacked two or three cars deep (or vertically stacked on mechanical lifts), parking needs can be satisfied in less than half the normal amount of space during peak hours. The cost of employing valets will be easily offset by the increased revenues and reduced costs of constructing parking (see chapter 21).

Privacy and Noise

When tall structures are clustered on a site, how far apart should they be to maintain the privacy of uses? There is no single answer, since personal space dimensions vary across cultures, and some uses, particularly housing and hotels, seek higher levels of privacy than others such as offices and retail spaces. Nonetheless, it has become conventional to set as a minimum space between buildings the typical dimensions across city streets, on the grounds that this has become an accepted distance. In most US situations this means spacing structures at least 50–65 ft (15–20 m) apart. Some cities regulate these dimensions: Vancouver requires a minimum distance between structures of 18.3 m (60 ft) if they are on the same block and 24.6 m (80 ft) if they are across a street. Even with this spacing, it may be desirable to orient residential buildings so that they do not directly face their neighbors, or provide privacy screens that limit views.

Residents generally prefer quiet environments, particularly during the evening hours, while commercial

39.28 Spacing of high-rise towers, North False Creek, Vancouver. (Gary Hack)

and entertainment uses often thrive on buzz. Even those residents who may wish to overlook events in spaces on the site may want their bedrooms oriented in quieter directions. At Sony Center in Berlin, where the central space is used for film festivals and performances, living rooms of residential units face on the active space while bedrooms face the opposite direction (see figure 39.26). Separating uses by tolerable noise levels is also possible, with a residential enclave located at a distance from entertainment and performance areas.

Service Areas

Building operators generally prefer having loading docks for each building located near each elevator core, which may be efficient from an operational standpoint but requires a large proportion of the frontage of the site to be devoted to loading areas. If at all possible, it is desirable to consolidate loading docks, which has the added benefit of reducing the total number of bays required. They may be paired for adjacent buildings, or a single large loading area may be created. In some cases, a large project may justify loading materials from large trucks to electric vehicles used to distribute goods to the various cores.

Collection of garbage is another important servicing consideration, particularly where waste materials are separated at their source for recycling. The use of vacuum collection facilities is one solution; another is special-purpose vehicles that can move from floors of buildings directly to storage and loading areas (see chapter 28).

Severability of Uses

Most mixed-use complexes need to be *severable* into a series of separate units for purposes of leasing, financing, and ultimately ownership. At the outset of planning, it is important to think through where the *demising lines* will be, both horizontally and vertically. Who will bear the long-term responsibility for maintaining the open spaces on the site? How will decisions be made on future replacement of heating or air conditioning systems that serve multiple types of tenants or owners? Since uses will change at different rates in the future, issues of access need to be considered. If retail

areas need renovation and need to be closed in the future, will this disrupt access routes between public transit and office lobbies or residential areas? There are solutions to each of these issues, and it is unfortunate if planners shy away from a mixed-use complex as a way of avoiding immediate problems.

One approach is to create a condominium or strata title scheme for the uses, clearly distinguishing between shared common spaces and systems and those that are individually controlled. Where there are residential uses or individually owned shops or office spaces, separate condominium entities may be necessary to distribute responsibilities within individual structures. Cross easements are a tested solution for access to or use of service facilities. A complicated formula for assessing (and agreeing on future assessments) may be necessary to avoid future conflicts over costs and arrangements. All of these arrangements need to be planned for from an early stage.

Mixed-Use Prototypes

Single-Building Mixed-Use Projects

Small mixed-use projects can lead the way to neighborhoods becoming active throughout the day and evening. They are especially appropriate as a seam between commercial and residential areas and near public transit stops, where there is a built-in market for commercial uses. Retail areas with shops and housing above existed in most US, Canadian, and European cities half a century ago, particularly along streetcar lines, but many hurdles need to be overcome to reproduce them today, including excessive parking demands of tenants, zoning restrictions, and the fear of adjacent residential neighbors that they will be impacted by the development. Several examples, however, illustrate how these may be addressed.

The Rockridge Market Hall in Oakland, California is a small mixed-use project (approx. 100,000 sq ft or 9,200 m²) that has been a commercial success and has had a transformative impact on the area around the Rockridge mass transit station. The motivation was a desire to create a market hall for fresh foods and other specialty food outlets that would entice potential shoppers exiting the transit station across the street (Childress 1990). Shops, including a market hall, occupy almost the entire ground floor, served by a common off-street loading area at the rear. With a three-story height limit and an unproved market for housing and offices, the upper floors were designed so that they could be lived in or easily converted to professional offices. Upper-story uses are entered through an outdoor lobby that leads to an elevator and stairway. An outdoor roof terrace above the market hall serves as an open space for the upper-floor units. A small parking area serves the retail customers, and parking near the adjacent transit station serves those who drive to the complex.

Introducing larger commercial outlets and office space in a low-scaled residential neighborhood requires the utmost sensitivity in siting and scaling a project. New automobile and pedestrian traffic will be attracted to the site, and will need to be handled so that they don't erode the quality of life in the residential neighborhood. The Rise, in Vancouver, is a project that offers lessons for the site planner (Urban Land Institute 2014). Three large-format stores are located on the site—a supermarket, a building supply outlet, and a home goods store—stores that are usually located as free-standing outlets some distance from residential areas. The idea of the development, occupying a full block in the transition zone between a commercial corridor and a rapidly intensifying residential neighborhood, was to promote walk-in patronage and ensure that the block did not become a dead zone after business hours. The program for the site, totaling 26,000 m² (280,000 sq ft) of gross leasable area, consists of retail anchor stores, smaller retail shops, offices for local services, 92 live-work townhouses arranged around a fourth-level rooftop open space, and 640 belowground parking spaces. The site planning challenge was to organize the access around the perimeter of the block so that each use had a pedestrian frontage. Major entrances to the large retail outlets face the commercial street. Residential lobbies were sited on the streets linking to the residential neighborhood. Parking access and loading for pickup of building materials are on a perpendicular street, out of sight of pedestrians. The U-shaped housing area was sited to take advantage of the magnificent views to downtown and the distant mountains. A masterful stroke!

In Philadelphia, the University of Pennsylvania transformed a full-block site adjacent to its campus

39.29 Aerial view, Rockridge Market Hall, Oakland, California. (Google Earth)

39.30 Street view, Rockridge Market Hall, Oakland. (Gary Hack)

39.31 Stairway to upper-level uses, Rockridge Market Hall, Oakland. (Gary Hack)

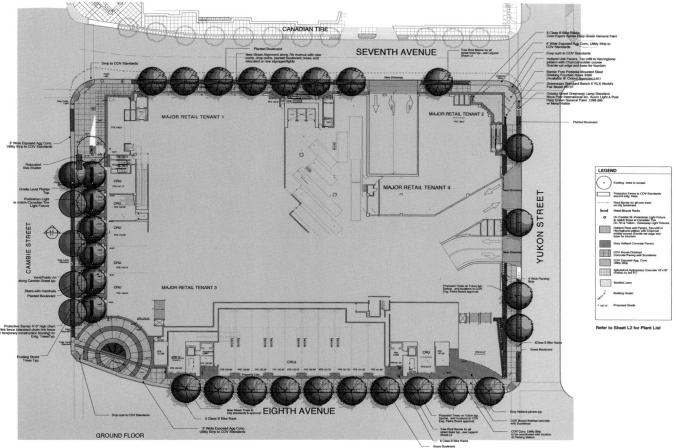

39.32 (top left) Street view, The Rise, Vancouver.
(Gary Fitzpatrick/Courtesy of Grosvenor Americas)

39.33 (bottom) Ground-level plan with entrances complementing surrounding streets, The Rise, Vancouver.
(Courtesy of Grosvenor Americas/Durante Kreuk Ltd.)

39.34 (top right) Housing courtyard on level 4, The Rise, Vancouver.
(Larry Goldstein/Courtesy of Grosvenor Americas)

Mixed-Use Development

that had been a parking lot for 25 years into a mixed-use shopping, restaurant, and hotel complex. Called University Commons, it consists of 300,000 sq ft (27,870 m²) devoted to a large bookstore, street-oriented shops, three restaurants, and a 228-room hotel with 18,000 sq ft (1,670 m²) of meeting space. The challenge of the project was to energize the main streets surrounding the site. This required a careful analysis of the potentials of the four block frontages. Contrary to intuition, the main entrance to the hotel was not located on the major pedestrian street but on the quieter alley street on the opposite side, to avoid cluttering the commercial frontage on Walnut Street with drop-off and loading activities. A secondary entrance is located on Walnut, allowing access to the conference and hotel facilities. A consolidated loading area was created for the complex on a dead end service street. Adjacent to the transit stop and bookstore entrance, a plaza was created and is active throughout the year as a casual meeting place,

39.35 (top left)   Aerial view, University Commons, Philadelphia. (Google Earth)

39.36 (top right)   Street view, University Commons, Philadelphia. (Courtesy of Inn at Penn)

39.37 (bottom left)   Automobile drop-off for hotel, University Commons, Philadelphia. (Courtesy of Inn at Penn)

39.38 (bottom right)   Plaza at entrance to bookstore, University Commons, Philadelphia. (Gary Hack)

outdoor dining area, farmers' market, and place for other activities. The height of the mixed-use structure was limited to 90 ft (27 m) to respect the scale of the campus and adjacent buildings. The project has not only been a commercial success, spurring other commercial developments, but has filled a large gap in the neighborhood with activity and life.

These three projects illustrate an important principle in designing small urban infill projects: they must be designed from the outside in, reflecting the scale and activity on surrounding streets. On larger sites it may be possible to create an independent center of activity away from the street, but it is usually a mistake to attempt this on small sites. The exception, of course, is when the street environment is noisy and hostile to pedestrians and there is a need to create a respite from the surrounding chaos. The Waterfall Lofts project in Vancouver is a fine example of how to do this: the street is lined with retail and studio office uses, while every housing unit faces on a quiet courtyard created within the block.

39.39 Street view, Waterfall Lofts, Vancouver.
(Courtesy of Stephen Hynes/Nick Milkovich Architects)

39.40 Central courtyard, Waterfall Lofts, Vancouver.
(Courtesy of Steven Hynes/Nick Milkovich Architects)

39.41 Aerial view, Renaissance Center, Detroit.
(Robert Thompson/Wikimedia Commons)

39.42 New city interface with people mover and pedestrian entrance, Renaissance Center, Detroit.
(Gary Hack)

39.43 Waterfront face, Renaissance Center, Detroit.
(Brosnhoj/Wikimedia Commons)

Vertical Mixed-Use Urban Complexes

Vertical mixed-use projects require ingenious architectural configurations to accommodate the several access, service, and parking needs. Site planning considerations sometimes take a back seat, and too often the result is a project with soaring internal spaces that turns its back on its surroundings. Examples that both resolve internal dynamics well and connect to adjacent areas are rare. The original Renaissance Center in Detroit had interesting (but disorienting) interior atria and was almost impossible to reach on foot from downtown. Between the two areas was a dead zone, cluttered with drop-off areas, air conditioning exhausts, and other barriers. Fortunately, creative additions to the perimeter and a reconfiguration of access patterns have brought life to the linkage, and made the project a more integral part of the city center. They have also opened up the complex to the adjacent waterfront, dispensing with a ring road that encircled the site. It would have been far better to design it properly at the beginning.

Sidebar 39.3

- -

Roppongi Hills, Tokyo, Japan

Built on a 115,000 m² (28.4 ac) site that had been assembled from 400 individual parcels, the project includes a 54-story tower containing offices, a hotel, and an art museum at its top, wrapped by a six-level retail and restaurant complex that also extends into the tower base. With the main shopping spine located adjacent to the main tower rather than under it, separate entrances and security checkpoints are maintained for each of the tower uses. Adjacent structures include two tall towers for housing and two mid-rise structures, a large cinema and theater, the Asahi Television main production facility, and additional office and retail spaces. The built space totals 724,000 m² (7.8 million sq ft).

Site planners: KPF and Jerde Partnership

39.44 Diagram of organization of Roppongi Hills, Tokyo. (Courtesy of Jerde Partnership)

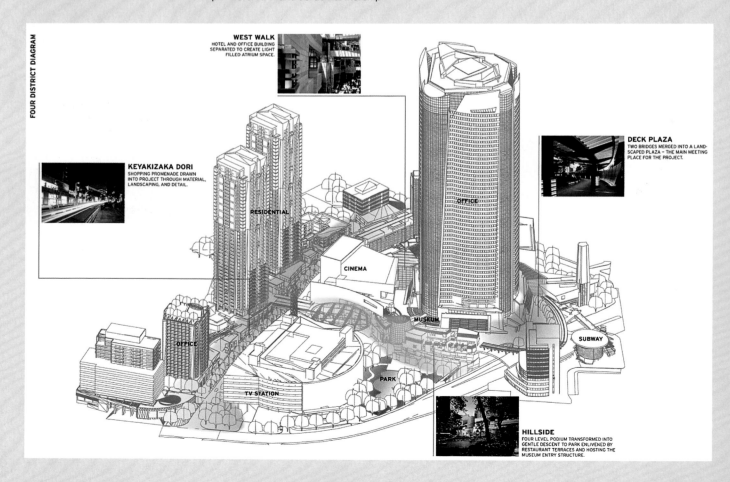

FOUR DISTRICT DIAGRAM

WEST WALK
HOTEL AND OFFICE BUILDING SEPARATED TO CREATE LIGHT FILLED ATRIUM SPACE.

KEYAKIZAKA DORI
SHOPPING PROMENADE DRAWN INTO PROJECT THROUGH MATERIAL, LANDSCAPING, AND DETAIL.

DECK PLAZA
TWO BRIDGES MERGED INTO A LANDSCAPED PLAZA – THE MAIN MEETING PLACE FOR THE PROJECT.

RESIDENTIAL

OFFICE

CINEMA

OFFICE

MUSEUM

SUBWAY

TV STATION

PARK

HILLSIDE
FOUR LEVEL PODIUM TRANSFORMED INTO GENTLE DESCENT TO PARK ENLIVENED BY RESTAURANT TERRACES AND HOSTING THE MUSEUM ENTRY STRUCTURE.

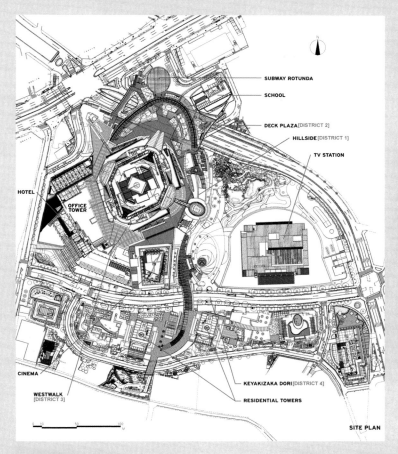

SUBWAY ROTUNDA

SCHOOL

DECK PLAZA [DISTRICT 2]

HILLSIDE [DISTRICT 1]

TV STATION

HOTEL

OFFICE TOWER

CINEMA

WESTWALK [DISTRICT 3]

KEYAKIZAKA DORI [DISTRICT 4]

RESIDENTIAL TOWERS

SITE PLAN

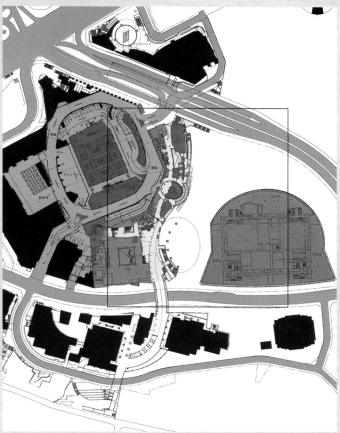

39.45 (top left)
Site plan, Roppongi Hills.
(Courtesy of Jerde
Partnership)

39.46 (top right)
Lower-level site plan,
Roppongi Hills.
(Courtesy of Jerde
Partnership)

39.47 (middle left)
Deck plaza, Roppongi Hills.
(Gary Hack)

39.48 (middle right)
West Walk shopping area,
Roppongi Hills.
(Gary Hack)

39.49 (bottom left)
Keyakizaka Dori entrance
to shopping.
(Gary Hack)

39.50 (bottom right)
Keyakizaka Dori, Roppongi
Hills.
(Gary Hack)

Roppongi Hills in Tokyo is a complicated project of interlocking uses that takes full advantage of approximately 25 m (80 ft) of topography in one of Tokyo's most desirable neighborhoods. The site plan is organized around four outdoor and indoor public spaces. People arriving via the metro travel by escalators through a rotunda to the Deck Plaza, a large hard-surfaced public space. From there they can enter the Mori Tower offices, the Mori Museum entry structure, and the West Walk, the second major space that arches around the tower and is the heart of the shopping complex. Taking advantage of the topographic differences, the Hillside is an outdoor park and performance area, with both programmed and

casual spaces. Keyakizaka Dori is the fourth public space, lined with shopping and restaurants and connecting to the fabric of the city. For special events and occasions (such as the city's film festival), it is closed to vehicles and extends the pedestrian realm. Roppongi Hills is an example of how a large mixed-use complex can fit comfortably in an existing urban district.

Horizontal Mixed-Use Urban Complexes
Many of the advantages of mixed-use development can be obtained by carefully organizing an array of uses side by side rather than vertically. The financing of a

---

Sidebar 39.4

- -

**University Park
at MIT, Cambridge,
Massachusetts**

39.51 Plan, University Park at MIT.
(Courtesy of Forest City Realty Trust)

39.52 Design guideline for open spaces at University Park.
(Koetter Kim Associates/MIT)

Planned and privately constructed on a 28 ac (11.3 ha) site that MIT assembled adjacent to its campus, University Park integrates 1.65 million sq ft (153,000 m²) of research and office facilities with more than 670 residential units, a hotel and conference center, a supermarket, and other retail facilities. The site is organized into city blocks, with all parking accommodated in structures on the perimeter. Residential uses are distributed and integrated throughout the development, with more family-oriented housing providing a buffer between the office and research uses and the adjacent Cambridgeport neighborhood.

Site planners: Koetter Kim Associates
Developers: Forest City Realty Trust

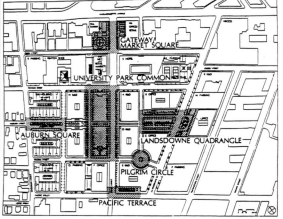

B. OPEN SPACES AND STREETSCAPE

OPEN SPACES AND STREETSCAPE

University Park is organized around a street system and interlocking open space system, which together constitute a framework around which development will occur.

The overall design goal is ease of pedestrian flow all the way from the Brookline Street neighborhood edge, through the new mixed-use development, across the railroad tracks where feasible, and to the Charles River open space system.

OPEN SPACES

Open spaces at University Park are to be developed in coordination with the street system and are intended to help support and focus the various activities which surround them. Design and programming of the open space should reflect the zoning ordinance requirement that such space be publicly beneficial and accessible.

These open spaces will be developed and programmed in detail as they are brought to realization individually over time. However, the following elements have been identified for the Gateway/Market Square, University Park Common, and Auburn Square.

The following illustrates some possible building facades:

BASIC WALL TYPE   GATEWAY   BUILDING ENTRY   BUILDING CORNER

BASIC WALL TYPE   GATEWAY   BUILDING ENTRY   BUILDING CORNER

39.53 Design guideline for building facades at University Park. (Koetter Kim Associates/ MIT)

39.54 (top left)   View of park, University Park.
(Gary Hack)

39.55 (top right)   Supermarket and other services integrated into office and research buildings.
(Gary Hack)

39.56 (middle left)   Research buildings, University Park.
(Gary Hack)

39.57 (middle right)   New residential loft building, University Park.
(Gary Hack)

39.58 (bottom)   New low-rise housing adjacent to Cambridgeport neighborhood.
(Gary Hack)

development is simplified when each use occupies its own site and the site can be easily parceled to allow individual ownership of buildings. Earlier we saw how Battery Park City adopted this strategy and has become a very successful new city neighborhood (chapter 2).

University Park at MIT, in Cambridge, Massachusetts, demonstrates how a clear pattern of blocks and consistent guidelines for development can result in an attractive moderately scaled inner-city development. The plan for the development emerged from a lengthy dialogue with the city and residents of the adjacent Cambridgeport neighborhood, an area with a long history of opposing new development. Design guidelines, which were adopted into the local zoning, called for a large open space, street-oriented buildings with limited heights, parking enclosed in structures, and housing adjacent to the existing neighborhood, among other rules. Other conditions were imposed by MIT, which leases the site to a master developer and ultimately to owners of individual buildings, and thus had a long-term interest in assuring the quality of the results.

University Park is a rare example of a development that follows the design guidelines but also goes beyond them to enrich the site. With limited frontage available on Massachusetts Avenue, the main commercial street in the area, the development's supermarket was sited one block away but designed to be visible from the avenue. It is located on the second floor of a mixed-use structure to allow other commercial uses to capture the ground-level flow, and is topped by three floors of housing. Buildings surrounding the central park have been designed so that the ground levels can be used as office space until the market for additional commercial space emerges, as the area reaches its full occupancy. Heights in the area were a contentious item in the negotiation of the plan. Old abandoned loft factories on the site were five stories, and it was agreed that new research and office structures would match that height, while housing adjacent to the neighborhood would be held to three stories. One residential structure, in the middle of the site facing the park, was allowed to rise to 17 stories. A standard palate of brick and an aesthetic of punched windows was adopted for the commercial buildings of University Park, while residential buildings were allowed to develop separate identities. Parking structures were carefully sited so that drivers could reach them without traveling on neighborhood streets. The overall result is a mixed-use district that takes advantage of synergies to support a lively, 24-hour community, serving the adjacent neighborhood, university, and new employees and residents.

Mixed Uses Connected by a Podium

A common prototype for developing mixed-use structures involves the creation of a podium (also called a *plinth*) of three to five levels of space for retail shops, food and beverage, and parking, above which rise individual towers for housing, offices, hotels, or other specialized uses. This pattern has been common in Asia for many years, and often the podium element fills an entire city block. The roof of the podium is typically devoted to recreation or green spaces, in effect replicating the ground level several levels above the street. A typical example is Landmark Centre in Hong Kong, constructed over 30 years ago and recently renovated, with high-end shopping on three levels in a podium, topped by a hotel structure and office building.

As projects have expanded in scale, podium development has become the organizing concept for some of the largest mixed-use complexes in the world. Perhaps the most impressive is the Union Square complex that includes the International Commerce Centre in West Kowloon, Hong Kong. It has exceptional access, constructed on a 13.5 ha (33.5 ac) site located over the Kowloon Station on the rail link to Hong Kong International Airport and a transfer point with other subway and regional rail lines. The podium consists of six levels: two levels belowground devoted to the rail station and parking, the ground level which accommodates all drop-offs, taxis, and loading, two levels of retail uses above, and a large park above it for the enjoyment of all who use the site. The podium provides 82,750 m² (891,000 sq ft) of retail space and over 6,000 parking spaces that serve the uses above. The 18 towers that rise above the podium include a 110-story office and hotel structure, additional offices, 5,866 housing units, 4,710 hotel and serviced apartment units, and a full range of recreational and service facilities needed for a district that attracts half a million people or more each day. The overall built area of the project totals 1.1 million m² (11.7 million sq ft) of space.

The site plan for Union Square is instructive. The high automobile flows to and from the complex and

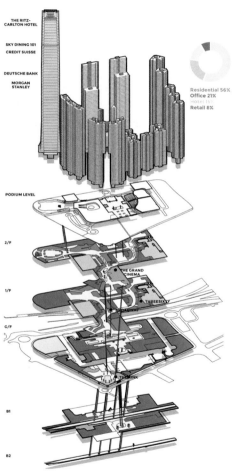

39.59 Podium at Landmark Centre, Hong Kong.
(Unidentified)

39.60 Interior atrium of podium retail space, Landmark Centre, Hong Kong.
(Courtesy of © China International Travel CA, Inc.)

the Kowloon Station require devoting a full level (the ground level) to circulation. Most of the tall towers are located on the perimeter of the site so that their foundations do not conflict with the station and rail lines below, which also allows for separate entrances for each tower around the edge of the site and a relatively uninterrupted floor area for the commercial complex. Generous skylights in the center of the complex admit light down through the commercial complex to the station, unifying the complex. However, the complex currently has little connection with its surroundings, since most pedestrians are two or three levels aboveground. Ultimately, the planners propose that bridge

39.61 View of International Commerce Centre, Union Square, Kowloon, Hong Kong.
(Ritz Carlton Hong Kong)

39.62 Plan and vertical layering, International Commerce Centre, Union Square, Kowloon, Hong Kong.
(Courtesy of Stefan Al)

39.63 Interior of retail area in podium, Union Square, Hong Kong.
(Gary Hack)

39.64 Rooftop park over the Union Square podium, Kowloon, Hong Kong.
(Gary Hack)

39.65 IDS Center atrium which connects upper-level pedestrian ways to the ground level, Minneapolis, Minnesota.
(Gary Hack)

39.66 Original Prudential Center complex, Boston, Massachusetts.
(Prudential Insurance Company)

connections be created to the waterfront and adjacent development projects.

Separation of pedestrians from the ground level is a common issue in cities with podium-based development linked by *skywalks*. Skywalks provide the rationale for creating a multistory retail space below towers in dense urban areas. In Minneapolis, upper-level pedestrian walkways function as the main circulation arteries during winter months, and podium developments such as that of the IDS Center provide the vertical connections to the street level. Differentiating the retail uses and activities between the street level and upper levels

is critical. In many cities, the street level becomes the domain of those taking mass transit, while pedestrian flows from block to block use the upper level *pedways* (see chapter 24).

The Prudential Center in Boston, Massachusetts is an unusual case because its elevated walkways were necessitated by site infrastructure. The development was built over a former rail yard with a datum less than 10 ft (3 m) below the level of surrounding streets; the continuing use of the rail tracks and the Massachusetts Turnpike parallel to them forced all roads and pedestrian walkways traversing the site to be about 18 ft (5 m) above the surrounding street level (which varies across the site). This allowed three levels of parking with 3,000 spaces to be constructed below the pedestrian ways in areas not occupied by rail lines and the Turnpike. The original Prudential Center complex, completed in 1968 on 23 acres (9.3 ha), consisted of 4.5 million sq ft (418,000 m²) of space divided among two office towers, three housing towers with 810 apartments, a 1,000-room convention hotel, two department stores, and a one-level outdoor commercial space of 190,000 sq ft (17,650 m²) occupying spaces between the towers. The

city's new convention center was built on a portion of the site. The Prudential Center was planned as a free-standing complex, with a ring road providing access to its garages and drop-off points, creating a separation of 150 ft (45 m) or more from active uses on the surrounding streets. It hardly seemed to be connected to the two vibrant neighborhoods, the Back Bay and the South End, that depended upon the Prudential deck as their main route between.

By the mid-1980s, the owners of the site believed it was underutilized and wished to add more towers

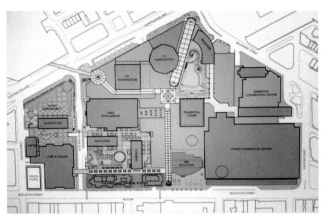

39.67 Prudential Center plan after redevelopment, Boston. (Boston Properties)

39.68 New entrance, office tower and condominiums along Huntington Avenue, Prudential Center, Boston. (Gary Hack)

39.69 New housing and hotel above retail lining Boylston Street, Prudential Center, Boston. (Gary Hack)

39.70 Interior, glass-covered arcades, Prudential Center, Boston. (Gary Hack)

while remedying its windswept commercial areas and open spaces. After a multiyear debate with residents of the apartments on the site, a new site plan was agreed upon which utilized the ring road areas for new housing, a hotel, offices, retail space, and apartments. Residents of adjacent areas got new commercial uses at ground level, including a new supermarket, and weather-enclosed 24-hour walkways between the neighborhoods. Prudential acquired the right to build a further 1.8 million sq ft (167,000 m²): two office structures, condominium housing, new open spaces, and an enclosed shopping arcade that has proved to be the city's highest-earning shopping area. The shopping arcades, limited to one story by the capacity of foundations, were modeled on the wonderful arcades in London and Melbourne, Australia, and have become one of the city's most popular walking destinations.

Entry points are graced by generous rotundas, which also provide indoor access to public transit (Hack 1994). A bridge connects the complex to Copley Place, an adjacent multilevel shopping mall with two hotels and office structures. After completing the project, Prudential sold the complex at a handsome profit, and its successor has added two additional office towers, filling small gaps in the perimeter.

The Prudential Center, and the other projects highlighted above, demonstrate how mixed-use complexes can add to the vitality of a city while respecting traditional patterns of streets and development. They need to be viewed both from the inside out and the outside in, regardless of scale. The best mixed-use projects blend seamlessly into the city fabric and also add new enclosed spaces that extend city life.

40 | Communities

Ultimately, a livable neighborhood, district, or city is more than a random collection of houses, shops, institutions, and mixed-use projects, however innovative and varied they may be. The form of a new residential community reflects attitudes toward nature, urbanity, neighboring, automobile use, social contact, and privacy. It must respond to the market for housing and other uses in its area and the prevailing economics of land and building. Every new development is also greatly affected by the standards for providing roadways and public services mandated by government agencies that must approve the project. Too often, large new community developments are the mindless result of responding to government demands and repeating patterns tried elsewhere. But the best new communities go beyond simple practicality and are a creative response to all the factors that make a place livable.

Components of a New Community

How large does a development need to be to qualify as a *new community* or a *new city*, *town*, *village*, or *neighborhood*? Generally, a large new development that contains most functions of everyday life—housing, shops, institutions, recreation opportunities and workplaces—is called a *new city* or *new town*. Post-World War II new towns built in the UK typically set as their target accommodating 75,000 residents with a full range of services and work opportunities, although this size proved too small to create the quality of life many residents desired, and the last of the new towns, Milton Keynes, was planned for 250,000. A survey of 30 new towns constructed in the US over the past 50 years indicates that

they have ranged in size from under 1,000 residents to over 88,000, and in area from 80 ac (32 ha) to 38,000 ac (15,400 ha) (Community Planning Laboratory 2002). At the low end, these might better be called *new villages* or *neighborhoods*.

Optimal size depends on what one means by community or neighborhood or town. The US *neighborhood unit* first found its form in Radburn, New Jersey, where a community was planned on 235 ac (95 ha) with 1,000 clustered housing units, 100 apartments, an elementary school, shared open spaces and play facilities, and shops for everyday needs. Only part of the development was built, but it has exerted a broad appeal as a planning module. The area required for such a self-contained neighborhood has grown in size as schools and supermarkets have become larger, densities of suburbs have declined and greater mobility has meant less dependence on local resources. However, the *danwei*, a living-working community that was the fundamental unit of Chinese society for 50 years, might house only a few thousand people but be a self-contained environment, providing shops, clinics, schools, and all the daily needs of those who live within the gates, subsidized by the business or institute it was built around (Bonino and De Pieri 2015). New developments, such as the SOHO MOMA residential complex in Beijing, have tried to reproduce this, although not always successfully, since there is an inherent conflict between the desire to support market-based functions such as shopping and the wish to internalize these in a *gated community*. Most new developments are simply not large enough to support a commercial complex alone. The size of a desirable community will also vary by density and layout: a high-density development with

40.1 Aerial view of
Livingston new town, West
Lothian, Scotland.
(Kim Traynor/Wikimedia
Commons)

40.2 Aerial view of central
Milton Keynes, England.
(Milton Keynes Council/
Green Digital Charter)

schools and services, such as Stuyvesant Town in New York, is a distinct neighborhood of 25,000 residents on an 80 ac (32 ha) site, while a lower-density sprawling suburban area may be four times that size and still not seem like a neighborhood.

Because the definitions are so slippery, we will use the term *community* to span across scales. Striving to create a community, rather than just a development, usually signals the desire to create a diverse area catering to a variety of types of households, and organizing its form and components so that they support face-to-face contact, neighboring, and local ties between residents through institutions they share. It also generally means encouraging walking by locating facilities so that they

40.3 Plan of Radburn, New Jersey, 1929.
(Clarence Stein and Henry Wright)

Medical services—clinics for routine and emergency visits, dentists, pharmacies.

Recreation places—playgrounds, playfields, parks for casual recreation; commercial recreation such as movie theaters, workout spaces, indoor tennis, water park; community gardens.

Local institutions—governmental service spaces; places for worship; community centers; cultural spaces; clubs and organizational spaces.

Work spaces—nearby employment centers; live-work areas; business incubator centers.

40.4 MOMA SOHO linked hybrid housing complex, Beijing.
(Courtesy of © Shue He/ Steven Holl, Architect)

40.5 Aerial view of Stuyvesant Town and Peter Cooper Village, New York.
(Melpomen/123RF Stock Photo)

are in easy range of most residents, also making possible chance contacts with friends and neighbors. A typical objective is ensuring that schools, shops, and public transportation are no more than a 10-minute walk from every home in a community, which translates to 1 km or half a mile. The typical components of a new community include:

Housing for a broad range of households—singles, families with and without children, seniors; those wishing autonomy and others seeking places which encourage neighboring; cohousing; a hotel or guest house if the area is large enough to support it.

Shops and services for everyday or weekly needs—groceries, laundries, bottle shops, restaurants, bars, shoe repair, hardware, gift and card shops, salons, pet care shops, and the like.

The number and amount of space for each of these components will depend upon the location, size of the project, market for spaces, and intentions of those developing the community. Not all of the spaces may materialize at the start, since *social capital* and institutions take time to form and businesses materialize as needs are sensed by entrepreneurs. Hence, flexibility for future development is important. A useful target is to think in terms of the kind of community being sought 10–15 years in the future.

Some Principles

Creating a community requires a mindset of striving for qualities of place that go beyond the value of the buildings that occupy a site. While it is easier to lease or sell space in a development that has a desirable environment, some of the virtues of a community only become obvious well after the initial developers of a site have departed. Fine communities share several attributes:

Identity—they are recognizable by their buildings and landscapes, and are different from other areas of the city.

Walkability—they minimize the distances that residents and workers need to travel for everyday needs. Promoting effective public transit within a 10-minute walk of homes and workplaces is essential.

Diversity—they accommodate a diverse set of residents and workers, and make it possible for people to remain in the community as they move through the life cycle.

Places for contact—the strength of community ultimately depends on forming traditions and institutions that bring people together in public; spaces where this can occur are essential.

Synergy—the uses reinforce each other. Shops and restaurants benefit from high-density housing and employment areas nearby; community buildings serve educational as well as social functions; open spaces double as casual and organized recreation areas.

Adaptability—the form of the community makes it possible to adapt uses over time. Parking areas in shopping areas can later be consolidated into structures, releasing land for new housing or offices; sites are deliberately held open for future development.

Maintenance and management—parks, public spaces, and shared facilities need long-term arrangements for maintenance. Creating the organizations and financial means for this is as essential as planning the site and will ultimately determine whether spaces are well used or avoided.

Each of these principles needs to be operationalized for a particular site. Integrating shops, workplaces, and housing in a single structure may be possible on one site but not another. The form of places for human contact will vary by climate and traditions. However, beginning with a list of aspirations is essential, and these need to be touchstones throughout the planning.

Form and Structure of Communities

A common point of departure in planning new communities is to think of them in organic terms, as a set of vital organs or cells connected by arteries and networks to central functions, much as the human body is organized. Victor Gruen's diagram for an ideal new city is composed of small compact local communities with neighborhood facilities at their center, connected by transit and roadways to major commercial centers and employment areas. Around the perimeter, separated from the residential areas by greenbelts, are industrial areas, airports, and other links to the larger world. This form of organization rationalizes commerce into three levels of facilities—local, district, and central shopping areas. The organic idea is easy to grasp and sell to others, which is part of why it has persisted for so long in thinking about designing communities.

The new city of Reston, Virginia, near Washington, DC, was organized in this manner, with five villages, two district centers, a dense city center, and several independent employment areas near the expressway. The form, not quite as neat as Gruen's diagram, has been fitted onto the topography of the site and the

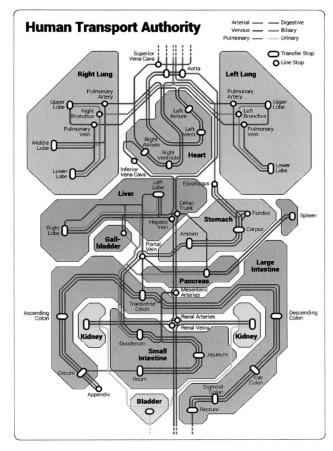

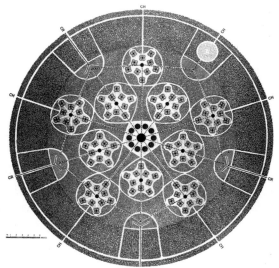

40.6 Human cardiovascular system diagram. (Jacob Larson)

40.7 Plan diagram for the perfect city. (Victor Gruen)

principal access routes that bisect the community. Much of Reston consists of low- and moderate-density housing clusters, separated by fingers of green spaces that preserve streams and watercourses and provide recreation trails throughout the community. The mixed-use city center provides an urbane counterpart to the sylvan neighborhoods.

Open-space networks often provide an armature for structuring new communities and providing separate identity to each of the neighborhoods. At Columbia, Maryland, also near Washington and built during the same period as Reston, fully 35% of the site was set aside for open spaces (5,000 ac, 2,025 ha), separating the community's five main villages, each of which has a local shopping area where religious structures, secondary schools, major playing fields, and community centers are also clustered. A regular system of arterial streets, landscaped as parkways, and collector streets provides access to local residential areas. Single-family detached housing and higher-density forms are never mixed on a local street; each has a separate entrance from a collector street. Open spaces and community facilities are managed by the Columbia Association, which also operates dozens of recreation facilities, provides social service programs, and organizes a myriad of arts and cultural activities for the city. These are paid for by an annual levy on all real estate in the city, including commercial properties, that amounts to approximately 0.35% of the value of each property. Without a local government for the new city—it relies upon the county for schools and other essential services—the Columbia Association has become an important social and political outlet for residents.

Open spaces that separate neighborhoods can also serve important ecological functions, storing stormwater runoff, providing a habitat for wildlife, and maintaining patches of the original environment of the site. They may be used for agriculture, growing fruits and vegetables for sale at farmers' markets or supermarkets, or for subscribers to a community-supported agriculture program. Creating small garden plots for residents will allow housing to be clustered more densely, creating a more walkable community. All of these functions may be seen at Prairie Crossing, and ecological community near Chicago.

At a totally different scale, on a site of 11.6 km² (2,866 ac), the Sino-German Eco-Park near Qingdao,

RESTON
MASTER PLAN

- Single Family
- Townhomes
- Apartments/Condominiums
- Parks/Open Space/Tennis/Pools
- Community Use/Schools/Churches/ Child Care
- Lakes
- Town Center District
- Town Center Urban Core Office/Retail/Hotels/Residential
- Business and R & D
- Village Centers/Convenience Retail

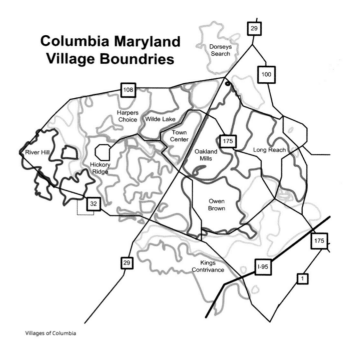

Columbia Maryland Village Boundries

Villages of Columbia

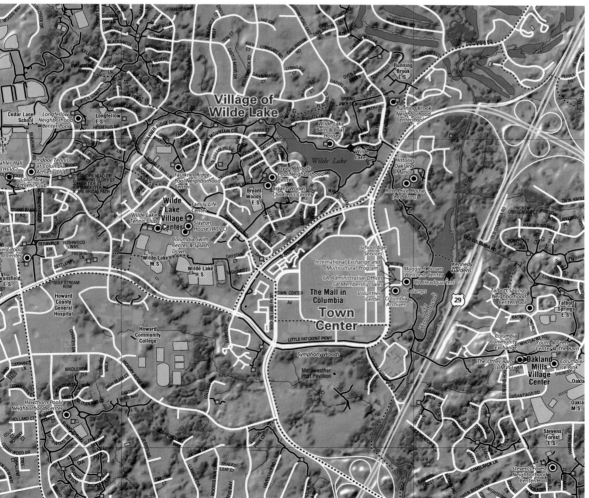

Prairie Crossing, Grayslake, Illinois

Located at the intersection of two major commuter rail lines, Prairie Crossing is an ecological community wonderfully endowed with open spaces and facilities. Over two-thirds of the site is dedicated to agriculture, recreation areas, and open prairie, reestablished on land that was farmed for generations. Osage orange hedgerows have been maintained and give structure to the site. The open spaces integrate the site through their walking and cycling paths and varied activities. An organic farm, incubator farms, allotment gardens, educational farm programs, and rain gardens complement the lush natural prairie landscape.

Housing is grouped in a series of differentiated clusters ranging from 35 to 120 units, each with common internal open spaces. The design is Midwest US vernacular, and all houses are energy-efficient. Although lots are small, virtually every housing unit looks out on

40.15 Site plan, Prairie Crossing, Grayslake, Illinois. (Courtesy of Prairie Holdings Corporation)

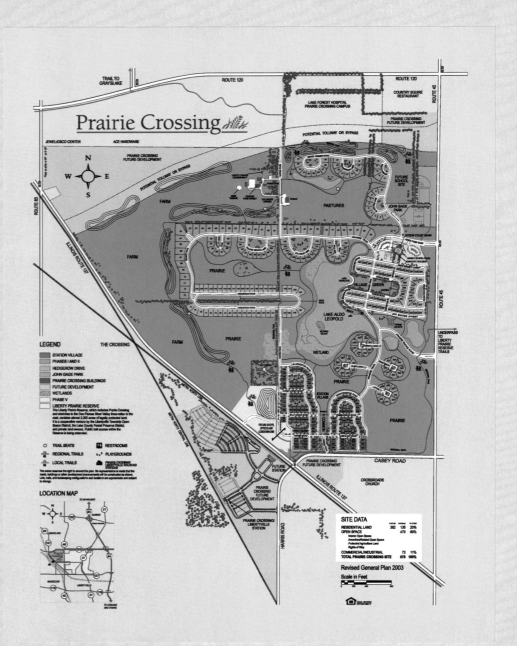

a large open space. A loop road connects the clusters and provides access to the surrounding arterial roads. Paved areas are minimized, and the site has zero net runoff.

Commercial areas are grouped near the commuter rail station, which is walkable from many of the houses. Approximately 30% of residents currently commute to work by train, several times the local average. Future development in the area of the station will add local employment and region-serving retail uses.

A homeowners' association is responsible for managing the open space, and several land trusts and nonprofit organizations are responsible for the farms and common facilities.

Location: Grayslake, Illinois, 65 km (40 mi) from Chicago
Site planners: William Johnson, Peter Calthorpe, Skidmore Owings and Merrill
Developer: Prairie Holdings Corporation, George Raney and Victoria Post Raney
Site area: 274 ha (678 ac)
Uses: 20% single-family housing (362 units); 11% mixed-use (113 units multifamily housing, commercial space, future employment areas); 69% open space (organic farms, meadows, lake, recreation a reas, buffers)
Facilities: charter school, commuter rail stops (2), shops, medical clinic, fitness and recreation center, community facilities, garden plots, stables

40.16 (top left)
Town Center viewed from Metra commuter rail station, Prairie Crossing.
(Gary Hack)

40.17 (top right)
Lake Aldo Leopold and wetlands, Prairie Crossing.
(Gary Hack)

40.18 (middle left)
House bordering on prairie landscape, Prairie Crossing.
(Gary Hack)

40.19 (middle right)
Residential rain garden.
(Gary Hack)

40.20 (bottom left)
Prairie Crossing Farm.
(Courtesy of Prairie Holdings Corporation)

40.21 (bottom right)
Prairie Crossing community center.
(Gary Hack)

China is planned as a series of oval-shaped *pods* that accommodate dense clusters of housing with local services, industrial areas, a city center, and a university town. Green spaces separate the pods and contain the highways, arterial roads, and mass transit lines that connect one to another and link to the larger metropolitan region. While the individual pod plans are intended to be walkable, an important issue is whether they have enough of a critical mass to support the commercial and service uses desired by the residents. At Anting New Town outside of Shanghai, which was also arranged to emulate a small German town, it has proved difficult to attract major commercial tenants to the center of the largely residential gated area, leaving the shops in the town center empty and pedestrian spaces devoid of activity.

Despite its difficulties, the self-contained community has been widely used as an organizing idea for large-scale development. It need not be planned

40.22 Sino-German Eco-Park, master plan, Qingdao, China.
(Courtesy of GMP Architekten)

40.23 Sino-German Eco-Park, first-phase development, Qingdao, China.
(Courtesy of GMP Architekten)

40.24 Anting New Town master plan, Shanghai, China.
(Albert Speer & Partner GmbH)

with curved streets and *organic forms*. Beginning in the 1970s, a prototypical 2 km (1.25 mi) square residential *superblock* was adopted as the basic unit of residential subdivision in Riyadh, and subsequently in much of Saudi Arabia. Organizing internal roadways in a pinwheel pattern minimizes the problems of through traffic. Larger blocks are included for open spaces and commercial uses near the center of each quadrant, and lot sizes are varied to allow for higher-density development along all 30 m (100 ft) rights-of-way. As in other locations, the prototype overestimated the amount of commercial space that could be supported locally by underestimating the growing popularity of large shopping centers, with the result that many commercial sites have been left vacant. Some have been converted to playgrounds, and others remain as flex space for the future.

A hierarchical roadway pattern is an essential component of the organic model for organizing communities. At the neighborhood level, local streets are kept discontinuous, making through traffic difficult. Collector roads gather the traffic and channel it to arterial roads, which usually have green space buffers, as in Columbia, or sometimes have commercial uses accessible from them. Arterial roads or highways or expressways link the community to the larger city. Major roadways become the edges of individual neighborhoods, often in tandem with a matrix of open spaces. Ironically, noisy roadways frequently occupy the quiet open spaces.

The organic-hierarchical model has largely dominated thought about how to organize large-scale communities since the invention of the garden city. The best older cities, however, are not structured so neatly. They evolve over time with layers of uses and facilities, changing as new groups inhabit a neighborhood, as shops arrive and leave and institutions are created and abandoned. As Christopher Alexander has famously asserted, "the city is not a tree" (Alexander 1965).

Consider the Glebe neighborhood in Ottawa, Canada, not far from downtown and Parliament Hill. Planned in the early twentieth century, the district is organized orthogonally, with green space around its perimeter and fingers of open space penetrating the neighborhood along historic creeks. A grid of residential streets and blocks runs in an east-west direction, each catering to a different housing type and price range. This allows residents to cluster along a street with others like themselves, but the full diversity of the

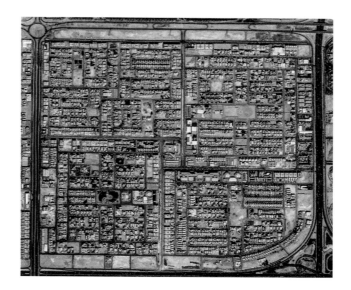

40.25 Typical neighborhood unit, Riyadh, Saudi Arabia. (Google Earth)

neighborhood is evident when one walks across the grain of streets, from modest row houses to large single-family houses. Running north-south is Bank Street, the neighborhood's shopping street and the location of public transit, within an easy 5–10-minute walk for all. And a chain of important local institutions—houses of worship, elementary schools, a tennis club, and small parks—are aligned on the quieter north-south streets in the middle of the neighborhood. The Glebe has been an attractive neighborhood for more than a century because it offers a matrix of opportunities to a diverse set of residents, and is organized in a legible way.

If an organic metaphor isn't the best way to conceptualize a city, what else is? Alexander has suggested that a better model of the good city is that of a *semilattice*, in which there is a complex set of relationships between neighborhoods, subcenters, and centers in the larger city. Translated into spatial form, the city is conceived of as a network of opportunities, with a transportation system (for pedestrians, cyclists, vehicles, and mass transit) providing access to a diverse set of choices. The form of the neighborhood does not predetermine social groupings, but enables the social relationships that develop spontaneously.

40.29 Bank Street shopping area, the Glebe, Ottawa.
(Gary Hack)

40.30 St James Tennis Club and Glebe Community Center in winter, Ottawa.
(Courtesy of the St James Tennis Club)

40.26 Aerial view of the Glebe neighborhood, Ottawa, Canada.
(Google Earth)

40.27 Semidetached houses in the Glebe, Ottawa.
(Gary Hack)

40.28 Single detached houses in the Glebe, Ottawa.
(Gary Hack)

One time-proven form for this kind of city is the gridiron plan, as in the Glebe. Towns built in a grid pattern date to antiquity: Miletus in Anatolia, based on the grid invented by the architect Hippodamus in the fifth century BC, and Chang An (now Xi'an) in China, which reached its height of one million residents in 750 AD, were planned grid cities. French bastide towns of the twelfth century and Florentine new towns two centuries later used grids as their structuring devices. Savannah, Georgia, one of the finest colonial cities in the US, follows a regular grid pattern, although its charm is not a result of regularity but of how the pattern is broken by green squares introduced into the grid. Most Spanish towns in the Americas were laid out with a grid of square blocks, and these remain at the

TREE

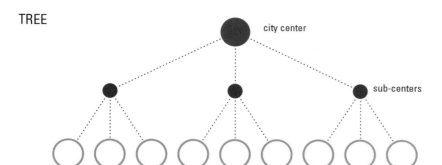

city center

sub-centers

neighborhoods

SEMI-LATTICE

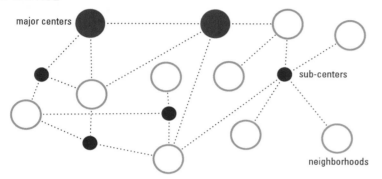

major centers

sub-centers

neighborhoods

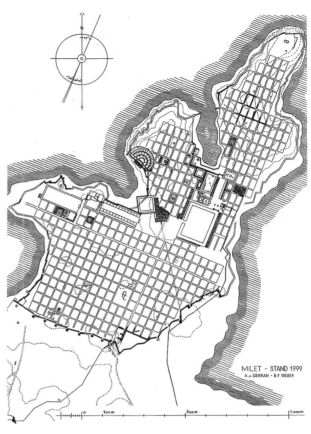

MILET – STAND 1999
A. v. GERKAN – B.F. WEBER

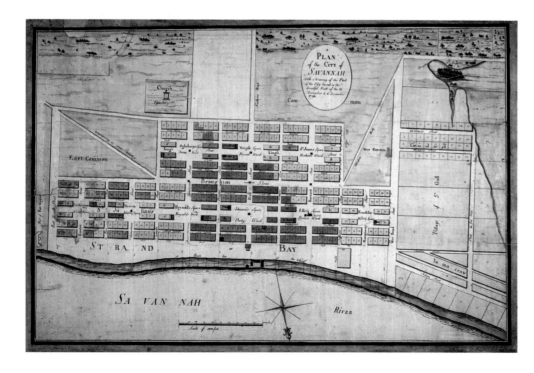

40.31 Tree versus
semilattice organization.
(Adam Tecza)

40.32 Miletus, Anatolia,
planned in the fifth century BC.
(A. van Gerken/B. F. Weber)

40.33 Plan of Savannah,
Georgia in 1796.
(City of Savannah)

center of many contemporary cities.In the mid-nineteenth century, the new towns established along the expanding network of railroads in the US and Canada adopted a regular orthogonal pattern keyed to the Northwest Survey (US) and Dominion Land Survey (Canada). Surveyors laid out the entire land area of the continent as a mile (1.6 km) square grid, dividing it into quadrants for easy distribution of the land. In Chicago and many other cities, the one-mile grid was further subdivided into 16 blocks in one direction and 8 blocks in the other (although in some areas the pattern of long and short blocks reverses each half mile). Allowing for rights-of-way of 50 ft (15 m) for streets, 25 ft (7.5 m) for rear alleys, and 80 ft (25 m) and 100 ft (30 m) on the half-mile and mile arterial roads, the resulting building blocks are 125 ft (38 m) deep by 600 ft (183 m) long. These dimensions have become the standard for many American gridiron cities. And the residential block with 8–12 houses (50–75 ft or 15–23 m lot widths) on each side of the street has become the typical social module for the traditional city. Shops and streetcars located on the mile or half-mile arterial streets are typically no more than a 10-minute walk from any home.

Orthogonal block patterns have seen a revival in many of the recent new urbanist developments of the US. Streets are minimized in width, and lots for housing are narrower than the norm, taking advantage of alleyways that provide access to garages. In some instances, alleyways have become the main access routes, with fronts of houses facing on green pedestrian areas. With higher densities than typical suburban subdivisions, walking is encouraged, and communities are planned to ensure that there are shops, schools, and other destinations within easy range. A good example of this approach may be found in the new Robert Mueller Community being developed on the site of a former airport in Austin, Texas. A new medical center anchors the area, along with offices, a range of commercial uses, schools, a variety of low-rise housing types, and active and passive recreation. It has become a new town, in town.

While land surveyors and real estate promoters were behind the grid cities of North America, in Europe engineers and architects searched for the ideal form of blocks and streets from a social and economic perspective. Ildefons Cerdà's 1859 plan for the expansion of Barcelona, l'Eixample, had broad influence on urban development plans in Europe and beyond.

40.34 Square mile module of development, with four quadrants, Chicago.
(Google Earth)

Designed to ensure light and air for all buildings, the grid is oriented at 45° from north-south, which means that all facades receive direct sunlight in the summer and winter. The blocks, or *manzanas* (*illes* in Catalan), are 113.3 m (372 ft) on a side, with corners chamfered (*chaflanes*) to assure smooth flow of traffic and provide enlarged public spaces at the intersections. Regular streets were 20 m (66 ft) wide, with the Gran Via at 50 m (165 ft) and Passeig de Gràcia as much as 60 m (197 ft). Development controls limited the heights of structures to 6–8 stories, and at least 800 m² (8,600 sq ft) was reserved in the center of each block for gardens. While the street pattern is uniform, the development of l'Eixample has become a rich array of imaginative buildings, and continues to be renewed with innovative modern structures that continue to observe the development envelope. Some central spaces have been dedicated to parking, with larger green spaces on top. Through good and bad times, l'Eixample has remained Barcelona's prime residential area.

It comes as no surprise that when Barcelona prepared for the 1992 Olympics, it chose to construct a modern version of l'Eixample for its Olympic Village.

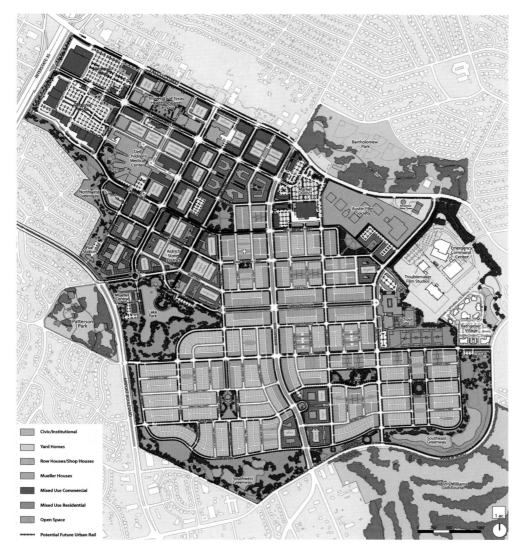

40.35 Robert Mueller
Community plan, Austin,
Texas.
(Courtesy of McCann
Adams Studio/Catellus
Austin, LLC)

Civic/Institutional

Yard Homes

Row Houses/Shop Houses

Mueller Houses

Mixed Use Commercial

Mixed Use Residential

Open Space

Potential Future Urban Rail

40.36 Mixed-use development in town center, Robert Mueller
Community, Austin.
(City of Austin)

40.37 Single-family homes, Robert Mueller Community, Austin.
(Garreth Wilcock, David Weekley Solar Home/Creative Commons)

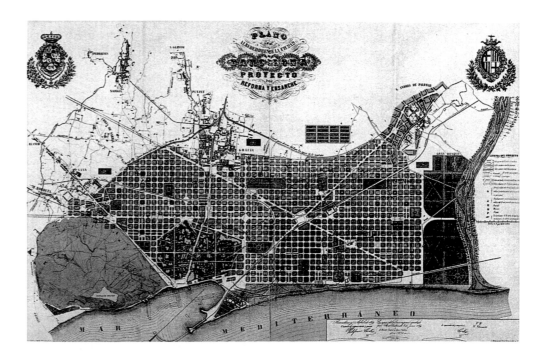

Replacing obsolete industrial areas and railway yards, 19 new blocks were created for housing, commercial uses, shops, and schools. The network of roadways continues the historical grid, and the block size is similar to the nineteenth-century plan, although adapted to account for remaining rail lines, major roadways, and other infrastructure. However, there are subtle differences in how the blocks are used, and a hierarchy of streets has been introduced. Major streets are lined with 6-story housing with commerce on the ground level, with occasional offices and hotels interspersed. Since many of the northwest-southeast streets dead-end at the waterfront park, they are less critical as movement channels, and have been reduced in size and importance. Lower-density forms of housing, schools, and institutions have been located in the centers of blocks, along with open spaces and recreation areas. In several locations, structures span the minor streets, adding to the developable area and reinforcing the continuity of the main streets. All of these moves add richness to the texture and activities of the area and reflect the functions of a modern city.

The Mueller community and Barcelona's Olympic Village provide networks of opportunities block by block for modest-sized developments. But it is also possible to apply this idea to larger-scaled developments.

The UK's last planned new city, Milton Keynes, is such a network city, providing for a rich mixture of activities and uses in every corner of the settlement. Three elements form the main structure of the city: a roadway network based on a 1 km square grid that provides accessibility across the site; green space corridors that follow the two main rivers on the site and cut across the grid; and a central zone that has been reserved for commercial and service uses.

Figure 40.39
Aerial view, l'Eixample, Barcelona.
(© Iakov Filimonov/dreamstime.com)

40.40 (top)
Plan, Olympic Village
community, Barcelona.
(Adam Tecza)

40.41 (middle left)
Paseo, Olympic Village
community, Barcelona.
(Gary Hack)

40.42 (middle right)
Housing fronting on park,
Olympic Village community,
Barcelona.
(Gary Hack)

40.43 (bottom left)
Minor street, Olympic
Village community,
Barcelona.
(Gary Hack)

40.44 (bottom right)
Internal space within block,
Olympic Village community,
Barcelona.
(Gary Hack)

Residential areas

Employment areas

Secondary & higher education

Centres

Services & community uses

Open spaces & recreation (Including buildings)

Lakes

Reserve sites

Brickfields

Railways

City road

Local road

Motorway

D A Boundary

0   2 kilometres

N

The subtleties of the Milton Keynes plan are important. The roadway grid is deliberately distorted to account for changes in topography and natural form, and to avoid impacts on several small preexisting villages. Each development cell is developed as a unique response to its site, location, and market at the time of development. The plans for the cells generally avoid crosscutting traffic, and pedestrians can get to each of the four adjacent areas via underpasses. The underpass locations are also the preferred sites for shops, schools, and other uses that serve larger areas than a single cell. Cells are joined in the city center to accommodate the large commercial complex, but blocks in the center are also subdivided to increase the frontages for commercial and office uses. Industry and office workplaces are

distributed across the city rather than concentrated in one area, to allow traffic to also be distributed throughout the day. Most of the 1989 plan has been developed, with 250,000 residents and an almost equal number of employees today. There is a great deal of variation from cell to cell in pattern and amenities, just as intended. Milton Keynes is an icon of new community development, considered by many the greatest success of the UK's new town program.

However, the city is not without its flaws. Notably, the grid does not make it easy to provide public transit because of the dispersed pattern of destinations and lack of separate transit rights-of-way. Bus service, operating on the grid roads, has been provided to the city center, railroad station, and some of the employment centers, but the many roundabouts and increasing congestion on some of the roadways compromise its efficiency. While there are many traffic-free pedestrian and cycle routes throughout the city, the underpasses below the main roads are dreary and often avoided by residents out of safety concerns. Densities are now considered too low in many of the cells, and both vacant and underdeveloped sites are being considered for a major expansion of the resident population. A new plan has been prepared for Milton Keynes, looking forward to 2031, which proposes higher-density sites for additional employment and residential construction, and the prospect of a fixed mass transit system. Plans are also afoot to introduce driverless vehicles on demand-responsive routes, which may take optimal advantage of the dispersed road system.

Rapid urbanization in Asian cities has led to a similar strategy of creating a network of arterial roads 0.5–1 km apart defining parcels for development, areas to be reserved for schools and institutions, and lands devoted to parks and open spaces. Superficially, this resembles the Milton Keynes approach, or even the older North American land development strategy. The Qunli community in Harbin, China is an example of this strategy. While there are a number of exemplary projects in Qunli, including two wetlands parks that serve as a sponge for runoff, it also illustrates that not every grid plan is an effective network of opportunities. Wide arterial roads serve as separators rather than connective tissue, and there are few active uses along them to encourage walking. Shopping areas have been constructed as independent projects, surrounded by parking and wide roadways, discouraging pedestrians. Generally each residential parcel is designed as a freestanding project, usually gated to prevent outsiders from passing through. And public spaces—parks, boulevards, cultural institutions—while creatively designed, are independent destinations rather than spaces used during daily routines.

The lesson for site planners from Qunli is that planning for infrastructure and parcels is not enough to ensure that a development meets the aspiration of becoming a fine community. The scale of roadways, the bordering uses along sidewalks and parks, and the distinctions between public and private realms will ultimately determine how a community functions and the opportunities for human interaction. The site planner's job does not end upon completion of the development plan.

40.46 Aerial view illustrating variation within the grid in 2012, Milton Keynes.
(Google Earth)

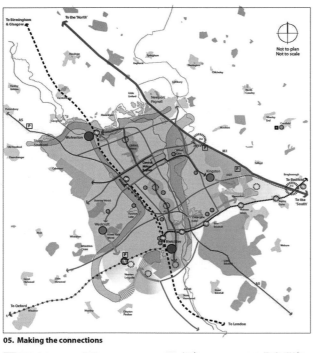

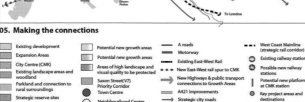

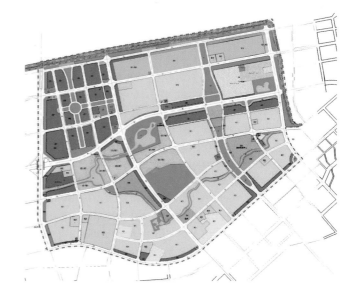

05. Making the connections

40.47 (top left) Plan for 2031, Milton Keynes. (Milton Keynes Commission)

40.48 (top right) Plan for the Qunli community, Harbin, China. (Courtesy of Turenscape)

40.49 (bottom) Aerial view of development in 2012, Qunli community, Harbin. (Google Earth)

Sustainable Communities

The terms "sustainable" and "eco" have become the obligatory adjectives for current new communities. However, planning and building large-scale developments that are truly resilient, that reduce carbon emissions and diminish our dependence on nonrenewable resources, is a challenging assignment. It requires significant initial investment in technologies that will be earned back over time, a market that is receptive to new ways of living, and changes in human attitudes and behavior. Only a few recently built communities have achieved these goals.

Start with the most important objectives:

Reducing carbon emissions directly attributable to the community—in its construction and operation, and as individuals live in the community. Among the large variables are fuels used for heating and electricity generation, the amount of energy used for mobility, the operation of public water and sewer systems, and maintenance of the public realm.

Lowering energy consumption by reducing the dependence on private automobiles, by encouraging walking, cycling, use of mass transit and shared vehicles. Movement is an *induced demand* that can be reduced by locating housing, shopping, and workplaces in closer proximity, and by increasing densities.

Creating energy from renewable and low-carbon sources on the site, such as solar, wind, and waste energy from industrial and building sources.

Reducing, reusing, and recycling disposable materials, both inorganic and organic. Creating closed loops of energy and materials on the site is one strategy.

40.50 View of Yuyang wetland park, Qunli community, Harbin.
(© loveharbin/dreamstime.com)

40.51 Shopping center along central spine, Qunli community, Harbin.
(Gary Hack)

40.52 Gated residential areas, Qunli community, Harbin.
(Gary Hack)

40.53 Central spine of Qunli community, Harbin.
(Gary Hack)

Retaining, treating, and reusing rainwater and
wastewater on the site. Water is too valuable to
be used only once, and can be too destructive
when discharged into streams after major storm
events. Exporting runoff simply shifts the
problems to others.

Protecting the community from severe weather
events, sea level rise, and extreme droughts,
landslide hazards, forest fires, and flooding. Mitigating the expected 2.5°C (5°F) temperature rise
and heat island effects.

Maintaining and extending the capacity of natural
systems to absorb water, filter it, recharge the
groundwater, and support terrestrial and marine
life, even in the face of greater climate extremes.

Other objectives, which may not seem directly relevant, can have important impacts on the sustainability
of a community. An example is providing a diverse
supply of housing for a broad band of incomes and
ages. Segregating communities can increase the need
for travel and make walking destinations less desirable.

A meaningful set of objectives must be accompanied by *metrics*—as the saying goes, if you can't
measure, you can't manage things. Some metrics are
obvious: the amount of energy consumed per capita,
the amount of energy produced on the site, the vehicle
miles traveled in private automobiles per capita, water
use per capita, the rate of recycling, the amount of food
produced locally, and so on (see chapter 18). But other
metrics are more qualitative and can only be scored
in relative terms. A community's participation in the
maintenance of its public realm is an example, as is
local membership in social organizations, both of
which are important to the social capital that will be
required in times of emergency.

The Tianjin Eco-City (formerly the Sino-Singapore
Eco-City) set down 26 quantitative and qualitative indicators to guide its development efforts and to be used
as measures of progress. The new community will ultimately house 350,000 residents on its 30 km² (11.6 sq
mi) site and provide an environment for technologically sophisticated industries. It is being built on land
that is largely reclaimed from the sea, having been
used as salt evaporation ponds for many years. The
plan includes extensive restoration of wetlands and the
construction of a new natural environment that will

buffer the city. While one of the project's objectives
is to have no net loss of wetlands, in reality the issue
is constructing wetlands that are sustainable in the
future in a densely packed environment. A mass transit
system will connect a series of five new centers with
a high-density mix of employment uses and housing.
The roadway network is largely a grid pattern, with
individual blocks housing gated compounds, much as
in the Qinli community discussed earlier. Massive solar
arrays have been installed along the edges of major
roadways, a solution that provides a noise barrier while
generating a significant amount of energy.

A close look at the indicators for Tianjin Eco-City
suggests that they are extremely ambitious—90% of
the trips are to be green trips; water consumption
levels are to be well below those of typical new developments, and the proposed waste generation and
recycling rates are also a stretch, as examples. Unfortunately, the infrastructure and first-phase development
patterns for the city do not match these expectations.
Wide arterial roadways, which conform to national
norms, encourage private auto use, and gated communities with no street presence discourage walking.
There is little evidence that people moving to the eco-
city are willing to part with their vehicles, and the delay
in creating mass transit systems has made private
automobiles obligatory. Generous landscaped areas
require large quantities of water for irrigation, and
few of the landscape patterns rely on natural runoff.
These contradictions highlight the importance of
implementation if sustainability targets are to be met.
An ecological community requires residents to adopt
habits that are conservation-minded.

An older eco-community in the Netherlands demonstrates how important it is for residents to share a
commitment to an ecologically attuned lifestyle. At the
Lanxmeer community in Culemborg, near Utrecht, a
core of prospective residents participated in the design
of their community, gaining a consensus on the life
patterns they would accept to live a sustainable lifestyle.
On a site that once was kept undeveloped to protect
water quality for the city's wells, the residents and planners agreed that the essential natural systems should
remain undisturbed. All rainwater would be maintained on the site and purified by natural processes so
that its quality was high enough for recreation use. An
orchard would be preserved to provide fruits for the

Key Performance Indicators (KPIs) for Sino-Singapore Tianjin Eco-City, Tianjin, China

Quantitative KPIs

(1) Good natural environment

KPI 1: Ambient air quality
The air quality in the Eco-city should meet at least China's National Ambient Air Quality Grade II Standard for at least 310 days. The SO_2 and NO_X content in the ambient air should not exceed the limits stipulated for China's National Ambient Air Quality Grade 1 standard for at least 155 days.

KPI 2: Quality of water bodies within the Eco-city
Water bodies in the Eco-city should meet Grade IV of China's latest national standards by 2020.

KPI 3: Quality of water from taps
Water from all taps should be potable.

KPI 4: Noise pollution levels
Noise levels must fully comply with China's standards for environmental noise in urban areas.

KPI 5: Carbon emission per unit GDP
The carbon emission per unit GDP in the Eco-city should not exceed 150 tonnes C per US$1 million.

KPI 6: Net loss of natural wetlands
There should be no net loss of natural wetlands in the Eco-city.

(2) Healthy balance in the man-made environment

KPI 7: Proportion of green buildings
All buildings in the Eco-city should meet green building standards.

KPI 8: Native vegetation index
At least 70% of the plant varieties in the Eco-city should be native plants/vegetation.

KPI 9: Per capita public green space
The public green space should be at least 12 square meters per person by 2013.

(3) Good lifestyle habits

KPI 10: Per capita daily water consumption
The daily water consumption per day each person should not exceed 120 liters by 2013.

KPI 11: Per capita daily domestic waste generation
The amount of domestic waste generated by each person should not exceed 0.8 kg by 2013.

KPI 12: Proportion of green trips
At least 90% of trips within the Eco-city should be in the form of green trips by 2020. Green trips refer to nonmotorized transport, i.e., cycling and walking, as well as trips on public transport.

KPI 13: Overall recycling rate
At least 60% of total waste should be recycled by 2013.

KPI 14: Access to free recreational and sports amenities
All residential areas in the Eco-city should have access to free recreational and sports amenities within a walking distance of 500 m by 2013.

KPI 15: Waste treatment
All hazardous and domestic waste in the Eco-city should be rendered nontoxic through treatment.

KPI 16: Barrier-free accessibility
The Eco-city should have 100% barrier-free access.

KPI 17: Services network coverage
The entire Eco-city will have access to key infrastructure services, such as recycled water, gas, broadband, electricity, and heating, by 2013.

KPI 18: Proportion of affordable public housing
At least 20% of housing in the Eco-city will be in the form of subsidized public housing by 2013.

(4) Developing a dynamic and efficient economy

KPI 19: Use of renewable energy
The proportion of energy utilized in the Eco-city in the form of renewable energy, such as solar and geothermal energy, should be at least 20% by 2020.

KPI 20: Use of water from nontraditional sources
At least 50% of the Eco-city's water supply will be from nontraditional sources such as desalination and recycled water by 2020.

KPI 21: Proportion of R&D scientists and engineers in the Eco-city workforce
There should be at least 50 R&D scientists and engineers per 10,000 workforce in the Eco-city by 2020.

KPI 22: Employment-housing equilibrium index
At least 50% of the employable residents in the Eco-city should be employed in the Eco-city by 2013.

Qualitative KPIs

KPI 23: Maintain a safe and healthy ecology through green consumption and low-carbon operations.

KPI 24: Adopt innovative policies that will promote regional collaboration and improve the environment of the surrounding regions.

KPI 25: Give prominence to the river estuarine culture to preserve history and cultural heritage and manifest its uniqueness.

KPI 26: Complement the development of recycling industries and promote the orderly development of the surrounding regions.

Source: Tianjin Eco-City, http://tianjinecocity.gov.sg/KPI.htm#2

40.54 Plan of Tianjin Eco-City, Tianjin, China.
(Sino-Singapore Tianjin Eco-City)

40.55 Aerial rendering of future development, Tianjin Eco-City, Tianjin.
(Keppel Corporation)

40.56 Reconstructed wetlands, Tianjin Eco-City, Tianjin.
(Courtesy of Richard Register/EcoCity Builders)

40.57 Solar array, Tianjin Eco-City, Tianjin.
(Sino-Singapore Tianjin Eco-City)

community, and areas would be set aside for residents to keep chickens and domesticated animals.

Housing in Lanxmeer was planned as a series of clusters, with common space for each, used as the residents of the cluster decide. A variety of accommodations are available, and each complex incorporates passive design or active solar panels providing up to 25% of the energy needs of their complex each year. In addition to schools and common facilities, the community also provides sites for employment—live-work accommodations, small offices, and larger sites for established firms.

Most of Lanxmeer is car-free. Residents park their cars at the edge of the complex, where individual storage areas are also located, and walk to their homes five minutes or less away. Those who commute to work elsewhere by train walk or cycle to the station, on the opposite side of the site. If large items need to be delivered, cars or small trucks are allowed to use the pedestrian pathways, traveling at pedestrian speeds.

Maintaining the collective lands, worrying about recycling and disposal, and overseeing the operations of the heating and energy systems require a significant commitment on the part of all residents. The buy-in to this participatory lifestyle began with the initial planning of the complex, and has been passed along to new residents as they arrive. In exchange for occasional hard work maintaining the public spaces and deciding upon the finances of the group, there is the satisfaction of being part of a caring community with an abiding commitment to their living environment.

Lanxmeer has demonstrated the virtue of an ecological community, but with fewer than 1,000 residents it is small enough that many residents know or recognize others when they meet them. Can this kind of commitment to ecological living be sustained at a much larger scale? Hammarby Sjöstad, Stockholm's new ecological community, offers some clues.

The site for Hammarby Sjöstad, 6 km (3.5 mi) from the center of the city, was a derelict industrial and waste disposal site when the city government acquired the lands and began its plans to create a model community. The aspiration was to create a highly livable, walkable, and sustainable community served by the most advanced technologies for infrastructure and movement. While the infrastructure would become the responsibility of the city government and local public utilities, Hammarby Sjöstad would be built by private developers, working within a parcel plan and design guidelines planned by the city. Competition and choice became the watchwords for developers and their architects, each trying to best their neighbors in terms of quality and price of the housing they offered. Densities are high, but are offset by the generous amount of open space in the form of semipublic courtyards and public parks and green spaces. The extraordinary waterfront site offers much more openness than the simple area of green.

Infrastructure systems at Hammarby Sjöstad were guided by the concept of creating closed systems—waste turned into supply. Wastewater is separated, with gray water recycled or used for irrigation and organic matter converted to fertilizer or feedstock for energy production. Garbage is separated at the source and transported via underground vacuum tubes to the energy center, where organic matter is burned for electricity or district heating and recyclables are packaged for transport to manufacturers. Rainwater that falls onto the site is channeled through natural filters until it is usable for irrigation. Natural vegetation on water's edges helps improve water quality while serving as a buffer for flood surges. Each system has been thought through, and is closely monitored to judge whether it meets expectations.

Before housing was constructed, a light rail system was put in place along the main boulevard of Hammarby Sjöstad. Buses also use the same right-of-way, radiating out beyond the transit routes. Residents have other choices for mobility as well: schools, local offices, and most shops they need are within a short walk; there are bicycle and car share services distributed through the community; and ferry services connect to central Stockholm and other areas. The high quality of these options means that only about 21% of the trips are by private automobile and only 45% of households own a vehicle (Foletta and Field 2011). Automobile CO_2 emissions are about half those of comparable areas in Stockholm, which as a city has one of the lowest emissions rates in the world.

Hammarby Sjöstad probably attracts those who wish to live a more sustainable lifestyle, but it also makes this possible through its physical plan, housing design, technological investments, and infrastructure. Conversations with residents suggest that they take great pride in both the quality of life and the commitment they have made to live responsibly in the environment.

Lanxmeer, Culemborg, Netherlands

40.58 (left)
Site plan for Lanxmeer, Culemborg, Netherlands. (Hyco Verhaagen/Courtesy of Stichting EVA)

40.59 (top right)
Entrance to auto-free zone, with school on right. (Gary Hack)

40.60 (middle right)
Housing cluster, created and maintained by surrounding residents. (Gary Hack)

40.61 (bottom right)
Seniors housing cluster. (Gary Hack)

The community of Lanxmeer has its origins in a participatory design process among prospective residents seeking to design a community that encouraged social interaction, minimized the demands on the land, reduced energy use and the disposal of water and wastes, and produced as much energy, food, and water locally as possible. The happy result is a unique environment, largely free of cars, with clusters of housing each fitting the preferences of its residents. There are apartment units, special units for the elderly, row houses and stacked row houses, individual houses, and specially designed live-work units. Residents of each cluster share common outdoor spaces and have more private spaces in the form of balconies and gardens. Each housing cluster incorporates passive and active solar energy providing up to 25% of its energy needs, and units are heated by a district heating system that employs geothermal energy. Recycling of solid wastes is mandated.

The site plan conserves an orchard and other gardening spaces, and provides wetlands to absorb storm runoff and treat gray water from units. The area is lushly planted and carefully tended, largely through volunteer efforts. Parking is largely confined to the outer edges of the community, where storage areas for residents are also located. The area nearest the

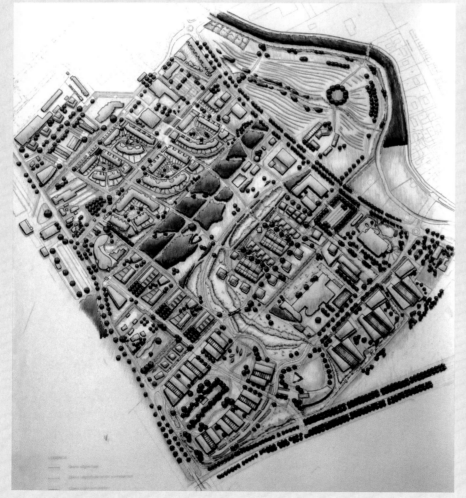

rail station is also the site of substantial offices and institutional uses, which balances the flow of commuters.

Residents of Lanxmeer remain deeply engaged in the management and operations of their community. They own and manage the district heating facility and assume responsibility for all site maintenance and collection of wastes. They have an active array of arts and social activities extending throughout the year. The community is remarkably diverse, but individuals share a common commitment to ecological living.

Location: Culemborg, The Netherlands, 18 km (10 mi) from Utrecht
Site planners: Marleen Kaptein, Jean Eigeman, Joachim Eble, Bugel Hajema
Developer: Stichting EVA, Marleen Kaptein
Site area: 24 ha (59 ac)
Uses: diverse housing types (400 units), including live-work units; mixed-use (institutional housing, 50,000 m² [538,000 sq ft], offices, modest commercial space); open space (farm, orchards, recreation areas, allotment gardens, buffers)
Facilities: elementary school, creche, art schools, commuter rail stop adjacent, convenience shops and services, district heating facility, local solar energy utility, common storage areas, car share

40.62 (top left)
Office area.
(Gary Hack)

40.63 (middle left)
Wetlands area with community orchard.
(Gary Hack)

40.64 (bottom left)
Montessori School and individually owned houses.
(Gary Hack)

40.65 (top right)
Live-work housing with space for residents' offices.
(Gary Hack)

40.66 (middle right)
Recreation pond fed by filtered runoff.
(Gary Hack)

40.67 (bottom right)
Environmental education boards.
(Gary Hack)

**Hammarby Sjöstad,
Stockholm Sweden**

Hammarby Sjöstad is a stellar example of an integrated, environmentally sustainable development on a brownfield site. Planned by Stockholm's City Planning Bureau, it anticipates having 24,000 residents of all ages and incomes, with residential areas averaging 130 persons/ha (320 persons per ac). Over 30% of the site is devoted to industry and commercial uses, employing over 5,000. It has the full range of educational and cultural facilities for a community of its size. Over 40 developers, with 30 architects, have constructed housing on the site, competing to provide the most attractive and energy-efficient units for sale (55%) and rent (45%). Mixed-use development lines the 37.5 m (123 ft) boulevard that is the spine of the community, with shops, schools, offices, and housing above, all within a few steps of public transit.

Hammarby set high targets in terms of energy efficiency, reuse of rainwater and wastewater, recycling of materials, and reduction of private automobile use. Its mantra is to create closed systems where materials are used to their maximum advantage: 50% of electricity and district heating is derived from recycled organic and combustible waste; solar energy panels on buildings provide half of the energy needed for hot water and contribute to electrical supply; 52% of residents use public transport and 27% commute by bicycle or walking; rainwater and gray water are filtered naturally and used for nonpotable water and irrigation; and biogas harvested from the former brownfields contributes to the supply of energy for heating. The green and technologically advanced infrastructure systems were installed from

40.68 Plan of Hammarby Sjöstad, Stockholm, Sweden.
(Stockholm City Planning Department)

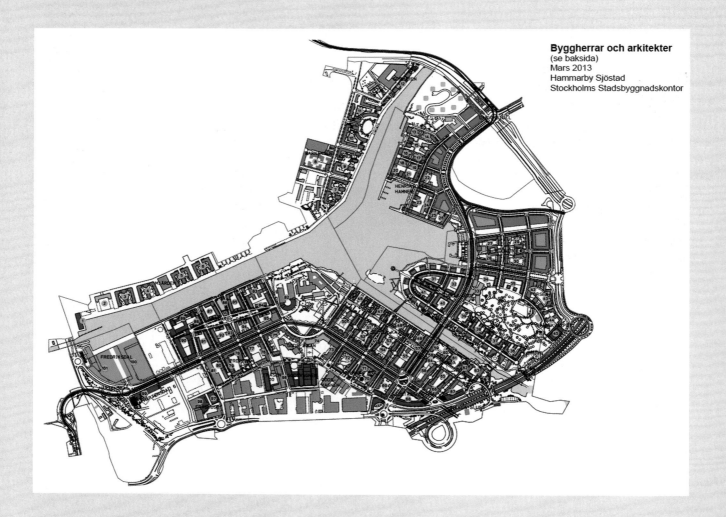

Byggherrar och arkitekter
(se baksida)
Mars 2013
Hammarby Sjöstad
Stockholms Stadsbyggnadskontor

the beginning. Notably, the light rail system serving Hammarby and connecting it to the Stockholm Metro was in place before the first residents arrived, obviating the need for purchasing cars. Car sharing and bicycle sharing further reduce the need for private automobiles.

Recreation opportunities are an important attraction of Hammarby. Located on an inlet of the city's archipelago, it offers opportunities for recreational boating, and no resident is more than 5 minutes' walk from the water. The water's edge is lined by promenades, cafés, and places to relax. The development goal is to provide 25 m² of public open space per apartment, and 15 m² additional open space in private courtyards. This is an equivalent of 18 m² per person, or 4.5 ac per 1,000 population in green space.

Location: Stockholm, Sweden
Site planner: Jan Inghe-Hagström, Stockholm City Planning Bureau
Developer: Hammarby Sjöstad Project Team, City Department of Streets and Real Estate Administration, with other city departments and public utility companies; housing and commercial uses by private or nonprofit developers
Site area (land): 160 ha (395 ac)
Uses: 10,800 apartments, 23% social housing, 29% privately owned, 37% cooperative; 290,000 m² (3,121,500 sq ft) office, light industry, and commerce; 30 ha (74 ac) green space
Facilities: preschools (10), schools (3), cultural institutions, health care centers, district energy facility, vacuum garbage collection system, car share and bicycle share systems

40.69 Aerial view of Hammarby Sjöstad. (Hammarby Sjöstad Ekonomisk Foerening)

**Hammarby Sjöstad,
Stockholm Sweden**

40.70 (top left)   Main boulevard with transit stop.
(Gary Hack)

40.71 (top right)   Housing courtyard with vacuum refuse ports.
(Courtesy of EnVac)

40.72 (bottom)   Waterfront view of Hammarby Sjöstad.
(Arild Vagen/Wikimedia Commons)

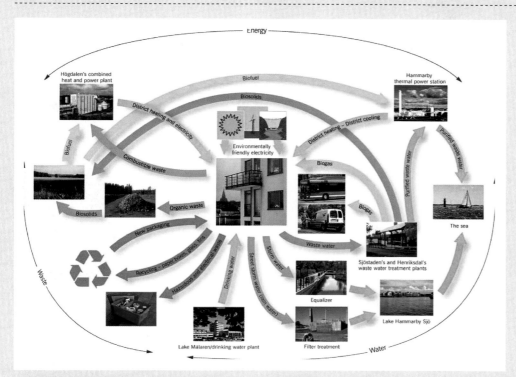

40.73 (top)
Closed-loop system
diagram, Hammarby
Sjöstad.
(Stockholm City Planning
Department)

40.74 (middle)
Sustainability strategies,
Hammarby Sjöstad.
(Courtesy of V. S. Gullapalli,
K. Keyimu, Roel M. Martinez,
R. Mittai, Mohd A. Naqvi,
C. Sichel, and M. A. Wanis
Walaa, Politecnico
di Milano)

40.75 (bottom left)
Rainwater detention park.
(Gary Hack)

40.76 (bottom right)
District energy plant.
(Courtesy of Urbed)

References

AASHTO. 1999. *Guide for the Development of Bicycle Facilities*. 3rd ed. Washington, DC: American Association of State Highway and Transportation Officials.

AASHTO. 2011. *A Policy on Geometric Design of Highways and Streets*. 6th ed. Washington, DC: American Association of State Highway and Transportation Officials.

Abu Bakar, Abu Hassan, and Soo Cheen Khor. 2013. A Framework for Assessing the Sustainable Urban Development. *Precedia—Social and Behavioral Sciences* 85: 484–492. http://www .sciencedirect.com/science/article/pii/S1877042813025044.

A. C. M. Homes. n.d. Silang Township Project. http://www .acmhomes.com/home/?page=project&id=23.

Acorn. 2013. Acorn UK Lifestyle Categories. http://www .businessballs.com/freespecialresources/acorn-demographics -2013.pdf.

Adams, Charles. 1934. *The Design of Residential Areas: Basic Considerations, Principles and Methods*. Cambridge, MA: Harvard University Press.

Adams, David, and Steven Tiesdell, eds. 2013. *Shaping Places: Urban Planning, Design and Development*. London: Routledge.

Adams, Thomas. 1934. *The Design of Residential Areas: Basic Considerations, Principles and Methods*. Cambridge, MA: Harvard University Press.

Adnan, Muhammad. 2014. Passenger Car Equivalent Factors in Heterogenous Traffic Environment: Are We Using the Right Numbers? *Procedia Engineering* 77:106–113. http://www .sciencedirect.com/science/article/pii/S1877705814009813.

Agili, d.o.o. 2017. Modelur Sketchup Tool. http://modelur.eu.

Agrawal, G. P. 2002. *Fiber-Optic Communication Systems*. Hoboken, NJ: Wiley.

Alexander, Christopher. 1965. The City Is Not a Tree. *Architectural Forum* 172 (April/May). http://www.bp.ntu.edu.tw/wp-content /uploads/2011/12/06-Alexander-A-city-is-not-a-tree.pdf.

Alexander, Christopher, and Serge Chermayeff. 1965. *Community and Privacy: Towards a New Architecture of Humanism*. Garden City, NY: Anchor Books.

Alexander, Christopher, Sara Ishikawa, Murray Silverstein, Max Jacobson, Ingrid Fiksdahl-King, and Shlomo Angel. 1977. *A Pattern Language: Towns, Buildings, Construction*. New York: Oxford University Press. See also https://www.patternlanguage.com/.

Al-Kodmany, Kheir. 2015. Tall Buildings and Elevators: A Review of Recent Technological Advances. *Buildings* 5:1070–1104. doi:10.3390/buildings5031070.

Al-Kodmany, Kheir, and M. M. Ali. 2013. *The Future of the City: Tall Buildings and Urban Design*. Southampton, UK: WIT Press.

Alonso, Frank, and Carolyn A. E. Greenwell. 2013. Underground vs. Overhead: Power Line Installation Cost Comparison and Mitigation. *PowerGrid International* 18:2. http://www.elp.com /articles/powergrid_international/print/volume-18/issue-2 /features/underground-vs-overhead-power-line-installation-cost -comparison-.html.

Alshalalfah, B. W., and A. S. Shalaby. 2007. Case Study: Relationship of Walk Access and Distance to Transit with Service, Travel and Personal Characteristics. *Journal of Urban Planning and Development* 133 (2): 114–118.

Alterman, Rachel. 2007. Much More Than Land Assembly: Land Readjustment for the Supply of Urban Public Services. In Yu-Hung Hong and Barrie Needham, eds., *Analyzing Land Readjustment: Economics, Law and Collective Action*, 57–85. Cambridge, MA: Lincoln Institute of Land Policy.

Altunkasa, M. Faruk, and Cengiz Uslu. 2004. The Effects of Urban Green Spaces on House Prices in the Upper Northwest Urban Development Area of Adna (Turkey). *Turkish Journal of Agriculture and Forestry* 28:203–209.

American Cancer Society. n.d. EMF Explained Series. http://www .emfexplained.info/?ID=25821.

American Institute of Architects. 2012. Insights and Innovations: The State of Senior Housing. Design for Aging Review 10. http:// www.greylit.org/sites/default/files/collected_files/2012-11/Insights -and-Innovation-The-State-of-Senior-Housing-AARP.pdf.

American Planning Association. 2006. *Planning and Urban Design Standards*. Hoboken, NJ: Wiley.

Andris, Clio. n.d. Interactive Site Suitability Modeling: A Better Method of Understanding the Effects of Input Data. Esri, ArcUser Online. http://www.esri.com/news/arcuser/0408/suitability.html.

Appleyard, Donald. 1976. *Planning a Pluralist City: Conflicting Realities on Ciudad Guayana*. Cambridge, MA: MIT Press.

Applied Economics. 2003. Maricopa Association of Governments Regional Growing Smarter Implementation: Solid Waste Management. https://www.azmag.gov/Documents/pdf/cms .resource/Solid-Waste-Management.pdf.

Aquaterra. 2008. International Comparisons of Domestic Per Capita Consumption. Prepared for the UK Environment Agency, Bristol, England.

Arbor Day Foundation. Tree Guide. http://www.arborday.org.

ArcGIS 9.2. n.d. http://webhelp.esri.com/arcgisdesktop/9.2/index .cfm?TopicName=Performing_a_viewshed_analysis.

Arch Daily. n.d. Shopping Centers. http://www.archdaily.com /search/projects/categories/shopping-centers.

Architectural Energy Corporation. 2007. Impact Analysis: 2008 Update to the California Energy Efficiency Standards for Residential and Nonresidential Buildings. California Energy Commission. http://www.energy.ca.gov/title24/2008standards /rulemaking/documents/2007-11-07_IMPACT_ANALYSIS.PDF.

Ataer, O. Ercan. 2006. Storage of Thermal Energy. In Yalcin Abdullah Gogus, ed., *Energy Storage Systems: Encyclopedia of Life Support Systems (EOLSS). Developed under the Auspices of UNESCO*. Oxford: Eolss Publishers; http://www.eolss.net.

Atkins. 2013. Facebook Campus Project, Menlo Park, EIR Addendum. City of Menlo Park, Community Development Department. https://www.menlopark.org/DocumentCenter /View/2622.

Audubon International. n.d. Sustainable Communities Program. http://www.auduboninternational.org/Resources/Documents /SCP%20Fact%20Sheet.pdf.

Austin Design Commission. 2009. Design Guidelines for Austin. City of Austin. https://www.austintexas.gov/sites/default/files /files/Boards_and_Commissions/Design_Commission_urban _design_guidelines_for_austin.pdf.

Ayers Saint Gross Architects. 2007. Comparing Campuses. http:// asg-architects.com/ideas/comparing-campuses/.

Bailie, R. C., J. W. Everett, Bela G. Liptak, David H. F. Liu, F. Mack Rugg, and Michael S. Switzenbaum. 1999. *Solid Waste*. Chapter 10. Boca Raton, FL: CRC Press. https://docs.google.com/viewer?url =ftp%3A%2F%2Fftp.energia.bme.hu%2Fpub%2Fhullgazd%2F Environmental%2520Engineers%27%2520Handbook%2FCh10.pdf.

Barber, N. L. 2014. Summary of Estimated Water Use in the United States in 2010. US Geological Survey, Fact Sheet 2014-3109. doi:10.3133/fs20143109.

Barker, Roger. 1963. On the Nature of the Environment. *Journal of Social Issues* 19 (4): 17–38.

Barr, Vilma. 1976. Improving City Streets for Use at Night – The Norfolk Experiment. *Lighting Design and Application* (April), 25.

Barton-Aschman Associates. 1982. *Shared Parking*. Washington, DC: Urban Land Institute.

Bassuk, Nina, Deanna F. Curtis, B. Z. Marrranca, and Barb Nea. 2009. Site Assessment and Tree Selection for Stress Tolerance: Recommended Urban Trees. Urban Horticulture Institute, Cornell University. http://www.hort.cornell.edu/uhi/outreach/recurbtree /pdfs/~recurbtrees.pdf.

Battery Park City Authority. n.d. Battery Park City. http://bpca.ny .gov/.

Bauer, D., W. Heidemann, and H. Müller-Steinhagen. 2007. Central Solar Heating Plants with Seasonal Heat Storage. CISBAT 2007, Innovation in the Built Environment, Lausanne, September 4–5. http://www.itw.uni-stuttgart.de/dokumente/Publikationen /publikationen_07-07.pdf.

Beatley, Timothy. 2000. *Green Urbanism: Learning from European Cities*. Washington, DC: Island Press.

Beckham, Barry. 2004. *The Digital Photographer's Guide to Photoshop Elements: Improve Your Photos and Create Fantastic Special Effects*. London: Lark Books.

Belle, David. 2009. *Parkour*. Paris: Éditions Intervista.

Ben-Joseph, Eran. n.d. Residential Street Standards and Neighborhood Traffic Control: A Survey of Cities' Practices and Public Official's Attitudes. Institute of Urban and Regional Planning, University of California at Berkeley. nacto.org/docs/usdg /residential_street_standards_benjoseph.pdf.

Benson, E. D., J. L. Hansen, A. L. Schwartz, Jr., and G. T. Smersh. 1998. Pricing Residential Amenities: The Value of a View. *Journal of Real Estate Finance and Economics* 16:55–73.

Bentley Systems, Inc. n.d. PowerCivil for Country. https://www .bentley.com/en/products/product-line/civil-design-software /powercivil-for-country.

Berger, Alan. 2007. *Drosscape: Wasting Land in Urban America*. New York: Princeton Architectural Press.

Berhage, Robert D., et al. 2009. *Green Roofs for Stormwater Runoff Control*. National Risk Management Research Laboratory, Environmental Protection Agency.

Beyard, Michael D., Mary Beth Corrigan, Anita Kramer, Michael Pawlukiewicz, and Alexa Bach. 2006. *Ten Principles for Rethinking the Mall*. Washington, DC: Urban Land Institute; http://uli.org /wp-content/uploads/ULI-Documents/Tp_MAll.ashx_.pdf.

Bidlack, James, Shelley Jansky, and Kingsley Stern. 2013. *Stern's Introductory Plant Biology*. 10th ed. New York: McGraw-Hill. http://www.mhhe.com/biosci/pae/botany/botany_map/articles /article_10.html.

Biohabitats. n.d. Hassalo on Eighth Wastewater Treatment and Reuse System. http://www.biohabitats.com/projects /hassalo-on-8th-wastewater-treatment-reuse-system-2/.

Bioregional Development Group. 2009. BedZED Seven Years On: The Impact of the UK's Best Known Eco-Village and Its Residents. http://www.bioregional.com/wp-content/uploads/2014/10/ BedZED_seven_years_on.pdf.

Blakely, Edward J., and Mary Gail Snyder. 1997. *Fortress America: Gated Communities in the United States*. Washington, DC: Brookings Institution Press.

Blondel, Jacques-François, and Pierre Patte. 1771. *Cours d'architecture ou traité de la décoration, distribution et constructions des bâtiments contenant les leçons données en 1750, et les années suivantes*. Paris: Dessaint.

Bloomington/Monroe County Metropolitan Planning Organization. 2009. Complete Streets Policy. https://www.smartgrowthamerica .org/app/legacy/documents/cs/policy/cs-in-bmcmpo-policy.pdf.

Bohl, Charles C. 2002. *Place Making*. Washington, DC: Urban Land Institute.

Bond, Sandy. 2007. The Effect of Distance to Cell Phone Towers on House Prices in Florida. *Appraisal Journal* 75 (4): 362. https:// professional.sauder.ubc.ca/re_creditprogram/course_resources /courses/content/appraisal%20journal/2007/bond-effect.pdf.

Bonino, Michele, and Filippo De Pieri, eds. 2015. *Beijing Danwei: Industrial Heritage in the Contemporary City*. Berlin: Jovis.

Botma, H., and W. Mulder. 1993. Required Widths of Paths, Lanes, Roads and Streets for Bicycle Traffic. In *17 Summaries of Major Dutch Research Studies about Bicycle Traffic*. De Bilt, Netherlands: Grontmij Consulting Engineers.

Bourassa, Steven C., and Yu-Hung Hong, eds. 2003. *Leasing Public Land*. Cambridge, MA: Lincoln Institute for Land Policy.

BRE Global Ltd. 2008. BREEAM GULF. http://www.breeam.org.

BRE Global Ltd. 2012. BREEAM Communities Technical Manual. http://www.breeam.org/communitiesmanual/.

Brewer, Jim, et al. 2001. *Geometric Design Practices for European Roads*. Washington, DC: US Federal Highway Administration.

British Water. 2009. Flows and Loads – Sizing Criteria, Treatment Capacity for Sewage Treatment Systems. http://www.clfabrication .co.uk/lib/downloads/Flows%20and%20Loads%20-%203.pdf.

Brooks, R. R. 1998. *Plants That Hyperaccumulate Heavy Metals*. New York: CAB International.

Brown, Michael J., Sue Grimmond, and Carlo Ratti. 2001. Comparison of Methodologies for Computing Sky View Factor in Urban Environments. Los Alamos National Laboratory. http://senseable.mit.edu/papers/pdf/2001_Brown_Grimmond _Ratti_ISEH.pdf.

Brown, Peter Hendee. 2015. *How Real Estate Developers Think: Design, Profits and the Community*. Philadelphia: University of Pennsylvania Press.

Brown, Sally L., Rufus L. Chaney, J. Scott Angle, and Alan J. M. Baker. 1995. Zinc and Cadmium Uptake by Hyperaccumulator Thlaspi caerulescens and Metal Tolerant Silene vulgaris Grown on Sludge-Amended Soils. *Environmental Science and Technology* 29:1581–1585.

Brown, Scott A., Kelleann Foster, and Alex Duran. 2007. Pennsylvania Standards for Residential Site Development. Pennsylvania State University. http://www.engr.psu.edu /phrc/Land%20Development%20Standards/PP%20 presentation%20on%20Pennsylvania%20Residential%20 Land%20Development%20Standards.pdf.

Bruun, Ole. 2008. *An Introduction to Feng Shui*. Cambridge: Cambridge University Press.

Bruzzone, Anthony. 2012. Guidelines for Ferry Transportation Services. National Academy of Sciences, Transit Cooperative Research Program Report 152.

Brydges, Taylor. 2012. Understanding the Occupational Typology of Canada's Labor Force. Martin Prosperity Institute, University of Toronto. http://martinprosperity.org/papers/TB%20 Occupational%20Typology%20White%20Paper_v09.pdf

Buchanan, Colin. 1963. *Traffic in Towns: A Study of the Long Term Problems of Traffic in Urban Areas*. London: Her Majesty's Stationery Office.

Burian, Steven J., Stephen J. Nix, Robert E. Pitt, and S. Rocky Durrans. 2000. Urban Wastewater Management in the United States: Past, Present, and Future. *Journal of Urban Technology* 7 (3): 33–62. http://www.sewerhistory.org/articles/whregion/urban_wwm_mgmt /urban_wwm_mgmt.pdf.

C40 Cities. 2011. 98% of Copenhagen City Heating Supplied by Waste Heat. http://www.c40.org/case_studies/98-of-copenhagen -city-heating-supplied-by-waste-heat.

Calabro, Emmanuele. 2013. An Algorithm to Determine the Optimum Tilt Angle of a Solar Panel from Global Horizontal Solar Radiation. *Journal of Renewable Energy* 2013:307547.

Calctool. n.d. http://www.calctool.org/CALC/eng/civil/hazen -williams_g.

California Department of Transportation. 2002. Guide for the Preparation of Traffic Impact Studies. Department of Transportation, State of California, Sacramento. http://www.dot .ca.gov/hq/tpp/offices/ocp/igr_ceqa_files/tisguide.pdf.

California Department of Transportation. 2011. California Airport Land Use Planning Handbook. http://www.dot.ca.gov/hq/planning /aeronaut/documents/alucp/AirportLandUsePlanningHandbook.pdf.

California School Garden Network. 2010. Gardens for Learning. Western Growers Foundation, California School Garden Network. http://www.csgn.org/sites/csgn.org/files/CSGN_book.pdf.

California State Parks. 2017. California Register of Historic Places. Office of Historic Preservation. http://ohp.parks.ca.gov/?page_id=21238.

Callies, David L., Daniel J. Curtin, and Julie A. Tappendorf. 2003. *Bargaining for Development: A Handbook of Development Agreements, Annexation Agreements, Land Development Conditions, Vested Rights and the Provision of Public Facilities.* Washington, DC: Environmental Law Institute.

Calthorpe, Peter. 1984. *The Next American Metropolis: Ecology, Community and the American Dream.* New York: Princeton Architectural Press.

Campanella, Thomas J. 2003. *Republic of Shade.* New Haven: Yale University Press.

Campbell Collaboration. n.d. http://www.campbellcollaboration.org.

Canada Mortgage and Housing Corporation. 2002. *Learning from Suburbia: Residential Street Pattern Design.* Ottawa: CMHC.

Canadian Environmental Assessment Agency. 2014. Basics of Environmental Assessment. https://www.ceaa-acee.gc.ca/default.asp?lang=en&n=B053F859-1.

Carmona, Matthew, Tim Heath, Taner Oc, and Steve Tiesdell. 2010. *Public Places, Urban Spaces: The Dimensions of Urban Design.* Abingdon, UK: Routledge.

Carr, Stephen, Mark Francis, Leanne G. Rivlin, and Andrew M. Stone. 1992. *Public Space.* Cambridge: Cambridge University Press.

Casanova, Helena, and Jesus Hernandez. 2015. *Public Space Acupuncture.* Barcelona: Actar.

Cascadia Consulting Group. 2008. Statewide Waste Characterization Study. California Integrated Waste Management Board. http://www.calrecycle.ca.gov/Publications/Documents/General%5C2009023.pdf.

Caulkins, Meg. 2012. *The Sustainable Sites Handbook: A Complete Guide to the Principles, Strategies, and Best Practices for Sustainable Landscapes.* New York: Wiley.

Center for Applied Transect Studies. n.d. (a) Resources & Links. http://transect.org/resources_links.html.

Center for Applied Transect Studies. n.d. (b) Smart Code. http://www.smartcodecentral.com.

Center for Design Excellence. n.d. Urban Design: Public Space. http://www.urbandesign.org/publicspace.html.

Cervero, Robert. 1997. *Paratransit in America: Redefining Mass Transportation.* New York: Praeger.

Cervero, Robert, and Erick Guerra. 2011. Urban Densities and Transit: A Multi-dimensional Perspective. UC Berkeley Center for Future Urban Transport, Working Paper UCB-ITS-VWP-2011-6. http://www.its.berkeley.edu/publications/UCB/2011/VWP/UCB-ITS-VWP-2011-6.pdf.

Chakrabarti, Vibhuti. 1998. *Indian Architectural Theory: Contemporary Uses of Vastu Vidya.* Richmond, UK: Curzon.

Chapin, Ross, and Sarah Susanka. 2011. *Pocket Neighborhoods: Creating Small Scale Community in a Large Scale World.* Newtown, CT: Taunton Press. See: http://www.pocket-neighborhoods.net/whatisaPN.html.

Chapman, Perry. 2006. *American Places: In Search of the Twenty-first Century Campus.* Lanham, MD: Rowman and Littlefield.

Chee, R., D. S. Kang, K. Lansey, and C. Y. Choi. 2009. Design of Dual Water Supply Systems. World Environmental and Water Resources Congress 2009. doi:10.1061/41036(342)71.

Chen, Liang, and Edward Ng. 2009. Sky View Factor Analysis of Street Canyons and Its Implication for Urban Heat Island Intensity: A GIS-Based Methodology Applied in Hong Kong. PLEA 2009 – 26th Conference on Passive and Low Energy Architecture, Quebec City, Canada, p. 166.

Chief Medical Officer of Health. 2010. The Potential Health Impact of Wind Turbines. Ontario Government, Toronto. http://www.health.gov.on.ca/en/common/ministry/publications/reports/wind_turbine/wind_turbine.pdf.

Childress, Herb. 1990. The Making of a Market. *Places* 7 (1). http://escholarship.org/uc/item/65g000cb#page-1.

Chrest, Anthony P., Mary S. Smith, and Sam Bhuyan. 1989. *Parking Structures: Planning, Design, Construction, Maintenance, and Repair.* New York: Van Nostrand Reinhold.

Chung, Chuihua Judy, Jeffrey Inaba, Rem Koolhaas, and Sze Tsung Leong, eds. 2001. *Harvard Design School Guide to Shopping.* Cologne: Taschen.

Cisco, Inc. 2007. How Cisco Achieved Environmental Sustainability in the Connected Workplace. Cisco IT Case Study. http://www.cisco.com/c/dam/en_us/about/ciscoitatwork/downloads/ciscoitatwork/pdf/Cisco_IT_Case_Study_Green_Office_Design.pdf.

City of Austin. n.d. Water Quality Regulations. https://www.municode.com/library/tx/austin/codes/environmental_criteria_manual?nodeId=S1WAQUMA_1.6.0DEGUWAQUCO_1.6.8RUIMTECOTARST.

City of Carlsbad. 2006. Design Criteria for Gravity Sewer Lines and Appurtenances. City of Carlsbad, California. http://www.carlsbadca.gov/business/building/Documents/EngStandVol1chap6.pdf.

City of Chicago. n.d. A Guide to Stormwater Best Management Practices. https://www.cityofchicago.org/dam/city/depts/doe/general/NaturalResourcesAndWaterConservation_PDFs/Water/guideToStormwaterBMP.pdf.

City of Fort Lauderdale. 2007. Building a Liveable Downtown. http://www.fortlauderdalegov/planning_zoning/pdf/downtown_mp/120508downtown_mp.pdf.

City of Portland. 1991. Downtown Urban Design Guidelines. City of Portland (Maine), Planning Department. http://www.portlandmaine.gov/DocumentCenter/Home/View/3375.

City of Portland. 2001. Central City Fundamental Design Guidelines. City of Portland (Oregon), Bureau of Planning and Sustainability. https://www.portlandoregon.gov/bps/article/58806.

City of Seattle. 2007. *Jefferson Park Site Plan Final Environmental Impact Statement*. Prepared by Adolfson Associates for the Department of Planning and Development.

City of Toronto. 2002. Water Efficiency Plan. Department of Works and Emergency Services, Toronto, and Veritec Consulting Limited. https://www1.toronto.ca/City%20Of%20Toronto/Toronto%20Water/Files/pdf/W/WEP_final.pdf.

City of Vancouver. n.d. Subdivision Bylaw. https://vancouver.ca/your-government/subdivision-bylaw-5208.aspx.

City of York Council. n.d. York New City Beautiful: Toward an Economic Vision. http://www.urbandesignskills.com/_uploads/UDS_YorkVision.pdf.

CityRyde LLC. 2009. Bicycle Sharing Systems Worldwide: Selected Case Examples. http://www.cityryde.com.

Claritas. n.d. Claritas PRIZM$_{NE}$ Lifestyle Categories. http://www.claritas.com.

Clark, Robert R. 2009 [1984]. General Guidelines for the Design of Light Rail Transit Facilities in Edmonton. http://www.trolleycoalition.org/pdf/lrtreport.pdf.

Clark, William R. 2010. Principles of Landscape Ecology. *Nature Education Knowledge* 3(10): 34. http://www.nature.com/scitable/knowledge/library/principles-of-landscape-ecology-13260702.

Claytor, Richard A., and Thomas R. Schueler. 1996. *Design of Stormwater Filtering Systems*. Ellicot City, MD: Center for Watershed Protection.

Clinton Climate Initiative. n.d. https://www.clintonfoundation.org/our-work/clinton-climate-initiative.

Cochrane Collaboration. n.d. http://www.cochrane.org.

Coleman, Peter. 2006. *Shopping Environments: Evolution, Planning and Design*. Oxford: Architectural Press. http://samples.sainsburysebooks.co.uk/9781136366512_sample_900897.pdf.

Collyer, G. Stanley. 2004. *Competing Globally in Architectural Competitions*. London: Academy Press.

Collymore, Peter. 1994. *The Architecture of Ralph Erskine*. London: Academy Editions.

Commission for Architecture and the Built Environment. n.d. Case Studies. http://webarchive.nationalarchives.gov.uk/20110118095356/http://www.cabe.org.uk/case-studies.

Commission on Engineering and Technical Systems. 1985. *District Heating and Cooling in the United States: Prospects and Issues*. Washington, DC: National Academies Press.

Community Planning Laboratory. 2002. New Towns: An Overview of 30 American New Communities. CRP 410, City and Regional Planning Department, California Polytechnic State University, Zeljka Pavlovich Howard, faculty advisor. http://planning.calpoly.edu/projects/documents/newtown-cases.pdf.

Condon, Patrick M., Duncan Cavens, and Nicole Miller. 2009. *Urban Planning Tools for Climate Change Mitigation*. Cambridge, MA: Lincoln Institute of Land Policy. http://www.dcs.sala.ubc.ca/docs/lincoln_tools%20_for_climate%20change%20final_sec.pdf.

Conference Board of Canada. 2017. Municipal Waste Generation. http://www.conferenceboard.ca/hcp/details/environment/municipal-waste-generation.aspx.

Consumer Product Safety Commission. 2010. Public Playground Safety Handbook. http://www.cpsc.gov/PageFiles/122149/325.pdf.

Corbin, Juliet, and Anselm Strauss. 2007. *Basics of Qualitative Research: Techniques and Procedures for Developing Grounded Theory*. 3rd ed. New York: Sage.

Corbisier, Chris. 2003. Living with Noise. *Public Roads* 67 (1). https://www.fhwa.dot.gov/publications/publicroads/03jul/06.cfm.

Cornell University. Recommended Urban Trees: Site Assessment and Tree Selection for Stress Tolerance. http://www.hort.cornell.edu/uhi/outreach/recurbtree/pdfs/~recurbtrees.pdf.

Correll, Mark R., Jane H. Lillydahl, and Larry D. Singell. 1978. The Effects of Greenbelts on Residential Property Values: Some Findings on the Political Economy of Open Space. *Land Economics* 54 (2):207–217.

Cotswold Water Park. n.d. http://www.waterpark.org.

Coulson, Jonathan, Paul Roberts, and Isabelle Taylor. 2015. *University Planning and Architecture: The Search for Perfection*. 2nd ed. Abingdon, UK: Routledge.

Crankshaw, Ned. 2008. *Creating Vibrant Public Spaces: Streetscape Design in Commercial and Historic Districts*. 2nd ed. Washington, DC: Island Press.

Craul, Phillip J. 1999. *Urban Soils: Applications and Practices*. New York: Wiley.

Creative Urban Projects. 2013. Cable Car Confidential: The Essential Guide to Cable Cars, Urban Gondolas, and Cable Propelled Transit. http://www.gondolaproject.com.

Crewe, Catherine, and Ann Forsyth. 2013. LandSCAPES: A Typology of Approaches to Landscape Architecture. *Landscape Journal* 22 (1): 37–53.

C.R.O.W. 1994. *Sign Up for the Bike: Design Manual for a Cycle-Friendly Infrastructure*. C.R.O.W. Record 10. The Netherlands: Centre for Research and Contact Standardization in Civil and Traffic Engineering.

DAN. 2013. Making a Site Model. SectionCut blog. http://sectioncut.com/make-a-site-model-workflow/.

Darin-Drabkin, H. 1971. Control and Planned Development of Urban Land: Toward the Development of Urban Land Policies. Paper presented at the Interregional Seminar on Urban Land Policies and Land-Use Control Measures, Madrid, November. ESA/HPB/AC.5/6.

Davenport, Cyndy, and Ishka Voiculescu. 2016. *Mastering AutoCAD Civil 3D 2016: Autodesk Official Press*. 1st ed. New York: Wiley.

Davison, Elizabeth. n.d. Arizona Plant Climate Zones. Cooperative Extension, College of Agriculture and Life Sciences, University of Arizona. http://cals.arizona.edu/pubs/garden/az1169/#map.

Del Alamo, M. R. 2005. *Design for Fun: Playgrounds*. Barcelona: Links International.

Denver Water. n.d. Water Wise Landscape Handbook. http://www.denverwater.org/docs/assets/6E5CC278-0B7C-1088-758683A48CE8624D/Water_Wise_Landscape_Handbook.pdf.

Department of Agriculture. n.d. Plant Hardiness Zone Map. Agricultural Research Service, US Department of Agriculture. http://planthardiness.ars.usda.gov/PHZMWeb/.

Department of Agriculture, Soil Survey Staff. 1975. Soil Taxonomy – A Basic System of Soil Classification for Making and Interpreting Soil Surveys. US Department of Agriculture, Agricultural Handbook 436.

Department of Agriculture, Soil Survey Staff. 2015. Illustrated Guide to Soil Taxonomy. Version 2.0. US Department of Agriculture, Natural Resources Conservation Service, National Soil Survey Center.

Department of Commerce. 1961. Rainfall Frequency Atlas of the United States. Prepared by David M. Hershfield. Technical Paper no. 40. http://www.nws.noaa.gov/oh/hdsc/PF_documents/TechnicalPaper_No40.pdf.

Department of Housing and Urban Development. n.d. 24 CFR Part 51 Environmental Criteria and Standards, Subpart B – Noise Abatement and Control. US Consolidated Federal Register. http://www.hudnoise.com/hudstandard.html.

Design Trust for Public Space. 2010. High Performance Landscape Guidelines: 21st Century Parks for New York City. http://designtrust.org/publications/hp-landscape-guidelines/.

Dezeen. n.d. (a). Playgrounds. https://www.dezeen.com/tag/playgrounds/.

Dezeen. n.d. (b). Shopping Centers. https://www.dezeen.com/tag/shopping-centres/.

Diepens and Okkema Traffic Consultants. 1995. *International Handbook for Cycle Network Design*. Delft, Netherlands: Delft University of Technology.

Dionne, Brian. n.d. Escalators and Moving Sidewalks. Catholic University of America. http://architecture.cua.edu/res/docs/courses/arch457/report-1/10b-escalators-movingwalks.pdf.

District Energy St Paul. n.d. http://www.districtenergy.com.

Ditchkoff, Stephen S., Sarah T. Saalfeld, and Charles J. Gibson. 2006. Animal Behavior in Urban Ecosystems: Modifications Due to Human-Induced Stress. *Urban Ecosystems* 9:5–12. https://fp.auburn.edu/sfws/ditchkoff/PDF%20publications/2006%20-%20UrbanEco.pdf.

Do, A. Quang, and Gary Grudnitski. 1995. Golf Courses and Residential House Prices: An Empirical Examination. *Journal of Real Estate Finance and Economics* 10 (10): 261–270.

Dober, Richard P. 2010 [1992]. Campus Planning. Digital Version. Society for College and University Planning. https://www.scup.org/page/resources/books/cd.

Doebele, William. 1982. *Land Readjustment*. Lexington, MA: Lexington Books.

Domingo Calabuig, Débora, Raúl Castellanos Gómez, and Ana Ábalos Ramos. 2013. The Strategies of Mat-building. *Architectural Review*, August 13. http://www.architectural-review.com/essays/the-strategies-of-mat-building/8651102.article.

Dorner, Jeanette. n.d. An Introduction to Using Native Plants in Restoration Projects. National Park Service, US Department of the Interior, Washington, DC. http://www.nps.gov/plants/restore/pubs/intronatplant/toc.htm.

Dowling, Richard, David Reinke, Amee Flannery, Paul Ryan, Mark Vandehey, Theo Petritsch, Bruce Landis, Nagui Rouphail, and James Bonneson. 2008. *Multimodal Level of Service Analysis for Urban Streets. NCHRP Report 616*. Washington, DC: Transportation Research Board; http://onlinepubs.trb.org/onlinepubs/nchrp/nchrp_rpt_616.pdf.

Downey, Nate. 2009. Roof-Reliant Landscaping: Rainwater Harvesting with Cistern Systems in New Mexico. New Mexico Office of the State Engineer. http://www.ose.state.nm.us/water-info/conservation/pdf-manuals/Roof-Reliant-Landscaping/Roof-Reliant-Landscaping.pdf).

Duany, Andres, Elizabeth Plater-Zyberk, and Robert Alminana. 2003. *New Civic Art: Elements of Town Planning*. New York: Rizzoli.

Dubbeling Martin, Michaël Meijer, Antony Marcelis, and Femke Adriaens, eds. 2009. *Duurzame stedenbouw: perspectieven en voorbeelden / Sustainable Urban Design: Perspectives and Examples*. Wageningen, Netherlands: Plauwdrukpublishers.

Duffy, Francis, Colin Cave, and John Worthington. 1976. *Planning Office Space*. London: Elsevier.

Dunphy, Robert T., et al. 2000. *The Dimensions of Parking*. 4th ed. Washington, DC: Urban Land Institute and National Parking Association.

EarthCraft Communities. n.d. http://www.earthcraft.org/builders/resources/.

East Cambridgeshire District Council. 2008. Percolation Tests. Technical Information Note 6. http://www.eastcambs.gov.uk/sites/default/files/Guidance%20Note%206%20-%20Percolation%20Tests.pdf.

Eden Project. n.d. www.edenproject.com.

Edwards, J. D. 1992. *Transportation Planning Handbook*. Washington, DC: Institute of Transportation Engineers.

Effland, William R., and Richard V. Pouyat. 1997. The Genesis, Classification, and Mapping of Soils in Urban Areas. *Urban Ecosystems* 1:217–228.

Egan, D. 1992. A Bicycle and Bus Success Story. In *The Bicycle: Global Perspectives*. Montreal: Vélo Québec.

Ellickson, Robert C. 1992–1993. Property in Land. *Yale Law Journal* 102:1315.

Energy Storage Association. n.d. Pumped Hydroelectric Storage. http://energystorage.org/energy-storage/technologies/pumped -hydroelectric-storage.

Engineering Tool Box. n.d. http://www.engineeringtoolbox.com /sewer-pipes-capacity-d_478.html.

Enright, Robert, and Henriquez Partners. 2010. *Body Heat: The Story of the Woodward's Redevelopment*. Vancouver: Blueimprint Press.

Envac. n.d. Waste Solutions in a Sustainable Urban Development: Envac's Guide to Hammarby Sjöstad. http://www.solaripedia.com /files/719.pdf.

Environmental Protection Agency. 1994. Composting Yard Trimmings and Municipal Solid Waste. http://www.epa.gov/ composting/pubs/cytmsw.pdf.

Environmental Protection Agency. 2000a. Constructed Wetlands Treatment of Municipal Wastewaters. http://water.epa.gov/type /wetlands/restore/upload/constructed-wetlands-design-manual.pdf.

Environmental Protection Agency. 2000b. Decentralized Systems Technology Fact Sheet: Small Diameter Gravity Sewers. http:// water.epa.gov/scitech/wastetech/upload/2002_06_28_mtb_small _diam_gravity_sewers.pdf.

Environmental Protection Agency. 2000c. Introduction to Phytoremediation. National Risk Management Research Laboratory, Cincinnati, US Environmental Protection Agency. EPA/600/R-99/107. http://www.cluin.org/download/remed /introphyto.pdf.

Environmental Protection Agency. 2002a. Collection Systems Technology Fact Sheet: Sewers, Conventional Gravity. http://water .epa.gov/scitech/wastetech/upload/2002_10_15_mtb_congrasew.pdf.

Environmental Protection Agency. 2002b. Wastewater Technology Fact Sheet: Anaerobic Lagoons. http://water.epa.gov/scitech /wastetech/upload/2002_10_15_mtb_alagoons.pdf.

Environmental Protection Agency. 2002c. Wastewater Technology Fact Sheet: Package Plants. http://water.epa.gov/scitech /wastetech/upload/2002_06_28_mtb_package_plant.pdf.

Environmental Protection Agency. 2002d. Wastewater Technology Fact Sheet: Sewers, Pressure. http://water.epa.gov/scitech /wastetech/upload/2002_10_15_mtb_presewer.pdf.

Environmental Protection Agency. 2002e. Wastewater Technology Fact Sheet: Slow Rate Land Treatment. http://water.epa.gov /scitech/wastetech/upload/2002_10_15_mtb_sloratre.pdf.

Environmental Protection Agency. 2002f. Wastewater Technology Fact Sheet: The Living Machine®. http://water.epa.gov/scitech /wastetech/upload/2002_12_13_mtb_living_machine.pdf.

Environmental Protection Agency. 2006. Biosolids Technology Fact Sheet: Heat Drying. http://water.epa.gov/scitech/wastetech /upload/2006_10_16_mtb_heat-drying.pdf.

Environmental Protection Agency. 2012a. Municipal Solid Waste Generation, Recycling and Disposal in the United States: Facts and Figures for 2012. http://www.epa.gov/waste/nonhaz/municipal /pubs/2012_msw_fs.pdf.

Environmental Protection Agency. 2012b. Part 1502 – Environmental Impact Statement. Code of Federal Regulations, Title 40. US Government Publishing Office. https://www.gpo .gov/fdsys/pkg/CFR-2012-title40-vol34/pdf/CFR-2012-title40 -vol34-part1502.pdf.

Environmental Protection Agency. 2014. Energy Recovery from Waste. http://www.epa.gov/epawaste/nonhaz/municipal/wte /index.htm.

Environmental Protection Agency. 2016. Heat Island Cooling Strategies. https://www.epa.gov/heat-islands/heat-island -cooling-strategies.

Environmental Protection Agency. 2017. Environmental Impact Statement Rating System Criteria. https://www.epa.gov/nepa /environmental-impact-statement-rating-system-criteria.

Environmental Protection Agency. n.d. (a). Electric and Magnetic Fields (EMF) Radiation from Power Lines. http://www.epa.gov /radtown/power-lines.html.

Environmental Protection Agency. n.d. (b). Mixed-Use Trip Generation Model. https://www.epa.gov/smartgrowth/mixed-use -trip-generation-model.

Envision Utah. n.d. http://www.envisionutah.org.

Enwave. n.d. http://www.enwave.com/disstrict_cooling_system.html.

EPA Victoria. 2005. Dual Pipe Water Recycling Schemes – Health and Environmental Risk Management. http://www.epa.vic.gov .au/~/media/Publications/1015.pdf.

Eppley Institute et al. 2004. Anchorage Bowl: Parks, Natural Open Space and Recreation Facilities Plan. Draft Plan. Land Design North; Eppley Institute for Parks and Public Lands, Indiana University; and Alaska Pacific University. http://eppley.org/wp -content/uploads/uploads/file/62/Anchorage.pdf.

Eppli, Mark J., and Charles C. Tu. 1999. *Valuing the New Urbanism: The Impact of New Urbanism on Prices of Single Family Homes*. Washington, DC: Urban Land Institute.

Eriksen, Aase. 1985. *Playground Design: Outdoor Environments for Learning and Development*. New York: Van Nostrand Reinhold.

Ernst, Michelle, and Lilly Shoup. 2009. Dangerous by Design: Transportation for America and the Surface Transportation Policy Partnership. http://culturegraphic.com/media/Transportation -for-America-Dangerous-by-Design.pdf.

Ervin, Stephen, and Hope Hasbrouck. 2001. *Landscape Modeling: Digital Techniques for Landscape Visualization*. New York: McGraw-Hill.

Esri. n.d. GIS Solutions for Urban and Regional Planning: Designing and Mapping the Future of Your Community with GIS. http://www .esri.com/library/brochures/pdfs/gis-sols-for-urban-planning.pdf.

Euroheat and Power. n.d. District Heating and Cooling Explained. http://www.euroheat.org.

Ewing, Reid. 1996. *Best Development Practices*. Washington, DC: Planners Press.

Ewing, Reid H. 1999. Traffic Calming: State of the Practice. Institute of Transportation Engineers, Washington, DC, Publication no. IR-098.

Faga, Barbara. 2006. *Designing Public Consensus: The Civic Theater of Community Participation for Architects, Landscape Architects, Planners and Urban Designers*. New York: Wiley.

Farvacque, C., and P. McAuslan. 1992. Reforming Urban Policies and Institutions in Developing Countries. Urban Management Program Paper No. 5. World Bank, Washington, DC.

Federal Communications Commission. 1999. Questions and Answers about Biological Effects and Potential Hazards of Radiofrequency Electromagnetic Fields. OET Bulletin 56, 4th ed. http://transition.fcc.gov/Bureaus/Engineering_Technology /Documents/bulletins/oet56/oet56e4.pdf.

Federal Emergency Management Agency. n.d. FEMA 100 Year Flood Zone Maps. http://msc.fema.gov.

Federal Highway Administration. 2000. Roundabouts: An Informational Guide. US Department of Transportation, FHWA Publication No. RD-00–067.

Federal Highway Administration. 2001. Geometric Design Practices for European Roads. https://international.fhwa.dot.gov/pdfs /geometric_design.pdf.

Federal Highway Administration. 2003. *Manual on Uniform Traffic Control Devices for Streets and Highways*. Washington, DC: US Department of Transportation.

Federal Highway Administration. 2006. Pedestrian Characteristics. https://www.fhwa.dot.gov/publications/research/safety/pedbike /05085/chapt8.cfm.

Federal Highway Administration. 2008. Traffic Volume Trends. http://www.fhwa.dot.gov/ohim/tvtw/08dectvt/omdex/cfm.

Federal Highway Administration. 2013a. Highway Functional Classification Concepts, Criteria and Procedures. https://www .fhwa.dot.gov/planning/processes/statewide/related/highway _functional_classifications/fcauab.pdf.

Federal Highway Administration. 2013b. Traffic Analysis Toolbox Volume VI: Definition, Interpretation and Calculation of Traffic Analysis Tools Measures of Effectiveness. http://ops.fhwa.dot.gov /publications/fhwahop08054/sect4.htm.

Federal Highway Administration. 2014. Road Diet Informational Guide. http://safety.fhwa.dot.gov/road_diets/info_guide/ch3.cfm.

Federal Highway Administration. n.d. (a). Noise Barrier Design – Visual Quality. http://www.fhwa.dot.gov/environment/noise/noise _barriers/design_construction/keepdown.cfm.

Federal Highway Administration. n.d. (b). Separated Bike Lane Planning and Design Guide. https://www.fhwa.dot.gov/environment /bicycle_pedestrian/publications/separated_bikelane_pdg /page00.cfm.

Ferguson, Bruce K. 1994. *Stormwater Infiltration*. Ann Arbor, MI: CRC Press.

Ferguson, Bruce K. 1998. *Introduction to Stormwater: Concept, Purpose, Design*. Hoboken, NJ: Wiley.

Ferguson, Bruce K. 2005. *Porous Pavements. Integrative Studies in Water Management and Land Development*. Ann Arbor, MI: CRC Press.

Fibre to the Home Council. 2011. FTTH Council – Definition of Terms. http://ftthcouncil.eu/documents/Publications/FTTH _Definition_of_Terms-Revision_2011-Final.pdf.

Field, Barry. 1989. The Evolution of Property Rights. *Kyklos* 42:319–345.

Fiorenza, S., C. L. Oubre, and C. H. Ward. 2000. *Phytoremediation of Hydrocarbon Contaminated Soil*. Boca Raton: Lewis Publishers.

Fischer, Richard A., and J. Craig Fischenich. 2000. Design Recommendations for Riparian Corridors and Vegetated Buffer Strips. US Army Engineer Research and Development Center, EDRC TN-EMRRP-SR-24. http://el.erdc.usace.army.mil/elpubs /pdf/sr24.pdf.

Fish and Wildlife Service. 2012. Land-Based Wind Energy Guidelines. http://www.fws.gov/windenergy/docs/WEG_final.pdf.

Fish and Wildlife Service. n.d. National Spatial Data Infrastructure: Wetlands Layer. http://www.fws.gov/wetlands/Documents/ National-Spatial-Data-Infrastructure-Wetlands-Layer-Fact-Sheet.pdf.

Fisher, Scott. 2010. How to Make a Contour Model Correctly. Salukitecture. http://siuarchitecture.blogspot.com/2010/10/how-to -make-contour-model-correctly.html.

Fitzpatrick, Kay, et al. 2006. Improving Pedestrian Safety at Unsignalized Crossings. NCHRP Report #562. Transportation Research Board, Washington, DC.

Fleury, A. M., and R. D. Brown. 1997. A Framework for the Design of Wildlife Conservation Corridors with Specific Application to Southwestern Ontario. *Landscape and Urban Planning* 37:163–186.

Florida, Richard. 2002. *The Rise of the Creative Class: And How It Is Transforming Work, Leisure, Community and Everyday Life*. New York: Basic Books.

Florida Department of Transportation. 2009. Quality/Level of Service Handbook. http://www.fltod.com/research/fdot/quality _level_of_service_handbook.pdf.

Foletta, Nicole, and Simon Field. 2011. Europe's Vibrant New Low Car(bon) Communities. Institute for Transportation and Development Policy, New York. https://www.itdp.org/europes-vibrant-new-low -carbon-communities-2/.

Foley, Conor. 2007. *A Guide to Property Law in Uganda*. Nairobi: United Nations Centre for Human Settlements (Habitat).

Fondación Metrópoli. 2008. Ecobox: Building a Sustainable Future. Fondación Metrópoli, Madrid. http://www.fmetropoli.org /proyectos/ecobox.

Forman, Richard T. T. 1995. *Land Mosaics: The Ecology of Landscapes and Regions*. Cambridge: Cambridge University Press.

Frank, L. D., and D. Hawkins. 2008. *Giving Pedestrians an Edge: Using Street Layout to Influence Transportation Choice*. Ottawa: Canada Mortgage and Housing Corporation.

Fregonese Associates. n.d. Envision Tomorrow: A Suite of Urban and Regional Planning Tools. http://www.envisiontomorrow.org /about-envision-tomorrow/.

Fruin, J. J. 1970. Designing for Pedestrians, a Level of Service Concept. PhD dissertation, Polytechnic Institute of Brooklyn.

Fujiyama, T., C. R. Childs, D. Boampomg, and N. Tyler. 2005. Investigation of Lighting Levels for Pedestrians — Some Questions about Lighting Levels of Current Lighting Standards. In *Walk21-VI, Everyday Walking Culture. 6th International Conference of Walking in the 21st Century*, 1–13. Zurich, Switzerland Walk21. https:// docs.google.com/viewer?url=http%3A%2F%2Fdiscovery.ucl.ac .uk%2F1430%2F1%2FWalk21Fujiyama.pdf.

Gaborit, Pascaline, ed. 2014. *European and Asian Sustainable Towns: New Towns and Satellite Cities in Their Metropolises*. Brussels: Presses Interuniversitaires Européennes.

Gaffney, Andrea, Vinita Huang, Kristin Maravilla, and Nadine Soubotin. 2007. Hammarby Sjöstad, Stockholm, Sweden: A Case Study. http://www.aeg7.com/assets/publications/hammarby %20sjostad.pdf.

Galbrun, L., and T. T. Ali. 2012. Perceptual Assessment of Water Sounds for Road Traffic Noise Masking. Proceedings of the Acoustics 2012 Nantes Conference. http://hal.archives-ouvertes.fr /docs/00/81/12/10/PDF/hal-00811210.pdf.

Gatje, Robert F. 2010. *Great Public Squares: An Architect's Selection*. New York: W. W. Norton.

Gautier, P-E, F. Poisson, and F. Letourneaux. n.d. High Speed Trains External Noise: A Review of Measurements and Source Models for the TGV Case up to 360 km/h. http://uic.org/cdrom/2008/11 _wcrr2008/pdf/S.1.1.4.4.pdf.

Gaventa, Sarah. 2006. *New Public Spaces*. London: Mitchell Beazley.

Gehl, Jan, and Lars Gemzøe. 1996. *Public Life—Public Space*. Copenhagen: Danish Architectural Press and Royal Academy of Fine Arts.

Gehl, Jan, and Lars Gemzøe. 2004. *Public Spaces, Public Life*. Copenhagen: Danish Architectural Press.

Gehl, Jan, and Lars Gemzøe. 2006. *New City Spaces*. Copenhagen: Danish Architectural Press.

Geist, Johann F. 1982. *Arcades: The History of a Building Type*. Cambridge, MA: MIT Press.

Geller, Roger. n.d. Four Types of Cyclists. http://www.portlandonline .com/transportation/index.cfm?&a=237507&c=44597.

Giannopoulos, G. A. 1989. *Bus Planning and Operation in Urban Areas*. Aldershot: Avebury Press.

Gibbs, Steve. 2005. A Solid Foundation for Future Growth. *Land Development Today* 1 (7): 8–10.

Giddens, Anthony. 1991. *Modernity and Self-Identity: Self and Society in the Late Modern Age*. Cambridge: Polity Press.

Glaser, Barney G., and Anselm L. Strauss. 1967. *The Discovery of Grounded Theory: Strategies for Qualitative Research*. Chicago: Aldine.

Global Designing Cities Initiative. 2016. *Global Street Design Guide*. Washington, DC: Island Press. https://gdci-pydi2uhbcuqfp9wvwe .stackpathdns.com/wp-content/uploads/guides/global-street-design -guide.pdf.

Global Legal Group. 2008. International Comparative Legal Guide to Real Estate. www.ilgc.co.uk.

GoGreenSolar.com. n.d. How Many Solar Panels Do I Need? https://www.gogreensolar.com/pages/how-many-solar-panels -do-i-need.

Gold, Martin E. 1977. *Law and Social Change: A Study of Land Reform in Sri Lanka*. New York: Nellen Publishing.

Gold, Martin E., and Russell Zuckerman. 2015. Indonesian Land Rights and Development. *Columbia Journal of Asian Law* 28 (1): 41–67.

Goldberger, Paul. 2005. *Up from Zero: Politics, Architecture and the Rebuilding of New York*. New York: Random House.

Gold Coast City Council et al. 2013. SEQ Water Supply and Sewerage Design and Construction Code: Design Criteria. http:// www.seqcode.com.au/storage/2013-07-01%20-%20SEQ%20 WSS%20DC%20Code%20Design%20Criteria.pdf.

Google. 2016. Google Charleston East Project. Informal Review Document, City of Mountain View. http://www.mountainview.gov /depts/comdev/planning/activeprojects/charleston_east.asp.

Google Earth Pro. n.d. https://support.google.com/earth/answer/3064261?hl=en.

Gordon, David L. A. 1997. *Battery Park City: Politics and Planning on the New York Waterfront*. Philadelphia: Gordon and Breach.

Gordon, Kathi. 2004. The Sea Ranch: Concept and Covenant. The Sea Ranch Association. http://www.tsra.org/photos/VIPBooklet.pdf.

GRASS. n.d. http://grass.osgeo.org/.

Grava, Sigurd. 2002. *Urban Transportation Systems: Choices for Communities*. New York: McGraw-Hill.

Great Lakes-Upper Mississippi River Board of State and Provincial Public Health and Environmental Managers. 2004. Recommended Standards for Wastewater Facilities. Health Research Inc. http://10statesstandards.com/wastewaterstandards.html.

Greenbaum, Thomas. 2000. *Moderating Focus Groups*. Thousand Oaks, CA: Sage.

Green Dashboard. n.d. Waste Diverted from Landfills. District of Columbia Government, Washington, DC. http://greendashboard.dc.gov/Waste/WasteDivertedFromLandfills.

GreenerEnergy. n.d. Tilt and Angle Orientation of Solar Panels. http://greenerenergy.ca/PDFs/Tilt%20and%20Angle%20Orientation%20of%20Solar%20Panels.pdf.

Greywater Action. n.d. How to Do a Percolation Test. http://greywateraction.org/content/how-do-percolation-test.

Gulf Organization for Research and Development. n.d. QSAS: Qatar Sustainability Assessment System Technical Manual, Version 2.1. http://www.gord.qa/uploads/pdf/GSAS%20Technical%20Guide%20V2.1.pdf.

Gustafson, David, James L. Anderson, Sara Heger Christopherson, and Rich Axler. 2002. Constructed Wetlands. University of Minnesota Extension. http://www.extension.umn.edu/environment/water/onsite-sewage-treatment/innovative-sewage-treatment-systems-series/constructed-wetlands/index.html.

Gustafson, David, and Roger E. Machmeier. 2013. How to Run a Percolation Test. University of Minnesota Extension. http://www.extension.umn.edu/environment/housing-technology/moisture-management/how-to-run-a-percolation-test/.

GVA Grimley LLP. 2006. Milton Keynes 2031: A Long Term Sustainable Growth Strategy. Milton Keynes Partnership. http://milton-keynes.cmis.uk.com/milton-keynes/Document.

Gyourko, Joseph E., and Witold Rybczynski. 2000. Financing New Urbanism Projects: Obstacles and Solutions. *Housing Policy Debate* 11 (3): 733–750.

Habraken, N. John. 2000. *Supports: An Alternate to Mass Housing*. Urban International Press.

Hack, Gary. 1994a. Discovering Suburban Values through Design Review. In Brenda Case Scheer and Wolfgang F. E. Preiser, eds., *Design Review: Challenging Aesthetic Control*. New York: Chapman and Hall.

Hack, Gary. 1994b. Renewing Prudential Center. *Urban Land*, November.

Hack, Gary. 2013. Business Performance in Walkable Shopping Areas. Active Living Research Program, Robert Wood Johnson Foundation. http://activelivingresearch.org/business-performance-walkable-shopping-areas.

Hack, Gary, and Lynne Sagalyn. 2011. Value Creation through Urban Design. In David Adams and Steven Tiesdell, eds., *Urban Design in the Real Estate Development Process*, 258–281. Hoboken, NJ: Wiley-Blackwell.

Hall, Edward. 1966. *The Hidden Dimension*. Garden City, NY: Doubleday.

Halprin, Lawrence. 2002. *The Sea Ranch ... Diary of an Idea*. Berkeley, CA: Spacemaker Press.

Hammer, Thomas R., Robert E. Coughlin, and Edward T. Horn. 1974. The Effect of a Large Urban Park on Real Estate Value. *Journal of the American Institute of Planners* 40 (4): 274–277.

Handy, Susan, Robert G. Paterson, and Kent Butler. 2003. Planning for Street Connectivity: Getting from Here to There. American Planning Association, Chicago, Planning Advisory Service Report 515.

Harris, P., B. Harris-Roxas, E. Harris, and L. Kemp. 2007. Health Impact Assessment: A Practical Guide. Centre for Health Equity Training, Research and Evaluation (CHETRE), University of New South Wales Research Centre for Primary Health Care and Equity, Sydney. http://hiaconnect.edu.au/wp-content/uploads/2012/05/Health_Impact_Assessment_A_Practical_Guide.pdf.

Haugen, Kathryn M. B. 2011. International Review of Policies and Recommendations for Wind Turbine Setbacks from Residences: Noise, Shadow Flicker and Other Concerns. Minnesota Department of Commerce, Energy Facility Permitting. http://mn.gov/commerce/energyfacilities/documents/International_Review_of_Wind_Policies_and_Recommendations.pdf.

Heaney, James P., Len Wright, and David Sample. 2000. Sustainable Urban Water Management. In Richard Feld, James P. Heaney, and Robert Pitt, eds., *Innovative Urban Wet-Weather Flow Management Systems*. Lancaster, PA: Technomic Publishing Company; http://unix.eng.ua.edu/~rpitt/Publications/BooksandReports/Innovative/achap03.pdf.

Heath, G. W., R. C. Brownson, J. Kruger, et al. 2006. The Effectiveness of Urban Design and Land Use and Transport Policies and Practices to Increase Physical Activity: A Systematic Review. *Journal of Physical Activity and Health* 3 (Suppl 1): S55–S76.

Hebrew Senior Housing. n.d. NewBridge on the Charles. http://www.hebrewseniorlife.org/newbridge.

Hegemann, Werner, and Elbert Peets. 1996 [1922]. *American Vitruvius: An Architect's Handbook of Civic Art*. New York: Princeton Architectural Press.

Heller, Michael, and Rick Hills. 2009. Land Assembly Districts. *Harvard Law Review* 121 (6): 1466–1527.

Hendricks, Barbara E. 2001. *Designing for Play*. Aldershot, UK: Ashgate.

Henthorne, Lisa. 2009. Desalination – a Critical Element of Water Solutions for the 21st Century. In Jonas Forare, ed., *Drinking Water—Sources, Sanitation and Safeguarding*. Swedish Research Council Formas. http://www.formas.se/formas_shop/ItemView .aspx?id=5422&epslanguage=EN.

Hershberger, Robert G. 2000. Programming. In American Institute of Architects, *The Architect's Handbook of Professional Practice*. 13th ed. http://www.aia.org/aiaucmp/groups/aia/documents/pdf /aiab089267.pdf.

Hershfield, David M. 1961. Rainfall Frequency Atlas of the United States: For Durations from 30 Minutes to 24 Hours and Return Periods from 1 to 100 Years. Technical Paper No. 40. US Department of Commerce; http://www.nws.noaa.gov/oh/hdsc /PF_documents/TechnicalPaper_No40.pdf.

High Tech Finland. 2010. District Heat from Nuclear. http://www .hightech.fi/direct.aspx?area=htf&prm1=898&prm2=article.

Hillier, Bill. 1996. *Space Is the Machine*. Cambridge: Cambridge University Press. See also http://www.spacesyntax.org /publications/commonlang.html.

Hirschhorn, Joel S., and Paul Souza. 2001. *New Community Design to the Rescue: Fulfilling Another American Dream*. Washington, DC: National Governors Association.

Hodge, Jessica, and Julia Haltrecht. 2009. *BedZED Seven Years On: The Impact of the UK's Best Known Eco-Village and Its Residents*. London: Peabody. http://www.bioregional.com /wp-content/uploads/2014/10/BedZED_seven_years_on.pdf.

Holl, Steven. 2011. *Horizontal Skyscraper*. Richmond, CA: William Stout Publishers.

Holsum, Laura M. 2005. The Feng Shui Kingdom. *New York Times*, April 25.

Hong, Yu-Hung, and Barrie Needham. 2007. *Analyzing Land Readjustment: Economics, Law and Collective Action*. Cambridge, MA: Lincoln Institute of Land Policy.

Hong Kong BEAM Society. 2012. BEAM Plus New Buildings, Version 1.2. http://www.beamsociety.org.hk/files/download/download -20130724174420.pdf.

Hong Kong Government. 1995. Sewerage Manual: Part 1, Key Planning Issues and Gravity Collection System. Drainage Services Department. http://www.dsd.gov.hk/TC/Files/publications_publicity /other_publications/technical_manuals/Sewer%20Manual%20 Part%201.pdf.

Hoornweg, Daniel, and Perinaz Bhada-Tata. 2012. What a Waste: A Global Review of Solid Waste Management. World Bank Urban Development Series. http://www-wds.worldbank.org/external/ default/WDSContentServer/WDSP/IB/2012/07/25/000333037 _20120725004131/Rendered/PDF/681350WP0REVIS0at0a0 Waste20120Final.pdf.

Horose, Caitlyn. 2015. Let's Get Digital! 50 Tools for Online Public Engagement. Community Matters. http://www.communitymatters .org/blog/let%E2%80%99s-get-digital-50-tools-online-public -engagement.

Horton, Mark B. 2010. A Guide for Health Impact Assessment. California Department of Public Health. http://www.cdph.ca.gov /pubsforms/Guidelines/Documents/HIA%20Guide%20FINAL%20 10-19-10.pdf.

Huat, Low Ing, Dadang Mohamad Ma'soem, and Ravi Shankar. 2005. Revised Walkway Capacity Using Platoon Flows. *Proceedings of the Eastern Asia Society for Transportation Studies* 5:996–1008.

Hughes, Philip George. 2000. *Ageing Pipes and Murky Waters: Urban Water System Issues for the 21st Century*. Wellington, New Zealand: Office of the Parliamentary Commissioner for the Environment.

Hunter, William W, J. Richard Stewart, Jane C. Stutts, Herman H. Huang, and Wayne E. Pein. 1998. A Comparative Analysis of Bicycle Lanes versus Wide Curb Lanes: Final Report. US Department of Transportation, Federal Highway Administration, Report #FHWA-RD-99-034, May.

Hwangbo, Alfred B. 2002. An Alternative Tradition in Architecture: Conceptions in Feng Shui and Its Continuous Tradition. *Journal of Architectural and Planning Research* 19 (2): 110–130.

Hyodo, T., C. Montalbo, A. Fujiwara, and S. Soehodho. 2005. Urban Travel Behavior Characteristics of 13 Cities Based on Household Interview Survey Data. *Journal of the Eastern Asia Society for Transportation Studies* 6:23–38.

IBI Group. 2000. *Greenhouse Gas Emissions from Urban Travel: Tool for Evaluating Neighborhood Sustainability*. Ottawa: Canada Mortgage and Housing Corporation. http://www.cmhc-schl.gc.ca /odpub/pdf/62142.pdf.

Illumination Engineering Society. 2014. Standard Practice for Roadway Lighting. ANSI/IES RP-8.

India Green Building Council. n.d. LEED-NC India. http://www.igbc.in.

Ingram, Gregory K., and Yu-Hung Hong. 2012. *Value Capture and Land Policies*. Cambridge, MA: Lincoln Institute of Land Policy.

Ingram, Gregory K., and Zhi Liu. 1997. Determinants of Motorization and Road Provision. World Bank Working Paper. http://www-wds .worldbank.org/external/default/WDSContentServer/WDSP/IB /2000/02/24/000094946_99031911113162/additional/127527322 _20041117172108.pdf.

Ingram, Gregory K., and Zhi Liu. 1999. Vehicles, Roads and Road Use: Alternative Empirical Specifications. World Bank Working Paper. www.siteresources.worldbank.org/Interurbantransport /resources/wps2038.pdf.

Institute for Building Efficiency. 2011. Green Building Asset Valuation: Trends and Data. http://www.institutebe.com /InstituteBE/media/Library/Resources/Green%20Buildings /Research_Snapshot_Green_Building_Asset_Value.pdf.

Institute of Transportation Engineers. 1999. *Traffic Engineering Handbook*. 5th ed. Englewood Cliffs, NJ: Prentice-Hall.

Institute of Transportation Engineers. 2004. *Parking Generation*. Washington, DC: ITE.

Institute of Transportation Engineers. 2006. Context Sensitive Solutions for Designing Major Thoroughfares for Walkable Communities. http://www.ite.org/css/.

Institute of Transportation Engineers. 2010. Designing Walkable Urban Thoroughfares: A Context Sensitive Approach. Institute of Transportation Engineers and Congress for the New Urbanism. http://www.ite.org/css/rp-036a-e.pdf.

Institute of Transportation Engineers. 2014. *Trip Generation Handbook*. 3rd ed. Washington, DC: ITE.

Institute of Transportation Engineers. 2017. *Trip Generation*. 10th ed. Washington, DC: ITE.

Intergovernmental Panel on Climate Change. 2007. Magnitudes of Impact. United Nations Environment Program and World Health Organization. http://www.ipcc.ch/publications_and_data/ar4/wg2 /en/spmsspm-c-15-magnitudes-of.html.

International Labor Organization. n.d. International Standard Classification of Occupations, ISCO-88. http://www.ilo.org/public /english/bureau/stat/isco/isco88/index.htm.

International Standards Organization. 2009. Environmental Management: The ISO 14000 Family of International Standards. http://www.iso.org/iso/theiso14000family_2009.pdf.

International Water Association. 2010. International Statistics for Water Services. Specialist Group – Statistics and Management, Montreal. http://www.iwahq.org/contentsuite/upload/iwa /document/iwa_internationalstats_montreal_2010.pdf.

Iowa State University, University Extension. 1997. Farmstead Windbreaks: Planning. Pm-1716.

Itami, Robert M. 2002. *Estimating Capacities for Pedestrian Walkways and Viewing Platforms: A Report for Parks Victoria*. Brunswick, Victoria, Australia: GeoDimensions Pty Ltd.

Jacobs, Allan B. 1993. *Great Streets*. Cambridge, MA: MIT Press.

Jacobs, Allan B., Elizabeth Macdonald, and Yodan Rofe. 2002. *The Boulevard Book*. Cambridge, MA: MIT Press.

Jacobs, Jane. 1992 [1962]. *The Death and Life of Great American Cities*. New York: Vintage Press.

Jacobsen, P. L. 2003. Safety in Numbers: More Walkers and Bicyclists, Safer Walking and Biking. *Injury Prevention* 9:205–209.

Jacquemart, G. 1998. *Modern Roundabout Practice in the United States*. National Cooperative Highway Research Program, Synthesis of Highway Practice 264. Washington, DC: National Academy Press.

James Corner Field Operations and Diller, Scofidio & Renfro. 2015. *The High Line*. London: Phaidon Press.

Japan Sustainable Building Consortium and Institute for Building Environment and Energy Conservation. 2017. CASBEE: Comprehensive Assessment System for Built Environment Efficiency. http://www.ibec.or.jp/CASBEE/english/.

Jarzombek, Mark M. 2004. *Designing MIT: Bosworth's New Tech*. Boston: Northeastern University Press.

Jefferson Center. n.d. Citizens Juries. http://jefferson-center.org/.

Jewell, Nicholas. 2015. *Shopping Malls and Public Space in Modern China*. London: Routledge.

Jim, C.Y., and Wendy Y. Chen. 2009. Value of Scenic Views: Hedonic Assessment of Private Housing in Hong Kong. *Landscape and Urban Planning* 91:226–234.

Katz, Robert. 1977. *Design of the Housing Site*. Champaign: University of Illinois Press.

Kayden, Jerold S. 1978. *Incentive Zoning in New York City: A Cost-Benefit Analysis*. Cambridge, MA: Lincoln Institute of Land Policy.

Kayden, Jerold S. 2000. *Privately Owned Public Space: The New York City Experience*. New York: Wiley.

Kelo. 2005. Kelo et al. v. City of New London et al., 545 U.S. 369.

Kenny, J. F., N. L. Barber, S. S. Hutson, K. S. Linsey, J. K. Lovelace, and M. A. Maupin. 2009. Estimated Use of Water in the United States in 2005. Geological Survey Circular 1344.

Kenworthy, Jeff. 2013. Trends in Transport and Urban Development in Thirty-Three International Cities 1995–6 to 2005–6: Some Prospects for Lower Carbon Transport. In Steffen Lehmann, ed., *Low Carbon Cities: Transforming Urban Systems*. London: Routledge.

Kenworthy, Jeff. 2015. Non-Motorized Mode Cities in a Global Cities Cluster Analysis: A Study of Trends in Mumbai, Shanghai, Beijing and Guangzhou since 1995. Working paper prepared for Hosoya Schaefer Architects AG.

Kenworthy, Jeff, and Felix B. Laube. 2001. *Millennium Cities Database for Sustainable Transport. Brussels: International Union of Public Transport*. Perth: Murdoch University Institute for Sustainability and Technology Policy.

Kenworthy, Jeff, and Craig Townsend. 2002. An International Comparative Perspective on Motorization in Urban China. *IATSS Research* 26 (2): 99–109.

Khan, Adil Mohammed, and Md. Akter Mahmud. 2008. FAR as a Development Control Took: A New Growth Management Technique for Dhaka City. *Jahangirnagar Planning Review* 6:49–54.

Khattak, Asad J., and John Stone. 2004. Traditional Neighborhood Development Trip Generation Study. Final Report. Center for Urban and Regional Studies, University of North Carolina at Chapel Hill.

Kittelson and Associates et al. 2003. Transit Capacity and Quality of Service Manual. 2nd ed. Transportation Research Board of the National Academies, Washington, DC, TCRP Report 100.

Klett, J. E., and C. R. Wilson. 2009. Xeriscaping: Ground Cover Plants. Colorado State University Extension. http://www.ext.colostate.edu/pubs/garden/07230.html.

Knoll, Wolfgang, and Martin Hechinger. 2007. *Architectural Models: Construction Techniques*. Plantation, FL: J. Ross Publishing.

Kohn, A. Eugene, and Paul Katz. 2002. *Building Type Basics for Office Buildings*. New York: Wiley.

Kost, Christopher, and Mathias Nohn. 2011. Better Streets, Better Cities: A Guide to Street Design in Urban India. Institute for Transportation and Development Policy and Environmental Planning Collaborative. http://www.itdp.org/documents/Better Streets111221.pdf.

Kroll, B., and R. Sommer. 1976. Bicyclists' Response to Urban Bikeways. *Journal of the American Institute of Planners* 42 (January): 41–51.

Kulash, Walter M. 2001. *Residential Streets*. 3rd ed. Washington, DC: Urban Land Institute.

Kulash, Walter M., Joe Anglin, and David Marks. 1990. Traditional Neighborhood Development: Will the Traffic Work? *Development* 21 (July/August): 21–24.

Kumar, Manish, and Vivekananda Biswas. 2013. Identification of Potential Sites for Urban Development Using GIS Based Multi Criteria Evaluation Technique. *Journal of Settlements and Spatial Planning* 4 (1): 45–51.

Kuusiola, Timo, Maaria Wierink, and Karl Heiskanen. 2012. Comparison of Collection Schemes of Municipal Solid Waste Metallic Fraction: The Impacts on Global Warming Potential for the Case of the Helsinki Metropolitan Area, Finland. *Sustainability* 4:2586–2610.

LaGro, James A., Jr. 2008. *Site Analysis: Linking Program and Concept in Land Planning and Design*. 2nd ed. New York: Wiley.

Lancaster, R. A., ed. 1990. *Recreation, Park and Open Space Standards and Guidelines*. Ashburn, VA: National Recreation and Park Association. http://www.prm.nau.edu/prm423/recreation _standards.htm.

Landcom. Inc. n.d. Street Tree Design Guidelines (Australia). http://www.landcom.com.au/publication/download/ street-tree-design-guidelines/.

LaPlante, John, and Thomas P. Kaeser. 2007. A History of Pedestrian Signal Walking Speed Assumptions. Third Urban Street Symposium, June 24–27, Seattle, Washington.

Larco, Nico and Kristin Kelsey. 2014. *Site Design for Multifamily Housing: Creating Livable, Connected Neighborhoods*. 2nd ed. Washington, DC: Island Press.

Larwood, Scott, and C. P. van Dam. 2006. Permitting Setback Requirements for Wind Turbines in California. California Wind Energy Collaborative. http://energy.ucdavis.edu/files/05-06-2013 -CEC-500-2005-184.pdf.

Law Handbook. 2017. Environmental Impact Assessment. Fitzroy Legal Services, Inc., Victoria, Australia. http://www.lawhandbook .org.au/2016_11_03_03_environmental_impact_assessment_eia/.

Leaf, W. A., and D. F. Preusser. 1998. Literature Review on Vehicle Travel Speeds and Pedestrian Injuries. National Highway Traffic Safety Administration, US Department of Transportation.

Lee, Jennifer H., Nathalie Robbel, and Carlos Dora. 2013. Cross Country Analysis of the Institutionalization of Health Impact Assessment. Social Determinants of Health Discussion Paper Series 8 (Policy and Practice). Geneva: World Health Organization; http://apps.who.int/iris/bitstream/10665/83299/1/9789241505437 _eng.pdf.

Leinberger, Christopher B. 2008. *The Option of Urbanism: Investing in a New American Dream*. Washington, DC: Island Press.

Lennertz, Bill, and Aarin Kutzenhiser. 2006. *The Charrette Handbook*. Chicago: American Planning Association Publishing.

Letema, Sammy, Bas van Vliet, and Jules B. van Lier. 2011. Innovations in Sanitation for Sustainable Urban Growth: Modernised Mixtures in an East African Context. On the Waterfront 2011. https://www.researchgate.net/publication/233740032 _Innovations_in_sanitation_for_sustainable_urban_growth_Modernised _mixtures_in_an_East_African_context.

Levlin, Erik. 2009. Maximizing Sludge and Biogas Production for Counteracting Global Warming. http://urn.kb.se/resolve?urn =urn:nbn:se:kth:diva-81528.

Li, Huan, and Robert L. Bertini. 2008. Optimal Bus Stop Spacing for Minimizing Transit Operation Cost. ASCE, Proceedings of the Sixth International Conference of Traffic and Transportation Studies Congress.

Lin, Zhongjie. 2014. Constructing Utopias: China's Emerging Eco-cities. ARCC/EAAE 2014 Architectural Research Conference, "Beyond Architecture: New Intersections & Connections." http://www.arcc-journal.org/index.php/repository/article/download /310/246.

Lincolnshire. n.d. Design Guide for Residential Areas. http://www .e-lindsey.gov.uk/CHttpHandler.ashx?id=1647&p=0.

Listokin, David, and Carole Walker. 1989. *The Subdivision and Site Plan Handbook*. New Brunswick, NJ: Rutgers Center for Urban Policy Research.

Locke, John. 1988 [1689]. *Two Treatises of Government*. Cambridge: Cambridge University Press.

Los Angeles County. 2011. Model Street Design Manual for Living Streets. http://www.modelstreetdesignmanual.com/.

Los Angeles Department of City Planning. 1983. Land Form Grading Manual. http://cityplanning.lacity.org/Forms_Procedures /LandformGradingManual.pdf.

Los Angeles Urban Forestry Division. n.d. Street Tree Selection Guide. http://bss.lacity.org/UrbanForestry/StreetTree SelectionGuide.htm.

Lowe, Will. n.d. Software for Content Analysis – A Review. http:// dl.conjugateprior.org/preprints/content-review.pdf.

Low Impact Development Center. n.d. Low Impact Development (LID): A Literature Review. US Environmental Protection Agency.

Lund, John W. 1990. Geothermal Heat Pump Utilization in the United States. Klamath Falls: Oregon Institute of Technology Geo-Heat Center.

Luttik, Joke. 2000. The Value of Trees, Water and Open Space as Reflected by House Prices in the Netherlands. *Landscape and Urban Planning* 48 (3–4): 161–167.

Lynch, Kevin. 1960. *Image of the City*. Cambridge, MA: MIT Press.

Lynch, Kevin. 1962. *Site Planning*. Cambridge, MA: MIT Press.

Lynch, Kevin. 1973. *Site Planning*. 2nd ed. Cambridge, MA: MIT Press.

Lynch, Kevin, and Gary Hack. 1984. *Site Planning*. 3rd ed. Cambridge, MA: MIT Press.

Lyndon, Donlyn, and Jim Alinder. 2014. *The Sea Ranch: Fifty Years of Architecture, Landscape, Place, and Community on the Northern California Coast*. New York: Princeton Architectural Press.

Macdonald, Elizabeth. n.d. Graphics for Planners: Tutorials in Computer Graphics Programs. http://graphics-tutorial.ced .berkeley.edu/photoshop.htm.

Mahmood, Qaisar, et al. 2013. Natural Treatment Systems as Sustainable Ecotechnologies for the Developing Countries. *BioMed Research International* 2013: 796373. doi:10.1155/2013/796373. http://www.ncbi.nlm.nih.gov/pmc/articles/PMC3708409/.

Malczewski, Jacek. 2004. GIS-Based Land-Use Suitability Analysis: A Critical Overview. *Progress in Planning* 62:3–65.

Marcus, Claire Cooper, and Carolyn Francis, eds. 1998. *People Places: Design Guidelines for Public Spaces*. 2nd ed. New York: Wiley.

Marcus, Clare Cooper, and Wendy Sarkissian. 1986. *Housing as if People Mattered: Site Design Guidelines for Medium-Density Family Housing*. Berkeley: University of California Press.

Marsh, William M. 2010. *Landscape Planning: Environmental Applications*. 5th ed. New York: Wiley.

Marshall, Richard. 2001. *Waterfronts in Post-industrial Cities*. Abingdon, UK: Taylor and Francis.

Marshall, Stephen. 2005. *Streets and Patterns: The Structure of Urban Geometry*. London: Spon Press.

Marshall, Wesley E., and Norman Garrick. 2008. Street Network Types and Road Safety: A Study of 24 California Cities. University of Connecticut, Storrs, CT. http://www.sacog.org /complete-streets/toolkit/files/docs/Garrick%20%26%20Marshall _Street%20Network%20Types%20and%20Road%20Safety.pdf.

Martens, Yuri, Juriaan van Meel, and Hermen Jan van Ree. 2010. *Planning Office Spaces: A Practical Guide for Managers and Designers*. London: Laurence King Publishing.

Martin, William A., and Nancy A. McGuckin. 1998. Travel Estimation Techniques for Urban Planning. NCHRP Report 365. Washington, DC: National Research Council, Transportation Research Board.

Maryland Department of the Environment. 2007 [2000]. Maryland Stormwater Design Manual. http://www.mde.state.md.us/programs /Water/StormwaterManagementProgram/MarylandStormwater DesignManual/Pages/Programs/WaterPrograms/Sedimentand Stormwater/stormwater_design/index.aspx.

Mateo-Babiano, Iderlina. 2003. Pedestrian Space Management as a Strategy in Achieving Sustainable Mobility. Working paper for Oikos PhD Summer Academy, St. Gallen, Switzerland. http:// citeseerx.ist.psu.edu/viewdoc/similar?doi=10.1.1.110.5978&type=sc.

Matsui, Minoru, and Chikashi Deguchi. 2014. The Characteristics of Land Readjustment Systems in Japan, Thailand and Mongolia and an Evaluation of the Applicability to Developing Countries. Proceedings of International Symposium on City Planning 2014, Hanoi, Vietnam. http://www.cpij.or.jp/com/iac/sympo/ Proceedings2014/3-fullpaper.pdf.

Maupin, Molly A., Joan F. Kenny, Susan S. Hutson, John K. Lovelace, Nancy L. Barber, and Kristin S. Linsey. 2014. Estimated Use of Water in the United States in 2010. US Geological Survey, Reston, VA, Circular 1405. http://pubs.usgs.gov/circ/1405/.

McCamant, Kathryn, and Charles Durrett. 2014. *Creating Cohousing: Building Sustainable Communities*. Gabriola, BC: New Society Publishers.

McCann, Barbara, and Susanne Rynne. 2010. Complete Streets. American Planning Institute, Washington, DC, PAS 559.

McDonough, William, and Michel Braungart. 2002. *Cradle to Cradle: Remaking the Way We Make Things*. New York: North Point Press.

McGovern, Stephen J. 2006. Philadelphia's Neighborhood Transformation Initiative: A Case Study of Mayoral Leadership, Bold Planning and Conflict. *Housing Policy Debate* 17:529–570.

McHarg, Ian L. 1971. *Design with Nature*. Philadelphia: Natural History Press.

McMonagle, J. C. 1952. Traffic Accidents and Roadside Features. *Highway Research Board Bulletin* 55:38–48.

Meachem, John. n.d. Googleplex: A New Campus Community. Clive Wilkinson Architects. http://www.clivewilkinson.com/pdfs /CWACaseStudy_GoogleplexANewCampusCommunity.pdf.

Melbourne Water Corporation. 2010. Constructed Wetlands Guidelines. Melbourne, Australia. http://www.melbournewater.com.au/Planning-and-building/Forms-guidelines-and-standard-drawings/Documents/Constructed-wetlands-guidelines-2010.pdf.

Metro Jacksonville Magazine. 2012. Sunflowers for Lead, Spider Plants for Arsenic. *Metro Jacksonville* Magazine, July 8. http://www.metrojacksonville.com/article/2010-jun-sunflowers-for-lead-spider-plants-for-arsenic.

Michael Sorkin Studio. 1992. *Wiggle*. New York: Monacelli Press.

Michelson, William. 2011. Influences of Sociology on Urban Design. In Tridib Banerjee and Anastasia Loukaitou-Sideris, eds., *Companion to Urban Design*. London: Routledge.

Miles, Mike, Laurence M. Netherton, and Adrienne Schmitz. 2015. *Real Estate Development*. 5th ed. Washington, DC: Urban Land Institute.

Miller, Norm. 2014. Workplace Trends in Office Space: Implications for Future Office Demand. Working Paper, University of San Diego, Burnham-Moores Center for Real Estate. http://www.normmiller.net/wp-content/uploads/2014/04/Estimating_Office_Space_Requirements-Feb-17-2014.pdf.

Ministry of Land, Infrastructure and Transport, Japan. n.d. Urban Land Use Planning System in Japan. http://www.mlit.go.jp/common/000234477.pdf.

Minnesota Pollution Control Agency. 2008. Minnesota Stormwater Manual. http://www.pca.state.mn.us/index.php/view-document.html?gid=8937.

Moeller, John. 1965. Standards for Outdoor Recreation Areas. American Planning Association, Chicago, Information Report No. 194. https://www.planning.org/pas/at60/report194.htm.

Montgomery, Michael R., and Richard Bean. 1999. Market Failure, Government Failure, and the Private Supply of Public Goods: The Case of Climate-Controlled Walkway Networks. *Public Choice* 99:403–437.

Moore, Robin C., Susan M. Goltsman, and Daniel S. Iacofano, eds. 1992. *Play for All Guidelines: Planning, Design and Management of Outdoor Play Settings for All Children*. 2nd ed. Berkeley, CA: MIG Communications.

Morar, Tudor, Radu Radoslav, Luiza Cecilia Spiridon, and Lidia Päcurar. 2014. Assessing Pedestrian Accessibility to Green Space Using GIS. *Transylvanian Review of Administrative Sciences* 42: E 116–139. http://www.rtsa.ro/tras/index.php/tras/article/download/94/90.

Morrall, John F., L. L. Ratnayake, and P. N. Seneviratne. 1991. Comparison of Central Business District Pedestrian Characteristics in Canada and Sri Lanka. *Transportation Research Record* (1294): 57–61.

Moudon, Anne Vernez. 2009. Real Noise from the Urban Environment: How Ambient Community Noise Affects Health and What Can Be Done about It. *American Journal of Preventive Medicine* 37 (2): 167–171.

Moughtin, Cliff, Rafael Cuesta, Christine Sarris, and Paola Signoretta. 2003. *Urban Design: Method and Techniques*. 2nd ed. Oxford: Architectural Press.

Mundigo, Axel, and Dora Crouch. 1977. The City Planning Ordinances of the Laws of the Indies Revisited, I. *Town Planning Review* 48:247–268. http://codesproject.asu.edu/sites/default/files/THE%20LAWS%20OF%20THE%20INDIEStranslated.pdf.

Murakami, Shuzo, Kazuo Iwamura, and Raymond J. Cole. 2014. CASBEE: A Decade of Development and Application of an Environmental Assessment System for the Built Environment. Japan Sustainable Building Consortium and Institute for Building Environment and Energy Conservation. http://www.ibec.or.jp/CASBEE/english/document/CASBEE_Book_Flyer.pdf.

Murdock, Steve H., Chris Kelley, Jeffrey Jordan, Beverly Pecotte, and Alvin Luedke. 2015. *Demographics: A Guide to Methods and Data Sources for Media, Business, and Government*. New York: Routledge.

Muthukrishnan, Suresh, et al. 2006. Calibration of a Simple Rainfall-Runoff Model for Long-Term Hydrological Impact Evaluation. *URISA Journal* 18 (2): 35–42.

NASA. n.d. ESRL Solar Position Calculator. US National Aeronautics and Space Administration. http://www.esrl.noaa.gov/gmd/grad/solcalc/azel.html.

Nasar, Jack L. 2006. *Design by Competition: Making Competitions Work*. Cambridge: Cambridge University Press.

National Association of City Transportation Officials. n.d. Urban Bicycle Design Guide. https://nacto.org/publication/urban-bikeway-design-guide/.

National Charrette Institute. n.d. http://www.charretteinstitute.org.

National Health and Medical Research Council. 2010. Wind Turbines and Health: A Rapid Review of the Evidence. Australian Government. http://www.nhmrc.gov.au/_files_nhmrc/publications/attachments/new0048_evidence_review_wind_turbines_and_health.pdf.

National Institutes of Health. n.d. Pubmed. http://www.ncbi.nim.nih.gov/pubmed.

National Oceanic and Atmospheric Administration. n.d. LIDAR Data Access Viewer. https://coast.noaa.gov/dataviewer/#/lidar/search/.

National Park Service. n.d. An Introduction to Using Native Plants in Restoration Projects. US Department of the Interior. http://www.nps.gov/plants/restore/pubs/intronatplant/toc.htm.

National Renewable Energy Laboratory. n.d. PVWATTS—A Performance Calculator for Grid Connected PV Systems. http://rredc.nrel.gov/solar/calculators/PVWATTS/version1/.

National Research Council. 2007. Elevation Data for Floodplain Mapping. National Research Council, Committee on Floodplain Mapping Technologies. http://www.nap.edu/catalog/11829.html.

National Research Council. 2011. Improving Health in the United States: The Role of Health Impact Assessment. National Research Council, Committee on Health Impact Assessment. Washington, DC: National Academies Press. http://www.nap.edu/download.php?record_id=13229.

National Weather Service. n.d. Precipitation Frequency Estimates. National Weather Service, US National Oceanic and Atmospheric Administration. http://www.nws.noaa.gov/oh/hdsc/index.html.

Natural Resources Canada. 2004. Micro-Hydropower Systems: A Buyer's Guide. https://docs.google.com/viewer?url=https%3A%2F%2Fwww.nrcan.gc.ca%2Fsites%2Fwww.nrcan.gc.ca%2Ffiles%2Fcanmetenergy%2Ffiles%2Fpubs%2Fbuyersguidehydroeng.pdf.

Natural Resources Canada. 2005. An Introduction to Micro-Hydropower Systems. http://www.nrcan.gc.ca/sites/www.nrcan.gc.ca/files/canmetenergy/files/pubs/Intro_MicroHydro_ENG.pdf.

Natural Resources Conservation Service. 2010. Field Indicators of Hydric Soils in the United States: A Guide for Identifying and Delineating Hydric Soils, Version 7.0. US Department of Agriculture. ftp://ftp-fc.sc.egov.usda.gov/NSSC/Hydric_Soils/FieldIndicators_v7.pdf.

Natural Resources Conservation Service. 2017. Wind Rose Data. US Department of Agriculture. http://www.wcc.nrcs.usda.gov/climate/windrose.html.

Needham, Barrie. 2007. The Search for Greater Efficiency: Land Readjustment in the Netherlands. In Yu-Hung Hong and Barrie Needham, eds., *Analyzing Land Readjustment: Economics, Law and Collective Action*, 127–128. Cambridge, MA: Lincoln Institute of Land Policy.

Nelesson, Anton. 1994. *Visions for a New American Dream: Process, Principles and an Ordinance to Plan and Design Small Communities.* 2nd ed. Chicago: Planners Press.

New Jersey Department of Environmental Protection. 2016. Stormwater Best Management Practices Manual. http://www.njstormwater.org/bmp_manual2.htm.

Newman, Oscar. 1972. *Defensible Space: Crime Prevention through Environmental Design.* New York: Macmillan.

Newman, Oscar. 1980. *Community of Interest.* Garden City, NY: Anchor/Doubleday.

New South Wales Roads and Traffic Authority. 2003. NSW Bicycle Guidelines. http://www.rms.nsw.gov.au/business-industry/partners-suppliers/documents/technical-manuals/nswbicyclev12aa.i.pdf.

New York City. 2017. Vision Zero Plan. http://www.nyc.gov/html/visionzero/pages/home/home.shtml.

New York City Department of Parks and Recreation. n.d. Approved Species List. http://www.nycgovparks.org/trees/street-tree-planting/species-list.

New York City Department of Transportation. 2009. Street Design Manual. http://www.nyc.gov/dot.

New York City Mayor's Office of Environmental Coordination. 2014. CEQR Technical Manual. http://www.nyc.gov/html/oec/html/ceqr/technical_manual_2014.shtml.

New York Department of City Planning. 2006. New York City Pedestrian Level of Service Study Phase I. http://www1.nyc.gov/assets/planning/download/pdf/plans/transportation/td_ped_level_serv.pdf.

Nijkamp, Peter, Marc van der Burch, and Gabriella Vindigni. 2002. A Comparative Institutional Evaluation of Public-Private Partnerships in Dutch Urban Land-Use and Revitalisation Projects. *Urban Studies* 39 (10): 1865–1880.

Noble, J., and A. Smith. 1992. Residential Roads and Footpaths – Layout Considerations – Design Bulletin 32. London: Her Majesty's Stationery Office.

North Carolina State University. n.d. Wetlands Identification. http://www.water.ncsu.edu/watershedss/info/wetlands/onsite.html.

Nowak, David J., and Daniel E. Crane. 2001. Carbon Storage and Sequestration by Urban Trees in the USA. *Environmental Pollution* 116:381–389.

OECD. 2006. Speed Management. Organisation for Economic Co-operation and Development and European Conference of Ministers of Transport.

Oke, T. R. 1987. *Boundary Layer Climates.* New York: Routledge.

Oke, T. R. 1997. Urban Climates and Global Environmental Change. In R. D. Thompson and A. Perry, eds., *Applied Climatology: Principles and Practices*, 273–287. London: Routledge.

Oldenburg, Ray. 1999. *The Great Good Place: Cafés, Coffee Shops, Bookstores, Bars, Hair Salons and Other Hangouts at the Heart of a Community.* Boston: Da Capo Press.

Oregon Department of Energy. n.d. Small, Low-Impact Hydropower. http://www.oregon.gov/ENERGY/RENEW/Pages/hydro/Hydro_index.aspx#Regulation.

Parolek, Daniel G., Karen Parolek, and Paul C. Crawford. 2008. *Form-Based Codes: A Guide for Planners, Urban Designers, Municipalities and Developers.* New York: Wiley.

Parsons Brinkerhoff Quade & Douglas, Inc. 2012. Track Design Handbook for Light Rail Transit. 2nd ed. National Academy Press, Transit Cooperative Research Program Report 155. http://onlinepubs.trb.org/onlinepubs/tcrp/tcrp_rpt_155.pdf.

Paschotta, Rudiger. n.d Optical Fiber Communications. In *RP Photonics Encyclopedia*. http://www.rp-photonics.com/optical_fiber_communications.html.

Pattern Language. n.d. http://www.patternlanguage.com.

Paulien and Associates. 2011. Utah System of Higher Education: Higher Education Space Standards Study. http://higheredutah.org/wp-content/uploads/2013/06/pff_2011_spacestandards_study.pdf.

Payne, Geoffrey. 1996. Urban Land Tenure and Property Rights in Developing Countries: A Review of the Literature. World Bank, Washington, DC. http://sheltercentre.org/sites/default/files/overseas_development_administration_1996_urban_land_tenure_and_property_rights.pdf.

PBC Geographic Information Services. n.d. http://www.pbcgis.com/viewshed/.

Pelling, Kirstie. 2009. Safety in Numbers. *iSquared* 8:22–26. http://www.crowddynamics.com.

Pennsylvania Department of Environmental Protection. 2003. Best Management Practices (BMP) for the Management of Waste from Land Clearing, Grubbing and Excavation (LCGE). http://www.elibrary.dep.state.pa.us/dsweb/Get/Document-49033/254-5400-001.pdf.

Philadelphia Water Department. 2011. Green City Clean Waters: The City of Philadelphia's Program for Combined Sewer Overflow Control. http://www.phillywatersheds.org/.

Planungszelle (Planning Cell). n.d. http://www.planungszelle.de/.

Play Enthusiast. n.d. *Play Enthusiast's Playground Blog*. https://playenthusiast.wordpress.com/.

Plummer, Joseph T. 1974. The Concept and Application of Life Style Segmentation. *Journal of Marketing* 38:35–42. http://bulatov.org.ua/teaching_courses/marketing_files/Lecture%2010%20ItM%20Life%20Style%20segmentation.pdf.

Poirier, Desmond. 2008. Skate Parks: A Guide for Landscape Architects and Planners. MLA thesis, Kansas State University, Manhattan. http://hdl.handle.net/2097/954.

Pollard, Robert. 1980. Topographic Amenities, Building Height and the Supply of Urban Housing. *Regional Science and Urban Economics* 10 (8): 181–199.

Pollution Control Systems. 2014. Wastewater Treatment Package Plants. Pollution Control Systems, Inc. http://www.pollutioncontrolsystem.com/Page.aspx/31/PackagePlants.html.

Pomeranz, M., B. Pon, H. Akbari, and S.-C. Chang. 2002. The Effect of Pavements' Temperatures on Air Temperatures in Large Cities. Paper LBNL-43442. Lawrence Berkeley National Laboratory, Berkeley, CA.

Portland Planning Department. 1991. Downtown Urban Design Guidelines. http://www.portlandmaine.gov/DocumentCenter/Home/View/3375.

Potter, Stephen. 2003. Transport Energy and Emissions: Urban Public Transit. In D. A. Hensher and K. J. Button, eds., *Handbook of Transport and the Environment*. Amsterdam: Elsevier.

Powell, Donald. 2011. Pillars of Design. *Urban Land*, October 18. http://urbanland.uli.org/development-business/pillars-of-design/.

Profous, George V. 1992. Trees and Urban Forestry in Beijing, China. *Journal of Arboriculture* 18 (3): 145–154. http://joa.isa-arbor.com/request.asp?JournalID=1&ArticleID=2501&Type=2.

Project for Public Spaces. 2009. What Makes a Successful Place? http://www.pps.org/reference/grplacefeat/.

Project for Public Spaces. n.d. Great Public Spaces. http://www.pps.org/places/.

Punter, John. 1999. *Design Guidelines in American Cities: A Review of Design Policies and Guidance in Five West Coast Cities*. Liverpool: Liverpool University Press.

Punter, John. 2003. *The Vancouver Achievement: Urban Planning and Design*. Vancouver: UBC Press.

Pushkarev, Boris, and Jeffrey M. Zupan. 1975a. Capacity of Walkways. *Transportation Research Record* (538).

Pushkarev, Boris, with Jeffrey Zupan. 1975b. *Urban Space for Pedestrians*. Cambridge, MA: MIT Press.

PWC Consultants. 2014. The Future of Work: A Journey to 2022. https://www.pwc.com/gx/en/managing-tomorrows-people/future-of-work/assets/pdf/future-of-rork-report-v16-web.pdf.

Ragheb, M. 2013. Vertical Axis Wind Turbines. http://mragheb.com/NPRE%20475%20Wind%20Power%20Systems/Vertical%20Axis%20Wind%20Turbines.pdf.

Rapoport, Amos. 1969. *House Form and Culture*. New York: Prentice Hall.

Ratti, Carlo, and Matthew Claudel. 2016. *The City of Tomorrow: Sensors, Networks, Hackers and the Future of Urban Life*. New Haven: Yale University Press.

Rees, W. G. 1990. *Physical Properties of Remote Sensing*. Cambridge: Cambridge University Press.

Reilly, William J. 1931. *The Law of Retail Gravitation*. New York: W. J. Reilly. https://www.scribd.com/doc/70608682/Reilly-s-law-of-retail-gravitation.

Reindel, Gene. 2001. Overview of Noise Metrics and Acoustical Objectives. AAAE Sound Insulation Symposium, 21–23 October 2001. http://www.hmmh.com/cmsdocuments/noise_metrics_emr.pdf.

Reiser + Umemoto. 2006. *Atlas of Novel Techtonics*. New York: Princeton Architectural Press.

Rios, Ramiro Alberto, Francisco Arango, Vera Lucia Vincenti, and Rafael Acevedo-Daunas. 2013. Mitigation Strategies and Accounting Methods for Greenhouse Gas Emissions from Transportation. Inter-American Development Bank. http://www10.iadb.org/intal/intalcdi/PE/2013/12483.pdf.

Roberts, Marion, and Clara Greed, eds. 2013. *Approaching Urban Design: The Design Process*. London: Routledge.

Robinson, Charles Mulford. 1911. *The Width and Arrangement of Streets*. New York: Engineering News Publishing Company.

Robinson, Charles Mulford. 1916. *City Planning, with Special Reference to the Planning of Streets and Lots*. New York: G. P. Putnam's Sons.

Rodrigue, Jean-Paul. 2013. *The Geography of Transport Systems*. 3rd ed. New York: Routledge. Summary at https://people.hofstra.edu/geotrans/index.html.

Rodrigues, Luis. n.d. Urban Design: Pedestrian-Only Shopping Streets Make Communities More Livable. Sustainable Cities Collective. http://www.smartcitiesdive.com/ex/sustainable citiescollective/pedestrian-only-shopping-streets-make -communities-more-livable/130276/.

Roger Bayley, Inc. 2010. The Challenge Series: The 2010 Winter Olympics: The Southeast False Creek Olympic Village, Vancouver, Canada. http://www.thechallengeseries.ca.

Rogers, Anthony L., James F. Manwell, and Sally Wright. 2006. Wind Turbine Acoustic Noise. Renewable Energy Research Laboratory, University of Massachusetts at Amherst. http://www.minutemanwind.com/pdf/Understanding%20Wind%20Turbine%20 Acoustic%20Noise.pdf.

Roper Center. n.d. Polling Fundamentals. Roper Center, Cornell University. http://ropercenter.cornell.edu/support/polling -fundamentals/.

Rosenberg, Daniel K., Barry R. Noon, and E. Charles Meslow. 1997. Biological Corridors: Form, Function, and Efficacy. *BioScience* 47 (10): 677–687 http://www.jstor.org/stable/view/1313208?seq=1.

Ross, Catherine L., Marla Orenstein, and Nisha Botchwey. 2014. *Health Impact Assessment in the United States*. New York: Springer.

Rossiter, David G. 2007. Classification of Urban and Industrial Soils in the World Reference Base for Soil Resources. *Journal of Soils and Sediments*. doi:10.1065/jss2007.02.208.

Rouphail, N., J. Hummer, J. Milazzo II, and P. Allen. 1998. Capacity Analysis of Pedestrian and Bicycle Facilities: Recommended procedures for the "Pedestrians" Chapter of the *Highway Capacity Manual*. Federal Highway Administration Report Number FHWA-RD-98-107. Office of Safety & Research & Development, US Federal Highway Administration.

Rudy Bruner Award. n.d. Winners and Case Studies. http://www.rudybruneraward.org/winners/.

RUMBLES. 2009. Vacuum Sewers: Technology That Works Coast-to-Coast. Rocky Mountain Section of AWWA and Rocky Mountain Water Environment Association. http://www.airvac.com/pdf /Western_States_E-print.pdf.

Russell, Francis P. 1994. Battery Park City: An American Dream of Urbanism. In Brenda Case Scheer and Wolfgang F. E. Preiser, eds., *Design Review: Challenging Aesthetic Control*. New York: Chapman and Hall.

Ryan, Zoe. 2006. *The Good Life: New Public Spaces for Recreation*. New York: Van Alen Institute/Princeton Architectural Press.

Sagalyn, Lynne B. 1989. Measuring Financial Returns When the City Acts as an Investor: Boston and Faneuil Hall Marketplace. *Real Estate Issues* 14 (Fall/Winter): 7–15.

Sagalyn, Lynne B. 1993. Leasing: The Strategic Option for Public Development. Paper prepared for the Lincoln Institute of Land Policy and the A. Alfred Taubman Center for State and Local Government, JFK School of Government, Harvard University.

Sagalyn, Lynne B. 2001. *Times Square Roulette: Remaking the City Icon*. Cambridge, MA: MIT Press.

Sagalyn, Lynne B. 2006. The Political Fabric of Design Competitions. In Catherine Malmberg, ed., *The Politics of Design: Competitions for Public Projects*, 29–52. Princeton, NJ: Policy Research Institute for the Region.

Sagalyn, Lynne B. 2007. Land Assembly, Land Readjustment and Public-Private Development. In Yu-Hung Hong and Barrie Needham, eds., *Analyzing Land Readjustment: Economics, Law and Collective Action*, 159–182. Cambridge, MA: Lincoln Institute of Land Policy.

Sagalyn, Lynne. 2016. *Power at Ground Zero: Money, Politics, and the Remaking of Lower Manhattan*. New York: Oxford University Press.

Sam Schwartz Engineering. 2012. Steps to a Walkable Community: A Guide for Citizens, Planners and Engineers. http://www.americawalks.org/walksteps.

Santapau, H. n.d. Common Trees (India). http://www.arvindguptatoys.com/arvindgupta/santapau.pdf.

Santos, A., N. McGuckin, H. Y. Nakamoto, D. Gray, and S. Liss. 2011. *Summary of Travel Trends: 2009 National Household Travel Survey*. Washington, DC: US Department of Transportation.

Sasaki Associates. 2015. Ananas Master Plan, Silang, Cavite, Philippines. Prepared for ACM Homes. http://www.sasaki.com /project/389/ananas-new-community/.

Sauder School of Business. 2011. Integrated Community Energy System: Southeast False Creek Neighborhood Energy Utility. Quest Business Case. http://www.sauder.ubc.ca/Faculty /Research_Centres/ISIS/Resources/~/media/AEE7D705491345 178C4568992FB87658.ashx.

Scheer, Brenda Case, and Wolfgang F. E. Preiser, eds. 1994. *Design Review: Challenging Aesthetic Control*. New York: Chapman and Hall.

Scheyer, J. M., and K. W. Hipple. 2005. *Urban Soil Primer*. Lincoln, NE: United States Department of Agriculture, Natural Resources Conservation Service, National Soil Survey Center. http://soils .usda.gov/use.

Schmidt, T., D. Mangold, and H. Müller-Steinhagen. 2004. Central Solar Heating Plants with Seasonal Storage in Germany. *Solar Energy* 76:165–174.

Schmitz, Adrienne. 2004. *Residential Development Handbook*. 3rd ed. Washington, DC: Urban Land Institute.

Schoenauer, Norbert. 1962. *The Court Garden House*. Montreal: McGill University Press.

Schwanke, Dean. 2016. *Mixed-Use Development: Nine Case Studies of Complex Projects*. Washington, DC: Urban Land Institute.

Senda, Mitsuru. 1992. *Design of Children's Play Environments*. New York: McGraw-Hill.

Seskin, Stefanie, with Barbara McCann. 2012. Complete Streets: Local Policy Workbook. Smart Growth America and National Complete Streets Coalition, Washington, DC.

Seskin, Stefanie, with Barbara McCann, Erin Rosenblum, and Catherine Vanderwaart. 2012. Complete Streets: Policy Analysis 2011. Smart Growth America and National Complete Streets Coalition, Washington, DC.

Shackell, Aileen, Nicola Butler, Phil Doyle, and David Ball. n.d. *Design for Plan: A Guide to Creating Successful Play Spaces.* Play England. Nottingham: DCSF Publications.

Sharky, Bruce G. 2014. *Landscape Site Grading Principles: Grading with Design in Mind*. New York: Wiley.

Sherman, Roger. 1978. Modern Housing Prototypes. Open Source Publication: https://ia800708.us.archive.org/7/items /ModernHousingPrototypes/ModernHousingPrototypesRoger Sherwood.pdf.

Shoup, Donald C. 1997. The High Cost of Free Parking. *Journal of Planning Education and Research* 17:3–20.

Shoup, Donald C. 1999. The Trouble with Minimum Parking Requirements. *Transportation Research Part A, Policy and Practice* 33:549–574.

Siegal, Jacob S. 2002. *Applied Demography: Applications to Business, Government, Law, and Public Policy*. San Diego: Academic Press.

Siegel, Michael L., Jutka Terris, and Kaid Benfield. 2000. *Developments and Dollars: An Introduction to Fiscal Impact Analysis in Land Use Planning*. Washington, DC: Natural Resources Defense Council; http://www.nrdc.org/cities/smartgrowth/dd/ddinx.asp.

Simpson, Alan. 2010. York: New City Beautiful: Toward an Economic Vision. City of York Council. http://www.urbandesign skills.com/_uploads/UDS_YorkVision.pdf.

Sinclair Knight Merz. 2010. Lane Widths on Urban Roads. Bicycle Network, Victoria, Australia. https://docs.google.com /viewer?url=https%3A%2F%2Fwww.bicyclenetwork.com .au%2Fmedia%2Fvanilla_content%2Ffiles%2FLane%2520Widths %2520SKM%25202010.pdf.

Singh, Varanesh, Eric Rivers, and Carla Jaynes. 2010. Neighborhood Pedestrian Analysis Tool (NPAT). *Arup Research Review*, 58–61 http://publications.arup.com/Publications/R /Research_Review/Research_Review_2010.aspx.

Sitkowski, Robert, and Brian Ohm. 2006. Form-Based Land Development Regulations. *Urban Lawyer* 28 (1): 163–172.

Sitte, Camillo. 1945. *The Art of Building Cities: City Building According to Artistic Principles*. Trans. C. T. Stewart. New York: Reinhold.

SketchUp. n.d. 3D Warehouse. https://3dwarehouse.sketchup.com/.

Slater, Cliff. 1997. General Motors and the Demise of Streetcars. *Transportation Quarterly* 51.

Smallhydro.com. n.d. Small Hydropower and Micro Hydropower: Your Online Small Hydroelectric Power Resource. http://www .smallhydro.com.

SmartReFlex. 2015. Smart and Flexible 100% Renewable District Heating and Cooling Systems for European Cities: Guide for Regional Authorities. Intelligent Energy Europe Programme of the European Union. http://www.smartreflex.eu/20151012 _SmartReFlex_Guide.pdf.

Smith, H. W. 1981. Territorial Spacing on a Beach Revisited: A Cross-National Exploration. *Social Psychology Quarterly* 44 (2): 132–137.

Society for College and University Planning. 2003. Campus Facilities Inventory Report, 2003. Executive Summary. http://www .scup.org/knowledge/cfi/.

Solar Electricity Handbook. 2013. Solar Angle Calculator. Coventry, UK: Greenstream Publishing; http://solarelectricityhandbook.com /solar-angle-calculator.html.

Solarge. n.d. http://www.solarge.org/uploads/media/SOLARGE _goodpractice_dk_marstal.pdf.

Solar Power Authority. n.d. How to Size a Solar PV System for Your Home. https://www.solarpowerauthority.com/how-to-size -a-solar-pv-system-for-your-home/.

Solidere. n.d. Beirut City Center: Developing the Finest City Center in the Middle East. http://www.solidere.com/sites/default/files/ attached/cr-brochure.pdf.

Solomon, Susan G. 2005. *American Playgrounds: Revitalizing Community Space*. Lebanon, NH: University Press of New England.

South Australia Health Commission. 1995. Waste Control Systems: Standard for the Construction, Installation and Operation of Septic Tank Systems in South Australia. http://greywateraction.org /content/how-do-percolation-test.

South East Queensland Healthy Waterways Partnership and Ecological Engineering. 2007. Water Sensitive Urban Design: Developing Design Objectives for Urban Development in South East Queensland. http://waterbydesign.com.au/techguide/.

Southworth, Michael, and Eran Ben-Joseph. 1997. *Streets and the Shaping of Towns and Cities*. New York: McGraw-Hill.

Souza, Amy. 2008. Pattern Books: A Planning Tool. *Planning Commissioners Journal* 72: 1–6. https://docs.google.com/viewer ?url=http%3A%2F%2Fplannersweb.com%2Fwp-content %2Fuploads%2F2012%2F07%2F210.pdf.

Sovocool, Kent A. 2005. Xeriscape Conversion Study, Final Report. Southern Nevada Water Authority. http://www.snwa.com/assets /pdf/about_reports_xeriscape.pdf.

Sprankling, John G. 2000. *Understanding Property Law*. Charlottesville, VA: Lexis Publishing.

Springfield Plastics. n.d. http://www.spipipe.com/Apps/PipeFlow Chart.pdf.

Steiner, Ruth Lorraine. 1997. Traditional Neighborhood Shopping Districts: Patterns of Use and Modes of Access. Monograph 54, BART@20, University of California at Berkeley. http://www.fltod .com/research/marketability/traditional_neighborhood_shopping _districts.pdf.

Stern, Robert A. M., David Fishman, and Jacob Tilove. 2013. *Paradise Planned: The Garden Suburb and the Modern City*. New York: Monacelli Press.

Steward, Julian. 1938. Basin-Plateau Aboriginal Sociopolitical Groups. Bureau of American Ethnology Bulletin 120.

Still, G. Keith. 2000. Crowd Dynamics. PhD dissertation, University of Warwick. http://wrap.warwick.ac.uk/36364/.

Strom, Steven, Kurt Nathan, and Jake Woland. 2013. *Site Engineering for Landscape Architects*. 6th ed. New York: Wiley.

Stucki, Pascal, Christian Gloor, and Kai Nagel. 2003. Obstacles in Pedestrian Simulations. Department of Computer Sciences, ETH Zurich. http://www.gkstill.com/CV/PhD/Papers.html.

Stueteville, Robert, et al. 2001. Urban and Architectural Codes and Pattern Books. In *New Urbanism: Comprehensive Report and Best Practices Guide*. Ithaca, NY: New Urban Pub.

Sullivan, Robert G., Leslie B. Kirchler, Tom Lahti, Sherry Roché, Kevin Beckman, Brian Cantwell, and Pamela Richmond. n.d. Wind Turbine Visibility and Visual Impact Threshold Distances in Western Landscapes. Argonne National Laboratory, University of Chicago. http://visualimpact.anl.gov/windvitd/docs/WindVITD.pdf.

SunEarth Tools. n.d. Sun Exposure Calcuator. http://www .sunearthtools.com/dp/tools/pos_sun.php.

Sunset Magazine. n.d. US Climate Zones. http://www.sunset.com /garden/climate-zones/climate-zones-intro-us-map.

Sustainable Sites Initiative. 2009. SITES Guidelines and Performance Benchmarks 2009. American Society of Landscape Architects, Lady Bird Johnson Wildflower Center at the University of Texas at Austin, and the United States Botanical Garden. http://www.sustainablesites.org/report/Guidelines%20and%20 Performance%20Benchmarks_2009.pdf.

Sustainable Sites Initiative. 2017. Certified Projects. http://www .sustainablesites.org/projects/.

Sustainable Sources. 2014. Greywater Irrigation. http://www .greywater.sustainablesources.com.

Suthersan, Suthan S. 1997. *Remediation Engineering: Design Concepts*. Boca Raton, FL: CRC/Lewis Press.

Suthersan, Suthan S. 2002. *Natural and Enhanced Remediation Systems*. Boca Raton, FL: Arcadis/Lewis Publishers.

Tal, Daniel. 2009. *Google SketchUp for Site Design: A Guide to Modeling Site Plans, Terrain and Architecture*. New York: Wiley.

Tang, Dorothy, and Andrew Watkins. 2011. Ecologies of Gold: The Past and Future Mining Landscapes of Johannesburg. *Places*. The Design Observer Group, posted February 24, 2011. http:// places.designobserver.com/feature/ecologies-of-gold -the-past-and-future-mining-landscapes-of-johannesburg/25008/.

Tangires, Helen. 2008. *Public Markets*. New York: W. W. Norton.

Telft, Brian C. 2011. Impact Speed and a Pedestrian's Risk of Severe Injury or Death. AAA Foundation for Traffic Safety, Washington, DC. https://www.aaafoundation.org/sites/default /files/2011PedestrianRiskVsSpeed.pdf.

Tertiary Education Facilities Management Association. 2009. Space Planning Guidelines. 3rd ed. Tertiary Education Facilities Management Association, Inc., Hobart, Australia. http://www .tefma.com/uploads/content/26-TEFMA-SPACE-PLANNING-GUIDELINES-FINAL-ED3-28-AUGUST-09.pdf.

Tetra Tech, Inc. 2011. Evaluation of Urban Soils: Suitability for Green Infrastructure and Urban Agriculture. US Environmental Protection Agency, Publication No. 905R1103.

Texas A&M University System. 2015. Facility Design Guidelines. Office of Facilities Planning and Construction. http://assets.system. tamus.edu/files/fpc/pdf/Facility%20Design%20Guidelines.pdf.

Thadani, Dhiru A. 2010. *The Language of Towns and Cities: A Visual Dictionary*. New York: Rizzoli.

Thomas, R. Karl, Jerry M. Melillo, and Thomas C. Peterson, eds. 2009. *Global Climate Change Impacts in the United States. United States Global Change Research Program*. New York: Cambridge University Press.

Thomas, Randall, and Max Fordham, eds. 2003. *Sustainable Urban Design: An Environmental Approach*. London: Spon Press.

Thomashow, Mitchell. 2016. *The Nine Elements of a Sustainable Campus*. Cambridge, MA: MIT Press.

Thompson, Donna. 1997. Development of Age Appropriate Playgrounds. In Susan Hudson and Donna Thompson, eds., *Playground Safety Handbook*, 14–27. Cedar Falls, IA: National Program for Playground Safety.

Thompson, Donna, Susan Hudson, and Mick G. Mack. n.d. Matching Children and Play Equipment: A Developmental Approach. *EarlychildhoodNews*. http://www.earlychildhoodnews.com /earlychildhood/article_print.aspx?ArticleId=463.

Thompson, F. Longstreth. 1923. *Site Planning in Practice: An Investigation of the Principles of Housing Estate Development*. London: Henry Frowde and Hodder & Stoughton.

Tiner, Ralph W. 1999. *Wetland Indicators: A Guide to Wetland Identification, Delineation, Classification and Mapping*. Boca Raton, FL: CRC Press.

Tonnelat, Stephane. 2010. The Sociology of Public Spaces. https://www.academia.edu/313641/The_Sociology_of_Urban _Public_Spaces.

Topcu, Mehmet, and Ayse Sema Kubat. 2009. The Analysis of Urban Features that Affect Land Values in Residential Areas. In Kaniel Koch, Lars Marcus, and Jesper Steen, eds., *Proceedings of the 7th International Space Syntax Symposium*, 26:1–9. Stockholm: KTH.

Transportation Research Board. 2003. Design Speed, Operating Speed and Posted Speed Practices. NCHRP Report 504. Transportation Research Board, Washington, DC.

Transportation Research Board. 2010. *Highway Capacity Manual*. 5th ed. Washington, DC: Transportation Research Board.

Tree Fund. Pottstown, Pennsylvania. n.d. Greening Our Cities and Towns. http://www.pottstowntrees.org/H2-Best-street-trees.html.

Turley, R., R. Saith, N. Bhan, E. Rehfuess, and B. Carter. 2014. The Effect of Slum Upgrading on Slum Dwellers' Health, Quality of Life and Social Wellbeing. The Cochrane Collaboration. http://www.cochrane.org/CD010067/PUBHLTH_the-effect-of-slum-upgrading-on-slum-dwellers-health-quality-of-life-and-social-wellbeing.

Turner, Paul Venable. 1984. *Campus: An American Planning Tradition*. New York: Architectural History Foundation; Cambridge, MA: MIT Press.

Tyrvainen, Liisa. 1997. The Amenity Value of the Urban Forest: An Application of the Hedonic Pricing Method. *Landscape and Urban Planning* 37:211–222.

Tyrvainen, Liisa, and Antti Miettinen. 2000. Property Prices and Urban Forest Amenities. *Journal of Environmental Economics and Management* 39:205–223.

UK Office of Water Services. 2007. International Comparison of Water and Sewerage Service. http://www.ofwat.gov.uk/regulating/reporting/rpt_int2007.pdf.

UN Centre for Human Settlements. 1999. Reassessment of Urban Planning and Development Regulations in African Cities. United Nations Centre for Human Settlements (Habitat), Nairobi. http://www.sampac.nl/EUKN2015/www.eukn.org/dsresource8b42.pdf?objectid=147674).

UN Department of Economic and Social Affairs. 1975. *Urban Land Policies and Land-Use Control Measures*. Vol. II, *Western Europe*. New York: United Nations.

UN Environment Programme. 2004. Constructed Wetlands: How to Combine Sewage Treatment with Phytotechnology. http://www.unep.or.jp/ietc/publications/freshwater/watershed_manual/03_management-10.pdf.

UN Environment Programme. 2005. International Source Book on Environmentally Sound Technologies for Municipal Solid Waste Management (MSWM). http://www.unep.or.jp/ietc/ESTdir/Pub/msw/index.asp.

UN Environment Programme. 2010. Waste and Climate Change: Global Trends and Strategy Framework. http://www.unep.or.jp/ietc/Publications/spc/Waste&ClimateChange/Waste&ClimateChange.pdf.

United Nations. 1989. The Convention on the Rights of the Child. UN Office of the High Commissioner for Human Rights. http://www.ohchr.org/EN/ProfessionalInterest/Pages/CRC.aspx.

United States Housing Authority. 1949. *Design of Low-Rent Housing Projects: Planning the Site*. Washington, DC: Government Printing Office.

University at Buffalo. n.d. Rudy Bruner Award Digital Archive. http://libweb1.lib.buffalo.edu/bruner/?subscribe=Visit+the+archive.

University at Buffalo and Beyer Blinder Belle Architects & Planners. 2009. Building UB: The Comprehensive Physical Plan. Buffalo, NY. See also http://www.buffalo.edu/facilities/cpg/Space-Planning/AttachmentA.html.

University of California at Berkeley. 1994. Electrophobia: Overcoming Fears of EMFs. *Wellness Letter*, November.

University of Florida. n.d. Street Tree Design Solutions. http://hort.ifas.ufl.edu/woody/street-trees.shtml.

University of Oregon Solar Radiation Monitoring Laboratory. n.d. Sun Path Chart Program. http://solardat.uoregon.edu/SunChartProgram.html.

University of Wisconsin. n.d. Suggested Trees for Streetside Planting in Western Wisconsin, USDA Hardiness Zone 4. http://www.dnr.wi.gov/topic/urbanforests/documents/treesstreetside.pdf.

Urban Design Associates. 2004. *The Architectural Pattern Book: A Tool for Building Great Neighborhoods*. New York: W. W. Norton.

Urban Design Associates. 2005. A Pattern Book for Gulf Coast Neighborhoods. Mississippi Renewal Forum. http://www.mississippirenewal.com/documents/rep_patternbook.pdf.

Urban Development Institute of Australia. 2013. EnviroDevelopment: National Technical Standards Version 2. http://www.envirodevelopment.com.au/_dbase_upl/National_Technical_Standards_V2.pdf.

Urban Land Institute. 2004. *Residential Development Handbook*. 3rd ed. Washington, DC: Urban Land Institute.

Urban Land Institute. 2005. Shanghai Xintiandi. Urban Land Institute Case Studies. https://casestudies.uli.org/wp-content/uploads/sites/98/2015/12/C035012.pdf.

Urban Land Institute. 2014. The Rise. Urban Land Institute Case Studies. http://uli.org/case-study/uli-case-studies-the-rise/.

Urstadt, Charles J., with Gene Brown. 2005. *Battery Park City: The Early Years*. Bloomington, IN: Xlibris Corporation.

US Army Corps of Engineers. 1992. Bearing Capacity of Soils. Engineer Manual no. 1110-1-1905, October 30.

US Army Corps of Engineers. 2003. Engineering and Design-Slope Stability. http://140.194.76.129/publications/eng-manuals/em1110-2-1902/entire.pdf.

US Green Building Council. 2013. LEED 2009 for Neighborhood Development (Revised 2013). Congress for New Urbanism, US Natural Resources Defense Council, and US Green Building Council. http://www.usgbc.org/resources/leed-neighborhood -development-v2009-current-version.

US Green Building Council. n.d. (a). Directory of LEED-ND Projects. http://www.usgbc.org/projects/neighborhood-development.

US Green Building Council. n.d. (b). Regional Credit Library. http:// www.usgbc.org/credits.

Valentine, K. W. G., P. N. Sprout, T. E. Baker, and L. M. Lawkulich, eds. 1978. The Soil Landscapes of British Columbia. British Columbia Ministry of Environment, Resource Analysis Branch. http://www.env.gov.bc.ca/soils/landscape/index.html.

Vandell, Kerry D., and Jonathan S. Lane. 1989. The Economics of Architecture and Urban Design: Some Preliminary Findings. *AREUEA Journal* 17 (2): 235–260.

Van Meel, Juriaan. 2000. *The European Office: Office Design and National Context*. Rotterdam: 010 Publishers.

Van Melik, Rianne, Irina van Aalst, and Jan van Weesep. 2009. The Private Sector and Public Space in Dutch City Centres. *Cities* (London) 26:202–209.

Van Uffalen, Chris. 2012. *Urban Spaces: Plazas, Squares and Streetscapes*. Salenstein, Switzerland: Braun Publishers.

Vasconcellos, Eduardo Alcantara. 2001. Urban Transport, Environment and Equity – The Case for Developing Countries. Earthscan. http://www.earthscan.co.uk.

Vision Zero Initiative. n.d. http://www.visionzeroinitiative.com.

Voss, Jerold. 1975. Concept of Land Ownership and Regional Variations. In *Urban Land Policies and Land-Use Control Measures*, vol. VII, *Global Review*. New York: UN Department of Economic and Social Affairs.

Voss, Judy. 2011. Revisiting Office Space Standards. Haworth, London. http://www.thercfgroup.com/files/resources/Revisiting -office-space-standards-white-paper.pdf.

Vrscaj, Borut, Laura Poggio, and Franco Ajmone Marsan. 2008. A Method for Soil Environmental Quality Evaluation for Management and Planning in Urban Areas. *Landscape and Urban Planning* 88:81–94.

Vuchic, Vukan R. 1999. *Transportation for Livable Cities*. New Brunswick, NJ: Center for Urban Policy Research.

Vuchic, Vukan R. 2007. *Urban Transit: Systems and Technology*. Hoboken, NJ: Wiley.

Wagner, J., and S. P. Kutska. 2008. Denver's 128-Year-Old System: The Best Is Yet to Come. *District Energy* (October), 16.

Walker, M. C. 1992. Planning and Design of On-Street Light Rail Transit Stations. *Transportation Research Record* (1361).

Walton, Brett. 2010. The Price of Water: A Comparison of Water Rates, Usage in 30 US Cities. Circle of Blue. http://www .circleofblue.org/waternews/2010/world/the-price -of-water-a-comparison-of-water-rates-usage-in-30-u-s-cities/.

Washington Metropolitan Area Transit Authority. 2006. 2005 Development-Related Ridership Survey, Final Report. http://www .wmata.com/pdfs/business/2005_Development-Related_Ridership _Survey.pdf.

Washington State Department of Commerce. 2013. Evergreen Sustainable Development Standard, Version 2.2. http://www .comerce.wa.gov/Documents/ESDS-2.2.pdf.

Weast, R. C. 1981. *Handbook of Chemistry and Physics*. 62nd ed. Boca Raton, FL: CRC Press.

Weggel, J. Richard. n.d. Rainfalls of 12 July 2004 in New Jersey. Working Paper, Drexel University. http://idea.library.drexel.edu /bitstream/1860/772/1/2006042020.pdf.

Weiler, Susan K., and Katrin Scholz-Barth. 2009. *Green Roof Systems: A Guide to the Planning, Design and Construction of Landscapes over Structure*. Hoboken, NJ: Wiley.

Wheeler, Stephen M., and Timothy Beatley, eds. 2014. *Sustainable Urban Development Reader*. 3rd ed. London: Routledge.

Wholesale Solar. n.d. Off-Grid Solar Panel Calculator. https://www .wholesalesolar.com/solar-information/start-here/offgrid-calculator #systemSizeCalc.

Whyte, William H. 1979. A Guide to Peoplewatching. In Lisa Taylor, ed., *Urban Open Spaces*. New York: Cooper-Hewitt Museum.

Whyte, William H. 1980. *The Social Life of Small Urban Spaces*. Washington, DC: Conservation Foundation.

Wikipedia. n.d. List of 3D Rendering Software. https://www .wikipedia.com/en/List_of_3D_rendering_software.

William Lam Associates. 1976. New Streets and Cityscapes for Norfolk: A Master Plan for Lighting, Landscaping and Street Furnishings. Norfolk Redevelopment and Housing Authority. https://books.google.com/books/about/New_Streets_and _Cityscapes_for_Norfolk.html?id=MPKUHAAACAAJ.

Wilson, James E. 1999. *Terroir: The Role of Geology, Climate and Culture in the Making of French Wines*. Berkeley: University of California Press.

Wolf, Kathleen L. 2004. Public Value of Nature: Economics of Urban Trees, Parks and Open Space. In D. Miller and J. A. Wise, eds., *Design with Spirit: Proceedings of the 35th Annual Conference of the Environmental Design Research Association*. Edmond, OK: Environmental Design Research Association.

World Bank. 1999. Municipal Solid Waste Incineration. Technical Guidance Report. http://www.worldbank.org/urban/solid_wm/erm /CWG%20folder/Waste%20Incineration.pdf.

World Bank. 2002. Cities on the Move: A World Bank Urban Transport Strategy Review. World Bank, Washington, DC. https:// openknowledge.worldbank.org/handle/10986/15232.

World Health Organization. 2013. Pedestrian Safety: A Road Safety Manual for Decisionmakers and Practitioners. World Health Organization, Geneva. http://www.who.int/roadsafety/en/.

World Health Organization. 2014a. Health Impact Assessment. http://www.who.int/hia/tools/process/en/.

World Health Organization. 2014b. Working across Sectors for Health: Using Impact Assessments for Decision-Making. http://www.who.int/kobe_centre/publications/policy_brief_health .pdf?ua=1.

World Health Organization. n.d. Electromagnetic Fields and Public Health. http://www.who.int/peh-emf/publications/facts/fs322/en/.

Wyle. 2011. Updating and Supplementing the Day-Night Average Sound Level (DNL). Wyle Report 11-04 prepared for the Volpe National Transportation Systems Center, US Department of Transportation. https://www.faa.gov/about/office_org /headquarters_offices/apl/research/science_integrated_modeling /noise_impacts/media/WR11-04_Updating&SupplementingDNL _June%202011.pdf.

Yang, Bo. 2009. Ecohydrological Planning for The Woodlands: Lessons Learned after 35 Years. PhD dissertation, Texas A&M University.

Yang, Bo, Ming-Han Li, and Shujuan Li. 2013. Design-with-Nature for Multifunctional Landscapes: Environmental Benefits and Social Barriers in Community Development. *International Journal of Research in Public Health.* 10:5433–5458.

Zeisel, John. 2006. *Inquiry by Design: Environment/Behavior /Neuroscience in Architecture, Interiors, Landscape and Planning.* New York: W. W. Norton.

Zhang, Henry H., and David F. Brown. 2005. Understanding Urban Residential Water Use in Beijing and Tianjin, China. *Habitat International* 29:469–491.

Zhu, Da, P. U. Asnani, Christian Zurbrugg, Sebastian Anapolsky, and Shyamala K. Mani. 2007. Improving Municipal Solid Waste Management in India: A Sourcebook for Policymakers and Practitioners. World Bank, WBI Development Series.

Zinco, Inc. n.d. System Solutions for Thriving Green Roofs. http://www.zinco-greenroof.com/EN/downloads/index.php.

Zonneveld, Isaak S. 1989. The Land Unit – A Fundamental Concept in Landscape Ecology and Its Applications. *Landscape Ecology* 3 (2): 67–86. doi:10.1007/BF00131171.

Glossary of Site Planning Terms

Academical village: Thomas Jefferson's plan for living and learning at the University of Virginia, which has become the prototype for the American college campus   591–592, 604

Academies (or **institutes** or **grandes écoles**): specialized institutions of higher learning and research devoted to particular fields   592–593

Accessory units: additional units built on a residential site, such as garages, granny flats, or home workspaces   488

Acidification: changes to the chemical composition of water bodies resulting from the absorption of CO_2 from the atmosphere or other sources   71

Activity programming: organizing and producing events, festivals, performances, and other activities in public spaces   634

Adaptability: the ability to accommodate changes to the form of the built environment over time   1, 10–11, 487, 497, 503, 600, 601, 672

Adaptation to climate change: adjustment in natural systems or the built environment to actual or expected changes to temperature, sea level, or weather conditions   231, 236

Adventure playground: a play area constructed by children, sometimes with adult assistance, that develops skills while satisfying the desire for recreation activities   485, 578

Adverse possession: the right to continued use of land established by occupying it for a long period of time, without actions by the rightful owner to prohibit such use   94

Aerial tramway (or **cable car**, **ropeway**, or **aerial tram**): a passenger compartment used for transportation, suspended from one or two stationary cables, propelled by a moving cable   320, 330–331

Aerobic biological processes: treatment of wastewater or solids through contact with oxygen from the atmosphere or through injection into or contact with soils, such as in composting, wetlands, or mechanical treatment basins   396, 462

Air rights: the right conferred by regulations to extend construction vertically, a right often transferrable from one site to another   325

Albedo: the proportion of light falling on a surface that is reflected   55–56

Alternating current: electric current that changes direction many times each second, typically used to supply power to sites   417

Anchor stores: large retail outlets that draw customers to a shopping center, providing patrons for smaller stores   508, 514, 527, 531, 533, 656

Ancient lights: English common law principle that an owner or occupier of an adjoining structure cannot block light to a building that has enjoyed it continuously for at least 20 years   57

Angle of repose: the steepest angle at which a specific loose material is stable   39, 466

Animateur: a person who enlivens and orchestrates a dialogue   122

Annual plants: plants with a life cycle of a single year that must be replaced each year   474, 478

Appraisal: an estimate of the value of a site or structure, generally based on sales of comparable properties, their revenue potential, and replacement costs   204, 207

Aquifer: a geological formation that contains or conducts groundwater   42–43, 191, 385

   confined aquifer: an area saturated by water that has impermeable materials above and below, and is generally under pressure so that water will rise to the top of the aquifer if the strata are penetrated by a well   43

   unconfined aquifer: an area saturated by water where the upper surface (water table) is open to the atmosphere through permeable material   42

Arcade: a covered passageway, generally lined by shops on one or both sides   164, 166, 342, 354–355, 509, 510, 522, 523–526, 530, 667, 668

Artificial intelligence: computer systems designed to perform tasks that normally require human intelligence, such as visual perception, speech recognition that guides action, translation of languages, and autonomous behavior   454, 543

As-of-right development: the form and amount of development permitted on a site without special exceptions or permits   102–103

Aspirational criteria: goals and objectives that serve as tests of the adequacy of a plan   176–177

Atrium: a large central space, often covered by a roof, that serves as a gathering space while providing access to bordering uses   532, 545–546, 549, 551–552, 613, 626, 648, 650, 665–666

Automated production: manufacturing processes that function with minimal human direction and control   408, 543, 564

Automated traffic control (ATC) systems: computer-controlled traffic signal systems that determine the timing of signals using time-based algorithms and data obtained by sensors   452

Automated waste collection systems (AWCS): systems that collect wastes via vacuum tubes, generally below ground, connecting the sources of waste and disposal locations   404, 407–411, 655

Automatic dumping hoppers: arms mounted on waste collection vehicles that lift and empty containers into the vehicle for transport to a disposal site   406

Autonomous vehicles: self-driving vehicles that require minimal or no human direction   307–309, 687

driverless buses: small buses, generally traveling on custom routes, that will pick up passengers when called and transport them to a point near their destination   308, 312

driverless cars: self-driving personal vehicles that will navigate to destinations, then to parking areas   307–309, 328

driverless taxis: self-driving vehicles that will pick up passengers when called on cell phones or other devices, take them to their destination, then move on to collect other passengers   307, 311

Average costs per capita: total capital and operating costs divided by the number of people served by a facility   228

Average daily traffic (ADT) volumes: the average total number of vehicles (or vehicle equivalents) that travel on a roadway link each day   81, 278

A-weighted scale decibels (dBA): the relative loudness of sounds as perceived by a human ear, in which the decibel values of low-frequency sounds are discounted   85–87

Bächle: water-filled runnels that transport runoff through the dense built-up areas of a city   360–361, 366

Balanced ecology: a state of dynamic equilibrium in an ecological community in which genetic, species, and ecosystem diversity remains relatively stable, changing only gradually through natural succession   4, 367, 691

Bal tashchit: a basic ethical principle in Jewish law, not to destroy or waste, to preserve the planet and improve lives both physically and spiritually   176–177

Bandwidth: the volume of information per unit of time that a transmission medium such as an Internet connection can handle   446, 543

Base transceiver station (BTS): equipment, generally mounted on a tower or tall building, that facilitates wireless communication between a mobile device and a network   448

Beauty: the combination of qualities, such as shape, color, or form, that please the aesthetic senses, particularly visual   7, 8, 173, 257, 366, 472, 478

Bedrock: solid rock underlying more permeable soils   26, 34–37, 39, 42, 53, 393

Behavior setting: physical settings that mediate between the dynamic behavior of individuals and more stable social structures   133–134

Bicycle garage: a protected space for storage of bicycles   342–343

Bicycle path: a designated or dedicated pathway aimed at promoting safe use of bicycles for travel or recreation   337, 340, 674

Bicycle sharing system: a system in which bicycles are made available for use by subscribers for short-term use   343–344

call-a-bike system: a bicycle share system coordinated with Intercity Express rail transportation, employing a system of authentication codes to automatically lock and unlock bikes   344

commercial bicycle sharing: a privately operated bicycle sharing system charging fees for use, with either fixed rental/return locations or GPS devices mounted on bicycles that allow tracking of locations   343

community bicycle sharing: a community-owned and operated bicycle sharing system, often restricting locations for rental and return to the area   343

OV-fiets bicycle rentals: prepaid bicycle and scooter rental systems in the Netherlands that allow bicycles to be rented in over 300 locations and used in concert with public transit   344

Big box retailers: large branded retail stores specializing in specific lines of products (furniture, clothing, building supplies, toys, etc.), generally preferring freestanding locations or clustering with other large outlets   361, 533, 535

Biogeoclimatic zones: large geographic areas with relatively uniform macroclimate, soils, vegetation, and animal life   65–66

Biomass: organic matter such as wood, agricultural crops, or wastes capable of being burned   401, 422, 432, 439–441

Biomass conversion to energy: technology for conversion of biomass materials into heat or other forms of energy   422, 439–441

combustion: burning biomass in a chamber and converting the heat into steam used to produce electricity, mechanical energy, heating, or cooling   439

gasification: converting solid biomass fuel into gaseous combustible gas (producer gas) through a sequence of thermochemical reactions   406, 439

pyrolysis: decomposition of biomass in the absence of oxygen, producing biochar, bio-oil, and gases including methane, hydrogen, carbon monoxide, and carbon dioxide   406, 439

Biosolids: organic matter recycled from sewage, generally used as a soil conditioner for agricultural uses   397

Biotic community: a group of independent organisms inhabiting the same region and interacting with each other   64–66

Blackwater tank: holding tank for wastewater from toilets, often used for settling of solids before disposal   392–393, 395–396

Borrowed landscape (or scenery): the principle of incorporating background landscape or distant scenic elements into the composition of a garden or park (Japanese: **shakkei**)   79

Branching layouts of roadways: treelike layout of streets with many local streets originating from higher-capacity roadways   292–293

Branded retailers: shops specializing in a single brand of merchandise, sometimes referred to as boutiques   506, 533, 535

Broadband communication: cable communication lines including coaxial cable, optical fiber, radio, or twisted-pair lines, allowing wide-bandwidth data transmission, supporting multiple signals and traffic types   446–447, 691

Brownfields: sites that are affected by real or perceived environmental contamination, often the result of prior industrial or commercial uses   48, 100, 188, 207, 458, 460–465, 696

Building control regulations: regulations that determine the maximum dimensions of structures (Thailand)   97

Building footprint: the ground-level coverage of a site by a building   2, 15, 73, 306, 497, 500–501, 514, 546–549, 646

Build-to line: a regulation that prescribes the location for all or a large fraction of a building's face, generally along a street   100

Buses: large motor vehicles for carrying passengers on roads, generally operating on a fixed route   139, 258, 263, 270, 272–274, 282, 286, 293, 307–309, 313–315, 317–318, 322, 335, 338, 349–350, 364, 516, 527–528, 693

articulated buses (bendy buses, bending buses, tandem buses, stretch buses, double buses, accordion buses): two-element buses connected by a pivot joint, allowing a vehicle to turn more sharply   314

double-articulated megabuses: three-element buses, connected by pivot joints   310, 314

Routemaster double-decker buses: two-story buses used for public transportation in the UK, Europe, Asia, and other countries   314

standard buses: rigid-body buses used in public transportation, generally with two sets of doors   314

tourist buses: Large buses designed to accommodate touring, generally with a single entrance, elevated seating with luggage compartments below, and internal toilet   312

trolley buses: electric buses that draw power from overhead cables, suspended by catenaries   310, 315

Bus rapid transit (BRT) system: a system of dedicated bus lanes (**busways** or **transitways**) and transit stops designed to increase the capacity and speed of bus transit   313–314, 316, 318–320

Bus stops: dedicated zones for passenger waiting and boarding of buses   82, 134, 139, 179, 258, 272, 313–315

BRT station: bus boarding area adjacent to a dedicated bus lane, designed to accept fares from passengers before boarding buses   319

bus bulb: curb extension that allows passengers to board buses in a moving lane, obviating the need for buses to pull into a parking lane   314–315

bus shelter: weather protection for passengers waiting to board buses   314, 354

far side stop: zone located after an intersection   314

near side stop: zone located before an intersection   314

Buy-out: a technique of assembling land in which offers are made to multiple owners in an area conditional on all owners accepting   206

Cabling systems: building or campus telecommunications infrastructure generally consisting of several components: an entrance portal that connects to the wider system; equipment rooms for equipment and consolidation points; backbone cabling with connections to data centers; horizontal cabling through wiring or plenums; telecommunication enclosures; and end user components such as telephones and workspace computers   446

Cadastral system (cadaster): a system of demarcation on the ground and recording property interests in land   91, 95–96

deed registration system: a system by which the transfer document (the deed) is registered in a publicly accessible place   95–96

private conveyance system: a system in which land is conveyed through private deeds or other transfer documents that are generally not recorded or registered, common in many developing countries   96

title registration system: a system in which the certificate (deed) is the proof of ownership, and registration is not compulsory   96

Torrens system: a system in which a register of landholdings is maintained by the state guaranteeing indefeasible title to those included on the register, and landownership is transferred through registration of title rather than deeds   96

Capacitance: the ability of a system to collect and store an electrical charge, such as in a battery   420

Capital costs or **expenditures**: financial resources dedicated to the creation of fixed assets, such as buildings, infrastructure, and landscape   228, 254, 403, 421, 444, 508

Capitalize: to record the amount of an item in a balance sheet account as a long-term asset, rather than as an expense   207

Carbon emission: the release of carbon into the atmosphere, generally in the form of CO_2, as a result of burning oil, coal, and gas for energy use, or through decay of natural products   4–5, 233–234, 236, 262, 314, 441–443, 601, 689

Carbon footprint: the quantity of carbon emitted by an individual, event, product, organization, or community, the geographic area over which these impacts are felt, or the area required to serve an urban settlement   5, 440, 601

Car-free zone: an area of settlement where automobiles are generally banned, either throughout the day or during specific hours   359, 362, 693–694

Catenaries: wires or ropes hanging freely between two points, conveying electricity (for use by trams or trains) or power (for ropeways or cable cars)   316–317, 320, 322–324, 360

Cell tower: a vertical structure for antennas and electronic communications equipment to create a cellular network   448–450

Centralized electrical generation: large facilities for electric power generation that serve entire communities or wider areas   417

Cesspool or **blackwater tank**: a tank for holding toilet wastes or other contaminated substances until they are removed for disposal   393

Chaflanes: chamfered corners on streets designed to improve the visibility and turning flows at intersections   682

Charrette: a brief, intense set of meetings in which professionals, stakeholders, and citizens collaborate on agreeing on objectives, sketching out a plan for an area, and reaching a consensus on its desirability   122–126

Chartered real estate investment companies or trusts (REICOs): real estate companies chartered by the state that have the capacity to aggregate property, often by offering shares to owners, installing infrastructure, redeveloping sites, and operating revenue-producing properties   206

Cistern: a structure used to collect rainwater, often belowground, to be used as needed   17, 236, 366, 377, 382–385, 387–388

Citizens' jury: a meeting involving a cross section of residents that debates goals or reviews plans   123

Civic spaces: public areas that belong to all in a city, which go by several names: **civic square**, **city or town square**, **people's (renmin) square**, **piazza**, **plaza mayor**, **campo**, and **zócalo**, among others   165, 635–639

Civil law traditions or **Napoleonic law**: a comprehensive system of law that is codified (in contrast to common law) covering substantive law, procedural law, and punishments, that has its origins in Europe, has spread to many of the colonies of France, Holland, Spain, and other countries, and is the underpinning of legal systems in Russia, China, and other countries   89–91

Clay: a natural very fine-grained material that is plastic when wet, consisting mainly of hydrated silicates of aluminum   36–39, 42–43, 48–49, 69, 72, 377, 379, 467, 580

Clients: individuals or organizations that commission and pay for professional work   10, 112, 114, 115, 119–121, 126–128, 137, 141, 145, 157, 160, 164, 174, 175, 237, 240, 574

Climate impact assessment: any of several methods for estimating the likely impacts of site plans and developments on the climate, both locally and in terms of global concerns   224, 231–236

Climax ecology: the final stage of ecological succession that remains relatively unchanged until destroyed by human interference, fire, or other events   65, 458

Closed-loop ecology: an ecosystem that does not rely on matter or exchanges from outside the system, typically where waste products are reused by one or more species   64, 367

Closed-loop infrastructure systems: systems designed to recycle waste materials or products on a site, such as **water loops**, **energy loops**, **carbon loops**, and **material loops**   4, 253, 261, 436, 439, 443, 689, 699

Cofferdam: a watertight enclosure pumped dry to permit construction work below the waterline   50

Cogeneration plant, combined heat and power (CHP): a facility that produces electricity and useful heat at the same time   422, 432, 436–437

   micro combined heat and power installation: small-scale facilities for CHP that serve a single site   422

Colleges: institutions that focus on undergraduate education, usually centered on teaching in the liberal arts tradition   590–593, 597–609, 616–618

   college houses: living units with spaces for dining, seminars, and activities that promote dialogue   591

   residential colleges: institutions where teaching is combined with living accommodations for students and faculty masters   591–592, 602–604

Combustion: creation of energy through burning   438

Comminutors: grinders or macerators that are used to reduce the size of wastewater solids   401

Common land or **property**: land that is owned by two or more individuals or an entity such as a homes association   92, 198–200

Common law traditions: a system of uncodified legal doctrines, based on precedents that are memorialized in collections of case law, that has its origins in British traditions and is widely practiced in its former colonies, including the US   57, 89–90, 94, 179

Commons: land or public spaces owned by an entire community   83, 92, 642

Common trench: an excavated area along a street shared by several utilities, which may be contained in a continuous box structure   257, 260

Communications systems: the full range of media for communication, each with its devices for transmission and switching   82, 114, 153, 254–255, 257, 260, 446–455, 594

   very-high-bit-rate subscriber line (VSDL): technology that allows faster data transmission over relatively short distances (up to 1,500 m) by employing multiple channels   447

   wired: the use of cables and wires for transmission of data, such as telephone networks, cable television and Internet access, fiber-optic data lines, and waveguide (electromagnetic) lines used for high-power applications   264, 446

   wireless: signals transmitted through the air between transmission towers and receivers, typically using radio waves   263–264, 446, 448–451, 453

Community: a locally based social group that shares facilities and participates in common activities and institutions   454, 479, 484, 486–487, 489–491, 512, 516, 521–522, 527, 529–530, 569, 571, 578, 581–582, 587, 594, 601, 606, 620, 627, 664, 669–699

Comparables: the value of a site or structure based on comparison with recent sales of properties with similar characteristics in a similar location that have been freely exchanged   207, 219

Compatibility with surroundings: of buildings or landscapes, a sharing of characteristics with those on nearby sites in terms of uses, form, heights, scale, materials, color, and/or details   8–9, 173, 178–179, 226

Complete streets: street patterns that balance the amount of space for flows by motor vehicles, bicycles, public transit, and pedestrians   258–260

Composting wastes: the process of accelerating the decomposition of organic materials through aerobic bacteria, fungi, and other organisms, producing materials that can be used as fertilizer   4, 261, 404, 406, 411, 413–415, 463

Comprehensive plan: a long-range municipal plan that synchronizes land use, infrastructure, transportation, public facilities, housing, and other elements essential to creating a beautiful, healthy, and economically successful community   81

Concurrency requirement: a requirement that the timing of any development approved conform to the schedule for extending infrastructure to the site   81

Condominium, strata title, commonhold, syndicate of co-ownership, or **co-propriété**: a form of ownership in which portions of a building or complex of buildings are owned by separate individuals or companies while the site is held in undivided ownership of the collectivity   79, 93, 198–201, 222, 422, 494, 647, 655, 667–668

   condominium corporation, strata council, commonhold association, body corporate, owners' corporation, or **syndic**: the entity selected by owners to manage the combined assets of the site, with responsibility for proposing or deciding upon charges to pay for operations and improvements   199

Connected node ratio (CNR): an index of the connectivity of a roadway pattern, computed by dividing the number of real intersections by the number of dead-end roadway points   294

Connectivity: the ease of making connections between blocks in a district or neighborhood, without taking circuitous routes   294–296

Conservation easement: a restriction on a property that prohibits building or development in perpetuity   94

Consistency requirements: requirements that development regulations and any projects approved conform to an adopted community plan   81

Constructed wetland: an artificial wetland constructed for the purpose of detaining or treating municipal and industrial wastewater, graywater, or stormwater runoff   70–71, 397–399, 682

Contour map: a map that locates equal elevation lines on a site   45–47, 64, 149, 156, 368–369, 396, 466, 468–470, 612

Controlled intersection: an intersection with traffic control devices that determine flows of vehicles and pedestrians   81, 273

Cooperative corporation, co-op, or **coop**: an association created to collectively own property, typically housing, in which individuals holding shares have proprietary leases for portions of the property they occupy, and the board of the entity has the right to approve all transfers of shares   93, 198, 200, 343, 503, 697

   asunto-osakeyhtio (Finland): a form of cooperative ownership for approximately one quarter of the apartments in the country, regulated by the Housing Companies Act, aimed at ensuring that housing is well maintained and retains its value   200

   borettslag (Norway): a housing association that is the common form of housing cooperative in the country, organized in similar ways to other countries in Scandinavia   200

   bostadsrättsförening (Sweden): a housing association with cooperative ownership, mandated by the National Board of Housing to balance the maintenance and improvements of a property with the ability of shareholders to pay the annual costs, in which appreciation upon resale is taxed as capital gain   200

   cooperative housing societies (India): associations promoting housing ownership in India   200

   limited equity or limited dividend cooperative (Canada): a cooperative in which the price of purchasing shares is low and owners must sell their shares back to the cooperative when leaving, realizing appreciation that is proportional to the amount they invested   200

mutual housing associations (UK): self-managed cooperative entities that date to the nineteenth century, in which shareholders pay a modest deposit upon entry, have perpetual leases while residing in their unit, and do not benefit from appreciation upon exit   200

Covenants: restrictions on the use of property placed by the seller and recorded on the deed   94–95, 97, 116, 185, 198, 206, 488

Cross easements: reciprocal rights for use or passage across property, recorded on a deed   94, 325, 655

Cultural landscape: an area recognized as special because of its association with a historic event, activity, or person, or exhibiting special cultural or aesthetic value   85

Danwei: live-work compounds in post-1949 China that were the basic unit of urban development   293, 669

Data center: a high-capacity computer installation serving organizations or cloud computing for multiple users   454, 558

Day-night average sound level (DNL): the average noise level over a 24-hour period, in which the noise level between 10 pm and 7 am is artificially increased by 10 dB to account for the decrease in community background noise during that period   86

Debt service costs: interest and amortization payments made to cover a mortgage   228

Decibel: a logarithmic unit used to measure sound levels, which expresses the ratio of the pressure of a given sound to a reference pressure, usually 0.0002 microbar   85, 232

Dedicated bicycle lane: a pathway restricted to bicycles   336

Dedicated bus lane: a lane or pathway restricted to buses (exclusive bus lane) or where buses have priority   314–315

Dedicated transit right-of-way: usually an off-roadway pathway restricted to transit, where crossings are minimized   257, 260, 310, 317–318

Dedication of property: the transfer of lands by a site developer to the local government, typically roadways, parks, and open spaces   30, 198, 565, 567, 572, 676

Deep lake water cooling (DLWC): a form of cooling for occupied spaces in which water is drawn from deep areas of a lake at 4–10°C and provided to a heat exchanger for cooling   439

Demising line: a boundary that separates one tenant's space from another's, sometimes by a party wall   655

Demographic analysis: analysis of existing and projected population characteristics for an area   130–131, 137, 226, 228, 480, 484, 504, 514

Density: a measure of the amount of occupied space, or number of households or people occupying it, divided by the area of a defined site or district   6, 13, 97–99, 100, 103, 133, 175, 218, 313, 332–333, 481–482, 587, 600

   gross density: a measure of density in which the denominator is the complete area without accounting for streets and unoccupied spaces   481–482

   net density: a measure of density in which the denominator is the area of the occupied site(s) only   481–482

Desalination systems: methods for converting seawater to freshwater, including distillation, ion exchange, reverse osmosis and other membrane processes, and solar desalination   382–383, 386

Design, plan, or development competition: a method of seeking ideas or plans by inviting professionals to submit proposals   30, 122, 124, 126–129, 141–142, 185, 419, 611

competition jury: a group appointed to assess competition entries, which may consist of distinguished professionals and representatives of the sponsor   127

definitive competition: a contest in which the program is sufficiently precise, and the sponsor expresses the intention to carry out the winning plans   126–127

developer-design competition: here developers and designers form joint ventures and make both plans and financial proposals for carrying out a project   128

idea competition: here the purpose is to enlarge the pool of ideas, not necessarily to select a plan or planner   122, 127

invited competition: here the sponsor selects a number of professionals or teams to submit proposals, and may provide stipends for preparation of proposals   126

mediated competition: here representatives of the sponsor work with a short list of competitors to ensure that proposals are as responsive as possible to the client's aspirations   127

open competition: here the contest is open to all who register, and the results are typically assessed by a jury   126

team selection competition: a process in which competitors are asked to submit ideas and qualifications to assist the sponsor in selecting a team to work with in preparing site plans   127–128

Design guidelines: statements of intent, **quantitative rules**, or **graphic suggestions** intended to guide the design or planning of a site, which may be suggestive or mandatory   25, 30–31, 81, 116, 175–185, 217, 597, 664, 693

Design review: the process of reviewing plans and architectural designs in terms of their suitability, which may be conducted by a **panel of experts** or through a **public inquiry** (UK)   178–179, 184–185

Design review commission or **architectural review commission**: a formal body created by a government to review projects in terms of their appropriateness; it may be **advisory** or have **decision authority**   184–185

Design speed: the selected speed used to determine the geometric and dimensional features of a roadway, generally set 10–15% higher than the posted speed limit, or by adding 8–16 kph (5–10 mph) to the posted speed limit   274–277, 289, 319, 321, 341, 467

Design vehicle: a frequently used vehicle that is used as the basis for computing turning radii and other requirements in the design of streets   272

Development agreement: an agreement between a local government or entity and a developer spelling out what may be built on a site, its form, any contributions to mitigate impacts, and the timing of development   102, 117, 197

Development concept plan or **master site plan**: a conceptual plan for a large site that will be developed in phases, serving as a reference as individual segments are approved   18–19, 102, 194, 197, 205, 217, 241, 558–559, 561, 587, 594–597, 637, 678

Development control plan (Australia): a plan that provides detailed planning and design guidelines to support the planning controls in the local environmental plan   97

Development or project impact report: a report prepared by the developer of a site that outlines the positive and negative impacts of the proposed site development   224–225

Development permit: a permit authorizing development (in locations where there is **discretionary review**), usually with a list of conditions that must be met   102–103, 118

Development regulations: public controls on the uses, density, form, massing, and other characteristics of permitted development   81, 92, 97–103, 117, 174, 220, 385, 644–645

Development rights or **entitlements**: the amount of development permitted by zoning or other development controls, or by special exceptions or development agreements   18, 20, 93–94, 101–102, 117, 217–219, 221–222

Direct current (DC): electric current flows in one direction, such as in photovoltaic instillations or locally generated electricity, now used in some large data centers   417

Direct observation: the technique of studying human behavior by observing and recording activities in spaces   133

Disaggregated per capita costs: cost accounting broken down to demonstrate the incidence of individuals and groups in the relevant population   228

Discharge locations: locations where overland runoff is released into streams, detention areas, lakes, or other water bodies   5, 42–43, 89, 262, 366–367, 373, 397–398, 401, 690

Discount rate: the interest rate used to value future revenues to arrive at the present value of an investment   6, 210–214, 421

Discretionary review: a process of reviewing plans and proposals relative to objectives or guidelines   100, 102, 179, 196

Displays: digital signboards or video installations   122, 264, 453–454

Disposable materials: materials that are used once, are contaminated or do not decompose easily, and therefore cannot be recycled   689

Disposal field: a specially prepared area belowground where wastewater flows from a septic tank for further purification   43, 386, 392–393, 411

Distributed antenna system (DAS): a network of spatially separated antenna nodes connected to a common source, providing wireless service within a building or area   449

Distributed electrical generation: electrical generation from a set of local sources that may include **solar panels**, **wind turbines**, and **local generators**, connected in a network   264, 307, 418, 422

Distributional impacts: how individuals or social classes are impacted by a change in the environment   231

District heating (and cooling) system: hot water or steam (and chilled water) distributed within a district through **insulated pipes** from an **energy source**; the system may also include **heat or cooling storage**   5, 82, 114, 140, 188–189, 263, 397, 416, 431, 441–442, 444–445, 693–696

District identity: defining characteristics of a district, which may be its layout, natural features, built forms, or landscape   11, 18, 21, 83, 177, 222–223, 250, 283, 362, 506, 530, 533, 600–601, 618, 630, 661, 672–673

District plan: a subarea plan, or **secondary plan**, that defines in greater detail the desired form of a community   81, 100

Diversity: the social and economic mix of residents in an area   164, 504, 672, 679

Dockless shared bicycles: a bicycle sharing system in which individual cycles are controlled by transponders on the bicycle that locate, lock, and charge for their use   344

Dollar bill shape: a typical rectangular office building shape, with a central core   546

Double-deck elevators: elevator cabs that are stacked so that they can serve two floors simultaneously   545

Dredging: removing spoils from the base of a water body, typically by vacuum pumping or scooping   50, 205, 206

Drip irrigation system: a form of irrigation that saves water by allowing it to drip slowly from a perforated tube on or below the surface   381, 382, 475

Driverless taxis. See **Autonomous vehicles**

Drosscape: areas reshaped by human action that have made them largely unusable, such as unconsolidated landfill areas, quarries, slag heaps, and tailings mounds or ponds   48–50, 85

Drought: a prolonged period with low rainfall frequency, often associated with a **100-year-occurrence drought**   4, 65, 73, 191, 384, 431, 690

Dry well: an underground structure that disposes of unwanted water, typically runoff and stormwater, by injecting it into the water table   378

Dual-pipe water system: a water distribution network with separate pipes for potable water and gray water, the latter used mainly for agriculture, irrigation, and industrial uses   380

Dumpsters: containers for refuse that can be automatically dumped into collection vehicles or transported directly to a disposal site   404, 406–407

Dunes: mounds or ridges of sand or loose sediment formed by wind, typically on seacoasts or in deserts   52–53, 68–69

Dwelling unit: a self-contained living unit with a kitchen and bathroom or toilet   266, 313, 480

Easement: the right to use, pass across, or gain benefits from an adjacent property, registered on the deed of that property   81, 90, 94–96, 97, 108, 114, 116, 120, 207, 255, 260, 325, 420, 655

   conservation easement: restrictions on the use and development of property that have been given to an outside agency such as a land trust   94
   cross easement: reciprocal rights for use or passage across property, recorded on deed   325
   facade easement: restrictions on changes to the facade of a structure without permission from the holder of the easement, such as a historical society   94
   maintenance easement: the right to enter another's property for the purpose of maintaining facilities, such as the wall of a house located on a property line (as in zero lot line housing) or a sewer line that crosses another's property   94, 420, 488, 655
   prescriptive easement: an easement on another's property acquired by continued use without permission from the owner for a period defined by local law, such as for a pathway   94
   privacy easement: a prohibition against creating windows or views to an adjacent property   94
   solar easement: a prohibition against shading an adjacent property, or specific elements such as an open space, windows, or solar collector   94
   view easement: a prohibition against blocking views across a property   94

Eco-city: a new or existing settlement dedicated to principles of sustainable development, reduction of energy usage, reduction of travel, and integration of natural and manmade systems   425, 690–692

Ecological corridor: a thin strip of vegetation used by wildlife to move between two areas and allowing exchange of biotic factors between them   66, 241, 249

Ecological patch: a relatively homogeneous area in terms of landscape that changes largely through internal dynamics, the basic unit of landscape   64–65, 167

Ecology: the relationships of organisms to each other and to their physical environment   4, 52, 64–74, 193, 265, 367, 387, 439, 456, 458–459, 691

Economic unit: one of the three basic units of an economy: the firm, the household, and the government   9

Economic value: a measure of the benefit provided by a good or service to an economic agent, such as the maximum amount of money an agent is willing to pay for a good or service   9–11, 100, 207–223

Ecotone: the transition between two biomes, where two communities meet and integrate   65

Efficient use: the optimized use of a device or space by extending the hours of use, range of users, or type of activities   5, 306, 475, 493

Effluent: liquid waste or sewage discharged into the environment   43, 226, 392, 396, 399, 401–402, 500, 564, 584

Electrical distribution lines: the final stage in the distribution of electric power from the transmission system to individual consumers, usually at medium voltage on electric poles or in conduits below ground   226, 417–422

Electromagnetic fields (EMF): a combination of invisible electric and magnetic fields of force caused by AC devices   386, 417, 447–449

> **radio frequency radiation (RFR)**: radio waves and microwaves at the low end of the energy spectrum, from broadcast antennas, portable radio systems, microwave antennas, satellites, and radar   449

Elevator systems: mechanical vertical transportation in buildings, driven either by motors and counterbalanced ropes or by hydraulic lifts   329, 365, 482, 497–500, 546–547, 647, 648, 650

> **skip-floor elevators**: buildings configured with access corridors every two or three floors, with units reached via stairways from the common corridor   502
> **sky lobbies**: transfer levels where passengers move from an express elevator to a local elevator to reach floors above   546, 648
> **stacked or double-deck elevators**: a single elevator shaft occupied by two independent elevators, one above the other   546

Embedded intelligence: the ability of a product, process, or service to analyze its performance and adopt new methods that improve performance   263, 446, 454, 543

Embodied energy: the energy consumed by all the processes involved in the construction of a building or site   169, 415, 441

Energy consumption: the amount of energy consumed in a process or system or by an organization, settlement, or society   5, 187, 234, 262, 308–309, 422, 432, 439, 443, 453, 504, 689, 694

Energy sources for district heating: sources of heat distributed by a district heating system, such as conventional fuels, cogeneration, geothermal transfer, biomass, sewer heat recovery, landfill waste gas, industrial process heat, nuclear power heat, and solar energy   435–445

Engineered reed bed or **engineered wetland**: a planted wetland that harnesses ecological processes for the breakdown of organic matter in wastewater   397–399

> **free water surface (FWS) wetland**: a wetland system where the water surface is exposed to the atmosphere   397
> **vegetated submerged bed (VSB) wetland**, or **subsurface flow (SSF) wetland**: a bed or channel containing rocks, gravel, and appropriate plant media where wastewater is treated or polished below the surface   397–399

Entitlement. See Development rights

Environmental impact assessment: processes by which the impacts of proposed changes to the environment of a site are analyzed and compared to other alternatives, including taking no action. The name, process, and contents vary significantly: **environmental impact assessment** (US, Hong Kong, India), **environment assessments** (Australia, Canada, China), **strategic environmental assessment** (EU), **assessment of environmental effects** (New Zealand), **environmental effects statement** (Victoria, Australia), **state environmental quality review** (New York, US), **California environmental quality assessment** (California, US), **uniform land use review procedure** (New York, US), **project impact report** (Boston, US). Changes to proposals may require a **supplemental environmental impact statement**   116, 193, 224–227

Environmental trace: signs in the environment that reveal pathways or use patterns   134

Equitable development: site changes or development in which the costs and benefits are distributed equally or fairly across all groups   11

Equity: a measure of the equality or fairness of the distribution of impacts or benefits from changes to a site, with special attention to groups with few resources   79

Equity (in finance): the value of an ownership interest in a property in excess of all claims or liens against it; the equity position in a property investment is the riskiest interest   212–213

Escalators: mechanical stairways for indoor or outdoor use   322, 325, 329–330, 333, 356, 510, 522, 536, 662

Esquisse: a conceptual approach to making a plan for a site or building   124

Estate: the legal position or status of ownership of property, the bundle of rights belonging to an owner   88–94

> **fee simple absolute**: freehold estate that is the highest possible ownership interest in a site   94
> **life estate**: ownership of land and structures for the duration of a person's life   89

Eutrophication: excessive nutrients in a lake or other body of water, frequently due to runoff of fertilizers from agricultural or urban lands, visible by the presence of algae or plant life on the surface of the water   71, 226, 397

Exaction: a payment required in exchange for acquiring a permit or development rights   14, 227

Exchange center: a location where participants dispose of items not needed, and take home items that they will find useful   415

Expropriation: involuntary taking of property from its owner for public use or benefit, generally with compensation. Similar terms include **compulsory taking**, **compulsory purchase**, **eminent domain**, **condemnation**   88, 204–206

Ex-situ treatment of hazardous wastes: extracting and treatment of contaminants through chemical processes, then returning treated materials to their previous location   461–462

Extended aeration process: a method of sewage treatment using modified activated sludge procedures, in which suspended-growth microorganisms are applied to break down wastes   399

Extra high voltage lines: cables transmitting electricity at voltages above 765 kV, carrying bulk power over long distances   417

Fair market value: the amount that a motivated seller and buyer would agree upon for a property in an open exchange   207

Farmers' market: a zone or structure where local farmers offer produce, foods, or goods for sale on a seasonal or year-round basis   515, 626, 628, 634, 639, 658, 673

FAR value: the amount that would be paid by a buyer of a site per FAR of development rights (see also **Floor area ratio**) 214–215

Feng Shui: a Chinese philosophical system of harmonizing people with their environment, focusing on orientation, forms, and relationships of buildings to natural landmarks 169–170, 172

Ferry system: a water-based transportation system connecting fixed terminals 331–332, 693

Fiber optic communication lines: a method of transmitting information from one place to another by sending pulses of light through an optical fiber 260, 446–448

   fiber to the curb (FTTC): providing service to the curb, with responsibility for further distribution falling to the owner of the site 447
   fiber to the home or premises (FTTH): providing fiber cables from a central point directly to the home or building 447
   fiber to the network or node (FTTN): providing service to central points, from which wireless service or distribution via cables is provided 447

Filter drain or **French drain:** a trench filled with gravel or rock or containing perforated pipe that redirects surface water and groundwater 378

Financial plan: a multiyear plan that identifies costs and revenues for development of a site, including both hard costs (construction) and soft costs (services, interest on construction, etc.) 112, 117, 202, 214–215, 217

Financial pro forma: an accounting of projected costs and revenues of a project by year that allows an analysis to be made of its value as an investment 114–115, 141–142, 144, 209–216

Fines: fine-grained crushed rock, often used as a surface for walkways 352, 565

Fiscal impact assessment: an analysis of the impacts of site development on the costs and revenues of government units, and the distribution of these to specific operating entities 116, 224, 227–229

Flag lots: building lots generally set behind others that are connected to the street by a narrow driveway 489

Flat: an apartment in a building with a common entrance to several units 480, 497–501

Floor area ratio (FAR) or **floor space index:** the occupied space on a site divided by the site area (see also **FAR value**) 98–101, 193, 214, 218–219, 482, 598–599

Focus group: a group of representative users assembled to preview or offer comments on a proposal 137

Food court: an area, typically in a shopping center, with food outlets and a common eating area 507, 516, 531, 535

Form-based zoning: land development regulation that prescribes the physical form of structures, rather than their use 100

Fractional ownership: a method by which several unrelated parties can each own and occupy a site or building for specific periods of time over the year 93, 200

Freelancers: self-employed independent workers who work on contract for organizations either in their own spaces or embedded within others' spaces 544

Freeze-thaw cycles: 24-hour periods with temperatures both below and above freezing 38, 351, 368, 379, 478

Frost line: the depth below the surface that typically freezes during winter 43, 394

Funicular, cliff railway, or **cog railway:** cars that ascend steep slopes guided by rails and propelled by either ropes or moving cogs between the rails 328–329

Galleria: a covered passageway, usually with a glass roof, lined by shops along its length 506, 524–526, 531

Gasification: a process that converts organic or fossil-fuel-based biomass materials into syngas and CO_2, accomplished by subjecting the material to high temperatures (>700°C) without combustion. The process combined with use of the syngas can be a source of energy 416, 439

Gated community: an area protected by a perimeter fence or wall, where all entering the enclosure must use a pass or be interviewed by guards 669

General plan. See Comprehensive plan

Geographic information system (GIS): computer software designed to capture, store, manipulate, analyze, manage, map, and present spatial or geographic data 35, 40, 45, 80, 108–110, 153–154, 163, 368

Geomancy: the art of placing or arranging buildings on a site to take account of natural forces or signs from the earth (see also **Feng Shui; Vastu Shastra**) 169

Geomorphology: the geological science that deals with the structure, origin, and processes of creating topography and other earth features 33, 34

Geothermal energy: the use of relatively constant subsurface temperatures to heat or cool building spaces, typically by pumping water from belowground or by tapping the releases of steam from the magma 4, 16–17, 43, 177, 417, 437–439, 444, 691, 694

   closed-loop system: water in enclosed tubes is circulated from belowground, exchanged in heating or cooling devices within the structure, and returned 438
   open-loop system: groundwater is pumped to an exchanger, then returned to the groundwater or wasted 438

Gradient: a measure of the slope of a site or roadway, typically expressed as a ratio of height to distance, or as a percentage 47–48, 73, 274, 319, 321, 328, 341, 348, 380–381, 395, 456, 466

Gravel: a loose aggregation of small water-worn stones or crushed rock, typically between ¼ in (6 mm) and ¾ in (19 mm) in diameter 38, 42, 47, 49–50, 297, 303–304, 352, 375, 378, 381, 392, 397, 444, 460, 467

Gravity model: a model that can predict the flow or attraction of people, goods, or communication based on Newton's Law of Gravitation, accounting for mass and distance 507

Gravity sewer system: a system that depends on downhill flow to move effluents to a disposal site 379–381, 393–397, 402

   collector lines aggregating discharges from many sources 380, 394
   lateral lines from occupied buildings to the public sewer lines 379, 380, 389
   manholes at critical junction points to allow for cleanout of the system 380–381, 394, 395
   sewage treatment plants that remove impurities before discharging or recycling water 393, 394, 396–397
   trunk lines transporting the waste to the sewage treatment plan 379, 381, 392, 394, 396

Gray water: relatively clean wastewater without fecal contamination, from baths, sinks, washing machines, and kitchen appliances 261, 368, 390–391, 392, 693–694, 696

Greenhouse gas (GHG) emissions: discharge of gases that contribute to the greenhouse effect by absorbing infrared radiation produced by solar warming of the Earth's surface, including carbon dioxide (CO_2), methane (CH_4), nitrous oxide (NO_2), and water vapor   4–5, 233–236, 308, 441, 443, 601

Green infrastructure: use of natural systems to collect, filter, detain, and transport water, improve air quality, recycle wastes, and perform other essential functions   16, 114, 116, 178, 188, 260–262, 379

Green roof (also **living roof**): a roof covered by a waterproofing membrane, growing medium, and plants designed to absorb rainfall and cool the temperature of the roof   367, 371, 375–376, 553, 564–565

> **extensive green roof**: a roof in which the building is partially or fully covered by planting   376
> **intensive green roof**: a roof in which portions of the building are planted more extensively and used for outdoor living or recreation   376

Gridiron plan: a rectilinear pattern of streets and blocks in a settlement   76, 168, 290–292, 303, 561, 680, 682

Grid parity: a situation in which an alternative energy source such as solar panels or wind turbines can generate power that is less than or equal to the price of purchasing power generated from conventional sources   422

Ground cover: horizontally spreading planting that protects a surface from erosion and inhibits weeds   2, 69, 71–72, 226, 368, 370, 381, 457, 463, 466, 477–478

Groundwater: water that is found below the surface in the cracks and spaces in soil, sand, and rocks, the source of 20% of the freshwater on the earth   3, 34, 36, 42–43, 51, 69–71, 108, 226, 303, 305, 367–368, 374–375, 377, 379, 383–384, 386, 392, 402, 414, 437–438, 444, 460–462, 690

Habitat corridor. See **Ecological corridor**

Halophyte species: plants that grow in waters of high salinity or in areas of salt spray, including mangrove swamps, saline semideserts, coastal marshes, and seashores   68

Hazards: situations or conditions that increase risk or danger   4, 7, 43, 50, 63, 68, 72, 231, 260, 278, 296, 368, 373, 427, 443, 461, 478, 513, 582, 690

Headhouse: areas of a transportation system designed to accommodate persons waiting for boarding, such as ferry terminals, waiting rooms, loading areas   325, 381

Headways: the average interval between vehicles or trains moving in the same direction on a route   311, 314–315, 318

Health: the condition of being sound in body, mind, or spirit, the relative absence of diseases or maladies   85, 116, 191–192, 224, 230–232, 259, 335, 397, 416–418, 427, 449, 460, 552, 567, 691

Health impact assessment: an analysis of the health effects and distribution of the effects of a project or development, such as hazards created, effects on air and water quality, and displacements   116, 224, 230–231

Health indicators: quantifiable characteristics of a population used to measure or predict likely impacts of a development   231

Heat exchanger: a device for transferring heat from one medium to another, such as between piped steam and circulating air   425, 438–439, 441–442

Heat island effect: a situation in which the densely built-up portions of an urban area are significantly warmer than the surrounding countryside, because of the absorption and retention of heat by hard-surfaced materials   55–57, 188, 193, 226, 231, 236, 303, 375, 475, 530, 639, 690

Height limits: regulations setting maximum heights for buildings   98, 102, 498, 501

Height planes: sloped planes that limit building heights, typically requiring buildings to step back from the street to allow the penetration of sunlight   99, 179

Heliostat array and collector: mirrored surfaces that reflect sunlight onto a single collector containing a medium such as water or molten salt that drives turbines to generate electricity   425–426

High-capacity information networks: trunk circuits with high capacity (backbones) that can carry all forms of data, typically dedicated to Internet traffic   543

Highest and best use: a legally permitted use of land or property that is likely to yield the highest economic return   207

Historic commission, landmark commission, or heritage commission: a committee or commission created to serve as a steward of historic properties or districts, reviewing any proposals for change   102

Historic preservation: the process of cataloging, researching, and designating structures, places, and districts for special protection, and encouraging wise use of them   25, 102

Historic tax credits: a credit against income for expenditures for rehabilitating or improving historic income-producing properties (the credit may be sold to others to obtain capital for improvements)   84

Homeowners' association, property owners' association, property board, property committee, property trust, owners' corporation, or common interest realty association: an entity created to manage commonly owned aspects of a site, with power to charge owners a pro-rata share of the expenses   95–96, 185, 198, 422, 677

Horizontal mixed uses: different uses, such as housing, offices, or a hotel, organized side by side within a single building   662–664

Housing density: the number of housing units per unit of land area (**gross density** if the denominator is the entire site, **net density** if only residential sites are included)   97, 332, 480–482, 487–488, 669

Housing types: prototypical housing forms based on whether units have their own site or share land with other units, have independent or shared entrances, or are in a shared structure   480–482, 487–502

> **apartments** (or **flats**): units with common entrances and access ways, including **walkup apartments**, **garden apartments**, **high-rise apartments**, **street bar housing**, and **tall thin towers**   480, 497–501
> **attached housing**: individual housing units with separate entrances joined up with other units through party walls, usually on both sides, including **semidetached houses**, **duplexes**, **quads**, **row houses**, **town houses**, **terrace houses**, **court garden houses**, **stacked row houses**, **back-to-back stacked row houses**, and **maisonettes**   198, 211, 480, 492–497, 680
> **cohousing** or **congregate housing**: structures that combine individual living units with shared kitchens and social spaces   503–504
> **detached housing**: freestanding single-household units on their own sites, including **bungalows**, **villas**, **small lot housing**, and **zero lot line houses**   198, 211, 480, 487–492, 673

extended-care housing: buildings or complexes that provide living opportunities at varying levels of care from independent living to assisted care to full nursing care   12–18, 503
   mixed housing forms: units that combine two or more housing types or housing with other uses such as shopping, working, or social service spaces with living (one example being **loft housing**)   480, 501–503

Human contact: meeting or greeting others, participating in shared activities, or simply observing strangers in public spaces   7, 133, 482, 484, 599, 601, 618, 622, 672

Human development stages: the stages of cognitive and motor skill development from first steps to independent teenage years, distinctions useful in planning play facilities, typically differentiated as **early childhood**, **exploration years**, **imaginative play years**, **collaborative years**, and **teamwork years**   574–578

Humus: the organic component of soil, formed by decomposition of leaves and other plant material by soil microorganisms   37, 65, 413

Hutongs: narrow residential streets in Asian cities that date from preindustrial times   140, 497–498

Hydric soils: soils formed under conditions of saturation, flooding, or ponding that last long enough during the growing season to develop anaerobic conditions in the upper part   68

Hydrophytic vegetation: wetland plant species adapted for life in habitats that have permanent or alternating dry and inundated or saturated soil conditions; also known as **obligate wetland species**   399

Identity. See **District identity**

Imhoff tank or **septic tank:** a chamber suitable for holding and processing sewage either by simple settling and sedimentation or anaerobic digestion of extracted sludge   391–392, 396

Incentive zoning: development regulations that award higher FARs to property owners if they provide public benefits, such as creating additional public open space, affordable housing, or public facilities   100, 218

Induced demand (for travel) or **induced activity:** travel required because of the separation of common destinations, such as work and housing or shopping   689

Infiltration basin or zone (or **bioretention** or **recharge basin**): an area devoted to holding stormwater runoff or floods, allowing them to slowly seep into the groundwater   16, 377

Infrastructure: the basic facilities and systems required to support use of a site, including utilities, transportation, communications, and social facilities   253–264

In-situ remediation: the application of natural landscape and bioremediation techniques to absorb harmful materials in the soil   461–462
   bioattenuation: biodegradation processes for chlorinated solvents, generally an anaerobic process sometimes referred to as **reductive dechlorination**   461
   natural attenuation: a variety of physical, chemical, and biological processes that act without human intervention to reduce the mass, toxicity, mobility, volume, or concentration of contaminants in the soil or groundwater   461
   natural remediation: removal of pollution or contaminants from soil, groundwater sediment, or surface water using natural processes   461

Insolation: the amount of solar radiation reaching a given area   58–59

Intelligent cities: settlements provided with human and social infrastructure to support sustainable development and promote innovation in jobs, social interchanges, and transportation; also referred to as **smart cities** and **smart connected cities**   262–264, 448, 452–454

Interest groups: groups beyond the owners of a site and the professionals working for them that are concerned with the outcomes of site development, or wish to promote facilities or uses on a site   103, 111, 120–122, 125, 176, 185

Internal rate of return (IRR): a discount rate that makes the net present value of all income or loss flows from a project equal to zero   215

Internet platforms for engagement: Internet programs that facilitate public participation in the design and review of development projects   122

Intersection types: configurations of roadway connection points   287–290
   four-way intersections: generally two roadways crossing   288
   roundabout or **traffic circles:** continuous-flow intersections with circulation around a central round-point   288–289
   three-way intersections: generally T-shaped connections with one through route and one dead end route   288
   underpass or **overpass configurations:** connections that allow free flow of through traffic; may include connections configured as **diamond**, **cloverleaf**, or **directional ramps**   289

Intertidal zone: the area on a shoreline that is between the low and high tide lines, also known as the **foreshore** or **littoral zone**   25, 51, 67, 226, 641

Intrinsic value: the actual value of a site in terms of tangible and intangible factors   207

Just-in-time supply chains: supply networks that provide components or finished products when needed, rather than storing large quantities at the user's location   544

Laboratories: special-purpose structures built for chemical, biological, or medical experimentation   557–562, 592–594, 597, 599, 604–605, 609–611, 618

Land assembly district: a district of property owners that has the power by majority vote to approve or disapprove the sale of their land   202, 205–206

Landfill or **tip:** an area for disposing of waste materials by burying them and covering with soil   5, 36, 48, 50, 233, 261, 393, 397, 404, 406, 411–413, 415–416, 443, 460–461, 463

Landform grading: a method of modifying steep slopes so that erosion is minimized, by channeling runoff to protected drainage ways   73

Land grant colleges: universities created or designated by state governments or the US government to receive the benefits of the Morrill Acts, which provided land and resources for institutions specializing in agriculture and the mechanic arts, later extended to support African-American colleges and American Indian colleges   597, 604–605

Landmark. See **Historic preservation**

Land pooling: assembly, resubdivision, and redistribution of land parcels owned by several owners, who benefit by the rationalization of parcels and infrastructure (Australia, India), also known as **land sharing** (Thailand) and **land readjustment**   202, 204, 206

Land readjustment: formal processes for combining parcels owned by a number of owners, replanning and resubdividing them, installing infrastructure, and returning somewhat smaller parcels to the original owners; also called **land pooling**, **land sharing**, **compulsory land readjustment procedure**, **public taking of lands**, and **land assembly districts** 202–204, 206

Landscape: all the visible features of the land, including topography, vegetation, ground surfaces, and manmade improvements, also referred to as **landschap** (Dutch), **landsceap** (Old English), or **landschaft** (German) viii, 1–2, 11, 43, 45, 52, 60, 76, 79, 85, 112, 114–117, 149–150, 156–158, 176–178, 185, 190, 193, 234, 237, 257–258, 261, 283, 286, 291, 296, 298, 305, 341, 352, 362, 375–376, 400, 417, 427, 449, 456–465, 471–478, 505, 549, 555, 559, 588, 601, 605–606, 609, 622, 630, 672, 673, 676, 690

Landscape ecology: the pattern and interaction between ecosystems within a region, especially the unique effects of spatial heterogeneity 64–66

Landscape matrix: the background ecological system in which landscape patches and corridors exist 64

Landscape traditions: longstanding cultural approaches to shaping the landscape, including the desire for the **picturesque**, the idea of **compressing** larger landscapes in gardens, and constructing **symbolic** landscapes that refer to broader contexts 2, 9, 168–173, 457–460, 485

Land tenure: the legal regime under which land is controlled by an individual who is said to "hold" the land, commonly differentiated between outright **ownership** and **leasehold** 88–93, 96

Lateral sewer lines: privately owned pipes connecting occupied structures to a public sewer line 379–380, 389, 394

Law of the Indies: a body of laws issued by the Spanish Crown in the sixteenth to eighteenth centuries for the American and Philippine possessions of its empire, which specifies the form of settlements 170–173

Layover area: a location for buses and other vehicles to idle while waiting for their scheduled travel time 318

Leasehold: a contract between an owner (lessor) and a tenant (lessee) that conveys certain rights to use a property for a defined period. Interest in property held under such a contract may be paid for by **periodic payments** or through a **prepaid leasehold** 18, 21, 25, 30, 32, 89–96, 185, 195, 198, 200–201, 206, 214, 550, 664, 672

Ledge: a narrow horizontal surface projecting from a wall or cliff 14, 34, 383, 395, 402

LEED: **Leadership in Energy and Environmental Design**, a sustainability-oriented building certification run under the auspices of the US Green Building Council (USGBC); includes **LEED-ND** designed to assess sustainability in site development 22, 185–190, 192–194, 565

Legacy structures: sites or buildings, generally over 50 years in age, that have special meaning because of their distinctive design, persons or institutions that have inhabited them, or events that have occurred there; also referred to as **historic structures**, **landmarks**, **cultural monuments**, and **heritage structures and sites** 83–85

Level of service (LOS): a qualitative measure used to predict the quality of movement based on traffic flow, speed, and delays; common usage includes **vehicular LOS**, **bicycle LOS**, and **pedestrian LOS** 272–274, 318, 332, 349, 569, 636, 693

LIDAR survey: light detection and ranging, a remote sensing method that uses light in the form of a pulsed radar to measure distances and construct topographic maps 46, 466

Life cycle costs: total costs incurred over the lifetime of use of a facility, often expressed as the sum of annual costs discounted at an appropriate interest rate reflecting the value of money 6, 254, 265, 435

Lifestyle: way of life or style of living that reflects the attitudes and values of a person or group 116, 130–133, 235, 382, 404, 480, 482, 484, 535, 540, 690–691

Lighting fixtures: lighting units generally mounted on poles in streets, with light technologies including **light-emitting diode (LED)**, **high-pressure sodium (HPS)**, and **compact ceramic metal halide (CCMH)** 139, 258, 287, 352, 430–434

Light rail transit (LRT) systems: multiple-unit self-powered vehicles that travel on rails within street rights-of-way or on dedicated corridors, offering an intermediate level of transit between high-capacity rail and individual streetcars; also referred to as **trolleys**, **trams**, **munis**, **subway-surface lines**, or **interurbans** 320–323

Liminal pond: a space occupied by seasonal water, dry in other parts of the year 71

Limited mobility: diminished capacity to walk or move unaided by others, which may be the result of disease, congenital disorder, accident, or neuromuscular and orthopedic impairments 8, 47, 301, 303, 312

Linear systems: patterns of streets following a single alignment for movement, with all secondary streets accessible from it 168, 241, 290, 293–294, 324

Liquefaction: a phenomenon whereby a saturated or partially saturated soil substantially loses strength in response to external stress, such as an earthquake, causing it to behave like a liquid 51

Live-work buildings: structures accommodating residential units as well as work spaces such as home offices, independent office space, or maker spaces 234, 293, 480–481, 499, 502–503, 646–647, 651, 656, 671, 693–695

Loading dock: a dedicated area for loading or unloading trucks, generally with a platform that is elevated to the height of the truck floor 6, 407, 512–513, 655

Loam: soil with roughly equal proportions of sand, silt, and clay, typically also containing humus 38–42, 391

Logistics warehouses: large usually automated warehouses that inventory goods or components and transfer them to shipping lines or end users as needed 544

Loss leader: a site or building space sold or leased at less than the cost of producing it, intended to serve as an attraction to other buyers or lessors 10

Low-carbon energy sources: sustainable sources of energy production, including solar, wind, tidal, and nuclear, although each needs to account for energy consumed in constructing and assembling the infrastructure and devices used in production 689, 691

Low-frequency infrasound: sounds below 20 Hz, lower than the threshold of human hearing, which may affect the feelings and health of humans and animals 428

Low-head hydropower: the use of stream flow or tidal flows with a head of 20 m (66 ft) or less to produce energy, also referred to as **micro hydropower** 422, 430–431

Mandala: a geometric figure representing the universe in Hindu and Buddhist symbolism, often circular with nested squares   169–170

Mandatory homes association: an organization of homeowners in which membership is automatic upon purchasing a home, which has responsibility for managing shared spaces, may have approval powers over changes to the exteriors of homes, and may levy charges to pay for common expenses   199

Mangrove: coastal swamps with trees or shrubs that are partly flooded at high tide and serve as a barrier to flood surges, the vegetation having tangled roots aboveground forming dense thickets   67–68

Manhole: a small covered opening in a walkway or roadway leading to a sewer or vault that allows a person to enter   380–381, 384, 395, 403

Manufactured homes: housing units prefabricated in a factory and moved to a site in components or complete units, sometimes referred to as **mobile homes**   490

Manzanas or **illes:** square blocks in l'Eixample, Barcelona, with chamfered corners (**chaflanes**) to assure smooth flow of traffic at intersections   682

Mass transit systems: generically, public transit systems of all modes, but also referring more specifically to heavy rail-based systems on separate rights-of-way above or belowground, variously designated Metro, rapid transit, Metropolitaine, subway, subterraneo, U-Bahn, S-Train, underground, rapid railway, T, MTA, CTA, SkyTrain, MRT, MetroTrain, MetroRail, MARTA, WMATA, the El   47, 82, 85, 87, 226, 234, 257, 293, 298, 309, 318, 323–327, 344, 360, 364, 527, 537, 637, 678–679, 687–690

Master control plan: a comprehensive set of regulations affecting development that derive from an areawide or citywide plan   81

Master plan: an overall spatial plan for an area that serves as a guide for development   18–19, 81, 102–103, 197, 206, 217, 558–559, 561–562, 587, 594–596, 637–638, 678

Material recovery station: a location for separation and recycling of solid wastes that have potential for reuse, also referred to as **recycling station** or **transfer station**   412

Membrane bioreactor (MBR): the combination of a membrane process like microfiltration or ultrafiltration with a suspended-growth bioreactor, widely used for municipal and industrial wastewater treatment   396, 399

Mental map: the spatial understanding of an area used for orientation and navigation   75–76

Metrics: measures of performance that allow objectives to be monitored and managed   4, 115, 122, 212, 680

Micro hydropower. See **Low-head hydropower**

Mitigation of climate change: efforts to reduce the emission of greenhouse gases (GHG)   231

Mitigation measures: steps a site developer is required to take to offset negative environmental impacts of developing a site   191, 196, 224–225, 227, 296, 461

Mixed-use structure: a structure containing two or more uses within a single envelope   479, 481, 530, 644–668

Mobile information devices: handheld personal communication devices with the capability of linking to Internet resources, such as smartphones   454

Monorail system: typically an elevated system of transit guided and powered from a single rail   309, 326

Morphological analysis: the study of the overall form of an area, from which generalizations are derived; as a design method, exploring exhaustively all the possible forms that respond to a multiobjective program   163

Moving eyeballs: the number of people passing a storefront or attraction   509

Moving sidewalks: automated belts or links carrying pedestrians along a route   327, 329–330

Multilevel retail center: a shopping area with stores on two or more levels   325, 365, 507, 510

Multiplier effects: second-order and further expenditures that flow from an initial investment, such as expenditures by new employees of a business that moves to an area   228

Multiuse infrastructure: infrastructure that serves purposes beyond the utilitarian, such as a drainage way that is also a recreation corridor or a detention area that is used as a playfield when dry   6

Natural experiment: findings that may be derived by analyzing a normal change to the environment, such as changes in automobile volumes on streets in an area when bus service is extended to it   139

Neighborhood: a defined area where individuals share social ties, use of facilities, or values   7, 9, 14, 25, 30–31, 75, 125, 130–132, 135, 138, 185, 187–188, 215–217, 222, 268, 283, 290–298, 333, 381, 420, 454, 475, 484, 492, 500–501, 527–529, 569, 571–572, 579–582, 587–588, 614, 618–620, 630, 632, 644–645, 655–656, 662–664, 668, 669–674, 679–680

Neighborhood plan: a plan for improvements to a defined area as well as regulations for future development, also known as a **subarea** or **secondary plan**   81, 100

Neighborhood unit: the proposed form for a residential area guided by the number of households needed to support an elementary school and recreation facilities at its center, and restricting heavy and high-speed traffic to the perimeter of the area   669, 679

New city: a planned new settlement large enough to support a range of commercial and employment facilities and provide diverse housing, recreation, and cultural activities, also referred to as **new town** and **new community**   314, 425, 637, 669, 672–673, 684

New urbanism: an urban design movement that promotes mixed-use walkable neighborhoods and diverse communities, containing a wide range of uses and jobs, and built with coherent character   163, 165, 222–223, 294, 298, 488, 491, 682

New urbanist town centers: areas with street-oriented commerce and housing or office uses above, on-street parking with larger lots behind shops, and generous sidewalks and public space   645

New village or **neighborhood:** a smaller-scale new development often centered on a school or local shopping area, planned to encourage local interaction   30, 475, 669

NIMBY: "not in my back yard," the rallying cry of groups that resist what they consider undesirable development (too large, too much traffic, too many outsiders, etc.) near where they live   9

No-build alternative: the option of not changing the status quo, which forms a benchmark for comparing the impacts of changes to the environment   116, 225

Noise impact area: the area, defined by type of noise source, within which incompatible land uses such as residences, schools, hospitals, or places of worship should not be located; for airports in most jurisdictions, this is the 65 dB community noise equivalent level (CNEL)   86

Occupation classifications: a typology of occupations, ranging from precise (International Labor Organization [ILO] three-digit classifications) to generalized (**white-collar, blue-collar, no-collar, creative, freelancer,** etc.) 543

Offices: areas for administrative, professional, and clerical work, such as occurs in **office parks, business parks, high-tech office parks,** and **headquarters campuses** 22–23, 26, 200, 220, 301, 359, 404–405, 499, 502, 518, 524–529, 543–557, 561, 597–599, 646, 648–650, 653–656, 660–668, 682–684, 693–696

Open-air markets: seasonal, temporary, or occasional markets where merchants bring their items for sale, such as **green markets, farmer's markets, flea markets, antiques markets, flower markets, crafts fairs, night markets,** and **holiday marketplaces** 515

Open space premium: the value added to bordering uses by the presence of an open space 79, 219–220, 485

Open space ratio: the fraction of the site area that is devoted to open space, sometimes including open spaces on roofs 98

Operating and maintenance expenditures: annual expenses for lighting, heating, cooling, gas, maintenance, cleaning, and other activities required to use a space or infrastructure element 6, 228, 254, 263, 310, 403, 435, 504–505

Opportunity costs: the income forgone by not taking an action, such as not leasing, selling, or using a property 10, 540

Organic forms: forms that flow from or mimic natural forms, often curvilinear, branched, or pod-shaped 167–168, 679

Organizational form: the diagrammatic structure of relationships in an organization, typically described as **flat** (little hierarchy, equal status of most members), **matrix-** or **lattice-like** (members have both line and reporting functions), **hierarchical** (extensive vertical reporting), or **Taylorist** or **studio** (organized around production chains) 543–544, 546

Orientation elements: fundamental vocabulary for orientation in the city; Lynch proposed **landmarks, nodes, paths, edges,** and **districts** 75–76

Orthogonal block pattern: a rectilinear pattern of streets bounding development areas (see also **Gridiron plan**) 146, 164, 168, 292, 611, 679, 681–682

Ownership: the bundle of rights that an owner possesses for use and enjoyment of a property (conventional forms include fee simple, fractional, life estate, condominium ownership, cooperative ownership); ownership may include mineral rights, development rights, air rights, and water rights 1, 10, 88–96, 116, 173, 195, 198–202, 330, 491–494, 655, 664

Oxidation ditch: an activated sludge biological treatment process for sewerage that utilizes long solids retention times (SRT) to remove biodegradable organics 399

Package plants for sewage treatment: premanufactured small treatment facilities used to treat wastewater in limited areas or on individual sites, typically treating flows of 0.01–0.25 MGD; they may integrate aeration, sequencing batch reactors, oxidation ditches, membrane bioreactors, chlorination, or ultraviolet ray treatment 393, 399–402

Parabolic reflector array: an array of reflector troughs that are straight horizontally and curved vertically to concentrate energy on a collector filled with fluid on the reflector's focal line 425

Parametric modeling: a process based on algorithmic thinking that enables the production of complex geometries and the optimization of forms that respond to specific parameters 154, 168

Paratransit: public or group transit, often privately operated, that provides rides as needed, including carpooling, dial-a-ride services, airport shuttles, party vehicles, commuter vans, handicapped access vehicles, touring vehicles, jitneys, jeepneys, públicos, colectivos, and minibus taxis 309–310, 312–313

Parking access: the status of individual parking spaces, which may be:

> **dedicated parking:** reserved for specific individuals or vehicles 486, 651, 654
> **public parking:** available to all, free or upon payment of a fee 305–306
> **shared parking:** reserved for individuals in a group 300–301, 333, 486, 494, 518, 621, 650, 654

Parking configurations: basic layouts of parking spaces that respond to flow patterns, dimensions available, and operations of parking areas, including parallel, angled, valet, dedicated, and shared parking 302–303

Parking garage: a structure for accommodating vehicles when not in use, including self-park, valet park, and automated parking garages, flat-floor garages with ramps, and sloped-floor garages where driving lanes serve as ramps; also referred to as **multilevel carparks, parking structures, parking ramps, parking decks, parking podiums,** or **parkades** 298, 304–307, 359–360, 424, 495–496, 510, 514, 549

Parking requirements: the estimated demand for parking, based on conventions, regulations, or driver surveys 98, 175, 300, 302, 513

Parkour: a training discipline and recreational activity that involves mastering obstacle courses 580–582

Passenger car equivalents or **passenger car units:** a metric used in assessing traffic flow on a roadway that normalizes the flow of different types of vehicles by comparing them to single cars 270

Pattern book: a collection of desirable plan configurations, site arrangements, and building types for a specific climate and context 116, 162, 165

Pattern Language: a vocabulary for community, site, and building design, based on tried and true practices, compiled originally by Alexander and colleagues 146, 164

Peak sun hours: the solar insolation that a location would receive if the sun were shining at its maximum value for a number of hours 423

Pedestrian area module: the dimension of a lane of pedestrians moving along a sidewalk 349

Pedestrian bridge: an overpass for pedestrians to allow safe passage across a busy street 286, 354–357, 365

Pedestrian concourse: a walkway system located above or below the streets, or at ground level without vehicular traffic, usually lined by shops and building entrances, sometimes referred to as a **skyway, catwalk, sky bridge, skywalk, plus-15 pedestrian area, underground city, ville souterraine, 地下城, catacomb, pedway,** or **underground shopping street** 261, 330, 363–365, 666

Pedestrian cordon studies: studies of the number of pedestrians crossing specific lines drawn across a walkway 135

Pedestrian density: the number of pedestrians per square meter or other dimension of space 345–349

Pedestrian promenade: a pedestrian way for pleasure walking along the water's edge, along a ridge with views (belvedere), or in a wide median such as Barcelona's La Rambla 357–359, 531

Pedestrian zone: an area largely or exclusively reserved for pedestrians, also called a **car-free zone**, **pedestrian precinct**, or **pedestrian mall**   285, 296, 354, 359–363, 533, 536, 622

People-mover systems: small automated vehicles on a track or free range that take pedestrians to a destination on demand, such as **personal rapid transit (PRT) systems** (see also **Autonomous vehicles**)   326–328, 659

Perennial plants: plants that live for more than two years   51, 376, 472–474, 478, 588

Performance bond: cash, securities, or a letter of credit posted by a developer, landowner, or contractor certifying that terms of a contract will be fulfilled, to be released when the obligation is certified as complete   196

Permeable pavement: a ground surface that is strong enough to support vehicles while allowing moisture to pass through it, including **permeable concrete**, **porous asphalt**, **compacted gravel**, **unit pavers**, **recycled-glass porous pavement**, and **reinforced grass**   375

Photovoltaic (PV) panels: panels that convert energy from the sun directly into electricity by creating flow electrons by the photovoltaic effect   422–425

Phytoremediation: direct use of living green plants for in-situ removal, degradation, or containment of contaminants in soils, sludges, sediments, surface water, and groundwater   462–465

> **hyperaccumulation**: absorbing heavy metals through the roots of plants, which are then removed   463–464
> **phytoaccumulation** (or **phytoextraction**): extraction and storage of contaminants in plants, which are then removed   462
> **phytodegradation** (or **phytotransformation**): the process by which substances taken by a plant are broken down   462–464
> **phytovolatilization**: release into the air of harmful substances from the soil, sometimes after they have been broken down into volatile components   462, 464
> **rhizodegradation** (or **phytostimulation**): the degradation of contaminants in the rhizosphere (area of soil surrounding the roots of plants) by microbial activity which is enhanced by the roots   462–464

Pilot project: a project undertaken as a test of concept for the purpose of improving future projects   139, 189, 452

Place: a specific location on a site, often filled with activities, where the occupant has a sense of being somewhere   1, 3, 8, 11, 21, 57, 75–76, 78–80, 83–85, 133–135, 164, 176–177, 241, 298, 357–364, 400, 432–434, 454, 456, 478, 484–485, 506, 516, 540, 544, 549, 567–569, 578, 587, 594, 600, 604, 616, 618, 622–643, 658, 672

Planned unit development (PUD) or **planned development (PD) area**: a multiphase development project in which densities have been modified from as-of-right development rules in favor of a contract that specifies site-specific requirements for facilities, open spaces, site arrangements, and timing of development, and optimizes the use of the site   102, 197, 266

Planning cell (Planungszelle): a process that engages approximately 25 randomly selected people who work as public consultants for a limited time (such as a week) on a planning or policy problem, moderated by two process guides, and then summarize their proposals in a citizen report; a process devised by Peter Dienel   123

Planning conditions and obligations: development approval granted subject to the applicant meeting specific conditions and making good on obligations   103

Planning permission (England and Wales): permission granted by a local authority for building or development, based on an application that may trigger a planning inquiry (pubic review process); also known as **planning obligation**   103, 179

Planning values: aspirations or objectives that underlie public plans   1–11

Plant classification: the formal naming of plants, based on genus, species, variety, and cultivar, such as *Ulmus americana* 'Princeton'   475

Plant hardiness zones: zones that help determine which plants are most likely to thrive at a location, based on average minimum winter temperature divided into 10°F intervals   472

Plot ratio. See Floor area ratio

Pod: a unit of development without through roads   26–27, 678

Podium or **plinth**: lower levels of a mixed-use development that cover the entire site, usually with retail uses, topped by housing, offices, hotels, or other uses, a common form of development in Hong Kong   500–501, 513, 650, 664–668

Polytechnics: universities that focus on science and engineering research and teaching   591–592, 609–613

Pop-up stores or outlets: short-term or seasonal stores intended to test retailing ideas or capitalize on short-term demand (such as a Halloween store)   514

Precinct traffic pattern: neighborhood traffic circulation organized so that there are limited routes into and out of the area, and neighborhood cross traffic is prevented   291, 296, 298

Preinsulated heating and cooling pipes: pipes for transporting hot water, steam, or chilled water, surrounded by insulation that minimizes heat loss or gain   444–445

Present value: the amount that an investor would pay today for an investment that returns money in the future, discounting future revenues based on the time value of money to the investor   208–214, 254–255, 421

Privacy: separation from others through control of visual, sound, and human presence   94, 135, 226, 345–346, 471, 481–485, 489–490, 493, 624, 627, 629, 646, 654–655, 669

Privacy gradient: the range of levels of privacy of spaces, from **public spaces** (anyone may enter) to **group public or semipublic spaces** (anyone may enter but with scrutiny) or **group private or semiprivate spaces** (open only to the owners or those invited) or **private** spaces (restricted to the owners)   483–484

Productivity of locations: comparison of the relative returns for the same product sold in different locations, varying because of differing sales volumes, personnel costs, or real estate costs   9

Product lines: groups of related products under a single brand sold by the same companies; may be sourced from several companies   644

Pro forma financial analysis: an accounting of projected cost and revenues of a project by year that allows an analysis to be made of its value as an investment   114–115, 141–142, 144, 209–218

Program (or **brief** or **project scope**): a written statement of the scope, purposes, and qualities of site improvements being sought   9, 14, 18–20, 26–27, 103, 114–117, 127–128, 131, 141–148, 150, 161, 164, 173, 175, 211, 244, 250, 301, 504, 543, 574, 606, 609, 622, 656

Property: the status of land based on ownership, including **no property** (belongs to nobody), **common property** (belongs to a group of owners or residents of an area), **state property** (belongs to a government), or **private property** (belongs to individuals or corporations)   91–93

Proprietary lease: a lease that accompanies a form of ownership, such as the proprietary lease for a residential unit to owners of shares in a cooperative   93, 198, 200

Prototype: a common form of building or site development, as opposed to structures that have a totally unique program   115, 140, 161–162, 287, 479–699

Proxemics: the branch of knowledge that deals with the amount of space that people in a specific culture feel it necessary to set between themselves and others, distinguishing between **intimate space**, **personal space** with acquaintances, and **social space** in groups   345

Public engagement: processes that bring people together to address issues of common importance, usually including both average citizens, stakeholders, and professionals   112, 121–126

Public inquiry (England and Wales): the process of soliciting input from the public and affected parties before ruling on planning permission   103, 123

Public markets: generally permanent locations for sale of locally produced foods and products   515–518

Pumping stations: locations where water or sewerage is lifted from one elevation to another, often created in relatively flat terrain   380, 395, 402

Pyrolysis: decomposition of materials at high temperatures in the absence of oxygen   406, 439

Quick response codes (QR): a type of matrix barcode that is machine readable and contains or connects to information about the item to which it is attached   454–455

Racetrack circulation pattern: circular pattern of movement in a shopping center, with parallel connections lined by shops   531

Radial form: roads spread outward from a common point of origin; may also be coupled with circumferential roadways forming a **radial-concentric** pattern   292–293

Radio frequency radiation (RFR): electromagnetic radiation, both radio waves and microwaves, that occupy the frequency range of 3Khz to 300 GHz, used for all forms of communication   449

Rainfall: water falling from the sky, for different reasons:

  convection rainfall: the sun heats the ground, moisture evaporates, cooling as it rises, vapor condenses forming clouds, falling to earth as surfaces cool   61
  frontal rainfall: a cold polar air mass meets a warmer tropical air mass forming a front; when the air becomes fully saturated it rains   61
  relief rainfall: rain is formed when air is forced to cool as it rises over relief features such as mountains and hills   61

Rainfall maps: maps providing data on frequency and intensity of rain events for local areas   368–370

Rain garden: a shallow depressed area use to collect rainwater from impervious areas such as roofs, driveways, roads, walkways, parking lots, and compacted lawn areas, planted with species that quickly absorb water   116, 260, 374–375, 487, 676–677

Rain shadow: an area having little rainfall because it is sheltered from prevailing rain-bearing winds by a range of hills or mountains   61

Raster-based graphics (or **bitmapped graphics**): digital images created by specifying each coordinate (or pixel) on an **x-y** grid, commonly used for photographic images, renderings, or graphic design   152

Rational choice: decisions made in self-interest based on information available to decision makers   174

Rational method for computing runoff: a simple technique for estimating a peak stormwater discharge from a site based on storm intensity, area, and a coefficient reflecting the absorptive capacity of the land   371–372

Real property: fixed property, principally land and buildings, as distinguished from **personal property** (books, cars, or other movable objects), **intangible personal property** (stocks, bonds, or licenses), or **intellectual property** (such as patents or trademarks)   93

Reclamation: filling of land or creating polders to allow its use for cultivation or development   49–51, 85, 402

Recontouring: adjusting the surface profile of land through grading, filling, and extraction of soils   50, 73

Recreation areas: a broad-ranging category of facilities or sites designed for exercise, public and family events, team competition, and relaxation   7, 15, 30, 48–49, 71–72, 83, 130, 132, 190, 198–199, 245–246, 267, 351, 381, 484, 490, 567–589, 594, 599, 606–609, 620, 639–643, 671–673, 676–677, 690–695

Recycling points. See Material recovery station

Regulatory taking: the imposition of government regulations that limit the uses of private property to such a degree that it cannot be used or developed   89

Remediation: mitigating the presence of pollutants on a site, through **containment**, **removal**, **ex-situ treatment**, or **in-situ remediation**   114, 460–465

Render: the process of making a drawing that is easily read by lay individuals, usually by creating a three-dimensional sketch or pictorial image (a **rendering**)   138, 150–160

Renewable energy sources: energy from sources that are not depleted when used, such as wind or solar power   188, 422–431, 691

Residual value: the salvage value or the remaining value of an asset after it has been fully depreciated. Also known as **terminal value**   209

Resilience: the capacity of a place to return to its original form after a major weather event, flooding, or a manmade disaster   4–5, 689–692

Return on investment (ROI): the benefit (return, gain or loss) generated by an investment relative to the amount of money invested, usually expressed as a percentage   212–214

  leveraged ROI: gain or loss relative to the equity invested after accounting for loans taken out to execute the project, also known as **return on equity (ROE)**   212–213
  return on cost (ROC): the ratio of the gain or loss from sales of a project to its total cost   210–212
  unleveraged ROI: gain or loss, assuming that all of the capital needed for a project is equity, that is sourced from the investors   212–213

Right-of-way: lands used for passage of vehicles, pedestrians, and infrastructure, acquired by the public through purchase, dedication, or easements   81, 87, 94, 195, 198, 255, 257–258, 279, 281–291, 317–323, 340–341, 361, 390

Riparian corridor: the land that borders either side of a stream or the edges of lakes or other water bodies   52, 66, 71–72, 462

Roadway density (RD): the number of km (mi) of roadways per unit of area (typically km^2 or sq mi), alternatively the **link:node ratio (LNR)** computed by dividing the number of link segments per unit area by the number of intersections in the same area   294–296

Roadway hierarchy: a functional classification system that differentiates roadways by type, each with its own standards   278–287

  arterials: main arteries of a city, emphasizing flow of through traffic, usually restricting access to adjacent properties to locations that don't interfere with traffic flow; includes **parkways, multiway boulevards**, and **grand avenues**   283–286
  collector streets: streets that transport vehicles from local streets to citywide arterial roadways; may also provide access to adjacent properties   281–283
  limited-access highways: roadways for long-distance movement with limited locations to enter and exit; includes **expressways, freeways**, and **motorways**   286–287
  local access streets: streets providing access to adjacent properties; includes **grid streets, loops, cul-de-sacs, alleys, mews**, and **auto courts**   278–281

Rumble strip: a series of raised strips across a road or along its edge, warning drivers of speed restrictions or danger ahead   296–297, 338

Runoff: the portion of precipitation that is not absorbed by the soil but travels by gravity to ponds, streams, or lakes   5, 13, 16, 64, 67–73, 114–118, 145, 158, 173, 226, 236, 241, 254–258, 260, 303, 360, 366–381, 383, 385–386, 390, 393, 456, 466, 470, 487, 565, 677, 687, 690, 694–695

Safety: an environment that is largely free of danger, risk, or injury   7, 82, 85, 120, 135, 231, 236, 258–259, 265, 274–275, 277, 287, 294–297, 316, 322–323, 335–338, 347, 378, 387, 432, 574, 582, 687

Sales kiosks or **pushcarts**: small booths or carts for sale of specialized items in the public spaces of shopping areas   354, 357, 361, 531

Salt marsh: an area of coastal grassland that is regularly flooded by seawater   68

Sand: small particles of disintegrated rock, often rounded by water motion, typically .0625–2 mm in size   25, 36–39, 42, 49, 52, 56, 68–69, 260, 368, 371, 378, 386, 391, 399, 458–459, 467, 574–576, 580

Sanitary wastes: nonhazardous and nonradioactive liquid or solid waste materials from agricultural, commercial, domestic, or industrial sources   393

Sankey diagram: a graphic illustration of flows, like those of energy, material, or money, in which the width of the arrows is proportional to the size of the represented flow   563–564

Secondary plan (Canada): a detailed area plan that is an elaboration of the citywide plan   81, 100, 123, 197

Security: an environment that is relatively free of crime, personal assaults, and threats   7, 134–135, 201, 245, 249, 294, 334, 342, 353, 362, 364–365, 432–433, 482, 484–485, 490, 523, 554, 618, 629–630, 650, 654, 660

Semilattice structure: a distributed set of nodes with nonhierarchical relationships   681

Sense of place or **topophilia**: a strong identity and character (in buildings or places) that is deeply felt by local inhabitants and many visitors   2, 3, 11, 115, 177, 240–241, 456

Sensors: devices located in the environment that are capable of recording, transmitting, and in some instances analyzing environmental conditions; they may collect **video, numeric data, binary data**, or **metering data**   264, 308, 407, 452–455

Septage or **sludge**: liquid and solid material pumped from a septic tank, cesspool, or other primary treatment source   393

Septic system: a system for separation and settling of solids in a **septic tank** or **Imhoff tank**, then distributing liquid wastes for further treatment in a belowground **septic disposal field** of perforated drain tiles   226, 392–393

Septic tank effluent pumping (STEP) system: a settling tank from which gray water effluent is pumped to a community low-pressure sewer system   396

Sequencing batch reactors: a technology that treats wastewater in batches by bubbling oxygen through it to reduce the biochemical oxygen demand (BOD), then discharging the higher-quality effluent for further treatment   399

Serial notation techniques: notation systems that record the sequence of spaces, activities, and features experienced by a person moving though a space   135–136

Service courtyard: an enclosed area large enough to accommodate trucks for receiving and loading goods and materials   512–513

Setback plane: an angled plane defining the outer limit of a building, requiring stepbacks from the street for higher floors. Also called a **slant plane**   99, 648

Severability of uses: the capacity to separate portions of a building for the purpose of obtaining separate mortgages or loans   655

Shared parking: parking spots that are shared among uses, such as for offices during the day and housing at night   300–301, 486, 494, 518, 650, 654

Sharrow: a shared-lane marking for joint use of street space, for bicycles and other vehicles   338–339

Sheet drainage: flowing water that spreads widely in relatively shallow sheets over gently sloping areas   371

Shop houses or **chop houses**: traditional houses with shops on the ground floor and storage, production, and living spaces above, common in older Asian cities   164, 522, 644–645

Shopping center: a collection of shops that attracts patrons because of the convenience of making multiple purchases in a defined location   518–520, 526–541

  community shopping center: a structure for comparison shopping, anchored by some combination of a large supermarket, drugstore, discount store, or department store   507, 526–530
  convenience shopping center: an individual freestanding store or a small cluster of them, often open late hours, for everyday purchases   518
  entertainment-based center: a center dominated by food and entertainment outlets; may also include gifts and specialty items   538–541
  fashion center: a center focused on designer-branded clothing, shoes, and accessories   518
  power center: a collection of large branded outlets sometimes called **category killers**, each drawing patrons to the center   518, 533, 535
  regional shopping center: a center with a full array of shops in each category, including fashion outlets, home goods, department stores, food and beverage areas, and often a cinema   518, 530–537

shopping village: a collection of small-scale unique shops, often locally owned, located along streets   518–520

superregional shopping center: a huge concentration of shops including multiple anchor stores, entertainment areas, and food and beverages   511–512, 518

town center: a center with a broad range of goods and services that serves a large community, usually street-oriented   533–535

Shopping streets: streets lined by a continuum of shops, most successful if both sides have shops and the street is easy to cross   364, 509–510, 521–524

Sidewalk: a pedestrian way for passage along a street, generally with three zones: the **curb zone** or **furniture zone** for lighting poles, utilities, or seating; the **pedestrian zone** for passage; and the **interface** or **frontage zone**, often adopted by merchants for display of goods or signage; also known as a **pathway, platform, footway,** or **footpath**   346–348, 352–355, 363, 432, 451, 467, 521, 629

Silt: fine clay or other material carried by running water and deposited as sediment   4, 36, 38–39, 41–42, 377, 379, 466, 487

Site coverage ratio: the total area occupied by buildings on a site divided by the site area   98

SITES®: a sustainability-focused rating system for sites that promotes climate mitigation, flood protection, reduced energy consumption, improved health, and increased outdoor recreation activities   187, 190–193

Sky cover: the extent to which the sky is obscured by clouds, usually expressed as an average over the year   58

Sky lobbies: high floors in buildings where passengers can transfer from express to local elevators serving floors above, or from low-zone to high-zone elevators   546, 648

Sky view factor (SVF): the fraction of the sky that is visible from the ground up, usually a dimensionless value ranging from 0 to 1. Also known as **sky plane exposure**   55–56

Skywalk or **upper-level pedestrian walkway**. See **Pedestrian concourse**

Sludge: semisolid slurry that is the result of sewage treated in a tank or treatment facility   392, 396–397, 402, 462

Slurry wall: a belowground wall at the edge of a building site, usually constructed by trenching and filling the cavity with concrete, which protects a site from intrusion of soil and groundwater   43, 461

SmartCode: a model transect-based planning and zoning document focusing on all scales of planning from the region to the community to the block and building   164, 166

Social capital: economic and social relationships in which social networks are central; the underpinning of local institutions   672, 690

Social infrastructure: facilities and spaces for social needs of communities, such as schools, civic buildings, community centers, recreation facilities, and religious places   83, 100, 193

Soil: the upper layer of the earth in which plants grow, typically a mixture of organic remains, clay, loam, and rock particles   2–3, 34, 36–43, 48, 51, 53, 56, 63–73, 108–110, 114, 191, 192, 226, 303, 352, 367–368, 370–373, 375–379, 392–394, 397–399, 460–469, 475

Soil horizons: layers of soil distinguished by color, texture, and material composition   37

Soil salinity: the salt content of a soil   61, 67–68

Soil surcharging: preloading or mounding of water-laden soils, often reclaimed land, to compact and remove water before developing, sometimes with the help of wick drains, vacuum consolidation, or electro-osmosis   61

Soil test boring: a vertical sample of the soil profile at a location, collected using a hand tool or drill rig   36

Solar array: a connected set of solar panels or reflectors that power a solar furnace or generate electricity for the grid or local consumption   5, 307, 423, 425, 443, 464, 690–692

Solar rights: the right to benefit from sunlight without obstruction by neighbors   57, 100

Solidification: the process of creating a solid mass from liquid or gaseous materials   462

Solid waste reduction strategies: strategies to reduce the output of solid waste in an area or jurisdiction, which may include **reducing** the original use of materials (such as by eliminating paper plates or not printing messages received in computers); **reusing** materials (such as by substituting reusable bottles for disposable ones or burning combustible wastes to produce energy); or **recycling** (reusing materials by crushing or melting and reforming them into new materials)   406

Solid wastes: items disposed of by residential, commercial, agricultural, or industrial uses, also called **garbage, refuse,** or **trash**   226, 234, 404–416, 443, 694

Solstice: the two times in the year when the sun reaches its highest point in the sky at noon (**summer solstice**) or lowest point (**winter solstice**), marking the longest and shortest periods of sunlight in the year   53–54

Sound attenuation: the use of barriers to reduce sound levels on adjacent sites, such as **sound barriers** or **berms** lining highways   86–87, 226

Souq (or **souk, soq, esouk,** or **suk**): a dense marketplace or commercial quarter in Asian, Middle Eastern, or North African cities   516

Source separation: the separation of recyclable materials in the solid waste stream before collection   406, 413

Space Syntax: a set of theories and techniques for analysis of spatial configurations, emphasizing geometric relationships   168

Specific area plan. See **District plan; Neighborhood plan; Secondary plan**

Specific heat: the amount of heat needed to raise the temperature of one gram of a material 1°C   55

Stable ecology. See **Balanced ecology**

Stakeholders: those with a direct financial or other tangible interest in a site   112, 115, 117, 119–127, 176, 237

Standard-gauge track: railway with a gauge of 1,435 mm (4 ft 8½ in), though standard gauges depart from this in some countries   321

Statement of intent: a proposal by a landowner to complete specific improvements on a site, generally within an agreed timetable   178

Storm frequencies or **events**: the expected size and frequency of maximum rainfall events, usually stated in terms of the largest storm that recurs on average in a specified number of years, such as a 10-year storm event or 100-year storm event   61–64

Street-oriented housing: housing where each unit has a front door facing a street   10

Structured survey: a method for collecting data on behavior and preferences using a survey with defined questions   137

Subdivision plan: a plan for dividing a site into multiple properties, providing for access roadways and other forms of infrastructure; a **draft or preliminary plan of subdivision** generally must be approved before any site work begins, and the **final plan of subdivision** is filed when the developer has completed all obligations for staking, creating roads, and installing infrastructure   116–117

Subdivision regulations: rules and requirements of the local government or utility districts that specify minimum property sizes, dimensions of rights-of-way, and specifications for infrastructure   93, 97, 195–197

Subsidence: the gradual sinking of an area of land, often the result of extraction of groundwater, mining, or petroleum activities   43, 50–51, 100, 226, 385

Sump tank: a bottomless tank sunk into the ground that allows for extraction of water in an area with a high-water table   402

Sunlight: sun moving across the sky and falling on a site, its location generally defined by **altitude** (the angle from the ground) and **azimuth** (its compass direction)   53–55

Superblock: a large block through which direct cross traffic is not possible   293, 609, 679

Supply chains: ordering and logistics systems for acquiring components from a variety of locations for assembly or sale   508, 512, 543–544

Surface form: the topography of a site   34

Surficial geology: the shape and materials of a site, including unconsolidated terrain   34–36

Sustainability: in site development, the goal of avoiding depleting natural resources to maintain an ecological balance, minimizing the effects on climate and the larger environment, and fostering a site's ability to rebound after extreme stress (see also **Resilience**)   2, 4–5, 12, 16, 175, 185–194, 262, 601, 690, 699

Sustainability metrics: measures that allow tracking of the draw on resources, emissions, induced travel, and other aspects of sustainability   4, 690, 691

Sustainability rating systems: local, regional, and national standards for development of sites, usually coupled with a certification system, the most common being those administered by LEED, BREEAM, CASBEE, and BEAM   185–194

Swale or swail: a shallow depression of the land, usually intended to collect and detain runoff; **vegetated swales** or **bioswales** also absorb some of the runoff and filter it, improving the water quality   16, 73, 116, 241, 254, 373–375, 377–378, 380–381, 466

Take part workshop: a community engagement process in which participants act out creative life patterns to arrive at understandings of a site, originated by Lawrence Halprin   176

Taking. See **Expropriation**

Taxi queue, cab stand, or **hack stand:** a zone where taxis are allowed to wait for passengers   311–312

Taylorism: a scientific approach to management, originated by Frederick W. Taylor, that analyzed each step in the work process and sought to optimize how it was carried out   546

Technical colleges: educational institutes specializing in practical training in technical fields, also known as **vocational schools, trade schools, career schools** or **colleges, community colleges, business academies, Berufsfachschulen, technicums,** and **senmon gakko**   591, 593

Terroir: the unique characteristics of a location, a subtle blend of landform, soils and subsoils, rainfall, climate, and human traditions   2–3, 79, 104, 118, 456, 459

Thermal mass: the ability of a material to absorb and store heat energy, with high-density materials like concrete and brick holding energy longer than lightweight materials such as timber   56

Thermal storage systems: systems for storing energy overnight or seasonally, using materials that include water, ice, rocks, gravel, or salts, or by injecting water into the rocks below   443–445

Tikkun olam: a Jewish concept defined by acts of kindness performed to perfect or repair the world   176

Time of use (TOU) tariffs: pricing electricity or other commodities to discourage peak use   443

Topography: the surface form of land   2, 13, 15, 43–48, 60, 65, 67, 81–82, 104–106, 149–150, 156–157, 167–170, 226, 277, 279, 286, 290–293, 304, 328, 341, 348, 357, 380, 399, 402, 448–449, 466, 468, 470–471, 491, 498, 540, 662, 686

Town common: lands owned by all residents of the town, usually in the center, originally used for grazing of animals in New England   8, 92

Townscape: the form and visual appearance of a town or urban area, a term popularized by Gordon Cullen   135–136

Traditional neighborhood development (TND): a neighborhood pattern consisting of streets, blocks, modest-sized lots, parks, and local services that promotes walkability through linkages and density   215–217, 268

Traditional sewage (or sewer or sewerage) system: a system for collecting, treating, and disposing of liquid wastes; its components may include **lateral sewer, collector** or **main sewer, interceptor sewer, primary treatment, secondary treatment,** and **tertiary treatment** (see also **Gravity sewer system**)   255, 367–368, 383, 393–396

Traffic calming measures: elements in the design and detailing of streets that slow traffic and improve the safety of pedestrians crossing the roadway (also referred to as **Verkehrsberuhigung, traffic mitigation, traffic abatement, stille veje, tempo 30 zones,** and **local area traffic management**); measures may include **speed bumps, speed humps or tables, rumble strips, narrowing lane widths, road diets, curb extensions** or **pinchers** or **chokers, chicanes** or **diverters,** and **medians**   278–279, 291, 296–298

Transect: a cross section through a typical settlement from dense urban center to the countryside, identifying prototypical development patterns   164, 166–167

Transfer of development rights (TDR): the ability to sell or otherwise transfer unused rights to develop a site to an adjacent site, or to a receiving zone   94, 101–102, 222

Transformer (electrical): a device used to transfer power from one circuit to another, changing voltages but not frequency   82, 260, 354, 417, 420–421

Transit-oriented development (TOD): a pattern of higher-density development around transit stops, encouraging walking and transit use rather than driving; also called a **transit village**   178, 314, 332–334, 527–529

Transit platforms: loading areas for mass transit, configured either as side loading platforms (serving one direction), or center loading platform (serving two directions)   321–323, 325

Trolleybuses: rubber-tired electrically powered buses, drawing energy from overhead electrical lines   310–311

Underground solid waste storage chambers: belowground storage areas emptied either by lifting the container and dumping or by vacuum suction   406–407

Underground storm drainage system: piped system to remove excess runoff from a site; components include **catch basins**, **trapped inlets** or **drainage boxes** for receiving water, **lateral lines** for transporting it from private properties to **collector sewer** lines running in public rights-of-way, **manholes** at junction points, **pumping stations** to lift water in relatively flat terrain, and **outfalls** for releasing water into larger water bodies   379–381

Underspace: the area below elevated expressways, rail lines, or transit lines   324

Undivided interest in property: property owned by two or more individuals with shared interest and responsibility   93, 198–199

Unearned increment: the rise in property value beyond general inflation and improvements made to it, attributed to actions of others and the community at large   201

Universities: institutions of higher learning that generally combine undergraduate education with postgraduate research and study and professional schools   10, 147, 184, 201, 260, 343, 404, 436, 449, 472, 477, 590–621

Unstructured dialogue: conversation without a strict agenda   135

User: an individual who uses a site but may have no ownership interest in it   5, 7, 9–10, 78, 112, 119–123, 130–135, 138–140, 163, 259, 296, 299, 307, 314, 328, 336, 340, 350, 389, 405, 408, 444, 450, 453, 456, 484, 513, 574, 587–588, 625, 630, 632

User advocate: an individual charged with speaking for or promoting the interests of users   140

Usufruct rights: a limited real right in civil law jurisdictions to use or enjoy a site or thing possessed without altering it   90

Utility corridors: conduits or structures created for multiple use by several infrastructure components, sometimes doubling as service connections   192, 445, 596

Vacuum sewer system: an underground system for waste collection in which solid wastes are drawn from **local holding tanks** via **pressure-sealed collection lines** to a **collection tank** for disposal or reuse   402–403

Valet parking: an arrangement in which valets take vehicles from a dropoff point to a parking area, retrieving them on call when needed   299, 303, 313, 523, 540, 654

Value creation: the value of a property that is greater than the cost of creating and selling it by virtue of the quality of the environment in which it sits   216–223

Value recapture: reclaiming a portion of the increased value of private properties when public improvements are made, such as construction of a transit line or park   201

Vastu Shastra: a traditional Hindu system of principles that guide the design, layout, measurements, and spatial geometry of sites   169–170

Vector-based graphics: the use of polygons, created by points or nodes, connected by lines, customarily used in CAD programs   152

Vegetated swales: open-air channels lined with vegetation that helps filter and slow runoff before it is released into storage areas   16, 373, 377

Vending carts. See **Sales kiosks**

Vernalization: exposure of plants or seeds to cold to stimulate flowering, usually expressed in terms of days of cold   472

Vertical mixed-use structures: structures containing two or more distinct uses vertically layered, such as housing over offices over shops   660–662

Very-high-bit-rate digital subscriber line (VDSL): a local subscriber technology that can operate over twisted pair copper telephone lines and provide data service at an upstream rate of 12 Mbps and downstream at 52 Mbps   447

View easement or **view plane**: an area where development is restricted by contract or regulation so that views are not obstructed   94

Viewshed: the surroundings that are visible from a single point on a site, often natural features   79–80

Virtual universities: teaching institutions in which students receive the majority of their instruction via the Internet or through materials mailed to them, meeting faculty face to face only occasionally; also known as open universities and Internet universities   593, 618–619

Vision Zero: a road improvement and traffic safety program that aims to achieve a system with no fatalities or serious injuries   275

Visualization: a method of portraying the form and character of a proposed development; it can range from a quick sketch to a model to a watercolor rendering to a computer-generated image   115, 138, 151, 152, 154–158

Visual preference study: a method for eliciting viewer preferences by asking them to make pairwise comparisons of structures or scenes   138

Vulnerable populations: groups likely to bear the greatest impacts of environmental change, who do not have the resources or means to counteract them   231, 259

Walkability: the ability to conduct daily life on foot, fostered in part by nearby destinations and the presence of safe walkways and absence of threats, partially quantified by computing WalkScore   187, 257, 672

Walkable commercial areas: shopping areas that are sustained by a significant number of walk-in patrons and have a desirable range of shops   644

Walking buffer zone or **shy distance**: the distance between pedestrians as they pass each other on a pathway   346

Walking speed: the speed of pedestrians on a path, culturally determined and affected by bordering opportunities   348–350

Waste-to-energy systems: systems for converting wastes to energy, including **incineration**, **pyrolyzation** (combustion in the absence of oxygen), **anaerobic digestion** (decomposition by microorganisms), **gasification** (high-temperature treatment with controlled oxygen or steam), and **plasma arc gasification** (use of plasma to create synthetic gas)   415–416, 417, 422

Waste transfer station: a solid waste receiving station where items are sorted by those delivering materials (in small local facilities), or by mechanized operations within the station (in larger facilities)   404, 406, 408, 411–412

Water conservation: strategies for reducing the use of water, such as low-water planting, reuse of gray water, and elimination of evaporative chillers   194, 381

Water pressure or **hydrostatic pressure**: the fluid pressure created by the weight of water above the elevation where it is measured; may also be created by pressure pumps   43, 387, 390

Water quality: the chemical, physical, biological, and radiological characteristics of water, with standards generally prescribing the minimum qualities for specific purposes   71–72, 231, 237, 368, 381, 385–387, 393, 396–397

Water rights: rights to withdraw water from groundwater sources or watercourses based on the size of a property; rights may be sold to or acquired from other property owners   94

Water sources: origins of water used for potable or irrigation purposes   374–375, 383–386, 390–391

  desalination: processes for removing salt from seawater   383, 386, 691

  gray water: recycled water treated to remove harmful impurities and used for irrigation and other nonpotable purposes   368, 390–391, 693, 696

  groundwater: water drawn from subsurface wells   42–43, 383–385

  surface water: water from rainfall and snowmelt   366, 374–375

Water storage system: methods of collecting and holding water for use   387–388

  cisterns: generally underground water tanks   17, 377, 383–384, 387–388

  reservoirs: holding areas open to the air   368, 382, 384–387, 389, 425

  storage tanks: enclosed aboveground structures, often elevated to increase water pressure in distribution lines   387–388, 444

Water table: the upper level of soil saturated by water   36, 39, 42–43, 50, 69, 228, 237, 297, 367–368, 378–379, 402, 414

Water treatment systems: a variety of techniques for assuring that water supply is safe for consumption   386–387

  coagulation and flocculation: adding chemicals with a positive charge that neutralize the negative charge of dirt and other dissolved particles forming floc   387

  disinfection: adding chemicals to the water or treating it with electromagnetic radiation (UV) to kill any remaining parasites, bacteria, and viruses   387

  filtration: passing water through filters to dissolve particles such as dust, parasites, bacteria, viruses, and chemicals   386–387, 400–401

  fluoridation: addition of fluoride that helps protect against dental cavities   386

  reverse osmosis systems: systems to remove impurities by pushing water through a semipermeable membrane   386

  sedimentation: removal of floc by settlement due to its weight   386, 402

Wayfinding: the legibility of routes through a city, often aided by maps and other devices   363, 365, 432

Wetland: an area characterized by permanent or seasonal standing water, with plant materials adapted to wet conditions and hydric soils (see also **Constructed wetland; Engineered reed bed**)   69–70

Wide curb lane (WCL): a curb lane on a roadway that has been widened to permit loading or as a buffer for bicycles   337

Wind break or shelter belt: a row of trees planted to provide shelter on the lee side   60

Wind chill factor: the perceived air temperature on a cold day, accounting for wind speed that makes exposed skin feel colder   59

Wind power: electric power generated by wind turbines of various kinds, including the conventional **horizontal axis** turbine, **vertical axis** turbine (vertical blades that spin around a vertical shaft), **Darrieus rotor** turbine (curved airfoil blades on a vertical shaft), and **Savonius rotor** turbine (cupped vertical blades on a vertical shaft)   426–429

Wind rose: a diagram of wind speed and direction for a particular time, or averaged over the season or year   69–70

Woonerf or **living street** or **home zone**: a local street designed to slow or restrict traffic so that the street can also be used for recreation or social activities   280–281

Xeriscaping (or **zeroscaping** or **xeroscaping**): landscape forms, materials, and practices that reduce or eliminate the need for irrigation   475

Zero net criterion: a target of having on-site production or offsets equal to or greater than on-site consumption, such as zero net energy, zero net runoff, or zero net carbon emissions   5, 367, 380, 677

Zoning regulations: development rules that prescribe the uses, area, form, and other characteristics of buildings on a site   13, 57, 81, 481, 644, 648, 655, 644

Index of Places, Projects, Persons, and Organizations

China Vanke headquarters, Shenzhen, China, 477
Church Street Marketplace, Burlington, Vermont, 362
Cincinnati, Ohio, 157, 572
Cincinnati Urban Design Review Board, 185
Cinque Terre, Italy, 359
Circular Quay, Sydney, Australia, 331–332
City Center, Las Vegas, Nevada, 645
City Hall Plaza, Boston, Massachusetts, 622–623, 636, 639
Civano, Tucson, Arizona, 489, 492
Civic Center Plaza, San Francisco, California, 622, 635
Civic Design Commission, Boston, Massachusetts, 185
Cleveland Arcade, Cleveland, Ohio, 524
CN Tower, Toronto, Canada, 449
Cochrane Collaboration, 231
Cochrane Street Escalator, Hong Kong, China, 330
Cohasset, Massachusetts, 92
Colby College, Waterville, Maine, 604
College of William and Mary, Williamsburg, Virginia, 604
Colonel By Drive, Ottawa, Canada, 286
Colorado River Aqueduct, 385
Colorado Springs, Colorado, 300
Columbia, Maryland, 199, 514, 530, 673–674, 679
Columbia Association, Columbia, Maryland, 673
Columbia University, New York, New York, 615–616
Columbus Circle, New York, New York, 265
Columbus Circle–Coliseum redevelopment (Time Warner Center),
    New York, New York, 128
Commonwealth Avenue, Newton and Boston, Massachusetts,
    24–27, 75, 220, 285
Commonwealth Avenue Mall, Boston, Massachusetts, 357–358
Community Bicycle Network, Toronto, Canada, 344
Congress of New Urbanism, 187
Constitution, US, 88–89
Convention on the Rights of the Child, UN, 567
Cooper Eckstut Associates, 32
Copenhagen, Denmark, 293, 335, 343, 359, 383, 416, 436, 452,
    485, 495, 509–510, 572, 574, 642
Copenhagen Bicycle Snake, Copenhagen, Denmark, 340
Copley Square, Boston, Massachusetts, 624–625
Cotswold Water Park, Gloucestershire and Wiltshire, UK, 48
Country Club Plaza, Kansas City, Missouri, 527
Cours Mirabeau, Aix-en-Provence, France, 476
Covent Garden Market, London, UK, 517
Crailsheim-Hirtenwiesen, Germany, 444
Crescent Park, Richmond, California, 424
Cullen, Gordon, 135–136
Cumberland Harbour, St. Mary's, Georgia, 197
Cumbernauld, Scotland, UK, 293
Cummings Corporation Park, Columbus, Indiana, 476
Curitiba, Brazil, 314, 318–319, 569
Cyclecross course, Gloucester, Massachusetts, 581

Dagenham South Brownfield, UK, 465
Dallas Arts Square, Dallas, Texas, 628
Dallas-Fort Worth, Texas, 293, 423
Dallas-Fort Worth International Airport, Texas, 293
Davos-Parsenn Bahnen, Switzerland, 329
Debrashtica village, Bulgaria, 390
Deere and Co. headquarters, Moline, Illinois, 552–553
Delecarlia Reservior, Washington, DC, 367
Delhi Pike, Ohio, 157
Denmark, 90, 296, 383, 429–430, 443
Denver, Colorado, 321–323, 382–383, 435, 475, 540

Department of Agriculture (USDA), US, 40, 472
Department of Housing and Urban Development (HUD), US, 85–86
Desert Ridge Marketplace, Phoenix, Arizona, 533, 535–536
Detroit, Michigan, 293, 326, 376, 573–574, 659–660
Detroit International Airport, Wayne County, Michigan, 326
Dhaka, Bangladesh, 98, 272, 313, 354
Dharavi, Mumbai, India, 387
Dilworth Plaza, Philadelphia, Pennsylvania, 515
Diplomatic Quarter, Riyadh, Saudi Arabia, 475
Disney theme parks, 170, 326, 408, 540
District Energy St. Paul, St. Paul, Minnesota, 441, 443
District Hall, Boston Innovation District, Boston, Massachusetts, 544
Dornbush Street, Pittsburgh, Pennsylvania, 276
Dortmund, Germany, 327
Douro Valley, Portugal, 52
Dover College, Dover, UK, 579
Duany, Andres, 163
Duany Plater-Zyberk Associates (DPZ Partners), 162–163, 519
Dubai, UAE, 50
Dublin, Ireland, 316
Dubrovnik, Croatia, 359
Duquesne Incline, Pittsburgh, Pennsylvania, 328–329
Düsseldorf, Germany, 327

East Cambridge Redevelopment Project, Cambridge,
    Massachusetts, 204
Eastern Harbor development, Amsterdam, Netherlands, 495
Easton Town Center, Columbus, Ohio, 533–535
East Roy Street, Seattle, Washington, 276
Eaton Centre, Toronto, Canada, 325, 507, 526
Eckstut, Stanton, 32, 108, 177
ECO-Box, Fondación Metrópoli, Madrid, Spain, 444
Ecologische Hoofdstructuur, Netherlands, 66
ECO-Springfield Treatment Facility, Springfield, Massachusetts, 397
Eden Project, Cornwall, UK, 48
Edificio Pluriusi, Rome, Italy, 646
Edinburgh, Scotland, UK, 359
Ehrenkranz Group & Eckstut, 32
Eixample, Barcelona, Spain, 56, 255, 682, 684
Elburn, Illinois, 235–236
Embarcadero, San Francisco, California, 287, 647
Empire State Building, New York, New York, 449
England, 96, 102, 485, 492, 494, 496
Enschede cogeneration facility, Delft, Netherlands, 436
Envac, 409–411, 696
Envision Utah, 178
Equitable Building Plaza, Chicago, Illinois, 622–623
Erskine, Ralph, 168–169
Esplanade, Chico, California, 285
European Convention on Human Rights, 88
European Green Belt, 66
European Union, 224

Facebook West Campus, Menlo Park, California, 553, 556
False Creek community, Vancouver, Canada, 486, 496
Faneuil Hall Market, Boston, Massachusetts, 516–517, 538
Fargo Street, Los Angeles, California, 276
Federal Aviation Administration (FAA), US, 86
Federal Courthouse plaza, Minneapolis, Minnesota, 459
Federal Emergency Management Agency, US, 63
Fells Point, Baltimore, Maryland, 106
Fellsway, Boston, Massachusetts, 286

Oak Bluffs, Martha's Vineyard, Massachusetts, 481
Ocean and Eastern Parkways, Brooklyn, New York, 285
Ocean City, New Jersey, 450
Octavia Street, San Francisco, California, 285
O'Hare International Airport, Chicago, Illinois, 326, 356–357
Ohio State University, Columbus, Ohio, 592, 605
Olana House, Columbia and Greene Counties, New York, 80
Old Market Hall, Helsinki, Finland, 517
Old Town Square, Prague, Czech Republic, 636
Olin Partnership (Laurie Olin), 32, 150
Olmsted, Frederick Law, vii, 167, 457
Olmsted and Vaux, 167, 292, 457–458
Olympic Sculpture Park, Seattle, Washington, 7, 457–458
Olympic site, Beijing, China, 172
Olympic Village, Barcelona, Spain, 682, 684–685
Oman, 386, 402
Omote-Sando Avenue, Tokyo, Japan, 506
One World Trade Center, New York, New York, 546–547
Ontario Greenbelt, Canada, 66
Ontario Municipal Board, Canada, 123
Orange County, Florida, 449
Ørestad, Copenhagen, Denmark, 293, 324, 485–486
Orlando, Florida, 409, 489, 529, 540
Ottawa, Canada, 164, 286, 318, 320, 517, 679–680
OV-fiets system, Netherlands, 344
Oxford Covered Market, Oxford, UK, 516
Oxford University, Oxford, UK, 590–591, 601, 604

P & T Architects, 25
Pacific Northwest, US, 57
Pacific Palisades, California, 292
Paju Book City, Seoul, Korea, 185
Pakistan, 96
Palatine, Illinois, 449
Paley Park, New York, New York, 87, 622–623, 626
Palm Jumeirah, Dubai, UAE, 403
Palo Alto Research Park, Palo Alto, California, 619
Panama, 68
Paris, France, 283, 285, 306, 325, 339, 343, 354–355, 359, 482,
    485, 499, 506, 515, 523, 569, 590, 593, 622–623, 640
Park City, Utah, 329
Park Meadows Shopping Center, Littleton, Colorado, 533
Park Place apartments, Mountain View, California, 496–497
Park Street Church, Boston, Massachusetts, 76
Paseo Verde, Philadelphia, Pennsylvania, 189
Passeig de Gràcia, Barcelona, Spain, 285, 682
Paul Revere Mall, Boston, Massachusetts, 622
Paunacussing Wetlands, Buckingham, Pennsylvania, 69
Peabody Terrace, Harvard University, Cambridge, Massachusetts,
    501–502
Pearl District, Portland, Oregon, 316
Pearl Street Mall, Boulder, Colorado, 361
Pedlow Field skateboard park, San Fernando Valley, California, 580
Peets, Elbert, 165
Pei Cobb Fried Associates, 32
Perkins Eastman, ix, 12–18
Perugia, Italy, 326
Peter Walker and Partners (PWP), 25, 561–562
Petronelli Way, Brockton, Massachusetts, 159
Philadelphia, Pennsylvania, 41, 59, 62, 77, 164, 205, 220, 279, 285,
    291, 306, 315–316, 320–321, 354, 367, 369, 370, 374, 378,
    382–383, 435, 483, 492, 494–495, 500–501, 515–516, 521, 557,
    619, 630, 642

Philadelphia alley streets, 257–258, 278–279
Philadelphia Historical Commission, Philadelphia, Pennsylvania, 185
Philippines, 170, 237–252
Phipps Conservatory, Pittsburgh, Pennsylvania, 375
Phoenix, Arizona, 286, 382–383, 385, 412, 533, 535–536
Phoenix North Gateway Transfer and Materials Recovery Station,
    Phoenix, Arizona, 412
Piano, Renzo (Renzo Piano Building Workshop), 329, 615
Piazza at Schmidts, Northern Liberties, Philadelphia,
    Pennsylvania, 500
Piazza di Spagna, Rome, Italy, 622–623
Piazza Matteotti, Treviso, Italy, 450
Piazza Navona, Rome, Italy, 515
Piazza San Marco, Venice, Italy, 522, 625, 628–629
Pier 45, New York, New York, 347
Pike Place Market, Seattle, Washington, 515–517, 542
Pioneer Square, Portland, Oregon, 622
Pisgah Forest, North Carolina, 44
Pittsburgh, Pennsylvania, 276, 320, 328–329, 375, 611, 626, 642
Plaça de Catalunya, Barcelona, Spain, 367, 628
Place de Furstemberg, Paris, France, 485
Place Georges-Pompidou, Paris, France, 622–623
Plater-Zyberk, Elizabeth, 164
Playa Vista, Los Angeles, California, 421
Plaza Bolivar, Bogotá, Colombia, 636
Plaza Mayor, Madrid, Spain, 522
Pleasanton Center, Pleasanton, California, 549
Plus 15 System, Calgary, Canada, 365
Poland, 90, 92
Ponte Vecchio, Florence, Italy, 367
Poplar Street neighborhood, Philadelphia, Pennsylvania, 492
Portland, Maine, 55, 179, 188
Portland, Oregon, 179, 182, 298, 310, 315–317, 331, 336, 343,
    399–400, 427, 617–618, 622
Portland State University, Portland, Oregon, 617–618
Potsdammer Platz, Berlin, Germany, 308
Potters Field, London, UK, 168
Pottstown, Pennsylvania, 420
Power and Light District, Kansas City, Missouri, 540–541
Prairie Crossing, Grayslake, Illinois, 352, 481, 487, 673, 676–677
Price Tower, Bartlesville, Oklahoma, 646
Prince William Street, St. John, New Brunswick, Canada, 260
Project for Public Spaces, 163, 624
Prospect New Town, Longmont, Colorado, 492
Providence Estate, Greenvale, Victoria, Australia, 70
Prudential Center, Boston, Massachusetts, 121–122, 145, 152, 428,
    509–510, 523, 650, 653, 666–668
PS 124, Brooklyn, New York, 579
Puebla, Mexico, 173
Puerto Madero, Buenos Aires, Argentina, 84
Puerto Rico, 90, 312
Puligny, France, 3, 304
Purdue University, West Lafayette, Indiana, 590, 594–596
Purdy's Wharf, Halifax, Nova Scotia, 439

Qatar, 187, 193, 452
Qian'an Sanlihe Greenway, Qian'an, Hebei Province, China, 373
Qingdao, China, 134, 673, 678
Quarry Village, San Antonio, Texas, 49
Quartier des Spectacles, Montreal, Canada, 409
Quebec, Canada, 90
Quebec City, Canada, 493
Queen Victoria Market, Melbourne, Australia, 515